barbri®

AF870528

Multistate Testing Practice Questions: Volume 2

INCLUDES

Step 5: Simulated Final Exam

Multistate Advantage™

To be used in conjunction with the Summer 2011 and Winter 2012 BARBRI Bar Review Courses

MPQ2

BARBRI gratefully acknowledges the assistance of the National Conference of Bar Examiners in granting permission to reprint released Multistate questions that have appeared on actual Multistate Bar Examinations: All Released Multistate Questions and original versions of the following questions modified by BARBRI in the Full Day Exam: 10, 12, 13, 15, 16, 17, 25, 30, 33, 35, 38, 39, 41, 42, 43, 45, 46, 49, 52, 54, 55, 57, 58, 60, 63, 64, 69, 73, 75, 77, 80, 81, 84, 85, 86, 87, 88, 89, 90, 93, 94, 95, 98, 102, 107, 108, 110, 115, 116, 118, 123, 124, 127, 128, 129, 130, 131, 133, 134, 135, 137, 141, 143, 144, 145, 147, 148, 149, 150, 152, 154, 159, 160, 165, 167, 169, 175, 176, 181, 182, 183, 188, 189, 191, 193, 195, 197.

All other questions and ***all*** analytical answers were prepared by BARBRI.

TABLE OF CONTENTS

HOW TO USE THE MULTISTATE PRACTICE QUESTIONS BOOKS

The Multistate Testing Practice Questions books are the backbone of BARBRI's ***Multistate Advantage***™ program—an unparalleled collection of workshops and workbooks that give you ***everything you need*** to succeed on the Multistate Bar Exam.

There are two Practice Questions books—MPQ 1 and MPQ 2. Together they contain over 2,000 MBE-type multiple choice questions. However, we do ***NOT*** recommend that you do all of the questions offered, ***especially at the expense of reading through the outlines and working on essay questions.*** Your course will probably provide a Paced Program™ with specific assignments from these books, or you can follow the suggested approach below to focus your MBE preparation.

First: After you've had the substantive lecture on an MBE subject, do the ***Step 3: MBE Drills*** workshops in the front of the MPQ 1 book. If you haven't yet done so, start with the Introductory Workshop, which contains the National Conference of Bar Examiners subject matter outlines showing topics tested on the MBE. Then do the question set for the subject that you have just studied. Finally, access the corresponding lecture in the Enrolled Student Center to review the questions and learn test-taking techniques for that subject.

Second: Do the ***question sets*** arranged by subject in MPQ 1 assigned in your Paced Program™. If you want to obtain a more detailed diagnostic analysis of your performance, ***including a ranking of your performance against that of other students taking the course at this time,*** do these questions using the BARBRI StudySmart© software or the BARBRI Mobile app (choose the Paced Program™ mode to do the questions arranged by question set).

Third: Once you have had the substantive lectures on all six MBE subjects, you will participate in the ***Step 4: Simulated MBE*** workshop, in which you will take a simulated Multistate Bar Exam under timed conditions and have it computer graded. We strongly recommend that you take this exam when it is scheduled by your course. There is no substitute for experiencing the time pressures imposed by a pace of 1.8 minutes per question.

Fourth: Your Paced Program™ may also assign the ***Half Day Practice Exam*** or the ***Full Day Practice Exam*** in this book. If you can, do these questions under timed conditions; *i.e.*, set aside a block of time (*e.g.*, one hour per 34 questions) and try to answer that set of questions within that time period. There are also ***Released Questions*** in the back of this book which you may want to look at, but remember that these older questions are not as representative of the current format of the exam as the newer questions developed by BARBRI.

Fifth: As a final tune-up before the exam, you will take the ***Step 5: Simulated Final Exam***, which is in ***the shaded section in the back of this book***. This 100 question test is designed to give you more practice in handling variations of commonly tested issues and is representative of some of the more difficult questions that you will see on the MBE.

Sixth: ***Don't panic***. If you are like many students, you will come out of the MBE remembering only the questions that you struggled with and not the many more questions that you answered correctly, so keep these two thoughts in mind:

1. Even if you get just the ***average score*** on the exam, you will have answered ***two-thirds*** of the questions correctly.

2. ***Thousands of students pass*** with a score ***lower*** than the average score.

As long as you keep on a reasonable schedule and follow BARBRI's guidelines, ***you will be prepared for the MBE***.

QUESTION SET GOALS

Introduction
The goals listed below are based on the average performance of previous BARBRI students on these questions. Use these goals to check your performance as you work through these questions, but remember that your scores on these sets of questions are ***raw*** scores; on the actual MBE, the bar examiners will add points to your raw score to obtain a ***scaled*** score, which is what states use to compute overall passing grades. The bottom line is that you can miss a lot of questions and still pass the exam.

Half Day Exam (100 questions)
50 correct (50%)

Full Day Exam (200 questions)
116 correct (58%)

Mixed Subject Set 1 (36 questions)
25 correct (69%)

Mixed Subject Set 2 (50 questions)
34 correct (68%)

Mixed Subject Set 3 (50 questions)
35 correct (70%)

Mixed Subject Set 4 (50 questions)
35 correct (70%)

Mixed Subject Set 5 (50 questions)
35 correct (70%)

Mixed Subject Set 6 (50 questions)
36 correct (72%)

Mixed Subject Set 7 (50 questions)
36 correct (72%)

Mixed Subject Set 8 (50 questions)
36 correct (72%)

Step 5: Simulated Final Exam

Overall: 57 (out of 100)
Constitutional Law: 9 (out of 17)
Contracts: 10 (out of 17)
Criminal Law: 10 (out of 16)
Evidence: 10 (out of 16)
Real Property: 9 (out of 17)
Torts: 9 (out of 17)

Half Day Practice Exam and Analytical Answers

Multistate Practice Exam

HALF DAY EXAM

Time—3 hours

You will be given three hours to work on this test. Be sure that the question numbers on your answer sheet match the question numbers in your test book. You are not to begin work until the supervisor tells you to do so.

Your score will be based on the number of questions you answer correctly. It is therefore to your advantage to try to answer as many questions as you can. Give only one answer to each question; multiple answers will not be counted. If you wish to change an answer, erase your first mark completely and mark your new choice. Use your time effectively. Do not hurry, but work steadily and as quickly as you can without sacrificing your accuracy.

YOU ARE TO INDICATE YOUR ANSWERS TO ALL QUESTIONS ON THE SEPARATE ANSWER SHEET PROVIDED.

DIRECTIONS

Each of the questions or incomplete statements in this test is followed by four suggested answers or completions. You are to choose the ***best*** of the stated alternatives. Answer all questions according to the generally accepted view, except where otherwise noted.

For the purpose of this test, you are to assume that Articles 1 and 2 of the Uniform Commercial Code have been adopted. You should assume that the 2001 amendments to Article 1 have been adopted, but that the 2001 and 2003 proposed amendments to Article 2 have not been adopted.

The Federal Rules of Evidence are deemed to control.

The terms "Constitution," "constitutional," and "unconstitutional" refer to the federal Constitution unless indicated to the contrary.

You are also to assume that there is no applicable statute unless otherwise specified; however, survival actions and claims for wrongful death should be assumed to be available where applicable. You should assume that joint and several liability, with pure comparative negligence, is the relevant rule unless otherwise indicated.

DO NOT OPEN THE TEST UNTIL YOU ARE INSTRUCTED TO DO SO.

Half Day Exam

1. Ⓐ Ⓑ Ⓒ Ⓓ	26. Ⓐ Ⓑ Ⓒ Ⓓ	51. Ⓐ Ⓑ Ⓒ Ⓓ	76. Ⓐ Ⓑ Ⓒ Ⓓ
2. Ⓐ Ⓑ Ⓒ Ⓓ	27. Ⓐ Ⓑ Ⓒ Ⓓ	52. Ⓐ Ⓑ Ⓒ Ⓓ	77. Ⓐ Ⓑ Ⓒ Ⓓ
3. Ⓐ Ⓑ Ⓒ Ⓓ	28. Ⓐ Ⓑ Ⓒ Ⓓ	53. Ⓐ Ⓑ Ⓒ Ⓓ	78. Ⓐ Ⓑ Ⓒ Ⓓ
4. Ⓐ Ⓑ Ⓒ Ⓓ	29. Ⓐ Ⓑ Ⓒ Ⓓ	54. Ⓐ Ⓑ Ⓒ Ⓓ	79. Ⓐ Ⓑ Ⓒ Ⓓ
5. Ⓐ Ⓑ Ⓒ Ⓓ	30. Ⓐ Ⓑ Ⓒ Ⓓ	55. Ⓐ Ⓑ Ⓒ Ⓓ	80. Ⓐ Ⓑ Ⓒ Ⓓ
6. Ⓐ Ⓑ Ⓒ Ⓓ	31. Ⓐ Ⓑ Ⓒ Ⓓ	56. Ⓐ Ⓑ Ⓒ Ⓓ	81. Ⓐ Ⓑ Ⓒ Ⓓ
7. Ⓐ Ⓑ Ⓒ Ⓓ	32. Ⓐ Ⓑ Ⓒ Ⓓ	57. Ⓐ Ⓑ Ⓒ Ⓓ	82. Ⓐ Ⓑ Ⓒ Ⓓ
8. Ⓐ Ⓑ Ⓒ Ⓓ	33. Ⓐ Ⓑ Ⓒ Ⓓ	58. Ⓐ Ⓑ Ⓒ Ⓓ	83. Ⓐ Ⓑ Ⓒ Ⓓ
9. Ⓐ Ⓑ Ⓒ Ⓓ	34. Ⓐ Ⓑ Ⓒ Ⓓ	59. Ⓐ Ⓑ Ⓒ Ⓓ	84. Ⓐ Ⓑ Ⓒ Ⓓ
10. Ⓐ Ⓑ Ⓒ Ⓓ	35. Ⓐ Ⓑ Ⓒ Ⓓ	60. Ⓐ Ⓑ Ⓒ Ⓓ	85. Ⓐ Ⓑ Ⓒ Ⓓ
11. Ⓐ Ⓑ Ⓒ Ⓓ	36. Ⓐ Ⓑ Ⓒ Ⓓ	61. Ⓐ Ⓑ Ⓒ Ⓓ	86. Ⓐ Ⓑ Ⓒ Ⓓ
12. Ⓐ Ⓑ Ⓒ Ⓓ	37. Ⓐ Ⓑ Ⓒ Ⓓ	62. Ⓐ Ⓑ Ⓒ Ⓓ	87. Ⓐ Ⓑ Ⓒ Ⓓ
13. Ⓐ Ⓑ Ⓒ Ⓓ	38. Ⓐ Ⓑ Ⓒ Ⓓ	63. Ⓐ Ⓑ Ⓒ Ⓓ	88. Ⓐ Ⓑ Ⓒ Ⓓ
14. Ⓐ Ⓑ Ⓒ Ⓓ	39. Ⓐ Ⓑ Ⓒ Ⓓ	64. Ⓐ Ⓑ Ⓒ Ⓓ	89. Ⓐ Ⓑ Ⓒ Ⓓ
15. Ⓐ Ⓑ Ⓒ Ⓓ	40. Ⓐ Ⓑ Ⓒ Ⓓ	65. Ⓐ Ⓑ Ⓒ Ⓓ	90. Ⓐ Ⓑ Ⓒ Ⓓ
16. Ⓐ Ⓑ Ⓒ Ⓓ	41. Ⓐ Ⓑ Ⓒ Ⓓ	66. Ⓐ Ⓑ Ⓒ Ⓓ	91. Ⓐ Ⓑ Ⓒ Ⓓ
17. Ⓐ Ⓑ Ⓒ Ⓓ	42. Ⓐ Ⓑ Ⓒ Ⓓ	67. Ⓐ Ⓑ Ⓒ Ⓓ	92. Ⓐ Ⓑ Ⓒ Ⓓ
18. Ⓐ Ⓑ Ⓒ Ⓓ	43. Ⓐ Ⓑ Ⓒ Ⓓ	68. Ⓐ Ⓑ Ⓒ Ⓓ	93. Ⓐ Ⓑ Ⓒ Ⓓ
19. Ⓐ Ⓑ Ⓒ Ⓓ	44. Ⓐ Ⓑ Ⓒ Ⓓ	69. Ⓐ Ⓑ Ⓒ Ⓓ	94. Ⓐ Ⓑ Ⓒ Ⓓ
20. Ⓐ Ⓑ Ⓒ Ⓓ	45. Ⓐ Ⓑ Ⓒ Ⓓ	70. Ⓐ Ⓑ Ⓒ Ⓓ	95. Ⓐ Ⓑ Ⓒ Ⓓ
21. Ⓐ Ⓑ Ⓒ Ⓓ	46. Ⓐ Ⓑ Ⓒ Ⓓ	71. Ⓐ Ⓑ Ⓒ Ⓓ	96. Ⓐ Ⓑ Ⓒ Ⓓ
22. Ⓐ Ⓑ Ⓒ Ⓓ	47. Ⓐ Ⓑ Ⓒ Ⓓ	72. Ⓐ Ⓑ Ⓒ Ⓓ	97. Ⓐ Ⓑ Ⓒ Ⓓ
23. Ⓐ Ⓑ Ⓒ Ⓓ	48. Ⓐ Ⓑ Ⓒ Ⓓ	73. Ⓐ Ⓑ Ⓒ Ⓓ	98. Ⓐ Ⓑ Ⓒ Ⓓ
24. Ⓐ Ⓑ Ⓒ Ⓓ	49. Ⓐ Ⓑ Ⓒ Ⓓ	74. Ⓐ Ⓑ Ⓒ Ⓓ	99. Ⓐ Ⓑ Ⓒ Ⓓ
25. Ⓐ Ⓑ Ⓒ Ⓓ	50. Ⓐ Ⓑ Ⓒ Ⓓ	75. Ⓐ Ⓑ Ⓒ Ⓓ	100. Ⓐ Ⓑ Ⓒ Ⓓ

Question 1

A tanker truck driver delivering gasoline to filling stations parked on the street in front of a building to get a cup of coffee after his deliveries. Contrary to company regulations, he parked in an area clearly marked as a no parking zone. Just as the driver went across the street, a minor quake jolted the area and caused a collapse of the walls of the building, which was extremely run-down and unstable. The front wall fell on top of the truck, causing gasoline to leak from the truck and stream down the street. A pedestrian walking two blocks away lit a cigarette and tossed a match in the street, causing the gasoline to ignite. The flames spread to a nearby commercial building and an explosion occurred, causing many windows in a neighboring apartment building to be blown inward. Flying glass was propelled into a tenant's apartment. The tenant suffered multiple cuts and a serious eye injury from the flying glass. The tenant brought a negligence action against the tanker company that employed the driver.

If the court finds in favor of the tanker company it will be because:

(A) The court follows the majority view regarding unforeseeable plaintiffs.

(B) The driver was acting outside the scope of his employment when the tenant was injured.

(C) The owner of the unstable building was a legal cause of the tenant's injuries because his building was in an unreasonably dangerous condition.

(D) The company had a rule against illegal parking on streets.

Question 2

A fashion student at a prestigious fashion design school bought a new sewing machine for $1,000 so that she would be more than adequately equipped for her design assignments. One day, her roommate loaned her sewing machine to their neighbor, as she had done on several prior occasions. Unfortunately, the neighbor caused extensive damage to the machine. The cost to repair the sewing machine was $400.

If the fashion student sues her roommate for the damage the neighbor caused to the sewing machine, what will be the result?

(A) The fashion student will recover $1,000.

(B) The fashion student will recover the fair market value of the sewing machine.

(C) The fashion student will recover $400.

(D) The fashion student will recover nothing, because her roommate did not damage the machine and the neighbor's conduct was not intentional.

Question 3

A landowner conveyed his land to a famous guitarist. The guitarist put the deed in his guitar case and took off for a three-week band tour. While the guitarist was out of town, the landowner offered to sell the same land to his neighbor for $5,000. Although the neighbor knew that the guitarist had already bought the land, the neighbor paid the landowner $5,000 and promptly recorded the deed she received. Thereafter, the neighbor conveyed the land to her ex-husband for $15,000. The ex-husband knew nothing about the guitarist's deed and promptly recorded the deed he received. Two weeks later, the guitarist returned and recorded his deed to the land. A month after that, the ex-husband conveyed the land to a buyer for $17,000. The buyer knew that the guitarist held a deed to the land, but paid the ex-husband $17,000 anyway. The buyer immediately recorded and filed an appropriate action against the guitarist and the ex-husband to determine ownership of the land. The land is situated in a state with the following statute: "No conveyance or mortgage of an interest in land is valid against any subsequent purchaser for value without notice thereof whose conveyance is first recorded."

The court will most likely rule that:

(A) The guitarist has superior rights to both the ex-husband and the buyer.

(B) The ex-husband has superior rights to both the guitarist and the buyer.

(C) The buyer has superior rights to both the guitarist and the ex-husband.

(D) The buyer has superior rights to the ex-husband, but the guitarist has superior rights to the buyer.

Question 4

Which of the following will the court not take judicial notice of?

(A) The birthdate of the plaintiff's son is June 14, 1984.

(B) The defendant has filed 25 frivolous lawsuits in the same court in which the case is being tried.

(C) It rained in the city in which the parties reside on March 28, 2007.

(D) Independence Day is July 4, and it is a state holiday.

GO ON TO THE NEXT PAGE

Question 5

For many years, civil service rules have provided that any member of the city's police department must serve a one-year probationary period before he or she will be considered a permanent employee. However, because the rules were enacted before the city's police academy was established, a prospective police officer now spends six months in the academy before being hired by the city. A graduate of the police academy was with the city police department for eight months after graduation when she was terminated. There were no city ordinances or state laws that required that she be given either a reason for the termination or a hearing, and she was given neither. The graduate brought suit against the city in state court because of the termination of her employment, alleging a violation of her due process rights.

Which of the following would most likely give her a constitutional basis to require the city to give her a statement of reasons for the termination and an opportunity for a hearing?

(A) No police officer had ever been terminated during probation except where there was actual cause.

(B) The six months she spent in the academy must be considered as part of her probationary period.

(C) The budget of the police department was recently increased to allow for the hiring of additional officers.

(D) She was the only female police officer on probation and the only officer not given permanent employment.

Question 6

A gambler owed his uncle $9,000, which was due on January 1. On January 15, the gambler offered to pay the uncle $8,000 if he would agree to accept the amount in full satisfaction of the $9,000 debt. The uncle agreed and the gambler paid him the $8,000.

If the uncle then sues the gambler for $1,000, the uncle will:

(A) Win, because the gambler had an obligation to pay $9,000 on January 1.

(B) Lose, because of the uncle's agreement to accept $8,000.

(C) Lose, because there was an accord and satisfaction.

(D) Lose, because the uncle agreed to the $8,000 after the January 1 due date.

Question 7

A parachute company marketed a new parachute with the warning that the parachute should be discarded after 150 jumps. The designer of the new parachute took several of the chutes to an independent laboratory for testing. The scientists concluded that there was a 1% failure rate on the chutes for jumps 100 through 150 due to a design defect. The designer did not report this problem to his superiors at the company. Several months later a skydiver used one of the new chutes. The chute failed, and the skydiver hurtled to the ground to his death. An investigation established that the designer knew of the design defect.

If the parachute manufacturer is charged with manslaughter in a common law jurisdiction, the verdict should be:

(A) Guilty, because the designer was the parachute manufacturer's employee and he designed the instrumentality of death.

(B) Guilty, because the skydiver died as a result of the failure of a product manufactured and sold by the parachute manufacturer.

(C) Not guilty, because a corporation cannot be found guilty of manslaughter.

(D) Not guilty, because there was only a 1% chance of parachute failure.

Question 8

A homebrewing supplier entered into a written five-year lease to rent a unit in a strip mall from a landlord. The rent was payable in monthly installments on the first of each month. Two months before the end of the five-year term, the landlord sent a letter to all of her tenants providing that those tenants wishing to renew their leases could do so at a rent increase of 10%. The homebrewing supplier did not respond to the letter, but continued to send checks for the original amount of rent to the landlord. Each check was marked "new rent payment," and the landlord deposited every one. Six months later, the landlord notified the homebrewing supplier that he was four months' in arrears in his rent.

Is the homebrewing supplier liable for the 10% difference in rent over the last four months?

(A) Yes, because he has a month-to-month tenancy for the increased rent amount.

(B) Yes, because he has a year-to-year tenancy for the increased rent amount.

(C) No, because he has a month-to-month tenancy for the original rent amount.

(D) No, because he has a year-to-year tenancy for the original rent amount.

Question 9

The plaintiff sued the defendant on a breach of contract theory. A witness testified for the plaintiff.

On cross-examination, which of the following questions is the trial judge most likely to rule improper?

(A) "Weren't you convicted last year of forgery?"

(B) "Isn't it true that you and the plaintiff have been best friends for many years?"

(C) "Isn't it true that you are known in the community as an alcoholic?"

(D) "Didn't you cheat your business partner out of a large amount of money last month?"

GO ON TO THE NEXT PAGE

Question 10

A classic car hobbyist attended a classic car show where he found a particular car he had always dreamed of owning. The owner of the car told him the car was for sale. He said that he had restored the classic car himself using nothing but genuine original parts. The owner also said that "this is the finest restoration of this type of car in the United States, and one of the two best in the world." After negotiating a price, the hobbyist agreed to purchase the car for a considerable sum. Later, the hobbyist discovered that the owner had not been truthful about the restoration.

In his action for deceit, assuming that all the other elements of deceit are proven, which statement will support the hobbyist's claims?

(A) The first statement regarding using genuine original parts, because it is a statement of material fact on which the hobbyist relied in making his decision to buy the classic car.

(B) The second statement regarding the car being the finest restoration in the United States and one of the two best in the world, because it is a statement of material fact on which the hobbyist relied in making his decision to buy the classic car.

(C) Both statements, because they were the type of statements a buyer of classic cars would materially rely on in making a decision to buy the car.

(D) Neither statement, because the hobbyist had a duty to inspect the car to make sure what the owner was saying was true.

Question 11

The driver of a tractor-trailer lost control of his vehicle after driving onto an icy bridge in excess of the speed limit and slid off the road. A state trooper responding to the accident got out of his squad car and walked toward the vehicle on the roadway. Before he could set up warning flares or safety cones, a delivery van approached the bridge in the oncoming lane. The van slid on the ice and spun out of control, striking and injuring the trooper. The trooper brought an action against the driver of the delivery van and the driver of the tractor-trailer.

Will the trooper prevail as against the driver of the tractor-trailer?

(A) Yes, because the trooper's injuries were a foreseeable result under the circumstances.

(B) Yes, because the "firefighters' rule" does not apply in this case.

(C) No, because the delivery van striking the trooper was the actual cause of his injuries.

(D) No, because the trooper was injured during the course of his job.

Question 12

The state legislature enacted a statute authorizing all state agencies having legal departments or employing lawyers to subscribe to a specific computerized legal research service provided by a legal research corporation. A contract was duly entered into between the state and the corporation. Before the corporation could begin installing the necessary equipment in state offices, it was revealed that the state university system had exhausted its budgeted resources and would not be able to operate without additional money. The legislature then repealed the statute authorizing use of the computer legal service and reallocated these funds to the university.

In an action by the corporation against the state to enforce the contract, the trial court should rule that the repealed statute is:

(A) Invalid, because it violates the constitutional prohibition against impairment of contracts.

(B) Invalid, because the state is equitably estopped to renounce a valid bid it has accepted.

(C) Valid, because the legislature has constitutional power to repeal its own enactments.

(D) Valid, because the sovereign may not constitutionally be sued without its own consent.

Question 13

A pedestrian was walking home when she saw a man waving what looked to be a police badge pursuing another man with a wallet in his hand. The pursuer yelled, "Don't let him get away. I'm a police officer and he just mugged someone!" The pedestrian immediately put out her leg and tripped the man, injuring him. The pursuing police officer arrested the man for the mugging, a felony in the jurisdiction. Subsequent investigation revealed that the man had just picked the victim's pocket, a misdemeanor, rather than mugged him, as the victim had told the officer.

If the man sues the pedestrian for battery, the pedestrian will have:

(A) A valid defense, because she saw the badge and therefore had reasonable grounds to believe that the pursuer was a police officer.

(B) A valid defense, because the police officer had reasonable grounds to arrest the man.

(C) No valid defense, because the pedestrian did not witness the crime.

(D) No valid defense, because a felony had not in fact been committed.

Question 14

In response to a tremendous increase in begging in the downtown area of a city, the city council enacted an ordinance that required anyone soliciting for charitable contributions of any sort in any public place to wear an identity card issued by the local police department. Identity cards could be obtained by completing an affidavit providing the applicant's identification and address information and further affirming that the applicant was not soliciting for personal use and belonged to a recognized charitable organization.

A member of an anti-tobacco charitable organization wishes to solicit contributions by similarly minded persons for use in his organization's campaign against public smoking. He does not want to comply with the identity card ordinance. He comes to you for legal advice and asks whether he should challenge the ordinance in federal court.

You should advise that the ordinance is probably:

(A) Unconstitutional, because it violates the First Amendment's prohibition of government infringement of the right of free speech.

(B) Unconstitutional, because it prevents religious organizations from obtaining contributions from their members, and thus interferes with the free exercise of religion.

(C) Constitutional, because it represents a reasonable balancing of the state's police power interest in protecting its citizens from fraud and annoyance against the right of people to seek charitable contributions.

(D) Constitutional, because preventing fraud in the solicitation for charitable contributions is a compelling interest.

Question 15

Two police officers noticed a car was weaving and generally being driven in an erratic manner. They pursued the vehicle and curbed it. When the driver emerged from the car, he was obviously intoxicated. The officers arrested him and put the driver in their squad car to take him to the station house. The driver's wife was in the passenger seat, and the other officer drove her in the car to the local precinct.

As the driver was being booked, one officer took a standard police inventory sheet and began searching the car. Beneath the passenger seat he found the passenger's purse. He opened the purse and found a plastic zip-lock bag containing a small amount of marijuana. The passenger was charged with possession of marijuana. Prior to trial, her attorney moved to suppress the admission of the marijuana seized from the passenger's purse into evidence.

Should the court rule favorably on the motion?

(A) Yes, because when conducting a search incident to an arrest the police may not open a closed container.

(B) Yes, because the police lacked probable cause to search the passenger's purse.

(C) No, because the search was incident to the lawful arrest of the driver.

(D) No, because the marijuana was discovered during the course of a valid inventory search.

Question 16

A builder of racing cars entered into a contract with a buyer to sell him a hand-built car for $25,000. The price was to be paid and the car was to be delivered one week later. Unbeknownst to the buyer, the builder's wife had a one-half interest in the car. The day after the contract was signed, the builder called the buyer and told him about his wife's half interest in the car, and that she would not go along with the sale at $25,000 but would agree to a sale for $40,000.

If the buyer sues the builder for breach of contract, will the court find that there is an enforceable contract for $25,000?

(A) No, because the car cannot be sold unless both owners convey title.

(B) Yes, because the buyer was unaware of the interest of the builder's wife when he signed with the builder.

(C) Yes, regardless of the fact that the buyer was unaware of the interest of the builder's wife at the time he signed.

(D) Yes, but the contract is discharged by prospective inability of performance.

Question 17

A homeowner orally agreed to sell her land to a buyer for $79,000. As a condition of the sale, the buyer orally agreed to pay $5,000 of the purchase price to a creditor of the homeowner. The buyer asked his secretary to prepare a formal, typewritten copy of the contract and, in so doing, the buyer's secretary accidentally left out the condition to pay the $5,000 to the creditor. Both the buyer and the homeowner read the document before signing, but neither noticed the oversight. The buyer refuses to pay the $5,000 to the creditor, and the creditor sues the buyer for the $5,000.

In the creditor's suit against the buyer for $5,000, who will prevail?

(A) The buyer, because an agreement to pay the debt of another must be in writing, and the buyer's promise to pay $5,000 of the land sale purchase price to the homeowner's creditor was not included in the written buyer-homeowner agreement.

(B) The buyer, because a promise concerning an interest in land must be in writing, and the buyer's promise to pay $5,000 of the land sale purchase price to the homeowner's creditor was not included in the written buyer-homeowner agreement.

(C) The buyer, because oral statements are inadmissible to vary the terms of an unambiguous writing.

(D) The creditor, because his rights as a third-party beneficiary have vested.

Question 18

A testator died, leaving a valid holographic will that provided: "I want my only son to have my house when I die and to live there as long as he wants. After that, I want it to go to my grandchildren." At the time of the testator's death, her son was married and had a daughter, the testator's only grandchild, who was also married. Both the son and his wife moved into the house, but about six months later they separated and the wife moved out. The following year, the son and the granddaughter were involved in an airplane crash in which the son was immediately killed. Several weeks later, the granddaughter died, leaving her husband as her only heir. The son's wife brings a suit against the granddaughter's husband claiming an interest in the house as the son's widow. There is no statute in this jurisdiction that governs the issue of the right of an estranged spouse to inherit property from a decedent spouse, but if the son is found to own property at the time of his death, it is possible that the son's wife could inherit one-half as his surviving spouse.

In this suit, the son's wife should most likely:

(A) Prevail, because the testator's will gave the son a fee simple interest in the property.

(B) Prevail, because the devise to the testator's grandchildren in her will is invalid as it violates the Rule Against Perpetuities.

(C) Not prevail, because the granddaughter had a vested remainder interest subject to open, which became indefeasibly vested.

(D) Not prevail, because the granddaughter had a contingent remainder interest by reason of the testator's will, and the contingency occurred.

Question 19

A privately held manufacturing corporation was a major employer in a local town. The chief executive officer ("CEO") of the marketing division of the corporation was a respected figure with a good reputation in the community. The CEO was suddenly fired by the executive vice president of the main corporation, prompting rumors about the financial health of the marketing division. A reporter from the town newspaper interviewed the vice president and asked him why the CEO had been dismissed. The vice president said: "The CEO was fired because he was a bad manager and the marketing division lost money because of the CEO's stewardship." The vice president's statement was printed in the town newspaper, and was picked up by business-oriented publications.

If the CEO sues the town newspaper for defamation, which of the following statements with regard to damages is correct?

(A) To prevail, the CEO must plead and prove pecuniary damages, such as an inability to find a position with another company.

(B) To prevail, the CEO must show evidence of actual injury, such as mental distress.

(C) Damages are presumed because the written repetition of a slander is characterized as libel.

(D) Damages are presumed if the court determines that the CEO is not a public figure.

Question 20

In a medical malpractice action, a surgeon was called as an expert witness by the plaintiff and testified that the surgical procedure utilized by the defendant was so new and experimental as to constitute negligence under the accepted standard of practice in the relevant medical community. On cross-examination by the defendant's counsel, the surgeon was asked whether *Modern Surgical Procedures* was a reliable authority in his area of specialty. The surgeon said that it was and the defense counsel then asked if the surgeon had relied upon the treatise in reaching the conclusion that the defendant was negligent. The surgeon stated that he did not. Defense counsel now proposes to read a passage from the treatise stating that the surgical procedure at issue is widely accepted by responsible medical practitioners. The plaintiff's counsel objects.

How should the court rule?

(A) For the defendant, but it should also caution the jury that the evidence may be considered only in impeachment of the surgeon.

(B) For the defendant.

(C) For the plaintiff, because the surgeon did not rely upon the treatise in forming his expert opinion.

(D) For the plaintiff, because the passage from the treatise is inadmissible hearsay.

Question 21

Congress enacted a law requiring all civil service employees to retire by age 75, except when such employees are employed by the armed services. Civil service employees of the armed services are required to retire by age 65. An employee of the armed services just turned 65 years old. He files suit in the federal district court seeking a declaratory judgment that would prevent his employer from requiring him to retire before age 75.

The employee's strongest argument in support that the statute's provisions regarding civil service employees of the armed services are invalid is that this provision:

(A) Denies him the privileges and immunities of national citizenship.

(B) Denies him a property right without just compensation.

(C) Is invidious discrimination on the basis of age in violation of the Fifth Amendment.

(D) Is not within the enumerated powers of Congress under Article I, Section 8.

Question 22

On returning home from a bar at night, a drunk man passed by a building construction site on which were left several cranes and similar vehicles. Being an operator of heavy equipment, the man was familiar with the operation of such vehicles, and soon was driving a concrete transport truck through the aisles of the site and then out into the city. A curious police officer followed the truck for a few blocks, then pulled alongside in an attempt to determine whether it was operating for the purposes of construction. At that moment, the man swerved the truck to the left, crushing the police car as it ground to a halt. The police officer inside was killed.

In this jurisdiction, manslaughter is statutorily defined as "the killing of a human being in a criminally reckless manner." Criminal recklessness is "consciously disregarding a substantial and unjustifiable risk resulting from the actor's conduct." The man is tried for manslaughter in connection with the death of the city police officer.

The prosecution's best reply to the man's defense of intoxication in the charged manslaughter is that:

(A) Whether the man was intoxicated is not the crucial issue; whether the manner in which he was operating the truck was criminally reckless is determinative.

(B) Conscious risk-taking refers to the man's entire course of conduct, including drinking with the knowledge that he might become intoxicated and perform an act that might severely injure or kill someone.

(C) Intoxication is a defense to a crime only if the intoxication is involuntary.

(D) Intoxication is not a defense to the crime charged, because at common law manslaughter is a general intent crime.

Question 23

A landowner gratuitously conveyed his interest in land to a friend by quitclaim deed. The friend promptly and properly recorded her deed. Six months later, the landowner conveyed his interest in the same land to an investor for $50,000 by warranty deed, which was promptly and properly recorded.

As between the friend and the investor, who has the superior right to title to the land?

(A) The friend, regardless of the type of recording statute.

(B) The friend, because she recorded prior to the investor's recording.

(C) The investor, regardless of the type of recording statute.

(D) The investor, because it took by warranty deed rather than quitclaim deed.

Question 24

The defendant is on trial for fraudulently signing a check for $10,000. The defendant has denied that she signed the check. The prosecutor calls the landlord of the apartment building in which the defendant has resided for three months before her arrest. The landlord intends to testify that it is the defendant's signature on the check, and he bases his opinion of the authenticity of her signature on the ground that he saw her sign the lease to his apartment.

The trial court should find this testimony:

(A) Admissible, because there was only a short period of time between when the landlord saw her sign the lease and the time of trial.

(B) Admissible, because any person can testify to the authenticity of another's signature, if that witness has previously seen that person's signature.

(C) Inadmissible, because the landlord has seen the signature only once and is not acting as a handwriting expert.

(D) Inadmissible, because the testimony is inherently unreliable.

Question 25

A city ordinance makes it the misdemeanor of disorderly conduct to smoke on a city bus. A defendant boarded a city bus and lit a cigarette. The bus driver asked the defendant to put out her cigarette. The defendant ignored the driver and took a seat. The driver flagged down a passing police officer and told him that the defendant was smoking on the bus. Meanwhile, the defendant quickly extinguished the cigarette and put the butt in her purse before the officer had boarded the bus. The officer told the defendant that she was charged with disorderly conduct, and then he searched the purse that she was carrying. The officer found not only the recently extinguished cigarette butt, but also a marijuana cigarette in her purse. The defendant was then charged with possession of marijuana.

At the defendant's trial for possession, should the marijuana cigarette be admitted over the defendant's objection?

(A) Yes, because it was obtained in a search incident to a valid arrest.

(B) Yes, because the purse was within the defendant's "wingspan" or reach.

(C) No, because the arrest was invalid.

(D) No, because the police officer did not give the defendant *Miranda* warnings.

Question 26

A state statute provides a remedy for victims of employment discrimination. The statute requires complainants to bring charges before the state's fair employment commission within 180 days of the alleged unlawful employment practices. The commission then has 120 days to convene a fact-finding conference to obtain evidence, ascertain the parties' positions, and explore settlement possibilities. An employee was discharged from his job purportedly because of a physical handicap unrelated to his ability to perform his job. The employee filed a timely complaint, alleging unlawful termination of employment, as required by the statute. However, through inadvertence, the commission scheduled the fact-finding conference five days after the 120-day statutory period expired. At the conference, the employer moved that the charge be dismissed for lack of a timely conference. The commission denied the motion. The employer petitioned the state supreme court. The court held for the employer, stating that the failure to comply with the 120-day requirement deprived the commission of jurisdiction to consider the employee's charge. On appeal to the United States Supreme Court, the employee argues that his right to due process will be violated if the commission's error is allowed to extinguish his cause of action.

Which of the following best describes the viability of the employee's due process claim?

(A) The claim fails, because the employee had no protected property interest in his job.

(B) The claim fails, because the state legislature, having conferred on claimants a remedy for claims of unfair employment practices, has the prerogative to establish limiting procedures for such claims.

(C) The claim succeeds, because the employee had a protected property interest in the remedy.

(D) The claim succeeds, because of the fundamental unfairness of leaving the employee without a remedy.

Question 27

A plaintiff sued a defendant for personal injuries that the plaintiff suffered as a result of a battery committed on the plaintiff by the defendant. The defendant admits that the plaintiff was beaten up, but claims he had nothing to do with the plaintiff's injuries. At trial, the defendant testified in his own behalf that on the date that the plaintiff suffered his injuries, he (the defendant) was on an extended vacation in England, 2,000 miles away from the place where the battery occurred. The plaintiff's attorney did not cross-examine the defendant regarding that testimony. In rebuttal, the plaintiff's attorney calls a witness, who is willing to testify that one week after the plaintiff suffered his injuries, the defendant said to the witness, "I haven't been out of the country in five years."

The witness's testimony is:

(A) Admissible as a statement against interest by the defendant.

(B) Admissible as a prior inconsistent statement of the defendant.

(C) Admissible as an admission by the defendant.

(D) Inadmissible, because the defendant was not given an opportunity to comment on the statement prior to the witness's testimony.

Question 28

A suspect was arrested for a misdemeanor battery and was not provided *Miranda* warnings at that time. He was placed in a "holding pen" while waiting to post bond. Before he could do so, a detective in charge of investigating a string of burglaries noticed that the suspect matched the description of the serial burglar. The detective brought the suspect from the holding pen into a room specifically reserved for interrogation. The detective had the suspect take a seat next to the door, which the detective left open. The detective gave him *Miranda* warnings and then began questioning him about the burglaries. Caught by surprise that he was being questioned for the burglaries rather than the battery, the suspect signed the rights waiver and provided a statement confessing to the burglaries.

On proper motion, should the suspect's statement be suppressed?

(A) No, because the suspect was not arrested for burglary and was thus free to leave the interview.

(B) No, because proper *Miranda* warnings were given.

(C) Yes, because the detective failed to inform the suspect that the questioning would be about the burglaries.

(D) Yes, because he should have been provided *Miranda* warnings when he was arrested.

Question 29

A wealthy philanthropist designed and constructed a playground for children and dedicated the property to the city to be used as a public park. One day, while playing at the park, a 10-year-old boy fell off the monkey bars and broke his leg. The boy's parents filed a suit on his behalf against the philanthropist and the city, on the grounds of negligence in the design of the monkey bars. At the trial, the philanthropist was granted a directed verdict, because the city now owns the park. The boy's parents appealed.

The appellate court will most likely hold that:

(A) The decision to grant the directed verdict should be upheld, because the philanthropist was relieved of liability when he dedicated the park to the city.

(B) The decision to grant the directed verdict should be upheld, because the philanthropist designed and constructed the park in the public interest.

(C) The decision to grant the directed verdict should be overturned if the plaintiffs introduced evidence that the philanthropist dedicated the park to the city in an effort to avoid liability for the park's negligent design.

(D) The decision to grant the directed verdict should be overturned, because the philanthropist's liability for negligence was not affected by the dedication of the park to the city.

Question 30

The defendant was on trial for murder. The defendant called a witness to testify to an alibi. On cross-examination of the witness, the prosecutor asked, "Weren't you on the jury that acquitted the defendant of another criminal charge?"

The best reason for sustaining an objection to this question is that:

(A) The question goes beyond the scope of direct examination.

(B) The probative value of the answer would be substantially outweighed by its tendency to mislead.

(C) The question is a leading question.

(D) Prior jury service in a case involving a party renders the witness incompetent.

Question 31

An online search engine corporation wishing to acquire a smaller website entity hired a law firm to perform its target's audit for a bundled fee of $2.5 million. A first fee installment of $1 million was to be paid on completion of the data collection process, which was to be completed within three weeks. A second installment was to be paid on receipt of a valuation of the target website entity's liabilities, due after another five weeks. The contract provided in part that "any amendments to this agreement must be in writing signed by both parties."

On completion of data collection after 25 days, the law firm demanded payment of the first installment payment of $1 million. The client refused, but negotiations conducted between the parties resulted in an oral agreement that the client would pay $750,000 immediately, and then the $1.5 million second installment as originally agreed, after valuation of all liabilities.

Was the oral agreement that the client pay $750,000 to the law firm after 25 days a valid modification of the original agreement?

(A) Yes, because the Statute of Frauds does not bar subsequent oral modification of a written agreement to which it is applicable.

(B) Yes, because contracts for services may be orally modified, if consideration is present, despite the existence of a no-oral-modification clause.

(C) No, because it was not in writing.

(D) No, because it was not supported by consideration.

Question 32

The father of a girl whose horse crashed through a neighbor's fence told the neighbor that he would have the fence repaired immediately at his cost. The father hired a local contractor to do the work. The contractor did a poor job and did not fix the fence properly.

Assuming that there was an enforceable agreement between the father and the neighbor, would the neighbor have an action against the contractor?

(A) No, because there was no agreement between the contractor and the neighbor with regard to the repairs on the fence.

(B) No, because the neighbor was only an incidental beneficiary of the contract between the contractor and the father.

(C) Yes, because the neighbor was a creditor beneficiary of the contract between the contractor and the father.

(D) Yes, because the neighbor was a donee beneficiary of the contract between the contractor and the father.

Question 33

An investor and a farmer purchased a tract of land, taking title as joint tenants. The investor orally agreed to the farmer's planting crops on the southern half of the property. Subsequently, the farmer died, leaving his entire estate to his daughter.

In an action for partition, if the investor is adjudged to be the owner of all of the property, it will most likely be because:

(A) The Statute of Frauds prevents the enforcement of the investor's oral agreement.

(B) The record title of the property as a joint tenancy can be changed only by a duly recorded instrument.

(C) The farmer could not unilaterally sever the joint tenancy.

(D) The farmer's expenditure of funds in planting the crops in reliance on the investor's oral promise estops the investor from denying the oral permission.

GO ON TO THE NEXT PAGE

Question 34

A state statute makes it a crime to operate a motor vehicle while intoxicated. Another state statute provides that a blood alcohol level of .10 raises a presumption of intoxication. A state police officer spotted the defendant's pickup weaving from lane to lane on the highway and stopped the truck. The defendant took a breathalyzer test that indicated a .12 blood alcohol level. He was charged with operating a motor vehicle while intoxicated.

At trial, at the close of all the evidence, and over the defendant's objection, the judge instructed the jury: "If you are convinced that, at the time the defendant was pulled over, his blood alcohol level was .10 or greater, you must presume that he was intoxicated." The defendant was convicted, and he is appealing on the ground that the judge's instruction was improper.

The appellate court should:

(A) Affirm, because the judge may instruct the jury on the law, and he merely cited the state statute.

(B) Reverse and remand, because the jury should have been left to draw its own conclusion without the judge's instruction.

(C) Reverse and remand, because the presumption might lead the jury to believe that the prosecution did not have to meet its burden of proving the defendant guilty beyond a reasonable doubt.

(D) Reverse and remand, because the instruction was substantially more prejudicial than probative.

Question 35

A city ordinance prohibits the distribution of pamphlets "on public sidewalks or other public areas when foot traffic is sufficiently heavy and the manner of distribution of the pamphlets causes obstruction of the foot traffic so as to result in spillover onto public streets where vehicular traffic creates a danger to human life." The state fair is held at fairgrounds whose entrances lie along a busy multilane street. A demonstrator was distributing pamphlets advocating repeal of the federal milk price support program at the state fair. He attracted a crowd of about 10 farmers and children outside the fairgrounds entrance at which he stood, but most of the few fairgoers entering the fair at that late afternoon time simply ignored him. When one of the dairy farmers became irate and threatened to "knock his block off," the demonstrator was arrested by a fair security guard and subsequently prosecuted under the city ordinance.

Which of the following statements is correct regarding the city ordinance and the demonstrator's prosecution?

(A) The ordinance is void on its face and void as applied to the demonstrator.

(B) The ordinance is valid on its face but void as applied to the demonstrator.

(C) The ordinance is valid on its face and valid as applied to the demonstrator.

(D) The ordinance is void on its face but valid as applied to the demonstrator.

Question 36

The defendant is on trial for embezzlement. He does not take the stand.

Which of the defendant's previous convictions is most likely to be admitted into evidence against him?

(A) A seven-year-old conviction for arson, a felony.

(B) A 12-year-old conviction for embezzlement, a felony.

(C) A six-month-old conviction for disorderly conduct, a misdemeanor.

(D) A two-year-old conviction for felonious sexual assault.

Question 37

A farmer asked his adjoining neighbor if he could build an irrigation ditch from the neighbor's natural fresh-water spring to his property to provide water for his cattle. Because the spring supplied more than enough water to meet the neighbor's needs, she agreed, provided that the farmer construct the ditch in such a manner that it would need the least maintenance possible so that he did not need to continually enter her land. The farmer constructed a concrete irrigation ditch from the spring to the land at a cost of $25,000. The only maintenance required on the ditch was a semiannual cleaning. Three years later, the neighbor informed the farmer that her water needs had increased, and he could no longer take water from the spring. In addition, the neighbor did not allow the farmer onto her land to do the semiannual cleaning, resulting in the blocking of the ditch. The farmer wishes to keep water flowing through the irrigation ditch to his land.

Which of the following would be the farmer's strongest argument?

(A) The farmer owns a valid easement appurtenant to the neighbor's property.

(B) Because the neighbor has allowed the farmer to construct the irrigation ditch, the neighbor would be estopped from preventing the farmer from coming onto her land.

(C) The farmer, although a licensee, has expended such a substantial sum of money in constructing the irrigation ditch that the neighbor may not terminate the farmer's license now.

(D) The farmer, although a licensee, may continue to enter the neighbor's property to clean and maintain the ditch until he is able to acquire another source of water.

Question 38

A professor had his laptop computer stolen from his office. He went to a computer resale shop to find a replacement and saw what he mistakenly thought was his computer. He questioned the owner of the shop, who told him that someone had just sold her the computer, but she refused to give him any information about the seller and refused to let him inspect the computer more closely. That night, after the shop was closed, the professor forced open the back door. After turning over the laptop to check the serial number, the professor realized that it was not the one that was stolen from his office. Nonetheless, he decided to keep it. The owner's clerk, who, unbeknownst to the professor lived in a room in the back of the shop, heard someone breaking in and called the police. The professor was arrested as he was exiting the shop and is charged with larceny and burglary in a common law jurisdiction.

Of which crimes may he be convicted and sentenced?

(A) Larceny, but not burglary.

(B) Burglary, but not larceny.

(C) Neither burglary nor larceny.

(D) Both burglary and larceny.

Question 39

An owner of a rental property that generated steady income properly executed a will devising the property: "To my trustee in trust to pay the educational expenses of my children, but if any of them do not graduate from the state university by the age of 30, then for the benefit of the state university's scholarship fund for local town residents." When the owner died, he had three young children, all under the age of five. The jurisdiction in which the parties and property are located retains the common law Rule Against Perpetuities.

Is the gift in trust to the state university valid?

(A) Yes, because the gift is a valid charitable trust.

(B) Yes, because the doctrine of cy pres is applicable.

(C) No, because the gift is not for a valid charitable purpose.

(D) No, because the gift violates the Rule Against Perpetuities.

Question 40

The plaintiff sued the defendant for damages and injuries after the defendant's car struck the plaintiff's car in an intersection. The plaintiff wanted a witness who lived on the corner and had seen the accident to testify on his behalf. However, the witness's recollection of the accident was very fuzzy because the trial did not take place until almost three years after the accident. The night before she was scheduled to testify, the witness consulted her diary, in which she had noted at the time that the defendant's car did not come to a complete stop at the stop sign and entered the intersection, striking the car driven by the plaintiff after the plaintiff's car had already entered the intersection. The plaintiff's attorney called the witness to the stand, and she testified to those details.

On cross-examination, the defendant's attorney asked the witness if she had consulted any materials to prepare for her testimony. The witness admitted that her recollection of the accident had been fuzzy and that she had consulted her diary the night before her testimony. The defendant's attorney immediately moved that the witness's testimony be stricken from the record.

The court should rule that:

(A) The witness's testimony is admissible, because, after reviewing her notes, she had an independent recollection of the event.

(B) The witness's testimony is admissible, because the contents of her diary are protected under the work product rule.

(C) The witness's testimony should be stricken, because her diary was not made available to the opposing party prior to trial.

(D) The witness's testimony should be stricken, because it is not the best evidence.

Question 41

While investigating the most recent of a series of murders, the detective in charge of the crime scene was approached by an onlooker who seemed to have detailed knowledge of the murders. The detective remembered seeing the onlooker at other murder scenes and became suspicious. He told the onlooker not to leave until the detective had the opportunity to ask him a few questions. After finishing with the crime scene, the detective started to question the onlooker at the scene of the crime without giving the onlooker the *Miranda* warnings. The onlooker eventually revealed details of the crime that were never made available to the public. As a result, the onlooker was arrested and charged with several murders. At trial, the onlooker testified that he believed that he could not leave until he had spoken with the detective. The onlooker's defense counsel moves to suppress the statements made to the homicide detective.

What is the most likely result?

(A) The motion will not be granted because the onlooker was not in custody.

(B) The motion will not be granted because the onlooker initiated the contact with the homicide detective.

(C) The motion will be granted because the onlooker believed he was not free to leave.

(D) The motion will be granted because the detective was required to give the onlooker *Miranda* warnings once the detective suspected the onlooker of having committed the crime.

Question 42

A grantor executed a deed conveying a tract of land to a private school "for the life of my wife, and then to my children, their heirs and assigns, in equal shares; provided, however, that the school shall use the premises for educational purposes only." The school then erected a temporary building on the land and conducted certain classes within the building for several years. Three years ago, a geological survey of the area revealed that there were valuable minerals beneath the surface of the land. The school granted a mining company the right to remove the minerals from a one-acre portion of the land upon the payment of a royalty. The mining company has conducted mining operations on the one-acre portion of the land while the school has continued to conduct classes in the temporary building located on the land. Although both the grantor and his wife are still alive, both of their children file suit against the school and the mining company seeking damages for the removal of minerals, an injunction to prevent further removal, and all other appropriate remedies.

Which of the following would be the most likely result?

(A) The injunction should be granted, and damages should be recovered but impounded for future distribution.

(B) The injunction and damages should be granted, because the interest of the school terminated with the first removal of minerals from the land.

(C) The injunction should be granted, but damages should be denied because the grantor and his wife are not parties to the action.

(D) The injunction should be denied, but damages should be awarded.

Question 43

A state legislator was the chairman of a committee that disbursed funds to schools in the state for various projects. The federal government supplied a portion of the funds as part of a federal revenue sharing plan. The legislator was charged with a violation of federal law when he and his committee made a $10,000 grant for textbooks to a private school for whites only. The legislator's defense is that as chairman of this committee he was acting in the course of his legislative duties, and thus, immune from federal interference.

The best argument that would support the legislator's constitutional claim is:

(A) If the state law authorizes the legislator's action, he cannot be prosecuted for violation of a federal law.

(B) The doctrine of federalism forbids the federal government from restricting the state's rights regarding the education of minor children within the state.

(C) The Tenth Amendment prevents the federal government from interfering with a member of the state's legislature in the performance of his legislative duties.

(D) As long as the private school is not a parochial school, federal law cannot limit a state's rights regarding the education of minor children within the state.

Question 44

The owner of a cookie factory contracted with an industrial oven manufacturer for the installation of new baking equipment. The written contract included the following provisions: "On installation of the new cookie baking system, the owner will pay to the oven manufacturer a total price of $120,000. Installation must be completed by January 15."

Installation of the new system at the client's plant was completed on January 30 and resulted in a great increase of cookie production through faster baking. The oven manufacturer sent his bill to the cookie factory owner, stating that the new baking equipment system was in place and operating as promised, and demanding the $120,000 payment. The owner refused to make any payment, noting in her reply letter that the system had not been installed by January 15, as promised.

If the oven manufacturer is found to be in breach because of the late installation of the baking equipment system, may he successfully bring an action to recover the reasonable value of his services?

(A) No, because failure of an express condition precedent would excuse the factory owner of her duty to pay the oven manufacturer.

(B) No, because a claim for reasonable value of services would be inconsistent with a claim by the factory owner against the oven manufacturer for breach of contract.

(C) Yes, because the factory owner continued to use the new baking system and was aware that the oven manufacturer expected to be paid for his services.

(D) Yes, because the factory owner continued to use the new baking system and realized increased production as a consequence of the contractual relationship between the parties.

Question 45

A large dairy regularly supplied milk to local grocery stores. A large grocery store located in the same city as the dairy had not previously done business with the dairy. It sent a written order to the dairy for 50 cases of homogenized whole milk at the wholesale market price of $10 per case for prompt shipment. The warehouse clerk at the dairy facility negligently shipped 50 cases of low-fat milk instead of the grade that was ordered.

When the milk is delivered at the grocery store by a common carrier, which of the following is the most appropriate statement of the parties' rights and duties?

(A) The store must accept the delivery, even though it is nonconforming, because a contract was formed when the dairy shipped it.

(B) A contract was formed but breached by the dairy when it shipped nonconforming goods, which the store has no obligation to accept.

(C) Because the goods are nonconforming, the store can treat the delivery as a counter-offer and refuse acceptance.

(D) The dairy's shipment of the milk is a counteroffer, but the store is under an obligation to reship it to the dairy at the dairy's expense if it decides not to accept the delivery.

Question 46

After negotiations, a painting contractor agreed with a homeowner to paint the exterior of her house for $20,000. The painter further agreed to use only top quality paint because the homeowner wanted the paint to last for many years. The painter filled out his standard form contract, but deliberately did not include a brand name for the paint that he would use. After telling the homeowner that the contract contained the terms agreed to, she signed without reading it. On completion of the job, the homeowner saw some empty paint cans in the painter's truck and realized that top quality paint had not been used.

If the homeowner sues the paint contractor for misrepresentation, any statements made by the painter before the contract was signed:

(A) Would be barred by the parol evidence rule.

(B) Would not be barred by the parol evidence rule.

(C) Would be admitted if the contract was proved to be an incomplete agreement of the parties.

(D) Would not be admitted because they occurred prior to the signing of the contract.

Question 47

A son was furious when his father sold some property that he had promised to bequeath to the son in his will. The son instituted proceedings to have his father committed to a psychiatric facility. The son testified falsely at trial that his father was addicted to prescription medicines and had abused the son and other family members when the son was a child. The administrative judge presiding over the trial did not believe the son's testimony and found the father competent. As a result of the testimony, the father suffered severe distress and anxiety.

If the father sues his son for intentional infliction of emotional distress due to the son's testimony, who is likely to prevail?

(A) The father, because the son acted with knowledge of falsity or reckless disregard as to the truth or falsity of his statements.

(B) The father, because the son's statements were extreme and outrageous.

(C) The son, because the father did not suffer physical injury.

(D) The son, because his testimony is privileged.

Question 48

A father purchased the largest model rocket that he could find, hoping to interest his daughter in space engineering. Several days later, the father and daughter went to an open area in a state park to fire the rocket. The father was in such a rush to fire the rocket that he failed to remove the safety key from the launch system. Upon connecting the launch system to the rocket motor, the motor exploded, seriously injuring the father and daughter.

A negligence action was brought on behalf of the daughter against the rocket manufacturer. At trial, evidence shows that the explosion resulted from a manufacturing defect in the motor. Evidence also shows that the motor would not have exploded while they were connecting the launch system if the father had removed the safety key.

Will the daughter recover for her injuries?

(A) No, because she did not purchase the rocket.

(B) No, because the father was negligent in failing to remove the safety key before connecting the motor.

(C) Yes, if the trier of fact determines that the defect in the motor could have been discovered by the rocket manufacturer in the exercise of reasonable care.

(D) Yes, unless the manufacturer shows that the defect in the motor could have been discovered by the rocket retailer in the exercise of reasonable care.

Question 49

A standard commercial unit for widgets is one gross, *i.e.,* 144 widgets. A buyer ordered from a seller 50 gross of widgets at $100 per gross, with the widgets to be delivered on or before October 3. On September 15, 50 boxes arrived from the seller. Each box was labeled, "Widgets—one gross."

On finding that one of the boxes contains 143 widgets, the buyer can:

(A) Seek cover.

(B) Immediately sue for breach.

(C) Reject the entire shipment of widgets.

(D) Do nothing because one less widget is not material.

Question 50

To buy a house, an investor secured a $10,000 mortgage from a bank. The bank promptly and properly recorded its mortgage. Subsequently, the investor financed certain improvements to the house with a $2,000 mortgage on the land from a finance company. The finance company promptly and properly recorded its mortgage. Before the investor made a payment on either mortgage, the federal government announced that it would begin storing nuclear waste products in the area. The value of property, including the investor's house, plummeted. The investor did not pay either the bank or the finance company, and the bank brought a proper action to foreclose, notifying both the investor and the finance company. A buyer bought the house at the foreclosure sale for $6,000, which was its fair market value. There are no special statutes in the jurisdiction regarding deficiency judgments.

The investor owes:

(A) $5,000 to the bank and $1,000 to the finance company.

(B) $4,000 to the bank and $2,000 to the finance company.

(C) Nothing to the bank and $2,000 to the finance company.

(D) $4,000 to the bank and nothing to the finance company.

Question 51

A defendant was convicted of burglary after the prosecution established at a jury trial that the defendant broke into the victim's house at night by cutting open a window screen and climbing into a bedroom. The evidence also established that the defendant was frightened into leaping out the window when the victim pulled a gun from beneath her pillow. The defendant testified in his own defense, stating that he entered the house merely to use the telephone. His lawyer thus argued that the defendant lacked the required intent for burglary. The trial court, after instructing the jury on the elements of burglary, said, "If you find that by a fair preponderance of the evidence the defendant has shown that he intended to use the telephone when he entered the victim's home, then you must find him not guilty."

If the defendant appeals his conviction, will he likely obtain a reversal?

(A) Yes, because the trial court's instruction permitted the jury to use a preponderance standard rather than beyond a reasonable doubt standard.

(B) Yes, because the trial court's instruction placed the burden of proof on the defendant.

(C) No, because any error in instructions was harmless, because it is more likely than not that the jury would have convicted him anyway.

(D) No, because the trial court is permitted to comment upon the evidence.

Question 52

A city that lies astride a major interstate highway recently passed a referendum declaring itself a "nuclear free zone." The referendum included a provision making criminal any importation of specified nuclear materials into the city limits. The law was immediately challenged in federal court by an interstate trucking firm that regularly transported prohibited nuclear materials through the city on the highway. The case ultimately reached the United States Supreme Court, which held in a 5-4 decision that the challenged ordinance was constitutional because the city had a rational basis for concluding that the citizens of the city would be safer if the prohibited materials were kept outside of town, and because the ordinance did not unduly burden interstate commerce. Many other towns and cities throughout the nation considered similar enactments after the Supreme Court decision was announced. You are a lobbyist hired by the trucking industry to persuade Congress that a federal statute prohibiting the state regulation of interstate transportation of nuclear materials must immediately be enacted. One congressman has tentatively agreed to sponsor such legislation, but wants to know whether such a federal statute would pass constitutional muster.

You should advise the congressman that the proposed statute would probably be held:

(A) Unconstitutional, because the Supreme Court has already ruled that local governments may prohibit specified nuclear materials from crossing their borders.

(B) Unconstitutional, because the disparate treatment of interstate versus intrastate carriers of nuclear materials would violate the Equal Protection Clause of the Fourteenth Amendment.

(C) Constitutional, because Congress has plenary power to regulate interstate commerce.

(D) Constitutional, because the Supremacy Clause requires that state enactments bow to conflicting federal legislation.

Question 53

A motorist was driving along a narrow, winding road when his car ran out of gas. Because the road had no shoulders, the motorist pushed his car onto the driveway of a landowner. Finding no one home at the house, the motorist started walking toward a gas station he had passed a mile back. While he was gone, the landowner returned and found the car in his driveway, with two of its wheels partially on his flower garden. Although the landowner had not posted any "no trespassing" signs, he believed he had the right to remove the car from his property. The car was unlocked, so he released the parking brake and carefully pushed the car back onto the road, and then reset the brake. Before the motorist could return, a truck had sideswiped the car, damaging it.

Can the motorist recover against the landowner for the damage to his car?

(A) Yes, because the landowner had not posted any "no trespassing" signs on his property.

(B) Yes, because the motorist was privileged to leave his car there.

(C) No, because the motorist's car damaged the landowner's property.

(D) No, because the landowner reasonably believed that he had a right to remove the car from his property.

Question 54

A licensed real estate broker and a homeowner entered into a written listing agreement in which the homeowner promised, among other things, to pay the real estate broker a 6% commission of the selling price of the homeowner's home if the real estate broker obtained a buyer ready, willing, and able to purchase it. The homeowner's home was listed for $180,000 in a service made available to real estate professionals.

A prospective buyer, after going to the real estate broker's office and viewing the homeowner's home, submitted a written offer to purchase the home for $180,000. The homeowner rejected this offer by not accepting it within the stated period. The buyer brings an action against the homeowner for specific performance, seeking to compel him to sell the home.

What is the probable outcome of this litigation?

(A) The homeowner will win, because no writing or writings constitute a memorandum sufficient to satisfy the Statute of Frauds.

(B) The homeowner will win, because the buyer's remedy at law is adequate.

(C) The buyer will win, because he is a third-party beneficiary of the agreement between the homeowner and the real estate broker.

(D) The buyer will win, because there is a memorandum that satisfies the Statute of Frauds.

GO ON TO THE NEXT PAGE

Question 55

A physics teacher at the local college was also a model rocket enthusiast. He owned a large parcel of land in the country, and on many occasions he would launch one of his rockets from the back area of his property. Although none of the teacher's rockets ever came near his neighbor's property, the neighbor complained to the teacher several times about his hobby and the fact that the teacher stored flammable fuels in his house. Once, his neighbor complained to the county sheriff, whereupon the teacher was charged with violating a local ordinance that prohibits the improper storage of flammable liquids on residential property. He was given a warning and told that he must have proper storage permits and facilities if he intended to keep the fuels for his model rockets on his property. Although the teacher obtained the proper permits to build underground storage tanks for his fuels, he continued to store them in 55-gallon drums in a shed located on the edge of his property farthest away from his neighbor.

Eventually, his neighbor brought a suit based on public nuisance against the teacher, seeking an injunction against the teacher to prevent him from storing flammable liquids on his property and launching model rockets.

The teacher's best defense is that:

(A) He obtained a permit from the city to build storage tanks for the fuels.

(B) There is no showing that his neighbor suffered any special damage.

(C) This is not a residential neighborhood.

(D) There is no specific ordinance that prohibits the teacher from launching model rockets on his own property.

Question 56

A couple going through a divorce proceeding was contesting the value of their house. The husband, a realtor, was very familiar with property values in the area and had personally prepared an appraisal shortly before commencement of the divorce proceedings. The appraisal document, which was subsequently destroyed by the husband, stated that the house was worth $200,000. Their next-door neighbor had seen this appraisal document prior to its destruction.

During settlement negotiations, the husband maintained that the house was worth $180,000. When negotiations proved to be fruitless, the parties proceeded to trial. At trial, the wife called the neighbor to testify as to the value placed on the house in the appraisal document. The neighbor's only knowledge as to the house's value comes from having read the document. The husband's attorney objects.

May the neighbor testify as to the value stated in the appraisal document?

(A) Yes, because she has personal knowledge of the contents of the document.

(B) Yes, because the husband has destroyed the document.

(C) No, because the appraisal document is the best, and thus the only admissible, evidence.

(D) No, because the neighbor's testimony would be inadmissible hearsay.

Question 57

During a gang shootout in a city, a gangbanger looked for a rival among the combatants because he wanted to kill him. Believing a bystander to be the rival, the gangbanger shot at the bystander and missed. The bullet passed through a window and killed a homeowner, who was asleep on her sofa.

The gangbanger may properly be convicted of:

(A) Attempted murder of the rival.

(B) Attempted murder of the bystander.

(C) Attempted murder of the bystander and murder of the homeowner.

(D) Manslaughter of the homeowner.

Question 58

The defendant is being tried for murder. A witness to the crime had aided the police artist in making the composite picture by which the defendant was identified. This witness disappeared before trial, and the prosecutor now wants to offer the sketch into evidence.

The sketch is:

(A) Inadmissible, under the best evidence rule.

(B) Inadmissible, as hearsay not within any exception.

(C) Admissible, as a record by a public employee.

(D) Admissible, as a prior identification.

Question 59

During an arson trial, the defendant took the stand in her own defense and denied committing the crime. Her attorney asked her what she said to the police when she was first arrested, and she replied that she had told them that she knew nothing about the arson because she was in another state at the time.

Her answer should be:

(A) Stricken, because it is self-serving.

(B) Stricken, because it is hearsay.

(C) Admissible, because she can competently testify to statements she made herself.

(D) Admissible, as a prior consistent statement.

Question 60

While a driver was driving someone else's car, he hit a plaintiff who was walking in a pedestrian right-of-way. The plaintiff sued both the driver and the owner of the car, alleging that the driver had negligently driven the car and that the owner had negligently permitted an unfit driver to use her car. At trial, the plaintiff calls his first witness. The witness testifies that within the last several months he is aware of three instances in which the driver has engaged in reckless driving. Both the driver and the owner object to the admission of this evidence.

The objection should be:

(A) Sustained, because the driver's character is not in issue.

(B) Sustained, because specific evidence of misconduct is not admissible to establish evidence of character.

(C) Overruled as to the case against the owner, but sustained as to the case against the driver.

(D) Overruled, because the evidence goes to the issue of the driver's criminal negligence.

GO ON TO THE NEXT PAGE

Question 61

The police, suspecting that the defendant was dealing drugs, observed several people walk up to the defendant's door, knock on his door, and then exchange cash for small packages that the police believed contained drugs. Two uniformed police officers then walked up to the door and knocked. The defendant answered the door, and one police officer asked if they could come in and take a look around. The defendant, believing that he had no other choice but to let the officers inside, agreed. Once inside, they discovered equipment used for making methamphetamine and several tablets of methamphetamine that were sitting on a table covered by a bed sheet. One officer promptly arrested and handcuffed the defendant while the other seized the equipment and tablets. Prior to his trial for the illegal manufacture and possession of methamphetamine, the defendant moved to suppress the evidence as having been illegally seized.

The motion should be:

(A) Denied, because the defendant allowed the police officers to enter his home and look around.

(B) Denied, because exigent circumstances existed for the warrantless seizure of the evidence.

(C) Granted, because the police should have secured the area and obtained a warrant to seize the evidence.

(D) Granted, because the defendant's consent was not voluntary.

Question 62

Congress enacted a statute, over the President's veto, that granted Congress the power to compel the President to remove United States troops from foreign territory when such troops have for 60 days been engaged in hostilities and there has been no formal declaration of war. The statute also provided that Congress may force the President to withdraw the troops before the 60 days have elapsed if Congress passes a joint resolution to that effect.

Which of the following statements best describes the likely result of judicial review of the constitutional validity of this statute?

(A) The statute is a valid exercise of Congress's authority under the war power.

(B) The statute is constitutionally suspect as an infringement on the President's exclusive power, as commander in chief, over matters relating to war.

(C) The statute is a valid exercise of Congress's foreign relations powers.

(D) The statute is constitutionally suspect, because the joint resolution is not subject to a presidential veto.

Question 63

In response to lobbying, Congress passed legislation appropriating $200 million for grants-in-aid to domestic horse liniment manufacturers and providing some degree of protection from foreign competition. However, because of concern about inefficiencies in the industry, the legislation was amended to allow the Secretary of Commerce the authority to deny grants to horse liniment manufacturers who failed to meet certain "management efficiency standards" outlined in the legislation.

One liniment manufacturer and a member of the trade association petitioned the Secretary of Commerce for a $15 million grant. This figure equaled the amount it would be entitled to under the legislation, based on the number of its employees, plants, and upon its average production of horse liniment over a 10-year period. The Secretary of Commerce refused to award the funds, because she determined that the liniment manufacturer was making no attempt to improve its management efficiency. The liniment manufacturer filed suit against the Secretary of Commerce, asserting that the power granted to the Secretary was unconstitutional.

Is the legislation constitutional?

(A) Yes, because the Secretary of Commerce, as a representative of the executive branch, may be granted regulatory authority.

(B) Yes, because the executive branch, represented by the Secretary of Commerce, shares power with Congress in the field of foreign commerce.

(C) No, because there was an improper delegation of legislative power.

(D) No, because the executive branch may not impound funds appropriated by Congress.

Question 64

A seller received a written offer in the mail signed by a buyer to purchase the seller's land for $50,000. The written offer was legally sufficient to form a written contract for the sale of the land. The seller called the buyer and said that the offer was acceptable, but that she wanted her attorney to review it. The seller asked her attorney to prepare a formal contract for the sale of the land according to the same terms and conditions in the written offer. When the attorney had finished, the seller signed the contract and mailed it to the buyer. Later that day, before the buyer had received the contract, a developer called the seller and offered to buy the land for $60,000, which the seller accepted immediately over the phone. The seller called the buyer and told him that she had received and accepted a higher offer. The seller then signed a written contract to sell the land to the developer. When the developer received the contract, he signed it and then promptly and properly recorded it, and sent the seller the specified down payment. The buyer received the written contract from the seller the next day. The recording statute in the jurisdiction provides: "Any conveyance of an interest in land, other than a lease for less than one year, shall not be valid against a subsequent purchaser for value, without notice thereof, whose conveyance is first recorded."

In an appropriate action brought by the buyer against the seller and the developer for specific performance and to quiet title, the buyer will:

(A) Win, because the buyer's written offer satisfies the Statute of Frauds.

(B) Win, because the contract of sale prepared by the attorney satisfies the Statute of Frauds.

(C) Lose, because the buyer never entered into a binding contract with the seller.

(D) Lose, because the recording statute protects the developer.

Question 65

An entrepreneur who owned a small bed-and-breakfast sold the establishment to a retired couple for $500,000. The couple paid $200,000 in cash and agreed to pay the balance to the entrepreneur in equal monthly installments over a 10-year period. A few years later, when his son started law school, the entrepreneur sent a letter to the couple (with a copy to his son) instructing them to send his son $500 a month from the money they owed to him until he instructed them to do otherwise. When the son finished law school three years later, the entrepreneur sent the couple another letter (again, with a copy to his son) telling them to stop sending the $500 monthly payment to his son and resume sending the full monthly installments to him. Two years after that, the entrepreneur died, leaving his entire estate (including the balance due on the note from the couple) to his new bride. The entrepreneur's son sues the couple, claiming he is entitled to receive $500 per month from the time he finished law school until all sums due to the entrepreneur had been paid.

Who will prevail?

(A) The son, because his rights were vested when the couple was instructed to make the payments to him.

(B) The son, because he had changed his position in reliance on the entrepreneur's agreement.

(C) The couple, because the entrepreneur had the right to stop making payments to his son at any time.

(D) The couple, because the son was only a gratuitous assignee and had no protected rights against the couple.

Question 66

The federal Food Safety Act provides for sporadic inspections of produce in order to prevent illness among consumers. After several widespread outbreaks of illness involving escarole, a new and more accurate procedure for determining the presence of harmful bacteria was developed. The new procedure was used in a limited area on escarole shipped locally within a large escarole-producing state to determine its effectiveness. Subsequently, Congress enacted an additional provision to the Act, levying a one cent tax on each crate of escarole so inspected.

This provision is:

(A) Constitutional, under the Supremacy Clause.

(B) Constitutional, because it is a proper exercise of congressional power to raise revenue.

(C) Unconstitutional, because the escarole subject to the inspection is not being sold in interstate commerce.

(D) Unconstitutional, because it interferes with state sovereignty.

Question 67

A landowner owned two adjoining parcels of land, a ranch and a farm. She contracted to sell the ranch to her brother, who promptly and properly recorded the deed. Because the ranch had no direct access to a public road, the landowner wrote into the deed, "my brother, his heirs and assigns shall have the right to use the existing dirt path along the eastern border of the farm for ingress and egress to the ranch." A few years later, the landowner sold the farm to a developer, who decided to subdivide the farm into lots for single-family residences. Because no street in the proposed subdivision would align with the dirt path mentioned in the deed from the landowner to the brother, the brother would be without ingress and/or egress to his land. The brother instituted an appropriate action to enjoin the blocking of the dirt path.

The most likely result is that judgment will be for:

(A) The brother, because the owner of the servient tenement cannot obstruct an express easement.

(B) The brother, because he has a way by necessity.

(C) The developer, because there has been a significant change in conditions and circumstances.

(D) The developer, because the appropriate remedy for the brother is damages, not injunction.

Question 68

A testator wanted to give his home to his brother. The testator executed a warranty deed conveying the home to his brother. The testator then wrote a letter to his brother saying, "Dear brother, my home is now yours." He put the letter and deed in an envelope and wrote the following on the outside of the envelope and signed it: "Cousin, you are to give this deed to my brother when I die. Until then, you should safeguard this envelope and the documents inside." The testator delivered these items to his cousin and continued to live in his home by himself. Two years later, the testator executed a will leaving all of his property to his sister. Seven years later, the testator died. Shortly thereafter, the cousin delivered the envelope containing the deed to the testator's brother, who promptly recorded the deed. The testator's will has been admitted to probate and his executor has brought an appropriate action against the brother to determine the title to the testator's home.

The court should rule:

(A) For the sister, because the deed was not effectively delivered before the testator died.

(B) For the sister, because the deed was not recorded before the grantor died.

(C) For the brother, because the deed effectively conveyed title when it was executed.

(D) For the brother, because the testator no longer owned his home when he died.

Question 69

A plaintiff brought an action in federal court against a state government, seeking monetary damages. The state moved to have the case dismissed for lack of jurisdiction, citing the Eleventh Amendment of the United States Constitution.

Which of the following facts would support a denial of the state's motion?

(A) The plaintiff is a private citizen of the defendant state.

(B) The plaintiff is a Native American tribe.

(C) The plaintiff is a neighboring state.

(D) The plaintiff is a foreign government.

Question 70

A federal statute designed to stop organized crime enumerated certain activities as crimes and provided that, in addition to charging these activities as the crimes they constitute, the activities would also constitute the criminal act of intentional furtherance of the goals of organized crime. Among the enumerated activities was the interstate distribution of cocaine. The statute's constitutionality has been upheld by the Supreme Court.

The defendant was arrested by federal agents after having driven a truck containing cocaine from Florida to Illinois, where he delivered his illicit cargo as directed. At trial, the defendant is convicted of interstate distribution of cocaine in violation of federal law, and convicted of a violation of the federal statute above.

The defendant may be sentenced:

(A) Under either statute, but not both.

(B) Under both statutes.

(C) Only under the statute that carries a lesser maximum sentence.

(D) Only under the statute that carries a greater maximum sentence.

Question 71

A decedent died without having executed a will, leaving a substantial estate to be distributed by the probate court. The jurisdiction's applicable statute provides that where a decedent leaves neither issue nor spouse, nor parents, his estate goes to his brothers and sisters and their descendants. The decedent was never married, had no children, and both of his parents are dead. A woman whose birth certificate was destroyed by fire seeks to establish that she is the daughter of the decedent's only sibling, who is now also deceased. The woman offers into evidence a statement in a properly recorded trust instrument. The instrument was executed by the decedent's father and recited that certain specified real property conveyed by the decedent's father into the trust should be held for her benefit, as "my loving granddaughter." The document actually offered is an enlarged print photocopy of microfilm records, authenticated by an employee of the county.

The trial court should:

(A) Exclude the evidence, because it is not the best evidence.

(B) Exclude the evidence, because it is inadmissible hearsay not within any recognized exception.

(C) Admit the evidence, because it is a record of a document affecting an interest in property.

(D) Admit the evidence, because it constitutes a past recollection recorded.

Question 72

A man was staying overnight at a small hotel when he received a phone call telling him that his child had been severely injured and was being rushed to the hospital. The man quickly booked a flight to his home in another part of the state and rushed out to the lobby to check out. He discovered, however, that there was a long line ahead of him and only one clerk on duty. The man realized that he would never make it to the airport in time for his flight if he continued to wait in line, so he left without paying his bill and flew home. That evening, he wrote a letter to the hotel, apologizing for his swift departure and enclosing payment for two nights' lodging; he also added an extra $25 "to cover any inconvenience and billing expense" he may have caused. Meanwhile, the hotel's manager discovered that the man had left without paying. On the hotel's behalf, the hotel manager signed a complaint with the state police, charging the man with theft of services. The police had a warrant sworn out for the man's arrest. The day after the man left the hotel, the hotel received the man's letter and payment. However, no one notified the police that the man had paid his bill. Three days after the man left the hotel, the state police, armed with a warrant, came to the man's office and arrested him. Although he repeatedly told the police that he had paid his bill and suggested that they call the hotel, they refused to do so. After holding the man for several hours, the police called the hotel. The manager confirmed that the man had paid his bill and the police released the man. The man sued the hotel for false imprisonment.

Who will prevail?

(A) The hotel, because the hotel reasonably believed that the man stole services.

(B) The hotel, because the police were not employees of the hotel.

(C) The man, because the hotel failed to promptly notify the police that it had received the man's check.

(D) The man, because the hotel failed to have an adequate number of clerks on duty when the man wanted to check out.

Question 73

Twenty years ago, an uncle conveyed his real property to his niece and nephew as tenants in common. The niece and nephew were estranged, however, so only the niece moved onto the property. Last year, the nephew sued the niece for an accounting for the years that she had exclusive possession of the property. The statutory period for adverse possession in this jurisdiction is 15 years.

The accounting will most likely be:

(A) Granted, because the niece occupied or controlled more than half of the land.

(B) Granted, because the niece ousted the nephew from possession.

(C) Denied, because the nephew had the right to use the property but chose not to do so.

(D) Denied, because the niece has held the property for the statutory period required for adverse possession.

Question 74

A federal statute imposed criminal penalties for killing certain specified animals that have been determined by Congress to be of importance to the tourism industry in the region in which the animal was located. Among the animals protected was the red fox. However, a state in which the red fox was located classified the animal as a varmint that could be destroyed at will by anyone with a general hunting license. A rancher who possessed a valid state general hunting license regularly shot and killed red foxes that ate his artichoke plants.

If the rancher is prosecuted under the federal statute and challenges the constitutionality of the law, which of the following is the strongest constitutional argument in support of the federal statute?

(A) The commerce power.

(B) The Necessary and Proper Clause.

(C) The police power.

(D) The power to regulate federal lands.

Question 75

An employee of a garden supply store recently moved from an apartment to a house with a large yard, and he needed a mower. He could not afford the one he wanted, even with his employee discount, so one day at work he took the mower from the mower department and hid it behind some crates on the loading dock. He planned to take the mower home with him that night. At the end of the day, however, the employee became afraid that he would be caught, so he returned the mower to the mower department and went home as usual.

The employee has most likely committed:

(A) Larceny.

(B) Attempted larceny.

(C) Embezzlement.

(D) No crime.

Question 76

A well-regarded paving contractor entered into a written contract with a store owner to pave the parking lot behind his store. The contract contained no provision regarding assignment. A few days after they entered into the contract, the contractor encountered scheduling difficulties and assigned the job to another paving contractor who had a comparable reputation and would do the job for the contract price.

With regard to this assignment by the contractor, which of the following statements is true?

(A) The assignment is valid only if the store owner agrees to accept performance by the competitor.

(B) The contractor breached his contract with the store owner by assigning it to the competitor without his prior consent.

(C) The store owner must accept performance by the competitor.

(D) The assignment is valid, even if the store owner objects, as long as the contractor supervises the performance of the contract by the competitor.

Question 77

An orchard and grocer had a written contract providing that the orchard would supply the grocer with a specified amount of apples and apple cider during the fall season. During the summer, the orchard's apple trees were damaged by apple blight that diminished the fall apple yield. Subsequently, the orchard assigned the contract to another orchard without notifying the grocer. The grocer discovered the substitution after he had received two deliveries of apples and cider, but said nothing. After the assignee orchard made a third delivery, it failed to make the last two deliveries called for in the contract between the grocer and the first orchard.

The grocer:

(A) Has a cause of action only against the assignee orchard for damages.

(B) Has a cause of action against the assignee orchard and the first orchard for damages.

(C) Has no cause of action against the assignee orchard because he and it are not in privity of contract.

(D) Has no cause of action against the first orchard because he accepted performance from the assignee orchard.

Question 78

A developer owned a large tract of land that she had surveyed by a licensed surveyor and then subdivided into numerous lots. At the time of the survey, the surveyor drove wooden stakes into the ground to mark the boundaries. The surveyor then made a plat of the survey and recorded the plat in the county recorder of deeds office. Shortly thereafter, a buyer purchased one of the lots from the developer. Prior to the purchase, the developer had shown the buyer the wooden stakes, and the buyer accepted such stakes as marking the boundaries of the lot. After taking possession of the lot, the buyer built a house thereon and enclosed it with a fence. A few months later, an investor purchased the adjacent lot from the developer. After taking possession of her lot, the investor hired a licensed surveyor to survey it. This surveyor discovered that, according to the recorded plat, the buyer's fence extended two feet onto the adjacent lot. On learning this, the investor demanded that the buyer remove his fence. The buyer refused.

If the investor sues the buyer, who will prevail?

(A) The buyer, because he bought his lot first.

(B) The buyer, because the surveyor's stakes are controlling.

(C) The investor, because the recorded plat controls.

(D) The investor, because the adverse possession period has not run.

Question 79

During the defendant's prosecution for burglary, the prosecution called a witness to the stand and asked: "After the defendant left the room, what did the defendant's friend say to you, if anything?" Previous evidence had established that the defendant and his friend had agreed, prior to the time the defendant left the room, to burglarize a jewelry store. The defense counsel said "Objection!" but the court overruled the objection. The witness then testified about what the friend said.

If the defense counsel wishes to complain about the court's ruling in this matter on appeal, what more should she do before the trial concludes?

(A) Nothing.

(B) Ask the court for the reasons that the objection was overruled.

(C) Restate the objection for the record, stating the grounds therefor.

(D) Request the trial court to order the prosecution to make an offer of proof.

Question 80

On a public sidewalk adjacent to an open parking lot, the defendant accidentally bumped into a passerby. The passerby responded by trying to punch the defendant but missed. The passerby wound up as if to take another swing, so the defendant grabbed the passerby in a bear hug and wrestled him to the ground. The passerby hit his head on the sidewalk and suffered serious injury.

May the defendant be convicted of battery?

(A) Yes, because the defendant initiated the contact by bumping into the passerby.

(B) Yes, because the defendant could have easily retreated.

(C) No, because the defendant did not intend to cause serious bodily harm.

(D) No, because the defendant reasonably feared a battery.

Question 81

A defendant lost some money while playing poker with several people at his friend's house. When the defendant accused his friend of cheating, his friend asked him to leave. The defendant became abusive and refused to leave, so his friend and a couple of other players forced him to go. Angry and determined to get back his money, the defendant went to his home and picked up his pistol. He headed back to his friend's house, intending to shoot his friend if he did not give back the money. However, due to the altercation at the house, his friend had called the police. Just as the defendant was about to step onto his friend's property, the police pulled up and stopped him. They frisked him, found the pistol in his pocket, and arrested him. A state statute prohibits entry onto the property of another with the intent to commit violence thereon.

If charged with attempt under this statute, most likely the defendant will be found:

(A) Not guilty, because this is an "attempt" statute, and there cannot be an attempt of an attempt.

(B) Not guilty, because it would be an attempt to convict a person for a guilty mind.

(C) Guilty, because the defendant was trying to enter the property and he had the necessary state of mind.

(D) Guilty, because the statute was designed to protect the public from violence, and the defendant is dangerous.

Question 82

A state enacted a sales tax on specified items purchased within the state. A subdivision of the federal government purchased from a dealer in the largest city in the state 100 new automobiles for use by federal agencies operating within the state.

Must the federal government pay the sales tax applicable to the new auto purchase?

(A) No, unless Congress has consented to such a tax.

(B) No, because the tax unfairly discriminates against interstate commerce.

(C) Yes, because the tax is nondiscriminatory.

(D) Yes, because there is a rational basis for the tax and it does not appear to be a disguised penalty.

Question 83

A landlord leased a 40-acre tract of land to a tenant for a 15-year period. After five years had expired, the government condemned 15 acres of the property for road construction and allocated the compensation award to the landlord and the tenant according to their respective interests. It so happened, however, that the tenant had used the 15 acres taken by the government to store vehicles necessary in the tenant's work. The tenant knew of no other place nearby where he could store the vehicles. There is no applicable statute in the jurisdiction where the property is located, nor any provision in the lease relating to the condemnation. The tenant quit possession, claiming that he could no longer live on the premises if he could not park the vehicles needed in his work close to where he lived. The landlord brought suit against the tenant to recover rent.

The most likely result of this suit is that the landlord will:

(A) Prevail, because the relationship of landlord and tenant was unaffected by the condemnation, thus leaving the tenant still obligated to pay rent.

(B) Prevail, because of the implied warranty on the part of the tenant to return the demised premises in the same condition at the end of the term as it was at the beginning.

(C) Not prevail, because there has been a breach of the implied covenant of quiet enjoyment by the landlord's inability to provide the tenant with possession of the whole of the property for the entire term.

(D) Not prevail, because there has been a frustration of purpose that excuses the tenant from further performance of his contract to pay rent.

Question 84

Another driver and the defendant were racing along a two-lane road. While the other driver tried to pass in the lane to the left of the center line, the plaintiff's car came into view, heading directly at the driver's vehicle. The driver lost control of his vehicle and collided with the plaintiff's car. The defendant's car, having already passed the plaintiff's car, was not involved in the collision. The plaintiff brings suit against the defendant for damages suffered in the collision.

Which of the following would be the defendant's best course of action?

(A) Seek dismissal of the claim, because the defendant did not cause the plaintiff damage.

(B) Seek indemnity from the other driver, if the plaintiff recovers a judgment against the defendant.

(C) Ask the court to limit his liability to one-half of the plaintiff's damages.

(D) Seek contribution from the other driver, if the plaintiff recovers a judgment against the defendant.

Question 85

A state suffering from a severe loss of tax revenues, due to an initiative that cut state sales taxes in half, enacted legislation that ended cost-of-living increases in all state employees' pensions. A state organization of employees brought suit against the appropriate state official in the federal court to reinstate the increase.

The most likely result will be that:

(A) The employees' organization will prevail, because the statute violates the prohibition against the impairment of the obligations of contracts by a state.

(B) The employees' organization will prevail, if it can show that the statute violates the state's constitution.

(C) The employees' suit will be dismissed, because the Eleventh Amendment prohibits a state's citizens from suing a state official for official acts in a federal court.

(D) The employees' organization will not prevail, because the state always has the power to amend its own legislation.

Question 86

A gambler lived in a state where gambling was illegal. Nevertheless, he gambled on a regular basis. He asked his friend to lend him $5,000 to bet on a football game. His friend agreed to lend him $5,000 if the gambler would bet half of it on the friend's behalf. The gambler agreed, took his friend's $5,000, and placed the bet. The gambler won on 4-to-1 odds. He gave his friend his $5,000 back but refused to tender any winnings.

If his friend sues the gambler to recover the winnings due under the contract, who will prevail?

(A) His friend, because he fully performed his part of the bargain.

(B) His friend, because the court will not allow the gambler to unfairly profit from his illegal contract.

(C) The gambler, because the contract was illegal and the court will not enforce an illegal contract.

(D) The gambler, because the contract was illegal and the court will only act to put the parties in the status quo ante, and his friend already has his money back.

Question 87

A restaurant patron looked up from her dinner and saw that another woman had taken her coat and was walking out the door with it. The patron quickly left and followed the woman, and saw the woman enter a nearby house. Later, when the patron knew that nobody was in the house, she opened a window to the house, climbed in, and got what she thought was her coat out of the front closet. When she put the coat on, however, she noticed for the first time that the coat was not her coat. But, because it was so cold outside, she decided to wear this coat home and to return it the next day. The following day she changed her mind and decided to keep the coat.

The patron is guilty of:

(A) Larceny.

(B) Burglary.

(C) Both larceny and burglary.

(D) Neither larceny nor burglary.

GO ON TO THE NEXT PAGE

Question 88

A young child was using real fireworks to blow up his toy tanks in his backyard during a pretend game of war while his father was in the house. The child was severely injured when one firework exploded in his hand. The child's mother, as guardian ad litem, brought an action against the fireworks manufacturer to recover for the child's injuries and medical expenses. The fireworks manufacturer defended on the ground that the child's father was negligent in supervising the child. The jurisdiction has abolished parent-child tort immunity.

Any negligence on the father's part will:

(A) Have no effect, because the father's negligence is not imputed to the child.

(B) Have no effect, because the jurisdiction has abolished parent-child tort immunity.

(C) Reduce the mother's recovery, because the mother's action is derivative of the child's cause of action.

(D) Reduce the mother's recovery, because the jurisdiction has abolished parent-child tort immunity.

Question 89

On Halloween night, a 12-year-old boy dressed up as a bandit by wearing dark clothes and a pair of panty hose over his head and went trick or treating. The boy wanted to impress the homeowners with his costume, so his method of operation was to go up to a house and ring the bell. When the person answered, he pointed a toy gun at the person's face and said, "Your money or your life," and then shouted, "Trick or treat!" At the fifth house he went to, the boy began his routine, but before he could say "trick or treat," the homeowner screamed and slammed the door in the boy's face. Still shaken by the experience, the homeowner suffered a heart attack five minutes later.

Is the homeowner likely to recover damages for the boy's conduct?

(A) Yes, for intentional infliction of emotional distress.

(B) Yes, for assault.

(C) No, because the boy is only 12 years old.

(D) No, because the homeowner should have known that the gun was a toy because it was Halloween.

Question 90

A landowner conveyed her property "to my only daughter, her heirs and assigns, as long as the premises are used for noncommercial purposes, then to my only grandson, his heirs and assigns." The jurisdiction in which the property is located follows the common law Rule Against Perpetuities.

The landowner's interest in the property, if any, is:

(A) Nothing.

(B) A reversion in fee simple absolute.

(C) A possibility of reverter.

(D) A right of entry based on a condition subsequent.

Question 91

To discourage the consumption of alcohol, a city adopted an ordinance prohibiting any advertisements of liquor prices except within the stores in which alcoholic beverages are sold. After the ordinance was adopted, a store located within the city that had regularly advertised its liquor prices experienced a 30% decrease in sales. The owner was not given personal notice of the city council meeting at which the ordinance was adopted. If he had been, as the owner of the city's largest volume dealer of alcoholic beverages, he would have spoken against the adoption of the ordinance.

If the store owner brings suit to have the ordinance declared unconstitutional, how should the court rule?

(A) Uphold the ordinance, because states have the power to ban and regulate liquor sales under the Twenty-first Amendment.

(B) Uphold the ordinance, because the ban does not favor local economic interests or unduly interfere with interstate commerce.

(C) Declare the ordinance unconstitutional as applied to the store owner, because the failure to give the owner notice violated the Fourteenth Amendment Due Process Clause.

(D) Declare the ordinance unconstitutional, because it amounts to an absolute ban on advertising a lawful product in violation of the First Amendment.

Question 92

A businesswoman sold the resort hotel she owned to a speculator for $250,000. The speculator paid $100,000 down and agreed to pay the balance in equal monthly installments over the next 15 years. Two years later, the speculator sold the hotel to a conglomerate in exchange for the conglomerate's agreement to assume all of his obligations. The conglomerate agreed, and assumed the contract that the speculator had with the businesswoman. The following year, when her daughter decided to go to graduate school, the businesswoman wrote a letter to the speculator instructing him that the full payment should now go to her daughter until the businesswoman told him otherwise. The daughter was given a copy of this letter. Two years later, the conglomerate sold the hotel and all of the obligations back to the speculator. About this time, the daughter graduated and the businesswoman promised her niece that she would help her finance her studies in veterinary medicine, and she sent another letter to the speculator telling him to send the monthly installments to the niece. A year later, the businesswoman died, leaving all her cash (and the balance due on the note from the speculator) to her daughter.

If the daughter were to sue the conglomerate to recover the sums paid to the niece, who would prevail?

(A) The daughter, because she was a creditor beneficiary, had notice, and had changed her position in reliance on the contract.

(B) The daughter, because she was a donee beneficiary and had assented to the agreement.

(C) The conglomerate, because the daughter's rights had not vested before being extinguished by the subsequent assignment.

(D) The conglomerate, because the daughter was only an incidental beneficiary of its agreement with the speculator.

Question 93

In which of the following cases would an objection to a leading question most likely be upheld?

(A) When asked on direct examination of a disinterested witness.

(B) When asked on direct examination of a minor.

(C) When asked on cross-examination of an expert witness.

(D) When related to the name, address, or occupation of the witness.

Question 94

On November 7, a painter agreed with a homeowner to paint his house for $10,000, payment to be made upon completion of the job. On November 14, while the job was still incomplete, the painter told her paint supplier that if he would give her the paint she needed, she would have the homeowner pay to him directly the $3,000 for paint that she owed him. The paint supplier agreed, and the painter sent the homeowner a letter setting forth this agreement. On December 1, the painter had completed the job, but the homeowner refused to pay the paint supplier any money.

In a suit by the paint supplier against the homeowner, what would be the homeowner's best defense?

(A) The paint supplier had already supplied the paint before the agreement, and therefore he had not relied on the homeowner's promise.

(B) The paint supplier was not an intended beneficiary of the agreement between the homeowner and the painter.

(C) The painter had not painted the house in a proper, workmanlike manner.

(D) The painter attempted to assign her rights before completion and an assignment to receive money before personal services are performed is inoperable.

Question 95

A defendant got into a fight with his former roommate over some money that the defendant claimed his old roommate owed for some long distance telephone calls. When his old roommate refused to pay the money, the defendant took two tickets that the roommate had purchased for a playoff college basketball game, intending to give them back the day after the game. The defendant is charged with larceny.

Most likely the defendant will be found:

(A) Not guilty, because he intended to return the tickets to his old roommate.

(B) Not guilty, because he believed that his old roommate owed him money.

(C) Guilty, because he intended to deprive his old roommate of the value of the tickets.

(D) Guilty, because the intent to return is never a good defense.

Question 96

A defendant was one of a group of persons who were engaged in a demonstration against the discriminatory practices of a private club. During the demonstration, the defendant threw a bomb containing highly toxic gas through the window of the club. At the time he threw the bomb, he knew that the club's president was inside the building. Unbeknownst to the defendant, the club's treasurer was also inside. Each inhaled some gas and were injured, but neither died. The defendant is charged with attempted murder of both the club's president and treasurer. At trial, the defendant testified that the reason he threw the bomb was that he wanted to make sure that nobody would be able to use the club, and that he did not intend to hurt anyone.

Presuming that the jury believes the defendant, he can be convicted of the attempted murder of:

(A) The club's president.

(B) The club's treasurer.

(C) Both the club's president and the club's treasurer.

(D) Neither the club's president nor the club's treasurer.

Question 97

A mother's will left her farm to her son and daughter "jointly, as tenants in common." The son and the daughter, having had no interest in farming, had long since moved to a large city about 150 miles from the farm. However, after the mother's death the son decided to move back to the farm. The son rented various parts of the farm to sharecroppers and regularly sent half of any profits from the farm to the daughter. A few years later the daughter died, leaving a will devising all of her property to a friend. The son, however, refuses to pay any of the profits of the farm to the friend and claims an exclusive interest in the farm.

If the friend sues the son, how will a court most likely rule?

(A) For the son, because he actively managed the use of the farm and the daughter never showed any interest in it.

(B) For the son, because he survived the daughter, the other joint tenant.

(C) For the son, because the unities of time, title, and interest have been destroyed by the daughter's death.

(D) For the friend, because he inherited the daughter's interest.

Question 98

A bank notified the police that an audit had revealed that one of its tellers had been embezzling money. After a bank officer signed a complaint on behalf of the bank, the police obtained a warrant from a magistrate and arrested the teller named in the complaint. The teller protested, asserting that she had stolen nothing. After the teller had been in jail overnight, the bank discovered that the auditor had named the wrong teller and immediately notified the police. The arrested teller was released with apologies from the police department. The teller sued the city and the police department for false imprisonment.

Will the teller prevail against the police?

(A) Yes, because of the teller's protestations of innocence.

(B) Yes, because the teller had not embezzled from the bank.

(C) No, because the police acted pursuant to a valid warrant.

(D) No, because the bank had reasonable grounds for signing a complaint against her.

Question 99

In July of last summer a grape grower contracted with a winery to deliver "500 tons of premium quality pinot chardonnay grapes grown on my ranch." The price was to be $1,000 per ton and delivery was to be on or before September 15. In August of the same year, the grape grower entered into an identical contract with a vineyard to sell 300 tons of premium quality pinot chardonnay grapes.

The grape grower completed his harvest by September 10 and had 800 tons of premium quality grapes. On September 11, an unexpected rain ruined 400 tons, and the grape grower notified the winery and the vineyard on that day that he would only be able to deliver 250 tons to the winery and 150 tons to the vineyard. On September 14, the vineyard purchased an additional 150 tons of premium quality pinot chardonnay grapes from a different grape farmer, one of several other available sources for premium quality pinot chardonnay grapes. These grapes along with the 150 tons from the grape grower gave the vineyard the 300 tons it needed.

On September 15, what is the winery's legal position with regard to the grape grower's failure to deliver the 500 tons of grapes required by his contract?

(A) If the winery has given the grape grower a written notice of termination, the winery will have the right to refuse to accept the 250 tons of grapes but will have no cause of action for damages against the grape grower.

(B) Even if the winery has given the grape grower a written notice of termination, the winery must accept the 250 tons of grapes and will have no cause of action for damages against the grape grower.

(C) Because the vineyard's purchase establishes that it is possible for the grape grower to perform by obtaining additional grapes from other available sources, the winery may accept the 250 tons from the grape grower and recover damages for the grape grower's failure to deliver the balance of the amount specified by the contract.

(D) Because the grape grower's contract with the winery was entered into before his contract with the vineyard, the grape grower is bound to deliver the entirety of his grape crop to the winery.

Question 100

The owner of a small dry cleaning business wanted to expand his business to include tailoring jobs. A local sewing machine retailer recommended a certain model of sewing machine for that purpose to the business owner, so the owner purchased the machine from the retailer for the use of one of his employees, an experienced seamstress. The machine had a defect that caused an injury to his employee's fingers, putting her out of work for several weeks. As a result, the business had to turn away all tailoring requests for that time period. The business owner asserted a claim based on strict liability in tort against the retailer of the sewing machine, seeking damages for loss of business because of the injury to his worker.

The business owner will probably:

(A) Recover, because the sewing machine was the actual and proximate cause of the business owner's loss of business.

(B) Recover, because the retailer knew that the sewing machine was to be used in the tailoring business.

(C) Not recover, because economic loss from injury to an employee is not within the scope of the retailer's duty.

(D) Not recover, because the retailer was not the manufacturer of the sewing machine.

STOP

ANSWER KEY AND SUBJECT KEY

Answer		Subject	Answer		Subject
1.	A	Torts	51.	B	Criminal Law/Procedure
2.	B	Torts	52.	C	Constitutional Law
3.	C	Real Property	53.	B	Torts
4.	A	Evidence	54.	A	Contracts
5.	A	Constitutional Law	55.	B	Torts
6.	A	Contracts	56.	B	Evidence
7.	C	Criminal Law	57.	C	Criminal Law
8.	B	Real Property	58.	B	Evidence
9.	C	Evidence	59.	B	Evidence
10.	A	Torts	60.	C	Evidence
11.	D	Torts	61.	A	Criminal Law/Procedure
12.	A	Constitutional Law	62.	D	Constitutional Law
13.	B	Torts	63.	A	Constitutional Law
14.	A	Constitutional Law	64.	D	Real Property
15.	B	Criminal Law/Procedure	65.	C	Contracts
16.	C	Contracts	66.	B	Constitutional Law
17.	D	Contracts	67.	A	Real Property
18.	C	Real Property	68.	D	Real Property
19.	B	Torts	69.	C	Constitutional Law
20.	B	Evidence	70.	B	Criminal Law/Procedure
21.	C	Constitutional Law	71.	C	Evidence
22.	B	Criminal Law	72.	B	Torts
23.	A	Real Property	73.	C	Real Property
24.	B	Evidence	74.	A	Constitutional Law
25.	C	Criminal Law/Procedure	75.	A	Criminal Law
26.	C	Constitutional Law	76.	C	Contracts
27.	C	Evidence	77.	B	Contracts
28.	B	Criminal Law/Procedure	78.	B	Real Property
29.	D	Torts	79.	C	Evidence
30.	B	Evidence	80.	D	Criminal Law
31.	B	Contracts	81.	C	Criminal Law
32.	C	Contracts	82.	A	Constitutional Law
33.	A	Real Property	83.	A	Real Property
34.	C	Evidence	84.	D	Torts
35.	B	Constitutional Law	85.	A	Constitutional Law
36.	B	Evidence	86.	C	Contracts
37.	C	Real Property	87.	A	Criminal Law
38.	A	Criminal Law	88.	A	Torts
39.	A	Real Property	89.	D	Torts
40.	A	Evidence	90.	C	Real Property
41.	A	Criminal Law/Procedure	91.	D	Constitutional Law
42.	A	Real Property	92.	C	Contracts
43.	C	Constitutional Law	93.	A	Evidence
44.	D	Contracts	94.	C	Contracts
45.	B	Contracts	95.	C	Criminal Law
46.	B	Contracts	96.	D	Criminal Law
47.	D	Torts	97.	D	Real Property
48.	C	Torts	98.	C	Torts
49.	C	Contracts	99.	A	Contracts/Sales
50.	B	Real Property	100.	C	Torts

Answer to Question 1

(A) If the tanker company prevails, it will be because the court follows the majority approach to duty questions. Under the majority approach articulated by Justice Cardozo in *Palsgraf v. Long Island Railroad*, a plaintiff can recover for the defendant's breach of duty only if she can establish that a reasonable person would have foreseen a risk of injury to her in the circumstances; *i.e.,* that she was located in a foreseeable zone of danger. Here, even assuming that the tanker driver breached a duty by parking his truck on the street, the tenant was not within a foreseeable zone of danger and would not be able to recover damages under this view. (B) is incorrect because the tanker driver's stopping for a cup of coffee after making deliveries does not take him outside the scope of the employment relationship. Hence, if the tanker driver breached a duty to the tenant, the tanker company would be vicariously liable for her injuries. (C) is incorrect because even if the owner of the unstable building were a legal (proximate) cause of the tenant's injuries, that would not preclude the tanker driver and the tanker company from being a legal cause as well. (D) is wrong because the fact that the tanker driver violated company rules by parking on the street would not prevent the tanker company from being liable for the tanker driver's actions, because he was still acting within the scope of his employment relationship.

Answer to Question 2

(B) The fashion student will recover the fair market value of the machine because her roommate is liable for conversion. Conversion is the intentional interference with the plaintiff's right of possession in the chattel that is serious enough to warrant that the defendant pay the full value of the chattel. Conversion will be found if the defendant was using the chattel without permission and it was accidentally damaged, as in this case. The remedy for conversion is the fair market value of the chattel at the time and place of conversion. Thus, (B) is correct and (A) is incorrect. (C) is incorrect because that would be the remedy for trespass to chattels, which is a less serious interference than conversion. Here, an unauthorized use that resulted in damages equaling almost half the chattel's original cost is too serious an interference in nature and consequences to be only trespass to chattel. (D) is incorrect because her roommate's lending the sewing machine without permission satisfies the intent requirement. Even though the damage was accidental, her roommate is liable for conversion.

Answer to Question 3

(C) The buyer has superior rights to both the guitarist and the ex-husband. Under a race-notice statute such as the one in this question, a subsequent purchaser is protected only if he purchases without notice of prior conveyances and records first. However, even though the neighbor had notice of the guitarist's deed and was therefore not a bona fide purchaser, and could not have prevailed against the guitarist, that does not mean that a bona fide purchaser from her would not prevail against the guitarist. The ex-husband was a subsequent bona fide purchaser from the neighbor and recorded before the guitarist. Thus, the ex-husband would prevail over the guitarist. The buyer, who had notice of the guitarist's deed when she subsequently acquired her deed from the ex-husband, will also prevail over the guitarist. This is due to the "shelter doctrine," which is applied to the recording acts. Under that doctrine, once a bona fide purchaser enters the chain of events, he can subsequently deed the land to a party who had notice of the prior deed and that party is also accorded the status of a bona fide purchaser. Thus, once the ex-husband, a bona fide purchaser, enters the picture and gets the protection of the act, he can sell to the buyer, who gets the protection of the act even though she purchased with notice.

The buyer comes under the shelter doctrine. The theory behind the shelter doctrine is that it extends full protection to bona fide purchasers in that it does not limit their ability to market the property. Otherwise, if they could not sell to parties with notice, their ability to market the property would be impaired. The exception to the shelter doctrine is that it does not apply to the first purchaser with notice—the neighbor. Thus, if the ex-husband had subsequently sold the land back to the neighbor, she would not have been accorded the status of a bona fide purchaser. The reason for the exception is obvious—to discourage fraud. Note also that because the buyer has a deed from the ex-husband, she prevails over the ex-husband. Therefore, (A), (B), and (D) are all incorrect.

Answer to Question 4

(A) The court will not take judicial notice of the birthdate. A birthdate (other than that of a famous person such as George Washington) is not the type of fact that a court will recognize as true without formal presentation of evidence (*e.g.*, presentation of a certified copy of a birth certificate). Under the Federal Rules, courts may judicially notice a fact that is (i) generally known within the territorial jurisdiction of the court or (ii) capable of accurate and ready determination by resort to sources whose accuracy cannot reasonably be questioned. Records of any state or federal court may be judicially noticed; they are easily verifiable. Thus, (B) is incorrect. (C) can be determined by consulting an almanac. It is therefore a manifest fact and can properly be noticed. The grounds for judicial notice of (D) are several: it is common knowledge, it is easily verifiable by reference to a calendar, and the state holiday is subject to judicial notice as a state law.

Answer to Question 5

(A) The fact that no police officer has been terminated during probation except for cause may be enough for the graduate to show that she has a right to a hearing. Continued public employment may be a protected property interest if there is a clear practice or mutual understanding that an employee can be terminated only for "cause." If the graduate can establish this, she will be able to force the city to give her a reason for her termination and a hearing. (C) is incorrect because a general increase in police officer positions does not establish a specific right to employment for the graduate. (B) is wrong because there is nothing in the Constitution that requires that a city follow any particular method of employment practice, as long as the method chosen by a city does not violate some constitutional prohibition. The fact that the city's civil service law was not changed to reflect the additional period of time a police officer spends in the police academy does not create a right protected by the Fourteenth Amendment. (D) states facts that could give rise to an equal protection, rather than due process, claim.

Answer to Question 6

(A) The uncle will win because consideration generally is required for modification of a contract, and the gambler's preexisting debt cannot serve as valid consideration. Consideration generally is necessary to modify a contract. Payment of a smaller sum than due will not be sufficient consideration for a promise by a creditor to discharge a debt unless the consideration is in some way new or different (*e.g.*, payment before maturity or to one other than the creditor) or the amount of debt is subject to an honest dispute (and so the parties are giving up the right to litigate the amount, which is consideration sufficient to support a modification in and of itself).

Here, nothing indicates that the gambler gave anything new or different in exchange for the lower payment. Moreover, the amount was not in dispute. Therefore, there is no consideration supporting the modification, so the modification is unenforceable. (Note that even if the money was owed on a contract under the U.C.C., which permits modification without consideration, the modification still would be unenforceable because the modification must still have a good faith purpose and nothing in the facts indicates that the modification was made in good faith.) (B) is incorrect because the agreement was not supported by consideration. As discussed above, consideration is required to support the gambler and the uncle's agreement. Payment by the gambler of a smaller sum than due is not sufficient consideration. Therefore, the uncle is not bound by the agreement, and he may recover the $1,000. (C) is incorrect because accord and satisfaction require that the amount of the debt be in ***dispute***. A contract may be discharged by an accord (an agreement, supported by consideration, to accept some other performance in lieu of the performance required under the existing contract) and satisfaction (the performance of the accord agreement). A partial payment of an original debt will suffice for an accord and satisfaction where there is a "bona fide dispute" as to the claim. However, because the amount of the gambler's debt was not in dispute, his payment of $8,000 was not valid consideration for an accord agreement. Therefore, the gambler's original debt has not been discharged by an accord and satisfaction, and the uncle may recover the $1,000. (D) is incorrect because it is irrelevant. A contract can be modified before or after the date of performance if the modification is supported by consideration. As discussed above, the gambler's payment of a preexisting debt is not valid consideration for the new agreement. Therefore, the uncle is entitled to the $1,000 owed from the original contract, even though he agreed after the due date to settle for $8,000.

Answer to Question 7

(C) The parachute manufacturer will not be guilty of manslaughter because, at common law, a corporation is not responsible for the criminal acts of its employees. Common law took the position that because the corporation had no mind, it could not form the mens rea necessary for a traditional crime, and because the corporation could not be imprisoned, there was no criminal liability imposed on the corporation for the common law crimes committed by its agents. Although the common law rule has been changed by statute in many jurisdictions, the question does not indicate the existence of such a statute. Absent a statute, the parachute manufacturer will not be guilty of manslaughter. (A) is wrong because, as stated above, at common law a corporation would not be liable for a common law crime. Additionally, at common law, an employer is not responsible for the unauthorized criminal conduct of his employees. (B) is wrong. Even if criminal liability could be imposed on the parachute manufacturer for the crimes of the designer, there would have to be a showing that the designer was at least ***reckless*** in causing the death. (B) seems to impose liability on the parachute manufacturer without regard to the mental state of the designer. (D) is wrong. The fact that there was only a 1% chance of parachute failure would be a factor for the jury to consider in deciding whether a person acted "recklessly"; it would not as a matter of law negate criminal liability.

Answer to Question 8

(B) The homebrewing supplier is liable for the 10% rent difference over the last four months because he has a year-to-year tenancy for the increased rent amount. When a tenant continues in possession after the termination of his right to possession, the landlord has two choices of action: She may treat the hold-over tenant as a trespasser and evict him under an unlawful detainer statute, or she may, in her sole discretion, bind the tenant to a new periodic tenancy. In a commercial lease, if the original lease term was for a year or more, a year-to-year tenancy results. If the landlord notifies the tenant before termination of the tenancy that occupancy after termination will be at an increased rent, the tenant will be held to have acquiesced to the new terms if he does not surrender. The tenant will be held to the new terms ***even if he objects*** to the increased rent, provided that the rent increase is reasonable. Here, the original lease was a commercial lease for a five-year term, so the landlord's decision to hold the homebrewing supplier to a new tenancy makes it a year-to-year tenancy. Because the landlord notified the homebrewing supplier of the 10% rent increase prior to the termination of the original five-year term, the new tenancy is at the increased amount of rent. Note that the landlord's depositing of the homebrewing supplier's checks would not create an accord and satisfaction even though they were marked "new rent payment." In addition to the requirement that a bona fide dispute must exist as to the amount owed, the check must conspicuously state that it is in full satisfaction of the debt before an accord and satisfaction can occur. (A) and (C) are incorrect because the new tenancy is year-to-year, not month-to-month. Most courts would rule a ***residential*** hold-over tenant a month-to-month tenant, irrespective of the term of the original lease, but the homebrewing supplier is a commercial tenant. (C) is also incorrect because the homebrewing supplier had notice that if he stayed beyond the original five-year term, the rent would be increased by 10%. (D) is incorrect for the same reason.

Answer to Question 9

(C) Asking if the witness is known as an alcoholic is most likely improper. This answer can best be understood by examining the permissible questions first. (A) asks about a prior conviction for forgery. Under Federal Rule 609, prior convictions of crimes requiring proof or admission of an act of dishonesty or false statement may be inquired into if they are less than 10 years old. This crime is one of dishonesty and is not too old; therefore, the question is proper. (B) is also a proper question. It goes to bias, which is always a permissible line of inquiry. (D) relates to prior bad acts for which there is no conviction. Federal Rule 608(b) permits cross-examination concerning prior bad acts if, in the discretion of the court, they are probative of truthfulness. Cheating a business partner is dishonest, and the witness is not a party; therefore, this question is proper. That leaves alternative (C). If the ability to observe, relate, or recall were at issue, then this question could be a permissible line of inquiry, especially because the witness is not a party and is not likely to be prejudiced by the question. On the other hand, the probative value of the other questions is obvious. Because the other questions are all obviously right, this is the one most likely to be ruled improper.

Answer to Question 10

(A) The owner's first statement regarding using genuine original parts was a false representation of material facts and therefore actionable. To establish a prima facie case of intentional misrepresentation (deceit), a plaintiff must establish (i) a misrepresentation made by the defendant, (ii) scienter, (iii) an intent to induce plaintiff's reliance on the misrepresentation, (iv) causation (*i.e.,* actual reliance), (v) justifiable reliance, and (vi) damages. Usually, there is a requirement that the false representation be of a material past or present fact; whether the restoration was accomplished with genuine original parts is a statement of fact that would be very material to a potential buyer of classic cars. Hence, assuming that all the other elements of deceit are proved, this statement can be the basis of the hobbyist's claim. The second statement, on the other hand, will not support the hobbyist's misrepresentation claim because he cannot show justifiable reliance on the statement. As a general matter, reliance on false statements of opinion, value, or quality will be viewed as unjustified. The owner's claims that this is the "finest" restoration and "one of the two best" are statements of opinion as to quality. An exception to this rule might apply if the hobbyist were purchasing the car to enter into competition, or if the owner had superior knowledge of the subject matter, but here there is no indication what the hobbyist's plans are, and his experience with classic cars would make his reliance on the owner's opinion unjustified. Thus, (B) is incorrect; only the first statement would support the claim. Therefore, (C) and (D) are also incorrect.

Answer to Question 11

(D) The trooper will not prevail. As a general rule, a defendant is liable if he negligently puts himself in peril and the plaintiff is injured in attempting a rescue. However, the "firefighters' rule" will bar firefighters and police officers, on public policy or assumption of risk grounds, from recovering for injuries caused by the risks of a rescue. Here, it was an inherent and foreseeable risk of the job that the trooper might be struck by another vehicle at an accident site. Hence, the trooper probably will not be able to recover, and (A) is incorrect. (B) is incorrect because the rule applies to firefighters and police officers who are injured from the unique risks that are inherent in the type of work they do, and therefore would apply in this case. (C) is incorrect. Although it is true that the delivery van was an actual cause of the trooper's injuries, it is not a superseding cause that would cut off the liability of the tractor-trailer driver. It is foreseeable that a state trooper, in the roadway responding to an emergency call, might be struck by another vehicle. If not for application of the firefighters' rule, the driver of the tractor-trailer would be liable to the trooper.

Answer to Question 12

(A) As a general rule, a state may not retroactively alter a contract to which it is a party. While that prohibition is not absolute, legislation that reduces the contractual burdens on the state will be strictly scrutinized. Here, the legislature is simply making a choice about how to distribute resources to meet competing needs, and the impairment will be stricken. A state may repeal its own enactments, but may not do so when repeal violates a constitutional prohibition. Thus, (C) is incorrect. Sovereign immunity is not a constitutional doctrine, nor is equitable estoppel, except as subsumed in the Due Process Clause in a manner not as directly applicable under these circumstances as the impairment of contracts doctrine. Therefore, (B) and (D) are incorrect.

Answer to Question 13

(B) The pedestrian will have a valid defense to her use of force. A felony arrest without a warrant by a police officer or a private citizen acting at the officer's direction is privileged if the officer has reasonable grounds to believe that a felony has been committed and that the person arrested has committed it. In such a case, force reasonably necessary to make the arrest is permitted. Here, the police officer had reason to believe he was chasing someone who had committed a felony, and the pedestrian can rely on the officer's privilege because she was acting at the officer's direction. (A) is incorrect because her belief that the pursuer was a police officer is not relevant here. The pursuer was a police officer, so the pedestrian was entitled to the same privilege as he had because she was acting at his direction. (C) is wrong because the pedestrian need not have been a witness to make an arrest for a felony, and can rely on the police officer's privilege even though the crime committed was a misdemeanor. (D) is wrong because the pedestrian was acting at the officer's direction, and the officer need only have a reasonable belief that a felony has been committed. Had she been acting on her own initiative, she would not have had a defense because the man in fact did not commit a felony.

Answer to Question 14

(A) The ordinance is probably unconstitutional because it violates free speech rights under the First Amendment. The Supreme Court has held that a charitable appeal for funds involves a variety of speech interests protected by the First Amendment. In one case, an ordinance that prohibited door-to-door solicitation by organizations that did not use at least 75% of their receipts for charitable purposes was struck down by the Court. The present ordinance would probably run afoul of the same rule, because in effect it prohibits all charitable solicitation absent relatively burdensome compliance with its registration provisions. The ordinance is also vulnerable because it limits the right of solicitation to those who belong to "a recognized charitable organization." (B), while a correct statement of law, does not apply in these circumstances. The question is directed toward the challenge the organization member would mount, not one that a religious organization might pursue. (C) is incorrect. Because the First Amendment rights at issue here are fundamental, a "reasonable balance" is not enough; the government ordinance is a direct, content-based regulation, and will be subjected to strict scrutiny. (D) is incorrect because even if the prevention of fraud is a compelling state interest, the statute is not narrowly tailored to achieve that interest, which is required under the strict scrutiny standard.

Answer to Question 15

(B) The motion to suppress the evidence will be granted because the police did not have probable cause to search the car. When the police place the driver of an automobile under arrest, there are a number of alternatives with respect to a search of the car: (i) Regardless of the crime for which the defendant is arrested, the police can search the entire passenger area of the car as a search incident to an arrest. However, the search incident to an arrest must be conducted at the time of the arrest. (ii) If the police have probable cause to search the car—*i.e.,* reasonable grounds for believing that a legitimate item of seizure is in the car—a search of the entire car can be made without a warrant. The search based on probable cause can be made at the time of the arrest or at a later time. (iii) If the police take the car under their control for an administrative reason (such as to get the car off the highway), they can "inventory" the items in the car under certain circumstances. In this question, the search of the car at the police station would have been valid ***if*** the police had probable cause to search the car. The question does not provide any facts that could form the basis for probable cause to search. Thus, the motion to suppress will be granted because of the lack of probable cause. (A) is wrong for two reasons: The search could not be justified as a search incident to an arrest because the arrest had been completed. Also, when conducting a valid search incident to an arrest, the police ***may*** open up a closed container within the arrestee's "wingspan." (C) is wrong because, as stated, a search incident to an arrest must occur at the time of the arrest. (D) is wrong. The police can conduct an administrative inventory if the car has been impounded by the police, and the police are, in fact, conducting an inventory of the items in the car. In this question, the car had not been impounded by the police, nor would it need to be because the passenger could drive it home. Also, it is clear from the facts that a traditional search was taking place.

Answer to Question 16

(C) The builder's unconditional promise to sell created a contract even if the buyer knew of the builder's wife's interest. When a promise is unconditional, the failure to perform according to its terms is a breach of contract. By not making his promise conditional on his wife's consent to convey her interest, the builder impliedly undertook to obtain her consent. Therefore, the contract is enforceable. (Note that this does not necessarily mean that the buyer will be able to get the car;

he may have to settle for damages because of the builder's wife's interest.) (A) is incorrect although partially true. It is true that the builder cannot sell his wife's half of the car without her consent; however, that does not make the contract here unenforceable. As stated above, by making his promise unconditional, the builder undertook a duty to obtain his wife's consent to sell the car. His failure to do so is a breach of contract, but a breach does not negate a contract; it merely gives the nonbreaching party a right to certain remedies. Therefore, the contract is enforceable, even if the builder's wife refuses to sell her interest. (B) is incorrect because the buyer's knowledge of the builder's wife's interest is irrelevant to the issue of the contract's enforceability. As discussed above, the builder's unconditional promise implied that the builder would obtain his wife's consent to convey her interest in the car. Therefore, the contract is enforceable regardless of whether the buyer was aware of the builder's wife's interest at the time he signed. (D) is incorrect because "prospective inability" is not a ground for discharge. Prospective failure of consideration occurs when a party has reasonable grounds to believe that the other party will be unable or unwilling to perform when due. The prospective inability of performance does not discharge the contract; rather, it allows the innocent party to suspend further performance until he receives adequate assurances that performance will be forthcoming. Therefore, the contract between the builder and the buyer is not discharged because of prospective inability of performance.

Answer to Question 17

(D) The creditor will prevail. Once a third-party beneficiary's rights vest, he may enforce the contract, and here the creditor's rights vested when he brought suit. He is seeking reformation of the contract, because the written terms do not reflect the original agreement of the parties. Here, the original agreement called for a $5,000 payment to the creditor. Because the buyer will not be able to successfully claim the defense of the Statute of Frauds (*see* below), the creditor should recover the $5,000. (A) is wrong because the buyer is not promising to act as a surety when he promises to pay some of the money to the debtor. Generally, contracts do not have to be in writing to be enforceable; however, under the Statute of Frauds, certain contracts will not be enforceable unless they are evidenced by a writing signed by the party to be charged. One such contract is to pay the debt of another. In this case, the buyer is not promising to pay another's debt, if the debtor fails to repay the debt to his creditor, but is merely paying part of the purchase price to the seller's creditor rather than to the seller himself, pursuant to the contract. Thus, this is not a surety situation, and no writing is required on that ground. (B) is wrong because the buyer's oral promise to pay part of the land sale purchase price to the debtor does not itself concern an interest in land. Under the Statute of Frauds, a promise creating an interest in land must be in writing. An agreement that concerns only to whom payment of part of a land sale purchase price is to be made does not create an interest in land, but rather is a promise that is collateral to the land sale and would not fail because it was not in writing. (C) is wrong because reformation is available even if the written document is unambiguous, as long as it fails to reflect the terms originally agreed upon.

Answer to Question 18

(C) The son's wife will not prevail because the granddaughter had a vested remainder interest subject to open, which became indefeasibly vested. It seems clear that the testator intended her grandchildren to inherit the property at some time, and that the only thing she desired was that her son be able to live there as long as he wanted. Because the son could conceivably live there all his life, this devise would be deemed a life estate in the son, with a vested remainder in the granddaughter. The granddaughter's interest would, however, be subject to open (partial defeasance) because it was possible that the son could have other children. At the son's death, the granddaughter's interest became indefeasibly vested. (A) is incorrect because the language of the will clearly does not express an intent that the son take a fee simple absolute. (B) is incorrect because however many children the son may have, his life would be the measuring life, and the grandchildren would inherit upon his death. Thus, this would not violate the Rule Against Perpetuities. (D) is incorrect because the granddaughter's interest was vested on her birth. It is true that it was subject to open and the time of possession was contingent on the son's decision to live in the house, but the granddaughter's basic remainder interest was always vested.

Answer to Question 19

(B) To prevail, the CEO must show evidence of actual injury. When a defamatory statement involves a matter of public concern, the plaintiff must provide competent evidence of actual injury (*i.e.,* presumed damages are not permitted absent a showing of knowledge of falsity or reckless disregard of truth). Actual injury is not limited to out-of-pocket loss; it may include impairment of reputation, personal humiliation, and mental anguish. Here, the reasons for the firing of the CEO of a town's largest employer, and the financial health of that employer, are matters of public concern for the readership of the town newspaper. Hence, the CEO will have to prove actual injury to prevail. (A) is incorrect because pecuniary damages are not necessary in libel cases. If not for the fact that a matter of public concern was involved, damages would be presumed. (C) is wrong even though it is a true statement. The common law rule of presumed damages is supplanted by the constitutional rules because a matter of public concern is involved. (D) is wrong because even if the CEO is not a public figure, the article involved a matter of public concern, so damages will not be presumed.

Answer to Question 20

(B) The court should rule for the defendant and allow the treatise to be read and considered by the jury as substantive evidence. Although the treatise constitutes hearsay because it is an out-of-court statement offered to prove the truth of the matter asserted (that the surgical procedure was accepted), it falls within one of the exceptions to the hearsay rule. Under Federal Rule 803(18), information in treatises can be read into evidence if the treatise is: (i) relied upon by the expert or is called to his attention during cross-examination; and (ii) is established as reliable by the witness, another expert, or judicial notice. The treatise itself is not admitted into evidence, but rather the relevant section is read in. Thus, (B) is correct and (D) is incorrect. (A) is incorrect because the Federal Rules allow such evidence to be used substantively and do not limit the information to impeachment, as a number of state courts do. (C) is incorrect because the information in a learned treatise is admissible as long as it is established to be reliable; however, if the opposing party did rely on the treatise, the offering party need not otherwise establish reliability.

Answer to Question 21

(C) The strongest possible argument here is (C), because equal protection claims are made against the federal government pursuant to the Fifth Amendment's Due Process Clause. The Supreme Court has held that this provision implicitly includes a requirement for equal protection. Although the employee has little chance of prevailing because only a rational basis test is used for age discrimination claims, this answer is the only possible basis for challenging the law. (A) is wrong because both constitutional provisions referring to privileges and immunities apply to ***state*** government conduct and are never used against the federal government. The Fourteenth Amendment provides that no state shall deny any citizen the privileges or immunities of national citizenship. Article IV provides that no state shall deny citizens of other states the privileges and immunities it accords its own citizens. (B) is wrong because a "just compensation" claim will only provide him compensation for his loss of property. Even if his job is considered to be a property right, the just compensation claim would not provide him the relief he wants, which is reinstatement in his job. (D) is wrong because even though there is no express provision in Article I, Section 8, concerning this legislation, it certainly is within congressional powers.

Answer to Question 22

(B) The prosecution's best reply is that conscious risk-taking refers to the man's entire course of conduct. Voluntary intoxication has historically been treated as the equivalent of recklessness for the reasons outlined in (B). (A) is wrong because intoxication ***is*** the crucial issue; drinking was a major part of the man's conscious risk-taking. (C) is wrong because voluntary intoxication is a defense to some crimes. (D) is wrong; it is irrelevant what the common law definition of manslaughter is because here there is a statute defining the crime.

Answer to Question 23

(A) Because the friend recorded prior to the subsequent conveyance, she has the superior right to title regardless of the type of recording statute. A conveyance that is recorded can never be divested by a subsequent conveyance through operation of the recording statutes. By recording, the grantee gives constructive (or "record") notice to everyone. Hence, proper recording prevents anyone from becoming a subsequent bona fide purchaser ("BFP"). Because the landowner's conveyance to the friend was recorded at the time of the landowner's conveyance to the investor, the investor cannot prevail. The investor will clearly lose under a pure race statute because the friend recorded first. The investor will also lose under notice and race-notice statutes because the conveyance to the friend was recorded at the time of the conveyance to the investor. The investor, therefore, had record notice and cannot claim the protection that these types of statutes provide for subsequent purchasers for value who take ***without*** notice. Thus, (A) is correct and (C) is incorrect. The fact that the friend is merely a donee rather than a BFP does not mean that her recording has no effect. It is only the ***subsequent*** taker who has to be a BFP rather than a donee to utilize the recording statute. The prior grantee, regardless of her status, protects her interest by recording because it prevents anyone from becoming a subsequent BFP. (B) is incorrect because, as noted above, the friend will prevail under any type of recording act, but not necessarily because she recorded prior to the investor's recording. If the jurisdiction has a notice statute, whether the friend recorded prior to the investor's recording is irrelevant. Rather, it is the fact that the friend recorded prior to the investor's ***purchase*** that gives the friend superior title in a notice jurisdiction, because the investor would have record notice of the conveyance and thus would not qualify as a BFP. (D) is incorrect because the quitclaim/warranty deed distinction does not affect who has title to the land; that status merely affects the parties' respective causes of action and ability to recover against the landowner.

Answer to Question 24

(B) The court should find this testimony admissible. Any person can testify to the authenticity of another's signature as long as that witness has seen the person's signature and can express an opinion regarding its authenticity. There is no requirement that the witness have seen the signature recently; thus, (A) is not the best answer, even though the length of time since the witness last saw the signature in question may go to the weight that should be given the witness's testimony. Nor is it decisive that the witness testifying regarding the signature has seen it only once. Under this circumstance, the witness's testimony may lack reliability, but that is a fact for defense counsel to bring out. Thus, (C) is incorrect. The testimony is of sufficient reliability to permit its admission. Thus, (D) is wrong.

Answer to Question 25

(C) The cigarette should not be admitted. There are six exceptions to the warrant requirement. The only exception applicable to this case is a search incident to a lawful arrest. However, if an arrest is unlawful, then any search incident to that arrest is also unlawful. At common law, a police officer could not make a warrantless arrest for a misdemeanor unless it was committed in his presence. While it is unclear whether a warrantless arrest for a misdemeanor not committed in the officer's presence would violate the Fourth Amendment, practically all states follow the common law rule. Because the defendant did not commit the misdemeanor of disorderly conduct in the presence of the officer, his arrest and accompanying search were invalid. It follows that (A) is incorrect. (B) is incorrect because it simply states the geographic scope of a search incident to a lawful arrest. (D) is incorrect because *Miranda* warnings, which protect a person's Fifth Amendment right against self-incrimination, do not generally affect seizure of evidence, and would not affect the seizure in this case.

Answer to Question 26

(C) The employee has more than an abstract interest in redressing his grievance. His right to redress, guaranteed by the state through its statutory enactment, is itself a property right. Although the legislature may elect not to confer a property interest, it may not constitutionally authorize the deprivation of such an interest, once conferred, without appropriate procedural safeguards. [Logan v. Zimmerman Brush (1982)] Thus, the state statute cannot be applied so as to deprive the employee of his property interest in using the statutory procedure for possible redress of unfair employment practices without at least affording him an opportunity for an appropriate hearing. It follows that (A) and (B) are incorrect, both because they state the wrong result and because they misstate the applicable rules. As indicated, the employee has a property interest and thus (A) is wrong. (B), in turn, describes a valid general rule but does not describe this case. The state can enact specific procedures, expect the employee to follow them, and bar the claim if he fails to do so. That is, however, not what happened here. Rather, the state itself failed to act in a timely manner, and the statutory time limit operated indiscriminately to extinguish the employee's claim. Finally, (D) is incorrect because it is too general. What happened to the employee was "unfair" because it deprived him of a property right, not because the state is required to provide any remedy, or a specific remedy.

Answer to Question 27

(C) The defendant's statement is an admission—an out-of-court statement by a party being offered into evidence by an opposing party. [Fed. R. Evid. 801(d)(2)] Because it is not considered hearsay evidence and is obviously relevant to the underlying question of who committed the battery against the plaintiff, it would be admissible. (A) is incorrect because the "statement against interest" exception to the hearsay rule provides that a declarant's out-of-court statement is admissible ***if it is against the declarant's interest when made***. [Fed. R. Evid. 804(b)(3)] The defendant's out-of-court statement ("I haven't been out of the country in five years") was not clearly against his interest when it was made. It is vastly different, for example, than if the defendant had confided to the witness that he had beaten the plaintiff; that would be a statement against interest at the time the statement was made. That the defendant's actual statement to the witness was ultimately used against the defendant does not qualify it as a statement against interest. Also, and equally important, (A) is incorrect because the "statement against interest" exception to the hearsay rule comes into play only ***if the declarant is unavailable to testify*** (*e.g.*, because the declarant is dead or cannot be found). [Fed. R. Evid. 804(a)] The question makes clear that the defendant not only is available to testify, but he actually does testify. Hence, the "unavailability" requirement of the "statement against interest" exception has not been satisfied. (B) is a plausible answer, but not as good as (C) because it contains several ambiguities. The answer is ambiguous as to the purpose for which the defendant's prior inconsistent statement is offered into evidence. If offered for the purpose of proving the truth of the matter asserted in the statement, it would be inadmissible hearsay evidence; it would not meet the specific requirements of Rule 801(d)(1)(A) to qualify as nonhearsay evidence: the defendant's prior inconsistent statement was not made ***under oath*** at ***another proceeding***. If offered for the purpose of impeaching the defendant's testimony, however, the prior inconsistent statement might be admissible. Proving the prior inconsistent statement of a witness is a well-accepted method for impeaching the testimony of that witness. In this case, though, ***extrinsic evidence*** (the testimony of the witness) is being offered to prove the defendant's prior inconsistent statement. Extrinsic evidence can be used to show a prior inconsistent statement of a witness, for purposes of impeachment, only if the inconsistency goes to a ***material*** issue in the case. It would, at best, be a judgment call as to whether the defendant's not having left the country in five years is a material issue in the plaintiff's suit against the defendant for battery. Thus, (C) is a better answer than (B). (D) is incorrect because, since the defendant's statement is an admission, its admissibility is not dependent on the defendant's having the opportunity to comment on it. Moreover, even if the defendant's statement were analyzed solely from the standpoint of being a prior inconsistent statement offered to impeach, (D) would be incorrect. The Federal Rules have abolished the common law requirement that a witness be given an opportunity to explain a prior inconsistent statement ***before*** extrinsic evidence of the statement can be admitted; the opportunity may be provided after introduction of the statement.

Answer to Question 28

(B) The statement should not be suppressed. Under the Fifth Amendment, a suspect must be provided with *Miranda* warnings prior to interrogation. The *Miranda* warnings and a valid waiver are prerequisites to the admissibility of any statement made by the suspect during custodial interrogation. Here, the detective provided the suspect with valid *Miranda* warnings; thus, the statement should not be suppressed due to a failure to provide *Miranda* warnings. (A) is incorrect because the facts state that the suspect had been arrested and was waiting to post bond. Thus, even though it was for a different charge, he was not free to leave. (C) is also incorrect. Under *Miranda*, there is no requirement for the police to advise the suspect of the offense they wish to question him about. (D) is incorrect because *Miranda* warnings must be given prior to interrogation, not after arrest.

Answer to Question 29

(D) The trial court's decision should be overturned because the city's ownership of the park does not cut off the philanthropist's liability for negligent design of the playground equipment. The prevailing rule is that in performing services of designing and constructing improvements on property eventually deeded to the city, a developer must accept responsibility for prededication negligence. Hence, the trier of fact should be permitted to consider evidence of the philanthropist's negligence. To hold otherwise would allow the developer to avoid liability merely by dedicating the grounds to a city. Thus, (A) and (B) are incorrect. (C) is incorrect because presenting evidence of a bad motive on the philanthropist's part is not necessary to find him liable.

Answer to Question 30

(B) This question raises several different issues: competency of witnesses, use of leading questions on cross-examination, the proper scope of cross-examination, and the probative value/prejudicial impact balancing test. Through a process of elimination, (B) emerges as the correct answer. (D) is incorrect. Under the Federal Rules, ***virtually all*** witnesses with personal knowledge are competent to testify. [Fed. R. Evid. 601] A witness is not rendered incompetent simply by having served on a jury in a prior case involving a party to the current suit. Such prior jury service might render the witness's testimony ***unpersuasive***, but it would not make it ***inadmissible***. (C) is incorrect because ordinarily, leading questions are permitted ***on cross-examination***. [Fed. R. Evid. 611(c)] The prosecutor's question is a leading question, but that is perfectly permissible, especially in a case like this, where the alibi witness is not "friendly" toward the prosecution. (A) is incorrect because cross-examination is generally limited in scope to the subject matter of the direct examination ***and matters affecting the credibility of the witness*** [Fed. R. Evid. 611(b)], and the prosecutor's question is, in a roundabout way, an attempt to impeach the witness's credibility. The implication behind the question is that if the witness had served on a jury that acquitted the defendant of another criminal charge, the witness would be inclined to think the defendant innocent of the pending charge. Alternatively, the implication behind the question could be that the witness is the kind of person who is "soft on crime" and for that reason is not a credible witness. In either event, because the question is an attempt to impeach the witness's testimony, it is within the proper scope of cross-examination. This leaves (B) as the remaining correct answer. (B) is not unquestionably correct, because the probative value/prejudicial impact balancing test found in Rule 403 is weighted heavily toward admission of evidence. For evidence to be excluded under this balancing test, its probative value must be substantially outweighed by its prejudicial impact. Nevertheless, in this case, a plausible reason for sustaining an objection to the prosecutor's question is that the probative value of the answer would be substantially outweighed by its tendency to mislead. The question and answer would inevitably let the jury know that the defendant had been previously charged with a crime. This information could be highly prejudicial to his defense. Because the question and answer have little probative value (the negative inferences pertaining to the witness's credibility being very weak), it is reasonable to sustain an objection to the question on the basis that its probative value is substantially outweighed by its prejudicial impact.

Answer to Question 31

(B) The oral agreement was a valid subsequent modification because the parties may orally waive the contract provision limiting amendment to a writing; thus (B) is correct and (C) is incorrect. (D) is incorrect because the law firm was in breach by not completing the data collection within three weeks, so the client's decision to compromise rather than sue for breach is consideration for the oral agreement. (A) is incorrect because the Statute of Frauds may bar subsequent oral modification of contracts to which it is applicable, but it is not applicable to the services contract here.

Answer to Question 32

(C) The neighbor, as third-party creditor beneficiary of the agreement to repair the fence, has an action against the contractor. A third party is a creditor beneficiary of a contract if the promisee's primary intent in contracting is to discharge an obligation to the third party. Here, the father bargained with the contractor to do repair work on the neighbor's fence in discharge of an obligation that the father had to the neighbor. Therefore, the neighbor was the third-party creditor beneficiary of the agreement to repair the fence and could sue the contractor on this agreement. (A) is wrong because a third-party beneficiary who is an intended beneficiary (*i.e.,* one to whom performance is given under the contract and upon whom the right to performance had been conferred by the promisee) may sue the promisor on the contract even though there is no agreement between the third-party beneficiary and the promisor. (B) is wrong because the neighbor was an intended, not an incidental, beneficiary; the contract between the father and the contractor provided that performance be made directly to the neighbor in discharge of an obligation that the father had to the neighbor (*i.e.,* to fix his fence, which the father's daughter had damaged). (D) is wrong because the neighbor was a creditor, and not a donee, beneficiary; the father's promise to have the neighbor's fence fixed was not gratuitous, but was in discharge of an obligation that the father had to the neighbor.

Answer to Question 33

(A) If the investor is adjudged the owner of all of the property, it will most likely be because the Statute of Frauds prevents the enforcement of an oral agreement concerning an interest in land. If the Statute of Frauds did not apply, the farmer could argue that the investor's statement resulted in a conveyance (severing the joint tenancy in all jurisdictions) or a lease (which severs the joint tenancy in some jurisdictions). (B) is wrong because there is no issue as to the record title to the land. The agreement between the investor and the farmer, if it had been reduced to writing, would have been perfectly valid as between them. (C) is wrong because a joint tenancy can be unilaterally severed. (D) is wrong because this would rebut rather than support the investor's ownership of the entire piece of land.

Answer to Question 34

(C) The appellate court should reverse and remand. When the existence of a presumed fact is submitted to the jury in a criminal case, the judge must instruct the jury that it ***may*** regard the basic facts as sufficient evidence of the presumed fact, but that it is not ***required*** by law to do so. If, as here, the presumed fact (intoxication) is an element of the offense, its existence must be proved beyond a reasonable doubt. Thus, the judge should have instructed the jury that it may regard a blood alcohol concentration of .10 or more as sufficient evidence of intoxication, not that it must do so. The instruction appears to relieve the prosecution of its burden of proving intoxication beyond a reasonable doubt. It follows that (A) is incorrect. (B) is incorrect because a jury should be instructed on the applicable law—*e.g.,* permissible inferences as to intoxication. (D) is incorrect because an instruction is supposed to inform the jury of the law, not be probative. The term "probative" applies to relevance of evidence, not jury instructions.

Answer to Question 35

(B) Substantially overbroad or vague statutes regulating First Amendment rights are void on their face, and persons may not be prosecuted for their violation even if their conduct might otherwise be subject to valid regulation. Conversely, statutes that reasonably regulate the time, place, and manner of speech in public forums may be unconstitutional if applied in situations where the First Amendment activity is unreasonably infringed. Here, the statute is a valid time, place, and manner restriction because it is content neutral, it is narrowly tailored to serve an important government interest, and it leaves open alternative channels of communication. It is not too vague when read as a whole, because pedestrian traffic is "sufficiently heavy" when the foot traffic spills over into public streets because of the obstruction. However, it is being applied to circumstances that do not provide any reasonable basis for regulation of the speech. Thus, (B) is correct: While the demonstrator's conduct can be regulated, it is the threat by the farmer that triggers the demonstrator's arrest, not his violation of the statute. (A) and (D) are incorrect because the statute itself is valid on its face. (C) is incorrect, in turn, because it wrongly asserts that the demonstrator may be prosecuted under these circumstances.

Answer to Question 36

(B) The defendant's conviction for embezzlement is most likely to be admitted. Because the defendant did not take the stand, this evidence is not being offered for impeachment and, thus, the 10-year time limit does not apply. Evidence of other crimes is admissible against an accused in a criminal case if it is relevant to some issue other than the defendant's character or disposition to commit the crime charged. Where, as here, the crime charged is embezzlement, evidence that the defendant committed embezzlement before might be admissible to establish fraudulent intent. The crimes in (A), (C), and (D) are not relevant to any issue other than character and propensity to commit a crime; therefore, they are inadmissible. The fact that (A) and (D) are felonies would be important only if this were impeachment evidence, which it is not.

Answer to Question 37

(C) The farmer's strongest argument would be that he has an irrevocable license. The original grant by the neighbor to the farmer was a license, which is a personal privilege to go upon the land belonging to the licensor. When the farmer expended a substantial sum of money in reliance on the license, the license became irrevocable under the doctrine of estoppel. (A) is wrong because the neighbor was estopped from terminating the license, not just from preventing the farmer from coming onto her land. (B) is wrong because the estoppel is based not on the mere construction of the ditch but the expenditure of a substantial sum of money in reliance on the license. Therefore, (C) is a better answer than (B). (D) is wrong because the duration of the irrevocable license is based on what the parties contemplated would be the duration when the oral license was granted and the facts do not indicate that they intended it to exist until the farmer acquired another source of water.

Answer to Question 38

(A) The defendant may be convicted of and sentenced for larceny only. At common law, burglary was the breaking and entering of the dwelling house of another at nighttime with the intent to commit a felony therein. The intent to commit a felony must exist at the time of the breaking and entering. Given that common law burglary requires the breaking and entering to be of the dwelling of another, an awareness of the building's use as a dwelling is a component of the mens rea for the crime. The professor's ignorance or mistake regarding the building's use as a dwelling negates the mens rea for that element of the crime of burglary. Furthermore, the professor did not have the intent to commit a felony at the time he broke into and entered the shop/dwelling. At that time, his only intent was to retrieve his own property, which would not have been sufficient for larceny (*see* below). For both of these reasons, the professor could not be convicted of and sentenced for burglary, thus making (B) and (D) incorrect answer choices. At common law, larceny was the taking and carrying away of the tangible personal property of another by trespass with the intent to permanently deprive the person of his interest in the property. In the instant case, the professor, at the time he broke into and entered the structure, did not have the intent to permanently deprive ***another*** of his interest of the laptop, given that he believed the laptop was the one stolen from his office. However, after turning over the laptop, the professor realized it was not his laptop, but he took it and carried it off anyway. This is sufficient for larceny. Thus, the professor may be convicted and sentenced for larceny, making (A) correct and (D) incorrect.

Answer to Question 39

(A) The gift in trust to the state university is a valid charitable trust. To be valid, a charitable trust must have an indefinite group of beneficiaries. The beneficiaries must be reasonably numerous and not individually identified. The trust may be for the benefit of an established charity or for a group of persons, as long as it is for a charitable purpose. Here, a trust for the benefit of a university to pay for the educational expenses of residents of a town qualifies as a charitable trust. Thus, (A) is correct and (C) is incorrect. (B) is incorrect because the doctrine of cy pres applies only when the purposes of a charitable trust are impossible to fulfill, are illegal, or have been completely fulfilled, allowing a court to redirect the trust to a different purpose that is as near as may be to the settlor's original intent. Here, because the trust purposes can be fulfilled, the doctrine does not apply. (D) is incorrect because the gift to the state university is certain to vest within the perpetuities period. The Rule Against Perpetuities applies to the equitable future interests of the beneficiaries in a private trust just as it does to legal future interests. The owner's three children are lives in being at the time the trust becomes effective, which is the owner's death. The executory interest in trust held by the state university is certain to either take effect or fail during those lives in being.

Answer to Question 40

(A) The witness's testimony is admissible. This question involves testimony by a witness whose recollection has been refreshed by reference to a document (her diary). Under the Federal Rules, any materials can be used to refresh one's recollection, and the Rules do not prohibit the use of such materials before trial. Thus, (A) is correct. (B) can quickly be discarded as incorrect. The contents of the witness's diary are not remotely protected under the work product rule. The work product rule involves a product, such as a document, ***prepared in anticipation of litigation or preparation for trial***, by or on behalf of ***a party***. The witness is not a party, and her diary was not prepared in anticipation of litigation or preparation for trial. It is, presumably, merely a collection of private thoughts transcribed for the witness's personal edification. (D) is also incorrect. The best evidence rule does not literally require a party to produce the best evidence possible to prove a point. Rather, it requires the production of the original document ***when attempting to prove the contents of a document***. [Fed. R. Evid. 1002] Although the witness used a document to refresh her recollection and enable her to testify, her testimony concerned the details of an auto accident, ***not the contents of the document***. Because the witness was testifying about an event, as opposed to the contents of her diary, her testimony was proper, notwithstanding the failure to produce the diary. (C) is a tempting answer, but ultimately incorrect. If a witness's recollection has been refreshed prior to trial by reference to a document, the court has discretion to require that the document be disclosed to the opposing party. [Fed. R. Evid. 612] The court is not ***required*** to order disclosure. In this case, there is no indication that the court ordered disclosure of the diary or that the plaintiff failed to comply with an order to produce the diary. All that is known is that, upon learning through cross-examination of the witness that she had consulted her diary the night before, the defendant's attorney immediately moved that the witness's testimony be stricken from the record. Because there is nothing improper about a witness's refreshing her recollection prior to trial, the defendant's motion should be denied and the witness's testimony should remain on the record.

Answer to Question 41

(A) The statements that the onlooker gave to the homicide detective most likely will not be suppressed for failure to provide a *Miranda* warning. Prior to custodial interrogation, the person being questioned must be informed that he has the right to remain silent, that anything he says can be used against him in court, that he has the right to the presence of an attorney, and that, if he cannot afford an attorney, one will be appointed for him if he so desires. The interrogation must also take place in a custodial setting. The test to determine whether a person is in custody is an objective test; the subjective beliefs of the interrogator or the accused are not determinative. Essentially, the issue is whether the person's freedom is being constrained in a significant way. Here, the onlooker had not been arrested, had not been placed in handcuffs, nor was he even at a police station. Being unconstrained at a crime scene probably would not constitute being "in custody"; as a result, *Miranda* warnings were not required. Thus, (A) is correct. (B) is incorrect because who initiates the contact is not really relevant to determine whether the person is "in custody," although it may be a factor to be considered when determining whether the defendant was free to leave. (C) is incorrect because it falsely states that the test for custody is a subjective one. The test is an objective test. (D) is also incorrect. *Miranda* warnings are required prior to custodial interrogation. The subjective beliefs of the interrogator as to who may have committed the crime are irrelevant.

Answer to Question 42

(A) Both an injunction and damages would be in order. The school has a life estate ***pur autre vie*** while the grantor's children have a vested remainder subject to open. Absent an "open mine" in existence at the creation of the life estate and remainder, a life tenant cannot extract minerals from the land because it depletes the corpus and constitutes waste. Thus, the remaindermen could recover damages and obtain an injunction for the unlawful waste. (B) is wrong because the school's action did not terminate its interest. The school's interest is not a defeasible one at all because the language that purports to restrict its use to educational purposes is only precatory and provides for no termination or forfeiture if the school fails to comply. (C) is wrong because it is entirely unnecessary for the grantor and his wife to be parties because neither of them has any interest in the land. (D) is wrong because the injury to the land is permanent and therefore should be prevented by an injunction.

Answer to Question 43

(C) The general principles of intergovernmental immunity prevent federal interference with state governmental functions. Though there is not a great deal of bite left in the Tenth Amendment under current case law, particularly with regard to congressional conditions on expenditures of federal money, this is still the best argument presented. (B) is not the best answer because it goes too far; the doctrine of federalism relates to the ***functions*** of state government, not to all the ***actions*** of the state government. Clearly, the federal government could prevent the state from exercising its power in such a manner as to deprive its citizens of their federal rights, including those rights with regard to public education. (A) is obviously wrong, because the doctrine of federal preemption prevents the states from interfering with the effect and purposes of federal law. (D) is wrong because it is too narrow. Aside from the problem of separation of church and state, there are many reasons why the federal government could limit a state's rights in this area.

Answer to Question 44

(D) The oven manufacturer will likely succeed because the factory owner otherwise will be unjustly enriched by getting the system without having to pay the price. A party who has breached a contract (and therefore cannot enforce it) can recover restitution under the modern view to prevent unjust enrichment of the other party. Hence, neither the failure of the express condition (A) nor the breach of contract claim (B) would preclude the oven manufacturer from recovering restitution for the reasonable value of his services. (C) is not as good a choice as (D) because all that is necessary to recover in a breached contract situation is that the other party would otherwise be unjustly enriched. Where there is no contractual relationship between the parties, the party seeking restitution in a quasi-contract action must specifically show that his expectation of being compensated is reasonable and that the benefits were conferred at the express or implied request of the defendant. Those elements are assumed when the unjust enrichment occurs in a breached contract situation. Hence, (D) states the rule in this situation more accurately than (C).

Answer to Question 45

(B) A contract was formed and breached by the shipment. The seller's act of shipping goods constitutes an acceptance of the offer, but, because the goods are nonconforming, the grocery store can reject them under the Uniform Commercial Code and avail itself of the remedies available to a buyer when the seller breaches a sales contract. Under the U.C.C., a buyer who receives nonconforming goods has a choice of rejecting them or accepting them. If the buyer chooses to accept the nonconforming goods, she may recover damages from the seller resulting from the breach, but only if she gives notice to the seller within a reasonable time after she discovers or should have discovered the breach. (A) is incorrect because the grocery store need not accept the milk. If the buyer chooses to reject the goods under the rule stated above, the rejection must be accomplished within a reasonable time after their delivery, and the seller must be notified of the rejection. Thus, the grocery store has the option of rejecting the milk within a reasonable time after its delivery. (C) is incorrect. When a buyer orders goods from a seller, and the seller complies with the order and ships goods, a contract has been formed under the U.C.C. The seller is liable for breach of contract if it ships nonconforming goods, unless it specifically states that it is shipping them as an accommodation, in which case it has made a counteroffer. In this case, the shipment constitutes an acceptance rather than a counteroffer, because there was no notice that this nonconforming tender was shipped only as an accommodation. (D) is incorrect because the dairy's nonconforming shipment was not a counteroffer. As discussed above, the shipment here constitutes an acceptance rather than a counteroffer, because there was no notice that this nonconforming tender was shipped only as an accommodation. In addition, if the grocery store rejects the nonconforming goods but has possession of the goods at the time of rejection, it need only hold them for a reasonable time for the dairy to remove them. If the dairy did not have an agent or office at the place of rejection, the grocery store would be obligated to sell the milk, which is perishable, for the account of the dairy. Because the dairy has an office in the same city as the grocery store, the grocery store need not sell the milk for the dairy's account. The grocery store has no responsibility to reship the milk to the dairy, even at the dairy's expense, if it decides not to accept delivery.

Answer to Question 46

(B) Statements made by the painting contractor before the contract was signed would not be barred by the parol evidence rule. This rule provides that a writing that constitutes a complete and final expression of the bargain may not be varied by prior written or oral statements or contemporaneous oral statements. However, the parol evidence rule does not bar prior statements when the cause of action is for misrepresentation, which is attacking the validity of the agreement. Thus, (A) and (D) are wrong. While (C) is true, it is not as good an answer as (B) because the statements could be admitted even if the contract was not proved to be an incomplete agreement.

Answer to Question 47

(D) The son is likely to prevail because his testimony is privileged. The privilege that is given to statements made as part of a judicial proceeding is a defense to civil liability, in order to ensure that witnesses will testify freely and truthfully without fear of lawsuits by those unhappy with the testimony. The privilege typically is applied when the plaintiff is suing in defamation, but will also apply when he uses another tort such as infliction of emotional distress to attack statements protected by a privilege. (A) is incorrect. Reckless disregard of the truth or falsity of statements is a definition of malice that can defeat a qualified privilege; however, statements made as part of a judicial proceeding are absolutely privileged, so even the son's knowledge of the falsity of his statement would not defeat the privilege. (B) is incorrect because, even assuming that the statements rose to the level of outrageousness sufficient to state a cause of action for intentional infliction of emotional distress, the statements were privileged. (C) is incorrect because physical injury is not an element of intentional infliction of emotional distress. To prevail, the plaintiff must show severe emotional distress, in addition to extreme or outrageous conduct by the defendant, intent or recklessness, and causation.

Answer to Question 48

(C) The rocket manufacturer will be liable for negligence if it should have discovered the defect in the motor. To establish a prima facie case for negligence in a products liability case, the plaintiff must show the existence of a legal duty owed by the defendant to that particular plaintiff, breach of that duty, actual and proximate cause, and damages. To prove breach of duty, plaintiff must show (i) negligent conduct by the defendant leading to (ii) the supplying of a defective product by the defendant. The call of the question indicates that the rocket manufacturer supplied a defective product. If the defect could have been discovered by the manufacturer in the exercise of reasonable care, it was negligent in not discovering the defect and preventing the rocket from being sold. Choice (A), which addresses the duty element, is incorrect because a manufacturer of rocket models is a "commercial supplier" owing a duty of due care to any foreseeable plaintiff. Although the daughter did not purchase the rocket (and so was not in privity with the manufacturer), she was the daughter of the purchaser and was standing nearby when her father connected the launch system and the rocket exploded, causing her injuries. (B) is incorrect because the father's negligence would be imputed to the daughter only where she and her father stand in such a relationship to each other (*e.g.,* an employer-employee relationship) that the courts would find it proper to charge the daughter with her father's negligence (such that she would be vicariously liable for her father negligent conduct if a third party had sued her). Here, there are no facts to impute the father's negligence in failing to remove the safety key to his daughter. Choice (D), which addresses the causation element, is incorrect because an intermediary's negligent failure to discover a defect is foreseeable negligence and therefore ***not*** a superseding cause. The rocket manufacturer is the defendant whose original negligence created the defect and will still be liable.

Answer to Question 49

(C) Under the "perfect tender rule," the buyer may reject the entire shipment. This power to reject is tempered by the U.C.C.'s provisions allowing a seller to "cure" defects. Although "cure" is not mentioned as an option, (C) remains a better answer than the others because (A) and (B) are not permissible options for the buyer at this time. With regard to (A), the contract's delivery date has not yet arrived and the seller must be given an opportunity to "cure" before the buyer seeks "cover." (B) is not an option because the delivery date has not yet arrived and there is no reason to anticipate that the seller will not make good before the date in question. There is no breach until delivery date, and an anticipatory breach situation does not exist. Hence, (A) and (B) are incorrect. (D) is incorrect because 143 widgets is not a gross and is a breach of the contract.

Answer to Question 50

(B) Absent any anti-deficiency statutes, the investor remains personally liable to pay for any shortfall arising from the foreclosure sale. Proceeds from the sale are used to satisfy the loan that was foreclosed first. Hence, all of the proceeds ($6,000) went to the bank. Thus, the investor must pay the balance still due the bank ($4,000) and the entire amount of the finance company's mortgage ($2,000), which is terminated by the foreclosure of the senior mortgage. (A) is wrong because foreclosure sales are not allotted proportionally between senior and junior interests. (C) is wrong because foreclosure does not extinguish the underlying debt. (D) is wrong because the finance company's mortgage does not remain on the land after foreclosure of the senior mortgage; hence, the investor is liable for that debt as well.

Answer to Question 51

(B) The defendant will likely obtain a reversal. Burglary is the breaking and entering of the dwelling house of another in the nighttime with the intent to commit a felony inside the house. The prosecution must prove every element of the offense, including intent, beyond a reasonable doubt.

Given that the trial court's instructions placed the burden of proving lack of intent on the defendant, they were in error. Thus, (B) is correct, and (D) is incorrect. (A) is incorrect because it focuses on the standard of proof, when the burden of proof is the issue. (C) is incorrect because it is impossible to make the harmless error analysis without knowing more about the state of the evidence, and the test for constitutional error is "harmless beyond a reasonable doubt," not by a preponderance, as suggested by the answer.

Answer to Question 52

(C) Congress's power over interstate commerce is broad, and the federal statute is clearly authorized by that power. The Court's 5-4 decision has no bearing here, because it was simply explaining what the standard was in the absence of any express congressional action. (A) is wrong because the fact that a state regulation does not burden interstate commerce in the absence of federal regulation does not preclude the federal government from subsequently enacting conflicting regulations which void the state law. (B) is wrong because the Fourteenth Amendment does not bind the federal government, and because a regulation of interstate commerce would rarely be classified as violating equal protection as to intrastate commerce. (D) is not the best answer because the Supremacy Clause alone does not speak to the validity of a federal statute, merely to its precedence over conflicting state enactments. The Supremacy Clause would operate, accordingly, only ***after*** the new statute is enacted, and would render the city ordinance invalid.

Answer to Question 53

(B) The motorist can recover against the landowner because the privilege of private necessity applied. A person may interfere with the real or personal property of another when the interference is reasonably and apparently necessary to avoid threatened injury from a natural or other force and the threatened injury is substantially more serious than the invasion that is undertaken to avert it. Here, it was necessary for the motorist to push the car into the landowner's driveway to avoid the threat of other vehicles colliding with it on the narrow road, which would be a substantially more serious harm than any damage to the landowner's property. Hence, the landowner was not entitled to move the car back into the road, and the motorist can recover from the landowner the damages that resulted from doing so. (A) is wrong because the absence of "no trespassing" signs is irrelevant. Even if the landowner had posted "no trespassing" signs and the motorist saw them, the signs do not negate the privilege, which supersedes any right of the landowner to protect his property. (C) is similarly incorrect; the fact that the motorist's car damaged the landowner's property does not extinguish the privilege. The motorist will be required to pay for the damage to the landowner's flower bed because the privilege of private necessity is not absolute, but the landowner was not entitled to move the car off of his land and back into danger. (D) is incorrect. A landowner's reasonable belief that he had a right to defend his property generally is not a defense to the entrant's exercise of a privilege, such as necessity, that supersedes the defense of property right. Here, the landowner's reasonable mistake that he had a right to remove the car is no defense.

Answer to Question 54

(A) The buyer cannot obtain specific performance against the homeowner because the absence of a written memorandum signed by the homeowner and containing the essential terms of an agreement between the buyer and the homeowner means that there is no enforceable contract. To obtain specific performance, there must be an enforceable contract between the parties. Pursuant to the Statute of Frauds, a contract for the sale of land is not enforceable unless it is evidenced by a writing signed by the party sought to be bound. In addition to this signature, the writing should contain a recital of consideration, the terms and conditions of the agreement, the identity of the party sought to be charged, and an identification of the contractual subject matter. The buyer is attempting to obtain specific performance of a contract to purchase the homeowner's house. Thus, the buyer must show the existence of a contract through a writing sufficient to satisfy the Statute of Frauds. The only writings mentioned in the facts are the buyer's written offer to purchase the house and the real estate listing agreement between the homeowner and the real estate broker. The latter reflects only an agreement between the homeowner and the real estate broker as to the terms of the real estate broker's services as a broker in connection with the sale of the homeowner's house. This in no way constitutes written evidence of an agreement between the homeowner and the buyer. The buyer's written offer was never signed by the homeowner and was, in fact, rejected by the homeowner in a manner consistent with its terms. Thus, this writing does not memorialize an agreement between the homeowner and the buyer for the sale of the homeowner's house; no agreement was ever reached. Therefore, there is no enforceable contract that can be the subject of specific performance. (D) is incorrect because, as explained above, there is no memorandum signed by the homeowner that lists the essential terms of an agreement between the homeowner and the buyer. In fact, there was never any such agreement, much less a writing reflecting its terms. (B) is incorrect because a purchaser of land is almost always deemed to have an inadequate remedy at law. Each parcel of land is always considered unique; *i.e.,* unlike any other that could be purchased with the same sum of money. Thus, if the buyer did have a cause of action against the homeowner, he would not have an adequate remedy at law. (C) is incorrect because the facts do not indicate that the real estate broker and the homeowner intended that the buyer or any other third person benefit by their agreement. Application of the factors that courts use to determine whether a third party is an intended beneficiary who can enforce a contract between the contracting parties or an incidental beneficiary who has no rights under the contract indicates that the buyer is not an intended beneficiary. The agreement did not: (i) expressly designate a third party; (ii) indicate that performance was to be made directly to a third party; or (iii) state that a third party had any rights under the contract. Also, there is no relationship between the buyer and either the homeowner or the real estate broker from which it could be inferred that either the homeowner or the real estate broker wished to make the agreement for the buyer's benefit. Thus, the buyer is not an intended beneficiary of the agreement between the homeowner and the real estate broker and cannot recover on that agreement.

Answer to Question 55

(B) The best defense is that there is no showing of special injury. A public nuisance exists when a property owner is using his property in such a manner that it creates an unreasonable risk to the public in general. The owner need not be violating a specific statute in order to be a public nuisance; hence, (D) is incorrect. Nor is it determinative that the owner has a permit to engage in the activity if the owner's use otherwise constitutes a public nuisance, making (A) incorrect. (Albeit, in many cases it would be hard to show a public nuisance if the owner did have a permit to use his property in a certain manner. But the facts of this case show that the teacher had not complied with the provisions of the permit.) The teacher would be correct in arguing that it is not a nuisance per se in storing the flammable liquids on his property because this is not a residential neighborhood; however, (C) is not the best answer because it still could be shown that under this particular situation it was a nuisance. Nevertheless, it is generally the duty of the local district attorney to bring actions to enjoin public nuisances, and private citizens will generally have no standing to bring such suit unless the private citizen can show that he suffers some special injury in addition to that sustained by the general public. The facts in this case fail to show such special injury, so (B) would be the teacher's best defense.

Answer to Question 56

(B) Under the best evidence rule, in proving the terms of a writing, where the terms are material, the original writing must be produced. Secondary evidence of the writing, such as oral testimony regarding the writing's contents, is permitted only after it has been shown that the original is unavailable for some reason other than serious misconduct of the proponent. Here, the value of the house is of major importance, and the contents of the document are closely related to this central issue. Consequently, the neighbor, whose only knowledge of this significant litigated issue comes from having read the document, is precluded from testifying as to the contents of the document unless the unavailability of the writing is established. Destruction of the original without fault of the party offering the secondary evidence constitutes a satisfactory explanation for nonproduction of the original and justifies the admissibility of secondary evidence. Thus, (B) is a better answer than (C). (A) is incorrect because personal knowledge of the contents does not in and of itself justify admissibility of the testimony. (D) is incorrect because the appraisal document, personally prepared by the husband, constitutes an admission by a party-opponent; *i.e.,* a prior acknowledgment by a party of one of the relevant facts. Under the Federal Rules, such statements are nonhearsay.

Answer to Question 57

(C) The gangbanger may be convicted of attempted murder of the bystander and murder of the homeowner. The gangbanger's actions with respect to the rival never rose to the level of attempt under either the traditional "proximity test" or the modern Model Penal Code test. Here, there is no evidence that the rival was even present. Thus, (A) is incorrect. Even though the gangbanger thought the bystander was the rival, he intended to kill the person at whom he aimed (the bystander). His actions with regard to the bystander fulfill the test for attempt under every approach. Therefore, the gangbanger could be convicted of the attempted murder of the bystander. Furthermore, the gangbanger's intent to kill the bystander is transferred to the homeowner, making the gangbanger guilty of murder, not manslaughter. Therefore, choice (C) is correct and (B) and (D) are incorrect.

Answer to Question 58

(B) The sketch is inadmissible. Under Rule 801 of the Federal Rules, prior identification can be admissible and the sketch could be deemed a prior identification. However, to be admissible, the witness must be there to testify at trial and be subject to cross-examination. The witness in this case is unavailable; hence, this exception does not apply. (D) is therefore incorrect. (A) applies to documentary evidence and has no relevance to this question. (C) is likewise not applicable, because this exception applies only to information within the personal knowledge of the public employee. In this case, the public employee gained the knowledge from the hearsay statement of an absent witness.

Answer to Question 59

(B) The defendant's answer should be stricken as hearsay. Prior consistent statements are admissible to rebut a charge that the witness is lying or exaggerating because of some motive; however, because the facts in this question do not indicate that such a charge has been made against the defendant, the statement is no more than hearsay. Hence, (D) is wrong. (C) is wrong because an out-of-court statement made by a witness is hearsay without regard to who made the statement. (A) is wrong because all evidence given by a witness in her own defense should be self-serving. This may go to the weight of the evidence, but it has nothing to do with its admissibility.

Answer to Question 60

(C) The witness's testimony of three instances of reckless driving by the driver would be considered character evidence. Character evidence is not admissible in a civil case if offered to show that a party probably acted in conformity with that character. Character evidence is admissible in a civil case when the character of a person is an issue in the case. The plaintiff is suing the owner on a negligent entrustment theory, and thus the driver's character as a safe driver is in issue in the case against the owner, but not in the case against the driver himself. (A) is wrong; as stated, the driver's character is in issue in determining whether the owner was negligent. (B) is wrong because specific instances of conduct may be used to prove character when character is an issue in the case. [Fed. R. Evid. 405(B)] (D) is wrong because this is not a criminal case.

Answer to Question 61

(A) The evidence should not be suppressed because the defendant consented. To be reasonable under the Fourth Amendment, most searches must be pursuant to a warrant. The warrant requirement serves as a check against unfettered police discretion by requiring the police to apply to a neutral magistrate for permission to conduct a search. A search conducted without a warrant will be invalid (and the evidence discovered during the search generally must be excluded from evidence) unless the search and seizure falls within an exception to the warrant requirement. One exception to the warrant requirement is when the police have valid consent to search the premises. The police may conduct a valid warrantless search when they have a voluntary and intelligent consent to do so. Knowledge of the right to withhold consent, while a factor to be considered, is not a prerequisite to establishing a voluntary and intelligent consent. In the instant case, there are no facts that indicate that the police put any undue pressure on the defendant to consent to the search. Although it is a factor to be considered in determining whether the consent was voluntary and intelligent, the defendant's subjective mistake about being able to withhold consent would probably not, by itself, be sufficient to deem the consent involuntary and unintelligent. As a result, (A) is the correct answer, and (D) is incorrect. (B) is incorrect. The Supreme Court has made it clear that there is no general "emergency" exception to the warrant requirement, although the police may seize "evanescent" evidence in certain circumstances. That said, there is no indication that evidence here would disappear, as it seems that the defendant's operation was ongoing, thus giving the police time to get a warrant. (C) is incorrect because the police may conduct a warrantless search with the defendant's permission, as they did in this question.

Answer to Question 62

(D) Action having the purpose and effect of altering the legal rights, duties, and relations of persons, including executive branch officials, must be subjected to the possibility of presidential veto. [Immigration & Naturalization Service v. Chadha (1983)] Although the President (or his predecessor) had the opportunity to veto the statute, the adoption of a joint resolution that shortens the time that the President may use the troops would have the purpose and effect of altering the rights and duties of the President, which accrue to him by virtue of his rather extensive military powers, and would not be subject to a presidential veto. For this reason the statutory provision may be an unconstitutional legislative veto of executive action. It follows that (A) and (C) are therefore incorrect. (B) is incorrect because the President does not have ***exclusive*** power over matters relating to war. Such power is shared with Congress.

Answer to Question 63

(A) Congress may delegate many of its powers to executive agencies, provided adequate standards are established to govern exercise of the delegated power. The power was properly delegated to the Secretary of Commerce because the statute "outlines" the "management efficiency standards" to be followed. (B) is incorrect because Congress has sole authority over foreign commerce; the authority is not shared with the executive branch. (C) is incorrect because the delegation is proper if adequate standards are established; as determined above, there are adequate standards here. (D) is incorrect because there is no executive impoundment here, merely a refusal to grant funds based upon standards established by Congress. Such standards are proper where, as here, Congress acts pursuant to its spending power and the standards are specified in advance.

Answer to Question 64

(D) The buyer will lose because the race-notice recording statute protects the developer. The developer paid a fair price for the land and had no knowledge of the buyer's claim to the land at the time he purchased the property. He would thus qualify as a bona fide purchaser for value and, because he was the first to record, he would have priority over the buyer. (A) and (B) are incorrect because the recording act determines priority among purchasers of property while the Statute of Frauds deals only with the validity of an individual contract. (C) is incorrect because the seller's signing the contract, which contained the same terms and conditions as the buyer's offer, constituted an acceptance, which became effective upon dispatch under the "mailbox rule" of contract law.

Answer to Question 65

(C) The couple will prevail, because the son was a gratuitous assignee of the contract between the entrepreneur and the couple, and the entrepreneur had expressly reserved the right to stop the payments at any time, which he did when his son finished law school and he told the couple to resume making the full payments to him. (A) is wrong because the son's right to receive the funds was limited to the period in which the entrepreneur told the couple to send the funds. (B) is wrong because the facts do not show a change in position in reliance upon the entrepreneur's actions. (D) is wrong because the son had rights under the contract that he could enforce against the couple until the entrepreneur revoked the assignment.

Answer to Question 66

(B) The provision is constitutional. A tax, even though enacted for a regulatory rather than a revenue-raising purpose, can be upheld as a "necessary and proper" exercise of Congress's power to tax under Article I, Section 8, Clause 1. This will be especially true if the revenues derived from the measure are used to cover the expenses associated with the federal regulatory scheme. Because the question does not involve the attempted exercise of a state's sovereignty, there is no issue of the Supremacy Clause, and (A) is wrong. (C) is incorrect because Congress has broad power to regulate commerce, and the sale of the escarole could probably be said to have a substantial economic effect on interstate commerce even if it was not actually being sold in interstate commerce. (D) is wrong because the states do not have the exclusive right to tax within their boundaries.

Answer to Question 67

(A) Judgment will be for the brother because the owner of the servient tenement cannot obstruct an express easement. The language in the deed from the landowner to the brother creates an express easement with the landowner's farm as the servient estate and the brother's ranch as the dominant estate. As such, the developer has no right to obstruct the brother's use of the easement. (B) is incorrect because the brother has an express easement, not an easement by necessity. While it is true that, in the absence of an express easement, the brother may have had a claim of an easement by necessity, an easement by necessity will not be implied when an express easement is provided. (C) is incorrect because a change in conditions and/or circumstances will not terminate an express easement. (D) is incorrect because injunctive relief is possible where a property right is involved.

Answer to Question 68

(D) Because the testator did not retain a right to revoke the escrow, his delivery of the deed to his cousin completes the conveyance. Title passes to the brother automatically on the testator's death and "relates back" to the date of delivery to the cousin. Thus, the testator's home was not his property at his death, and it cannot pass to the sister. Thus, (A) is incorrect. (B) is incorrect because recording is a form of protection; it is not required to convey property. (C) is incorrect because execution of the deed alone is not enough to convey title; delivery is also required for a valid conveyance.

Answer to Question 69

(C) The state's motion should be denied if the plaintiff is a neighboring state. The Eleventh Amendment does not bar actions by one state government against another state government. (A) is incorrect. As a general rule, under the Eleventh Amendment, a federal court may not hear a private party's or a foreign government's claims against a state government. A private state citizen is a private party. As such, the Eleventh Amendment generally bars a private citizen from suing a state government in federal court. (B) is incorrect because the Supreme Court has held that, for Eleventh Amendment purposes, a Native American tribe is treated as a private party, and so it is barred from bringing an action against a state government in federal court. (D) is incorrect because the Eleventh Amendment bars actions brought by a foreign government against a state government.

Answer to Question 70

(B) The defendant may be sentenced under both statutes. Double jeopardy does not prohibit the imposition of cumulative sentences for two or more statutorily defined offenses specifically intended by the legislature to carry separate punishments, even though constituting the "same" crime under the *Blockburger* test (*i.e.,* each offense does not require proof of some additional fact that the other does not) when the punishments are imposed at a single trial. Absent a clear intention, it is presumed that multiple punishments are not intended for offenses constituting the same crime under *Blockburger*. Here, it is clear that Congress, in enacting the statute, intended that certain offenses, such as interstate distribution of cocaine, be subject to separate punishments. (B) is the only alternative that expresses the view that the defendant may be sentenced under both statutes. Thus, it is the correct answer, and (A), (C), and (D) are incorrect.

Answer to Question 71

(C) The court should admit the evidence. Statements in a document affecting an interest in property are admissible, pursuant to Federal Rule 803(15), if they are relevant to the purpose of the document. Thus, (B) is incorrect. (A) is incorrect because properly authenticated copies of recorded writings may be used in lieu of originals. [Fed. R. Evid. 902(4)] (D) is incorrect because the trust instrument cannot qualify as a recorded recollection; there is no witness testifying that he made or adopted the writing while the events were fresh in his mind and he has no present recollection.

Answer to Question 72

(B) The hotel will prevail because the swearing out of a complaint that was proper at the time may not serve as a basis for a false imprisonment action despite the failure to cancel the complaint (although in some circumstances such swearing out may give rise to an action for malicious prosecution). Thus, (C) is incorrect. (A) is incorrect because the reasonableness of the hotel's belief that the man stole services is irrelevant. Even if the hotel's belief was unreasonable, it does not establish the intent required for false imprisonment. (D) is wrong because the absence of an adequate number of clerks is not an act confining one within fixed boundaries, as required for false imprisonment.

Answer to Question 73

(C) The niece had the right to possess and enjoy the whole of the property subject to the equal right of the nephew to do the same. The fact that the nephew chose not to exercise his right does not make the niece's possession wrongful. Therefore, an accounting is not warranted here. (A) is wrong because, as stated, the niece may enjoy the whole of the property. (B) is wrong because there is nothing in the facts to indicate an ouster. (D) is wrong because the niece cannot take by adverse possession unless there has been an ouster; her possession was not hostile to the nephew's interest.

Answer to Question 74

(A) The commerce power is the strongest argument. Congress has the power, under the Commerce Clause, to regulate any activity that, taken cumulatively, has substantial economic or commercial effect on interstate commerce. Although there are limits on the power of Congress to regulate commerce, in only a few cases has the Court invalidated a federal law as exceeding the scope of Congress's commerce power. Because Congress has concluded that the animal is important to the region's tourism industry, and given the comparative weakness of the other answers, (A) is the strongest argument. (B) is incorrect because the Necessary and Proper Clause must be linked with another constitutional power of Congress. Here it is presented by itself, not in connection with another power, and thus it is incorrect. (C) is incorrect because there is no federal police power. (D) is wrong. The facts of this question do not offer any facts suggesting that the animals are on federal lands. Thus, the power to regulate federal lands is irrelevant.

Answer to Question 75

(A) Larceny is the taking and asportation of the personal property of another by trespass and with the intent to permanently deprive the person of his interest in the property. Here, the moving of the mower to the loading dock constituted the taking and carrying away. Because the employee did not have express or implied permission to move merchandise in this way, it was trespassory. Clearly, he intended to permanently deprive the store of its interest in the mower. Thus, the larceny was complete when the employee moved the mower to the loading dock, and (B) and (D) are therefore incorrect. (C) is incorrect because to be guilty of embezzlement, the employee would have had to have been in possession of the mower when he converted it. Because the employee did not have especially broad power over the mower and it was not given to him by a third party, he merely had custody, not possession, of the mower.

Answer to Question 76

(C) The store owner must accept the competitor's performance. The assignment by the contractor of the contract involved a delegation of her duties to the competitor. While generally all contractual duties may be delegated to a third person, duties involving personal judgment and skill may not be delegated. However, a contract for paving generally would not be regarded as involving a personal subject matter; hence, the contractor could delegate the duties to another competent contractor without the store owner's consent and the store owner must accept performance. Thus, (A) and (B) are wrong. (D) is a misstatement of law. The contractor need not supervise. The store owner may sue the contractor if the competitor fails to perform under the contract.

Answer to Question 77

(B) The grocer has a cause of action against both orchards. The delegator remains personally liable for performance of the agreement even though the delegatee is performing the contract. Hence, (A) is incorrect. (C) is incorrect because although the grocer and the assignee orchard are not in privity of contract, the grocer is a third party beneficiary of the agreement between the two orchards. When there is a delegation of duties, both the delegator and delegatee are liable for performance of the agreement. (D) is wrong because if the services to be performed are not personal, the obligee has no choice but to accept performance, and it would be unfair that if by accepting performance, the obligee waives his rights as against the delegator.

Answer to Question 78

(B) The buyer prevails. The plat is only intended to be a representation of the actual survey as made on the land itself. The plat is in the nature of a certified copy of an instrument that will be controlled by the original. Where a survey as made and marked on the ground conflicts with the plat, the survey prevails. Thus, the buyer had a right to rely on the surveyor's stakes as establishing the boundaries of his lot. Thus, (B) is correct and (C) is incorrect. (A) is incorrect because priority in purchase would not entitle the buyer to take land that was not part of the lot. (D) is incorrect because, while it is true that the adverse possession period has not run, the buyer need not rely on adverse possession to prevail.

Answer to Question 79

(C) The record on appeal must show that a specific objection was made and that the challenged evidence was inadmissible on that ground, before the trial court's action can be considered error. (A) is wrong because the defense counsel's objection did not state specific grounds for the objection. (B) is wrong; the court is never required to state the reason for overruling an objection. (D) makes no sense at all. The objection was overruled and the evidence was received. "Offers of proof" are sometimes made when evidence is held inadmissible.

Answer to Question 80

(D) The defendant should not be convicted of battery. The issue in this question is the type of force one may use in self-defense, and whether retreat is necessary. Generally, a person who is without fault may use such force as reasonably necessary to protect himself from the imminent use of unlawful force upon himself. There is no duty to retreat before using nondeadly force, even if retreat would result in no further harm to either party. In the instant case, the defendant was not at fault for creating the conflict, as he had merely accidentally bumped into the passerby. Furthermore, the amount of force that he used most likely will be considered reasonable. The passerby had already attempted to commit a battery on his person—battery being the unlawful application of force to the person of another resulting in either bodily injury or an offensive touching—and it appeared that the passerby was about to attempt it again. As stated, no attempt to retreat is required before using nondeadly force. Thus, the defendant was privileged in his use of force in self-defense. (A) is incorrect because the initial contact between the passerby and the defendant was accidental. Such a minor occurrence would not be considered sufficient to place the defendant "at fault" for the subsequent attempted battery by the passerby. (B) is incorrect because, as stated, no retreat is necessary before using nondeadly force. (C) is incorrect because the defendant need not intend to cause serious bodily injury to commit a battery. An offensive touching generally is sufficient for a battery. Furthermore, battery is generally considered to be a general intent crime; no intent to injure, whether serious or not, is required.

Answer to Question 81

(C) The defendant will likely be found guilty. An attempt requires both a specific intent to commit the crime and an overt act in furtherance of that intent. Given that the defendant intended to enter his friend's property and was apprehended just before doing so, both requirements for attempt can be established. (A) is incorrect because the defendant is not being charged with the attempt to commit violence, but with the attempt to enter onto the property with the intent to commit violence. (B) is also wrong because the statute prohibits not only the state of mind, but also an act (entering onto another's property). (D) is a poor answer because the defendant cannot be convicted unless it is proved that he committed the offense with which he has been charged, and this answer does not require that the elements of the crime be proved.

Answer to Question 82

(A) As a direct tax on the federal government, the sales tax is invalid unless Congress has consented to such a tax. (B) is wrong because the tax is on all autos purchased in the state, regardless of their source, and thus, there is no burden on interstate commerce. (C) is wrong because direct state taxation of the federal government is invalid whether or not discriminatory, absent the consent of Congress. (D) is wrong because, as stated, unless Congress consents, a direct tax on the federal government is invalid. Thus, the fact that there is a rational basis and that the tax is not a penalty does not matter: The question is one of the ***power*** to tax, not whether the tax itself is appropriate.

Answer to Question 83

(A) The landlord likely will prevail. In a partial condemnation case, the landlord-tenant relationship continues, as does the tenant's obligation to pay the entire rent for the remaining lease term. (B) is wrong because, while the tenant generally is obligated to return the premises in the same condition as when received, that obligation would not be considered breached by the actions of a third party such as the government. (C) is wrong because the covenant of quiet enjoyment can be breached only by actions of the landlord and not those of a third party, such as the government. (D) is wrong because the law of landlord and tenant traditionally refuses to recognize frustration of purpose as grounds for termination of a lease.

Answer to Question 84

(D) The defendant should seek contribution from the other driver. The other driver and the defendant are joint tortfeasors who are each jointly and severally liable for the plaintiff's injuries. As such, either may be sued for the entire amount of damages suffered. (C) is therefore incorrect. However, if the defendant is found to be liable to the plaintiff, he may seek contribution from the other driver to force the driver to pay a portion of the recovery. He would have no right to indemnity because he is actively negligent in causing the plaintiff's injuries. (B) is therefore incorrect. (A) is incorrect because the defendant was a substantial factor in causing the plaintiff's injuries.

Answer to Question 85

(A) The employees' organization likely will prevail. The Constitution prohibits the impairment of contractual obligations by a state except in certain narrow circumstances. The sort of "emergency" normally required for such state action is arguably present here, given the loss in tax revenues. But it is unlikely that the state would prevail because the termination of annual cost-of-living adjustments is permanent and appears to be the sort of self-interest driven choice to reduce the state's contractual burdens that the Court has found suspect in comparable cases. (B) is wrong because federal courts do not have the jurisdiction to decide questions regarding an individual state's own constitution. (C) is wrong because the Eleventh Amendment does not bar suits against state officials unless retroactive relief is sought. (D) is wrong because although a state may amend its own statutes, it cannot do so in such a manner as to violate constitutional prohibitions.

Answer to Question 86

(C) The gambler will prevail. The general rule is that a court will not enforce a contract if its subject matter or consideration is illegal; the court will leave the parties as it finds them. Here, the subject matter of the contract, placing gambling bets, is illegal in the state. Thus, (A) is wrong because his friend's performance is irrelevant. (B) is wrong because the court will refuse to help either party to an illegal contract, even where one party has gained unfairly. (D) is wrong because the court will not put the parties back into the position they were in prior to entering into the contract, but rather will leave them where they stand.

Answer to Question 87

(A) The patron is guilty of larceny, but not burglary. When the patron took the coat, knowing it was not her own, she committed a trespassory taking. However, the facts state that she did not intend to permanently (or for an unreasonably long time) deprive the other woman of her possessory interest in the coat. Thus, ***at that time***, she did not have the intent to commit larceny. However, under the continuing trespass doctrine, if a defendant takes property with a wrongful state of mind, but without the intent to commit larceny, and later, while still in possession of the property, forms the intent to steal it, the trespass involved in the initial wrongful taking is regarded as "continuing," and the defendant is guilty of larceny. Here, the patron's initial taking of the coat was wrong, in that she knew the coat did not belong to her when she borrowed it without permission. Thus, when she later formed the intent to permanently keep the coat, she committed larceny under the continuing trespass doctrine. However, she did not commit burglary. Burglary is the breaking and entering into the dwelling of another at nighttime with the intent to commit a felony therein. The intent to commit a felony must exist at the time of the breaking and entering. In the instant case, when the patron broke and entered into the woman's home, the only intent she had was to retrieve her own property, which would not be a felony. Without the intent to commit a felony at the time of the breaking and entering, the patron would not be guilty of burglary. Thus, (A) is correct, and (B), (C), and (D) are wrong.

Answer to Question 88

(A) The father's negligence will have no effect because a parent's contributory negligence is not imputed to the child. Nor is the father's negligence imputed to the mother because the contributory negligence of one spouse is not imputed to the other spouse. (B) and (D) are incorrect because parent-child immunity would be relevant only if the child were suing a parent for negligence; it is inapplicable here. (C) is incorrect even though a parent's action for his child's medical expenses is a derivative action. Recovery in a derivative action (such as for loss of services or recovery of medical expenses) depends on the potential success of the injured child's own action. Hence, any defense against the child would affect recovery, as would any defense against the family member seeking recovery in the derivative action. Here, however, no defense has been raised against either the child or the mother, and (as discussed above) the father's negligence is not imputed to either of them.

Answer to Question 89

(D) The homeowner is not likely to recover. The reasonableness of the homeowner's apprehension of immediate harmful or offensive contact is determined by the reasonable person standard. Thus, although it may be a close question here because of the boy's appearance and the authentic appearance of the gun, the fact that four other homeowners had not been frightened by the boy's routine indicates that a reasonable person would have recognized that this was just a youngster engaging in traditional Halloween activity. The boy could also argue that the homeowner should be deemed to have impliedly consented to this type of conduct by opening the door on Halloween. Because all of the other choices are clearly wrong, (D) is the best option. (B) is wrong because if the homeowner's apprehension of immediate harm was unreasonable, the homeowner does not have a cause of action for assault. Furthermore, the boy did not have the requisite intent for assault. While he may have intended to momentarily startle the person answering the door, he did not intend to cause apprehension of immediate harmful or offensive contact. (A) is wrong because the homeowner does not have a cause of action for intentional infliction of emotional distress; dressing up as a bandit and carrying a toy gun while trick or treating is not extreme and outrageous conduct so as to transcend all bounds of decency. (C) is wrong because minors may be liable for their intentional torts.

Answer to Question 90

(C) The landowner has a possibility of reverter in the property. The grandson's interest would be void under the Rule Against Perpetuities because his interest could (and most likely would) vest more than 21 years after a life in being. Hence, the instrument would be read as if the executory interest to the grandson did not exist. The daughter's interest is a fee simple determinable; thus, the grantor, the landowner, retains a possibility of reverter. (A) is therefore incorrect. (B) is incorrect because a possibility of reverter rather than a reversion arises upon a conveyance of a fee simple determinable. (D) is incorrect because the estate created was a fee simple determinable, not a fee simple subject to a condition subsequent. Moreover, rights of entry must be expressly raised in the conveyance.

Answer to Question 91

(D) The court should find the ordinance unconstitutional. Regulation of truthful advertising of a lawful activity is valid only if it serves a substantial government interest, directly advances that interest, and is narrowly tailored to achieve that interest. The consumption of alcohol is a valid activity and the ordinance here does not address deceptive advertising. While the city may argue that discouraging drinking is a substantial government interest, it might have a difficult time proving that the ordinance here advances that interest. More importantly, given that the ordinance amounts to a total ban on advertising outside of stores selling liquor, the city would have a difficult time arguing that the ordinance is narrowly tailored. (A) is incorrect because the Supreme Court has held that while the Twenty-first Amendment gives states power to regulate liquor commerce, it does not give them power to override First Amendment protections. (B) is incorrect because while it may be true that the ordinance does not favor local economic interests or unduly interfere with interstate commerce (and so does not violate the Commerce Clause), it nevertheless is unconstitutional for the reasons stated above. (C) is incorrect because the store owner did not have a right to personal notice. Such a right arises only when there is personalized adjudication—when the government seeks to deprive a specific individual of life, liberty, or property. Here, the government adopted a city-wide ordinance affecting all liquor sellers.

Answer to Question 92

(C) The conglomerate will prevail. The businesswoman had reserved the right to reassign the proceeds at any time, and had assigned them to her niece before she died. The daughter's initial interest in the proceeds was subject to the businesswoman's right to revoke by a subsequent assignment, which the daughter was aware of. During the time the conglomerate sold back the hotel and obligations to the speculator, the proceeds were assigned to the niece; therefore, the daughter's rights were not vested. (A) and (B) are wrong because there was no vesting when the conglomerate was an obligor. The daughter was not a third-party beneficiary of the original agreement between the businesswoman and the speculator; she was a subsequent assignee of the businesswoman's rights. While she may have been a third-party beneficiary of the agreement between the speculator and the conglomerate, she did not assent to it or change her position in reliance on it; hence, her rights did not vest. (D) is wrong because the contract between the conglomerate and the speculator expressly required the conglomerate to assume the speculator's obligations. The daughter was an intended beneficiary of that agreement, but her rights did not vest before they were extinguished by the subsequent assignment.

Answer to Question 93

(A) Leading questions are allowed on the direct examination of a "hostile" witness. There is no rule that allows leading questions on the direct examination of a "disinterested" witness. A leading question is normally permitted on cross-examination whether the witness is a layperson or an expert. Therefore, (C) is wrong. (B) is wrong because leading questions may be asked of very young or very old witnesses at the discretion of the court. (D) is wrong because a leading question may be asked of any witness on preliminary matters not in dispute.

Answer to Question 94

(C) The best defense is the quality of the partner's work. The painter assigned part of her claim against the homeowner to the paint supplier, and, as a general rule, the assignee is subject to the same defenses that the obligor has against the assignor. If the painter, the assignor, had not done the work properly, a homeowner would have a defense against her, hence he can use this defense against the paint supplier. (A) is immaterial, because this is not a third-party beneficiary agreement, but an assignment of the right to receive money. Thus, (B) must also be ruled out. (D) is wrong because an assignment of a future claim is not inoperable.

Answer to Question 95

(C) The defendant will be found guilty of larceny. The only value his tickets will have to anyone is if they are used for admission to the basketball game. Consequently, because the defendant did not intend to return the tickets to his old roommate until after the game, the defendant intended to deprive his old roommate of the value of the tickets for an unreasonable amount of time, and thus most likely would be found guilty of larceny. (A) is not a correct answer because, although the intent to return the tickets may be a valid defense in some situations, his old roommate would have been effectively permanently deprived of their value when they were returned, and thus the deprivation would be for an unreasonable time. Therefore, the defendant's intent would not be a valid defense. (B) is a tempting answer, but it is not the most likely. There are no facts that indicate the relative value of the tickets to the money that the defendant claims his old roommate owes him. (D) is not the most likely answer, because the intent to return may be a valid defense in some instances.

Answer to Question 96

(D) The defendant ***cannot*** be convicted of the attempted murder of either the club's president or treasurer. All attempts require the specific intent to commit the crime. Thus, the defendant must have had the specific intent to kill the president and the treasurer, despite the fact that a defendant may be guilty of common law murder on the showing that the defendant acted with a high degree of recklessness. As a result, if the jury believes that the defendant had no intent to kill either the club's president or treasurer, he cannot be convicted of attempted murder of either. Thus, (D) is correct, and (A), (B), and (C) are wrong.

Answer to Question 97

(D) The friend will prevail because he inherited the daughter's interest. Although the language in the mother's will uses the word "jointly," the grant also states "as tenants in common." Because no right of survivorship is mentioned, the court will most likely find that this language establishes a tenancy in common, rather than a joint tenancy. The daughter can pass her interest in the farm by will, and thus the friend now holds the farm as a tenant in common with the son. (A) is wrong because the son's management of the use of the farm does not entitle him to an exclusive interest in it. (B) is wrong because the interest created by the mother's will was a tenancy in common, not a joint tenancy. (C) is wrong because the unities only apply to a joint tenancy.

Answer to Question 98

(C) It is a defense to false imprisonment that the police acted under a ***valid*** arrest warrant. The warrant was valid here, and that should serve as a complete defense. Mere statements by a defendant that she is innocent do not compel the police to follow the defendant's suggestions. It follows that (A) is incorrect. (B) is incorrect because the police acted under a valid warrant and are not charged with knowing whether the teller actually committed the crime with which she was charged. (D) is incorrect because the reasonableness of the bank's actions will not affect the liability of the police. Even if the bank did not have reasonable grounds for signing the complaint, the police will not be liable because they acted pursuant to a valid warrant.

Answer to Question 99

(A) The winery may refuse the shipment if notice of termination is given but will not recover damages for breach. This problem is governed by U.C.C. sections 2-615 and 2-616. A crop failure resulting from an unexpected cause excuses a farmer's obligation to deliver the full amount as long as he makes a fair and reasonable allocation among his buyers. The grape grower has done this by allocating pro rata between the winery and the vineyard. Nevertheless, under U.C.C. section 2-616, the buyer may either accept the proposed modification or terminate the contract. Thus, (B) is wrong. (C) is wrong because even though alternative sources are available, the grape grower is not obligated to use them because the contract was tied to a designated parcel of land—"my [the grape grower's] ranch." (D) is wrong because it is contrary to the provision of U.C.C. section 2-615, which permits the farmer to make an allocation.

Answer to Question 100

(C) The business owner will not recover, because economic loss from injury to an employee is not within the scope of the retailer's duty. Most courts have refused to extend strict products liability to cases in which plaintiff suffers only economic loss when not accompanied by physical harm to the plaintiff, requiring the plaintiff instead to bring an action for breach of warranty to recover such damages. (In contrast, the employee would probably be successful in her strict liability action because the product's defect caused her injuries.) Here, the business owner's only loss is economic; hence, he cannot recover in a strict liability action. (A) is therefore wrong. (B) is wrong because it would have no bearing on a strict liability in tort action; it would be relevant only in an action based on breach of implied warranty. (D) is wrong because strict liability extends to retailers, because they are commercial suppliers of products.

Full Day Practice Exam and Analytical Answers

Note: This exam is ***not*** part of the Simulated MBE Workshop and is ***not*** computer graded

Multistate Practice Exam

A.M. EXAM

Time—3 hours

You will be given three hours to work on this test. Be sure that the question numbers on your answer sheet match the question numbers in your test book. You are not to begin work until the supervisor tells you to do so.

Your score will be based on the number of questions you answer correctly. It is therefore to your advantage to try to answer as many questions as you can. Give only one answer to each question; multiple answers will not be counted. If you wish to change an answer, erase your first mark completely and mark your new choice. Use your time effectively. Do not hurry, but work steadily and as quickly as you can without sacrificing your accuracy.

YOU ARE TO INDICATE YOUR ANSWERS TO ALL QUESTIONS ON THE SEPARATE ANSWER SHEET PROVIDED.

DIRECTIONS

Each of the questions or incomplete statements in this test is followed by four suggested answers or completions. You are to choose the ***best*** of the stated alternatives. Answer all questions according to the generally accepted view, except where otherwise noted.

For the purpose of this test, you are to assume that Articles 1 and 2 of the Uniform Commercial Code have been adopted. You should assume that the 2001 amendments to Article 1 have been adopted, but that the 2001 and 2003 proposed amendments to Article 2 have not been adopted.

The Federal Rules of Evidence are deemed to control.

The terms "Constitution," "constitutional," and "unconstitutional" refer to the federal Constitution unless indicated to the contrary.

You are also to assume that there is no applicable statute unless otherwise specified; however, survival actions and claims for wrongful death should be assumed to be available where applicable. You should assume that joint and several liability, with pure comparative negligence, is the relevant rule unless otherwise indicated.

DO NOT OPEN THE TEST UNTIL YOU ARE INSTRUCTED TO DO SO.

A.M. Exam

1. Ⓐ Ⓑ Ⓒ Ⓓ
2. Ⓐ Ⓑ Ⓒ Ⓓ
3. Ⓐ Ⓑ Ⓒ Ⓓ
4. Ⓐ Ⓑ Ⓒ Ⓓ
5. Ⓐ Ⓑ Ⓒ Ⓓ

6. Ⓐ Ⓑ Ⓒ Ⓓ
7. Ⓐ Ⓑ Ⓒ Ⓓ
8. Ⓐ Ⓑ Ⓒ Ⓓ
9. Ⓐ Ⓑ Ⓒ Ⓓ
10. Ⓐ Ⓑ Ⓒ Ⓓ

11. Ⓐ Ⓑ Ⓒ Ⓓ
12. Ⓐ Ⓑ Ⓒ Ⓓ
13. Ⓐ Ⓑ Ⓒ Ⓓ
14. Ⓐ Ⓑ Ⓒ Ⓓ
15. Ⓐ Ⓑ Ⓒ Ⓓ

16. Ⓐ Ⓑ Ⓒ Ⓓ
17. Ⓐ Ⓑ Ⓒ Ⓓ
18. Ⓐ Ⓑ Ⓒ Ⓓ
19. Ⓐ Ⓑ Ⓒ Ⓓ
20. Ⓐ Ⓑ Ⓒ Ⓓ

21. Ⓐ Ⓑ Ⓒ Ⓓ
22. Ⓐ Ⓑ Ⓒ Ⓓ
23. Ⓐ Ⓑ Ⓒ Ⓓ
24. Ⓐ Ⓑ Ⓒ Ⓓ
25. Ⓐ Ⓑ Ⓒ Ⓓ

26. Ⓐ Ⓑ Ⓒ Ⓓ
27. Ⓐ Ⓑ Ⓒ Ⓓ
28. Ⓐ Ⓑ Ⓒ Ⓓ
29. Ⓐ Ⓑ Ⓒ Ⓓ
30. Ⓐ Ⓑ Ⓒ Ⓓ

31. Ⓐ Ⓑ Ⓒ Ⓓ
32. Ⓐ Ⓑ Ⓒ Ⓓ
33. Ⓐ Ⓑ Ⓒ Ⓓ
34. Ⓐ Ⓑ Ⓒ Ⓓ
35. Ⓐ Ⓑ Ⓒ Ⓓ

36. Ⓐ Ⓑ Ⓒ Ⓓ
37. Ⓐ Ⓑ Ⓒ Ⓓ
38. Ⓐ Ⓑ Ⓒ Ⓓ
39. Ⓐ Ⓑ Ⓒ Ⓓ
40. Ⓐ Ⓑ Ⓒ Ⓓ

41. Ⓐ Ⓑ Ⓒ Ⓓ
42. Ⓐ Ⓑ Ⓒ Ⓓ
43. Ⓐ Ⓑ Ⓒ Ⓓ
44. Ⓐ Ⓑ Ⓒ Ⓓ
45. Ⓐ Ⓑ Ⓒ Ⓓ

46. Ⓐ Ⓑ Ⓒ Ⓓ
47. Ⓐ Ⓑ Ⓒ Ⓓ
48. Ⓐ Ⓑ Ⓒ Ⓓ
49. Ⓐ Ⓑ Ⓒ Ⓓ
50. Ⓐ Ⓑ Ⓒ Ⓓ

51. Ⓐ Ⓑ Ⓒ Ⓓ
52. Ⓐ Ⓑ Ⓒ Ⓓ
53. Ⓐ Ⓑ Ⓒ Ⓓ
54. Ⓐ Ⓑ Ⓒ Ⓓ
55. Ⓐ Ⓑ Ⓒ Ⓓ

56. Ⓐ Ⓑ Ⓒ Ⓓ
57. Ⓐ Ⓑ Ⓒ Ⓓ
58. Ⓐ Ⓑ Ⓒ Ⓓ
59. Ⓐ Ⓑ Ⓒ Ⓓ
60. Ⓐ Ⓑ Ⓒ Ⓓ

61. Ⓐ Ⓑ Ⓒ Ⓓ
62. Ⓐ Ⓑ Ⓒ Ⓓ
63. Ⓐ Ⓑ Ⓒ Ⓓ
64. Ⓐ Ⓑ Ⓒ Ⓓ
65. Ⓐ Ⓑ Ⓒ Ⓓ

66. Ⓐ Ⓑ Ⓒ Ⓓ
67. Ⓐ Ⓑ Ⓒ Ⓓ
68. Ⓐ Ⓑ Ⓒ Ⓓ
69. Ⓐ Ⓑ Ⓒ Ⓓ
70. Ⓐ Ⓑ Ⓒ Ⓓ

71. Ⓐ Ⓑ Ⓒ Ⓓ
72. Ⓐ Ⓑ Ⓒ Ⓓ
73. Ⓐ Ⓑ Ⓒ Ⓓ
74. Ⓐ Ⓑ Ⓒ Ⓓ
75. Ⓐ Ⓑ Ⓒ Ⓓ

76. Ⓐ Ⓑ Ⓒ Ⓓ
77. Ⓐ Ⓑ Ⓒ Ⓓ
78. Ⓐ Ⓑ Ⓒ Ⓓ
79. Ⓐ Ⓑ Ⓒ Ⓓ
80. Ⓐ Ⓑ Ⓒ Ⓓ

81. Ⓐ Ⓑ Ⓒ Ⓓ
82. Ⓐ Ⓑ Ⓒ Ⓓ
83. Ⓐ Ⓑ Ⓒ Ⓓ
84. Ⓐ Ⓑ Ⓒ Ⓓ
85. Ⓐ Ⓑ Ⓒ Ⓓ

86. Ⓐ Ⓑ Ⓒ Ⓓ
87. Ⓐ Ⓑ Ⓒ Ⓓ
88. Ⓐ Ⓑ Ⓒ Ⓓ
89. Ⓐ Ⓑ Ⓒ Ⓓ
90. Ⓐ Ⓑ Ⓒ Ⓓ

91. Ⓐ Ⓑ Ⓒ Ⓓ
92. Ⓐ Ⓑ Ⓒ Ⓓ
93. Ⓐ Ⓑ Ⓒ Ⓓ
94. Ⓐ Ⓑ Ⓒ Ⓓ
95. Ⓐ Ⓑ Ⓒ Ⓓ

96. Ⓐ Ⓑ Ⓒ Ⓓ
97. Ⓐ Ⓑ Ⓒ Ⓓ
98. Ⓐ Ⓑ Ⓒ Ⓓ
99. Ⓐ Ⓑ Ⓒ Ⓓ
100. Ⓐ Ⓑ Ⓒ Ⓓ

Question 1

The defendant robbed a bank and fled in a getaway car driven by an accomplice, not realizing that one of the bundles of money he took had the serial numbers recorded and had a tiny tracking device attached to the wrapper. The bank's security consultant obtained portable tracking equipment and was able to trace the bundle of money to the defendant's house. The police were notified and they arrived at the defendant's house a few hours after the robbery. They knocked on the door, announced their presence, and saw someone matching the description of the robber in the hallway. They entered and arrested the defendant, and then conducted a protective sweep of the house for the accomplice, who they believed had a gun. They did not find him, but while checking a closet, they discovered several of the bundles of money from the bank and a gun the defendant had used in the robbery. The police also discovered two clear plastic bags of what appeared to be marijuana sitting on top of a dresser. They seized the money, the gun, and the two bags. Later testing confirmed that the substance in the bags was marijuana.

The defendant was charged with the bank robbery and with possession of the marijuana. At a preliminary hearing, he moves to suppress introduction of the money, gun, and marijuana.

The court should:

(A) Grant the motion as to the marijuana but not as to the money or the gun because the money and gun were found as a result of the protective sweep for the defendant's accomplice.

(B) Grant the motion as to the money and the gun but not as to the marijuana because the bags containing the marijuana were clearly visible on the dresser during the search.

(C) Grant the motion as to all of the evidence seized.

(D) Deny the motion as to all of the evidence seized.

Question 2

A contractor gave the low bid for some electrical repairs to a homeowner's house. Based on this bid, the contractor and the homeowner entered into a contract stating that the contractor would perform the electrical repairs for $6,000. Before beginning work on the project, the contractor notified the homeowner that he would lose money on the job at that price, and would not proceed with the work unless the homeowner would agree to increase the price to $9,000. The homeowner thereupon, without notifying the contractor, entered into a contract with an electrician to make the repairs for $7,500, which was the fair market cost of the work to be done. The electrician finished the house on schedule and then showed the homeowner that he (the electrician) had spent $8,500 on the job. The homeowner thereupon paid the electrician the full balance of their contract price plus an additional $1,000, so that the electrician would not lose money on the job.

In a contract action by the homeowner against the contractor, the homeowner will recover:

(A) The difference between the fair market cost of the repairs and the contractor's original contract price.

(B) $3,000, the difference between the contractor's original contract price and the amount the contractor demanded.

(C) $2,500, the difference between the contractor's original contract price and the total amount the homeowner paid the electrician for the repairs.

(D) $1,500, the difference between the contractor's original contract price and the electrician's contract price.

Question 3

A singer entered into a contract with a hairstylist. The stylist agreed to accompany the singer on her six-month world tour and to fix her hair for each performance, in exchange for a large fee to be paid on completion of the tour. Two months into the tour, the stylist grew tired of life on the road and assigned "all his rights and duties" under the contract to his assistant. When the singer learned that the stylist had made the assignment and left the tour, she was distraught, but since she needed someone to style her hair for that night's show she allowed the assistant to take over. The next night, without legal excuse, the assistant abandoned the tour, leaving the singer without anyone to style her hair before that night's concert.

Which of the following legal conclusions is correct?

(A) Both the stylist and the assistant are liable to the singer for legal damages, if any, caused by the assistant's default.

(B) Only the assistant is liable to the singer for legal damages, if any, caused by the assistant's default, while the stylist is not liable because the singer allowed the assistant to style her hair after the assignment.

(C) Only the stylist is liable to the singer for legal damages, if any, caused by the stylist's default, while the assistant is not liable to the singer because he was not a party to a contract with the singer and thus his services were "at will."

(D) Neither the stylist nor the assistant are liable to the singer for legal damages, if any, caused by either the stylist or the assistant's default because enforcing a contract for personal services would be tantamount to involuntary servitude.

Question 4

A delivery company employed several messengers to deliver packages by car to nearby towns. The company also allowed some employees to use company cars for personal use from time to time. A clerical employee had her car in a body shop because she had run a red light and been broadsided by another vehicle. This was the second time she had run a light and been hit. She borrowed a company car for the weekend and was using it to do some grocery shopping. The employee negligently went through a red light and crossed the path of a rented van. The man driving the van swerved to avoid the employee and struck a light post and several parked cars, severely damaging the van. At the time of the accident, the driver of the van was exceeding the posted speed limit; he would have been able to avoid hitting the light post and the cars had he been going the proper speed.

The leasing company that had rented the van to the driver brought a lawsuit against the delivery company employee and the delivery company. The jurisdiction retains traditional contributory negligence rules.

If the delivery company prevails in the lawsuit, it will be because:

(A) The delivery company had no reason to know that its employee had a poor driving record.

(B) The driver of the van had the last clear chance to avoid the accident.

(C) The driver of the van exceeded the posted speed limit.

(D) The employee had agreed to assume all liability when she borrowed the delivery company's car.

Question 5

A shopper was in a large department store that was remodeling its menswear department and had hired a contractor to do the work. A carpenter employed by the contractor was working on the remodeling job. When the carpenter left the store to take her lunch break, she left a carpenter's level projecting out into one of the aisles, unbeknownst to any store employees. Shortly before she returned from lunch an hour later, the shopper came down that aisle and tripped over the level. He fell and struck his head on the sharp corner of a display case. The shopper required hospitalization and sued the store for his injuries.

Will the shopper prevail in his suit against the store?

(A) Yes, because the contractor's employee left the level in the aisle.

(B) Yes, because the store's employees had a reasonable time to discover the level before the shopper fell.

(C) No, because the store's employees did not leave the level in the aisle.

(D) No, because the store's employees were unaware that the level was in the aisle.

Question 6

The federal Fair Opportunity Act provided that an employer whose products are in any way used by or sold to the federal government must meet certain very specific standards for the hiring of women in traditional male jobs. One city has since enacted an ordinance requiring that any employer doing business with the city have a workforce consonant with the gender composition of the population of the city. A private janitorial service located in the city does contract cleaning for both the city jail and some local federal government offices. The gender makeup of the company's workforce violates the city's ordinance, but is in compliance with the federal Fair Opportunity Act. The janitorial service brings an action in state court to enjoin enforcement of the city ordinance. It argues that the local rule is invalid since it conflicts with the federal statute by creating more stringent standards.

The trial court should rule:

(A) There is no conflict, because Congress intended that the Fair Opportunity Act apply only to employers who dealt exclusively with the federal government.

(B) There is no conflict, because the city is permitted to impose more strict requirements to deal with a local problem than those established by the federal government.

(C) The federal act preempts the local ordinance and thus the latter cannot be enforced.

(D) The federal act preempts the local ordinance only insofar as it attempts to regulate employers who do business with the federal government, so the ordinance may not be enforced only as to the janitorial company, but is otherwise valid.

Question 7

Congress has enacted a statute that requires all companies engaging in business with the federal government to enact certain affirmative action programs in hiring. A small diner has been providing catering services for a local branch office of the United States Department of Agriculture. At lunch one day, a senior enforcement officer of the Department of Agriculture happens to notice the racial makeup of the diner's workforce, and informs the diner that it is in violation of the affirmative action statute, and files charges against the diner.

If the diner challenges the validity of the federal statute, what is the government's best response to the argument that Congress has exceeded its legitimate powers?

(A) The act is a valid enforcement of the Due Process Clause of the Fifth Amendment and a valid exercise of the Enabling Clause of the Thirteenth Amendment.

(B) The act is a valid exercise of the commerce power and a valid exercise of the Enabling Clause of the Thirteenth Amendment.

(C) The act is a valid enforcement of the Due Process Clause of the Fifth Amendment and a valid exercise of the commerce power.

(D) The act is a valid exercise of the federal police power.

Question 8

The plaintiff, an electrical contractor, sued the defendant homeowner for refusal to pay for extensive wiring repairs performed on his home by the plaintiff's employee. The plaintiff called the employee to the stand. The employee, under oath, testified that he did not perform any work at the defendant's home. The employee also denied writing a letter to a friend telling the friend that the employee was going to do electrical work on the home. Without releasing the employee as a witness, the plaintiff offers into evidence the letter written by the employee to his friend.

If the employee's letter to his friend is properly authenticated, the trial court should:

(A) Admit the letter for impeachment purposes only.

(B) Admit the letter as both substantive and impeachment evidence.

(C) Exclude the letter because a party may not impeach his own witness.

(D) Exclude the letter because it is inadmissible hearsay.

Question 9

Believing that state law made it illegal to purchase a certain drug without providing identification and signing a log book, a defendant purchased the drug without doing so. Unbeknownst to the defendant, the state legislature had repealed the statute, and the drug could be legally purchased without providing identification or a signature.

May the defendant be charged with attempting an illegal purchase of drugs?

(A) No, because the repeal of the statute made it factually impossible for the defendant to be guilty of the charge.

(B) No, because the repeal of the statute made it legally impossible for the defendant to be guilty of the charge.

(C) Yes, because factual impossibility is not a defense to attempt.

(D) Yes, because legal impossibility is not a defense to attempt.

Question 10

A city adopted an ordinance providing that street demonstrations involving more than 15 persons may not be held in commercial areas during "rush" hours. "Exceptions" may be made to the prohibition "on 24-hour advance application to and approval by the police department." The ordinance also imposes sanctions on any person "who shall, without provocation, use to or about someone and in his presence, opprobrious words or abusive language tending to cause a breach of the peace." No court has as of yet interpreted the ordinance.

Which of the following is the strongest argument that both parts of the ordinance are facially unconstitutional?

(A) No type of prior restraint may be imposed on speech in public places.

(B) Laws, regulating by their terms expressive conduct or speech, may not be overbroad or unduly vague.

(C) The determination as to whether public gatherings may be lawfully held cannot be vested in the police.

(D) The right of association in public places without interference is ensured by the First and Fourteenth Amendments.

Question 11

A chef agreed in writing to lease a restaurant from the owner of the property. The term of the tenancy was two years, and rent was payable in monthly installments at the beginning of each month. At the end of the second year, there had been no discussions between the chef and the owner regarding renewal or termination. The chef did not vacate the premises at the end of the term; instead, she sent a check for the next month's rent to the owner. The owner cashed the check after the term had expired but informed the chef that his acceptance of the check did not mean that he was going to renew the lease or let the chef stay. At the end of that month, the owner seeks advice on whether he can evict the chef.

How should the owner be advised to proceed?

(A) The owner must give the chef a full 30 days' notice before beginning eviction proceedings because a month-to-month periodic tenancy has been created.

(B) The owner may begin eviction proceedings as soon as the additional month has expired.

(C) The owner may not evict the chef for 11 months and must give six months' notice before beginning eviction proceedings because a year-to-year periodic tenancy has been created.

(D) The owner may not evict the chef for 11 months but need not give any notice prior to eviction because a tenancy for years for a term of one year has been created.

Question 12

The defendant broke into a woman's house one night. As he was collecting valuables, he was surprised by the woman. He struck her on the head with a candlestick and tied her up, then finished filling his sack and left. The police discovered the woman several hours later and rushed her to the hospital. The defendant was apprehended by the police early the following morning with the loot still in his possession. He was taken to police headquarters, given *Miranda* warnings, and asked if he wished to make a statement about the prior evening's events. The police did not mention that the woman had been seriously injured and was in the hospital. The defendant said he understood his rights and was willing to talk. He then admitted that he committed the burglary of the woman's house. The following day, the woman died from injuries caused by the blow to her head. The defendant was charged with murder.

If the defendant moves to prevent introduction of the confession into evidence, his motion should most probably be:

(A) Denied, because failure of the police to advise the defendant of the woman's condition was harmless error since felony murder does not require intent to kill or injure.

(B) Denied, because the defendant's waiver of his rights did not depend on the nature of the charges that were later filed against him.

(C) Granted, because the defendant could not make a knowing and intelligent waiver unless he was informed concerning the woman's condition.

(D) Granted, because the use of a confession to burglary in a prosecution for murder violates due process where the police withheld information about the potential seriousness of the offense.

Question 13

A witness in a contract case testified on direct examination that four people attended a meeting. When asked to identify them, she gave the names of three, but despite trying, was unable to remember the name of the fourth person. The attorney who called her as a witness seeks to show her his handwritten notes of the part of his pretrial interview with her in which she provided all four names.

The trial court is likely to consider the showing of the notes taken as:

(A) A proper attempt to introduce recorded recollection.

(B) A proper attempt to refresh the witness's recollection.

(C) An improper attempt to lead the witness.

(D) An improper attempt to support the witness's credibility.

Question 14

A retail seller of lawn and garden equipment entered into a written contract with a manufacturer of wheelbarrows. The terms of the contract called for the seller to deliver 100 fifteen-pound-capacity wheelbarrows to the buyer by March 1. On February 28, the buyer received from the seller 90 fifteen-pound-capacity wheelbarrows and 10 twenty-pound-capacity wheelbarrows. A letter accompanying the shipment stated, "We no longer make fifteen-pound-capacity wheelbarrows. We are sending the last 90 we have in stock along with 10 twenty-pound-capacity wheelbarrows. The twenty-pound-capacity were sent as an accommodation to you."

Which of the following is ***not*** a correct statement?

(A) The buyer can reject the entire shipment.

(B) The buyer can accept the 90 conforming wheelbarrows, reject the 10 nonconforming wheelbarrows, and sue the seller for damages.

(C) The buyer can accept the entire shipment and sue the seller for damages.

(D) The buyer can accept or reject the seller's accommodation offer.

Question 15

A franchised United States dealer of a very popular German car contracted with a doctor to sell him the car for $29,000 cash, the sale to be consummated after delivery to the dealer of the car, which the dealer ordered from the manufacturer specifically for the doctor. The average retail markup in such sales is 30%. The signed retail contractual document was a form drafted by the dealer's lawyer, and the doctor did not question or object to any of its terms. When the car arrived from Germany, the doctor repudiated the contract. The dealer at once sold the car for $29,000 cash to another buyer, for whom the dealer had also ordered from the manufacturer a car identical to the doctor's.

In an action against the doctor for breach of contract, the dealer will probably recover:

(A) $29,000 minus what it cost the dealer to purchase the car from the manufacturer.

(B) $29,000 minus the wholesale price of an identical car in the local wholesale market among dealers.

(C) Nominal damages only, because the dealer resold the car to the other buyer without lowering the retail price.

(D) Nothing, because the parties' agreement was an adhesion contract and therefore unconscionable.

Question 16

The plaintiff sued the defendant, who had constructed the plaintiff's house, for breach of warranty of habitability. At trial, in cross-examination of the plaintiff, the defendant's attorney asked whether the plaintiff had sued another contractor 30 years earlier, claiming similar defects in another house built for the plaintiff. The question was not objected to and the plaintiff answered that she had had some "water problems" with the first house she ever purchased, but no suit was filed.

The defendant then called as a witness the contractor of 30 years earlier to testify that the plaintiff had brought suit against him for defects in the earlier house, many of which were like those now claimed to be found in the home the defendant built, but that the case was settled without trial.

The trial court should rule the witness's offered testimony:

(A) Admissible as proper impeachment because the plaintiff will have an opportunity to explain or deny the witness's statement.

(B) Admissible, because the plaintiff failed to object to the defendant's questions on cross-examination relative to the prior suit.

(C) Inadmissible, because the best evidence of the former suit is the court record.

(D) Inadmissible, because its probative value is substantially outweighed by the danger that it will confuse the issues and waste time.

Question 17

A husband decided to kill his wife by poisoning her. He asked his friend, a pharmacist, to obtain some deadly poison, and to give it to him without recording the transaction. Because the pharmacist suspected the husband's motive, she supplied the husband with a small quantity of an antibiotic, instead of the poison. The antibiotic is harmless if administered in small quantities, except for the less than 1% of the population who are allergic to the drug. The husband injected his wife with the drug while she slept, and she died from an allergic reaction.

The pharmacist is an accomplice to:

(A) Murder.

(B) Manslaughter.

(C) Criminally negligent homicide.

(D) No degree of criminal homicide.

GO ON TO THE NEXT PAGE

Question 18

A husband was arrested for domestic violence against his wife. His wife agreed to testify against him. Shortly after the jury had been sworn in, but before any evidence could be presented, the couple reconciled and the wife refused to testify. Believing that the case was not strong without the wife's testimony, the prosecution dropped the charges and the husband was released. A few weeks later, the couple split up again and the wife filed a battery action for damages against her husband based on the original incident. The husband has filed a motion asking the court to dismiss the wife's case on double jeopardy grounds.

The court should:

(A) Deny the husband's motion because jeopardy had not yet attached during the first trial since the prosecution had not yet presented any evidence against the defendant.

(B) Deny the husband's motion because this is an action for damages and not a criminal proceeding.

(C) Grant the husband's motion because battery is a lesser included offense of domestic violence.

(D) Grant the husband's motion because the prior case was not discontinued due to a manifest necessity.

Question 19

A married couple was leaving a nightclub at closing. The wife forgot her jacket and went back in to the club to retrieve it while her husband looked for a cab outside. Her husband saw a cab sitting across the street and ran for it, cutting off one of the club's bouncers who was also looking for a ride home. The bouncer became angry at the husband for "stealing his cab." The cab departed while they were arguing. Seeing no one else around, the bouncer began to punch and kick the husband, causing him severe injury. The wife watched the entire episode from across the street and became greatly distressed. The husband sued the bouncer for his injuries.

If the wife also sues the bouncer, alleging intentional infliction of emotional distress, will she recover?

(A) No, because the bouncer did not intend to inflict emotional distress on the wife.

(B) No, because the bouncer did not know that the wife was watching from across the street.

(C) Yes, because the bouncer's conduct was extreme and outrageous.

(D) Yes, because the bouncer's conduct caused the wife to be severely emotionally disturbed.

Question 20

A mall leased one of its retail units to a clothing store for a period of five years. The lease agreement provided that the clothing store would pay to the mall, as additional rent, $1,000 a month in maintenance fees for the upkeep of the common areas in the mall. The agreement also permitted assignments and subleases. For four years, the clothing store timely paid all rent and maintenance fees. At the end of the fourth year, the clothing store properly assigned the lease to a discount shoe outlet. At the time it assigned the lease, the clothing store owed $3,000 in maintenance fees for the last three months of its occupancy. The shoe outlet paid its rent but did not pay any maintenance fees to the mall for the first six months. The shoe outlet then abandoned the property. The mall made reasonable efforts during the last six months of the term to relet the unit but was unable to do so. After applying the security deposit to satisfy the balance of the rent, the mall wishes to collect the unpaid maintenance fees for the last 15 months of the lease, totaling $15,000.

Who is liable for those fees and in what amount?

(A) The clothing store and the shoe outlet are jointly and severally liable for the $15,000 in fees.

(B) The clothing store is solely liable for $3,000 in fees, and the clothing store and the shoe outlet are jointly and severally liable for $12,000 in fees.

(C) The clothing store is solely liable for $3,000 in fees, the shoe outlet is solely liable for $6,000 in fees, and the clothing store and the shoe outlet are jointly and severally liable for $6,000 in fees.

(D) The clothing store is solely liable for $3,000 in fees, and the shoe outlet is solely liable for $12,000 in fees.

Question 21

A dentist rented office space in a medical building for a period of five years. The lease provided that the building's owner would maintain all common areas of the building, including the parking lot. Three years into the lease, the building was sold to an investor. The investor took subject to all of the leases, including the dentist's lease, but did not assume any of the original owner's obligations under it. Five months after the sale, a contractor, hired by the original owner, who was reconstructing the building's parking lot, walked off the job because he had not received any progress payments from either the original owner or the investor during the past five months. After notifying the original owner and the investor and receiving no response, the dentist agreed to pay the contractor $20,000 up front to finish the job. The dentist then withheld his rent payment of $2,000 for that month and brought an action against the original owner and the investor to recover the balance of the payment to the contractor.

Is either the original owner or the investor liable to the dentist?

(A) Neither the original owner nor the investor is liable to the dentist because the dentist is in breach of his covenant to pay rent.

(B) The original owner is liable to the dentist, but the investor is not, because the investor did not assume the original owner's obligations.

(C) The investor is liable to the dentist, but the original owner is not, because the sale by the original owner to the investor severed any privity of estate between the original owner and the dentist.

(D) Both the original owner and the investor are liable to the dentist because the maintenance duties constitute an independent covenant that is part of the lease and that runs with the land.

GO ON TO THE NEXT PAGE

Question 22

The federal government contracted with a number of communications utilities to install fiberoptic communication lines between major federal offices across the country. The utilities, which maintained ownership of the lines, contracted with the federal government to install the lines on a "cost plus fixed fee" basis, whereby all installation costs would be reimbursed by the government. One such line was installed in a state's capital city, where the Department of the Interior maintained its western regional office. The state imposes a tax on the installation of all communication lines in the state, including fiberoptic cable lines. It seeks to impose the tax on the line running to the federal office.

Will the state be permitted to impose the tax?

(A) Yes, because the tax is indirect and nondiscriminatory.

(B) Yes, because the tax is a valid exercise of state power under the Tenth Amendment.

(C) No, because the tax burdens the activities of the federal government.

(D) No, because the activity taxed involves interstate commerce.

Question 23

In an action by the plaintiff against the defendant, one of the issues is whether the defendant is a licensed physical therapist. Normally, the names of all licensed physical therapists are registered with the office of the state Department of Professional Registrations. The plaintiff wishes to introduce a certified document, signed by the chief registrar of the department (who cannot be located), stating that an examination of the department's rolls does not disclose the defendant's name.

Should the document be admitted?

(A) Yes, because a statement of absence from public record is admissible.

(B) Yes, because the chief registrar is unavailable.

(C) No, because the document is hearsay not within an exception.

(D) No, because the document is not self-authenticating.

Question 24

A shopping center contracted with a security service to provide nighttime monitoring of mall property. An employee of the security service, without the manager's permission, began placing several of his pet rattlesnakes in the shopping center at night as a deterrent to burglars, and posted signs at night saying, "Beware of poisonous snakes."

The shopping center was conducting a contest to guess the number of jelly beans that filled a car. A student at a local college broke into the shopping center to take a sample of the jelly beans in a given volume of the car's interior so that, using the manufacturer's figures for interior volume, he could calculate the number of beans in the car. As the student was carefully opening a vent window to take his sample of jelly beans, one of the security service employee's rattlers that had been lying under the car bit him on the ankle. The student, who had not seen the warning signs about snakes, was hospitalized for two weeks and had to miss a semester of school as a result of the snakebite.

If the student brings an action against the shopping center, will he likely recover?

(A) No, because he was a trespasser on shopping center property.

(B) No, because he was guilty of breaking and entering.

(C) Yes, because the use of poisonous snakes for security amounted to unreasonable force.

(D) Yes, because he had not seen the signs warning of the poisonous snakes.

Question 25

On a wholly random basis, a state agency has given a few probationary employees who were not rehired at the end of their probationary period a statement of reasons and an opportunity for a hearing, but the agency has very rarely done so. No statute or rule of the agency required such a statement of reasons or a hearing. The employment of a probationary employee was terminated without a statement of reasons or an opportunity for a hearing. The agency did not even consider whether it should give him either.

A suit by the employee requesting a statement of reasons and a hearing will probably be:

(A) Successful, on the grounds that failure to give the employee reasons and an opportunity for a hearing constituted a bill of attainder.

(B) Successful, on the grounds that an agency's inconsistent practices, even if unintentional, deny adversely affected persons the equal protection of the laws.

(C) Unsuccessful, because the employee does not have a right to be rehired that is protected by procedural due process.

(D) Unsuccessful, because the conditions of state employment are matters reserved to the states by the Tenth Amendment.

Question 26

A manufacturing company was in the business of making copper tubing. A retail seller telephoned the manufacturing company's sales department and placed an order for 10,000 linear feet of copper tubing at a sale price of $2 per foot. The tubing was to be used in the production of a custom order for one of the retail seller's customers. The manufacturing company installed special equipment for the manufacture of the tubing to the retail seller's specifications and had completed a portion of the order when the retail seller again telephoned the sales department. This time, however, the retail seller canceled its order, saying it no longer had need of the tubing because its customer had been declared bankrupt and refused to pay for the order.

If the manufacturing company sues for breach, it will:

(A) Win, because the contract is fully enforceable.

(B) Win, because the contract is enforceable to the extent of the portion of the order completed.

(C) Lose, because a contract for the sale of goods over $500 must be in writing.

(D) Lose, because the parol evidence rule would preclude testimony about the initial telephone call.

Question 27

Police investigating a homicide had probable cause to believe that the defendant had committed it. They then learned from a reliable informant that, a short while ago, the defendant had gone to a friend's house to obtain a false driver's license from the friend, a convicted forger. Believing that the defendant might still be there, the police, without obtaining a warrant, went to the friend's house. They entered the house and found the defendant hiding in the basement. He was arrested and given his *Miranda* warnings. At the police station, he confessed to the homicide.

At a preliminary hearing, the defendant's attorney contends that the confession should be suppressed on Fourth Amendment grounds.

Is the court likely to agree?

(A) Yes, because the police did not have a search warrant to enter the friend's house and there were no exigent circumstances.

(B) Yes, because the police did not have an arrest warrant for the defendant and there were no exigent circumstances.

(C) No, because a reliable informant told police that the defendant was in the friend's house.

(D) No, because the police had probable cause to arrest the defendant.

Question 28

All of the deeds for the lots on a city block contained a restrictive covenant requiring that all houses built on the lots be set back a minimum of 50 feet from the sidewalk. Local zoning regulations required that all homes on the block be set back a minimum of 35 feet from the sidewalk. A man purchased a lot on the block on which it would be possible to build a home with a 50-foot setback. However, the man applied to the city zoning commission for a variance reducing the setback to 30 feet from the sidewalk. In his petition, the man cited the unusual shape of the lot and asserted that it would cause hardship for him to build in compliance with the 35-foot setback required by the zoning regulations. The zoning commission granted the man the variance. A woman whose home was located on the block noticed surveyors putting up ropes 30 feet from the sidewalk on the man's lot, and she discovered that the man planned to build a home with only a 30-foot setback. The woman brings suit to enjoin the man from building a residence with a setback of less than 50 feet.

Who will prevail?

(A) The man, because zoning regulations take precedence over restrictive covenants as a matter of public policy.

(B) The man, because equity will not impose a hardship.

(C) The woman, because the man will be unjustly enriched if he is permitted to build a 30-foot setback.

(D) The woman, because a zoning variance does not affect the enforcement of a restrictive covenant.

Question 29

A mother conveys her land to an irrevocable trust "to pay the income to my daughter for life, then to my daughter's children for their lives, and upon the death of the last survivor of my daughter's children, the trustee shall distribute the principal to my daughter's grandchildren, if any; otherwise, to my church." At the time of the conveyance, the daughter has two children and no grandchildren.

The church's interest can best be described as:

(A) A contingent remainder.

(B) A vested remainder subject to total divestment.

(C) An executory interest.

(D) Nothing.

GO ON TO THE NEXT PAGE

Question 30

In a writing signed by both parties, a renowned architect agreed to design and supervise construction of a new house for a buyer. The architect's fee was to be paid on completion of the house. When the design plans were about two-thirds complete, the architect assigned to a newly licensed architect "all of my rights and duties under my design and construction-supervision contract with the buyer." The novice architect expressly promised the architect to carry out the work to the best of her ability. The buyer, on learning of the assignment, refused to allow the novice architect to proceed on the project and brought an action against the architect to compel him to resume and complete performance of the contract.

Is the buyer entitled to such relief?

(A) Yes, because the architect's services under the contract are unique.

(B) Yes, because the architect has personally completed two-thirds of the design work.

(C) No, because the architect-buyer contract is one for personal services by the architect.

(D) No, because the architect effectively delegated his remaining duties under the architect-buyer contract to the novice architect.

Question 31

A foreign correspondent wished to purchase a parcel of land from a developer that was not yet on the market. Before he left the country, he gave his attorney $100,000 and his power of attorney. He instructed the attorney that, should the land be put up for sale, she was authorized to: offer up to $100,000 for it, enter into a binding contract to purchase it on the correspondent's behalf, and if he did not return in time, close on the property. In early January, the developer put the land on the market. The attorney offered $75,000 for it, which the developer readily accepted. On January 15, the attorney, on the correspondent's behalf, entered into a written contract to purchase the land for $75,000. Closing was set for February 15. During this time, the attorney heard nothing from the correspondent. When he had not returned by the date of closing, the attorney attended the closing and tendered the $75,000. The developer tendered a deed made out to the correspondent as the grantee. On February 20, news was received that the correspondent had been killed by a stray bullet on January 14. The correspondent's will left his entire estate to his niece. The developer believes the conveyance to the correspondent is invalid, and brings a suit to quiet title to the land.

The court will most likely find that the owner of the land is:

(A) The niece, because the attorney held the deed on constructive trust for the correspondent's estate.

(B) The niece, because of the operation of the doctrine of equitable conversion.

(C) The developer, because a deed to a nonexistent person is void and conveys no title.

(D) The developer, because the risk of loss is on the buyer.

Question 32

The plaintiff sued the defendant for injuries suffered when her car collided in an intersection with one driven by the defendant. At trial, the plaintiff testified that she had had the right-of-way over the defendant to enter the intersection. The defendant did not cross-examine her. The plaintiff then called a witness to testify that, shortly after the collision, as she pulled the plaintiff from the car, the witness heard the plaintiff say, "I think I'm dying! Didn't the other driver see I had the right-of-way?" The witness's testimony was admitted over defense counsel's objections. On appeal from a verdict for the plaintiff, the defendant challenges the admission of the witness's testimony.

Should the trial court's ruling be upheld?

(A) Yes, because the plaintiff's statement was made under belief of impending death.

(B) Yes, because the plaintiff's statement was an excited utterance.

(C) No, because the plaintiff's credibility had not been attacked.

(D) No, because the plaintiff's belief that she had the right-of-way had already been established without contradiction.

Question 33

There is high and persistent unemployment in an industrialized state. Its legislature therefore enacted a statute requiring every business with annual sales in the state of over $1 million to purchase each year goods and/or services in the state equal in value to at least half of its sales in the state.

Which of the following parties most clearly has standing to contest the constitutionality of this state statute in federal court?

(A) A business in another state that supplies from that other state 95% of the goods and services bought by a corporation that has annual sales in the industrialized state of $20 million.

(B) A corporation selling $300,000 worth of goods in the state but presently purchasing only $10,000 in goods and services in the state.

(C) The governor of an adjacent state on behalf of that state and its residents.

(D) The owner of high-grade, secured bonds issued by a corporation with sales in the state of $10 million that currently purchases only $1 million in goods and services in the state.

Question 34

A pedestrian was in a hurry and he crossed the street in the middle of the block rather than walking to the corner crosswalk. A police officer stopped the pedestrian and asked to see his driver's license. The pedestrian did not have a driver's license. When he told the officer this, she said, "All right, I'm taking you in for jaywalking," and seized his wrist, twisting it up and behind him in a personnel control lock. A black belt in judo, the pedestrian easily slipped the officer's grasp. The officer pulled her baton from her belt and attempted to strike the pedestrian, who moved swiftly to the side, chopped at her arm, and caused the baton to fall from her grasp to the pavement. At that point two other officers arrived on the scene and arrested the pedestrian.

Jaywalking (crossing a street outside of a crosswalk or not at an intersection) is punishable in the jurisdiction by a fine. There is no other applicable statute.

If the pedestrian brings an action against the first officer for battery, what is the probable outcome?

(A) He will lose, because he struck the officer.

(B) He will lose, because the offense was committed in the officer's presence.

(C) He will lose, because he is guilty of jaywalking.

(D) He will win, because the officer was not privileged to arrest him.

Question 35

The defendant drug company developed a new drug for treatment of a genetic disease. The defendant extensively tested the drug for several years on animals and human volunteers and had observed no undesirable side effects. The federal Food and Drug Administration ("FDA") then approved the drug for sale as a prescription drug. Five other drug companies, each acting independently, developed drugs identical to the defendant's drug. Each of these drugs was also approved by the FDA for sale as a prescription drug. A wholesaler bought identically shaped pills from all six of the manufacturers and sold the pills to drugstores as a branded product.

This drug had a long-delayed side effect. Sons of male users of the product are sterile. One such son, the plaintiff, brought an action against the defendant for his damages. The defendant, through the wholesaler, supplied about 10% of the branded product sold in the state where the plaintiff lived. It is not possible to establish which of the five companies supplied the particular pills that the plaintiff's father took.

If the plaintiff asserts a claim against the defendant based on strict liability in tort, which of the following will be a decisive question in determining whether the plaintiff will prevail?

(A) Does the res ipsa loquitur doctrine apply?

(B) Can liability be imposed on the defendant without proof that the defendant knew that the drug had an undesirable side effect?

(C) Is the defendant relieved of liability by the FDA approval of the drug?

(D) Can liability be imposed on the defendant without showing that its pills were used by the plaintiff's father?

Question 36

After becoming intoxicated one evening, the defendant went to a used car lot to try to find a car that he could use to drive home. On discovering that none of the cars had keys in the ignition, he broke into the main office of the used car lot to get a key. As he left the office with a key, a security guard tried to apprehend the defendant. The defendant pushed the guard to the ground. The guard hit his head hard on the pavement and died. Relevant statutes extend burglary to include buildings not used as a dwelling. First degree murder is defined as "the premeditated and intentional killing of another or a killing committed during the commission of a rape, robbery, burglary, or arson." Second degree murder is defined as all murders that are not first degree murder.

If the defendant is charged with first degree murder for the death of the security guard, the court should charge the jury on the issue of the defense of intoxication that:

(A) Voluntary intoxication is no defense to the crime of first degree murder as defined by the statute.

(B) Voluntary intoxication is a defense to the crime of first degree murder if the defendant would not have killed the security guard but for the intoxication.

(C) Voluntary intoxication is a defense to the crime of first degree murder if it prevented the defendant from forming the intent to commit a burglary.

(D) Voluntary intoxication is a defense to first degree murder if it prevented the defendant from forming the intent to kill the security guard.

Question 37

A police officer spent several hours using binoculars to observe an older man loitering on a college campus. The man, who was shabbily dressed and carrying a backpack, would approach certain students as they walked by him, and after a brief conversation with them, discreetly pass the students a small envelope in exchange for cash. The officer stopped the man under suspicion that he was dealing drugs. The man was not dealing drugs, but instead had been soliciting donations for a known radical and sometimes violent political group. The man grew irate when the officer opened one of the envelopes in question and discovered that they only contained literature about the group. The officer then frisked the man and discovered an illegal weapon taped to his leg. The officer immediately arrested the man.

Which of the following best describes the situation?

(A) The officer's actions were unlawful because the officer initially failed to get an arrest warrant before approaching the man, even though he had ample time to do so because the surveillance had been going on for several hours.

(B) The man's arrest was unlawful because the officer was mistaken about the man selling drugs and thus the weapon would be inadmissible as fruit of the poisonous tree.

(C) The officer's actions were lawful in stopping the man because the officer had reasonable ground to believe that the man was dealing drugs, but the subsequent search was unlawful once the officer realized his mistake about the drug dealing.

(D) The stop, search, and subsequent arrest were lawful.

Question 38

An area of grasslands is owned by the United States and is located in the center of a large western state. Acting pursuant to a federal statute authorizing such action, the United States Bureau of Land Management leased the grazing rights in the grasslands to ranchers located nearby. A company owns a vast amount of rangeland adjacent to the grasslands and leases its land for livestock grazing purposes to the same ranchers, but at prices higher than those charged by the Bureau. The company sued the Bureau in an appropriate federal district court to restrain the Bureau from competing with that company by leasing the grasslands.

Which of the following constitutional provisions may most easily and directly be used to justify the federal statute authorizing this leasing program of the Bureau of Land Management?

(A) The General Welfare Clause of Article I, Section 8.

(B) The Federal Property Clause of Article IV, Section 3.

(C) The Commerce Clause of Article I, Section 8.

(D) The Supremacy Clause of Article VI.

Question 39

In the plaintiff's antitrust suit against the defendant manufacturers of insulation, the plaintiff's interrogatories asked for information concerning total sales of insulation by each of the defendants in a particular year. The defendants replied to the interrogatories by referring the plaintiff to an insulation manufacturer's journal for the information.

If, at trial, the plaintiff offers the journal as evidence of the sales volume, this evidence is:

(A) Admissible, as an adoptive admission of the defendants.

(B) Admissible, as a business record.

(C) Inadmissible, as hearsay not within any exception.

(D) Inadmissible, as lacking sufficient authentication.

Question 40

In a written agreement between a manufacturer of quality red cheese and a retail seller of fine quality foods, the manufacturer agreed to sell all output of its red cheese to the retail seller, and the retail seller agreed to sell the manufacturer's red cheese exclusively. The agreement went on to state that the retail seller would pay $150 for each 10-wheel container of red cheese ordered from the manufacturer.

Under the above facts, what are the relative obligations of the parties?

(A) The manufacturer has to sell all of its output to the retail seller; the retail seller has to buy all of the manufacturer's output.

(B) The manufacturer has to sell all of its output to the retail seller; the retail seller has to sell exclusively the manufacturer's red cheese.

(C) The manufacturer has to sell all of its output to the retail seller; the retail seller has to sell exclusively the manufacturer's red cheese, but it does not have to buy any.

(D) The manufacturer has to sell all of its output to the retail seller; the retail seller has to buy all of the manufacturer's output and has to sell exclusively the manufacturer's red cheese.

Question 41

A farmer owned land in fee simple. He executed two deeds, the first conveying an undivided one-half interest in the land to a husband and a wife as joint tenants with right of survivorship, and the second conveying an undivided one-half interest in the land to the husband's only child. The child was 13 years old at the time. The common law joint tenancy is unmodified by statute. The farmer handed the two deeds to the husband. The husband promptly and properly recorded the deed to himself and his wife and put the deed to his child in a safe-deposit box without recording it. No actual consideration was paid for the deeds. The same year, the husband, the wife, and the child were killed simultaneously in an airplane crash. They all died intestate.

The applicable statute in the jurisdiction provides that "when title to property or its devolution depends on priority of death and there is insufficient evidence that the persons have died otherwise than simultaneously, the property of each person shall be disposed of as if he had survived."

An appropriate action was instituted by the heirs of the husband, the wife, and the child. The farmer, who is not an heir of any of the deceased, is a party to the action.

The court should determine that title to the land is:

(A) Entirely in the farmer.

(B) One-half in the heirs of the husband and one-half in the heirs of the wife.

(C) One-half in the farmer, one-quarter in the heirs of the husband, and one-quarter in the heirs of the wife.

(D) One-half in the heirs of the child, one-quarter in the heirs of the husband, and one-quarter in the heirs of the wife.

Question 42

A privately owned corporation contracted with the United States to construct a dam across a river in a state other than that in which it was incorporated. The state imposed a gross receipts tax on all business conducted within it. The state sued the corporation to collect that tax on the receipts the corporation received under this federal contract. No federal statutes or administrative rules are applicable, and the contract between the United States and the corporation does not mention state taxation.

The court should hold the state tax, as applied here, to be:

(A) Constitutional, because a state has exclusive jurisdiction over all commercial transactions executed wholly within its borders.

(B) Constitutional, because private contractors performing work under a federal contract are not immune in these circumstances from nondiscriminatory state taxation.

(C) Unconstitutional, because it violates the Supremacy Clause.

(D) Unconstitutional, because it imposes an undue burden on interstate commerce.

GO ON TO THE NEXT PAGE

Question 43

A lawyer sued a client for his fee, based on an agreed hourly rate. The client subpoenaed the lawyer's time records for the days on which he purported to have worked for the client to show that the lawyer had billed an impossible number of hours to the client and others on those days. The client's subpoena provided that any information concerning the matters handled for other clients be deleted or masked. The lawyer moved to quash the subpoena on the ground of attorney-client privilege.

The subpoena should be:

(A) Upheld, because the information about hours billed is not within the privilege.

(B) Upheld, because a lawyer has no right to invoke his client's privilege without instructions from the client.

(C) Quashed, because a lawyer is entitled to a right of privacy for the work product in his files.

(D) Quashed, because no permission was obtained from the other clients to divulge information from their files.

Question 44

A landowner was estranged from his son and three small grandchildren. The landowner owned a valuable piece of property that he wanted to pass on to his grandchildren, without his son's involvement. The landowner conveyed the property to his own sister, "for life, remainder to all of my grandchildren who ever attain the age of 25."

The grandchildren's interest can best be described as:

(A) A contingent remainder.

(B) A vested remainder.

(C) An executory interest.

(D) Nothing.

Question 45

On January 1, a builder and a landowner agreed in writing that the builder would build a house on the landowner's lot according to the landowner's plans and specifications for $160,000, the work to commence on April 1. The landowner agreed to make an initial payment of $20,000 on April 1, and to pay the balance on completion of the work.

On February 1, the builder notified the landowner that he (the builder) would lose money on the job at that price, and would not proceed with the work unless the landowner would agree to increase the price to $190,000. The landowner thereupon, without notifying the builder, agreed in writing with a competing building company for the building company, commencing April 1, to build the house for $175,000, which was the fair market cost of the work to be done.

On April 1, both the builder and the building company showed up at the building site to begin work, the builder telling the landowner that he had reconsidered and would build the house for $160,000 as originally agreed. The landowner dismissed the builder and allowed the building company to begin work on the house.

In a contract action by the builder against the landowner, which of the following would the court decide under the prevailing American view?

(A) The landowner will win because the builder in legal effect committed a total breach of contract.

(B) The landowner will win because the building company's contract price was $15,000 lower than the $190,000 demanded by the builder on February 1.

(C) The builder will win because the landowner did not tell him before April 1 about the contract with the competing building company.

(D) The builder will win because he attempted to perform the contract as originally agreed.

Question 46

A state law provides free school lunches for elementary school students whose family incomes are below poverty level. A local white supremacist group has organized a private elementary school that denies admission to all non-Caucasians. Most of the school's students are living below poverty level and the school officials have demanded that free lunch service be provided by the state.

Which of the following is the strongest argument against the constitutionality of the state law as applied to providing free lunch to the students at the school?

(A) No legitimate educational function is served by the free lunch program.

(B) The state may not in any way aid private schools.

(C) The Constitution forbids private bias of any kind.

(D) Segregation is furthered by the distribution of lunch to these students.

Question 47

Buyers of a house with an old above-ground pool wanted it removed, so the current homeowners agreed that they would arrange to have the pool moved to their new home, but since the sale was occurring in winter, the pool would have to be moved at a later date. The parties therefore agreed that the buyers would pay all but $5,000 of the home's sale price at closing, and then pay the final $5,000 six months after the sale. The contract further stated:

> It is understood and agreed that the purchasers' obligation to pay the $5,000 six months after the sale shall be voided if the current homeowners have not, within three months after the aforesaid sale, removed the existing pool in the rear of the house.

The homeowners' removal of the pool from the backyard of the house is:

(A) A condition subsequent in form but precedent in substance to the buyers' duty to pay the $5,000.

(B) A condition precedent in form but subsequent in substance to the buyers' duty to pay the $5,000.

(C) A condition subsequent to the buyers' duty to pay the $5,000.

(D) Not a condition, either precedent or subsequent, to the buyers' duty to pay the $5,000.

Question 48

An electrician was employed by an electrical services company that had contracts with a number of large office and condominium buildings to provide emergency electrical services and repairs at any hour of the day or night. Hence, he was required to be "on call" 24 hours a day and to drive his company van, which had all of his tools, to his home each night. One afternoon, the electrician left the company's office at 4 p.m. as usual. However, when he left the main highway, he did not turn left toward his home but instead turned right toward the supermarket a few blocks away to pick up some items for dinner. While leaving the supermarket parking lot, the electrician drove negligently and struck a pedestrian. The pedestrian suffered serious injuries and required several operations and a lengthy hospital stay. The pedestrian filed suit against the company for $100,000.

Is the pedestrian likely to recover from the company?

(A) Yes, because the electrician's trip to the market was only a slight deviation from the direct route to his home.

(B) Yes, but only if the company knew that the electrician had proclivities to drive negligently.

(C) No, because turning in the opposite direction from his home constituted a "frolic" by the electrician.

(D) No, because an employer is not liable for the torts of an employee traveling to and from work.

Question 49

A defendant, who had been previously hospitalized at a mental institution, was charged with the murder of his wife. In his defense, he testified that, at the time he killed her, he believed that his wife was planning to destroy the world by detonating a massive explosive device that she had developed and built in the basement of their home. He also said that he had concluded that the only way to prevent her scheme was to kill her, and that he had become so obsessed with the importance of doing so that he could think of nothing else. One day when he saw her open the door to the basement, he lunged at her and pushed her down the steps to her death.

The best defense raised by the defendant's testimony is:

(A) Lack of the requisite mental element.

(B) Lack of the requisite act element.

(C) Insanity.

(D) Belief that the situation justified his actions.

Question 50

The academic dean of a college was well liked and considered a competent scholar and a fine teacher. However, six months after her appointment as dean, she received a certified letter from the provost of the college, summarily dismissing her. No reasons were given in the letter for her dismissal. She had her lawyer contact the provost to discover the basis for her dismissal. Two days later, the lawyer received a letter from the provost stating, in relevant part, "The dean was dismissed from her employment at our college because I received an anonymous telephone call informing me that she had purchased drugs from a student." The provost had, in fact, received such a phone call, but the basis of the statement was untrue, because the dean had never even used illegal drugs, much less bought them from a student.

If the dean files suit against the provost for libel:

(A) The dean will lose, because the provost was merely repeating the defamatory communication of another.

(B) The dean will lose, because by having her attorney ask the reason for the dismissal, the dean impliedly consented to the statement in the letter.

(C) The dean will win, because the provost should have verified the anonymous statement before repeating it to the lawyer.

(D) The dean will win, because the dean was not buying drugs.

Question 51

A homeowner purchased a riding lawn mower from a lawn mower dealer. During his first use of the mower, the homeowner noticed that the mower was vibrating when he turned, but he was able to finish mowing. A few days later, the homeowner lent the mower to his neighbor. The neighbor was driving the mower back to his yard when he made a turn and a wheel broke off, causing the neighbor to be thrown off the lawn mower and onto the sidewalk. The neighbor was injured.

The neighbor brought a negligence action against the dealer for his injuries. At trial, the neighbor presented evidence that the wheel broke because of a manufacturing defect. The dealer presented evidence that the homeowner could have discovered the defect after the mower began vibrating when he used it for the first time.

In this action, who is likely to prevail?

(A) The neighbor, because the lawn mower was sold by the dealer with an unreasonably dangerous defect.

(B) The neighbor, because the defect in the wheel would not likely have occurred in the absence of negligence.

(C) The dealer, because the homeowner should have discovered the defect when the mower first started vibrating.

(D) The dealer, because there is no evidence that the dealer had reason to know that the lawn mower was defective.

Question 52

Two states that permit the hunting and trapping of snipe are separated from each other by a middle state that strictly forbids it in order to protect snipe, a rare species of animal, from extinction. A middle state statute provides, "Possession of snipe traps is prohibited. Any game warden finding a snipe trap within the state shall seize and destroy it." A snipe hunter from the one state that permitted trapping traveled across the middle state to purchase a new snipe trap from a manufacturer in the other state that permitted it. On the way back with the trap in her car, she stopped in a state park in the middle state to camp. A game warden saw the trap on the front seat of her car. The warden seized the trap and destroyed it in accordance with the state statute after the hunter admitted that the seized item was a prohibited snipe trap.

The hunter challenges the application of the statute to her on the basis of a denial of equal protection. The hunter has demonstrated that common carriers are permitted to transport snipe traps as cargo across the middle state for delivery to another state and that, in practice, the statute is enforced only against private individuals transporting those traps in private vehicles. No federal statutes or federal administrative regulations apply.

Application of the statute to the hunter will probably be found:

(A) Constitutional, because the traps constitute contraband in which the hunter could have no protected property interest.

(B) Constitutional, because there is a rational basis for differentiating between the possession of snipe traps as interstate cargo by common carriers and the possession of snipe traps by private individuals.

(C) Unconstitutional, because the state cannot demonstrate a compelling public purpose for making this differentiation between common carriers and such private individuals.

(D) Unconstitutional, because interstate travel is a fundamental right that may not be burdened by state law.

GO ON TO THE NEXT PAGE

Question 53

A state statute forbids the use of radar detecting devices while driving. A driver passing through the state while on vacation received a ticket for operating such a device. A valid federal administrative rule, adopted under a federal consumer product safety act, regulates the design of radar detection systems. The rule was issued to limit consumers' exposure to electromagnetic fields. No other federal law applies.

Which of the following best states the effect of the federal rule on the state statute?

(A) The federal rule preempts the state statute, because the federal rule regulates the same subject matter—radar detectors.

(B) The federal rule preempts the state statute, because the federal rule does not contain affirmative authorization for continued state regulation.

(C) The federal rule does not preempt the state statute, because the state statute regulates local traffic rules, a field of exclusive state power.

(D) The federal rule does not preempt the state statute, because the purposes of the federal rule and the state statute are different.

Question 54

The defendant is tried on a charge of driving while intoxicated. When the defendant was booked at the police station, a videotape was made that showed him unsteady, abusive, and speaking in a slurred manner.

If the prosecutor lays a foundation properly identifying the tape, should the court admit it in evidence and permit it to be shown to the jury?

(A) Yes, because it is an admission.

(B) Yes, because its value is not substantially outweighed by unfair prejudice.

(C) No, because the privilege against self-incrimination is applicable.

(D) No, because specific instances of conduct cannot be proved by extrinsic evidence.

Question 55

A rancher entered into a contract to sell her land to a developer for $60,000. The contract provided that the rancher agreed to convey a good and marketable title to the developer 60 days from the date of the contract. At the time set for closing, the rancher tendered a deed in the form agreed to in the contract. The developer's examination of the record prior to the date of closing disclosed, however, that the owner of record was not the rancher, but a farmer. Further investigation by the developer revealed that, notwithstanding the state of the record, the rancher had been in what the developer concedes is adverse possession for 15 years. The period of time to acquire title by adverse possession in the jurisdiction is 10 years. The developer refuses to pay the purchase price or to take possession because of the "inability" of the rancher to transfer a marketable title.

In an appropriate action by the rancher against the developer for specific performance, the rancher will:

(A) Prevail, because she has obtained a "good and marketable title" by adverse possession.

(B) Prevail, because the rancher's action for specific performance is an action in rem even though the farmer is not a party.

(C) Not prevail, because the developer cannot be required to buy a lawsuit even if the probability is great that the developer would prevail against the farmer.

(D) Not prevail, because the rancher's failure to disclose her lack of record title constitutes fraud.

Question 56

An architectural historian bought a house, financing $150,000 of the purchase price with a loan from a bank, secured by a mortgage on the property. The bank recorded its mortgage. Ten years later, the historian borrowed $5,000 from a finance company, using the house as security. The finance company recorded its mortgage on the property. Five years later, the historian obtained a $40,000 mortgage from a savings and loan association to pay for an addition to the house. The savings and loan association did not record its mortgage. Subsequently, the historian lost her job and was unable to make payments on either the finance company or the savings and loan mortgages. The finance company filed foreclosure of its mortgage, and the house was sold to a buyer at the foreclosure sale.

After acquiring the property at the sale, what is the buyer's obligation regarding the bank's and the savings and loan association's mortgages?

(A) The buyer takes the property subject to both mortgages.

(B) The buyer takes the property subject to neither mortgage.

(C) The buyer takes the property subject to the savings and loan association's mortgage, but not subject to the bank's mortgage.

(D) The buyer takes the property subject to the bank's mortgage, but not subject to the savings and loan association's mortgage.

Question 57

A brother and a sister made a written contract pursuant to which the brother promised to convey a specified apartment house to his sister in return for his sister's promise (i) to convey a 100-acre farm to the brother and (ii) to pay the brother $1,000 in cash six months after the exchange of the apartment house and the farm.

Which of the following statements concerning the order of performances is ***least*** accurate?

(A) The brother's tendering of good title to the apartment house is a condition precedent to the sister's duty to convey good title to the farm.

(B) The sister's tendering of good title to the farm is a condition precedent to the brother's duty to convey good title to the apartment house.

(C) The sister's tendering of good title to the farm is a condition subsequent to the brother's duty to convey good title to the apartment house.

(D) The brother's tendering of good title to the apartment house and the sister's tendering of good title to the farm are concurrent conditions.

Question 58

To provide consistency in education in the state, a state law provides for the free distribution of textbooks on secular subjects to students in all public and private schools. A local private religious school accepts the secular textbooks for core academic subjects and supplements its students' education with religious texts.

Which of the following is the strongest argument in favor of the constitutionality of free distribution of textbooks to the students at the private religious school?

(A) Private religious schools, like public nonsectarian schools, fulfill an important educational function.

(B) Religious instruction in private schools is not constitutionally objectionable.

(C) The purpose and effect of the free distribution of these textbooks is secular and does not entangle church and state.

(D) The Free Exercise Clause requires identical treatment by the state of students in public and private schools.

Question 59

A company operated a fleet of touring buses. It owned its own garage for repairing and maintaining its fleet. Behind this garage was a large vacant lot in which the company stored old, discarded, and wrecked buses, which it salvaged for parts or sold for scrap. This area was fenced in by a five-foot-high chain link fence, but the company was aware that children from the neighborhood would climb the fence and play among the junked buses. Consequently, the company would have one of its employees walk through the storage area during the day to chase away any children who may have scaled the fence.

One Saturday afternoon, when the company's garage had closed for the weekend, a group of children climbed over the storage area's fence to play army among the junked buses. One of the children (who had been chased away from the lot before and who also had been warned by his parents not to play in these buses) was trying to climb onto the roof of one of the old buses, when he slipped on the front bumper of the bus and his arm broke through the front windshield, causing severe lacerations. Through an appropriate guardian, the child brought suit against the company for his injury.

Which of the following, if established, would most aid the child in showing that the company breached a duty owing to him?

(A) It would have been economically feasible to remove the windows from all of the abandoned buses.

(B) This area would be classified more as a residential neighborhood than an industrial area.

(C) The company could have eliminated the risk of injury without unduly interfering with its normal operations.

(D) The company improperly maintained the fence that surrounded the lot with the discarded and abandoned buses.

Question 60

Cars driven by the plaintiff and the defendant collided, and the defendant was charged with driving while intoxicated in connection with the accident. She pleaded guilty and was merely fined, although, under the statute, the court could have sentenced her to two years in prison.

Thereafter, the plaintiff, alleging that the defendant's intoxication had caused the collision, sued the defendant for damages.

At trial, the plaintiff offers the properly authenticated record of the defendant's conviction.

The record should be:

(A) Admitted as proof of the defendant's character.

(B) Admitted as proof of the defendant's intoxication.

(C) Excluded, because the conviction was not the result of a trial.

(D) Excluded, because it is hearsay not within any exception.

Question 61

A defendant was owed $500 by his bookie. The defendant went to the bookie's house one night to get his money, but the bookie was not at home. So, the defendant opened an unlocked window and entered the house to see if he could find the $500 due him. He could not find the cash, so he decided to take a painting that he knew was worth substantially more than $500. He later sold it for $1,000 and kept the proceeds. The defendant is charged with burglary. The jurisdiction in which the bookie's house is located retains the common law requirements for burglary.

The defendant should be found:

(A) Not guilty, because there was no breaking, since he did not use force to enter the house.

(B) Not guilty, because he did not have the intent to commit a felony when he entered the house.

(C) Guilty, because he did have the intent to commit a felony when he entered the house.

(D) Guilty, because the painting was worth substantially more than $500.

Question 62

In a contract action between the plaintiff and the defendant, brought in federal court on the basis of diversity jurisdiction, the major issue is the value of a parcel of land. The plaintiff's attorney calls a realtor to the stand and qualifies her as an expert on property valuation. Since the realtor had not personally inspected the property, the plaintiff's attorney was prepared to ask the realtor a hypothetical question based on evidence adduced at the trial. However, the trial had already dragged on longer than expected, and to save time, the plaintiff's attorney merely asks the realtor, "In your expert opinion, how much is the land worth?" The defendant's attorney objects.

The objection should be:

(A) Sustained, because an expert may not render an opinion on an ultimate issue.

(B) Sustained, because an expert must disclose the basis for her opinion.

(C) Overruled, because qualification as an expert creates a presumption of a proper basis for the opinion.

(D) Overruled, because the defendant is entitled to immediate cross-examination of the realtor.

GO ON TO THE NEXT PAGE

Question 63

A brother and a sister leased a house from a landlord. During the term of the lease, the sister verbally invited a friend to share the house with her and her brother. The friend agreed to pay part of the rent to the landlord, who did not object to this arrangement, despite a provision in the lease that provided that "any assignment, subletting, or transfer of any rights under this lease without the express written consent of the landlord is strictly prohibited, null, and void." The brother objected to the friend's moving in. When the friend moved in, the brother brought an appropriate action against the landlord, the sister, and the friend for a declaratory judgment that the sister had no right to assign. The sister's defense was that she and the brother were tenants in common of a term for years, and that she had a right to assign a fractional interest in her undivided one-half interest.

In this action, the brother will:

(A) Prevail, because a co-tenant has no right to assign all or any part of a leasehold without the consent of all interested parties.

(B) Prevail, because the lease provision prohibits assignment.

(C) Not prevail, because he is not the beneficiary of the nonassignment provision in the lease.

(D) Not prevail, because his claim amounts to a void restraint on alienation.

Question 64

A singer has denied his purported signature on a letter that has become critical in a breach of contract suit between him and a record producer. At trial, the record producer's counsel calls a teacher who testifies that she taught the singer mathematics in school 10 years earlier, knows his signature, and proposes to testify that the signature to the letter is that of the singer. The singer's counsel objects.

The trial judge should:

(A) Sustain the objection on the ground that identification of handwriting requires expert testimony and the teacher does not, per se, qualify as an expert.

(B) Sustain the objection on the ground that the best evidence of the singer's handwriting would be testimony by a person who had examined his writing more recently than 10 years ago.

(C) Overrule the objection on the ground that a schoolteacher qualifies as an expert witness for the purpose of identifying handwriting.

(D) Overrule the objection on the ground that a lay person may identify handwriting if he has seen the person in question write, and has an opinion concerning the writing in question.

Question 65

A man and a woman, once married to each other, had gone through a bitter divorce. The divorce decree awarded custody of the couple's four-year-old son to the woman, with the man receiving visitation rights. On the first opportunity that the man had to take his son for the weekend, the man disappeared with him. The woman was greatly distressed and called the man's parents on a weekly basis, always asking if they knew anything about the whereabouts of their son and grandson. The man's parents knew quite well where their son and grandson were, and they often sent money to help support their son while he was on the run. However, they always insisted that they knew nothing about the child. Four years after the child was abducted, the police arrested the man and returned the child to his mother.

If the woman files an action against the man's parents, alleging infliction of emotional distress, will she prevail?

(A) Yes, because the man's parents acted in deliberate disregard of a high probability that their actions would cause the woman to suffer emotional distress.

(B) Yes, because the man's parents enabled their son to stay on the run by supporting him.

(C) No, because the woman has not suffered physical harm.

(D) No, because the woman never was in a zone of danger.

Question 66

A lawyer was appointed as an administrative judge to review claims against the federal government made by Native Americans under a congressional statute. For 20 years, the lawyer heard, reviewed, and arbitrated disputed claims made against the government by various Indian tribes and their citizens. When the lawyer found a claim to be valid, he would make a recommendation to the Bureau of Indian Claims that the claim be paid. If the lawyer found the claims to be without merit, or if the Bureau decided against his recommendation, the claimant would have the right to bring suit in a federal court. Last year, a presidential commission recommended the abolition of the Bureau of Indian Claims as a cost-cutting measure. Congress acted on this recommendation and repealed the statute. The lawyer was offered a position as an attorney in the Department of Transportation, but he turned it down and brought suit against the government.

What is the likely result of this suit?

(A) The lawyer prevails, because it violates the doctrine of separation of powers for the executive branch to interfere with a congressional act by recommending its repeal.

(B) The lawyer prevails, because it violates the Constitution to terminate the tenure of a federal judge during good behavior.

(C) The government prevails, because it established the lawyer's position and it can terminate it at will.

(D) The government prevails, because the lawyer had no judicial discretion or powers in his position with the Bureau.

Question 67

A woman belonged to an extremist political group that advocated the overthrow of the United States government. Among the woman's grievances against current government was a belief that young people were being brainwashed by public school curricula. To end this practice, the woman decided to run for the local school board in the next general election so that she would have a voice in future curricula decisions. The election laws of the city where the woman resided required all candidates for the school board to sign a loyalty oath and file it with the town clerk in order to have their names placed on the ballot for the next school board election. When the woman arrived at the clerk's office to file her candidacy, she was informed of the loyalty oath requirement and was shown the oath. The woman read the oath and objected to the requirement that she sign it.

Which of the following statements is correct as to whether the city may constitutionally require the woman to sign the oath in order to have her name placed on the ballot?

(A) The loyalty oath requirement is valid if the candidate must merely affirm that she does not advocate the violent overthrow of the state or federal governments.

(B) The loyalty oath requirement is valid if the candidate must merely affirm that she will oppose the violent overthrow of the state or federal governments.

(C) The loyalty requirement is valid if the candidate must merely affirm that she has never been a member of any organization dedicated to the violent overthrow of the state or federal governments.

(D) No oath is constitutionally permissible as a condition for ballot qualification.

Question 68

A state prohibits publication of the identity of victims of sexual crimes, but allows trials of such cases to be televised, as long as the victim's face is blocked out. Recently, the nephew of a United States Senator was accused of raping a woman at his family's estate in the state. Because of the notoriety of the senator's family, the press was eager to enlighten the public as to all aspects of the case. A reporter for a metropolitan newspaper published in the state discovered the name of the nephew's victim from a police report that inadvertently included the victim's name, and the newspaper published the victim's identity in the next edition of the paper. The reporter and the paper were fined $2,500 for violating the statute.

If the reporter and the paper challenge the fine, the court should rule:

(A) For the state, because it has a compelling interest in protecting the privacy of its citizens.

(B) For the state, because inclusion of the victim's identity in the police report was inadvertent.

(C) For the reporter and the paper, because the state does not have a compelling interest in prohibiting the dissemination of the lawfully obtained information here.

(D) For the reporter and the paper, because the First Amendment allows the press to print any information that it legally obtains.

Question 69

The inventor of a laser-beam vegetable chopper ran a television ad that described the chopper and said, "This chopper is yours for only $49.99 if you send your check or money order" to a specified post office box. The owner of a retail specialty shop wrote to the inventor, "What's your best, firm price for two dozen choppers?" The inventor sent a written reply that said in its entirety, "We quote you for prompt acceptance $39.99 per unit." The shop owner subsequently mailed a check to the inventor in the appropriate amount, with a memo enclosed saying, "I accept your offer for 24 choppers."

A contract would arise from these communications only if:

(A) Both parties were merchants.

(B) The inventor had at least 24 choppers in stock when the shop owner's check and memo were received.

(C) The shop owner's check and memo were mailed within three months after his receipt of the inventor's letter.

(D) The shop owner's check and memo were mailed within a reasonable time after his receipt of the inventor's letter.

Question 70

An aspiring chef who made homemade hot sauce posted a notice on a bulletin board in a local grocery store stating: "Get a bottle of the hottest hot sauce on earth for only $5 directly from the maker. Not available in stores." The ad listed the man's home mailing address at the bottom. An entrepreneur wrote a letter to the address asking, "What's your price for a case of hot sauce?" The man sent a written reply that said in its entirety, "I can do 12 bottles for $50. Sound good?" The entrepreneur subsequently mailed a check to the man in the appropriate amount, with a memo enclosed saying, "I accept your offer for a case of hot sauce." The man shipped the case to the entrepreneur after receiving his check and memo, and with the shipment sent the entrepreneur an invoice that conspicuously stated the following lawful provision: "These items shall not be offered for resale at retail." The entrepreneur received and read, but disregarded, the invoice restriction and began reselling the bottles for double the price he paid.

The man has a cause of action against the entrepreneur for breach of contract only if:

(A) The man, as a maker of homemade hot sauce, was not a merchant.

(B) The invoice restriction was a material alteration of preexisting terms.

(C) The man's written reply that quoted 12 bottles for $50, but did not contain a restriction on retail sales, was not an offer that the entrepreneur accepted by ordering the case.

(D) The entrepreneur was consciously aware when taking delivery of the goods that the store ad had said, "Not available in stores."

Question 71

A state legislature revised its tax laws to reclassify inherited money as "income," making it subject to the state's high income tax. The legislation was exceedingly complicated and difficult for laypersons, or even trained professionals, to comprehend. Additionally, a provision stated: "Any person who knowingly fails to declare as income any monies received during a tax year shall be guilty of a felony."

During the first tax year in which the new tax law was in effect, a woman inherited $3,500 from her uncle. When the woman received her tax forms, she was confused because of all the complicated computation schedules and fine print. The State Department of Revenue had planned to include a supplemental booklet explaining the new law along with the tax forms. However, a computer glitch caused the booklet not to be included in the mailings. The woman called her attorney and asked him if the inherited money needed to be included on her income tax return. The attorney assured her that the income tax applied only to earned income, interest, and dividends. The woman also called the regional branch of the State Department of Revenue. The telephone operator transferred her call to a part-time intern in the revenue department, who, after explaining who he was, told the woman that inherited funds were not "income" for purposes of the income tax. The woman filed her state income tax return, but did not declare the $3,500 inherited from her uncle.

If the woman is subsequently charged with a felony pursuant to the statute quoted above, which of the following represents the woman's best defense?

(A) The woman's mistake regarding the law's coverage negates the state of mind required by the statute.

(B) The woman never received a booklet explaining the law from the Department of Revenue.

(C) The woman relied on the intern's advice.

(D) The woman relied on her attorney's advice.

Question 72

The plaintiff entered a hunting area dressed in a deer costume, in hopes of getting deer to come within range of his gun. The defendant, who had consumed numerous alcoholic beverages before embarking on his hunt, caught sight of the deer costume and fired, injuring the plaintiff. The plaintiff brought an action against the defendant to recover for his injuries. The jurisdiction retains traditional contributory negligence.

Which of the factors below is not relevant for the plaintiff to prevail?

(A) Whether the plaintiff's conduct in dressing as a deer in a hunting area was more negligent than the defendant's act of hunting while intoxicated.

(B) Whether the defendant had the last clear chance to avoid injuring the plaintiff.

(C) Whether the defendant's act of hunting while intoxicated was willful and wanton.

(D) Whether the defendant's act of hunting while intoxicated was negligent.

Question 73

A state statute provides that persons moving into a community to attend a college on a full-time basis may not vote in any elections for local or state officials that are held in that community. Instead, the statute provides that for voting purposes all such persons will retain their residence in the community from which they came. In that state the age of majority is 18.

Which of the following is the strongest argument to demonstrate the unconstitutionality of this state statute?

(A) A state does not have an interest that is sufficiently compelling to justify the exclusion from voting of an entire class of persons.

(B) There are less restrictive means by which the state could assure that only actual residents of a community vote in its elections.

(C) Most persons moving to a community to attend college full-time are likely to have attained the age of majority under the laws of this state.

(D) On its face this statute impermissibly discriminates against interstate commerce.

Question 74

A seller entered into a contract to sell his land to a buyer for $100,000, with the closing to take place in 30 days. The following week, the seller died in an automobile accident. His will left his personal property to his son and his real property to his sister.

At closing, who is entitled to the proceeds of the sale?

(A) Neither the son nor the sister, because death, an eventuality for which the parties could have provided, terminates the agreement if they did not so provide.

(B) Neither the son nor the sister, because title was rendered unmarketable by the seller's death.

(C) The son.

(D) The sister.

Question 75

A businessman entered into a contract to sell his office complex to a purchaser for $1 million. The purchaser paid the businessman $100,000 in earnest money. The day before the date set for closing, the purchaser died intestate, leaving her niece as her only heir. The niece showed up at the closing with a certified check for $900,000.

Which of the following is correct?

(A) The niece may specifically enforce the agreement.

(B) The businessman may return the $100,000 down payment and cancel the contract.

(C) Death terminates the agreement.

(D) Any title acquired would be unmarketable by reason of the purchaser's death.

Question 76

At the trial of the plaintiff's battery action, arising from an incident in which the defendant allegedly bit off the plaintiff's ear, a witness testified that he was taking a shortcut through an alley one morning and heard someone cry "Help!" Rushing around the corner of a building, the witness saw the plaintiff lying on the sidewalk in a pool of blood, with his left ear missing. The defendant was standing nearby. During cross-examination of the witness by the defendant's counsel, the following question was asked: "If you arrived on the scene after the alleged ear biting, how can you possibly know my client is the one who bit off the plaintiff's ear?" The witness responded: "Because I read in the newspaper the next day that another witness to the event told police that he saw the defendant spit the ear out after I left." The defendant moved to have the witness's last remark stricken from the record.

If the trial court denies the defendant's motion, that ruling is most strongly supported by which of the following?

(A) The report of the eyewitness was an excited utterance.

(B) The report of the eyewitness was a statement of recent perception.

(C) The error in admitting the statement could not be cured by an appropriate jury instruction.

(D) The remark was invited by the cross-examiner's questions.

Question 77

A bicycle manufacturer manufactured a bicycle that it sold to a retail dealer. The bicycle had a serious manufacturing defect in its brakes, but the dealer did not discover the defect before putting it on the sales floor despite a careful inspection of the bicycle. The retail dealer sold the bicycle to a bicycle messenger. Shortly thereafter, while the messenger was riding the bicycle along a busy city street, he saw a traffic light facing him turn from green to yellow. He sped up, hoping to cross the intersection before the light turned red. However, the messenger quickly realized that he could not do so and applied the brake, which failed and caused him to crash. The messenger sustained injuries. Assume that the jurisdiction follows traditional contributory negligence rules.

If the messenger asserts a claim against the retail dealer based on strict liability in tort, will the messenger prevail?

(A) Yes, because the brake failed because of a dangerous defect present when the bicycle left the factory of the manufacturer.

(B) Yes, because the brake failed while the messenger was riding the bicycle.

(C) No, because the messenger contributed to his own injury by speeding up.

(D) No, because the retail dealer carefully inspected the bicycle before selling it.

Question 78

A manufacturer built a speedboat that it sold through an independent dealership. One day, the boat's owner was racing the boat dangerously close to shore in a misguided effort to impress some sunbathers on the beach. The owner was heading straight for the beach and then attempted to turn quickly away, but the steering failed and the boat crashed onto shore, injuring a sunbather. The sunbather asserts a claim based on negligence against the manufacturer. At trial, she presents evidence of the above facts and evidence that the steering failure resulted from a defect in the boat that was present when it left the manufacturer. At the end of the sunbather's case, the manufacturer moves for a directed verdict.

The court should:

(A) Grant the motion, because the sunbather failed to present evidence of negligence on the part of the manufacturer.

(B) Grant the motion, because the sunbather's uncontroverted evidence established that the boat owner's negligence was a superseding cause of the accident.

(C) Deny the motion, because the defect is not something that would ordinarily occur in the absence of negligence.

(D) Deny the motion, because the manufacturer placed a dangerously defective boat into the stream of commerce.

Question 79

While hiking through an area that had been recently devastated by a fire, a hiker discovered a sign that stated: "Now Entering State Wilderness Area." Thinking that the sign would make a nice decoration, the hiker took the sign home with him. He was arrested and charged with violating a state statute that provides, "Any person who appropriates to his own use property owned by the state shall be guilty of a crime." At trial, the hiker admitted taking the sign, but claimed that he believed the sign had been abandoned, given that the area had recently been devastated by a fire. In fact, the sign had not been abandoned.

If the jury believes the hiker, he will most likely be found:

(A) Guilty, because this is a strict liability offense.

(B) Guilty, because intent is not placed in issue by this statute.

(C) Not guilty, as long as the jury finds that the hiker's belief as to the sign's abandonment was reasonable.

(D) Not guilty, because the hiker honestly believed that the sign had been abandoned.

Question 80

The plaintiff was hit by a car driven by the defendant that she had not seen when crossing the street. The plaintiff sued the defendant for her injuries. At trial, the plaintiff calls a police officer to testify that, 10 minutes after the accident, a driver stopped him and said, "Officer, a few minutes ago I saw a hit-and-run accident involving a blue convertible, which I followed to the drive-in restaurant at the corner," and that a few seconds later the officer saw the defendant sitting alone in a blue convertible in the drive-in restaurant's parking lot.

The officer's testimony about the driver's statement should be:

(A) Admitted as a statement of recent perception.

(B) Admitted as a present sense impression.

(C) Excluded, because it is hearsay not within any exception.

(D) Excluded, because it is more prejudicial than probative.

Question 81

An investor entered into a contract with a winery. The contract provided that the investor would invest $1 million in the winery and, in return, the winery would produce and market at least 500,000 bottles of wine each year for five years under a specified label. The contract included a provision that, if feasible, the wine would be distributed by the winery only through a certain wholesale distributor of fine wines. Neither the investor nor the winery had previously dealt with the distributor. The distributor learned of the contract two days later from reading a trade newspaper. In reliance thereon, he immediately hired an additional sales executive and contracted for enlargement of his wine storage and display facility.

If the winery refuses to distribute the wine through the distributor and the distributor then sues the winery for breach of contract, is it likely that the distributor will prevail?

(A) Yes, because the winery's performance was to run to the distributor rather than to the investor.

(B) Yes, because the investor and the winery could reasonably foresee that the distributor would change his position in reliance on the contract.

(C) No, because the investor and the winery did not expressly agree that the distributor would have enforceable rights under their contract.

(D) No, because the investor and the winery, having no apparent motive to benefit the distributor, appeared in making the contract to have been protecting or serving only their own interests.

Question 82

A contract between an investor and an inventor stated that the investor will finance all of the inventor's expenses for the next six months in exchange for half of the profits from any inventions that the inventor develops during that time. During those six months, the investor runs into financial problems and borrows $200,000 from a bank. The investor executes a written instrument providing that the bank "is entitled to collect the debt from my share of the profits, if any, under the inventor contract." The bank gave prompt notice of this transaction to the inventor.

If the inventor thereafter refuses to account for any profits to the bank and the bank sues the inventor for the investor's share of profits then realized, the inventor's strongest argument in defense is that:

(A) The investor-inventor contract did not expressly authorize an assignment of rights.

(B) The investor and the inventor are partners, not simply debtor and creditor.

(C) The bank is not an assignee of the investor's rights under the investor-inventor contract.

(D) The bank is not an intended third-party beneficiary of the investor-inventor contract.

Question 83

To satisfy customer demand for ketchup from organically grown tomatoes, a major restaurant chain agrees to give its ketchup manufacturer a $4 million upfront investment in exchange for the manufacturer's switching all of its current tomato farming techniques to satisfy organic standards. The contract further states that the restaurant chain will then be able to purchase all its needs for organic ketchup from the ketchup manufacturer at a certain price.

Soon after entering into this contract, the ketchup manufacturer, without the restaurant chain's knowledge or assent, sold all its tomato farms, but not its manufacturing plants, to a large agricultural corporation. Under the terms of this sale, the agricultural corporation agreed to sell to the tomato grower all tomatoes grown on the land for 20 years. The agricultural corporation's employees have no experience in organic farming, and the agricultural corporation has no reputation in the farming industry as a successful tomato producer. The restaurant chain-ketchup manufacturer contract was silent on the matter of the ketchup manufacturer's selling any or all of its business assets.

If the restaurant chain seeks an appropriate judicial remedy against the ketchup manufacturer for selling its tomato farms, is the restaurant chain likely to prevail?

(A) Yes, because the sale transaction created a significant risk of diminishing the supply of organic ketchup that the ketchup manufacturer will be able to sell to the restaurant chain under the contract.

(B) Yes, because the restaurant chain-ketchup manufacturer contract did not contain a provision authorizing a delegation of the ketchup manufacturer's duties.

(C) No, because the ketchup manufacturer remains in a position to perform under the restaurant chain-ketchup manufacturer contract.

(D) No, because the ketchup manufacturer, as a corporation, must necessarily perform its contracts by delegating duties to others.

Question 84

A bar owner applied to the state liquor board for transfer of the license of his bar to a new site. The board held a hearing on the application. At that hearing, a woman appeared without being subpoenaed and stated that the bar owner had underworld connections. Although the woman did not know this information to be true, she had heard rumors about the bar owner's character and had noticed several underworld figures going in and out of his bar. In fact, the bar owner had no underworld connections. The liquor board ultimately granted the bar owner's application.

In a claim against the woman based on defamation, the bar owner will:

(A) Not recover, if the court finds that the woman's belief was reasonable.

(B) Not recover, because the board granted the bar owner's application.

(C) Recover, because the woman's statement was false.

(D) Recover, because the woman appeared before the board voluntarily.

Question 85

A brother and a sister inherited their childhood home from their father, taking title as tenants in common. The brother moved into the home, while the sister returned to her residence in a distant city. Although there was no discussion between the brother and the sister concerning their common ownership, the brother paid all taxes, insurance, and other carrying charges on the home. He paid no rent or other compensation to the sister, nor did the sister request any such payment. Thirty years later, a series of disputes arose between the brother and sister concerning their respective rights to the home. The jurisdiction where the land is located recognizes the usual common law types of cotenancies, and has an ordinary 20-year adverse possession statute.

If the brother brings an action against the sister to quiet title to the home in himself, the decision should be for:

(A) The brother, because he has acquired title by adverse possession.

(B) The brother, because the acts of the parties indicate the sister's intention to renounce her right to the inheritance.

(C) The sister, because there is no evidence that the brother has performed sufficient acts to constitute her ouster.

(D) The sister, because one co-tenant cannot acquire title by adverse possession against another.

Question 86

A drug dealer is being tried in federal court for criminal conspiracy with a friend to violate a federal narcotics law. At trial, the prosecutor calls the drug dealer's new wife and asks her to testify about a meeting between the drug dealer and the friend that she observed before she married the drug dealer.

Which of the following is the most accurate statement of the applicable rule concerning whether the wife may testify?

(A) The choice is the wife's.

(B) The choice is the drug dealer's.

(C) The wife is permitted to testify only if both the wife and the drug dealer agree.

(D) The wife may be compelled to testify even if both the wife and the drug dealer object.

Question 87

A defendant held up a gasoline station. During the robbery, he shot and killed a customer who attempted to apprehend him. The defendant was prosecuted for premeditated murder and convicted. Thereafter, he was indicted for armed robbery of the station. Before the trial, his attorney moved to dismiss the indictment on the ground that further proceedings were unconstitutional because of the defendant's prior conviction.

The motion to dismiss should be:

(A) Granted, because once the defendant was convicted on any of the charges arising out of the robbery, the prosecution was constitutionally estopped from proceeding against the defendant on any charge stemming from the same transaction.

(B) Granted, because the Double Jeopardy Clause prohibits a subsequent trial on what is essentially a lesser included offense.

(C) Denied, because there is no constitutional requirement that all known charges against a defendant be brought in the same prosecution.

(D) Denied, because estoppel does not apply when a defendant is charged with violating two different statutes.

Question 88

An appropriations act passed by Congress over the President's veto directs that $1 billion "shall be spent" by the federal government for the development of a new military weapons system, which is available only from one company. On the order of the President, the Secretary of Defense refuses to authorize a contract for purchase of the weapons system. The company sues the Secretary of Defense, alleging an unlawful withholding of these federal funds.

The strongest constitutional argument for the company is that:

(A) Passage of an appropriation over a veto makes the spending mandatory.

(B) Congress's power to appropriate funds includes the power to require that the funds will be spent as directed.

(C) The President's independent constitutional powers do not specifically refer to spending.

(D) The President's power to withhold such funds is limited to cases where foreign affairs are directly involved.

Question 89

A building contractor sued a homeowner for failure to pay on a small cost-plus construction contract. At trial, the contractor, who personally supervised all of the work, seeks to testify to what he remembers about the amount of pipe used, the number of workers used on the job, and the number of hours spent.

The homeowner objects on the ground that the contractor had routinely recorded these facts in notebooks, which are in the contractor's possession.

The contractor's testimony is:

(A) Admissible as a report of regularly conducted business activity.

(B) Admissible as based on firsthand knowledge.

(C) Inadmissible, because it violates the best evidence rule.

(D) Inadmissible, because a summary of writings cannot be made unless the originals are available for examination.

Question 90

A grand jury was investigating a bank robbery. The only information known to the prosecutor was a rumor that a certain ex-convict might have been involved. The grand jury subpoenaed the ex-convict. He refused to answer questions about the robbery and was granted use immunity. He then testified that he and a friend had robbed the bank. The grand jury indicted both the ex-convict and his friend for the bank robbery. The prosecutor permitted the friend to enter a plea to a lesser offense in exchange for the friend's agreement to testify against the ex-convict. The prosecutor had no evidence as to the identity of the robbers except the testimony of the friend and the ex-convict.

At the ex-convict's trial, his objection to his friend's being permitted to testify should be:

(A) Sustained, because the prosecutor may not bargain away the rights of one co-defendant in a deal with another.

(B) Sustained, because the friend's testimony was acquired as a result of the ex-convict's grand jury testimony.

(C) Overruled, because the police suspected the ex-convict even before he testified in the grand jury hearing.

(D) Overruled, because a witness cannot be precluded from testifying if his testimony is given voluntarily.

Question 91

A driver purchased a new automobile from a car dealer. Within a few days of the purchase, the driver returned the car to the dealer for repairs because the car kept pulling to the left whenever the driver applied the brakes. The dealer's mechanic readjusted the brakes but did not detect any other problem with the brake system. The dealer's mechanic assured the driver that the brakes were fixed and, even if they did pull the car to the left again, the brakes would still allow the car to stop.

The car worked fine for two days, but then the brakes started pulling to the left again. As the driver was driving the car back to the dealer's shop for further repair, he saw a pedestrian crossing the street. The driver pressed his foot down on the brake pedal, but the master cylinder failed, and the car would not stop. The driver's car struck the pedestrian, injuring him.

If the pedestrian sues the driver for his injuries:

(A) The pedestrian will prevail, because the driver knew that there was a problem with his brakes.

(B) The pedestrian will prevail, because drivers have a duty to maintain their vehicles in safe working order.

(C) The driver will prevail, because he had no reason to know that his brakes would not stop the car.

(D) The driver will prevail, because he diligently had his brakes repaired.

Question 92

A woman purchased a new toaster, manufactured by a well-known appliance manufacturer, from an appliance store. The first morning the woman had the toaster, the toaster burnt the woman's toast, so she took the toaster back to the store to complain. The store's technician adjusted the toaster's darkening dial and assured the woman that the toaster should work properly in the future. The next morning, the woman's sister came over for breakfast and decided to try the new toaster. When the sister went to retrieve her toast from the toaster, she received an electrical shock and was injured.

The sister sued the appliance manufacturer on a theory of strict liability for her injuries. At trial, the parties stipulated to the above facts. The sister presented evidence that the electrical shock was caused by a defective power cord. At the close of evidence, the manufacturer moved for a directed verdict.

The court should:

(A) Deny the motion, because manufacturers are strictly liable for injuries that result from defects in their products.

(B) Deny the motion, because the trier of fact could find that the toaster was defective when it left the manufacturer's control.

(C) Grant the motion, because the technician at the store made adjustments to the toaster.

(D) Grant the motion, because the sister presented no evidence that that model of toaster had a history of electrical defects.

Question 93

A defendant was convicted in federal court of possession of one kilogram of heroin with intent to distribute. She was sentenced to a prison term. Subsequently, the defendant was indicted by a federal grand jury for conspiracy to distribute the same kilogram of heroin. She moved to dismiss the indictment.

Her motion should be:

(A) Denied, because the Double Jeopardy Clause does not apply when the second prosecution is for violation of a separate statute.

(B) Denied, because each prosecution requires proof of an element that the other does not.

(C) Granted, because the Double Jeopardy Clause protects her against a second prosecution for the same criminal conduct.

(D) Granted, because the Due Process Clause protects her against double punishment for the same criminal conduct.

Question 94

A realty company developed a residential development encompassing single-family dwellings, town houses, and high-rise apartments. Included in the deed to each unit was a covenant under which the grantee and the grantee's "heirs and assigns" agreed to purchase electrical power only from a plant that the realty company had constructed within the development. The plant did not supply power outside the development. After constructing and selling half of the units, the realty company sold its interest in the development to an investment firm. The investment firm operated the power plant and constructed and sold the remaining units. Each conveyance from the investment firm contained the same covenant relating to electrical power that the realty company had included in the conveyances it had made.

A woman bought a dwelling unit from a man who had purchased it from the realty company. Subsequently, the woman, whose lot was along the boundary of the development, ceased buying electrical power from the investment firm and began purchasing power from a power company that provided such service in the area surrounding the development. The investment firm instituted an appropriate action against the woman to enjoin her from obtaining electrical power from the power company. Both the power company and the investment firm have governmental authorization to provide electrical services to the area.

If judgment is for the woman, it most likely will be because:

(A) The covenant does not touch and concern the land.

(B) The mixture of types of residential units is viewed as preventing one common development scheme.

(C) The covenant is a restraint on alienation.

(D) There is no privity of estate between the woman and the investment firm.

Question 95

A state college instructor was discharged because of her refusal to comply with a state statute requiring public employees to swear or affirm that they will (i) "uphold and defend" the state and federal constitutions, and (ii) "oppose the overthrow" of the state or federal governments "by force, violence, or by any improper method." The statute had previously been held constitutional by the state supreme court. The instructor filed a complaint in federal district court, alleging the unconstitutionality of the statute and seeking an injunction and damages.

Which of the following is the state's strongest argument for sustaining the validity of the statute?

(A) Government employment is a privilege, not a right.

(B) The oath as a whole is only a commitment to abide by constitutional processes.

(C) The First and Fourteenth Amendments permit a state to fix the conditions of state employment.

(D) The state has a compelling need to keep disloyal persons out of governmental positions of trust.

Question 96

A buyer entered into a contract with a retail seller to purchase three computers of a specific brand for $4,500 for use in his business office. However, when the computers arrived at his office, the buyer saw that they were a different brand of computers. Because he was short of computers, the buyer asked his secretaries to use the computers. One week later, however, his secretaries complained about the computers, and therefore the buyer wrote to the seller that he was "rejecting" the three computers that were sent to him, and asked for the return of the $4,500. The seller refused to do so.

The legal effect of the buyer's retention and use of the computers for one week before notifying the seller was:

(A) An acceptance of the three computers, because the buyer was aware that the computers were not the brand he ordered.

(B) An acceptance of the three computers if the buyer's use thereof was more than reasonably required to test whether the computers were acceptable substitutes for the ones he ordered.

(C) Not an acceptance, because the computers were nonconforming.

(D) A waiver of any claim for damage against the seller on account of nondelivery of the computers he ordered.

Question 97

A wholesale distributor of electronic poker games served the entire state in which it had its headquarters. There were no plants manufacturing the types of machines that the distributor sold within 1,000 miles of the state, and electronic poker games were in scarce supply. A retail seller sold mechanical and electronic games to taverns and convenience stores in the area. On August 3, the distributor sent a letter to the retail seller, which the retail seller received on August 5. The letter stated, in relevant part: "I now have in stock those 20 electronic poker games that you wanted for your business. I can guarantee delivery until September 2 at $2,000 per machine." On August 16, the distributor sold the 20 electronic poker games to an arcade owner at a price of $2,300 per machine. On August 17, the distributor faxed the retail seller: "Am revoking offer regarding poker machines; have already sold same at higher price." The retail seller received the fax the same day.

During the month of August, a special session of the state legislature passed a bill declaring the sale of electronic gambling machines to be illegal in the state. The definition of electronic gambling machines included the electronic poker games distributed by the distributor. The governor signed the bill into law on August 28, and it became effective immediately. On August 30, the retail seller faxed the distributor: "Accept your offer to sell me 20 poker games at $2,000 per machine." The distributor received the fax the same day.

If the distributor is not obliged to sell 20 electronic poker machines to the retail seller at $2,000 each, it will be because:

(A) The distributor had already sold the machines at a higher price.

(B) The state law banning the sale of such machines operated to revoke the offer.

(C) The distributor revoked his offer before the retail seller accepted.

(D) The state law banning the sale of such machines renders the performance of the distributor's duties impossible.

Question 98

Acting on an anonymous telephone call, police went to the defendant's apartment, knocked on the door, and demanded to search it for narcotics. When the defendant refused, the police forced the door open and placed him under arrest. As they were removing him from the apartment, the defendant offered to give the officers "valuable information" in exchange for his release. Before he could say anything else, the defendant was given *Miranda* warnings by the police. Thereafter, he told the police that he had stored some heroin in his friend's apartment and that he and his friend had been going to sell it. The heroin was recovered, and the defendant was prosecuted for conspiracy to sell narcotics and for possession of narcotics. At his trial, the defendant moved to suppress his statements.

Which of the following is the defendant's best argument in support of the motion to suppress?

(A) The defendant is entitled to know the identity of his accuser, and the state cannot supply this information.

(B) The police should have given the defendant *Miranda* warnings prior to entry into the apartment, and the warnings were ineffectual once the defendant offered to give the police information.

(C) The defendant was intimidated by the forced entry into the apartment, and because the statements were involuntary and coerced, their use against him would violate due process of law.

(D) The statements were fruits of an unlawful arrest, and though the *Miranda* warnings may have been sufficient to protect his right against self-incrimination, they were not sufficient to purge the taint of the illegal arrest.

Question 99

A resident being interviewed live by a television reporter stated that, "The biggest problem in this city is corruption in city government, particularly the mayor." The mayor has now brought an action for defamation against the resident. At trial, the mayor has produced testimony as to his honesty and good character. As part of his defense, the defendant seeks to offer into evidence the fact that the mayor was convicted two years ago of taking a bribe to award a city contract for solid waste disposal.

Is the evidence admissible?

(A) No, because character evidence is not admissible in civil cases.

(B) No, because character can be proved only by opinion or reputation testimony.

(C) Yes, because the mayor's character is directly in issue.

(D) Yes, because there was an actual conviction for the crime.

Question 100

A developer entered into a written contract to buy a parcel of land from a farmer at a price of $160,000. At the time the contract was entered into, the developer gave the farmer $10,000 earnest money. The closing date was set for April 29. On April 17, the developer's attorney conducted a title search, during which the attorney discovered that the farmer's distant cousin had a legitimate claim to a one-tenth undivided interest in the land. On April 26, the developer paid the cousin $10,000, and the cousin gave the developer a quitclaim deed, surrendering any and all interest the cousin had in the land. The developer informed the farmer of the situation. On April 29, the developer appeared at the title company's office and tendered a certified check to the closing officer, but the farmer never appeared at the closing. The developer asked the closing officer to place the certified check in escrow and promptly sued the farmer for specific performance.

Will the developer prevail in his specific performance action?

(A) Yes, if the certified check is for $150,000.

(B) Yes, if the certified check is for $140,000.

(C) No, because the developer should have informed the farmer of the title defect to allow the farmer to obtain marketable title, but the farmer must return the developer's earnest money.

(D) No, because the developer has become a co-tenant of the farmer and an action for partition rather than specific performance is appropriate.

STOP

Multistate Practice Exam

P.M. EXAM

Time—3 hours

You will be given three hours to work on this test. Be sure that the question numbers on your answer sheet match the question numbers in your test book. You are not to begin work until the supervisor tells you to do so.

Your score will be based on the number of questions you answer correctly. It is therefore to your advantage to try to answer as many questions as you can. Give only one answer to each question; multiple answers will not be counted. If you wish to change an answer, erase your first mark completely and mark your new choice. Use your time effectively. Do not hurry, but work steadily and as quickly as you can without sacrificing your accuracy.

YOU ARE TO INDICATE YOUR ANSWERS TO ALL QUESTIONS ON THE SEPARATE ANSWER SHEET PROVIDED.

DIRECTIONS

Each of the questions or incomplete statements in this test is followed by four suggested answers or completions. You are to choose the ***best*** of the stated alternatives. Answer all questions according to the generally accepted view, except where otherwise noted.

For the purpose of this test, you are to assume that Articles 1 and 2 of the Uniform Commercial Code have been adopted. You should assume that the 2001 amendments to Article 1 have been adopted, but that the 2001 and 2003 proposed amendments to Article 2 have not been adopted.

The Federal Rules of Evidence are deemed to control.

The terms "Constitution," "constitutional," and "unconstitutional" refer to the federal Constitution unless indicated to the contrary.

You are also to assume that there is no applicable statute unless otherwise specified; however, survival actions and claims for wrongful death should be assumed to be available where applicable. You should assume that joint and several liability, with pure comparative negligence, is the relevant rule unless otherwise indicated.

DO NOT OPEN THE TEST UNTIL YOU ARE INSTRUCTED TO DO SO.

P.M. Exam

101. Ⓐ Ⓑ Ⓒ Ⓓ	126. Ⓐ Ⓑ Ⓒ Ⓓ	151. Ⓐ Ⓑ Ⓒ Ⓓ	176. Ⓐ Ⓑ Ⓒ Ⓓ
102. Ⓐ Ⓑ Ⓒ Ⓓ	127. Ⓐ Ⓑ Ⓒ Ⓓ	152. Ⓐ Ⓑ Ⓒ Ⓓ	177. Ⓐ Ⓑ Ⓒ Ⓓ
103. Ⓐ Ⓑ Ⓒ Ⓓ	128. Ⓐ Ⓑ Ⓒ Ⓓ	153. Ⓐ Ⓑ Ⓒ Ⓓ	178. Ⓐ Ⓑ Ⓒ Ⓓ
104. Ⓐ Ⓑ Ⓒ Ⓓ	129. Ⓐ Ⓑ Ⓒ Ⓓ	154. Ⓐ Ⓑ Ⓒ Ⓓ	179. Ⓐ Ⓑ Ⓒ Ⓓ
105. Ⓐ Ⓑ Ⓒ Ⓓ	130. Ⓐ Ⓑ Ⓒ Ⓓ	155. Ⓐ Ⓑ Ⓒ Ⓓ	180. Ⓐ Ⓑ Ⓒ Ⓓ
106. Ⓐ Ⓑ Ⓒ Ⓓ	131. Ⓐ Ⓑ Ⓒ Ⓓ	156. Ⓐ Ⓑ Ⓒ Ⓓ	181. Ⓐ Ⓑ Ⓒ Ⓓ
107. Ⓐ Ⓑ Ⓒ Ⓓ	132. Ⓐ Ⓑ Ⓒ Ⓓ	157. Ⓐ Ⓑ Ⓒ Ⓓ	182. Ⓐ Ⓑ Ⓒ Ⓓ
108. Ⓐ Ⓑ Ⓒ Ⓓ	133. Ⓐ Ⓑ Ⓒ Ⓓ	158. Ⓐ Ⓑ Ⓒ Ⓓ	183. Ⓐ Ⓑ Ⓒ Ⓓ
109. Ⓐ Ⓑ Ⓒ Ⓓ	134. Ⓐ Ⓑ Ⓒ Ⓓ	159. Ⓐ Ⓑ Ⓒ Ⓓ	184. Ⓐ Ⓑ Ⓒ Ⓓ
110. Ⓐ Ⓑ Ⓒ Ⓓ	135. Ⓐ Ⓑ Ⓒ Ⓓ	160. Ⓐ Ⓑ Ⓒ Ⓓ	185. Ⓐ Ⓑ Ⓒ Ⓓ
111. Ⓐ Ⓑ Ⓒ Ⓓ	136. Ⓐ Ⓑ Ⓒ Ⓓ	161. Ⓐ Ⓑ Ⓒ Ⓓ	186. Ⓐ Ⓑ Ⓒ Ⓓ
112. Ⓐ Ⓑ Ⓒ Ⓓ	137. Ⓐ Ⓑ Ⓒ Ⓓ	162. Ⓐ Ⓑ Ⓒ Ⓓ	187. Ⓐ Ⓑ Ⓒ Ⓓ
113. Ⓐ Ⓑ Ⓒ Ⓓ	138. Ⓐ Ⓑ Ⓒ Ⓓ	163. Ⓐ Ⓑ Ⓒ Ⓓ	188. Ⓐ Ⓑ Ⓒ Ⓓ
114. Ⓐ Ⓑ Ⓒ Ⓓ	139. Ⓐ Ⓑ Ⓒ Ⓓ	164. Ⓐ Ⓑ Ⓒ Ⓓ	189. Ⓐ Ⓑ Ⓒ Ⓓ
115. Ⓐ Ⓑ Ⓒ Ⓓ	140. Ⓐ Ⓑ Ⓒ Ⓓ	165. Ⓐ Ⓑ Ⓒ Ⓓ	190. Ⓐ Ⓑ Ⓒ Ⓓ
116. Ⓐ Ⓑ Ⓒ Ⓓ	141. Ⓐ Ⓑ Ⓒ Ⓓ	166. Ⓐ Ⓑ Ⓒ Ⓓ	191. Ⓐ Ⓑ Ⓒ Ⓓ
117. Ⓐ Ⓑ Ⓒ Ⓓ	142. Ⓐ Ⓑ Ⓒ Ⓓ	167. Ⓐ Ⓑ Ⓒ Ⓓ	192. Ⓐ Ⓑ Ⓒ Ⓓ
118. Ⓐ Ⓑ Ⓒ Ⓓ	143. Ⓐ Ⓑ Ⓒ Ⓓ	168. Ⓐ Ⓑ Ⓒ Ⓓ	193. Ⓐ Ⓑ Ⓒ Ⓓ
119. Ⓐ Ⓑ Ⓒ Ⓓ	144. Ⓐ Ⓑ Ⓒ Ⓓ	169. Ⓐ Ⓑ Ⓒ Ⓓ	194. Ⓐ Ⓑ Ⓒ Ⓓ
120. Ⓐ Ⓑ Ⓒ Ⓓ	145. Ⓐ Ⓑ Ⓒ Ⓓ	170. Ⓐ Ⓑ Ⓒ Ⓓ	195. Ⓐ Ⓑ Ⓒ Ⓓ
121. Ⓐ Ⓑ Ⓒ Ⓓ	146. Ⓐ Ⓑ Ⓒ Ⓓ	171. Ⓐ Ⓑ Ⓒ Ⓓ	196. Ⓐ Ⓑ Ⓒ Ⓓ
122. Ⓐ Ⓑ Ⓒ Ⓓ	147. Ⓐ Ⓑ Ⓒ Ⓓ	172. Ⓐ Ⓑ Ⓒ Ⓓ	197. Ⓐ Ⓑ Ⓒ Ⓓ
123. Ⓐ Ⓑ Ⓒ Ⓓ	148. Ⓐ Ⓑ Ⓒ Ⓓ	173. Ⓐ Ⓑ Ⓒ Ⓓ	198. Ⓐ Ⓑ Ⓒ Ⓓ
124. Ⓐ Ⓑ Ⓒ Ⓓ	149. Ⓐ Ⓑ Ⓒ Ⓓ	174. Ⓐ Ⓑ Ⓒ Ⓓ	199. Ⓐ Ⓑ Ⓒ Ⓓ
125. Ⓐ Ⓑ Ⓒ Ⓓ	150. Ⓐ Ⓑ Ⓒ Ⓓ	175. Ⓐ Ⓑ Ⓒ Ⓓ	200. Ⓐ Ⓑ Ⓒ Ⓓ

Question 101

An ex-convict, who spent nine years in prison for car theft, vowed to get even with the prosecutor of his trial. While in prison, the ex-convict was told by another prisoner, a drug dealer, that when the prosecutor was in private practice as a criminal defense attorney, he had represented the drug dealer in a drug charge. The drug dealer claimed that because he did not have the cash to pay the prosecutor his fees, he offered to pay his fees with five ounces of cocaine, and the prosecutor accepted.

Although the ex-convict had no independent reason to know whether what the drug dealer said was true, he believed that it was. When he got out of prison he learned that the prosecutor was running for district attorney. The ex-convict went to one of the local papers and sold them the story for $1,000. In the article that resulted, the ex-convict was quoted as saying, "I only hope that the prosecutor suffers like I had to suffer for the last nine years." Although the allegation was false, the prosecutor withdrew from the race as a result of the article.

In a suit by the prosecutor against the ex-convict for defamation, the probable result would be:

(A) The prosecutor prevails because the ex-convict acted with deliberate malice toward the prosecutor.

(B) The prosecutor prevails if the ex-convict should have known that the story was false.

(C) The ex-convict prevails because the story was a matter of public concern.

(D) The ex-convict prevails because he honestly believed the truth of the assertion made by the drug dealer.

Question 102

A statute in the jurisdiction makes it a crime to sell ammunition to a person under the age of 18. The courts have interpreted this statute as creating a strict liability offense that does not require knowledge of the age of the purchaser and as creating vicarious liability. A 16-year-old boy, who looked four or five years older, entered a store and asked a clerk for a box of .22-caliber shells. The store owner had instructed her employees not to sell ammunition to anyone under the age of 18 and to always ask for identification. The clerk asked the boy his age. The boy said he was 20. The clerk then placed a box of shells on the counter and asked, "Anything else?" The boy said that was all he wanted but then discovered he did not have enough money to pay for the shells, so the clerk put the box back onto the shelf.

If the owner of the store is charged with attempting to violate the statute, her best argument would be that:

(A) It was impossible for the sale to have occurred.

(B) She had strictly instructed her employees not to sell ammunition to minors.

(C) The boy lied about his age.

(D) The clerk did not have the mental state needed for the crime charged.

Question 103

A manufacturer that produces the most up-to-date, high-speed mainframe computers on the market contracted with a company that is on the cutting edge of data storage technology for the sale/purchase of a "Yellow Giant" computer. The written contract stated that the company would purchase one of the manufacturer's "'Yellow Giant' computers at a price of $175,000." At the time, the going price for Yellow Giant computers was $150,000. When the manufacturer delivered a Yellow Giant on the specified date, the company refused to accept delivery and refused to pay. The manufacturer sued the company for breach, claiming that its expensive computers were manufactured to order and so it was forced to dispose of the Yellow Giant at a price far below fair market value. In defending the suit, the company's president wishes to testify that the company rejected the Yellow Giant because both parties knew that the company really wanted a "Purple Giant," a machine much faster than the Yellow Giant, but which the parties agreed would be called a "Yellow Giant" in the contract to keep competitors in the dark as to the company's new capabilities, and that the parties had executed contracts in the past that had specified a less powerful computer than the model that was actually delivered.

Should the testimony of the company's president be admitted?

(A) Yes, because the company is entitled to reformation of the contract.

(B) Yes, because the president's testimony would explain the meaning of a disputed contract term.

(C) No, because the parol evidence rule applies and the president's testimony contradicts a term in the written contract.

(D) No, because the Statute of Frauds applies, since the contract is for a large amount of money.

Question 104

Due to a notable increase in prostitution arrests in the state, the state legislature has enacted new regulations for massage parlors. The new law requires that all workers at any massage parlor or similar business be licensed by the state attorney general.

This requirement is:

(A) Constitutional, because it is within the proper scope of the exercise of the police powers of the state.

(B) Constitutional, because the attorney general is designated as the proper person to enforce the law.

(C) Unconstitutional, as a burden on interstate commerce.

(D) Unconstitutional, as a violation of the Privileges and Immunities Clause of Article IV.

Question 105

A state enacted a statute to regulate the use of independent contractors in the state by major garment makers, most of whom were headquartered out of state, because it had led to the hiring of illegal aliens to work under conditions reminiscent of 19th-century sweatshops. The statute provides that any garment-making subcontractor must have been a citizen of the United States for five years and a resident of the state for one year.

This clause of the legislation is subject to a constitutional challenge based on:

(A) The Equal Protection Clause of the Fourteenth Amendment.

(B) The Privileges or Immunities Clause of the Fourteenth Amendment.

(C) The Due Process Clause of the Fifth Amendment.

(D) The Tenth Amendment reserved powers of the state.

Question 106

The plaintiff sued the defendant for injuries received in an automobile accident. There was only one neutral eyewitness to the accident, and the lawyers for the plaintiff and the defendant mutually agreed on a time and place to depose the witness. The lawyers and the witness appeared as scheduled, but the court reporter who had been ordered for the occasion failed to show up. Because rearranging the deposition would be time-consuming and difficult, the lawyers decided to go ahead with the deposition. The witness was not required to give oath or affirmation prior to his testimony, but neither lawyer had any reason to believe that the witness had any motivation to lie. During the deposition, the lawyers tape recorded their questions and the witness's responses. Each lawyer received a copy of the tape of the deposition. The witness suffered a heart attack and died two months after the deposition. Shortly thereafter, the case came to trial.

Assuming proper notice is given, what evidence of the witness's deposition is admissible at trial?

(A) An authenticated copy of the tape of the deposition only.

(B) The testimony of the lawyers who conducted the deposition regarding the witness's statement only.

(C) Either an authenticated copy of the tape or the testimony of the lawyers.

(D) Neither a copy of the tape nor the testimony of the lawyers.

Question 107

An unmarried couple purchased a condominium as tenants in common. Subsequently, the man and the woman made an oral agreement that, on the death of either of them, the survivor would own the entire condominium, and, as a result, they decided they did not need wills. Two years later, the man and the woman were involved in the same automobile accident. The man was killed immediately. The woman died one week later. Both died intestate. The man's sole heir is his brother. The woman's sole heir is her mother. The brother claimed one-half of the condominium, and the mother claimed all of it. The jurisdiction has no applicable statute except for the Statute of Frauds, and it does not recognize common law marriages.

In an appropriate action by the mother, claiming the entire ownership of the condominium, the court will find that:

(A) The mother owns the entire interest, because the man and the woman did not make wills in reliance upon their oral agreement.

(B) The mother owns the entire interest, because she is entitled to reformation of the deed to reflect the oral agreement.

(C) The brother and the mother each own an undivided one-half interest, because the man and the woman each died as the result of the same accident.

(D) The brother and the mother each own an undivided one-half interest, because the Statute of Frauds applies.

Question 108

A state statute provides that only citizens of the United States may be employed by that state. In an action brought in a federal court, a resident alien who was prevented from obtaining state employment as a garbage collector solely because of his alien status challenged the statute's constitutionality as applied to his circumstances.

Which of the following statements concerning the burden of persuasion applicable to this suit is correct?

(A) The alien must demonstrate that there is no rational relationship between the citizenship requirement and any legitimate state interest.

(B) The alien must demonstrate that the citizenship requirement is not necessary to advance an important state interest.

(C) The state must demonstrate that there is a rational relationship between the citizenship requirement and a legitimate state interest.

(D) The state must demonstrate that the citizenship requirement is necessary to advance a compelling state interest.

Question 109

A landowner's piece of property was located on the corner of a busy intersection. People walking past the intersection often cut across the landowner's property rather than walk along the sidewalk, despite a "keep off" sign that the landowner erected. The landowner had captured a young bobcat several months earlier and had decided to keep him as a pet. In an effort to stop people from cutting across his yard, the landowner erected a large sign that read, "Beware of Bobcat." Knowing that a bobcat attacks using its claws, he took it to a vet to have its claws removed. The vet failed to remove one of the bobcat's claws, but the landowner was not aware of this. The landowner kept the bobcat on a leash in the front yard. The leash was long enough to allow the bobcat access to most of the landowner's property; however, the bobcat could not reach the sidewalk that ran adjacent to the landowner's property. The next day, a woman was walking home from the market. When she came to the intersection, she cut across the landowner's property rather than staying on the sidewalk. The bobcat charged at the woman and slashed her legs severely with its one remaining claw.

If the woman brings suit against the landowner for her injuries caused by the bobcat and establishes that she did not see the warning sign, the woman will:

(A) Recover, because the bobcat was not a domesticated animal.

(B) Recover, because the woman was not aware of the sign on the landowner's property.

(C) Not recover, because the woman was a trespasser.

(D) Not recover, because the vet was the cause of the injury.

Question 110

The plaintiff used aluminum brackets in her business. On the telephone listed as hers in the telephone book, the plaintiff received a call in which the caller said, "I own the hardware store downtown. We have a special on aluminum brackets this week at 30% off." The plaintiff ordered brackets from the caller. When the brackets were never delivered, she sued the defendant, owner of the hardware store, for breach of contract.

At trial, the defendant, who denies having made the telephone call, objects to the plaintiff's testimony concerning it. When asked, the plaintiff testifies that, aside from the telephone call, she had never heard the defendant speak until she met him in the judge's chambers before the trial and that, in her opinion, the voice on the telephone was the defendant's.

The strongest argument for admission of the plaintiff's testimony concerning the telephone call is that:

(A) The call related to business reasonably transacted over the telephone.

(B) The call was received at a number assigned to the plaintiff by the telephone company.

(C) After hearing the defendant speak in chambers, the plaintiff recognized his voice as that of the person on the telephone.

(D) Self-identification is sufficient authentication of a telephone call.

Question 111

A man owned a small warehouse that he leased to a florist, who used it as a storage and distribution center for fresh cut flowers being shipped to other florists in the area. The man wanted to put the florist out of business so that he could lease the warehouse to someone else at a higher rent. He entered the warehouse one night using a master key and, to ensure that all of the florist's inventory would be destroyed, he deployed several kerosene space heaters to raise the temperature of the storeroom and destroy the flowers. While he was filling one, a small amount of kerosene spilled and was ignited by an ash from his cigarette. Although the fire that started was small at first, the man panicked when he saw the flames and ran out of the building. The fire eventually spread to the walls of the building and heavily damaged it before being extinguished by firefighters. The jurisdiction follows the common law except that arson covers structures in addition to dwellings.

If the man is charged with arson, can he be found guilty?

(A) Yes, because the man caused the fire during the commission of a malicious felony.

(B) Yes, because the man did nothing when the kerosene caught on fire.

(C) No, because the man did not intend to set the building on fire.

(D) No, because the man cannot be liable for arson of a building that he owned.

Question 112

A woman and her boyfriend worked together as pickpockets. The woman approached a man from the front to distract him, holding a small camera and asking him to take a picture, while her boyfriend came up from behind with a knife to slice open the back pocket of the man's pants and remove his wallet. The man was drunk and believed that the woman had a gun and was trying to rob him, but he was unaware of the boyfriend behind him. The man reached into his back pocket to hand over his wallet and was cut by the boyfriend's knife as it was slicing through his pocket. The wallet dropped to the ground as the man clutched his hand. The boyfriend picked it up, and he and the woman fled while the man knelt on the ground in pain. The woman was apprehended shortly thereafter and charged with robbery.

Should the woman be found guilty?

(A) Yes, because her boyfriend obtained the property by means of force.

(B) Yes, because the man believed that the woman would shoot him if he did not give up his wallet.

(C) No, because neither the woman nor her boyfriend intended to use force against the man to obtain the property.

(D) No, because the man's belief that the woman was robbing him was unreasonable.

Question 113

A professor who was an expert on American history conducted full-day tours through the historic sites of Philadelphia. The professor's fee for his services was $105, which did not include the entrance fees for several of the historical sites. A law student took a day off school and "hung around" the Liberty Bell monument, where the professor's tour started. That day the professor was conducting 27 persons on the tour. Most of the participants had paid in advance, but the professor was holding up a sign with information about the tour and handing out brochures, one of which the law student took. The professor accepted a few additional participants who signed up on the spot, but the law student was not among them. All day long, the law student hung around at the fringe of this group, paying the entrance fees separately but following the group through the different historical sites. However, he always positioned himself close enough to the professor's group so that he could hear virtually every word of the professor's lecture, although the law student did not ask the professor any questions. The law student signed his name and address on the register at Independence Hall. The professor noted this and took down the information. Two days after the tour concluded, the law student received a bill from the professor in the amount of $105.

The law student will most likely be required to pay the professor:

(A) $105, because that is the contract price for the tour.

(B) $105, because the amount of the contract was less than $500, making the Statute of Frauds inapplicable.

(C) $105, if that is a reasonable fee for the lectures based on the professor's expertise.

(D) Nothing, because the historical sites were open to the public and the law student paid his own way.

Question 114

In compliance with a federal statute requiring buildings to be made accessible to persons with disabilities, a lawyer installed wheelchair ramps at both entrances to his office building located on a parcel of land that he had owned for many years. One year later, the lawyer entered into a contract with an accountant to sell the parcel of land, including the office building. After having the property surveyed, the accountant notified the lawyer that she was not going to complete the sale because the wheelchair ramp on the south side of the building extended over the property line and into the adjoining tract of land, making the title unmarketable. The lawyer insisted that the accountant proceed with the sale, and brought an action to compel her performance.

If the court were to find that title is marketable, it will be because:

(A) The wheelchair ramp is required by federal law.

(B) The lawyer currently owns the adjoining tract of land and acquired it and the office building land as part of a larger parcel.

(C) The wheelchair ramp extends only 10 inches over the property line.

(D) The contract between the lawyer and the accountant requires the lawyer to convey only a quitclaim deed.

Question 115

An ordinance of a city makes it unlawful to park a motor vehicle on a city street within 10 feet of a fire hydrant. At 1:55 p.m., a man, realizing he must be in the bank before it closed at 2 p.m. and finding no other space available, parked his automobile in front of a fire hydrant on a city street. The man then hurried into the bank, leaving his elderly neighbor as a passenger in the rear seat of the car. About five minutes later, and while the man was still in the bank, a woman was driving down the street. The woman swerved to avoid what she mistakenly thought was a hole in the street and sideswiped the man's car. The man's car was turned over on top of the hydrant, breaking the hydrant and causing a small flood of water. The man's car was severely damaged and the elderly neighbor was badly injured.

If the elderly neighbor asserts a claim against the man, the most likely result is that the elderly neighbor will:

(A) Recover, because the man's action was negligence per se.

(B) Recover, because the man's action was a continuing wrong that contributed to the elderly neighbor's injuries.

(C) Not recover, because a reasonably prudent person could not foresee injury to the elderly neighbor as a result of the man's action.

(D) Not recover, because a violation of a city ordinance does not give rise to a civil cause of action.

Question 116

A father had made a legally binding promise to furnish his son and his fiancée with a house on their wedding day, planned for June 10 of the following year. Pursuant to that promise, the father and a contractor-friend entered into a contract for the building of a home on a piece of undeveloped land that the father owned. The contractor began building the house but breached the contract by abandoning the house unfinished on March 1. The contractor was aware when the agreement was made of the purpose for which the father wanted the completed house.

Which of the following, if true, would best support the father's claim for consequential damages on account of the house not being finished by June 10?

(A) The son and his bride, married on June 10, would have to pay storage charges on their wedding gifts and new furniture until the house could be completed.

(B) The son's fiancée jilted him on June 10 and ran off with another man who had a new house.

(C) The father was put to additional expense in providing the son and his bride, married on June 10, with temporary housing.

(D) On June 10, the father paid a $5,000 judgment obtained against him in a suit filed March 15 by an adjoining landowner on account of the father's negligent excavation, including blasting, in an attempt to finish the house himself after the contractor's repudiation.

Question 117

On October 1, a siding installer sent a letter to a builder stating, "I am offering to install siding on one or up to all of the 12 houses that you are currently building. This offer remains open until November 1." On October 13, the builder e-mailed the installer, "We accept your offer with respect to the house on Main Street." There was only one house on Main Street that the builder was constructing, so the installer promptly began the siding installation. On October 25, the installer telephoned the builder to inform him that she had accepted other work and so would not be able to install siding on the builder's other houses. The builder thereafter faxed the installer, "We would like you to do the siding on the other houses."

In an action by the builder against the installer for breach of contract, the builder will probably:

(A) Succeed, because the installer had promised that the offer would remain open until November 1.

(B) Succeed, because the installer's attempted revocation was by telephone.

(C) Not succeed, because the builder's power of acceptance was terminated by the installer's contract with another party.

(D) Not succeed, because the builder's power of acceptance was terminated by effective revocation.

Question 118

A landlord heard that a company was looking for old buildings to purchase and raze to make room for new development. On July 1, the landlord sent a letter to the company stating, "I own two adjacent apartment buildings that might meet your needs. One is located on 123 Main Street and the other property is right behind it on 123 Wood Street. I will sell you one or both of the apartment buildings for $250,000 each. This offer remains open until August 1." On July 15, the company faxed the landlord, "Accept your offer with respect to the apartment building on Main Street." On July 18, the company faxed the landlord, "Will also take the building on Wood Street." On July 22, the landlord discovered that he did not have good title to the Wood Street property.

Which of the following would provide the best legal support to the landlord's contention that he was not liable for breach of contract as to the Wood Street property?

(A) Impossibility of performance.

(B) Unilateral mistake as to basic assumption.

(C) Termination of the offer by the company's having first contracted to buy the Main Street property.

(D) Excuse by failure of an implied condition precedent.

Question 119

A man defeated a woman in a close election to determine the president of the State Carpenters' Union. Shortly after the election, the woman discovered that the man had been a member of the Communist Party 15 years ago. The United States has a statute that prohibits a member of the Communist Party from serving as an officer of a labor union. The woman revealed this information to the executive board of the Carpenters' Union, which declared the man's election as president invalid. The man brings suit in federal court, challenging the constitutionality of the United States statute.

The court will most likely hold the statute to be:

(A) Constitutional, because the statute bears directly on the internal security of the United States.

(B) Constitutional, if the government can show a rational basis for the adoption of the statute.

(C) Unconstitutional, because the federal government may never discriminate among persons on the basis of political affiliation.

(D) Unconstitutional, as a bill of attainder.

Question 120

The plaintiff, who was formerly married to the defendant's wife, sued the defendant, claiming that they had entered into an oral agreement whereby the defendant agreed to hire the plaintiff as chief engineer and the plaintiff agreed to take the job at a specified salary, and that the defendant had subsequently breached their employment contract by refusing to hire the plaintiff. At the trial of the plaintiff's suit, the defendant took the stand and denied having any contract with the plaintiff for employment or otherwise. In response, the plaintiff offers into evidence a properly authenticated phone message to the defendant's wife that the defendant had left with the switchboard operator at her office soon after the agreement. The message stated, "I know you won't be happy, but I've offered the chief engineer position to your ex-husband and he's accepted." The defendant's attorney objects.

The phone message should be ruled:

(A) Admissible, because it is the statement of a party-opponent.

(B) Admissible, because it is a recent perception.

(C) Inadmissible, because it is a privileged communication between husband and wife.

(D) Inadmissible, because it is hearsay not within any recognized exception to the hearsay rule.

Question 121

A salesman was staying at a hotel for a convention. Hotels in the area near the convention had been experiencing a series of robberies where the robber would break into the locked hotel room and then rob his victim by threatening the victim with a gun. In response, the hotel where the salesman was staying had recently re-inspected its rooms to ensure that its hotel room locks were secure and in compliance with state requirements. Nevertheless, one night during the convention, the robber broke into the salesman's room in the same manner as his other robberies. Instead of threatening to shoot, however, the robber hit the salesman over the head with a blackjack, seriously injuring him.

If the salesman sues the hotel for his injuries and does not prevail, it will be because:

(A) The hotel's management reasonably believed that the hotel room locks were adequate.

(B) The hotel is not vicariously liable for the intentional torts of unrelated third parties.

(C) The use of force by the robber was unforeseeable and therefore a superseding intervening cause.

(D) The hotel was in compliance with a state statute setting minimum standards for hotel room locks.

Question 122

A husband and wife were going through a nasty divorce. The wife hired a private detective to spy on her husband. The detective followed the husband to a hotel, where he saw the husband meet a woman and go into her hotel room. The detective checked into the adjoining room, placed an electronic listening device on the wall, and listened to and recorded the activities of the husband and the woman in the next room. He did nothing with the information he gathered, however, because the wife's retainer check to the detective bounced. Both adultery and electronic eavesdropping are crimes under state law.

If the husband sues the detective for invasion of privacy:

(A) The husband will win, because he had an expectation of privacy in the woman's hotel room.

(B) The husband will win, because the detective's electronic eavesdropping was illegal.

(C) The husband will lose, because adultery is illegal.

(D) The husband will lose, because the detective published nothing about the husband's activities.

Question 123

Fifteen years ago, a homeowner executed his will, devising his home "to my surviving widow for life, remainder to such of my children as shall live to attain the age of 30 years; but if any child dies under the age of 30 years survived by a child or children, such child or children shall take and receive the share which his, her, or their parent would have received had such parent lived to attain the age of 30 years." At the date of writing his will, the homeowner was married to an actress, and they had two adult daughters. The actress died 10 years ago, and the homeowner married a dancer two years later. At his death last year, the homeowner was survived by the dancer and three children, the two daughters from his marriage to the actress, and a son. The son, who is six years old, was the homeowner's child by the dancer. The jurisdiction recognizes the common law Rule Against Perpetuities unmodified by statute.

The result of the application of the Rule is:

(A) The remainder to the children and to the grandchildren is void, because the homeowner could have subsequently married a person who was unborn at the time he executed his will.

(B) The remainder to the children is valid, but the substitutionary gift to the grandchildren is void, because the homeowner could have subsequently married a person who was unborn at the time he executed his will.

(C) The gift in remainder to the daughters or their children is valid, but the gift to the son or his children is void.

(D) The remainder to the children and the substitutionary gift to the grandchildren are valid.

Question 124

A defendant was indicted in state court for bribing a public official. During the course of the investigation, police had demanded and received from the defendant's bank the records of the defendant's checking account for the preceding two years. The records contained incriminating evidence. On the basis of a claim of violation of his constitutional rights, the defendant moves to prevent the introduction of the records in evidence.

His motion should be:

(A) Granted, because a search warrant should have been secured for seizure of the records.

(B) Granted, because the records covered such an extensive period of time that their seizure unreasonably invaded the defendant's right of privacy.

(C) Denied, because the potential destructibility of the records, coupled with the public interest in proper enforcement of the criminal laws, created an exigent situation justifying the seizure.

(D) Denied, because the records were business records of the bank in which the defendant had no legitimate expectation of privacy.

GO ON TO THE NEXT PAGE

Question 125

After a bitter custody battle, the court dissolving a marriage ordered that the mother had sole custody of her three-year-old son. The father was allowed to have his son for visitation purposes, which included two weeks every summer. During the first summer visitation period, the father took his son to stay with the father's parents. When the two-week period ended, both the father and his son disappeared from sight. Under an assumed name, the father leased a poultry farm in a rural area and kept his son there. His son enjoyed living on the farm and helping collect eggs and doing other activities with his dad. The mother tried to find the father but was unable to learn of his whereabouts. Two years after the son and the father's disappearance, one of the father's neighbors saw the son's picture in a television program about missing children. The neighbor notified local police and the son and his mother were reunited.

If the mother files suit on her son's behalf seeking damages from the father for false imprisonment, who will prevail?

(A) The son, because the father did not have legal custody of him.

(B) The son, because the father deprived him of his mother's care for two years.

(C) The father, because the son did not realize he was confined.

(D) The father, because the son enjoyed living on the farm.

Question 126

The defendant was arrested and charged with the battery of a co-worker. At trial, the defendant testified that he struck the co-worker only in self-defense because the co-worker had threatened to kill him. The defendant further testified without objection that he had told the arresting officer that he had acted in self-defense. In rebuttal, the prosecutor called the officer to testify that the defendant made no such statement to him.

The officer's testimony is:

(A) Admissible, as an admission by silence of a party-opponent.

(B) Admissible, because it contradicts the defendant's assertion.

(C) Inadmissible, because it is extrinsic evidence on a collateral matter.

(D) Inadmissible, because the defendant had a constitutional right to remain silent.

Question 127

A federal statute set up a program of dental education. The statute provided that the Secretary of Health and Human Services "shall, on a current basis, spend all of the money appropriated for this purpose" and "shall distribute the appropriated funds" by a specified formula to state health departments that agree to participate in the program. In the current year, Congress appropriated $100 million for expenditure on this program.

To ensure a budget surplus in the current fiscal year, the President issued an executive order directing the various Cabinet secretaries to cut expenditures in this year by 10% in all categories. He also ordered certain programs to be cut more drastically because he believed that "they are not as important to the general welfare as other programs." The President identified the dental education program as such a program and ordered it to be cut by 50%. Assume that no other federal statutes are relevant.

To satisfy constitutional requirements, how much money must the Secretary of Health and Human Services distribute for the dental education program this year?

(A) $50 million, because the President could reasonably determine that this program is not as important to the general welfare as other programs.

(B) $50 million, because as chief executive the President has the constitutional authority to control the actions of all of his subordinates by executive order.

(C) $90 million, because any more drastic cut for the program would be a denial of equal protection to beneficiaries of this program as compared to beneficiaries of other programs.

(D) $100 million, because the President may not unilaterally suspend the effect of a valid federal statute imposing a duty to spend appropriated monies.

Question 128

A farmer executed and delivered to a developer a quitclaim deed purporting to convey to the developer all of the right, title, and interest of the farmer in his land. The developer accepted the deed and placed it in his safe deposit box. Four years later, the farmer, who was indebted to his cousin in the amount of $35,000, executed and delivered to the cousin a warranty deed purporting to convey the land in exchange for a full release of the debt. The cousin immediately recorded her deed. The following month, the developer recorded his deed to the land and notified the cousin that he claimed title. There is no evidence of occupancy of the land, and the jurisdiction where the land is situated has a recording statute that requires good faith and value as elements of the junior claimant's priority.

Which of the following best describes the conflicting claims of the developer and the cousin?

(A) The developer cannot succeed, because the quitclaim deed through which he claims prevents him from being bona fide (in good faith).

(B) The outcome will turn on the view taken as to whether the cousin paid value within the meaning of the statute requiring this element.

(C) The outcome will turn on whether the developer paid value (a fact not given).

(D) The developer's failure to record until four years after the conveyance estops him from asserting title against the cousin.

Question 129

A plaintiff contended that a defendant owed him $6,000. The defendant denied that he owed the plaintiff anything. Tired of the dispute, the defendant eventually signed a promissory note by which he promised to pay the plaintiff $5,000 in settlement of their dispute.

In an action by the plaintiff against the defendant on the promissory note, which of the following, if true, would afford the defendant the best defense?

(A) Although the plaintiff honestly believed that $6,000 was owed by the defendant, the defendant knew that it was not owed.

(B) Although the plaintiff knew that the debt was not owed, the defendant honestly was in doubt whether it was owed.

(C) The original claim was based on an oral agreement, which the Statute of Frauds required to be in writing.

(D) The original claim was an action on a contract, which was barred by the applicable statute of limitations.

Question 130

An electrical engineer designed an electronic game. The engineer entered into a licensing agreement with a manufacturer under which it agreed to manufacture the game according to the engineer's specifications and to market it and pay a royalty to the engineer. A girl whose parents had purchased the game for her was injured while playing with the game. The girl recovered a judgment against the manufacturer on the basis of a finding that the game was defective because of the engineer's improper design. Evidence was also presented that the manufacturer could have discovered the defect by reasonable inspection.

In a claim for indemnity against the engineer, will the manufacturer prevail?

(A) Yes, because as between the engineer and the manufacturer, the engineer was responsible for the design of the game.

(B) Yes, because the manufacturer and the engineer were joint tortfeasors.

(C) No, because the manufacturer was strictly liable to the girl.

(D) No, because the manufacturer, by a reasonable inspection, could have discovered the defect in the design of the game.

Question 131

A defendant was charged with murder. His principal defense was that he had killed in hot blood and should be guilty only of manslaughter. The judge instructed the jury that the state must prove guilt beyond a reasonable doubt, that the killing was presumed to be murder, and that the charge could be reduced to manslaughter, and the defendant accordingly found guilty of this lesser offense, if the defendant showed by a fair preponderance of the evidence that the killing was committed in the heat of passion on sudden provocation. The defendant was convicted of murder. On appeal, he seeks a new trial and claims error in the judge's instructions to the jury.

The defendant's conviction will most probably be:

(A) Affirmed, because the judge carefully advised the jury of the state's obligation to prove guilt beyond a reasonable doubt.

(B) Affirmed, because the defendant's burden to show hot blood was not one of ultimate persuasion but only one of producing evidence to rebut a legitimate presumption.

(C) Reversed, because the instruction put a burden on the defendant that denied him due process of law.

(D) Reversed, because presumptions have a highly prejudicial effect and thus cannot be used on behalf of the state in a criminal case.

GO ON TO THE NEXT PAGE

Question 132

While walking on patrol in a commercial district in the early evening, a police officer noticed that a light was on in the back window of a machine shop. Curious about what was going on inside, the officer went to the back of the building and tried to look through the window of the shop, but it had been painted on the inside so that only a strip about three inches at the top, eight feet above ground level, was still transparent. The officer quietly brought two trash cans from a neighboring business over to the window, stood on them and saw, through the strip of unpainted window, that the shop owner's son was inside with a friend, sucking white powder into his nose through a rolled-up tube of paper from off a small mirror. Recognizing that the shop owner's son was snorting cocaine, the officer knocked at the front door to the shop, and the son let him in. The officer immediately arrested the owner's son and his friend. In the back room of the shop through whose window he had peered, the officer found and seized several grams of cocaine, a razor blade, and a mirror. In the subsequent prosecution of the shop owner's son for possession of cocaine, the owner's son seeks to bar introduction of the cocaine, mirror, and razor blade into evidence.

His motion will probably be:

(A) Granted, because the officer could not have known that the owner's son was snorting cocaine absent a chemical test of the substance being snorted.

(B) Granted, because the officer violated the owner's son's reasonable expectation of privacy.

(C) Denied, because the search was incident to a valid arrest.

(D) Denied, because the owner's son consented to the officer's entry into the shop.

Question 133

The plaintiff sued the defendant in an automobile collision case. At trial, the plaintiff wishes to show by extrinsic evidence that the defendant's primary witness is the defendant's partner in a gambling operation.

This evidence is:

(A) Admissible as evidence of the witness's character.

(B) Admissible as evidence of the witness's possible bias in favor of the defendant.

(C) Inadmissible, because criminal conduct can be shown only by admission or record of conviction.

(D) Inadmissible, because bias must be shown on cross-examination and not by extrinsic evidence.

GO ON TO THE NEXT PAGE

Question 134

A landowner nearing retirement hired a company to clear all the trees from a specified portion of a plot of land he owned in the woods and to build a rustic log cabin on the property with those trees. Under the contract, the landowner was to make payments to the company of $10,000 on the first of every month for nine months beginning August 1, on monthly presentation of a certificate by an environmental protection group certifying that construction was proceeding in an ecologically sound manner. The company cleared the trees in July and began working on the cabin. The landowner made three $10,000 payments for the work done in July, August, and September, without requiring a certificate. The company worked through October, but no work was done from November 1 to the end of February because of bad weather, and the landowner made no payments during that period. The company did not object. On March 1, the company demanded payment of $10,000; but the landowner refused on the grounds that no construction work had been done for four months and the environmental protection group had issued no certificate. The company thereupon abandoned work and repudiated the agreement.

Assuming that the company committed a total breach on March 1, what would be the probable measure of the landowner's damages in an action against the company for breach of contract?

(A) Restitution of the three monthly installments paid in August, September, and October.

(B) What it would cost to get the cabin completed by another builder, minus installments not yet paid to the company.

(C) The difference between the market value of the partly built cabin, as of the time of the company's breach, and the market value of the cabin if completed according to specifications.

(D) In addition to other legally allowable damages, an allowance for the landowner's mental distress if the house cannot be completed in time for his retirement.

Question 135

On May 1, a landowner faxed a potential buyer, "Will sell you any or all of the lots in my subdivision at $5,000 each. Details follow in letter." The letter described the 50 lots in the subdivision and contained all of the necessary details concerning terms of payment, insurance, mortgages, etc. On May 2, after she had received the fax but before she had received the letter, the buyer faxed the owner, "Accept your offer with respect to lot 101." On May 3, the owner telephoned the buyer and stated that because he had just discovered that a shopping center was going to be erected adjacent to the subdivision, he would "need to have $6,000 for each of the lots, including lot 101." The buyer agreed to pay him $6,000 for lot 101, and, on May 6, she faxed, "Accept your offer with respect to the rest of the lots."

The buyer will most likely be required to pay:

(A) Only $5,000 for each of the 50 lots.

(B) Only $5,000 for lot 101, but $6,000 for the remaining 49 lots.

(C) $6,000 for each of the 50 lots.

(D) $6,000 for lot 101, but only $5,000 for the remaining 49 lots.

Question 136

An amusement park entered into a contract with an engineering firm to construct a new roller coaster for the park. The contract provided that the amusement park would make monthly payments to the engineering firm and that the engineering firm would submit a monthly report from an independent safety inspector that all state-mandated safety guidelines were being met during construction. Construction began and the amusement park made three monthly payments, but the engineering firm failed to provide any monthly safety reports. The amusement park did not object. Construction was then halted for two months during hurricane season, and the amusement park made no payments during that period. The engineering firm did not object. On the day construction was set to resume, the engineering firm demanded a monthly payment. The amusement park refused on the grounds that no progress on the project had been made in two months and no safety reports had been submitted. The engineering firm thereupon abandoned work and repudiated the agreement.

What was the probable legal effect of (i) the engineering firm's failure to object to the amusement park's failure to make payments during the hurricane season and (ii) the amusement park's making three monthly payments without requiring submission of a safety report?

(A) Estoppel-type waiver as to both.

(B) Waiver of delay in payment and revocable waiver as to the safety reports.

(C) Mutual rescission of the contract.

(D) Discharge of the amusement park's duty to make the payments and estoppel-type waiver as to the safety reports.

Question 137

A landowner gave his lawyer a power of attorney containing a provision that specifically authorized the lawyer to sell and convey any part or all of the landowner's real property. The lawyer conveyed part of the landowner's land to a developer by deed in the customary form containing covenants of title. The developer sues the landowner for breach of a covenant.

The outcome of the developer's suit will be governed by whether:

(A) Deeds without covenants are effective to convey realty.

(B) The jurisdiction views the covenants as personal or running with the land.

(C) The developer is a bona fide purchaser.

(D) The power to "sell and convey" is construed to include the power to execute the usual form of deed used to convey realty.

Question 138

Responding to an open bid solicitation from the procurement office of the Defense Department, a technologies company submitted a bid for the development of a new flame-resistant fabric. On review of the bids, the company was notified that it was the low bidder; however, its bid for the contract was denied because of its failure to meet guidelines on minority representation that the procurement office imposed on firms contracting with the Defense Department. Several months later, the project was rebid. Although the company did not participate, company officials later learned that the contract had been awarded to another regional company after the procurement office waived its minority representation guidelines for that project. The company whose bid had previously been rejected filed an action in federal district court seeking only to enjoin performance of the contract.

The court should:

(A) Dismiss the action, because the company cannot show a relationship between the procurement office's award of the contract and any injury that it may be claiming.

(B) Dismiss the action, because the federal government may enter into contracts under whatever conditions it chooses.

(C) Decide the case on the merits, because the procurement office must show that its waiver of the minority representation guidelines was necessary to further a compelling government interest.

(D) Decide the case on the merits, because the company can claim that the unequal treatment of the two bidders violated its rights under the Due Process Clause of the Fifth Amendment.

Question 139

A woman was crossing the street at a crosswalk, but did not look both ways. The woman was hit by a truck, and immediately afterwards, she was struck by a car. As a result of these collisions with the vehicles, the woman suffered severe injuries. Although it was impossible to determine which portion of the woman's injuries was caused by the driver of the car and which was caused by the truck driver, at the trial of the woman's suit, the jury determined that the driver of the car was 20% negligent, that the truck driver was 40% negligent, and that the woman was 40% negligent. It was further determined that the woman had suffered $100,000 in damages. The woman had already received $10,000 from her group medical insurance plan. The driver of the car had a $500,000 auto liability insurance policy, and the truck driver is now insolvent.

How much will the woman recover in damages from the driver of the car?

(A) $90,000.

(B) $60,000.

(C) $50,000.

(D) $20,000.

Question 140

A developer contracted to buy a parcel of land from a landowner, with deed to be delivered and money paid on August 1. The developer planned to build a high-rise building on the land. The developer had visually inspected the land, but did not take any special notice of the fact that a stream flowed up to the eastern property line of the land and reappeared just beyond the western property line. In fact, there was a conduit under the surface of the land through which the waters of the stream were diverted. On July 28, one of the developer's friends mentioned the existence of the conduit to the developer. When the landowner tendered a deed to the land on August l, the developer refused to accept it, stating that she would not have tried to buy the land if she had known about the conduit. The landowner files suit, demanding performance by the developer or damages for breach.

Who should prevail?

(A) The landowner, because the developer had ample opportunity to discover the existence of the conduit before she agreed to buy the land.

(B) The landowner, because the purpose for which the developer intended to use the land is irrelevant.

(C) The developer, because the landowner had a duty to provide a marketable title.

(D) The developer, because of the doctrine of frustration of purpose.

Question 141

A student broke into her professor's office to look at examination questions without taking them. Once in the office, the student was unable to locate the examination questions, as they were locked in a desk drawer. The student mistakenly believed that looking at examination questions was a felony in the jurisdiction; in fact, such conduct would be a misdemeanor at most. The jurisdiction includes offices as structures that could be burglarized.

If the student were to be apprehended and charged with burglary, she should be:

(A) Acquitted, because she did not complete the crime and she has not been charged with attempt.

(B) Acquitted, because what she intended to do when she broke in was not a felony.

(C) Convicted, because she had the necessary mental state and committed the act of breaking and entering.

(D) Convicted, because factual impossibility is not a defense.

Question 142

A man was negligently driving down the road, not paying attention to where he was going. Because of this, he hit and seriously injured a pedestrian who was lawfully crossing the street. The accident was witnessed by a friend of the woman who was standing on the sidewalk. The friend suffered extreme emotional distress that physically affected her nervous system. The friend brings suit against the driver for negligent infliction of emotional distress in a jurisdiction that has adopted the majority approach in bystander cases.

The friend will:

(A) Win, because she witnessed the pedestrian being seriously injured by the driver.

(B) Win, because severe shock to the nervous system constitutes a physical injury.

(C) Lose, because she was not crossing the street with the pedestrian.

(D) Lose, because she was not a close relative of the pedestrian.

Question 143

An issue in the plaintiff's action against the defendant for causing the plaintiff's back injury was whether the plaintiff's condition had resulted principally from a similar occurrence five years before, with which the defendant had no connection.

The plaintiff called as a witness his treating physician, who offered to testify that when she saw the plaintiff after the latest occurrence, the plaintiff told her that before the accident he had been working full-time, without pain or limitation of motion, in a job that involved lifting heavy boxes.

The physician's testimony should be:

(A) Admitted, because it is a statement of the plaintiff's then-existing physical condition.

(B) Admitted, because it is a statement made for purposes of medical diagnosis or treatment.

(C) Excluded, because it is hearsay not within any exception.

(D) Excluded, because the plaintiff is available as a witness.

Question 144

A state statute requires the permanent removal from parental custody of any child who has suffered "child abuse." That term is defined to include "corporal punishment of any sort." A father gently spanks his six-year-old son on the buttocks whenever he believes that spanking is necessary to discipline him. Such a spanking has never physically harmed the child. The state files suit under the statute to terminate the father's parental rights solely because of these spankings. The father defends only on the ground that the statute in question is unconstitutional as applied to his admitted conduct.

In light of the nature of the rights involved, which of the following is the most probable burden of persuasion on this constitutional issue?

(A) The state has the burden of persuading the court that the application of this statute to the father is necessary to vindicate a compelling state interest.

(B) The state has the burden of persuading the court that the application of this statute to the father is rationally related to a legitimate state interest.

(C) The father has the burden of persuading the court that the application of this statute to him is not necessary to vindicate an important state interest.

(D) The father has the burden of persuading the court that the application of this statute to him is not rationally related to a legitimate state interest.

Question 145

The defendant and her boyfriend went into a drugstore. While in the store, the defendant reached into the cash register and took out $200. The owner of the store came out of a back room, saw what had happened, and told the defendant to put the money back. The defendant's boyfriend then took a revolver from under his coat and shot and killed the store owner.

The defendant claims that the store owner owed her $200 and that she went to the drugstore to try to collect the debt. She said that she asked her boyfriend to come along just in case the store owner made trouble, but that she did not plan on using any force and did not know that her boyfriend was armed.

If the defendant is prosecuted for murder on the basis of felony murder and the jury believes her claim, she should be found:

(A) Guilty, because her boyfriend committed a homicide in the course of a felony.

(B) Guilty, because her taking the boyfriend with her to the store created the risk of death that occurred during the commission of a felony.

(C) Not guilty, because she did not know that her boyfriend was armed and thus did not have the required mental state for felony murder.

(D) Not guilty, because she believed she was entitled to the money and thus did not intend to steal.

Question 146

In which of the following scenarios does a defendant have a constitutional right to be represented by counsel?

(A) During a photo identification.

(B) During a post-charge lineup.

(C) During a taking of a voice exemplar.

(D) During a blood sampling.

Question 147

The defendant was charged with aggravated assault. The defendant did not testify at trial; however, he sought to offer opinion evidence of his good character for truth and veracity.

This testimony should be:

(A) Admitted, because a criminal defendant is entitled to offer evidence of his good character.

(B) Admitted, because a party's credibility is necessarily in issue.

(C) Excluded, because evidence of character is not admissible to prove conduct in conformity therewith.

(D) Excluded, because it is evidence of a trait not pertinent to the case.

Question 148

A landowner conveyed a parcel of land "to my brother, his heirs and assigns, but if my brother dies and is not survived by children by his present wife, then to my cousin and his heirs and assigns." Shortly after taking possession, the brother discovered rich metal deposits on the land, opened a mining operation, and removed and sold a considerable quantity of valuable ore without giving the cousin any notice of his action. The brother has no children. The brother, his wife, and the cousin are all still living. The cousin brought an action in equity for an accounting of the value of the ore removed and for an injunction against further removal.

If the decision is for the brother, it will be because:

(A) The cousin has no interest in the land.

(B) The right to take minerals is an incident of a defeasible fee simple.

(C) The right to take minerals is an incident of the right to possession.

(D) There was no showing that the brother acted in bad faith.

Question 149

After being notified by a doctor that her employment with his office was terminated, a nurse applied for a position with a hospital. In her application, the nurse listed her former employment with the doctor, with the understanding that the doctor might be contacted. The doctor, in response to a telephone inquiry from the hospital, stated that the nurse "lacked professional competence." Although the doctor reasonably believed that to be a fair assessment of the nurse, his adverse rating was based on an episode of malpractice for which he blamed the nurse but which in fact was chargeable to another doctor. Because of the doctor's adverse comment on her qualifications, the nurse was not employed by the hospital.

If the nurse asserts a claim based on defamation against the doctor, will the nurse prevail?

(A) Yes, because the doctor was mistaken in the facts on which he based his opinion of the nurse's competence.

(B) Yes, because the doctor's statement reflected adversely on the nurse's professional competence.

(C) No, because the nurse authorized the hospital to make inquiry of her former employer.

(D) No, because the doctor had reasonable grounds for his belief that the nurse was not competent.

Question 150

A 10-lot subdivision was approved by the proper governmental authority. The authority's action was pursuant to a map filed by the developer, which included an undesignated parcel in addition to the 10 numbered lots. The shape of the undesignated parcel is different and somewhat larger than any one of the numbered lots. Subdivision building restrictions were imposed on "all the lots shown on said map." The developer contracts to sell the undesignated parcel, described by metes and bounds, to an investor.

Is title to the parcel marketable?

(A) Yes, because the undesignated parcel is not a lot to which the subdivision building restrictions apply.

(B) Yes, because the undesignated parcel is not part of the subdivision.

(C) No, because the undesignated parcel has never been approved by the proper governmental authority.

(D) No, because the map leaves it uncertain whether the undesignated parcel is subject to the building restrictions.

Question 151

On March 15, a vineyardist entered into a written agreement with a winery that provided that the vineyardist would sell 1,600 tons of tokay grapes to the winery for $750 per ton, delivery to be no later than November 1 of the same year. By November 1, the vineyardist had delivered only 700 tons of grapes and had informed the winery by fax that she had used the remainder of her crop in the production of wine for her own shop. The winery purchased an additional 900 tons of tokay grapes from other growers at the then-prevailing market price of $800 per ton. The vineyardist has submitted an invoice to the marketing department of the winery for $525,000.

Ignoring incidental costs of cover, the winery should:

(A) Pay the $525,000, since by accepting delivery of the 700 tons of grapes, the winery waived an objection to the vineyardist's breach.

(B) Pay the vineyardist the market value of her 700 tons of grapes as of November 1, less the cost of cover for the remaining 900 tons.

(C) Pay the vineyardist $480,000, which represents the contract price for the grapes she delivered less the cost of cover for the remaining 900 tons.

(D) Pay the vineyardist nothing, since she will be unable to enforce any claim for payment in court.

Question 152

The defendant was prosecuted for bank robbery. At trial, the bank teller was unable to identify the defendant, now bearded, as the bank robber. The prosecutor then showed the teller a group of photographs, and the teller testified that she had previously told the prosecutor that the middle picture (concededly a picture of the defendant before he grew a beard) was a picture of the bank robber.

The teller's testimony is:

(A) Inadmissible, because it is hearsay not within any exception.

(B) Inadmissible, because it is a violation of the defendant's right of confrontation.

(C) Admissible as prior identification by the witness.

(D) Admissible as past recollection recorded.

Question 153

A yogurt manufacturer sold one of its small, underperforming dairy farms to a farmer for a reduced price. The sale contract provided that the yogurt manufacturer would purchase all of the milk produced by the farm during the next five years at the current market price at time of delivery, delivery and payment to be made at weekly intervals, and the farmer agreed to supply in any event a minimum of 1,000 gallons of milk per month during that period. When the sale was closed, the yogurt manufacturer's lawyer handed the farmer's lawyer a letter stating: "This is to notify you that we will take all of your milk production until further notice."

For one year, the farmer delivered to the yogurt manufacturer and the yogurt manufacturer paid for all of the milk produced at the farm. During that year, the farmer increased his milk production by 100% by increasing the number and productivity of the cows. The farmer then proposed to the yogurt manufacturer that, since he had doubled production, it would only be fair that he supply the yogurt manufacturer with half of his new total, but in any event a minimum of 1,000 gallons per month, leaving the farmer free to sell the remainder of the milk at higher prices for other uses. The yogurt manufacturer, in a signed writing, agreed to the proposal by the farmer for the remaining period of the original contract.

The modification between the yogurt manufacturer and the farmer reducing the contractual amounts by 50% was:

(A) Enforceable in all respects.

(B) Enforceable only to the extent of milk tendered by the farmer.

(C) Unenforceable, because there was no consideration for the yogurt manufacturer's promise to take only one-half of the production.

(D) Unenforceable, because of the indefiniteness as to the quantity of the goods.

Question 154

A manufacturer of men's neckties received the following order from a retail store: "Ship 500 two-inch ties, assorted stripes, your catalogue No. V34." The tie manufacturer instead shipped 500 three-inch ties. The store manager immediately faxed the tie manufacturer: "Reject your shipment. Order was for two-inch ties." The store, however, did not ship the ties back to the tie manufacturer.

Did the store properly reject the ties?

(A) Yes, because the ties were nonconforming goods.

(B) Yes, because the tie manufacturer did not notify the store that the ties were shipped as an accommodation to the store.

(C) No, because the tie manufacturer could accept the store's offer by prompt shipment of either conforming or nonconforming goods.

(D) No, because the store waived its right to reject the ties by not returning them promptly to the tie manufacturer.

Question 155

A state statute permits the state to seize and dispose of real property that was used to commit or facilitate the commission of a felony drug offense. After a drug dealer's arrest for selling cocaine out of his home, a felony, the state instituted an action of forfeiture against the drug dealer's house and property. After notice to the drug dealer and a hearing, a judge granted the order and the state seized the property. Six months later, after the time for any appeals had expired, the property was sold at a public auction to a third party. It was only when the third party brought an action to quiet title that a bank holding a properly recorded mortgage on the drug dealer's property learned of the forfeiture. Because the bank's mortgage payments were automatically deducted from an account the drug dealer had under a different name, no one at the bank was aware that the property had been seized. The only notice provided to parties other than the drug dealer was a public notice published for three weeks in a general circulation newspaper. The bank defends the quiet title action on the ground that it did not receive the notice required under the United States Constitution to protect its interest in the property.

If the court rules that the bank's rights under the Due Process Clause of the Fourteenth Amendment were violated by the state's seizure of the property, it will be because:

(A) In any judicial proceeding affecting rights to real property, a claimant is required to provide notice and an evidentiary hearing to all parties with a legal interest in the property before taking actions affecting their rights.

(B) The government itself was the party that seized the property, rather than a private party using governmental processes.

(C) The notice was not adequate under the circumstances to apprise a party with a properly recorded legal interest in the property.

(D) The jurisdiction treats the mortgagee as having title to the property rather than merely a lien.

Question 156

A defendant's car was stopped by an officer for a minor traffic violation. The officer recognized the defendant as a suspect in a multimillion-dollar bank fraud scheme that had just been discovered by the authorities. She placed the defendant under arrest and gave him *Miranda* warnings. She then asked for permission to search the trunk of the car. The defendant nodded and unlocked the trunk. The officer searched the trunk and discovered a bag containing what appeared to be cocaine in a compartment in the trunk. When later tests determined that it was cocaine, the authorities added a charge of transporting illegal narcotics to the defendant's indictment. At a preliminary hearing, the defendant moved to have evidence of the cocaine excluded as the result of a search in violation of the Fourth Amendment.

Should the court grant the defendant's motion?

(A) Yes, because one taken into custody cannot give valid consent to a search that would otherwise require a warrant.

(B) Yes, because the search exceeded the scope of a permissible search incident to a lawful arrest.

(C) No, because it appears that the defendant's consent was voluntary under the circumstances.

(D) No, because persons have a lesser expectation of privacy in their vehicles for purposes of the Fourth Amendment.

Question 157

With the owner's permission, a defendant took the owner's car with the intention of driving it three miles to a grocery store and back. While on his way to the store, the defendant decided to keep the car. Two days later, he changed his mind and returned the car. The defendant is charged with larceny of the car.

The defendant should be found:

(A) Guilty of larceny, because he kept the car for two days.

(B) Guilty of larceny, because he had the requisite intent.

(C) Not guilty of larceny, because he returned the car two days later.

(D) Not guilty of larceny, because he lacked the requisite intent.

Question 158

A bill collector for a store came to a consumer's house at 7 p.m. on a summer evening while many of the consumer's neighbors were seated on their porches. When the consumer opened the door, the bill collector, who was standing just outside the door, raised an electrically amplified bullhorn to his mouth. In a voice that could be heard a block away, the bill collector called the consumer a "deadbeat" and asked him when he intended to pay his bill to the store. In fact, the consumer did not owe any money to the store.

If the consumer asserts a claim based on defamation against the bill collector and prevails, it will be because:

(A) The bill collector was negligent in failing to discover that the consumer owed no money to the store.

(B) The bill collector's conduct was extreme and outrageous.

(C) The bill collector knew that the consumer owed no money to the store.

(D) The consumer suffered some pecuniary damage.

Question 159

A homeowner is suing a motorcyclist, alleging that the motorcyclist destroyed her rose garden by riding his motorcycle through her yard. The homeowner seeks to introduce in evidence a photograph of her garden to depict the nature and extent of the damage done. The photograph was taken by an insurance adjustor, who was not called as a witness, four days after the alleged incident.

The judge should rule the photograph:

(A) Admissible, because the homeowner can testify that it fairly and accurately portrays the condition of the garden after the damage was done.

(B) Admissible, because the photograph was taken within a week after the alleged occurrence.

(C) Inadmissible, because the homeowner failed to call the photographer to testify concerning the circumstances under which the photograph was taken.

(D) Inadmissible, because it is possible to describe the damage to the garden through direct oral testimony.

Question 160

Pursuant to a state statute, a student applied for tuition assistance to attend a state university. He was qualified for such assistance in every way except that he was a resident alien who did not intend to become a United States citizen.

The state's restriction of such grants to United States citizens or resident aliens seeking such citizenship is probably:

(A) Valid, because aliens are not per se "a discrete and insular minority" specially protected by the Fourteenth Amendment.

(B) Valid, because the line drawn by the state for extending aid was reasonably related to a legitimate state interest.

(C) Invalid, because the justifications for this restriction are insufficient to overcome the burden imposed on a state when it uses such an alienage classification.

(D) Invalid, because the Privileges and Immunities Clause of Article IV does not permit such an arbitrary classification.

Question 161

A carpenter purchased an old house, planning to slowly fix it up. He financed the purchase by taking out a mortgage on the property with a bank, which recorded the mortgage. The carpenter purchased some custom-made windows from a retail dealer. The modern windows were easily removable from the window frames to make cleaning them easier. The carpenter had lacked sufficient funds to pay the $10,000 the dealer wanted for a complete set of new windows, so the dealer had agreed to sell the windows to the carpenter on an installment payment plan, with the windows as security. The carpenter installed the windows himself and stored the old windows in the basement of the house. The carpenter made three payments to the bank on the $30,000 mortgage, and he made two payments to the dealer on the windows. The carpenter then lost his job and ceased making payments to the bank and the dealer. The carpenter has departed to parts unknown and the dealer wishes to remove the windows from the house. The bank objects and the matter winds up in court.

How should the court rule on the dealer's request to remove the windows?

(A) The dealer may remove the windows, because the old windows are available for the bank to restore the house to its original condition.

(B) The dealer may remove the windows, because the windows are designed to be removable.

(C) The dealer may not remove the windows, because regardless of their form, windows are an integral part of the house.

(D) The dealer may not remove the windows, because the bank's lien is senior to the dealer's.

Question 162

The owner of a small antique shop had purchased a 200-year-old powder horn inscribed with the name of a Revolutionary War hero. The curator of a nearby museum, which displays numerous other artifacts owned by the war hero, offered to buy the powder horn from the shop owner. The price offered was slightly higher than what the shop owner had been planning to ask for it when he offered it for sale and was a very fair price for an item of that nature. The shop owner, however, refused to sell to the curator because he did not like the way she had done business with other antique dealers in the past. The curator then turned to threats, saying that she had a power of attorney from the heirs of the war hero and that the law allowed her to bring a replevin action to seize it from the shop owner if he did not accept her offer. In fact, her statements were false and she knew that she had no power to obtain the powder horn. However, the shop owner believed her and reluctantly agreed to sell her the item for the price that she had offered.

Can the shop owner recover damages in a misrepresentation suit against the curator?

(A) No, because the shop owner had no right to rely on the curator's statements regarding the law.

(B) No, because the shop owner suffered no pecuniary harm.

(C) Yes, because the shop owner would not have made the transaction with the curator if not for her false statements.

(D) Yes, because the curator knew that her statements were false when she made them.

Question 163

Pursuant to its power under the Commerce Clause, Congress adopted legislation prohibiting employers from requiring any employee to work more than a 12-hour day. The legislation also provided that any employee whose rights under the legislation were violated by his employer could bring a cause of action for damages against the employer in the federal district court in the district where the employee resided. The legislation defined "employer" to include "all commercial employers, all charities that compensate workers for their time, and all state and local governments."

A state required its police department's paramedics to work a 24-hour shift because of the nature of the job. They would then be off for 48 hours. A paramedic for the state's police department was unhappy with this arrangement and preferred to work a regular 10- or 12-hour day. A friend of the paramedic told him about the federal legislation discussed above, and the paramedic immediately brought an action against the state in federal district court.

The district court should hold:

(A) In favor of the paramedic, because under the Commerce Clause, Congress can create a federal court cause of action for damages against state governments.

(B) In favor of the paramedic, because Congress has the power to regulate the jurisdiction of the federal courts pursuant to Article III.

(C) Against the paramedic, because the federal legislation was not enacted pursuant to Congress's power to enforce the Fourteenth Amendment.

(D) Against the paramedic, because Congress has no power to remove the states' Eleventh Amendment immunity from suit in federal court.

Question 164

An employee of a convenience store was indicted and put on trial for robbery of the store. At the trial, the employee took the stand in his own defense. He stated, "I didn't have anything to do with that robbery, but I know who did. The robber was the evening cashier." The jury acquitted the employee of the robbery charge.

The prosecutor became convinced that the cashier had, in fact, committed the robbery in question, and successfully argued that the grand jury should indict him for the crime. At the cashier's trial, the prosecution called the employee to the stand, with the expectation that he would incriminate the cashier. Instead, to the prosecutor's surprise, the employee testified, "the cashier didn't have anything to do with that robbery, but I know who did, because I committed the robbery myself." When asked about his testimony at his own trial, the employee refused to answer, claiming his privilege against self-incrimination. Finding her case in a shambles, the prosecutor wishes to call to the stand as a witness one of the jurors in the employee's robbery trial, who is prepared to testify that the employee said the cashier committed the robbery.

If the defense objects, the court should rule that the witness's testimony is:

(A) Admissible to impeach the employee's credibility, but not as substantive evidence of the cashier's guilt.

(B) Admissible to impeach the employee's credibility and as substantive evidence of the cashier's guilt.

(C) Inadmissible, because former jurors are not competent to testify concerning cases on which they served as jurors.

(D) Inadmissible, because a transcript of the employee's testimony at his robbery trial is the best evidence.

Question 165

A driver was traveling through an area plagued with a high incidence of burglaries and assaults. Acting pursuant to a police department plan to combat crime by the random stopping of automobiles in the area between midnight and 6 a.m., a police officer stopped the driver and asked him for identification. As the driver handed the officer his license, the officer directed a flashlight into the automobile and saw what appeared to be the barrel of a shotgun protruding from under the front seat on the passenger side of the car. The officer ordered the driver from the car, searched him, and discovered marijuana cigarettes and a shotgun.

At the driver's trial for unlawful possession of narcotics, his motion to suppress the use of the marijuana as evidence should be:

(A) Sustained, because the marijuana was discovered as a result of the unlawful stopping of the driver's automobile.

(B) Sustained, because the use of the flashlight constituted a search of the interior of the driver's automobile without probable cause.

(C) Denied, because the officer's conduct was consistent with the established police plan.

(D) Denied, because the discovery of the gun in plain view created the reasonable suspicion necessary to justify the arrest and search of the driver.

Question 166

A professional wrestler entered into a written agency contract with an agent, who agreed to try to get the wrestler's picture on a variety of food products. The wrestler promised that the agent would have the exclusive right to promote the wrestler on food product lines. They agreed that the wrestler would receive 70% of the proceeds and that the agent would receive 30%. The agent was able to persuade a breakfast cereal company to put the wrestler's picture on their cereal boxes. Shortly after the agent confirmed the cereal deal with the cereal manufacturer, the wrestler and the agent agreed orally that henceforth the wrestler would receive 50% of the proceeds, including proceeds from the cereal deal, and the agent would receive the other 50%. The wrestler received a $10,000 check from the cereal manufacturer, and he promptly sent the agent a check for $3,000. The agent demanded an additional $2,000, but the wrestler refused to pay.

If the agent sues the wrestler for the $2,000, the party likely to prevail is:

(A) The agent, because consideration is not required for a modification.

(B) The wrestler, because of the parol evidence rule.

(C) The wrestler, because the agent had a preexisting legal duty to secure food product promotions for the wrestler.

(D) The wrestler, because an exclusive contract requires that the party given the privileges of exclusivity use his best efforts.

Question 167

At a time when a homeowner held title to a subdivision lot in fee simple, the developer executed a warranty deed conveying the same lot to a purchaser. The deed was promptly and duly recorded. Subsequently, the homeowner conveyed the lot to the developer by a warranty deed that was promptly and duly recorded. Later, the developer conveyed the lot to an investor by a warranty deed, which was promptly and duly recorded. The investor paid the fair market value of the lot and had no knowledge of any claim of the purchaser. In an appropriate action, the investor and the purchaser contest title to the lot.

In this action, judgment should be for:

(A) The purchaser, because the purchaser's deed is senior to the investor's.

(B) The investor, because the investor paid value without notice of the purchaser's claim.

(C) The purchaser or the investor, depending on whether a subsequent grantee is bound, at common law, by the doctrine of estoppel by deed.

(D) The purchaser or the investor, depending on whether the purchaser's deed is deemed recorded in the investor's chain of title.

Question 168

The plaintiff sued the defendant for making a slanderous statement that greatly embarrassed the plaintiff. The defendant denied that he ever made such a statement. At trial, the plaintiff called a witness to the stand, and the witness testified that he heard the defendant make the statement on August 4. The defendant discredited the witness, and the plaintiff offers evidence of the witness's good reputation for truthfulness.

The rehabilitation is most likely to be permitted if the discrediting evidence by the defendant was testimony that:

(A) The witness and the plaintiff had known each other since childhood.

(B) The witness had been convicted of perjury in an unrelated case.

(C) The witness had attended a school for mentally retarded children.

(D) The witness disliked the defendant.

Question 169

In a trial between a farmer and his neighbor, an issue arose about the farmer's ownership of a horse, which had caused damage to his neighbor's crops. The neighbor offered to testify that he looked up the farmer's telephone number in the directory, called that number, and that a voice answered, "This is [the farmer] speaking." At this, the neighbor asked, "Was that your horse that trampled across my cornfield this afternoon?" The voice replied, "Yes." The neighbor had not spoken to the farmer prior to the phone conversation.

The judge should rule the testimony:

(A) Admissible, because the answering speaker's identification of himself, together with the usual accuracy of the telephone directory and transmission system, furnishes sufficient authentication.

(B) Admissible, because judicial notice may be taken of the accuracy of telephone directories.

(C) Inadmissible, because the neighbor was not familiar with the farmer's voice and is unable to verify that it was in fact the farmer to whom he spoke.

(D) Inadmissible, because the farmer was not first asked whether the conversation had taken place and given the opportunity to admit, deny, or explain.

Question 170

A wife discovered that her husband was having an affair with his assistant and decided to seek revenge. One night, the wife drove to the assistant's house, drove onto her lawn, and began blowing her horn and yelling obscenities out her window. The wife was so loud that the assistant's family and all of her neighbors were awakened and heard the wife's accusations.

If the assistant asserts a claim based on intentional infliction of emotional distress against the wife, will the assistant prevail?

(A) Yes, because the wife's conduct was extreme and outrageous.

(B) Yes, because the wife was intruding on the assistant's property.

(C) No, because the assistant suffered no physical harm.

(D) No, because the assistant was guilty of adultery.

Question 171

A missionary was travelling door to door hoping to convert others to his church. At one house, a devout elderly woman answered the door and the two began discussing their religious differences. The conversation took a disagreeable turn, and the woman, greatly offended, slammed her door shut. The missionary had been leaning with his hand on the doorway during their conversation, and as a consequence, his fingers were pinched in the door, causing him injury.

If the missionary asserts a claim based on battery against the woman and prevails, it will be because:

(A) The woman had not first asked the missionary to leave the property.

(B) The woman knew that the door was substantially certain to pinch the missionary's fingers.

(C) The woman acted in anger by slamming the door shut.

(D) The missionary was not trespassing when he came to the woman's door.

Question 172

A freshman beat out a senior for the starting middle linebacker position on their college football team. After practice, the senior came up behind the freshman and shoved him in the back. When the freshman turned around, the senior punched him in the jaw, knocking out a tooth and giving him a split lip. Before the freshman could retaliate, the two were quickly separated by other players. The senior taunted him, "The next time I see you I won't go so easy on you." That night the freshman was at a bar frequented by the football players, some of whom were teasing him about the altercation that afternoon. The freshman was enraged but did not respond. He then saw the senior enter the room but kept his back to him. Suddenly he felt someone shove him in the back. Pulling out his pocketknife, he whirled and stabbed the person behind him, believing it to be the senior. In fact, it was an intoxicated patron who had stumbled and fallen into the freshman. The knife severed a major artery, and the patron died on the way to the hospital.

The freshman is charged with murder for the patron's death. At trial, the freshman testified that he honestly believed that the senior was going to kill him the next time he saw him. On cross-examination, he admitted that such a belief was unreasonable. The freshman's attorney requests the judge to instruct the jury on voluntary manslaughter, both on an "imperfect self-defense" theory and on a "heat of passion" basis.

How should the judge respond?

(A) The judge should give both an "imperfect self-defense" instruction and the "heat of passion" instruction.

(B) The judge should give the "imperfect self-defense" instruction, but not the "heat of passion" instruction.

(C) The judge should give the "heat of passion" instruction, but not the "imperfect self-defense" instruction.

(D) The judge should refuse to give both instructions.

Question 173

When the latest generation of interactive video games reached the video arcades in their state, community groups and civic leaders complained to the state legislature that the most popular games among young teenagers had graphic displays of violence and sexual themes. With the stated aim of protecting minors from the perceived evils of offensive but not necessarily obscene materials, the legislature enacted a statute banning the commercial licensing of video arcade games with a specifically defined degree of graphic violent or sexual content.

Under the statute, the owner of a chain of shopping mall video arcades in the state was denied licenses for a number of video games that he wanted to install at his arcades. He challenges the statute in federal district court.

The court will probably find the statute:

(A) Constitutional, because for materials accessible to minors, the state may adopt a different standard for determining whether the material is offensive or obscene than the standard it applies for adults.

(B) Constitutional, because the statute precisely defines the type of content that is prohibited in the video games.

(C) Unconstitutional, because narrower means are available to deny minors access to the objectionable material without affecting rights of adults.

(D) Unconstitutional, because some of the banned video games may have serious literary, artistic, political, or scientific value, as determined by contemporary community standards, and thus do not fall within the definition of obscenity.

Question 174

Two brothers were playing golf when the elder brother left to take a telephone call. When he returned, he told the younger brother, "My wife was just involved in an accident. She ran a red light and hit another car. I need to leave." After arriving at the scene of the accident, the elder brother, after talking with bystanders, determined that his wife had not driven through a red light. The driver of the other car brought suit against the wife for injuries suffered in the accident. To help establish liability, the driver of the other car seeks to have the younger brother testify as to the elder brother's statements on the golf course.

The younger brother's testimony is:

(A) Admissible as an admission.

(B) Admissible as a statement against interest.

(C) Inadmissible, because it is hearsay not within any recognized exception.

(D) Inadmissible, because it constitutes opinion.

Question 175

An owner by his will specifically devised his real property "to my daughter, her heirs and assigns, but if my daughter dies survived by a husband, a child, or children, then to her husband during his lifetime with remainder to my daughter's children, their heirs and assigns. However, if my daughter dies survived by a husband and no child, the property is specifically devised to my niece, her heirs and assigns."

While the owner's will was in probate, the niece quitclaimed all her interest in the property to the daughter's husband. Three years later the daughter died, survived by her husband but no children. The daughter left a will devising her interest in the property to her husband. The only applicable statute provides that any interest in land is freely alienable. The niece instituted an appropriate action against the husband to establish title to the property.

Judgment should be for:

(A) The niece, because her quitclaim deed did not transfer her after-acquired title.

(B) The niece, because the husband took nothing under the owner's will.

(C) The husband, because the niece had effectively conveyed her interest to the husband.

(D) The husband, because the doctrine of after-acquired title applies to a devise by will.

Question 176

A candlemaker who owned a bee farm sold the farm to a beekeeper. Because the candlemaker was still interested in making beeswax candles, the contract provided that the candlemaker reserved the right to purchase all of the beeswax produced by the beekeeper during the next five years at the current market price at time of delivery, and the beekeeper agreed to supply "in any event a minimum of 100 pounds of beeswax per month during that period." For one year, the beekeeper delivered to the candlemaker and the candlemaker paid for all of the beeswax produced by the beekeeper. As the first year of the contract ended, the beekeeper was stung by a bee and, due to an allergy, became so seriously and permanently ill and impaired as to be unable to attend to the bees. He gave the candlemaker prompt notice that he would be unable to continue, and from that time on he never made another delivery of beeswax to the candlemaker.

Assuming that contractual obligations existed between the candlemaker and the beekeeper, the beekeeper's refusal to perform was:

(A) Justifiable, because the parties had not agreed to a specific amount of beeswax in the contract.

(B) Justifiable, because his performance was excused because of his permanent disability.

(C) Justifiable, because he gave the candlemaker reasonable notice so that the candlemaker could buy beeswax elsewhere.

(D) Not justifiable and constituted a breach of contract.

Question 177

On June 1, a jeweler placed an order for 10 classic yellow gold ring settings with a goldsmith. The jeweler's order called for delivery by July 1. On June 2, the goldsmith shipped 10 white gold ring settings that arrived at the jeweler's place of business on June 3. The jeweler immediately faxed the goldsmith rejecting the shipment because the rings were white gold instead of the classic yellow gold he had requested. The goldsmith replied by fax: "Will deliver proper ring settings before July 1." The jeweler received this fax on June 4, but did not reply to it.

On June 30, the goldsmith tendered 10 classic yellow gold ring settings, but the jeweler refused to accept them.

Did the jeweler properly reject the ring settings tendered on June 30?

(A) Yes, because the goldsmith's shipping the white gold settings on June 1 was a present breach of contract.

(B) Yes, because the goldsmith's shipping the white gold settings on June 1 was an anticipatory repudiation.

(C) No, because the goldsmith cured the June 1 defective delivery by his tender of conforming goods on June 30.

(D) No, because a contract for the sale of goods can be modified without consideration.

Question 178

A woman was in the process of moving out of the apartment that she had shared with a roommate. She collected numerous items of hers from her roommate's room that the roommate had borrowed. As she was leaving the apartment, she grabbed what she believed to be her laptop computer, which her roommate had often borrowed. Because it was an older, slower machine, she planned to trade it in for a different model at a computer resale store. She noticed that the laptop was much lighter than usual, but she reasonably attributed this to her diligence in following a weight-lifting regimen at her gym. When she arrived at the computer store, she discovered that she had taken a brand new, state-of-the-art laptop that her roommate had recently purchased. She then kept the laptop rather than buying a new one.

Is the woman guilty of common law larceny?

(A) No, because she mistakenly believed that the computer she had picked up was hers.

(B) No, because her mistake as to whose computer she had picked up was reasonable.

(C) Yes, because she intended to keep the computer when she took it.

(D) Yes, because she decided to keep the computer when she discovered the mistake.

Question 179

A defendant was on trial for murder. At the trial, the defendant put forth the defense of self-defense, claiming that the victim was about to kill him when he shot the victim. To help establish that he was in fear of the victim, the defendant called a witness to testify that she heard a third party tell the defendant that the victim, "is a mean, vicious killer; he has murdered three people in the past year."

The witness's testimony is:

(A) Admissible under the state of mind exception to the hearsay rule.

(B) Admissible nonhearsay.

(C) Inadmissible, because it is hearsay not within any recognized exception.

(D) Inadmissible, because it does not help establish that the defendant acted in self-defense.

Question 180

A small village had a population of 400, and 90% of the inhabitants belonged to the same church. The village council consisted of five members, all of whom were members of that church. The council unanimously appropriated $350 to pay a landscaper to mow their church's lawn for a year. An atheist in the village, who lived in a tiny house and paid only $200 per year in village and county property taxes, was incensed that any of it should go to support the church. The atheist filed suit in federal district court to strike down the council's appropriation to mow the church lawn.

Should the court entertain the atheist's suit?

(A) No, because the atheist paid so little in taxes that his interest in the matter, if any, is too minimal.

(B) No, because taxpayers lack standing to sue over appropriations by duly constituted legislative bodies.

(C) Yes, because a taxpayer may sue under the authority of the First Amendment's Establishment Clause if a fund into which he has paid is being used for religious purposes.

(D) Yes, because taxpayers have standing to sue when questions involving constitutional rights are at issue.

Question 181

Two companies manufacture pesticide and have plants located along the same river. During a specific 24-hour period, each plant discharged pesticide into the river because of negligence in their operations. A rancher operated a cattle ranch downstream from the plants. The rancher's cattle drank from the river and were poisoned by the pesticide. The amount of the discharge from either plant alone would not have been sufficient to cause any harm to the rancher's cattle.

If the rancher asserts a claim against the two companies, what, if anything, will the rancher recover?

(A) Nothing, because neither company discharged enough pesticide to cause harm to the rancher's cattle.

(B) Nothing, unless the rancher can establish how much pesticide each plant discharged.

(C) One-half of the rancher's damages from each company.

(D) The entire amount of the rancher's damages, jointly and severally, from the two companies.

Question 182

For valuable consideration, the owner of a parcel of land signed and gave to her neighbor a duly executed instrument, which provided that the owner retained the right to sell the property during her lifetime, but at her death, or if she earlier decided to sell, the property would be offered to her neighbor at $500 per acre. The neighbor had to exercise this right, if at all, within 60 days of receipt of said offer to sell. The neighbor recorded the instrument. The instrument was not valid as a will.

Is the neighbor's right under the instrument valid?

(A) Yes, because the instrument is recorded.

(B) Yes, because the neighbor's right to purchase will vest or fail within the period prescribed by the Rule Against Perpetuities.

(C) No, because the neighbor's right to purchase is a restraint on the owner's power to make a testamentary disposition.

(D) No, because the neighbor's right to purchase is an unreasonable restraint on alienation.

Question 183

In a contract suit by the plaintiff against the defendant, the plaintiff offers into evidence a document purporting to have the defendant's signature.

Which of the following will the court ***not*** accept as a method of authenticating the defendant's signature?

(A) A nonexpert who, in preparation for trial, has familiarized himself with the defendant's usual signature testifies that, in his opinion, the questioned signature is genuine.

(B) The jury, without the assistance of an expert, compares the questioned signature with an admittedly authentic sample of the defendant's handwriting.

(C) A witness offers proof that the signature is on a document that has been in existence for at least 20 years, that was in a place where it would likely be if it was authentic, and that has no suspicious circumstances surrounding it.

(D) A witness testifies that the defendant admitted that the signature was his.

Question 184

A carload of gang members, armed with automatic rifles, sped into the rival gang's neighborhood looking for a store that its rival gang used as a hangout. The gang members knew that the store closed at 6 p.m. and that the rival gang went elsewhere after nightfall. As the gang members drove by, they sprayed the store with bullets. One of the bullets struck and killed a six-year-old girl who was asleep in an apartment located on the second floor above the corner store. A few days later, the police arrested the defendant, who admitted to being a member of the gang and to having been in the car when the gang members shot up the store. The defendant was placed on trial for the girl's murder.

If the defendant takes the stand in his own defense, and the jury believes the defendant's testimony, which of the following assertions by the defendant would be his best defense to the murder charge?

(A) "I was the driver of the car and did not actually shoot into the building."

(B) "I took a lot of drugs that night, and I was so high that I don't even remember the incident; I did not intend to kill somebody."

(C) "Another member of my gang pointed a gun at me. I was really scared that if I didn't shoot into the building, I would be seriously injured or killed myself."

(D) "I believed that the building was abandoned and had no idea that there would be people inside it."

Question 185

Neighbors of an apparently destitute couple bought a month's supply of food and gave it to them. Later, the wife confided in the neighbors that she and her husband did have money and that, because they had been so kind, she was leaving them money in her will. When the wife died, at the neighbors' request the husband gave the neighbors the following signed instrument: "In consideration of my wife's promise to our neighbors, and their agreement not to sue her estate, I agree to pay them the sum of $5,000." When the husband died of a heart attack several days later, the neighbors asked the administrator of his estate to pay them the $5,000. The administrator refused on the ground that there was no consideration for the agreement.

On which of the following theories would it be most likely that the neighbors would recover?

(A) The husband's written instrument was a binding unilateral contract.

(B) The husband's acceptance of the food was fraudulent.

(C) The husband is bound by promissory estoppel.

(D) The husband and the neighbors entered into a valid compromise.

GO ON TO THE NEXT PAGE

Question 186

An entrepreneur purchased a piece of undeveloped land with plans to build a luxury spa. He financed the purchase with a loan from a bank, secured by a mortgage on the land. The land contained a mineral hot spring. The entrepreneur hired builders to harness the spring's water into a soaking pool. The spa was not a success and the entrepreneur ran out of money. He entered into a contract that purported to transfer his inventory and all his interests in the soaking pool to a buyer by a document that was sufficient as a bill of sale to transfer personal property but was insufficient as a deed to transfer real property. The bank soon after foreclosed on its mortgage and the land was sold at auction to a bidder, who took title in fee simple.

Title to the soaking pool is in:

(A) The bidder, as fee simple owner of the land.

(B) The buyer, as purchaser of the soaking pool under the bill of sale.

(C) The person who owns the water rights as an incident thereto.

(D) The entrepreneur, as the builder of the soaking pool.

Question 187

As part of the Domestic Security Act, Congress established a permanent commission to evaluate the security of federal government buildings located in the District of Columbia. The commission would have the authority to evaluate current security conditions, establish new security guidelines, and coordinate security procedures among various governmental agencies. The legislation provided that three members of the commission were to be appointed by the President, two members by a committee of the House of Representatives, and two members by the United States Supreme Court. The President had the authority to veto any of the selections to the commission made by the congressional committee or the Supreme Court.

If a party with the requisite standing challenges the legislation and it is found unconstitutional, it will most likely be because:

(A) The President's power to veto a particular selection made by the congressional committee constitutes an improper exercise of the veto power.

(B) The commission will be exercising administrative powers.

(C) The judiciary does not have the power to make appointments to an advisory commission.

(D) The legislation does not provide for Senate confirmation of the presidential appointees.

Question 188

A brother and a sister owned real property as joint tenants with the right of survivorship. The sister executed a mortgage on the property with a bank to secure a loan. Subsequently, but before the indebtedness was paid to the bank, the sister died intestate with her daughter as her only heir at law. The jurisdiction in which the property is located recognizes the title theory of mortgages.

In an appropriate action, the court should determine that title to the property is vested:

(A) In the brother, with the entire interest subject to the mortgage.

(B) In the brother, free and clear of the mortgage.

(C) One-half in the brother free of the mortgage, and one-half in the daughter subject to the mortgage.

(D) One-half in the brother and one-half in the daughter, with both subject to the mortgage.

Question 189

An owner conveyed her parcel of land to her church "for the life of my son, and from and after the death of my said son to all of my grandchildren and their heirs and assigns in equal shares; provided that the church shall use the premises for church purposes only." In an existing building on the property, the church immediately began to conduct religious services and other church activities. Subsequently, the church granted a construction company the right to remove sand and gravel from a one-half acre portion of the property on payment of a royalty. The construction company has regularly removed sand and gravel since and paid a royalty to the church. The church has continued to conduct religious services and other church activities on the property. All four of the living grandchildren of the owner, joined by a guardian ad litem to represent unborn grandchildren, instituted suit against the church and the construction company seeking damages for the removal of sand and gravel and an injunction preventing further acts of removal. There is no applicable statute.

Which of the following best describes the likely disposition of this lawsuit?

(A) The injunction and damages should be granted, because the interest of the church terminated with the first removal of sand and gravel.

(B) The injunction should be granted, and damages should be recovered but impounded for future distribution.

(C) The injunction should be granted, but damages should be denied because the owner and her son are not parties to the action.

(D) The injunction should be denied, but damages should be awarded.

Question 190

A woman who had befriended a four-year-old girl told the girl that her mother had to go out of town and that her mother had asked the woman to take care of her for the day instead of going to the preschool. Although the girl had been taught to never talk to strangers, she did not consider the woman to be a stranger and readily believed her. The woman took the girl to the zoo. She had a fun day with the woman, and then the woman returned the girl to her mother's porch and drove off. After the girl's mother found out what happened, the woman was arrested and charged in a jurisdiction that maintains a traditional, common law definition of criminal false imprisonment and has a typical, modern kidnapping statute.

The woman can be properly convicted of and sentenced for:

(A) Kidnapping only.

(B) Either kidnapping or false imprisonment.

(C) Both kidnapping and false imprisonment.

(D) Neither kidnapping nor false imprisonment.

Question 191

The defendant, charged with murder, was present with her attorney at a preliminary examination when a witness, who was the defendant in a separate prosecution for concealing the body of the murder victim, testified for the prosecution against the defendant. When called to testify at the defendant's trial, the witness refused to testify, although ordered to do so.

If the prosecution offers evidence of the witness's testimony at the preliminary examination, the evidence is:

(A) Admissible as former testimony.

(B) Admissible as past recollection recorded.

(C) Inadmissible, because it would violate the witness's privilege against self-incrimination.

(D) Inadmissible, because it is hearsay not within any exception.

Question 192

A small town had a municipal auditorium that all groups were permitted to use. Lately, a local preacher has begun to hold recruiting seminars for his religious cult at the auditorium. Sensing the displeasure of the voting public and fearing that the auditorium would become a mecca for fringe religious groups, the town council adopted the following ordinance: "Effective immediately, no religious groups will be permitted to use the municipal auditorium for meetings, speeches, or other public gatherings." The preacher, who was having great success recruiting followers in the town, challenged the constitutionality of the ordinance in federal court.

Based on the above facts, his challenge should:

(A) Fail, because the ordinance treats all religions equally.

(B) Fail, because continuing to allow religious groups to use the auditorium would violate the Establishment Clause of the First Amendment.

(C) Succeed, because "religious groups" is an unconstitutionally vague term.

(D) Succeed, because the town cannot show that the ordinance serves a compelling government interest.

Question 193

An electric company is the sole distributor of electrical power in the city. The company owns and maintains all of the electric poles and equipment in the city in compliance with government standards. The electric company has had to replace insulators on its poles repeatedly because unknown persons regularly shoot at and destroy them, which causes the power lines to fall to the ground. On one of these occasions, a five-year-old child who had wandered out of his yard intentionally touched a downed wire, and was seriously burned.

If a claim on the child's behalf is asserted against the electric company, the probable result is that the child will:

(A) Recover, if the electric company could have taken reasonable steps to prevent the lines from falling when the insulators were destroyed.

(B) Recover, because a supplier of electricity is strictly liable in tort.

(C) Not recover, unless the electric company failed to exercise reasonable care to stop the destruction of the insulators.

(D) Not recover, because the destruction of the insulators was intentional.

Question 194

A woman conveyed her real property to a buyer for $90,000. The buyer never recorded his deed. A year later, the woman drew up a deed of conveyance for the property and gave it to her son as a gift. The son knew nothing of the prior conveyance to the buyer, and the son recorded his deed. The following year, the son sold the property to a friend via an installment land sale contract. The full purchase price was $100,000, and the friend made her first installment payment of $40,000 to the son. The friend received a deed from the son and promptly and properly recorded it. According to the terms of the installment agreement, the friend was to make two further payments of $30,000 each. The first of these payments was due a year after the closing date and the second payment a year after that. The buyer learned about the son's conveyance to the friend and filed suit against the friend, seeking to oust her from the property and to quiet title in the buyer. The recording statute in the state where the property is located and where all the parties reside reads in relevant part: "No conveyance shall be good against a subsequent purchaser for value, without notice, unless it be recorded."

Which of the following judicial orders would it be ***inappropriate*** for the court to make?

(A) Award the friend a 40% share of the property as a tenant in common with the buyer.

(B) Grant the property to the buyer, but order the buyer to pay the friend $40,000.

(C) Grant the property to the friend, but order the friend to pay the buyer the remaining $60,000 in payments.

(D) Grant the property solely to the friend, based on the recording statute, without any compensation to the buyer.

Question 195

According to statute, a candidate for state office may have his name placed on the official election ballot only if he files with the appropriate state official a petition containing a specified number of voter signatures. A candidate failed to get his name placed on the state ballot as an independent candidate for governor because he failed to file a petition with the number of voter signatures required by state statute. In a suit against the appropriate state officials in federal district court, the candidate sought an injunction against the petition signature requirement on the ground that it was unconstitutional.

Which of the following, if established, constitutes the strongest argument for the candidate?

(A) Compliance with the petition signature requirement is burdensome.

(B) The objectives of the statute could be satisfactorily achieved by less burdensome means.

(C) Because of the petition signature requirement, very few independent candidates have ever succeeded in getting on the ballot.

(D) The motivation for the statute was a desire to keep candidates off the ballot if they did not have strong support among voters.

Question 196

Acting on a hunch, a police officer went to a young woman's apartment, broke in, and searched it. The officer found exactly what she was looking for under the woman's bed: a sack filled with jewels. The attached note read, "Sweetheart, here are the goods from the estate heist. Your loving boyfriend." It was well known in the community that the woman's boyfriend was a jewel thief. The officer also knew that the estate of a local socialite had been burglarized three days ago. Just as the officer finished reading the note, the woman returned. The officer immediately placed the woman under arrest as an accessory to the estate burglary. Based on the evidence obtained from the woman's apartment, a search warrant was issued for her boyfriend's apartment. The search yielded burglar tools and more jewels from the estate. The boyfriend was immediately arrested and charged with the estate burglary. At the boyfriend's trial for the estate burglary, his attorney files a motion to suppress the evidence consisting of the bag of jewels and note, the tools, and the jewels from the boyfriend's apartment.

The court should:

(A) Grant the motion as to the bag of jewels and note, but deny it as to the evidence found in the boyfriend's apartment.

(B) Grant the motion, because all of this evidence is fruit of the poisonous tree.

(C) Deny the motion, because the police would have caught the boyfriend with the goods eventually.

(D) Deny the motion, because the police had a warrant to search the boyfriend's apartment.

Question 197

A car owner left her car with the mechanic to have repair work done. After completing the repairs, the mechanic took the car out for a test drive and was involved in an accident that caused damages to the plaintiff. A statute imposes liability on the owner of an automobile for injuries to a third party that are caused by the negligence of any person driving the automobile with the owner's consent. The statute applies to situations of this kind, even if the owner did not specifically authorize the mechanic to test-drive the car.

The plaintiff sued the owner and the mechanic jointly for damages arising from the accident. In that action, the owner cross-claims to recover from the mechanic the amount of any payment the owner may be required to make to the plaintiff. The trier of fact determined that the accident was caused solely by negligent driving on the mechanic's part, and that the plaintiff's damages were $100,000.

In this action, the proper outcome will be that:

(A) The plaintiff should have judgment for $50,000 each against the owner and the mechanic; the owner should recover nothing from the mechanic.

(B) The plaintiff should have judgment for $100,000 against the mechanic only.

(C) The plaintiff should have judgment for $100,000 against the owner and the mechanic jointly, and the owner should have judgment against the mechanic for 50% of any amount collected from the owner by the plaintiff.

(D) The plaintiff should have judgment for $100,000 against the owner and the mechanic jointly, and the owner should have judgment against the mechanic for any amount collected from the owner by the plaintiff.

Question 198

A man fed a lost cat and returned it to its owner. She was so happy to see her cat that she promised to leave the man money in her will. When the cat owner died a few days later, the man visited the owner's daughter demanding his share of the estate. All of the cat owner's bank accounts had been held in joint tenancy with her daughter. The daughter reluctantly signed a document stating that she would pay the man $500 in exchange for his agreement not to sue her mother's estate. She later had second thoughts and refused to pay the man on the ground that there was no consideration for the agreement.

Besides the consideration stated in the daughter's written instrument, what other fact would strengthen the man's claim?

(A) He never would have fed and returned the cat had he known that he would not receive any payment for his efforts.

(B) He believed he could sue the cat owner's estate.

(C) The majority of the funds in the cat owner's bank account were royalties from a series of television commercials starring the cat.

(D) The cat owner's promise to him was in writing.

Question 199

A landowner held title to a tract of land in fee simple. Without the landowner's knowledge, a rancher entered the tract with his herd of cattle. The cattle drank and fed from the land for 12 years, at which time the rancher gave possession of the tract to a friend. The following year, the friend entered into a lease with the landowner to lease the tract for a period of five years. After the end of the five-year term of the lease, the friend remained on the tract for an additional three years and then left the tract. At that time, the landowner conveyed the tract by a quitclaim deed to her nephew. The period of time to acquire title by adverse possession in the jurisdiction is 10 years.

After the landowner's conveyance to her nephew, title to the tract was in:

(A) The rancher.

(B) The landowner.

(C) The friend.

(D) The nephew.

Question 200

A man was engaged in a telephone conversation with his son. At one point in the conversation, he said to his son, "My accountant is at my door. I'll have to hang up. Talk to you later." The next morning, the man's housekeeper found him dead and obviously the victim of foul play. The accountant was arrested and charged with the murder. The prosecution seeks to have the son testify at the accountant's trial as to his telephone conversation with his father. The prosecution's attempt is met by an objection from the defense.

How should the court rule on the son's testimony?

(A) Admissible, as a present sense impression.

(B) Admissible, as evidence of the victim's state of mind.

(C) Admissible, as a prior identification.

(D) Inadmissible, as hearsay not within any recognized exception.

ANSWER KEY AND SUBJECT/TOPIC KEY

Answer		Subject Matter
1.	C	Criminal Law/Procedure—search and seizure
2.	D	Contracts—measure of damages
3.	A	Contracts—assignment and delegation
4.	A	Torts—vicarious liability
5.	A	Torts—duty of owners and occupiers of land
6.	B	Constitutional Law—preemption
7.	B	Constitutional Law—legislative power
8.	B	Evidence—impeachment
9.	B	Criminal Law—attempt/impossibility
10.	B	Constitutional Law—freedom of expression
11.	B	Real Property—landlord-tenant
12.	B	Criminal Law/Procedure—*Miranda* rights
13.	B	Evidence—refreshing recollection
14.	D	Contracts/Sales—buyer's remedies
15.	A	Contracts/Sales—measure of damages
16.	D	Evidence—probative value/impeachment
17.	D	Criminal Law—parties to crime
18.	B	Criminal Law/Procedure—double jeopardy
19.	B	Torts—intentional infliction of emotional distress
20.	B	Real Property—assignment of leasehold interest
21.	D	Real Property—transfer of leased property
22.	A	Constitutional Law—intergovernmental immunity
23.	A	Evidence—hearsay
24.	A	Torts—duty of owners and occupiers of land
25.	C	Constitutional Law—procedural due process
26.	A	Contracts/Sales—Statute of Frauds
27.	D	Criminal Law/Procedure—warrantless arrest
28.	D	Real Property—equitable servitude
29.	D	Real Property—Rule Against Perpetuities
30.	C	Contracts—specific performance
31.	C	Real Property—delivery of deeds
32.	B	Evidence—hearsay exceptions
33.	A	Constitutional Law—standing
34.	D	Torts—battery/privilege of arrest
35.	D	Torts—proof of fault/products liability
36.	C	Criminal Law—murder/intoxication
37.	D	Criminal Law/Procedure—search and seizure
38.	B	Constitutional Law—legislative powers
39.	A	Evidence—admissions of party-opponent
40.	C	Contracts—consideration/requirements contract
41.	D	Real Property—tenancy in common
42.	B	Constitutional Law—intergovernmental immunities
43.	A	Evidence—attorney-client privilege
44.	D	Real Property—Rule Against Perpetuities
45.	A	Contracts—excuse of condition/anticipatory repudiation

46.	D	Constitutional Law—Equal Protection Clause
47.	A	Contracts—conditions
48.	A	Torts—vicarious liability
49.	C	Criminal Law—insanity
50.	B	Torts—defamation
51.	D	Torts—negligence
52.	B	Constitutional Law—equal protection
53.	D	Constitutional Law—preemption
54.	B	Evidence—probative value
55.	C	Real Property—marketable title
56.	D	Real Property—priority of mortgages
57.	C	Contracts—conditions
58.	C	Constitutional Law—Establishment Clause
59.	C	Torts—duty of owners and occupiers of land
60.	B	Evidence—public records exception to hearsay rule
61.	B	Criminal Law—burglary
62.	D	Evidence—expert testimony
63.	C	Real Property—assignments and subletting
64.	D	Evidence—lay opinions
65.	A	Torts—intentional infliction of emotional distress
66.	D	Constitutional Law—judicial power
67.	B	Constitutional Law—freedom of belief
68.	C	Constitutional Law—freedom of the press
69.	D	Contracts/Sales—offer and acceptance
70.	C	Contracts/Sales—"battle of the forms"
71.	B	Criminal Law—state of mind
72.	A	Torts—contributory negligence
73.	B	Constitutional Law—regulation of voting rights
74.	C	Real Property—equitable conversion
75.	A	Real Property—equitable conversion
76.	D	Evidence—scope of cross-examination
77.	A	Torts—strict products liability
78.	C	Torts—products liability based on negligence
79.	D	Criminal Law—larceny
80.	C	Evidence—hearsay
81.	D	Contracts—third-party beneficiaries
82.	C	Contracts—assignment of rights
83.	A	Contracts—delegation of duties
84.	A	Torts—defamation
85.	C	Real Property—adverse possession
86.	A	Evidence—husband-wife privilege
87.	C	Criminal Law/Procedure—double jeopardy
88.	B	Constitutional Law—separation of powers
89.	B	Evidence—personal knowledge requirement
90.	B	Criminal Law/Procedure—immunized testimony
91.	C	Torts—duty of care
92.	B	Torts—strict products liability
93.	B	Criminal Law/Procedure—double jeopardy
94.	A	Real Property—equitable servitude
95.	B	Constitutional Law—freedom of expression

96.	B	Contracts/Sales—acceptance
97.	B	Contracts—offer and acceptance
98.	D	Criminal Law/Procedure—exclusionary rule
99.	C	Evidence—character evidence
100.	B	Real Property—marketable title/specific performance
101.	D	Torts—defamation
102.	D	Criminal Law—attempt
103.	B	Contracts/Sales—parol evidence rule
104.	A	Constitutional Law—state regulation of commerce
105.	A	Constitutional Law—Equal Protection Clause
106.	C	Evidence—hearsay rule
107.	D	Real Property—Statute of Frauds
108.	D	Constitutional Law—equal protection
109.	C	Torts—strict liability
110.	C	Evidence—lay opinions
111.	B	Criminal Law—arson
112.	A	Criminal Law—robbery
113.	A	Contracts—implied-in-fact contract
114.	B	Real Property—easements/marketable title
115.	C	Torts—proximate cause
116.	C	Contracts—consequential damages
117.	D	Contracts—offer and acceptance
118.	C	Contracts—offer and acceptance
119.	D	Constitutional Law—individual rights
120.	A	Evidence—privileged communications/admissions
121.	A	Torts—duty of innkeepers
122.	A	Torts—invasion of privacy
123.	D	Real Property—Rule Against Perpetuities
124.	D	Criminal Law/Procedure—search and seizure
125.	B	Torts—false imprisonment
126.	C	Evidence—impeachment
127.	D	Constitutional Law—executive power
128.	B	Real Property—recording
129.	B	Contracts—mistake
130.	A	Torts—indemnity
131.	C	Criminal Law/Procedure—burden of proof
132.	B	Criminal Law/Procedure—search and seizure
133.	B	Evidence—impeachment/bias
134.	B	Contracts—measure of damages
135.	B	Contracts—consideration
136.	B	Contracts—discharge of duties
137.	D	Real Property—covenants for title
138.	A	Constitutional Law—standing
139.	B	Torts—comparative negligence
140.	A	Real Property—marketable title
141.	B	Criminal Law—burglary/impossibility
142.	D	Torts—negligent infliction of emotional distress
143.	B	Evidence—hearsay rule
144.	A	Constitutional Law—fundamental rights
145.	D	Criminal Law—felony murder

146.	B	Criminal Law/Procedure—right to counsel
147.	D	Evidence—character evidence
148.	B	Real Property—executory interests
149.	D	Torts—defamation
150.	D	Real Property—marketable title
151.	C	Contracts/Sales—buyer's remedies
152.	C	Evidence—prior identification by witness
153.	A	Contracts/Sales—consideration
154.	A	Contracts/Sales—rejection of nonconforming goods
155.	C	Constitutional Law—procedural due process
156.	C	Criminal Law/Procedure—consent to search
157.	D	Criminal Law—larceny
158.	D	Torts—defamation
159.	A	Evidence—authentication
160.	C	Constitutional Law—equal protection
161.	D	Real Property—fixtures
162.	B	Torts—misrepresentation
163.	C	Constitutional Law—judicial power
164.	B	Evidence—impeachment
165.	A	Criminal Law/Procedure—search and seizure
166.	C	Contracts—consideration/preexisting duty rule
167.	D	Real Property—conveyancing
168.	B	Evidence—rehabilitation of impeached witness
169.	A	Evidence—authentication
170.	A	Torts—intentional infliction of mental distress
171.	B	Torts—battery
172.	A	Criminal Law—manslaughter
173.	C	Constitutional Law—obscenity/overbreadth
174.	C	Evidence—hearsay/admission of party opponent
175.	C	Real Property—transfer of executory interest
176.	D	Contracts—impossibility
177.	C	Contracts/Sales—remedies for breach
178.	A	Criminal Law—larceny
179.	B	Evidence—hearsay/relevance
180.	C	Constitutional Law—taxpayer standing/Establishment Clause
181.	D	Torts—causation/joint and several liability
182.	B	Real Property—right of first refusal
183.	A	Evidence—authentication
184.	D	Criminal Law—homicide/malice aforethought
185.	D	Contracts—consideration
186.	A	Real Property—fixtures
187.	B	Constitutional Law—separation of powers
188.	C	Real Property—mortgage of joint tenancy
189.	B	Real Property—life estates
190.	B	Criminal Law—kidnapping
191.	A	Evidence—former testimony
192.	D	Constitutional Law—Equal Protection Clause/freedom of speech
193.	A	Torts—proximate cause
194.	D	Real Property—conveyancing/recording
195.	B	Constitutional Law—ballot restrictions

196.	D	Criminal Law/Procedure—search and seizure
197.	D	Torts—indemnity
198.	B	Contracts—consideration
199.	A	Real Property—adverse possession
200.	A	Evidence—hearsay/present sense impression

Answer to Question 1

(C) The court should suppress all of the evidence because it was the fruit of an unconstitutional arrest. As a general rule, the police must have an arrest warrant to effect an arrest of an individual in his own home. There is no general "emergency" exception to the warrant requirement. While police officers in hot pursuit of a fleeing felon or trying to prevent the destruction of evidence may sometimes make a warrantless search and seizure, the burden is on the government to show that one of those exceptions applies. Here, the police did not arrive at the defendant's house in hot pursuit of the defendant, and there was no indication that the defendant might be destroying the money or other evidence; *i.e.,* there were no circumstances precluding them from keeping the house under surveillance while they obtained a warrant. Hence, the arrest was unconstitutional. Because an arrest constitutes a seizure under the Fourth Amendment, the exclusionary rule applies, and evidence that is the fruit of the unconstitutional arrest may not be used against the defendant at trial. Here, all of the evidence was seized without a warrant, and none of the other exceptions to the warrant requirement are applicable. While the protective sweep that turned up the money and gun probably would have been within the bounds of a search incident to an arrest because the police had reason to believe an armed accomplice was present, the arrest in violation of the Fourth Amendment makes the search unlawful. Similarly, while the bags of marijuana were discovered in plain view, the police have to be legitimately on the premises for that exception to apply. Thus, (C) is correct; (A), (B), and (D) are incorrect.

Answer to Question 2

(D) The homeowner can recover $1,500, the difference between the contractor's contract price and the contract price of the substitute performance. Here, while the homeowner actually paid $2,500 more than the contractor's contract price to have the house repaired, he was obligated to pay only $1,500 more because the electrician had a legal duty to make the repairs to the house for his contract price and no more. The homeowner will not be able to recover the $1,000 difference because he has a duty to mitigate damages, and paying more than he was actually obligated to pay breaches the duty. (A) and (B) are incorrect because they do not apply the proper measure of damages formula. (C) is incorrect because the "cost of completion" does not include the additional $1,000 the homeowner gave the electrician to save the electrician from having performed the job at a loss. As explained above, the homeowner was not required to pay the electrician the $1,000 to complete the repairs and the homeowner's paying the extra amount breaches his duty to mitigate damages. Thus, the homeowner cannot recover the extra $1,000.

Answer to Question 3

(A) Both the stylist and the assistant are liable on the contract. (B) is incorrect because when contractual duties are delegated, the delegator remains liable on the contract, even if the delegate assumes the duties. The result might be different if the obligee expressly consented to the delegation of duties and released the original obligor (a novation), but that did not happen here. Here, the singer allowed the assistant to style her hair, but that does not, without more, constitute a novation. (C) is also incorrect. The liability of a delegate turns on whether there has been a mere "delegation" or delegation plus an "assumption of duty." Here the delegate, the assistant, "assumed the duties" by making a promise to perform supported by consideration (*i.e.,* the right to collect the stylist's fees). Thus, the nondelegating party (the singer) can sue the assistant for nonperformance. (D) is incorrect. Contracts for personal services are not subject to specific performance, but the courts will award money damages for their breach.

Answer to Question 4

(A) If the delivery company prevails, it will be because it entrusted its car to its employee without having reason to know that she had a poor driving record. In the absence of negligence on the delivery company's part, it will not be liable for its employee's negligent driving either as her employer or as the owner of the automobile she was driving. An employer will be vicariously liable for tortious acts committed by its employee only if the tortious acts occur within the scope of the employment relationship. Here, although the employee was using the company car, she was not conducting any business for the delivery company. Her use of the car to go grocery shopping was a personal errand outside the scope of her employment for which the delivery company is not vicariously liable. The delivery company is also not vicariously liable for permitting its employee to drive its car—the general rule absent a statute to the contrary is that an automobile owner is not vicariously liable for the tortious conduct of another driving the owner's automobile. However, the owner may be liable for its own negligence in entrusting the car to a particular driver. If the delivery company knew or should have known that its employee had a poor driving record, its furnishing the employee with a car would constitute a breach of its duty to other drivers. However, if it is determined that the delivery company had no reason to know of the employee's poor driving record, it will not be liable. (B) is incorrect because the fact that the driver of the van had the last opportunity to avoid the accident is irrelevant to the leasing company's right to recover from the delivery company. The doctrine of last clear chance does not apply because it is essentially ***plaintiff's rebuttal*** against the defense of contributory negligence; it would not be raised by the delivery company as a defense (*i.e.,* if the delivery company asserted that the driver of the van was contributorily negligent, the leasing company could rebut by asserting that ***the delivery company employee*** had the last clear chance to avoid the accident). (C) is incorrect. Even though the driver of the van's violation of the posted speed limit probably constituted contributory negligence, it will not be imputed to the leasing company. Just as an automobile owner generally would not be vicariously liable for the driver's negligence, a driver's ***contributory*** negligence will not be imputed to the automobile owner who is suing the other driver. Because there is no indication that the leasing company was itself negligent in leasing the van to the driver, the driver's conduct in exceeding the speed limit will not prevent the leasing company from recovering. (D) is incorrect because the fact that the delivery company had the employee assume all liability may allow it to seek indemnification against the employee if the leasing company prevails against it; however, such an assumption of liability does not affect its liability to the leasing company.

Answer to Question 5

(A) The shopper will prevail because the employee of the contractor hired by the store left the level in the aisle. The general rule that a principal will not be vicariously liable for the acts of its independent contractor's agent is subject to several broad exceptions, including one for duties that are nondelegable because of public policy considerations. One of these duties is the duty of a business to keep its premises safe for customers. Hence, a business would be liable for the negligence of an employee of an independent contractor to the same extent as for the negligence of its own employee. Here, the carpenter was employed by the contractor, which was hired by the store. The carpenter breached the duty owed to business invitees such as the shopper by leaving the level projecting out into one of the aisles. The shopper was injured as a result, so he will prevail in a suit against the store. (B) is wrong. As part of the duty owed to business invitees, the store employees have a duty to make reasonable inspections of their premises to discover unsafe conditions (such as if a customer had spilled something slippery in an aisle). However, regardless of whether they had a reasonable time to discover the level, the store is liable because it is responsible for the carpenter's conduct. (C) is wrong because, as discussed above, the store is liable under these circumstances for the conduct of its independent contractor's employee. (D) is wrong because the store is liable regardless of the knowledge of its employees.

Answer to Question 6

(B) There is no conflict between the two provisions. If the federal legislation does not address the issue of preemption, and a problem is uniquely local, the local government is permitted to enact rules more strict than the federal standards. The Court has made it clear that for preemption, either the federal statute must ***expressly*** preempt state measures, or its preemptive force must be clear by either "occupying the field" or posing a conflict that makes compliance with both measures impossible. Because the facts do not indicate that the federal measure expressly preempts state regulation, and because neither of the implied preemption conditions are met, (B) is the correct answer and (C) and (D) are incorrect. (A) is not supported by the facts.

Answer to Question 7

(B) Congress has addressed the problem of racial discrimination primarily under the commerce power, but the Thirteenth Amendment does contain an enabling clause that would authorize this type of statute because it is not limited to governmental action. [*See* Patterson v. McLean Credit Union (1989)] While the Due Process Clause of the Fifth Amendment has been applied to the federal government in the same way that the Equal Protection Clause of the Fourteenth Amendment has been applied to states in racial segregation cases, the diner is not a government agency. Therefore, the Fifth Amendment argument would not be very effective, because it is not the government itself that is being accused of discrimination. Thus, (A) and (C) do not offer the best response. (D) is incorrect because it misstates the law: There is no general federal police power.

Answer to Question 8

(B) The letter is admissible as substantive evidence as well as for impeachment purposes. For the purpose of impeaching the credibility of a witness, a party may show that the witness has, on another occasion, made statements that are inconsistent with some material part of his present testimony. This may be done by first cross-examining the witness as to the prior inconsistent statement that he has made. If the witness denies having made the statement or fails to remember it, the making of the statement may be proved by extrinsic evidence. A proper foundation must be laid by giving the witness an opportunity to explain or deny the statement, and it must be relevant to some issue in the case. Here, the plaintiff's employee has denied on cross-examination that he wrote the letter to his friend. The plaintiff can then impeach the employee by offering the letter into evidence. Because the employee has not been released as a witness, he will have an opportunity to explain or deny the statement, and it is relevant to whether any work was done at the home. Because prior inconsistent statements are generally hearsay, they often are admissible only for purposes of impeachment. In this case, however, the statement is admissible as substantive evidence because it falls within an exception to the hearsay rule. Under Rule 803(3), a statement of a declarant's then-existing state of mind is admissible as a basis for a circumstantial inference that the declarant acted in accordance with his state of mind. [*See also* Mutual Life Insurance Co. v. Hillmon] The employee's statement that he was going to do electrical work on the home is admissible as circumstantial evidence tending to show that he followed through with his plans and did the electrical work, which is what the statement is being offered to establish. In this case, therefore, the letter should be admissible as both substantive and impeachment evidence, making (B) correct and (A) incorrect. (C) is incorrect because the Federal Rules provide that the credibility of a witness may be attacked by any party, including the party calling him. [Fed. R. Evid. 607] (D) is incorrect. The letter is hearsay because it is being offered to prove the truth of the matter asserted—that the employee was going to do electrical work on the home—as a basis for inferring that the employee did do the work. However, as discussed above, it falls within the "present state of mind" exception to the hearsay rule.

Answer to Question 9

(B) The defendant may not be charged with attempt. To prove attempt, the government must establish that the defendant had a specific intent to commit the crime and committed an act beyond mere preparation for the offense. There can be no attempt, however, if there is no crime on the books to cover either the defendant's behavior or his intended behavior. This is known as the doctrine of legal impossibility. Here, the defendant could not be charged with attempting to purchase a certain drug without providing an identification or signature because it was not illegal to do so. (D) is wrong because legal impossibility is a defense to attempt. (C) is wrong because, although it is a correct statement of law, factual impossibility is not present here. Factual impossibility involves a defendant who has set out to do something that would, if accomplished, constitute a crime, but because of factors of which he is unaware, there is no chance he will succeed in doing it. Here, the defendant was able to do what he set out to do—purchase the drug without an identification or signature. Thus, (A) is also wrong.

Answer to Question 10

(B) A regulation will not be upheld if it is overbroad (*i.e.*, if it prohibits substantially more speech than is necessary). If a regulation punishes a substantial amount of protected speech, judged in relation to the regulation's plainly legitimate sweep, the regulation is facially invalid unless a court has limited construction of the regulation so as to remove the threat to constitutionally protected expression. If a criminal law or regulation fails to give persons reasonable notice of what is prohibited, it may violate the Due Process Clause on vagueness grounds. This principle is applied somewhat strictly when First Amendment activity is involved in order to avoid the chilling effect a vague law might have on speech (*i.e.*, if it is unclear what speech is regulated, people might refrain from speech that is permissible for fear that they will be violating the law). The ordinance at issue here is overbroad in banning all street demonstrations of more than 15 people in commercial areas during rush hour. This regulation bans far more speech than is necessary. This regulation is also unduly vague because "rush" hour is apparently not defined in the ordinance. The section of the ordinance referring to certain types of prohibited language is also so vague as to be facially invalid. (A) is incorrect because prior restraints may be imposed on speech in public places if such restraints are granted under narrowly and clearly defined standards. (C) is incorrect because the police have powers to prevent breaches of the peace. (D) is incorrect because the state may interfere with the right of association, where, for example, there is an imminent danger to public health and welfare.

Answer to Question 11

(B) The owner may begin eviction proceedings at any time. When a tenant continues in possession after the termination of her right to possession, the landlord has two choices of action: He may treat the hold-over tenant as a trespasser and evict her under an unlawful detainer statute, or he may, in his sole discretion, bind the tenant to a new periodic tenancy, in which case the terms and conditions of the expired tenancy apply to the new tenancy. Here, while the owner accepted the check sent by the chef, he informed her that he was not electing to bind her to a new tenancy. The owner may keep the check because he is entitled to rent for the month that the chef was a hold-over tenant, but at the end of that month he has the right to evict her because no periodic tenancy was created and the chef's right to possession has terminated. (A) is incorrect because the owner did not elect to create a periodic tenancy. Furthermore, had he done so, the tenancy would have been a year-to-year tenancy rather than a month-to-month tenancy because it is a commercial lease for more than one year, rather than a residential lease. (C) is incorrect because, as discussed above, the owner did not elect to create a periodic tenancy when the chef held over. (D) is incorrect because no tenancy for years is created when a tenant holds over. If the landlord elects to bind the tenant to a new tenancy, it will be a periodic tenancy, regardless of whether the original tenancy was a tenancy for years.

Answer to Question 12

(B) The defendant's motion should be denied because his waiver of his *Miranda* rights was valid. Even though the prosecution must show, by a preponderance of the evidence, that a defendant's waiver of his *Miranda* rights was knowing, voluntary, and intelligent, the suspect need not have been informed of all subjects of an interrogation to effect a valid waiver. The police were not required to tell the defendant of the woman's condition. (A) is incorrect because no error was involved. (C) is incorrect for the reasons described above, *i.e.,* the police need not inform the subject of all aspects of the interrogation for the waiver to be considered valid. (D) is incorrect because due process requires only that confessions be voluntary, *i.e.,* not the product of official compulsion. Withholding information about the potential seriousness of the offense does not violate due process.

Answer to Question 13

(B) Showing the witness the notes is a proper attempt to refresh her recollection. A witness may use any writing or thing for the purpose of refreshing her present recollection. This is known as "present recollection revived." Under most circumstances, she may not read from the writing while she actually testifies because the writing is neither authenticated nor in evidence. Here, the writing was shown to her solely to refresh her recollection and is, therefore, proper. (A) is incorrect because it describes "past recollection recorded," which is a hearsay exception [Fed. R. Evid. 803(5)] allowing the writing itself to be introduced into evidence if a proper foundation is laid for its admissibility. Here, there is no attempt to enter the notes into evidence. (C) is incorrect because what the attorney is asking to do does not constitute a traditional "leading question," which generally calls for a "yes" or "no" answer or is framed to suggest the desired answer. Furthermore, the ordinary rules on leading questions may be waived when the witness needs help to respond because of loss of memory. (D) is incorrect because aiding a witness's present recollection has nothing to do with bolstering the witness's credibility (which generally may not be done until the witness has been impeached).

Answer to Question 14

(D) The statement in (D) is not an accurate statement because the seller has not made a proper accommodation offer. If there had been no prior contract and the seller had attempted to accept by shipment, shipment of the "accommodation" units would be a counteroffer and if the buyer accepted them, she could not sue for damages. However, here there was a prior written contract. (A) is a true statement. The buyer has a contract for 100 wheelbarrows; she is not required to accept anything less. (B) is also a correct statement. The buyer can accept if she wants less than the full order and hold the seller responsible for damages. (C) too is a correct statement. Under the U.C.C., if a valid contract existed, the buyer can accept the entire shipment and sue the seller for damages.

Answer to Question 15

(A) The dealer can collect his lost profits, *i.e.,* the difference between the contract price ($29,000) and what the dealer paid to purchase the car from the manufacturer. In a contract for the sale of goods, a seller can collect his lost profits when the buyer breaches if the seller cannot be made whole by a subsequent sale of the item contracted for. This occurs where the seller can obtain or manufacture as many goods as it can sell (*e.g.,* a car dealership), because in such a situation, the seller would have been able to sell to the subsequent purchaser anyway. This is known as a lost volume situation, and in such a situation, the U.C.C. allows the seller to sue for his lost profits. Generally, lost profits are measured by the difference between the cost of goods and the contract price, less the seller's saved expenses. (B) is incorrect because it uses the wrong measure for lost profits. The cost of a similar car in the local wholesale market is irrelevant because the dealer did not purchase the car on the wholesale market, but rather purchased the car from the manufacturer. The dealer's actual price will be used to determine his lost profits. (C) is incorrect because although the dealer resold the car, the resale has not made him whole since he could have sold a car to the other buyer anyway. Thus, the resale does not put the dealer in as good a position as he would have been in had the doctor performed (the goal of contract remedies). Thus, the dealer will be allowed to recover his lost profits, as explained above. (D) is incorrect because contracts of adhesion are not unconscionable per se, and there is nothing in the facts to indicate a degree of unconscionability that would render the contract voidable at the buyer's option.

Answer to Question 16

(D) The trial court should rule the witness's testimony inadmissible because its probative value is substantially outweighed by the danger that it will confuse the issues and waste time. Where a witness makes a statement not directly relevant to the issues in the case, the rule against impeachment (other than by cross-examination) on a collateral matter applies to bar the opponent from proving the statement untrue either by extrinsic contradictory facts or by a prior inconsistent statement. The purpose of the rule is to avoid the possibility of unfair surprise, confusion of issues, and undue consumption of time. An issue is considered collateral if it would not be admissible other than to contradict the testimony. Evidence that a person has previously filed similar claims is generally inadmissible to show the invalidity of the present claim. At best, this evidence shows the plaintiff's tendency toward litigation. Unless there is evidence that the previous claim was false, the probative value of such evidence is deemed outweighed by the risk of confusion of the issues. Because the prior suit would not be the subject of proof independent of impeachment, it is a collateral matter, and extrinsic evidence, such as the witness's testimony, is inadmissible. (A) is wrong because the testimony is not proper impeachment and is inadmissible. Further, this choice states the foundational requirement for introducing a prior inconsistent statement. This is not a prior inconsistent statement and, if the testimony were admissible, the opportunity to explain or deny would not be required. (B) is wrong because the failure to object merely meant that the plaintiff's answer to the question was admitted into evidence; it does not change the fact that the matter is collateral. Because it is a collateral matter, extrinsic evidence will not be permitted. (C) is wrong for two reasons: First, the suit is a fact that exists independently of the court record, and thus, the best evidence rule would not apply. Further, as stated above, extrinsic evidence of any kind is not admissible on a collateral matter; the defendant is limited to cross-examination for impeachment in these circumstances.

Answer to Question 17

(D) The pharmacist is not an accomplice to criminal homicide because intent is required to invoke accomplice liability. To be convicted as an accomplice, a person must have given aid, counsel, or encouragement with the intent that an offense be committed or, in some cases, with knowledge that she was contributing to the commission of a crime. The pharmacist supplied the apparently benign antibiotic to prevent the possible commission of a crime of homicide rather than to aid or abet the commission of such crime by the husband. The pharmacist lacked intent to commit any of the homicide crimes. (A) is incorrect because murder is the unlawful killing of a human being with malice aforethought and the pharmacist lacked any of the states of mind required to establish malice. (B) is incorrect because voluntary manslaughter involves a killing after adequate provocation, and "unlawful act" involuntary manslaughter requires a killing in the course of a felony or a malum in se misdemeanor. None of these situations is present here. (C) is incorrect because criminal negligence requires negligence of a greater degree than the "reasonable person" standard for torts. The pharmacist did not reach this degree of negligence by supplying the husband with the usually harmless antibiotic.

Answer to Question 18

(B) The court should deny the motion because jeopardy generally does not attach in civil proceedings, other than juvenile proceedings. Here, the wife is bringing a civil battery action for damages against her husband. The prior trial was based on a criminal charge of domestic violence. Thus, double jeopardy is inapplicable under these facts. Thus, even though simple battery may be a lesser included offense of domestic violence, it would not prevent the wife from bringing a civil action against the husband. Furthermore, even if the state were not allowed to retry the husband on the domestic violence charge under the "manifest necessity" concept, that would not prevent the wife from bringing a civil action against her husband. Thus, (C) and (D) are wrong. (A) is also wrong because jeopardy attaches in a jury trial at the empanelling and swearing in of the jury.

Answer to Question 19

(B) Because the bouncer was unaware that the wife was watching, the bouncer could not have the requisite intent to inflict emotional distress. For intentional infliction of emotional distress based on conduct directed at a third person, recovery is ordinarily limited to plaintiffs who are not only present at the time, but are known by the defendant to be present, so that the mental distress is likely to have been anticipated by the defendant. (A) is not as good an answer, because the bouncer need not intend to inflict emotional distress. Liability for this tort may be based on recklessness. (C) and (D) state elements of the tort, but are meaningless without the necessary awareness of the presence of the wife.

Answer to Question 20

(B) The clothing store is liable for the total amount on privity of contract grounds, and the shoe outlet is liable for $12,000 on privity of estate grounds. When a leasehold interest is assigned, the assignor and the landlord are no longer in privity of estate; the assignee is now in privity of estate with the landlord. Hence, each is liable to the other on all covenants in the lease that "run with the land." Here, the agreement to pay a maintenance fee for upkeep of the common areas of the mall is a covenant that runs with the land because it burdens the tenant and benefits the landlord with respect to their interests in the property (*i.e.*, it "touches and concerns" the land). The shoe outlet is therefore liable for the maintenance fees for the 12-month term of its tenancy. However, because the shoe outlet was not in privity of estate prior to the assignment, it is not liable for the $3,000 in maintenance fees that the clothing store owed; thus, (A) is incorrect. (C) and (D) are incorrect because the clothing store continues to be liable for the maintenance fees after the assignment. While the original tenant is no longer in privity of estate with the landlord after assignment, the tenant can still be held liable on its original contractual obligation in the lease, *i.e.*, on privity of contract. This allows the landlord to sue the original tenant where the assignee has disappeared, is judgment-proof, etc. Here, the clothing store is liable for the period the shoe outlet occupied the property as well as the period the property was abandoned. Thus, the mall has the choice of suing either the clothing store (under privity of contract) or the shoe outlet (under privity of estate) for the $12,000 in maintenance fees, as provided in (B).

Answer to Question 21

(D) Both the original owner and the investor are liable to the dentist. A landlord's assignment of the rents and reversion interest, such as through a sale of the property, is subject to the same rules as a tenant's assignment of the leasehold interest. The assignee is liable to the tenants for performance of all covenants made by the original landlord in the lease, provided that those covenants touch and concern the land. The burdens of those covenants run with the landlord's estate and become the burdens of the new landlord. The original landlord also remains liable (on privity of contract grounds) on all covenants that he made in the lease. Here, the duty to maintain the parking lot touches and concerns the land because it benefits the tenant and burdens the landlord with respect to their interests in the property. Thus, regardless of who hired the contractor, the investor had a duty to ensure that the contractor completed the work, and is liable to the dentist for the costs the dentist incurred to have the work completed. (A) is incorrect because the failure of the dentist to pay rent does not excuse the prior breach of the covenant to maintain the parking lot. As a general rule, covenants in a lease are independent of each other. Thus, if one party breaches a covenant, the other party can recover damages, but must still perform his promises under the lease. Absent application of constructive eviction, an implied warranty of habitability, or some other statutory provision, the dentist may not have had authority to withhold rent despite the breach of the maintenance covenant, and the investor may now have the option to terminate the lease as a result. Even if that were the case, however, both landlords would remain liable to the dentist for the damages incurred from the breach of the maintenance agreement while the lease was in force. (B) is incorrect because the fact that the investor did not contractually assume the original owner's obligations does not alter its liability to the dentist under privity of estate principles. Had the investor contractually assumed the obligations, the dentist could have also proceeded against the investor on a contractual basis as a third-party beneficiary of the assumption agreement. Even without the assumption, the investor is liable to the dentist on privity of estate grounds. (C) is incorrect because the fact that privity of estate between the original owner and the dentist was severed by the sale does not alter the original owner's privity of contract obligations. Because the original owner made a covenant in the lease to maintain the parking lot, he is contractually obligated to fulfill that covenant regardless of the sale of the property to the investor.

Answer to Question 22

(A) The state may impose a tax on the fiberoptic line. A state tax levied directly against the property or operation of the federal government without the consent of Congress is invalid. However, nondiscriminatory, indirect taxes on the federal government or its property are permissible if they do not unreasonably burden the federal government. Because this tax is not levied directly against the government, but rather against the provider of a service that the government is obtaining, and is levied on all communications lines in the state, the tax is valid. The fact that the economic burden of the tax will ultimately be borne by the government under the "cost plus" contract does not invalidate the tax. (B) is wrong because the Tenth Amendment provides that powers not delegated to the United States, nor prohibited to the states, are reserved to the states. This limits Congress's power to regulate the states but does not serve as an independent grant of power to the states. Both the federal government and the state government have the power to tax, but the federal law is supreme in this area. (C) is wrong because not every state tax that burdens the federal government is invalid. A nondiscriminatory tax on a service provided to the federal government by a private entity does not appear to be an unreasonable burden on the operation of the federal government. (D) is wrong because the fact that interstate commerce is involved does not invalidate the tax. Power over commerce is concurrent, belonging to both the states and the federal government. While federal law is supreme in the area of interstate commerce, state legislation that affects interstate commerce is not automatically invalidated.

Answer to Question 23

(A) The document should be admitted. Related to the exception to the hearsay rule for public records and other official writings, Federal Rule of Evidence 803(10) provides that evidence in the form of a certification or testimony from the custodian of public records that she has diligently searched and failed to find a record is admissible to prove that a matter was not recorded, or, inferentially, that a matter did not occur. Here, the defendant's status as a licensed physical therapist would normally be revealed in the records of the department. The document here at issue is admissible, under the foregoing hearsay exception, as a means of proving that the defendant is in fact not licensed. (B) is incorrect because this hearsay exception does not require unavailability of the declarant. (C) is incorrect because, as explained above, the statement of absence from public record forms an ***exception*** to the hearsay rule. (D) is incorrect because a public document that has been signed and certified is self-authenticating under Rule 902; hence, no testimonial sponsorship for the document is required.

Answer to Question 24

(A) The student's status as a trespasser on shopping center property precludes his recovery against the shopping center. This question does not identify the basis for the student's action against the shopping center; therefore, you have to consider all of the shopping center's potential grounds for liability. Because the security service is an independent contractor, something more than simple vicarious liability is needed to make the shopping center liable for the security service employee's torts. And because the shopping center did not authorize the use of snakes to guard the stores, it is not liable for an intentional tort, even though the use of poisonous snakes would otherwise be unreasonable force in defense of property. Another potential basis for liability is the shopping center's status as owner or occupier of the property. The general rule is that a landowner owes no duty to a trespasser whose presence is undiscovered to warn of or make safe concealed dangerous conditions or dangerous activities on the land. However, trespassers who are discovered or whom the landowners should anticipate because they habitually and routinely enter the land are owed a higher duty. The landowner will be liable for concealed, dangerous, artificial conditions known to the landowner and negligently conducted active operations, including those of third persons whom the landowner has the ability and authority to control. Here, the student was neither discovered nor anticipated. No one actually noticed him before his injury, and nothing in the facts indicates that people habitually broke into the mall—the mere fact that the shopping center had a security guard is not sufficient to make someone breaking in an anticipated trespasser. Thus, even if the shopping center should have supervised the security service employee more closely, it owed no duty to the student because he was a trespasser. (B) is incorrect because the fact that the student was guilty of breaking and entering is irrelevant. Had the student been a discovered or anticipated trespasser, the shopping center might be liable to the student for, *e.g.*, negligent supervision of the security service, even though the student broke into the building. (C) is incorrect because the shopping center did not authorize use of the poisonous snakes. If it had, (C) would be correct because a landowner may only use reasonable force to defend his property, and may not use indirect force that will cause death or serious bodily harm, such as a spring gun or deadly animal, when he could not use such force directly, such as here. (D) is incorrect because it is irrelevant. Undiscovered trespassers need not be warned of the dangers on the land; the landowner owes no duty to them.

Answer to Question 25

(C) The employee's suit will be unsuccessful because he has no right to a hearing here because he has no life, liberty, or property interest at stake. The Due Process Clause requires a hearing only when a life, liberty, or property interest is at stake. The employee clearly is not at risk of losing his life or liberty, and the Supreme Court has made clear that neither is a property interest involved here. To have a property interest in continued government employment, there must be a statute, regulation, contract right, or clear policy that the employee can be dismissed only for cause. Absent such a right to employment, the employee is an at-will employee and may be terminated without a hearing. Here, there was no law, contract, or policy giving the employee a right to a job absent cause for firing him. Therefore, no hearing was required. (A) is incorrect because bills of attainder involve criminal or otherwise punitive measures inflicted without judicial trial. Nothing here indicates that the employee is being punished; rather he is not being retained as an employee. (B) is incorrect because while the Equal Protection Clause prohibits government from discriminating between similarly situated persons unreasonably, where, as here, no fundamental right or suspect or quasi-suspect class is involved, the discriminatory government action will be upheld as long as it is rational. The random hearing policy here could be rational (*e.g.,* it might provide a sufficient sample to ensure that probationary employees are not being terminated for improper reasons); thus, it will be upheld. (D) is incorrect because it is too broad. Not every aspect of state government employment is protected by the Tenth Amendment. [*See, e.g.,* Garcia v. San Antonio Metropolitan Transit Authority (1985)]

Answer to Question 26

(A) The manufacturing company will win because the contract is fully enforceable under the U.C.C. Tubing is a good, so Article 2 of the U.C.C. applies. The contract is for the sale of goods over $500 (10,000 linear feet at $2/foot), so ordinarily section 2-201 would require a writing. However, section 2-201(3) provides that a writing is not required where the contract is for "specially manufactured" goods not suitable for resale in the ordinary course of the seller's business and the seller has made a substantial beginning of their manufacture or commitments for their procurement. Because the tubing is a custom order of unique specifications and the manufacturing company has begun manufacturing it, this exception to the U.C.C. Statute of Frauds applies. (B) is incorrect because the contract is fully enforceable. While the manufacturing company is required to mitigate damages, it is entitled to the full range of contract remedies to put it in the position it would have been in had the retail seller not breached (*i.e.,* benefit of the bargain damages on the entire contract). (C) is incorrect because while it is true that a contract for the sale of goods over $500 must ordinarily be evidenced by a signed writing, the "specially manufactured goods" exception (*see* above) applies here. (D) is incorrect because the parol evidence rule bars admissibility of evidence that varies an integrated writing; here, there is no writing at all.

Answer to Question 27

(D) The court is not likely to agree to suppress the confession for two reasons: The defendant probably has no standing to raise a violation of the friend's Fourth Amendment rights, and even if he did, the confession would not be excluded because it was not the fruit of the Fourth Amendment violation. Under the Fourth Amendment, the police generally can arrest, without a warrant, anyone that they have reasonable grounds to believe has committed a felony. There are two exceptions, however, when a warrant is required: Absent exigent circumstances, the Fourth Amendment requires the police to have a warrant to arrest a person in his own home or to search the premises of a third person for an arrestee. Here, the police had probable cause to arrest the defendant and the arrest did not occur in the defendant's home. Although the arrest did take place in the friend's home and the police did not obtain a warrant to search the friend's home, this will not help the defendant because the warrant requirement for a third person's premises is intended to protect the third person's expectation of privacy; while the search may have violated the friend's Fourth Amendment rights, the friend is not being charged with an offense. The Supreme Court has held that a person can have evidence excluded on Fourth Amendment grounds only if that person's Fourth Amendment rights were violated; a person has no standing to raise a violation of another's Fourth Amendment rights. A person has standing to object to the search of a place only if the person has an ownership or possessory interest in the place searched or is an overnight guest in the place searched. Here, the police entered the friend's home, and the facts indicate that the defendant was there only to obtain a forged license. Thus, the defendant probably has no standing to raise the Fourth Amendment violation. Furthermore, even if he had standing, his confession could still be used against him. While the exclusionary rule generally provides that evidence obtained or derived from exploitation of illegally obtained evidence must be excluded, the Supreme Court has held that where the police have probable cause to arrest a defendant and improperly arrest him in his home without a warrant, a confession made by the defendant at the police station is admissible because it is not the fruit of the unlawful arrest (because the police could have lawfully arrested the defendant the moment he stepped outside of the house). [New York v. Harris (1990)] Here, even if the arrest were unlawful because of the absence of a warrant, the police had probable cause to arrest the defendant and so could have waited until he left the friend's house. Hence, the confession at the police station was not a fruit of the unlawful arrest and should not be suppressed. (A) is wrong because, as discussed above, it is unlikely that the defendant can establish that the warrantless entry by itself was a violation of his own reasonable expectation of privacy. (B) is wrong because the absence of an arrest warrant, even if it would have made the arrest unlawful under the circumstances, would not require suppressing the confession. As discussed above, the confession was not the fruit of the unlawful arrest because the police had probable cause to arrest the defendant as soon as he left the house. (C) is wrong because it is irrelevant. The fact that a reliable informant gave them the defendant's location, even assuming that it would have helped establish probable cause for searching there, does not excuse the requirement that a magistrate make an independent evaluation of probable cause before issuing a warrant.

Answer to Question 28

(D) The woman will be able to enforce the restrictive covenant as an equitable servitude. Zoning regulations and restrictive covenants in private deeds are completely separate concepts. Both must be complied with, and neither provides any excuse for violating the other. Thus, a variance from the government regulation does not prevent enforcement of the private covenant. The court will enforce the covenant as an equitable servitude because the woman is seeking an injunction. An equitable servitude is a covenant that, regardless of whether it runs with the land at law, equity will enforce against the assignees of the burdened land who have notice of the covenant. Here, all of the deeds contained the restrictive covenant. There is no indication that the man did not have notice of the restriction, and it is both possible and reasonable for him to comply with the restriction at this stage. Privity of estate is not required because the majority of courts enforce the servitude as an equitable interest in the land itself. Hence, the woman will obtain the injunction.

(A) is incorrect because, as noted above, zoning regulations and covenants in deeds are completely separate; thus, the zoning regulation would not take precedence over the covenant. The only time a zoning regulation might prevent enforcement of such a covenant is where enforcement would result in a zoning violation (*e.g.*, covenant calls for single family residential housing only, while the land is zoned strictly commercial). (B) is an incorrect statement of law. Equity will impose a hardship, although it will try to balance the hardships between the parties. Here, the hardship on the man is not unreasonable because it is possible for him to build a house that complies with the setback restriction and he has not yet dug the foundation for the house he was planning. (C) is incorrect because nothing in the facts indicates that the man will be unjustly enriched by building his home in violation of the covenant; *e.g.*, there is no indication that his home or property will be worth more simply because it has a 30-foot setback rather than a 50-foot setback.

Answer to Question 29

(D) The purported contingent remainder to the church violates the Rule Against Perpetuities and consequently it takes nothing. Under the Rule Against Perpetuities, an interest in property is not valid unless it will vest, if at all, not later than 21 years after a life in being at the creation of the interest. The perpetuities period for irrevocable trusts begins to run on the date the trust is created. Under the "all-or-nothing" rule, if it is possible that a disposition to a class might vest remotely with respect to any member of the class, the entire class gift is invalid. Here, at the time the trust was created, the daughter had a life estate and the daughter's two children had a vested remainder subject to open in a life estate. The remainder to the daughter's grandchildren, however, is void because every member of the class will not be ascertained until the death of the survivor of the daughter's children, and that surviving child might be born to the daughter after the trust's creation. Then the daughter's two children who are lives in being might die, and 21 years after their deaths this afterborn child might give birth to an afterborn grandchild, whose interest would vest remotely. Thus, the interest to the daughter's grandchildren violates the Rule Against Perpetuities and, hence, any interest being conveyed subsequent in time, such as that to the church, will automatically violate the Rule. Like any other gift, a gift for charitable purposes is void for remoteness if it is contingent upon the happening of an event that may not occur within the perpetuities period. The only exception to this rule is that if there is a gift to a charity, followed by a gift over to another charity upon a possibly remote event, the gift over is valid. Remember, this is a charity-to-charity exception; the Rule Against Perpetuities still applies to dispositions over from an individual to a charity on a remote condition. In this case, there is a disposition over from an individual to a charity on a remote condition in violation of the Rule. (A) would be the correct answer if the Rule did not apply because the church's interest is contingent on the daughter having no grandchildren. (B) is incorrect because a vested remainder subject to total divestment arises when: (i) the remainderman is in existence and ascertained, (ii) its interest is not subject to any condition precedent, but (iii) its right to possession and enjoyment is subject to being defeated by the happening of some condition subsequent. The remainder here at all times remains subject to the condition precedent that the daughter have no grandchildren and therefore the remainder can never be vested. Furthermore, there is no condition subsequent that would ever divest the church of its interest once it acquired such interest. (C) is incorrect because without regard to the Rule, any interest that the church would ever take would not divest the daughter or her children of their life estates. Thus, its interest could not be described as an executory interest.

Answer to Question 30

(C) The buyer cannot compel the architect to resume performance. Contracts for personal services are not subject to specific performance notwithstanding the fact that damages might be inadequate or difficult to assess or the services to be performed are unique. The courts reason that specific performance of personal service contracts is tantamount to involuntary servitude and would present enforcement problems. At most, the buyer would be able to obtain an injunction to prevent the architect from working on another project at the times the architect agreed to work for the buyer. Thus, (C) is correct and (A) is incorrect. (B) is incorrect because it is irrelevant. Whether specific performance is available at all generally depends on whether the subject matter is unique, but even a contract for unique services cannot be enforced by specific performance. The fact that a party has begun performance is irrelevant. (D) is incorrect because duties involving personal skill and judgment may not be delegated absent consent by the obligee (the buyer). The architect did not have the buyer's consent, so there was no valid delegation.

Answer to Question 31

(C) The developer owns the land because a deed to a nonexistent person is void and conveys no title. Because the correspondent was dead when the deed was delivered, the deed passed nothing and was a nullity. Note that the developer will be required to return the $75,000 to the correspondent's estate to avoid unjust enrichment. (A) is wrong because title never passed from the developer. Furthermore, even if it had, it would not have passed even bare legal title to the attorney because she was not a grantee and the developer did not intend to pass title to her. (B) is wrong because the correspondent was killed before the contract was formed. Had he been alive at that time, the contract would have been valid and executory on his death. If a buyer dies after the contract for sale was entered into but before it has been completed, his heirs or devisees can demand a conveyance of the land at the closing. Because the correspondent was dead when the contract was entered into, however, the attorney's agency was no longer valid and there was no contract. (D) is wrong because the term "risk of loss" refers to risk of the property's being destroyed after the contract is signed but before closing. Here, the property was not destroyed. Moreover, there was no valid contract because the correspondent died before the contract was signed. Therefore, the risk of loss is irrelevant.

Answer to Question 32

(B) The testimony was properly admitted under the excited utterance exception to the hearsay rule. Statements made under the stress of some exciting event and relating to that event are admissible as an exception to the hearsay rule. (A) is incorrect because the Federal Rules require the maker of a dying declaration to be unavailable for the declaration to be admissible. (C) is incorrect; even though the statement bolsters the credibility of the plaintiff, it still qualifies as an exception to the hearsay rule and is admissible substantive evidence. (D) is incorrect because it is up to the broad discretion of the trial judge under Federal Rule 403 whether to exclude relevant evidence based on needless presentation of cumulative evidence. There is nothing to indicate that admission of the testimony constituted an abuse of discretion.

Answer to Question 33

(A) The party in (A) is the only one that clearly meets the "injury in fact" requirement for standing. The plaintiff should "have such a personal stake in the outcome of the controversy as to ensure the concrete adversariness that sharpens the presentation of issues." The business will be clearly injured if its customer is required to drastically reduce purchases to comply with the statute of the industrialized state. In addition, the fact that the proposed plaintiff is not a citizen of the industrialized state indicates the interstate impact of the state's legislation. (B) is incorrect because the corporation's sales are not large enough to fall within the ambit of the state statute, so no injury in fact has been suffered. (C) is incorrect because the general rule is that a plaintiff must have standing in his own right, he cannot assert the rights of another to obtain standing, and nothing here indicates that the governor has a concrete stake here. (D) is incorrect because the potential plaintiff's claim is far too tenuous. While the corporation whose bonds the potential plaintiff owns will be subject to the law, it is not likely that the potential plaintiff will suffer any injury because he has no interest in the corporation's profitability (a bondholder does not share in a corporation's profits, but is only entitled to repayment, and because the owner's bonds here are secured, his investment is protected no matter what happens to the corporation).

Answer to Question 34

(D) The pedestrian will win because the officer was not privileged to arrest him. For purposes of tort liability, a police officer is privileged to make an arrest without a warrant for a felony or for a breach of the peace committed in her presence, but not for a misdemeanor not involving a breach of the peace absent a statute providing otherwise. If the arrest is privileged, the officer may use only that degree of force necessary to effect the arrest, but never deadly force. Here, the pedestrian's offense of jaywalking was a misdemeanor that did not involve a breach of the peace, so the officer did not have a privilege of arrest and committed a battery by grabbing the pedestrian. (A) is incorrect because the fact that the pedestrian struck the officer after she came at him with a baton would not affect her liability for the initial battery. (B) is incorrect because an ordinary misdemeanor cannot be the basis of an arrest at common law even if it is committed in the presence of the officer; it must also constitute a breach of the peace. (C) is incorrect because it is irrelevant whether the pedestrian is guilty of jaywalking—the officer was not privileged to arrest him for it absent a statutory privilege of arrest broader than the common law privilege.

Answer to Question 35

(D) The decisive question in this case involves establishing causation in a strict products liability action. A cause of action based on strict liability for products requires: (i) absolute duty owed by a commercial supplier; (ii) production or sale of a defective product; (iii) actual and proximate cause; and (iv) damages for a prima facie case. (D) goes to the question of actual causation (*i.e.,* whether the defendant was the cause-in-fact of the plaintiff's injuries), which is an essential element in strict liability cases. The issue here is whether the court will apply an "enterprise liability" theory (which has been done in negligence cases). In these cases, courts use an alternative causes approach, which shifts the burden of proof to each of the several defendants to establish that its negligence was not the actual cause of the plaintiff's injury. (A) is incorrect because res ipsa loquitur, which allows the trier of fact to infer a breach of duty on the part of the defendant, is only applicable in negligence cases. (B) is incorrect because in strict liability cases the supplier can be held liable even if it was unaware of the harm the product could cause. (C) is incorrect because FDA approval would not affect the defendant's liability in a strict liability action. A product may comply with FDA regulations but still be defective under state products liability law.

Answer to Question 36

(C) The court should instruct the jury that the defendant is not liable for first degree murder if he did not form the intent to commit the crime of burglary, because a defense to the underlying felony precludes a conviction for felony murder. Voluntary intoxication is a defense to specific intent crimes, such as burglary, if it prevents the defendant from formulating the requisite intent. In the absence of the defendant's liability for burglary, he cannot be convicted of first degree murder based on the facts presented here. (A) is incorrect because voluntary intoxication may be a defense to first degree murder under the circumstances here. (B) is an incorrect statement of law; the intoxication must negate a specific intent for the underlying felony for it to serve as a defense.

(D) is incorrect; while premeditated murder is a specific intent crime for which voluntary intoxication may be a defense, nothing in the facts suggests that the charge is based on premeditation. Here, the first degree murder charge is based on commission of a burglary.

Answer to Question 37

(D) All of the officer's actions were lawful. A police officer has the authority to briefly detain a person for investigative purposes if he has a reasonable suspicion supported by articulable facts of criminal activity. Here, the officer watched the man engage in what reasonably appeared to be drug transactions and he was justified in stopping and detaining the man to investigate. Furthermore, if a police officer has a reasonable suspicion to believe that a detainee is armed and dangerous he may also conduct a frisk to ensure that the detainee has no weapons. Here, the man grew irate when he was stopped, and it was reasonable for the officer to briefly frisk him for weapons for both the officer's safety and for the safety of the students around him. (A) is incorrect. Police generally need not obtain a warrant before arresting a person in a public place, even if they have time to get a warrant. A police officer may arrest a person without a warrant when he has reasonable grounds to believe that a felony has been committed and that the person before him committed it. (B) is incorrect. If during an investigatory detention, the officer develops probable cause for arrest, the officer can proceed on that basis. Although the officer was incorrect in his initial suspicions of drug dealing, the illegal weapon he discovered during the patdown was sufficient to establish probable cause for the man's arrest. (C) is incorrect because, as stated above, an officer has a right to subject a detainee to a brief frisk for weapons to ensure his own safety.

Answer to Question 38

(B) The property power of Article IV, Section 3 of the federal Constitution is directly on point. The Property Clause contains no express limit on Congress's power to dispose of property owned by the United States. Such property includes all species, such as leasehold interests and electrical energy as well as ordinary realty and personalty. Disposal may include direct competition with private enterprise (such as grasslands) and has never been invalidated on that ground. (A) is incorrect because the General Welfare Clause allows Congress to spend for the general welfare, and here Congress is not spending, but disposing of property. (C) is not as good an answer as (B) because it is not direct. The Commerce Clause gives Congress the power to regulate interstate commerce, which encompasses any activity that either in itself or in combination with other activities has a substantial economic effect on, or effect on movement in, interstate commerce. When this power is combined with the Necessary and Proper Clause, it might allow Congress to regulate disposition of federal lands in a specified manner, but the property power is much more direct. (D) is incorrect because the Supremacy Clause merely states that federal law takes precedence over conflicting state law, but no state law is involved here. A private company is suing because the federal government is undercutting the company's price.

Answer to Question 39

(A) The annual is admissible as an adoptive admission of the defendants. Admissions of party opponents are nonhearsay under Federal Rule 801(d)(2) and are an exception to the hearsay rule under the common law. Furthermore, a party may expressly adopt someone else's statement as his own, thus giving rise to an "adoptive" admission. The defendants have done this by referring the plaintiff to the figures in the journal as accurate in their response to the interrogatory. The defendants are estopped, at trial, from denying their admissibility. (B) is incorrect because the journal does not clearly contain entries made in the ordinary course of business. (C) is incorrect because admissions of party opponents are nonhearsay under the Federal Rules. (D) is incorrect because party admissions waive the authentication requirement.

Answer to Question 40

(C) The agreement between the parties is a type of requirements contract that obligates the retail seller to buy from the manufacturer all of the red cheese that it will sell and obligates the manufacturer to supply the retail seller's needs up to the manufacturer's entire output. The retail seller does not have to buy any of the manufacturer's red cheese if it acts in good faith. Requirements contracts (a promise by the buyer to buy all of his requirements from the seller, who promises to sell that amount to the buyer) and output contracts (a promise by the seller to sell all of his output to the buyer, who agrees to buy that amount from the seller) are enforceable under section 2-306 of the Uniform Commercial Code. Consideration exists on both sides in these contracts. In a requirements contract, the buyer's consideration is the good faith operation of his business and the promise that he will only buy from the seller; the seller's consideration is the promise to sell at an agreed-upon per unit price whatever the buyer requires. In an output contract, the seller's consideration is the good faith operation of business and the promise to sell the goods only to the buyer, and the buyer's consideration is the promise to buy at an agreed-upon unit price whatever the seller produces. The agreement here is essentially a requirements contract that puts an upper limit on what the retail seller can require—the total output of the manufacturer—and also requires the manufacturer to sell its red cheese only to the retail seller. It is not an output contract because the retail seller is not required to buy all of the manufacturer's output even though it has retained the right to do so. Under the U.C.C., the buyer in a requirements contract is required to conduct his business in good faith and according to commercial standards of fair dealing in the trade so that his requirements will approximate a reasonably foreseeable figure. However, good faith variations from prior requirements are permitted even when the variation may be such as to result in discontinuance. Thus, a shutdown by a requirements buyer for lack of orders may be permissible if the buyer is acting in good faith. [U.C.C. §2-306, comment 2] In this case, then, (C) best states the obligations of the parties: the retail seller is not obligated to buy any red cheese from the manufacturer as long as it acts in good faith, but any red cheese it sells must come from the manufacturer.

Answer to Question 41

(D) The court should determine that title to the land is one-half in the heirs of the child, one-quarter in the heirs of the husband, and one-quarter in the heirs of the wife. The husband and the wife held the one-half interest in the land as joint tenants with right of survivorship. Thus, had one of them survived, he or she would own the entire one-half interest. The operation of the simultaneous death statute in the jurisdiction, which disposes of property as if each survived, results in their property being distributed as though they were tenants in common; *i.e.*, one-half of their interest passes through the husband's estate as though he survived and one-half of their interest passes through the wife's estate as though she survived. The child always held her one-half interest as a tenant in common, so her one-half interest clearly passes to her heirs without any need to resort to the simultaneous death statute. (A) is wrong because the farmer effectively conveyed his entire interest in the land to the wife, the husband, and the child, and the farmer is not the sole heir of the decedents. No consideration is required for a valid conveyance, and both deeds were properly delivered. Acceptance is presumed. (B) is wrong because it ignores the child's interest. The husband and wife never owned the whole of the land; therefore, they cannot pass the whole of the land to their respective heirs. (C) is wrong because it implies that the one-half interest was not effectively conveyed to the child. The delivery of the deed to the child's parent during the time that she was a minor is effective delivery. The fact that the deed was not recorded has no effect on its effectiveness.

Answer to Question 42

(B) The court should find the tax constitutional because it is nondiscriminatory. Nondiscriminatory, indirect taxes on the federal government or its property are permissible if they do not unreasonably burden the federal government. The tax here is a nondiscriminatory "doing business" tax directed at the gross receipts of ***all*** business conducted within the state, and there is no indication that the tax unreasonably burdens the transaction of business by the federal government. Hence, the fact that the corporation was acting as a federal contractor will not immunize it from liability for the tax. (A) is incorrect because it is too broad. A state's power over purely intrastate commercial transactions is subject to the Due Process Clause and, where the federal government is involved, such as here, the Supremacy Clause. However, the tax here does not violate the Supremacy Clause, as (C) states, because it is not targeted at, nor does it unreasonably burden, the federal government. (D) is incorrect because, even if interstate commerce is involved here, the three factors evaluated by a court in determining whether an undue burden exists (substantial nexus, fair apportionment, and fair relationship) do not appear to be lacking in this case.

Answer to Question 43

(A) The subpoena should be upheld because the information about hours billed is not within the privilege. There is no privilege regarding a communication that is relevant to an issue of breach of duty by the lawyer to his client or by the client to her lawyer. Thus, the billing data does not fall within the ambit of the privilege. (B) is incorrect because the information here is not covered by the privilege. Furthermore, if the privilege were applicable, the lawyer would be able to invoke the privilege on behalf of his clients. The lawyer's authority to do this is presumed in the absence of any evidence to the contrary. (C) is a correct statement of law, but the work product rule does not apply to these facts. Documents prepared by the lawyer for his own use ***in prosecuting his client's case*** are protected by this rule. Time records are not prepared for litigation purposes; they are not related to the substance of the client's case. (D) is incorrect because the other clients are protected by the blacking out of confidential information. Moreover, because the time records are not communications to or from the client and the identity of clients is often not considered to be within the privilege, the billing records of other clients may not be privileged and their consent may not have been necessary even without the deletions.

Answer to Question 44

(D) The grandchildren take nothing because the purported conveyance to them violates the Rule Against Perpetuities. Under the Rule Against Perpetuities, an interest in property is not valid unless it will vest, if at all, not later than 21 years after a life in being at the creation of the interest. The validity of interests under the Rule is determined at the time the interests are created, taking into account the facts then existing. The "lives in being plus 21 years" period begins to run, and the measuring lives used to show the validity of an interest must be in existence, at that time. The problem in this case is that there is an age contingency beyond age 21 in an open class. The perpetuities period begins to run on the date the landowner conveyed the property to his sister. After that date, the landowner's son could have additional children, shortly after which the lives in being (the son and the three older grandchildren) might all die. The additional children's interest would vest when they reach age 25, which is more than 21 years after lives in being. (A) is wrong because the interest violates the Rule Against Perpetuities. Except for the Rule, the grandchildren's interest would be classified as a contingent remainder. It is contingent because of the condition precedent of their reaching a certain age before taking an interest. (B) is wrong because, even if the Rule Against Perpetuities had not been violated, the grandchildren's interest would not have been vested because their taking was subject to a condition precedent. (C) is wrong because, even if the Rule Against Perpetuities had not been violated, the grandchildren's interest would be a remainder rather than an executory interest. Their interest follows a life estate and as a rule of thumb, remainders always follow life estates. An executory interest is an interest that divests the interest of another, and under these facts, the sister would not have been divested of her interest; she was entitled to retain the property for the remainder of her life.

Answer to Question 45

(A) The landowner will win because the builder's notice constituted an anticipatory repudiation, which can be treated as an immediate and total breach of contract. If a contract is executory on both sides and one party ***unequivocally*** notifies the other party that he will not perform when his duty is due, the nonrepudiating party has the option of treating the repudiation as an immediate and total breach and suing for damages. Although the repudiator can retract the repudiation, this must be done before the nonrepudiating party relies on the repudiation. Here, the contract was wholly executory (because neither party had performed) when the builder said that he would not perform at the agreed price. Because the builder's statement was unequivocal, it constitutes an anticipatory repudiation. Thus, the landowner was free to find someone to substitute for the builder. Because the landowner did find a substitute, he relied on the repudiation and so the builder's attempted revocation was invalid. (B) is incorrect because the difference in price between the builder's demand and the competing building company's price is irrelevant. Under the common law, the builder had a contractual duty to perform at the price he agreed to, and his statement that he would not do so constituted an anticipatory repudiation regardless of the price the builder was attempting to obtain. (C) is incorrect because the landowner had no duty to inform the builder of the contract with the competing building company. The repudiating party is the wrongful party in an anticipatory repudiation situation, and so the law does not impose a duty of notification on the nonrepudiator. If the repudiator suffers harm by his repudiation, it is his own fault. (D) is incorrect because, as stated above, a repudiator can revoke the repudiation only if the nonrepudiating party has not relied on the repudiation. Here, the landowner had relied (by hiring the competing building company). Thus, it is too late for the builder to revoke the repudiation.

Answer to Question 46

(D) The strongest argument against the constitutionality of providing the lunches is that state provision of free lunch to this segregated private school would violate the Equal Protection Clause by giving state support to a racially segregated educational process. The practice amounts to significant state involvement in these activities. Note that a party challenging the state involvement here would also have to show a discriminatory motive, because the distribution of lunch to all students living below poverty level is neutral on its face. (A) is incorrect because it is nonsensical. Providing lunch to hungry students serves a legitimate educational function; and even if it did not, there is no requirement that a state serve such a function in the exercise of its power to tax and spend. For example, denial by the Internal Revenue Service of tax-exempt status to racially discriminatory religious schools does not violate the Constitution because the governmental interest in ending racial discrimination outweighs the burden on these religious schools. (B) is incorrect because a state may aid anyone as long as its acts are not constitutionally prohibited. (C) is incorrect because the Constitution does not forbid any private bias; it only forbids discriminatory state action. To the extent that private discrimination is forbidden under various federal civil rights acts, the source of the prohibition is legislative, not constitutional.

Answer to Question 47

(A) A condition subsequent is one the occurrence of which cuts off an already existing duty of performance. The ***form*** of the condition requiring removal of the pool is that of a condition subsequent because, under the language of the contract, failure to do so will cut off the buyers' duty to pay the $5,000. A condition precedent is one that must occur before an absolute duty of immediate performance arises in the other party. The ***substance*** of the pool removal provision is that of a condition precedent because no duty to pay $5,000 arises until ***after*** the sellers have removed the pool. (B) and (C) are wrong because the buyers are not under a duty to pay the $5,000 before the sellers are required to remove the pool. (D) is wrong because removal of the pool is a condition precedent to the buyers' duty to pay the $5,000.

Answer to Question 48

(A) The company probably will be vicariously liable to the pedestrian because the electrician's deviation did not take him outside the scope of the employment relationship. Under the doctrine of respondeat superior, an employer will be vicariously liable for tortious acts committed by its employee if the tortious acts occur within the scope of the employment relationship. What the scope of employment is in a particular case is a question of fact determined by factors such as the specific authorization by the employer, the employee's motivation, and the normal routines of the employee. Ordinarily, an employee heading home after work is no longer within the scope of employment. Here, however, the electrician was required to be "on call" 24 hours a day, and was required to drive the company van to his home so he would be ready to provide emergency service whenever a call would come in. Most likely, then, the electrician was still within the scope of his employment when he was driving the van home. The next issue is whether his deviation from his route home took him outside the scope of his employment. Most courts today consider the foreseeability of the deviation to be the most important factor in determining whether the employee was still within the scope of employment or was on a "frolic" of his own. Thus, minor deviations in time and geographic area from the employer's business are still within the scope of employment because they are foreseeable. Here, the electrician's deviation of a few blocks from his normal route home to pick up some groceries was not a substantial enough departure from his employment purposes so as to be unforeseeable, and therefore the company can be held vicariously liable for the electrician's negligence. (B) is incorrect because the pedestrian can recover even without showing that the company knew of the electrician's potential for negligence. While that might make the company independently liable for its own negligence in allowing the electrician to drive a company van, the company is vicariously liable even without the assumption stated in (B). (C) is incorrect because, as discussed above, a minor deviation of a few blocks is not considered a "frolic" by most courts unless it is unforeseeable. (D) is incorrect even though it is a true statement as a general rule. While an employee traveling to and from work ordinarily is not acting within the scope of his employment, the electrician was "on call" for his employer under the facts in this question even while he was driving home from work.

Answer to Question 49

(C) The best defense that the defendant's testimony offers is insanity. Under the *M'Naghten* test for insanity, a defendant must show that (i) a disease of the mind (ii) caused a defect of reason (iii) such that the defendant lacked the ability at the time of his actions to either know the wrongfulness of his actions or understand the nature and quality of his actions. Under the A.L.I./Model Penal Code test for insanity, the defendant is entitled to acquittal if the proof shows that he suffered from a mental disease or defect and as a result lacked substantial capacity to either: (i) appreciate the criminality (wrongfulness) of his conduct; or (ii) conform his conduct to the requirements of law. In the instant case, the defendant believed that his wife was out to destroy the world, which would (to a mentally unbalanced person) make her killing justified. Given that the defendant believed his actions to be justified, this defendant thus would not have the ability to know the wrongfulness of his actions (under the *M'Naghten* test) or to appreciate the wrongfulness of his conduct (under the A.L.I./Model Penal Code test). His hospitalizations indicate a mental disease exists. (A) is incorrect because the defendant intended to kill his wife; hence, the mens rea required for homicide, malice aforethought, is satisfied. (B) is incorrect because the defendant performed the act that killed his wife. (D) is incorrect because the defendant's belief was not a reasonable one.

Answer to Question 50

(B) The dean will lose because the provost can raise consent as a complete defense to her libel action. A defamation action at common law required the plaintiff to prove (i) defamatory language on the defendant's part that is (ii) "of or concerning" the plaintiff, (iii) publication of the defamatory language to a third person, and (iv) damage to the reputation of the plaintiff. (Because the defamation here does not refer to a public figure or likely involve a matter of public concern, the elements of falsity and fault do not need to be proved.) In this case, the provost uttered a statement to a third person, the lawyer, that linked the dean to the purchase of drugs; this satisfies the first three elements of the prima facie case. Because the statement was libel (uttered in a writing), general damages will be presumed by law; the dean does not need to show actual damages from the statement. Hence, the dean can establish a prima facie case for libel against the provost. As with all torts, however, consent, whether express or implied, is a complete defense to a defamation action. Implied consent includes apparent consent, which is consent that a reasonable person would infer from the plaintiff's conduct. Here, it was reasonable for the provost to infer that the dean's dispatch of her lawyer to request the reasons for her dismissal included a consent for the provost to make defamatory statements to the lawyer as long as they related to the reasons for the dean's dismissal. Thus, the dean impliedly consented to the statement in the letter and will not prevail in her suit against the provost. (A) is incorrect because the fact that the provost did not originate the statement does not provide a defense. One who repeats a defamatory statement will be held liable on the same general basis as the primary publisher even though the repeater states the source or makes it clear that he does not believe the defamation. (C) is incorrect even though the provost should have verified the statement before repeating it. His defense is that the dean impliedly consented to the statement rather than that he did not originate the statement. (D) is incorrect because whether the dean was buying drugs only affects whether the provost can also raise the defense of truth in this defamation action. The provost will win by raising the defense of consent; the fact that the dean was not buying drugs does not change this result.

Answer to Question 51

(D) The dealer will prevail because there is no evidence that it should have discovered the defect. To prove breach of duty in a products liability action based on negligence, the plaintiff must show (i) negligent conduct by the defendant leading to (ii) the supplying of a defective product by the defendant. However, a dealer who buys from a reputable manufacturer with no reason to anticipate that the product is dangerous need make only a cursory inspection of the goods to avoid liability for manufacturing defects. Here, there is no evidence that the dealer should have known that the wheel was defective; hence the dealer will likely prevail. (A) is incorrect because merely selling the lawn mower with an unreasonably dangerous defect, without knowing or being expected to know of the defect, will not subject the dealer to liability for negligence. The statement in (A) is more appropriate in an action based on strict liability. (B) is incorrect because the use of res ipsa loquitur suggested by that choice would be directed at the manufacturer rather than the dealer, and the dealer is not liable for the manufacturer's negligence. (C) is incorrect because the negligent failure of an intermediary to discover a defect is not a superseding cause. If the dealer were otherwise liable, the negligent failure of the homeowner to discover the defect in the wheel would not cut off the dealer's liability.

Answer to Question 52

(B) Application of the statute to the hunter is constitutional. Where a statutory classification is challenged as violating the Equal Protection Clause, one of three tests is used. If the classification relates to exercise of a fundamental right or is based on a suspect trait, a compelling state interest must justify the classification. If a quasi-suspect classification is involved (*i.e.,* one based on gender or legitimacy), the law will be upheld if it is substantially related to an important government interest. In other cases, the classification is valid if there is a rational basis for the classification. This rational basis test is used for classifications that relate to matters of economics or social welfare. The state statute does not infringe on a fundamental right, nor is it based on a suspect or quasi-suspect trait. Thus, it is judged under the rational basis test. (C) is incorrect because the compelling state interest test is inapplicable here. (A) is incorrect because the existence of a protected property interest is a consideration more appropriate to a due process argument than to one based on equal protection. (D) is incorrect because, although interstate travel is a fundamental right subject to the compelling state interest test, not every restriction on the right to cross state lines is an impairment of the right to travel. Prohibiting possession of snipe traps would not penalize or unduly burden the right of interstate travel.

Answer to Question 53

(D) The federal rule does not preempt the state statute. A valid federal statute or regulation may expressly or impliedly occupy the entire field regulated, so as to preclude even nonconflicting state or local regulation of the same general subject. Here, the federal rule relates to the subject of consumer product safety, while the state statute relates to traffic safety. Thus, even if the federal rule is deemed to occupy the entire field that it regulates, that field differs from the field to which the state statute relates. Consequently, there is no preemption. It follows that (A) is incorrect. (B) is incorrect because the mere absence of affirmative authorization for continued state regulation does not establish preemption. (C) is simply an incorrect statement of the law; it is much too broad.

Answer to Question 54

(B) This videotape, after being properly authenticated, would be considered to be real evidence going to show the intoxicated state of the defendant shortly after he was driving. It would be admitted as relevant because its value would not be substantially outweighed by undue prejudice. (A) is wrong because the videotape is not being offered to prove the truth of any statements that the defendant made; it is offered to prove only that he was intoxicated. Thus, there is no statement being made that would constitute an admission. (C) is wrong because the defendant is not being asked to give any testimony. Rather, the matter in question is the introduction of real proof. (D) is wrong because a videotape of the defendant at the time in question has nothing to do with specific instances of conduct, which have to do with past actions of the defendant.

Answer to Question 55

(C) The seller of land is obligated to deliver a title that is free from reasonable doubt either in fact or law. This does not require a perfect title, but rather one that is free from questions that might present an unreasonable risk of litigation. Title is marketable if a reasonably prudent buyer would accept it in the exercise of ordinary prudence. An inability to establish a record chain of title will generally render the title unmarketable. If the seller attempts to rely on adverse possession to show that defects have been cleared, courts traditionally do not favor such an argument, because proof of adverse possession normally rests on oral evidence, which might not be available to the buyer at a later time. Here, although the rancher may have acquired title by adverse possession, the developer should not be faced with the prospect of having to prove this in court in the future. Thus, (A) is incorrect. (If the rancher had written proof or a quiet title judgment, title would be marketable.) (D) is incorrect because it does not appear that the rancher's conduct amounted to fraud. (B) is nonsensical.

Answer to Question 56

(D) The buyer takes subject to the bank's mortgage. A foreclosure sale wipes out all junior mortgages (those that came later in time than the mortgage that was foreclosed) but does not wipe out senior mortgages (those that came earlier). Because the bank's mortgage preceded the finance company's, it is senior and is not wiped out. The buyer takes subject to this mortgage. Thus, (B) is wrong. Although the buyer is not personally liable on this debt (he did not sign the note, the historian did), he must pay the mortgage or face foreclosure by the bank. Because the savings and loan association's mortgage came later than the finance company's, it is junior and is wiped out. Thus, (A) and (C) are wrong. If, after paying the cost of the foreclosure and paying off the finance company's mortgage, there is money left over from the sale, it will first go to paying off the savings and loan association's mortgage. But regardless of whether the savings and loan association is paid off or not, the buyer takes completely free of this obligation.

Answer to Question 57

(C) The least correct statement refers to a condition subsequent because a condition subsequent is one the occurrence of which cuts off an already existing absolute duty of performance. The sister's tendering of good title would not cut off the brother's duty to perform. (A) and (B) are wrong because they are not inaccurate statements. A condition precedent is one that must occur before an absolute duty of immediate performance arises in the other party. When conditions are concurrent as they are here (as discussed below), it can be said that each condition is a condition precedent to the other. (D) is wrong because conditions concurrent are those that are capable of occurring together (which describes the brother and sister's relationship regarding the exchange of the farm and the apartment house) and the parties are bound to perform at the same time. In effect, each is a condition precedent to the other.

Answer to Question 58

(C) If it can be shown that there is neither a religious purpose nor an effect on religion, and that there is not excessive entanglement between government and religion, then the government is not involved in an establishment of religion. The fact that private sectarian schools fulfill an important function (A) would not justify a violation of the Establishment Clause. That religious instruction in private schools is not objectionable (B) is true—but the issue here is whether the government is involved in the establishment of religion, not whether what is being taught is objectionable or unobjectionable. The Free Exercise Clause (D) does not require identical treatment of public and private schools and, furthermore, the relevant issue here involves the Establishment Clause, not the Free Exercise Clause.

Answer to Question 59

(C) A land occupier has an affirmative duty to warn or protect children against dangerous artificial conditions on the land. Thus, the best answer to the question is what the company should have done to best protect the children in this factual situation. (B) is thus easily eliminated, because it has nothing to do with this particular issue; regardless of the neighborhood, the company was aware that children played among the buses. (A) is not the best answer because the company must do what is necessary to protect the children, consistent with the business it is operating on the premises. This answer only goes to one narrow possibility of injury. There are many other ways the children could have been injured playing with these abandoned and wrecked buses. Due care could also have required installation of a higher fence or more diligent patrol of the yard. (D) is also not the best answer because the maintenance of the fence is not in issue; the facts indicate that the children were able to climb the fence without a problem. Hence, (C) is the best answer because it states a breach of duty in the broadest terms. The child would be best able to show a breach of duty by proving that the company could have taken precautionary steps to prevent any injury to children who were tempted to come onto the premises.

Answer to Question 60

(B) The record should be admitted because its direct relevance to the ultimate issue of the case outweighs the danger of prejudice against the defendant. (A) is wrong because evidence of this prior conviction would not be admissible as character evidence against the defendant. (C) is wrong because the process leading to the conviction is irrelevant. (D) is wrong because an exception to the hearsay rule applies. Federal Rule 803(22) provides that judgments of felony convictions are admissible in both criminal and civil actions to prove any fact essential to the judgment. Felony convictions are those for which the ***potential*** punishment is imprisonment in excess of one year; hence, the hearsay exception applies here.

Answer to Question 61

(B) The defendant will not be guilty of burglary because he did not have the intent to commit a felony at the time he entered the bookie's house. At common law, the elements of burglary are (i) a breaking (ii) and entry (iii) of a dwelling (iv) of another (v) at nighttime (vi) with the intent of committing a felony therein. Here, the defendant entered the bookie's house with the intent only to obtain repayment of a debt, which does not satisfy the intent required for larceny. Given that the defendant believed he was entitled to take the money as repayment of the debt, he did not intend to permanently deprive the bookie of his property. The fact that he later decided to steal the painting will not establish the requisite intent; it must exist at the time of the breaking and entering. Thus, both (C) and (D) are wrong. (A) is wrong because, although actual breaking requires some use of force to gain entry, minimal force is sufficient, as when the burglar opens an unlocked window.

Answer to Question 62

(D) The defendant's objection should be overruled because the opportunity for immediate cross-examination protects the defendant's rights. Federal Rule 705 provides that a hypothetical question need not be asked. Examining counsel may ask the expert for an opinion and then immediately allow the opposing side to cross-examine, without any disclosure of the data underlying the opinion (unless the trial court requires advance disclosure). It follows that (B) is incorrect. (A) is incorrect because the Federal Rules repudiate the ultimate issue limitation. (C) is simply an incorrect statement of the law—no presumption is created by the qualification of an expert.

Answer to Question 63

(C) The landlord, as the beneficiary of the nonassignment clause, could have taken positive action to avoid the transfer, but by accepting rent from the friend, he waived his right to avoid the transfer. The brother has no such right to contest the transfer because he was not the beneficiary of the nonassignment clause. (A) is wrong because one co-tenant generally does not need the consent of other co-tenants to assign her interest. Only the landlord's consent was necessary under the lease clause. Because the landlord waived his right to avoid the transfer, the transfer became valid. (B) is wrong because the right to enforce this lease provision was waived by the landlord. (D) is wrong because nonassignment clauses in leases are valid. They are not considered to be void restraints on alienation.

Answer to Question 64

(D) The judge should overrule the objection because lay opinion is permissible (and often essential) to identify handwriting. A foundation must first be laid to establish familiarity with the handwriting. (A) is wrong because expert testimony is not necessary to identify handwriting. (B) is wrong because only a proper foundation is required for the admission of testimony identifying handwriting. The fact that there are other individuals who may be more familiar with or in more recent contact with the handwriting does not, of itself, preclude admissibility of the teacher's testimony. The fact that the teacher has not seen the singer's handwriting for 10 years goes to the credibility of her testimony but not to its admissibility. (C) is wrong because expert testimony is not required for handwriting identification and, therefore, the witness need not be qualified as an expert.

Answer to Question 65

(A) The woman will prevail on a theory of intentional infliction of emotional distress. To establish liability for intentional infliction of emotional distress, the defendants must have intended to cause severe emotional distress (*i.e.,* either acted with the goal of bringing about such distress or knew with substantial certainty that such distress would result from their conduct). It is also sufficient if the defendants acted recklessly, *i.e.,* in deliberate disregard of a high probability that their conduct would cause emotional distress. Here, the man's parents caused the woman to spend four years not knowing where her young son was. The man's parents acted in deliberate disregard of the high probability that a mother would be severely distressed by being kept from her child, not knowing whether he was safe or even alive. (A) correctly states the requisite intent for this tort. (B) is not as good a choice as (A) because their support was not what makes them liable to the woman for this tort; rather, it was their lies as to her child's whereabouts and failure to let the woman know anything about how her child was doing that constituted the extreme and outrageous conduct here. (C) is incorrect because it is not necessary to prove physical injuries to recover for intentional infliction of emotional distress. (D) is incorrect because the "zone of danger" is more appropriately used in determining liability for ***negligent*** infliction of emotional distress. Here, the woman has a cause of action for intentional infliction of emotional distress.

Answer to Question 66

(D) The government will most likely prevail because the lawyer had no judicial discretion or powers in his position. Under Article III of the Constitution, a federal judge is protected from termination of tenure during good behavior. This necessarily requires that a person who seeks protection under this provision be able to show that he is a federal "judge." From the facts, the lawyer was clearly no more than an administrative hearing officer, without discretion or power. Thus, he would not be a judge within the meaning of this article, and its provisions would not apply to him. Therefore (B) is wrong. (A) is wrong because anybody can recommend that Congress enact or repeal a statute. Just because an executive branch's commission does so does not mean that there is a violation of the separation of powers doctrine. (C) is factually incorrect and does not explain the proper reason for the result.

Answer to Question 67

(B) The loyalty oath is valid if it merely requires the candidate to affirm that she will oppose the violent overthrow of the government. The government may require employees and other public officers to take a loyalty oath. Such an oath must not be overbroad, so as to prohibit constitutionally protected activities, nor can it be vague. An oath has been upheld that requires state employees to oppose the overthrow of the government by force, violence, or by an illegal or unconstitutional method. [Cole v. Richardson (1972)] This type of oath (which is virtually the same as that set forth in (B)) was deemed to be similar to an oath requiring the taker simply to commit herself to live by the constitutional processes of our system. (D) is incorrect because, as noted above, a requirement for a loyalty oath as a condition of holding public office or employment is valid, as long as the oath is within constitutionally acceptable limits. (A) is incorrect because it has been held that a loyalty oath that disavows ***advocating*** the violent overthrow of the government as an abstract doctrine is invalid. The First Amendment prohibits statutes regulating advocacy that are not limited to advocacy of action. [Communist Party v. Whitcomb (1974)] The oath in (A) appears to be overbroad in that it regulates mere advocacy of violent overthrow of the government, rather than regulating only advocacy of action. Therefore, the oath is invalid. (C) is incorrect because only knowing membership in an organization with specific intent to further unlawful aims is unprotected by the First Amendment. [Keyishian v. Board of Regents (1967)] The oath in (C) would in effect punish mere membership in an organization, without showing knowledge of, or a specific intent to further, any unlawful aims of the organization.

Answer to Question 68

(C) The reporter and the paper should prevail. The Constitution prohibits Congress or the states from abridging freedom of the press. While this freedom is no greater than the freedom of speech granted to all citizens, the information printed by the paper here is protected. The media may not be punished for publishing a true fact once it is lawfully obtained from the public records or is otherwise released to the public. It does not matter that the release was inadvertent. Therefore, (C) is correct and (B) is incorrect. [*See* The Florida Star v. B.J.F. (1989)] (A) is partially true—a state might have a compelling interest in protecting the privacy of its citizens—but the state generally cannot protect the interest by prohibiting publication of public information; the most that the state may do is keep such records sealed. (D) is incorrect because it is too broad; freedom of the press is not absolute. For example, the press would not be allowed to reprint copyrighted material regardless of whether it was legally obtained.

Answer to Question 69

(D) An offer must be accepted within a reasonable time. The inventor's reply letter constituted an offer to sell 24 choppers for $39.99. The shop owner accepted this offer by a memo plus full performance. If this occurred within a reasonable time, a contract was formed. (A) is incorrect because contracts may be formed by nonmerchants. (B) is incorrect because the contract would have already been formed by the shop owner's acceptance; it is irrelevant whether the inventor has enough stock on hand. (C) is incorrect because the inventor's offer called for prompt acceptance and so did not constitute a firm offer, which must be kept open for a reasonable time, not to exceed three months.

Answer to Question 70

(C) If the man's original reply was not an offer, then the entrepreneur's sending the check and memo would have been an offer and the man's shipment of the hot sauce would have been an acceptance. The acceptance would have included terms altering the offer (the no resale provision), but under the U.C.C., between merchants such terms generally become part of the contract. Thus, the entrepreneur could be held liable for breaching the no resale provision. (A) is wrong because under Article 2, the status of the man does not change the result. (B) is wrong because if the invoice by the man was a material alteration, the man would not prevail. (D) is wrong because the phrase "not available in stores" is not sufficient to restrict subsequent resale. It merely indicates that the hot sauce was not currently available in stores.

Answer to Question 71

(B) The woman's best defense is that the statute was not reasonably available because she did not receive the explanatory booklet. Generally, it is not a defense to a crime that the accused was unaware that her acts were prohibited by the criminal law or that she mistakenly believed that her acts were not prohibited. However, the accused has a defense if the statute proscribing her conduct was not published or made reasonably available prior to the conduct. The statute under which the woman is charged was presumably published prior to her filing her income tax return. However, the statute was exceedingly complicated, as were the computation schedules and other information accompanying the tax forms. Consequently, the failure of the state to include the explanatory booklet with the tax forms may amount to a situation in which the pertinent statute was not made reasonably available to the woman prior to filing her return. If this is the case, then the woman will have a defense. (C) is incorrect. At common law, it was no defense that the defendant relied on an official interpretation of the law by the public officer or body responsible for its interpretation or administration. Under modern law, it is a defense if the defendant relies upon an erroneous official statement of the law by one charged by law with responsibility for the interpretation, administration, or enforcement of the law. However, even under this rule the woman would not have a strong defense because the intern, who was working at the revenue department part-time, is not the type of public officer charged by law with responsibility for interpreting or enforcing the statute, on whose advice the woman would be entitled to rely. (D) is incorrect because generally it is no defense that a defendant simply relied on the erroneous advice of counsel. An emerging trend provides that if reasonable reliance on the advice of counsel negates the necessary state of mind for the crime, such reliance may be a defense. However, (D) focuses on the woman's reliance on her attorney's advice rather than her lack of intent, so (B) is the better answer. (A) is incorrect because the woman's mistake as to the scope of the law does not negate the required state of mind. If the mental state for a crime requires a certain belief concerning a collateral aspect of law, ignorance or mistake as to that aspect of law will negate the requisite state of mind. Such a situation involves ignorance of some aspect of the ***elements*** of the crime rather than the ***existence*** of the statute making the act criminal. The statute here simply penalizes one who knowingly fails to declare monies received that fall within the statute. The woman knew that she was not declaring certain money that she received; her ignorance that the law applied to those funds does not negate her state of mind and is not a defense.

Answer to Question 72

(A) It is not relevant in a contributory negligence jurisdiction that the plaintiff's negligence was greater than the defendant's. Any negligence on the part of the plaintiff will prevent his recovery, unless one of the factors discussed below is applicable. (B) is not the best answer because it is relevant to the plaintiff's recovery. If the defendant had the last clear chance to avoid injuring the plaintiff, the plaintiff will prevail because the doctrine of last clear chance overcomes the plaintiff's contributory negligence. (C) is incorrect. It is relevant to the plaintiff's claim that the defendant's conduct was willful and wanton, because the plaintiff's contributory negligence is no defense to willful and wanton behavior. (D) is incorrect because the first step for the plaintiff to recover is to establish that the defendant acted negligently, thereby breaching his duty of care.

Answer to Question 73

(B) A state may require that those enrolled to vote be bona fide residents of the community. However, any law regulating the right of persons over age 18 to vote must be narrowly tailored to promote a compelling interest. (A) is incorrect because a state ***does*** have a compelling interest in the integrity of the voting process that will support narrowly tailored restrictions. (C) is incorrect because whether persons have attained the age of majority has nothing to do with their status as bona fide residents. (D) is incorrect because there does not appear to be any discriminatory effect on interstate commerce. (B) is correct because it is the only answer that recognizes that the state may limit ballot access to actual residents, albeit with safeguards against over-inclusiveness; *e.g.*, the state should provide means by which the students can show that they are bona fide residents.

Answer to Question 74

(C) The son is entitled to the proceeds of the sale because, under the doctrine of equitable conversion, a deceased seller's interest generally passes as personal property. If the seller dies, "bare" legal title passes to the takers of his real property, but they must give up the title to the buyer when the contract closes. When the purchase price is paid, the money passes as personal property to those who take the seller's personal property (unless the seller ***specifically*** devises the land in question to a devisee). Thus, the son, as the personal property devisee, is entitled to the proceeds of the sale and (D) is incorrect. (A) is incorrect as a matter of law. A real estate contract survives the death of either party unless the agreement itself provides otherwise. (B) is incorrect because marketable title is title reasonably free from doubt. Generally, this involves either defects in the chain of title or encumbrances that might present an unreasonable risk of litigation. Such problems are not present in these facts.

Answer to Question 75

(A) The niece may specifically enforce the agreement. Under the doctrine of equitable conversion, if the buyer dies, the takers of her real property can demand a conveyance of the land at the closing of the contract. (B) is wrong because the death of either the seller or the buyer does not render the agreement cancellable at the will of either party. (C) is wrong because a real estate contract survives the death of either party unless the agreement itself provides otherwise. (D) is wrong because marketable title is title reasonably free from doubt. Generally, this involves either defects in the chain of title or encumbrances that might present an unreasonable risk of litigation. Such problems are not present in these facts.

Answer to Question 76

(D) The remark was invited by cross-examination. By process of elimination: (A) is not the best answer because it cannot be determined whether the eyewitness was under the influence of the exciting event when he spoke to the police, and there are multiple levels of hearsay involved. (B) suffers from the same defects. (C) is wrong because inability to cure an error by jury instruction is not a valid reason for denying a motion to strike. Therefore, (D) must be the best answer—because the defendant's counsel asked how the witness knew a certain fact, the specific response to counsel's question might be admitted as precisely what counsel asked for.

Answer to Question 77

(A) The messenger will prevail. In a strict liability action, the plaintiff must prove that a product was so defective that it is unreasonably dangerous. The defect causing the harm must have existed when the product left the defendant's control. The defendant must be a commercial supplier of the product in question. Brake failure on a bicycle is an unreasonably dangerous defect. If this defect existed when the bicycle left the factory of the manufacturer, then the messenger has a viable cause of action sounding in strict liability against the retail dealer, a supplier in the distributive chain. Thus, (A) is correct. (B) is wrong because it implies ***absolute*** liability, not ***strict*** liability; *i.e.,* the retail dealer is not liable simply because the brakes failed. It must be established that the brakes were defective when placed in commerce. (C) is wrong because, in jurisdictions retaining traditional contributory negligence rules, ordinary contributory negligence does not bar recovery in strict liability cases where the plaintiff fails to discover the defect or to take steps to guard against its existence. (D) is wrong because a careful inspection would be relevant to a negligence action, but not to one based on strict liability.

Answer to Question 78

(C) The court should deny the motion because the sunbather can rely on res ipsa loquitur to get the case to the jury. To prevail on a negligence claim, the sunbather must show negligent conduct by the manufacturer, leading to the supplying of a dangerously defective product by the company. The failure to exercise reasonable care, which is the critical distinction between a products liability action based on negligence and one based on strict liability, can be established by res ipsa loquitur in a case such as this, because the steering defect at the manufacturing stage would not usually occur without some negligence on the part of the manufacturer. Hence, (C) is correct and (A) is wrong. (B) is wrong because any negligence on the part of the owner is reasonably foreseeable and will not relieve the manufacturer of the consequences of its negligence. (D) is wrong because simply placing a defective boat into the stream of commerce would present grounds for a strict liability action, but not one for negligence. Some negligence must be shown.

Answer to Question 79

(D) The hiker will most likely be found not guilty if the jury believes the hiker's claim. Although the statute does not clearly indicate what state of mind is required, the statute appears to be a larceny-type offense. Larceny requires a specific intent to steal. Therefore, if the hiker honestly believed that the sign was abandoned property, he did not have the intent to steal and so will be found not guilty. (A) and (B) are wrong because a statute that closely resembles a traditional common law offense requiring mens rea is seldom held to be a strict liability offense; rather, it is interpreted to require the mens rea of the common law crime. (C) is wrong because, even if the hiker's belief was not reasonable, the hiker would not be guilty if he honestly believed that the sign had been abandoned. A mistake of fact need not be reasonable when offered as a defense to a specific intent crime.

Answer to Question 80

(C) The officer's testimony is hearsay because it relates to a statement made by the driver, while not testifying at the trial, and it is offered in evidence to prove the truth of the matter asserted; *i.e.,* that the blue convertible was involved in the hit-and-run accident. (B) is incorrect because the fact that the driver's statement came 10 minutes after the accident probably indicates that the statement was not made close enough to the time of receipt of the sense impression to qualify for the present sense impression exception. (A) is incorrect because there is no "recent perception" exception to the hearsay rule. (D) is incorrect because the evidence is very probative and would not be excluded as prejudicial simply because its receipt in evidence would disadvantage the defendant.

Answer to Question 81

(D) The distributor is not an intended beneficiary of the contract between the investor and the winery. Although the distributor was mentioned in the contract, it seems clear that the investor and the winery did not intend to confer any benefits or rights on the distributor. Rather, the parties seem to have been simply expressing a preference as to the distributor of the wine, with no indication that the validity of the contract depended on use of the distributor. (A) is incorrect because the winery was contractually bound to perform only with regard to the investor, rather than to the distributor. (B) is incorrect because the investor and the winery could not foresee that the distributor would act in reliance on a contract that conferred no rights on him. (C) is incorrect because an express agreement between the investor and the winery would not have been necessary to a determination that the distributor had some rights under the contract. For example, if the distributor stood in such a relationship to the investor that one could infer that the investor wished to make an agreement for his benefit, then it would be more likely that the contract was primarily for the benefit of the distributor. (D) is the best answer because the key factor is that the investor and the winery were simply protecting their own interests, with no thought of conferring a benefit on the distributor.

Answer to Question 82

(C) The only theory under which the bank can recover the investor's share of the profits is that the bank is an assignee of the investor's rights. (D) would not provide a strong defense for the inventor, because it is clear that the bank was not an intended beneficiary of the investor-inventor contract. (A) is incorrect because there is no presumption that an assignment is invalid absent express authorization in the contract. (B) is incorrect because, even if the investor and the inventor are partners, the investor would still be able to assign his rights to profits. (C) is the best answer, because the bank's only hope of prevailing is for it to be considered an assignee of the investor's rights. It appears that the written instrument executed by the investor lacks the present words of assignment necessary to manifest the intent of the assignor to transfer his rights under the contract completely and immediately to the assignee. The instrument merely allows the bank to collect the debt from the investor's share of the profits. Thus, the inventor has a fairly strong argument that the bank is not an assignee of the investor's rights under the investor-inventor contract.

Answer to Question 83

(A) The restaurant chain is likely to prevail. A contractual duty may not be delegated if performance by the delegate will materially change the obligee's expectancy under the contract. Here, substitution of the agricultural corporation, a company with no experience in the tomato growing business, for the ketchup manufacturer, an established entity in the business, greatly decreases the probable success of the supply of organic ketchup for which the restaurant chain, the obligee, contracted. Thus, a court should rule that the attempted delegation by the ketchup manufacturer of its duty to grow organic tomatoes for the venture is invalid. It follows that (C) is incorrect. (B) is incorrect because a delegation can be effective absent a contractual provision authorizing the same. (D) is incorrect because, although the ketchup manufacturer certainly must delegate duties to its individual employees, here it is attempting to delegate duties to an entirely different company, one with no experience or reputation in the industry.

Answer to Question 84

(A) In defamation actions involving a private person plaintiff and a defamatory statement relating to a matter of public concern, the plaintiff must show that the defendant acted, if not with malice, then at least negligently as to truth or falsity. This principle applies where the defamatory potential of the statement was apparent. Here, the bar owner is a private person plaintiff. His application for transfer of a liquor license, as the subject of a public hearing held by a governmental entity, is a matter of public concern, particularly if the bar owner potentially has underworld connections. The defamatory potential of the woman's accusations of the bar owner's underworld connections is apparent. Therefore, the woman must have, at the very least, been negligent as to truth or falsity for the bar owner to recover; *i.e.,* no strict liability. If the woman's belief in the truth of the rumors was reasonable, as stated by (A), she would not be liable. (B) is incorrect because the bar owner's reputation could have been damaged even though his application was granted. (C) is incorrect because it implies liability without fault, simply because a false statement was made. (D) is incorrect because, even if the woman's appearance was voluntary, there still must be a showing of fault.

Answer to Question 85

(C) The sister will prevail in a quiet title action brought by the brother because there is no evidence that he has performed sufficient acts to constitute her ouster. Actual possession of property held in concurrent ownership by one concurrent owner for the statutory adverse possession period will not be sufficient to give that possessor title to the whole estate to the exclusion of his co-tenant, unless there has been an ouster. Here, the brother occupied the home under unity of possession with the sister. Thus, his possession is not adverse to that of the sister, and (A) is incorrect. (B) is incorrect because the facts do not indicate that the sister intended to renounce her rights in the property. (D) is incorrect because, had the brother ousted the sister prior to possessing the land for the required period, he could claim title to the home because his possession would have been adverse.

Answer to Question 86

(A) The choice to testify will be the wife's. In federal court, one spouse may testify against the other in a criminal case, with or without the consent of the party-spouse. Thus, the witness-spouse may not be compelled to testify, but neither may she be foreclosed from testifying (except as to a confidential communication made between the spouses while they were husband and wife). Here, the wife is being asked to testify about a meeting in which her husband participated that took place before her marriage to him. Thus, the privilege for confidential marital communications is inapplicable, making (C) incorrect. Of (A), (B), and (D), only (A) reflects the fact that the wife may not be compelled to testify, nor may she be foreclosed from testifying.

Answer to Question 87

(C) The motion to dismiss should be denied. For purposes of the Double Jeopardy Clause, two crimes do not constitute the "same offense" if each crime requires proof of an additional element that the other crime does not require, even though some of the same facts may be necessary to prove both crimes. Here, even though the same facts are involved for both crimes, the robbery charge requires proof of a taking by force but not a death, while the murder charge requires proof of a death but not of a taking of property. Thus, (C) is correct and (A) is incorrect. (B) is incorrect because armed robbery is not a lesser included offense of premeditated murder. (D) is incorrect because the prosecution would be estopped if violation of one statute constituted a lesser included offense of the other statute.

Answer to Question 88

(B) Under Article I, Section 8, Congress may spend to "provide for the common defense and general welfare," which means, in effect, that spending may be for any public purpose. Furthermore, the Necessary and Proper Clause grants Congress the power to make all laws appropriate for carrying into execution any power granted to any branch of the federal government. The power to require that the weapons system be purchased falls within this rubric. Furthermore, the President has no constitutional authority to "impound" (*i.e.,* refuse to spend) funds whose expenditures Congress has expressly mandated. The President's duty is to take care that the laws are faithfully executed. (A) is incorrect as a matter of law. Whether a bill is passed with the President's signature or over his veto is not relevant to the question of whether spending is permissive or mandatory. (C) is incorrect because even though the President's powers do not expressly refer to spending, the President has extensive military powers as commander in chief that could include spending for military necessities in the event of actual hostilities against the United States. (D) is incorrect because, in the event of actual hostilities, the President, as commander in chief of the armed forces and militia, could exercise his inherent power to allocate funds. There is also some case law implying that the President has some inherent powers, even in internal affairs, to meet national emergency needs.

Answer to Question 89

(B) The contractor can testify as to any firsthand knowledge he has and need not rely on any written records if he presently remembers the facts. Firsthand knowledge is considered to be reliable testimony. (A) is wrong because the records themselves are not being introduced. (C) is wrong because the best evidence rule applies only in situations where the content of the writing is in issue. Here, the contractor is testifying about facts he perceived, facts that exist apart from the writing. The notebooks merely describe what the contractor saw and knows personally. (D) is wrong because no such summary is sought to be introduced, and even if it were, (D) is an incorrect statement of the law.

Answer to Question 90

(B) Testimony obtained by a promise of immunity is by definition coerced and therefore involuntary. Thus, immunized testimony may not be used for impeachment of the defendant's testimony at trial. The friend's testimony will not be permitted to be used against the ex-convict because it resulted from the ex-convict's immunized testimony. (A) is wrong because it is an inaccurate statement of the law. Prosecutors can bargain away the rights of co-defendants. (C) is wrong because police suspicion is not the equivalent of actual testimony. (D) is wrong. Even though a witness wants to testify, various privileges such as lawyer/client, doctor/patient, etc., may bar the testimony. Here, the grant of immunity to the ex-convict is a bar to the friend's derived testimony because use immunity bars use of one's testimony or anything derived from it.

Answer to Question 91

(C) The driver will prevail under the facts given. The driver owed to a foreseeable plaintiff a general duty to behave as a reasonable person would under the same or similar circumstances. Continuing to drive the car with knowledge of an attendant danger would create an unreasonable risk of injury to people such as the pedestrian, and would constitute a breach of the driver's duty of care. However, the driver had no reason to know of the dangerous underlying problem (the defective master cylinder), and he had been assured by the dealer's mechanic that the car was safe to drive. Thus, the driver has not breached his duty of care here. (A) is incorrect because the driver had been assured by the dealer's mechanic that a recurrence of the problem would not result in total brake failure. Thus, the driver had a reasonable belief that he could safely drive the car to the dealer. (B) is incorrect because the driver's duty to maintain his car's brakes does not make him strictly liable for a brake failure. The driver reasonably relied on the advice of the dealer's mechanic in believing that the car was safe to drive. It is true that, as (D) states, the driver had diligently had his brakes repaired, but if he had reason to know, subsequent to the repairs, that the brakes were dangerous, he should not have driven the car. Because the driver reasonably relied on the advice of the dealer's mechanic, the driver had no reason to know of the danger involved in continuing to drive the car. Thus, (C) is a better answer than (D).

Answer to Question 92

(B) The court should deny the motion. To hold a manufacturer strictly liable for a defect in a product, the product must have reached the consumer without substantial change in the condition in which it was supplied. The jury could find that the toaster was defective when it left the manufacturer's control, so that the manufacturer produced a product that is so defective as to be unreasonably dangerous. This defective product actually and proximately caused the sister's injuries; hence, the manufacturer's motion should be denied. (A) is wrong because, unlike (B), it ignores the requirement that the defect be attributable to the manufacturer. (C) is wrong because the sister's strict liability action is based on a defect in the electrical cord of the toaster. The facts do not establish that the technician's adjusting of the darkening dial had any effect on the toaster's power cord. Thus, the technician's input does not preclude the success of the sister's action against the manufacturer. (D) is wrong because a history of defects in this model of toaster would show that the manufacturer should have had notice of the problem. Such notice would be relevant to a negligence action, but not to an action for strict liability.

Answer to Question 93

(B) The defendant's motion should be denied because a prosecution for conspiracy is distinct from a prosecution for any substantive offense involving the same conduct as the conspiracy. The Fifth Amendment provides that no person shall be twice put in jeopardy for the same offense. The general rule is that two crimes do not constitute the same offense if each crime requires proof of an additional element that the other crime does not require, even though some of the same facts may be necessary to prove both crimes. [Blockburger v. United States (1932)] Furthermore, a prosecution for conspiracy is not barred merely because some of the alleged overt acts of that conspiracy have already been prosecuted. [United States v. Felix (1992)] Here, both the conspiracy charge and the possession charge require proof of an element that the other charge does not; hence, there is no double jeopardy problem with the indictment. (A) is incorrect because it is too broad a statement. The fact that separate statutes are involved does not establish that these are not the "same offense" for purposes of double jeopardy. (C) is incorrect because the "same conduct" test is not currently used by the Supreme Court to evaluate a double jeopardy claim. (D) is incorrect because the question involves the defendant's motion to quash an indictment and not her ultimate punishment.

Answer to Question 94

(A) If the woman prevails, it will be because the covenant does not touch and concern the land. The investment firm is seeking to enforce the covenant by means of an equitable remedy. Thus, this question concerns an equitable servitude. An equitable servitude relates to a promise that touches and concerns the land. A covenant touches and concerns the land when it makes the land itself more useful or valuable to the benefited party. Here, an agreement to purchase electrical power only from a specified source probably does not touch and concern the land. (B) is incorrect because a common development scheme is not necessary for an equitable servitude. Generally, equitable servitudes are created by covenants contained ***in a writing*** that satisfies the Statute of Frauds. Negative equitable servitudes that may be implied from a common scheme for development are one exception to the writing requirement. (C) is incorrect because the covenant here does not restrain alienation. (D) is incorrect because privity of estate is not required for enforcement of an equitable servitude. In any event, privity is present here because (i) at the time the promisor (the man) entered into the covenant with the promisee (the realty company), the two shared some interest in the land independent of the covenant—*i.e.,* grantor-grantee (horizontal privity); and (ii) the successor in interest to the covenanting party (the woman) holds the entire durational interest held by the covenantor (vertical privity).

Answer to Question 95

(B) The Supreme Court has specifically upheld requirements that public employees take an oath to "support the Constitution of the United States" and the state constitution [Connell v. Higgenbotham (1971)] and that state employees take an oath "to oppose the overthrow of the government . . . by force, violence, or by an illegal or unconstitutional method" [Cole v. Richardson (1972)]. The Court held that such oaths merely required the takers "to commit themselves to live by the processes of our system." (B) is, therefore, correct because it reflects these Supreme Court precedents involving loyalty oaths. (A) is wrong because the Supreme Court has moved away from the old privilege versus right analysis, and, in any case, there is no justification based upon "privilege" that would permit oaths that are overbroad or vague, resulting in a chilling effect on First Amendment activities. (C) is wrong because it is overbroad. States may not infringe on First Amendment rights in employment. (D) is wrong. It is doubtful that a college instructor position would be considered to be a position of governmental trust.

Answer to Question 96

(B) The buyer's use of the computers is an acceptance only if the use was more than reasonably necessary to determine whether they were suitable, since they did not conform to the contract. The U.C.C. gives a buyer the right to reject goods that do not conform to the contract until he has accepted the goods. Acceptance occurs when the buyer: (i) indicates that he will keep the goods, after reasonable inspection, even though they are nonconforming; (ii) fails to reject within a reasonable time after tender or delivery of the goods or fails to seasonably notify the seller of his rejection; or (iii) does an act inconsistent with the seller's ownership. Thus, the buyer is allowed a reasonable time to inspect the goods before accepting or rejecting them. Here, the buyer used the computers for a week and then found them to be unacceptable substitutes for the computers that he ordered. If this trial period was reasonable, he did not accept the goods and therefore may reject them. If the period is more than what reasonably would be required to test them, the buyer will be seen as having accepted them and can no longer reject them. (A) is wrong because it does not provide for the buyer's right to reasonably inspect. It is not enough that the buyer simply knew that the computers he received were nonconforming; he is entitled to inspect them to determine whether he will keep them even though they are not what he ordered. (C) is wrong because even nonconforming goods can be accepted. After reasonable inspection, a buyer may decide to keep the goods despite the nonconformity, and this is an acceptance. (D) is wrong because, under the U.C.C., if a buyer accepts nonconforming goods, he may still sue for damages. Here, as explained above, it is unclear whether the buyer accepted the computers that were sent to him (he did so only if the week trial period was unreasonable). But even if there was an acceptance, the buyer could still recover damages due to the nonconforming shipment. Thus, he has not waived a claim for damages due to the nondelivery of the three computers that he ordered.

Answer to Question 97

(B) Because the subject matter of the contract became illegal after the distributor's offer but before the retail seller's acceptance, the supervening illegality is deemed to revoke the offer. It will be a defense to enforcement of a contract if either the consideration or the subject matter is illegal. If the illegality is present at the time of the offer, there is no valid offer. If the illegality arises after the offer but before acceptance, the illegality operates to revoke the offer. If the illegality arises after formation of a valid contract, it discharges the contract because performance has become impossible. Here, the retail seller received the distributor's offer to sell the games on August 5. Generally, an offer not supported by consideration can be revoked at will, even if the offeror has promised not to revoke for a certain period. However, an offer by a merchant to buy or sell goods in a signed writing that, by its terms, gives assurances that it will be held open is not revocable for lack of consideration during the time stated. The distributor is a merchant who deals in goods of the kind being sold. Its offer contained in the letter of August 3 assured the retail seller that its terms would be open until September 2. Thus, the offer was not revocable until September 2, and the distributor's purported revocation of August 17 was ineffective. The legislation rendering illegal the sale of the type of machines to be sold by the distributor to the retail seller took effect on August 28, two days before the retail seller's acceptance. Thus, the illegality arose after the distributor's offer and before the retail seller's acceptance. Hence, the state law serves to revoke the offer. (C) is incorrect because, as explained above, the distributor's attempted revocation was ineffective. (D) is incorrect because the state law would only create a condition of impossibility of performance if it became effective after formation of a valid contract. Here, the law was effective before the retail seller's acceptance. (A) is incorrect because if the state law had not been enacted, the distributor would have been bound by the terms of its offer until September 2. The fact that the distributor was able to obtain a higher price for the machines would not permit it to revoke its offer prior to expiration of the specified period.

Answer to Question 98

(D) The entry into the defendant's apartment and his arrest, without a warrant, probable cause, or circumstances permitting an exception from these requirements, were unconstitutional. The statements he made thereafter were fruits of the original unconstitutional arrest and must be suppressed unless the taint was purged. The giving of *Miranda* warnings was not sufficient.

Hence, (D) is the best answer. If probable cause for a warrant is based on information from an informer, usually that informer's identity need not be revealed. Thus, (A) is incorrect. (B) is a misstatement of law. There was no interrogation by the police to trigger the *Miranda* requirements. (C) is attractive but not as accurate an answer as (D). If the police had been acting with probable cause to arrest, their forced entry into the apartment would not have made the defendant's statements involuntary.

Answer to Question 99

(C) The evidence is admissible because the mayor's character is directly in issue. The general rule is that evidence of character to prove the conduct of a person in the litigated event is not admissible in a civil case. However, when a person's character itself is one of the issues in the case, character evidence is not only admissible, but in fact is the best method of proving the issue. Where the plaintiff brings a defamation action for injury to reputation and the defendant pleads as an affirmative defense that his statements were true, the plaintiff's character is directly at issue in the case. Under the Federal Rules, any of the types of evidence (reputation, opinion, or specific acts) may be used to prove character when character is directly in issue. [Fed. R. Evid. 405(b)] Here, the mayor's character is at issue and the resident is offering character evidence to show that his assertion that the mayor is corrupt is a true statement. Thus, (C) is correct and (A) is incorrect. (B) is incorrect because, as stated above, any of the types of evidence can be used to prove character when it is directly in issue. (D) is incorrect because an actual conviction is required for impeachment purposes, but not for the purpose of establishing character—evidence of an arrest or indictment would have been equally admissible.

Answer to Question 100

(B) The developer will be entitled to obtain specific performance. If the vendor of land cannot give marketable title but the purchaser wishes to proceed with the transaction, the purchaser can usually obtain specific performance with an abatement of the purchase price in an amount representing the title defect. Here, the cousin's legitimate claim to one-tenth of the property constituted a defect that would make title unmarketable. The title defect was cured by the developer at a cost of $10,000. Thus, an abatement will be applied to the purchase price. The certified check for $140,000 in choice (B) represents the purchase price ($160,000) less the earnest money already paid ($10,000) less the abatement to obtain marketable title ($10,000), leaving the amount to be tendered as $140,000. (A) is wrong because either the abatement or the earnest money is not taken into account with that figure. (C) is wrong because the developer acted reasonably in clearing the title defect himself. The rule that a buyer must notify a seller of title defects is intended to prevent the buyer from avoiding the closing by raising a title defect problem at the last minute. Here, the developer was trying to facilitate the closing by resolving the title problem himself, which he did. Prior notice to the farmer was not necessary in this case. (D) is wrong because the action is based on a contract that was signed before any potential co-tenancy occurred, and there is no rule that precludes a co-tenant from obtaining specific performance from another co-tenant on an otherwise valid contract.

Answer to Question 101

(D) The ex-convict prevails because he believed the truth of the assertion. The prosecutor is a candidate for public office and, as such, to recover he must establish (i) falsity, and (ii) "actual malice"—*i.e.*, knowledge of falsity or reckless disregard of truth or falsity. Thus, if the ex-convict honestly believed the truth of his statement, the prosecutor could not show actual malice, and the ex-convict would prevail. (A) is wrong because it goes to malice in the sense of "ill will." That type of malice is not the standard for defamation; it is irrelevant that defendant wanted to "get even" with the prosecutor. (B) is wrong because a showing of negligence is not sufficient to recover for defamation of a public official or figure; knowledge of falsity or reckless disregard of truth or falsity is required. (C) is wrong because even if the story is a matter of public concern, the prosecutor might still prevail if he can show fault on the part of the ex-convict—such as the ex-convict's reckless disregard for whether the statement was true.

Answer to Question 102

(D) The store owner will not be convicted of an attempt to violate the statute if her employee did not have the requisite intent. Although the statute has been interpreted to create a strict liability crime, which does not require proof of criminal intent, an attempt of a strict liability crime requires proof that the defendant acted with the intent to bring about the proscribed result. Therefore, for the store owner to be charged vicariously with attempt, her employee must have acted with the requisite intent; he must have intended to sell the ammunition to a minor. If he did not so intend, the store owner will not be convicted of attempt. (A) is incorrect because this is a case of factual impossibility, which is not a defense to attempt. (B) is incorrect because careful instructions will not, in and of themselves, absolve an employer from vicarious liability. (C) is incorrect because the strict liability elements of the underlying offense make it clear that knowledge of the age of the purchaser is not an element of the underlying offense. Thus, the clerk (and the store owner) can be liable for selling ammunition to a minor no matter how old the purchaser looked or how old he claimed to be. The boy's lie may have bearing on the clerk's lack of intent, but this is not as direct an answer as (D).

Answer to Question 103

(B) The testimony should be admitted. Where a dispute exists as to the meaning of a written agreement's terms, parol evidence can be received to aid the fact finder in reaching a correct interpretation of the agreement. The Uniform Commercial Code, which governs the contract here, follows the modern approach that permits evidence of interpretation even when the terms are not patently ambiguous. [*See* U.C.C. §2-202, comment 1] Here, the terms may be explained by the previous course of dealing between the parties, because it suggests that the parties understood that specifying "Yellow Giant" in the contract did not mean that a Yellow Giant was being ordered. In addition, the fact that the purchase price for the "Yellow Giant" is $25,000 more than the going price for a Yellow Giant creates enough uncertainty to warrant admission of testimony explaining what the parties meant by the term "Yellow Giant." While the company will have the burden of proving that the term meant something different from what it appears to mean, any evidence it offers will be considered by the trier of fact. (A) is incorrect because reformation is generally available only when a writing incorrectly reflects a valid antecedent agreement, such as where a mistake was made in transcribing the agreement. Here, the writing correctly reflects the antecedent agreement, because the parties agreed to use the words "Yellow Giant"; the problem now lies in determining what was meant by "Yellow Giant." Also, this answer overconfidently states the outcome of the controversy, because the manufacturer may have evidence of its own that contradicts the company's. (C) is incorrect on these facts because the president is seeking to explain, not contradict, the terms of the written contract. Before it can be determined that testimony is being offered to contradict the terms of a written agreement, the meaning of the terms must be resolved. Thus, the parol evidence rule does not bar admission of this testimony. (D) is incorrect because the requirements of the Statute of Frauds [U.C.C. §2-201] are satisfied here. The U.C.C. requires only (i) a writing sufficient to indicate that a contract was formed, (ii) a quantity term, and

(iii) the signature of the party to be charged. All other terms of the contract, including the meaning of a contract term, can be established by parol evidence without implicating the Statute of Frauds.

Answer to Question 104

(A) The licensing requirement is constitutional. The state may "within the proper purpose of the exercise of its police powers" require licensing of anyone who deals with the public in general, and the Supreme Court has been particularly liberal when the state is attempting legislation that is remedial in effect to cure a social evil that exists within the state. (B) is wrong because the designation of the attorney general does not affect the constitutionality. (C) is wrong because this is a permissible burden (if it is one at all). (D) is wrong because there is no indication that the state is treating nonresidents differently than those residing in the state. (Note also that the Interstate Privileges and Immunities Clause does not protect corporations.)

Answer to Question 105

(A) It is unlikely that this provision could survive even the traditional rationality test. There is no apparent rational relationship between the classifications of citizens and noncitizens, and particularly residents and nonresidents, and the proper state purpose of discouraging the hiring of illegal aliens. Furthermore, state alienage classifications are suspect and will be upheld only if necessary to promote a compelling state interest. The classification in this case is not necessary because there are less burdensome means available to accomplish the state's purpose. (B) is wrong because the Fourteenth Amendment Privileges or Immunities Clause is limited to rights arising out of national citizenship. (Note that the durational residence requirement, but not the United States citizenship requirement, may violate the Article IV Privileges and Immunities Clause.) (C) is wrong because the Due Process Clause of the Fifth Amendment applies only to federal government action. (D) is wrong because the Tenth Amendment reserves power to the states; it does not include restrictions on state power.

Answer to Question 106

(C) Either an authenticated copy of the tape or the testimony of the lawyers is admissible. Hearsay is a statement, other than one made by the declarant while testifying at the trial or hearing, offered to prove the truth of the matter asserted. The witness is obviously not testifying at the current trial, and his statements are being offered for their truth. Thus, his deposition testimony is hearsay. The next issue is whether it falls within an exception to the hearsay rule. Ordinarily, a now-unavailable declarant's statements made in a deposition are admissible under the former testimony exception to the hearsay rule. That rule, however, requires that the statements be made under oath. Because the witness was not under oath when he testified, this exception would not apply. When a declarant is unavailable, a statement not specifically covered under the specific hearsay exceptions but having equivalent guarantees of trustworthiness is admissible if: (i) it is offered as evidence of a material fact; (ii) it is more probative of the issue than any other evidence the proponent can procure with reasonable efforts; (iii) the purposes of the rules of evidence and the interests of justice will best be served by admission of the statement; and (iv) the proponent gives the adverse party sufficient notice of his intention to use the statement and the statement's particulars. [Fed. R. Evid. 807—the "catch-all" exception] Here, the witness's statements are being offered as evidence of the material fact—the accident. Clearly, because the witness was the only neutral eyewitness, his statements are more probative of the issue than any other evidence that can be produced. Because the witness was the only neutral eyewitness and because the statement comes with guarantees of trustworthiness (*e.g.,* the witness was subject to cross-examination by the parties involved in this trial), the interests of justice would best be served by admission of the testimony. Because both sides agree that the witness had no motive to lie, the oath is a less important guarantee of trustworthiness, and the lack of an oath should not affect the admissibility of the statements. Because both parties were present (in the form of their lawyers) when the statements were made and knew that the witness was being questioned for the purpose of this suit, the notice requirement was probably satisfied. Therefore, the witness's deposition is admissible. Because the witness's statements exist independently of the recording, the best evidence rule, which requires that the original "document" be produced to prove its terms, does not apply, and either the authenticated recording or the lawyers' testimony would be admissible. Thus (A) and (B) are both true but not as good as (C) because (C) contains both options. (D) is incorrect because, as stated, the tape or the testimony is admissible. (D) would have been the correct choice were it not for the unusual set of circumstances making this declarant's statements extraordinarily useful and trustworthy.

Answer to Question 107

(D) The brother and the mother each own an undivided one-half interest because the Statute of Frauds applies. The Statute of Frauds requires that any transfer of an interest in land be in writing. The right of survivorship the man and the woman tried to create by their oral agreement is an interest in land. As such, it must be in writing to be enforceable. Furthermore, to create a joint tenancy with right of survivorship, the unities of time, title, interest, and possession must be present; *i.e.*, a tenancy in common cannot be converted to a joint tenancy by agreement. Therefore, the man and the woman remained tenants in common at their deaths, with each undivided one-half interest passing through their respective estates. (A) is incorrect because reliance on a mistake of law cannot convert a tenancy in common to a joint tenancy, and for the mother to take the entire interest, the woman would have to have a right of survivorship. (B) is incorrect because, as discussed above, the man and the woman's mistake as to the operation of law is an insufficient basis to reform the deed. A joint tenancy is not created without the four unities and the use of the specific language required by the jurisdiction. (C) is incorrect because the deaths of the man and the woman, resulting from the same accident, are irrelevant. The deaths were not simultaneous and it would not have mattered if they were. The share of each tenant in common goes to each tenant's heirs, and death resulting from the same accident or simultaneous death would not entitle the other co-tenant to take as if he or she had survived because a tenancy in common is involved.

Answer to Question 108

(D) The state must demonstrate that the requirement is necessary to advance a compelling state interest. The Equal Protection Clause requires that similarly situated persons not be discriminated against unreasonably. Where a suspect class is involved, it is unreasonable to discriminate unless the government can show that the discrimination is narrowly tailored to achieve a compelling governmental interest. As to state government regulation, alienage is a suspect class. Thus, (D) is correct. (A) is incorrect because it states the wrong test (rational basis). (B) is incorrect because it places the burden on the wrong party (the alien). (C) is incorrect because it states the wrong test (rational basis). This test applies only to laws restricting alien participation in the functioning of the state government.

Answer to Question 109

(C) The woman will not recover, because she was a trespasser on the landowner's land. The general rule is that one who possesses an animal not customarily domesticated in that area is strictly liable for all harm done by the animal as a result of its harmful or dangerous characteristics. For trespassers, however, strict liability is not imposed against landowners. Trespassers cannot recover for injuries inflicted by the landowner's wild animals in the absence of negligence, such as where the landowner knows that trespassers are on the land and fails to warn them of the animal. Under this standard, even though the landowner could anticipate that trespassers like the woman would cross his property, he will not be liable because he exercised reasonable care by posting a sign warning about the bobcat and by attempting to make the animal less dangerous. (A) is incorrect because, as discussed above, the landowner is not strictly liable to the woman, a trespasser. (B) is incorrect because the woman cannot recover regardless of whether she saw the sign. With regard to the landowner's exercise of reasonable care, it does not matter that the woman did not see the sign as long as the sign was noticeable enough that it could have been seen. (D) is incorrect because the vet's negligent conduct is the type of foreseeable intervening cause that would not supersede any fault on the landowner's part. If the landowner were negligent, he could be jointly liable with the vet for the woman's injuries.

Answer to Question 110

(C) The strongest argument for admission of the plaintiff's testimony concerning the telephone call is that, after hearing the defendant speak in chambers, the plaintiff recognized his voice as that of the person on the telephone. Aural voice identification is not a subject of expert testimony; *i.e.,* lay opinion is sufficient. Familiarity with the voice may be acquired before ***or after*** the speaking that is the subject of the identification. Thus, the fact that the plaintiff became familiar with the defendant's voice later, in the judge's chambers, does not disqualify the identification. That identification, coupled with the defendant's self-identification during the call, is sufficient to authenticate the telephone conversation. (A) and (B) are wrong because they state requirements for identifying the person called, not the caller. (D) is wrong because self-identification of the caller is insufficient evidence of identity; additional evidence of identity, such as the testimony in (C), is required.

Answer to Question 111

(B) The man can be guilty of arson because his failure to put out the fire that he started establishes the malice necessary for arson. Arson at common law consists of the malicious burning of the dwelling of another. All that malice requires is that the defendant acted with the intent or knowledge that the structure would burn, or with reckless disregard of an obvious risk that the structure would burn. Here, it is not enough that the man accidentally or negligently caused the fire to start. However, because he was the cause of the fire, he had a duty to take reasonable steps to try to prevent it from spreading. His failure to do anything when the fire was probably small enough to put out would suffice as reckless disregard of an obvious risk that the building would burn, which it did. With regard to the dwelling requirement, the jurisdiction has extended the crime of arson to structures other than dwellings. The requirement that the building be "of another" pertains to possession rather than ownership. Thus, a landlord could be guilty of arson for burning down his own building if his tenants were in possession of it rather than him; hence, (D) is wrong. (A) is wrong because the malice requirement is not established by the fact that the man harbored ill will against the florist, and there is no "felony arson" doctrine comparable to the felony murder doctrine. (C) is wrong because, as discussed above, the man need not have intended to set the building on fire; all that must be shown is a reckless disregard of an obvious risk that the structure would burn.

Answer to Question 112

(A) The woman should be found guilty of robbery because her accomplice obtained the wallet by means of force. Robbery consists of (i) a taking (ii) of personal property of another (iii) from the other's person or presence (iv) by force or intimidation (v) with the intent to permanently deprive him of it. Thus, robbery is basically an aggravated form of larceny in which the taking is accomplished by force or threats of force. The force must be used either to gain possession of the property or to retain possession immediately after such possession has been accomplished, but the defendant need not have intended to use force to complete the crime; the only intent required is the intent to permanently deprive the victim of his property. Here, the woman and her boyfriend had such intent, and they were able to carry out that intent in part because the boyfriend slashed the man's hand with the knife, incapacitating him. The fact that the boyfriend did not intend to injure the man is irrelevant; hence, (C) is wrong. (B) is wrong because the man's erroneous belief that he was being threatened does not establish the element of threat or intimidation. The woman's conduct was merely an attempt to distract the man and did not constitute a threat or intimidation; the fact that the man's intoxication caused him to believe otherwise does not change that result. (D) is wrong because the unreasonableness of the man's belief does not change the fact that the woman is liable as an accomplice to the robbery by her boyfriend, because robbery (the use of force) was a foreseeable consequence of the pickpocketing.

Answer to Question 113

(A) The law student will probably be required to pay the professor $105 under an implied-in-fact contract. An implied-in-fact contract is a contract formed by manifestations of assent other than oral or written language, *i.e.*, by conduct. Even if there is no subjective "meeting of the minds," the parties will be bound if their conduct objectively appears to manifest a contractual intent. Where an offeree silently takes the benefit of offered services with reasonable opportunity to reject them and reason to know that they were offered with the expectation of compensation, the offeree's inaction may constitute an acceptance. [Restatement (Second) of Contracts §69(1)(a)] Here, the student's silence in the face of the professor's offer and his conduct in staying within earshot of the group is a sufficient objective manifestation of contractual intent for the court to find an implied-in-fact contract. Hence, a court will probably allow the professor to recover the contract price. (B) is wrong because it states the wrong rationale. The Statute of Frauds would not be applicable even if the cost of the tour were over $500; the $500 provision of the Statute of Frauds is applicable only to the sale of goods. (C) is wrong because it states a restitutionary remedy available in a quasi-contract action. A quasi-contract action for restitution is a legal remedy to prevent unjust enrichment where an enforceable contract is not present, and allows the claimant to recover the reasonable value of the benefits that he rendered to the other party. While the professor probably could pursue a quasi-contract action for restitution because he rendered services with a reasonable expectation of being compensated, he is not limited to that remedy because he can establish an implied-in-fact contract. Hence, he can recover the contract price for the tour without having to establish that it was a reasonable fee for the lectures. (D) is wrong because, as stated above, the law student's conduct would be sufficient for a court to find the existence of an implied-in-fact contract here, or, at a minimum, to grant restitution in a quasi-contract action.

Answer to Question 114

(B) The court could find the title marketable by finding that an implied easement for the benefit of the office building land was created from the existing use when that parcel of land was severed from the adjoining tract of land by the sale. The requirement that the seller provide the buyer with marketable title means that the title must be free from questions that present an unreasonable risk of litigation. A significant encroachment constitutes a title defect, regardless of whether an adjacent landowner is encroaching on the seller's land or vice versa. However, under the circumstances in (B), a court will be able to avoid the encroachment problem by implying an easement from the existing use (a quasi-easement). If a use exists on the "servient" part of the tract that is reasonably necessary for the enjoyment of the "dominant" part, and a court determines that the parties intended the use to continue after division of the property, an easement will be implied. Given that title will not be marketable otherwise, the court will deem that the parties intended for the use to continue. (A) is incorrect because the fact that the law requires a ramp would not prevent the adjacent property owner from bringing a lawsuit to have the encroachment removed. (C) is incorrect because an encroachment of 10 inches is significant enough to make title unmarketable. Whether an encroachment is significant enough to make title unmarketable is ultimately a question of fact; however, structures that encroach more than a few inches over the property line are generally found by the courts to be significant encroachments. (D) is incorrect because the type of deed required by the contract does not establish marketability. Also, the fact that a contract calls for a quitclaim deed, which does not contain any covenants for title, does not eliminate the implied warranty to provide marketable title.

Answer to Question 115

(C) The elderly neighbor will not recover because the man did not breach a duty owed to him when he parked the car. This question can be analyzed in terms of either the extent of the duty of care or proximate cause. Where a defendant's conduct creates an unreasonable risk of injury to persons in the position of the plaintiff, the general duty of care extends from the defendant to the plaintiff. However, no duty is imposed on a person to take precautions against events that cannot reasonably be foreseen. And in terms of proximate cause, intervening forces that produce unforeseeable results (results not within the increased risk created by the defendant's negligence) will be deemed to be unforeseeable and superseding, and thus break the causal connection between the defendant's negligent act and the ultimate injury. Here, the man's allegedly negligent parking did not increase the risk that the woman would sideswipe his car; the woman's conduct was an unforeseeable intervening force that cuts off the man's liability for his conduct. (A) is incorrect for two reasons. For breach of a statute to establish negligence per se, the plaintiff must show that the statute was designed to prevent the type of harm that occurred, which does not seem to be the case with the fire hydrant ordinance here. Furthermore, proving breach of an applicable statute establishes only duty and breach of duty. Actual and proximate cause must still be established for recovery, and proximate cause is lacking here. (B) is incorrect because the fact that the man's conduct was a cause in fact of the elderly neighbor's injury, even assuming that leaving the car there was negligent, does not establish the necessary element of proximate cause. (D) is incorrect because violation of an ordinance may establish negligence per se if the statutory standard is applicable to the situation.

Answer to Question 116

(C) The father's additional expense in providing temporary housing would be the best basis for a claim of consequential damages. In addition to the standard measure of damages, consequential damages may be awarded for further losses resulting from the breach that any reasonable person would have foreseen would occur from a breach ***at the time of entry*** into the contract. Temporary housing expenses would have been foreseeable at the time the contractor and the father entered into the contract. (A) is incorrect because it would be consequential damage to the son rather than the father, because it is the son who will incur the expense. (B) is incorrect because the fiancée's jilting of the son is not a foreseeable consequence of the breach. (D) is incorrect because at the time the contractor and the father entered into the contract, both parties would have reasonably assumed that the house would be built and completed by experienced construction personnel. The father's attempt to complete the house himself and the ensuing negligence were not foreseeable.

Answer to Question 117

(D) The builder probably will not succeed because the builder was notified of the installer's other jobs. Notice to an offeree that the offeror has made an inconsistent contract with a third party operates as a revocation of the offer. (A) is incorrect because there was apparently no consideration given by the builder for the installer's promise to keep the offer open until November 1. (C) is not as good an answer as (D) because it is the notice to the offeree that constitutes the revocation (rather than the inconsistent contract with the third party). (B) is incorrect because it is irrelevant that a telephone was used; an offer may be revoked by any means informing the offeree that it has been revoked.

Answer to Question 118

(C) Arguably, the company's fax on July 15 could reasonably be interpreted as a rejection of the landlord's offer as to the Wood Street building, *i.e.,* having accepted only the Main Street property, the company was impliedly rejecting the rest. Once rejected, the offer is terminated and the offeree's power of acceptance is extinguished; thus, the July 18 attempt to accept would be ineffective. None of the other alternatives makes sense. For impossibility of performance in (A) to apply, the impossibility must be "objective"; *i.e.,* the duties could not be performed by anyone. Also, the impossibility must arise ***after*** the contract has been entered into. (D) is wrong because a condition precedent must be distinguished from a promise. A condition is the occurrence of an event that will create, limit, or extinguish the absolute duty to perform. In this case, it would probably be determined that the intention of the parties was an exchange of promises. (B) is wrong because a unilateral mistake in most cases will not prevent formation of a contract. Only mutual mistake going to the heart of the bargain may prevent the formation of the contract.

Answer to Question 119

(D) The court will likely find that the statute is a bill of attainder. A bill of attainder is a legislative act that inflicts punishment without a judicial trial on individuals who are designated either by name or in terms of past conduct. Past conduct acts to define who those particular persons are. The prohibition against bills of attainder mandates the use of judicial machinery for trial and punishment of crime as well as the drafting of the definition of criminal conduct in such general terms that it will not single out a particular individual or small group for punishment because of past behavior. In *United States v. Brown* (1965), the Court found that a provision making it a crime for an officer of a labor union to have been a member of the Communist Party was an unconstitutional bill of attainder. Hence, (A) is wrong. (B) is wrong because regardless of whether a rational basis exists for the adoption of the statute, if it constitutes a bill of attainder it cannot be upheld. (C) is wrong because it is too broad. While the right to join together with other persons for political activity is protected by the First Amendment, infringements on that right may be justified by compelling government interests.

Answer to Question 120

(A) The phone message is admissible because it is an admission by a party-opponent. An admission is a statement made or an act done that amounts to a prior acknowledgment by one of the parties to an action of one of the relevant facts in dispute. The statement may be in writing and need not be against that party's interest at the time it was made. Here, the plaintiff is offering a statement made by the defendant that is directly relevant to the issue in the lawsuit. The phone message should therefore be ruled admissible. (B) is incorrect. While statements of a declarant's then-existing intent are admissible as an exception to the hearsay rule to allow an inference that the intent was probably carried out, statements of memory or belief are not admissible to prove the truth of the fact remembered or believed. Thus, even though the defendant left the message shortly after he made the agreement with the plaintiff, it would not be admissible under the state of mind exception to the hearsay rule. (C) is incorrect because the privilege for confidential communications between a husband and wife does not extend to routine communications of a business nature that were not made in confidence. Here, the defendant gave the message to the switchboard operator to relay to his wife. Thus, the communication was not made in reliance on the intimacy of the marital relationship. (D) is incorrect because the statement is admissible as an admission of a party-opponent, which is not hearsay under the Federal Rules.

Answer to Question 121

(A) If the salesman does not prevail, it will be because the hotel's management did not breach its duty of care. Innkeepers have a duty to use a high degree of care to aid or assist their guests and to prevent injury to them from third persons. Included in this duty is the duty to take reasonable precautions against foreseeable criminal acts of third parties. As stated in (A), the fact that the hotel's management had reason to believe that the locks were adequate after inspection is a basis for finding that the hotel has satisfied its duty of care. (B) is incorrect because any liability on the part of the hotel would not be vicarious liability, but rather direct liability for its failure to take security precautions. (C) is incorrect because the robbery would be a superseding intervening force only if it was unforeseeable. Given the string of robberies, the fact that this robber used a blackjack does not make the crime a superseding force. If the hotel's management had reason to believe the locks were inadequate, any criminal conduct by the robber would likely be deemed to be a foreseeable risk of the inadequate locks. (D) is incorrect because compliance with the statute is not determinative. The statute sets forth a minimum standard of conduct regarding installation of locks in hotel rooms. Despite compliance with this statute, a careful hotel proprietor might be required to take additional precautions to satisfy the duty of care under the circumstances.

Answer to Question 122

(A) The detective is liable for the type of invasion of privacy of intrusion upon the plaintiff's private affairs or seclusion. The husband could reasonably expect that what he did in the woman's hotel room would be free from intrusion. The detective violated the husband's seclusion by listening to the activities in the room. This intrusion would be highly offensive to a reasonable person. (D) is wrong because the viability of this cause of action does not depend on publication by the defendant; the interest protected by this type of invasion of privacy is the plaintiff's right to be let alone, rather than his interest in not having the information disseminated. (B) is wrong because illegality of the defendant's actions is not an element of the prima facie case for this form of invasion of privacy. Even if the eavesdropping were legal, the detective's conduct would still be an actionable intrusion upon the husband's private domain. Finally, the fact that the husband may have been engaging in illegal adulterous conduct does not justify a private individual's intrusion on his solitude. (The situation might be different if the detective were a law enforcement officer acting pursuant to previously obtained judicial authorization.) Thus, (C) is wrong.

Answer to Question 123

(D) The gifts are valid under the Rule. The homeowner's will created a life estate in the dancer, contingent remainders in the class consisting of the homeowner's children (contingent upon their attaining age 30), and contingent remainders in the class consisting of any children of the homeowner's children (contingent on their surviving their parent, and the parent dying before attaining age 30). There are two keys to understanding the question. The first is that a will speaks at death, no matter when it was executed. Here, the homeowner's will became an effective conveyance only when he died last year. The second key is that the grandchildren (*i.e.,* the children of the daughters or the son) do not themselves have to survive to any particular age to take their gifts. The wording of the question is somewhat confusing on this point, but it is clear when read carefully. Because there are two future interests in the question, each must be analyzed separately under the Rule Against Perpetuities. The gift to the homeowner's children is a class gift, and the Rule makes class gifts entirely void unless it is certain that the gift will vest or fail as to all members of the class within the perpetuities period. However, it is clear that this will be true here. The three children (the daughters and the son) are all alive when the will speaks. Hence, they are all lives in being. (If the dancer had been pregnant when the homeowner died, that child, when born, would also have been considered a "life in being" as of the homeowner's death.) The gift is certain to vest as to each of the homeowner's children when each reaches age 30, which is obviously within each child's lifetime. Likewise, if one of the children dies before age 30, his or her interest will fail; again, that is certain to happen within his or her lifetime. Because this is so, the class gift to the children of the homeowner is certain to vest or fail as to each member within "lives in being." The gift is therefore valid under the Rule. It is not even necessary to add the 21-year period as permitted by the Rule. As to the class gift to the grandchildren of the homeowner, a similar analysis follows. If any grandchild's interest ever becomes vested, it will do so immediately on the death of that grandchild's parent (one of the daughters or the son) prior to reaching age 30. Because those three persons are "lives in being" at the homeowner's death, the grandchildren's interests are certain to vest or fail in every case at the end of a life in being. Again, it is not necessary to add the 21-year period as permitted by the Rule. (A) is wrong because the time of execution of the will is irrelevant; it is the date of the testator's death that commences the running of the perpetuities period. (B) is wrong for the same reason. (C) is wrong for the reasons discussed above.

Answer to Question 124

(D) The defendant's motion should be denied. To have a Fourth Amendment right, a defendant must have a reasonable expectation of privacy in the object seized. A person does not have such an expectation in objects held out to the public, such as account records held by a bank. Thus, (D) is correct. (A) is incorrect because a search warrant is not required where the defendant does not have a Fourth Amendment right. (B) is incorrect because the defendant did not have a Fourth Amendment right in the records. Also, the period covered by the records was not necessarily overextensive. It could be that the defendant was suspected of being involved in bribery for the preceding two years. (C) is incorrect because, even if the facts here presented describe an exigent situation, such a situation is actually an exception to the warrant requirement; and, like the warrant requirement, will not arise unless and until the defendant has a Fourth Amendment right.

Answer to Question 125

(B) The father will be liable for false imprisonment because he deprived the son of access to the person that the court had determined should be his primary caretaker. This question is testing your knowledge of the issue of awareness in a false imprisonment action. A prima facie case for false imprisonment consists of: (i) an act or omission to act by the defendant that confines or restrains the plaintiff; (ii) intent on the part of the defendant to confine; and (iii) causation. Under the general rule, confinement is not present unless the plaintiff is aware of the confinement at the time. However, most courts recognize an exception to the awareness requirement if the plaintiff is actually injured by the confinement. Here, there is no indication that the son was aware of any confinement. However, even though the son enjoyed living on the farm, he has been deprived of his mother's custody and care for two years during a time in which the divorce court had decided that his best interests would be served by having his mother as the primary custodial parent. Even though the son was not physically harmed, the mother would have little difficulty establishing that her son's lengthy separation from his mother during his formative years constituted harm to her son. [*See* Restatement (Second) of Torts, §42, illus. 4] (A) is wrong because it implies that a person with legal custody cannot be liable for false imprisonment. An intentional confinement of a child by his legal custodian could constitute false imprisonment if the other requirements for the tort are met. (C) is wrong because the fact that the son was not aware of his confinement will not prevent recovery for false imprisonment if he was harmed by the confinement. (D) is wrong because the fact that the son enjoyed living on the farm does not establish that he was not harmed by the confinement. As discussed above, the deprivation of contact with his mother for two years constituted harm to her son.

Answer to Question 126

(C) The officer's testimony is not admissible because the defendant's statement that he told the officer that he acted in self-defense is extrinsic evidence on a collateral matter. A witness's statement on a collateral matter may be impeached only by cross-examination. A collateral matter is one that is not directly relevant to the issues in the case. Here, the officer's testimony is being offered to disprove the defendant's claim that he told the officer that he acted in self-defense, which the defendant related just to bolster his self-defense claim. While the ***circumstances*** of the defendant's altercation itself are relevant to a self-defense claim and could be the proper subject of testimony, his ***statement*** to the officer is just an assertion of his innocence and is not directly relevant to whether his self-defense claim was proper. (The prosecution could have objected to the defendant's statement as irrelevant, and could have challenged it on cross-examination, but it cannot impeach the statement with extrinsic evidence.) (A) is incorrect because for silence to be an admission, the party must have remained silent when faced with an accusatory statement. Here, the defendant was not confronted with an accusatory statement at his arrest. (B) is incorrect because, as discussed above, the testimony constitutes impeachment by extrinsic evidence on a collateral matter. While it may cast doubt on the defendant's overall credibility, it is not directly relevant to the issue of self-defense in the case. (D) is incorrect. The Fifth Amendment privilege against self-incrimination would prevent the prosecution from using the defendant's silence for substantive purposes as an admission. Here, however, the defendant's silence is not being offered as an admission, but only for the limited purpose of impeaching his claim that he made a statement to the officer.

Answer to Question 127

(D) The Secretary must distribute $100 million, because the President's executive order constitutes an attempted exercise of legislative power. Although the Supreme Court has not fully resolved the scope of the President's power over internal affairs, it has held that the President has no power to refuse to spend appropriated funds when Congress has expressly mandated that they be spent. Congress has the power to spend money for the general welfare under Article I, and the President's action here infringes on that power. It follows that (A) and (B) are incorrect. (C) is incorrect because, although it presupposes a less drastic spending cut than (A) or (B), the President may not unilaterally impose even a cut of 10% when Congress has clearly required the spending of the full amount.

Answer to Question 128

(B) The outcome will turn on the definition of "value," because the cousin, having received her deed after the developer, is the junior claimant. The cousin's recordation prior to the developer's will protect the cousin's right to the land only if she took the deed in good faith and for value. Here, the farmer apparently gave the deed to the cousin in exchange for a release from the antecedent debt. If the jurisdiction in question considers this "value," the cousin will benefit from the recording act because she is a subsequent bona fide purchaser for value, the very person the recording acts seek to protect. (A) is wrong because the form of deed has no effect on bona fide purchaser status. A quitclaim deed merely means the seller is not making any warranties of title. (C) is wrong because whether the developer paid value is irrelevant. The developer is not the subsequent purchaser. The recording act protects subsequent purchasers, so the developer's interest depends on whether the cousin benefits from the protection of the act. (D) is wrong because the developer's title is good as against anyone except a subsequent bona fide purchaser for value. Thus, unless the cousin is shown to qualify for the protection of the recording act, the developer's title is good. There is no estoppel component to the recording acts.

Answer to Question 129

(B) The scenario in (B) provides the best defense because it would enable the defendant to rescind based on unilateral mistake. Rescission of a contract is available when one party is mistaken about material facts relating to a contract, the mistake adversely affects that party, and the other party knows of the mistake. (A) is wrong because in this case it is the nonmistaken party who is adversely affected. (Note that under choices (A) and (B) it is unclear whether the plaintiff's claim is based on a contract. If it is, the promissory note will be treated as a modification. The modification could be rescinded as discussed above, but there also is an issue of whether there was valid consideration for the modification under the preexisting duty rule. (B) is still the best answer. Under the preexisting legal duty rule, past consideration is valid consideration if there is an honest dispute as to duty owed. There would be no honest dispute under (B) because the nonmistaken party is taking advantage of the mistaken party, but this is not true in (A).) (C) is wrong. The Statute of Frauds is not a problem here because the plaintiff is seeking to enforce the promissory note—which complies with the Statute of Frauds—and not the original agreement. Neither does the preexisting legal duty rule negate the consideration here because there is an exception to the rule for reaffirmations of voidable promises (*e.g.,* promises unenforceable under the Statute of Frauds, promises by infants, promises based on fraud, etc.). (D) is wrong because the statute of limitations would run anew on the note that the plaintiff is trying to enforce, and there is no preexisting legal duty consideration problem because of the exception to the rule for "technical defense bars"—a new promise to pay a legal obligation barred by a technical defense (such as the statute of limitations) is enforceable according to the terms of the new promise.

Answer to Question 130

(A) The manufacturer will prevail. Generally, a joint tortfeasor may recover indemnification from another joint tortfeasor where there is a considerable difference in the degree of fault. Here, the engineer, the person whose improper design actually caused the girl's injuries, is a "more wrongful" tortfeasor than the manufacturer. Thus, the manufacturer should prevail in its claim against the engineer, which result is reflected in (A). (B) is incorrect because indemnity is not available simply because the manufacturer and the engineer are joint tortfeasors. (C) is incorrect because the manufacturer's liability to the girl does not preclude it from obtaining indemnity from the engineer. (D) is incorrect because, even though the manufacturer was negligent in failing to discover the defect, it may still be entitled to indemnity from the person who negligently designed the game as the "more wrongful" tortfeasor.

Answer to Question 131

(C) The conviction should be reversed. The Due Process Clause has been interpreted as requiring the prosecution to prove each element of the crime charged beyond a reasonable doubt. The "malice aforethought" element of murder has traditionally been defined as encompassing the absence of provocation engendering a passion. Putting the burden of persuasion as to the existence of provocation and passion on the defendant relieves the prosecution of its burden as to their absence. Therefore, (C) is the best answer and (A) is incorrect on the facts. (B) is incorrect because the presumption of "malice aforethought" is not a legitimate presumption. (D) is incorrect as a matter of law. Presumptions are permitted as long as they are not mandatory for the jury.

Answer to Question 132

(B) The shop owner's son had a reasonable expectation of privacy, as evidenced by the obscuring of the window so that neighbors could not see into the shop. Hence, the officer's search would have to be based on a valid warrant or qualify under one of the exceptions to the warrant requirement. Putting trash cans next to a back window to climb upon and peering into the window through a narrow opening eight feet above the ground would be considered a violation of the owner's son's Fourth Amendment rights and not a "plain view" of criminal activity. Because the seizure of the cocaine, mirror, and razor was based on the illegal search, the evidence could not be used by the state. (A) is wrong; absolute certainty of illegal activity is not required for a valid search. A reasonable belief is required. (C) is wrong. The arrest itself is probably invalid, and in any event a search of the next room would not be an area within the immediate control of the defendant. (D) is wrong. Consent to enter the shop is not a consent to search the back room.

Answer to Question 133

(B) The evidence is admissible as evidence of the witness's possible bias in favor of the defendant. Evidence that a witness is biased tends to show that the witness has a motive to lie. A witness may always be impeached by extrinsic evidence of bias, provided a proper foundation is laid. Bias may be shown by evidence of a business relationship or friendship with a party. Here, the fact that the witness is the defendant's partner in a gambling operation is admissible to impeach the witness for bias. (A) is wrong because the only relevant facet of the witness's character in this case is his veracity, and extrinsic evidence of bad acts is not admissible to impeach a witness. Under the Federal Rules, instances of a witness's conduct may be inquired into on cross-examination if they are probative of truthfulness (*i.e.,* acts of deceit or lying), but extrinsic evidence is not allowed. It is doubtful that running a gambling operation would be found to be probative of the witness's truthfulness. Even if it were, extrinsic evidence would be inadmissible. (C) misstates the law. Criminal conduct can be shown by means other than admission or record of conviction. As discussed above in (A), a witness may be impeached by instances of bad or criminal conduct (even if it does not result in a conviction) if it is probative of truthfulness and it is brought out on cross-examination (no extrinsic evidence). (D) is wrong because extrinsic evidence of bias is admissible. (Note, however, that many states require that the bias be inquired into on cross-examination before extrinsic evidence is admissible.)

Answer to Question 134

(B) Cost of completion minus installments is the correct measure of damages because the facts give us the breach of a construction contract by the builder during construction. In such cases where the builder breaches after partially performing, the owner of the land is entitled to the cost of completion plus reasonable compensation for any delay in performance. Courts generally allow the builder to offset or recover for work performed to date to avoid the unjust enrichment of the owner. Hence, the unpaid installments should be deducted. Although this option does not mention reasonable compensation for delay, it is clearly a more accurate statement of the correct measure of damages than the other options. (A) is incorrect because the landowner's damage relates to the cost of having the cabin completed. This cost could either exceed or be less than the restitution of the installments. If the amount is less, the landowner would be unjustly enriched. (C) is incorrect because damage relates to cost of completion and not market value. The house might have minimal market value in its partially completed state, and to measure damages based on the differences between such minimal value at the time of breach and market value when completed according to specifications could dramatically overstate the landowner's real damages. (D) is incorrect because damages for mental distress are too speculative and are not awarded in a contract situation.

Answer to Question 135

(B) The buyer probably will be required to pay $6,000 for all but lot 101. The facts indicate that there was an enforceable contract at $5,000 as to lot 101 as of May 2, so there was no consideration for the buyer's agreeing to pay more for that lot; hence, that promise is unenforceable. (C) and (D) are therefore incorrect. However, as to the other lots, the owner's telephone call would act as a revocation of the original offer, and a new offer at $6,000; the buyer's fax occurred after revocation of the original offer and therefore was an acceptance of this new offer and bound the buyer to pay the raised price. Thus, (B) is correct and (A) is incorrect.

Answer to Question 136

(B) The legal effect of the two circumstances is best stated by (B). When a condition or duty of performance (*i.e.,* payment) is broken, the beneficiary of the condition or duty has an election: it may (i) terminate its liability; or (ii) continue under the contract. If it chooses the latter course, it will be deemed to have waived the condition or duty. Because the engineering firm did not terminate its liability to complete construction of the roller coaster, but rather treated the contract as ongoing, it is deemed to have waived the delay in payment. The amusement park's failure to require a safety report would be deemed a revocable waiver. At any time the amusement park could insist on the safety report before making a monthly payment. Because the safety report represents that the work performed during a particular month met safety guidelines, the amusement park would always retain the right to condition its payment for a particular month on receipt of the report. (A) is incorrect because there was no estoppel waiver as to either the failure to pay or the failure to provide safety reports. Whenever a party indicates that it is "waiving" a condition before it is to happen, or some performance before it is rendered, and the person addressed detrimentally relies on such an indication, the courts will hold this to be a binding (estoppel) waiver. The engineering firm never indicated in advance that it was waiving the payments during hurricane season and there was no detrimental reliance by the amusement park. Likewise, the amusement park never indicated in advance that it was waiving the safety report requirement and there was no detrimental reliance by the engineering firm. (C) is incorrect because mutual rescission requires an ***express agreement*** between the parties to rescind. The agreement to rescind is itself a binding contract supported by consideration (the giving up by each party of its right to counterperformance from the other). The parties did not rescind the contract here. (D) is incorrect because, as noted above, there was no estoppel waiver as to the safety reports. Also, there was never any discharge of the amusement park's duty to make the payments during the hurricane season. (Although the amusement park's duty might be excused because no work was done during that time, this does not necessarily follow from the terms of the contract.)

Answer to Question 137

(D) The outcome of the developer's suit will be governed by whether the power to "sell and convey" is construed to include the power to execute the usual form of deed used to convey realty. If the lawyer lacked the authority to include covenants for title, the landowner will probably not be bound by those covenants. (A) is wrong because the deed included covenants. It may be slightly relevant on the issue of how the power of attorney should be construed, but the outcome of the case will not be governed by this determination. (B) is wrong for a couple of reasons. Covenants for title are not like real covenants; they are not characterized as personal or running with the land. Covenants for title are either present or future. Even if the terminology "personal" or "running with the land" were used, (B) would be incorrect because the suit concerns the original parties; thus, whether the covenant runs with the land would be irrelevant. (C) is wrong because bona fide purchaser status is irrelevant to the enforcement of covenants for title. This status is important mostly for purposes of the recording statute.

Answer to Question 138

(A) The court should dismiss the action because the company whose bid had been rejected cannot show that any injury it allegedly suffered will be remedied by a decision enjoining performance of the contract with the company that was later awarded the contract. Even if a federal court has jurisdiction over the subject matter of a case, it will not decide a constitutional challenge to a government action unless the party challenging the action has "standing" to raise the constitutional issue, *i.e.,* a concrete stake in the outcome of the controversy. This requires plaintiff to show an injury in fact—caused by the government—that will be remedied by a decision in its favor. Here, the company cannot establish that whatever injury it might have suffered by having its bid rejected will be remedied by an injunction preventing the other company from performing its contract with the government; hence, it does not have standing to bring this action. (B) is wrong because it is too broad; even in the absence of express constitutional limitations, the government is restricted by the Bill of Rights in the exercise of its contracting power. (C) is wrong because the company does not have standing to raise a claim on behalf of minorities potentially affected by the waiver. Even if the court were to consider the merits of the case, the government, while it might have had to show a compelling government interest to ***institute*** its affirmative action policies, would not have to show a compelling interest to ***suspend*** the policies. (D) is wrong because the company does not have standing to assert a violation of its rights in an action to enjoin another party's performance of a contract with the government.

Answer to Question 139

(B) The woman will recover $60,000. Under pure comparative negligence, which you should assume is the rule unless the question specifies otherwise, the plaintiff may recover no matter how great her negligence. In this case, the woman has suffered damages of $100,000. Because she was 40% negligent, she may recover only $60,000 ($100,000 less $40,000). Therefore, (B) is correct, and (A) is wrong. Absent a statute, damages are not reduced or mitigated because of benefits received from collateral sources (*e.g.,* health insurance). Thus, the woman's receipt of $10,000 under her insurance plan does not diminish her recovery. (C) is therefore wrong. The driver of the car and the truck driver are jointly and severally liable for the woman's injuries because their negligent acts combined to proximately cause an indivisible injury to the woman. Because the driver of the car and the truck driver are jointly and severally liable, the woman may recover the entire $60,000 from the driver of the car. Thus, (D) is wrong.

Answer to Question 140

(A) The landowner will prevail because the developer, who is apparently a purchaser at arm's length, had ample opportunity to inspect the property and discover the conduit. The law will not protect a party in the developer's situation who failed to protect herself. The landowner, in the absence of a fiduciary relationship with the developer or of any affirmative representations that the landowner knows or discovers to have been false, has no duty to disclose the existence of the conduit except (in some jurisdictions) if he knows that the developer is laboring under a misapprehension as to a basic assumption and the act of nondisclosure is made in bad faith. The facts do not support either of these exceptions. It does not appear that the landowner acted in bad faith, particularly because the landowner permitted an inspection and the developer had ample opportunity to discover the truth. Furthermore, it does not appear that the developer will be unable to build the high-rise simply because of the presence of the conduit. (B) is incorrect because the developer's purpose is not irrelevant; if the landowner knew about the developer's purpose, the landowner may have a duty to disclose any fact that would preclude that purpose. (C) is incorrect because the existence of the conduit does not make title unmarketable. (D) is incorrect because nothing in the facts indicates that the developer could not build the high-rise on the property despite the existence of the conduit; there are no facts indicating that the developer will experience grossly excessive costs in attempting to do so; and the existence of the conduit, which was discoverable, is not the sort of unforeseeable supervening event that would give rise to a frustration defense.

Answer to Question 141

(B) The student should be acquitted. Burglary requires a breaking and entering with the intent to commit a felony therein. Because what the student intended to do when she broke in was not a felony, it cannot be said that she entered with the intent to commit a felony. For this reason, she should be acquitted of burglary. It follows that (B) is correct and (C) is incorrect. (D) is incorrect. The fact that the student was unable to retrieve the exams would not have been a defense to the burglary charge, as that would raise a factual impossibility scenario, and factual impossibility is not a defense to a charge of an attempt of a crime. (A) is incorrect because the crime of burglary would have been complete at the moment of breaking and entering with intent to commit a felony therein. However, because looking at exam questions was not a crime, the student could not be convicted of either burglary or attempted burglary.

Answer to Question 142

(D) The friend will lose because she was not a close relative of the pedestrian. If a bystander suffers distress from seeing injury to another, a majority of courts now allow recovery if (i) the plaintiff and the person injured by the defendant are closely related, (ii) the plaintiff was present at the scene of the injury, and (iii) the plaintiff personally observed or perceived the event. Here, the friend is not related to the pedestrian; hence, she cannot recover for her distress. (A) is incorrect because witnessing the injury to another is not sufficient. (B) is incorrect even though the friend did suffer physical symptoms from the distress. As discussed above, she has not met the requirements to recover. (C) is incorrect because the friend's proximity to the pedestrian is only relevant in the minority of jurisdictions that have retained the "zone of danger" requirement for bystander recovery. Here, the jurisdiction has adopted the majority approach.

Answer to Question 143

(B) The testimony of the physician should be admitted as a statement to a physician made for purposes of diagnosis or treatment. The Federal Rules allow the admission of statements not only of past symptoms and medical history, but also of the cause or source of the condition as reasonably pertinent to diagnosis or treatment. This is an exception to the hearsay rule. (A) is incorrect because this is not a statement of ***present*** bodily condition, which falls under a different exception to the hearsay rule. (C) is incorrect because, as explained above, this testimony is admissible under an exception to the hearsay rule. (D) is incorrect because this hearsay exception does not require unavailability of the declarant.

Answer to Question 144

(A) If a law burdens a fundamental right, the state must demonstrate that the law is necessary to promote a compelling state interest. In all other cases, a law is valid if it rationally relates to a legitimate end of government. Where the "rational basis" test applies, the law is presumed valid and the burden is on the challenging party to prove its invalidity. The statute at issue infringes on the father's right of parental custody, which is almost certainly a fundamental right. Thus, the state bears the burden of showing that this statute is needed to promote a compelling state interest. (A) is correct. (B) and (D) are wrong because showing a rational relationship is not enough because a fundamental right is involved. (C) and (D) are wrong because the burden is on the state, not the father.

Answer to Question 145

(D) The defendant should be found not guilty. A conviction for felony murder requires that the defendant have had the intent to commit the underlying felony. Here, because the defendant believed that the $200 rightfully belonged to her, she did not have the intent to permanently deprive the store owner of his money. Thus, the defendant lacked the intent required for conviction of the underlying felony, and she cannot be found guilty of felony murder. (A) is wrong because it fails to account for the necessary intent to commit the underlying felony. (B) is wrong because taking the boyfriend to the store did not in and of itself create a risk of death. Also, (B), like (A), fails to account for the necessary intent to commit the underlying felony. (C) is wrong because the required mental state for felony murder (*i.e.,* intent to commit the underlying felony) has nothing to do with knowledge that the boyfriend was armed.

Answer to Question 146

(B) A defendant has the right to be represented by privately retained counsel, or to have counsel appointed for him by the state if he is indigent, during a post-charge lineup. [Moore v. Illinois, 434 U.S. 220 (1977)] This is not the case in (A)—during a photo identification [United States v. Ash, 413 U.S. 300 (1973)]; (C)—during a taking of a voice exemplar [Gilbert v. California, 388 U.S. 263 (1967)]; or (D)—during a blood sampling [Schmerber v. California, 384 U.S. 757 (1966)].

Answer to Question 147

(D) The testimony should be excluded. The accused in a criminal case may introduce evidence of a ***pertinent*** character trait because it may tend to show that he did not commit the crime charged. But here, evidence of the defendant's character for truth is not pertinent to a charge of a violent crime (aggravated assault). (A) is wrong because the character evidence is admissible only if it is pertinent to the charged crime. (B) is wrong because the defendant's credibility is not in issue, as he did not testify. (C) is wrong because in a criminal trial such evidence may be admitted, if pertinent, at the initiative of the accused.

Answer to Question 148

(B) If the decision is for the brother, it will be because the right to take minerals is an incident of a fee simple interest. The owner of a defeasible fee has the same right to possession and privileges of use as the owner of a fee simple absolute. Only unconscionable conduct by the owner that substantially reduces the value of the land could possibly be enjoined by the person who would take the land should the current owner's estate terminate. (A) is incorrect because the cousin has an executory interest. (C) is an incorrect statement of the law. A person in possession (*e.g.*, a life tenant), absent other circumstances, does not have the right to exploit mineral resources. (D) is incorrect because it is irrelevant. The brother's mental state of "good faith" or lack thereof has no bearing on his right to take minerals from his fee estate.

Answer to Question 149

(D) The nurse will not prevail because the doctor had reasonable grounds for his statement. As a former employer responding to queries of a prospective employer about a job applicant, the doctor has a qualified privilege. Such a privilege is not absolute; it exists only if exercised in a reasonable manner and for a proper purpose. The privilege may be lost if the speaker made a statement not within the scope of the privilege or if the speaker acted with "malice" (*i.e.,* knowledge that the statement was untrue or with reckless disregard as to its truth or falsity). Because the doctor had reasonable grounds for his belief, he was not acting with malice. (A) is incorrect because of the reasons stated in the analysis above. A statement of opinion may be actionable if it appears to be based on specific facts which, if expressly stated, would be defamatory. However, because of the qualified privilege, the doctor will not be liable for his mistake as long as his belief was reasonable. (B) is incorrect because the fact that the statement was in a category that is slander per se (*i.e.,* adversely reflecting on the nurse's abilities to practice her profession) goes to whether the nurse must plead special damages. It does not, however, undermine the qualified privilege. (C) is incorrect because permission to make inquiry is not tantamount to consent to be defamed.

Answer to Question 150

(D) Title to the undesignated parcel is unmarketable because the map leaves it uncertain whether the parcel is subject to the building restrictions. Marketable title is one that is free from reasonable doubt in fact or in law. Here, there is confusion because the building restrictions apply to all the lots shown on the map, but the parcel at issue is not one of the 10 numbered lots. Thus, it is unclear whether the parcel is subject to restrictions that will reduce the uses of the lot or its market value. (A) is wrong because it is not clear that the undesignated parcel is not subject to the subdivision restrictions. It was included on the map and the restrictions apply to "all lots shown." (B) is wrong because even though the undesignated parcel is not one of the 10 lots, it may be bound by the restrictions. Because this is unclear, title is not marketable. (C) is wrong because there could be marketable title without government approval.

Answer to Question 151

(C) The vineyardist is entitled to the contract price for the grapes delivered and accepted, but the winery is entitled to cover—to purchase grapes at the market price prevailing at the time of performance and to deduct any increase over the contract price. (A) is wrong because the winery is entitled to cover and does not "waive" the breach by accepting a part performance. (B) is wrong because the price for the grapes delivered is the contract price, not the prevailing market price. (D) is wrong because the vineyardist is entitled to payment for the grapes she delivered and would be able to enforce her claim through litigation, if necessary.

Answer to Question 152

(C) The teller's testimony is admissible as prior identification by the witness. Under the Federal Rules of Evidence, a statement of prior identification of another person by the witness is nonhearsay. Thus, (A) is incorrect. (B) is incorrect because the teller is testifying at the trial and is subject to cross-examination. Thus, the defendant's right of confrontation is not violated. (D) is incorrect because past recollection recorded is an ***exception*** to the hearsay rule, and the statement here at issue is nonhearsay. Also, past recollection recorded involves use of a writing made when the events were fresh in the mind of the witness. There is no such writing involved here.

Answer to Question 153

(A) The modification is fully enforceable. Although there was no consideration for the yogurt manufacturer's promise to take only half of the bargained-for production, none is required because this is a contract for the sale of goods and hence subject to U.C.C. section 2-209(1), which provides that a good faith modification is enforceable regardless of lack of consideration. Hence, (C) is wrong. (B) and (D) are wrong because they imply that the original agreement was not fully enforceable. The agreement between the yogurt manufacturer and the farmer is basically an output contract and is fully enforceable under the U.C.C. Although generally the subject matter of a contract must be definite and certain, an agreement to buy or sell all of one's requirements or output is deemed capable of being made certain by reference to objective, extrinsic facts. It is assumed that the parties will act in good faith.

Answer to Question 154

(A) The store properly rejected the ties. In single delivery contracts, the buyer can reject goods for any defect in the goods, even if the breach is not material. Here, the ties sent by the tie manufacturer were nonconforming goods. Thus, the store properly rejected the ties. (B) is incorrect because even if the tie manufacturer had notified the store that the ties were shipped as an accommodation, this would merely be a counteroffer, and the store would not have been obligated to accept the ties. (C) is incorrect because acceptance of an offer by shipment of nonconforming goods results in a breach of the contract, giving the buyer the right to reject. (D) is incorrect because, after rejection of goods in his possession, the buyer's obligation is to hold the goods with reasonable care at the seller's disposition for a time sufficient to permit the seller to remove them. The buyer is not obligated to promptly return the goods to the seller in order to preserve his remedies.

Answer to Question 155

(C) The basis for finding that the bank's due process rights have been violated is that it should have received notice through personal service or by mail. When the government seeks to use a judicial or administrative process to take or terminate property interests, it must give notice to those persons whose property interests may be taken by that process. The form of notice must be reasonably designed to insure that those persons will in fact be notified of the proceedings. Here, the bank had recorded its mortgage and presumably could have been notified by mail that the property was being seized by the government. Being deprived of the opportunity to protect its interest in the property violated the bank's due process rights under the three-part test of *Mathews v. Eldridge*. *Mathews* lists three criteria that the courts should weigh in determining what constitutes fair process: (i) the importance of the individual interest involved, (ii) the value of specific procedural safeguards to that interest, and (iii) the governmental interest in fiscal and administrative efficiency. Here, the bank has an important property right that is being terminated, the procedure of publishing a general notice was not sufficient to safeguard its interests, and the government interest in efficiency would not have been overburdened by requiring notice by mail to parties with a recorded interest in the property. (A) is incorrect because it is too broad. Under *Mathews*, the government is not required to provide personal notice to all parties if it is not feasible, nor is it required to provide a preseizure hearing if exigent circumstances make it impracticable. (B) is incorrect because even when a private party is seeking to use a judicial or administrative process, state action is involved and the Due Process Clause must be satisfied; hence, notice to a record mortgage holder would be required even if a private party were seeking to seize the property through judicial means. (D) is incorrect because the state's characterization of the mortgagee's interest is not critical; the mortgagee has legal rights to the property that are protected by the Due Process Clause, regardless of how the rights are characterized.

Answer to Question 156

(C) The court should deny the defendant's motion because it appears that he voluntarily consented to the search that revealed the drugs. The police may conduct a valid warrantless search of an area otherwise protected by the Fourth Amendment if they have a voluntary and intelligent consent to do so. The scope of the search is governed by the scope of the consent, but consent extends to all areas to which a reasonable person under the circumstances would believe it extends. The fact that a defendant has been placed under arrest does not mean that he cannot otherwise give valid consent to a search, and the search that led to the discovery of the cocaine in this case was within the scope of the consent that the defendant provided. Thus, he has no Fourth Amendment grounds to exclude evidence of the cocaine. (A) is incorrect because the fact that the defendant was arrested did not mean that his consent was not voluntary. Whether consent is voluntary is judged by the totality of the circumstances. He does not necessarily need to be told that he has a right to withhold consent or be informed of the specific items being sought in the search. As long as his consent was not the product of express or implied coercion, it will be valid. (B) is incorrect even though it is a true statement. A valid arrest of the occupant of an automobile does not permit the police to conduct a warrantless search of the trunk of the automobile. Here, however, the search of the trunk was based on the defendant's consent rather than as incident to his arrest. (D) is incorrect. The lesser expectation of privacy in vehicles permits the police to search a vehicle without a warrant if they have probable cause to believe that the vehicle contains contraband or evidence of a crime. However, the facts in this question do not indicate that the officer had probable cause to search the trunk of the defendant's car. The more certain basis for upholding the validity of the search is the consent given by the defendant.

Answer to Question 157

(D) The defendant is not guilty of larceny because he lacked the intent to deprive the owner permanently of his car at the time of the taking. Larceny consists of: (i) a taking (ii) and carrying away (iii) of tangible personal property (iv) of another (v) by trespass (vi) with intent to permanently (or for an unreasonable time) deprive the person of his interest in the property. The intent to deprive must exist at the time the property is taken. Here, the defendant is not guilty of larceny because, at the time of the taking, he intended to return the car within a reasonable time and had a substantial ability to do so. Thus, (A) and (B) are incorrect. (C) is incorrect because if the defendant had the requisite intent at the time of the taking, he would be guilty of larceny even though he later returned the car.

Answer to Question 158

(D) If the consumer prevails, it will be because he suffered pecuniary damage. This question involves spoken defamation (slander). Ordinary slander is not actionable in the absence of pleading and proof of special damages. The defamation here does not fall within one of the slander per se categories (adverse reflection on the plaintiff's abilities in his profession, loathsome disease, crime involving moral turpitude, unchastity of a woman). Thus, the consumer will not prevail without a showing of special damages. (A) and (C) are incorrect because proof that the defendant knew of the falsity of the defamatory statement, or was negligent in that regard, is not required in cases involving a private person plaintiff and a matter of private concern. (B) is incorrect because "extreme and outrageous conduct" is part of the prima facie case for intentional infliction of emotional distress, not for defamation.

Answer to Question 159

(A) The judge should rule the photograph admissible. Photographs are admissible only if identified by a witness as a portrayal of certain facts relevant to the issue and verified by the witness as a correct representation of those facts. The witness who identifies the photograph need only be familiar with the scene or object that is depicted. It is not necessary to call the photographer to authenticate the photograph. The homeowner is familiar with the garden that is depicted. Thus, she may testify to the photograph as an accurate portrayal of the condition of the garden after the damage was done. (B) is incorrect because, if the photograph accurately depicts the damage, the photograph need not have been taken within a week after the occurrence. The fact that it was taken within a week does not establish that it was an accurate portrayal of the damage to the garden. (C) is incorrect because, as noted above, it is not necessary to call the photographer. (D) is incorrect because, as long as the photograph is properly authenticated, it is admissible.

Answer to Question 160

(C) The state's restriction is probably invalid. State laws based on alienage are subject to strict scrutiny, meaning that a compelling state interest must be shown to justify the disparate treatment. However, if the law discriminates against alien participation in the self-governance process, the "rationality" test is applied. Here, the student's application for tuition assistance does not relate to participation in the governmental process; thus, the strict scrutiny test applies. (B) is incorrect because it is based on the assumption that the "rationality" test is appropriate. (C) is the only answer that addresses the fact that the state must demonstrate a compelling interest to justify the restriction. It follows that (A) is incorrect. (D) is incorrect because aliens are excluded from the protection of the Privileges and Immunities Clause of Article IV.

Answer to Question 161

(D) The dealer may not remove the windows because they are fixtures and the bank's mortgage on the real property takes priority. Under the concept of fixtures, a chattel that has been annexed to real property is converted from personalty to realty. As an accessory to the real property, it is subject to any mortgage on the real property. In all common ownership cases (*i.e.*, those in which the person who brings the chattel onto the land owns both the chattel and the realty), whether an item that is not incorporated into a structure is a "fixture" (*i.e.*, part of the realty) depends upon the objective intention of the party who made the "annexation." This intention is determined by considering: (i) the nature of the article, (ii) the manner in which it is attached to the realty, (iii) the amount of damage that would be caused by its removal, and (iv) the adaptation of the item to the use of the realty. Under this analysis the windows are fixtures. It should first be noted that the carpenter is the fee simple owner of the house rather than a tenant and intended to make numerous permanent improvements to the house in future years; the state-of-the-art windows were simply the first step in what he believed would be a long-term process. The fact that the windows were easily removable (and therefore would cause minimal damage in the event of removal) would ordinarily indicate less of an intention to permanently improve the freehold, but here the facts indicate that they were easily removable to make it easier to clean them. Another important factor indicating that the windows are fixtures is that they cannot readily be used at any other house unless the window sizes happen to correspond to those at the carpenter's house. They were custom-made specifically for that house and therefore they were specially adapted to the use of the realty. They serve both functional and aesthetic purposes, they are an integral part of the house, and are necessary and appropriate to the use of the premises. Thus, in view of factors (i) and (iv) above, and considering the carpenter's fee simple ownership and long-term plans for the house, they should be deemed fixtures.

The fact that the windows are fixtures does not resolve the dispute between the dealer and the bank, however. Under Article 9 of the Uniform Commercial Code ("U.C.C."), a seller of a chattel that will become a fixture can grant a security interest in the chattel for a portion of the purchase price and protect its interest by making a "fixture filing" even though the real property has a mortgage. Under U.C.C. section 9-313(4), a seller who provides a purchase money security interest in an affixed chattel will prevail (to the extent of its claim) over a prior recorded mortgage on the land as long as the chattel interest is recorded within 20 days after the chattel is affixed to the land; this allows the seller to remove the chattel without having to reimburse the mortgagee for any diminution in the property's value. However, if this exception does not apply, the general rule that the first interest to be recorded prevails will be applied by the court. Here, while the dealer has a purchase money security interest in the windows, there is no indication that it made a fixture filing within 20 days of when the windows were installed. Thus, the bank's recorded mortgage interest is superior to the dealer's security interest, so the dealer will not be permitted to remove the windows. (A) is incorrect. In determining whether a chattel is a fixture in landlord-tenant cases, courts will generally allow the tenant to remove any chattel that he installed (*i.e.*, deem it not to be a fixture) if removal does not cause substantial damage to the premises or the virtual destruction of the chattel. However, that reflects the probable intent of the tenant who purchased the chattel, because he has no interest in permanently improving the freehold. Here, however, the carpenter was the fee simple owner of the house. The fact that he saved the old windows does not negate his intent to permanently improve the real estate with the new ones. (B) is incorrect because, as discussed above, the ease of removing the windows was for purposes of cleaning and does not negate an intent to permanently improve the real estate. (C) is incorrect even though it states an important factor for concluding that the windows are fixtures. As discussed above, the fact that windows are an integral part of the house would not have precluded the dealer from prevailing had he recorded his security interest in them.

Answer to Question 162

(B) The shop owner cannot recover damages in a misrepresentation action against the curator because he has suffered no pecuniary loss as a result of reliance on the false statement. An action for intentional misrepresentation requires the plaintiff to show (i) a misrepresentation by the defendant, (ii) scienter, (iii) an intent to induce the plaintiff's reliance on the misrepresentation, (iv) causation (*i.e.,* actual reliance on the misrepresentation), (v) justifiable reliance by the plaintiff on the misrepresentation, and (vi) damages. The damages element permits the plaintiff to recover only if he has suffered actual pecuniary loss as a result of reliance on the false statement. Here, the shop owner received a fair price for the powder horn and would not have obtained a higher amount had he sold it to someone else. His distress over selling it to the curator because of her false statement does not satisfy the damages requirement for intentional misrepresentation. (A) is wrong because statements of law are viewed as statements of opinion that cannot be justifiably relied on only when they are merely predictions as to the legal consequences of facts. In contrast, a statement of law that includes an express or implied misrepresentation of fact is actionable. Here, the curator's assertions that she had a power of attorney and the legal right to seize the horn through a replevin action are fact-based assertions that the shop owner had the right to rely upon. (C) is wrong even though it correctly states the causation element of intentional misrepresentation. Without the element of pecuniary harm, the prima facie case is not complete. (D) is wrong because the shop owner suffered no actionable damages. Also, the curator need not ***know*** that her statements were false. The element of scienter also encompasses statements that were made with reckless disregard as to their truth or falsity.

Answer to Question 163

(C) The court should hold against the paramedic because the Supreme Court has permitted Congress to remove the states' Eleventh Amendment immunity from suit only when it acts to enforce the Fourteenth Amendment. The Eleventh Amendment generally prohibits a federal court from hearing private parties' claims against the government, including claims for damages such as the paramedic's claim here. While Congress's power to prevent discrimination under the Fourteenth Amendment has enabled it to abrogate state immunity, it has no such power under the Commerce Clause. [*See* Seminole Tribe of Florida v. Florida (1996)] Hence, the court should dismiss the action as barred by the Eleventh Amendment, and (A) is therefore incorrect. (B) is incorrect because while Congress does have the power to regulate the jurisdiction of the federal courts, it does not have the power to grant jurisdiction in violation of another constitutional provision, such as the Eleventh Amendment in this case. (D) is incorrect because Congress does have power under certain circumstances to remove the states' Eleventh Amendment immunity. Under the power given to Congress in the enabling clause of the Fourteenth Amendment (and perhaps the Thirteenth and Fifteenth Amendments), it could pass antidiscrimination legislation that permits a state to be sued in federal court.

Answer to Question 164

(B) The witness's testimony is admissible to impeach the employee's credibility and as substantive evidence of the cashier's guilt. As long as the defendant is given an opportunity to explain or deny the statement, extrinsic proof of a prior inconsistent statement is admissible to impeach the defendant's testimony. If the prior inconsistent statement was made under oath at a prior trial, hearing, or other proceeding, it is admissible nonhearsay; *i.e.,* it is admissible as substantive evidence. In this case, the prior inconsistent statement was made under oath at the employee's trial and thus is admissible for its substance as well as for impeachment. (A) is incorrect because, as discussed above, the witness's testimony is admissible as substantive evidence of the cashier's guilt. (C) is incorrect because jurors are incompetent to testify only (i) before the jury on which they are sitting, and (ii) in post-verdict proceedings as to certain matters occurring during jury deliberations. Because the witness is not testifying before the jury on which she was sitting and is not testifying about jury deliberations, she is a competent witness. (D) is incorrect because the best evidence rule does not apply to this situation. The witness is not being called to prove the terms of a writing or to testify about knowledge she gained from reading a writing. The facts as to which she is testifying exist independently of any writing; thus, the best evidence rule does not apply.

Answer to Question 165

(A) The driver's motion to suppress should be sustained. Because stopping a car is a seizure for Fourth Amendment purposes, police generally may not stop a car unless they have at least a reasonable suspicion that a law has been violated. However, even absent that suspicion, police may set up roadblocks to stop cars if (i) the cars are stopped on the basis of some neutral, articulable standard, and (ii) the stops are designed to serve a purpose closely related to a particular problem arising from automobiles and their mobility. [*See* Indianapolis v. Edmund (2000)] The use of a checkpoint to detect evidence of ordinary criminal wrongdoing unrelated to use of cars or highway safety, such as the conduct here, was improper and thus the marijuana would be inadmissible under the exclusionary rule. (B) is wrong because if the car had been properly stopped, the use of the flashlight would not have been improper. (C) is wrong because the established police plan cannot overcome the constitutional objection to the random stopping. (D) is wrong because the stopping of the car was improper. If it had been proper, the subsequent search would have been proper because it would have been based on probable cause.

Answer to Question 166

(C) The wrestler is likely to prevail because of the preexisting duty rule. At common law, a modification of a contract required consideration because the parties were under a preexisting legal duty to perform. Because there was no consideration for the modification, the agent is not entitled to the $2,000. (A) would be correct if the U.C.C. applied, but it does not apply to this fact situation. (B) is wrong; the parol evidence rule does not apply to subsequent modifications. (D) is wrong. It is a true statement but it is not the reason the wrestler will prevail. There is nothing in the facts to indicate that the agent did not use his best efforts.

Answer to Question 167

(D) Judgment could be for either the purchaser or the investor, because there is a split of authority as to whether a recorded deed, obtained from a grantor who had no title at that time, but who afterwards obtains title, is constructive notice to a subsequent purchaser from the same grantor. Thus, the answer to this question turns on whether the deed from the developer to the purchaser constitutes constructive notice to the investor. (A) is incorrect because it does not address the issue of the investor's notice of the prior deed. (B) is incorrect because of the possibility that the deed to the purchaser should have put the investor on notice of the purchaser's claim. (C) is incorrect because it does not address the issue of notice.

Answer to Question 168

(B) The rehabilitation will most likely be permitted to rebut testimony of the witness's perjury conviction. Under Federal Rule 608(a), a witness can be rehabilitated with evidence of his good reputation for truthfulness after the character of the witness for truthfulness has been attacked by "opinion or reputation evidence or otherwise." The commentary to Rule 608 specifically states that impeachment through a prior conviction is covered by the "or otherwise" provision and therefore will give rise to rehabilitation through reputation for truthfulness evidence. (A) and (D) are wrong because the commentary to Rule 608 specifically states that impeachment through bias does not allow rehabilitation with reputation for truthfulness evidence. (C) is possible. It could be argued that the impeachment in (C) qualifies under the "or otherwise" provision. (C) is not, however, as good an answer as (B), where the rehabilitation through good reputation evidence would clearly be allowed.

Answer to Question 169

(A) The testimony should be admissible as sufficiently authenticated. Where the identity of the speaker of an oral statement is important, authentication as to the speaker's identity is required. A statement made during a telephone conversation may be authenticated by a party to the call who testifies that: (i) he recognized the other party's voice; (ii) the speaker had knowledge of certain facts that only a particular person would have; or (iii) he called a certain person's telephone number, and a voice answered, "This is (the person whose number was called)." Here, the identity of the person with whom the neighbor spoke on the telephone is important because the speaker admitted that his horse caused the damage. Thus, authentication is required. Because the neighbor called the listed phone number for the farmer, and the answering voice identified itself as the farmer, authentication is proper under (iii) above. (B) is incorrect because the accuracy of phone books is not an accurately verifiable fact or a matter of common knowledge. (C) is incorrect because, as noted above, familiarity with the speaker's voice is only one means of authentication. (D) is incorrect because there is no requirement of corroboration by the speaker.

Answer to Question 170

(A) The assistant will likely prevail. Extreme and outrageous conduct is an element of the prima facie case for intentional infliction of emotional distress. Because the wife's conduct was extreme and outrageous, intentional, and likely caused the assistant severe distress, the assistant will probably prevail. (B) is incorrect because mere intrusion on the plaintiff's property does not constitute intentional infliction of emotional distress. (C) is incorrect because physical injury is not required to recover for this tort. (D) is incorrect because, even though the assistant may be guilty of adultery, this would not justify the wife's extreme and outrageous behavior.

Answer to Question 171

(B) If the missionary prevails, it will be because the woman knew that the door would likely pinch his fingers. The requisite intent for intentional torts (such as battery) is satisfied if the actor knows with substantial certainty that the consequences of her conduct will result. Here, by slamming the door shut, the woman set in motion a force that brought about harmful contact to the missionary. (A) is wrong because a request to leave the property would not have justified commission of the battery. Generally, one may use reasonable force to prevent the commission of a tort against her property, if use of force is preceded by a request to desist. The missionary was not engaged in the commission of a tort against the woman's property. Thus, the woman's use of force was not justified, with or without a request to leave the property. (C) is wrong because the woman's anger is not determinative as to whether she had the requisite intent to commit a battery. (D) is wrong because the fact that the missionary was not trespassing when he came to the door is not determinative. Nothing in the facts indicates that the woman had the right to use force against the missionary at the time she slammed the door.

Answer to Question 172

(A) The judge should give both manslaughter instructions and allow the jury to consider both theories of manslaughter in determining whether the intentional killing should be reduced to voluntary manslaughter. In a "heat of passion" killing, provocation will reduce a killing to voluntary manslaughter if four requirements are met: (i) the provocation was a type that would arouse sudden and intense passion that would cause a reasonable person to lose self-control, (ii) the defendant in fact was provoked, (iii) there was not sufficient time between the provocation and the killing for the passion of a reasonable person to cool, and (iv) the defendant in fact did not cool off between the provocation and the killing. Although some provocations were defined as inadequate as a matter of law at common law, modern courts are more likely to submit to the jury the question of what constituted adequate provocation. Similarly, whether there has been a sufficient time for a reasonable person to cool off is a factual question that depends on the nature of the provocation and the attendant circumstances. Here, the freshman's belief that he was being shoved again by the senior and set up for another punch in the face may have rekindled his rage at the earlier punch and taunting by the senior. The jury should be allowed to consider all of the circumstances, including the earlier altercation, to decide whether there was a sufficient provocation or a sufficient time for a reasonable person to cool off. Hence, the judge should agree to give the "heat of passion" manslaughter instruction. Some states recognize, as this state apparently does, an "imperfect self-defense" doctrine under which a murder may be reduced to manslaughter even though the defendant unreasonably but honestly believed in the necessity of responding with deadly force. Such a defense appears to also have been raised by the facts. Thus, the judge should instruct the jury on both theories, making (A) the correct answer choice and (B), (C), and (D) incorrect.

Answer to Question 173

(C) The statute will probably be found to violate the First Amendment because it is overbroad. The state can adopt a specific definition of obscenity applying to materials sold to minors, even though the material might not be obscene in terms of an adult audience. However, government may not prohibit the sale or distribution of material to adults merely because it is inappropriate for children. Here, there is no indication that the state has attempted less restrictive means of keeping minors from the objectionable video games, such as requiring arcade operators to put these games in a limited access area and monitor their use. While an outright ban on these games may be the most certain means of denying minors access to them, the denial of adult access to them indicates that the statute will probably be found unconstitutional. (A) is incorrect even though it is a true statement. As indicated above, a statute designed to protect minors must be narrowly drawn to avoid a First Amendment violation. (B) is incorrect because the fact that the statute precisely defines the content that is prohibited indicates only that it probably is not unconstitutionally vague; it does not affect its overbreadth problem. (D) is incorrect because, as indicated above, restrictions on materials available to minors do not necessarily have to satisfy the constitutional test for obscenity. In addition, (D) misstates the test: the element of serious social value is determined by a national standard, rather than community standards.

Answer to Question 174

(C) The younger brother's testimony is inadmissible hearsay because it is an out-of-court statement by the declarant (the elder brother) offered to prove that the elder brother's wife had driven through a red light, and no hearsay exceptions apply here. (A) is wrong because the elder brother is not a party to the litigation, and the husband-wife relationship does not suffice to allow the use of the statement against his wife as a vicarious admission. (B) is wrong because there is no indication that the elder brother is unavailable as a witness, which is required for the statement against interest exception to apply. (D) is wrong because the elder brother's statement was a statement of fact, rather than opinion; further, even if it were opinion, that would not make it inadmissible if it otherwise qualified as an admission.

Answer to Question 175

(C) Judgment should be for the husband. The niece, by quitclaim deed, conveyed to the husband her future ***interest*** in the property; technically, it is an executory interest. When the daughter died survived by a husband and no children, the niece would have taken title to the property pursuant to the owner's will. However, because of the quitclaim deed, the husband takes title to the property. (A) is incorrect because no after-acquired title is involved; the niece had her future interest from the moment of the owner's death, and that is what her deed transferred. (B) is incorrect because, although it is true that the husband took nothing under the owner's will, the niece chose to convey her interest in the property to the husband, as permitted by the applicable statute. (D) is incorrect because after-acquired title is inapplicable to these facts. Moreover, the after-acquired title doctrine applies to conveyances by warranty deed. The conveyance here was effected by quitclaim deed.

Answer to Question 176

(D) The beekeeper's refusal to perform was a breach of contract. Discharge of contractual duties by impossibility must be objective; *i.e.,* the duties could not be performed by anyone. Generally, physical incapacity of a person necessary to effectuate the contract only excuses performance where the services are deemed "unique." That would not be the case here. The beekeeper's allergy to the bees does not constitute objective impossibility of performance because his duties are delegable. Hence, his failure to deliver is not excused. (B) is wrong because his performance would be excused only if the parties had entered into a contract for personal services. (A) is wrong because the beekeeper promised to supply at least 100 pounds per month. (C) is wrong because such notice would not excuse a breach.

Answer to Question 177

(C) The jeweler did not properly reject the ring. When a buyer has rejected goods because of defects, the seller may, within the time originally provided for performance, cure by giving reasonable notice of intention to do so and making a new tender of conforming goods, which the buyer must then accept. The goldsmith took all of the steps necessary to cure. Consequently, the jeweler's rejection of the ring settings tendered on June 30 was improper. It follows that (A) is incorrect. (B) is incorrect because the goldsmith's prompt sending of a fax on June 4, indicating his intention to cure the defect, does not indicate a clear unwillingness or inability to perform, as is required for anticipatory repudiation. (D) is incorrect because modification of the contract is not at issue here. By curing the defective delivery, the goldsmith is simply performing according to the terms of the contract.

Answer to Question 178

(A) The woman is not guilty of common law larceny of the computer because her mistake prevented her from having the requisite mens rea for larceny. Larceny requires the intent to permanently deprive another of her interest in the property taken. The woman did not have such intent, given that she believed that the computer was her own and that her roommate had no possessory interest in it. Therefore, she did not have the intent required for larceny. (B) is wrong because the woman's mistake need not have been reasonable. When mistake is offered to negate the existence of general intent or malice, it must be a reasonable mistake. However, any mistake of fact, reasonable or unreasonable, is a defense to a specific intent crime, and larceny is a specific intent crime. (C) is wrong because, as stated above, she did not have the intent to deprive her roommate of her roommate's computer; her mistake negates such intent. (D) is wrong because the "continuing trespass" doctrine is inapplicable. Although larceny generally requires the intent to deprive another person of her interest in the property at the moment of taking, the continuing trespass doctrine provides that if a defendant takes property with a wrongful state of mind, but without the intent to steal, and then he later forms the intent to steal it, the trespass involved in the initial wrongful taking is regarded as "continuing" and the defendant is guilty of larceny. However, this doctrine has no application if the defendant's initial taking of the property, although trespassory, was not motivated by a wrongful state of mind. Here, the woman took her roommate's computer as a result of an innocent mistake. Even though she decided to keep the computer, she will not be guilty of larceny because her initial taking was done with an innocent state of mind.

Answer to Question 179

(B) The witness's testimony is admissible to show the effect of the statement on the defendant's state of mind. A statement is hearsay if it is offered to prove the truth of the matter asserted in the statement. If the statement is offered for another purpose, it is not considered a hearsay statement. Statements offered for the purpose of showing the effect on the listener are generally not classified as hearsay. Thus, (B) is correct, and (C) is wrong. (A) is wrong; the statements are not hearsay, and the state of mind exception applies to the state of mind of the speaker. (D) is wrong. Clearly, if the defendant heard the statement, that would tend to establish the fear necessary for a self-defense claim.

Answer to Question 180

(C) Because the appropriation by the village council implicates the Establishment Clause and a portion of the atheist's taxes are paying for the appropriation, the court should entertain his suit. To raise a constitutional challenge to a government action, the person who is challenging it must have standing to raise the constitutional issue. To have standing, a person must be able to assert that he is injured by a government program. This injury must be more than the merely theoretical injury that all persons suffer by seeing their government engage in unconstitutional actions. In cases where a taxpayer is claiming injury from the use of his taxes for an unconstitutional appropriation or expenditure of public funds, the Supreme Court has required the taxpayer to show that the challenged measure (i) was enacted under the governmental body's power to tax and spend (rather than as an incidental expenditure in the administration of an essentially regulatory statute), and (ii) exceeds some specific limitation on that power. The only specific limitation that the Court has recognized when an appropriation measure has been challenged is the First Amendment's Establishment Clause. [*See* Flast v. Cohen (1968)] Here, the atheist is challenging a specific appropriation of money by the village council that has been earmarked to benefit the property of the local church. The Establishment Clause, which is applicable to the states through the Fourteenth Amendment, requires that government programs (i) must have a secular purpose, (ii) must have a primary effect that neither advances nor inhibits religion, and (iii) must not produce excessive government entanglement with religion. Because the council's appropriation may violate these requirements, the atheist has standing as a taxpayer to sue the council. (A) is incorrect even though the portion of the atheist's taxes that would be used for the appropriation is minimal. While this factor has been relied on by the Supreme Court in its general refusal to grant federal and state taxpayers standing, it has not been used to deny municipal taxpayers standing in federal courts. [*See* Asarco, Inc. v. Kadish (1989)] Furthermore, the Court has carved out a narrow exception for federal taxpayers to challenge an appropriation, despite the fact that any one taxpayer's contribution would be minute and indeterminable, where the measure was enacted under Congress's taxing and spending powers and violates the Establishment Clause (as discussed above). This exception would be equally applicable to the village council's appropriation here if the court were to follow the federal taxpayer approach. Thus, the minimal contribution by the atheist's taxes would be irrelevant. (B) is incorrect because it does not recognize the limited exception discussed above. (D) is incorrect because generally taxpayers do not have standing to sue on constitutional grounds. The Supreme Court has not expanded the standing rules beyond what *Flast v. Cohen* had established.

Answer to Question 181

(D) The rancher can recover all of his damages. Where two or more tortious acts combine to proximately cause an indivisible injury to a plaintiff, each tortfeasor will be jointly and severally liable for that injury. This is so even though each defendant acted entirely independently. Here, the tortious acts of the two companies combined to proximately cause the poisoning of the rancher's cattle. Thus, each company will be jointly and severally liable for the entire amount of the rancher's damages. Thus, (D) is correct. (A) is wrong. Where two or more acts combine to cause the injury, but none of the acts standing alone would be sufficient, each of the acts is an actual cause of the injury (because but for either of the acts, the injury would not have occurred). Thus, the rancher can recover because the combined actions of the defendants caused his injury. (B) is wrong because the rancher need not show the amount of fault of each defendant to recover; they are both joint tortfeasors. (C) is wrong because, as mentioned, in this type of case the defendants are jointly and severally liable for the entire injury.

Answer to Question 182

(B) The neighbor's right to purchase the land is valid because it will vest or fail within the period prescribed by the Rule Against Perpetuities. The neighbor's right to purchase is a preemptive option, which is subject to the Rule Against Perpetuities. If the option could be exercised more than 21 years after some life in being at its creation, it is void. Obviously, the neighbor's right to purchase will vest or fail within 21 years after the owner's death. Thus, the Rule's provisions are satisfied. (A) is incorrect because recordation is not essential to the validity of the instrument, as between the grantor and grantee. Recordation merely gives notice to the world that an interest affecting title has been conveyed. (C) is incorrect because there is no prohibition against the owner of property conveying her property so that it will pass outside of her will. Here, the owner has chosen freely to dispose of the property in the manner described, and her choice will be given effect. (D) is incorrect because a preemptive right, such as is held by the neighbor, is not so onerous a restriction on transfer of property as to constitute an unreasonable restraint on alienation.

Answer to Question 183

(A) Pretrial familiarization of a signature by a nonexpert is not an accepted method of authentication because lay opinion as to the authenticity of handwriting must be based on personal familiarity with the handwriting. Here, the nonexpert's only familiarity with the defendant's usual signature has come from pretrial preparation. An expert witness or the trier of fact can determine the genuineness of a writing by comparing the questioned writing with another writing proved to be genuine. Thus, (B) would be an accepted method of authenticating the defendant's signature. (C) is an accepted method of authentication because it describes the requirements under the Federal Rules for authentication of an ancient document. (D) is acceptable as an admission by a party-opponent—*i.e.,* a prior acknowledgment by one of the parties of a relevant fact.

Answer to Question 184

(D) If the defendant believed that the building was abandoned, he probably will not be found to have had the requisite mens rea for murder. Murder is the unlawful killing of another human being with malice aforethought. Malice aforethought exists when the defendant has (i) intent to kill, (ii) intent to inflict great bodily injury, (iii) reckless indifference to an unjustifiably high risk to human life ("abandoned and malignant heart"), or (iv) intent to commit a felony (under the felony murder doctrine). Here, the jury could find that spraying a building with gunfire from a submachine gun demonstrates a reckless indifference to an unjustifiably high risk to human life even though the defendant was not intending to shoot anyone. However, if the jury accepts his assertion that he believed that the building was abandoned and had no idea that there would be any people inside it, the jury will probably find that he did not have a sufficient awareness of an unjustifiably high risk to human life to be liable for murder. (A) is not as strong a defense as (D) because the defendant may still be found liable for the murder as an accomplice. The defendant will be an accomplice to the drive-by shooting even if he was only the driver because he assisted the principal in the commission of the crime and had the intent to do so. An accomplice is liable not only for the crime he intended to aid but also for any other crimes committed during commission of the intended crime if the other crimes were probable or foreseeable. Here, even though the gang members knew that the store was closed, a jury could find that it was foreseeable that someone would be killed when they sprayed the building with gunfire. Even if the defendant was only the driver, his best defense would be his belief that the building was abandoned. (B) is incorrect because the defendant's voluntary intoxication would not be a defense to a murder charge that was based on reckless indifference to an unjustifiably high risk to human life. Voluntary intoxication caused by alcohol or drugs is a defense to a crime that requires purpose (intent) or knowledge as long as the intoxication prevents the defendant from formulating the purpose or obtaining the knowledge. It is no defense to crimes involving recklessness or negligence, however. Even though recklessness requires a conscious disregard of the risk, and the defendant's intoxication may make him unaware of the risk, courts hold him liable for recklessness offenses because his initial act of becoming voluntarily intoxicated was reckless. Thus, for murder based on a reckless indifference to an unjustifiably high risk to human life, voluntary intoxication would not be a defense. (C) is incorrect because duress is not a defense to murder. A criminal offense may be excused if the defendant does the act under threat of imminent infliction of death or great bodily harm, as long as the defendant reasonably believes that the threat will be carried out. However, no threat will suffice as a defense to a homicide crime. The defendant may still be liable for murder if he acted with an awareness of an unjustifiably high risk to human life.

Answer to Question 185

(D) The most likely theory is that the husband and the neighbors entered into a valid compromise. If the neighbors have given up a good faith claim, their agreement with the husband is a compromise supported by valid consideration. Thus, there is an enforceable contract. (A) is wrong because the husband was requesting a promise from the neighbors, not an act. (B) is wrong because the husband was under no obligation to reject a gift if he did not deliberately induce the neighbors to give it. (C) is wrong because there is no evidence that the neighbors gave the food in reliance on any promise made by the husband.

Answer to Question 186

(A) Title to the soaking pool resides in the bidder, the fee simple owner of the land. Under the concept of fixtures, the soaking pool was converted from personalty into realty. The soaking pool is an accessory to the land and passes with the ownership of the land. (B) is incorrect because the document purporting to transfer the entrepreneur's interest in the soaking pool to the buyer was insufficient to transfer real property. (C) is an incorrect statement of the law. (D) is incorrect because the soaking pool, as an accessory to the land, belongs to the owner of the land.

Answer to Question 187

(B) If the legislation is found to be unconstitutional, it will be because the commission will be exercising administrative powers. Under Article II, Section 2, Congress may not appoint members of a body with administrative or enforcement powers. Such persons are "officers of the United States" and must be appointed by the President with senatorial confirmation unless Congress has vested their appointment in the President alone, in federal courts, or in heads of departments. Here, selection of two members of the commission by a committee of the House of Representatives would violate the Appointments Clause because the commission has investigative and administrative powers. (A) is incorrect because the problem with the legislation is not that the President is infringing on the legislative branch's power by being able to veto congressional appointments, but rather that the congressional appointments are infringing on the executive branch appointment power. (C) is incorrect because Congress may by law vest appointment power of inferior officers in the federal courts. Hence, the judiciary has been properly granted the power by Congress to appoint members of the commission. (D) is incorrect because only Cabinet-level officers require Senate confirmation for their appointment. Inferior officers, which would include members of this commission, may be appointed by the President without Senate approval if provided for by Congress, as is the case here.

Answer to Question 188

(C) Title to the property is vested one-half in the brother free of the mortgage, and one-half in the daughter subject to the mortgage. Because the jurisdiction in which the property is located recognizes the title theory of mortgages, execution of the mortgage on the property effected a severance of the joint tenancy, by passing a title interest from the sister to the bank. Following severance of the joint tenancy, the brother and the sister held title as tenants in common, with no right of survivorship. The interest of a tenant in common passes by succession. When the sister died, the brother could not take the property by right of survivorship because of the severance of the joint tenancy. Thus, (A) and (B) are incorrect. Upon her mother's death, the daughter succeeded to her interest in the property, subject to the mortgage. However, the brother's interest in the property, as a tenant in common, is not subject to the mortgage. Therefore, (D) is incorrect and (C) is correct.

Answer to Question 189

(B) Both an injunction and damages should be ordered. The church has a life estate pur autre vie, and a life tenant as a general rule is not entitled to consume or exploit natural resources on the property; this constitutes affirmative (voluntary) waste that injures the interests of the future interest holders. Any award of damages will be held until the class gift to the grandchildren closes at the son's death. (A) is wrong because the church's action did not terminate its interest. The "provided that" language creates a condition subsequent. An estate subject to a condition subsequent does not terminate automatically on the happening of the condition. To terminate, the grantor must exercise a right of entry, and here no right of entry was reserved. (C) is wrong because it is entirely unnecessary for the owner and her son to be parties, because neither of them has any interest in the land. The owner has given up her interest entirely, and the son is present in the conveyance only to serve as a measuring life for the life estate; he owns no interest in the land itself. (D) is wrong because the injury to the land is permanent and therefore should be prevented by an injunction.

Answer to Question 190

(B) The woman can be convicted of either kidnapping or false imprisonment, but not both. False imprisonment consists of unlawful confinement of a person without her valid consent. Confinement requires that the victim either be compelled to go where she does not wish to go or to remain where she does not wish to remain. A confinement is unlawful unless specifically authorized by law or by the victim's consent. Any consent must be freely given by one with capacity to give such consent; *i.e.,* consent is invalidated if obtained by coercion, threats, deception, or incapacity arising from mental illness, retardation, or youth. Here, the woman compelled the girl to go with her to the zoo by lying to her about her mother's having to go out of town and asking the woman to care for the girl. This constitutes a confinement because, despite the fact that the girl enjoyed her time with the woman, the girl was only four years old and incapable of validly consenting to go and remain with the woman. Such confinement was not authorized by law. Consequently, the woman could be convicted of and sentenced for false imprisonment. Kidnapping under modern statutes is confinement of a person that involves either some movement of the victim or concealment of the victim in a secret place. As with false imprisonment, consent freely given by a person competent to do so precludes a confinement or movement from being kidnapping. However, a young child is incapable of giving valid consent to her detention or movement. The woman "moved" the girl by taking her to the zoo. This was a confinement because the girl was compelled to go where she would not otherwise have gone. The fact that the experience apparently was totally enjoyable for the girl does not mean that there was a valid consent that would preclude a conviction for kidnapping. As explained above, the girl is incapacitated by her age from giving a valid consent to the woman's actions. For the foregoing reasons, the woman can be properly convicted of and sentenced for kidnapping. However, the woman cannot be convicted of ***both*** kidnapping and false imprisonment, because false imprisonment is a lesser included offense of kidnapping (*i.e.,* kidnapping is a form of aggravated false imprisonment). A lesser included offense is one that consists entirely of some, but not all, elements of the greater crime. A person may not be convicted of both the greater offense and a lesser included offense. False imprisonment and kidnapping both consist of unlawfully confining a person against her will, with kidnapping containing the added elements of either moving or concealing the victim. Thus, false imprisonment is a lesser included offense of kidnapping. Consequently, the woman may be convicted of and sentenced for ***either*** of these offenses, but ***not both*** of them. (A) is incorrect because kidnapping is not the only crime of which the woman can be convicted. (C) is incorrect because, as discussed above, there can be a conviction and sentence for either of these crimes, but not for both of them. (D) is incorrect because these facts support a conviction for either of the crimes mentioned.

Answer to Question 191

(A) Because the witness persists in refusing to testify as to matters covered in his earlier testimony, he should be considered "unavailable" at the defendant's trial. Thus, his former testimony should be admissible as an exception to the hearsay rule. It will be considered to be trustworthy because it was given during formal proceedings, under oath, and subject to cross-examination. (B) is wrong because this is not the applicable exception to the hearsay rule. In this case, there is no evidence that the witness does not presently remember the facts in question. (C) is wrong because the witness could have asserted his privilege against self-incrimination when the former testimony was given. He can assert his privilege at present to keep from testifying. (D) is wrong because there is an applicable exception to the hearsay rule.

Answer to Question 192

(D) The preacher's challenge should succeed. Having created a forum generally open for use by all groups, the town must justify its exclusions therefrom under applicable constitutional norms. To justify discriminatory exclusion from a public forum based on the religious content of a group's intended speech, the town must show that the ordinance is necessary to serve a compelling state interest, and that it is narrowly drawn to achieve that end, and nothing in the facts indicates that the town will be able to do so. (B) suggests that the ordinance serves the compelling interest of maintaining separation of church and state. However, the former "equal access" policy did not offend the Establishment Clause. The former policy had a secular purpose (providing a forum in which citizens can exchange ideas); it avoided excessive entanglement with religion; and it did not have a primary effect of either advancing or inhibiting religion (permitting religious groups to use the auditorium would result in, at most, an incidental benefit). Thus, (B) is incorrect. (A) is incorrect because an unjustified content-based exclusion of religious speech is not made more acceptable by virtue of the fact that it treats all religions equally. (C) is incorrect because, although there is no authoritative constitutional definition of religion, it is unlikely that the term "religious groups" will be deemed to be impermissibly vague.

Answer to Question 193

(A) The child will recover under the conditions stated in (A). The electric company had notice that the insulators were being destroyed, causing the power lines to fall. Certainly, it was foreseeable that children, or anyone else, in the vicinity of a fallen line might be injured by such a dangerous condition. Consequently, the electric company had a duty to take reasonable steps, if possible, to prevent the lines from falling. Breach of this duty will lay the foundation for a recovery by the child. (B) is simply an incorrect statement of the law; a supplier of electricity is not subject to strict liability. (C) is incorrect because, even if the company took measures to stop the destruction of the insulators, it also had a duty to take precautions against the danger of falling power lines. (D) is incorrect because the electric company had a duty to make its operations safe in light of the destruction of which it had notice. This is true even though the destruction was intentional. Criminal acts and intentional torts of third persons are not superseding forces where they are foreseeable, such as here.

Answer to Question 194

(D) It would not be appropriate to grant the property solely to the friend without compensation to the buyer. When a purchaser has paid only part of the purchase price under an installment land contract, most courts hold that the purchaser is protected by the recording acts only to the extent of payment made. Depending on the equities involved in the case, the court has three options: (i) create a tenancy in common in the property, with the contract purchaser receiving a share of the property equal to the proportion of payments made; (ii) award the land to the prior claimant, but give the contract purchaser a right to recover the amount she paid (with interest), secured by a lien on the property; or (iii) award the land to the contract purchaser, but require the contract purchaser to make the remaining payments to the prior claimant. This last obligation is also secured by a lien on the property. Thus, (A), (B), and (C) are all appropriate actions for the court. (D) is not appropriate because it misstates the law. When only partial payment of the purchase price has been paid, the subsequent purchaser is protected only to the extent of payment. Thus, even if the equities favored the friend and she was allowed to retain the property, the buyer would be entitled to the remaining payments.

Answer to Question 195

(B) Restrictions on the ability of persons to be candidates may violate the First Amendment rights of speech and political association or the Fourteenth Amendment Equal Protection Clause. The Supreme Court uses a balancing test in determining whether a regulation of the electoral process is valid: if the restriction on First Amendment activities is severe, it will be upheld only if it is

narrowly tailored to achieve a compelling interest, but if the restriction is reasonable and nondiscriminatory, it generally will be upheld on the basis of the state's important regulatory interests. Thus, if the ballot restriction here is deemed to be a severe and unreasonable burden on independent candidates, the candidate's best argument is (B)—that the objectives of the statute could be satisfactorily achieved by less burdensome means. [*See* Norman v. Reed (1992)] A state may require that independent candidates obtain a reasonable number of signatures. Although such a requirement may be burdensome, that factor alone does not make it invalid. Thus, (A) is not as strong an argument as (B). (D) is incorrect because signature requirements may be justified by a state interest in assuring that candidates have at least minimal support before they are allowed to appear on the ballot. (C) is incorrect because the fact that few independent candidates have obtained ballot status may simply reflect the absence of even the minimal popular support which the state may legitimately require.

Answer to Question 196

(D) The court should deny the motion to suppress because the police had a warrant to search the boyfriend's home. The boyfriend's expectation of privacy extended only to his own home, which was searched under a warrant. He does not have standing to assert a Fourth Amendment claim regarding the search of his girlfriend's apartment because her apartment was not his home, and he did not own it or have a right to possession of it. Thus, (A) is incorrect. Because the boyfriend cannot object to the search that provided the probable cause for the search of his apartment, (B) is also incorrect. (C) is not a valid justification because there is nothing to indicate that the seizure would fall under the "inevitable discovery" exception to the exclusionary rule.

Answer to Question 197

(D) The mechanic is liable by virtue of his negligence, and the owner is vicariously liable for the mechanic's negligence by virtue of the statute. Where such joint liability exists, the plaintiff may recover the entire judgment amount from either defendant. Further, where one is held liable for damages caused by another simply because of his relationship to that person (*i.e.,* vicarious liability), such person may seek indemnification from the person whose conduct actually caused the damage. Applying the foregoing principles to the facts of this question, the plaintiff may recover the entire $100,000 from the owner and the mechanic jointly. This eliminates (A) and (B). Because the owner is only liable vicariously, she is entitled to indemnification from the mechanic for any amount collected from the owner by the plaintiff. Therefore, (D) is the correct answer and (C) is incorrect.

Answer to Question 198

(B) If the man had a reasonable *(i.e.,* good faith) belief in the enforceability of his claim, his surrender of the claim is valid consideration. (A) is wrong because his motive for feeding and returning the cat is immaterial. (C) is wrong. The source of the cat owner's money is irrelevant. In addition, the accounts were held in joint tenancy and any interest the cat owner may have had in the funds ended when she died. (D) is wrong because there was no consideration given for the cat owner's promise and the fact that it was in writing does not change the lack of consideration.

Answer to Question 199

(A) The rancher acquired title to the tract by adverse possession. He possessed the property for longer than the required 10 years. Although the rancher entered the tract without the landowner's knowledge, he dealt with the property in such a manner as to put the true owner and the community on notice of the fact of his possession. Also, the rancher's possession was continuous, exclusive, and hostile. Thus, the elements of adverse possession are present. Because the landowner lost title to the land due to the rancher's adverse possession, it follows that (B) is incorrect. (C) is incorrect because the friend never possessed the land for the requisite statutory period. Also, she did not hold the land in a hostile manner for a continuous period. (D) is incorrect because the nephew, who supposedly took title to the tract by a quitclaim deed from the landowner, cannot take title from someone who had none to convey.

Answer to Question 200

(A) The son's testimony, although hearsay, should be admissible under the exception for present sense impressions. Hearsay is defined under the Federal Rules as "a statement, other than one made by the declarant while testifying at the trial or hearing, offered in evidence to prove the truth of the matter asserted." The son's testimony as to what his father said on the phone is hearsay: the father's statement that "my accountant is at my door" is being offered in evidence by someone other than the father to prove that the accountant was present at the father's house shortly before he was killed. The son's testimony is therefore not admissible under Fed. R. Evid. 802 unless an exception to the hearsay rule applies. Rule 803(1) recognizes an exception for a statement "describing or explaining an event or condition made while the declarant was perceiving the event or condition, or immediately thereafter." Because the statement is made concurrently with the event it is describing, it is safe from defects in memory and there is usually little or no time for calculated misstatements. Here, the father's statement that "my accountant is at my door" was made to his son immediately after he perceived the accountant to be there. Thus, the statement is the father's present sense impression that his son may testify to at trial. (B) is incorrect because the father's statement is not being offered to show his state of mind or his intent to do something in the future. The prosecution is using the father's statement simply to establish the accountant's presence at his house the day he was killed. (C) is incorrect because the prior identification must be by the witness testifying at trial to be admissible. Had the father survived an attempted homicide and testified at the accountant's trial, Fed. R. Evid. 801(d)(1)(C) would permit his prior statement to the lawyer identifying the accountant to be admitted as nonhearsay and substantive evidence. (D) is incorrect. While the testimony is hearsay, it falls within the exception to the hearsay rule for present sense impressions.

Mixed Subject Practice Questions and Analytical Answers

Mixed Subject Set 1 Answer Sheet

1.	Ⓐ	Ⓑ	Ⓒ	Ⓓ	19.	Ⓐ	Ⓑ	Ⓒ	Ⓓ
2.	Ⓐ	Ⓑ	Ⓒ	Ⓓ	20.	Ⓐ	Ⓑ	Ⓒ	Ⓓ
3.	Ⓐ	Ⓑ	Ⓒ	Ⓓ	21.	Ⓐ	Ⓑ	Ⓒ	Ⓓ
4.	Ⓐ	Ⓑ	Ⓒ	Ⓓ	22.	Ⓐ	Ⓑ	Ⓒ	Ⓓ
5.	Ⓐ	Ⓑ	Ⓒ	Ⓓ	23.	Ⓐ	Ⓑ	Ⓒ	Ⓓ
6.	Ⓐ	Ⓑ	Ⓒ	Ⓓ	24.	Ⓐ	Ⓑ	Ⓒ	Ⓓ
7.	Ⓐ	Ⓑ	Ⓒ	Ⓓ	25.	Ⓐ	Ⓑ	Ⓒ	Ⓓ
8.	Ⓐ	Ⓑ	Ⓒ	Ⓓ	26.	Ⓐ	Ⓑ	Ⓒ	Ⓓ
9.	Ⓐ	Ⓑ	Ⓒ	Ⓓ	27.	Ⓐ	Ⓑ	Ⓒ	Ⓓ
10.	Ⓐ	Ⓑ	Ⓒ	Ⓓ	28.	Ⓐ	Ⓑ	Ⓒ	Ⓓ
11.	Ⓐ	Ⓑ	Ⓒ	Ⓓ	29.	Ⓐ	Ⓑ	Ⓒ	Ⓓ
12.	Ⓐ	Ⓑ	Ⓒ	Ⓓ	30.	Ⓐ	Ⓑ	Ⓒ	Ⓓ
13.	Ⓐ	Ⓑ	Ⓒ	Ⓓ	31.	Ⓐ	Ⓑ	Ⓒ	Ⓓ
14.	Ⓐ	Ⓑ	Ⓒ	Ⓓ	32.	Ⓐ	Ⓑ	Ⓒ	Ⓓ
15.	Ⓐ	Ⓑ	Ⓒ	Ⓓ	33.	Ⓐ	Ⓑ	Ⓒ	Ⓓ
16.	Ⓐ	Ⓑ	Ⓒ	Ⓓ	34.	Ⓐ	Ⓑ	Ⓒ	Ⓓ
17.	Ⓐ	Ⓑ	Ⓒ	Ⓓ	35.	Ⓐ	Ⓑ	Ⓒ	Ⓓ
18.	Ⓐ	Ⓑ	Ⓒ	Ⓓ	36.	Ⓐ	Ⓑ	Ⓒ	Ⓓ

MIXED SUBJECT QUESTIONS - SET 1

Question 1

A friend knew that a man and a woman cared deeply for each other and encouraged the man to ask the woman to marry. Unbeknownst to the friend, the man was already married. Finally, after continued encouragement by the friend, the man went through a marriage ceremony with the woman, and the friend was the man's best man at the ceremony.

If the friend is charged with being an accessory to bigamy, he should be found:

(A) Guilty, because he encouraged the man, and his mistake as to the existence of a prior marriage is no defense to a charge of bigamy.

(B) Guilty, because he was present when the crime occurred and is thus a principal in the second degree.

(C) Not guilty, because he did not have the mental state required for aiding and abetting.

(D) Not guilty, because his encouragement and assistance was not the legal cause of the crime.

Question 2

A dump truck driver was driving a dump truck at a safe speed. From the other direction a semitrailer driver came around a curve and was confronted with a very slow-moving steamroller just in front of him. To avoid colliding with the steamroller, the semitrailer driver pulled his wheel to the left and crossed the center lane, where he bore down on the dump truck driver, who was coming from the other direction. The semitrailer driver did not yield, and there were other vehicles to the dump truck driver's left. The dump truck driver's only option was to turn his truck to the right, onto another person's land. The truck caused damage to the landowner's lawn.

Which of the following best describes the dump truck driver's liability to the landowner?

(A) The dump truck driver is liable for the damage to the lawn.

(B) The dump truck driver is liable for private nuisance, because he has interfered with the landowner's use and enjoyment of the land.

(C) The dump truck driver is liable for both trespass and public nuisance.

(D) The dump truck driver is liable for nothing, because the incident was not his fault, and he acted in a reasonable and responsible manner.

Question 3

The police set up an undercover "sting" operation in which they posed as fences of stolen property and bought and sold such property to anyone who came into their warehouse. A defendant is being prosecuted for receiving stolen property in connection with his arrest by the undercover police officers, and the prosecution attempts to introduce a videotape showing the defendant offering to sell a television set to one of the undercover police officers.

If this evidence is held to be inadmissible, the most likely reason is that:

(A) It is hearsay not within any exception.

(B) It violates the defendant's privilege against self-incrimination.

(C) A proper foundation was not established for its introduction into evidence.

(D) Criminality may not be proven by specific instances of misconduct.

Question 4

A woman and a man had lived together for several years but had never married because the man was already married. During the time the woman and the man lived together, they had accumulated property. One day, the man told the woman to move out.

The state in which they lived recognized in general the validity of property agreements entered into by unmarried couples who lived together, but there was a statute that provided that such agreements were void as being against public policy when one of the parties living together was married to another. The woman brought suit against the man, alleging that they had an agreement to share equally all property accumulated by them during the time they lived together, and challenging the constitutionality of the statute.

Will the woman prevail in her challenge to the statute?

(A) Yes, if the state fails to prove that the statute is rationally related to a legitimate state purpose.

(B) Yes, if the woman can prove that the statute is not necessary to effectuate a compelling state interest.

(C) No, if the woman fails to prove that the statute is not rationally related to a legitimate government purpose.

(D) No, if the state proves that the statute was necessary and proper.

Question 5

A state statute required all persons operating a catering business within the state to be licensed by the state board of health. The statute further provided that licenses will be granted only to applicants who have resided in the state for five years and who are citizens of the United States. A long-time resident of the state who was not a United States citizen challenges the requirement that applicants for licenses must be citizens of the United States.

This provision is most likely:

(A) Constitutional, as an exercise of the state's police power.

(B) Constitutional, as an effort to protect the health and welfare of the residents of the state.

(C) Unconstitutional, as a denial of equal protection.

(D) Unconstitutional, as a bill of attainder.

Question 6

A mother and her son were walking through a park where dog owners frequently exercised their dogs and sometimes unleashed them. Suddenly, a large black dog attacked the mother, seriously injuring her. The son suffered minor injuries when he tried to drive the dog away from his mother. The mother and the son filed a personal injury suit against the dog owner. The dog owner denies that the attacking animal was his dog. At trial, the son is called as a witness to testify that he was looking directly at the dog owner when the dog owner unleashed the dog, which immediately ran up to them and attacked the mother.

Should this testimony be admitted over the dog owner's objection that the son is not competent to testify?

(A) No, because the son is a close relative of a party, and therefore may not testify on that party's behalf.

(B) No, because the son is a party-plaintiff, and therefore may not testify as to the facts of the accident.

(C) Yes, because the son appears to be over the legal age to testify.

(D) Yes, because there is nothing to indicate that the son is incompetent to testify.

Question 7

Acting on an anonymous telephone call, the police went to a woman's apartment, pounded on the door, and demanded to search it for possible stolen property. The woman refused. The police then kicked open the door and placed the woman under arrest. The woman then offered to give the officers some inside information in exchange for her release. Before she could say anything else, the woman was given *Miranda* warnings by the police. Thereafter, she told the police that she knew of a large supply of stolen property stored at a nearby warehouse and said that she and a friend had been selling the stolen property out of the warehouse for years. The police raided the warehouse and recovered the stolen property. The woman was charged with conspiracy to sell stolen property and for possession of stolen property. At her trial, the woman moved to suppress the statements.

Which of the following is the woman's best argument in support of the motion to suppress?

(A) The woman was intimidated by the forced entry into her home and, because her statements were involuntary and coerced, their use against her would violate due process of law.

(B) The woman is entitled to know the identity of her accuser, and the state cannot supply this information.

(C) The woman's statements were fruits of an unlawful arrest, and although the *Miranda* warnings may have been sufficient to protect her right against self-incrimination, they were not sufficient to purge the taint of the illegal arrest.

(D) The police should have given the woman *Miranda* warnings prior to entry into her home, and the warnings were ineffectual once the woman offered to give information.

Question 8

A geologist was studying the land formations in and around a mountain. One day, he opened a newspaper to find that he was in an ad for a brand of cigarettes. The ad headline "quoted" the geologist as saying, "They make you feel like you're in the mountains." The geologist is certain that it is his picture, but he never posed for the ad for the cigarettes. The geologist brings an action to recover damages against the cigarette company.

Most likely his best cause of action is:

(A) Defamation.

(B) Invasion of privacy.

(C) Intentional infliction of emotional distress.

(D) Negligent infliction of emotional distress.

Question 9

Twenty-five years ago, a man purchased a vacant tract of land from a woman. Unbeknownst to the man, the woman did not own the land. Someone else owned the land in fee simple. Shortly after the purchase, the man built a house on the northwest corner of the tract, leaving the rest of the tract vacant. Recently, the actual owner of the tract died, still without knowledge that the man had built a house on the northwest corner of the tract. The actual owner's will left all of his property to his son. The relevant statutory period for adverse possession is 20 years.

If the man brings suit to quiet title to the tract he had purchased 25 years ago, the court should decide that:

(A) The man is the owner of the entire tract.

(B) The son is the owner of the entire tract, because as to him, adverse possession began when the actual owner died.

(C) The son is the owner of the entire tract, because the man only occupied a portion of the tract.

(D) The son is the owner of the entire tract, if the man did not pay the property taxes on the entire tract.

Question 10

A man owned a tract of land in fee simple. Fifteen years ago, he built a barn on five acres that he believed were part of his property. One year later, the man discovered that the five acres on which he had built his barn were not part of his property. The five acres actually belonged to a woman. The next year, the woman died, leaving all of her property to her one-year-old daughter. Now the man brings a quiet title action against the daughter. The statutory period for adverse possession in this jurisdiction is 10 years.

Who will prevail?

(A) The daughter, because the man did not pay the property taxes on the five acres.

(B) The daughter, because her status as a minor would toll the adverse possession statute until she reached her majority.

(C) The man, because he honestly believed that the five acres were part of his land.

(D) The man, because he was in continuous possession of the five acres for the statutory period.

Question 11

A woman purchased a tract of land from a man by warranty deed. Unbeknownst to the woman, the man was not the actual owner of the tract. The woman built a home on the tract and moved into it. Two years later, the actual owner learned of the man's transaction with the woman and prevented the woman from entering the tract from that point forward. This led to a costly court battle. When the woman notified the man and told him that she thought it was his duty to straighten this out, he ignored her.

The woman would succeed in a suit for damages against the man for breach of which of the following covenants of title?

(A) The covenant of quiet enjoyment only.

(B) The covenants of seisin, right to convey, quiet enjoyment, warranty, further assurances, and the covenant against encumbrances.

(C) The covenants of seisin, right to convey, quiet enjoyment, warranty, and further assurances.

(D) The covenants of seisin and right to convey only.

Question 12

A police officer saw an unarmed thief grab a coat off the rack of a store and run. As the police officer gave chase, the thief ducked into an alley. When the police officer came to the alley, she saw movement behind some boxes. She yelled for the thief to come out or she would shoot. When the thief did not, the police officer shot at the boxes. A bag lady had been asleep behind them, and she was killed. The police officer is charged with homicide.

A jury should find the police officer:

(A) Not guilty of homicide, because she was attempting to catch a thief who was fleeing from a crime, and the police officer had the right to use deadly force.

(B) Not guilty of homicide, because she saw the thief commit a misdemeanor, and therefore she had the right to use deadly force if necessary to arrest him.

(C) Guilty of homicide, unless she had reason to believe that the thief was a felon.

(D) Guilty of homicide, because she was not entitled to use deadly force.

Question 13

A plaintiff sues a defendant for breach of contract. The existence and terms of the contract are in dispute. The plaintiff's lawyer calls the plaintiff to the witness stand and seeks to elicit testimony that the plaintiff and the defendant met on a certain date and reached an agreement, which was reduced to a writing. The plaintiff then intends to testify, "The writing, which was subsequently inadvertently destroyed, provided that the defendant would purchase 300 widgets from me at a price of $1,000."

The quoted testimony is admissible only if:

(A) The judge finds that the writing is unavailable, through no fault of the plaintiff.

(B) The judge finds that the plaintiff is accurately relating the contents of the writing.

(C) The jury finds that the writing is unavailable, through no fault of the plaintiff.

(D) The jury finds that the plaintiff is accurately relating the contents of the writing.

Question 14

Congress determined that there should be a uniform law for handgun registration throughout the United States and enacted the Federal Firearms Act.

Which of the following constitutional provisions could most easily be considered the basis of such enactment?

(A) The Equal Protection Clause of the Fourteenth Amendment.

(B) The Second Amendment.

(C) The Commerce Clause.

(D) The Necessary and Proper Clause.

Question 15

A store sold office equipment and supplies to various businesses in the area. The store entered into a written agreement with an electronics company to purchase all of its monthly requirements of printers for a period of five years at a specified unit price. The agreement contained a nonassignment clause. Shortly thereafter, the electronics company assigned the contract to a finance company as security for a loan. The store subsequently ordered the printers from the electronics company and paid the electronics company the agreed price for the printers for the first month of the agreement.

Which of the following accurately states the legal effect of the covenant not to assign the contract?

(A) The covenant as properly interpreted was not breached, and the assignment was effective.

(B) The covenant made the assignment to the finance company ineffective.

(C) The electronics company's assignment was a breach of its contract with the store but was nevertheless effective to transfer to the finance company the electronic company's rights against the store.

(D) The covenant is effective if the parties can establish a rational reason for including the covenant into their agreement.

Question 16

A retailer and a supplier entered into a supply agreement. The supplier then assigned the agreement to a wholesaler for consideration. The retailer, unaware of the assignment, made payment to the original supplier.

Which of the following is correct?

(A) The retailer and the supplier are each liable to the wholesaler for half the amount paid.

(B) The supplier is liable to the wholesaler for the full amount.

(C) The retailer is liable to the wholesaler for the full amount.

(D) Neither the retailer nor the supplier is liable to the wholesaler for any amount.

Question 17

A store and a company entered into an agreement under which the store would make payment to one of the company's creditors. The creditor did not become aware of the agreement between the store and the company until the store paid the company directly. The creditor sues the company for payment.

Which of the following is correct?

(A) The creditor, as an incidental beneficiary of the agreement between the store and the company, can sue the company for payment.

(B) The creditor has a prior right to payment against the company.

(C) The creditor has no right to payment because its rights have not yet vested.

(D) The creditor cannot sue for payment because the original agreement is in violation of the Statute of Frauds.

Question 18

A vineyard and a wine distributor enter into a valid written agreement whereby the vineyard is to supply the wine distributor with all of the distributor's requirements of wine for a period of five years. The agreement contains a nonassignment clause. Nonetheless, a few months after the agreement is entered into, the vineyard assigns its rights under the contract to one of its creditors. After one year, the wine distributor decides that it wishes to purchase its wines from a different vineyard and terminates its contract with the original vineyard.

If the creditor of the vineyard sues the distributor, will it prevail?

(A) Yes, because the distributor did not terminate the contract in good faith, because it still had a requirement for the wine.

(B) No, because the vineyard's "assignment of the contract" to its creditor would normally be interpreted as a delegation of duties under the contract as well as an assignment of its rights, and its duties owed to the distributor were personal and therefore nondelegable.

(C) The vineyard's rights under its agreement with the distributor were personal and therefore nonassignable.

(D) The original contract between the vineyard and the wine distributor was unenforceable by either party for want of a legally sufficient consideration for the vineyard's promise to supply the wine distributor's requirements of wine.

Question 19

A pilot was flying his airplane, which he always kept well-maintained. Due to a flock of birds that suddenly got in his way, the pilot was forced to seek an emergency landing area and glided toward a field where children were playing. As the pilot made his landing, he was unable to avoid striking and injuring one child.

If the child brings an action for personal injuries against the pilot, what is the pilot's best defense?

(A) He did not act willfully and wantonly.

(B) He could not reasonably foresee that he would have to make an emergency landing.

(C) He used reasonable care in the maintenance of his aircraft.

(D) His conduct was not the cause of the injury to the child.

Question 20

A woman took her car in for scheduled maintenance. The mechanic certified that the car was in perfect working order. Later that day, the woman was driving beyond the posted speed limit when her brakes failed, causing her car to strike a pedestrian.

If the pedestrian brings an action against the mechanic who certified the woman's car as operable, what will be the probable outcome?

(A) Judgment for the mechanic, because the pedestrian was legally a bystander.

(B) Judgment for the mechanic, because the woman's negligence was an independent, superseding cause.

(C) Judgment for the pedestrian if the mechanic was negligent in inspecting the car.

(D) Judgment for the pedestrian, because the mechanic was strictly liable in tort.

Question 21

A man was arrested by a police officer when he was found carrying an ice pick concealed in his pants. The man stated that he carried the ice pick only for protection. The man was convicted of violating a state statute prohibiting the carrying of a concealed "knife or dagger." The man appealed his conviction on the basis that an ice pick is not a "knife or dagger" as defined in the statute under which he was convicted.

The appellate court will hold that:

(A) The man's conviction should be upheld if the appellate court finds that the statute sought to outlaw the classic instruments of violence and their homemade equivalents, such as an ice pick.

(B) The man's conviction should be upheld, because an ice pick is a weapon, by the man's own admission.

(C) The man's conviction should be overturned, because he was carrying the ice pick for protection only.

(D) The man's conviction should be overturned, because he harbored no malicious intent.

Question 22

A buyer is interested in buying the northern half of a large tract of land from its current owner. The land has a stream running across it that eventually flows into a river on the northern half of the land. The buyer and seller eventually agree on the price, and the seller conveys by deed to the buyer according to the following description: "The upper portion of my land, from the northern boundary to the stream."

In determining the exact boundaries of the portion of the land purchased by the buyer, which of the following would be the most accurate?

(A) The seller retained the entire stream as part of her portion of the land.

(B) The seller and the buyer each own one-half of the stream bed.

(C) The buyer owns the entire stream because of the rule interpreting the words of a deed most stringently against the grantor.

(D) Because the description is invalid, the ownership interest of the seller and the buyer in the stream cannot be determined.

Question 23

A woman's car was stolen while parked. The car was never recovered. Following all required procedures, she filed a claim with her insurer. The insurer refused to pay, claiming that the loss was not covered because the woman had not locked her car as required by her policy. In a declaratory judgment action, the woman seeks to testify that she always locks her car when she gets out of it.

The judge should find the woman's offer to testify:

(A) Objectionable, because it calls for a self-serving declaration.

(B) Objectionable, because it is not relevant.

(C) Unobjectionable, because it calls for evidence of habit.

(D) Unobjectionable, if it is offered as impeachment evidence.

Question 24

The President of the United States and the leader of a bordering foreign nation agreed that each should appoint three members to a special joint commission to deal with a wildlife problem. The President of the United States, acting in concert with the foreign leader, named the joint commission as a permanent enforcement agency for the regulations that were adopted by both nations. Although the President received prior congressional authorization to enter into this agreement, the Senate did not ratify the agreement by a two-thirds vote. The President then entered into an executive agreement with the foreign leader whereby the joint commission was granted adjudicative as well as enforcement powers with respect to a particular issue.

The executive agreement by the President is:

(A) Valid, because the President has unlimited powers in entering into executive agreements.

(B) Valid, because the agreement is within the President's powers in the area of foreign affairs.

(C) Invalid, because the Senate did not ratify the executive agreement by a two-thirds vote.

(D) Invalid, because wildlife is not an area left solely to presidential discretion.

Question 25

Congress passed a law making it a crime to hunt a particular animal during certain months. The animal regularly migrated among several states and a federal wilderness area during the months that hunting was banned. One of the states adopted a statute allowing unlimited hunting of that animal during these months, because an overabundance of the animal was causing damage to the land. An entity that has been found to have standing in such matters filed an action in federal district court seeking to overturn the state statute.

The district court most likely would declare the state statute to be:

(A) Constitutional, because the conservation of wildlife is an issue best left to the states in which the wildlife is located.

(B) Constitutional, because a state statute protecting its land takes precedence over any federal laws.

(C) Unconstitutional, because a federal law is the law of the land, and any acts by a state inconsistent therewith are null and void.

(D) Unconstitutional, because the conservation of wildlife is not within the police powers of the state.

Question 26

While in a department store, a man picked up a sweater and slipped it under his shirt. The man then started for the door. A woman, who also was shopping in the store, saw the man take the sweater. The woman grabbed a baseball bat from the sporting goods aisle and chased the man into the parking lot. The woman began swinging the bat at the man's head, hoping to knock him out and thus prevent the theft. The man pulled a knife from his pocket and stabbed the woman, killing her. The man was arrested and charged with murder.

At trial, the man will most likely be found:

(A) Guilty, because the evidence shows that he provoked the assault on himself by his criminal misconduct.

(B) Guilty, because the evidence shows that the man intended to kill or cause serious bodily harm.

(C) Not guilty, because the jury could find that the man acted recklessly and not with the intent to cause death or serious bodily harm.

(D) Not guilty, because the man was acting in self-defense.

Question 27

A wife is on trial for the murder of her husband. She is accused of pushing him from the window of their thirteenth-floor apartment; she claims he committed suicide. The wife called an operator for a suicide-prevention clinic to testify that the deceased husband had called the clinic on more than one occasion threatening to "end it all."

The judge should rule the testimony:

(A) Admissible, because the statement was made in "contemplation" of death.

(B) Admissible, because it tends to show that the husband intended to commit suicide.

(C) Inadmissible, because it violates the psychiatrist-patient privilege.

(D) Inadmissible, because no phone calls were made to the clinic by the husband on the day he died.

Question 28

A large tract of land was located in a jurisdiction that has adopted the following statute:

> No conveyance or mortgage of an interest in land is valid against a subsequent purchaser for value without notice thereof whose conveyance is first recorded.

The man who owned the land owed money to a woman, and in satisfaction of this debt, the man conveyed the property to her. Although the woman intended to have the deed recorded, she mistakenly failed to do so. Two years later, the man borrowed money from a bank and, to secure the loan, executed a mortgage deed on the property. The bank promptly recorded this mortgage. Three months later, the man, just before he died, donated the property by general warranty to his son, who did not know about the prior events. The son recorded the deed and entered into a contract with his friend to sell him the property. The next month, the woman discovered that the deed in her safe was not recorded, and so without notice of any of the prior transactions, the woman recorded the deed. A month after that, the friend paid the son full value for the property, and without actual knowledge of any of the other transactions regarding the property, the friend had the deed duly recorded. By the end of the next year, the friend had expended substantial sums of money on the property. However, when he put up the property as security for a loan from the bank, he learned for the first time of the woman's claim.

In a suit between the friend and the woman, which of the following statements most accurately describes the probable outcome?

(A) The friend would prevail, because the money he paid for the property, along with the money expended since then, was far in excess of what the woman paid, and under equity, the friend would be deemed the owner; however, he would have to reimburse the woman for what she paid for the property.

(B) The friend would prevail, because under the doctrine of equitable conversion, his "right" to the property preceded the woman's recordation, and thus whatever right she may have had would have been terminated before she could record.

(C) The friend would prevail, because he purchased from the son, whose deed was recorded before the woman's deed.

(D) The woman would prevail, because she recorded first.

Question 29

A woman owned a tract of land. The jurisdiction in which the land was located had a statute providing that no conveyance or mortgage of an interest in land is valid against a subsequent purchaser for value without notice thereof whose conveyance is first recorded.

The following events occurred:

December 2007: The woman owed money to a man, and in satisfaction of this debt, the woman conveyed the property to him. Although the man intended to have the deed recorded, he mistakenly failed to do so.

August 2008: The woman borrowed money from a bank and, to secure the loan, executed a mortgage deed on the property. The bank promptly recorded this mortgage.

December 2008: The man discovered that the deed from the woman's property was still in his safe and had not yet been recorded. He immediately went and recorded it.

In February 2009, the woman defaulted on her loan, and the bank therefore instituted proceedings to foreclose on the property.

The bank will:

(A) Not prevail, because the woman conveyed her entire interest to the man, and therefore had no property left that she could have mortgaged.

(B) Prevail, because to not enforce the bank's claim would reward the woman for perpetrating a fraud on the bank.

(C) Prevail, because the bank loaned the woman the money without notice of the man's interest, and it recorded the mortgage deed first.

(D) Prevail, because the instrument that is recorded first under this type of statute always prevails over the unrecorded or subsequently recorded instrument.

Question 30

An author was addressing a community group on the disparate treatment afforded non-whites by the police as compared to their treatment of whites. He said, "I'll bet that two kids, one white and one black, could do exactly the same thing at some suburban shopping center, and the cops would bust the black kid and not even bother the white one."

A group of teenagers of various races who were attending the address decided to test the author's theory at a nearby shopping mall. In pairs of varying racial composition, they approached shoppers and asked if they could carry their packages for a nominal fee. An elderly shopper who had recently been the victim of a purse snatching was so frightened by the approach of two teenagers that she dropped her packages and screamed for assistance. She was so distraught that she had to be taken home by ambulance. She later sued the teenagers on a theory of negligence and prevailed.

If she then seeks recovery from the author, is she likely to prevail?

(A) No, because the teenagers were not employees of the author.

(B) No, because the author did not authorize the teenagers' acts.

(C) Yes, because the teenagers would not have acted as they did but for hearing the author's comments.

(D) Yes, because her claim against the teenagers prevailed on a theory of negligence.

Question 31

A defendant is on trial for aggravated assault. The defendant claims that he was merely a bystander and that another person was the actual aggressor. The defendant calls a witness to testify that the defendant has a reputation for being a "good and loving person who would never hurt anyone."

The trial judge should rule the testimony:

(A) Admissible, because it is not hearsay.

(B) Admissible, because this is a criminal matter, and it tends to show the defendant's relevant good character.

(C) Inadmissible, because the prosecution has not introduced evidence concerning the defendant's reputation.

(D) Inadmissible, because character evidence is not permissible to show that an accused has acted in conformity with the character.

Question 32

A father did not like his daughter's boyfriend. One night the father came home and found the daughter and the boyfriend in the den with the lights out. The father grabbed the boyfriend and told him to get out of the house and threatened to beat the boyfriend up if he did not leave immediately. When the boyfriend did not leave, the father grabbed a poker from the den fireplace and raised it above his head in a threatening manner. The boyfriend threw a heavy ashtray at the father, hitting him in the side of the head and killing him. The boyfriend was charged with murder.

The jury should find the boyfriend:

(A) Guilty, because he had refused to immediately leave the house.

(B) Guilty, because his presence in the father's home with the daughter provoked the father to attack him.

(C) Not guilty, because a poker is a dangerous weapon.

(D) Not guilty, because it was the daughter's home also, and she invited the boyfriend into it.

Question 33

A city amended its ordinance to require that "adult theaters" could not be located either within 100 feet of each other or within 500 feet of any residential area. This zoning requirement was passed to protect the residential character of neighborhoods from destruction. A company owns two adult theaters in the city. One is about 1,000 feet from another adult theater. The second theater is adjacent to a residential area, in violation of the zoning ordinance. The company has filed an action to have the zoning requirement declared unconstitutional.

The court should hold that the zoning ordinance is:

(A) Invalid, because it violates the First Amendment.

(B) Invalid, because it is a form of spot zoning.

(C) Valid, in that it covers the entire city.

(D) Valid, because the protections afforded by the First Amendment are subject to zoning and licensing requirements.

Question 34

A woman was jogging along a jogging path. Suddenly, a driver pulled out of an alley perpendicular to the jogging path and failed to stop at a stop sign. He hit her with his car, injuring her. The woman sued the driver. A city code provided that drivers must stop at all stop signs perpendicular to the jogging path.

On the basis of which standard of care will the driver be judged?

(A) Strict liability, because an automobile is an inherently dangerous instrument.

(B) That of a reasonable and prudent person under the facts of this situation.

(C) The standard set by the city code.

(D) The doctrine of res ipsa loquitur, because it can be presumed that nobody would fail to stop at a stop sign in the absence of negligence.

Question 35

A woman was driving carefully but with an expired driver's license, in violation of a statute requiring license renewal. When she stopped at a stop sign, another driver, who was speeding, crashed into her car. The woman suffered injuries and sued the other driver.

The fact that the woman had an expired driver's license would not affect her claim against the other driver because:

(A) The other driver's negligence occurred after the woman's.

(B) The driver should have known that there are some unlicensed drivers on the road.

(C) The prevention of accidents of this sort is not the reason that drivers are required to renew their driver's licenses.

(D) There is a greater chance of causing injury when a driver speeds than when a person drives with an expired license.

Question 36

A husband was infuriated because he found out that another man was having an affair with his wife. The husband saw a person whom he believed to be that other man walking down the street ahead of him. The husband struck the man with a staggering blow. The husband was arrested and charged with battery upon the man. It turned out that the man the husband struck was only someone who strongly resembled the man who was having the affair.

Which of the following best states the rule to be applied?

(A) The husband is not guilty of battery if a reasonable person would have made the same mistake as to the man's identity.

(B) The husband is not guilty of battery if a reasonable person would have made the same mistake as to the man's identity and also would have been so provoked under the circumstances to strike him.

(C) The husband is guilty of battery even if he honestly and reasonably believed that the person he struck was the man who was having an affair with the wife.

(D) The husband is guilty of battery only if he realized whom it was that he was striking.

MIXED SUBJECT SET 1 SUBJECT GUIDE

1. Criminal Law
2. Torts
3. Evidence
4. Constitutional Law
5. Constitutional Law
6. Evidence
7. Criminal Law
8. Torts
9. Real Property
10. Real Property
11. Real Property
12. Criminal Law
13. Evidence
14. Constitutional Law
15. Contracts
16. Contracts
17. Contracts
18. Contracts
19. Torts
20. Torts
21. Criminal Law
22. Real Property
23. Evidence
24. Constitutional Law
25. Constitutional Law
26. Criminal Law
27. Evidence
28. Real Property
29. Real Property
30. Torts
31. Evidence
32. Criminal Law
33. Constitutional Law
34. Torts
35. Torts
36. Criminal Law

MIXED SUBJECT ANSWERS - SET 1

Answer to Question 1

(C) To hold a person liable as an accessory to a crime, the state must show that his assistance or encouragement was given with intent to aid the principal in the commission of the crime. The facts indicate that the friend did not have this state of mind. The friend did not know that the man was already married, and thus, the friend is not guilty because he did not have the mental state required for aiding and abetting. (A) is wrong because it involves a mistaken legal premise insofar as liability as an accessory is concerned. (B) is accurate in part, but ignores the requirement of a mental state. (D) is wrong because the accessory can be liable even if he did not "cause" the crime.

Answer to Question 2

(A) Even if the dump truck driver can assert the defense of private necessity, he would still be liable for the damage to the landowner's lawn. The dump truck driver's entrance onto the landowner's land constituted a prima facie case of trespass to land. The following elements must be proved for trespass to land: (i) an act of physical invasion of plaintiff's real property by defendant; (ii) intent on defendant's part to bring about a physical invasion of the plaintiff's real property; and (iii) causation. Intent to trespass is not required—intent to enter onto the land is sufficient. Thus, even though the dump truck driver did not intend to trespass onto the landowner's land, he did intend to drive onto it to avoid hitting the semitrailer driver. Under the defense of private necessity, however, a person may interfere with the property of another where it is reasonably and apparently necessary to avoid threatened injury and where the threatened injury is substantially more serious than the invasion that is undertaken to avert it. Where the act is solely to benefit a limited number of people (rather than to benefit the public as a whole), the defense is qualified; *i.e.,* the actor must pay for any injury he causes. Here, the dump truck driver was acting to avoid serious injury. However, he must pay for the damage to the lawn. (D) is therefore incorrect because negligence concepts are irrelevant to an action based on trespass to land. (B) is incorrect because a private nuisance is a substantial and unreasonable interference with another private individual's use and enjoyment of his land. Even if the dump truck driver interfered with the landowner's use of his lawn, the interference was neither substantial nor unreasonable. (C) is incorrect because there is no public nuisance in this case. A public nuisance unreasonably interferes with the health, safety, or property rights of the community. The dump truck driver's actions affected a limited number of people rather than the community.

Answer to Question 3

(C) A proper foundation was not established for the videotape's introduction into evidence. Videotape evidence is treated the same as photographic and tape-recorded evidence. If it is properly authenticated, it is admissible, but it may not be properly admitted without the proper foundation first being established. (A) is wrong because the tape constitutes an admission and, therefore, is not hearsay. (B) is wrong because the privilege against self-incrimination applies only to testimonial evidence. (D) is nonsensical.

Answer to Question 4

(C) Property rights are tested on a rational basis standard. Under the rational basis test, the burden of proof is on the plaintiff, not the state. Thus, the woman will not prevail if she fails to prove that the statute is not rationally related to a legitimate government purpose. Hence, (A) is wrong. (B) is wrong because it uses the wrong standard and because the burden of proof is on the plaintiff, not the state. (D) is incorrect; the Necessary and Proper Clause has nothing to do with state statutes.

Answer to Question 5

(C) The provision is most likely unconstitutional as a denial of equal protection. Alienage is a suspect class when used by the states; therefore, strict scrutiny will be applied to determine if there is a compelling state interest, unless the law discriminates against alien participation in the functioning of the state government. This is not that type of law, and no compelling interest is demonstrated by these facts. (A) and (B) are, therefore, wrong because the state has not and could not allege a compelling interest in support of this measure. (D) is wrong because the statute would not qualify as a bill of attainder, which imposes punishment on specific individuals without a judicial trial.

Answer to Question 6

(D) The testimony should be admitted because nothing indicates that the son is incompetent. All witnesses are competent unless physically or mentally impaired in some fashion not applicable here, or unless they are too young to understand the oath and the need to testify truthfully. Therefore, (A) and (B) are incorrect. (C) is wrong because there is no precise age at which an infant is deemed competent to testify; it depends on the capacity and intelligence of the particular child.

Answer to Question 7

(C) The statements were the fruits of an unlawful arrest, because the police did not have an arrest warrant, but they entered the woman's house even though she had expressly refused to allow them entry. Although the *Miranda* warnings may have been sufficient to protect the woman's right against self-incrimination, they were not sufficient to purge the taint of the illegal arrest. Thus, the entry into the woman's apartment and her arrest without a warrant, probable cause, or circumstances permitting an exception from these requirements were illegal. The statements she made thereafter were fruits of the original illegality and are to be suppressed unless the taint is purged. The giving of *Miranda* warnings is not sufficient. (A) is wrong because the facts indicate that the statements were voluntarily made. (B) is a correct statement of the law, but it is irrelevant under these facts. (D) is wrong because *Miranda* warnings are only required prior to custodial interrogation.

Answer to Question 8

(B) A cause of action for invasion of privacy—specifically, commercial misappropriation—would apply here because the defendant made unauthorized use of the geologist's picture for the defendant's commercial advantage. Thus, the geologist's best cause of action is for invasion of privacy. The facts do not show that he was defamed, nor do the facts indicate that he suffered any type of severe emotional harm. Thus, (A), (C), and (D) are wrong. The only cause of action would be for an invasion of privacy, specifically for commercial appropriation, because the defendant made unauthorized use of his picture for its commercial advantage.

Answer to Question 9

(A) The man would be declared the owner of the tract on the basis of constructive adverse possession. Constructive adverse possession is applicable when a claimant goes into actual possession of some portion of the property under color of title; in such a case, he will be deemed in adverse possession of the entire property described in the instrument on the basis that his adverse possession is constructive possession of the extended parts of the property not actually occupied. Thus, (C) is incorrect. (B) is incorrect because a transfer in ownership does not interrupt the statutory period for adverse possession. (D) is incorrect because only a minority of states require the adverse possessor to pay taxes on the property.

Answer to Question 10

(D) Because the man was in continuous possession for the statutory period and has met all of the other requirements of adverse possession, he would be declared the owner of the five acres. (A) is incorrect because only a minority of states require the adverse possessor to pay property taxes. (B) is incorrect because the disability of the woman's successor in the interest will not toll the running of the statute. For a disability, such as status as a minor, to stop the clock, the disability must have been in existence on the day the adverse possession began. Here, the daughter was not yet alive when the adverse possession began. Thus, her status as a minor will not toll the running of the statute. (C) is incorrect because the man's state of mind is irrelevant under the majority view. Even if he had possessed the land knowing he was trespassing, he could still claim it by adverse possession.

Answer to Question 11

(C) A general warranty deed gives the grantee six covenants of title: the right to seisin, the right to convey, a covenant against encumbrances, the covenant of quiet enjoyment, the covenant of further assurances, and a general warranty. Under the covenants of quiet enjoyment, warranty, and further assurances, the man promised that (i) the woman would not be disturbed in her possession of the tract; (ii) he would defend the woman's title against lawful claims; and (iii) he would perform whatever acts are necessary to perfect the woman's title. Because the man neither owned the tract of land nor was acting as the actual owner's agent, he breached the covenants of seisin and right to convey at the time of the conveyance to the woman. When the actual owner prevented the woman from re-entering the property, this interfered with the woman's quiet enjoyment, and the man's refusal to "straighten this out" was a breach of the covenant of further assurances. Thus, (C) is the correct answer. Hence, (A) is incorrect because quiet enjoyment was not the only covenant breached. There is nothing in the facts to suggest the property is encumbered; thus, the man did not breach the covenant against encumbrances, and (B) is therefore incorrect. (D) is incorrect because seisin and right to convey were not the only covenants that the man breached.

Answer to Question 12

(D) The Supreme Court has held that it is unconstitutional for an officer to use deadly force to arrest an unarmed escaping felon unless the officer has probable cause to believe that the suspect poses a significant threat of death or serious physical injury to the officer or others. In jurisdictions following this approach, the use of deadly force to apprehend a fleeing felon is reasonable only where it is necessary to prevent the felon's escape ***and*** where the felon threatens death or serious bodily harm. Other jurisdictions allow use of deadly force whenever necessary to prevent a fleeing felon's escape. Regardless of the approach used, here it does not appear that shooting at the thief was necessary to prevent his escape or that the thief threatened serious bodily injury. Thus, (A), (B), and (C) are incorrect.

Answer to Question 13

(A) Under the best evidence rule, when a document is unavailable but is central to the resolution of a dispute (*i.e.*, not collateral) and there is an attempt to enter the contents of that document into evidence through testimony, the judge must first find that the document itself is not available through no fault of the proponent (here, the plaintiff), in order for testimony on the issue to be admissible. Thus, (A) is the correct answer. (B) is wrong because, as stated, the document itself must be produced unless it is not available. (C) and (D) are wrong because the judge, not the jury, makes these types of determinations.

Answer to Question 14

(C) This statute deals with activities that have an effect on interstate commerce and, therefore, is within the commerce power. (B) is wrong because the Second Amendment is prohibitory; therefore, it could not be the basis of enactment, but could only prohibit some types of enactments. (A) is wrong because the Fourteenth Amendment Equal Protection Clause applies only to the states, not the federal government. (D) is wrong because the Necessary and Proper Clause only broadens congressional power authorized under some other provision; it does not itself create the power to act.

Answer to Question 15

(A) The assignment was effective. Under U.C.C. section 2-210(3), which governs this sale-of-goods case, "unless the circumstances indicate the contrary, a prohibition of assignment of 'the contract' is to be construed as barring only the delegation to the assignee of the assignor's performance." Here, the electronics company assigned to the finance company the right to receive payment on its contract with the store. There were no delegations of duties to the finance company (the assignee). Therefore, when the electronics company "assigns the contract" to the finance company, because the electronics company has assigned only the right to payments, it has not breached its contract with the store. (B) and (C) are therefore wrong. (D) is wrong because the covenant would not stand or fall on its rationale.

Answer to Question 16

(B) When an assignment has been made, but the obligor on the contract (here, the retailer) has not been informed of the assignment, it is still obligated to pay the party with whom it originally dealt. Here, the retailer paid the original supplier in full, and therefore, the original supplier is liable to the wholesaler for the full amount of payment, and (A) and (C) are therefore wrong. (D) is wrong because the original supplier is liable to the wholesaler.

Answer to Question 17

(C) A third party beneficiary of a contract can enforce a contract only when its rights have vested. Vesting occurs when (i) the third party manifests assent to the promise; (ii) brings suit to enforce the promise; or (iii) materially changes its position in reliance on the promise. Prior to vesting, the original parties are free to modify or rescind the third party beneficiary's rights. Here, the third party beneficiary (the creditor) did not become aware of the original contract until after payment was made by the store to the company, indicating that the original parties modified their agreement, thereby modifying or rescinding the creditor's rights. (A) is wrong because the creditor is a creditor beneficiary, not an incidental beneficiary. (B) is wrong because it is an incorrect statement of the law. (D) is wrong both because there is nothing in the facts to indicate that the original agreement was in violation of the Statute of Frauds; even if it were, that is irrelevant to the rights of the creditor, who can sue the promisee on the original obligation between them.

Answer to Question 18

(A) Under the U.C.C., a buyer in a requirements contract must act in good faith. Here, when the distributor terminated the contract in order to purchase wine from another vineyard, it still had a requirement for wine. Thus, the distributor did not act in good faith. (B) and (C) are wrong, because the rights involved here are clearly assignable because the payment of money does not involve personal responsibilities. (D) is wrong because the U.C.C. regards requirements contracts as being supported by sufficient consideration.

Answer to Question 19

(C) The pilot's best defense is that he was not negligent, because the pilot used reasonable care and caution in the maintenance of his airplane. A forced landing is unforeseeable, and the pilot need not have foreseen the presence of anyone in particular on the ground, because this was an emergency situation that did not come about due to any negligence on the part of the pilot. Thus, (B) is wrong. (A) is wrong because the pilot need not have acted willfully or wantonly to be liable. (D) is wrong because the pilot's conduct was the cause in fact of the child's injury; *i.e.*, the child would not have been injured but for the pilot's landing of the plane. The pilot is also a proximate cause of the injury because an injury to someone on the ground is a foreseeable result of an emergency landing. However, causation alone is not enough to impose liability; there must also be a breach of duty, and the pilot did not breach his duty of reasonable care.

Answer to Question 20

(C) The pedestrian will prevail if the mechanic was negligent in inspecting and certifying the car. Because the brakes failed soon after the mechanic certified the car, it is highly likely that the mechanic was negligent. There is no strict liability in tort for service transactions, so (D) is wrong. Privity of contract is not required to find liability for negligence, and the pedestrian's presence on the street makes her a foreseeable plaintiff, so (A) is wrong. (B) is incorrect because this is not a superseding cause situation; the mechanic's potential negligence would not be cut off by the woman's foreseeable negligent driving.

Answer to Question 21

(A) The question here is one of statutory interpretation. The status of the man's conviction will rest on how the appellate court interprets the statute. If the court interprets the statute to include the ice pick, the man's conviction is proper. Thus, (A) is correct. (B) is wrong because it does not reach the issue of statutory interpretation; the statute prohibits a concealed "knife or dagger," not merely a concealed "weapon." Thus, the man's "admission" is not enough to convict him under this statute. (C) and (D) are wrong because the man's motive or intent is irrelevant; the statute makes carrying a concealed knife or dagger a crime regardless of the intent.

Answer to Question 22

(B) The seller and the buyer each own one-half the stream bed. The general rule is that where a stream is a boundary, abutting owners each own one-half of the stream bed. Thus, (B) is the correct answer and (C) and (A) are wrong. (D) is incorrect; the description is sufficiently detailed to be valid.

Answer to Question 23

(C) Under Rule 406 of the Federal Rules of Evidence, evidence of a person's habit or of the routine practice of an organization, whether corroborated or not and regardless of the presence of eyewitnesses, is relevant to prove that the conduct of the person or organization on a particular occasion was in conformity with the habit or routine practice. If the woman "always" locks her car upon exiting it, the evidence is offered as habit and is admissible. (D) is wrong, because the evidence is admissible to establish habit even if it is not offered for impeachment. (B) is wrong because the evidence may tend to show that the insurer is required to cover the woman's loss. (A) is wrong because "self-serving" is not a valid objection.

Answer to Question 24

(B) The Supreme Court has long accepted that the President has broad power to enter into executive agreements with foreign states, and this would be true especially where Congress has authorized the agreement, according to Justice Jackson's opinion in *Youngstown Sheet & Tube v. Sawyer* (1952), which was adopted by the Court in *Medellin v. Texas* (2008). (A) is wrong because there are some limits on the President's powers to enter into executive agreements. (C) is wrong because a two-thirds vote is not required for an executive agreement. (D) is a correct statement, because Congress has authority to act to preserve wildlife. That authority does not, however, deprive the President of the power to enter agreements of this sort.

Answer to Question 25

(C) Under the Supremacy Clause of the United States Constitution, federal laws are the law of the land unless they are found to be inconsistent with the Constitution. The federal statute is not inconsistent with the Constitution because Congress can adopt laws that are necessary and proper to protect animals that move on federal land. The state statute must be declared unconstitutional inasmuch as it is in conflict with the federal law, because the federal law restricts hunting of the animal, while the state statute allows unlimited hunting of the animal. Thus, (B) is incorrect because even this type of state statute does not take precedence over a federal law. (A) is incorrect, because the issue is not whether the question is "best" left to the states, but rather whether the federal government has the authority to enact these laws. (D) is incorrect because even if wildlife is within the police powers of the state, the Supremacy Clause renders this inconsistent state statute unconstitutional.

Answer to Question 26

(D) A person is privileged to use deadly force to prevent a crime only if it is an ***inherently dangerous*** felony. Shoplifting is not an inherently dangerous felony; thus, the woman's use of deadly force was not privileged. Therefore, the man was entitled to defend himself against the woman's improper use of deadly force by using deadly force himself. (A) is wrong because the man did not initiate an assault. (B) is wrong because even if the man intended to kill the woman, his action was justified. (C) is a misstatement of the law and of the facts.

Answer to Question 27

(B) Under the Federal Rules of Evidence, the testimony is admissible as a nonhearsay state of mind, as circumstantial evidence that the declarant acted in accordance with his intention. (A) is incorrect because a "dying declaration" must be made while in fear of "impending" death. (C) is incorrect because the operator is not a psychiatrist, and there is no evidence that the husband assumed her to be one. (D) is wrong because the state of mind need not be as of the time of the incident to be relevant.

Answer to Question 28

(D) The woman would prevail because she recorded her deed before the friend recorded his deed. The jurisdiction in this question has a race-notice statute, under which a subsequent bona fide purchaser is protected only if she records before the prior grantee. While the friend was a bona fide purchaser, he did not record his interest in the property before the woman did; thus the woman will prevail. (A) is incorrect because priority under a race-notice recording act, such as the one in this question, is determined by the subsequent purchaser's status as a bona fide purchaser and on the basis of who records first. Courts do not determine ownership by balancing the equities on the basis of who spent the most money. (B) is wrong because the doctrine of equitable conversion, wherein equity regards the purchaser in a land sale contract as the owner of the real property, does not change the result under the recording statute. The woman will prevail because she recorded first. (C) is incorrect because the friend cannot rely on the son's recording of his deed; the woman recorded her interest before the friend recorded his. Furthermore, even if the issue were whether the friend had actual notice of the woman's interest, the friend could not rely on the "shelter rule" that protects transferees from a bona fide purchaser, because the son was not a purchaser for value and therefore not protected by the recording statute.

Answer to Question 29

(C) The bank will prevail under the recording statute. The jurisdiction in this question has a race-notice statute, under which a subsequent bona fide purchaser is protected only if he records before the prior grantee or mortgagee. Here, the bank recorded its mortgage prior to the man's recording of his deed; thus, the man will take the property subject to the bank's mortgage. (A) is incorrect because even though at common law the woman would not have had any title to mortgage to the bank after the conveyance to the man, the race-notice statute nullifies that priority as to the subsequent bona fide purchaser who first records. (B) is wrong because the issue is not whether the woman would be rewarded, but which innocent party will be protected by the recording act. (D) is incorrect because it more accurately describes a pure race jurisdiction. In a race-notice jurisdiction, only the bona fide purchaser for value will prevail over a prior unrecorded deed or mortgage interest; hence, a purchaser who records first under this statute would not prevail if he had actual notice of a prior unrecorded interest.

Answer to Question 30

(B) The elderly shopper will not likely prevail because the author did not authorize the teenagers' conduct. Cause in fact is not a sufficient basis to find liability. Here, although the teenagers would not have acted as they did but for the author's lecture, the elderly shopper must also demonstrate ***proximate*** causation, in order for the author to be liable. Proximate causation requires that the teenagers' actions and the shopper's response must have been foreseeable by the author. Because the author did not authorize their actions, the harm that the shopper suffered is not likely to be foreseeable. Thus, (C) and (D) are wrong. (A) is not as good a choice as (B) because the mere fact that they were not his employees does not alone insulate the author from liability.

Answer to Question 31

(B) In a criminal matter, the accused is permitted, at any time during the trial, to introduce evidence of his good character for the trait involved in the case to support the probability that he did not commit the crime alleged. Here, the crime in question involves violence. Therefore, evidence of the defendant's good character for nonviolence may be admitted. Thus, (C) and (D) are wrong as misstatements of the law. (A) is wrong because just the fact that evidence is not hearsay is no reason to admit it.

Answer to Question 32

(C) Clearly the boyfriend was acting in self-defense, and even if throwing a heavy ashtray could be deemed to be deadly force, the boyfriend had the right to defend himself against the unprivileged attack with the use of deadly force (*i.e.*, the poker). (A) and (B) are incorrect because the boyfriend's presence in the house and failure to leave immediately did not give the father a privilege to use deadly force against him. (D) is irrelevant.

Answer to Question 33

(D) The court should hold that the zoning ordinance is valid under the First Amendment. In *Young v. American Mini Theaters* (1986), the Court held that the mere fact that the commercial exploitation of certain material was protected by the First Amendment does not prevent the city from zoning or imposing other licensing requirements, as long as the businesses are not totally banned. The Court has upheld zoning ordinances such as the one here as reasonable regulations of the secondary effects of the speech involved. [*See* City of Renton v. Playtime Theaters (1986)]

Answer to Question 34

(C) When an applicable statute establishes the due care, the defendant's conduct is governed by the special statutory standard rather than the usual "reasonable person" standard. The statute is applicable because the woman appears to be within the class of persons to be protected and the type of harm that occurred is what the statute (the city code) was intended to prevent. Thus, (B) is wrong. (A) is wrong because an automobile is not an inherently dangerous instrument. (D) is a misstatement of law.

Answer to Question 35

(C) A statutory standard of care will replace the general common law duty of care if the statute was designed to prevent the type of harm suffered by the plaintiff. Here, the woman was driving carefully and stopped at a stop sign when she was hit by a car driven negligently by the other driver. The fact that she was driving with an expired license could not prevent the type of harm that she suffered. Hence, (C) is the best answer because it precludes applicability of the statute altogether. (A) is incorrect because it is irrelevant that the driver's speeding came after the woman's failure to renew her license. (B) is incorrect because it is irrelevant whether the driver knew that there are unlicensed drivers on the road. (D) does not state a legally recognized basis for this result.

Answer to Question 36

(C) The husband is guilty of battery regardless of his belief. Battery is an unlawful application of force to the person of another resulting in either bodily injury or an offensive touching. Here, the husband made a mistake as to the identity of the person whom he struck, but there was no mistake as to the intention of the husband to strike this person. Mistake of fact affects criminal guilt only if it shows that the defendant did not have the state of mind required for the crime. Although battery need not be intentional (*i.e.,* it can result from criminal negligence), it is clear from the facts that the husband intended to strike the man. Thus, the mistake made by the husband (who apparently believed that he was striking the man having the affair with the wife) does not show the absence of the state of mind required for battery, and will therefore not affect the husband's guilt. (A) is incorrect because, even if a reasonable person would have made the same mistake of identity, the fact remains that the husband committed a battery against the man he struck. A case of mistaken identity provides no defense to the battery that was committed. (B) is incorrect for the same reason as (A), and also because it implies that a battery against the man having an affair with the wife would be excused by adequate provocation (presumably resulting from the affair with the wife). It is true that a killing that would otherwise be murder may be reduced from murder to voluntary manslaughter if the defendant acted under a legally adequate provocation, and finding one's spouse in the act of adultery is deemed to be adequate provocation. However, there is no rule of law that excuses a battery on the ground that the victim committed adultery with the defendant's wife. (D) is incorrect because it also is based on the premise that the husband is not guilty if he thought that he was striking the man who was having an affair with the wife. As explained previously, regardless of whom the husband thought he was striking, the significant point is that he unlawfully struck a man, and this constitutes a battery.

Mixed Subject Set 2 Answer Sheet

1.	Ⓐ	Ⓑ	Ⓒ	Ⓓ	26.	Ⓐ	Ⓑ	Ⓒ	Ⓓ
2.	Ⓐ	Ⓑ	Ⓒ	Ⓓ	27.	Ⓐ	Ⓑ	Ⓒ	Ⓓ
3.	Ⓐ	Ⓑ	Ⓒ	Ⓓ	28.	Ⓐ	Ⓑ	Ⓒ	Ⓓ
4.	Ⓐ	Ⓑ	Ⓒ	Ⓓ	29.	Ⓐ	Ⓑ	Ⓒ	Ⓓ
5.	Ⓐ	Ⓑ	Ⓒ	Ⓓ	30.	Ⓐ	Ⓑ	Ⓒ	Ⓓ
6.	Ⓐ	Ⓑ	Ⓒ	Ⓓ	31.	Ⓐ	Ⓑ	Ⓒ	Ⓓ
7.	Ⓐ	Ⓑ	Ⓒ	Ⓓ	32.	Ⓐ	Ⓑ	Ⓒ	Ⓓ
8.	Ⓐ	Ⓑ	Ⓒ	Ⓓ	33.	Ⓐ	Ⓑ	Ⓒ	Ⓓ
9.	Ⓐ	Ⓑ	Ⓒ	Ⓓ	34.	Ⓐ	Ⓑ	Ⓒ	Ⓓ
10.	Ⓐ	Ⓑ	Ⓒ	Ⓓ	35.	Ⓐ	Ⓑ	Ⓒ	Ⓓ
11.	Ⓐ	Ⓑ	Ⓒ	Ⓓ	36.	Ⓐ	Ⓑ	Ⓒ	Ⓓ
12.	Ⓐ	Ⓑ	Ⓒ	Ⓓ	37.	Ⓐ	Ⓑ	Ⓒ	Ⓓ
13.	Ⓐ	Ⓑ	Ⓒ	Ⓓ	38.	Ⓐ	Ⓑ	Ⓒ	Ⓓ
14.	Ⓐ	Ⓑ	Ⓒ	Ⓓ	39.	Ⓐ	Ⓑ	Ⓒ	Ⓓ
15.	Ⓐ	Ⓑ	Ⓒ	Ⓓ	40.	Ⓐ	Ⓑ	Ⓒ	Ⓓ
16.	Ⓐ	Ⓑ	Ⓒ	Ⓓ	41.	Ⓐ	Ⓑ	Ⓒ	Ⓓ
17.	Ⓐ	Ⓑ	Ⓒ	Ⓓ	42.	Ⓐ	Ⓑ	Ⓒ	Ⓓ
18.	Ⓐ	Ⓑ	Ⓒ	Ⓓ	43.	Ⓐ	Ⓑ	Ⓒ	Ⓓ
19.	Ⓐ	Ⓑ	Ⓒ	Ⓓ	44.	Ⓐ	Ⓑ	Ⓒ	Ⓓ
20.	Ⓐ	Ⓑ	Ⓒ	Ⓓ	45.	Ⓐ	Ⓑ	Ⓒ	Ⓓ
21.	Ⓐ	Ⓑ	Ⓒ	Ⓓ	46.	Ⓐ	Ⓑ	Ⓒ	Ⓓ
22.	Ⓐ	Ⓑ	Ⓒ	Ⓓ	47.	Ⓐ	Ⓑ	Ⓒ	Ⓓ
23.	Ⓐ	Ⓑ	Ⓒ	Ⓓ	48.	Ⓐ	Ⓑ	Ⓒ	Ⓓ
24.	Ⓐ	Ⓑ	Ⓒ	Ⓓ	49.	Ⓐ	Ⓑ	Ⓒ	Ⓓ
25.	Ⓐ	Ⓑ	Ⓒ	Ⓓ	50.	Ⓐ	Ⓑ	Ⓒ	Ⓓ

MIXED SUBJECT QUESTIONS - SET 2

Question 1

As a man walked out of a store, he saw a friend under the hood of a car trying to get it started. When the man asked what was wrong, the friend told him that she had lost the keys to her car and was trying to "hotwire" it. The man told his friend to get behind the steering wheel, and when she was ready, the man started the car by "hotwiring" it. In fact, the friend did not own the car, and the man is charged with being an accessory to larceny.

The man should be found:

(A) Guilty, because his actions enabled his friend to steal the car.

(B) Guilty, because he had no reason to believe that the car was really his friend's.

(C) Not guilty, because he did not intend to aid his friend in stealing a car.

(D) Not guilty, because his friend would have probably stolen the car without his help.

Question 2

An inventor operated a shortwave radio in his home. The inventor maintained a large radio antenna on the rear part of his lot. One day the inventor noticed that the guide wires holding the antenna in place were frayed. He hired a contractor to replace the guide wires with new, stronger wire. The contractor replaced all of the guide wires as per his agreement with the inventor. Four days after the contractor finished his work and the inventor had paid him, the antenna fell over onto the inventor's neighbor's house, causing severe damage.

If the neighbor brings suit against the inventor for damages to his home, the neighbor is most likely to prevail against the inventor because:

(A) Of respondeat superior.

(B) He assumed responsibility when he paid the contractor for the repair.

(C) He was in possession of the property from which the antenna fell.

(D) The contractor was engaged in an inherently dangerous activity.

Question 3

A homeowner called a tree trimmer to his house to trim some branches on a large pine tree in the homeowner's backyard. The tree trimmer trimmed off several large branches and pruned several others. The homeowner paid the tree trimmer, who left and did not return. A week after the tree trimmer trimmed the tree, one of the pruned branches split from the trunk of the tree and landed on a neighbor's car.

If the neighbor brings suit against the tree trimmer for damage to his car, the best defense for the tree trimmer is that:

(A) He was relieved of liability when the homeowner paid for the tree trimming.

(B) He could not reasonably foresee that the branch would split off and fall.

(C) He did all the work under the direction of the homeowner.

(D) The pine tree was on the property of the homeowner.

Question 4

A homeowner was helping his neighbor clean out her garage. As the homeowner and the neighbor were moving some boards out of the garage, the neighbor ran into the overhead door's hinge, causing it to fall and hit the homeowner on his head, killing him. The homeowner's wife sued the neighbor for the wrongful death of her husband, seeking damages of $100,000. The wife, who was present when the accident occurred, is called to testify that at the time of the accident, the homeowner was carrying the boards on his shoulder, and he therefore was unable to see that the neighbor had hit the door hinges.

As a witness, the wife is:

(A) Competent, if she is testifying as the personal representative of her husband's estate.

(B) Competent, in spite of the fact she is the plaintiff.

(C) Incompetent, because she is unqualified to give opinion evidence.

(D) Incompetent, because she cannot testify for her husband in a civil case.

Question 5

Congress enacted legislation that was intended to open up federal lands to private industry to explore for, and extract, oil and coal deposits. The act established the Federal Lands Exploitation Commission to supervise the exploration and extraction of fossil fuels from federal lands, and empowered the Commission to enter into contracts on behalf of the federal government with the private companies that wish to mine for coal and drill for oil. The Commission members were also required to investigate safe and sound methods of exploiting the oil and coal deposits without doing unnecessary harm to the environment and to make recommendations to Congress for new laws that would govern the exploitation of federal lands. Further, the commissioners were given the power to make the rules and regulations concerning the contracts with the companies and to appoint administrative law judges to conduct hearings regarding violation of the Commission's rules and disputes concerning the contracts.

The authority for the establishment of the Federal Lands Exploitation Commission is most likely:

(A) The Commerce Clause.

(B) The taxing and spending power.

(C) Congress's authority to regulate federal land.

(D) The war and defense power.

Question 6

Congress enacted legislation intended to protect children from unsafe car seats. The act established a commission to supervise the manufacturing and sale of car seats, and empowered the commission to promulgate car seat safety regulations. The commission members were also required to investigate safe and sound methods of installing child car seats. The commission's chairperson was designated as an Undersecretary of Health and Safety; the President appointed two commissioners from child safety groups; and the three major car seat manufacturers chose one commissioner each, who were then appointed by Congress to the commission.

For its violation of the commission's rules with regard to car seat manufacturing, a car seat manufacturer was fined $5,000, to be paid immediately without a trial on the merits. The manufacturer files suit in the federal court to enjoin the commission's enforcement of this rule.

The manufacturer's best argument in support of its contention that the rule was illegal is:

(A) Regulations concerning criminal conduct cannot be made by agency rules, but must be made by federal statute.

(B) The appointment of the commissioners was illegal; therefore, the rules promulgated by the commission are invalid.

(C) Because the fine was potentially $5,000 for violation of the rule, the manufacturer had a right to a trial by jury.

(D) The presumptive fine violated the manufacturer's rights of equal protection as guaranteed by the Fourteenth Amendment.

Question 7

Congress established a vaccination review commission to supervise the manufacturing and administration of childhood vaccinations. An administrative law judge had been appointed to his position by the commission chairperson. When a new administration came into office, the new commission chairperson removed the judge from his position as the ALJ, but offered the judge a position as an attorney in the enforcement division. The judge brought suit in federal court to enjoin the commission chairperson from removing him from his position.

The judge should:

(A) Prevail, because a judge cannot be removed from office after appointment.

(B) Prevail, if it is shown that at all times he maintained good behavior.

(C) Not prevail, because he was not a judge within the meaning of Article III.

(D) Not prevail, because the appointing authority had changed.

Question 8

Two friends were on their way to a football game when they were injured as their car was sideswiped and driven off the road by a large truck belonging to a delivery company. The friends brought an action against the truck driver and the delivery company, alleging negligence by the truck driver in driving too fast. The delivery company answered and asserted the affirmative defense that the driver of the car had been on cocaine and was intoxicated at the time of the accident.

The delivery company's counsel seeks to have the highway patrolman who investigated the accident state that he overheard the car driver tell his passenger, "This was probably all our fault; we shouldn't have been on coke."

Assuming the trial judge takes judicial notice that "coke" means "cocaine," the judge should rule that the tender of evidence is:

(A) Admissible, as an admission of a party.

(B) Admissible, to save time because the same statement could be admitted by way of the accident report.

(C) Inadmissible, because if he had been intoxicated, he would not be capable of making a rational decision as to fault.

(D) Inadmissible, because it is hearsay not within any exception.

Question 9

The plaintiff was injured when her car was hit head on by a pickup truck belonging to a landscaping company. The plaintiff brought an action against the truck driver and the landscaping company, alleging negligence by the truck driver in driving too fast. Counsel for the plaintiff seeks to introduce the statement of a former employee of the landscaping company, who said to the truck driver just before the accident, "You had better slow down. You've been warned by the boss many times not to go this fast."

The judge should rule the statement admissible only if:

(A) The statement was made immediately after the accident, and was made under oath.

(B) The former employee is unavailable to testify to the matters in the statement.

(C) Plaintiff's attorney produces a record of three citations that the truck driver received in the last year for speeding, driving the same truck.

(D) Plaintiff's attorney first proves as a preliminary question of fact that during the trip the former employee was an agent of the landscaping company and that the statement concerned the scope of his employment.

Question 10

An architect, who had been a lawyer's roommate and lover for several years, decided to leave the lawyer and move in with a doctor. On the day that the architect was to move into the doctor's condominium, the lawyer shot the architect in the neck, intending to kill him. The architect was not severely wounded, but he was hospitalized for several days. During his stay at the hospital, it was discovered that the architect had developed a form of cancer that was invariably fatal. Three weeks after being shot, the architect died of pneumonia caused by an infection resulting from the bullet wound in his neck. The doctor had been killed when his condo burned down as he slept. The fire occurred two days after the lawyer shot the architect.

Is the lawyer guilty of a criminal homicide?

(A) No, because his actions merely constituted attempt.

(B) No, because the architect was already suffering from an incurable disease.

(C) No, because the lawyer actually prolonged the architect's life because he prevented his probable death in the fire that destroyed the doctor's condo.

(D) Yes, because the lawyer's act was the proximate cause of the architect's death.

Question 11

A young woman went to her local shoe shop and selected a pair of shoes. She gave the salesperson cash for the shoes. As the salesperson was putting the shoes into a bag, a robber brandishing a gun entered the store, forced the salesperson to put all of the money in the register into the bag with the shoes, and fled with the bag, the money, and the shoes. After the police had come, the young woman asked the salesperson to get her another pair of shoes. He told the young woman that she would have to pay for them again. The young woman refused.

If the young woman sues the shoe shop for another pair of shoes, who will prevail?

(A) The young woman, because she did not yet have possession of the shoes.

(B) The young woman, because the purpose of the contract had been made impossible by an unforeseen event.

(C) The shoe shop, because title to the shoes had already passed to the young woman.

(D) The shoe shop, because the contract goods had already been identified.

Question 12

A woman went to her local department store and told the salesperson that she wanted a coat that was extremely warm. The salesperson went into his stockroom and brought out four different styles of very warm coats. The woman tried on each of the four but did not like the way any of them looked. While walking around the store, however, the young woman saw a coat she did like and told the salesperson to bring one in her size. The salesperson brought her the coat and he said that it was made of the finest cashmere and would probably last for years. The young woman tried on the coat and told the salesperson that she would take it and paid him. After wearing the coat twice, however, she decided it was not warm enough for her climate. She took the coat back to the department store and demanded her money back. The store refused.

If the woman sues to get her money back, under which theory would she most likely prevail?

(A) Breach of the implied warranty of fitness for particular purpose.

(B) Breach of the implied warranty of merchantability.

(C) Breach of express warranty.

(D) None of the listed warranties.

Question 13

A man went to his local sporting goods store and told the salesperson that he wanted a tennis racket that was very high-end. The salesperson showed him a racket that he said was made of the finest titanium and would probably last for years. The man bought the racket and left the store. He then played with the racket for six days, but after a week the rim of the racket was dented. He took it to the pro shop at his club and was told that the racket was painted plastic.

If the man sues the sporting goods store for a refund, under which theory would he most likely prevail?

(A) Breach of an express warranty that the racket was titanium.

(B) Breach of an express warranty that the racket would last for years.

(C) Breach of the implied warranty of merchantability.

(D) Breach of the warranties in both (A) and (C).

Question 14

A customer selected a new wallet at a local department store that the salesperson said was made of the finest calfskin and was stitched by hand. The customer bought the wallet and left the store. A few moments later, he took out the wallet to transfer his cash and credit cards into it. On close inspection, he noticed a small nick in the leather. He immediately went back to the department store and demanded a refund. The salesperson refused.

If the customer sues for a refund, who will prevail?

(A) The customer, because there was a breach of contract.

(B) The customer, because he had a reasonable time after purchase in which to inspect.

(C) The department store, because the customer accepted the goods.

(D) The department store, because the customer did not give written notice of the breach.

Question 15

A con artist asked his friend to introduce him to the town's banker so that he could apply for a loan to set up a hardware business. The friend, also a friend of the banker, arranged a meeting and later gave the con artist a glowing recommendation based on their long and deep friendship. When the banker approved a $25,000 loan, the friend was present at the signing of the loan papers and co-signed on the con artist's behalf. Unbeknownst to the friend, the con artist intentionally misrepresented his intentions as to the proceeds of the loan and his financial status, forging some documents used to verify his solvency. The con artist has been tried and convicted of obtaining money by false pretenses (a felony) and sentenced to state prison.

If the friend is charged as an accessory to obtaining money by false pretenses, he should be found:

(A) Guilty, because he was present when the crime was committed and was thus a principal in the second degree.

(B) Guilty, because he encouraged and aided the con artist, and his ignorance of the con artist's insolvency is no defense to the charged crime.

(C) Not guilty, because he lacked the requisite mental state to be an aider and abettor.

(D) Not guilty, because his encouragement and aid was not the legal cause of the offense.

Question 16

A man gave a friend a deed purporting to give to the friend "My property known as Twelve Oaks, with its five acres of land and the stable and dressage course located thereon." The man told the friend that he was giving the property to her, but because he did not have a better description, he wanted to keep the deed until his attorney could review them. The friend agreed and gave it back to him. Unfortunately, the man suffered a heart attack the next day and died without seeing his attorney. However, when the friend spoke with the administrator of the man's estate, she learned that the man had, as part of another deed 12 years before, sold that part of

Twelve Oaks on which was located the stable and dressage course.

The man's heirs bring an action for declaratory relief against the friend, asserting that the deed to Twelve Oaks is void because it contained an inaccurate and ambiguous description.

A trial court would enter judgment:

(A) Against the friend, because the deed failed to give an accurate description of the property owned by the man at the time of his death.

(B) Against the friend, because the man informed the friend that he did not know the description of his property and he wanted his attorney to prepare the deed.

(C) Against the friend, because the deed purports to transfer more property than the man owned and thus is void as a matter of law.

(D) For the friend, because the error in description was not sufficient to put in doubt what the man intended to convey to her.

Question 17

The owner of a parcel of land gave his sister a deed to the land that said, "I convey to you six acres of my developed land located at 123 Maple Street, Riverton, Delaware County." The land at 123 Maple Street consisted of 22 acres. The original owner then died. His will devised all of his real property to his children.

If, in a suit for declaratory relief, the original owner's children attempt to void the deed to the Maple Street property, the sister will:

(A) Prevail, because the original owner intended for his sister to choose the appropriate acreage, and she can therefore select the six acres that satisfy her needs.

(B) Prevail, because the deed clearly states what property the original owner intended to grant to his sister.

(C) Not prevail, because the phrase "developed land" is too uncertain.

(D) Not prevail, because the description is too vague.

Question 18

A man owned a parcel of land and gave his friend a typed and signed deed to the property. The man told the friend that he was giving the property to her, but that because he had not had a chance to make copies of the deed, he needed it back until the next day. The friend agreed and gave it back to him. Unfortunately, the man was hit by a bus that evening and died.

Assuming that the court finds the description in the deed to be sufficient, which of the following findings is a court likely to make with regard to the friend's interest in the property?

(A) An interest was transferred to the friend, because even though there was no actual delivery, the deed can be treated as a will.

(B) An interest was transferred to the friend, because there was a valid deed and a valid delivery.

(C) No interest was transferred to the friend, because the owner kept the deed; thus, there was no delivery.

(D) No interest was transferred to the friend, because the owner did not have the chance to make copies of the deed.

Question 19

An owner of land gave his friend a deed for a specified parcel of property. After the owner's death, the friend discovered that the owner had sold part of the property. The purchaser had been given an easement to cross over the owner's property to get to the property she had purchased, although there is no evidence that the purchaser had ever used the "right of way."

If the purchaser does have the right of way over the property the owner gave to his friend, the owner's estate would be liable for breach of the covenant:

(A) Against encumbrances.

(B) Of quiet enjoyment, if such a right of way exists whether or not the purchaser is using it.

(C) Of right to convey, because the owner, by not mentioning the right of way in the friend's deed, implied that there were no easements.

(D) Of right to convey, because the existence of the right of way by the purchaser is inconsistent with the owner's alleged title.

Question 20

An owner of land gave his valet a deed which conveyed a specified piece of property. He then died. The owner's son introduces evidence that the owner had promised him in writing that, if he was ever going to get rid of that piece of property, the son would have the right to purchase it first.

The trial court will:

(A) Void the deed to the valet.

(B) Require the valet to convey to the son if he tenders market price for the property.

(C) Do nothing to the valet's deed, but the son may have a cause of action against the owner's estate.

(D) Do nothing to the valet's deed, because the son has no claim against either the valet or the owner's estate.

Question 21

A mechanic was tried for the aggravated assault of a nurse. The mechanic called a witness to the witness stand. The witness was to testify that the night before the alleged crime, the mechanic stated to the witness that he was going to visit his mother in a distant city some 1,000 miles away.

The testimony is:

(A) Admissible, because it is a declaration of intent to do a future act.

(B) Admissible, because of the verbal acts exception.

(C) Inadmissible, because it is not relevant.

(D) Inadmissible, because it is hearsay not within any exception.

Question 22

A man was a permanent resident alien of the United States who was awaiting an opportunity to become a citizen. He filed an application to become an instructor in the local public high school but was denied the position solely on the ground that he was not a citizen. The man now brings suit, alleging that his status as a resident alien was not a proper ground for denying him a position as an instructor.

May the state deny a permanent resident alien employment as an instructor in the public high school?

(A) Yes, because employment by the state is a privilege, not a right.

(B) Yes, because citizenship bears some rational relationship to the interest that is being protected.

(C) No, to do so would be a denial of equal protection.

(D) No, because the evidence presented was uncontroverted that he was awaiting the opportunity to become a citizen.

Question 23

A bank was robbed by a short man (under 5' 5") who was wearing a purple jumpsuit with a red hood and green gloves. The next day, the police received a tip from a neighbor of a short man that the man treated the entire apartment complex to breakfast and flashed a huge roll of bills. When questioned by police, the short man, no taller than 5'2", explained that a friend had paid off an old debt that the man had long ago written off. Later that day, sanitation workers found a purple jumpsuit and green gloves in the apartment complex's dumpster and called the police. The police arrested the short man and executed a search warrant for his apartment, which turned up nothing. At the short man's trial for bank robbery, the prosecution seeks to introduce into evidence the clothing recovered from the dumpster.

The clothing is:

(A) Admissible, as circumstantial evidence that the short man committed the robbery.

(B) Admissible, as direct evidence that the short man committed the robbery.

(C) Inadmissible, because it is irrelevant.

(D) Inadmissible, unless the prosecution proves beyond a reasonable doubt that it is the same clothing the robber wore.

Question 24

In a property settlement after a divorce, the wife was awarded all personal property that had been accumulated during the marriage, including the husband's classic 19-inch black-and-white TV set. In order to get his prized TV set back, the husband lied to his friend, telling him that the wife took the TV set in violation of the property settlement. The friend remembered that the wife gave the friend's wife a key to her new home, and he volunteered to go with the husband to get the TV back while the wife was at work. The husband and the friend went to the wife's house, but, unknown to them, the wife had taken the day off work. After the friend noisily opened the back door with his wife's key, the wife called the police, who quickly arrived and arrested the husband and the friend.

As to a charge of common law conspiracy to commit larceny, the friend should be found:

(A) Not guilty, because he did not intend to steal.

(B) Not guilty, because he did not have a corrupt motive.

(C) Guilty, because there was an agreement, and the opening of the locked door was sufficient for the overt act.

(D) Guilty, because good motives are not a defense to criminal liability.

Question 25

A state passed a statute that provided for direct reimbursement from public funds to nonpublic schools, including religious schools, of the cost of performing various testing services required of all schools by state law. The three state-prepared tests involved consisted of a student evaluation test, a comprehensive achievement test, and scholarship and college qualification tests. The law also provided for payment to the nonpublic schools for the grading of the tests, which are graded objectively.

On review by the Supreme Court, the statute should be held:

(A) Constitutional, because objective grading standards are used and reimbursement covers only secular services.

(B) Constitutional, if the state interest is great enough to justify the burden on religion, and no alternative means are available.

(C) Unconstitutional, because direct payment to nonpublic schools is a violation of the Establishment Clause of the First Amendment.

(D) Unconstitutional, because the statewide administration of the test for nonpublic as well as public schools entangles the state with religious schools.

Question 26

A fashionista purchased a wardrobe closet at an antique auction. Three days later, while cleaning the inside of the closet, she discovered a small quantity of a white powder inside a box.

She showed the box to her boyfriend, a paralegal. He identified the powder as driscamine, a controlled substance. He told her that it was illegal to buy driscamine, but because she did not know that it was in the closet when she purchased it, it was okay to keep it, which she did. A state statute prohibits "willful and unlawful possession of a controlled substance."

If the fashionista is charged with violating this statute, she should be found:

(A) Guilty, because she knowingly possessed the driscamine.

(B) Guilty, because she acquired the driscamine when she intentionally purchased the wardrobe closet and, in doing so, committed the requisite unlawful act.

(C) Not guilty, because she thought she was acting lawfully.

(D) Not guilty, because she did not willfully acquire the driscamine and, hence, committed no unlawful act.

Question 27

A truck driver is suing a car driver for injuries he suffered when their vehicles collided at an intersection controlled by stoplights. The truck driver called a witness to the accident to testify that he saw the driver of the car drive through a red light. On cross-examination, the car driver's attorney asks the witness, "Isn't it true that the car driver's ex-wife is paying $500 for your testimony today?" The truck driver's attorney objects.

The objection should be:

(A) Overruled, because the question gives the witness an opportunity to explain or deny the allegation.

(B) Overruled, because the question is a proper form of impeachment.

(C) Sustained, because the question addresses a collateral issue.

(D) Sustained, because it is a leading question.

Question 28

A property owner owned a tract of commercial property that he conveyed in joint tenancy to his twin sons as a birthday present. Unfortunately, a few years after the conveyance, the property owner and his sons had a serious falling out over how to run the family business. The property owner no longer wished the sons to control valuable commercial property, and so he demanded that they return the deed with which he conveyed the property to them. The sons returned the deed, and the property owner destroyed it. A few months later, one of the twins learned that he was seriously ill and not likely to live much longer. He executed a quitclaim deed conveying "any interest I have in the commercial property conveyed to me and my brother from my father" to his daughter. The twin who conveyed the property subsequently died.

Who owns the property?

(A) The living twin.

(B) The property owner.

(C) The living twin and the deceased twin's daughter as tenants in common.

(D) The living twin and the deceased twin's daughter as joint tenants.

Question 29

A property owner owned a tract of land that he leased to a baker for 27 years. The baker built a large bakery on the property. The baker then sold the bakery building to a buyer, assigning the lease with the property owner's approval. The buyer has failed to make a rent payment for several months and has also failed to build the cafe that the baker had agreed to build in the original lease.

The landlord of the property has a cause of action against:

(A) The buyer for the rent only, because the rent covenant runs with the land.

(B) The buyer for the rent and the cafe, but only if the buyer expressly assumed performance of all covenants.

(C) The buyer and the baker for both the rent and the cafe.

(D) The buyer for the rent only, and the baker for the cafe only.

Question 30

A property owner conveyed commercial property in joint tenancy to his two daughters as a birthday present. The deed from the property owner to his daughters was never recorded. After a few years, the property owner no longer wished the daughters to control valuable commercial property, and so he demanded that they return the deed with which he conveyed the property to them. The daughters returned the deed, and the property owner destroyed it. The property owner then sold and conveyed the property to a third party. The jurisdiction's recording act states the following: "No conveyance or mortgage of an interest in land is valid against any subsequent purchaser for value without notice thereof whose conveyance is first recorded."

If the third party brings a quiet title action and is successful, which of the following best explains this result?

(A) As owner of the property, the property owner was entitled to convey it to the third party.

(B) The daughters failed to record the deed they took from their father.

(C) The daughters failed to record their deed, and the third party was unaware of their interest when she paid the property owner market value for the property.

(D) The daughters failed to record their deed, the third party was unaware of their interest when she purchased the property, and the third party recorded her deed.

Question 31

A consumer purchased a portable electronic device from a retailer. The device was in the manufacturer's original packaging when the consumer purchased it. Shortly thereafter, the consumer was using the device appropriately when it generated an electrical shock. The shock injured the consumer and caused the circuits of the device to overheat and melt, destroying the device.

The consumer brought an action based on strict liability against the manufacturer of the device. At trial, the consumer established the above facts. The consumer's expert testified that the product was in a defective condition unreasonably dangerous to users. However, because the device was destroyed, the expert could not determine whether the accident was caused by a design defect or a manufacturing defect. The manufacturer's expert testified that the device was not defective.

If the manufacturer moves for a directed verdict at the close of the evidence, how should the court rule?

(A) Grant the motion, because the consumer did not show that the retailer was not at fault.

(B) Grant the motion, because the consumer's expert could not determine the exact nature of the defect.

(C) Deny the motion, because the jury could decide that the harm was caused by a dangerous defect present in the device when it left the manufacturer.

(D) Deny the motion, because the consumer was injured by the device.

Question 32

A 12-year-old girl's parents went out of town for the day, leaving her home until 5 p.m. At 2 p.m., the girl went out rollerblading and saw that a neighbor was growing prize roses in her yard. The girl entered the yard and cut all of the prize roses off the rose bushes and rollerbladed over a rose bush, causing the rose bush to die. The jurisdiction has no statute regarding parental liability.

In a suit by the neighbor against the girl's parents for the damage caused to her rose bush, the neighbor should:

(A) Prevail, because a minor's parents are vicariously liable any time the minor commits a tortious act.

(B) Prevail, because the girl's parents left the girl alone during the day.

(C) Not prevail, unless she can show that the girl's parents were aware that the girl has done this sort of act before.

(D) Not prevail, because the jurisdiction has no statute regarding parental liability.

Question 33

A car manufacturer entered into contracts with various refineries to purchase the gasoline they produced for the manufacturer's dealerships. One agreement with an oil dealer provided that the car manufacturer was given the right to purchase all gasoline refined by the oil dealer for the next five years at a price set at 95% of the domestic market price at the time of delivery. The car manufacturer agreed to purchase no less than 5,000 gallons a week and to use its own tankers to transport the gasoline from the oil dealer's refinery to its storage facilities. At the time the contract was signed, the car manufacturer gave written notice to the oil dealer that it intended to buy all gasoline produced by the oil dealer until further notice.

This agreement between the car manufacturer and the oil dealer was:

(A) Unenforceable because of the failure to set a specific price for the gasoline.

(B) Unenforceable because it was for an unreasonable period of time.

(C) Enforceable as to price, but not as to the amount of gasoline the oil dealer agreed to sell.

(D) Enforceable in all respects.

Question 34

A shoe manufacturer entered into a contract to purchase all cowhide refined by a tannery for the next five years at a price set at 95% of the domestic market price at the time of delivery. The shoe manufacturer agreed to purchase no less than 500 pounds of cowhide a week. At the time this contract was signed, the shoe manufacturer gave written notice to the tannery that it intended to buy all cowhide produced by the tannery until further notice. For the first year, the shoe manufacturer continued to purchase all cowhide produced by the tannery. However, by the end of that year, the tannery doubled its production of cowhide. At a meeting between the tannery and the shoe manufacturer, the tannery's president noted that the shoe manufacturer was getting as much cowhide as it needed, and that the tannery intended to sell the extra cowhide it was producing on foreign markets at a higher price than the shoe manufacturer was paying. The shoe manufacturer agreed to maintain its purchases at the first year's level and signed an addendum to the original agreement reflecting this change.

The modification of this contract made by the addendum was:

(A) Enforceable to the extent that the shoe manufacturer purchased the cowhide.

(B) Enforceable in all respects.

(C) Unenforceable, because there was no consideration for the shoe manufacturer's agreement to take only one-half of the cowhide produced.

(D) Unenforceable, because the contract did not state the amount of cowhide that the tannery would produce.

Question 35

In anticipation of pending domestic agriculture regulations that would make growing corn less profitable, a candy company entered into a contract with a corn farmer who grew a particularly good variety of corn, whereby the candy company was given the right to purchase all high fructose corn syrup refined by the corn farmer for the next five years at a price set at 95% of the domestic market price at the time of delivery. The candy company agreed to purchase no less than 1,000 liters of corn syrup a week and to use its own trucks to transport the corn syrup to its storage facilities. At the time this contract was signed, the candy company gave written notice to the corn farmer that it intended to buy all high fructose corn syrup produced by the corn farmer until further notice. Thereafter, the candy company continued to purchase one-half of the corn farmer's total corn syrup capacity until the following year. At that time, the corn farmer, by letter, notified the candy company that it could no longer deliver corn syrup to it in accordance with their agreement because the new domestic agriculture regulations had rendered growing corn unprofitable.

The corn farmer's refusal to deliver corn syrup to the candy company is:

(A) Justifiable, because corn is widely available.

(B) Justifiable, because its performance was excused because of the lack of profitability.

(C) Justifiable, because the candy company was aware of the possibility of new government regulations when it entered into the agreement.

(D) Not justifiable and a breach of contract.

Question 36

A publisher entered into a contract with a paper manufacturer who used very fine materials, whereby the publisher was given the right to purchase all paper refined by the paper manufacturer for the next five years at a price set at 95% of the domestic market price at the time of delivery. The publisher agreed to purchase no less than 1,000 pounds of paper a week. At the time this contract was signed, the publisher gave written notice to the paper manufacturer that it intended to buy all paper produced by the paper manufacturer until further notice. The paper manufacturer then sold its plant to a lumber-processing company.

What is the effect of this sale on the paper manufacturer's obligation to the publisher?

(A) The sale discharges its obligation to the publisher because there has been a full performance.

(B) The paper manufacturer is liable for damages if the lumber processing plant fails to deliver paper to the publisher.

(C) The paper manufacturer is excused from further performance because it no longer has a factory to produce paper.

(D) The paper manufacturer breached its contract with the publisher.

Question 37

Two robbers planned to commit armed robberies targeting older victims. However, when the time came to actually commit the robbery, one of the robbers, thinking that the potential victim looked too much like his grandmother, backed out and told his cohort that he was going home. The second robber went ahead with the plan and robbed the elderly victim, who died of a heart attack due to the stress of the robbery. The second robber was arrested and implicated the first robber.

The first robber is guilty of:

(A) No crime.

(B) Conspiracy.

(C) Murder.

(D) Murder and conspiracy.

Question 38

The defendant, who formerly worked for a construction company, became intoxicated one night and decided to move some heavy construction equipment that was parked at a construction site. Ignoring "no trespassing" signs, the defendant jumped the fence and climbed into a large dump truck and started it up. However, due to his intoxication, he quickly lost control of the truck. It rumbled a short distance and crashed into a trailer housing the main office of the construction site. The defendant is prosecuted for recklessly damaging property.

The defendant should be found:

(A) Guilty, because his actions constituted an unlawful taking of the construction equipment.

(B) Guilty, because he was intoxicated while attempting to move the construction equipment.

(C) Not guilty, because at most he could be found guilty of criminal negligence.

(D) Not guilty, because he must have been aware that his conduct would cause the damage to the trailer in order to be found guilty of reckless damage.

Question 39

A Congressional committee was formed to conduct an investigation. The committee subpoenaed a man to appear before it to answer certain questions. The man appeared before the committee but refused to answer any questions. The committee notified the Speaker of the House of the man's refusal to cooperate. The Speaker called a special session of the House. At the special session, a majority of the members of the House voted to order the Attorney General of the United States to prosecute the man pursuant to a federal statute that establishes the penalties for contempt of Congress.

Is the Attorney General constitutionally obligated to prosecute the man pursuant to the congressional order?

(A) No, if the man is an appointive official of the executive branch, because he would then be immune from prosecution for acts performed in the course of his duties.

(B) No, because the decision to prosecute is exclusively within the discretion of the executive branch.

(C) Yes, because the Attorney General may not lawfully disobey a directive from Congress to punish a contempt.

(D) Yes, because the Attorney General may not refuse to prosecute one who has violated federal law.

Question 40

The legislature of a state enacted a statute that provides for loaning certain textbooks on secular subjects to students in all public and private schools. In accordance with the statute, the state board of education distributed textbooks to a private school that offers religious instruction and admits only Caucasian students.

Which of the following is the strongest argument against the constitutionality of free distribution of textbooks to the students at the private school?

(A) A state may not constitutionally aid private schools through distribution of textbooks.

(B) Segregation is furthered by the distribution of textbooks to these students.

(C) The distribution of textbooks advances religion because it is impossible to separate their secular and religious uses.

(D) The distribution of textbooks fosters excessive government entanglement with religion.

Question 41

A truck driver collided with a motorcyclist in a busy intersection. A police officer present at the scene cited the trucker for running a red light. At the preliminary hearing, the trucker initially pleaded guilty, but he withdrew his plea when the judge told him what she had in mind for a sentence. The judge let the trucker change his plea to not guilty. The trucker, however, had no success at his trial and was convicted. The motorcyclist is now suing the trucker in a civil action for the injuries he sustained in the accident.

If the motorcyclist tries to introduce evidence of the trucker's original guilty plea, on proper motion, this evidence will be:

(A) Excluded, because it is hearsay not within any exception.

(B) Excluded, because the plea was withdrawn.

(C) Admitted, because an admission is not hearsay.

(D) Admitted, because it described the trucker's state of mind.

Question 42

A pedestrian was lawfully crossing the street when he was struck and seriously injured by a car that had run a red light. At the time, the driver was on his way home from a local tavern. The pedestrian brings suit against the tavern for his injuries, claiming that the driver was permitted to drink too much liquor at the tavern before leaving. The pedestrian calls a witness to the stand. The witness testifies that she and a friend had visited the tavern on the night in question. The witness seeks to testify that she remarked to her friend, "Look at that guy. He's so drunk he can't even stand up."

The witness's testimony concerning her remark to her friend is:

(A) Admissible as a prior consistent statement.

(B) Admissible as a statement by the witness regarding the condition she observed, made while she was observing it.

(C) Admissible as relevant nonhearsay testimony.

(D) Inadmissible as hearsay not within any exception.

Question 43

An unmarried couple lived together for 10 years as husband and wife. During this time, the woman identified herself as the man's wife, and the couple maintained a joint checking account and filed joint income tax returns as husband and wife. During this period of cohabitation, the man decided to buy a home. The deed identified the grantees as the man and the woman, "his wife, and their heirs and assigns forever as tenants by the entirety." The man made a down payment of $20,000 and executed a mortgage for the unpaid balance. Both he and the woman signed the note for the unpaid balance as husband and wife. The man continued to make the monthly payments as they became due until he and the woman had an argument and decided to separate. The man abandoned the woman and the house. The woman then made the payments for six months. At the end of this period, the woman brought an action against the man for partition of the land in question. The jurisdiction does not recognize common law marriages, and has no applicable statute on the subject.

The woman's request for partition should be:

(A) Granted, because the estate created by the deed was not a tenancy by the entirety.

(B) Granted, because the tenancy by the entirety that was created by the deed was severed when the man abandoned the woman.

(C) Denied, because a tenant by the entirety has no right to partition.

(D) Denied, because the man has absolute title to the property.

Question 44

A tenant leased an apartment from a landlord for a period of one year. At the end of the year, the tenant continued occupying the apartment, paying the landlord the $250 rent in advance each month. The tenant had continually complained to the landlord about the facilities provided for trash disposal behind the apartment building. Finally, after receiving no response from the landlord, the tenant complained to the health department, who in turn mandated that the landlord substantially improve the trash facilities for the apartment building. Shortly thereafter, the landlord notified the tenant that his rent was being increased to $400 per month. The tenant protested and pointed out that all of the other tenants in the apartment building paid rent of $250 per month. The landlord then gave the tenant the required statutory notice that the tenancy was being terminated at the earliest possible time. By an appropriate action, the tenant contested the landlord's right to terminate.

If the tenant succeeds, it will be because:

(A) The doctrine prohibiting retaliatory eviction is part of the law of the jurisdiction.

(B) A periodic tenancy was created by implication.

(C) A landlord must generally charge the same rent for all units located in one complex.

(D) The landlord failed to establish a valid reason why the tenant's rent needed to be raised.

Question 45

Two neighbors owned summer homes adjacent to each other on the lake. After a week-long stay by the son of one of the property owners, the neighbor called the owner and said that his boat dock had been badly damaged and was told by another resident that the owner's son and some friends had gotten drunk and accidentally crashed their boat into his dock. The owner was surprised at the accusation because he was sure that if his son had caused the damages, he would have told him. However, he did not want to get into a dispute with his neighbor, so he told his neighbor that he would have the dock repaired and pay for the repairs if the neighbor agreed not to bring a claim against his son for the damage to the dock. The neighbor agreed, and the owner hired a local carpenter to do the work. Later, however, the owner discovered that his son did not damage the dock because the damages occurred after his son had returned to college.

Is the owner obligated to pay for the repairs?

(A) No, because the owner never really believed that his son caused the damage.

(B) No, because his son in fact did not cause the damage.

(C) No, because the neighbor was wrong when he accused his son of causing the damage and it would be unfair to enforce an agreement when there was a mutual mistake of fact.

(D) Yes.

Question 46

A defendant was convicted after a jury trial of violation of federal statutes prohibiting the sale of automatic weapons to foreign nationals. It was established at trial that the defendant had purchased a number of stolen United States Army heavy machine guns and attempted to ship them abroad. The trial court expressly based its imposition of the maximum possible sentence for the conviction on the defendant's refusal to reveal the names of the persons from whom he purchased the stolen weapons. His counsel argues that this consideration is reversible error.

In the defendant's appeal of the sentence imposed, the appeals court should:

(A) Reverse the trial court, because the consideration of the defendant's silence violates his Fifth Amendment privilege against self-incrimination.

(B) Reverse the trial court, because the consideration of collateral circumstances in sentencing violates his due process rights.

(C) Affirm the trial court, because the right to silence of the Fifth Amendment does not include the right to protect others from incrimination.

(D) Affirm the trial court, because citizens must report violations of the criminal statutes.

Question 47

A man kept a small printing press in his home. His son's girlfriend had been in the man's home on many occasions to visit with his son and had seen the printing press. She decided to print a one-page newsletter critical of the local school board's policies and distribute it around town. On an evening when she knew that her boyfriend and his family were out, she broke into their home intending to use the printing press to print her newsletter. The girl believed that the unauthorized use of the printing press constituted a crime, but she was mistaken in this belief. The girl was discovered in the house and charged with burglary. The jurisdiction defines burglary as the breaking and entering of the dwelling house of another at nighttime with the intent to commit a crime.

The girl should be found:

(A) Guilty, because her mistake was one of law, not of fact.

(B) Guilty, because she broke and entered the family's home believing she was going to commit a crime.

(C) Not guilty, because even if she had been successful, no crime would have occurred.

(D) Not guilty, because there was no dangerous proximity to success.

Question 48

A homeowner lived in a house on a large corner lot located a few hundred feet from a convenience store that was frequented by many people in the neighborhood. Everyone took a shortcut across the homeowner's front yard rather than staying on the sidewalk that bordered her lawn. The heavy foot traffic wore a path through her lawn, and people left soft drink cans and candy wrappers strewn all over her front yard. Fed up, the homeowner hired a local contractor to build a fence around her front lawn. The next afternoon, the contractor started the job by surveying the property and digging post holes, but left to do another small job in that area. He left behind a wheelbarrow with a shovel leaning against it. After noticing the items, the homeowner called the contractor's office and spoke to his wife. The contractor's wife said that he was on another job in the area and would pick up the wheelbarrow and shovel on his way back, but he never did.

A neighbor who was walking to the convenience store to pick up a six-pack of beer after work took his usual shortcut when he came to the neighbor's corner. As he was walking by the wheelbarrow, a police car with siren wailing went by on the main street, distracting him. As he followed the police car with his eyes, he tripped over the shovel leaning against the wheelbarrow and fell, breaking his arm.

Is the homeowner liable to the neighbor for his broken arm and related damages?

(A) No, because she did not create the condition that harmed him.

(B) No, because the danger to which he was exposed was open and obvious.

(C) Yes, because she was aware of the condition that harmed him.

(D) Yes, because she knew that he frequently cut across her lawn on the way to the convenience store.

Question 49

A pet owner left his dog in his yard while he went to work. The dog's constant barking greatly annoyed his neighbor. When the pet owner came home that evening he found the dead body of his beloved dog in the yard, with blood around its nose and mouth. He was very upset because the dog had been his pet for many years. A subsequent investigation revealed that his neighbor had given the dog a treat with rat poison in it during the day because she could not stand the barking.

If the pet owner brings an action against the neighbor to recover for his emotional distress, he likely will:

(A) Prevail, if he suffered physical injury from his distress.

(B) Prevail, if the neighbor was aware that it was very likely that the pet owner would suffer severe emotional distress.

(C) Not prevail, unless the neighbor intended to cause the pet owner severe emotional distress.

(D) Not prevail, because the neighbor did not kill the dog in the presence of its owner.

Question 50

After months of bilateral talks, the President entered into a treaty with a foreign nation previously designated by the President as a terrorist state. Under the treaty, the foreign nation agreed to curtail its nuclear testing program and the United States agreed to lift trading sanctions against the foreign country. The treaty was approved by a vote of more than two-thirds of the Senate. Subsequently, it was revealed that the government of the foreign nation had been sponsoring the copying and black market trade of products patented in the United States and protected by international law. Outraged, Congress approved a bill purporting to repeal the treaty. When the bill was presented to the President, he vetoed it, citing national security interests. Both houses of Congress then repassed the bill by a more than two-thirds vote.

As a result of the foregoing, which of the following statements is correct?

(A) The treaty is still valid, because it was both negotiated by the President and passed by Congress.

(B) The treaty is still valid, because the President still supports the treaty and the President's power over foreign affairs is paramount.

(C) The treaty was effectively repealed, because acts of Congress are the supreme law of the land, and any United States treaty in conflict with a congressional act is invalid.

(D) The treaty was effectively repealed, because the repeal was approved over the President's veto after the treaty was made.

MIXED SUBJECT SET 2 SUBJECT GUIDE

1. Criminal Law
2. Torts
3. Torts
4. Evidence
5. Constitutional Law
6. Constitutional Law
7. Constitutional Law
8. Evidence
9. Evidence
10. Criminal Law
11. Contracts
12. Contracts
13. Contracts
14. Contracts
15. Criminal Law
16. Real Property
17. Real Property
18. Real Property
19. Real Property
20. Real Property
21. Evidence
22. Constitutional Law
23. Evidence
24. Criminal Law
25. Constitutional Law
26. Criminal Law
27. Evidence
28. Real Property
29. Real Property
30. Real Property
31. Torts
32. Torts
33. Contracts
34. Contracts
35. Contracts
36. Contracts
37. Criminal Law
38. Criminal Law
39. Constitutional Law
40. Constitutional Law
41. Evidence
42. Evidence
43. Real Property
44. Real Property
45. Contracts
46. Criminal Law
47. Criminal Law
48. Torts
49. Torts
50. Constitutional Law

MIXED SUBJECT ANSWERS - SET 2

Answer to Question 1

(C) To hold a person liable under the theory of accessory or accomplice liability, the prosecution must show that the defendant helped with the crime with the intent to see the crime committed. Unless the prosecution can establish the unlawful mental state, there can be no criminal liability. Because the man did not have the intent to see a larceny committed, he cannot be guilty. (A) is wrong because he did not have the necessary mental state. (B) is wrong; the issue is not whether he had reason to believe the car was the friend's, but whether he intended a larceny to take place. (D) is wrong because the fact that the friend would probably have stolen the car anyway will not relieve the defendant from liability if he helped with the necessary intent.

Answer to Question 2

(C) The inventor's duty as possessor of land makes him liable to the neighbor for the damage from the antenna. The fact that an independent contractor may have negligently created the danger does not relieve the duty the inventor owes to adjoining landowners. [*See* Restatement (Second) §422] (A) is not correct because respondeat superior refers to an employer-employee relationship; the contractor was an independent contractor. (B) is wrong because no shifting of responsibility was created by the payment under these facts. (D) is wrong because there are not enough facts to establish that the contractor's work was an inherently dangerous activity.

Answer to Question 3

(B) If the tree trimmer could not reasonably foresee that the tree branch would fall, then he was not negligent. (A) is wrong because payment does not relieve an independent contractor from liability. (C) is wrong because even if the tree trimmer did do the work under the direction of the homeowner, he would then be liable along with the homeowner. (D) is wrong because the location of the pine tree would not affect the tree trimmer's liability.

Answer to Question 4

(B) The wife is competent to testify. Persons interested in a lawsuit are not disqualified as witnesses. (A) is wrong because the wife need not be the personal representative of her husband's estate to testify. (C) is incorrect because she is testifying as to what she saw, not as to her opinion. In any event, a lay witness may testify as to an opinion if she is a percipient witness. (D) is wrong because the common law spousal incapacity has been abolished.

Answer to Question 5

(C) Congress is specifically given the power to regulate federal lands in Article IV. Because there is no other authority that can regulate the use of federal lands but Congress, this is all the authority Congress would need to enact this type of statute. Thus, (B) and (D) are wrong. (A) is wrong because although Congress has broad powers under the Commerce Clause, this is not a matter falling under that clause.

Answer to Question 6

(B) The Appointment Clause of the Constitution permits Congress to vest appointments of inferior officers only in the President, the courts, or the heads of departments. Enforcement is an executive act; therefore, Congress cannot appoint its own members to the commission to exercise enforcement powers. A duly appointed commission does have the power to make rules and regulations governing the subject matter for which it is appointed. Those rules are not "criminal" statutes in this case. Thus, (A) is wrong. (C) is wrong because Congress may establish new public rights and actions that may be adjudicated by agencies, without juries. (D) is wrong because there is no discrimination.

Answer to Question 7

(C) The administrative law judge is not a judge within the sense of Article III, and only such judges are protected by the provisions of that article. Thus, (A) and (B) are incorrect. (D) makes no sense. The statutory authority for appointments remains the same, and only the person holding the office has changed.

Answer to Question 8

(A) An admission by a party-opponent is the party's own statement offered against him by the opposing side, and under the Federal Rules, it is not hearsay. Thus, (D) is incorrect. (B) does not state a proper basis for admissibility; besides, the only way the statement could be admitted by way of the report is as an admission. (C) is wrong. If the statement qualifies as an admission—made by a party, offered by the opponent and relevant—it will be admissible even if the admitting party had no rational basis for the statement.

Answer to Question 9

(D) Under Federal Rule 801(d)(2), an out-of-court statement of an agent or an employee can be introduced as an admission against the principal or employer if it concerns a matter within the scope of the agency or employment, made during the existence of the relationship. Given the establishment of that preliminary fact, the statement here constitutes an admission by a party-opponent and is not hearsay. (A) and (C) state requirements for admissibility that have no basis in law. Admissibility of an admission is not conditioned on the availability of the declarant; (B) is therefore incorrect.

Answer to Question 10

(D) The lawyer shot the architect, intending to kill him, and the architect died. The only issue is whether the lawyer's act was the proximate cause of the architect's death. Proximate cause is found when the results are the natural and foreseeable results of the defendant's acts. Infections and negligent medical treatment are deemed to be a foreseeable risk in homicide cases; since the architect died of pneumonia that resulted from the bullet, most courts would conclude that proximate cause has been established. (A) would be correct if proximate cause could not be established. (B) and (C) are wrong. The fact that the architect already had an incurable disease or would likely have died from another cause will not negate proximate cause.

Answer to Question 11

(A) The young woman will prevail. Where the seller is a merchant, the risk of loss does not pass to the buyer until the buyer takes physical possession of the goods. (B) is wrong because performance was not impossible; the young woman had already performed and the shoe store could perform by tendering another pair of shoes. (C) is wrong because passage of title does not shift the risk of loss in this case. (D) is wrong because while a buyer gains some rights once the goods are identified, identification does not shift the risk of loss.

Answer to Question 12

(D) An implied warranty of fitness for particular purpose arises where a seller knows that the buyer is relying on the seller to pick suitable goods for the buyer and the buyer relies on the seller's expertise. Here, the woman asked the seller to pick suitable goods, but declined the seller's advice and picked out her own coat. Therefore, this warranty did not arise. The implied warranty of merchantability arose but was not broken. This warranty arises in every sale of goods by a merchant and ensures, generally, that goods shall be fit for ordinary purposes. Nothing in the facts indicates that the coat is not fit for ordinary purposes. The only express warranties here arose from the statement that the coat was cashmere and, perhaps, from the sample coat on the sales floor. However, nothing in the facts indicates that there has been a breach of either of these express warranties. Therefore, (D) is the correct answer.

Answer to Question 13

(D) An express warranty will arise from any statement of fact or promise. Here, the salesperson said that the racket was made of titanium and would last for years. The former is a statement of fact that will give rise to a warranty; thus, (A) is a good theory. The latter is not a statement of fact, but a prediction of the future. Moreover, it is not specific—how long is "years"? This statement amounts to mere puffery and will not give rise to a warranty. Therefore, (B) is not a good theory. An implied warranty of merchantability will arise in every sale by a merchant unless disclaimed. To be merchantable, goods must be fit for ordinary purposes, and arguably a racket that dents right away because it is made of plastic is not fit for ordinary purposes. Therefore, (C) is a good theory, making (D) the correct choice.

Answer to Question 14

(C) Once a buyer has accepted goods, his right to reject for nonconformance generally lapses and his only remedy is a suit for damages. Acceptance usually occurs when the buyer takes possession of the goods. In some cases, the buyer can revoke acceptance, but the breach must be substantial and the buyer must have a good reason for accepting the goods (*i.e.*, something more than not taking the time to carefully inspect). Here, the customer accepted the goods and the breach appears minor. (A) entitles the customer only to damages, not a full refund. (B) is a misstatement of the law. (D) is wrong because written notice is not required; oral notice is acceptable.

Answer to Question 15

(C) To be liable as an aider and abettor (*i.e.*, an accomplice), the defendant must encourage or aid in commission of the underlying crime with intent that the crime be committed or, in certain cases, with knowledge that it was to be committed. Because the friend had no knowledge of the crime, he could not be an aider and abettor. (A) is wrong because mere presence at the scene of the crime is not enough to make the friend a principal in the second degree. (B) is wrong because, as stated, there must be intent or knowledge to be an aider and abettor. (D) is wrong because if the requisite intent is present, the defendant can be liable even though he did not "cause" the crime.

Answer to Question 16

(D) The court should find for the friend, because the error in description was not sufficient to put in doubt what the man intended to convey to her. A description in a deed is sufficient if it furnishes a good lead as to the identity of the property. Hence, (A) is wrong. (C) is incorrect because a deed purporting to convey more land than the grantor owns does not invalidate the deed. (B) fails to conform to the facts.

Answer to Question 17

(D) The sister will not prevail. The description is too vague in its entirety; there may be difficulty determining ***which*** six acres are meant. Thus, (B) is wrong. (C) is wrong because the "developed land" language is not the only vague part; which six acres of the property is also a problem. (A) is wrong because whatever the original owner's actual intent, he failed to accomplish it with this deed.

Answer to Question 18

(B) A court is likely to find that the deed was valid and properly delivered. (A) is wrong because an undelivered deed cannot be sustained as a valid testamentary disposition under the Statute of Wills. (C) is wrong because the original giving of the deed to the friend constituted "delivery" and she accepted; the fact that she returned the deed to the owner temporarily does not change the fact that a delivery was made. (D) is irrelevant.

Answer to Question 19

(A) The existence of the easement breaches the covenant against encumbrances and the owner's estate is in breach of this covenant. (B), (C), and (D) are incorrect because the existence of an easement burdening the land does not breach the covenant of quiet enjoyment or right to convey, respectively. The covenant of quiet enjoyment is breached when the grantee is evicted by a third party with ***paramount*** title, *i.e.,* title or ownership of the estate conveyed that is superior to the grantor's title. The covenant of right to convey is breached if the grantor lacks title, *i.e.,* ownership of the estate conveyed, at the time of the grant.

Answer to Question 20

(C) The trial court will do nothing with the valet's deed, but the son may have a cause of action against the father's estate. If a "right of first purchase" is found to be valid, the agreement is merely a promissory restraint, the breach of which may give the son a cause of action against his father's estate, but will not affect the valet's interest unless he had knowledge of the agreement at the time he acquired her deed from the owner. Thus, alternatives (A), (B), and (D) are incorrect.

Answer to Question 21

(A) The testimony would be hearsay, but it would be admissible under the exception of a declaration of an intent to do a future act, sometimes referred to as a declaration of present mental state. [Fed. R. Evid. 803(3)] (D) is therefore incorrect. The trip provides an alibi defense and is therefore relevant; so (C) is thus incorrect. (B) is wrong because this is not a verbal act; verbal acts are out-of-court statements that when spoken have legal significance, *e.g.*, words of contract or defamation.

Answer to Question 22

(B) Although state classifications based on alienage are generally suspect, a state may reserve a government position for citizens if it is related to self-governance, involves policymaking, or requires exercise of important discretionary power over citizens. In these cases, only a rationality test is used. A public school teacher at the primary and secondary school level performs an important governmental function (*e.g.*, he influences students' attitudes about government, the political process, citizenship, etc.), and therefore the exclusion of aliens is rationally related to the state's interest in furthering educational goals. [Ambach v. Norwick (1979)] (C) is, accordingly, incorrect. The principle articulated in (A) is correct, but has no bearing here, where the question is whether a distinction based on alienage is permissible. (D) is true, but irrelevant; the state may deny the man's application regardless of his ultimate intentions, so long as he remains an alien.

Answer to Question 23

(A) The clothing is circumstantial evidence because the trier of fact is being asked to draw an inference that the clothes are the short man's based on the proven fact that the clothes were found in a dumpster at the short man's building. Direct evidence is evidence that, if believed, will by itself establish one of the propositions in the case; no inference will be necessary. Thus, (B) is incorrect. (C) is incorrect because finding the clothing matching the description of the robber's clothes near the short man's apartment tends to make it more probable that the short man committed the robbery than it would be without the clothing. (D) is incorrect because it states the standard for proving guilt, not for the admissibility of evidence.

Answer to Question 24

(A) The friend should be found not guilty because he did not intend to steal. The friend did not intend to achieve the objective of the conspiracy—to permanently deprive the owner of her property—because the friend thought the husband was the true owner of the TV. (C) is incorrect because there must be an agreement to reach an ***unlawful*** objective. Because the friend thought he was achieving a ***lawful*** objective, he did not have the intent required for conspiracy. (B) is incorrect because a "corrupt motive" is not an element of a crime. A person could be found guilty of a crime even if he did not have a corrupt motive, assuming all required elements for a crime are present. (D) is incorrect for a similar reason. "Good motive" is largely irrelevant; the intent, or lack thereof, is what is important.

Answer to Question 25

(A) The statute should be held constitutional. The nature of the aid provided by the statute has a secular purpose, is of legitimate interest to the state, and does not present any risk of being used to aid the transmission of religious views. (B) misstates the test; this is a test that was used for the Free Exercise Clause, and this is an Establishment Clause case. (C) is incorrect because not all aid to religious schools violates the Establishment Clause. (D) has no basis in the facts given.

Answer to Question 26

(A) She should be found guilty. As soon as her boyfriend informed her that driscamine was a controlled substance and she decided to keep it, she violated the statute, because she willfully possessed a controlled substance. (B) is incorrect because the statute does not punish mere possession; the possession must be "willful." (C) is incorrect because ignorance of the law is generally no excuse. It clearly does not negate the mental state required for this statutory crime. (D) is incorrect because the statute does not punish willful acquisition but willful possession.

Answer to Question 27

(B) The objection should be overruled. It is proper to impeach a witness by showing that the witness has a possible bias. Evidence that the witness is being paid to testify would be proper impeachment through bias. (A) states the requirement for introduction of a prior inconsistent statement; this is obviously inapplicable here. The credibility of a witness is not collateral, and so (C) is incorrect. Leading questions are proper on cross-examination; thus (D) is incorrect.

Answer to Question 28

(C) The living twin and the deceased twin's daughter own the property as tenants in common. A conveyance of a co-tenant's interest in joint tenancy property severs the joint tenancy, and that interest is subsequently held as a tenancy in common with the other co-tenants. Thus, (D) is incorrect. Because the joint tenancy with right of survivorship was severed before the deceased twin's death, (A) is incorrect. Returning the deed to the property owner did not return ownership of the property to him; that would require a reconveyance. Thus, (B) is incorrect.

Answer to Question 29

(C) An assignment does not release the tenant from his contractual obligations to the landlord; thus, the baker is still liable for all of the lease provisions. Thus, (D) is incorrect. An assignee is in privity of estate with the landlord and is liable on all covenants in the lease that run with the land. His assumption of these duties is implied; it need not be expressed in the assignment. Covenants to pay money run with the land, as do covenants to perform physical acts on the property. Therefore, the buyer is liable for both the rent and the cafe even if it did not expressly assume performance of the covenants. Thus, (A) and (B) are incorrect.

Answer to Question 30

(D) The third party's success will be because the daughters failed to record their deed, the third party was unaware of their interest when she purchased the property, and the third party recorded her deed. The property owner had no interest in the property that he conveyed to the third party; thus, (A) is wrong. However, if the third party is a bona fide purchaser for value who records first, the deed to the daughters would not be good against the third party's deed. (B) and (C) are incorrect because they do not contain every element necessary for the third party to prevail.

Answer to Question 31

(C) The court should deny the motion. Strict liability requires proof only that an unreasonably dangerous defective condition in the defendant's product caused the plaintiff's injury. The consumer presented sufficient evidence that the product was dangerously defective and that the defect was the cause of her injury so that the case should go to the jury. If a defect is difficult to trace (such as when a product is destroyed), the plaintiff may rely on an inference that this type of product failure ordinarily would occur only as a result of a product defect. (A) is wrong both because the consumer does not need to show absence of fault by the retailer and because the retailer's negligence would not cut off the manufacturer's liability for supplying a defective product. (B) is wrong because, regardless of the absence of evidence on the exact nature of the defect, the jury could conclude, based on all of the facts, that the device was dangerously defective. (D) is wrong because showing that the consumer was injured by the device is not enough to establish liability. The jury must still determine that the device was in a defective condition unreasonably dangerous to users when it left the manufacturer, as stated by (C).

Answer to Question 32

(C) The only basis on which to hold the parents liable here is if they had notice of their child's destructive tendencies. (C) is a better answer than (D) because it holds out the possibility, not negated by the facts, that the girl's parents were on notice of her tendency to misbehave, in which case they would be liable even absent a statute. (A) misstates the law; in the absence of a statute, parents are not vicariously liable for the torts of their minor children. (B) is wrong because the mere failure to be home with their daughter would not by itself amount to negligence with respect to the neighbor.

Answer to Question 33

(D) The contract is enforceable in all respects. This is an output contract. (A) is wrong because there is a price term, although it is dependent on future events. (B) is wrong because there are no facts that show the five years to be "unreasonable" and even if there were, parties are free to enter into unreasonable contracts. (C) is wrong because the car manufacturer agreed to buy at least 5,000 gallons a week by the original agreement, and all the gasoline by its notice. Such output contracts are enforceable.

Answer to Question 34

(B) Although there was no consideration for the shoe manufacturer to take only one-half of the bargained-for production, none is required because this is a contract for the sale of goods, and subject to U.C.C. section 2-609 (which provides that good-faith modification is enforceable regardless of lack of consideration). (C) is therefore wrong. (A) makes no sense. (D) is wrong because the agreement indicates the amount of cowhide that the shoe manufacturer will purchase.

Answer to Question 35

(D) The corn farmer's refusal to deliver the corn syrup is nonjustifiable and a breach of contract. The lack of profitability did not constitute an objective impossibility of performance, because the corn farmer could still grow corn. (A) and (B) are therefore wrong. (C) is wrong because the candy company's knowledge of the new regulations was not a condition of the contract, but the purpose for entering into it.

Answer to Question 36

(B) The paper manufacturer is liable for damages if the lumber processing plant fails to deliver paper to the publisher. Because delivery of paper is not personal in nature, that duty can be assigned. The quantity will be measured by the paper manufacturer's original output. However, when a duty is delegated to a delegate, the delegator remains liable should the delegate fail to perform. (A) is incorrect because the contract was for five years, and five years have not yet elapsed. (C) would be correct only if the paper manufacturer went out of business without delegating its duties to another by selling the other the business, not the case here. (D) is wrong because, as indicated above, such a delegation is proper.

Answer to Question 37

(B) The first robber is guilty of conspiracy but not murder. The conspiracy was complete when the robbers agreed to commit the robbery and targeted their first victim. The first robber's withdrawal is no defense to the conspiracy charge. Hence, (A) is incorrect. The first robber is not guilty of murder, however, because of his withdrawal. The murder charge would be based on felony murder, because the second robber caused the foreseeable death of the elderly victim from the heart attack during the commission of the felony. However, a conspirator may limit his liability for subsequent acts of other conspirators by performing an affirmative act that notifies the other members of the conspiracy. Here, the first robber told the second robber that he was going home in time for the second robber to abandon his plans. Hence, he is not liable for felony murder arising from the robbery, making (C) and (D) incorrect.

Answer to Question 38

(B) The defendant should be convicted because he was intoxicated when he damaged the trailer. The defendant is being charged with reckless damage to property. A person acts recklessly when he consciously disregards a substantial and unjustifiable risk that a prohibited result will follow, and this disregard constitutes a gross deviation from the standard of reasonable care. Attempting to move a large piece of construction equipment while intoxicated should be considered to be reckless conduct because of the great potential for destruction arising from the size and destructive power of the construction equipment. Therefore, (B) is correct. (A) is incorrect because merely driving the equipment in violation of the law would not necessarily be reckless. For instance, here, the statute likely was enacted to prevent untrained persons from driving dangerous equipment, but the defendant was trained to operate the truck in question; thus, if not for the fact that he was drunk, his action would not necessarily have been reckless. Violating the statute may be evidence of negligence, but negligence is insufficient to establish recklessness. (C) is incorrect for the same reason that (B) is correct—driving the equipment while intoxicated constitutes reckless conduct. Although voluntary intoxication is a defense to a crime that requires purpose or knowledge, it is no defense to crimes involving recklessness. Even though the defendant's condition may in fact have precluded him from being consciously aware of the risk, his initial act of becoming voluntarily intoxicated was sufficiently reckless to justify holding him liable for his conduct while intoxicated. (D) is incorrect because it states the mental state for knowing conduct—if the defendant is aware that his conduct will necessarily or very likely cause a certain result, he acts knowingly with respect to that result. Recklessness is a lesser standard of fault.

Answer to Question 39

(B) The Attorney General is not obligated to prosecute the man, regardless of whether the man is an appointive official of the executive branch. The doctrine of separation of powers prohibits legislative interference with the executive discretion as to whether to prosecute. Here, the legislative branch is mandating that the Attorney General—a member of the executive branch—prosecute the man. Thus, (C) and (D) are incorrect. (A) is incorrect because officials of the executive branch are not immune from prosecution relating to their duties.

Answer to Question 40

(B) State provision of textbooks to the segregated private school violates the Equal Protection Clause by giving state support to a racially segregated school. Here, the private school only admits Caucasian students and is thus segregated. (A) is wrong because a state may, under certain situations, aid a private parochial school. (C) and (D) are parts of the test for violation of the Establishment Clause. The Supreme Court has held that a state lending textbooks on secular subjects to all students, including those at religious schools, does not violate the Establishment Clause. Thus, (C) and (D) are incorrect.

Answer to Question 41

(B) A plea of guilty which is later withdrawn may not be used against the defendant who made the plea, except in special cases not applicable to this fact pattern. [Fed. R. Evid. 410] (A) is wrong;

because the trucker's statement would be considered an admission, it cannot be excluded by the hearsay rule. It will be excluded under Rule 410, which prohibits the use of the withdrawn guilty plea, even if it does qualify as an admission. (C) is wrong because, although an admission is not hearsay, this evidence is excluded by Rule 410. (D) is wrong. While the trucker's state of mind might be relevant in the civil suit, the evidence will still be excluded under Rule 410.

Answer to Question 42

(B) The witness's remark is admissible under the present sense impression exception to the hearsay rule. [Fed. R. Evid. 803(1)] (A) is wrong. A prior consistent statement can be used to rebut evidence that the trial testimony is a lie or an exaggeration because of some motive to falsify that has arisen since the event. The facts do not indicate such a claim was made. The statement is hearsay because the witness is relating an out-of-court statement that she made; therefore, (C) is wrong. (D) is wrong because the statement comes within the present sense impression exception to the hearsay rule.

Answer to Question 43

(A) The woman's request for partition should be granted. The estate could not have been a tenancy by the entirety because that estate can exist only between a legally married husband and wife. The estate created would probably be considered either a joint tenancy with right of survivorship or a tenancy in common, either of which may be partitioned. (B) is wrong because, even if the estate had been by the entirety, abandonment by one spouse does not cause a severance. (C) is wrong because although a tenant by the entirety cannot obtain a partition, that is not the type of tenancy involved here. (D) is wrong because the man could not have absolute title under these facts.

Answer to Question 44

(A) If a tenant exercises the legal right to report housing or building code violations or other rights provided by statute, the landlord is not permitted to terminate the tenant's lease in retaliation. The landlord is also barred from penalizing the tenant in other ways, such as raising the rent. This protection is recognized by residential landlord-tenant acts in nearly half the states. In the present case, the landlord is attempting to evict the tenant for retaliatory purposes. Thus, if the jurisdiction prohibits such evictions, the tenant will succeed in his action. (B) is wrong. The fact that this is very likely a periodic tenancy will not save the tenant from eviction, because the proper statutory notice has been given to terminate it. (C) is wrong because the amount of rent charged each tenant is a function of "freedom of contract," and a landlord is free to charge differing amounts of rents for the units. (D) is wrong because a landlord generally does not need to establish a valid reason to raise rent.

Answer to Question 45

(D) Modern courts would hold that a promise to forbear suit on a claim that the promisor ***honestly and reasonably*** believes to be valid is good consideration to support an agreement, even if the claim ultimately turns out not to be valid. Hence, (A) and (B) are wrong. (C) is wrong because the mutual mistake was only as to the reason for entering the contract, not the terms of the contract. There is no reason why a contract should not be enforced when the parties were mistaken as to the need for the contract if the contract is otherwise valid. Additionally, it is not "unfair" to enforce it because the owner always had the right to investigate the truth of the facts before he agreed to pay for the dock.

Answer to Question 46

(C) The defendant was not privileged to refuse revealing the names of the stolen weapon sellers. The United States Supreme Court held, in *Roberts v. United States* (1980), that a defendant's refusal to cooperate with an investigation of the criminal conspiracy of which he was a member may properly be considered in imposing sentence. This is because the Fifth Amendment right to silence does not afford a privilege to refuse to incriminate others. (C) is therefore correct and (A) is incorrect. (B) is incorrect because the court's consideration of the defendant's refusal to cooperate does not violate due process. (D) is not an accurate statement of the law.

Answer to Question 47

(C) The girl should be found not guilty. Under the statute, the girl could not be convicted of burglary unless she actually intended to commit a crime when she entered the home. Because what she intended to do was not a crime, there can be no burglary, even though she thought she was committing a criminal act. (A) and (B) are therefore incorrect. (D) is incorrect because she had "broken" and "entered," which, except for the mental element, is all that is required to complete the crime.

Answer to Question 48

(B) The neighbor cannot recover because the cause of his injury was not a highly dangerous concealed artificial condition. Generally, the owner or occupier of land does not owe a duty to an ordinary trespasser to warn of dangerous conditions on the land or to make the land safe. Where the trespasser is an anticipated trespasser—*i.e.,* where the landowner knows that people habitually intrude on a particular part of her land—a duty to warn of or make safe highly dangerous concealed artificial conditions known to the landowner arises. However, there is no duty to warn of conditions so apparent that the trespasser should be able to discover them himself. Here, even though the neighbor qualifies as an anticipated trespasser, the wheelbarrow and shovel were neither concealed nor highly dangerous. Thus, (B) is correct. (A) is incorrect because it would be irrelevant whether the landowner created the artificial condition if she were otherwise liable because she allowed the condition to remain on her land. (C) is incorrect because mere knowledge of the dangerous condition does not impose a duty to warn. (D) is incorrect because, as stated above, the homeowner had no duty to warn of obvious artificial conditions.

Answer to Question 49

(B) The pet owner will prevail if the neighbor was aware that it was very likely that the pet owner would suffer severe emotional distress. An action for intentional infliction of emotional distress requires (i) an act by the defendant amounting to extreme and outrageous conduct, (ii) intent on the part of the defendant to cause the plaintiff to suffer severe emotional distress, or recklessness as to the effect of the defendant's conduct, (iii) causation, and (iv) damages—*i.e.*, severe emotional distress. Here, intentionally killing someone's pet by giving it poison would be considered extreme and outrageous conduct by most courts, and the pet owner appears to have suffered severe emotional distress. If, as (B) states, the neighbor was aware that it was very likely that the pet owner would suffer severe distress, she has acted with the mental state of recklessness, completing the prima facie case. (A) is wrong because, unlike for negligent infliction of emotional distress, a showing of physical injury is not necessary for intentional infliction of distress—severe emotional distress will suffice. (C) is incorrect because it is too narrow. It is not essential for the pet owner to show an intent to cause severe emotional distress—a reckless disregard of a high probability that emotional distress will result satisfies the state of mind element. (D) is incorrect because it is not essential to recover for this tort that the neighbor have killed the dog in the pet owner's presence. Given the circumstances of the dog's death and the pet owner's discovery of the dog's body, the conduct is likely to be found extreme and outrageous.

Answer to Question 50

(D) The treaty was effectively repealed because the bill was passed over the President's veto. Valid treaties are on a "supremacy parity" with acts of Congress, meaning that they are both considered to be the "supreme law of the land." If a conflict exists between them, it is resolved by order of adoption—the last in time prevails. Here, the bill to repeal the treaty was approved by Congress over the President's veto by a more than two-thirds vote. Thus, the President's veto was overridden, and because the bill was passed after the treaty, the bill prevails. (A) is incorrect because, as stated above, acts of Congress and treaties are on a supremacy parity—the fact that a treaty is approved by both the President and the Senate does not make it supreme over conflicting legislation that is validly enacted at a later point. (B) is incorrect because of the parity rule discussed above. It is true that the President's power over foreign affairs is paramount, and the President might be able to enter into an executive agreement to get around the repeal of the treaty, but such a possibility does not change the status of the treaty in question. (C) is incorrect because, although it states the correct result, its rationale is too broad. Acts of Congress are on parity with treaties; they do not automatically invalidate all treaties; *e.g.,* treaties that are entered into after the act of Congress is approved.

Mixed Subject Set 3
Answer Sheet

1. Ⓐ Ⓑ Ⓒ Ⓓ
2. Ⓐ Ⓑ Ⓒ Ⓓ
3. Ⓐ Ⓑ Ⓒ Ⓓ
4. Ⓐ Ⓑ Ⓒ Ⓓ
5. Ⓐ Ⓑ Ⓒ Ⓓ
6. Ⓐ Ⓑ Ⓒ Ⓓ
7. Ⓐ Ⓑ Ⓒ Ⓓ
8. Ⓐ Ⓑ Ⓒ Ⓓ
9. Ⓐ Ⓑ Ⓒ Ⓓ
10. Ⓐ Ⓑ Ⓒ Ⓓ
11. Ⓐ Ⓑ Ⓒ Ⓓ
12. Ⓐ Ⓑ Ⓒ Ⓓ
13. Ⓐ Ⓑ Ⓒ Ⓓ
14. Ⓐ Ⓑ Ⓒ Ⓓ
15. Ⓐ Ⓑ Ⓒ Ⓓ
16. Ⓐ Ⓑ Ⓒ Ⓓ
17. Ⓐ Ⓑ Ⓒ Ⓓ
18. Ⓐ Ⓑ Ⓒ Ⓓ
19. Ⓐ Ⓑ Ⓒ Ⓓ
20. Ⓐ Ⓑ Ⓒ Ⓓ
21. Ⓐ Ⓑ Ⓒ Ⓓ
22. Ⓐ Ⓑ Ⓒ Ⓓ
23. Ⓐ Ⓑ Ⓒ Ⓓ
24. Ⓐ Ⓑ Ⓒ Ⓓ
25. Ⓐ Ⓑ Ⓒ Ⓓ
26. Ⓐ Ⓑ Ⓒ Ⓓ
27. Ⓐ Ⓑ Ⓒ Ⓓ
28. Ⓐ Ⓑ Ⓒ Ⓓ
29. Ⓐ Ⓑ Ⓒ Ⓓ
30. Ⓐ Ⓑ Ⓒ Ⓓ
31. Ⓐ Ⓑ Ⓒ Ⓓ
32. Ⓐ Ⓑ Ⓒ Ⓓ
33. Ⓐ Ⓑ Ⓒ Ⓓ
34. Ⓐ Ⓑ Ⓒ Ⓓ
35. Ⓐ Ⓑ Ⓒ Ⓓ
36. Ⓐ Ⓑ Ⓒ Ⓓ
37. Ⓐ Ⓑ Ⓒ Ⓓ
38. Ⓐ Ⓑ Ⓒ Ⓓ
39. Ⓐ Ⓑ Ⓒ Ⓓ
40. Ⓐ Ⓑ Ⓒ Ⓓ
41. Ⓐ Ⓑ Ⓒ Ⓓ
42. Ⓐ Ⓑ Ⓒ Ⓓ
43. Ⓐ Ⓑ Ⓒ Ⓓ
44. Ⓐ Ⓑ Ⓒ Ⓓ
45. Ⓐ Ⓑ Ⓒ Ⓓ
46. Ⓐ Ⓑ Ⓒ Ⓓ
47. Ⓐ Ⓑ Ⓒ Ⓓ
48. Ⓐ Ⓑ Ⓒ Ⓓ
49. Ⓐ Ⓑ Ⓒ Ⓓ
50. Ⓐ Ⓑ Ⓒ Ⓓ

MIXED SUBJECT QUESTIONS - SET 3

Question 1

A state requires that applicants for a particular professional license reside there for at least one year before applying for the license. A man holding a similar professional license from another jurisdiction moves to the state and immediately proceeds to work in his profession. The state department of justice brings an action in state court to enjoin the man's business and for civil penalties.

If the man attacks the provision of the state legislation that requires that licensees be residents of the state for a year prior to the application, his challenge should be based upon:

(A) The Privileges and Immunities Clause of Article IV.

(B) The Commerce Clause.

(C) The Equal Protection Clause of the Fourteenth Amendment.

(D) The Privileges or Immunities Clause of the Fourteenth Amendment.

Question 2

A patient sought psychiatric treatment from a psychiatrist. During the treatment, the psychiatrist, unbeknownst to the patient, videotaped her. No sound recording was made of the sessions, but the psychiatrist was conducting a study on "body language" and planned to use the videotapes in those experiments. The patient learned that the psychiatrist had been videotaping their analysis sessions and brought an action against him for battery.

If the patient does not prevail as to this theory, it will probably be because:

(A) She did not suffer any injury as a result of the psychiatrist's actions.

(B) The psychiatrist had an implied consent to take the actions he did as part of the patient-physician privilege.

(C) She did not suffer an offensive touching.

(D) The psychiatrist intended that his actions would foster medical research.

Question 3

A businessman agreed with an accountant to lease to the accountant a small business computer system. Their oral agreement included that the lease would be for a term of five years, and that the accountant would pay a monthly charge of $500 for the system. The businessman and the accountant further agreed that $200 of the monthly charge would be paid by the accountant directly to a third party, in satisfaction of a debt the businessman owed the third party.

The businessman prepared a written copy of the agreement on his computer, but accidentally did not include the agreement that called for the direct payment to the third party in the written copy. The businessman sent the copy of the written agreement, signed by him, to the accountant, who also signed it without noticing that the provision calling for the direct payment to the third party was missing.

If the accountant refused to make any payments to the third party, and the latter brings an action against the accountant for damages as a consequence, which of the following, if true, would be most harmful to the third party?

(A) The obligation of the businessman to the third party was subject to a statute of limitations that had run prior to the date the agreement between the businessman and the accountant was first discussed.

(B) The third party never notified the businessman or the accountant that he accepted their agreement to have the accountant make payments to him.

(C) No consideration supported the obligation owed by the businessman to the third party.

(D) Before the third party learned of the agreement between the businessman and the accountant, they agreed that the accountant would pay the entire $500 directly to the businessman.

Question 4

On January 1, a golf pro shop mailed an order for $1,000 worth of golf balls to a golf supply distributor, specifying that it would pay for the balls within 30 days of delivery. The golf balls were delivered on February 15. Two days later, the distributor learned that the pro shop had been insolvent for at least a month and immediately made a demand on the pro shop to reclaim the golf balls, despite the pro shop's assurances that it would still make the payment before March 15.

May the distributor reclaim the golf balls?

(A) No, because the latest date specified for payment of the account has not yet passed.

(B) No, because the pro shop assured the distributor that it will make payment before March 15.

(C) Yes, because the pro shop was insolvent when the golf balls were delivered.

(D) Yes, because the pro shop had an affirmative duty to tell the distributor of its insolvency when it placed its order.

Question 5

A new college graduate entered into an oral agreement with a freshman to lease the freshman her mini-refrigerator for a term of four years. The freshman was to pay the graduate $20 a month, of which $10 of the monthly charge was to be paid directly to the graduate's parents, in satisfaction of a debt the graduate owed her parents. While the graduate was putting the agreement into writing she accidentally did not include the agreement to pay her parents directly. The freshman also failed to notice that the direct payment provision was missing before she signed the contract, which the graduate signed.

If the parents bring an action against the freshman, which of the following will have the greatest effect on the outcome?

(A) Whether the parents were a party to the agreement between the graduate and the student.

(B) Whether the agreement between the graduate and the freshman was completely integrated.

(C) Whether the graduate was negligent in not discovering that the agreement omitted mention of the payment of money directly to her parents.

(D) Whether the freshman was negligent in not discovering that the agreement omitted mention of the payment of money directly to the parents.

Question 6

A farmer orally agreed to lease a tractor from a company for $500. However, when the company's secretary put the agreement into writing she accidentally typed in a charge of $300. Both the company and the farmer signed the contract without noticing the mistake in the price. When it came time for payment, the farmer refused to pay more than $300 for the rental of the tractor.

If the company brings an action for the difference between the payment as orally agreed and as memorialized in the contract, which of the following, if proven, would most benefit the company?

(A) The parties made a mistake in integration.

(B) The writing was only a partial integration.

(C) The writing was intended as a sham.

(D) The company or the farmer misunderstood the amount the rental payment was to be.

Question 7

The owner of 10 acres of undeveloped grassland decided to open a public park. The entrance to the park was to be by a street that he planned to construct on the edge of his property. The owner's plan was approved and recorded, but construction of the street has been delayed awaiting permits.

After the plans for the park were announced to the public, a family purchased an adjacent plot from another party, planning to build a home. The family applied for a building permit that would allow them to gain access to their plot from the planned yet still undeveloped street, which was referenced in their deed. The owner of the grassland objects to the granting of the building permit on the ground that he never granted any rights to anyone to use the street. There are no applicable statutes dealing with this situation. The family brings an appropriate action to determine their rights to build an access connecting the adjacent plot and the street.

The best argument for the grassland owner in this action is that:

(A) The Statute of Frauds prevents the introduction of evidence that might prove the necessity for the family to use the street.

(B) The family would be unjustly enriched if they were permitted to use the street.

(C) The family's right must await the action of appropriate public authorities to open the street as a public street, because no private easement arose by implication.

(D) The family's right to use the street is restricted to the assertion of a way by necessity, and the facts preclude the success of such a claim.

Question 8

Two farmers owned adjacent tracts of farmland. Both relied on an old gravel road to get their vehicles onto the nearest highway. After many years, one of the farmers decided to develop his property, including a paved access ramp directly from his land to the highway. His development plan, which outlined the proposed public access ramp, was fully approved by all necessary governmental agencies and duly recorded.

Meanwhile, the adjacent farmer sold his farm to a corporation. The description used in the deed from the adjacent farmer to the corporation fully referenced the first farmer's development plan and recording data. The corporation now seeks a building permit that would allow it to construct access from the adjacent land to the planned highway access ramp. The farmer objects to the granting of the building permit on the ground that he never granted any rights to the adjacent farmer or the corporation to use the access ramp. The corporation brings an appropriate action to determine its rights to build an access connecting the adjacent land and the access ramp. There are no applicable statutes.

The best argument for the corporation in this action is that:

(A) The deed from the adjacent owner to the corporation referred to the recorded plan and therefore created rights to use the access ramp delineated in the plan.

(B) The recording of the plan is a dedication of the access ramp shown on the plan to public use.

(C) There is a way by necessity over the land to gain access to the highway.

(D) The fact that the corporation could only gain access to the adjacent land by expending a large amount of money to repair and improve the gravel road creates a sufficient need for an easement across the land to gain access to the access ramp to the highway.

Question 9

The defendant, angered because a rival gang member had twice beaten him up after school, obtained a heavy lead pipe and waited in a deserted alleyway which he knew the rival took as a route home every day after school. When his enemy came walking down the alley, the defendant leapt out behind him and smashed the pipe into the victim's head, knocking him to the ground. The defendant then rolled the victim over and pounded his face with 15 to 20 heavy blows with the lead pipe, killing him. The jurisdiction defines first degree murder as murder committed with premeditation and deliberation. All other murders are defined as second degree murders.

If the defendant is convicted of first degree murder (as opposed to second degree murder), it will be because:

(A) The nature of the acts causing death distinguishes the defendant's action as first degree murder.

(B) The degree of causative relationship between the defendant's acts and the death of the victim renders it murder of the first degree.

(C) The relationship between the defendant and the victim requires that a finding of first degree murder be made.

(D) The defendant's mental state up to and including the moment of the attack determines that the act is first degree murder.

Question 10

A defendant is on trial for arson of a restaurant. Chemical tests by the fire department indicate that gasoline was used as the igniting agent of the fire. The prosecution calls to the stand a waitress who works at a diner near the burned restaurant. She will testify that on the night of the fire, the defendant came into the diner smelling like gasoline.

Should the court admit this testimony over the defendant's objection?

(A) No, it is inadmissible as the opinion of a nonexpert witness.

(B) No, it is inadmissible because the best evidence is the result of the chemical tests.

(C) Yes, it is admissible lay opinion testimony.

(D) Yes, it is admissible expert testimony because everyone who drives a car is an expert as to the smell of gasoline.

Question 11

In certain parts of a state, single-family residences had become so expensive that the vast majority of families could no longer afford to buy a home. To alleviate this problem, the legislature enacted statutes creating a housing agency. The agency, organized along the lines of a private corporation, was authorized to act as general contractor and build homes in counties where the average cost of a new home exceeded by 50% the national average cost of a new home, then to sell the homes at the cost of materials and labor to first-time homebuyers. In one medium-sized city in the state, the average cost of a new home exceeded the national average by 15%, while in a nearby large city, the average cost of a new home exceeded the average by 50%. The agency began building and selling homes in the large city, but did not operate in the medium city. About 35% of the population of the medium city is of Armenian ethnicity. A citizen of Armenian heritage brings a class action against the state, seeking to have the agency's failure to operate in the medium city declared a violation of the right to equal protection of the Armenian citizens of that city.

What fact would be most helpful for the citizen in challenging the statute?

(A) The state could have permitted the agency to build and sell homes in all areas of the state.

(B) Armenian citizens experience difficulty in affording single-family residences.

(C) The legislation setting up the agency was intended to discriminate against Armenian citizens.

(D) The percentage of Armenian citizens is much higher in the medium city than in the large city.

Question 12

A state conducted a study in which it found that many parents were moving out of certain areas of the state because they could not find affordable daycare. As a result, the state legislature enacted a statute that created an agency to operate subsidized daycare centers throughout these areas. These daycare centers would charge parents a nominal fee compared to private daycare centers in the area. A private daycare center has discovered that its business has fallen off about 30% since the agency started operating a daycare center in its city. It brings an action seeking to enjoin the operation of the agency.

What will be the probable outcome of this litigation?

(A) The center will win, because operation of a state agency in competition with a private business violates the Due Process Clause of the Fourteenth Amendment.

(B) The center will win, because permitting some citizens to do business with a state business while others do business with a private business violates the Equal Protection Clause of the Fourteenth Amendment.

(C) The center will lose, because it lacks standing to challenge the legislation, having suffered no direct injury.

(D) The center will lose, because the agency is a valid exercise of the state's powers.

Question 13

As part of a new environmental policy, a state legislature enacted a statute creating a farmland development agency. The agency was organized along the lines of a private corporation. The agency's purpose was to restore and cultivate polluted land in the state, making the land suitable for farmers. Once the agency cultivated the land, it would sell the land to new farmers at a reduced price. The agency began cultivating and selling farmland in one county where the pollution levels were high, but did not operate in a neighboring county with slightly lower pollution levels. A group of residents in the second county bring an action in federal court against the agency director, seeking to compel the agency to begin operations in their county.

What will be the probable outcome of this litigation?

(A) The action will be dismissed, because the state is immune from litigation under the Eleventh Amendment.

(B) The action will be dismissed, because the agency is organized as a private business and thus does not engage in any state action.

(C) The state will prevail, because it has a rational basis for not operating in the neighboring county.

(D) The citizens will prevail, because the state cannot show a compelling state interest in not operating in their county.

Question 14

To encourage economic development in areas of a state currently underdeveloped, state legislation created an agency to build retail buildings in those parts of the state and then to sell the stores to buyers at the cost of materials and labor. The federal government has enacted legislation in effect for the relevant period that regulates the manner in which building contractors conduct business.

Is the state agency subject to these federal regulations?

(A) No, because its activities take place entirely within the state.

(B) No, because as an agency of state government, it is immune from federal regulation.

(C) No, because the federal government is not empowered to enact legislation regulating state governments or their agencies.

(D) Yes.

Question 15

A city ordinance required that all dogs be leashed when taken outside of an enclosed area. One dog owner often allowed his dog to run loose in front of his house. One clear and sunny day when the dog was running loose, a pizza delivery driver was driving carefully on that street at a speed somewhat below the posted limit. The dog dashed out into the street from between two parked cars. The delivery driver alertly applied her brakes, but could not avoid striking the dog. A man driving directly behind the delivery driver promptly applied his brakes as soon as he saw the delivery driver brake. However, the man's vehicle struck the rear of the delivery driver's car. Both of the vehicles suffered damage and both drivers suffered minor personal injuries.

If the man sues the delivery driver for his vehicle damage and personal injuries, the man will:

(A) Prevail, because the ordinance was designed to prevent dogs from being hit by cars.

(B) Prevail, because the delivery driver was a proximate cause of the accident.

(C) Not prevail, because the delivery driver obeyed the traffic laws.

(D) Not prevail, because the delivery driver was not negligent.

Question 16

A renter rented a house from a landlord. The renter and the landlord entered into a written lease providing that the renter was to pay a fixed monthly rent plus all taxes. A month later, the renter was offered a job in another state and the renter assigned her lease to a friend by written agreement. The renter forgot to tell the friend that he was liable to pay the taxes on the residence during the period of the lease. As a result, the friend failed to pay the taxes on the house. The landlord was informed that there was a tax lien on the residence. She paid the lien and brought suit against the friend for the amount.

Judgment for:

(A) The friend, because under the terms of his assignment with the renter he is not liable for the taxes.

(B) The friend, because the agreement to pay taxes was collateral, and thus is not a covenant running with the land.

(C) The friend, because in order for the agreement to be a covenant running with the land it must be expressly stated in the original agreement.

(D) The landlord, because payment of property taxes touches and concerns the land.

Question 17

A woman entered into a written lease with the owner of a condominium unit. Under the terms of the condominium building's bylaws, no pets were permitted in any of the units. Thus, a "no pet" clause was contained in the woman's lease. A few months later, the condominium unit's owner died, leaving his entire estate to his sister. Several days before his death, the woman had assigned her lease to a young couple by written agreement. The woman failed to properly state that no pets were permitted in the building. The couple became very upset on learning of the pet prohibition and abandoned the unit.

Can the sister bring a suit against the woman for this breach of the lease?

(A) No, because she is no longer a tenant.

(B) No, because she was not a tenant at the time the sister gained her interest in the property.

(C) Yes, because the woman's assignment to the couple did not terminate her obligations.

(D) Yes, because the woman had caused the problem by failing to include the pet provision in her assignment.

Question 18

An entrepreneur entered into a written lease-option to purchase an office building. The option to purchase the building could be exercised at any time during the five-year term of the lease by giving the building's owner a written 30-day notice of the intent to exercise the option. A few months later, the entrepreneur assigned his lease-option to a dentist looking for office space by written agreement.

If the dentist fully performs under the lease, can the dentist exercise the option to purchase that was given to the entrepreneur?

(A) Yes, because both the burden and benefit of the covenant to convey run with the land.

(B) No, because the covenant to convey does not touch or concern the land.

(C) No, because the option to purchase was personal to the entrepreneur.

(D) No, because the burden of the covenant to convey given in a lease does not run with the land.

Question 19

A college student assigned her apartment rental lease, by written agreement, to one of her sorority sisters. The sorority sister, in turn, assigned the lease to a classmate.

If the classmate fails to pay the rent, can the landlord bring suit against the sorority sister to recover this money?

(A) Yes, because the sorority sister remains in privity of estate with the landlord.

(B) Yes, because the sorority sister remains in privity of contract with the landlord.

(C) No, because the sorority sister is no longer in privity of estate with the landlord.

(D) No, because the fact that the college student was allowed to assign the lease means that the sorority sister is allowed to assign it also.

Question 20

A consultant operated a consulting firm from an office in his home. An employee asked if she could stay late one night to use one of the firm's computers. The consultant replied that she could consider the computer hers. The employee mistakenly believed that the consultant was giving her the computer. Late the next night, when the employee could borrow her roommate's car, she drove to the consultant's house to pick up the computer. She went to the door leading directly to the office, which was unlocked. She let herself in and took the computer. The next day, the consultant reported the computer as stolen, and the police arrested the employee.

The employee can be convicted of:

(A) Burglary.

(B) Attempted burglary.

(C) Larceny.

(D) None of the above.

Question 21

In a civil action for personal injuries, a plaintiff asserts that on the previous July 15 he was injured when the defendant negligently operated her motor vehicle and caused it to strike his vehicle when both cars were being driven along a principal north-south arterial street in a small town.

Concerning the following facts that arise during the trial, to which is it most appropriate for the judge trying the case to apply the doctrine of judicial notice?

(A) The pavement on the street was wet on July 15, based on the judge's recollection that it was raining heavily that day.

(B) The street runs in a north-south direction, based on information generally known by residents of the town.

(C) The brakes on the defendant's car were faulty, based on the uncontroverted testimony of her auto mechanic and an automotive engineer testifying as an expert for the plaintiff.

(D) The defendant was exceeding the speed limit when the accident occurred, based on the testimony of the plaintiff, two credible eyewitnesses, and the police officer who examined the skid marks, but controverted by the testimony of the defendant and a passenger in her car.

Question 22

A state's penal statutes contain the following: "Any person who commits a battery on a state official knowing that the victim is a state official shall be punished by imprisonment in the county jail for not more than one year or fined not more than $5,000, or both." While picking up her unemployment check at the state office building, a woman got into an argument with a man wearing a brown suit and angrily shoved him against the wall, causing him no injuries. The man she shoved was the director of the state department of unemployment, and the woman is prosecuted under the penal statute quoted. The woman admits that she shoved the victim intentionally, but denies that she knew the man was a state official.

The jury should return a verdict of:

(A) Not guilty, if they find that the state should have warned the woman that the victim was an official, even though they do not believe her testimony.

(B) Not guilty, if they believe the woman's testimony.

(C) Guilty, even if they believe the woman, because this is a public welfare offense.

(D) Guilty, regardless of whether they believe the woman, because she admitted that she intentionally shoved the victim.

Question 23

In a college student's civil suit for personal injuries against her stepfather, arising from acts of sexual abuse allegedly committed by him against her when she was a minor, the student calls as a witness a police officer who will testify that, 11 years ago, the stepfather confessed to the witness that he had committed the acts complained of by the student.

Should the trial court admit the police officer's testimony over the stepfather's objection?

(A) Yes, because past instances of misconduct may be used to impeach a witness.

(B) Yes, because the stepfather's confession is an admission of a party-opponent.

(C) No, because the best evidence of a conviction is the judgment of the court that convicted him.

(D) No, because the sexual assault that is the subject of the evidence is more than 10 years old.

Question 24

Before the conclusion of a beauty pageant, the judges announced the first runner-up and the winner. As the auditorium quieted for the winner's acceptance remarks, the runner-up loudly said that the winner only won because she slept with all of the judges. The winner immediately slapped the runner-up forcefully in the face.

If the runner-up brings an action for battery against the winner, who will prevail?

(A) The winner, because she was provoked by the runner-up's comment.

(B) The winner, because a reasonable person would have slapped the runner-up under the circumstances.

(C) The runner-up, unless the winner's slap was spontaneous.

(D) The runner-up, because the winner intentionally caused an offensive touching.

Question 25

A producer hired a violinist to play in an orchestra that was to leave on a 10-week tour. The violinist turned down another job opportunity in order to accept the producer's job offer. One week after the start of the tour, the violinist was hospitalized with a bad back and was unable to perform. The producer hired another musician to take her part in the orchestra. Four days later, the violinist recovered but the producer refused to allow her to rejoin the orchestra or to complete the tour. She then sued the producer for breach of contract.

Which of the following is the violinist's best legal theory?

(A) Her reliance on the job offered by the producer by declining another job opportunity created an estoppel against the producer.

(B) Her failure to perform with the orchestra for four days was not a material failure so as to discharge the producer's duty to perform.

(C) Her performance with the orchestra for the four-day period was physically impossible.

(D) She was never told that an injury might jeopardize her continued employment with the orchestra.

Question 26

An actor was hired by a director to perform in a three-month run of a play that the director had written. Two weeks after the play's opening night, the actor fainted and could no longer perform because of a resulting concussion. After a week of treatment, the actor returned to the theatre to resume his role but the director refused him admission, having hired someone else to replace the actor.

In his action against the director for breach of contract, which of the following, if true, would adversely affect the actor's rights?

(A) Most of the theatre members felt that the replacement was a better performer than the actor.

(B) The director had offered the actor a job in the ticket office at a higher salary but the actor had declined.

(C) The director could not find any substitute except for the replacement actor, who demanded a contract for a minimum of two and a half months if he was to perform at all.

(D) The actor did not wish to continue to be employed by the director.

Question 27

A developer owned a 10-acre tract of land that was covered by a number of small trees. The first step in his development was the removal of the trees. The developer's neighbor knew that the developer intended to remove the trees from his property. The day before development was to start, the neighbor went onto the developer's land, cut down a number of trees for firewood and moved them onto his property. The developer brought an appropriate action against the neighbor for damages.

The developer most likely will:

(A) Recover only nominal damages, because the value of the land was not diminished.

(B) Recover nominal damages and the value of the trees removed.

(C) Not recover, because removal of the trees saved him money in the development of the land.

(D) Not recover, because the value of the land was not diminished by the removal of the trees.

Question 28

A plaintiff has brought an action for personal injuries against a store, in connection with an incident in which he slipped and fell after the store's linoleum floors had been mopped. A major issue at trial is the degree of moisture that remained on the floor, because it had been mopped 45 minutes before the plaintiff walked on it. The store offers the testimony of an expert, who will testify about an experiment he conducted measuring thc amount of time necessary for a linoleum floor to dry completely after having been mopped.

Under what condition should the court admit this testimony?

(A) A representative of the plaintiff was present when the experiment was conducted.

(B) It is shown that the conditions of the expert's experiment were substantially similar to the conditions of the store's floor when the plaintiff slipped.

(C) The plaintiff was given an opportunity to conduct his own experiment with the same type of linoleum used by the expert.

(D) It is shown that the expert is not an employee or otherwise related in interest to the store.

Question 29

A teenager ordered a custom-made prom dress from a tailor for $175, although she knew she could not afford to pay that amount. On the day the dress was ready, the teenager phoned her best friend and promised her friend that if she would collect the dress, that night she could dance with the teenager's boyfriend at the prom. The teenager knew that the tailor would be gone by the afternoon and that the always-intoxicated clerk at the tailor's shop would willingly hand the dress over. The teenager forged a claim ticket and gave it to her friend to show to the clerk. The friend did as the teenager asked. She picked up the dress and gave it to the teenager.

The friend will be found not guilty of taking the dress from the tailor's shop because:

(A) The teenager was the principal in the conspiracy to obtain the dress without payment.

(B) She was acting under the teenager's direction.

(C) The clerk, whom the friend knew was intoxicated, willingly handed over the dress.

(D) She believed that the tailor was expecting the dress to be picked up without money changing hands.

Question 30

A homeowner heard a strange noise one night. She took a handgun from her nightstand and began to inspect her home. The homeowner's neighbor had also heard the strange noise. He walked out of his house and onto the homeowner's front lawn, thinking that the sound came from the homeowner's home. He stood silently on her lawn, listening. When the homeowner was near the front door, her cat playfully charged into her, causing her to drop the gun. The gun hit the floor and discharged. The bullet went through the homeowner's front window and struck the neighbor in the shoulder.

If the neighbor sues the homeowner on a battery theory, he will:

(A) Prevail, because handguns are highly dangerous instrumentalities.

(B) Prevail, because the cat's actions are imputed to the homeowner.

(C) Lose, because the firing of the gun was a nonvolitional act.

(D) Lose, because the neighbor was a trespasser.

Question 31

The defendant was walking down a street when he realized that a long-lost friend was walking in the opposite direction. The defendant started waving his arms in a desperate attempt to get his friend's attention. The defendant did not notice an old woman, who was walking past him, and negligently struck her with his elbow with sufficient force to cause her to stumble to the pavement. The fall did not, however, cause her any major injury.

If the defendant is prosecuted for criminal battery, he will probably be found:

(A) Not guilty, because his act did not cause serious bodily injury.

(B) Not guilty, because he did not have the mental state required for criminal battery.

(C) Guilty, because he failed to exercise due care in flailing his arms about near a public sidewalk.

(D) Guilty, because he caused an offensive touching.

Question 32

A contractor for a large multistory building used an excavation subcontractor to dig the excavation for the foundation, and a structural subcontractor to begin structural work on the foundation. Just after the foundation was completed, an employee of the structural subcontractor was killed when the walls of the excavation collapsed.

The employee's survivors brought an appropriate action against all of the involved parties. At trial, the structural subcontractor calls a civil engineer licensed by the state to testify that he examined the geologist's reports of the soil conditions surrounding the construction site, as well as a report by the investigator who examined the site of the collapse, and that it is his (the engineer's) opinion that the collapse was caused by the excavation subcontractor's failure to take into consideration the composition of the soil being excavated.

Is the engineer's testimony admissible?

(A) Yes, if civil engineers in his field rely on such materials as reports by geologists and others in reaching conclusions such as his.

(B) Yes, if he was not professionally negligent in his analysis.

(C) No, because his opinion relates to an ultimate issue that must be determined in the case.

(D) No, because his opinion was based on facts not personally within his knowledge.

Question 33

Congress created a tribunal by statute, which was empowered to review claims made by clients of a federal agency and make recommendations to the agency regarding their merits. A lawyer was properly appointed to the tribunal. Six years later, the tribunal was abolished by repeal of the authorizing legislation, and the lawyer was offered an administrative position in the transportation department at a lower salary. The lawyer brought an action against the federal government on the grounds that Congress may not remove a federal judge from office during good behavior, nor decrease his salary during continuance in office. Counsel for the government made a motion to dismiss.

The trial court should rule:

(A) For the government, because the lawyer was not an Article III judge and is not entitled to life tenure.

(B) For the government, because the lawyer lacked standing to raise the question.

(C) For the lawyer, because he has established a property right to his position on the tribunal.

(D) For the lawyer, because of the independence of the federal judiciary constitutionally guaranteed by Article III.

Question 34

Shortly after a series of rapes took place within a city, the city council approved the offering of a $25,000 reward for the arrest and conviction of the perpetrator of the rapes. Information concerning the reward was published in the local newspaper.

In which of the following ways could the city's reward offer be effectively accepted?

(A) Only by an offeree's making the arrest and assisting in the successful conviction of a rapist within the scope of the offer.

(B) Only by an offeree's return promise to make a reasonable effort to bring about the arrest and conviction of a rapist within the scope of the offer.

(C) By an offeree's communication of assent through the same medium (local newspaper) used by the city in making its offer.

(D) By an offeree's supplying information leading to arrest and conviction of a rapist within the scope of the offer.

Question 35

A city council passed an ordinance providing that residents who had their car's exhaust pipes replaced by modern models reducing gas emissions would receive a partial refund of the expense incurred. Information concerning the refund was telecast once daily for a week over the local television station. The next year, the city council passed a resolution repealing its refund offer. The city council caused this resolution to be broadcast by the city's sole radio station once daily for one week. The local television station, meanwhile, had ceased operations.

If the city's refund offer was revocable, revocation could be effectively accomplished only:

(A) In the same manner as made or by a comparable medium and frequency of publicity.

(B) In the same manner as made only.

(C) By simply passing the resolution, because the events that transpired at the city council meeting are considered to be of public notice.

(D) By notice mailed to all residents of the city and all other reasonably identifiable potential offerees.

Question 36

During a shooting at the scene of a robbery, a police officer was shot and killed. The city's police department announced a reward of $10,000 for information leading to the arrest of the individual who caused the death of the police officer. The next year, the police department made a public announcement repealing its reward offer. One month later, a man confessed to a local bartender of having committed the shooting. The bartender reported the information to the police and the man was arrested and ultimately convicted of the robbery and shooting. A friend suggested to the bartender that he claim the police department's $10,000 reward, of which he had been previously unaware. The bartender immediately made the claim but the police department refuses to pay him.

If the bartender sues the city to recover the $10,000 reward, which of the following would be most helpful to him?

(A) The city was benefited by the bartender's services.

(B) The attempted revocation of the reward was against public policy.

(C) The city's offer was in the nature of a bounty so that the elements of contract are not essential to the city's liability.

(D) The city is estopped from denying the reward to the bartender because he acted in the public interest.

Question 37

A woman lost her dog. She posted signs for a $500 reward to whomever would find and return her pet on many trees and poles throughout her neighborhood. The woman eventually purchased a new puppy and published an ad in the local newspaper stating that she repealed her previous reward offer. The ad was printed once daily for a week.

Meanwhile, a dogcatcher had found the woman's dog, and, because it had no tags, he sent it to the local pound. One day a volunteer at the pound recognized the woman's dog from one of her reward postings and suggested that the dogcatcher claim the woman's $500 reward.

If the dogcatcher sues the woman to recover the $500 reward, which of the following would not be helpful to the woman's defense?

(A) The consideration furnished by the dogcatcher, if any, for the woman's reward promise was legally insufficient under the preexisting duty rule.

(B) The dogcatcher was already compensated by the pound for his capturing services.

(C) The woman's offer had effectively been revoked prior to the dogcatcher's attempted acceptance.

(D) The dogcatcher failed to communicate his acceptance of the offer to the woman.

Question 38

A gardener purchased a new riding lawn mower from a gardening store. The gardener used the lawn mower that afternoon to mow her lawn. Although the instructions recommended against it, she ran the mower at full throttle around her yard because she was in a hurry to finish. As she was nearing the edge of her property, she attempted to turn the mower. However, the steering wheel locked and she was unable to turn, hitting into a low wall on the border of her property. The collision caused the mower to overturn and the gardener was injured. The gardener asserts a claim against the gardening store based on strict liability in tort in a jurisdiction that follows traditional contributory negligence rules. At trial, the gardener presents evidence that the steering locked because of a defect present when the mower left the manufacturer's factory. The gardening store presented evidence that it carefully inspected the mower before selling it.

Will the gardener likely prevail?

(A) Yes, because the steering locked while the gardener was riding the mower.

(B) Yes, because the steering locked as a result of a defect present when the mower left the manufacturer's factory.

(C) No, because the gardener contributed to her own injury by running the mower at full throttle.

(D) No, because the gardening store carefully inspected the mower before selling it.

Question 39

A man purchased a new power boat with an inboard engine from a boating supply store. The boating supply store properly inspected the boat before delivery, but did not detect a virtually invisible manufacturing defect in the boat's steering mechanism. Later that summer, the man was entertaining some friends on his boat on a lake near a dam. There were some warning pylons near the dam, warning boaters to stay clear. The man decided to show off for his friends by weaving his boat in and out of the warning pylons. As he rounded the last of them, the steering mechanism of his boat jammed, and the boat crashed into the dam. The man was severely injured. The man brings an action for damages against the boating supply store on a theory of strict liability in tort in a jurisdiction that does not apply its comparative fault rules to strict liability actions.

Who will prevail?

(A) The boating supply store, because it properly inspected the boat before selling it to the man.

(B) The boating supply store, because the man was negligent in weaving in and out of the pylons.

(C) The man, because the steering failed due to a defect present when the boat left the manufacturer.

(D) The man, because the steering mechanism failed while he was operating the boat.

Question 40

A driver drove into an intersection and struck a pedestrian. The driver immediately left his car and ran to the pedestrian. Before the ambulance arrived, the driver said to the pedestrian, "It was all my fault; I'm sorry I ran a red light." The driver then said, "I'll pay for all your medical expenses." The pedestrian sued the driver for his injuries and, at the resulting trial, the pedestrian wished to testify to the two statements made by the driver. The defense objected.

The court should rule that:

(A) Both of the driver's statements are admissible.

(B) The driver's statement acknowledging that he ran a red light is admissible, but his promise to pay the pedestrian's medical expenses is inadmissible.

(C) The driver's statement acknowledging that he ran a red light is inadmissible, but his promise to pay the pedestrian's medical expenses is admissible.

(D) Neither of the driver's statements is admissible.

Question 41

Shortly before their wedding, a man and a woman bought a tract of land, taking title in both names. They had intended to build a summer cottage there, but many years after their marriage the land was still a vacant lot. The man decided that their introverted son would have more confidence if he were a landowner; thus, the man drew up a deed conveying a one-quarter interest in the land to him. Not wanting to show favoritism, two weeks later the man drew up a deed conveying a one-quarter interest in the same land to their daughter.

Who owns the land?

(A) The man and woman share ownership of the land with rights of survivorship, and the son and daughter have no interests.

(B) The son has a one-quarter interest, the daughter has a one-quarter interest, and the woman has a one-half interest.

(C) The son has a one-quarter interest, the daughter has a one-quarter interest, and the woman has a one-half interest, with rights of survivorship.

(D) The woman owns the land.

Question 42

As a woman was walking home on a dark cloudy night, a man came upon her from behind and stole her purse. A suspect was arrested nearby shortly thereafter. After the suspect had been booked, the police took his photograph. They then showed his photograph, along with the photographs of four people who had the same general features as the arrested man, to the woman. The woman identified the suspect as the culprit. At trial, after the woman had identified the suspect as the person who stole her purse, the suspect's attorney objects to the prosecution's introduction into evidence of the photographic identification.

The objection will most likely be:

(A) Denied.

(B) Sustained, because the suspect's right to counsel was violated at the showing of the photograph to the woman.

(C) Sustained, because the woman did not have a good opportunity to observe the culprit.

(D) Sustained, because a photographic identification must be considered a critical stage of the proceeding.

Question 43

A state requires all businesses engaged in any form of retail sales to be licensed. The state legislature amended the statutes governing licensing so that any business seeking a retail sales license must establish that at least 40% of the items sold will be manufactured or produced within the state.

Which of the following constitutional provisions will provide the best basis on which to attack the validity of the state licensing provision requiring a minimum percentage of local goods?

(A) The Privileges or Immunities Clause of the Fourteenth Amendment.

(B) The Commerce Clause.

(C) The Equal Protection Clause.

(D) The Due Process Clause of the Fourteenth Amendment.

Question 44

While on routine patrol late one night, a police officer noticed that a car was weaving recklessly across several lanes of traffic. He stopped the driver, believing that he was driving while intoxicated. By state law, the officer was empowered to arrest the driver and take him to the nearest police station for booking. As he approached the vehicle, the officer saw the driver put what appeared to be a bottle in the glove compartment. The officer arrested the driver and then searched his vehicle. In the glove compartment, the officer discovered a vial containing a small amount of cocaine. The driver was charged with possession of cocaine. At a preliminary hearing, the driver's attorney moves to prevent introduction of the cocaine into evidence on the grounds that the search violated his client's federal constitutional rights.

This motion will most likely be:

(A) Denied, because the officer was acting under a fear for his personal safety.

(B) Denied, because the search was incident to a constitutionally valid custodial arrest.

(C) Granted, because the officer needed a warrant to search the glove compartment.

(D) Granted, because there was no reasonable or proper basis on which to justify conducting the search.

Question 45

A woman was injured when the car she was driving was struck by a moving truck. The woman brings an action for personal injuries against the moving company. The complaint alleges that the driver was drunk at the time of the accident and that the moving company was negligent in hiring him and permitting him to drive knowing that he had a drinking problem and convictions for drunk driving. The driver is called as a witness by the moving company and is expected to testify that he was not drunk at the time of the accident. Instead, the driver states on direct examination that he had had several beers as he drove his truck that evening and was under the influence of drugs when his truck struck the woman's car. The counsel for the moving company wants to confront the driver with his deposition testimony that he was completely sober at the time of the accident.

Will this evidence be permitted?

(A) No, the statement is hearsay not within any recognized exception.

(B) No, the moving company cannot impeach its own witness.

(C) Yes, but it may be used only to refresh the driver's recollection.

(D) Yes, it can be used to impeach and as substantive evidence that the driver was sober.

Question 46

A federal statute was enacted that provided federal funds to open child health care centers in inner-city areas.

The strongest constitutional basis for this enactment is the:

(A) Commerce Clause.

(B) Equal Protection Clause.

(C) Taxing and Spending Clause.

(D) General federal police powers.

Question 47

A patient suffering from a life threatening blood disorder could be saved only by undergoing a new treatment only offered by a physician in another city. It was therefore arranged that the patient would fly to the city where the physician would perform the treatment. The day before the patient was to leave, his sole heir, who stood to inherit from him, poisoned him. The poison produced a reaction that required postponement of the journey. Meanwhile, the plane on which the patient was to have flown crashed and all aboard were killed. The next day the patient died from the combined effects of the poison and the blood disorder. His heir was arrested and charged with criminal homicide.

The heir should be found:

(A) Not guilty, because the poison was not the sole cause of death.

(B) Not guilty, because the patient would have died anyway if the heir had not poisoned him.

(C) Not guilty, because the heir's actions resulted only in postponing the patient's death by one day.

(D) Guilty.

Question 48

A woman is suing a fast-food restaurant for injuries she suffered when she fell after slipping on a wet spot on the floor of the restaurant. At trial, the woman introduced evidence that someone had spilled a drink on the floor and that an employee had just finished mopping up the spill before she walked over the wet spot and fell, injuring her back. The woman then calls the restaurant's manager, as a hostile witness, and attempts to elicit testimony that, after her fall, the restaurant instituted a policy requiring that bright yellow signs with red warnings be placed after mopping the floor.

Will this evidence be permitted?

(A) Yes, to establish that the restaurant was negligent in not warning customers that the floor was wet.

(B) Yes, to show that the restaurant was aware that a wet floor creates a hazardous condition.

(C) No, because its admission would discourage other tortfeasors from taking remedial measures.

(D) No, because it is not a proper form of impeachment.

Question 49

A farmer willed his farm to his daughter. The will stated that the property would go to the daughter for her life with a remainder to each of her children living at the time of the farmer's death. The will further provided that "The interest of any child who attempts to mortgage or sell his or her interest shall immediately terminate and shall pass to and become the property of the remaining children of my daughter who are alive at the time of my death, in equal shares." Several weeks later the farmer died. One of the daughter's three children wants to sell his interest in the farm. The daughter and the two other children object to the sale.

In an action for declaratory relief by the grandson that the stated restriction on the sale is void, what would be the probable result?

(A) The suit would be dismissed, because the grandson has no interest in the property.

(B) The gift to the daughter's children is void in its entirety, because it violates the Rule Against Perpetuities.

(C) The restriction would be stricken, because it unlawfully restricts the alienation of real property.

(D) The restriction is proper, because all the grandson has is a defeasible estate.

Question 50

In response to a number of accidents involving pedestrians in the local business district, a city enacted a statute making it illegal for a pedestrian to walk through the central business district anywhere other than on the sidewalk. The city also enacted a statute making it illegal for any business to obstruct the sidewalk in front of its establishment. As a man was walking along the sidewalk in the central business district, he discovered that a shopkeeper had stacked a pile of boxes in front of his establishment in such a way that it totally obstructed the sidewalk. The man stepped into the street to walk around the obstruction of boxes and was struck by a cab driver driving negligently. The jurisdiction follows traditional contributory negligence rules.

If the man asserts a claim against the cab driver, the man's act of leaving the sidewalk and walking into the street will have which of the following effects?

(A) It will bar the man's recovery as a matter of law.

(B) It will bar the man's recovery unless the cab driver saw the man in time to avoid the impact.

(C) It may be considered by the trier of fact on the issue of the cab driver's liability.

(D) It is not relevant in determining the man's rights.

MIXED SUBJECT SET 3 SUBJECT GUIDE

1. Constitutional Law
2. Torts
3. Contracts
4. Contracts
5. Contracts
6. Contracts
7. Real Property
8. Real Property
9. Criminal Law
10. Evidence
11. Constitutional Law
12. Constitutional Law
13. Constitutional Law
14. Constitutional Law
15. Torts
16. Real Property
17. Real Property
18. Real Property
19. Real Property
20. Criminal Law
21. Evidence
22. Criminal Law
23. Evidence
24. Torts
25. Contracts
26. Contracts
27. Torts
28. Evidence
29. Criminal Law
30. Torts
31. Criminal Law
32. Evidence
33. Constitutional Law
34. Contracts
35. Contracts
36. Contracts
37. Contracts
38. Torts
39. Torts
40. Evidence
41. Real Property
42. Criminal Law
43. Constitutional Law
44. Criminal Law
45. Evidence
46. Constitutional Law
47. Criminal Law
48. Evidence
49. Real Property
50. Torts

MIXED SUBJECT ANSWERS - SET 3

Answer to Question 1

(C) If a law discriminates based on a suspect classification or impacts a fundamental right, strict scrutiny applies (*i.e.*, the law will be upheld only if the government can show that the law is necessary to achieve a compelling interest). Generally, government action cannot meet the strict scrutiny test. Moreover, the Supreme Court has indicated that any discrimination between citizens of the same state does not even meet the rational basis test under the Equal Protection Clause. (A) is incorrect because the Privileges and Immunities Clause of Article IV prohibits discrimination against nonresidents, and here, the complaint is by a new resident rather than by a nonresident. (B) is incorrect because the Commerce Clause generally is not violated by licensure requirements. There is an exception to the Commerce Clause (which prohibits state discrimination against interstate commerce) for state action that furthers an important, non-economic state interest (*e.g.*, health or safety). Generally, state professional licensing laws fall within the exception. (D) is incorrect because the Privileges or Immunities Clause of the Fourteenth Amendment prohibits states from denying their citizens the right of national citizenship (*e.g.*, the right to vote). The right to practice a profession is not within such rights.

Answer to Question 2

(C) The patient cannot make out a case for battery because she did not experience an offensive touching. To make out a prima facie case for battery, the plaintiff must show an intentional act by the defendant that caused harmful or offensive contact to the plaintiff's person. Here, nothing indicates that the patient was touched in any way; thus, (C) is correct. (A) is incorrect because injury is not an element of battery; battery can be established even absent a showing of injury or damages. (B) is incorrect because if the elements of battery were present, the physician-patient privilege would not protect the psychiatrist here because the patient did not impliedly consent to the taping. When a patient consents to a doctor's treatment, she impliedly consents to all necessary touching that goes along with the treatment. However, when the doctor goes beyond the scope of the acts consented to and does something substantially different, the defense of consent is no longer available. Here, the patient consented to talk with the psychiatrist, but that is substantially different from agreeing to be the subject of an experiment. Thus, if taping the patient were a battery, the psychiatrist could not rely on implied consent to relieve him of liability. (D) is incorrect because a benevolent motive is not a defense to a battery. If the other elements of battery were present, the fact that the battery occurred to foster medical research would not be a defense—that would allow psychiatrists to physically strike their patients merely to study their reactions!

Answer to Question 3

(D) The new agreement between the businessman and the accountant would be most harmful to the third party. The parties to a contract that benefits a third party may validly modify the contract before the beneficiary learns of the contract and relies on it to his detriment. (A) and (C) are incorrect because, if the businessman intended to confer a benefit on the third party by entering into the contract with the accountant, the third party could enforce the agreement as a donee third party beneficiary whether or not an enforceable obligation existed between the businessman and the third party. (B) is incorrect because a third party beneficiary is not obligated to notify the parties that he accepts the benefit of their agreement, especially when the agreement merely calls for the payment of money to him.

Answer to Question 4

(C) The distributor may reclaim the golf balls because the pro shop is insolvent. U.C.C. section 2-702 permits a seller to reclaim goods upon demand within 10 days after the buyer receives them if the seller discovers that the buyer received the goods on credit while insolvent. Here, the distributor made a demand to reclaim the golf balls two days after the pro shop received them, so (C) is the correct answer. (A) is incorrect because it does not matter whether the time for payment has not yet passed. As explained above, the demand to reclaim the goods must be made within 10 days of receipt, which in this case would be February 25. Thus, if the distributor waited until the latest date for payment, it would be too late to reclaim the golf balls. (B) is incorrect because, when the buyer is actually insolvent, the U.C.C. allows the seller to do more than merely demand assurances. (D) is an incorrect statement of law.

Answer to Question 5

(B) The most critical factor will be whether the agreement was completely integrated. The effect of a completely integrated agreement, meaning that the writing embodies the entire agreement of the parties, is that evidence could not be introduced to show a prior or collateral oral agreement. (A) is incorrect because the parents need not be a party to the contract; they have rights as third-party beneficiaries. (C) and (D) are incorrect because the negligence of either of the parties has no bearing on whether the collateral oral agreement can be proved or enforced.

Answer to Question 6

(A) The most beneficial scenario is if the parties made a mistake in integration. Where the parties make a mistake in integrating their agreement into a writing, the courts will permit the error to be corrected. (B) is not helpful to the company because a writing that is a partial integration cannot be contradicted, it may only be supplemented by proving up consistent additional terms. (C) is wrong because if the writing were a sham, no rights would arise from it. (D) is wrong because if one of the parties made a mistake as to the payment amount, he would not necessarily be entitled to relief.

Answer to Question 7

(C) The best argument of the grassland owner is that the family's rights clearly depend on the existence of a public street. (A) is wrong because no issue of the Statute of Frauds is present. There has been no purported conveyance to the family of rights in the street by anyone who owns such rights. (B) is wrong because there is no legal objection to the enrichment that results if persons other than the dedicator are permitted to use a public street. (D) is wrong because, if a public street exists, the family need not assert a way by necessity.

Answer to Question 8

(B) The best argument is that the recording of the plan is a dedication of the access ramp shown on the plan to public use. Generally, a governmental agency accepts a dedication when it approves the plans. (A) is wrong because a simple referral to a recorded plan does not automatically create rights. (C) is wrong because the corporation does not need a way of necessity because it has other access to the land. (D) is wrong because the alternative access exists, and the amount of money required to improve the access does not determine need for an easement by necessity.

Answer to Question 9

(D) The degree of murder under the statute is determined by the defendant's mental state—whether the killing was intentional and accomplished after premeditation and deliberation. The defendant's relationship with the victim and the manner of killing may have evidentiary significance with regard to the defendant's mental state, but do not themselves distinguish first from second degree murder. Thus, (A) and (C) are incorrect. The causal relationship between the defendant's act and the death of the victim may determine whether the act is murder, but once that analytical hurdle has been passed, it has no further significance as to the degree of murder. Therefore, (B) is incorrect.

Answer to Question 10

(C) The witness should be allowed to testify as to what she perceived. To be admissible under the Federal Rules, evidence must be probative of a material issue in the case and must be competent (*i.e.*, not otherwise excludable). Evidence is material if it relates to an issue in the case, and it is probative if it tends to prove the fact for which it is offered. Evidence is competent if it does not violate a specific exclusionary rule. At issue here is whether the defendant started the restaurant fire. If gasoline was used to start the fire, the fact that the defendant was seen near the fire and smelled like gasoline makes it more likely that he started the fire; so the proffered evidence is material and relevant. It is also competent: under the Federal Rules, opinion testimony by lay witnesses is admissible when (i) it is rationally based on the perception of the witness, and (ii) it is helpful to a clear understanding of her testimony or to the determination of a fact in issue. Matters involving sense recognition, such as what something smelled like, are common subjects of opinion testimony. Here, the witness's testimony satisfies both elements of the test and should be admitted. Thus, (C) is correct and (A) is incorrect. (D) is incorrect because to testify as an expert one must have special knowledge, skill, experience, or education as to the subject of her testimony, and if everyone who drives a car knows the smell of gasoline, there is nothing special about that knowledge. (B) is incorrect because the best evidence rule requires that the original document be produced only when the terms of the document are material and sought to be proved. The fact to be proved—that gasoline was used—exists independently of any written record of the chemical tests; therefore, the best evidence rule does not apply.

Answer to Question 11

(C) The most helpful fact would be an intent to discriminate. State action that is facially neutral will nevertheless be struck down if it can be shown that it was intended to discriminate on the basis of race or national origin and does in fact have that effect. The citizen must show that the legislature selected the specific cost guidelines with full knowledge of the population characteristics in the medium city and with the specific intent to disqualify that city from participation in the program because of its high concentration of Armenians. If he proves that intent, he will prevail, and (C) is accordingly his best argument. (A) would not be as helpful because the state could show a rational basis for not operating in the medium city—that housing costs were not high enough to warrant state intervention—which would suffice to justify different treatment not based upon purposeful discrimination. (B) is not a good answer because the difficulty experienced by Armenian citizens in obtaining housing may have nothing to do with state action and may be experienced by other groups as well. (D) is not the best answer because, while it is arguably some evidence of purposeful discrimination, it does not state it as clearly as (C).

Answer to Question 12

(D) Providing daycare centers for its citizens is clearly within the reserved police powers of the state. Because this is facially neutral economic and social legislation, the state simply needs a rational basis for its actions, and that is present. (A) and (B) are, accordingly, wrong. A state may undertake traditionally private business activities, and the analysis for both due process and equal protection purposes is rational basis review, under which the state will prevail. (C) is not a good answer because the center has suffered a direct injury (lost business) caused by the state government action. It has standing to challenge the legislation, but standing has nothing to do with the merits of the claim, which it will lose.

Answer to Question 13

(C) The state will prevail. Because this is economic legislation not involving fundamental rights or suspect classifications, it will be upheld if it has a rational basis. The higher pollution levels justify intervention in certain areas, and so the legislation would probably be valid. (A) is wrong because while the Eleventh Amendment immunizes states from suit in federal courts, that immunity does not authorize a state to violate the Constitution; a suit alleging such a violation may be filed against the responsible officials. (B) is an incorrect statement of law; as an agency of the state, the agency's operations are state action. (D) is wrong because it applies the wrong standard of review.

Answer to Question 14

(D) The state agency is subject to federal regulation. In theory, the Tenth Amendment prohibits federal regulation of state activities if the regulation would virtually eliminate the state's local functions. As a practical matter, the Court's holding in *Garcia v. San Antonio Metropolitan Transit Authority* (1985) gives Congress broad authority when it acts pursuant to its enumerated powers. Accordingly, a federal regulation that controls the states as well as private persons is valid. Thus, the state agency would have to follow the federal regulations, which control due to the Supremacy Clause. Thus, (D) is correct, and (B) and (C) are wrong. (A) is wrong because even intrastate activities are subject to federal Commerce Clause regulation if they substantially affect interstate commerce.

Answer to Question 15

(D) The man will not prevail because the delivery driver was not negligent. Even though the delivery driver may have been a cause of the accident, she is liable only if she was negligent. Thus, (B) is incorrect, and (D) is correct. (A) is incorrect because the delivery driver did not violate the applicable statute. (C) is incorrect because obeying a law does not preclude negligent conduct; *i.e.,* even though she obeyed the traffic laws, she would be liable if she had been negligent in some way (*e.g.,* driving within the speed limit but going too fast on a day when the streets were icy).

Answer to Question 16

(D) Judgment should be for the landlord, because payment of property taxes touches and concerns the land. An assignee is in privity of estate with the lessor, and is liable for those covenants in the original lease that run with the land. Hence, (A) is wrong. (B) and (C) are wrong because an agreement to pay taxes touches and concerns the land, and thus runs with the land.

Answer to Question 17

(C) The sister can sue the woman for breach of the lease. The assignor (here the woman) remains in privity of contract with the lessor and is liable for the rent reserved in the lease. (A) and (B) are incorrect because the woman's status as a tenant is immaterial. (D) is incorrect because the woman's failure to include the "no pet" provision in her assignment to the couple does not affect her liability as the assignor under privity of contract.

Answer to Question 18

(A) The dentist can exercise the option to purchase. A covenant to convey touches and concerns both the leasehold and reversion, and therefore runs with those respective interests in the land. Thus, (B) is incorrect. (C) is incorrect because there is nothing about the option in the facts that shows it to be personal. (D) is incorrect because, as explained above, the burden of the covenant to convey does run with the land.

Answer to Question 19

(C) The landlord cannot bring suit against the sorority sister. Absent an express assumption, an assignee is not liable on the original covenants once she reassigns. Hence, (A) is wrong. (B) is wrong because an assignee is not in privity of contract with the lessor unless the assignee expressly assumes the lease obligations. (D) is incorrect because the sorority sister's ability to subsequently assign the lease is unrelated to the issue of liability. The sorority sister, as an assignee of the college student, is liable for covenants running with the land on the basis of privity of estate. Once the sorority sister assigned the lease to her classmate, the privity of estate ends and the sorority sister's liability is terminated.

Answer to Question 20

(D) The employee is guilty of none of the listed crimes. To be guilty of burglary, a person must have the intent to commit a felony in the structure at the time of entry. Attempted burglary requires the same specific intent. Because the employee merely intended to retrieve what she believed was her own property, she did not intend to commit a felony. Thus, (A) and (B) are wrong. Likewise, (C) is wrong because, since the employee believed the computer was her own, she lacked the intent to permanently deprive the consultant of his interest, which would be necessary for her act to constitute larceny. Thus, (D) is correct.

Answer to Question 21

(B) The fact that the street runs in a north-south direction is the most appropriate item for the judge to apply the doctrine of judicial notice to because it is a matter of common knowledge in the community. The Federal Rules conform to the existing state rules governing judicial notice. Federal Rule 201(b) defines a fact that may be noticed as "one not subject to reasonable dispute in that it is either (i) generally known within the territorial jurisdiction of the trial court, or (ii) capable of accurate and ready determination by resort to sources whose accuracy cannot reasonably be questioned." To be considered generally known within the community, the fact must be something that well-informed people generally know and accept. Although usually facts of common knowledge are known everywhere, it is sufficient for judicial notice if they are known in the community where the court is sitting. Because the fact that the street runs in a north-south direction is generally known by the community in which the court sits, judicial notice may be taken of it. (A) is incorrect because judicial notice may not be taken of a fact solely because it is personally known by the judge. A judge may have to ignore facts that he knows as a private person if those facts are neither commonly known in the community nor capable of certain verification by resort to easily accessible sources of indisputable accuracy. Therefore, the judge may not take judicial notice of the wet pavement based solely on his recollection. (C) is incorrect because the fact that the brakes were faulty is subject to reasonable dispute. As discussed above, judicial notice may only be taken of matters of common knowledge in the community where the court sits or facts capable of certain verification. Here, the fact that the defendant's brakes were faulty was not a matter of common knowledge in the town. They were only faulty in the opinion of two witnesses. Also, the condition of the brakes is not easily verified by resorting to well-established sources. Even though their testimony was uncontroverted, the auto mechanic and engineer would not be considered such sources because their conclusions could be reasonably questioned. Therefore, the condition of the brakes would be considered to be subject to reasonable dispute and not appropriate for judicial notice. (D) is also incorrect because the defendant's speed at the time of the accident was subject to reasonable dispute. As discussed above, judicial notice may only be taken of facts not subject to reasonable dispute—*i.e.,* matters of common knowledge in the community or facts capable of certain verification. Whether the defendant exceeded the speed limit is not a matter of common knowledge in the community. In fact, there was conflicting testimony concerning her speed. The speed also was not a fact capable of certain verification from well-established sources. The skid marks would not be considered certain enough to be such a source.

Answer to Question 22

(B) The jury should return a verdict of not guilty if they believe the woman's testimony. The statute punishes a battery committed against a victim the defendant ***knows*** is a state official. Therefore, if the jury believes the woman's testimony that she did not know the man was a state official, they must find her not guilty of the charged violation. This is not a public welfare offense, but a particular form of battery. Thus, (C) is incorrect. (D) is incorrect because the statute requires knowledge of the status of the victim. (A) is wrong. There is no duty on the part of the state to warn the woman. If she knew, she will be guilty; if she did not know, she will not be guilty.

Answer to Question 23

(B) The officer's testimony should be admitted because it is an admission by a party-opponent. Generally, evidence is admissible if it is relevant, *i.e.,* if it has a tendency to prove any fact of consequence to the action. The testimony here is relevant because it makes it more likely that the defendant committed the acts complained of. It is also competent because its admission does not violate any exclusionary rule of evidence. Evidence law generally prohibits admission of hearsay—out-of-court statements offered to prove the truth of the matter asserted—but the rule does not apply to admissions by party-opponents—they are treated as nonhearsay under the Federal Rules. Thus, the testimony is admissible and (B) is correct. (A) may be a true statement—past instances of misconduct may be used to impeach a witness, at least if they are probative as to whether he is worthy of belief—but it is an incorrect answer because it focuses on impeachment, and the defendant is not being impeached here. (C) is incorrect because the best evidence rule is not applicable here. The rule requires that when the contents of a writing are sought to be proved, the writing itself should be admitted if it is available. Here, however, the witness is not trying to prove that the defendant has been convicted, but rather that he made the admission. (D) is incorrect for reasons similar to why (C) is incorrect. It is true under the Federal Rules that convictions generally are not admissible for impeachment of a witness if more than 10 years old, but the officer is not trying to admit the defendant's conviction here (and is not trying to impeach the defendant, who may not even have testified). Rather, the student is seeking to admit the defendant's confession. The confession is an admission by a party-opponent and is admissible as substantive evidence.

Answer to Question 24

(D) The runner-up will prevail because the winner intentionally caused an offensive touching. To make out a prima facie case for battery, the runner-up need only show an act by the winner that brings about harmful or offensive contact, intent by the winner to bring about the contact, and causation. These elements are present here, and no defense is available (provocation is not a defense—insulting words do not give one the privilege to strike another). Therefore, (D) is correct. (A) and (B) are incorrect because, as indicated above, neither actual provocation nor reasonable provocation is a defense to battery. (C) is incorrect because even spontaneous acts are volitional movements, and that is all that is required to meet the "act" requirement. As long as the act is triggered by the conscious mind, it will be considered a volitional movement.

Answer to Question 25

(B) Her best argument is that her failure to perform with the orchestra for four days was not a material failure so as to discharge the producer's duty to perform. The contract extended for a 10-week period. Missing only four days of a performance to run for 10 weeks would not be considered a material breach of the contract. (A) is wrong because this would tend to go more to a formation problem. Here the contract has already been validly formed. (C) is wrong because a claim of impossibility could conceivably discharge the entire contract, and, therefore, the violinist would have no claim. (D) is wrong because the violinist need not be warned of the consequences of a breach.

Answer to Question 26

(C) The director is entitled to find a substitute to perform in the actor's absence. If the only way the director could acquire a substitute was to agree to the extended term, then the director's actions would be proper. (A) is wrong because this would not relieve the director from liability to the actor. (B) is wrong because the actor does not have to accept any job under the contract, only the job that was the subject of the contract or a similar job to mitigate damages. (D) is wrong because this factor would not excuse the director from his liability under the contract.

Answer to Question 27

(B) The developer can recover nominal damages and the value of the trees removed. The neighbor trespassed onto the developer's land and took the trees, which belonged to the developer. However, the developer is entitled to receive only nominal damages for the act of trespass, because the trespass caused no damage. The developer is also entitled to receive the value of the trees removed by the neighbor since this amounted to a taking of the developer's property. (A) and (D) are therefore incorrect. (C) is incorrect because the fact that the neighbor's actions benefited the developer would not diminish his right of recovery.

Answer to Question 28

(B) The expert's testimony is only relevant if the conditions of the experiment were substantially similar to the conditions at the time and place of the accident. Evidence of pretrial experiments that does not require expert testimony is treated no differently under the Federal Rules from other evidence. It will be admissible if it is relevant (*i.e.,* if it has any tendency to prove or disprove a fact that is of consequence to the action) and if it is not barred by a specific exclusionary rule or the general balancing test of Rule 403. To the extent that the conditions of the expert's experiment replicated the conditions of the accident, the experiment is relevant because whether the expert's linoleum was wet after 45 minutes tends to establish whether the store's floor was wet when the plaintiff walked on it, and this fact is of major consequence to the plaintiff's personal injury action. To the extent that the conditions of the expert's experiment are not similar, the minimal probative value of his testimony probably would be outweighed under Rule 403 by considerations of unfair prejudice or waste of time. (A) is incorrect because the Federal Rules do not require a representative of the adverse party to be present at the experiment; the plaintiff's attorney can subject the conditions of the experiment to scrutiny through cross-examination of the expert. (C) is incorrect for the same reason: the plaintiff's attorney can effectively cross-examine the expert even without having conducted his own experiments. (D) is incorrect because the person conducting the experiment need not be an independent observer. If the expert is an employee, his potential bias can be elicited on cross-examination.

Answer to Question 29

(D) The friend will be found not guilty if she sincerely believed that the tailor was expecting the dress to be picked up without money changing hands. The crime of larceny requires an intent to steal. The friend was operating under an honest mistake of fact. (A) is incorrect because there was no conspiracy; if there were a conspiracy, the friend would be guilty. (B) is incorrect because a person can be guilty of a crime even though someone else directs her to do it. (B) does not state the reason why the friend would not be guilty. (C) is incorrect because the fact that the clerk handed it over would not absolve the friend of liability.

Answer to Question 30

(C) The neighbor will lose because the firing of the gun was not volitional. To prevail in an action for battery, the neighbor must show that the homeowner engaged in volitional conduct with knowledge or desire to cause a battery. Here, the gun discharged without any volitional act, and so the neighbor will lose. (A) is incorrect because even if a gun is considered to be a dangerous instrumentality, that fact is not relevant to a battery action, which is based on intent rather than strict liability. A cat's actions are not imputed to its owner; thus, (B) is incorrect. (D) is incorrect because the neighbor's status as a trespasser would not necessarily prevent him from prevailing in an action for battery; the homeowner did not have a right to use deadly force to protect her property here.

Answer to Question 31

(B) The defendant will probably be found not guilty. The mental state necessary for criminal battery is either intentional or criminally negligent conduct. Clearly, the defendant did not intend to have bodily contact with the old woman, and in light of the circumstances it will be unlikely that his conduct will be considered such an extreme deviation from ordinary behavior as to establish criminal negligence. (A) is wrong; a serious injury is not required for battery. (C) is wrong because criminal negligence requires a greater deviation from ordinary behavior than simply a "failure to exercise due care," which is the tort standard. (D) is not as accurate as (B). It does not address the critical issue in the case—the mental state of the defendant.

Answer to Question 32

(A) The engineer's testimony is admissible as relevant opinion testimony by an expert witness. The Federal Rules permit witnesses qualified as experts to testify in the form of an opinion if the subject matter is one where scientific, technical, or other specialized knowledge will assist the jury in understanding the evidence or determining a fact in issue. [Fed. R. Evid. 702] Under Federal Rule 703, the expert may base his opinion on facts not known personally but supplied to him outside the courtroom (*e.g.,* reports of other experts). Such facts need not be admissible in evidence as long as the facts are of a kind reasonably relied on by experts in the particular field. Here, the engineer, who was licensed by the state, probably qualifies as an expert on the subject of his testimony and therefore can state his opinion as to the cause of the collapse of the excavation wall. As choice (A) states, he may base his opinion on the geologist's and the investigator's reports if civil engineers in his field rely on this type of data in reaching conclusions such as his. Thus, choice (D) is incorrect. Choice (B) is incorrect because whether this analysis is negligent is irrelevant to its admissibility; this fact can be brought out by cross-examination. A prudent analysis will still be inadmissible if it was based on materials that experts in his field did not reasonably rely on. Choice (C) is incorrect; Federal Rule 704(a) provides that otherwise admissible opinion testimony is not objectionable because it embraces the ultimate issue to be decided by the trier of fact.

Answer to Question 33

(A) Only Article III judges enjoy the constitutional grant of life tenure, and the lawyer is not an Article III judge. The tribunal is an administrative agency with limited jurisdiction, and while the lawyer exercises some adjudicatory powers, all persons with some adjudicatory functions are not judges within the meaning of Article III. (A) is thus correct and (D) is wrong. (C) is also wrong, because the Constitution does not recognize property rights in employment. The lawyer could show some kind of wrongful discharge only if he could claim that he was deprived of something "in the nature of a property right." (B) is incorrect because the lawyer clearly has standing; he alleges a specific injury to himself and brings the claim in his own right, alleging the violation of a constitutional right.

Answer to Question 34

(D) Offers of this type normally require only that the offerees supply information leading to the arrest and conviction of the culprit. The language of the reward offer should not be read with total literalness, but rather in the context of what the city was seeking to obtain and the normal duties required to accept an offer of this kind. Therefore, (A), which would require that the offeree actually participate in the arrest, can be eliminated. (B) and (C) can be ruled out without difficulty because they would envision a bilateral contract under which the offeree would be promising or assenting to the city's proposal. In this context the offer is obviously a unilateral proposal that can be accepted only by performance.

Answer to Question 35

(A) This kind of refund offer can be revoked by comparable publicity as to the revocation by the offeror. Here, publicity through means of the city's radio station would be comparable to the initial offer publicized over the television station. (B) is wrong because the facts make it impossible to use the same manner to revoke the offer. (C) does not go far enough in communicating the revocation effectively to anyone who heard the offer originally. (D) would be too onerous a task.

Answer to Question 36

(C) The bartender cannot successfully recover on a contract theory because he was unaware of the offer when he provided the police the information. An offeree must be aware of the offer before he can, by his actions, accept it. The police department, therefore, would not be liable on a contract theory. The bounty idea has sometimes been used in reward cases when the offeror is a governmental agency. Therefore, (C) is the best answer. (A) does not go far enough because a party will not be liable for benefits gratuitously lavished upon it. (B) is wrong because public policy cannot limit a party's right to revoke an offer. (D) is incorrect because estoppel requires detrimental reliance on the other party's conduct, and here the bartender could not rely on the offer since he was unaware of it.

Answer to Question 37

(D) Noncommunication of acceptance would be least helpful because the contract with the woman was unilateral and did not require a notice of acceptance; rather, performance was sufficient. (A) is helpful because the fact that the dogcatcher was already under contract might have impact with respect to the preexisting duty rule. (B) is helpful because the fact that the dogcatcher had been compensated already would not have a bearing on a contract theory but might on a quasi-contractual theory. (C) is helpful because the publication of the revocation in the local newspaper may have effectively revoked the woman's offer.

Answer to Question 38

(B) The gardener will likely prevail because the steering locked because of a defect present when the mower left the manufacturer. A retailer is strictly liable for injuries caused by a dangerous defect in a product sold by that retailer. This is true even if the retailer carefully inspects the product before selling it. (D) is therefore incorrect. (A) is incorrect because the fact that the steering locked is not enough to create liability without evidence that it was the result of a defect in the mower. (C) is incorrect because contributory negligence is not a good defense to strict liability in tort in jurisdictions retaining traditional contributory negligence rules.

Answer to Question 39

(C) To recover on a theory of strict tort liability, the man must show that his injuries were caused by an unreasonably dangerous defect in the boat that existed when the boat left the boating supply store's control; (C) is the only alternative that reflects this requirement. A prima facie case in products liability based on strict tort liability consists of: (i) an absolute duty owed by a commercial supplier; (ii) production or sale of a defective product; (iii) actual and proximate cause; and (iv) damages. Examples of commercial suppliers include manufacturers, retailers, wholesalers, and assemblers. The second element is established by proving that the product is in a defective condition unreasonably dangerous to users. A plaintiff need not prove that the defendant was at fault in selling or producing a dangerous product. To prove actual cause, a plaintiff must trace the harm suffered to a defect in the product that existed when the product left the defendant's control. Here, because the steering failed due to a defect present when the boat left the manufacturer, that defect must also have been present when the man bought the boat from the boating supply store, the retailer. This defect rendered the boat unreasonably dangerous to users such as the man. The boating supply store sold the boat in this defective condition, and the defect actually and proximately caused the man to incur severe personal injuries. Thus, (C) states why the man will prevail. (A) is incorrect because the inspection of the boat by the boating supply store prior to sale would be relevant to a ***negligence*** action, but not to one based on strict liability. Strict liability will still lie because the boat left the boating supply store's control with a defect that rendered it unreasonably dangerous. (B) is incorrect because ordinary contributory negligence is not a defense in strict liability actions in jurisdictions that do not apply comparative fault rules in these cases. To the extent that the man is "misusing" the boat by weaving in and out of the pylons, it is a reasonably foreseeable misuse that the commercial supplier must take into account. To avail itself of the man's conduct as a defense, the boating supply store must show that the man voluntarily and unreasonably encountered a known risk. The facts herein do not indicate any such knowing assumption by the man of the risk of harm from the defective steering mechanism. (D) is incorrect because it does not establish the causation element. The boating supply store's strict tort liability depends on whether the steering mechanism failed because of a defect present at the time it sold the boat to the man. If the boat was not defective at the time of sale, or if any defect that was present had nothing to do with the failure of the steering mechanism, the boating supply store will not be liable for a subsequent failure of the steering mechanism from some other cause.

Answer to Question 40

(B) The court should rule the driver's statement acknowledging that he ran a red light is admissible; but his promise to pay the pedestrian's medical expenses inadmissible. The driver's statement acknowledging that he ran a red light is admissible as an admission by a party-opponent, while his promise to the pedestrian is inadmissible as an offer to pay medical expenses. An admission is a statement made or act done that amounts to a prior acknowledgment by one of the parties to an action of one of the relevant facts. The Federal Rules of Evidence treat such statements as nonhearsay. In his first statement, the driver acknowledges that he ran the red light, and that the accident resulting in the pedestrian's injuries was his fault. This statement clearly amounts to an acknowledgment of relevant facts (*i.e.,* that the driver was at fault) and qualifies as an admission by a party-opponent. Evidence that a party paid (or offered to pay) an injured party's medical bills is not admissible to prove liability for the injuries. Such payment (or offer to pay) might be prompted solely by humanitarian motives. The driver's second statement is clearly an offer to pay the medical bills of the pedestrian, an injured party. Thus, the statement is not admissible to prove liability for the pedestrian's injuries (and proving liability appears to be the only reason the pedestrian has for attempting to introduce the statement into evidence). Note that had this been a single statement, the outcome would have been the same, because an admission of fact accompanying offers to pay medical expenses is admissible. (A) is wrong because, as explained above, the driver's second statement is inadmissible. (C) is wrong as to both statements because the admission is admissible and the offer to pay is inadmissible. (D) is wrong because the admission is admissible evidence.

Answer to Question 41

(B) The son has a one-quarter interest, the daughter has a one-quarter interest, and the woman has a one-half interest. There is a presumption that the man and woman are tenants in common. For a joint tenancy to exist, there must be an express creation of such tenancy; thus, there is a presumption of tenancy in common unless the conveyance is to a husband and wife in a state that recognizes tenancy by the entirety. Here, the man and woman were not married when they took title to the land. Each tenant in common has an undivided interest, which may be conveyed by inter vivos transfer. The man started with an undivided one-half interest, one-half of which he conveyed to his son and the other half of which he conveyed to his daughter. The man has thus conveyed all of his interest in the land, and so (A) is incorrect. There is no right of survivorship in a tenancy in common; therefore, (C) is incorrect. (D) is not supported by the facts.

Answer to Question 42

(A) The objection will likely be denied. Under the Federal Rules of Evidence, after a witness has testified, statements of prior identification are admissible to prove their truth unless the defendant can show that the circumstances of the identification were unnecessarily suggestive and likely to result in irreparable misidentification. There is no evidence of that in the facts. (B) is wrong because there is no right to counsel at a photo display. (C) is wrong because it goes to the weight to be given the evidence rather than its admissibility. (D) is wrong because the photograph identification would not be considered a critical stage.

Answer to Question 43

(B) The Commerce Clause provides the best basis for a challenge to the provision. The statute burdens interstate commerce by diverting purchase of items from interstate to intrastate commerce, discriminating against interstate commerce. (A) is incorrect because the Privileges or Immunities Clause does not apply: The sale of products does not fall within the limited number of "privileges" the Court has recognized under the Fourteenth Amendment. (C) is incorrect because the statute applies to all businesses, so it does not create the sort of classification that triggers equal protection analysis. Because the license requirement is well within the traditional state police powers, and would be reasonable except for the Commerce Clause problems, (D) is incorrect.

Answer to Question 44

(B) The motion will be denied because the search was incident to a constitutional arrest. After arresting the occupant of an automobile, the police may search the interior of the auto if the police reasonably believe that evidence of the offense for which the person was arrested may be found in the vehicle. The court is likely to find that, based on what he saw, the officer reasonably believed that he would find evidence of alcohol consumption. Thus, (B) is correct and (D) is wrong. (A) is wrong because the police officer need not fear for his safety to make a valid search incident to a constitutional arrest under the circumstances above. (C) is wrong because a valid search incident to arrest encompasses the area within the defendant's "wingspan." This includes the glove compartment.

Answer to Question 45

(D) The evidence will be permitted. Under the Federal Rules of Evidence, this prior inconsistent statement may be used to impeach and as substantive evidence. A prior inconsistent statement made while under oath and subject to penalty of perjury in a deposition or prior hearing is not hearsay under the Federal Rules. (A) is therefore incorrect. (B) is incorrect because the Federal Rules permit a party to impeach its own witness, even if not "surprised." (C) is incorrect because it is too narrow.

Answer to Question 46

(C) The strongest basis for the enactment is the Taxing and Spending Clause. The federal government has the power to tax and spend funds for the general welfare of the citizens of the United States. (A) is arguable because, under the Commerce Clause, Congress has enacted a wide variety of social legislation. However, since this legislation is strictly dealing with welfare, the act would most probably be based on the Taxing and Spending Clause. (B) is incorrect because the facts do not indicate that any citizen is being deprived of any federal right. There is no general federal police power, so (D) is wrong.

Answer to Question 47

(D) The heir should be found guilty. The heir's act was not only the "but for" cause, but also, because the death was the natural foreseeable result, the "proximate" cause. The fact that other preexisting conditions contributed to the death does not absolve the heir. (A) is wrong; there is no requirement that the defendant's acts be the sole cause of the result. Most results have more than one cause. (B) is wrong; everyone dies at some point.

Answer to Question 48

(C) The evidence should not be admitted. Under the Federal Rules of Evidence, evidence of subsequent remedial measures is inadmissible to show negligence. This is based on the public policy of safety. The law wants to encourage people to make repairs or take other remedial measures after an accident without being held back by a fear of liability. Thus, (A) and (B) are incorrect. (D) is wrong because the woman is not trying to impeach the manager or anyone else.

Answer to Question 49

(D) The restriction would likely be held valid. There are two gifts to the farmer's grandchildren. The first is a vested remainder that follows the daughter's life estate, and the second is the executory interest that is given to the other grandchildren if one purports to sell or mortgage his interest.

This interest is valid because the forfeiture restraint imposed in the will is valid. While a forfeiture restraint on a fee simple is void, a forfeiture restraint on the transferability of a future interest, during the period when the interest is a future interest, is valid. Thus, (C) is incorrect. (A) is incorrect because the grandson and the other grandchildren have interests that are vested at the farmer's death. (B) is incorrect for the same reason. The grandchildren's interests vested and their class closed at the time of the farmer's death; thus, they are not subject to the Rule Against Perpetuities.

Answer to Question 50

(C) The man's conduct may be considered by the trier of fact. Because the man was not where the cab driver might have expected him to be, it would be relevant in judging the reasonableness of the cab driver's conduct. For this reason, (D) is wrong. (A) and (B) are wrong because the man's violation would probably be excused under the circumstances. While (B) raises the issue of last clear chance, which would negate a contributory negligence defense, the facts do not establish that the man was contributorily negligent.

Mixed Subject Set 4 Answer Sheet

1.	Ⓐ	Ⓑ	Ⓒ	Ⓓ	26.	Ⓐ	Ⓑ	Ⓒ	Ⓓ
2.	Ⓐ	Ⓑ	Ⓒ	Ⓓ	27.	Ⓐ	Ⓑ	Ⓒ	Ⓓ
3.	Ⓐ	Ⓑ	Ⓒ	Ⓓ	28.	Ⓐ	Ⓑ	Ⓒ	Ⓓ
4.	Ⓐ	Ⓑ	Ⓒ	Ⓓ	29.	Ⓐ	Ⓑ	Ⓒ	Ⓓ
5.	Ⓐ	Ⓑ	Ⓒ	Ⓓ	30.	Ⓐ	Ⓑ	Ⓒ	Ⓓ
6.	Ⓐ	Ⓑ	Ⓒ	Ⓓ	31.	Ⓐ	Ⓑ	Ⓒ	Ⓓ
7.	Ⓐ	Ⓑ	Ⓒ	Ⓓ	32.	Ⓐ	Ⓑ	Ⓒ	Ⓓ
8.	Ⓐ	Ⓑ	Ⓒ	Ⓓ	33.	Ⓐ	Ⓑ	Ⓒ	Ⓓ
9.	Ⓐ	Ⓑ	Ⓒ	Ⓓ	34.	Ⓐ	Ⓑ	Ⓒ	Ⓓ
10.	Ⓐ	Ⓑ	Ⓒ	Ⓓ	35.	Ⓐ	Ⓑ	Ⓒ	Ⓓ
11.	Ⓐ	Ⓑ	Ⓒ	Ⓓ	36.	Ⓐ	Ⓑ	Ⓒ	Ⓓ
12.	Ⓐ	Ⓑ	Ⓒ	Ⓓ	37.	Ⓐ	Ⓑ	Ⓒ	Ⓓ
13.	Ⓐ	Ⓑ	Ⓒ	Ⓓ	38.	Ⓐ	Ⓑ	Ⓒ	Ⓓ
14.	Ⓐ	Ⓑ	Ⓒ	Ⓓ	39.	Ⓐ	Ⓑ	Ⓒ	Ⓓ
15.	Ⓐ	Ⓑ	Ⓒ	Ⓓ	40.	Ⓐ	Ⓑ	Ⓒ	Ⓓ
16.	Ⓐ	Ⓑ	Ⓒ	Ⓓ	41.	Ⓐ	Ⓑ	Ⓒ	Ⓓ
17.	Ⓐ	Ⓑ	Ⓒ	Ⓓ	42.	Ⓐ	Ⓑ	Ⓒ	Ⓓ
18.	Ⓐ	Ⓑ	Ⓒ	Ⓓ	43.	Ⓐ	Ⓑ	Ⓒ	Ⓓ
19.	Ⓐ	Ⓑ	Ⓒ	Ⓓ	44.	Ⓐ	Ⓑ	Ⓒ	Ⓓ
20.	Ⓐ	Ⓑ	Ⓒ	Ⓓ	45.	Ⓐ	Ⓑ	Ⓒ	Ⓓ
21.	Ⓐ	Ⓑ	Ⓒ	Ⓓ	46.	Ⓐ	Ⓑ	Ⓒ	Ⓓ
22.	Ⓐ	Ⓑ	Ⓒ	Ⓓ	47.	Ⓐ	Ⓑ	Ⓒ	Ⓓ
23.	Ⓐ	Ⓑ	Ⓒ	Ⓓ	48.	Ⓐ	Ⓑ	Ⓒ	Ⓓ
24.	Ⓐ	Ⓑ	Ⓒ	Ⓓ	49.	Ⓐ	Ⓑ	Ⓒ	Ⓓ
25.	Ⓐ	Ⓑ	Ⓒ	Ⓓ	50.	Ⓐ	Ⓑ	Ⓒ	Ⓓ

MIXED SUBJECT QUESTIONS - SET 4

Question 1

A state contains major deposits of natural gas. In an effort to support this industry, and at the same time save its citizens substantial sums for the cost of heating their homes and businesses, the legislature enacted a substantial tax on out-of-state suppliers of natural gas. In addition, the state required state-licensed public utilities to buy no less than 75% of their natural gas needs from sources within the state as long as their needs could be met. An out-of-state supplier ("the supplier") brought suit against the state challenging this statute.

The best constitutional argument the supplier could make is that the statute violates:

(A) The Due Process Clause of the Fourteenth Amendment.

(B) The Equal Protection Clause of the Fourteenth Amendment.

(C) The Privileges and Immunities Clause of Article IV.

(D) The Commerce Clause.

Question 2

The defendant was at work when her husband called her and said, "The neighbor just tripped over those roots I told you to take out. He's badly hurt and I'll bet he sues us for all we're worth." The defendant then told her secretary, "The neighbor just got hurt because I forgot to do my yard work." On returning home, however, the defendant discovered that the neighbor had actually tripped over roots from his own tree in his own yard. The neighbor disagreed and sued the defendant and her husband. At trial, the neighbor called the defendant's secretary to testify as to the defendant's statement to him.

The secretary's testimony will be:

(A) Excluded, because the defendant had no firsthand information when she made her statement to the secretary.

(B) Excluded, because it is inadmissible lay opinion.

(C) Admitted, because it is not hearsay.

(D) Admitted to impeach the defendant's expected testimony as to the result of her own investigation.

Question 3

A woman whose car was in the shop wanted to meet her friend at a restaurant a mile away from the woman's home. She noticed that her neighbor had forgotten to lock his bicycle upon returning home. The woman took her neighbor's bicycle and began riding it to the restaurant, intending to bring it back in the trunk of her friend's car after her dinner. She had ridden the bicycle a distance of two blocks when she was hit by a car that had gone through a red light. The bicycle was destroyed in the collision.

If charged with larceny of the bicycle, the woman will most likely be found:

(A) Guilty, because she intended to take the bicycle without permission.

(B) Guilty, because she was responsible for the permanent loss of the bicycle.

(C) Not guilty, because she did not ride the bicycle far enough away from where she took it.

(D) Not guilty, because what she planned to do with the bicycle did not create a substantial risk of permanent loss.

Question 4

A plaintiff purchased a new car manufactured by a corporation from a local dealership. While the plaintiff was driving home from the dealership, she stopped at a stop sign. She was struck from behind by a jeep driven by a driver who had negligently failed to stop. On impact, the plaintiff was injured when she hit her head on the front windshield. The plaintiff was wearing a seat belt at the time of the impact which should have prevented this, but the seat belt buckle was defective and failed to hold the plaintiff. Assume that a state law requires all automobiles to be equipped with seat belts that will prevent drivers from hitting their heads on windshields on impact.

If the plaintiff asserts a claim against the driver, the plaintiff will:

(A) Prevail, unless the corporation was negligent in the manufacture of the car that the plaintiff was driving.

(B) Prevail, because the driver's negligent driving was a cause in fact of the collision.

(C) Not prevail, because the seat belt in the plaintiff's car violated a state law.

(D) Not prevail, because the plaintiff would not have been injured but for the failure of the seat belt buckle.

Question 5

A plaintiff driving his new sports car was stopped at a red light when he was struck from behind by a truck driven by a driver who had negligently failed to stop. On impact, the door on the driver's side of the car flew open because of a latent defect in the latch that could not have been detected during the ordinary manufacturing process. The plaintiff, who was not wearing a seat belt, fell out the open door and was injured. The jurisdiction retains traditional contributory negligence rules; however, evidence of nonuse of a seat belt is not admissible in a civil action.

If the plaintiff asserts a claim against the corporation that manufactured the car, will the plaintiff prevail?

(A) Yes, because the plaintiff could not reasonably have discovered the defect.

(B) Yes, because the car he was driving was dangerously defective.

(C) No, because the truck driver's negligent driving was the cause of the plaintiff's injuries.

(D) No, because the corporation did not know or have reason to know of the defect.

Question 6

A state's legislature passed a statute that required every used car sold in the state to be tested prior to sale to determine whether it was in compliance with a set of strict exhaust emission standards that were also included in the legislation. Used cars would have to be brought up to standard and pass the emissions test prior to sale. Certain persons in the state object to the legislation because one of its results will be to raise the average price of used cars in the state. Only cars to be sold for junk are exempt from the statute.

Among the following, who would be most likely to have standing to raise a constitutional challenge to the legislation?

(A) A state resident who was thinking about selling used cars in the state.

(B) A state resident who was thinking about buying a used car in the state.

(C) An out-of-state dealer of used cars who had a contract to sell cars to a large dealer in the state.

(D) An out-of-state manufacturer who might be required to indemnify its dealers in the state for costs arising from the statute.

Question 7

Growers of potatoes in the state recently began spraying a pesticide onto their crops to prevent the spread of a pest that can destroy young potato plants. The pesticide is manufactured exclusively by one company at its plant. When the plant is producing the pesticide it emits a fine, sticky, harmless mist as a byproduct. The mist drifts over a plaintiff's property, which is adjacent to the company's plant. Although the company uses the best technology available, it is unable to prevent the release of the mist. The plaintiff brings suit against the company on the theory of private nuisance to enjoin the production of the pesticide at the company's plant.

Which of the following facts, if established, will be most helpful to the company's defense?

(A) The company commenced the manufacture of the pesticide at its plant three years before the plaintiff acquired the land adjacent to the plant.

(B) Federal, state, and local agencies approved the design of the plant and equipment used to produce the pesticide.

(C) The principal users of the pesticide are state and federal departments of agriculture.

(D) The pesticide is the only type of pesticide that can safely and effectively kill the pest, which, if not controlled, would destroy the state's potato crop, its principal product.

Question 8

While cross-examining a defendant on trial for robbery and assault with a deadly weapon, the prosecutor asks him whether he was convicted of fraud within the previous year.

This question is:

(A) Improper, because fraud is not probative of a tendency to commit violence.

(B) Improper, unless the proper foundation was laid.

(C) Proper, because fraud is a form of stealing, and so it will tend to show that the defendant could commit robbery.

(D) Proper, because it tends to show that the defendant would lie.

Question 9

While a driver was driving an owner's car, he hit a plaintiff who was walking in a pedestrian right-of-way. The plaintiff sues the owner, alleging that that owner had negligently permitted an unfit driver to use her car. As part of her defense, the owner calls her husband to testify for her. The husband offers testimony that the owner rarely loans her automobile to anybody, but that when she does loan it, the owner invariably checks to see whether the driver is careful and law abiding. The plaintiff objects to the admission of this evidence.

The plaintiff's objection should be:

(A) Sustained, because there is no evidence to corroborate the husband's testimony.

(B) Sustained, because it seeks to prove conduct in conformity with the character evidence.

(C) Overruled, because the owner's character is in issue.

(D) Overruled, because it tends to establish the owner's habit.

Question 10

An owner and a builder executed a contract providing that the builder was to construct a residence on a specified location according to plans and specifications. The total contract price was $500,000. The lot on which the residence was to be built was located on the seashore and there was an existing wood frame structure that had to be demolished before the residence could be built. No date was included in the contract for completion of the home. The contract between the owner and the builder stated that construction would begin within two weeks after the existing structure was demolished and the rubble removed from the lot. The day after the preexisting structure was demolished and the rubble removed, a hurricane eroded the seashore, resulting in the owner's lot being now under water.

The builder will not need to perform the contract because:

(A) The contract is void because the subject of the contract was destroyed through no fault of the parties.

(B) The builder is discharged of his obligation because of impossibility of performance.

(C) The increased costs of construction would bankrupt him.

(D) The contract is void because of mutual mistake.

Question 11

A homeowner and a contractor duly executed a contract providing that the contractor was to construct a residence on a specified lot. No date was included in the contract for completion of the home. After the contractor completed 5% of the residence, a tornado demolished the construction but left the lot undamaged.

Must the contractor still perform the contract?

(A) No, the contract is void because the subject of the contract was destroyed through no fault of the parties.

(B) No, the contractor is discharged of his obligation because of impossibility of performance.

(C) Yes, but he is entitled to a quantum meruit recovery for the work done prior to the destruction of the construction.

(D) Yes, the contractor must perform the original contract without any compensation for the destruction of the construction.

Question 12

An owner and a builder executed a contract providing that the builder was to construct a residence on a specified lot according to plans and specifications. The total contract price was $800,000. No date was included in the contract for completion of the home. After the builder completed 60% of the residence, a flash flood from a nearby river partially eroded the lot but left the construction undamaged. The builder determined that it would cost an additional $1.2 million to repair the lot so that the residence can be constructed according to the plans. Without the additional lot repair work, the residence cannot be constructed at all.

Must the builder perform the contract?

(A) No, if the increased costs of construction would bankrupt him.

(B) No, the contract is void because of mutual mistake.

(C) No, the builder is discharged of his obligation because of impracticability of performance.

(D) Yes, but he may bring an action against the owner for the increased costs of construction.

Question 13

An owner and a contractor executed a contract providing that the contractor was to construct a three-story, castle-like structure on a specified location according to plans and specifications drawn up by an architect. The total contract price was $900,000. No date was included in the contract for completion of the home but the builder was to begin construction one week after the contract was signed. The day after the contract was signed by the parties, the state development commission declared the land encompassing the owner's lot part of a natural wilderness area, requiring that all residences constructed therein be single story and have plans approved by the development commission. The original plans for the three-story structure are totally incompatible with the commission's guidelines for residences in a wilderness area.

Must the builder perform the contract?

(A) No, the contract is void because of mutual mistake.

(B) No, and he may recover his lost profits in an action against the owner.

(C) No, the contractor is discharged of his obligation because of supervening illegality.

(D) Yes, if the owner and the architect supply new plans approved by the development commission.

Question 14

Fifty-one years ago, an owner conveyed land to a taker for "so long as the land is used solely for residential purposes, otherwise, the interest in land shall revert to the owner and his heirs." The taker used the land as her personal residence for 20 years, but 31 years ago, she began operating a children's day camp on the land. The owner knew of this operation, but he took no action.

Two years ago, the aged taker decided to get out of the camp business. She closed her business and once again began to use the land solely as her personal residence. Also two years ago, the owner died, survived by his son and only heir. Now the son is laying claim to the conveyed land. The jurisdiction in which the land is located has a seven-year adverse possession statute and another statute that bars enforcement of possibilities of reverter 55 years after their creation.

May the son validly claim title to the land?

(A) Yes, because less than 55 years has elapsed since the creation of the possibility of reverter.

(B) Yes, because the adverse possession period began to run when the taker returned the property to residential status, and the taker has not held for the requisite seven years.

(C) No, because the adverse possession period began 31 years ago, and the taker has held the property for more than the requisite seven years.

(D) No, because the owner did not assert his possibility of reverter; thus, no cause of action arose in the owner or his heirs.

Question 15

One night when a man was very drunk, he took one of his rifles, loaded it, and fired a bullet through his front door. Unbeknownst to him, at the time he fired the rifle, someone was driving by the house. The bullet went through the front door, through the window of the car, and killed the driver. The shooter was convicted of murder and appeals. He contends that there was insufficient evidence to support a finding of murder.

The court of appeals should rule that the evidence is:

(A) Sufficient to prove that the killing was intentional.

(B) Sufficient to prove that the killing was done with malice aforethought.

(C) Insufficient, because the shooter did not know that the driver was driving by his house and therefore he could not have acted intentionally.

(D) Insufficient, because at most the shooter's conduct constituted gross negligence and involuntary manslaughter.

Question 16

Logging has long been one of the major industries of a state. To protect the logging industry, which was being harmed by the too rapid depletion of the wood in the forests of the state, and to promote the general welfare of the state's citizens, the state legislature enacted statutes for the first time requiring licenses for commercial logging. To receive a license, the applicant must pay a $500 fee and establish by acceptable evidence that he has been engaged in commercial logging in the forests of the state for the past 15 years. A limited number of special licenses are available for those who do not meet the requirements of the regular licenses, and these special licenses are expressly reserved for citizens who have resided in the state for at least three years prior to the date of the application. A legally admitted alien who has been residing in the state for 10 years brings suit in federal court to enjoin enforcement of the licensing statute as to himself and all other similarly situated non-citizen legal residents of the state.

Which of the following doctrines will probably be determinative of his claims?

(A) The powers reserved to the states by the Tenth Amendment to the federal Constitution.

(B) The Equal Protection Clause of the Fourteenth Amendment.

(C) The Due Process Clause of the Fifth Amendment to the federal Constitution.

(D) The Privileges and Immunities Clause of Article IV.

Question 17

Commercial fishing has long been one of the major industries of a coastal state. To protect the fishing industry and to promote the general welfare of the state's citizens, the legislature of the state enacted statutes requiring licenses for commercial fishing. An applicant for the license must pay a $300 fee and establish that he has been engaged in commercial fishing in the waters of the state for 10 years. A commercial fisherman residing in a neighboring state frequently takes his fishing boat up the coast. His favorite spot is approximately two miles off the coast of the legislating state.

If the commercial fisherman challenges the constitutionality of the legislating state's statutes, the court should find the statutes:

(A) Constitutional, because Congress has not enacted legislation regarding the subject matter of the statutes.

(B) Constitutional, because economic and social regulations are presumed valid.

(C) Unconstitutional, because less restrictive means are available.

(D) Unconstitutional, because Congress has exclusive power to regulate foreign commerce, which includes commercial ocean fishing.

Question 18

The owner of a ranch in fee simple died and left the property to his daughter, "my daughter, her heirs and assigns; but if my son is living 25 years from the date of my death, then to my son, his heirs and assigns." At the time of the owner's death, his son was one year old. The common law Rule Against Perpetuities is unmodified in the jurisdiction.

The grant in the will to the owner's son is:

(A) Valid, because the interest vests, if at all, within a life in being.

(B) Valid, because it grants the son a reversionary interest.

(C) Invalid, because the will grants the daughter the complete interest in the property, so there is nothing to be left to the son.

(D) Invalid, if this jurisdiction does not recognize a testator's ability to convey a possibility of reverter by will.

Question 19

A defendant is charged with the arson of a house. At trial, prosecution offers evidence that when the defendant was arrested, shortly after the crime had been committed, she had a large amount of cocaine hidden in the trunk of her car.

This evidence should be:

(A) Admitted to prove the defendant's propensity to commit crimes.

(B) Admitted to prove the defendant's general bad character.

(C) Excluded because such evidence may be offered only to rebut evidence of good character offered by the defendant.

(D) Excluded because its probative value is substantially outweighed by the danger of unfair prejudice.

Question 20

A defendant is charged with the burglary of a warehouse. At the request of the police investigating the burglary, the night watchman at the warehouse who had seen the thief leaving the premises wrote out a description of the thief, who bore a strong likeness to the defendant. However, the night watchman died of a heart attack before the defendant was arrested and brought to trial. The prosecution attempts to offer the description written out by the night watchman into evidence.

The description is:

(A) Admissible as a past recollection recorded.

(B) Admissible as an identification of a person the night watchman knew committed the crime in question.

(C) Inadmissible as hearsay not within an exception.

(D) Inadmissible as an opinion of a non-expert.

Question 21

A defendant is charged with theft of a car. On cross-examination of the defendant, the prosecution asked her whether she had been convicted of fraudulent business practices six months earlier.

This question is:

(A) Proper to show that the defendant has a bad character.

(B) Proper to show that the defendant is inclined to lie.

(C) Improper because the probative value of the evidence is outweighed by the danger of unfair prejudice.

(D) Improper because the conviction has insufficient similarity to the crime charged.

Question 22

A defendant is charged with larceny. His principal defense was that he had no intent to permanently deprive the victim of her property. The judge instructs the jury that the State had to prove beyond a reasonable doubt that the defendant was guilty of larceny and that the evidence tended to show that the defendant had taken some jewels belonging to the victim; but if they believed that the defendant had proven by a fair preponderance of the evidence that he did not intend to keep the jewels, but to return them, they should find him not guilty. The defendant was convicted of larceny. He appeals the conviction, contending that the judge erred in his instructions to the jury.

The defendant's conviction will probably be:

(A) Affirmed, because the jury has the power to ignore the defendant's testimony if they do not believe him.

(B) Affirmed, because the defendant had failed to rebut the State's evidence tending to show that he intended to keep the jewels.

(C) Reversed, because the judge cannot comment at all on the evidence.

(D) Reversed, because the instructions put some of the burden of proof on the defendant.

Question 23

A large delivery truck collided with a car. At the time of the accident, the driver of the truck said to the car driver, "The accident was my fault; I wasn't paying any attention. Don't worry, my company will make it right." The delivery company had not authorized the truck driver to make that statement. The subsequent investigation of the accident by the delivery company revealed that the truck driver had been drinking on the day of the accident. He was fired. The car driver brings an appropriate action against the delivery company for damages resulting from the accident. The truck driver has disappeared. The car driver now seeks to testify as to what the truck driver said at the time of the accident.

The evidence is:

(A) Admissible, as an admission by an employee of the defendant.

(B) Admissible, as an excited utterance.

(C) Inadmissible, because the truck driver is no longer employed by the delivery company.

(D) Inadmissible, because the delivery company had not authorized the truck driver to speak on its behalf.

Question 24

Two landowners owned adjacent lots A and B. Both lots were located in State Red, which has a 20-year adverse possession statute. Thirty years ago, the lot A owner married and left State Red to reside in State Blue. The lot A owner did not return to view the property during her period of residence in State Blue. One year after the lot A owner left, the lot B owner built a driveway on his land. The driveway extended three feet over onto lot A. The lot B owner mistakenly believed that this three-foot strip of land was his property. The lot B owner regularly used the driveway and was continuing to use it when the lot A owner, having been widowed, recently returned to State Red. The lot A owner discovered the encroachment on her return.

What are the lot A owner's rights against the lot B owner?

(A) The lot A owner has no action against the lot B owner, because the lot B owner's title to the three-foot strip has been established by adverse possession.

(B) The lot A owner has no action against the lot B owner, because her prolonged absence from State Red establishes a presumption of abandonment of her rights in the property.

(C) The lot A owner has an action against the lot B owner, because the lot A owner had no knowledge of the lot B owner's encroachment.

(D) The lot A owner has an action against the lot B owner, because the lot B owner mistakenly thought he owned the three-foot strip.

Question 25

A nonunion carpenter went to work on a construction project that was involved in a labor dispute. Every morning when he arrived at work, he would be accosted by the picketers who would try to persuade him not to continue to work. One morning while the carpenter was trying to get to work, one of the union workers stopped him at the gate and told him that he should not go to work. When the carpenter insisted that the striker get out of the way, the striker said, "Try to make me, scab!" The carpenter, intending to frighten the striker, swung his hammer at him. The head on the hammer, however, was defective and it flew off, hitting the striker in the face.

If the striker sues the carpenter for battery, most likely he will:

(A) Prevail, because he was struck by the hammer head.

(B) Prevail, unless he intended to provoke the carpenter.

(C) Not prevail, because the negligence of the manufacturer of the hammer was the direct cause of the injury.

(D) Not prevail, if a reasonable person would have been angered by what the striker had said.

Question 26

A local physician who was prominent in the community and beloved by his patients died suddenly of a heart attack. A reporter with the local newspaper was assigned to write an obituary before the next day's edition went to press. The reporter talked briefly with the physician's widow, and then called the state medical school, from which the physician had always said he had graduated. As it was late in the afternoon, the reporter did not speak with any professors but with a secretary in the office of the dean. When asked about the physician, the secretary replied that she did not think the physician ever graduated.

The local newspaper printed this information in the next day's edition. On reading the obituary, the physician's widow became very angry, as the physician had, in fact, graduated with high honors. She demanded a retraction from the newspaper. The next day, on the front page, the newspaper admitted its error and stated that the physician graduated with high honors from the state's medical school. They also fired the reporter. Nonetheless, both the executor of the physician's estate and his widow sued the local newspaper for defamation.

What is the local newspaper's best defense?

(A) There was no malice on the part of the defendant.

(B) The newspaper's retraction negated any harm.

(C) The reporter got his information from a secretary at the medical school.

(D) The physician is dead.

Question 27

A student and her boyfriend were going away to college and had quite a few personal belongings to transport. The student drove in her car while her father and her boyfriend rode in the father's van. About halfway to the college, while the van and the car were driving down the freeway, the van suddenly swerved out of control and ran off the highway, ending up on its side in the center divider. When the student ran to the van, she discovered to her horror that her father was dead, and her boyfriend appeared to be injured, but not severely. Because her father previously had heart trouble, the student assumed that he had had a heart attack while driving. Filled with remorse, the student told her boyfriend, "I'm so sorry about this. I'll make good any losses you suffer because of this accident."

The boyfriend learned that he had suffered an injury to his spinal column that would prevent him from ever playing basketball again. He had been a scholarship athlete in basketball at the college and was considered to be a certain high draft selection for a professional basketball league when he graduated. The boyfriend brought an action against the student for several million dollars in damages. A subsequent investigation revealed that the accident was caused solely by a defect in the steering mechanism of the van.

Which of the following is the best defense the student could assert against her boyfriend's claim?

(A) There was no consideration supporting the student's promise to her boyfriend to "make good any losses."

(B) The student did not intend to offer to pay the boyfriend for the loss of his professional career when she said she would "make good any losses."

(C) The student was in error when she assumed that her father's heart attack was the cause of the accident.

(D) The student did not know that her boyfriend would not be able to play basketball when she offered to "make good any losses."

Question 28

A homeowner was postponing shoveling the snow off her driveway one Saturday morning because it was so cold outside. When she heard a scream and ran outside, she found the neighborhood newspaper delivery boy injured, lying by his bicycle in her driveway. Feeling terribly guilty, she took the boy to a local doctor and wrote a note to the doctor that she would cover all the subsequent costs.

The boy later admitted that he was attempting to ride the bicycle with his eyes closed, and that his fall had nothing to do with the snow in the homeowner's driveway. After treating the boy for his injuries until he recovered, the doctor sent the homeowner a bill for his services. When the homeowner refused to pay, the doctor brought an action to recover the amount of his bill.

Who will prevail?

(A) The doctor, because he gave medical treatment to the boy after receiving the homeowner's note.

(B) The doctor, because the homeowner's promise to pay the boy's medical expenses was in writing.

(C) The homeowner, because there was no consideration for her promise to the doctor.

(D) The homeowner, because she derived no benefit from the medical services rendered to the boy.

Question 29

By mutual agreement, a brother and sister purchased a 10-acre parcel of land and took title as joint tenants. Three years after the purchase, the brother asked if he could build an apartment house on his half of the property; the sister agreed. He then built an apartment house on the eastern five acres of the property. Two years later, the brother died, leaving his entire estate to his son.

In an action for partition, if the brother's estate is judged the owner of the eastern five acres, it will be because:

(A) The sister's conduct during the brother's lifetime estopped her from asserting title to the eastern half of the property.

(B) The taking of title as joint tenants does not conclusively presume that the property is held as joint tenants.

(C) The joint tenancy was terminated at the time the oral agreement was made.

(D) A joint tenant may will away his interest in property to a lineal descendant.

Question 30

A landowner conveyed her parcel of land to a buyer. The buyer placed the deed in her safe deposit box but did not record the instrument before leaving town. Six months later, the landowner conveyed the same parcel of land to a farmer, who promptly recorded his deed. The farmer had heard that the landowner previously sold the land to a different buyer, but he was sure that the landowner would not sell him property she had already sold to someone else. Six months later, the buyer returned to the land and found the farmer there. A statute of the jurisdiction in which the land is located provides: "No conveyance or mortgage of an interest in land is valid against any subsequent purchaser for value without notice thereof whose conveyance is first recorded." The buyer now sues the farmer in ejectment.

Who owns the land?

(A) The farmer, because his recording cured any possible defect of his knowing of the earlier sale.

(B) The farmer, because he recorded first.

(C) The buyer, because the farmer is not protected by the recording act.

(D) The buyer, because her deed from the landowner came earlier than the farmer's.

Question 31

The state legislature of state A enacted legislation prohibiting the use of tractor-trailer rigs weighing more than 100,000 pounds gross, on the basis that superheavy trucks rapidly degrade the state's roadways and pose a greater safety danger than smaller trucks. A trucking firm that frequently uses state A's highways for trips between state B and state C purchased several tractor-trailer rigs weighing over 100,000 pounds when loaded. The trucking firm brings an action for declaratory relief in federal court in state B, seeking to have the state A legislation declared unconstitutional. It presents expert testimony that the heavier trucks are no less safe than smaller models. State A produces no evidence, but asserts that the legislation is justified as an exercise of its police power.

The trial court should rule:

(A) That the legislation is an unconstitutional violation of the trucking firm's Fourteenth Amendment rights to due process of law.

(B) That the legislation is unconstitutional because it violates the Commerce Clause.

(C) That the legislation is a valid exercise of the state's police power to regulate highway safety.

(D) That the evidence of the damage done to the state's highways by the superheavy trucks is sufficient to uphold the legislation independently of the safety argument.

Question 32

A bartender promised to pay her friend $100 if he would take her color television and stereo from her house, so that she could report the items as being stolen to collect a settlement from the insurance company. Although the friend had visited the bartender's house on two previous occasions, he mistakenly broke and entered her neighbor's house and took the neighbor's color television and stereo. When he returned to the bar where the bartender was waiting for him, both were arrested by the police.

If the bartender and her friend are tried for conspiracy, the court will find them:

(A) Not guilty, because the friend failed to take the bartender's property.

(B) Not guilty, because the friend, being in the wrong house, could not take the bartender's property.

(C) Guilty, because they actually took the neighbor's property.

(D) Guilty, because they intentionally agreed to defraud the insurance company.

Question 33

In order to get some quick cash to pay off a gambling debt, an acquaintance of the defendant asked him to pretend to break into the acquaintance's home, take some silverware, and return the silverware to the acquaintance. The acquaintance believed that he could both collect the insurance proceeds for the "theft" of the silverware, and sell the silverware on the black market. The acquaintance provided the defendant with his address: "46 Maple Avenue." However, due to a strong windstorm, the house number "9" for "49 Maple Avenue" became detached and slid out of position, making it look like "46 Maple Avenue." Thinking that "49 Maple Avenue" was the acquaintance's home due to the mispositioned house number, the defendant slid open a window that was slightly ajar, entered, and took some silverware he found in the kitchen. The silent burglar alarm alerted the police, who arrived and arrested the defendant a short time later.

If the defendant is charged with burglary, the court would find him not guilty because:

(A) He acted under a mistake of law.

(B) There was no breaking.

(C) There was no entry.

(D) He reasonably thought that he was in the acquaintance's home.

Question 34

A landowner invited some friends, including his neighbor, to a party in his backyard. All the friends showed up, except for the neighbor. That evening, a guest produced and lit a large skyrocket. The skyrocket failed to climb properly and crashed into the neighbor's garage, burning the garage to the ground. A local ordinance made it a misdemeanor to sell fireworks within the city limits.

If the neighbor sues the landowner for the damage to his garage, the theory on which he is most likely to prevail is:

(A) The landowner failed to exercise due care to control the acts of his guests.

(B) The landowner is strictly liable for harm resulting from abnormally dangerous activities performed on his land.

(C) Because he had been invited to the landowner's party, the neighbor, as an invitee, was owed by the landowner a duty to discover and guard against activities on his land involving an unreasonable risk of harm.

(D) The landowner is liable on a negligence per se theory because of the local ordinance banning the sale of fireworks within the city.

Question 35

The class president invited his class to his home to celebrate homecoming. When the sun began to set, a student built a bonfire in the backyard. The student continued to feed the flames until the bonfire was quite large. Suddenly, a gust of wind blew the flames to a neighboring property, igniting the neighbor's shed.

If the neighbor sues the student for the damage to his shed on a theory of negligence, under which of the following arguments, if sustained by the facts, would the student avoid liability?

(A) The lighting of bonfires on homecoming is an accepted custom in the community.

(B) The bonfire was positioned by the student in the center of the backyard to avoid damaging the neighbor's shed.

(C) The fire that started would have burned itself out but for the fact that the neighbor's shed was built out of substandard, highly flammable material.

(D) The student was a guest on the class president's property and entitled to the same restricted scope of liability as the property owner.

Question 36

The complainant was robbed by a man wielding an unusual knife with a pearl-studded handle. The defendant was arrested and charged with armed robbery of the complainant. At trial the prosecution calls a witness to testify that, three days after the robbery of the complainant, she was robbed by the defendant with a knife that had a pearl-studded handle.

The court should hold that the witness's testimony is:

(A) Admissible, as showing habit.

(B) Admissible, as establishing an identifying circumstance.

(C) Inadmissible, because it is improper character evidence.

(D) Inadmissible, because its probative value is substantially outweighed by the danger of unfair prejudice.

Question 37

A state penal statute makes it a misdemeanor to willfully shut off the gas, electricity, or any other form of power to an inhabited dwelling, unless strictly outlined procedures for notice and hearing are met. A landowner rented a furnished house to a young married couple for several months when she failed to receive the monthly rent check. The couple did not answer any of the owner's calls, and the neighbors confirmed that they had not seen the couple for weeks. The owner therefore concluded that the couple had abandoned the rental. She called the power company and had the electricity and gas shut off until she could find another tenant. A week later, the couple returned from an overseas tour. They reported to the authorities that their power had been turned off, and the owner was prosecuted under the misdemeanor statute. At trial it was established that, while they were abroad, the couple had inadvertently failed to place the proper postage on the rent check, which was returned to their tour guide.

The owner will probably be:

(A) Convicted, because the charged crime is a violation of a public safety statute, and she is strictly liable for her action in turning off the power.

(B) Convicted, because she did not undertake a more thorough inquiry or wait a more reasonable length of time before concluding that the house had been abandoned.

(C) Acquitted, if the trier of fact concludes that the owner was reasonable in believing that the house had been abandoned.

(D) Acquitted, if the trier of fact concludes that the young couple was negligent in not placing proper postage on the rent check mailed from abroad.

Question 38

A high school graduate was asked by his elderly aunt to live with her in her large brownstone and attend to the household activities for the rest of her life, in exchange for the house. The graduate agreed, and moved from his parents' home to the brownstone. For eight years, he attended to his aunt's personal needs, and maintained the household. No further discussion was ever had between the graduate and his aunt regarding conveyance of the brownstone.

Shortly after his aunt died, the graduate was contacted by the aunt's estranged daughter, who stated that in the aunt's last will and testament, she had devised the house to her. When the graduate refused to vacate the brownstone, the daughter brought action for possession of the house.

If the graduate prevails in the action, it will be because:

(A) He can successfully assert the doctrine of "unclean hands" to prevent the daughter from pressing her claim under the will.

(B) The Statute of Frauds need not be satisfied as between family members.

(C) The Statute of Frauds will not bar enforcement of the aunt's promise because her promise induced the graduate to perform, and injustice can be avoided only by enforcement.

(D) The Statute of Frauds will not be applied where there has been part performance and where that performance is such as can be explained by the existence of the asserted contract and in no other way.

Question 39

While dating, a man and woman purchased a parcel of land for $100,000, each contributing half the purchase price, and took title as joint tenants with right of survivorship. Two years after the couple were married, they separated. The man then quitclaimed all of his interest in the land to his brother, who duly recorded the deed. The jurisdiction has no applicable statute.

The land is now held by:

(A) The woman and brother, as joint tenants with right of survivorship.

(B) The woman and brother, as tenants in common.

(C) The man and woman, as tenants by the entirety.

(D) The man and woman, as joint tenants with right of survivorship.

Question 40

A boy was arrested for shoplifting. His mother was consoling him at the police station when a reporter for a daily newspaper took her picture. The photograph appeared on the front page of the next day's edition of the paper, above the story of the boy's arrest. A caption to the photograph identified her as the boy's mother. Later that week, the mother lost her job as a result of the story in the paper.

If the mother asserts a claim against the newspaper for invasion of privacy, she will:

(A) Recover, if she was not involved in the events that led to the boy's arrest.

(B) Recover, because the photograph and news story caused her to be discharged from her employment.

(C) Not recover, because her photograph was taken in a public place.

(D) Not recover, because the caption was accurate.

Question 41

A motorist drove home from work late one night, and fell asleep behind the wheel of his car. His car drifted across the middle of the road and struck another car. The other driver was killed instantly in the collision. Angered by the noise of the collision, a homeowner fired a gun out the window of his house at the car. The bullet struck and killed a bystander. Both the motorist and the homeowner were arrested and charged with common law murder.

Which of the defendants likely would be found guilty?

(A) Both the motorist and the homeowner.

(B) The motorist.

(C) Neither the motorist nor the homeowner.

(D) The homeowner.

Question 42

The federal accounting office issued a call for competitive bids for a contract to supply 3,000 four-wheel drive utility vehicles without antipollution devices and with engines with a displacement of 4,000 cubic centimeters. A supplier in a state won the contract as low bidder and began manufacture of the vehicles. However, the state's statutes require that automobiles manufactured in that state be equipped with antipollution devices and have a maximum displacement of 2,500 cubic centimeters. The supplier files suit in state court, seeking a judicial declaration that the state statute may not be enforced as to it.

The court should rule:

(A) The statute may not constitutionally be applied to the supplier because to do so would violate the Supremacy Clause.

(B) The statute may not constitutionally be applied to the supplier because to do so would violate the Contracts Clause.

(C) The statute may not constitutionally be applied to the supplier because to do so would violate the Commerce Clause.

(D) The statute may constitutionally be applied to the supplier.

Question 43

A driver was operating his vehicle along a residential street at the posted speed limit when he saw a ball roll across the street. The driver did not slow down because the ball cleared his path before he reached it. A few seconds later, a child darted out into the street after the ball without looking for cars. The driver's car struck the child, and the child was injured.

The child's parents brought an action on the child's behalf against the driver in a jurisdiction that follows traditional contributory negligence rules. At trial, the above facts were established. At the close of the evidence, the driver moved for a directed verdict.

The court should:

(A) Deny the driver's motion, because it will be up to the jury to determine whether he should have slowed down to below the speed limit.

(B) Deny the driver's motion, because it will be up to the jury to determine whether the child's parents were negligent in supervising the child.

(C) Grant the driver's motion, because the child was negligent in darting into the street without looking out for traffic.

(D) Grant the driver's motion, because he was going no faster than the posted speed limit.

Question 44

A banker was driving along a two-way road when a girl ran into his lane. A pedestrian saw the banker's vehicle bearing down on the girl. Concerned that she would be hurt, the pedestrian rushed into the street to try to save her. Just as he reached her, the pedestrian tripped and fell down in the street. The banker's vehicle collided with both the pedestrian and the girl. The jurisdiction follows traditional contributory negligence rules.

If the pedestrian sues the driver for personal injuries, who will prevail?

(A) The banker, because he could not have expected an adult to run into the street.

(B) The banker, if he was traveling no faster than the posted speed limit.

(C) The banker, because the pedestrian was unrelated to the girl.

(D) The pedestrian, if the banker had the last clear chance to avoid the accident.

Question 45

A couple was engaged and looking for a lot on which to build their first house. They purchased a piece of land, taking title as joint tenants with right of survivorship. Before construction of the house could begin, the man discovered that the woman was having an affair, and the engagement was called off. Wanting to obtain the money to run off with her lover, the woman wanted to sell the land, but the man refused to sell. The woman put the land up for sale anyway, and when a buyer agreed to purchase it, the woman forged the man's signature on the deed conveying the land to the buyer.

Who owns the land?

(A) The man only.

(B) The buyer only.

(C) The man and the buyer as tenants in common.

(D) The man, the woman, and the buyer as tenants in common.

Question 46

A state law grants each county great autonomy in setting the health standards governing the preparation, packaging, transportation, and sale of food items. A county council recently enacted an ordinance, valid under the constitution and statutes of the state, prohibiting the packaging and sale of any food item in any non-biodegradable material; the ordinance defines non-biodegradable and specifically lists as prohibited all forms of plastics, cellophane, or similar materials. The ordinance specifically exempts from its terms sales of food to public institutions such as hospitals, jails, and schools. A retail food seller in the county files an appropriate court action attacking the county ordinance on the grounds that it violates the Equal Protection Clause of the Fourteenth Amendment.

The court should rule:

(A) For the food seller, because the state's interests could be effectuated by alternative methods less intrusive upon the food seller's constitutional rights.

(B) For the food seller, because no compelling state interest is served by the challenged ordinance.

(C) For the county, because the state may regulate in this area as Congress has not entered the field.

(D) For the county, because the ordinance is rationally related to a legitimate state interest—the health and safety of its citizens.

Question 47

A grantor executed and delivered a deed to his daughter conveying his ranch as follows: "To my daughter for life, but if my daughter dies survived by her husband and children, then to my daughter's husband for life, with the remainder in fee simple to my daughter's children; but if my daughter dies survived by her husband and no children, then to my son in fee simple." A few months later, the daughter married a husband; as a wedding gift, the grantor quitclaimed his interest in the ranch to the daughter's husband. Assume that the jurisdiction does not follow the doctrine of destructibility of contingent remainders.

A year later, the daughter died without children and without a will. The applicable law of intestate succession provides that the husband is the daughter's only heir. The son claims that the husband has no interest in the land.

Title to the ranch is held by whom?

(A) The husband, because of the doctrine of merger.

(B) The husband, because the daughter died intestate and her fee simple passed to him as her intestate heir.

(C) The son, because the interest granted to the daughter's spouse is void under the Rule Against Perpetuities.

(D) The son, because the daughter, although survived by her spouse, died without children.

Question 48

A grantor executed and delivered a deed to his son conveying his land as follows: "To my son for life, but if my son dies survived by his spouse and children, then to my son's spouse for life, with the remainder in fee simple to my son's children."

A year later, the son died survived by his spouse and two offspring, a girl and a boy. The boy died intestate two days after the son, leaving one child as his only heir.

What are the respective interests of the spouse, the girl, and the child in the land?

(A) The spouse has a life estate, the girl has an absolutely vested remainder, and the child has nothing.

(B) The spouse has fee simple ownership of the land, and the girl and the child have nothing.

(C) The spouse has a life estate, and the girl and the child have absolutely vested remainders.

(D) The spouse has a life estate, and the girl has a vested remainder subject to open.

Question 49

A hunter who held a hunting license issued by the state was hunting elk in that state. The hunter was hunting on private land when he spied an elk. The elk was 200 yards away, inside a fence that surrounded a federal military base. The hunter shot the elk from where he was standing, but entered the military base to retrieve the carcass. A federal statute prohibits the removal of wild animals or the carcasses thereof from United States military bases. The hunter is prosecuted under the statute.

The best argument in favor of upholding the statute as constitutional would be based on:

(A) The Supremacy Clause.

(B) The Army and Navy Clause.

(C) The Commerce Clause.

(D) The Privileges or Immunities Clause of the Fourteenth Amendment.

Question 50

An owner of a 60-acre parcel of land bordered by a lake on its east side sold the western 50 acres to a fisherman. The recorded deed recited that the fisherman, his heirs and assigns had the right to use the single lane gravel road to the lake that ran along the southern border of the owner's property. Subsequently, the fisherman died and his son inherited the 50-acre parcel. The son wishes to build a resort on the property but would need to pave and widen the lake road so it could bear the increased traffic. The owner files an action for declaratory judgment seeking to enjoin improvement of the road.

If the owner prevails, it will be because:

(A) The proposed improvement exceeds the scope of an easement by necessity.

(B) The proposed improvement constitutes a burden that exceeds the scope of an express easement.

(C) The servient owner has the obligation for maintenance of an easement for right-of-way, and hence can control the nature of its improvement.

(D) The proposed resort so changes the nature of the use of the dominant tenement that any easement has been abandoned.

MIXED SUBJECT SET 4 SUBJECT GUIDE

1. Constitutional Law
2. Evidence
3. Criminal Law
4. Torts
5. Torts
6. Constitutional Law
7. Torts
8. Evidence
9. Evidence
10. Contracts
11. Contracts
12. Contracts
13. Contracts
14. Real Property
15. Criminal Law
16. Constitutional Law
17. Constitutional Law
18. Real Property
19. Evidence
20. Evidence
21. Evidence
22. Criminal Law/Procedure
23. Evidence
24. Real Property
25. Torts
26. Torts
27. Contracts
28. Contracts
29. Real Property
30. Real Property
31. Constitutional Law
32. Criminal Law
33. Criminal Law
34. Torts
35. Torts
36. Evidence
37. Criminal Law
38. Contracts
39. Real Property
40. Torts
41. Criminal Law
42. Constitutional Law
43. Torts
44. Torts
45. Real Property
46. Constitutional Law
47. Real Property
48. Real Property
49. Constitutional Law
50. Real Property

MIXED SUBJECT ANSWERS - SET 4

Answer to Question 1

(D) Clearly this statute burdens interstate commerce by diverting purchases that would otherwise be made from interstate businesses to intrastate suppliers and by imposing a tax on interstate suppliers. Both requirements have the purpose and effect of imposing a direct burden on interstate commerce and, especially in the case of the tax, do so in a facially discriminatory manner. As such, they would be subjected to strict scrutiny, and would fail. (D) is therefore the best answer. (A) is incorrect because the measures involve economic and social matters and would, under the usual due process analysis, be subjected to rational basis scrutiny, which they would survive. (B) is wrong because there is a rational basis for the classification and no suspect classification or fundamental right is involved. (C) is wrong because while a corporation as a legal entity may be considered a person for some purposes, corporations are not citizens for the purposes of the Article IV Privileges and Immunities Clause.

Answer to Question 2

(C) This question involves an admission—*i.e.,* a statement by a party (the defendant) being offered against her. An admission is ***not considered a hearsay statement***. [Fed. R. Evid. 801(d)(2)] Thus, (C) appears to be correct—that the secretary's testimony about the defendant's statement will be admitted because it is not hearsay. (C) is not an ideal answer, though, because it is so incomplete. The fact that an item of evidence is nonhearsay does not automatically render it admissible. For example, if nonhearsay evidence is irrelevant, it would not be admissible. Thus, deciding whether (C) is the ***best*** answer requires a thorough assessment of the alternatives. (D) can be quickly discarded as incorrect. Impeachment evidence is not admissible until ***after*** the witness to be impeached has testified. It would be improper to admit the secretary's testimony for the purpose of impeaching the defendant's ***expected*** testimony as to the result of her own investigation of the accident. (A) is tempting, but it is also incorrect. Normally, an out-of-court statement of a declarant, like the in-court testimony of a witness, is admissible only if it was made ***with personal knowledge***. This requirement, however, does not apply to admissions. Thus, although the defendant's statement ("The neighbor just got hurt because I forgot to do my yard work") was made without personal knowledge, it will be admissible. As a party, the defendant will have ample opportunity to explain why she made the statement even though she lacked personal knowledge about the accident that injured the neighbor. The persuasiveness of her explanation will determine whether the jury takes her admission seriously. (B) is also incorrect. The common law requirement that lay witnesses were not permitted to give opinions, but only allowed to state facts, has been rejected in favor of a ***helpfulness standard***. For example, Rule 701 allows lay witnesses to give testimony in opinion form as long as it is helpful to a clear understanding of the testimony or the determination of a fact in issue. Similarly, an admission is not rendered inadmissible merely because it is in opinion form. For example, a party's statement that "I was negligent" or "It was all my fault" will be admitted into evidence as an admission. Therefore, although (C) is not an ideal answer, it is basically correct, and (A), (B), and (D) are clearly incorrect.

Answer to Question 3

(D) The woman will most likely be found not guilty, because what she planned to do with the bicycle did not create a substantial risk of permanent loss. To be guilty of larceny, a defendant must intend to steal, which can be established either by intending to permanently deprive or intending to create a substantial risk of loss of the item involved. The woman intended to take the bicycle, but she also intended to safely return it. Thus, she did not have the specific mental state necessary to be guilty of larceny. (A) is therefore incorrect. (B) is incorrect because the key factor is the defendant's mental state, not what actually happened to the bicycle. (C) is incorrect because it does not address the intent requirement. Furthermore, it incorrectly implies that some specific distance is required to satisfy the asportation requirement for larceny; in fact, any slight movement of the property will be sufficient.

Answer to Question 4

(B) But for the driver's negligent act of colliding with the plaintiff's car, the plaintiff would not have been injured. The driver is thus a cause in fact of the plaintiff's injuries. (A) is incorrect because the corporation's negligence would not qualify as an intervening act because it occurred earlier in time than the driver's. (C) is incorrect because the failure of the seat belt is not the type of intervening force that would relieve the driver from liability. (D) is incorrect because the "but for" test is used to establish liability in concurrent cause cases, not limit another's liability.

Answer to Question 5

(B) The plaintiff's claim against the corporation, as a commercial supplier of the product, would be based on strict liability in tort. As such, he would only need to establish that the car was dangerously defective in order to recover. A defective door latch would be a dangerous defect. (A) is incorrect because it is irrelevant. Even if the plaintiff could have discovered the defect, his failure to discover it would be, at best, contributory negligence, which is not a defense to strict liability in tort in jurisdictions retaining traditional contributory negligence rules. (C) is incorrect because the truck driver's negligence would qualify as a foreseeable intervening force that would not relieve the corporation from liability. (D) is incorrect because the corporation is strictly liable even though it did not know or have reason to know of the defect.

Answer to Question 6

(C) Standing requires an allegation of such a personal stake in the outcome of the controversy as to assure that concrete adverseness which sharpens the presentation of issues. Abstract injury is not enough; the plaintiff must show that he has sustained or is immediately in danger of sustaining some direct injury as the result of the challenged official conduct. The injury or threat of injury must be real and immediate, not conjectural or hypothetical. Here, the potential plaintiffs in (A) and (B) are merely thinking about selling or buying used cars in the state. Thus, any injury or threat of injury to them is strictly hypothetical and abstract. Consequently, the potential plaintiffs in (A) and (B) are unlikely to have standing. Likewise, the out-of-state manufacturer in (D), who ***might*** be required to indemnify its dealers in the state, is at this point able to assert merely a hypothetical injury, not one that is real and immediate. On the other hand, the potential plaintiff in (C), who already has a contract to sell used cars to a state dealer, is immediately in danger of sustaining a direct economic injury as a result of the statute—*i.e.*, costs associated with testing each car and bringing up to standard those cars found to be deficient.

Answer to Question 7

(D) A private nuisance action requires a showing that the defendant's interference with the use and enjoyment of the plaintiff's property was unreasonable. To be characterized as unreasonable, the severity of the inflicted injury must outweigh the utility of the defendant's conduct. Here, the fact that the pesticide is the only means of preventing destruction of the state's principal agricultural product would be the most persuasive additional fact for the company's defense. (A) is incorrect because coming to the nuisance is generally not a good defense to a nuisance action. (B) and (C) are incorrect even though they state factors which may be considered by a court in determining whether an injunction should be issued. The main question is whether the severity of the injury outweighs the utility of the defendant's conduct, and these two factors do not speak as well to this point as (D).

Answer to Question 8

(D) The question is proper. The defendant has taken the stand in his own defense, and therefore the prosecutor can attack his credibility as a witness. Under Federal Rule 609, evidence of conviction of a crime requiring proof of an act of dishonesty or false statement can always be used to attack a witness's character for truthfulness. (A) is incorrect because even if fraud were probative of the tendency to commit violence, evidence of other crimes is not admissible to prove that a person has a propensity to commit criminal acts. (C) is incorrect for the same reason. (B) is wrong because no foundation is needed to show a prior conviction for impeachment purposes.

Answer to Question 9

(D) The plaintiff's objection should be overruled. The husband's testimony is a classic example of evidence regarding habit, and the owner's habit is relevant to the issue of negligent entrustment. (A) is wrong because neither the Federal Rules nor the prevailing common law requires the corroboration of habit evidence. (B) and (C) are wrong because the testimony is evidence of habit, not character.

Answer to Question 10

(B) Prevention of performance by an irresistible, superhuman cause is an excuse for nonperformance of a contract, unless the parties stipulate to the contrary. The destruction of the lot by the forces of nature rendered performance impossible, so the builder need not perform. (A) is wrong because destruction of the property does not make the contract void; it merely discharges the builder. (C) is wrong because the builder's bankruptcy is irrelevant for this purpose. (D) is wrong because there was no mutual mistake.

Answer to Question 11

(D) The general rule is that a contractor is responsible for destruction of the premises under construction prior to completion. Once the residence is completed, risk of loss shifts to the owner. The contractor must perform the original contract without compensation for the work that was destroyed by the storm. Thus, (D) is correct and (C) is wrong. (A) is wrong because the subject matter was not destroyed; and even if it were, the contract would not be void. (B) is wrong because performance is not impossible; he can rebuild the residence.

Answer to Question 12

(C) Modern courts recognize that impracticability due to excessive and unreasonable difficulty or expense is a defense to breach of contract for nonperformance. Since the cost to the builder to perform under the original contract would exceed more than double what he would be paid, under the modern view, he would be excused from performance by commercial impracticability. Unlike destruction of the building itself before completion, which will not discharge a contractor's duty, the erosion of the lot, which destroys the means of performing the contract, will generally not be one of the risks that a builder will be deemed to have assumed. Thus, (D) is wrong. (A) is wrong because the builder's bankruptcy is irrelevant for this purpose. (B) is wrong because there is no mutual mistake here.

Answer to Question 13

(C) Performance is excused where prevented by operation of law, despite any stipulation to the contrary. Because governmental interference made performance of the contract as contemplated illegal, the contractor is excused from performance, even though some performance is possible. Thus, (C) is correct, and (D) is incorrect. (A) is incorrect because there was no mutual mistake when the contract was formed. (B) is wrong because the owner did not breach the contract.

Answer to Question 14

(C) On the happening of the prohibited event (using the land for other than residential purposes), the taker's fee simple determinable automatically came to an end, and the owner was entitled to present possession. Not having claimed possession within the applicable seven-year period, and with the taker's possession being open, notorious, continuous, and adverse, any action by the owner or his heirs is now barred by adverse possession. Thus, (A) and (B) are incorrect. (D) is incorrect because a possibility of reverter becomes possessory automatically upon termination of the prior determinable estate. Unlike a right of entry, a grantor does not have to assert a possibility of reverter in order for a cause of action to arise.

Answer to Question 15

(B) Under the facts of this case, to support a finding of murder, the trial court would have to find that the shooter acted either intentionally or with malice aforethought. The facts clearly indicate that the shooter did not know of the car, so it cannot be said that he shot at it intentionally, and therefore (A) is not correct. "Malice aforethought" can mean that the defendant is acting with a "wanton" state of mind. There is little question that shooting a rifle through a front door can be considered "wanton." Thus, the question is whether the shooter's intoxication was sufficient to negate this state of mind. If a defendant's lack of awareness results from voluntary intoxication, his conduct will nevertheless be deemed wanton. (C) is not a correct analysis of the issue, because his intentional act was firing the rifle, not shooting at the car. (D) is not the best answer, because although there is the possibility that the shooter might have been able to show only gross negligence, there is sufficient evidence to support a finding of malice aforethought and murder.

Answer to Question 16

(B) This situation presents a possible violation of the Equal Protection Clause. A state may not favor established residents over new residents. To do so in an area that affects a person's ability to engage in his livelihood impedes migration from state to state. Interstate travel is a fundamental right, and a classification that burdens it would trigger a strict scrutiny analysis. In any case, the classification would be subjected to something more than the mere rationality test. (A) is incorrect because this is not an area reserved to the states, and even if it were, the United States Constitution would take precedence over state law. (C) is wrong because the Fifth Amendment applies only to federal, not state, government action. (D) is wrong because the Privileges and Immunities Clause does not apply to aliens.

Answer to Question 17

(C) The statutes violate the Privileges and Immunities Clause of Article IV, which prohibits discrimination against nonresidents with respect to essential activities (*e.g.*, pursuing a livelihood) unless (i) the discrimination is closely related to a substantial state purpose, and (ii) less restrictive means are not available. Here, other controls could be placed on fishing without discriminating against out-of-state fishermen. (A) is wrong because, even though Congress has not acted in this area, the statutes would still be unconstitutional in light of the negative implications of the "dormant" Commerce Clause. Congressional silence is, therefore, irrelevant. (B) states a due process test which, even if applicable, would not preclude a finding of unconstitutionality on other grounds. (D) is wrong because the activity here does not involve foreign commerce—this is a dispute between one state and a citizen of another state.

Answer to Question 18

(A) The grant is valid because the son was a life in being at the time the interest was created. (B) is incorrect because a reversionary interest is an interest remaining in the grantor. (D) is incorrect because a possibility of reverter is the interest left in the grantor after a conveyance of a fee simple determinable. Here, the owner did not create such an estate. (C) is obviously incorrect, because the language of the deed clearly shows that the owner was not giving his daughter the complete interest in this property; she received a fee simple subject to divestment by the son's executory interest.

Answer to Question 19

(D) In a criminal case, other crimes and wrongs of the defendant may be admissible even though they are not charged, but they are not automatically admissible. There are two basic principles: other crimes or wrongs are not admissible to show that the defendant is a bad person, nor are they admissible to show propensity of the defendant to commit this crime. Other crimes or wrongs may be admissible if they are relevant to show motive, intent, absence of mistake, identity or common scheme or plan, unless the judge determines that the probative value is substantially outweighed by prejudice. (A) and (B) are therefore wrong. (C) is wrong because extrinsic evidence of specific crimes is not admissible to rebut evidence of good character. While (D) calls for a determination on the part of the trial judge and could be debated, it is the best answer because (A), (B), and (C) are incorrect statements of the law.

Answer to Question 20

(C) The description is inadmissible as hearsay not within an exception. (B) is wrong. Under the Federal Rules of Evidence, prior identification can be admissible. The description is in the nature of prior testimony or prior identification. To be admissible, however, the declarant must testify at the trial and be subject to cross-examination. Since the night watchman died, this requirement cannot be satisfied. On these facts, there are no exceptions to the hearsay rule that would make the description admissible. (A) is wrong because before a document can be admitted as a past recollection recorded, the person whose statement appears in the document must be on the witness stand. (D) would have no bearing on the admissibility of the description.

Answer to Question 21

(B) The question is proper to show that the defendant is inclined to lie. Because the question involves a crime of dishonesty, and the conviction is less than 10 years old, the question is proper on cross-examination because it goes to the defendant's credibility. (A) is wrong because evidence is not admissible to show general bad character or propensity to commit crimes. (C) is wrong because this crime has plenty of probative value on the issue of credibility and because most courts hold that impeachment with a crime requiring proof or admission of an act of dishonesty or false statement cannot be excluded as too prejudicial. (D) is wrong because similarity to the crime charged is not required by the Federal Rules of Evidence.

Answer to Question 22

(D) The prosecutor is required by the Due Process Clause to prove each and every element of a crime beyond a reasonable doubt. One of the elements of larceny is an intent to permanently deprive a victim of his or her property, and the instructions in this case put the burden of proof on the defendant to show that there was no such intent. This relieves the prosecution of its burden because it implies that there is a presumption that the defendant intended to permanently deprive her of her jewels. (A) is wrong. The jury does have the power to ignore the defendant's testimony, but the conviction will be reversed because of the unconstitutional instruction on burden of proof. (B) is wrong. The defendant is not required to rebut the state's evidence; the state must prove each element beyond a reasonable doubt. (C) is not the best answer. While it is true that in some jurisdictions the judge cannot comment on the evidence in a criminal case, that prohibition would not be violated by an appropriate instruction on burden of proof.

Answer to Question 23

(A) This question raises the issue of whether an employee's out-of-court statement will be attributed to the employer, and thus considered an admission when the employer is a party. The statement can be attributed to the employer, provided it was made (i) while the person was employed by the employer (not before or after the period of employment) and (ii) provided the statement related to the employment. Thus (A) is correct. The truck driver's statement was made while he was employed by the delivery company, and it related to his employment since it pertained to an accident that occurred when he was driving a company truck, presumably in the course of employment. Thus, (C) is incorrect. That the truck driver is no longer employed by the delivery company does not bear on the admissibility of his statement; what counts is that he was employed at the time he made the statement. (D) is also incorrect. That the delivery company did not authorize the truck driver to make the statement does not preclude it from being admissible. Although one basis for attributing an employee's statement to the employer is the employer's authorization for the employee to speak on its behalf about the matter, that is not the only one. (B) is incorrect because there is little reason to conclude that the truck driver's statement was an "excited utterance" within the meaning of that hearsay exception. The question does not indicate that the truck driver spoke in an excited manner or that he was agitated. That the truck driver spoke shortly after the accident would not alone be sufficient to make his statement an "excited utterance."

Answer to Question 24

(A) The lot B owner had exclusive, continuous possession of the three-foot strip for the requisite statutory period. This possession was open and notorious; it was also hostile (adverse). The lot B owner's mistake as to the ownership of the three-foot strip is not determinative. The lot B owner has held adversely because his actions appear to the community to be a claim of ownership and he is not holding with permission of the owner. Thus, (D) is incorrect. (C) is incorrect because the open and notorious nature of the lot B owner's possession was sufficient to put the true owner on notice that a possession adverse to her title had been taken. (B) is an incorrect statement of the law; there is no such presumption.

Answer to Question 25

(A) The facts state that the carpenter swung the hammer at the striker "intending to frighten" him. Thus, the carpenter did an act with the intent of causing the apprehension of immediate harmful or offensive contact, *i.e.*, an "assault." Because the striker was actually hit by the hammer head, the trial court would utilize the ***transferred intent doctrine*** to supply the necessary intent for battery. It makes no difference that the carpenter may not have known that the hammer was defective, because he set in motion the force that injured the striker; hence, (C) is an improper answer. (B) and (D) are not correct answers because they both go to the issue of a defense, and a person is not privileged to use deadly force against another no matter how provoking the other's mere statements may have been. Clearly, being hit with a hammer would be considered deadly force.

Answer to Question 26

(D) The local newspaper's best defense is that the physician is dead. Only living persons can be defamed; defamation of a deceased person is not an actionable tort. Thus, because the physician is dead, the newspaper can obtain dismissal of the defamation action without having to establish any defamation defenses. Therefore, (D) is correct. (A) is not as good a defense as (D) because, in order to use the defense of absence of malice, the newspaper would have to establish that the physician was a public figure, which would be more difficult than showing that the doctor is dead. Moreover, it is not conclusive from the facts that the physician is a public figure because the facts merely state that he was prominent in the community. (B) is incorrect because a retraction, while it may show lack of actual malice in mitigation of damages, would not necessarily eliminate all of the harm to the physician's reputation. (C) is incorrect because the fact that the reporter got his information from a secretary at the medical school does not preclude liability for defamation. At most, that fact may be asserted to disprove malice if the physician was a public figure or negligence if the doctor's death was a matter of public concern.

Answer to Question 27

(A) The boyfriend did not promise to do anything he was not otherwise obligated to do in bargained-for exchange for the student's promise, so no consideration supported the latter's promise. If the agreement were otherwise enforceable, none of the other facts offered by the answers would prevent it from being carried out. (B) is incorrect because a court will not examine the promisor's intent when making a promise. (C) is incorrect because mistake as to a fact that motivated the contract is not a defense under these circumstances; the student had assumed the risk of mistake by making the promise without being certain of the cause of the accident. (D) is similarly incorrect. Mistake as to the value of the promise is generally a risk assumed by the parties.

Answer to Question 28

(A) The homeowner offered to pay the doctor if he treated the injured newspaper delivery boy. The doctor accepted by treating the boy; this treatment was also his consideration for the contract. Thus, the homeowner was contractually bound to pay for the medical expenses and (A) is correct. (B) is incorrect because the homeowner's promise need not have been in writing to be enforceable. The requirement of a writing under the Statute of Frauds for promises to pay the debt of another is not applicable here. The homeowner's promise was not a suretyship promise that was collateral to a promise of the boy; it was an independent promise by the homeowner to be primarily liable for the boy's medical expenses, and therefore need not be in writing to be enforceable. (C) is incorrect because the doctor's treatment is the consideration for the homeowner's promise to pay. There is nothing in the facts to suggest that the doctor had incurred a preexisting duty to treat the boy until he recovered; he treated the boy, sending the homeowner the bill in reliance on her promise. Hence, a court will find sufficient consideration here to avoid a preexisting duty issue. (D) is incorrect because the doctor's treatment was the benefit that the homeowner sought to derive from her bargain. Remember that the benefit need not have economic value; the homeowner's benefit here is her peace of mind.

Answer to Question 29

(A) Because the sister informed her brother that he could develop the eastern five acres of the land, and because he reasonably relied on her statement to his detriment, she probably will be estopped to deny its effect. (B) is incorrect. Where the language of the grant is clear and a joint tenancy is created, no presumption is needed or applies. The joint tenancy cannot later be changed by subsequent informal action. (C) is wrong because an oral agreement is not effective to terminate a joint tenancy. (D) is an incorrect statement of the law. A joint tenant may not pass an interest to anyone at death, due to the right of survivorship.

Answer to Question 30

(C) The buyer owns the land because the farmer is not protected by the recording act. In a race-notice jurisdiction such as described, a subsequent purchaser must have taken ***without notice*** of the earlier sale and must have been the first to record. Otherwise the recording act will not apply. The farmer was indeed the first to record, but he took with notice that the property had been sold before. It does not matter how the subsequent purchaser learns of the earlier sale; if that person knows about it, he loses. Because the recording act does not apply to protect the farmer, the common law rule of first-in-time, first-in-right gives title to the buyer. Thus, (C) is correct and (B) is incorrect. (A) is incorrect because recording does not cure the problem of the farmer taking with notice. (D) is not as good an answer as (C) because if the recording act did apply, the buyer's receiving a deed before the farmer would not give her superior rights to the land.

Answer to Question 31

(B) As a general matter, a state may regulate in ways that impact on interstate commerce as long as the regulation does so only indirectly and the benefits outweigh the burdens imposed by compliance with the regulation. [Kassel v. Consolidated Freightways Corp. (1981)] When, as here, only a bare assertion that the regulation would increase safety is involved, a court will generally find that the regulation is invalid. This does not mean that a state could not prevail if it proved that the benefits of the regulation do in fact outweigh the burdens. Indeed, the Court intimated that such would be the case in *Bibb v. Navajo Freight Lines, Inc.* (1959). But state A has not made a sufficient showing here, and the trucking firm has presented colorable "expert" evidence to the contrary.

(A) is incorrect because economic and social regulations are tested at the rational basis level for due process purposes, and even the minimal showing here would suffice for the state. (C) states a correct premise (*i.e.,* that the state is regulating for highway safety), but an incorrect result, and is wrong. (D) is wrong because the state has in fact made no such showing before the court. Thus, while there is a normal presumption of constitutionality, the state here has not met its burden in defending the measure in the face of contrary, expert evidence.

Answer to Question 32

(D) A conspiracy requires an agreement between two or more people to accomplish an unlawful act or objective. The parties must intend to enter into the agreement and intend to achieve the objective of the agreement. The bartender and her friend agreed to defraud the insurance company and had the requisite intent. They also committed an overt act in furtherance of that intent. Thus, they can be convicted of conspiracy. (A) is wrong because the crime is complete upon agreement with the requisite intent; the objective does not have to be accomplished. (B) is wrong because impossibility is not a defense to conspiracy. (C) is wrong. Taking the neighbor's property could make them guilty of some other crime, but it is not necessary to convict them of conspiracy.

Answer to Question 33

(D) Common law burglary is the breaking and entering of the dwelling house of another in the nighttime with the intent to commit a felony or larceny inside the house. However, in addition to the specific intent to commit a felony, the defendant also must have intended to break and enter the dwelling. If the defendant reasonably believed it was his acquaintance's home, he would not have the intent to break and enter, as he would believe he had permission to break into and enter the house. (A) is wrong because mistake of law generally is not a defense. Furthermore, the defendant did not appear to be acting under the impression that his acts were lawful. Thus, mistake of law is not an issue in the question. (B) is wrong; opening the window, even though it was ajar, would be considered a breaking under the better view. (C) is wrong; there clearly was an entry.

Answer to Question 34

(A) The neighbor's best theory is that the landowner negligently failed to control the conduct of his guests. A landowner has a duty to exercise reasonable care with respect to his own activities on the land and to control the conduct of others on his property so as to avoid unreasonable risk of harm to those outside the property. It was reasonably foreseeable that a large skyrocket might malfunction and cause injury or damage to the person or property of someone outside the landowner's land, especially to an adjoining landowner. By failing to prevent his guest from lighting the skyrocket, the landowner breached his duty to control the conduct of persons on his property so as to avoid an unreasonable risk of harm to those outside the property. This breach actually and proximately caused the damage to the neighbor's garage. Therefore, the neighbor would prevail under the theory set forth in (A). Regarding (B), it is questionable whether the setting off of fireworks constitutes an abnormally dangerous activity. However, even if this is deemed to be an abnormally dangerous activity, simply failing to control the guest's activities will not render the landowner strictly liable for harm that results. The landowner would owe an absolute duty to make safe an abnormally dangerous activity in which he was actually engaged (*e.g.,* if he himself was setting off the fireworks or if he had organized the party with a purpose of having his guests shoot fireworks out of his backyard). However, he was not so engaged. At most, he failed to prevent someone else from shooting fireworks. For this, the landowner can be held liable on a negligence basis, but not in strict liability. (C) is incorrect for two reasons. First, the neighbor's being invited to the landowner's party does not make the neighbor an "invitee." A social guest is deemed to be a licensee, *i.e.,* one who enters on land with the permission of the owner or possessor for his own purpose rather than for the benefit of the owner or possessor. Second, at the time of the damage to the garage, the neighbor was not even on the landowner's land. Thus, the neighbor is neither a licensee nor an invitee; the landowner's duty toward him is one of ordinary care because he is an adjoining property owner. (D) is incorrect because the landowner did not violate the ordinance. The precise standard of care in a common law negligence case may be established by proving the applicability to the case of a statute providing for a criminal penalty. Where the plaintiff is in the class intended to be protected by the statute and the statute was designed to prevent the type of harm suffered by the plaintiff, violation of the statute is negligence per se in most jurisdictions, *i.e.,* plaintiff will have established a conclusive presumption of duty and breach of duty. The ordinance here at issue proscribes the sale of fireworks within the city. The landowner did not engage in any transaction involving fireworks. Thus, he did not violate the ordinance, and negligence per se is inapplicable.

Answer to Question 35

(B) The student probably will be able to avoid liability if he can establish that he built the bonfire to avoid damaging the neighbor's shed. The element of breach of duty in a negligence case requires a showing that the defendant acted unreasonably, which is a question for the trier of fact. Assuming that the student owed a duty to avoid harm to the neighbor's shed, the student will be able to argue that he did not breach that duty because he positioned the bonfire to avoid damaging the neighbor's shed. If the facts support this argument, the student probably will be able to avoid liability to the neighbor. (A) is incorrect because customary methods of conduct do not conclusively establish the standard for determining whether a defendant's conduct amounted to negligence. Although it may have been an "accepted custom" in the community to light bonfires at homecoming, this custom may in fact present an unreasonable risk of injury to persons in the position of the neighbor. Thus, the argument in (A) does not enable the student to avoid liability. (C) is incorrect because all of the direct consequences of a negligent act are viewed as proximately caused by that act. If it was reasonably foreseeable that lighting the bonfire would cause damage to the neighbor's shed, then the student's conduct was negligent. If some damage to the shed from the bonfire was foreseeable, the student is liable for the total destruction that occurred, despite the fact that the shed would not have burned down if it were not built of highly flammable material (*i.e.,* the student must "take his plaintiff as he finds him"). (D) is incorrect because there really is no restricted scope of liability for the class president with respect to persons outside his property. A landowner has a duty to exercise reasonable care with respect to his own activities on the land so as to avoid unreasonable risk of harm to others outside the property. Thus, the class president would be liable to the neighbor if he had built the bonfire and thereby created an unreasonable risk of harm to the neighbor's shed, resulting in damage to the shed. The student's status as a guest on the property does not excuse the student from the duty to refrain from creating an unreasonable risk of harm to the person or property of a foreseeable plaintiff, such as the neighbor. Therefore, (D) presents nothing that will enable the student to avoid liability.

Answer to Question 36

(B) Other crimes and wrongs are generally not admissible to prove that a person acted in conformity with his bad character. They are sometimes admissible to establish the identity of the accused.

Other crimes are admissible on identity when they are committed in a very unique way that shows what amounts to a "signature" of the perpetrator. Theoretically, even signature crimes can be excluded if the judge determines that the probative value is substantially outweighed by prejudice. However, a crime qualifying as a signature crime is highly probative and would rarely be excluded under that theory. (C) and (D) are not wrong but, given the highly unique weapon, the court should hold that the evidence is admissible. (A) is wrong. One other crime could not establish habit.

Answer to Question 37

(C) The owner would be acquitted if the jury found that she was reasonable in believing that the house was abandoned. Under the terms of the statute, the actor must willfully shut off the gas to an inhabited dwelling. The requirement of an inhabited dwelling is a material element of the crime. A reasonable mistake about a material element will negate criminal liability for all crimes except strict liability offenses. This is not a strict liability offense because a mental state of willfulness is required. Thus, if the owner reasonably believed that the house was abandoned, she made a reasonable mistake about whether it was an inhabited dwelling, and she should be found not guilty. (A) is wrong because, as mentioned, this is not a strict liability offense; willfulness is required. (B) is not as good an answer as (C) because there is no specific amount of time that she must wait before reasonably concluding that the house has been abandoned. (B) assumes that the jury will find her actions unreasonable, but it is also possible that they will find her actions reasonable. (D) is wrong because if all the elements of the statute were present, the owner would not be excused from criminal liability simply because the couple had been negligent in mailing the rent check.

Answer to Question 38

(C) If the graduate prevails, it will be because the court has applied the promissory estoppel exception to the Statute of Frauds. [*See* Restatement (Second) of Contracts §§129, 139] Because the graduate relied on his aunt's promise by moving in with her and caring for her, and because the monetary value of his services is difficult to determine, specific enforcement of the aunt's promise is necessary to avoid injustice. [*See* Restatement (Second) of Contracts §129, illus. 10] (D) is wrong because the graduate's performance of the oral agreement is not such as could be explained only by the existence of an oral agreement to convey the brownstone. The daughter has done nothing but assert her legal rights, and a familial relationship does not obviate the Statute of Frauds. Thus, (A) and (B) are incorrect.

Answer to Question 39

(B) An inter vivos conveyance by one joint tenant of his interest in the property severs the joint tenancy and changes it to a tenancy in common. (A) is wrong because, as discussed above, severance results in a tenancy in common. The woman and brother could not hold as joint tenants because the unity of time is lacking. (C) is incorrect because a tenancy by the entirety can be created only in a husband and wife. The couple was not married until after the creation of the tenancy, and their marriage does not change the nature of their title to the land. (D) is wrong because the man's conveyance to his brother severed the joint tenancy.

Answer to Question 40

(C) The facts do not make out a claim for invasion of privacy in any of the four forms that invasion of privacy takes. The photograph was not an appropriation for commercial purposes because it was incidental to a legitimate news story and was not used in an advertisement. The photograph did not involve intrusion because it was taken in a public place. The news feature did not involve false light because the caption correctly identified her as the boy's mother and the facts do not indicate anything else to suggest that the photograph conveyed a false impression. Finally, the mother's appearance at the police station simply was not a private fact, because it is generally agreed that anything visible in a public place may be recorded and given circulation by means of a photograph. (A) and (B) are therefore incorrect. (D) is incorrect because truth is not a defense to most invasion of privacy actions. Even for false light invasion of privacy, the fact that the caption was true does not preclude recovery if the photograph otherwise conveyed a false impression. Thus, (C) is a better choice than (D).

Answer to Question 41

(D) The homeowner likely would be found guilty. At common law, murder was the unlawful killing of a human being with malice aforethought. Malice aforethought could be established with any one of the following states of mind: intent to kill; intent to cause serious bodily harm; the depraved heart killing (a reckless indifference to an unjustifiably high risk to human life); or the commission of a felony. The homeowner would be guilty of murder. Firing a gun out of his window at a car would demonstrate a reckless indifference to a high risk to human life. It is unlikely that the motorist would be guilty of murder. While his action might be classified as negligent or even reckless, it would not represent a depraved heart (reckless indifference to life) state of mind. Thus, (A), (B) and (C) are incorrect.

Answer to Question 42

(A) Because the state statute conflicts with the terms of the federal contract, the federal contract must take precedence, pursuant to the Supremacy Clause and principles of federal immunity from state regulation. (B) is not a good answer because there are no facts indicating that the statute was enacted after the contract was formed; in fact, the problem implies that the reverse is true. (C) is not the best answer because, although it is possible that a state's regulation of the manufacture of goods might affect interstate commerce so as to invoke the commerce power, the facts of this problem do not indicate any likelihood of such a circumstance and are insufficient to be conclusive anyway. (D) is incorrect. Thus, (A) is the only correct answer.

Answer to Question 43

(A) The court should deny the driver's motion because a jury could find that a reasonable person, observing a ball roll into the street, would slow down further to avoid the foreseeable risk of hitting a child darting into the street. (B) is wrong because the parents' potential negligence, even if it gave rise to a contribution claim by the driver against them, would not cut off the child's claim against the driver, because the driver's negligence would remain both an actual and a proximate cause of the accident—even if parental negligence was also a cause. A parent's negligence ordinarily is not imputed to a child, and no other basis appears from the fact pattern for doing so. Hence, the driver's motion would not be denied for that reason. (C) raises the possibility of a contributory negligence defense. A child, however, is usually held to the standard of a reasonable child of like age, intelligence, and maturity. The facts tell us nothing about the child's age, intelligence, and maturity, and it will be up to the jury to determine whether the child was negligent. (D) is wrong because reasonable care in the circumstances could require driving at less than the speed limit, as noted above.

Answer to Question 44

(D) The pedestrian had fallen and was in "helpless peril" when the banker's car struck him. If the banker had the "last clear chance" to avoid the accident, that would override any contributory negligence on the pedestrian's part. (A) is incorrect because "danger invites rescue," and it is foreseeable that an adult would rush out to aid a child in danger. (B) is incorrect because one may be negligent even if speed limits are observed. (C) is incorrect because relatives are not the only people who may be expected to be rescuers, even though the pedestrian did not have a ***duty*** to rescue the girl.

Answer to Question 45

(C) Because the land was held in joint tenancy, all of the interest in the land could only be conveyed by both of the joint tenants. The forgery of the man's signature on the deed is ineffective to convey his interest in the property. Thus, (B) is incorrect. However, the woman's signature on the deed will serve to convey her interest in the land. (D) is therefore incorrect. This conveyance of the woman's interest in the property terminates the joint tenancy, leaving the man and the buyer holding their interests as tenants in common. Thus, (A) is incorrect.

Answer to Question 46

(D) Where no suspect or quasi-suspect classification or fundamental rights are involved, the equal protection analysis uses the rational basis test: if the statute is rationally related to a legitimate state interest, it is valid. Because there appears to be a rational basis for the challenged legislation—protecting the environment and the citizenry from the effects of potentially permanent artificial materials—the law is valid. (A) is incorrect because it assumes that the state must use the least restrictive alternative, but that is not required except when strict scrutiny is used. There is no basis for such review under the facts of this question because there is neither a suspect classification nor a fundamental right. (B) is wrong for the same reason: under equal protection analysis, a "compelling purpose" is required only when strict scrutiny is used. Challenges to economic regulations are subjected only to a rational basis test. (C) is incorrect because whether Congress has entered the field is irrelevant to an equal protection analysis. The call of the question specifically asks for the determination of the equal protection challenge; federal preemption issues are irrelevant here.

Answer to Question 47

(D) The ranch will pass exactly as expressed by the grantor in the deed. Because the daughter died without children, the husband does not have a life estate. (A) is wrong because, absent applicability of the doctrine of destructibility of contingent remainders, merger occurs when a life estate and a vested remainder or reversion is held by the same person—not the case here because the husband has no life estate. The daughter's interest is a life estate; thus, she has no interest to pass to the husband by intestate succession. (B) is therefore wrong. (C) is wrong because the Rule Against Perpetuities is not violated; the spouse's interest will vest, if at all, within a life in being plus 21 years, because the daughter's spouse will be identifiable at her death.

Answer to Question 48

(C) The spouse has a life estate, the girl has an absolutely vested remainder, and the child, by intestate succession, will inherit the boy's absolutely vested remainder. The remainder to the son's children was vested subject to open upon the birth of his first child. Because the son cannot have any more children after his death, all members of the class are ascertained at that time and the remainder becomes indefeasibly vested. Because the grant was to the son's "children" rather than "issue" or "descendants," there is no unborn child problem. (A) is wrong because the boy's vested remainder is inheritable by the child. (B) is wrong because the spouse has only a life estate—not a fee simple absolute—and the girl and the child have absolutely vested remainders. (D) is wrong because the class gift in the limitation "to the remainder in fee simple to son's children" closes on son's death; no children thereafter can be born to him, which precludes the remainder's being "subject to open."

Answer to Question 49

(A) Absent consent or cession, a state retains jurisdiction over federal lands within its territory. However, Congress also retains the power to enact legislation respecting such lands, pursuant to the Property Clause. When Congress so acts, the federal legislation necessarily overrides conflicting state laws under the Supremacy Clause. Here, the laws of the state permit the hunter to hunt in the state. However, under the Supremacy Clause, the federal statute overrides the state law with respect to matters involving the federal military base, which is located in the state. The power to raise and maintain an army and navy does not necessarily include the right to regulate certain property. Thus, (B) is wrong. The Commerce Clause could possibly be a proper basis for upholding the statute, but there is nothing in the facts indicating that Congress has exercised the commerce power in this manner. (A) is therefore a better answer. (D) is wrong because the Privileges or Immunities Clause applies to state action.

Answer to Question 50

(B) If the owner prevails it will be because the proposed easement constitutes an excessive burden. The grant was for use of a single lane gravel road, not for a wider, paved road, and a court could easily find this burden excessive. (A) is incorrect because the easement involved is an express easement, not an easement by necessity. (C) is an incorrect statement of law; the owner of a servient estate does not have the obligation to maintain an easement and cannot unilaterally control the nature of its improvement. (D) is incorrect because a surcharging of the easement does not terminate the easement; it merely gives the owner of the servient estate the right to stop the additional use.

Mixed Subject Set 5 Answer Sheet

1.	Ⓐ Ⓑ Ⓒ Ⓓ	26.	Ⓐ Ⓑ Ⓒ Ⓓ
2.	Ⓐ Ⓑ Ⓒ Ⓓ	27.	Ⓐ Ⓑ Ⓒ Ⓓ
3.	Ⓐ Ⓑ Ⓒ Ⓓ	28.	Ⓐ Ⓑ Ⓒ Ⓓ
4.	Ⓐ Ⓑ Ⓒ Ⓓ	29.	Ⓐ Ⓑ Ⓒ Ⓓ
5.	Ⓐ Ⓑ Ⓒ Ⓓ	30.	Ⓐ Ⓑ Ⓒ Ⓓ
6.	Ⓐ Ⓑ Ⓒ Ⓓ	31.	Ⓐ Ⓑ Ⓒ Ⓓ
7.	Ⓐ Ⓑ Ⓒ Ⓓ	32.	Ⓐ Ⓑ Ⓒ Ⓓ
8.	Ⓐ Ⓑ Ⓒ Ⓓ	33.	Ⓐ Ⓑ Ⓒ Ⓓ
9.	Ⓐ Ⓑ Ⓒ Ⓓ	34.	Ⓐ Ⓑ Ⓒ Ⓓ
10.	Ⓐ Ⓑ Ⓒ Ⓓ	35.	Ⓐ Ⓑ Ⓒ Ⓓ
11.	Ⓐ Ⓑ Ⓒ Ⓓ	36.	Ⓐ Ⓑ Ⓒ Ⓓ
12.	Ⓐ Ⓑ Ⓒ Ⓓ	37.	Ⓐ Ⓑ Ⓒ Ⓓ
13.	Ⓐ Ⓑ Ⓒ Ⓓ	38.	Ⓐ Ⓑ Ⓒ Ⓓ
14.	Ⓐ Ⓑ Ⓒ Ⓓ	39.	Ⓐ Ⓑ Ⓒ Ⓓ
15.	Ⓐ Ⓑ Ⓒ Ⓓ	40.	Ⓐ Ⓑ Ⓒ Ⓓ
16.	Ⓐ Ⓑ Ⓒ Ⓓ	41.	Ⓐ Ⓑ Ⓒ Ⓓ
17.	Ⓐ Ⓑ Ⓒ Ⓓ	42.	Ⓐ Ⓑ Ⓒ Ⓓ
18.	Ⓐ Ⓑ Ⓒ Ⓓ	43.	Ⓐ Ⓑ Ⓒ Ⓓ
19.	Ⓐ Ⓑ Ⓒ Ⓓ	44.	Ⓐ Ⓑ Ⓒ Ⓓ
20.	Ⓐ Ⓑ Ⓒ Ⓓ	45.	Ⓐ Ⓑ Ⓒ Ⓓ
21.	Ⓐ Ⓑ Ⓒ Ⓓ	46.	Ⓐ Ⓑ Ⓒ Ⓓ
22.	Ⓐ Ⓑ Ⓒ Ⓓ	47.	Ⓐ Ⓑ Ⓒ Ⓓ
23.	Ⓐ Ⓑ Ⓒ Ⓓ	48.	Ⓐ Ⓑ Ⓒ Ⓓ
24.	Ⓐ Ⓑ Ⓒ Ⓓ	49.	Ⓐ Ⓑ Ⓒ Ⓓ
25.	Ⓐ Ⓑ Ⓒ Ⓓ	50.	Ⓐ Ⓑ Ⓒ Ⓓ

MIXED SUBJECT QUESTIONS - SET 5

Question 1

In a fraud trial, the prosecution alleges that the defendant invited the victims to become local investors/distributors for a supposed cosmetics manufacturer. The defendant claims she was brought into the scheme by the purported head of the manufacturer's sales department and was just following instructions with no knowledge of the fraud. The prosecution intends to call a witness to testify that the defendant convinced him to invest in a similar scheme involving household products five years ago.

Should the trial court admit this evidence over the defendant's objection?

(A) No, because evidence of other acts or wrongs is not admissible to prove character and action in conformity therewith.

(B) No, because it is irrelevant.

(C) Yes, because it is evidence of the defendant's character for dishonesty.

(D) Yes, because it is evidence of the defendant's state of mind.

Question 2

In an accountant's trial for filing fraudulent tax reports, the prosecution calls a former colleague of the accountant, and she testifies that the accountant's reputation in the community is for frequently participating in very questionable reporting, often resulting in unnecessary risk for his clients. She testifies further that she thinks the accountant is dishonest.

Should the trial court admit this evidence over the accountant's objection?

(A) No, because the prosecution cannot initiate evidence of the defendant's character.

(B) No, because use of the colleague's opinion is improper.

(C) Yes, because it is evidence of the defendant's character for dishonesty.

(D) Yes, because it is evidence of habit.

Question 3

In early January, a famous fast food restaurant chain entered into a contract with a consulting firm specializing in labor-intensive industries. This writing was signed by both parties, and provided that if at least 2,000 work-hours per restaurant are eliminated, the restaurant chain will pay to the consultants within 90 days of installation of new food production systems at the local restaurants a first installment of $1 million. It went on to provide that upon installation of new food processing systems nationwide, the restaurant chain will pay to the consultants a second and final installment of $1.5 million, that nationwide installation must be completed by January 15 of the following year, and that any amendments to the agreement must be in writing and signed by both parties.

The consultants immediately began work on the restructuring of their client's food processing methods. On September 5, the consultants had designed a radical change in the food production system that could be implemented by October 1, and they demanded payment of the first installment payment of $1 million.

Were the consultants entitled to payment of the first installment when they completed design work on the new system on September 5?

(A) No, because substantial completion of installation of the system in local restaurants would be a constructive condition precedent to the restaurant chain's duty to pay.

(B) No, because the phrase "within 90 days of installation" would be interpreted to mean within 90 days ***after*** installation.

(C) Yes, because September 5 was "within 90 days of installation" of the food processing system on October 1.

(D) Yes, because the consultants had completed work on designing the new system and could expect to install it within 90 days.

Question 4

After extensive negotiations, representatives for an automobile manufacturer and a tire maker orally agreed on the specifications for a supply of tires. The lawyer for the car manufacturer then drafted a written agreement and sent it to the tire maker's lawyer, who modified the draft and sent it back to the car manufacturer. This writing was signed by both parties. The tire maker now brings an action for breach of contract against the car manufacturer seeking damages. The car manufacturer attempts to introduce the testimony of its chief negotiator describing the oral agreement with the tire maker representatives that the tires would meet certain requirements of the car models. The tire maker objects, arguing that the parol evidence rule bars admission of this testimony.

Which of the following is the best argument supporting admission of the testimony?

(A) The memorandum signed by the parties was not a complete integration of their agreement.

(B) The parol evidence rule does not bar evidence interpreting a written agreement.

(C) The car manufacturer detrimentally relied on the oral agreement in signing the memorandum.

(D) The parol evidence rule does not exclude misrepresentations.

Question 5

An applesauce bottler wishing to redesign his factory entered into an agreement with a contractor. The contract provided that a new plastic bottle system, replacing the glass bottle system, would be installed by March 10. The agreement's only other provisions provide for a first payment of a specified amount on design and a second payment of the balance on successful testing of the new installation. Installation was completed on March 25.

Does the fact that the installation was not completed until March 25 justify the applesauce bottler's refusal to pay the second installment?

(A) No, because the agreement did not contain a liquidated damage clause providing for delay in completion.

(B) No, because neither party manifested an understanding that time was of the essence in the agreement.

(C) Yes, because installation by March 10 was an express condition of the agreement.

(D) Yes, because the doctrine of substantial performance does not apply to commercial contracts.

Question 6

A woman consulted with an acupuncturist regarding her intractable back pain. They entered into an agreement under which the acupuncturist promised to treat the woman for her back pain. However, no price was given for the treatment. Four months later, after weekly sessions with the acupuncturist, the woman's back pain was completely gone. The woman refused to pay the acupuncturist anything, and he brought suit against her for services rendered.

The acupuncturist will:

(A) Recover his normal fee for the treatment.

(B) Recover a reasonable price for his services.

(C) Not recover, because no price term was contained in the original contract.

(D) Not recover, because the acupuncturist cannot prove that he was the cause of the woman's pain disappearing.

Question 7

Faced with great increases in the price of gas, the owner of a building complex contracts with an energy specialist to insulate all walls and windows of his buildings in order to save heat and air conditioning. The agreement provided that the necessary supply of heating oil per building should be reduced by at least 800 gallons per year, whereupon the owner would pay the energy specialist a fee of $70,000. A subsequent measuring showed that, after insulation work was performed, the amount of heating oil needed decreased on average 650 gallons per building. This work saved the building owner $52,000 in heat and air conditioning costs per building each year.

The energy specialist sent a letter to the building owner requesting certification that the new insulation was in place and operating as promised, and demanding the $70,000 fee. The owner refused to so certify and refused to make any payment.

If the energy specialist brings an action against the building owner for breach of contract, what will be the likely outcome?

(A) The energy specialist will recover on the contract, because it substantially performed under the agreement.

(B) The energy specialist will recover on the contract, because its services saved the owner $52,000 per building each year in climate control costs.

(C) The energy specialist will not recover on the contract, because savings of 800 gallons of heating oil was an express condition that was not fulfilled.

(D) The energy specialist will not recover on the contract, because the owner would not certify that the new system was operating as promised.

Question 8

A newsstand owner leased space in an office building. An investor purchased the office building and told the newsstand owner that he wanted to negotiate a new lease. During the negotiations, the newsstand owner and the investor orally agreed that the newsstand owner would have the exclusive right to sell newspapers and magazines in the office building. The investor prepared a written lease outlining the agreement, but forgot to include the agreement that the newsstand owner would have exclusive rights in the office building. The newsstand owner was given a copy of the lease to read, but he merely glanced over the lease because he assumed that it reflected his agreement with the investor. The newsstand owner then signed the lease, which included a merger and integration clause. One month later, the investor leased space in the building to a drug store. The drug store's lease did not prevent it from selling newspapers or magazines. As a result of the competition, the newsstand owner lost substantial profits in his business. The newsstand owner brings suit to reform the contract to reflect his exclusive right to sell newspapers and magazines in the office building.

The most likely result of this suit is that:

(A) The newsstand owner will prevail.

(B) The newsstand owner will prevail only if he can prove a mutual mistake.

(C) The newsstand owner will not prevail because of the application of the parol evidence rule.

(D) The newsstand owner will not prevail because the mistake on his part was unilateral.

Question 9

A federal statute provided for federal grants to cities that desired to rebuild inner-city areas for residential housing. A city applied for funding to build housing and received a grant of $2.5 million. After the area was prepared for construction, however, the city council decided that it would greatly benefit the inner-city dwellers if, in addition to housing, commercial property were built. Thus, the council decided to use $1.5 million for housing and to "borrow" the remaining $1 million from the housing fund to build a commercial mall. The city resolution provided that 30% of the rental from the mall each year would go to a fund for maintenance of the housing and for funds to build additional housing. Construction had started on residential buildings and the commercial mall when the federal court, at the request of the federal government, froze the construction accounts containing the proceeds from the grant.

In a motion by the city to release the funds, the court would most likely:

(A) Grant the motion, because the city's plan for a fund to build more residential housing substantially complies with the terms of the grant.

(B) Grant the motion, because the doctrine of preservation of state sovereignty prevents the federal government from interfering with the state's discretion in this situation.

(C) Deny the motion, because the federal government can control the expenditure of the funds because it provided the funds.

(D) Deny the motion, because the doctrine of state sovereignty has no application in this situation; the action was by the city council and not the state legislature.

Question 10

While out drinking with friends one evening, a young man got into an argument with a soldier from the nearby Army base and was bested in a brief exchange of punches. Vowing revenge on the soldier who had beaten him, the young man, after further drinking, went to the Army base and surreptitiously approached what he believed to be the barracks where the soldier slept. As he was climbing through the window he had jimmied, a military police officer happened by and challenged him. In a tussle with the MP, the young man struck the MP with his own baton, killing him. Still extremely intoxicated, the young man abandoned the idea of finding and severely beating the soldier, and staggered home. The jurisdiction's statutes define murder as "the premeditated and intentional killing of another or the killing of another in the commission of robbery, rape, burglary, or arson." The statutory definition of burglary is identical to the common law. The jurisdiction's statutes provide that intoxication is not a defense to a crime unless it negates an element of the offense.

At the young man's trial for the murder of the MP, the court should instruct the jury on the issue of the defense of intoxication that:

(A) Voluntary intoxication is a defense to the crime of murder if the young man would not have killed the MP but for the intoxication.

(B) The young man is guilty of murder despite his intoxication only if the prosecution proves by clear and convincing evidence that he acted with premeditation and intentionally.

(C) Voluntary intoxication is no defense to the crime of murder.

(D) Intoxication is a defense to the crime of burglary if it prevented the young man from forming the intent to commit a crime inside the barracks, in which case he could only be convicted of murder on the requisite showing of intentional action and premeditation.

Question 11

The defendant demanded that her neighbor cut down bushes that blocked her view, but the neighbor refused. Furious, the defendant slapped the neighbor. In response, the neighbor grabbed a pistol from her purse and fired a shot at the defendant, but missed. Just as her neighbor cocked the pistol to fire another shot, the defendant grabbed a shovel and hit her neighbor over the head, killing her instantly. The defendant was charged with the common law murder of her neighbor. At trial, the defendant testified that she hit her neighbor because she believed that her neighbor would have shot and killed her if she did not.

If the jury believes the defendant, it should find her:

(A) Guilty of murder, because she did not retreat.

(B) Guilty of murder, because she was the original aggressor in the encounter and had not withdrawn.

(C) Not guilty of murder, because her neighbor was the first to resort to deadly force.

(D) Not guilty of murder, because she had no opportunity to premeditate.

Question 12

A 15-year-old boy living at home with his parents, who were having a dinner party, set up a practical joke where a bucket of water is balanced on a partially open door so that the next person to enter the room through that door is drenched. The boy set up the filled bucket on the partially open door of the guest bedroom, knowing that his father would take the guests' coats in there. The boy's father did not use the guest bedroom for the coats, but later that evening, an invited guest of the boy's parents mistakenly wandered into the room. As the guest opened the door to the guest bedroom, the bucket of water plunged down on him, opening a four-inch cut in his scalp that required stitches.

In an action by the guest against the boy and his parents for personal injuries, the court should determine the boy's culpability according to:

(A) The presumption against negligence afforded to all minors.

(B) The age, experience, and intelligence of an ordinarily prudent minor in circumstances similar to the boy's.

(C) The standard applicable to adults, since the boy is nearly grown.

(D) Strict liability, because the practical joke turned out to be so dangerous.

Question 13

A farmer in a rural area contracted with a power company to erect wind turbines on his property. While zoning codes permitted this use of the property, the foundation supports for the turbines were not at the depth required by a code provision intended to ensure that large structures could withstand hurricane force winds. When the wind turbines became operational, the noise bothered the farmer's neighbor, although other neighbors the same distance away were not bothered. The neighbor, who was a commercial beekeeper, also discovered that his bees were producing less honey after the turbines began operating.

If the beekeeper brings a private nuisance action against the farmer, is he is likely to prevail?

(A) Yes, because the noise from the wind turbines interfered with the beekeeper's use and enjoyment of his land.

(B) Yes, because the wind turbines were in violation of the zoning code.

(C) No, because the noise from the wind turbines apparently would not disturb a person of ordinary sensibilities in the community.

(D) No, because the zoning code regulation was not designed to prevent the type of harm that the beekeeper suffered.

Question 14

The owner of a large tract of land in fee simple subdivided 100 acres into 250 lots. She obtained all the necessary governmental approvals and recorded a plat of the planned development, and in a 12-year span sold 175 of the lots. The purchaser of one of the lots received a deed containing a provision that was in all the deeds to these 175 lots. It provided that the property conveyed shall be used for a single-family dwelling only and that no structure, other than a single-family dwelling, shall be erected or maintained. It further provided that occupancy in any dwelling built on the property shall be by a single family for residential purposes only and that the agreement is specifically made binding on the grantee and grantee's heirs, their assigns and successors.

Two years ago, the owner contracted with a water sport resort to sell an additional 100 acres that she owned contiguous to these lots. As part of this agreement, the owner also conveyed to the resort the 75 lots she had not previously sold. Nothing in the deeds for these 75 lots restricted their use to single-family residences, and in fact, the resort was planning to use all the property purchased for a resort and for multi-family dwellings.

If the purchaser of the first lot brought suit against the owner to establish that all the original 250 lots, including the 75 she had agreed to sell to the resort, had to be used only for single-family dwellings in a proper proceeding, what would be the most likely result?

(A) The owner will prevail, because the provision in the deed only binds the grantee.

(B) The owner will prevail, because the remaining 75 deeds did not contain this provision.

(C) The purchaser will prevail, because he can show that a common development scheme had been established for the entire subdivision.

(D) The purchaser will prevail, unless the evidence shows that the resort was not aware of this provision at the time of its agreement with the owner.

Question 15

A city council ordinance provided that city officials should automatically issue a parade permit to any group filing the proper papers with city authorities, except in situations where a prior group had already received permission to parade on the same street at the same time on the same day. Another city ordinance prescribed fines for persons conducting a parade in the city without a permit.

A religious leader filed appropriate papers with city officials to parade down the main street of the city at 1 p.m. on July 15. City officials noted that they had already issued a parade permit for another parade at the same place, date and time. The officials told the leader that he could not have a parade permit for the time and place requested and suggested that he select another day and/or location. The leader refused and insisted that he would conduct his parade when scheduled, even without a permit. On July 15 at 1 p.m., both organizations assembled on the main street and began to organize into parades. City officials asked the religious leader and his followers to desist, but they refused and were thereafter arrested, convicted, and fined under the city ordinance.

If the convicted members seek to have their convictions overturned by the federal courts, they will:

(A) Lose, because the religious leader should have gone to federal court to secure his organization's rights before violating the ordinance.

(B) Lose, because the city ordinances are a reasonable restriction on time, place, and manner of speech and were not applied in a discriminatory manner.

(C) Lose, because the city ordinances represented the will of the people as expressed through the city council.

(D) Win, because the city ordinances, on their face, violate the free speech guarantees of the First Amendment.

Question 16

In a defamation action, the plaintiff offers the testimony of a witness who will state that when she heard the defendant describe the plaintiff as "the biggest shyster in town," she understood him to mean that the plaintiff was an incompetent lawyer. The witness is the eleventh person the plaintiff has called to interpret the quoted statement.

Should the witness's testimony be admitted?

(A) No, because its probative value is substantially outweighed by needless presentation of cumulative evidence.

(B) No, because it is hearsay not within any exception.

(C) Yes, because it is relevant.

(D) Yes, as a present state of mind.

Question 17

A salesman was employed by a florist, who owned a retail shop adjacent to a large wholesale nursery. The owner of the nursery liked to use a brand-name artificial fertilizer for her plants, although other effective fertilizers were available at comparable prices. She stored a large quantity of the fertilizer in a heap on the nursery's property, as did many other nursery owners without incident. The fertilizer gave off fumes that caused the salesman to suffer lung irritation. Occasionally, the salesman's irritations became so bad that he had to take off from work and seek medical attention. After losing a few hundred dollars in wages and amassing a few hundred dollars in medical expenses, the salesman sued the nursery owner for damages.

The court is likely to rule in favor of:

(A) The salesman, because the nursery owner had equally effective fertilizers available at comparable prices to the fertilizer used.

(B) The salesman, because the nursery owner is strictly liable for injuries caused by emissions from her property.

(C) The nursery owner, because the selection of the fertilizer was reasonable and it was stored in a reasonable manner.

(D) The nursery owner, because the salesman is merely an employee of the florist and does not own the property on which the shop is located.

Question 18

A defendant is on trial in federal court, charged with having sold cocaine to an undercover agent. The defendant calls a witness to the stand who testifies that she was with the defendant in another state on the date of the alleged drug sale. Following her testimony, the prosecution seeks to introduce the record of judgment of the witness's seven-year-old embezzlement conviction. The defendant's attorney objects.

The court should rule the record of judgment:

(A) Admissible, as going to the witness's credibility.

(B) Admissible, provided no appeal is pending.

(C) Inadmissible, because the record is inadmissible hearsay.

(D) Inadmissible, because, for impeachment, a specific act of misconduct cannot be shown by extrinsic evidence.

Question 19

The United States entered into a treaty with a neighboring country whereby each country agreed to ban hunting of the red tailed raccoon, a species of raccoon indigenous to both. The raccoon had been placed on the endangered species list of various conservation groups. The raccoon freely crossed the international boundary between the countries, and state lines within the United States. Laws in three states in the United States permitted hunting of the raccoon.

After the treaty was fully ratified by both countries, a United States federal court would most likely hold that the state laws permitting hunting of the raccoons are:

(A) Unconstitutional, because a treaty is the supreme law of the land.

(B) Unconstitutional, because free roaming wildlife is federal property.

(C) Constitutional, because wild animals are natural inhabitants of the state, and the federal government may not take state property without consent of the state.

(D) Constitutional, under the rights reserved to the states by the Tenth Amendment.

Question 20

An elderly man wrote a note to a friend stating that he wanted her to have his house and land. The man then went to his lawyer and had her draft a deed conveying the property to his friend. The man validly executed the deed and gave both the note and the executed deed to the lawyer, telling her to give them to the friend on his death.

The man continued to live on the property until his death one year later. Shortly thereafter, his will was admitted to probate; it left all of his property to a cousin. Prior to the probate of the estate, the friend received the note and deed from the lawyer, and promptly recorded the deed. After probate, she brought an appropriate action to quiet title to the property conveyed by the deed.

In that action, the court should find for:

(A) The friend, because the deed as delivered constituted a valid conveyance of the property.

(B) The friend, because the man's note to her constituted a valid conveyance of the property.

(C) The cousin, because the deed conveying the property to the friend was not recorded until after the man's death and thus was not effective.

(D) The cousin, because the fact that the man remained in possession of the property rendered the conveyance in the deed to the friend ineffective.

Question 21

A woman attempted to charge a coat using a credit card that her friend had stolen. The store's electronic credit reporting system indicated the account was defunct, and the store clerk refused to complete the transaction. The woman left the store and held up a couple at gunpoint in a nearby park. However, the couple had just been robbed of all their valuables and was heading over to the police station to report the crime, so the woman got nothing. The woman was arrested and charged with attempting to obtain property by false pretenses and attempted robbery.

The court should find the woman:

(A) Not guilty of attempting to obtain property by false pretenses and not guilty of attempted robbery.

(B) Guilty of attempting to obtain property by false pretenses and guilty of attempted robbery.

(C) Not guilty of attempting to obtain property by false pretenses and guilty of attempted robbery.

(D) Guilty of attempting to obtain property by false pretenses and not guilty of attempted robbery.

Question 22

To protect the minor children living in the area, a town council enacted an ordinance that prohibited advertisements that include a depiction of a nude person, whether male or female. The owner of a local video rental shop often posts large posters to advertise movies he has available for rent. A substantial part of his business consists of the rental of adult movies, which are kept in a separate part of the shop. In the adult room he hangs movie advertisements, many of them depicting nude or partially nude people. He does not allow minors to enter the adult room.

If the owner challenges enforcement of the ordinance against him, how will the court most likely rule?

(A) For the town, because the ordinance is a valid exercise of the town's power to protect the morals of its minor citizens.

(B) For the town, because the posters may appeal to a minor's prurient interest in sex.

(C) For the owner, because prohibiting the posting of the movie advertisements violates his First Amendment rights.

(D) For the owner, because not all nudity is obscene.

Question 23

A plaintiff was injured when the car she was driving was struck by a truck owned by the defendant and driven by its employee. The employee was just finishing his deliveries for the defendant when the accident occurred. At the scene of the accident, a bystander heard the employee say, "I can't believe it . . . I shouldn't have had all those beers." The plaintiff sued the defendant for her injuries and asked the bystander to testify at trial as to the employee's statement.

The bystander's testimony should be ruled:

(A) Admissible, as a statement against interest.

(B) Admissible, as an admission of a party-opponent.

(C) Admissible, as an excited utterance.

(D) Inadmissible, as hearsay not within any exception.

Question 24

A freelance professional photographer was purchasing film at a store when he noticed that a well-known actress was browsing through the store's clothing department. He took a photograph of the actress in the store without her knowledge. Several days later, the photographer sold the photograph to the manager of the store, explaining that the actress had agreed that the store could use the photograph in an advertising campaign. The manager enlarged the photograph and hung it above the main entrance with a caption stating that the actress shops at the store. One month earlier, the actress had entered into a contract with a competing store, the terms of which provided that the competing store had the exclusive right to use her name and likeness for advertising purposes.

If the actress asserts a claim based on invasion of privacy against the store, will she prevail?

(A) Yes, because the store, without the actress's permission, used her picture for its advertisement.

(B) Yes, because the photographer had no right to take the actress's picture.

(C) No, because the store believed it had permission to display the actress's picture.

(D) No, because the actress would clearly qualify as a public figure.

Question 25

The owner of a tract of land with a house on it entered into a lease with a tenant for a term of three years. The tenant installed a batting cage, an automatic pitching machine, and electric lights in the backyard of the land for her son, an amateur baseball player. Six months after entering into the lease, the owner mortgaged the land to a bank to secure a loan. The tenant was not notified directly of the mortgage but the mortgage was recorded. Two months before the lease term was to end, the owner defaulted on his mortgage payments, and the bank began foreclosure proceedings, as it was entitled to do under the terms of the mortgage. The tenant, knowing her lease would soon end but not being aware of the foreclosure proceedings, began to remove all of the equipment she had installed in the backyard. The bank brought an action to enjoin the removal of the equipment, naming both the tenant and the owner as defendants in the suit.

If the court refuses the injunction, it would be because:

(A) The circumstances reveal that the equipment was installed for the tenant's (and her son's) exclusive benefit.

(B) The Statute of Frauds precludes the bank from claiming any interest in the equipment.

(C) The tenant was never given direct notice of the mortgage.

(D) In the absence of a contrary agreement, a residential tenant is entitled to remove any personal property she voluntarily brings upon the premises.

Question 26

A landlord leased an apartment to a friend for a term of five years. One year later, the landlord purchased a hot tub on credit, giving the seller a security interest in the hot tub in order to secure payment. The landlord had the hot tub installed on the rear balcony of the friend's apartment. One week later, the landlord mortgaged the apartment building to a bank to secure a loan. The bank recorded the mortgage the next day. Three days after that, the seller recorded a fixture filing evidencing its interest in the hot tub. Six months before the termination of the lease, the landlord defaulted on both her mortgage and the payments for the hot tub. The bank duly instituted foreclosure proceedings.

Who has the superior claim to the hot tub?

(A) The bank.

(B) The landlord.

(C) The friend.

(D) The seller.

Question 27

A city ordinance makes it unlawful for any group of individuals or organization in excess of 20 persons to demonstrate, march, or picket in the city's civic center without first posting a bond with the police department and receiving a permit. The permit procedure takes at least one working day, and costs $10. In addition to making a violation a misdemeanor, the ordinance authorizes the police department to terminate any demonstration if "any person in the demonstration, without provocation, uses, in the presence of other persons not a party to the demonstration, annoying, disturbing, opprobrious words and abusive language in such a manner as tending to cause a breach of the peace."

A group of demonstrators brings suit in the state court to enjoin the city from preventing their scheduled demonstration on Memorial Day without a permit, and to enjoin the city from using this ordinance to require them to have a permit.

The demonstrators' strongest contention for finding the provisions of this statute unconstitutional is that:

(A) The city's civic center is a place where demonstrations of this type normally occur, and the city cannot prevent citizens from demonstrating there.

(B) There is no showing by the city that the demonstrators are likely to become disruptive or unruly.

(C) The ordinance is overbroad and unduly vague.

(D) The First and Fourteenth Amendments ensure the right of association in public places without interference.

Question 28

An information technology ("IT") specialist spent one and a half years working for the county IT department when her employment was terminated without her being given a hearing or reason for the termination. The county rules required any member of the department to serve at least two years before being hired as a permanent employee. However, in recent years, the department director considered the rules outdated and only required a member of the department to serve one year before being hired. The county code does not require the county to give a hearing or reasons for a worker's termination of employment. The employee brought suit against the county in federal court because of the termination of her employment.

Which of the following facts, if shown, gives the county the strongest argument for refusing to give the employee a statement of reasons why her employment was terminated and for denying her the opportunity to contest the termination?

(A) The employee, a college graduate, did not perform as well as her graduate school counterparts.

(B) The employee had failed to include in her application the fact that during college she was a member of a radical student organization.

(C) The employee had not been granted permanent employment status.

(D) The employee had received the poorest performance evaluation in the department.

Question 29

A driver borrowed a car from a friend. When the driver picked up the car, the friend forgot to warn the driver that the brake fluid had a tendency to leak out of the brake system and needed to be replaced regularly. The friend telephoned the driver's wife and warned her about the brake fluid problem. The wife, however, forgot to tell the driver. Shortly thereafter, the driver was driving the wife to work in the borrowed car. The driver was proceeding along at a reasonable rate of speed and within the posted speed limit. As he approached an intersection, he saw another car run through the red light and into the intersection. The driver, on seeing the other car, stepped on the brakes, but the brakes failed and the two cars collided. If the proper amount of brake fluid had been in the brake system, the driver could have stopped in time to avoid the collision. The driver and the wife were injured. The jurisdiction has adopted "pure" comparative negligence.

If the driver asserts a claim against the operator of the vehicle that ran the red light, the driver will:

(A) Recover only a portion of his damages, because the wife was also at fault.

(B) Recover the full amount of his damages, because the driver himself was not at fault.

(C) Not recover, because the driver had the last clear chance to avoid the accident.

(D) Not recover, because the wife was negligent in not telling the driver about the defective brake condition, and the wife's negligence would be imputed to the driver.

Question 30

A father lent his car to his son so that he could take his girlfriend out to dinner. Before he left, the father warned the son that the gas gauge failed to indicate when the car ran out of gas and told him to fill up the tank on the way to dinner. Running late, the son decided he would pick up gas on the way home. At dinner the son had too much to drink and asked his girlfriend to drive on the way home because she did not have anything to drink. Because the son was drunk, he forgot to tell his girlfriend to stop for gas. While going through an intersection, the car stalled because it ran out of gas. A driver, who ran a stop sign, crashed into the car. If the car had not run out of gas, the car would not have stalled in the middle of the intersection. The son and his girlfriend were injured. The jurisdiction has adopted "pure" comparative negligence.

If the son asserts a claim against the driver, the son will:

(A) Recover in full for his injury, because his girlfriend, who was driving the car in which he was riding, was not herself at fault.

(B) Recover a portion of his damages, based on the respective degrees of his negligence and that of the driver.

(C) Not recover, because his girlfriend had the last clear chance to avoid the accident.

(D) Not recover, because the son was primarily at fault for the collision.

Question 31

A prisoner escaped from prison and stole a car. He picked up a hitchhiker and told her what he had done. Although the hitchhiker was emotionally disturbed and of borderline mental retardation, she understood what the prisoner had done and that the police were after him. The hitchhiker hated the police, and told the prisoner she would do anything she could to help him. To avoid the police, they drove to the mountains, with the prisoner doing much of the driving.

With respect to the stolen car, at common law, the hitchhiker is:

(A) Liable as a co-conspirator to car theft.

(B) Liable as an accessory after the fact to car theft.

(C) Liable for compounding a felony.

(D) Not liable for any common law crime.

Question 32

The defendant, over six feet tall and 250 pounds, became lost in an unfamiliar part of the city and did not have enough money for bus fare back to his house. He was scruffily dressed and appeared very unkempt. He approached a slightly built man who was standing alone at the bus stop and said in a gruff voice, "Do you have any money?" When the man replied, "Yes," the defendant said, "Give me five dollars!" The man reached into his pocket and handed the defendant a five-dollar bill. The man walked away from the bus and flagged down a passing patrol car, telling the police that he was just robbed. The defendant was arrested and charged with robbery. At the defendant's trial, he testified that he was not trying to rob anyone; he was just trying to beg for some money to get home.

If the jury believes his testimony, the defendant should be found:

(A) Not guilty of robbery, because the defendant lacked the requisite criminal intent.

(B) Guilty of robbery, because the defendant took the man's money after intimidating him, and the effect of the defendant's size on the man, rather than the defendant's intent, is controlling.

(C) Not guilty of robbery, but guilty of assault, because the defendant placed the man in reasonable apprehension of bodily harm.

(D) Guilty of both robbery and assault, because assault is not a lesser included offense of robbery.

Question 33

A brother and sister were in the middle of a very large lake on a fishing trip, out of sight of land, when their boat ran out of gas. The brother spotted a large fishing boat in the distance. Knowing that fishing boats carried extra gas cans on board, the brother and sister paddled toward the other boat. The brother told his sister to sneak onto the other ship and steal a gas can. The sister got onto the other boat and grabbed a gas can when a fisherman on the boat, who was 6'6" tall and weighed 250 pounds, grabbed her arm. The sister was terrified and picked up a heavy bucket and hit the fisherman on the head; he slumped to the ground apparently dead. The brother then ran up and told the sister that the fisherman was dead and that they had to put him in the water so it would look like he drowned after slipping and falling off the boat. They thereupon put the fisherman in the water without attempting to determine if he was alive or dead. Later, a medical examination showed conclusively that the blow only knocked the fisherman out; he died of suffocation due to water in the lungs. The brother was charged with causing the death of the fisherman.

If the jury believes the brother's story that he thought the fisherman was already dead before he and the sister put the body in the water, although he had made no effort to determine if the fisherman was alive, the killing was:

(A) Excusable homicide.

(B) Voluntary manslaughter.

(C) Involuntary manslaughter.

(D) Murder, if the jury finds that a reasonable person would have determined whether the fisherman was alive.

Question 34

A man spent the evening in the local bar and became inebriated. After leaving the bar, he got into a car that he thought was his, but was not. Because the keys were in the ignition, he was able to start the car and drive off. As he drove home, he pulled out his gun and fired randomly into a house, shooting and wounding a woman inside. In the resulting criminal trial, the man claims he was too drunk to know either that the car was not his or that there was anyone in the house.

The man will be found:

(A) Not guilty of larceny and not guilty of battery.

(B) Guilty of larceny and guilty of battery.

(C) Not guilty of larceny and guilty of battery.

(D) Guilty of larceny and not guilty of battery.

Question 35

A mom wished to buy her son an expensive car for a wedding present. On May 15, she visited a dealership where the salesman and the mom signed a writing providing for the sale of a specified car "if we can agree on a price on or before June 1." On May 20, the mom dispatched a letter to the salesman stating, "I will buy the car for $150,000." On the same day, the salesman dispatched a letter to the mom, stating, "I will sell the car for $150,000."

Has a valid contract been formed between the dealership and the mom?

(A) Yes, because the May 15 writing constitutes a contract with a missing price term, and that term was filled by the crossing offers.

(B) Yes, because when two crossing offers are identical in import, one will be treated as an offer and the other as an acceptance.

(C) Yes, because there was mutual assent; both parties agreed to a price of $150,000 for the car.

(D) No, because there were two crossing offers and no acceptance; hence there was no mutual assent.

Question 36

The legislature of a state passed a statute providing that "no newspaper in this state shall publish a political endorsement or an editorial favoring one political candidate or party over another on either the day of election or the day preceding the day of election." The stated purpose for the legislation was to prevent unfair attacks on candidates and to ensure that they would have time to respond to or rebut any published article prior to the election. A newspaper published in the state, which was distributed regionally and in states bordering the state, filed suit in federal court seeking to enjoin enforcement of the statute.

The newspaper's best argument for the invalidity of the statute is which of the following?

(A) The statute unduly burdens interstate commerce, because the newspaper is circulated in other states.

(B) The statute unduly interferes with the newspaper's property interest in distributing newspapers.

(C) The statute unduly restricts the newspaper's freedom of speech.

(D) The statute violates the Equal Protection Clause, because restrictions are imposed merely on the basis of the day the newspaper is printed, while the same material can be printed on other days.

Question 37

A witness was in a store when she heard a screeching of brakes and immediately rushed out of the store. She saw a car speeding off into the distance and found a victim, badly injured and lying in the street. The victim gasped to the witness, "I'm going to die. The car that hit me had license number DD666!" The victim then lapsed into unconsciousness. The witness gave her information to the police, including a description of the car and the victim's comment on the license plate. The police traced the registration to the defendant. The victim recovered from his injuries and filed suit against the defendant for his injuries. At the trial, the victim wants to have the witness testify as to the victim's statement regarding the defendant's license number.

The court should rule that such testimony by the witness is:

(A) Inadmissible, because it is more prejudicial than probative.

(B) Inadmissible, because it is hearsay not within any recognized exception to the hearsay rule.

(C) Admissible, as a declaration made in belief of impending death.

(D) Admissible, as an excited utterance.

Question 38

After a bomb explosion in an airport locker, a detective was told by a reliable informant that, three months before, the informant had been in the terrorist's apartment and saw what appeared to be some sticks of dynamite. Reasonably believing that the informant's information established probable cause, the detective prepared an affidavit for a search warrant. After the warrant was issued, the detective and a group of police raided the terrorist's apartment. No evidence connecting the terrorist with the bombing was discovered, but the police did discover several grams of cocaine during the search of the apartment.

At his trial for possession of narcotics, the terrorist's motion to suppress the evidence would probably be:

(A) Denied, because the informant was a reliable informant and the detective reasonably believed that the informant's information was accurate and that the warrant was properly issued.

(B) Granted, because in fact the police did not discover any evidence linking the terrorist to the bombings and, therefore, the seizure of the cocaine was fruit of the poisonous tree.

(C) Granted, if the court determines that the information supplied by the informant to the detective concerned information too remote in time to justify a claim of probable cause at the time the detective requested the search warrant.

(D) Granted, because the search warrant was not issued for the purpose of searching the terrorist's apartment for illegal drugs.

Question 39

A girlfriend and boyfriend decided to get married. The girlfriend was one month short of her 18th birthday, and the boyfriend was 19. They went to a jeweler who made wedding rings to order and described what they were interested in. The girlfriend and boyfriend then signed a purchase order for two rings, a woman's band for $500 and a man's for $650. After the girlfriend's 18th birthday, the rings were ready. The girlfriend went to the jeweler and told him that they would not be needing the rings because she and the boyfriend had broken up. When he protested that they were custom-made and would probably not sell to anyone else, the girlfriend said, "All right, I've got $400 in my savings account. I'll take my ring, but you'll have to find my boyfriend about the other one." The jeweler had the girlfriend sign another purchase order for the woman's band at $400, payment to be made by the end of the month.

When the jeweler did not hear from the girlfriend after another month, he brought an action for breach of contract against her. Evidence produced at trial established that the market value of the rings was $500 and $650 for the woman's and man's rings, respectively, and that the age of majority in the jurisdiction was 18.

Is the jeweler entitled to recover against the girlfriend?

(A) Yes, in the amount of $1,150.

(B) Yes, in the amount of $500.

(C) Yes, in the amount of $400.

(D) No.

Question 40

A seller entered into an enforceable written agreement to sell her home to a buyer for $150,000. The agreement provided that escrow would close on March 31, and on that date the seller would provide good and marketable title to the house, free and clear of all encumbrances. On March 10, the seller was notified by her insurance company that she had to renew her insurance policy by March 15. The seller immediately notified the company that she did not want the insurance renewed at that time. Consequently, when the house was destroyed by fire on March 25, it was uninsured. On March 31, the buyer refused to close and the seller immediately brought an action against him for specific performance.

In this jurisdiction, which has no applicable statute to govern this situation, the most probable result of this action would be:

(A) The buyer prevails, because an implied term of all conveyances is that the property at the time of closing will be in substantially the same condition as it was at the time the contract was entered into.

(B) The buyer prevails, because as the house was destroyed, the seller would have nothing to "sell" and, therefore, could not convey marketable title.

(C) The seller prevails, because under the doctrine of equitable conversion, the risk of loss was on the buyer.

(D) The seller prevails, but since the house was destroyed, she is only entitled to recover the fair market value of the land itself.

Question 41

A defendant is being tried for the murder of a victim, which occurred during the burglary of the victim's house. In its case-in-chief, the prosecution seeks to offer evidence that the defendant, who was arrested several days after the crime, had been caught with several grams of cocaine in his car.

This evidence will most likely be:

(A) Inadmissible, because the defendant has not offered evidence of good character.

(B) Inadmissible, because it has limited probative value and is unduly prejudicial.

(C) Admissible, because it tends to show what the defendant did with the money he stole.

(D) Admissible, because it tends to show that the defendant is capable of committing serious crimes.

Question 42

A defendant is being tried for the murder of a bank teller, which occurred during the robbery of a bank. At trial, a witness, who knew the defendant, is called to testify that on the day after the robbery he saw the defendant buying some groceries, and when the defendant removed a large roll of money, the witness had asked, "You didn't steal that from someone, did you?" The defendant nodded.

This evidence is:

(A) Admissible, as an excited utterance.

(B) Admissible, because it is not hearsay.

(C) Inadmissible, because it is hearsay not within any exception.

(D) Inadmissible, because the defendant had no reason to respond to this statement.

Question 43

The state police wished to infiltrate a racist organization devoted to the goal of creating an "all white America." The police decided to create a new undercover position for the person who would infiltrate the racist organization. The pay was substantially better than the salary of ordinary officers. The chief of police invited all white police officers to apply for the undercover position. A plaintiff had been a state police officer for eight years and had received many citations for efficiency, bravery, and public service. However, the plaintiff is black, and the chief refused to even accept his application for the undercover position, even though the plaintiff told the chief that he was very desirous of obtaining the position.

If the plaintiff sues to require the chief to give serious consideration to his application, should the court rule that the chief has acted in a manner in accordance with the principles of the United States Constitution?

(A) Yes, because the state has a rational basis for using race as a qualification for the job.

(B) Yes, because the state has a compelling interest in infiltrating the racist organization, to promote the general welfare of its citizens.

(C) No, because the chief's actions were discriminatory per se.

(D) No, if there is a chance that the plaintiff might be able to win the confidence of the racist organization leaders.

Question 44

A dealer had a contract with a city to supply the city with five computers a month for seven months. At the start of the fourth month, the dealer realized that his supply of computers had dwindled to one. The dealer immediately sent a fax to his supplier asking for a price quote for 20 computers to be delivered before the first of next month. The supplier responded by fax: "I can deliver 20 computers from my present stock at a cost of $1,000 per computer." The dealer responded the next day with another fax that stated: "I will buy 20 computers at a cost of $1,000 per computer."

Assuming no further communications between the parties, has a contract been formed at this point?

(A) Yes, because the dealer's fax ordering the computers was an acceptance of the supplier's offer.

(B) Yes, because the supplier's fax was an acceptance of the offer in the dealer's first fax.

(C) No, because the fax sent by the dealer was an offer that was never accepted by the supplier.

(D) No, because none of the communications were worded in such a way as to be definite and certain enough to be offers.

Question 45

A supplier had a contract with a store to supply the store with 10 iPods a month for 11 months. In order to fulfill that contract, the supplier entered into a contract with a seller for the sale of 20 iPods. The payment provisions were $2,000 on acceptance of the contract, $1,000 on delivery of the iPods, and $1,000 when the supplier receives his last payment from the store. The store defaulted on its payments to the supplier.

Is the supplier liable for the last payment of $1,000 to the seller?

(A) Yes, because the provisions only set a reasonable time for payment.

(B) Yes, because an obligor may not delegate the duty of payment.

(C) No, because an express condition for payment to the seller has not occurred.

(D) No, because the supplier has not received sufficient funds to make the payment to the seller.

Question 46

A lessee leased some land from a lessor for a period of 10 years. Five years later, the state took title to the land under proper eminent domain proceedings.

Which of the following statements is correct concerning the rights of the lessee?

(A) The lessee may continue to occupy the land, as eminent domain proceedings will not affect lessees.

(B) The lessee may continue to occupy the part of the land that the lessee cultivated, as eminent domain proceedings will not affect parts of land that a lessee has cultivated.

(C) The lessee may not continue to occupy the land, is relieved from his obligation to pay rent to the lessor, and will not share in the condemnation award.

(D) The lessee may not continue to occupy the land and is entitled to share in the condemnation award based on the value of the remaining five years, less rent that would have been paid during that period.

Question 47

The Social Security Act provided that surviving spouses and stepchildren would be denied benefits unless the decedent wage-earner spouse had been married at least nine months prior to death. A wife married her husband, who was in apparent good health, five months before his death. The wife was denied survivor benefits by the Social Security Administration. She now brings an action to compel the Social Security Administration to award her benefits.

The decision of the court should be that:

(A) The wife should be awarded benefits, because the nine-month period is arbitrary, capricious, and without any rational justification.

(B) The wife should be awarded benefits, because the classification is an invidious scheme and violates her rights to equal protection.

(C) The wife should not be given benefits, because the nine-month period in question is reasonably calculated to achieve a permissible governmental end.

(D) The wife should not be awarded benefits, because it would be an undue burden on the public treasury to allow all wives survivor benefits.

Question 48

An owner of a store heard several gunshots and rushed out into the street. He found a victim lying on the sidewalk, bleeding profusely. She gasped to the owner, "I'm going to die. My upstairs neighbor shot me." The victim lapsed into unconsciousness and died on the way to the hospital without uttering another word. The neighbor was arrested and charged with the murder of the victim. At the neighbor's trial, the prosecution seeks to have the store owner testify as to the victim's statement.

Such testimony should be ruled:

(A) Inadmissible, because it is more prejudicial than probative.

(B) Inadmissible, because it is hearsay not within any recognized exception to the hearsay rule.

(C) Admissible, as a declaration made in belief of impending death.

(D) Admissible, as an excited utterance.

Question 49

The workers for a municipal telephone company were sent out to install new cables at an intersection on a vacant lot where an old building that had been demolished had stood. The workers had to dig out the old cables, install new sheathing, and then connect and insert the new cables. The excavating took much longer than planned, and by the end of the day they had just finished digging a 30-foot long trench and removing the old cables. The foreman of the workers put up two barriers along the side of the trench and posted signs on each of the barriers warning individuals of the open trench.

A boy, who was in seventh grade, passed by the excavation with his friends on his way home. The boy could not quite make out what the signs on the barriers said in the deepening dusk, so he walked over to the nearest one and read it. His friends, who had continued walking, called for him to hurry along. As he ran to catch up with his friends, he moved along the edge of the excavation. The edge was soft and gave way, and the boy fell into the trench, severely injuring himself. The boy's mother brings an action against the company. The facts above are established. At the close of evidence, the company moves for a directed verdict.

If the court denies the directed verdict, it will be because:

(A) The trier of fact could determine that the boy was attracted to the excavation by the signs.

(B) The jurisdiction has rejected traditional contributory negligence and assumption of risk rules and applies comparative negligence.

(C) The trier of fact could determine that the workers were negligent in leaving the open trench without additional protection for passersby.

(D) The mother does not need to establish negligence against the company because it is strictly liable for the injuries to the boy.

Question 50

A defendant was arrested for carrying a concealed weapon in violation of his parole. The police had reason to believe that the defendant was part of a group that sold stolen automobile parts. The police interrogated the defendant continually for 10 hours. Finally, the police threatened to have the defendant's parole revoked if he did not cooperate. Fatigued from the lengthy interrogation and afraid of going back to jail, the defendant confessed to being a member of the group involved in the theft of automobile parts. The defendant gave the police the location of a friend's garage where the stolen parts were located. Based on this confession, the police obtained a search warrant to search the garage, where they discovered a large quantity of stolen automobile parts. The defendant was prosecuted for conspiracy to sell stolen automobile parts. Before trial, he moved to prevent use of the stolen parts as evidence.

The court will most likely rule that the evidence should be:

(A) Admitted, because it was obtained pursuant to a warrant.

(B) Admitted, because the defendant had no standing to object to the search of the garage.

(C) Suppressed, because the uncorroborated statements of a criminal suspect are not a sufficient basis for a warrant.

(D) Suppressed, because it is the fruit of the defendant's involuntary statements.

MIXED SUBJECT SET 5 SUBJECT GUIDE

1. Evidence
2. Evidence
3. Contracts
4. Contracts
5. Contracts
6. Contracts
7. Contracts
8. Contracts
9. Constitutional Law
10. Criminal Law
11. Criminal Law
12. Torts
13. Torts
14. Real Property
15. Constitutional Law
16. Evidence
17. Torts
18. Evidence
19. Constitutional Law
20. Real Property
21. Criminal Law
22. Constitutional Law
23. Evidence
24. Torts
25. Real Property
26. Real Property
27. Constitutional Law
28. Constitutional Law
29. Torts
30. Torts
31. Criminal Law
32. Criminal Law
33. Criminal Law
34. Criminal Law
35. Contracts
36. Constitutional Law
37. Evidence
38. Criminal Law/Procedure
39. Contracts
40. Real Property
41. Evidence
42. Evidence
43. Constitutional Law
44. Contracts
45. Contracts
46. Real Property
47. Constitutional Law
48. Evidence
49. Torts
50. Criminal Law/Procedure

MIXED SUBJECT ANSWERS - SET 5

Answer to Question 1

(D) The court should admit the evidence. Although evidence of other crimes, wrongs, or bad acts is not admissible to prove character and conformity therewith, such evidence may be admissible if it is relevant to some issue other than the defendant's character or disposition to commit the crime. Here, the testimony is relevant to counter the defendant's assertion that she lacked knowledge of a fraudulent scheme. (A) is therefore incorrect. (B) is incorrect because the testimony tends to make the fact that the defendant knew about the scheme more probably true than it would have been without the testimony. (C) is incorrect because the defendant has neither taken the stand nor introduced evidence of her good character.

Answer to Question 2

(A) The court should not admit this evidence because the prosecution cannot initiate evidence of the defendant's bad character. The prosecution may offer such evidence only after the accused has put his character in issue by either taking the stand (thus placing his credibility in issue) or offering evidence of his good character. Thus, (C) is incorrect. (B) is incorrect because, under the Federal Rules, character may be proven by opinion evidence. (D) is incorrect because this does not constitute a regular response to a specific set of circumstances; it is merely reputation and opinion evidence.

Answer to Question 3

(B) The consultants were not entitled to payment of the first installment. Within 90 days after installation is the most reasonable interpretation of the relevant contract language. The agreement is express, not constructive, on this point, and the normal situation would be that the parties expected payment to occur after installation, since a contrary interpretation would require a prediction as to when installation would be completed. Thus, (B) is correct, and (C) and (D) are incorrect. (A) is incorrect because it does not take into account the 90 days.

Answer to Question 4

(A) The best argument for admission of the testimony is that the memorandum does not cover the entire agreement between the parties and was thus not a complete integration. Because the writing contains no mention of the oral agreement to meet certain car models requirements, the testimony would not "interpret" it in any way. Thus, (B) is incorrect. (C) and (D) are wrong because there is no evidence that the car manufacturer detrimentally relied on the oral agreement in signing the memorandum, or that the tire supplier's promise constituted a misrepresentation at the time it was made.

Answer to Question 5

(B) The late installation does not justify the refusal to pay. Generally, late performance of a contract is treated as a minor breach that gives the nonbreaching party a right to damages but does not relieve him of his duty to perform. Late performance will be considered to be material only if the nature of the contract requires timely performance (such as in "goods" contracts within the U.C.C.) or if the contract provides that time is of the essence. Nothing in the contract here states that time is of the essence, and the contract does not by its nature require timely performance (it is a "services" contract rather than a "goods" contract under the U.C.C.). (A) is incorrect because absence of a liquidated damage clause does not have a bearing on whether delay in performance is a material breach. (C) is incorrect because the completion date is stated in terms of a promise rather than as an express condition. (D) is an untrue statement; the doctrine applies to commercial contracts for services.

Answer to Question 6

(B) The acupuncturist will be able to recover a reasonable price for his services. While the parties failed to agree on a material term, most courts today will imply reasonable terms if they are consistent with the parties' intent as otherwise expressed. Terms that can be supplied by a reasonableness standard include a price term for the performance of services. Unless the parties have shown at the time of contracting that they do not want a contract until they agree on a price, a reasonable price will be implied. (A) is wrong because the acupuncturist's fee is not necessarily reasonable although the court will take into account the acupuncturist's normal fee when it determines the reasonable fee. (C) is wrong because it fails to take into account that a court will imply a reasonable price term. (D) is wrong because it is irrelevant. In contract, a party need not prove that the "performing" party actually caused the performance. The patient received the performance she bargained for here—a cure.

Answer to Question 7

(C) The energy specialist will not recover on the contract because of failure of an express condition. The circumstances show that the requirement that the building owner realize a savings of 800 gallons of heating oil per building was an express condition of the contract. The energy specialist explicitly assumed the risk of meeting this condition. Because the actual savings achieved was less than promised, the substantial performance was not sufficient. Thus, (A) and (B) are wrong. (D) is wrong because certification by the owner was never made a condition of the contract.

Answer to Question 8

(B) The newsstand owner is likely to prevail only if he can prove a mutual mistake. A contract can be reformed to reflect the original intent of the parties where there has been a mutual mistake in the integration. The plaintiff's negligence is not a bar to reformation. Here, both parties were unaware that the written contract did not reflect their agreement. (A) is not as good an answer as (B) because it fails to mention the mutual mistake element. (C) is wrong because the parol evidence rule does not apply in an action for reformation; if it did, contracts could rarely be reformed. (D) is wrong because the mistake here was not unilateral. Both parties believed that the written lease contained the exclusivity provision.

Answer to Question 9

(C) The court will likely deny the motion because Congress generally has the power to condition federal spending if Congress reasonably finds that the spending program is for the general welfare. (A) is incorrect because the federal government determines how the funds are to be expended, not the recipient. Thus, while it may be arguable that the city's plan is a better way to use the money, the fact remains that the money was given for one purpose only and it must be expended for that purpose. Hence, (B) is wrong because the federal government in this situation does have the authority to control the spending of its funds and it is not an interference with the state's sovereign powers. (D) is wrong because the doctrine of sovereignty does not just extend to the state's executive or legislative branch, but to all governmental activities and entities within the state.

Answer to Question 10

(D) Burglary requires a specific intent to commit a crime and intoxication might negate the existence of that intent. In the circumstances of the problem, the young man could argue with some force that he did not intend to kill the MP or act with premeditation, but must account for the fact that the killing occurred in what could be characterized as a burglary, which would be murder under the statutes of the jurisdiction. Thus, if the young man did not have the requisite intent, he did not commit burglary and so the killing does not fall under the felony murder part of the statute. The young man can therefore be convicted only if he acted intentionally or with premeditation. (A) is incorrect because voluntary intoxication is not a defense unless it negates ***intent***; (A) concerns the issue of causation. (B) is wrong because it states the wrong standard of proof—the prosecution must prove all elements of the crime beyond a reasonable doubt. (C) is wrong because voluntary intoxication may be a defense to the felony murder definition of murder.

Answer to Question 11

(C) The jury should find the defendant not guilty of murder. If the victim of the initial aggression suddenly escalates a "minor" fight into one involving deadly force, and does so without giving the initial aggressor the chance to withdraw, the aggressor may use force in her own defense. Here, even though the defendant was the initial aggressor, she reacquired her right to self-defense because her neighbor responded to the defendant's slap (nondeadly force) by shooting at her (deadly force) without giving the defendant a chance to withdraw. Thus, the defendant regained the right to use deadly force in self-defense. (C) is therefore correct, and (B) is incorrect. (A) is incorrect because the majority of jurisdictions do not require a party to retreat before using deadly force. Furthermore, even in those jurisdictions that follow the retreat rule, a person is not required to retreat unless she can do so with complete safety. Here, given that the neighbor was cocking the pistol to fire again at close range, the defendant would not have been able to retreat in safety. (D) is incorrect because, under the common law, a defendant can be guilty of murder even if she did not premeditate. At common law, malice aforethought includes (i) the intent to kill; (ii) the intent to inflict great bodily injury; (iii) a reckless indifference to an unjustifiably high risk to human life ("abandoned and malignant heart"); and (iv) the intent to commit a felony for felony murder.

Answer to Question 12

(B) The boy's culpability should be determined under the general rule that a minor's conduct is judged by the standard applicable to an ordinarily prudent minor of the same age, experience, and intelligence in similar circumstances. Thus, (A) is wrong. The fact that the boy is almost an adult does not make this rule inapplicable, but would affect the level of care to which he would be held. Therefore, (C) is wrong. (D) is a misstatement of law; strict liability does not apply.

Answer to Question 13

(C) The beekeeper will not prevail because the noise apparently would not disturb a person of ordinary sensibilities. For a private nuisance action to lie, the interference with the plaintiff's use and enjoyment of his land must be substantial. This means that it must be offensive, inconvenient, or annoying to an average person in the community. It will not be characterized as substantial if it is merely the result of the plaintiff's hypersensitivity or specialized use of his own property. Here, the noise from the wind turbines does not disturb other neighbors similarly situated, indicating that the plaintiff's disturbance was based on hypersensitivity. Thus, the fact that the beekeeper is bothered by it and that it may interfere with the beekeeping operation on his property does not make it a substantial interference. Hence, the beekeeper likely will not prevail under the circumstances here. (A) is incorrect because it is not sufficient that the farmer's conduct interfered with the beekeeper's use and enjoyment of his land; the interference must be both substantial and unreasonable for the beekeeper to prevail. (B) is incorrect because the farmer's violation of the zoning code does not establish that an actionable nuisance is present, particularly because the regulation that was violated pertained to the stability of the structure rather than the noise that was generated. Conversely, (D) is incorrect because the fact that the zoning code regulation was not designed to prevent excessive noise does not establish that the farmer's activity was not a nuisance; it could constitute a nuisance even if the structures complied with the zoning code regulation.

Answer to Question 14

(C) The buyer will prevail. Because the owner had a scheme for an exclusively residential subdivision that included these lots when the sales began (as evidenced by the recorded plat), a court will imply a reciprocal negative servitude limiting the remaining lots to the same use. (A) is incorrect because the owner also covenanted to restrict the lots to single-family use. (B) is incorrect, because if there is a reciprocal negative covenant, it would apply whether or not the deeds specifically contained the provision. The resort's actual knowledge is not the issue; the resort must have had actual notice, record notice, or, as is likely here, inquiry notice (*e.g.*, the neighborhood appears to conform to common restriction). Thus, (D) is not the best answer.

Answer to Question 15

(B) The religious leader and his followers will lose. The government can place reasonable restrictions on time, place, and manner of speech in public forums. It would be difficult to envision more reasonable ordinances than the ones involved here. Therefore, (B) is correct, because it states the appropriate rule. (D) is wrong, since a facial challenge requires that there be no conceivable circumstances under which the ordinance could be constitutionally applied, and that is clearly not the case here. (A) is wrong; the unconstitutionality of the ordinance could be raised for the first time as a defense in the criminal case. Under accepted principles of comity, the religious leader does not have to go to federal court to litigate federal constitutional claims. (C) is wrong because even if the law represents the "will of the people," it could still be unconstitutional. The Supreme Court has emphasized repeatedly that constitutional rights are neither subject to, nor can be compromised by, a "vote of the people."

Answer to Question 16

(A) Under Federal Rule 401, relevant evidence is evidence having any tendency to make a material fact more or less probable than it would be without the evidence, and is always the starting point of admissibility of evidence. However, relevant evidence may be excluded if its probative value is substantially outweighed by the needless presentation of cumulative evidence. Here, the witness's testimony is clearly relevant; however, 10 other witnesses have already been called to interpret the same statement. Therefore, the judge can deny admissibility of the testimony of this witness because it amounts to the needless presentation of cumulative evidence. (B) is incorrect. Hearsay is an out-of-court statement offered to prove the truth of the matter asserted. Here, the plaintiff is not offering the statement to prove the truth of the matter asserted; *i.e.,* she is not trying to prove that she is the biggest shyster in town. Rather, the statement is being offered to show the effect on the hearer. The witness will be testifying as to what she believed the statement meant. Thus, the statement is not hearsay. (C) is an incomplete answer choice. As stated above, the evidence is relevant, but is nevertheless inadmissible because of the needless presentation of cumulative evidence. (D) is incorrect because present state of mind is an exception to the hearsay rule, and as discussed above, the statement is not hearsay. Thus, the exception does not apply.

Answer to Question 17

(C) The court is likely to rule in favor of the nursery owner. The only basis of liability that the salesman could use in his suit is negligence—*i.e.,* that the nursery owner negligently selected and stored the fertilizer. Because the nursery owner acted reasonably in selecting and storing the fertilizer, she will prevail. (A) is wrong because the nursery owner would not be liable simply because other fertilizers were available. (B) is wrong because property owners are not strictly liable for all emissions from their property. There is no suggestion that the storage of the fertilizer was an abnormally dangerous activity that would allow the salesman to bring a strict liability action. (D) is wrong. Despite the fact that the salesman's lack of property rights in the land would preclude him from maintaining a nuisance action, he could still maintain a negligence action as a foreseeable victim of negligent conduct. (C) is the best answer because it precludes this result.

Answer to Question 18

(A) The court should find the record admissible. A witness other than the accused may be impeached by (i) any felony conviction (unless the judge determines that its probative value is substantially outweighed by Rule 403 considerations) or (ii) conviction of any other crime requiring proof or admission of an act of dishonesty or false statement. [Fed. R. Evid. 609(a)] Embezzlement is both. The fact that an appeal is pending does not affect the admissibility of the conviction; thus, (B) is incorrect. The official record of judgment is always admissible proof that the judgment was entered; (C) is therefore incorrect. While the proposition in (D) is correct, it does not apply to proof of prior convictions. A prior conviction may be shown not only by cross-examination of the witness but also by introducing a record of judgment.

Answer to Question 19

(A) The state laws will likely be found unconstitutional because a treaty is the supreme law of the land, and state statutes that conflict with ratified treaties are invalid. (B) and (C) state incorrect rules of law. The federal government may exercise its property powers to acquire control of free-roaming animals on public land. The federal government does not, however, have inherent authority over or ownership of all "free-roaming wildlife." A state may, in turn, assert some rights over animals within its borders. That power must, nevertheless, give way in the face of a valid exercise of federal power. (D) is wrong because a treaty, being the supreme law of the land, takes precedence over the rights reserved to the state under the Tenth Amendment.

Answer to Question 20

(A) The court should find for the friend. A grantor may deliver a deed to an escrowee with instructions that it be delivered to the grantee when certain conditions (*e.g.,* death of the grantor) are met. When the conditions occur, title passes automatically to the grantee and relates back to the date of delivery to the escrowee. Thus, (D) is incorrect. (B) is not as good an answer because the facts given are insufficient to conclude that the note is a valid conveyance. To work a conveyance, the note would have to include the names of the grantor and grantee, operative words of conveyance (questionable here), a description of the land, and the grantor's signature. (C) and (D) are wrong because deeds may be effective to convey property although recorded after the grantor's death or although the grantor remains in possession after executing the deed.

Answer to Question 21

(B) The court should find the woman guilty of both crimes. To convict for attempt, the prosecutor must establish that the defendant (i) had the specific intent to commit the crime; and (ii) engaged in behavior that constituted a substantial step toward commission of the crime and was strongly corroborative of the defendant's criminal purpose. The woman could be found guilty of attempting to obtain property by false pretenses. She had the specific intent to commit the crime, and the jury could find she took a substantial step toward commission of it. Thus, (A) and (C) are incorrect. Similarly, the woman had the specific intent to commit the robbery and took a substantial step toward commission of the crime. It is no defense to attempt that it was factually impossible for the defendant to complete the plan; she did all the things she intended to do. Thus, (D) is incorrect and (B) is correct.

Answer to Question 22

(D) The court will rule for the owner because the ordinance is too broad. The Supreme Court has defined obscenity as a description or depiction of sexual conduct that taken as a whole, by the average person, applying contemporary community standards, appeals to the prurient interest in sex, portrays sex in a patently offensive way, and using a reasonable person standard, does not have serious literary, artistic, political, or scientific value. Thus, under this definition, not all nudity is obscene. (A) is incorrect because although the town may try to protect its minors, that purpose does not allow it to prohibit all such advertisements. The ordinance is too broad to be valid and its purpose will not save it. (B) is incorrect because the "average person" in the above definition does not include children. (C) is incorrect because if the posters fall within the Court's definition of obscenity, they could be prohibited because obscenity is not protected by the First Amendment.

Answer to Question 23

(B) The employee's statement is admissible as a vicarious admission by a party-opponent. The statement acknowledges significant consumption of alcohol, which could have contributed to the accident. Under the Federal Rules, statements by an agent concerning a matter within the scope of his agency, made during the existence of the relationship, is nonhearsay. Thus, the employee's admission of drinking is admissible against his employer, and (D) is therefore incorrect. (A) is incorrect because the statement against interest exception requires that the declarant be unavailable as a witness. The facts do not indicate that the employee is unavailable. (C) is incorrect because the excited utterance exception requires that the statement concern the immediate facts of the startling occurrence. The employee's admission of drinking does not concern the immediate facts of the accident. Moreover, (A) and (C) are hearsay exceptions, and the Federal Rules do not recognize the employee's statement as hearsay.

Answer to Question 24

(A) The actress will prevail on an invasion of privacy claim. Where plaintiff is well-known, so that her name and likeness have commercial value, using plaintiff's name or likeness for commercial purposes without permission is an invasion of privacy. (B) is wrong. There is generally no violation of one's right of privacy when her picture is taken in a public place. (C) is wrong. In the absence of actual consent or some other recognized privilege, the appropriation is actionable. The store's good faith belief that consent was obtained is no defense. (D) is wrong because the actress's status as a public figure bolsters this type of invasion of privacy charge (commercial appropriation) rather than diminishes it.

Answer to Question 25

(A) Because the tenant installed the equipment without any intention to benefit her landlord, the chattels have not become fixtures, and she is entitled to remove them at the end of the lease term if she repairs any damage done by the removal. (B) is wrong because the Statute of Frauds does not preclude the bank from claiming an interest in chattels that have become fixtures and thus part of the real estate and are nonremovable. (C) is wrong because the tenant's notice of the mortgage is immaterial. The mortgagee's rights are no greater than those of the landlord herself, so the same issue could arise even without any mortgage being involved in the question. (D) is wrong because personal property that a tenant attaches to the real property may become a fixture (and thus part of the real property) if the tenant intended to improve the realty.

Answer to Question 26

(D) The seller has the superior claim to the hot tub under U.C.C. fixture filing rules. (A) is wrong because the seller's interest prevails, even over a prior recorded mortgage on land, as long as the fixture filing is recorded within 20 days after the hot tub is installed. (B) is wrong because the seller has a purchase money security interest in the hot tub, allowing the seller to repossess the hot tub in the event the landlord defaults on her payments. (C) is wrong because the landlord had installed the chattel herself and there is no indication that it was guaranteed by the lease, so the friend would have no claim to the hot tub.

Answer to Question 27

(C) Although the First and Fourteenth Amendments severely limit the states' right to regulate public speech, reasonable regulations based on time, place, and manner are constitutionally permissible. (D) is thus wrong. (A) is wrong because the fact that the civic center is a place normally used for demonstrations of this type does not bar the city from restricting the demonstration; that is exactly why the city sought to impose certain limitations on these demonstrations. (B) is also incorrect, because a municipality does have the limited right to place certain limitations on a citizen's right of free speech in these circumstances, even when there is absolutely no reason to believe that the demonstration will be anything but peaceful and quiet. However, any such regulation by the city cannot be substantially overbroad (*e.g.,* censor protected speech) or vague (*i.e.,* be so unclear as to what is prohibited that a demonstrator is required to censor himself). The statute's provisions for terminating a parade and arresting demonstrators are overbroad and too vague to meet any legitimate state purpose. Absent any court decisions that have limited construction of the regulation so as to remove the threat to constitutionally protected expression, the statute's imprecise terms could be applied to protected speech and do not provide persons with reasonable notice as to what speech is prohibited.

Answer to Question 28

(C) The strongest argument for the county is that the employee had not been granted permanent employment status. During the two-year period, the employee was subject to being fired at any time. Thus, she had no right in the nature of a property right and, constitutionally, would not be entitled to a hearing. (A), (B), and (D) are all arguable reasons for terminating the employee's employment. However, just because the county might have had a valid reason for firing her, it does not follow that the county could forgo a hearing if she were otherwise entitled to one. (A), in addition, is not a good argument if the standard by which the employee was tested was an artificial standard, having no rational relationship to the needs of the job of the employee.

Answer to Question 29

(B) The driver will recover the full amount of his damages because there is no evidence that the driver was negligent. Thus, he can recover all of his damages regardless of the jurisdiction's adoption of comparative negligence. (A) and (D) are wrong because one spouse's negligence is ordinarily not imputed to the other. (C) is wrong because this is not the proper use of the last clear chance doctrine. That doctrine is used by plaintiffs to rebut a contributory negligence defense, not by defendants to defend a negligence claim, and is not applicable in comparative negligence jurisdictions.

Answer to Question 30

(B) The son will recover a portion of his damages. The son's negligence will proportionately reduce his recovery (even if greater than that of the driver). (A) is incorrect because the son's damages will be reduced by the amount of his own fault, regardless of whether the girlfriend was negligent. (C) is incorrect because the last clear chance doctrine is used by plaintiffs to counter a contributory negligence defense, not by defendants to defend a negligence claim, and is not applicable in comparative negligence jurisdictions. (D) is incorrect because pure comparative fault allocates liability based on the percentage of a tortfeasor's fault, not on the basis of who is "primarily" at fault.

Answer to Question 31

(B) The hitchhiker is liable as an accessory after the fact because she helped the prisoner to escape arrest. An accessory after the fact is one who receives, relieves, comforts, or assists another knowing that he has committed a felony, in order to help the felon escape arrest, trial, or conviction. The felony must be completed at the time the aid is rendered. The prisoner committed the felony of car theft. Although the hitchhiker was emotionally disturbed and of borderline mental retardation, she understood what the prisoner had done and that the police were after him. Knowing these things, the hitchhiker decided to help the prisoner escape the police, and she actively assisted him by doing some of the driving to the mountains to avoid the police. Thus, the hitchhiker knowingly assisted a felon in an effort to help him escape apprehension. This conduct renders the hitchhiker liable as an accessory after the fact. Because the hitchhiker is liable for the common law crime of being an accessory after the fact, (D) is incorrect. (A) is incorrect because the hitchhiker and the prisoner did not enter into an agreement to commit car theft. A conspiracy is a combination or agreement between two or more persons to accomplish some unlawful purpose, or to accomplish a lawful purpose by unlawful means. Conspiracy requires: (i) an agreement between two or more persons; (ii) an intent to enter into an agreement; and (iii) an intent to achieve the objective of the agreement. Each conspirator is liable for the crimes of all other conspirators if: (i) the crimes were committed in furtherance of the objectives of the conspiracy; and (ii) the crimes were a natural and probable consequence of the conspiracy. Here, there was no agreement between the hitchhiker and the prisoner to accomplish the theft of the car by mutual action. The hitchhiker did not even meet the prisoner until after he had stolen the car, at which time she agreed to help him escape capture. Helping the prisoner escape capture after the completion of the car theft does not make the hitchhiker a co-conspirator with regard to the theft itself. (C) is incorrect because compounding a felony consists of entering into an agreement for valuable consideration not to prosecute another for a felony or to conceal the commission of a felony or the whereabouts of a felon. Although the hitchhiker helped to conceal the whereabouts of the prisoner, she did so simply because of her dislike for the police. The hitchhiker did not agree to conceal the prisoner's whereabouts in exchange for valuable consideration. Therefore, the hitchhiker is not guilty of compounding a felony.

Answer to Question 32

(A) If the jury believes the defendant's testimony, he did not have the intent for robbery. A robbery consists of (i) a taking (ii) of personal property of another, (iii) from the other's person or presence, (iv) by force or intimidation, (v) with the intent to permanently deprive him of it. Thus, robbery is basically an aggravated form of larceny in which the taking is accomplished by force or threats of force. If the jury believes the defendant's testimony that he was only trying to beg for some bus money, his only intent was to accept money that the man voluntarily gave him. The defendant did not have the requisite criminal intent because the defendant believed that the man was freely transferring his interest in the property to the defendant. Thus, the jury should find him not guilty of robbery. (B) is incorrect because the defendant's intent, rather than the effect of his conduct, is the controlling factor. Without any other facts, the defendant's conduct was sufficiently intimidating that a jury could conclude that he had an intent to rob. If the jury believes the defendant's testimony, however, it should find that he did not have the intent necessary for robbery. (C) is incorrect because the defendant's testimony, if believed, would also negate the intent necessary for assault. Criminal assault is either (i) an attempt to commit a battery, or (ii) the intentional creation of a reasonable apprehension in the mind of the victim of imminent bodily harm. If the defendant had intended to create an apprehension of imminent bodily harm, he would be liable for robbery because he would have been using that apprehension to permanently deprive the man of his property. However, assuming that the defendant was just trying to beg rather than rob, he will not be found to have intended to create the apprehension that he did. (D) is incorrect not only because the defendant's testimony disproves the requisite intent of either offense, but also because the assault would be a lesser included offense of the robbery under these circumstances. A lesser included offense is one that consists entirely of some (but not all) of the elements of the greater crime. Under the constitutional prohibition against double jeopardy, lesser included offenses "merge" into the greater offenses, in the sense that one may not be convicted of both the greater offense and a lesser included offense. Here, the robbery would be by intimidation: conduct by the defendant that was intended to create apprehension of imminent bodily harm in the man's mind. This element of the robbery offense would be enough to establish liability for assault as well, but robbery has additional elements; hence, the defendant could not have been found guilty of both robbery and the lesser included offense of assault.

Answer to Question 33

(C) The killing was involuntary manslaughter if the jury believes the brother. The brother's failure to determine whether the fisherman was dead or alive when the brother and the sister threw the fisherman into the water constitutes criminal negligence, and when a death is caused by criminal negligence, it is involuntary manslaughter. Criminal negligence requires a greater deviation from the reasonable person standard than is required for civil liability. The defendant must have taken a very unreasonable risk in light of the utility of his conduct, knowledge of the facts, and the nature and extent of the harm that may be caused. The brother's conduct in throwing the fisherman into the lake was designed merely to disguise the fact that the fisherman had been hit on the head and apparently killed by the sister. Such conduct has no social utility. In addition, the brother was certainly aware that, if the fisherman was not actually dead, throwing him into the water would most likely result in his death by drowning. Thus, the brother acted with a sufficiently high degree of deviation from the reasonable person standard of care as to constitute criminal negligence. This negligence caused the death of the fisherman. Therefore, the killing is involuntary manslaughter. (A) is incorrect because an excusable homicide is one for which there is a defense to criminal liability, which is not the case here. The brother's commission of involuntary manslaughter means that the death of the fisherman is the result of criminal homicide rather than excusable homicide. (B) is incorrect because the killing of the fisherman was not intentional. An intentional killing is reduced from murder to voluntary manslaughter if the defendant committed the killing under a provocation that would arouse sudden and intense passion in an ordinary person such as to cause him to lose self-control, and there was insufficient time between the provocation and the killing for the passions of a reasonable person to cool. As noted above, the brother's act resulting in the death of the fisherman was not intentional, but was rather committed as a consequence of criminal negligence. In addition, the brother was not acting under any provocation that would have reduced an intentional killing to voluntary manslaughter. For these reasons, the killing is not voluntary manslaughter. (D) is incorrect because the brother did not act with malice aforethought. Murder is the unlawful killing of a human being with malice aforethought. Malice aforethought exists if the defendant: (i) intends to kill; (ii) intends to inflict great bodily injury; (iii) is aware of an unjustifiably high risk to human life; or (iv) intends to commit a felony. It is theoretically possible that the brother could be convicted of murder based on awareness of an unjustifiably high risk to human life (depraved heart). However, a finding that the brother acted unreasonably would not establish this state of mind. When the brother threw the fisherman into the water, believing that the fisherman was dead, he was most likely acting with criminal negligence rather than with any of the states of mind that would constitute malice aforethought. Therefore, the brother is not guilty of murder.

Answer to Question 34

(C) The man will be found not guilty of larceny and guilty of battery. Larceny is a specific intent crime that requires that the defendant intend to permanently deprive the owner of his property. If the defendant can show that he really believed the car to be his own, there is no intent to deprive the owner of his property. Therefore, the defendant is not guilty of larceny, and (B) and (D) are incorrect. (A) is wrong because battery is a general intent crime that can arise out of a showing of gross negligence. Shooting at a residence is gross negligence and can support a finding of battery even if the defendant does not know that anyone is home.

Answer to Question 35

(D) A contract has not been formed between the dealership and the mom. If offers stating precisely the same terms cross in the mail, they do not give rise to a contract. An offer cannot be accepted if there is no knowledge of it. The letters sent by the mom and the salesman constitute crossing offers, of which there was no acceptance. Thus, there is no contract. (C) is therefore incorrect. (B) is incorrect; it is a misstatement of the law. (A) is incorrect because, under the U.C.C., a reasonable price will be supplied by the court unless the parties have shown that they do not want a contract until they have agreed on price. Here, the May 15 writing indicates that the mom and the salesman did not intend to be contractually bound until they agreed on a price. As explained above, the crossing letters do not indicate an agreement on price.

Answer to Question 36

(C) The newspaper's best argument is based on freedom of speech. The validity of a law that regulates elections is determined by a balancing test. If the law regulates "core political speech," rather than the process surrounding elections, strict scrutiny is applied (*i.e.,* the law must be narrowly tailored to achieve a compelling interest). The Supreme Court has held that a state law prohibiting campaigning on election day is invalid as applied to a newspaper editorial urging voters to vote a certain way, because the right to comment on political issues is an essential element of free speech. The state statute at issue here is similar to the law that was held invalid by the Court; thus, its enforcement should be enjoined on free speech grounds. (A) does not offer a very good argument for the paper. It is true that the regulation affects interstate commerce because the newspaper is circulated in other states. However, because the regulation does not directly burden interstate commerce (*i.e.,* it does not discriminate against interstate commerce by favoring local economic interests), the newspaper must argue that the burden on interstate commerce outweighs the promotion of legitimate local interests. Here, the local interest of promoting fair elections is quite strong, and the burden on interstate commerce is very weak. Therefore, the Commerce Clause argument is not very strong. (B) is incorrect because the statute in fact does not affect the newspaper's right to distribute the paper; it merely prohibits the paper from containing certain material on certain days. (D) would not be a good argument because the Equal Protection Clause only prohibits setting up classes to treat similar persons or groups in a dissimilar manner. Here, all similar entities (newspapers) are treated alike—none is allowed to publish political editorials the day before and the day of an election. The fact that the same material can be printed on other days does not create an equal protection problem.

Answer to Question 37

(D) The testimony should be admissible. The witness's proposed testimony about the victim's statement ("I'm going to die. The car that hit me had license number DD666!") is hearsay evidence. Hearsay is an out-of-court statement offered in evidence to prove the truth of the matter asserted in the statement. [Fed. R. Evid. 801(c)] Because it appears that the victim's statement is being offered to establish that the car that hit him had license number DD666, it is hearsay. Nevertheless, it is admissible under the "excited utterance" exception to the hearsay rule. Hence, (D) is correct. At first glance it might seem that the "dying declaration" exception to the hearsay rule applies as well. [*See* Fed. R. Evid. 804(b)(2)] There is no indication, however, that the declarant (the victim) is ***unavailable*** to testify, a prerequisite for admitting evidence under the dying declaration exception. [Fed. R. Evid. 804(a)] The victim is a party and thus would seem to be available to testify. If the victim were to testify that he had no memory as to the license number, he would be considered unavailable [Fed. R. Evid. 804(a)(3)], but there is no indication that the victim has so testified. Therefore, the dying declaration exception does not apply, and (C) is incorrect. (B) is incorrect because the witness's proposed testimony is admissible under the hearsay exception for "excited utterances." [Fed. R. Evid. 803(2)] This hearsay exception, like most, does ***not*** require the declarant to be unavailable as a condition for the admission of hearsay evidence. It merely requires that the hearsay statement relate to a ***startling event or condition***, made while the declarant was under the ***stress of excitement*** caused by the event or condition. The victim's statement relates to a startling event (the car crash) that prompted the statement. Because the statement was made so soon after the crash, while the victim was badly injured, it probably constitutes an excited utterance. The witness's testimony is highly probative in establishing that the defendant was driving the car that struck the victim. (A) is incorrect in asserting that the witness's testimony is inadmissible because it is more prejudicial than probative. The witness's testimony is in no sense ***unfairly*** prejudicial to the defendant.

Answer to Question 38

(A) In order to issue a valid search warrant, the magistrate must determine that there exist reasonable grounds to believe that a legitimate item of seizure is located at the place to be searched, *i.e.,* "probable cause to search." However, a finding that the warrant was invalid because it was not supported by probable cause will not entitle a defendant to exclude the evidence obtained under the warrant if the police reasonably relied on the warrant's facial validity. Hence, (A) is correct.

(B) and (D) are wrong because once the police are in the defendant's apartment with a facially valid search warrant, it is immaterial that they are unable to find the items for which the search warrant was issued, and if in their legal search they turn up other contraband, evidence of this discovery is admissible. (C) is wrong. It is true that the length of time between the time an informant observed some facts and the time this information is given to the police is important, because the greater the time, the less chance that the facts still remain the same. Therefore, there is less probable cause to believe that the designated items are still in the place where the informant says they are. However, as discussed above, a determination that probable cause is absent will not necessarily require that the evidence be excluded.

Answer to Question 39

(C) The jeweler is entitled to recover $400 because, on attaining the age of majority, the girlfriend affirmed the contract as to her ring at that price. Infants generally lack legal capacity to incur binding contractual obligations. Contracts entered into by infants are voidable at this election unless the contract is for a "necessity." On reaching majority, an infant may affirm; that is, choose to be bound by her contract. Here, at the time of entering into the contract for the two rings, the girlfriend was not yet 18 years old (the applicable age of majority). Because a wedding ring is not a necessity, the girlfriend's contract was voidable at her option. However, when the girlfriend went back to see the jeweler, she had reached the age of 18. At that time, she chose to be bound by the contract, although her affirmation was limited to her ring (instead of both rings), and to a lower price for her ring than that which was originally agreed upon. When a voidable promise is reaffirmed, the promise will be enforced according to the terms of the reaffirmation rather than the original obligation. Thus, the girlfriend is now bound by her contract, but only for the purchase of ***her*** ring at a price of $400. (D) is incorrect because it ignores the fact that, having affirmed the contract (albeit on different terms), the girlfriend, who is no longer an infant, is bound to the terms of the reaffirmed contract. (A) is incorrect because $1,150 reflects the purchase price of both rings as contained in the original contract. On reaching majority, the girlfriend chose not to be bound by the original contract. Similarly, (B) is incorrect because $500 reflects the purchase price of the girlfriend's ring as contained in the original agreement (as well as the market value of the ring). On reaching majority, the girlfriend could have refused to pay anything. She is now bound only to the contract as affirmed by her, which is for $400.

Answer to Question 40

(C) The seller prevails because the doctrine of equitable conversion places the risk of loss on the purchaser as soon as the enforceable contract is entered into. (B) is wrong because "marketable" title does not refer to whether the seller would be able to sell a destroyed home or not. It refers to a deed free of any possible dispute as to who is the owner of the property. (A) is wrong because the doctrine of equitable conversion applies to the risk of loss and, thus, there is no such implied term in the conveyance or contract. (D) is wrong because the seller is entitled to receive the contract price in the specific performance action.

Answer to Question 41

(B) The evidence will likely be inadmissible. Other crimes and wrongdoings of a defendant are sometimes admissible to prove motive, opportunity, intent, preparation, plans, knowledge, identity, or absence of mistake [Fed. R. Evid. 404(b)], provided, however, that the probative value of the evidence is not substantially outweighed by prejudice or other Rule 403 considerations. On these facts, the probative value of possession of cocaine seems very slight and is highly prejudicial. Therefore, the evidence will probably be inadmissible. (A) is wrong. Other crime evidence is sometimes admissible to show motive, opportunity, etc., even if the defendant does not place his character in issue. Also, if the defendant offers evidence of good character, the prosecutor cannot for that reason alone offer extrinsic evidence of specific crimes. (C) is wrong. The issue is whether the defendant murdered the victim during a burglary, not what he did with the money. It is true that the evidence tends to show that the defendant had money, but the probative value that he committed the crime charged would be very slight and clearly outweighed by prejudice. (D) is wrong. If the evidence were offered to prove that the defendant is capable of committing serious crimes, it would be inadmissible character evidence.

Answer to Question 42

(B) The nod constitutes nonverbal conduct intended as an assertion and would thus be considered a "statement" for purposes of the hearsay rule. However, this statement constitutes an admission and hence is not hearsay under Federal Rule 801. (C) is therefore incorrect. Likewise, (A) is incorrect, because (i) an excited utterance is an exception to the hearsay rule and this is not hearsay, and (ii) even if it were hearsay, this does not constitute an excited utterance because the statement was not made during or soon after the startling event and under the stress of that event. (D) is incorrect. The defendant responded to the question with a nod. If the defendant had failed to respond and the prosecutor wished to introduce his silence as an adoptive admission, then it would be necessary to determine whether there was a reason to respond.

Answer to Question 43

(B) The court should rule in favor of the chief. This is one of the very rare situations in which a distinction based on race is likely to be upheld. The government, based on the facts, has a compelling interest in infiltrating the racist group. Due to the nature of the group, a white police officer is obviously necessary for this task. This means the action meets both elements of the strict scrutiny test: the interest is compelling and the means selected are narrowly tailored because no other nondiscriminatory action would work. The increased salary likely reflects the danger of the undercover task, and so is justifiable. (A) is incorrect because the rational basis test is never used for racial discrimination. Strict scrutiny always is employed. (C) is incorrect because even discriminatory conduct is permissible if it is necessary to achieve a compelling government interest and the means selected are narrowly tailored. (D) is incorrect because, based on the facts of the question, the group prohibits association with black persons. Thus, even if there is a slight chance that a black person could win the confidence of the group, the court would still likely hold that the chief had a compelling interest to impose that qualification.

Answer to Question 44

(A) A contract has been formed because the supplier's fax will be considered an offer and the dealer's second fax will be considered an acceptance of the offer. Although the dealer merely asked for a price quote, the supplier's fax in response will be construed as an offer because the language and surrounding circumstances make it reasonable for the dealer to expect that the supplier was willing to enter into a contract. "I can deliver 20 computers . . . [for] $1,000 per computer" coupled with the fact that the supplier knew that the dealer wanted to buy 20 computers makes it reasonable for the dealer to assume that the supplier was manifesting a promise, undertaking, or commitment to enter into a contract, especially because the terms were so specific here as to quantity, price, and delivery date. The dealer's response was an acceptance of the supplier's offer to sell the computers. (B) is wrong because the supplier's fax was the offer, not the acceptance.

The dealer's initial fax could not be construed as an offer because it did not manifest present contractual intent and was not definite as to the terms. Therefore, (C) is also wrong. (D) is wrong because the supplier's fax was definite enough to be an offer. The U.C.C. does not require the same degree of formality as the common law, and so a contract was clearly formed when the dealer responded with the fax.

Answer to Question 45

(A) The supplier is liable for the last payment. The fact that the supplier was to pay the $1,000 when he received his last payment from the store would be interpreted as a provision setting the time for payment rather than the source from which the payment was to come, because the price was clearly set at $4,000 and was not expressly made conditional on the store's paying the supplier. Therefore, the supplier could not claim that because he had not received payment from the store he did not have to pay the seller. Thus, (C) and (D) are incorrect. (B) is incorrect because it misstates the law.

Answer to Question 46

(D) Because the leasehold interest is a property interest, the lessee has a constitutional right to compensation for the property interest taken through eminent domain. Compensation will be determined by the value of the estate, less the rent the lessee no longer is required to pay. (A) is incorrect. The taking of land through eminent domain results in the taking of all interests in the land. (B) is wrong because cultivating land does not prevent a state from taking title under proper eminent domain. (C) is incorrect. It is true that the lessee may not continue to occupy the land and that he is free of his rent obligation, but he will share in the condemnation award.

Answer to Question 47

(C) The wife should not be given benefits. The Supreme Court in *Weinberger v. Salfi* (1975) held that the government does not have to show a compelling reason for denying noncontractual benefits. The wife's rights were noncontractual, and the only obligation of the government was to show that the classification of nine months served some proper governmental purpose. The Court stated that the purpose behind the requirement is to prevent sham marriages (*i.e.*, those solely to qualify for benefits). Thus, (A) and (B) are wrong. (D) is wrong. It implies that distinctions predicated on gender are appropriate in the face of a claim that more women than men would qualify for the benefits, a proposition the Court has rejected on numerous occasions.

Answer to Question 48

(C) The testimony should be ruled admissible. The store owner's proposed testimony about the victim's statement ("I'm going to die. My upstairs neighbor shot me.") is hearsay evidence. Hearsay is an out-of-court statement offered in evidence to prove the truth of the matter asserted in the statement. [Fed. R. Evid. 801(c)] Because it appears that the victim's statement is being offered to establish that the defendant did the shooting, it is hearsay. Nevertheless, it is admissible under the "dying declaration" exception to the hearsay rule. For a dying declaration to be admissible, two prerequisites must be met: (i) The declarant must be ***unavailable*** to testify. [Fed. R. Evid. 804(a)] The victim, being dead, obviously is unavailable to testify. (ii) A dying declaration can only be admitted ***in certain kinds of cases***—homicide prosecutions and civil cases.

[Fed. R. Evid. 804(b)(2)] This is an appropriate case, a murder prosecution. This hearsay exception further requires that the declarant's statement be made while believing her death to be ***imminent***, and that the statement concern the ***cause or circumstances*** of what the declarant believed to be impending death. [Fed. R. Evid. 804(b)(2)] The victim believed her death was imminent. She was bleeding profusely from being shot and gasped, "I'm going to die." In addition, her statement ("My upstairs neighbor shot me") pertained to the cause or circumstances of her death. The store owner's proposed testimony might also be admissible under the hearsay exception for "excited utterances." Rule 803(2) makes admissible a hearsay statement relating to a ***startling event or condition***, made while the declarant was under the stress of excitement caused by the event or condition. Certainly one could argue that the victim's statement was an excited utterance. But the question does not make clear that her statement was made while under the stress of excitement. Thus, while (D) is a plausible answer, (C) is better because the victim's statement fits so precisely within the dying declaration exception to the hearsay rule. (B) is clearly wrong because it asserts that the statement does not fit within any recognized exception to the hearsay rule. (A) is wrong. The store owner's testimony obviously would be highly probative in establishing that the defendant murdered the victim. (A) nonetheless asserts that the testimony should be inadmissible because it is more prejudicial than probative. This answer is incorrect because it fundamentally misconceives the concept of prejudice in the context of the Rule 403 probative value/prejudicial impact balancing test. The only kind of prejudice that can properly be balanced under this test is ***unfair*** prejudice. The "prejudice" surrounding the admission of the store owner's testimony is not in any sense unfair; it is merely the natural result of any evidence having such ***persuasive*** force. In other words, it is prejudicial only in the sense that it will harm the defendant's defense because it is highly probative of the fact that the defendant killed the victim.

Answer to Question 49

(C) If the court denies the motion, it will be because the jury could determine that the workers were negligent in leaving the open trench without additional protection for passersby. A finding of negligence establishes the prima facie elements of duty and breach in a negligence action. The other elements of actual cause, proximate cause, and damages are indicated by the facts, so the trier of fact should determine whether the company has breached its duty. (A) is incorrect because the fact that the boy appears to have been attracted to the trench by the warning sign, which was not readable from the street, does not establish negligence on the part of the company or that the trench was an attractive nuisance (which is a doctrine applicable to property owners). (B) is wrong because the boy could still recover even if the jurisdiction retains traditional contributory negligence and assumption of risk rules. His conduct in walking up to the sign was not contributorily negligent, nor did he knowingly and voluntarily assume any risk by reading the sign. Assumption of risk requires that the boy know of the risk as well as voluntarily assume it. The boy cannot be said to have known of a risk that the edge of the excavation would give way. Although knowledge may be implied where the risk is one that the average person would clearly appreciate, the court will take into account the boy's age and any other relevant circumstances. It is unlikely that a court would find that an average seventh-grader would appreciate the unstable nature of the edge of the trench in the dusk. (D) is incorrect because strict liability would only be imposed if excavations were considered abnormally dangerous activities. For an activity to be abnormally dangerous, it (i) must involve a risk of serious harm to persons or property even when reasonable care is exercised by all actors, and (ii) must not be a matter of common usage in the community. Although involving a risk of serious harm, an excavation generally is not classified as an abnormally dangerous activity because it can be done safely and is a fairly common activity.

Answer to Question 50

(D) The court will most likely rule that the evidence should be suppressed. A statement is only considered to be voluntary if it is the product of a free and rational choice. If from the surrounding circumstances it appears that the statement was produced by either physical or mental coercion, it will not be considered to be voluntary. While it is a judgment for the court as to whether the confession would be voluntary or involuntary, the lengthy interrogation would probably result in a finding that the confession was involuntary. If the confession is determined to be involuntary, the evidence obtained as a direct result of the confession will probably be suppressed as the fruit of the poisonous tree. (A) is incorrect because evidence obtained pursuant to a warrant is inadmissible if the warrant was improperly issued. (B) is incorrect because the defendant is not basing his motion to suppress on the search of the garage but on the illegally obtained statement. (C) is incorrect because a warrant may be issued on the basis of such uncorroborated statements.

Mixed Subject Set 6 Answer Sheet

1. Ⓐ Ⓑ Ⓒ Ⓓ	26. Ⓐ Ⓑ Ⓒ Ⓓ
2. Ⓐ Ⓑ Ⓒ Ⓓ	27. Ⓐ Ⓑ Ⓒ Ⓓ
3. Ⓐ Ⓑ Ⓒ Ⓓ	28. Ⓐ Ⓑ Ⓒ Ⓓ
4. Ⓐ Ⓑ Ⓒ Ⓓ	29. Ⓐ Ⓑ Ⓒ Ⓓ
5. Ⓐ Ⓑ Ⓒ Ⓓ	30. Ⓐ Ⓑ Ⓒ Ⓓ
6. Ⓐ Ⓑ Ⓒ Ⓓ	31. Ⓐ Ⓑ Ⓒ Ⓓ
7. Ⓐ Ⓑ Ⓒ Ⓓ	32. Ⓐ Ⓑ Ⓒ Ⓓ
8. Ⓐ Ⓑ Ⓒ Ⓓ	33. Ⓐ Ⓑ Ⓒ Ⓓ
9. Ⓐ Ⓑ Ⓒ Ⓓ	34. Ⓐ Ⓑ Ⓒ Ⓓ
10. Ⓐ Ⓑ Ⓒ Ⓓ	35. Ⓐ Ⓑ Ⓒ Ⓓ
11. Ⓐ Ⓑ Ⓒ Ⓓ	36. Ⓐ Ⓑ Ⓒ Ⓓ
12. Ⓐ Ⓑ Ⓒ Ⓓ	37. Ⓐ Ⓑ Ⓒ Ⓓ
13. Ⓐ Ⓑ Ⓒ Ⓓ	38. Ⓐ Ⓑ Ⓒ Ⓓ
14. Ⓐ Ⓑ Ⓒ Ⓓ	39. Ⓐ Ⓑ Ⓒ Ⓓ
15. Ⓐ Ⓑ Ⓒ Ⓓ	40. Ⓐ Ⓑ Ⓒ Ⓓ
16. Ⓐ Ⓑ Ⓒ Ⓓ	41. Ⓐ Ⓑ Ⓒ Ⓓ
17. Ⓐ Ⓑ Ⓒ Ⓓ	42. Ⓐ Ⓑ Ⓒ Ⓓ
18. Ⓐ Ⓑ Ⓒ Ⓓ	43. Ⓐ Ⓑ Ⓒ Ⓓ
19. Ⓐ Ⓑ Ⓒ Ⓓ	44. Ⓐ Ⓑ Ⓒ Ⓓ
20. Ⓐ Ⓑ Ⓒ Ⓓ	45. Ⓐ Ⓑ Ⓒ Ⓓ
21. Ⓐ Ⓑ Ⓒ Ⓓ	46. Ⓐ Ⓑ Ⓒ Ⓓ
22. Ⓐ Ⓑ Ⓒ Ⓓ	47. Ⓐ Ⓑ Ⓒ Ⓓ
23. Ⓐ Ⓑ Ⓒ Ⓓ	48. Ⓐ Ⓑ Ⓒ Ⓓ
24. Ⓐ Ⓑ Ⓒ Ⓓ	49. Ⓐ Ⓑ Ⓒ Ⓓ
25. Ⓐ Ⓑ Ⓒ Ⓓ	50. Ⓐ Ⓑ Ⓒ Ⓓ

MIXED SUBJECT QUESTIONS - SET 6

Question 1

A state enacted legislation providing for the testing of all high school students in the performance of certain adult-world tasks. In public schools, the test was administered at the school by government employees. In private schools—both religious and secular—the test was administered by school personnel, and the schools were reimbursed for the costs of administering the tests and reporting the results to the state.

An association with appropriate standing filed suit seeking to enjoin the reimbursement to the religious schools, claiming that the reimbursement violates the Establishment Clause of the First Amendment to the United States Constitution.

The trial court should:

(A) Grant the injunction, because direct state payment to religious schools violates the Establishment Clause.

(B) Grant the injunction, because the state may not require the religious schools to conduct tests that violate their religious principles.

(C) Deny the injunction, because the reimbursement has a secular purpose that neither advances nor inhibits religion and that will not entangle the state in religion.

(D) Deny the injunction, because the tests do not involve matters of religion.

Question 2

The owner of a used car dealership and his business had been under investigation by the IRS for several months because of suspected fraudulent tax returns. In addition, a police detective who had been investigating a stolen car ring uncovered evidence indicating that the car dealer might be a part of the ring. The detective went to the car lot and found evidence indicating that the ring was operating through there. The car dealer then agreed to accompany the detective to the station to make a statement on the evidence. On the way he voluntarily informed the detective about the fraudulently filed tax returns, because he believed that by revealing these facts he might receive a lighter sentence for his involvement in the stolen car ring.

At his trial for filing false tax returns, the car dealer's attorney moved to exclude the statement he made. The best argument for admitting the statement is that:

(A) The police detective was not an agent of the Internal Revenue Service.

(B) The car dealer had not been formally charged at the time that the statement was made.

(C) The statement was volunteered by the car dealer.

(D) The statement was made prior to the arrest of the car dealer.

Question 3

A housecleaning agency was given a key to a customer's house so that the agency could have its employees clean while the homeowner was away. After a maid sent by the agency had finished and left the homeowner's house, she went back because she had forgotten her cigarettes. She neglected to lock the door when she left the second time because she was already late for the next job. When the homeowner returned after a few days away, she discovered that her house had been ransacked and several items of jewelry stolen. The front door was open, and there were no signs of forced entry.

If the homeowner brings an action against the agency that employed the maid, she likely will:

(A) Not prevail, because she is limited to claims for breach of contract based on her agreement with the agency.

(B) Not prevail, because the act of the burglar was an independent supervening cause of the homeowner's loss.

(C) Prevail, because the maid's failure to lock the door created the risk that someone might enter and take the homeowner's valuables.

(D) Prevail, because when the maid returned after having completed her work, she was technically a trespasser, making the agency vicariously liable for any damage she caused to the premises.

Question 4

The owner in fee simple of a tract of land told his favorite nephew, "I've always liked you, so I'm going to leave you my land when I die." The nephew, who was being pressured by his friend to pay off an old debt, executed and delivered to her a general warranty deed to the tract of land. The friend immediately recorded the deed. The owner died shortly thereafter. His will left the tract of land to his nephew.

Which of the following best describes the effect of the nephew's deed to the friend at the time it was recorded?

(A) It was ineffective as a conveyance of either legal or equitable interest in the tract of land.

(B) It effectively conveyed legal title to the tract of land because it was recorded.

(C) It effectively conveyed equitable title to the tract of land.

(D) It effectively conveyed the nephew's expectancy of title.

Question 5

The owner of a small business had a written contract with a cleaning company to clean the business's building on a daily basis. One week prior to the contract's expiration date, the parties agreed to a new contract that would contain the same terms as the prior contract, which the owner would prepare. When the owner gave the new contract to the cleaner for his signature, the owner represented that it was the same as the old contract. However, the owner knew this was not true because he included new cleaning duties that were not in the earlier contract. Relying on the owner's representations, the cleaner signed the contract without reading it.

If the cleaner sues the business, he could obtain:

(A) Rescission.

(B) Reformation.

(C) Novation.

(D) Repudiation.

Question 6

A young couple agreed to break into an elderly woman's house to steal a painting, but they were arrested shortly after they pried open the house's back door. Both were charged with conspiracy to commit larceny, among other crimes. At her trial, the woman testified that she suspected the man of being a thief, that she agreed to the plan in order to catch him, and that she had made an anonymous telephone call to the police alerting them to the crime to enable them to make an arrest "in the act." The jurisdiction follows common law conspiracy rules.

As to a charge of conspiracy to commit larceny, if the jury believes the woman, it should find her:

(A) Not guilty, because she did not intend to steal.

(B) Not guilty, because she prevented the theft from occurring.

(C) Guilty, because there was an agreement, and the prying open of the back door was sufficient for the overt act.

(D) Guilty, because she is not a police officer, and thus cannot claim any privilege of apprehending criminals.

Question 7

A woman who was hospitalized with a serious case of salmonella poisoning after eating some chicken sued the grocery store that sold the chicken and the chicken plant that processed it. At trial, the woman called a biochemist and asked him whether, in his opinion, based on laboratory reports made concerning her illness and tests on the remainder of the chicken in her freezer, it was possible that the chicken was the source of the salmonella. The reports are relied on by biochemists, and the biochemist had the reports with him. Counsel for the chicken production plant objected to the biochemist's testimony on this point.

The court should rule that the testimony is:

(A) Admissible, because such reports are reasonably relied upon by biochemists in the course of their profession.

(B) Admissible, because the biochemist has the reports with him and can offer them into evidence.

(C) Inadmissible, because the biochemist's testimony embraces the ultimate issue in the case.

(D) Inadmissible, because the contents of the laboratory reports are hearsay and not admissible under any exception.

Question 8

A woman purported to convey a vacant parcel of land she did not own to a buyer by a general warranty deed. The buyer immediately recorded the deed, built a house on the land, and has resided there ever since. Six months later, the woman acquired title to the parcel of land from the true owner. The woman immediately sold the land to an investor by a general warranty deed, which the investor promptly recorded. The investor paid the woman a reasonable value for the parcel of land. Because the investor purchased the parcel of land solely as an investment and never visited it, she never knew that the buyer was living there.

Who has title to the parcel of land?

(A) The buyer, and the investor has no enforceable claim to the parcel of land.

(B) The buyer, but the investor can sue to recover title under the title covenants.

(C) The investor, and the buyer has no enforceable claim to the parcel of land.

(D) The investor, but the buyer can sue to recover title on an estoppel theory.

Question 9

While driving his car down the road, the defendant, who had no history of heart problems, experienced a heart attack. The defendant's car crossed the center line of the highway, in violation of a motor vehicle statute, and headed directly at a car driven by the plaintiff that was exceeding the speed limit. The plaintiff, seeing the defendant's car heading toward him, swerved to avoid the collision. In so doing, the plaintiff's car spun out of control and crashed into a ditch, causing the plaintiff injury. The plaintiff brought suit against the defendant for the injuries sustained in the accident. The jurisdiction retains traditional contributory negligence rules.

The plaintiff will:

(A) Prevail, because the defendant's act was a substantial factor in causing the plaintiff's car to swerve.

(B) Prevail, because the defendant violated a statute by crossing the center line.

(C) Not prevail, because the defendant had no prior history of heart trouble.

(D) Not prevail, because the plaintiff was exceeding the speed limit.

Question 10

The Drug Control Act is a federal law that seeks to control those substances that are dangerous to the health of the population in general. The statute provides substantial penalties for violations of the Act. The Food and Drug Administration has conducted a substantial number of tests on a new diet pill. The results of the studies show that the drug might have dangerous side effects when taken regularly, and the Food and Drug Administration now seeks to prohibit its distribution under the Drug Control Act. A major pharmaceutical company that desires to market the diet pill sues to have the statute declared unconstitutional.

The most likely result in this suit is that the statute will be declared to be:

(A) Constitutional, as a proper exercise of the general welfare power.

(B) Constitutional, as a proper exercise of Congress's power to regulate interstate commerce.

(C) Unconstitutional, because it interferes with the right of privacy of diet pill users.

(D) Unconstitutional, because it deprives the pharmaceutical company of property without just compensation.

Question 11

An indictment was filed in federal district court charging the defendant with violations of federal bank robbery statutes. At trial, the government attempted to introduce into evidence the testimony of the defendant's wife, who would testify that she had seen the defendant arm himself on several occasions with weapons identical to those used in the bank robberies, had seen him return to their home carrying sacks filled with money with the markings of the robbed banks, and had overheard, while serving meals, the defendant and his co-defendants discussing plans for robbing the various banks and concealing the loot. The defendant's attorney objected, and the district court judge ruled that the wife's testimony was within the spousal privilege and could not be admitted over the defendant's objection.

Was this ruling correct?

(A) No, because the spousal privilege may be asserted only by the testifying spouse—she may not be compelled to testify nor be foreclosed from testifying.

(B) No, because there is no federal common law, and the spousal privilege is a creation of the common law.

(C) Yes, because the privilege not to testify may be asserted by either the testifying or nontestifying spouse.

(D) Yes, because the defendant and his wife were married at the time and he can prevent her from disclosing the confidential communication.

Question 12

A man was driving very erratically when he was stopped by state troopers and arrested for drunk driving. He was advised of his constitutional rights and elected to remain silent. At trial for his drunk driving charge, the man testified in his own defense, stating that he had just left his doctor's office and had been administered medication without being told that it would seriously and immediately hamper his coordination. On cross-examination, the prosecutor asked whether the defendant just made up this medication story after the fact to evade legitimate liability for driving while intoxicated and the man said he had not. The prosecutor then asked why the defendant had not told the arresting officer about the medication, and defense counsel objects.

The trial court should rule that the question is:

(A) Improper, because to require the defense to inform the prosecution of defendant's testimony prior to trial would be unconstitutional pretrial discovery.

(B) Improper, because use of defendant's post-arrest silence violates his right to due process of law.

(C) Proper, because defendant's silence was not used as direct evidence but only for impeachment on cross-examination.

(D) Proper, because defendant's post-arrest silence is a prior inconsistent statement which is admissible to show recent fabrication.

Question 13

A new synthetic liquid was created that could safely double the output of electrical power plants. One byproduct of the production of the liquid was a hazardous chemical that was not biodegradable in the environment. A state-of-the-art manufacturing plant was built to produce this liquid, and the manufacturing plant secured an expert opinion on how to dispose of the hazardous chemical byproduct. The expert concluded that the earth beneath the disposal site was impermeable, and that there was no danger of contaminating the underground waters if the chemical were buried. Based on this expert opinion, the hazardous chemical was buried in a depression on the land because the head of the manufacturing plant reasonably believed that it was safe. The chemical, nonetheless, seeped through the underlying soil strata, and was carried by the flow of percolating water to a neighboring well used by the adjacent sheep farm to water the sheep. The chemical rendered the water in the well unfit for consumption by sheep.

The sheep farmer had bought the farm after the plant was built. While he was unaware of the hazardous chemical disposal underground when he bought the farm, the sheep farmer was later told his well may be contaminated, and he did nothing about it. The sheep were harmed by drinking from the contaminated well, and the sheep farmer asserts a claim against the manufacturing plant for damages to the sheep in a jurisdiction that follows traditional contributory negligence rules.

Which of the following is the manufacturing plant's best defense?

(A) Many companies converted their power plants so that they could utilize the synthetic liquid developed by the manufacturing plant.

(B) The sheep farmer did not do what a reasonable person would have done to prevent harm to his sheep after he learned that the well was contaminated.

(C) The sheep farmer was contributorily negligent.

(D) The manufacturing plant was in place and in operation before the sheep farmer purchased his property.

Question 14

A landowner and his neighbor owned adjoining tracts of land. The boundary line between the two properties was never properly determined or clearly known. Thirty years ago, the landowner installed a gas-powered generator on land he thought he owned, but which was in fact owned by the neighbor. Fifteen years later, the neighbor was found to be mentally incompetent. She died last year, and her executor filed suit to eject the landowner and quiet title. The statute of limitations for ejectment is 20 years.

With respect to the land on which the generator was installed:

(A) The landowner cannot claim title by adverse possession because the statute of limitations was tolled by the neighbor's incompetency.

(B) The landowner cannot claim title by adverse possession because his occupation was not hostile.

(C) The landowner has acquired title by adverse possession.

(D) The landowner has acquired title by acquiescence because there was original uncertainty as to the true boundary line.

Question 15

An aircraft manufacturer anticipating lengthy contract negotiations with a foreign country to sell military aircraft and parts entered into a written agreement with a highly skilled salesperson to act as its agent. Under the contract between the aircraft manufacturer and the sales agent, the agent was required to begin meetings with the representatives of the foreign country on August 1. However, on July 19, the sales agent accepted a job with a competing company, and could not thereafter represent the aircraft manufacturer. To fulfill her contractual obligations with the aircraft manufacturer, the sales agent called her friend, who was reputed to be "the best in the business," and orally assigned the aircraft manufacturer contract to him for a specified sum.

If the aircraft manufacturer does not want the sales agent's friend to represent it and sues the sales agent for damages for breach, who will prevail?

(A) The aircraft manufacturer, because the assignment was oral.

(B) The aircraft manufacturer, because the sales agent's performance was personal.

(C) The sales agent, because her friend is a better negotiator than the sales agent and so the aircraft manufacturer would not be damaged.

(D) The sales agent, because damages are speculative.

Question 16

To help stimulate the economy, Congress passed a law proscribing loans with interest rates higher than 10% per annum. A bank that had been lending money to high risk recipients had been charging 15% interest on its loans.

If the bank challenges the federal statute, claiming that Congress had no power to pass such a statute, it will most likely:

(A) Lose, because the General Welfare Clause coupled with the Necessary and Proper Clause gives Congress the power to pass legislation to limit interest rates.

(B) Lose, because the Commerce Clause gives Congress power to regulate interstate commerce, and the interest rates banks may charge affect interstate commerce.

(C) Win, because regulating interest rates of banks is not among the powers granted to Congress.

(D) Win, because the regulation interferes with the bank's rights under the Privileges and Immunities Clause of Article IV.

Question 17

An engineer is called as a witness in a professional malpractice action. During direct examination by the attorney for the party who called her, she is asked leading questions. The opposing party objects.

Which of the following will have no bearing on whether the trial court will permit leading questions?

(A) The question is necessary to refresh recollection.

(B) The questions relate to preliminary information, such as name, address, etc.

(C) The engineer was called as an adverse witness.

(D) The questions relate directly to an issue of ultimate fact in the lawsuit.

Question 18

A man was hired as a registered nurse by a hospital operated by the county and was given an information booklet explaining that during the first nine months of employment he would be on probationary status and could be dismissed for any reason and without an explanation. After six months, he was notified by hospital administrators that he was being dismissed. If he had been employed for over nine months, hospital regulations provided that he could be dismissed only for cause and after notice and a hearing.

Which of the following, if true, most strongly supports the man's dismissal without notice or hearing?

(A) He could be replaced with a more competent nurse.

(B) His performance as a nurse had been unsatisfactory.

(C) He had not been employed for at least nine months.

(D) He had violated hospital regulations by talking with a newspaper reporter about the hospital's policy of allowing registered nurses to dispense medication without doctor authorization.

Question 19

A 10-year-old boy playing with his friends at an abandoned construction site was struck in the face by a 10-year-old girl wielding a "sword" (a piece of sheet metal left as scrap by the builders). The blow seriously injured the boy's eye. The boy's parents brought an action against the girl and her parents for negligence and intentional tort. The insurance company representing the girl's family raised the defense of contributory negligence as to the negligence cause of action, alleging that the boy was engaged in a mock battle with the girl with his own pretend "sword," another piece of metal.

When the court instructs the jury as to the standard to be applied to the boy's conduct, it should state that:

(A) The boy's conduct is judged by what a person of ordinary prudence and caution would have done in the same circumstances.

(B) The boy's conduct is judged by what a child of similar age, experience, and intelligence would have done in similar circumstances.

(C) The boy's conduct is immaterial, because the girl committed an intentional tort when she purposely struck the boy in the eye.

(D) The boy's conduct is immaterial, because it is presumed that a child under the age of 14 cannot be negligent.

Question 20

A developer prepared and duly recorded a subdivision plan, dividing his 200-acre tract of land into 80 two-acre lots with a 40-acre tract in the center designated "future public golf course." He began to market the 80 two-acre lots by preparing and distributing a brochure promoting the subdivision. The developer sold 70 of the lots to individual purchasers. Each deed referred to the recorded plan. Years later, wishing to rid himself of the remaining acreage, the developer sold the remaining 20 acres and the 40-acre tract to an investor by a deed that referred to the plan. The investor sold the 10 two-acre lots to individual purchasers and the 40-acre tract to a partnership. None of the deeds from the investor referred to the plan. The partnership has announced its intention of erecting a shopping mall on the 40-acre tract. A golfer, an owner of a two-acre lot purchased from the developer, brings suit to enjoin the partnership.

If the golfer wins, it will be because:

(A) The partnership will be deemed to have taken with actual notice because of the location of the 40-acre tract.

(B) The golfer can sue in equity to enforce the plan against the partnership.

(C) The golfer is a creditor-beneficiary of the developer's promise with respect to the 40-acre tract.

(D) The golfer would be economically benefited by the existence of a golf course within the development.

Question 21

A vacant lot in a downtown area was condemned by the city council, which planned to establish a riverfront park on the site. During a proceeding to establish condemnation damages, counsel for the city called the lot owner to the stand, expecting him to say that he had been offered $250,000 for the property one month before it was condemned. However, on direct examination, the lot owner testified that he had received a $400,000 offer for his land a month before condemnation. Counsel for the city then seeks to confront the lot owner with his statement made at his deposition that the offer was for $250,000.

The statement contained in the deposition is:

(A) Inadmissible, because the city cannot impeach its own witness.

(B) Inadmissible, because it is hearsay not within any exception.

(C) Admissible for impeachment and as substantive evidence that the lot owner received an offer for $250,000.

(D) Admissible, but only for the purpose of impeachment.

Question 22

A boy planned to rob the local currency exchange, but he needed a getaway car and somebody to be a lookout. He asked his sister, who immediately refused and warned him against carrying it out. The boy showed his sister a gun, threatening to shoot her if she did not go along with the plan. The sister consented to help, and the pair left for the currency exchange, with the sister driving. When they arrived, the sister left the car running so that she could get away and contact the police while her brother was inside, but the boy ordered her to go inside with him. During the robbery attempt, the clerk pulled out a gun, and the boy and the clerk shot and killed each other.

If the sister is charged with the killing of the store clerk, should the jury find her criminally liable if it accepts the sister's version of the facts?

(A) Yes, because duress is not a defense to murder.

(B) Yes, because the clerk's death occurred in furtherance of and during the perpetration of a robbery in which the sister was participating.

(C) No, because the sister lacked the requisite intent.

(D) No, because the sister withdrew from the conspiracy to commit robbery and thus is not liable for any acts committed in furtherance of the conspiracy.

Question 23

A homeowner wanted to have his yard landscaped. He called a number of commercial establishments that do such work and received a bid for $5,000, a bid for $4,500, and a bid for $4,000. The homeowner entered into a contract with the low bidder to have the yard landscaped for $4,000.

Shortly before the low bidder was scheduled to begin work, he called the homeowner and told him that his secretary had made a mistake in adding the figures, and he could not possibly do the work for less than $4,600.

If the homeowner sues the low bidder for breach of contract, who will prevail?

(A) The homeowner, but only if it is too late for the homeowner to accept the bid of the next lowest bidder.

(B) The homeowner, because he did not have reason to know of the low bidder's mistake.

(C) The low bidder, because he had not yet commenced performance under the contract.

(D) The low bidder, because he can successfully assert the defense of mistake.

Question 24

Three thieves agreed to rob a bank. The first was to steal a car to be used for the getaway, the second agreed to procure weapons, and the third would check the bank for cameras. The car thief stole a car and parked it in a lot behind his girlfriend's apartment building. While visiting her the night before the robbery, the car thief suffered a series of convulsive seizures. He was rushed to the hospital where he was placed in the intensive care unit and heavily sedated. Meanwhile the two other thieves, unaware of their accomplice's illness, met and decided to rob the bank on their own, despite the absence of a getaway car and driver. They robbed the bank, but were quickly apprehended as they tried to escape and implicated the car thief under police questioning.

The car thief can be charged with:

(A) Theft of the car only.

(B) Conspiracy to commit robbery and theft of the car only.

(C) Robbery and theft of the car only.

(D) Theft of the car, conspiracy to commit robbery, and robbery.

Question 25

Two brothers inherited a tract of land as joint tenants from their parents. Only half of the acreage was planted with oranges, and the older brother decided that to increase productivity, the balance of the land should be planted with a different variety of oranges. The younger brother refused to participate in the project, and the older brother brought an action for declaratory relief alleging that he was entitled to be reimbursed for half of the cost of the improvement.

Which of the following correctly describes the result in the action?

(A) The older brother will be denied the requested judgment.

(B) The older brother will be granted the requested judgment.

(C) The result depends upon whether the younger brother will receive an economic benefit.

(D) The result depends upon whether the improvements will produce sufficient income to amortize their cost.

Question 26

Pursuant to statute, a state's department of education provides model lesson plans to any school or school district in the state requesting such plans. A private religious school whose curriculum is more than 50% religious matters applied for and received model lesson plans for the nonreligious subjects taught in its classrooms.

Which of the following is the best argument supporting the constitutionality of the state's statutory policy of providing model lesson plans to this private religious school?

(A) The teaching of religious matters in private schools is not constitutionally prohibited.

(B) The purpose and effect of the lesson plan program is secular and does not entangle government and religion.

(C) Private religious schools fulfill an important educational function.

(D) The state's refusal to provide lesson plans to private religious schools would violate the Free Exercise Clause of the First Amendment by discriminating against their students in favor of students in secular private and public schools.

Question 27

On September 1, a law school professor announced to his class that he would pay the tuition of the bar review course of the student's choice for the student who received the highest grade in his Constitutional Law class.

A week later, one student in the professor's class told the professor that he was giving his best effort to get the highest grade in class to win the prize and had already purchased every substantive Constitutional Law outline on the market.

Shortly thereafter, the dean of the law school learned of the contest and informed the professor that it was against school policy. On October 1, the professor told his class that he was withdrawing his offer.

Which of the following statements about the professor's October 1 announcement is correct?

(A) It had no legal effect, because no offer had been made.

(B) It was an effective revocation of the offer to all students who heard it because it was made in the same manner as the offer.

(C) It was an ineffective revocation as to any student who failed to hear it.

(D) It was ineffective as to the student who had begun performance prior to the withdrawal of the offer.

Question 28

The plaintiff instituted suit against a development firm and its employee for injuries suffered by the plaintiff when a basement stair collapsed as he was being shown one of the firm's buildings that it was leasing. At trial, the employee for the firm claims that he told the plaintiff about the defective stair. The plaintiff then offers evidence that after his fall, the CEO of the development firm called him at home and offered to pay all of the plaintiff's medical expenses, saying, "I guess I owe you that much after our employee didn't warn you about the broken stair."

The statement regarding the lack of warning is:

(A) Admissible, as a statement against interest.

(B) Admissible, as an admission by the CEO of the development firm that the employee had not warned the plaintiff about the defective stair.

(C) Inadmissible, as hearsay not within any exception.

(D) Inadmissible, on public policy grounds.

Question 29

A plaintiff's friend told her that she could use his lakeside cabin for the weekend. Her friend gave the plaintiff instructions on how to find his cabin, but once the plaintiff arrived at the lake, she found that all the cabins looked very similar. The plaintiff rechecked her friend's instructions and then entered the cabin that she thought belonged to her friend. In fact, the cabin belonged to a different cabin owner.

After the plaintiff unpacked her luggage, she realized that the cabin was quite cold. Thus, she gathered some wood from the woodpile and started a fire in the fireplace. Unbeknownst to the plaintiff, the fireplace flue was blocked and so an explosion ensued, and the plaintiff was injured by the explosion. The cabin owner had known that the flue was blocked, but he had not gotten around to having the problem fixed because he was not going to be at the cabin for several weeks.

If the plaintiff sues the cabin owner for her injuries, who will prevail?

(A) The plaintiff, because the cabin owner knew that the flue was defective.

(B) The plaintiff, because the cabin owner had a duty to warn of the defect.

(C) The cabin owner, because he had no reason to anticipate that anyone would be in the cabin.

(D) The cabin owner, because the plaintiff was a trespasser.

Question 30

Although they were never legally married, a couple had lived together for many years and had held themselves out to be husband and wife. They were driving through a sparsely populated area of a state when the wife complained to the husband of severe pains in her abdominal area. She asked her husband to stop in the next city to have a doctor at the city's hospital examine her. After the city, the next town was more than 100 miles away.

Thinking that the wife's condition was not serious, and because it was getting to be late in the afternoon and the husband had a reservation at the inn in the town that would be automatically canceled if they did not arrive before 6 p.m., he refused to stop at the city and drove on toward the town. In fact, the wife was suffering from an attack of acute appendicitis. Her appendix burst before they reached the town, and she was on the point of expiring when the husband arrived at the town's clinic. A nurse attended to the wife and called a doctor, the only physician in the county, and he arrived 30 minutes later. The doctor negligently concluded that it was too late to save the wife's life, and she died two hours later. The autopsy also revealed that the wife had a fatal form of cancer that would have caused her death in a few months. After a coroner's inquest into the death of the wife, the husband was charged with murder.

Which of the following is most beneficial to the husband's defense in a jurisdiction that follows the common law as to homicide crimes?

(A) The husband and the wife were never legally married.

(B) The doctor acted negligently when he concluded that the wife's life could not be saved.

(C) The wife would have died from cancer in a few months.

(D) The husband did not believe that the wife's complaints of abdominal pain signaled a serious medical problem.

Question 31

On May 1, a sales manager announced at a monthly sales meeting that he would give a $1,000 bonus to the salesperson with the highest sales at the end of the month.

The sales manager's announcement would best be interpreted as:

(A) Preliminary negotiations.

(B) A promise to make a conditional gift.

(C) A contractual offer, creating a power of acceptance.

(D) A mere statement designed to induce the salespersons to work harder and boost sales.

Question 32

A beekeeper sued the manufacturer of a specially designed helmet and faceguard that was designed to protect the wearer from bee stings. The beekeeper alleged that he was wearing the helmet and faceguard when he was stung on the left cheek by a bee that had entered through a small tear in the faceguard, and that, one hour later, the beekeeper suffered a heart attack. The beekeeper's physician, having listened to the beekeeper testify to the foregoing facts at trial, is called by the beekeeper and asked whether, assuming the truth of such testimony, the beekeeper's subsequent heart attack could have resulted from the bee sting.

The physician's opinion is:

(A) Admissible, because the physician was the beekeeper's treating physician.

(B) Admissible, as a response to a hypothetical question.

(C) Inadmissible, because a proper foundation has not been laid.

(D) Inadmissible, because an expert's opinion may not be based solely on information provided by lay persons.

Question 33

A rancher owned a large parcel of vacant land that motorcyclists frequently used for impromptu motorcross competitions on weekends. The rancher was aware of this use of his land but had no immediate plans for the parcel and so took no action against the motorcyclists. One weekend, the rancher drove out to the parcel to do some target shooting. He was shooting when a rider arrived at the area with his bike and began riding on the trails. The rider, who was intoxicated, tried a particularly dangerous stunt on his bike just as one of the rancher's shots struck a rock and ricocheted. The shot passed through the rider's leg, severing an artery. Fortunately, prompt medical attention saved his life.

If the rider brings an action for negligence against the rancher, he will probably:

(A) Recover all of his damages.

(B) Recover a portion of his damages, because he was negligent in driving his motorcycle while drunk and attempting the dangerous stunt.

(C) Not recover, because driving while drunk is gross negligence or worse.

(D) Not recover, because he was a trespasser on the rancher's land.

Question 34

The plaintiff brought suit against his former boss for a libelous letter received by the plaintiff's present employer. The former boss allegedly sent the letter. The authenticity and contents of the letter are disputed at the jury trial. In response to a question from the plaintiff's attorney, the present employer states that: "I received a letter from the plaintiff's former boss, which I seem to have lost, but I remember exactly what it said."

The plaintiff's present employer will be allowed to testify as to the contents of the letter if:

(A) The plaintiff's attorney lays a proper foundation by proving the present employer's good character for truth.

(B) The judge finds that the original letter is lost.

(C) The jury is satisfied that the original letter is unavailable.

(D) The present employer can recall the contents of the letter from memory without looking to any other document.

Question 35

An employer owned a tract of land in fee simple. As a bonus, the employer presented a deed conveying the tract to an employee. The deed was never recorded. Six months later, the employer found himself in dire financial straits and needed the tract back to complete its sale to a buyer. He asked the employee to please destroy the deed, which the employee dutifully and voluntarily did. Shortly thereafter, the employer and the employee were killed in an explosion in the factory where they both worked.

Each of the successors in interest claim title to the tract.

The probable outcome will be that:

(A) The employer owned the tract, because the employee voluntarily destroyed the deed.

(B) The employer owned the tract, because the destruction of the deed by the employee relates back and redates the present transfer of the deed to the employee.

(C) The employee owned the tract, because the deed was merely evidence of her title and its destruction was insufficient to cause title to pass back to the employer.

(D) The employee owned the tract, because her destruction of the deed to the tract was under the undue influence of the employer.

Question 36

Federal legislation required that state and local police departments receiving financial assistance from the Federal Law Enforcement Assistance Agency devote a specified amount of those resources to combatting "white-collar" crimes.

Which of the following would provide the best constitutional underpinning for this legislation?

(A) The power to enforce the penal statutes of the United States.

(B) The police power.

(C) The war and defense power.

(D) The power to tax and spend for the general welfare.

Question 37

A father of a boy preparing for his bar mitzvah ceremony entered into an oral contract with a professional photographer. The contract provided that the photographer would take photos of the boy's bar mitzvah celebration in two weeks in exchange for $1,000. The contract also provided that the father was to pay a named creditor of the photographer rather than the photographer herself. One week after making the contract, the father learned that his brother-in-law, a fairly good amateur photographer, would take the photographs free of charge. The father called the photographer that same day to tell her that their deal was off. The creditor to whom the father was to make payment had not become aware of any agreement between the father and the photographer.

Which of the following is true?

(A) The father can rescind the contract if the photographer and the creditor agree to the rescission.

(B) The father can rescind the contract if the photographer agrees to the rescission.

(C) The father has a valid Statute of Frauds defense, rendering the contract unenforceable, if the photographer chooses to sue him for breach.

(D) The photographer must wait until the date of the event to sue for breach of contract.

Question 38

An artist was adept at copying the paintings of famous artists. In need of money, he made a copy of a painting by a recently deceased artist, complete with her signature. The artist then contacted an art collector and asked whether he would be interested in purchasing this "recovered" painting. The art collector examined the painting and, still believing it to be an original, offered the artist $1 million for it, which the artist eagerly accepted. The art collector gave the artist a check and left with the painting. The artist promptly deposited the check, which cleared several days later.

At common law, the artist is guilty of:

(A) Forgery.

(B) False pretenses.

(C) Larceny by trick.

(D) No crime.

Question 39

A passenger suffered a broken arm from an automobile accident caused by his driver's negligence in running through a red light. The passenger was taken by ambulance to a nearby hospital for treatment. There, the emergency room physician negligently reset the bone in the passenger's arm. As a result, the passenger never recovered full use of his arm and his earnings as a carpenter were permanently reduced. The jurisdiction retains joint and several liability and traditional contribution rules based on equal shares.

If the passenger brings suit against the driver for the damage to his arm, the passenger will recover:

(A) All of his damages, including the permanent disability, from the driver.

(B) The portion of his damages attributable to a properly treated broken arm from the driver.

(C) Half of his damages from the driver under traditional contribution rules.

(D) All of his damages from the driver only if the passenger joins the negligent doctor as a defendant and the doctor fails to satisfy that portion of the judgment attributable to his negligence.

Question 40

In an action for breach of contract, which of the following questions, if asked of a witness for the plaintiff on cross-examination by counsel for the defendant, would most probably be ruled improper by the trial court?

(A) "Weren't you fired last year after your employer learned you had been using its computerized accounting system to divert company funds to your personal bank account?"

(B) "As a creditor of the plaintiff, isn't it true that you stand to gain several thousand dollars if the plaintiff prevails in this lawsuit?"

(C) "Isn't it true that you are currently a resident of the city detoxification hospital recovering from addiction to Valium?"

(D) "Weren't you convicted of forgery six years ago?"

Question 41

A man and a woman who were not married each put up 50% of the down payment on a home. They took title as tenants in common, and each orally promised the other that the survivor should take title to the home. They lived in the home for three years, equitably dividing mortgage payments and maintenance expenses. They were then involved in a serious car accident. The woman was killed almost instantly and the man died in the hospital one week later. Neither left a will. The woman was survived only by her mother. The man was survived only by his brother.

Who owns the home?

(A) The mother owns the whole.

(B) The brother owns the whole.

(C) The mother and the brother each have a one-half interest as tenants in common.

(D) The mother and the brother each have a one-half interest as joint tenants.

Question 42

A parent purchased for her teenage daughter a refurbished MP3 player from an online auction site. The seller of the player had purchased the MP3 player from a recycling center and reconditioned it with cheaper parts from a different manufacturer. One day while the teenager was listening to the MP3 player through its original headphones, the player shorted out and caused injury to the teenager's eardrum.

If the teenager asserts a claim based on strict liability in tort against the MP3 player's manufacturer, the teenager will probably:

(A) Recover, because the manufacturer put the player in the stream of commerce.

(B) Recover, because the headphones were a part of the MP3 player when it was new.

(C) Not recover, because the MP3 player had been refurbished by the seller.

(D) Not recover, because the teenager was not in privity of contract with the manufacturer.

Question 43

A cab driver filed a personal injury suit against a limo driver for injuries she sustained when their vehicles collided in an intersection controlled by stoplights. The cab driver's attorney seeks to have the police officer who investigated the accident and prepared the police report testify that she took the statement of a witness who told her that the limo driver "drove right through the red light."

The judge should rule the testimony:

(A) Inadmissible, because the police report is the best evidence.

(B) Inadmissible, because it is hearsay.

(C) Inadmissible as oral testimony, but the report may be introduced into evidence.

(D) Admissible, because the police officer was testifying as to past recollection recorded.

Question 44

An avid swimmer wished to install an in-ground swimming pool in her backyard and hired a contractor to do the installation. The swimmer chose to locate the pool close to the property line dividing her yard from her neighbor's property. Unfortunately, when the pool excavation was nearly completed, subsidence on the neighbor's property, caused by the excavation, caused part of the neighbor's backyard lawn to collapse.

If the neighbor sues the swimmer for the damage to his lawn, for whom will a court most likely rule?

(A) The neighbor, because the swimmer is absolutely liable for the damage to her neighbor's land.

(B) The neighbor, because installing an in-ground pool that close to the property line was negligent.

(C) The swimmer, because only the lawn was damaged, not any of the buildings located on the property.

(D) The swimmer, because she had no duty to provide support for her neighbor's land.

Question 45

At the defendant's trial for arson, the prosecution seeks to impeach the defendant through a record of the defendant's conviction of a misdemeanor robbery five years ago. The defendant objects.

Should the court admit this evidence over the defendant's objection?

(A) No, unless the prosecution shows that its probative value as impeachment evidence outweighs its prejudicial effect.

(B) No, because the conviction is a misdemeanor and the crime did not involve dishonesty.

(C) Yes, because the conviction is less than 10 years old.

(D) Yes, because a witness may be impeached by any crime.

Question 46

A doctor in one state wanted to obtain malpractice insurance from a reputable company located in another state. However, the laws of the state in which the doctor works require physicians to obtain malpractice insurance only from carriers located within that state. The doctor challenges this requirement in state court, alleging that the requirement violates the United States Constitution.

His challenge will most likely:

(A) Succeed, because the requirement that the insurer be located within the state violates the Due Process Clause of the Fourteenth Amendment.

(B) Succeed, because the requirement constitutes discrimination against interstate commerce.

(C) Fail, because the state can enforce its laws governing the sale of insurance only if the insurance company is located in the state.

(D) Fail, because the requirement is reasonably related to the legislation's purpose to protect patients.

Question 47

A state statute provided that directors of orphanages, homes for the developmentally disabled, and similar institutions stand in loco parentis to the children under their charge. A mentally disabled 11-year-old child lived in a state facility for the mentally disabled. The facility had no fence around it, because the children who lived there had been evaluated and judged not dangerous by behavioral health experts. One day, the child ran away from the premises. Despite the facility's prompt notification of the police, before the child was found he had beaten up a young boy he encountered on the street. The boy's parents filed suit against the director of the facility on the boy's behalf.

Assuming that no other liability statute applies, who will prevail?

(A) The boy, because under the statute the director has the responsibilities and duties of a parent.

(B) The boy, because the director is strictly liable for the disabled child's acts.

(C) The director, because vicarious liability does not apply since the 11-year-old child is not directly liable for his conduct.

(D) The director, because she did not know that the disabled child had dangerous propensities.

Question 48

A husband and wife were installing a swimming pool in their backyard with help from a local handyman and a family friend when one of the pool's walls collapsed, injuring the handyman. The handyman sued the husband and wife on a negligence theory. The handyman's attorney seeks to have a paramedic who had responded to the accident testify that the family friend, who was a construction worker, made a statement to her that "I told the two of them that they needed more reinforcement in the concrete."

The trial judge should rule this evidence:

(A) Inadmissible, because it is not relevant to the issues presented in the trial.

(B) Inadmissible, because it is a hearsay declaration.

(C) Admissible, because it is an admission.

(D) Admissible, because it is a statement against interest.

Question 49

A buyer agreed to buy a limited edition guitar from a seller for $12,000 and a contract memorializing the agreement was signed by both parties. The next day, after the seller received an offer of $20,000 for the guitar, he called the buyer and said that he could not sell the guitar to him for $12,000. The buyer did not respond. On the delivery date, the buyer fails to tender $12,000 and the seller does not deliver the guitar.

On these facts:

(A) The seller can recover from the buyer for breach of contract.

(B) The buyer can recover from the seller for breach of contract.

(C) Neither the seller nor buyer can recover until one of the parties tenders performance.

(D) The contract is terminated.

Question 50

The accused and an accomplice decided to burglarize a home. They agreed that the crime would be committed the following Saturday night. On Thursday, the accused shoplifted a crowbar from a department store, figuring he could use it for future crimes. On Friday, the accused was arrested and jailed for an unrelated crime. He was confined over the weekend. His accomplice decided to go ahead with the burglary. On Saturday night, as he was about to break open the front door to the home, he was arrested by a passing police officer.

Of which crimes, in a common law jurisdiction, is the accused guilty?

(A) Larceny of the crowbar only.

(B) Larceny of the crowbar and conspiracy only.

(C) Larceny of the crowbar and attempted burglary only.

(D) Larceny of the crowbar, conspiracy, and attempted burglary.

MIXED SUBJECT SET 6 SUBJECT GUIDE

1. Constitutional Law
2. Criminal Law
3. Torts
4. Real Property
5. Contracts
6. Criminal Law
7. Evidence
8. Real Property
9. Torts
10. Constitutional Law
11. Evidence
12. Criminal Law
13. Torts
14. Real Property
15. Contracts
16. Constitutional Law
17. Evidence
18. Constitutional Law
19. Torts
20. Real Property
21. Evidence
22. Criminal Law
23. Contracts
24. Criminal Law
25. Real Property
26. Constitutional Law
27. Contracts
28. Evidence
29. Torts
30. Criminal Law
31. Contracts
32. Evidence
33. Torts
34. Evidence
35. Real Property
36. Constitutional Law
37. Contracts
38. Criminal Law
39. Torts
40. Evidence
41. Real Property
42. Torts
43. Evidence
44. Real Property
45. Evidence
46. Constitutional Law
47. Torts
48. Evidence
49. Contracts
50. Criminal Law

MIXED SUBJECT ANSWERS - SET 6

Answer to Question 1

(C) In *Committee for Public Education and Religious Liberty v. Regan* (1980), the United States Supreme Court held that a similar statute passed by the state of New York did not violate the Establishment Clause because it had a secular legislative purpose. Its principal effect did not advance or inhibit religion, and it did not foster an excessive government entanglement with religion. Here, our facts show a state law that provides for secular testing and reimbursement for testing administration costs to religious schools. As such, the state law does not violate the Establishment Clause because it had a secular legislative purpose (namely, reimbursing schools for secular testing that was conducted in all schools—religious and secular alike), its principal effect did not advance or inhibit religion, and it did not foster an excessive government entanglement with religion. (A) is therefore incorrect; aid can be given to religious schools that pass this test. (B) is wrong. It misstates the facts given, which make no mention of a specific religious group. Rather, the suit was filed by an association challenging the reimbursement. (D) is irrelevant. The question is not whether the tests involve "matters of religion," but whether the reimbursement program impermissibly advances religion.

Answer to Question 2

(C) The best argument for admitting the statement is that it was volunteered by the car dealer. Generally, *Miranda* warnings and a valid waiver are prerequisites to the admissibility of any statement made by the accused during ***custodial interrogation***. If the defendant is not in custody, or if the police are not "interrogating" the defendant, *Miranda* warnings are not required. Thus, the best argument for admitting a statement made by the defendant who had not been provided *Miranda* warnings must be either that the defendant was not in custody at the time the statement was made or that the statement was not the result of police interrogation (*i.e.,* that the statement was volunteered). Thus, (C) is the best answer. (A) is wrong because the agency that the officer works for is not relevant. The fact that a confession offered in a federal prosecution was made to a police officer will not automatically allow it into evidence. It will be suppressed if it is the product of some violation of the defendant's constitutional rights by the police officer. (B) is wrong; if the car dealer had not been formally charged, his Sixth Amendment right to counsel would not be implicated by his confession to the police detective. However, this would not prevent suppression of the confession if his Fifth Amendment *Miranda* rights were violated. (D) is wrong because *Miranda* violations can occur before a formal arrest. The test is whether the defendant was "in custody" at the time the statement was made.

Answer to Question 3

(C) The homeowner will prevail because the maid's negligence increased the risk of criminal conduct by a third party. Criminal acts and intentional torts of third persons are foreseeable independent intervening forces if the defendant's negligence created a foreseeable risk that they would occur. Here, the maid's failure to lock the door was negligent because it created a risk of burglary; hence, the burglary does not cut off the agency's liability for the maid's negligence. As the maid's employer, the agency is vicariously liable under respondeat superior. (A) is wrong because there is nothing in the facts to indicate that the homeowner waived her right to bring tort claims against the agency; having a contractual relationship with a party does not automatically preclude bringing a tort action against the party. (B) is wrong because the burglary was not a superseding cause of the loss; it was within the increased risk caused by the maid's negligence. (D) is wrong because she reentered to retrieve a personal item that she had brought with her when she went to the job; her return just to get the item was within the scope of her employment and would not make her a trespasser.

Answer to Question 4

(A) At the time it was recorded, the nephew's deed to the friend was ineffective as a conveyance of either legal or equitable interest in the tract of land. Because the nephew did not acquire either legal or equitable title until after the owner died, he had nothing to pass on to his friend. Therefore, (B) and (C) are wrong. (D) is wrong because the doctrine of estoppel by deed does not apply to automatically inure title to the grantee's (the friend's) benefit until the grantor (the nephew) acquires title to the property. At the time the friend recorded her deed, the owner was still alive and held title to the tract of land.

Answer to Question 5

(A) The cleaner can obtain rescission in equity without waiting to be sued on the contract. The grounds for rescission would be the intentional misrepresentation by the business owner that the second agreement was the same as the first. (B) is incorrect because reformation requires that the agreement not reflect the intention of the parties. Here, there was never any intent on the part of the owner to agree to the terms of the old agreement. (C) would not apply to this fact situation—a novation substitutes another party for one of the original parties to the contract. (D) is incorrect because, as noted above, the cleaner need not repudiate the contract and wait to be sued for breach. He may immediately file an action in equity to obtain rescission.

Answer to Question 6

(A) The jury should find the woman not guilty of conspiracy because she did not intend to steal the painting. A conspiracy is a combination of or an agreement between two or more persons to accomplish some criminal or unlawful purpose, or to accomplish a lawful purpose by unlawful means. The elements of conspiracy are: (i) an agreement between two or more persons; (ii) the intent to enter into an agreement; and (iii) the intent to achieve the objective of the agreement. Here, if the jury believes that the woman agreed to the plan in order to have the man arrested, she must be found not guilty, given that she would not have had the intent to achieve the objective of the conspiracy. Thus, (A) is correct, and (C) is wrong. (B) is wrong because, at common law, withdrawal is not a defense to a conspiracy. Thus, her act of prevention would not have excused the conspiracy if she had the proper mental state. (D) is wrong because the privilege to apprehend criminals is not an issue here.

Answer to Question 7

(A) The basis of an expert's opinion need not be admissible into evidence for the expert's testimony to be admissible, provided that the information is of a type reasonably relied upon by experts in the particular field. [Fed. R. Evid. 703(B)] (B) is incorrect because the biochemist need not offer the reports into evidence in order to base his opinion on them. In fact, the proponent of the expert opinion is not permitted to disclose the reports if they are inadmissible, unless the court determines that their probative value in assisting the jury to evaluate the expert's opinion substantially outweighs their prejudicial effect. (C) is wrong because the Federal Rules reject the traditional prohibition on opinions embracing the ultimate issue in the case, as long as the opinion is helpful to the trier of fact. (D) is wrong because the biochemist is only relying on the reports as the basis of making his opinion; he is not offering the reports themselves into evidence. Hence, they would not be governed by the hearsay rule.

Answer to Question 8

(A) The buyer has title to the parcel of land. Under the estoppel by deed theory, if a grantor purports to convey an estate in property that she does not then own, her subsequent acquisition of title to the property will automatically inure to the benefit of the grantee, but only as against the grantor. If the grantor transfers her after-acquired title to a bona fide purchaser for value ("BFP"), the BFP gets good title. Here, when the woman acquired title to the parcel of land from the true owner, that title passed automatically to the buyer by operation of law. Although the investor paid a reasonable value for the parcel of land, she is not a BFP because she had at least inquiry notice of the buyer's interest in the land. Under the majority view, a recorded deed obtained from a grantor who had no title at that time but who afterwards obtains title is not in the chain of title and so does not give constructive (or record) notice to a subsequent purchaser. However, a subsequent purchaser is charged with knowledge of whatever an inspection of the property would have disclosed and anything that would have been disclosed by inquiring of the possessor. Here, an examination of possession would have revealed the buyer's interest in the parcel of land. Thus, the investor has no enforceable claim to the land and (C) is wrong. (B) is wrong because the investor's cause of action against the woman for breach of the covenants of seisin (*i.e.*, the grantor has the estate or interest that she purports to convey) and right to convey (*i.e.*, the grantor has the power and authority to make the grant) does not affect the buyer's title to the parcel of land. (D) is wrong because it states the minority position under estoppel by deed. Under the majority view, title passes to the buyer automatically; he need not bring suit to recover title.

Answer to Question 9

(C) The plaintiff will not prevail because the defendant had no history of heart problems. For the plaintiff to prevail in a claim against the defendant, the plaintiff must show (i) duty, (ii) breach of duty, (iii) actual and proximate cause, and (iv) damages. While drivers owe a duty of care to other drivers on the road, a driver would not be deemed to have breached that duty if he had a surprise heart attack while driving, given that he had no history of heart trouble. (A) is wrong because the fact that the defendant's car was a cause of the accident does not establish breach of duty. (B) is wrong because violation of an applicable statute, which may sometimes establish breach of duty, will be excused where compliance was impossible. Here, because the defendant suffered a sudden heart attack, he was unable to comply with the motor vehicle statute. (D) is wrong. The facts do not establish whether the accident would have happened regardless of the plaintiff's contributory negligence, but the trier of fact will not reach that issue because the plaintiff will not be able to establish the prima facie case.

Answer to Question 10

(B) The statute will likely be declared constitutional. Because Congress's power to regulate interstate commerce is plenary, Congress has the right to prohibit completely the transportation of "harmful" substances in the channels of commerce. Congress could also otherwise regulate the manufacture and use of harmful drugs as part of its regulation of commerce. (A) is wrong because this Act has nothing to do with Congress's right to expend federal tax revenues, and the general welfare power has to do with Congress's spending power. (C) is incorrect because the constitutional right of privacy does not include the right to ingest harmful drugs. (D) is incorrect because this Act is a restriction on property use that is considered harmful to the public health and welfare; consequently, it is considered regulation and not a taking within the meaning of the Fifth Amendment, and no compensation would be required.

Answer to Question 11

(A) Federal Rule 501 provides that federal courts shall apply rules of privilege developed at common law except in diversity cases, wherein state law controls, but this is not a diversity case. The United States Supreme Court has held that the privilege not to testify may be asserted only by the testifying spouse, and if she is willing to so testify against her husband, the marital relationship is so disharmonious that there is nothing left for the privilege to preserve. Thus, (A) is correct and (B) and (C) are incorrect. (D) is incorrect because it states the privilege for confidential marital communications, which is different from the spousal privilege. Further, the confidential communication was between the defendant and his co-defendants, not between the defendant and his wife.

Answer to Question 12

(B) The question was improper because it effectively comments on the defendant's post-arrest silence and thus violates his right to due process of law. A prosecutor may not comment on the defendant's silence after being arrested and receiving *Miranda* warnings. The warnings carry an implicit assurance that silence will carry no penalty. Thus, the defendant's invocation of his right to remain silent cannot be used as evidence against him at trial, nor can he be questioned or cross-examined about his decision to remain silent, even if he testifies at trial. Thus, (B) is the correct answer, and (C) is wrong. (*Distinguish:* If the defendant fails to disclose potential exculpatory evidence to the police ***after waiving*** his right to remain silent, he may be cross-examined at trial on that failure in an effort to show that it is a recent fabrication. In this case, however, the defendant ***invoked*** his right to remain silent.) (A) is wrong; the question is improper, but not because it would be unconstitutional pretrial discovery. (D) is also wrong. Although statements made without proper *Miranda* warnings can sometimes be used to impeach, the defendant's silence would not be classified as a prior statement.

Answer to Question 13

(B) Under the "avoidable consequences" rule, a plaintiff has a duty to mitigate damages to avoid further injuries from the defendant's conduct. Because the sheep farmer's property was damaged in this situation, the sheep farmer's claim would be based on strict liability. As such, simple contributory negligence would not be a good defense in jurisdictions following traditional contributory negligence rules. (C) is therefore incorrect. But if the plaintiff discovers the existence of the danger and fails to act reasonably to prevent further harm from occurring, the defendant would have a good defense, making (B) the best defense. (A) is incorrect because there is no balancing of utility and risk where abnormally dangerous activities are involved. (D) is incorrect because the sheep farmer would have had to have known of and appreciated the risk involved when he purchased the property to constitute assumption of the risk. Thus, (B) is the only correct answer.

Answer to Question 14

(C) The landowner has acquired title to the land on which the generator was installed by adverse possession. To establish title by adverse possession, the possession must be (i) actual and exclusive, (ii) open and notorious, (iii) adverse (hostile), and (iv) continuous throughout the statutory period. Exclusive possession generally means not sharing possession with the true owner or the general public. Possession is open and notorious when it is such as the usual owner would make of the land and is sufficient to put the true owner on notice of the fact of possession. Possession is hostile when it is without the owner's consent; by the large majority view, it does not matter whether the possessor believes he is on his own land or knows he is trespassing on someone else's land. Continuous possession is possession that the average owner would make of the property under the circumstances. Here, the landowner's possession of the neighbor's land was clearly actual and exclusive, as he did not share possession with the neighbor or the general public. His possession was open and notorious, as the installation of a gas-powered generator is a use that the usual owner would make of the land. Moreover, the generator was above ground and thus visible to the neighbor. The landowner possessed the property for 30 years, 10 beyond that required by the statue of limitations. Finally, although the landowner believed he was on his own land, his state of mind is irrelevant. Because he did not enter with the neighbor's permission, the landowner's possession was hostile. Thus, (B) is incorrect. (A) is incorrect because an intervening disability does not toll the statute of limitations. The statute is tolled only if the true owner was under some disability ***before*** the adverse possession began. (D) is incorrect because the doctrine of acquiescence does not apply to these facts. Most courts will fix ownership as per the agreed boundary line, provided it is shown that: (i) there was original uncertainty as to the true line; (ii) the agreed line was established (*i.e.*, agreed upon); and (iii) there has been lengthy acquiescence in the agreed line by the adjoining owners and/or their successors. Here, although there was original uncertainty as to the true boundary line, nothing in the facts indicates that the line was fixed by the agreement of the landowner and the neighbor.

Answer to Question 15

(B) The aircraft manufacturer will prevail in its suit against the sales agent for damages because the sales agent's performance was personal and, therefore, is nondelegable. Where a contract is assigned in total, such as the contract here, the assignment includes a delegation of duties. Although the general rule is that all contractual duties can be delegated to a third person, duties may not be delegated if they involve personal judgment and skill. Here, the sales agent's performance as a skilled negotiator involved personal judgment and skill and, thus, may not be delegated. (A) is wrong because delegations of contractual duties can be oral. (C) is wrong because the damage lies in taking away the sales agent that the aircraft manufacturer has chosen to be negotiator, which is not permitted when her duties involve personal judgment and skill. (D) is wrong because damages could be measured by the cost of hiring another negotiator of the aircraft manufacturer's choosing. Also, the question turns on whether the sales agent's duties are delegable, and not on how damages would be calculated.

Answer to Question 16

(B) Congress may regulate, under the Commerce Clause, anything that has a substantial economic effect upon interstate commerce. The rates that banks charge for interest certainly affect interstate commerce or may simply constitute commerce in its broad sense. In either case, the regulation is clearly within Congress's commerce power. Thus, (C) is incorrect. (A) is incorrect because the General Welfare Clause gives Congress the power to spend for the general welfare, and the regulation here is not related to any spending measure. (D) is incorrect because the Privileges and Immunities Clause of Article IV prohibits states from discriminating against nonresidents. Here, we have a federal statute. So the Privileges and Immunities Clause is inapplicable.

Answer to Question 17

(D) The substantive relation of the questions to the issues of the lawsuit has no bearing on whether leading questions are permitted. Use of leading questions on direct examination to refresh the recollection of a witness or to establish preliminary matters is permitted in the discretion of the trial court. Thus, (A) and (B) are incorrect. Where a witness is hostile to the party calling him, the examination is treated as cross-examination, and leading questions may be used. Thus, (C) is incorrect.

Answer to Question 18

(C) Because the man is an at-will employee, the hospital is not required to provide any justification for his dismissal. The facts indicate that he was dismissed after six months of his nine-month probationary period, and that after nine months, he could be dismissed only for cause after notice and a hearing. Thus, (C) is the hospital's strongest defense. (A) and (B) state grounds that the hospital could conceivably raise, but because the man had not completed the nine-month period, it is not required to raise these grounds. (D), in turn, raises the possibility of a First Amendment defense to the firing, but because grounds were not required here, this is an incorrect answer choice.

Answer to Question 19

(B) The court should instruct that a child's conduct is judged by the standard of care applicable to a child of similar age, experience, and intelligence in similar circumstances. Most jurisdictions apply this standard to a child's conduct unless the child was engaged in an adult activity. Thus, (A) is wrong. Formerly, many jurisdictions would conclusively presume that a very young child was incapable of negligence, and that an older child was rebuttably presumed not to have acted negligently. Most courts today, however, do not fix these presumptions at an arbitrary age. Thus, (D) is a misstatement of law. (C) is wrong because the question refers to the negligence cause of action. As to that action, the boy's conduct is material, because it will either reduce or bar his recovery in the negligence action.

Answer to Question 20

(B) The golfer can enjoin the partnership's actions only if she has an equitable servitude. An equitable servitude is a covenant that, regardless of whether it runs with the land at law, equity will enforce against the assignees of the burdened land who have notice of the covenant. The requisite notice may be acquired through actual notice (direct knowledge of the covenants in the prior deeds), inquiry notice (the neighborhood appears to conform to common restrictions), or record notice (if the prior deeds are in the grantee's chain of title it will, under the recording acts, have constructive notice of their contents). Here, the golfer will be able to enforce the restriction as an equitable servitude because the partnership has ***record*** notice of it: a deed in its chain of title referred to the recorded plan that designated the 40-acre tract as a golf course. (A) is wrong because the location of the 40-acre tract will not be sufficient to establish actual notice. However, as explained above, the partnership has record notice of the restriction. (C) is wrong because the golfer is not a third-party beneficiary of the developer's promise. Instead, she is a direct promisee because she dealt directly with the developer. (D) is not sufficient to grant the golfer an injunction against the partnership.

Answer to Question 21

(C) Under the Federal Rules, depositions can be used more broadly than under the rules in many states. Here, the prior inconsistent statement can be used for impeachment purposes and as substantive evidence. (A) is wrong because the Federal Rules permit impeachment of your own witness. (B) is wrong because under the Federal Rules, prior inconsistent statements, made under oath and subject to the penalty of perjury in a deposition or prior hearing, are admissible as nonhearsay. (D) is wrong because the statement can be used for more than impeachment.

Answer to Question 22

(C) The sister is not criminally liable for the store clerk's death. A defendant may, by virtue of her participation in a conspiracy, be liable for the crime of all other conspirators if the crimes were committed in furtherance of the objectives of the conspiracy and were a natural and probable consequence of the conspiracy (*i.e.,* were foreseeable). Furthermore, liability for felony murder would attach if the killing were committed during the course of a felony. Thus, the sister would be criminally liable for the killing of the clerk if she were a co-conspirator or if she were a principal to the underlying felony (the robbery). However, under the facts, the sister is neither because she lacked the requisite intent. Given the threat to her life, the sister did not freely enter into a conspiracy to commit robbery. (A) is incorrect because, while duress is not a defense to murder, it ***is*** a defense to the underlying felony, and thus is a defense to the felony murder charge. Here, the sister was acting under duress during the robbery, and thus she has a defense to the robbery charge. (B) is incorrect because, as stated above, under these facts duress is a good defense to the robbery charge and thus would be a good defense to the felony murder charge. (D) is also incorrect. Although a valid withdrawal would be a good defense to subsequent crimes of any co-conspirator, it is doubtful whether the sister in fact entered into a conspiracy in the first place. Because she never had the intent required for participation in the conspiracy, the jury would not be required to consider her defense of withdrawal.

Answer to Question 23

(B) The homeowner will prevail in his suit against the low bidder for breach of contract because the homeowner did not know or have reason to known of the low bidder's mistake with respect to the amount of its bid. Where only one of the parties entering into a contract is mistaken about facts relating to the agreement, the unilateral mistake will not prevent formation of the contract unless the nonmistaken party knew or had reason to know of the mistake. Here, the relatively small difference between the $4,000 bid and the next lowest bid of $4,500 (where there was also a $500 difference between the next lowest bid and the highest bid) probably would not have alerted the homeowner to the existence of a mistake. Therefore, (B) is correct, and (D) is incorrect. (A) is incorrect because it is irrelevant whether the nonmistaken party can make an alternative contract. (C) is incorrect because it is irrelevant that the contract is still executory.

Answer to Question 24

(D) The car thief can be charged with theft, conspiracy, and robbery. The facts clearly show that the car thief is guilty of the theft of the car that was to be used for the getaway. Conspiracy requires: (i) an agreement between two or more persons; (ii) the intent to enter into the agreement; and (iii) the intent to achieve the objective of the agreement. Most states also require an overt act in furtherance of the conspiracy. The car thief conspired to commit robbery, because he entered into an agreement with the two other thieves to rob the bank, intending both to enter into such an agreement and to achieve the objective thereof. The car thief's theft of the car constituted an overt act in furtherance of the conspiracy. Thus, the car thief can be charged with conspiracy. Furthermore, each member of a conspiracy is liable for the crimes of all other conspirators if: (i) such crimes were committed in furtherance of the objectives of the conspiracy; and (ii) such crimes were a natural and probable consequence of the conspiracy. A conspirator may ***limit his liability for subsequent acts*** of the other members of the conspiracy if he withdraws from the conspiracy by performing an affirmative act that notifies all members of the conspiracy in time for them to have the opportunity to abandon their plans. The car thief's absence from the robbery scene with the getaway car was due to his sudden illness, rather than any voluntary decision on his part to withdraw from the conspiracy. Thus, the car thief failed to make a legally effective withdrawal from the conspiracy. Certainly, the robbery of the bank, which was the sole object of the conspiracy, was a crime committed in furtherance of the conspiracy's objectives and was a natural and probable consequence of the conspiracy. Therefore, the car thief is liable for this robbery committed by his co-conspirators. Because the car thief can properly be charged with all three crimes, (A), (B), and (C) are incorrect.

Answer to Question 25

(A) The older brother will be denied the requested judgment. A co-tenant has no duty to improve the property and cannot force the other co-tenants to contribute to the cost of improvements made by him. Only in an action for partition can the value of improvements be recouped. Thus, (B) is wrong. (C) and (D) are wrong because the results of an improvement are irrelevant; a co-tenant cannot force his other co-tenants to contribute to the improvement.

Answer to Question 26

(B) The Establishment Clause prohibits the government from taking action respecting the establishment of religion. Where no sect preference is involved, government action will be upheld if it serves a secular purpose, its primary effect neither advances nor inhibits religion, and it does not produce excessive government entanglements with religion. (A) is a true statement—it is not unconstitutional to teach religious matters in private schools—but the Constitution prohibits government from providing much aid to such private schools. (C) is irrelevant for similar reasons—although private religious schools might fulfill an important educational function, they still will run afoul of the Constitution unless the above three-part test is met. (D) is incorrect because the state is compelled by the Establishment Clause not to provide certain types of aid to religious schools; in such cases, the Free Exercise Clause is not violated so long as the law is general in nature, which is the case here.

Answer to Question 27

(D) The professor's announcement was an ineffective revocation as to the student who had begun performance, because an offer to enter into a unilateral contract is not revocable once performance has begun. An offer to enter into a unilateral contract can be accepted only by performing the stipulated act. Here, the student's devoting his study time extensively to the subject of Constitutional Law and using substantive outlines that he purchased specifically so he would win the prize constitutes beginning performance, making the offer irrevocable. Thus, the offer is irrevocable as to the student, making (D) correct and (B) incorrect. (A) is incorrect, because the offer was valid. It created a reasonable expectation in the offeree that the offeror was willing to enter into a contract on the basis of the offered terms. There was an expression of a promise, undertaking, or commitment to enter into a contract; the terms were certain and definite; and they were communicated to the offeree. (C) is incorrect because a revocation need only be published in the same manner as the offer; it need not actually reach everyone who knew of the offer.

Answer to Question 28

(B) The offer to pay medical expenses in itself is not admissible as an admission. Here, however, there is a statement that follows such an offer. This statement is admissible as an admission by the CEO of the development firm that the employee had not warned the plaintiff about the dangerous condition of the stairs. Because this is an admission, it is not hearsay under the Federal Rules. (A) is an exception to the hearsay rule and is thus unnecessary. Furthermore, it is an exception requiring the unavailability of the declarant, and there is no indication in the facts that the employee is now unavailable. (C) is wrong because, as mentioned, the statement is not hearsay under the Federal Rules. (D) is a misstatement of the law; only the offer to pay medical expenses is inadmissible on public policy grounds.

Answer to Question 29

(C) The plaintiff was a trespasser in the cabin owner's cabin because she entered the cabin without permission or privilege. A landowner generally owes no duty to an undiscovered trespasser. However, if a landowner discovers or should anticipate the presence of a trespasser, he must exercise ordinary care to warn the trespasser of or to make safe concealed, unsafe, artificial conditions known to the landowner that involve a risk of death or serious bodily harm. Here, the cabin owner owed no duty to the plaintiff because he had no reason to anticipate the presence of someone in the cabin. Thus, (C) is a better answer than (D). (A) is wrong because the cabin owner's knowledge of the defect is important only if he owed a duty to the plaintiff, which he did not. (B) is wrong because, as stated, he had no duty to warn the plaintiff because he did not know of her presence.

Answer to Question 30

(D) If the husband did not believe that the wife's complaints indicated a serious medical problem, he did not have the mental state required for murder. Murder is the unlawful killing of a human being with malice aforethought. Malice aforethought is present if the defendant acts with: (i) intent to kill; (ii) intent to inflict great bodily injury; (iii) reckless indifference to an unjustifiably high risk to human life; or (iv) intent to commit a felony. Assuming that, as stated in (D), the husband did not believe that the wife's complaints of abdominal pain were indicative of a serious medical problem, it cannot be said that in bypassing the city emergency facility the husband acted with the intent to kill or seriously injure the wife, or that he even acted with reckless indifference to a high risk to the wife's life. If the husband did not believe there was a serious medical problem, he could not have thought he was placing the wife in great danger of death by driving on to the town. Under such circumstances, the husband lacked the mens rea required to sustain a murder conviction. (A) refers to the matter of whether the husband had a duty to assist the wife in her distress. A defendant's failure to act will not result in criminal liability unless the defendant has a legal duty to act under the circumstances. Such a duty may exist where there is a sufficiently close relationship between the defendant and the victim; *e.g.*, a spouse has a duty to prevent harm to his or her spouse. Even if the husband and the wife were not legally married, the fact that they had lived together for many years as if they were married indicates that they were in a relationship of such a close nature as to give rise to a duty to act to prevent harm to each other. Thus, the facts set forth in (A) will not be helpful to the husband. Regarding (B), a defendant is responsible for all results that occur as a natural and probable consequence of his conduct, even if he did not anticipate the precise manner in which they would occur. All such results are proximately caused by the defendant's act, and the chain of causation is broken only by a superseding factor. An intervening act will shield the defendant from liability if the act is a mere coincidence or is outside the foreseeable sphere of risk created by the defendant's conduct. Negligent medical care is a foreseeable risk. Being injured or even dying due to incompetent medical care was a risk to which the husband exposed the wife when he refused to stop at the city, thereby exacerbating an already serious situation. Although the husband may not have anticipated that the wife would die because of the doctor's incompetence, the wife's death was a natural and probable consequence of the husband's refusal to stop at the city. Thus, the additional fact of the doctor's incompetent treatment of the wife does not establish any defense for the husband. (C) is incorrect because an act that hastens an inevitable result is still considered a legal cause of that result. Although it may be true that the wife would have died of cancer within a relatively short time, the husband's failure to get her proper care as quickly as possible actually caused her death.

Answer to Question 31

(C) The sales manager's May 1 announcement would best be interpreted as a contractual offer that created a power of acceptance. The sales manager made an expression of a promise, undertaking, or commitment to enter into a contract; the terms were certain and definite; and they were communicated to the offerees (the salespeople at the meeting), creating a power of acceptance. Thus, (C) is correct, and (A) and (D) are incorrect. (B) is incorrect because there was an offer for a bargained-for exchange: the sales manager would pay a bonus to the top salesperson who, through diligent work, brought in the highest sales at the end of the month. Because there was consideration, this was not to be a gift, making (B) incorrect.

Answer to Question 32

(B) The physician's opinion is admissible. Under the Federal Rules, an expert witness may learn the basis for the opinion at or before the hearing. (A) is wrong because the basis for an expert's opinion need not be personal observation; here, the physician was asked his opinion about the beekeeper's testimony. (C) is wrong because under the Federal Rules, an expert witness may testify in the form of an opinion without prior disclosure of the underlying facts or data. In addition, here the basis of the expert's testimony was based on evidence already introduced at trial. (D) is wrong because expert opinion may indeed be based on information provided by lay persons.

Answer to Question 33

(A) The rider probably will recover all of his damages. The rancher owed the rider a duty of reasonable care in conducting activities on his land because the rancher was (or should have been) aware of the rider's presence, making the rider a discovered (or anticipated) trespasser. Hence,

(D) is incorrect. The rancher breached this duty of care by shooting while the rider was in the vicinity, and this duty was an actual and proximate cause of the rider's injury. (B) and (C) are incorrect because the rider's negligence, even if it was gross negligence, was not a substantial factor in causing his injuries because it did not create a foreseeable risk of being shot by the rancher (*i.e.*, a sober, careful rider who was in the same place at the same time would still have been shot). The rider's damages stem just from the bullet piercing the artery in his leg, which does not appear to be attributable to his negligence. Thus, his recovery from the rancher would be total.

Answer to Question 34

(B) This is a best evidence rule question; it is an attempt to prove the contents of a document that is the basis of the suit. The best evidence rule applies and therefore the party must produce the original document or offer a satisfactory excuse for not producing it. Under Rule 1004, if the original is lost, that is considered a reasonable excuse for not producing the original. Whether the letter is in fact "lost" would be a preliminary question of fact to be determined by the court under Rule 104(a), rather than the jury. Thus, (B) is correct and (C) is incorrect. (A) is incorrect; there is no such requirement under the Rules. (D) is incorrect; there is no such rule of law.

Answer to Question 35

(C) A court will likely determine that the employee owned the tract of land because the deed was merely evidence of her title and its destruction was insufficient to cause title to pass back to the employer. A deed, once it has been delivered, is merely evidence of title, and its destruction does not cause any change in the title. To transfer title, the employee would have had to deliver a new deed transferring title back to the employer. (A) and (B) are therefore wrong. (D) is wrong because the facts do not support a claim of undue influence.

Answer to Question 36

(D) The strongest support for the legislation would be the power to tax and spend for the general welfare. Prior to disbursement, the federal government may attach any reasonable condition to expenditures under the general welfare power. (A) is not a power of Congress enumerated in the Constitution. There is no general federal police power, the federal government being one of limited, enumerated powers. Thus, (B) is incorrect. (C) is incorrect because the war and defense power does not apply to the facts presented.

Answer to Question 37

(B) The photographer must agree to a rescission of the agreement. A party to a contract may not unilaterally rescind the contract. However, both parties to a contract may agree to rescind and discharge their contractual duties as long as the duties are still executory on both sides. Here, neither party has performed under the contract—the photographer has not shot the pictures and the father has not paid the photographer. Thus, the contract will be mutually rescinded if the photographer gives her assent to the father. (A) is incorrect because the creditor's rights as a third-party beneficiary of the contract have not yet vested; thus, his consent to the rescission is not needed. An intended beneficiary, such as the creditor, can enforce a contract only after his rights have vested, which will occur when he (i) manifests assent to the promise in a manner invited or requested by the parties; (ii) brings suit to enforce the promise; or (iii) materially changes position in justifiable reliance on the promise. Here, the creditor has not even become aware of the agreement between the father and the photographer, so his rights have not yet vested. (C) is not correct because this is primarily a services contract and not a sales contract. While contracts for the sale of goods valued at $500 or more are not enforceable unless evidenced by a writing signed by the party to be charged, the photographer is providing a service in taking photographs for the father, rather than just selling photographs. No other Statute of Frauds provisions apply, so the contract does not have to be evidenced by a writing. (D) is incorrect because the father made an anticipatory repudiation of the contract and the nonrepudiating party, in such a case, has the option of treating the anticipatory repudiation as a total repudiation and suing immediately. Here, the father's repudiation of the contract was unequivocal and the contract was bilateral with executory duties on both sides. Thus, the photographer may choose to sue for breach of contract immediately.

Answer to Question 38

(B) The artist is guilty of false pretenses. The offense of false pretenses consists of obtaining title to the property of another by an intentional false statement of past or existing fact, with the intent to defraud the other. Here, with intent to defraud the art collector, the artist knowingly and falsely represented to her that the painting in question was by a recently deceased artist. The art collector, deceived by this misrepresentation and relying thereon, paid money for the painting. Thus, the artist has committed the offense of false pretenses. It follows that (D) is incorrect. (A) is incorrect because a writing that derives its value from the mere fact of its existence (historical or artistic value) cannot be the subject of forgery. (C) is incorrect because larceny by trick involves obtaining ***possession***, not ***title***, by means of a false representation.

Answer to Question 39

(A) The passenger will recover all of his damages from the driver. Because the damage resulting from medical malpractice was a foreseeable result of the driver's negligence, the driver is liable for such damage even though the negligent doctor contributed to the passenger's damages; *i.e.*, the doctor's negligence is not a superseding cause and therefore does not cut off the driver's liability for the passenger's injuries. (B) is wrong because joint and several liability allows the plaintiff to recover all of his damages from one of the joint tortfeasors. (C) is wrong because contribution rules apply only to a defendant who has paid the full judgment to the plaintiff and is seeking contribution from another tortfeasor; they have no relevance to the plaintiff's recovery against the defendant. (D) is wrong because the passenger could maintain an action for all his damages directly against the driver with no need to join the doctor.

Answer to Question 40

(C) Federal Rule of Evidence 608(b) permits cross-examination relating to prior bad acts if, in the discretion of the trial court, they are probative of truthfulness. Thus, (A) is wrong. (D) is wrong because Federal Rule 609 permits inquiry into a prior crime less than 10 years old if conviction of the crime required proof or admission of an act of dishonesty or false statement. Because the bias involved in a pecuniary interest is always relevant and admissible, (B) is wrong. Only the question relating to drug abuse—a marginally relevant topic, relating possibly to the witness's ability to perceive or remember—appears improper.

Answer to Question 41

(C) The mother and the brother each have a one-half interest in the home as tenants in common. When the woman died, her one-half interest descended to her intestate heir, her mother; and likewise, when the man died, his one-half interest passed to his intestate heir, his brother. There is no right of survivorship in a tenancy in common, and the oral agreement between the man and the woman does not satisfy the Statute of Frauds or the Statute of Wills. The facts involving the closeness of the man's death to the woman's are a mere distraction, because no real simultaneous death issues arise here. It follows that (A) and (B) are incorrect. (D) is incorrect because a tenancy in common does not become a joint tenancy upon the death of the co-tenants.

Answer to Question 42

(C) The teenager will probably not recover because the MP3 player had been refurbished by the seller. To establish a prima facie case in products liability based on strict liability in tort, the plaintiff must prove: (i) absolute duty owed by a commercial supplier, (ii) production or sale of a defective product, (iii) actual and proximate cause, and (iv) damages. To hold the commercial supplier strictly liable for a product defect, the product must be expected to, and must in fact, reach the user or consumer without substantial change in the condition in which it is supplied. A product manufacturer is not strictly liable for defects that were not present when the product left the manufacturer's control. (A) is therefore wrong. (B) is wrong because the seller altered the player by refurbishing it with cheaper parts, and the facts indicate that the player shorted out; there was no apparent defect in the headphones. (D) is wrong because courts do not require privity of contract in a strict liability in tort action.

Answer to Question 43

(B) The judge should rule the testimony inadmissible. The witness's statement is hearsay because it is being offered for the truth of the matter asserted; it does not stop being hearsay just because it has become part of a police report. (A) and (C) are wrong because although the police report itself may qualify under some exception, the witness's statement contained in the report is still hearsay. (D) is wrong because the facts do not indicate that the police officer is testifying from her report, and it does not change the hearsay character of the testimony.

Answer to Question 44

(A) A court will most likely rule for the neighbor because the swimmer is absolutely liable for the damage to her neighbor's land. A property owner has a right to the support of his land without any buildings on it. An adjoining owner is absolutely liable for any withdrawal of support. Thus, if the swimmer's excavation withdrew support for her neighbor's land, she is absolutely liable for the damage. (B) is wrong because the swimmer's negligence is irrelevant to a claim for subsidence of land in its natural state; she is absolutely liable. Negligence would be relevant, however, if the land had been improved by buildings that were damaged as a result of the subsidence ***and*** their weight. But if the land would have collapsed in its natural state (*i.e.*, without the weight of the buildings), the landowner is strictly liable for damages to the buildings. (C) is wrong because damage to the land itself is recoverable if support has been withdrawn. (D) is wrong because, as indicated, adjoining landowners have a right of subjacent and lateral support.

Answer to Question 45

(B) Under the Federal Rules, a witness may be impeached by a record of conviction of any crime (felony or misdemeanor) if it can be readily determined that conviction of the crime required proof or admission of an act of dishonesty or false statement. A witness also may be impeached by any felony, whether or not it involves dishonesty or a false statement. In a criminal case in which the accused is being impeached, a felony conviction that does not involve dishonesty or a false statement will be admitted only if the government shows that its probative value as impeachment evidencc outweighs its prejudicial effect. Here, the evidence the prosecution is seeking to introduce is a misdemeanor that does not involve dishonesty or a false statement; thus, (B) is correct and (A) is incorrect. (C) is a correct statement of law—a conviction is generally admissible if it is less than 10 years old—but it is not as good of an answer as (B). (D) is incorrect because, as discussed above, a witness may not be impeached by any crime.

Answer to Question 46

(B) The Commerce Clause prohibits states from discriminating against interstate commerce in favor of local business. The requirement here—limiting acceptable malpractice carriers to insurance companies within the state—clearly discriminates against interstate commerce. Because the state seeks simply to protect its citizens, which will presumably occur if insurance is provided by a reputable company whether or not the company is located within the state, there are reasonable alternatives to the discriminatory regulation challenged here. Thus, the insurance regulation violates the Commerce Clause. (A) is incorrect. The requirement to obtain malpractice insurance only from in-state carriers is an economic burden. The Commerce Clause provides a stronger protection than the Due Process Clause, because economic regulations get rational basis analysis under the Due Process Clause. (C) is wrong because the state can enforce its regulations within the state even if the insurer is from out of state, provided it does not discriminate when it does so. (D) is incorrect, because even if there is a rational relationship between the state interest and the particular requirement that the doctor is challenging, there are reasonable nondiscriminatory alternatives available to regulate the out-of-state insurers.

Answer to Question 47

(D) Parents are not vicariously liable at common law for the intentional torts of their children (although many states have imposed limited liability for certain conduct by statute). However, a parent (or anyone else having care or custody of a child) can be held liable for injuries caused by the child where the parent herself was negligent. For example, the parent may be liable for failing to exercise reasonable care to protect against the child's known dangerous tendencies. Here, pursuant to statute, the director stood in loco parentis to the disabled child. Thus, the director could be held liable if she knew that the disabled child had dangerous propensities, and failed to take appropriate measures (*e.g.*, keeping a closer watch on the disabled child). The director then would be liable for her own negligence, not vicariously liable for the disabled child's intentional tort. Here, however, all of the children had been previously evaluated as not being dangerous, and there is no other indication of negligence on the part of the facility, so the director would not be liable. (A) is incorrect because it ignores the fact that the director's liability depends on her knowledge of any dangerous propensities on the part of the disabled child. (B) is incorrect because neither raising children generally nor operating a home for developmentally disabled children are abnormally dangerous activities giving rise to strict liability. (C) is incorrect because it is the wrong rationale. Regardless of whether the 11-year-old child is liable for his conduct, vicarious liability does not apply to parents absent a statute.

Answer to Question 48

(B) The statement is inadmissible hearsay because it is being offered to prove the truth of the matter asserted. (A) is wrong because the statement may tend to show a reason for the accident. (C) is wrong because the friend is not a party, and the statement is not attributable to either the husband or wife. (D) is wrong because the statement against interest exception requires that the declarant be unavailable to testify; nothing in the facts suggests that the friend is unavailable. Further, the statement by the friend does not appear to be against his interest.

Answer to Question 49

(B) The buyer can recover because the seller's phone call was an anticipatory repudiation. Anticipatory repudiation occurs where a promisor, prior to the performance time, unequivocally indicates that he cannot or will not timely perform, allowing the nonrepudiator the option of suspending performance and waiting to sue until the performance date, or to sue immediately. The seller's phone call was an unequivocal statement that he would not sell the guitar for $12,000. This repudiation excused the buyer's duty to tender $12,000 on the delivery date. (A) is incorrect because the seller's anticipatory breach excused the buyer's performance. (C) is incorrect because the seller's repudiation the day after the contract was signed gave rise to an immediate cause of action. (D) is wrong because the contract was not terminated; rather, it was anticipatorily breached by the seller.

Answer to Question 50

(D) The accused is guilty of larceny of the crowbar, conspiracy, and attempted burglary. At common law, larceny was the taking and carrying away of the personal property of another by trespass with the intent to permanently (or for an unreasonable time) deprive the person of his interest in the property. Here, the defendant shoplifted a crowbar, and he intended to keep the crowbar for future burglaries. Thus, he is guilty of larceny of the crowbar. At common law, the elements of conspiracy are: (i) an agreement between two or more persons; (ii) the intent to enter into the agreement; and (iii) the intent to achieve the objective of the agreement. In the instant case, the accused agreed with an accomplice to burglarize the home; thus, he is guilty of conspiracy. Furthermore, given that the accused never communicated a withdrawal from the conspiracy to his accomplice, he would be vicariously liable for the attempted burglary of the home. As a result, (A), (B), and (C) are incorrect, and (D) is correct.

Mixed Subject Set 7
Answer Sheet

1.	Ⓐ	Ⓑ	Ⓒ	Ⓓ	26.	Ⓐ	Ⓑ	Ⓒ	Ⓓ
2.	Ⓐ	Ⓑ	Ⓒ	Ⓓ	27.	Ⓐ	Ⓑ	Ⓒ	Ⓓ
3.	Ⓐ	Ⓑ	Ⓒ	Ⓓ	28.	Ⓐ	Ⓑ	Ⓒ	Ⓓ
4.	Ⓐ	Ⓑ	Ⓒ	Ⓓ	29.	Ⓐ	Ⓑ	Ⓒ	Ⓓ
5.	Ⓐ	Ⓑ	Ⓒ	Ⓓ	30.	Ⓐ	Ⓑ	Ⓒ	Ⓓ
6.	Ⓐ	Ⓑ	Ⓒ	Ⓓ	31.	Ⓐ	Ⓑ	Ⓒ	Ⓓ
7.	Ⓐ	Ⓑ	Ⓒ	Ⓓ	32.	Ⓐ	Ⓑ	Ⓒ	Ⓓ
8.	Ⓐ	Ⓑ	Ⓒ	Ⓓ	33.	Ⓐ	Ⓑ	Ⓒ	Ⓓ
9.	Ⓐ	Ⓑ	Ⓒ	Ⓓ	34.	Ⓐ	Ⓑ	Ⓒ	Ⓓ
10.	Ⓐ	Ⓑ	Ⓒ	Ⓓ	35.	Ⓐ	Ⓑ	Ⓒ	Ⓓ
11.	Ⓐ	Ⓑ	Ⓒ	Ⓓ	36.	Ⓐ	Ⓑ	Ⓒ	Ⓓ
12.	Ⓐ	Ⓑ	Ⓒ	Ⓓ	37.	Ⓐ	Ⓑ	Ⓒ	Ⓓ
13.	Ⓐ	Ⓑ	Ⓒ	Ⓓ	38.	Ⓐ	Ⓑ	Ⓒ	Ⓓ
14.	Ⓐ	Ⓑ	Ⓒ	Ⓓ	39.	Ⓐ	Ⓑ	Ⓒ	Ⓓ
15.	Ⓐ	Ⓑ	Ⓒ	Ⓓ	40.	Ⓐ	Ⓑ	Ⓒ	Ⓓ
16.	Ⓐ	Ⓑ	Ⓒ	Ⓓ	41.	Ⓐ	Ⓑ	Ⓒ	Ⓓ
17.	Ⓐ	Ⓑ	Ⓒ	Ⓓ	42.	Ⓐ	Ⓑ	Ⓒ	Ⓓ
18.	Ⓐ	Ⓑ	Ⓒ	Ⓓ	43.	Ⓐ	Ⓑ	Ⓒ	Ⓓ
19.	Ⓐ	Ⓑ	Ⓒ	Ⓓ	44.	Ⓐ	Ⓑ	Ⓒ	Ⓓ
20.	Ⓐ	Ⓑ	Ⓒ	Ⓓ	45.	Ⓐ	Ⓑ	Ⓒ	Ⓓ
21.	Ⓐ	Ⓑ	Ⓒ	Ⓓ	46.	Ⓐ	Ⓑ	Ⓒ	Ⓓ
22.	Ⓐ	Ⓑ	Ⓒ	Ⓓ	47.	Ⓐ	Ⓑ	Ⓒ	Ⓓ
23.	Ⓐ	Ⓑ	Ⓒ	Ⓓ	48.	Ⓐ	Ⓑ	Ⓒ	Ⓓ
24.	Ⓐ	Ⓑ	Ⓒ	Ⓓ	49.	Ⓐ	Ⓑ	Ⓒ	Ⓓ
25.	Ⓐ	Ⓑ	Ⓒ	Ⓓ	50.	Ⓐ	Ⓑ	Ⓒ	Ⓓ

MIXED SUBJECT QUESTIONS - SET 7

Question 1

A landowner owned two adjoining parcels of land. The landowner sold the western parcel to a buyer by a deed that contained the following clause: "Grantee promises for himself, his heirs, successors, and assigns to not erect a structure over two stories on the land." The buyer built a two-story house on the property and lived there for 30 years, after which he sold the land to a movie star by a deed that did not contain the structure height restriction. The movie star decided to tear down the existing house on the land and erect a three-story house. Her neighbor, who purchased the eastern parcel from the landowner 10 years earlier, discovers that the movie star's house will be larger than his and files suit to enforce the covenant.

Who will prevail?

(A) The neighbor, because the restrictive covenant in his deed runs with the land.

(B) The neighbor, because privity is not required to enforce an equitable servitude.

(C) The movie star, because her deed did not contain the restrictive covenant.

(D) The movie star, because she had no notice of the structure height restriction.

Question 2

A public school teacher was hired without a written contract. The school district handbook provides that all newly hired employees are at-will employees for their first year of service and may be dismissed for any reason or without reason. Six months after being hired, the teacher was dismissed without any prior notice or a hearing.

Which of the following, if true, most strongly supports the teacher's argument that she should have been afforded notice and a hearing before dismissal?

(A) She was the only newly hired teacher not to have survived the probationary period for the past three years.

(B) There is no evidence that teachers with permanent status are any more competent than this teacher.

(C) The teacher moved her household from out of state in reliance on an oral promise by the school board that the job would be permanent and that she could be dismissed only for cause.

(D) She was the only teacher there over the age of 50.

Question 3

The owner of a summer cottage contracted to put new vinyl siding on the cottage for $10,500. Two weeks before the work was to start, however, the contractor called to say that there was a clerical error in the bid and that he could not do the work for less than $12,000 or he would lose money. The cottage owner agreed to pay the additional $1,500 but told the contractor that he was being unfair. After the work was completed, the cottage owner handed the contractor a check for $10,500, telling the contractor that that was all he would pay him because he had no right to raise the price.

If the contractor sues the cottage owner for the additional $1,500, who will prevail?

(A) The cottage owner, because the contractor was already under a preexisting legal duty to replace the siding on the cottage for $10,500.

(B) The cottage owner, because the promise to pay the additional money was not in writing.

(C) The contractor, because he relied on the cottage owner's promise to pay the additional money to his detriment.

(D) The contractor, because there was a valid modification of the parties' original contract.

Question 4

One of the employees of a department store informed the chief of security that he suspected a customer of shoplifting. The employee pointed out the suspected shoplifter, but the security chief thought that the employee was pointing at a different woman. He waited until the woman had left the store and then followed her outside. He went up to the woman, pointed a gun at her, and told her she needed to return with him to the department store's security office. The woman did so, even though she insisted that she had not done anything wrong. The woman was kept waiting in the office for a few minutes until the employee informed the security chief that he had arrested the wrong woman.

If the woman sues the department store on the theory of false imprisonment, she will:

(A) Prevail, unless the security chief's belief that she was the shoplifter is judged to be reasonable.

(B) Prevail, because she was intentionally detained.

(C) Not prevail, because the period for which the woman was detained was the minimal period necessary to establish her identity.

(D) Not prevail, because the woman suffered no harm.

Question 5

To combat the problem of obesity among the nation's youth, a state adopted a statute providing funds to train a corps of nutritionists who could go to schools and run six-week seminars designed to encourage healthy eating and exercise habits. The administration of a private school that has a stated policy of admitting only white students has requested that a state nutrition corps member be sent to the school to run a six-week seminar.

Which of the following is the best constitutional argument supporting the state's rejection of the request?

(A) The Constitution prohibits private discrimination.

(B) The state may not aid private schools.

(C) Segregation would be furthered by the provision of the seminar.

(D) No legitimate educational function is served by giving nutrition seminars at private schools.

Question 6

In an attempt to induce her niece to improve her grades, an aunt told her niece that she would give her $50 for every "A" she earned in law school. Inspired by the opportunity to earn extra spending money, the niece studied like never before and ended up earning three "As" the following semester. Upon contacting her aunt with the news, the niece learned that her aunt was "only kidding" about paying her for every "A" earned in law school.

If the aunt's offer to her niece was held to be valid, it would be an offer for:

(A) A bilateral contract.

(B) A unilateral contract.

(C) A bilateral contract or a unilateral contract, according to the offeree's intentions.

(D) A unilateral contract that became a bilateral contract when the niece began to perform.

Question 7

A woman graduated from a law school in a state that does not require graduates from that state's law schools to take and pass the bar examination in order to practice law. She moved to another state and wished to practice law without taking and passing that state's bar examination. In state court, she challenges the constitutionality of that state's requirement that she pass the bar in order to practice law there.

She will probably:

(A) Lose, because the state has plenary power regarding commerce.

(B) Lose, because licensing is within the police power of the state and infringes on no specific constitutional prohibition.

(C) Win, because the license requirement substantially burdens interstate commerce.

(D) Win, because the license requirement violates the Equal Protection Clause of the Fifth Amendment.

Question 8

A zoologist decided to install an artificial koi pond in his backyard. He asked his neighbor, a landscaper, for advice on doing the installation himself. After the zoologist dug a trench for the drainpipe, the neighbor complained that her garage, located only 20 feet from the trench, had developed numerous cracks in the foundation and walls.

What is the zoologist's best defense to an action by the neighbor for the damage to her garage?

(A) The zoologist gave notice to the neighbor of his intention to excavate and she made no objection.

(B) A professional would have excavated in the same manner.

(C) The zoologist's excavation was done in a proper manner, and there would have been no subsidence except for the fact that the garage was there.

(D) The garage was made of solid concrete and thus was unusually heavy.

Question 9

A car owner was having problems with her car's brakes. The brake shop to which she brought her car told her that the entire hydraulic brake system needed to be replaced at a cost of $1,800. The car owner agreed to have the work performed, and the shop replaced the brake system. When the car owner picked up the car, she insisted on testing the brakes before paying for the work. During a test drive, the brakes squeaked when compressed but otherwise worked perfectly. The mechanic told the car owner that the squeak would disappear on its own in a few days. The car owner stated that she would pay the shop when the squeak disappeared and left with her car. A month later, the brakes still squeaked and the car owner refused to pay for the work. The shop files suit to collect the $1,800 contract price.

The court should find that:

(A) The car owner must pay the shop the $1,800 because she got the substantial benefit of her bargain.

(B) The car owner must pay the shop the $1,800, but she would be entitled to set off the amount it would take to fix the squeak.

(C) The car owner does not have to pay the shop anything, because the squeak amounted to a breach of contract that relieved the car owner of her duty to perform.

(D) The shop must "cure" by providing the car owner with a new set of brakes that do not squeak, after which the car owner must pay the shop the $1,800.

Question 10

The owner of a gardening service looking to purchase a lawnmower for his business asked a retailer if he would install a lightweight blade on a particular lawnmower that he liked, but which had a heavy duty blade on it designed for cutting thick weeds. The retailer agreed and installed a lightweight blade designed for lawn cutting, but the blade was not designed to be used on that style of lawnmower. Two weeks later, while a worker for the gardening service was using the lawnmower to cut through a patch of heavy weeds, the blade broke and a piece of it flew off the lawnmower and severely cut the worker's leg. Assume that the jurisdiction follows traditional contributory negligence rules.

If the worker asserts a claim based on strict liability in tort against the lightweight blade's manufacturer, the strongest defense is:

(A) The worker was not in privity of contract with the blade manufacturer.

(B) The worker was contributorily negligent in using the lightweight blade to cut heavy weeds.

(C) The blade manufacturer used every available means to inspect and discover defects in the blade.

(D) The blade manufacturer could not foresee that the grass blade might be used on heavy weeds.

Question 11

In compliance with all applicable laws, and after receiving all necessary permits, a developer constructed a new housing development consisting of 100 single-family residences. The developer wants to ensure that the housing development retains its residential character.

Which of the following methods, assuming it would be enforceable by a court, should the developer use to achieve her goal?

(A) All deeds should contain negative easements.

(B) All deeds should be subject to conditions subsequent.

(C) All deeds should include covenants.

(D) All lots should conform to the applicable zoning laws.

Question 12

While driving east on a two-lane highway, a pickup truck collided with a westbound motorcycle. The accident was observed by a cab driver. Because the cab driver had a passenger, she did not stay at the scene of the accident but made some notes shortly thereafter. She made her statement to the police the next day, in which she stated that just before the accident, the pickup swerved into the westbound lane, hitting the motorcycle. At the trial of the motorcyclist's personal injury action against the truck driver, the cab driver was having difficulty remembering some of the facts. The motorcyclist's attorney sought to let her review the notes she had made.

The court should rule this:

(A) Permissible, because it is a present recollection refreshed.

(B) Permissible, because it is a past recollection recorded.

(C) Impermissible, because the cab driver is required to report all accidents to her employer, and the record is thus privileged.

(D) Impermissible, because there is no showing that the cab driver had used her notes when she gave her statement to the police officer.

Question 13

A woman had a history of epileptic seizures which came without warning over the last five years. One day, as she was driving to town she had a seizure. She lost control of her car and struck a pedestrian who was lawfully crossing the street. The pedestrian died immediately thereafter as a result of his injuries. The woman is charged with involuntary manslaughter.

She will most likely be found:

(A) Guilty, because the law presumes that a person intends the natural and probable consequences of her acts.

(B) Guilty, because she knowingly and recklessly chose to drive her car.

(C) Not guilty, because her failure to control the car was not a voluntary act.

(D) Not guilty, because she had no intent to harm anyone.

Question 14

A homeowner contracted with a local heating company to install two baseboard heaters in an addition to his home for a total cost of $3,500. This figure included the heaters and labor costs for installation. Upon completion of the installation, the heating company sent an invoice to the homeowner for the $3,500. The homeowner did not immediately pay the bill because the heaters were too noisy. The heating company sent a repair worker to the home to service the heaters, but after several attempts to fix the problem, the heaters were still too loud.

The homeowner contacted a qualified repairman to find out how to fix the problem and was told it would cost an additional $300 for new blowers and $150 in labor costs to replace the faulty blowers. The homeowner mailed the heating company a copy of the repair estimate and a check for $3,050—the contract price less the cost of new blowers and labor to install them—and wrote prominently on the check "Payment in full for installation of two baseboard heaters." The heating company cashed the check upon receipt. The heating company then sued the homeowner for $450, the difference between the agreed contract price and the amount paid.

Will the heating company be successful in recouping the $450 from the homeowner?

(A) No, because the heating company failed to fix the problem after several attempts.

(B) No, because the heating company cashed the check.

(C) Yes, because the check did not represent payment in full (*i.e.,* the contract price) for the work done.

(D) Yes, because the heating company should have been given more time to cure the defect.

Question 15

Congress passed a law mandating standards for hybrid automobiles in an effort to encourage more citizens to purchase hybrid cars so as to improve environmental conditions. The same law established a commission, consisting solely of members of Congress, whose purpose was to obtain information from manufacturers of hybrid automobiles regarding the number, type, and costs to the consumer of hybrid automobiles used in the United States and report its findings on an annual basis to Congress. A manufacturer of hybrid cars objects to having to supply the government with any information about its cars and so resists a subpoena for its chief executive officer to testify before the commission.

Insofar as Congress's power to investigate is concerned, the general rule is that:

(A) The power of Congress is limited only by the concept of separation of powers.

(B) Congress's power to investigate is coextensive with its power to legislate.

(C) Congress's power to investigate is limited to the appointment of its own members to make such investigations.

(D) There are no limitations upon Congressional powers of investigation as to the domestic economy.

Question 16

The plaintiff sued the defendant for battery. The defendant claimed that he was attacked for no reason by the plaintiff and that he hit the plaintiff with a pipe in self-defense. A witness was called to testify that on the day in question she heard the defendant and his roommate talking outside their apartment. The witness testified that the roommate told the defendant that the plaintiff had been flirting with the defendant's girlfriend, and that the defendant seemed very angry. The defendant's attorney objected to this testimony.

The court should find the evidence:

(A) Admissible, to show provocation for the battery.

(B) Admissible, as a legally operative fact.

(C) Inadmissible, because it is hearsay.

(D) Inadmissible, because it is an opinion.

Question 17

A paraplegic woman was sitting in her wheelchair in the park when a disheveled man approached her and grabbed her tightly by her hands and began to pray. The man claimed that he was a faith healer and that he could heal the woman so that she could walk again. In actuality, the man was an outpatient at a local hospital's mental health section. The woman brought a suit against the man for battery. At trial, the trier of fact determined that the man knew she had not consented to his grasping her hands, but that he truly believed that he had the ability to heal her.

If the man asserts as a defense that he was mentally disabled, this defense is:

(A) Not valid, because he was only an outpatient.

(B) Not valid, because he had the requisite state of mind for battery.

(C) Valid, because mentally disabled patients cannot be held responsible for their actions.

(D) Valid, because the man really believed he was a healer.

Question 18

A doctor and a lawyer owned adjoining parcels of land. Ten years ago, the doctor installed a swimming pool on her land. The doctor obtained the lawyer's oral consent to run plumbing from the pool across part of the lawyer's land. Last year, the lawyer sold his land to a buyer. The buyer wants to plant a garden on the land under which the doctor's plumbing runs, and wants to eject the doctor and quiet title. The statute of limitations for ejectment is seven years.

With respect to the land under which the plumbing was laid:

(A) The doctor has acquired title by adverse possession.

(B) The doctor has acquired a prescriptive easement.

(C) The doctor has acquired both title by adverse possession and a prescriptive easement.

(D) The doctor has acquired neither title by adverse possession nor a prescriptive easement.

Question 19

A small computer company contracted with a community college to supply computer tech support for all of the college's faculty and staff beginning September 1. Two weeks before the date that performance was to begin, the computer company received a more lucrative offer at a large university. In order to fulfill its contract obligations to the community college, the company delegated its duties under the contract to another computer company for $1,000 above the contract price. The community college agreed to allow the replacement computer company to perform the services, but on September 1, the replacement company refused to perform.

If the community college sues the replacement company, what will the result be?

(A) The replacement company will prevail, because the community college's only remedy is against the computer company.

(B) The replacement company will prevail, because $1,000 is grossly inadequate consideration.

(C) The community college will prevail, because there has been a novation.

(D) The community college will prevail, because it is an intended third-party beneficiary of the computer company-replacement company contract, and the replacement company assumed the duty of performance under the contract.

Question 20

The owner of a garage and one of his mechanics had a dispute over the amount of wages due for work that the mechanic had done on cars. The owner alleged that he paid the mechanic for work that the mechanic did not perform, while the mechanic contended that she did the work. After arguing over the matter for over an hour, the mechanic quit. The owner did not allow the mechanic to take her tools with her, stating that he was keeping her tools until she repaid the money that he had overpaid her.

The mechanic met with a friend and discussed the situation with him. After hearing what had happened, the friend, believing that the owner was unlawfully retaining the mechanic's tools, suggested that he could pose as a garage client and retrieve the tools for the mechanic, and the mechanic agreed. The plan succeeded, except for the fact that the friend took tools that belonged to a new employee. The owner immediately realized what had happened, and he gave the friend's license number to the police. The friend was arrested before he could show the tools to the mechanic.

Of the following, which is the best argument for the friend as a defense to a charge of larceny in a common law jurisdiction?

(A) He had the consent of the tools' owner.

(B) He thought the tools belonged to the mechanic.

(C) He intended to return the tools to the mechanic rather than keeping them.

(D) He was apprehended by the police before the mechanic could inspect the tools.

Question 21

A state passes a law allowing terminally ill patients to use marijuana under limited circumstances. Federal law, however, provides that marijuana may not be used under any circumstances. The state sues in federal district court, arguing that marijuana is beneficial for the terminally ill and should be permitted under these circumstances, despite the federal prohibition of marijuana use throughout the United States.

The federal district court should rule that:

(A) The issue should be certified to the court of appeals immediately because of the importance of the issue.

(B) The issue is a peculiarly local one that is better addressed on a state level, and should enjoin enforcement of the federal law.

(C) The federal statute preempts the state medical marijuana law, and the state law is invalid pursuant to the Supremacy Clause.

(D) The federal court has no jurisdiction to hear the case, because a state is a party and original jurisdiction lies with the United States Supreme Court.

Question 22

A woman aboard an airplane informed a flight attendant that she had witnessed another passenger stealing several small bottles of alcohol from a serving cart. The flight attendant alerted the airline's private on-board security guard, dressed in plain clothes, who approached the passenger, displayed his gun, and demanded that the passenger step into a service area for further questioning. The accused passenger quickly complied. On further investigation, it was determined that the woman was mistaken, and what she had actually witnessed was another flight attendant from a different section of the plane getting more supplies for a serving cart.

If the passenger sues the airline on the theory of assault, he likely will:

(A) Prevail, because the guard displayed his gun.

(B) Prevail, because the airline's belief that he was stealing was unreasonable.

(C) Not prevail, because he suffered no injury.

(D) Not prevail, because the airline is not responsible for the woman's unreasonable mistake.

Question 23

A man was approached by his cousin, who planned to rob a bank, to act as the escape driver. The man pretended to agree, and he planned to report his cousin to the police before the crime was committed. On the day appointed for the crime, the man picked up his cousin and drove him to the bank, and they stopped at a convenience store on the way. He left the car running with his cousin inside and from the store he called the police to warn that a bank robbery was about to occur. The police officer answering the phone thought it was a prank call and hung up. After another unsuccessful attempt the man went back to the car to talk his cousin out of the bank robbery, but he found the car missing. The cousin had grown nervous after a few minutes, driven to the bank, and robbed it at gunpoint. He fled the scene, but was apprehended soon thereafter.

If the man is charged with conspiracy, the trial court is most likely to find him:

(A) Guilty, because his withdrawal was ineffective because it was not communicated to his cousin in time for him to change his plans.

(B) Guilty, because he provided his cousin with an instrumentality of the crime.

(C) Not guilty, because the man withdrew from any conspiracy.

(D) Not guilty, because the man lacked criminal intent.

Question 24

A landowner orally agreed to sell 100 acres of land to a buyer for $10,000. As a condition of the sale, the buyer agreed to pay $5,000 of the purchase price to the landowner's creditor. The buyer's attorney drafted the contract, which both the landowner and the buyer read before signing. The signed document made no reference to the payment to the landowner's creditor, and neither party noticed the oversight.

Which of the following would be most important for deciding the creditor's action against the buyer for $5,000?

(A) The buyer was negligent in not having carefully read the written agreement.

(B) The landowner-buyer agreement was completely integrated.

(C) The terms of the signed document are unambiguous.

(D) The omission of any reference to the creditor from the written document was accidental and, therefore, the contract may be reformed.

Question 25

Congress enacted legislation prescribing the specifications for various types of containers that all suppliers of nonprescription drugs were required to use in marketing their products.

Congress's power to pass this legislation is derived from:

(A) The Necessary and Proper Clause.

(B) The Commerce Clause.

(C) The General Welfare Clause.

(D) The Tenth Amendment.

Question 26

A couple suspected of fraud spent many hours at a police station for the purposes of investigation. Having fallen asleep on her chair, the wife was awakened by a police officer, and, still groggy, she thought that she was being attacked, and she punched the police officer in the face before she realized the truth. Later, the husband was being interrogated. The interrogation officer accidentally touched a live electrical wire to the husband's armpit, which caused his arm to involuntarily twitch and strike the interrogator in her face.

Which defendant(s) can be convicted of battery under these facts?

(A) The wife only.

(B) Both the wife and the husband.

(C) Neither the wife nor the husband.

(D) The husband only.

Question 27

A developer owned a 100-acre tract of land, which he subdivided into 200 single-family residences. All deeds contained a covenant that the property would be used only for residential purposes. Two years after the last lot was sold, the developer purchased the 50-acre tract of land adjoining the subdivision. The developer constructed another group of 100 single-family residences on this land. To ensure their marketability, the developer desired to sell them like homes in the original development, and to that extent, intended that the deeds to the new homes contain the same restrictions as those in the original development and be enforceable in the same manner by owners in both developments.

Will the developer be successful in this plan?

(A) No, zoning restrictions will control.

(B) No, because in order to have such restrictions, the entire project must have been built at the same time.

(C) Yes, the restrictions will be equally enforceable for this new project as they were for the original development.

(D) Yes, provided that a court considers this new project to be part of a common development scheme with the original development.

Question 28

A homeowner owed a contractor $1,400 for work that the contractor did on her home. Pursuant to the contract between the parties, the $1,400 was due on September 1. After the homeowner told the contractor that she probably would not be able to pay the $1,400 on September 1, the contractor agreed to extinguish the debt if the homeowner, who was the manager of an appliance store, purchased a washer and dryer that the contractor's mother wanted and had it delivered to the mother's home and set up by September 15. Because the homeowner's manager discount would allow her to pay only $1,000 for the washer and dryer, which had a list price of $1,200, she agreed and the parties signed a writing to that effect on August 26.

Is the new agreement between the homeowner and the contractor legally enforceable?

(A) No, because the new agreement did not constitute a discharge by novation.

(B) No, because the contractor's mother is a donee beneficiary.

(C) Yes, because the homeowner incurred a different obligation than she originally had.

(D) Yes, because the new agreement between the homeowner and the contractor is enforceable with or without consideration as long as it was made in good faith.

Question 29

Congress passed a statute that established a five-member commission to investigate issues relating to gun control and to make recommendations to Congress for new gun control laws.

All five members of the commission were appointed by Congress. An entity that has organizational standing brings a suit to enjoin the commission from investigating and recommending new gun control laws to Congress.

The appropriate decision for the court is to:

(A) Forbid the commission to take any action.

(B) Order that all members of the commission be appointed by the President by and with the advice and consent of the Senate.

(C) Allow the commission to investigate but not make recommendations regarding gun control.

(D) Allow the commission to continue investigating and making recommendations to Congress regarding gun control.

Question 30

A mother received a telephone call asking her to meet with the vice principal of her son's school because he was caught cheating. As she was waiting in the hallway to meet the vice principal, the school's janitor, a big man who was an amateur body builder, introduced himself as the vice principal and asked the mother to step into his office, closing the door behind him. For several minutes, the janitor asked the mother a series of flirtatious personal questions, causing the mother to grow very uncomfortable. However, she did not leave the office out of concern for her son's academic standing. The actual vice principal eventually returned to his office and ended the questioning.

If the mother sues the janitor for false imprisonment, she is most likely to:

(A) Prevail, because the janitor was a body builder who could have physically harmed her if she tried to leave the room.

(B) Prevail, because she would not have stayed in the room if the janitor had not pretended to be the vice principal.

(C) Not prevail, because the janitor would have let her leave if she wanted.

(D) Not prevail, because she had no reason to believe that she could not leave.

Question 31

The plaintiff was riding down a department store escalator when the escalator malfunctioned, causing the plaintiff to fall forward to the floor and injure himself. His companion, who has no medical training, tried to make the plaintiff comfortable. While waiting for the ambulance, the plaintiff said, "My left arm is numb and I have chest pains. I'm afraid I'm having a heart attack." Upon being taken to the hospital, it was determined that the plaintiff had not suffered a heart attack, but had sustained severe damage to his chest and to the nerves affecting feeling in his left arm. The plaintiff sued the department store for his injuries. At trial, the plaintiff called his companion to testify to the statement made by the plaintiff.

The companion's testimony as to the statement is:

(A) Admissible, to prove the extent of the plaintiff's injuries at the time.

(B) Inadmissible, because the plaintiff did not suffer a heart attack.

(C) Inadmissible, because the companion is not a doctor.

(D) Inadmissible, because it is hearsay not within any exception.

Question 32

A hunter saw what he thought to be a deer in a copse of trees. To approach the trees, the hunter had to climb over a fence posted with "no hunting" and "no trespassing" signs. He stalked the deer, fired, and discovered to his chagrin that he had just shot a large bull. The owner of the property, a rancher, heard the shot and grabbed his shotgun, fearing that hunters had shot another one of his cattle. When he arrived at the copse of trees and discovered that the hunter had killed his prize bull, he became enraged and ordered the hunter to get off his property in extremely abusive language. Instead of leaving immediately, the hunter said, "It's just a damn cow!" The rancher raised his shotgun and fired at the hunter, narrowly missing him. When the rancher operated the pump-action of the shotgun and raised it again, the hunter shot and killed him.

In the hunter's prosecution for murder, he should be found:

(A) Guilty, because he was a trespasser on the owner's land.

(B) Not guilty, because the owner attacked him with deadly force.

(C) Guilty, because the owner's attack was provoked by the hunter.

(D) Not guilty, because the owner had no right to defend his property with deadly force.

Question 33

A bakery owner entered into a one-year written contract with a chocolate chip manufacturer whereby the manufacturer agreed to ship to the bakery owner 5,000 pounds of premium chocolate chips on the first day of each month for $12,500 per shipment. When the bakery owner opened the first shipment of chips, he found that 60% of them were tainted with rat hairs. He immediately called the manufacturer and reported the breach. The manufacturer offered to send replacements, but the bakery owner refused the offer and canceled the entire contract.

Will the manufacturer prevail in an action against the bakery owner seeking contract damages?

(A) No, because the bakery owner was entitled to a perfect tender, and the manufacturer's failure to provide a perfect tender resulted in a breach of contract.

(B) No, because damages are speculative.

(C) Yes, because the bakery owner's notice of the manufacturer's breach was not in writing.

(D) Yes, because the manufacturer had a right to cure.

Question 34

The defendant is charged with the murder of his employer. At the trial, the prosecution offered the testimony of another employee who testified that he had accidentally picked up the phone when the defendant was talking to an unidentified man who said, "I hear your boss is going to confess about the money you and she embezzled from the company. What are you going to do about it?"

If the defendant's attorney objects to the employee's testimony on the ground that it is irrelevant, the judge should:

(A) Sustain the objection.

(B) Sustain the objection, on the grounds that whatever probative value the testimony has is substantially outweighed by the danger of unfair prejudice, confusion of the issues, or misleading the jury.

(C) Overrule the objection.

(D) Overrule the objection, but instruct the jury not to consider the employee's testimony as evidence of the defendant's involvement with any embezzlement of funds.

Question 35

A passenger on a cruise ship went to the ship's spa for a hot rock massage. A hostess had the passenger lie on her stomach and placed warm stones on her back. The hostess told the passenger that the ship's licensed masseuse would be in to begin her massage when the rocks cooled, in approximately half an hour. Only several minutes later, however, a man came into her room and began rubbing her back. Unbeknownst to the passenger, the man was not the masseuse but another passenger on the ship acting on a dare from his friends. The man continued to massage the passenger awkwardly for several minutes, at times pinching her back uncomfortably. When the passenger finally spoke up in protest, the man ran out of the room, laughing hysterically. The incident humiliated the passenger and caused her extreme distress.

If the passenger sues the cruise ship for negligence, which of the following defenses would most likely show that the cruise ship is not liable?

(A) The passenger had been told the masseuse would begin the massage in half an hour when the rocks had cooled; therefore, she was not justified in believing that the man was the masseuse.

(B) The man's conduct was an independent intervening cause that cuts off the cruise ship's liability.

(C) The cruise ship had no reason to believe that the man would impersonate a masseuse, and had otherwise taken reasonable precautions to insure privacy in the spa.

(D) The passenger was not really injured by anything the man did.

Question 36

An automobile manufacturer entered into a contract with a well-known tire distributor which provided that the distributor would deliver to the automobile manufacturer 1,000 tires on the 15th of each month for $50,000 per shipment, with payment due upon receipt.

The automobile manufacturer and the tire distributor properly fulfilled their contractual obligations for two months. The day after the third tire delivery, the tire distributor's president visited the automobile manufacturer and found the automobiles produced with his company's tires to be a "disgrace." To protect the tire distributor's reputation, the president announced that he will not send any additional tire shipments. The automobile manufacturer immediately brought a breach of contract action against the tire distributor.

Who will prevail?

(A) The tire distributor, because it was not in breach when the action was filed.

(B) The tire distributor, if it can show that the automobile manufacturer made disgraceful automobiles.

(C) The automobile manufacturer, because the president's action amounts to an anticipatory repudiation.

(D) The automobile manufacturer, because the president's action amounts to a prospective inability to perform.

Question 37

A woman elected to a state legislature is prosecuted in federal court for violating the civil rights of a member of the janitorial staff of the state legislature's building in connection with a sexual assault that occurred in her office. The woman raises as a defense the claim that the allegedly wrongful acts were committed in the course of legislative business, and she is immune from scrutiny by the federal courts.

Which of the following is the strongest constitutional argument in favor of the woman's defense?

(A) The application of federal civil rights statutes to state legislators would violate the Due Process Clause.

(B) A federal court must follow state law respecting the scope of legislative immunity.

(C) State legislators enjoy the protection of the Speech and Debate Clause of the United States Constitution.

(D) Because of the doctrine of federalism, federal law generally cannot be applied to state legislators acting in the course of their official duties.

Question 38

The owner of a large parcel of land subdivided it into 20 separate lots. He sold lots 1-19, retaining lot 20 for himself to live on. The deeds for each of the 19 lots sold by the owner contained the following restriction: "All lots within the subdivision shall be used for residential purposes only." The purchasers of lots 1-19 each built residences on their property. The owner lived on lot 20 until his death, when it was sold without any restrictions to a buyer. Subsequently, the buyer sold lot 20 to a grocer, furnishing him with an abstract of title and assuring him that the land was unrestricted. The abstract of title showed that lot 20 was not restricted. The following year, the grocer decided to build a grocery store on lot 20. A homeowner who owned adjoining property in the subdivision informed the grocer of the restriction and told him that he would be unable to build the grocery store.

If the homeowner brings suit seeking an injunction against the grocer's building of the grocery store, will she prevail?

(A) No, because the grocer had neither actual nor constructive notice of the restriction.

(B) No, because the grocer relied on the abstract of title and the buyer's representation in good faith.

(C) Yes, because the property owners in the subdivision have a right to keep the subdivision in the condition that they want it.

(D) Yes, because the grocer will be charged with notice as a result of the residential character of the subdivision.

Question 39

The defendant is charged with the murder of his accountant. At trial, the prosecution calls as a witness the defendant's business partner, who testifies that he overheard a telephone conversation between the defendant and the accountant, in which the accountant threatened to report him to the I.R.S. for cheating on his income tax return. The defendant's attorney objects to the business partner's testimony on the ground that it is hearsay.

The judge should:

(A) Sustain the objection.

(B) Overrule the objection because the testimony, although hearsay, is being introduced to show the defendant's state of mind, a hearsay exception.

(C) Overrule the objection because the testimony, although hearsay, qualifies as a business record since the call was made during business hours on a business phone.

(D) Overrule the objection because the evidence is offered to help prove the defendant's motive.

Question 40

Two mothers were talking outside of a school one afternoon. One of them asked the other for the phone number of the woman she employed in her home to take care of her children. That mother, knowing that reliable child care is hard to find, did not want to share the information with the other woman, so she instead said, "You don't want her number, we discovered that she was intoxicated last week when we came home from work." This accusation was false, but it quickly spread throughout the neighborhood.

If the woman sues the mother for defamation and establishes the above facts, the woman must also show:

(A) That she suffered special damages by reason of the mother's oral statement.

(B) That she lost other child care jobs because of the statement.

(C) That the statement was extreme and outrageous because any drinking of alcohol is against the woman's strict moral code.

(D) No additional facts.

Question 41

Two friends entered a bar looking to get money to pay off a loan shark, but with no plan how to do so. They struck up conversations with two women. The first friend left the bar, having induced one of the women to return home with him. Once in his house, the first friend told the woman that she would not be allowed to leave unless she gave him all of her money. Fearing for her safety, the woman gave him all of the cash she had in her possession. Meanwhile, the second friend remaining at the bar noticed that the other woman left her credit card on the counter. When the woman looked away, the friend picked up the credit card and put it into his pocket. Shortly thereafter, the woman realized her card was gone and accused the man of taking it. The man pretended to be insulted, slapped the victim, and went off with the credit card in his pocket.

Which of the two friends can be convicted for common law robbery?

(A) Both can be convicted.

(B) The first friend can be convicted, but the second cannot be convicted.

(C) The second friend can be convicted, but the first cannot be convicted.

(D) Neither of the two friends can be convicted of robbery.

Question 42

A woman entered a dress shop that had displayed in its window a red dress priced at $120 and told the salesperson that she wanted to purchase the dress in her size. The salesperson rang up the sale and handed the woman a box that contained the dress she had just purchased. When the woman got home, she opened the box and discovered a dress exactly like the one in the store window, except that it was yellow. The dress had a tag which read:

> This dress shop expressly warrants that this dress shall be free of manufacturing defects for five days. If a dress is defective, liability shall be limited to the cost of repair or replacement of defective merchandise.

The woman returned to the dress shop and demanded an exchange or refund. The salesperson refused on the grounds that the dress was not defective.

If the woman files suit for a refund, who will prevail?

(A) The woman, because in consumer transactions a consumer has an absolute right to return goods within 24 hours under the "buyer's remorse" laws.

(B) The woman, because an express warranty that the dress would be red arose and was breached.

(C) The dress shop, because the dress is not defective and the color does not affect the dress's function as clothing.

(D) The dress shop, because of the disclaimer on the dress tag.

Question 43

A landowner was the owner in fee simple of a tract of land. The landowner conveyed the tract to her neighbor, "for life and then to the first child of my neighbor's only sister who shall reach the age of 21." The sister was unmarried and childless at the time of the conveyance. Five years later, the sister married, and she gave birth to a son the following year. When the son reached the age of 21, he brought an action in ejectment against the neighbor, who is still alive and living on the tract of land.

The neighbor's best defense against the son's attempt to eject her is that:

(A) The neighbor's life estate was not subject to termination during her lifetime.

(B) The son has no claim to the tract, because he was not living at the time of the landowner's original conveyance.

(C) A conveyance of the tract to the son violates the Rule Against Perpetuities.

(D) The son's interest, if any, would be that of a contingent remainder, and the contingency is the neighbor's death.

Question 44

The president of a private college received a report that there was a great deal of cocaine use occurring on the second floor of the dormitory. The president persuaded the school security officers to place several concealed microphones in the second-floor student lounge. Conversations occurring in the lounge were monitored by the security officers and they recorded a conversation in which a sophomore at the college offered to sell cocaine to a freshman. A tape of the conversation was taken to the local police, who played it for a local judge. The judge issued a warrant to search the sophomore's room. While searching the room the police discovered a large amount of cocaine and the sophomore was arrested and charged with unlawful possession of narcotics. His attorney moved to prevent the introduction of the cocaine into evidence.

The motion will most likely be:

(A) Granted, because the sophomore's privacy was unreasonably invaded.

(B) Granted, because the electronic surveillance was "fundamentally unfair."

(C) Denied, because the police properly obtained a search warrant.

(D) Denied, because the college president was acting on behalf of the college population in general.

Question 45

An artist was on trial for burglary, defined in the jurisdiction as breaking and entering the dwelling of another with the intent to commit a felony. The artist's defense was that he was merely retrieving his own property, because he had sold a painting to a customer but the customer had refused to pay him for it or return it. A neighbor of the customer testified for the prosecution that he saw the artist carrying a painting from the customer's house. The artist attempts to call to the stand a witness who was in the gallery at the time of the sale to testify to the transaction between the artist and the customer. The prosecution objects to the testimony, claiming it is irrelevant.

The judge should rule that the witness's testimony is:

(A) Admissible, because it is relevant in determining whether the artist had the intent required for burglary.

(B) Admissible, because it is relevant in establishing the neighbor's credibility.

(C) Inadmissible as irrelevant, because it would tend to impeach the neighbor's testimony on a collateral matter.

(D) Inadmissible as irrelevant, because the probative value of the witness's testimony is substantially outweighed by the danger of unfair prejudice, confusion of the issues, waste of time, or needless presentation of cumulative evidence.

Question 46

A homeowner conveyed her home "to my friend for life, and then to my brother's heirs." The brother had a young child at the time of the conveyance. Subsequently, the friend died. The brother and his minor child are still alive. The jurisdiction has abolished the common law rule of destructibility of contingent remainders.

Who owns the home?

(A) The brother's child.

(B) The court-appointed guardian ad litem of the brother's child.

(C) The homeowner and her heirs in fee simple.

(D) The homeowner and her heirs would take the home until the brother died.

Question 47

A proud grandfather who planned to take pictures of his grandson's graduation purchased a camera from a camera store. He used the camera on several occasions over the next few weeks without incident, but when he used it on the day before his grandson's graduation, it caught fire and exploded, burning him and destroying an expensive coat he was wearing. Although the grandfather was in a great deal of pain because of his injuries, he insisted on attending his grandson's graduation. However, because he no longer had a workable camera, the grandfather hired a professional photographer to take pictures of the special day.

In a breach of warranty action, which of the following represents the most that the grandfather may recover?

(A) The difference between the value of the camera accepted and its value if it had been as warranted.

(B) The difference between the value of the camera accepted and its value if it had been as warranted, plus medical costs for treating the grandfather's burns.

(C) The difference between the value of the camera accepted and its value if it had been as warranted, medical costs for treating the grandfather's burns, and the cost to replace the grandfather's coat.

(D) The difference between the value of the camera accepted and its value if it had been as warranted, medical costs for treating the grandfather's burns, the cost to replace the grandfather's coat, and the cost of hiring the professional photographer.

Question 48

Hoping to help control a growing problem with violent all-male teenage gangs who frequented a youth center, a city council passed an ordinance forbidding any male between the ages of 13 and 19 to enter the center unless accompanied by a female.

An 18-year-old boy who was new to the city went to the youth center to try to meet new friends. He was refused admission because he was not escorted by a female.

Angered, the boy filed suit in federal district court seeking admission to the center and asking the court to strike down the ordinance as unconstitutional.

Which of the following standards should the court use in determining the validity of the ordinance?

(A) The boy must show that the ordinance is not rationally related to a legitimate state interest.

(B) The boy must show that the ordinance is not substantially related to an important government interest.

(C) The city must show that the ordinance is substantially related to an important government interest.

(D) The city must show that the ordinance is necessary to achieve a compelling interest.

Question 49

A recent law school grad was discussing his new job at lunch with a former classmate, who was unemployed, and told him about some missing funds currently being investigated at his law firm. He was shocked and upset when his classmate bitterly replied, "I always knew you were dishonest. You stole that money."

The new attorney may:

(A) Sue the classmate for intentional misrepresentation, because the classmate had no reason to believe that the accusation was true.

(B) Sue the classmate for defamation, because if the law firm learns of the allegation, the new attorney might be arrested for embezzlement.

(C) Sue the classmate for intentional infliction of emotional distress.

(D) Sue the classmate for negligent infliction of emotional distress.

Question 50

The plaintiff filed a personal injury action against a restaurant. The plaintiff alleges that she suffered food poisoning after consuming the restaurant's daily special—extra-strong coffee and chili over eggs. The restaurant defends by claiming that the special on the day in question was an exotic tea served with a yogurt and fruit blend and that the extra-strong coffee drink was not even on the menu that day. Counsel for the restaurant called a former waitress to testify as to whether the extra-strong coffee drink was on the menu that day. The former waitress, who lives with the plaintiff, testified that it was always on the menu. The restaurant's attorney then asked, "Didn't you in fact, at your deposition, state that the extra-strong coffee drink was not on the menu that day?" The plaintiff's attorney objects.

The question is:

(A) Proper, because the former waitress is hostile.

(B) Proper, because it constitutes refreshing the witness's recollection.

(C) Improper, because this is a leading question on direct examination.

(D) Improper, because the restaurant cannot impeach its own witness.

MIXED SUBJECT SET 7 SUBJECT GUIDE

1. Real Property
2. Constitutional Law
3. Contracts
4. Torts
5. Constitutional Law
6. Contracts
7. Constitutional Law
8. Real Property
9. Contracts
10. Torts
11. Real Property
12. Evidence
13. Criminal Law
14. Contracts
15. Constitutional Law
16. Evidence
17. Torts
18. Real Property
19. Contracts
20. Criminal Law
21. Constitutional Law
22. Torts
23. Criminal Law
24. Contracts
25. Constitutional Law
26. Criminal Law
27. Real Property
28. Contracts
29. Constitutional Law
30. Torts
31. Evidence
32. Criminal Law
33. Contracts
34. Evidence
35. Torts
36. Contracts
37. Constitutional Law
38. Real Property
39. Evidence
40. Torts
41. Criminal Law
42. Contracts
43. Real Property
44. Criminal Law
45. Evidence
46. Real Property
47. Contracts
48. Constitutional Law
49. Torts
50. Evidence

MIXED SUBJECT ANSWERS - SET 7

Answer to Question 1

(A) The neighbor will prevail because the restrictive covenant runs with the neighbor's land, which is benefited, and with the movie star's land, which is burdened. A covenant at law will run with the land and be enforceable against subsequent grantees if: (i) the contracting parties intended it to run; (ii) there is privity of estate between the original promisor and promisee (horizontal privity), as well as between the promisor and his successor (vertical privity); (iii) the covenant touches and concerns the property; and (iv) the burdened party has notice of the covenant. Here, the use of the words "heirs, successors, and assigns" in the covenant shows the intent for the covenant to run. The original parties were in horizontal privity because at the time the buyer entered into the covenant, he and the landowner shared an interest in the land independent of the covenant—as grantor and grantee. Because the neighbor and the movie star hold the entire interest in the parcels held by the landowner and the buyer, respectively, there is vertical privity. The covenant touches and concerns the land because it diminishes the movie star's rights in connection with her enjoyment of the western parcel. Finally, the movie star has notice of the covenant because it is contained in her chain of title (in the landowner-buyer deed). Thus, the covenant runs with the land. (B) is incorrect because although privity is not required to enforce an equitable servitude, the covenant here runs with the land at law. Moreover, privity does exist under these facts as explained above. (C) is incorrect because the fact that the structure height restriction was not contained in the movie star's deed does not shield her from enforcement of the covenant because it was contained in a previous deed relating to the property (record notice). (D) is incorrect because the movie star at least had record notice of the restriction.

Answer to Question 2

(C) Under the Due Process Clause, a person has a right to notice and a hearing if the government deprives the person of life, liberty, or property. The Supreme Court has held that a government employee will have a property interest in continued employment only if the employee has a legitimate claim to (as opposed to a mere expectancy of) continued employment. To have such a claim, there must be a contract, clear practice, mutual understanding, etc., that the employee can be terminated only for cause. If someone in a position of authority promised that the teacher could be dismissed only for cause and the teacher relied on this promise by moving, a case can be made that the teacher had a legitimate claim to continued employment despite the employee handbook. (A) would also support the contention of a legitimate claim to continued employment. If every teacher over the past three years has survived the probation period, an argument can be made that there was a policy of retaining all newly hired teachers. However, this argument is weaker, factually, than the contract argument and so is not as good an answer choice as (C). (B) and (D) are incorrect because they are irrelevant—whether other teachers are more or less competent or younger than the teacher involved here does not factor into whether the teacher here has a legitimate claim to continued employment. The teacher needs to point to a contract or policy providing for dismissal only for cause.

Answer to Question 3

(A) The cottage owner will prevail, because the contractor was already under a preexisting legal duty to replace the siding on the cottage for $10,500. Under the preexisting legal duty rule, the promise to perform or the performance of an existing legal duty will not be sufficient consideration. If the parties agree to modify their contract, consideration is usually found to exist where the obligations of both parties are varied. However, a modification solely for the benefit of one of the parties is unenforceable in contracts not governed by the U.C.C. Here, the contractor was already under a binding contract to replace the siding on the cottage for $10,500. The contract is primarily for services, and thus not governed by the U.C.C. Moreover, the obligations of both parties under the modified agreement are not varied; the modification (paying the contractor an additional $1,500) would benefit only the contractor. The contractor's performance of a duty that he was already obligated to perform does not constitute sufficient consideration to support the modification. Therefore, the cottage owner is obligated to pay only the originally agreed-upon $10,500. Thus, (A) is correct and (D) is incorrect. (B) is incorrect because contracts for services do not come within the Statute of Frauds unless by their terms they cannot be performed within one year of their making, and performance of this contract could be completed in less than a year. (C) is incorrect because, in replacing the siding on the cottage, the contractor was simply fulfilling his contractual obligation, rather than acting to his detriment in reliance on the cottage owner's promise to pay the additional money. Even where unsupported by consideration, a promise is enforceable under the promissory estoppel doctrine to the extent necessary to prevent injustice if: (i) the promisor should reasonably expect to induce action or forbearance of a definite and substantial character; and (ii) such action or forbearance is in fact induced. The contractor was legally bound to perform the work on the cottage regardless of whether the cottage owner agreed to pay the extra $1,500. Thus, the contractor did not incur a detriment in reliance on the cottage owner's promise.

Answer to Question 4

(B) The facts satisfy the requirements of false imprisonment. False imprisonment requires an act or omission that confines or restrains the plaintiff to a bounded area, intent, and causation. As discussed below, no privilege applies, so the store is vicariously liable for the actions of its security chief. (A) is wrong because reasonable belief is not sufficient by itself to establish a shopkeeper's privilege to detain a suspected shoplifter; the means of restraint must be reasonable and the use of force intended or likely to cause serious bodily harm may not be used. Here, the security chief pointed a gun at the woman. (C) is wrong because even if the period of confinement was reasonable for purposes of the shopkeeper's privilege, it is not available here because the detention was accomplished by the threat of deadly force. (D) is wrong because "harm" is not required.

Answer to Question 5

(C) If the state provides a nutritional corps member to a segregated school, it would represent a significant involvement in activities of a school that practices segregation and would thus violate the Equal Protection Clause. Thus, answer (C) is correct because segregation would be furthered by the provision of a nutritional corps seminar. (A) is incorrect because it is too broad. The Constitution prohibits slavery, and the Supreme Court has interpreted the enabling clause of the Thirteenth Amendment to give Congress the power to outlaw anything that it sees as an incident or badge of slavery. However, here we are dealing with state legislation, and nothing in the facts indicates that Congress has found the discrimination here to be a badge of slavery. (B) also is a gross overstatement. Government may aid private schools as long as such aid does not run afoul of the Constitution (*e.g.*, does not support ethnic, racial, or religious discrimination).

Answer to Question 6

(B) The aunt's offer to her niece was for a unilateral contract. In a unilateral contract, acceptance of an offer is possible only by performing a stipulated act, whereas in a bilateral contract, acceptance of an offer is accomplished by promising to do the stipulated act. The aunt's offer could be accepted by the niece only by completion of performance (*i.e.,* obtaining an "A" in the class), and when the niece received her three "A's", a unilateral contract was formed. Thus, (B) is correct and (A) and (C) are incorrect. (D) is incorrect because acceptance of an offer by performance of the stipulated act creates a unilateral contract, and such performance does not convert the contract into a bilateral contract, which is created by a promise to perform rather than by performance itself.

Answer to Question 7

(B) She will probably lose her challenge. Licensing of persons who deal with the general public is a valid exercise of the state's police power. Because attorneys deal with the general public, the licensing scheme as a general matter is valid because there are circumstances in which the licensing requirement could be rationally related to the state's interest in making sure that its attorneys have passed its bar examination. (A) is a misstatement of law; Congress, not the states, has plenary power over interstate commerce. (C) is not supported by the facts. While an argument could be made that the woman's activities have some impact on interstate commerce, there is nothing here to indicate that the requirement to pass the state bar examination burdens interstate commerce. (D) is wrong because the equal protection guarantee of the Fifth Amendment applies only to federal government action and because there is no "Equal Protection Clause" in the Fifth Amendment; rather, equal protection principles are taken from the Fifth Amendment's Due Process Clause.

Answer to Question 8

(C) The zoologist's best defense is that his excavation was done in a proper manner, and there would have been no subsidence except for the fact that the garage was there. A property owner is entitled to have her land supported in its natural state by adjoining land. If the land is improved by buildings and an adjacent landowner's excavation causes subsidence, the adjacent landowner will be strictly liable for damages to the buildings caused by the excavation only if it is shown that the land would have collapsed in its natural state (*i.e.*, in the absence of the buildings). Even if the land would not have collapsed except for the weight of the buildings, the excavating landowner is liable for damage to the buildings if his excavation is found to have been done negligently. Here, if the neighbor's land would not have subsided but for the weight of the garage, the zoologist is not absolutely liable. He would be liable only if he were negligent in excavating. (C) covers the lack of negligence and the fact that the weight of the garage contributed to its damage; it is therefore his best defense. (A) is wrong because notice of the excavation, and lack of objection, does not preclude recovery by the neighbor on the negligence. (B) is wrong because it concerns only the negligence issue, and not whether the weight of the garage contributed to its damage. (D) is not as good an answer as (C) because even if the garage was unusually heavy, the zoologist could still be liable if he were negligent in excavating.

Answer to Question 9

(B) Because the shop's breach of contract was minor, the car owner must pay the brake shop the $1,800, but she would be entitled to damages to remedy the squeak. A breach of contract is minor if the nonbreaching party gets the substantial benefit of her bargain, despite the other party's defective performance. A minor breach does not relieve the nonbreaching party of her duty to perform under the contract, although she will be entitled to remedial damages for the breach. Here, the brakes worked perfectly except for the squeak and, most importantly, stopped the car when compressed, as brakes are supposed to do. Thus, the breach was minor and would not relieve the car owner of her own duty to perform (*i.e.,* to pay the bill), although she could get damages, if the court so decided, for the squeak. Thus, (B) is correct, and (C) is wrong. (A) is wrong because it does not take into account the fact that the car owner could be entitled to damages for the shop's breach. (D) is wrong for a couple of reasons. First, a seller's right to cure when goods or their tender are not perfect may not apply here, because the facts do not establish whether the defect causing the brakes to squeak is in the product itself or in its installation. The U.C.C. rules regarding the right to cure do not apply to service contracts (*e.g.,* faulty installation of brakes). Second, the right to cure arises when the buyer has rejected goods because of defects, and here the car owner did not reject the brake system—she took the car home with her knowing of the squeaking brakes. Thus, it would be too late for a "cure."

Answer to Question 10

(D) The blade manufacturer's best defense is that it could not foresee that the grass blade might be used on heavy weeds. Manufacturers must foresee reasonably foreseeable misuses of a product, but a product manufacturer is not liable if the injury results from an unintended and unforeseeable misuse of the product. (A) is wrong because strict liability extends to foreseeable users; absence of privity is not a defense. (B) is wrong because the facts do not indicate that the worker knew about the lightweight blade, and, in any case, states retaining traditional contributory negligence rules hold that ordinary contributory negligence, including reasonably foreseeable misuse, is not a defense to strict products liability. (C) is wrong because the care exercised by the manufacturer is irrelevant in a strict liability action; the supplying of an unreasonably dangerous defective product satisfies the breach element of the tort.

Answer to Question 11

(C) To ensure that the housing development retains its residential character, all deeds should include covenants. The answer is best reached by the process of elimination. Negative easements are of too limited a use to ensure that the project retains its residential character, so (A) is wrong. (D) is wrong because a governmental authority may change zoning laws. (B) is possible, but it is unlikely a court will enforce a forfeiture of an owner's estate, particularly because the same result could be accomplished by the use of covenants in the deeds. In addition, buyers may be reluctant to purchase lots subject to a condition subsequent that could cause the loss of their interest. Thus, (C) is the best method.

Answer to Question 12

(A) The court should permit the cab driver to review her notes. Under the rule of present recollection refreshed, a witness may be shown any writing that may refresh her memory of an event. (B) is wrong because the doctrine of past recollection recorded refers to the admissibility of the contents of a writing, and a proper foundation must be laid. (C) is a misstatement of the law and makes no sense in this situation. (D) is wrong because the cab driver is not testifying to the contents of her statement, but to her recollection of the accident.

Answer to Question 13

(B) The woman will most likely be found guilty of involuntary manslaughter because she knowingly and recklessly chose to drive her car. Involuntary manslaughter is of two types: (i) a killing committed by the criminal negligence of another; or (ii) a killing occurring during the commission of an unlawful act. Criminal negligence requires a greater deviation from the "reasonable person" standard for civil liability. Some states require that the defendant have had a subjective awareness of the risk. Here, given that the woman was aware of the fact that she might experience a seizure while driving, her actions most likely constituted criminal negligence (also called recklessness). Thus, she will most likely be convicted of involuntary manslaughter. (A) is incorrect. A jury can infer the required general intent from the performance of an act. However, it would not relieve the prosecution of the burden of proving that the defendant acted in a criminally negligent manner, an essential element of the crime of involuntary manslaughter. (C) is incorrect because she voluntarily drove knowing that she might experience a seizure, which is sufficient for involuntary manslaughter. (D) is incorrect because the state of mind for involuntary manslaughter can be established by criminal negligence.

Answer to Question 14

(B) The heating company will not recoup the $450 from the homeowner because its cashing of the check from the homeowner amounted to an accord and satisfaction that discharged any further contractual duty of the homeowner to pay the heating company. The majority view holds that an accord and satisfaction is established where one who is owed payment under an existing obligation that is the subject of a bona fide dispute is offered, as payment in full, a check made out for a smaller amount, and he signs and cashes the check. Here, the heating company signed and cashed the check, the amount of which was subject to an honest dispute, where it was marked "Payment in full," and cannot now sue for additional monies. Thus, (B) is correct and (C) is wrong. (A) and (D) are wrong because it was the existence of an accord and satisfaction, and not the heating company's failure to adequately fix the problem, which foreclosed its options to recoup further monies.

Answer to Question 15

(B) The power of Congress to investigate is coextensive with the power to legislate created by Article I, Section 8 of the Constitution. (A) and (D) are accordingly incorrect statements of the limitations on this power. (A) is wrong because it postulates that "only" the separation of powers doctrine limits the investigative power. (D) is wrong because it is too sweeping. Congressional investigation is limited to matters over which the Congress has jurisdiction. (C) is simply wrong. Congress may use appropriate means to investigate, and Congressional investigative committees may be comprised of members appointed by the executive branch, provided that it is done in such a way as to not violate separation of powers principles.

Answer to Question 16

(A) The witness's testimony about the conversation between the defendant and his roommate is not being offered for its truth (*i.e.*, to prove that the plaintiff had been flirting with the defendant's girlfriend), but rather to show its effect on the defendant. Thus, it is not hearsay, and (C) is incorrect. When the words themselves are in issue (*e.g.*, words of contract, gift, defamation, etc.), they are legally operative facts. This concept does not apply to these facts, and so (B) is incorrect. (D) is incorrect because opinion testimony by lay witnesses is admissible if it is based on the perception of the witness, helpful in determining a fact in issue, and not based on scientific, technical, or other specialized knowledge. Here, the witness saw the defendant, and he appeared angry. Whether the defendant was angry could help determine whether he acted in self-defense or struck the first blow.

Answer to Question 17

(B) The defense is not valid because the man had the state of mind to commit battery. Battery requires an intent on the part of the defendant to bring about harmful or offensive (*i.e.*, unconsented-to) contact to the plaintiff's person. Under the majority view, minors and incompetents will be liable for their intentional torts. Mental incompetency does not preclude a showing that a defendant "intended" to inflict a harmful or offensive touching. Hence, (C) is wrong. (D) is wrong because it makes no difference who the man thought he was; it is only relevant that he intended to do what he did. Because he knew that he was committing a touching that was not consented to by the plaintiff, he had the state of mind for battery. (A) is irrelevant with regard to his intent for battery.

Answer to Question 18

(D) The doctor has acquired neither title by adverse possession nor a prescriptive easement in the land under which the plumbing was laid. To establish title by adverse possession, the possession must be (i) actual and exclusive, (ii) open and notorious, (iii) adverse (hostile), and (iv) continuous throughout the statutory period. Exclusive possession generally means not sharing possession with the true owner or the general public. Possession is open and notorious when it is such as the usual owner would make of the land and is sufficient to put the true owner on notice of the fact of possession. Possession is hostile when it is without the owner's consent. Continuous possession is possession that the average owner would make of the property under the circumstances. Acquiring a prescriptive easement is analogous to acquiring property by adverse possession; however, the use need not be exclusive. Here, although the doctor's use and possession of the lawyer's land was actual, exclusive, open, notorious, and continuous throughout the seven-year statutory period, the doctor used the land with the lawyer's consent, and there are no facts to indicate that the doctor in any way manifested an intention to claim the land as her own. Therefore, the "hostile" requirement is not met and (A), (B), and (C) are wrong.

Answer to Question 19

(D) The community college will prevail in its suit against the replacement company because there was a delegation of duties plus an assumption of duty on the part of the replacement company, supported by consideration, creating a third-party beneficiary situation in which the obligee can compel performance or bring suit for nonperformance. Because the replacement company has promised that it will perform the duty delegated and that promise is supported by consideration, an assumption of duty has occurred and a third-party beneficiary situation is created in which the community college can compel performance or bring suit for nonperformance. Thus, (D) is correct and (A) is incorrect. (B) is incorrect because a court would probably not even inquire into adequacy of consideration when the value of the consideration was satisfactory to the parties involved. (C) is incorrect because the facts do not clearly indicate a novation. A novation occurs where a new contract substitutes a new party to receive benefits and assume duties that had originally belonged to one of the original parties under the terms of the old contract. A novation discharges the old contract. A novation will be found when there is (i) a previous valid contract; (ii) an agreement among the parties, including the new party to the new contract; (iii) the immediate extinguishment of contractual duties as between the original contracting parties; and (iv) a valid and enforceable new contract. Here, the facts do not state or otherwise indicate that a new contract was created and the duties under the old contract were discharged. Thus, this is not a novation situation.

Answer to Question 20

(B) The friend's best argument is that he thought the tools belonged to the mechanic. Larceny is the taking and carrying away of the tangible personal property of another by trespass with the intent to permanently (or for an unreasonable time) deprive the owner (or person in possession) of his interest in the property. Thus, larceny is a specific intent crime, in that the defendant must intend to permanently deprive the person of his interest in the property. Importantly, this intent generally must exist at the time of taking (save for the continuing trespass doctrine). In this case, the friend believed that the mechanic was being unlawfully deprived of his property, and his intent was to return the tools to their rightful owner. Thus, when he took the tools, he lacked the intent to permanently deprive another of his interest in the property. This would be true even if the garage owner factually had a lawful right to retain the tools, as the mistake of law would negate the friend's intent to permanently deprive another of his interest in the property. (A) is wrong, of course, because he did not have the consent of the owner of the tools he took. (C) is wrong because it is not a defense to a charge of larceny that the defendant did not intend to keep the item taken for his own use. (D) is wrong because it prematurely raises the continuing trespass doctrine. Under the continuing trespass doctrine, a defendant may be convicted of larceny when he initially takes property with a wrongful state of mind, but without the intent to permanently deprive the owner of the property, and then later forms the intent to permanently deprive the owner of the property. Here, the friend had not yet had the opportunity to form that later intent (even assuming the initial taking was with a wrongful state of mind). Thus, (D) does not address the correct issue.

Answer to Question 21

(C) The court should rule that the federal statute preempts the state law. Under the Supremacy Clause, a valid federal regulation supersedes any state action that conflicts with it, as is the case here. (A) is wrong because there is no basis for certification under the facts presented. While (B) might state an alluring policy choice, it is both outside the purview of the court and inappropriate in the face of the express determination by Congress to preempt local control. (D) is incorrect because while the Constitution gives the Supreme Court original jurisdiction over cases in which a state is a party, that jurisdiction is not exclusive. Congress has given the lower federal courts concurrent jurisdiction over all cases in which the Supreme Court has original jurisdiction except those between states. This is a case between the United States and a state. Therefore, the Supreme Court's jurisdiction is not exclusive and the case can be heard in a lower federal court.

Answer to Question 22

(A) The airline could be liable to the passenger for assault. Assault is an act creating a reasonable apprehension in the plaintiff of immediate harmful or offensive contact, intent to bring about such apprehension, and causation. The demand by a man armed with a gun that the passenger accompany him was a conditional threat that caused a reasonable apprehension of harm, and the guard knew that the display of the gun would cause sufficient apprehension that the passenger would comply with his demand. No privilege was present here; the threat of deadly force is not permitted in making a misdemeanor arrest. Hence, the airline is vicariously liable for the intentional tortious conduct of its security guard because force is authorized in his employment (even though the force used here was excessive). (B) is incorrect because, regardless of whether the airline's belief was reasonable, it did not have the privilege to threaten deadly force. (C) is incorrect because there need be no actual injury for the passenger to recover for assault. He is entitled at least to nominal damages, and depending on the nature of the defendant's conduct, he might be entitled to punitive damages. (D) is wrong for the same reason as (B); regardless of the reasonableness of the woman's belief, the airline did not have a privilege to do what it did.

Answer to Question 23

(D) The man is not guilty of conspiracy because he never had the required mental state for conspiracy. Conspiracy requires: (i) an agreement between two or more persons; (ii) the intent to enter into an agreement; and (iii) the intent to achieve the objective of the agreement. The two intent elements indicate that conspiracy is a specific intent crime. Here, because the man planned to contact the police before his cousin could commit the crime, he never intended to achieve the criminal objective of robbing the bank. Thus, he cannot be found guilty of conspiracy. (A) is incorrect because the man never entered into the conspiracy to begin with since he lacked the requisite intent; thus, he did not need to withdraw. (B) is incorrect because merely providing the instrumentality to commit the crime is insufficient by itself to establish liability for conspiracy. There also must be some intent to facilitate the crime, which is absent here. (C) is incorrect because, as stated above, the man never entered into the conspiracy. If he had, (C) would still be incorrect because, at common law and in most states, withdrawal is not a defense to the conspiracy charge itself, merely a limitation on liability for the subsequent acts of the co-conspirators.

Answer to Question 24

(D) The omission of any reference to the creditor in the written document was accidental, and both parties' failure to notice the oversight was a mutual mistake that would allow reformation of the contract so that the contract would reflect the intent of the parties. A plaintiff who wants to obtain reformation of a contract must show that there was an antecedent agreement that is not correctly reflected in the writing (*e.g.,* by mistake). These requirements are met here, where the writing fails to include a provision that was included in the earlier oral agreement, concerning payment of part of the purchase price to the landowner's creditor. (A) is wrong because the negligence of either the buyer or the landowner should not adversely affect the creditor's claim where the facts do not suggest that either party assumed the risk of the mistake. (B) is wrong because, even if the landowner-buyer agreement was completely integrated, the contract could still be reformed for mutual mistake if the omission of any reference to the creditor from the written document was accidental. Under the parol evidence rule, completely integrated writings cannot be contradicted or supplemented by either written or oral expressions made prior to the writing or oral expressions made contemporaneously with the writing. But the parol evidence rule does not apply where a party to a written agreement alleges facts (*e.g.,* mistake) that entitle him to reformation of the agreement. (C) is wrong because the answer turns on a mutual mistake involving omission of a material term, and not on an ambiguity in the writing and, as explained above, such mutual mistake allows for reformation of the contract.

Answer to Question 25

(B) The Supreme Court has construed the scope of the Commerce Clause very broadly, so that it covers the regulation of drug packaging, which has a substantial economic effect on interstate commerce. (A) is wrong because this type of regulation definitely falls under the Commerce Clause, and there is no need to imply a power (under the Necessary and Proper Clause) when an enumerated power controls. Moreover, the Necessary and Proper Clause, by itself, does not grant Congress the power to do anything. (C) is wrong because the General Welfare Clause presents a limitation on Congress's spending and taxing powers, which are not relevant here. (D) is wrong because the Tenth Amendment is not a grant of power to Congress; rather, it reserves the powers not granted to Congress to the states.

Answer to Question 26

(A) Only the wife may be convicted of battery. Battery is the unlawful application of force to the person of another resulting in either bodily injury or an offensive touching. Battery is a general intent crime which may be committed recklessly or with criminal negligence. However, there still must be some voluntary act on the part of the defendant. The husband's act was involuntary, thus negating criminal liability. Thus, (B) and (D) are wrong. However, the wife's actions might result in a battery conviction. If the wife was reasonable in her belief that she was under attack, she would have the defense of self-defense. If she was unreasonable in that belief, she would be guilty of battery. It would be a jury question as to whether her belief was reasonable or unreasonable. This makes (C) and (D) wrong.

Answer to Question 27

(D) If a court considers this new project to be part of a common development scheme with the original development, the developer will be successful. Prior purchasers may enforce restrictions in subsequent deeds from a common grantor if there is a general scheme evidencing the developer's intent to benefit the entire subdivision. Hence, (B) is wrong. (A) is wrong because zoning regulations do not limit the enforceability of private covenants. (C) is wrong because it is too absolute; if a court finds there is no common development, the restrictions are not enforceable by the owners of homes in the original development.

Answer to Question 28

(C) The new agreement between the two parties is enforceable as an accord. An accord is an agreement in which one party to an existing contract agrees to accept, in lieu of the performance that he is supposed to receive from the other party, some other, different performance. Generally, an accord must be supported by consideration, but the consideration may be of a lesser value than the originally bargained-for consideration in the prior contract, as long as it is of a different type or the claim is to be paid to a third party. Here, the homeowner's obligation to provide the contractor's mother with a new washer and dryer was of a lesser value to the homeowner than the originally bargained-for consideration in the prior contract, but it was of a different type ***and*** the claim was to be paid to a third party (the contractor's mother). Thus, it was sufficient new consideration to form a valid accord. (A) is incorrect because, while the new agreement did in fact fail as a novation, it was legally enforceable as an accord, as discussed in (C) above. A novation requires (i) a previous valid contract, (ii) an agreement among all parties, including the new party to the new contract, (iii) the immediate extinguishment of contractual duties as between the original contracting parties, and (iv) a valid and enforceable new contract. Here, the contractor's mother did not agree to the new terms, so there was no novation. However, the new agreement was still legally enforceable, because it qualified as an accord. (B) is incorrect because the homeowner and the contractor, as the parties to the new agreement, may legally enforce the new agreement for the reasons explained in (C) above, so it is irrelevant to the call of the question whether the contractor's mother, as a third-party donee beneficiary, has any legal rights against either party. (D) is incorrect because the original agreement was not a sale of goods contract under the U.C.C., which provides that an agreement modifying a contract subject to Article 2 needs no consideration to be binding, as long as the parties were acting in good faith. Here, the original obligation was to pay the amount due on a service contract, so this provision does not apply. It is nevertheless enforceable as an accord, as (C) states.

Answer to Question 29

(D) Congress may establish legislative and investigative commissions, so long as all the members of the commission are appointed by Congress. In these facts, the commission is not exercising any enforcement powers but rather is merely investigating and making recommendations, and all of its members are appointed by Congress; therefore, for the limited purposes indicated, the Constitution is not violated. Thus, (B) is incorrect because this commission does not have any enforcement powers. Therefore, the President need not appoint any members of the commission. Furthermore, the advice and consent of the Senate is not required here. (C) is incorrect because Congressional commissions can both investigate and make recommendations to Congress. (A) is incorrect because forbidding the commission to take any action is too strong a remedy and is not constitutionally required.

Answer to Question 30

(D) The mother likely will not prevail in a false imprisonment action against the janitor because the mother was in the room willingly and no facts show that she was there against her will. For false imprisonment, a plaintiff must prove that the defendant intentionally confined or restrained plaintiff to a bounded area, and here there is no evidence of that. (A) is wrong because, although a plaintiff need not risk harm by trying to escape, the mother was not trying to escape. (B) is incorrect because, whatever the reason for her staying in the room, there are no facts showing that the janitor intended to falsely imprison her. (C) is not as good a choice as (D) because, while it is unlikely that the janitor would have attempted to keep her from leaving the room, the facts do not establish what his state of mind was.

Answer to Question 31

(A) The companion's testimony is admissible. Declarations of present bodily condition are admissible as an exception to the hearsay rule, even if not made to a physician. Such statements relate to symptoms, such as pain. Here, the plaintiff's statement was one of present bodily condition and is admissible to prove the extent of his injuries, which is an issue in the case. It follows that (D) is incorrect. (C) is incorrect because, as noted above, a declaration of present bodily condition is admissible even if not made to a physician. (B) is incorrect, because the plaintiff's statement is admissible as a declaration of present pain, not as proof that he had a heart attack.

Answer to Question 32

(B) The hunter is not guilty of murder because he acted in self-defense in response to the owner's deadly attack. At common law, murder is the unlawful killing of another with malice aforethought. Malice aforethought may be shown by (i) the intent to kill, (ii) the intent to inflict great bodily injury, (iii) a reckless indifference to an unjustifiably high risk to human life ("abandoned and malignant heart"), or (iv) the intent to commit a felony. In the instant case, it is clear that the hunter intentionally shot and killed the rancher. However, a killing that otherwise might constitute murder will be excused if the defendant was acting in self-defense. A person may use deadly force in self-defense is he is (i) without fault, (ii) confronted with unlawful force, and (iii) threatened with imminent death or great bodily harm. All three elements can be met here. Although the hunter was a trespasser and accidentally shot the rancher's bull, he did nothing to initiate or provoke the physical altercation, as the rancher would not be entitled to use deadly force against a trespasser. The hunter was also confronted with unlawful force when the rancher shot at the hunter and raised his rifle to take a second shot at the hunter. Clearly, this would also represent a threat of imminent death. Thus, the hunter was entitled to use deadly force in self-defense, making him not guilty of murder. This is not affected by the fact that the hunter was a trespasser (choice (A)) or that the owner was enraged by the hunter's negligence and attitude (choice (C)). (D) is a correct statement of the law, but inapplicable to the given facts, given that the hunter was not acting in defense of property, but rather in self-defense.

Answer to Question 33

(D) The manufacturer will prevail in an action to enforce the contract, because the manufacturer had the right to cure the defect and was prevented from doing so. In an installment contract, an installment can be rejected only if the nonconformity substantially impairs the value of that installment and cannot be cured. Moreover, the installment contract as a whole is deemed to be breached only if the nonconformity substantially impairs the value of the entire contract. Here, the contract is an installment contract because the deliveries are to be made in separate lots at different times. The delivery of tainted chocolate chips was the first of 12 deliveries that were to be made, and there is nothing in the facts to indicate that the manufacturer could not cure the problem with this delivery and with the rest of the deliveries for the year. Thus, the nonconformity did not substantially impair the value of the entire contract. As to this installment, the bakery owner must afford the chocolate chip manufacturer the right to cure, *i.e.,* to send replacement chips as the manufacturer had offered to do, and his failure to allow the manufacturer to do so will result in the manufacturer prevailing in an action to enforce the contract. (A) is wrong because the "perfect tender" rule, which allows a buyer to reject goods for "any defect" in the goods or tender, is not the rule for installment contracts, where a defective shipment cannot be rejected if the defect can be cured. (B) is wrong because damages could be measured by lost profits or by standard contract measure. (C) is wrong because a notification of rejection need not be in writing.

Answer to Question 34

(C) The judge should overrule the objection. Evidence is relevant if it tends to establish a material proposition in the case. This evidence, which would help establish a motive, which in turn would help establish the guilt of the defendant, would clearly be relevant. Therefore, an objection based solely on the relevance of the evidence should be overruled. Therefore (A) and (B) are wrong. (D) is wrong. On the facts of this case, the involvement of the defendant in embezzlement would be relevant, and since the objection was based on grounds of relevance, the limiting instruction would not be required. The statement might be hearsay when used for that purpose, but it might qualify as an admission by silence on the part of the defendant. In any event, the objection was not on hearsay grounds.

Answer to Question 35

(C) The best defense is that the cruise ship acted reasonably under the circumstances and had no reason to know of the man's conduct. The cruise ship owed a duty to its passenger to provide a private environment for the massage. If it took reasonable precautions to do so, it did not breach its duty. (A) is incorrect; it goes only to the issue of the passenger's conduct, not whether the cruise ship was negligent. (B) is wrong because the man's conduct is not "intervening" but is the circumstance by which the cruise ship's breach of its duty to the passenger may be shown. (D) is contrary to the facts—the passenger suffered at least some discomfort from the physical contact, which satisfies the damage element for negligence.

Answer to Question 36

(C) The refusal of the tire distributor's president to send any additional tire shipments to the automobile manufacturer amounted to an anticipatory repudiation which breaches the contract. An anticipatory repudiation arises where a promisor, by words or conduct, unequivocally indicates that he cannot or will not perform when the time comes. In such a case, the other party has several options, including treating the repudiation as an immediate breach and suing for damages. Thus, (C) is correct and (A) is incorrect. (B) is incorrect because the "disgraceful" quality of the automobiles would not be a defense under the contract because the contract made no provision regarding the quality of the automobile manufacturer's product. (D) is incorrect because the president's actions were an anticipatory repudiation, and not a prospective inability to perform, which involves conduct or words that merely raise doubts that the party will not perform and do not rise to the level of an unequivocal refusal to perform. Here, the president refused without equivocation to send any additional tire shipments to the automobile manufacturer.

Answer to Question 37

(D) The general principles of intergovernmental immunity prevent federal interference with state governmental functions. In these facts, although the assault occurred in the state legislator's office, there is no indication that she was conducting state governmental duties at the time of the assault and, therefore, while this would be her strongest constitutional defense, it would not be applicable under these facts. There is no indication of any violation of due process, and federal courts need follow state law only in cases where jurisdiction is based on diversity of citizenship or when a federal statute specifically incorporates state law. Thus, (A) and (B) are incorrect. (C) is incorrect because the protection of the Speech and Debate Clause extends only to federal legislators.

Answer to Question 38

(D) The homeowner will prevail because the grocer will be charged with notice as a result of the residential character of the subdivision. When a developer subdivides land into several parcels and some of the deeds contain negative covenants but some do not, negative equitable servitudes binding all the parcels in the subdivision may be implied if: (i) there exists a common scheme for development, and (ii) the grantee has notice of the covenant. The requisite notice may be acquired through actual notice (direct knowledge of the covenants in the prior deeds), inquiry notice (the neighborhood appears to conform to common restrictions), or record notice (if the prior deeds are in the grantee's chain of title he will, under the recording acts, have constructive notice of their contents). Here, the owner's common scheme is evidenced by the general pattern of prior restrictions: lots 1-19 were restricted to residential use. Because the facts state that the other purchasers of lots 1-19 each built residences on their property, the grocer would at least be charged with inquiry notice of the restriction. Thus, (A) is incorrect. (B) is incorrect because the grocer's reliance on the abstract of title and the buyer's representation would not negate the inquiry notice. (C)'s reasoning would not be sufficient to bind the grocer to the covenant.

Answer to Question 39

(D) The judge should overrule the objection. Out-of-court statements offered for the purpose of proving knowledge on the part of the listener, which in this case would establish motive, are not objectionable as hearsay. Therefore, (A) is incorrect. (B) is incorrect. The state of mind exception to the hearsay rule applies when the out-of-court statement helps establish the declarant's state of mind. (C) is incorrect. Phone calls during business hours on business phones do not qualify as a business record.

Answer to Question 40

(D) The woman need show no additional facts. A defamatory statement communicated to another constitutes slander per se if it adversely reflects on a person's abilities in her business or profession. At common law, damages are presumed for slander per se. The mother's statement to the other mother was defamatory and slander per se because she alleged that the woman was intoxicated while on the job, which adversely reflects on her reliability and trustworthiness in her child care work. Hence, the woman need not prove special damages, such as loss of child care jobs. Thus, (A) and (B) are incorrect. (C) might be relevant in an action for intentional infliction of distress, but it is irrelevant in a defamation action against the mother.

Answer to Question 41

(B) The first friend can be convicted of common law robbery, but the second cannot be convicted. Robbery is the taking and carrying away of the personal property of another from the other's person or presence by force or intimidation. In the instant case, the first friend committed a robbery when he threatened the woman and told her that she could not leave without giving him all of her money. The only issue would be whether the asportation element is satisfied. However, the asportation element is satisfied by any slight moving, and it is likely that the first friend moved the money at some point during the robbery. Thus, a jury could find the first friend guilty of robbery. This makes (C) and (D) wrong answer choices. In the case of the second friend, however, a conviction for robbery is unlikely. Although a close call, the taking or retention of the property was not by force or intimidation in the second case. The crime against the property was already completed when the man slapped the victim. Furthermore, the slap was not to prevent the woman from physically taking the credit card back; rather, it was a ruse used to deflect the accusation that the second friend took the credit card. Thus, (A) is wrong, and this provides a second reason why (C) is incorrect.

Answer to Question 42

(B) The woman will prevail in her suit for a refund, because the dress shop breached an express warranty. An express warranty will arise from any affirmation of fact or promise made by the seller to the buyer, or from any description of the goods, and any sample or model if the statement, description, sample, or model is part of the basis of the bargain. Here, the woman reached her decision to buy by viewing the dress in the window; thus, an express warranty arose that the dress she purchased would conform to the dress in the window. This warranty was not negated by the attempted disclaimer on the dress tag because that came too late to be part of the parties' contract. Thus, (B) is correct and (D) is wrong. (A) is a misstatement of the law. (C) is wrong because the dress is, in fact, "defective" (it is the wrong color), and the express warranty was breached for the reasons discussed above.

Answer to Question 43

(A) The neighbor's best defense against the son's attempt to eject her is that her life estate was not subject to termination during her lifetime. The usual life estate is measured by the life of the grantee. Although a life estate may be made defeasible (*e.g.*, determinable, subject to a condition subsequent, or subject to an executory interest), the conveyance here created an indefeasible life estate (*i.e.*, one that will end only when the life tenant dies) in the neighbor. (B) is incorrect because the son did not have to be alive at the time of the original conveyance in order to now claim an interest in the tract. (C) is incorrect because the son's interest would vest within 21 years of a life in being (his mother, the sister). (D) is incorrect because the son's interest would be a vested rather than contingent remainder. A remainder is contingent if it is created in favor of unborn or unascertained persons. Because the sister was childless at the time of the conveyance, the remainder to the sister's "first child . . . who shall reach the age of 21" was a contingent remainder. It remained contingent at the son's birth because he had to reach age 21 to take. However, the son has reached age 21, and thus his remainder is vested. It is indefeasibly vested because it is not subject to being defeated, divested, or diminished in size.

Answer to Question 44

(C) The motion to suppress should be denied because a valid search warrant was obtained. A search warrant must be based on probable cause. Here, there was sufficient information for a judge to conclude that there was probable cause to believe that evidence of a crime would be found in the sophomore's room. Thus, the warrant was properly obtained. (A) is wrong because the sophomore had only a limited expectation of privacy in a dormitory's lounge. Also, even if his privacy had been invaded, any invasion here was done by private persons, not the state, and thus would not prevent introduction of the evidence. (B) is wrong because it is untrue as a matter of law. (D) is wrong because it is not a sufficient basis to deny the sophomore's motion. It is irrelevant that the college president acted on behalf of the college population.

Answer to Question 45

(A) The judge should admit the witness's testimony. Evidence that the artist was retrieving his own painting from the customer's wrongful possession would help negate the intent required for burglary. Therefore, it would be relevant. The testimony would have no effect on the neighbor's credibility, so (B) and (C) are incorrect. (D) is not a very good answer. First, the objection is on relevancy, not on Rule 403. In addition, rejecting the evidence on Rule 403 grounds would be extremely unlikely on the facts presented.

Answer to Question 46

(D) The homeowner and her heirs would take the home until the brother died. At common law, a contingent remainder had to vest prior to or upon termination of the preceding freehold estate or it was destroyed. Here, the remainder in the brother's heirs is contingent because one does not have "heirs" until his death. Because the jurisdiction has abolished the rule of destructibility, the homeowner's reversion would take over, and would give way to a springing executory interest in the brother's heirs on his death. Thus, (C) is wrong. (A) is wrong because the brother's child is not entitled to possession until her father's death, at which time she would qualify as his "heir." (B) is wrong because the brother's child has no right to possession; thus, a guardian cannot possess for her.

Answer to Question 47

(C) When a buyer accepts goods that turn out to be defective, he may recover as damages any "loss resulting in the normal course of events from the breach," which includes the difference between the value of the goods accepted and the value they would have had if they had been as warranted, plus incidental and consequential damages. Incidental damages resulting from the seller's breach include expenses reasonably incurred in inspection, receipt, and transportation, care, and custody of goods rightfully rejected. In this case, the grandfather incurred no incidental damages. Consequential damages resulting from the seller's breach include any loss resulting from general or particular requirements and needs of which the seller at the time of contracting had reason to know and which could not reasonably be prevented by cover or otherwise, and injury to person or property proximately resulting from any breach of warranty. Here, the grandfather is entitled to breach of warranty damages for the loss of the camera—the difference between the value of the camera accepted and its value if it had been as warranted—plus damages for injury to his person (*e.g.,* medical costs for treating the grandfather's burns) and property (*i.e.,* the cost to replace his coat) because they were proximately caused from the breach of warranty. Thus, (C) is correct, and (A) and (B) are wrong. (D) is wrong because the cost of hiring the professional photographer was not foreseeable. The seller was not told of any particular requirements and needs of the grandfather at the time of contracting nor would the seller have reason to know that the grandfather planned to use the camera to take pictures of his grandson's graduation and would hire a professional photographer if he lost the use of the camera.

Answer to Question 48

(C) Classifications based on gender are quasi-suspect and are therefore subject to intermediate scrutiny. Ordinances and statutes based on gender will violate the Equal Protection Clause unless the government shows by exceedingly persuasive justification that the ordinance is substantially related to an important government objective. (A) is incorrect because it puts the burden on the boy and states the wrong level of scrutiny (rational basis test). (B) is incorrect because while it states the correct test, it puts the burden on the boy. (D) is incorrect because while it places the burden on the correct party (*i.e.*, city), it states the strict scrutiny test rather than the intermediate scrutiny test.

Answer to Question 49

(C) The new attorney may sue the classmate for intentional infliction of emotional distress. The scope of that tort is broad enough to allow recovery for emotional distress caused by a defendant's intentional insults and indignities. However, the attorney has to establish that the classmate's statements were extreme and outrageous, so it is by no means certain that the new attorney would prevail. Nevertheless, it is the only theory that offers the new attorney a chance of recovering. (A) is incorrect because intentional misrepresentation is inapplicable here; there is no reliance on the false statement or intent to induce reliance. Defamation requires a publication to third persons; hence (B) is incorrect because there is no other party in the facts. (D) is incorrect because negligent infliction of emotional distress requires a showing by the plaintiff that the defendant created a foreseeable risk of physical injury to the plaintiff, typically by causing a threat of physical impact that leads to emotional distress. No such risk was present here.

Answer to Question 50

(A) The question is proper. Under the Federal Rules, either party may impeach a witness, and leading questions are permitted when a witness is hostile. Thus, (C) and (D) are incorrect. (B) is incorrect because the examiner is not trying to refresh the former waitress's recollection of whether the drink was on the menu; rather, he is talking about a deposition and is trying to impeach her with an inconsistent statement.

Mixed Subject Set 8 Answer Sheet

1. Ⓐ Ⓑ Ⓒ Ⓓ
2. Ⓐ Ⓑ Ⓒ Ⓓ
3. Ⓐ Ⓑ Ⓒ Ⓓ
4. Ⓐ Ⓑ Ⓒ Ⓓ
5. Ⓐ Ⓑ Ⓒ Ⓓ
6. Ⓐ Ⓑ Ⓒ Ⓓ
7. Ⓐ Ⓑ Ⓒ Ⓓ
8. Ⓐ Ⓑ Ⓒ Ⓓ
9. Ⓐ Ⓑ Ⓒ Ⓓ
10. Ⓐ Ⓑ Ⓒ Ⓓ
11. Ⓐ Ⓑ Ⓒ Ⓓ
12. Ⓐ Ⓑ Ⓒ Ⓓ
13. Ⓐ Ⓑ Ⓒ Ⓓ
14. Ⓐ Ⓑ Ⓒ Ⓓ
15. Ⓐ Ⓑ Ⓒ Ⓓ
16. Ⓐ Ⓑ Ⓒ Ⓓ
17. Ⓐ Ⓑ Ⓒ Ⓓ
18. Ⓐ Ⓑ Ⓒ Ⓓ
19. Ⓐ Ⓑ Ⓒ Ⓓ
20. Ⓐ Ⓑ Ⓒ Ⓓ
21. Ⓐ Ⓑ Ⓒ Ⓓ
22. Ⓐ Ⓑ Ⓒ Ⓓ
23. Ⓐ Ⓑ Ⓒ Ⓓ
24. Ⓐ Ⓑ Ⓒ Ⓓ
25. Ⓐ Ⓑ Ⓒ Ⓓ
26. Ⓐ Ⓑ Ⓒ Ⓓ
27. Ⓐ Ⓑ Ⓒ Ⓓ
28. Ⓐ Ⓑ Ⓒ Ⓓ
29. Ⓐ Ⓑ Ⓒ Ⓓ
30. Ⓐ Ⓑ Ⓒ Ⓓ
31. Ⓐ Ⓑ Ⓒ Ⓓ
32. Ⓐ Ⓑ Ⓒ Ⓓ
33. Ⓐ Ⓑ Ⓒ Ⓓ
34. Ⓐ Ⓑ Ⓒ Ⓓ
35. Ⓐ Ⓑ Ⓒ Ⓓ
36. Ⓐ Ⓑ Ⓒ Ⓓ
37. Ⓐ Ⓑ Ⓒ Ⓓ
38. Ⓐ Ⓑ Ⓒ Ⓓ
39. Ⓐ Ⓑ Ⓒ Ⓓ
40. Ⓐ Ⓑ Ⓒ Ⓓ
41. Ⓐ Ⓑ Ⓒ Ⓓ
42. Ⓐ Ⓑ Ⓒ Ⓓ
43. Ⓐ Ⓑ Ⓒ Ⓓ
44. Ⓐ Ⓑ Ⓒ Ⓓ
45. Ⓐ Ⓑ Ⓒ Ⓓ
46. Ⓐ Ⓑ Ⓒ Ⓓ
47. Ⓐ Ⓑ Ⓒ Ⓓ
48. Ⓐ Ⓑ Ⓒ Ⓓ
49. Ⓐ Ⓑ Ⓒ Ⓓ
50. Ⓐ Ⓑ Ⓒ Ⓓ

MIXED SUBJECT QUESTIONS - SET 8

Question 1

In response to a telephone call, a report went out over the police radio requesting an ambulance because of a shooting. Several officers who heard the broadcast arrived at the subject residence and knocked on the front door, identifying themselves as police officers. Believing that someone inside the house had been shot, one of the officers entered the building through an unlocked window and opened the front door for the other officers to enter. While searching for victims, the officers saw, in plain view, several containers of cocaine. A defendant, the occupant of the house, was arrested and charged with possession of narcotics. At his trial, the defendant moved to suppress the evidence of the narcotics on the ground that the police officers' warrantless entry into his residence was improper.

Did the police officers have a right to enter the building without a warrant?

(A) Yes, because exigent circumstances existed as a result of the shooting.

(B) Yes, because the police officers were acting in their official function.

(C) No, because there were no factors to indicate that there was not enough time to obtain a warrant.

(D) No, because there was no probable cause to enter without a warrant.

Question 2

The defendant was on trial for driving while intoxicated and injuring a pedestrian. The pedestrian claimed that the defendant was driving the car; however, the defendant's spouse testified at trial that she had been driving the car at the time of the accident and had not consumed any alcohol that evening. In response, the prosecution calls a friend of the defendant's spouse to testify that the spouse told the friend that she and the defendant had changed seats in the car after the incident and that she remained in the driver's seat until the police arrived.

The testimony is:

(A) Admissible for impeachment purposes only.

(B) Admissible to show bias.

(C) Inadmissible, because a witness who is available to testify can be impeached only through cross-examination.

(D) Inadmissible, because the witness must be given an opportunity to explain or deny the statement.

Question 3

A child lost her lunch on the way to elementary school. She walked to the local grocery store and explained her predicament to the manager. He told her that if she agreed to pay him back the following day, she could have a pre-packaged lunch. The child accepted the manager's offer, picked up her lunch, and promised to pay the manager the following day.

If the child refuses to pay and the grocery store sues her for the cost of the lunch and wins, it will be because:

(A) A third party witnessed the child's promise.

(B) The child cannot return the lunch so she cannot return the store to the status quo ante.

(C) The child needed the food.

(D) The contract did not have to be in writing.

Question 4

A landowner embarked on an expedition into a remote jungle, leaving no means to communicate with him. Because property values suddenly began plummeting in the landowner's neighborhood, his son believed that it was imperative to sell his father's property before it became worthless. Having no way to speak to his father ahead of time, the son prepared a deed conveying the property to a buyer, but left the line for the buyer's name blank. He then signed his father's name on it as the grantor, and handed the deed to the buyer. The deed, however, did not include any language regarding the amount the father was to receive in exchange for the property. The buyer believed that the son was the owner of the property. When the father returned, he was happy that the property had been sold.

If the buyer changed his mind and now wishes to have the conveyance set aside, which of the following would be his best argument?

(A) The deed was not valid because the rapidly declining property values amounted to extreme duress.

(B) The deed was not valid because the buyer was not identified in the writing.

(C) The deed was not valid because the consideration for the deed was not contained in the writing.

(D) The deed was not valid because the son signed it.

Question 5

To protect ready access to its capitol building, a state statute provides:

> The distribution and sale of any written material within 100 feet of the State Capitol Building shall be prohibited except where:
>
> (i) The person or organization intending to distribute the material first obtains a permit from the State Administrator's Office, which shall be issued at no charge to the first 10 persons or organizations requesting a permit each day, and
>
> (ii) The person or organization does not distribute or sell written materials within 10 feet of any entrance to the State Capitol Building.

A state citizen who was unhappy with a law that was recently enacted went to the main entrance of the capitol building and handed out leaflets criticizing the law. He was soon approached by the building's security guards, who asked to see his permit. When he was unable to produce one, they cited him for leafleting without a permit.

If the citizen challenges his citation on the basis that the permit statute is unconstitutional under the First Amendment, the court should decide that:

(A) The statute is unconstitutional because 10 permits a day is too few.

(B) The statute is unconstitutional because 10 feet from a doorway is unreasonable.

(C) The statute is constitutional because it is content neutral, narrowly tailored to serve an important government interest, and leaves open alternative channels of communication.

(D) The statute is constitutional because the grounds and walkways of the capitol building are not public forums.

Question 6

Late one night two brothers took the older brother's new all-terrain vehicle for an off-road test drive on some trails at a county park, even though a county ordinance prohibited vehicle traffic on any of the trails, limiting their use to hikers, bike riders, and horse riders. While on a trail, the vehicle's tires slipped and the vehicle fell down a steep incline. As it fell, it turned over several times, but landed on its tires when it reached the bottom of the incline. However, the vehicle's roll bar, which was intended to protect passengers in the event the vehicle turned over, collapsed due to some cracks in the welded area of the brace. The older brother was killed in the accident, and the younger brother suffered severe head and back injuries. The younger brother brought a negligence action against the vehicle's manufacturer. The manufacturer cited as a defense the violation of the county ordinance by the older brother.

Depending on the jurisdiction's contributory negligence rule, this violation of the ordinance will:

(A) Bar or reduce recovery by the younger brother.

(B) Bar or reduce recovery by the younger brother if the jury finds that he was aware of the ordinance.

(C) Not bar or reduce recovery by the younger brother, because at the time he and the older brother went into the park it was closed and no one else was on the trails.

(D) Not bar or reduce recovery by the younger brother.

Question 7

A man loaned $10,000 to his good friend who was heavily in debt. He told his friend that he could have until the following June to repay the loan and to make repayment directly to the man's grandson. The man knew that his grandson, who would be graduating from law school in June, was hoping to buy a new car upon graduation and could use the money as a down payment on the car. Neither the man nor his friend told the grandson of this agreement. Before the friend repaid the $10,000 loan, the grandson went out and bought his dream car, cashing some savings bonds to make the down payment. A week later, the grandfather suffered a reversal of fortune and told his friend to pay the $10,000 to him after all, which the friend did. A short time later, the grandson learned of the aborted plan to pay the $10,000 to him.

If the grandson sues the friend for the $10,000, will he prevail?

(A) Yes, because he was the intended beneficiary of the contract between his grandfather and the friend.

(B) Yes, because he detrimentally relied on the promise between his grandfather and the friend by purchasing the car.

(C) No, because his rights had not yet vested when the contract was modified.

(D) No, because the man intended the repayment of the $10,000 to the grandson to be a gift.

Question 8

A landowner owned a tract known as Section 35. He subdivided Section 35, and sold a lot to a neighbor. The warranty deed that conveyed the property included the following language:

COVENANTS

* * *

Purchaser shall have a privilege to hunt and fish on all lands owned by Seller in Section 35.

* * *

These covenants shall run with the land.

Years later, the landowner sold the remaining land in Section 35 to a builder. Shortly thereafter, the neighbor died, leaving the lot to her granddaughter. The builder posted "no trespassing" signs on his land. The granddaughter brought an action for declaratory judgment against the builder to enforce the granddaughter's ability to hunt and fish on the builder's land.

What would be the likely result?

(A) The granddaughter will win, because the warranty deed granted her an easement.

(B) The granddaughter will win, because the warranty deed granted her an irrevocable license.

(C) The granddaughter will win, because the warranty deed granted her a profit.

(D) The builder will win, because the warranty deed granted a revocable license.

Question 9

At the defendant's trial for arson, a witness for the defense is asked whether the defendant has a reputation for honesty and veracity. The prosecution objects.

How should the court rule on the objection?

(A) Sustained, because the evidence is hearsay.

(B) Sustained, because the evidence is irrelevant.

(C) Overruled, because the prosecution put the defendant's character at issue by filing charges against him.

(D) Overruled, because the reputation evidence is admissible to establish a character trait.

Question 10

A defendant is arrested and tried for battery. At trial, the prosecution offers evidence showing that the defendant lightly punched the victim in the stomach. The victim was not injured in any way. The defendant claims that he was suffering from a seizure and had no control over his actions.

If the jury believes him, should he be convicted of battery?

(A) Yes, because being lightly punched in the stomach is an offensive touching.

(B) Yes, because battery is a general intent crime.

(C) No, because the defendant did not act voluntarily.

(D) No, because the victim was not injured.

Question 11

An investor owned a large tract of land. To the east of the land was a city-owned parking lot. The investor used a driveway across the eastern part of the land to provide the western part with access to the parking lot. Subsequently, the investor sold the western parcel to a bakery and the eastern parcel to a coffee shop. By a written instrument, the coffee shop granted the bakery and its customers the right to use the driveway to access the parking lot. The only other way to enter the parking lot is over land to the north of the western parcel. The bakery has been unsuccessful in obtaining access to the parking lot over this land.

The bakery's right to use the driveway is:

(A) An easement in gross.

(B) An easement appurtenant.

(C) An easement by necessity.

(D) An easement by implied reservation.

Question 12

A builder and a wealthy landowner entered into a written contract whereby the builder would build on the grounds of the landowner's estate a mausoleum, using imported Italian granite, to hold the remains of the landowner's recently deceased wife. The cost of the mausoleum was set at $100,000. After the contract was signed but before construction began, the builder learned that an unforeseen embargo prevented him from getting the granite he planned to use to build the mausoleum. He could get the granite from another source, but it would cost an additional $25,000. The builder explained the situation to the landowner, who agreed to pay $125,000 to have the mausoleum built. The builder prepared a writing stating that the price for the mausoleum was now $125,000. Both the builder and the landowner signed the writing. After the work was completed, the landowner gave the builder a certified check for $100,000 and refused to pay one penny more.

If the builder brings suit against the landowner to recover the additional $25,000, will the builder likely prevail?

(A) No, because the builder had a preexisting duty to do the work for $100,000.

(B) No, because the 25% increase in price that the builder was trying to force on the landowner is unconscionable.

(C) Yes, because the later agreement was in writing and signed by the parties.

(D) Yes, because the modification was made by the parties in good faith because of the unforeseen circumstances.

Question 13

The plaintiff is suing the defendant to recover for damage to the plaintiff's garage, which burned down from a fire that started in the defendant's bakery. The plaintiff alleged that the fire was started by one of the bakery's employees, who was known to come into the bakery after an evening of drinking at a nearby bar to experiment with recipes. The defendant denied the allegation and claimed that the fire was the result of arson by a local gang member. At trial, the plaintiff called to the stand a court reporter, who will testify that he recorded the testimony of the now-deceased manager of the bakery at a preliminary hearing on a criminal charge of arson against the gang member, and the manager testified that the fire was the result of the employee's drunkenly experiments. The defendant objects to the court reporter's testimony.

The court should rule that the testimony is:

(A) Admissible, as substantive evidence of the cause of the fire.

(B) Admissible, under the former testimony exception to the hearsay rule.

(C) Inadmissible, because the court transcript would be the best evidence.

(D) Inadmissible, because it is hearsay not within any exception.

Question 14

A state adopted a statute requiring all public school students to recite the Pledge of Allegiance. A parent of a public school student objected to the requirement because the Pledge includes the words, "under God." The parent brought suit in state court, seeking an injunction based on an alleged violation of the Establishment Clause of the First Amendment, as applied to the states through the Due Process Clause of the Fourteenth Amendment.

In deciding the substance of the parent's claim, which of the following factors would be most relevant?

(A) Whether the statute constitutes a law of general application.

(B) Whether the student involved sincerely believes that reciting the Pledge is against the tenets of his faith.

(C) Whether requiring students to recite the Pledge is narrowly tailored to promote a compelling interest.

(D) Whether requiring students to recite the Pledge has a secular purpose, has a primary effect that neither advances nor inhibits religion, and does not produce excessive entanglement between government and religion.

Question 15

A wife wanted to have her husband murdered in order to collect the proceeds from a life insurance policy. The wife solicited the services of a hitman, agreeing to split the insurance proceeds with him. The plan was for the hitman to shoot the husband at home and make it look like a botched burglary attempt, while the wife would be at her church hall playing bingo that night. However, when the hitman broke into the apartment, the husband was able to subdue him and call the police. The hitman was arrested and implicated the wife, who was arrested in the parish priest's office just after she had confessed the plan to the priest. The wife is charged with attempted murder and conspiracy to commit murder in a state that retains the common law definitions of these crimes. A psychiatric evaluation of the hitman after he was arrested revealed that he was legally insane, and he later committed suicide while awaiting trial.

As to the conspiracy charge against the wife, which of the following would be her most promising defense?

(A) She cannot be tried for both offenses; the prosecutor must choose between them.

(B) The hitman was insane when the conspiracy was formed.

(C) The hitman died in jail before trial.

(D) She had second thoughts about the plan while playing bingo and had revealed it to her priest.

Question 16

A brother and a sister held record title to a home as joint tenants with right of survivorship. The brother moved out of the home shortly after conveying his interest in the home to his friend by quitclaim deed. The friend did not record his deed. Several years later, the sister died, leaving her adopted daughter as her sole heir. Shortly after the sister died, the brother asked his friend to return his deed and give up his interest in the home. The friend agreed and returned the deed, which the brother destroyed.

Who has title to the home?

(A) The friend and the daughter as co-tenants.

(B) The brother and the daughter as co-tenants.

(C) The brother as sole owner.

(D) The friend as sole owner.

Question 17

A homeowner contracted for construction of a custom-built, elevated deck in his backyard. The deck's designer supervised the construction, which was carried out by several employees of a local building company. The homeowner was pleased with the appearance of the deck, but the first time he stepped on it, a support on one side of the deck gave way, causing the homeowner to fall and be injured. The homeowner brought an action joining the building company and the deck's designer as defendants, alleging negligence. In his complaint, he alleged that he does not know which of the defendants is responsible for the damages.

Which of the following doctrines would be most helpful against the designer?

(A) Respondeat superior.

(B) Res ipsa loquitur.

(C) Contribution.

(D) Indemnity.

Question 18

The plaintiff sued the defendant in a contract dispute. At trial, the plaintiff's sister testifies as a witness on behalf of the plaintiff, stating that the defendant agreed to sell a computer to the plaintiff for $250. To prove that the sister is telling the truth, plaintiff's counsel asks the sister on direct examination about a conversation she had with her mother, in which she told her mother that the defendant agreed to sell a computer to the plaintiff for $250. The defendant objects to the testimony.

How should the court rule?

(A) Admissible, because it is a prior consistent statement.

(B) Admissible, because it is not hearsay.

(C) Inadmissible, because leading questions cannot be asked on direct examination.

(D) Inadmissible, because the sister has not been impeached.

Question 19

A woman whose child attended a charter school learned that the children of the woman's neighbor who attended a parochial school received a hot lunch paid for, in part, through federal expenditures enacted under Congress's spending power. The charter school received no funding from the federal government. The woman challenged this federal expenditure as a violation of the Establishment Clause.

For her to bring the suit, at the very least the woman must allege that:

(A) She is exempt from paying federal income taxes and has children who are of school age.

(B) She pays federal income taxes and the use of federal funds in this manner is an improper taxing and spending method.

C) She pays federal income taxes and has children who are of school age.

(D) She pays federal income taxes and has children who are of school age, and the use of federal funds in this manner is an improper taxing and spending method.

Question 20

A contactor agreed to build a plant for a manufacturer. The contract required the contractor to use lighting fixtures from a specific company. Inadvertently, the contractor installed fixtures from a different company. The installed fixtures are generally considered to be of a slightly greater quality than the fixtures specified in the contract. The mistake was not discovered until the manufacturer did a final inspection of the building. As built, the plant is worth $2,000 more than it would be worth had the specified fixtures been used. Because of a downturn in the economy, the manufacturer no longer wants to move into the new plant and refuses to pay the contractor because of the breach regarding the light fixtures. It would cost the contractor $20,000 to replace the fixtures with the ones specified in the contract.

If the contractor sues the manufacturer for specific performance, which of the following doctrines will be most important to a court's decision?

(A) Perfect tender.

(B) Waste.

(C) Substantial performance.

(D) Quasi-contract.

Question 21

A landowner conveyed a vacant tract of land to a developer by quitclaim deed. The developer did not record its deed. Prior to the start of construction, the developer abandoned the project and returned the deed to the landowner. The landowner then executed and delivered a general warranty deed conveying the land to a buyer. The buyer promptly and properly recorded his deed. Subsequently, the developer decided to proceed with its original development of the land it had purchased from the landowner. The jurisdiction has the following recording act: "A conveyance of an interest in land shall not be valid against any subsequent purchaser for value, without notice thereof, unless the conveyance is recorded."

In a suit between the developer and the buyer, the buyer will prevail, if at all, because:

(A) The buyer recorded his deed.

(B) The developer's interest terminated when it returned its deed to the landowner.

(C) A general warranty deed has priority over a quitclaim deed.

(D) The buyer is a bona fide purchaser.

Question 22

The plaintiff sued the defendant for injuries resulting from a car accident. At trial, the plaintiff's witness testified that the defendant ran a red light and then hit the plaintiff's car.

Which of the following is the court most likely to allow to impeach the credibility of the witness?

(A) A record of a juvenile offense.

(B) A question on cross-examination asking whether the witness lied on the job application for his present job.

(C) A certified copy of a conviction for robbery five years ago for which the witness has since been proved innocent and pardoned.

(D) A record of an arrest one week ago for criminal trespass.

Question 23

Congress provided funds to a group of young scouts. A person believed that this particular scouting group practiced racial discrimination and brought suit to enjoin the federal provision of funds to this group.

Assuming the factual allegation regarding racial discrimination is correct and that the person has standing to challenge the expenditure, how should the court rule?

(A) Deny the injunction, because the discrimination is by a private entity.

(B) Deny the injunction, because the scouts have a First Amendment right to associate.

(C) Grant the injunction, because the scouts are violating the Equal Protection Clause.

(D) Grant the injunction, because by providing the funds, Congress is promoting segregation.

Question 24

A defendant was charged with robbing and murdering a store clerk. A security camera had recorded the incident, clearly showing that the defendant shot the store clerk at point blank range, and that the defendant dropped the handgun immediately after shooting the store clerk. The gun, with the defendant's fingerprints on it, was recovered. Two eyewitnesses also were able to conclusively identify the defendant as the robber/murderer. After the defendant had been validly arrested, the police conducted a warrantless search of the defendant's home, and several items from the store were found. The items from the store were introduced at trial over the defendant's objection. The defendant was convicted after a nonjury trial. On appeal, the appellate court ruled that the warrantless search was unconstitutional under the circumstances.

Must the appellate court also overturn the defendant's conviction?

(A) No, because the error in admitting the evidence was harmless.

(B) No, because the tainted evidence would not have affected a judge's decision as much as that of a jury.

(C) Yes, because the police should have obtained a warrant before searching his home.

(D) Yes, because a violation of a constitutional right is never harmless.

Question 25

A landowner and his friend owned a tract of land as joint tenants with right of survivorship. The landowner executed a deed conveying his interest in the land to his grandson. The landowner gave the deed to his attorney with instructions to deliver it to the grandson upon the landowner's death. The grandson first learned of the deed at the landowner's funeral the following year. The next day, the grandson recorded the deed.

Who owns the land?

(A) The friend and the grandson, as joint tenants.

(B) The friend and the grandson, as tenants in common.

(C) The friend.

(D) The grandson.

Question 26

In lieu of a snack vending machine, a small company put candy bars into a box in the office kitchen. Using the honor system, employees were asked to put a dollar into an envelope in the box if they took out a candy bar. The office manager would periodically take the money collected in the envelope and use it to purchase new candy. One night while cleaning the kitchen, the company's night janitor impulsively took all the money from the envelope. His actions were recorded on the company's newly installed security camera. The janitor later admitted that he took the money to fund illegal dogfights.

Which of the following crimes did the janitor commit?

(A) Embezzlement, because the janitor took money that rightfully belonged to his employer.

(B) Larceny, because he did not intend to purchase replacement candy with the money.

(C) Robbery, because the theft was motivated by an underlying felony.

(D) No crime, because the money in the envelope was voluntarily abandoned by his co-workers.

Question 27

A state statute made it unlawful to sell soft drink beverages in any type of container except refundable glass containers. A violation of the statute constituted a misdemeanor, subjecting the violator to a fine of up to $1,000.

An out-of-state corporation manufacturing and selling aluminum soft drink cans in the above state brought suit in federal district court contesting the constitutionality of the statute as an undue burden on interstate commerce under the Commerce Clause.

The court should:

(A) Deny a hearing, because the Eleventh Amendment forbids the exercise of judicial power by the federal government in a suit prosecuted against any state by a citizen of another state.

(B) Deny the hearing, because only state courts may decide the constitutionality of state laws.

(C) Grant a hearing, because a federal question is involved.

(D) Grant a hearing, because jurisdiction exists on the basis of diversity.

Question 28

In a personal injury action, a doctor sat in court and listened to all of the evidence regarding the plaintiff's injuries. The defense subsequently calls that doctor to testify as to his opinion about whether the plaintiff's injuries will prevent the plaintiff from ever working again.

May the doctor testify to this?

(A) No, because he has not examined the plaintiff.

(B) No, because whether the plaintiff will work again is an issue for the jury.

(C) Yes, because an expert's opinion can be based on facts made known to him at the trial.

(D) Yes, because the doctor is not testifying as an expert because he has not examined the plaintiff.

Question 29

A patient complaining of pain in his side underwent a physical exam and x-rays, which showed that the patient had a small surgeon's clamp lodged in his left side. It had been left in the patient during an operation nine years previously. The patient brought an action against the hospital and the surgeon who operated on him, alleging negligence.

The hospital and the surgeon filed a general denial and a special affirmative defense alleging that the statute of limitations is a bar to the action. Recovery for negligence in the jurisdiction is limited to two years. The patient's attorney makes a motion to strike the special affirmative defense.

The motion should be:

(A) Granted, because the statute of limitations is tolled under the circumstances.

(B) Granted, because of the common law rule that one must know of a wrong in order to have a remedy.

(C) Denied, because the facts do not present an exception to the statute of limitations.

(D) Denied as to the surgeon, but granted as to the hospital.

Question 30

A minor entered a liquor store and asked the cashier to let him purchase a case of beer for a party even though he was underage. The cashier agreed as long as he paid double the retail price for the beer as compensation for the risks of the sale. As the cashier started to ring up the transaction, an undercover officer who overheard them intervened and arrested them. The state criminal code provides that it is a felony to knowingly provide alcohol to any person under the age of 21.

If the state follows the unilateral theory of conspiracy:

(A) The minor can be convicted of solicitation and the cashier can be convicted of conspiracy to violate the statute.

(B) Both the minor and the cashier can be convicted of conspiracy to violate the statute.

(C) The minor cannot be convicted of either solicitation or conspiracy, but the cashier can be convicted of conspiracy to violate the statute.

(D) The minor cannot be convicted of either solicitation or conspiracy, and the cashier cannot be convicted of conspiracy.

Question 31

A landowner died, validly devising her land "to my son for life, then to my brother and sister in fee simple." Without obtaining the brother and sister's consent, the son borrowed $20,000 from a bank, secured by a mortgage on the land, to make improvements to the land. Five years later, the son died. The brother and sister took possession of the land, but failed to make any mortgage payments.

If the bank sues to recover the delinquent payments, the court should render judgment for:

(A) The bank, because a life tenant is obligated to make repairs.

(B) The bank, because the remaindermen are obligated to pay the principal of a debt.

(C) The brother and sister, because the son committed ameliorative waste.

(D) The brother and sister, because the mortgage does not encumber the fee simple.

Question 32

A state passed a law providing that legislative staff members in the state legislature were to receive an hourly wage that was less than the federal minimum wage. A legislative staff member filed suit in federal court challenging this state law.

Which of the following is the strongest argument in support of the staff member's constitutional challenge?

(A) Congress may extend federal minimum wage requirements to legislative staff members by virtue of the Necessary and Proper Clause.

(B) The minimum wage law applies to private sector employees as well as state employees.

(C) Congress may extend federal minimum wage requirements to state legislative staff members as a means of guaranteeing a republican form of government.

(D) Congress has plenary power to extend federal minimum wage requirements under the General Welfare Clause.

Question 33

The father of a young child whose life was saved by doctors at a hospital emergency room called the president of the hospital and told her that he will donate $50,000 to the hospital, payable in 90 days, in consideration of the doctors' saving his child's life. The president recognized the father's name as a wealthy philanthropist who had donated generously to other worthy causes, and accepted the offer. The president promptly informed the hospital's board of directors of the father's offer and her acceptance of the offer. The board approved the purchase of a new respirator for $50,000 and authorized the president to enter into a written contract with a medical devices company to make the purchase, which she did. Once the child recovered, the father changed his mind and refused to give the hospital the $50,000.

If the hospital sues the father, what would the hospital's best theory be to recover the $50,000?

(A) The father's offer was supported by consideration.

(B) The father was estopped from not performing under a theory of detrimental reliance.

(C) The father's offer constituted fraud in the inducement.

(D) The terms of the father's offer were definite and certain.

Question 34

The plaintiff was injured when she slipped at the defendant restaurant. The defense attorney asked the manager on duty at the time of the incident to prepare a report of the accident. This report was given to the defense attorney prior to trial. During discovery, the plaintiff demands that a copy of the report be produced.

Will the court order the defendant to produce the report?

(A) Yes, because business reports are not privileged.

(B) Yes, because it is the best evidence.

(C) No, because it is covered by the attorney-client privilege.

(D) No, because it is hearsay.

Question 35

An attorney won a large medical malpractice verdict against a doctor for a botched liposuction procedure performed on a patient. The patient was unaware that the doctor was board-certified only in dermatology but not in plastic surgery. In a televised interview in which he discussed the trial, the attorney stated that "doctors who are not board-certified need to notify their patients regarding their true qualifications." The doctor brought a defamation action against the attorney based on the statement.

Who will prevail?

(A) The attorney, because the attorney's statement is related to judicial proceedings and thus is privileged.

(B) The attorney, because the doctor was not board-certified in plastic surgery.

(C) The doctor, because he was board-certified in dermatology.

(D) The doctor, because the statement clearly referred to him.

Question 36

Congress adopted a law granting a state university $2.5 million to study the properties of snowflakes. An outraged taxpayer filed suit to challenge the appropriation.

Which of the following is the best argument against this challenge?

(A) The legislation is a valid exercise of the federal taxing and spending powers.

(B) The federal court lacks jurisdiction to enjoin such expenditures voted by Congress, under the doctrine of separation of powers.

(C) The taxpayer lacks standing to challenge the expenditure.

(D) There is no diversity in this suit because the spending appropriation being challenged is federal, and the plaintiff is a citizen of the United States.

Question 37

A carjacker pulled a gun on a motorist at a stoplight, intending to force her out of her car so he could steal it. The motorist, however, was carrying a gun and shot the carjacker, killing him. The motorist was charged with violation of a concealed weapons statute, a felony in the jurisdiction, and with common law murder.

Assuming that the motorist has committed a felony with regard to the gun, will she be found guilty of murder?

(A) Yes, because one cannot use deadly force in defense of property.

(B) Yes, because the defendant committed a felony by carrying the handgun.

(C) No, because one may use deadly force in defense of property.

(D) No, because she was defending herself against an imminent threat of deadly force.

Question 38

A homeowner lived next door to a vacant lot owned by another neighbor. From the time the homeowner purchased his own property, he told other people that he owned the vacant lot. The homeowner had an underground dog fence installed under the vacant lot without the neighbor's knowledge. The homeowner also mowed the vacant lot regularly in the summer. When he had landscaping services performed on his own property, the landscapers dug up vegetation beds, which extended three feet into the neighbor's lot. After the statutory period for bringing a trespass action had passed, the homeowner brought an action to quiet title, claiming ownership of the vacant lot.

Which of the following additional facts, if true, would be most helpful to the homeowner's case?

(A) One of the people that the homeowner often told about owning the vacant lot was the neighbor herself.

(B) The neighbor occasionally saw the homeowner's dog on the vacant lot, but never demanded that the homeowner keep the dog in the homeowner's yard.

(C) The vegetation beds continued to exist with the same dimensions, and were regularly maintained by the homeowner, for the entire statutory period.

(D) When he told people that he owned the vacant lot, the homeowner believed that it was true.

Question 39

In litigation over whether a holographic will and codicil were prepared by the testator, the defendant, in a challenge to the validity of the instruments, calls the testator's former business partner to testify that he has seen the testator's handwriting on many business documents and that the handwriting on the will and codicil is that of the testator. The plaintiff objects to the testimony of the business partner.

How should the court rule?

(A) The testimony is inadmissible because the witness has not been qualified as a handwriting expert.

(B) The testimony is inadmissible because a proper foundation has not been laid.

(C) The testimony is admissible because the witness is familiar with the testator's handwriting.

(D) The testimony is admissible because the witness is not interested in the outcome of the case and therefore is competent to testify.

Question 40

A recent college graduate landed her dream job teaching kindergarten at the same elementary school she had attended as a child. The woman's contract provided that she would be paid $40,000 for the school year, and that she could only be fired for just cause. Days before the woman was to begin teaching, the school's principal fired the woman, without cause, so that she could hire her cousin for the job instead. The woman submitted her resume to an employment agency, but was so depressed over the loss of her dream job that she turned down another school's offer for a similar job paying a $30,000 salary, and instead spent the rest of the school year miserably unemployed.

If the woman successfully sues the school for breach of contract, how much can she recover?

(A) $40,000, her full contract salary.

(B) $30,000, the going rate for other teacher positions in the area.

(C) $10,000, the difference between her contract salary and the salary of other position she was offered.

(D) Nothing, because the woman failed to mitigate her damages.

Question 41

A driver picked up his cousin and his best friend to go to a concert. The friend sat in the front seat, and the cousin sat in back. On the way to the concert, the friend pulled out a water pipe with which to smoke marijuana. He handed it to the driver, and then grabbed the steering wheel in order to steer the vehicle while the driver lit up the water pipe. The driver continued to operate the brake and gas pedals with his feet. As the driver smoked the water pipe, the steering wheel slipped from the friend's hand, and the car smashed into a tree. The cousin in the back seat was injured, incurring a broken wrist and a broken ankle. She sued both the driver and the friend for damages. Following a trial, the jury found the driver 60% negligent and the friend 40% negligent, and awarded the cousin a total of $10,000 for medical expenses and $100,000 for pain and suffering. Because the driver is insolvent, the cousin wants to collect all of the damages from the friend.

In the absence of a statute on the issue, may she do so?

(A) No, because tortfeasor liability is proportional to fault in the case of noneconomic damages.

(B) No, because the driver and the friend did not act in concert.

(C) Yes, because the injuries to the cousin are divisible.

(D) Yes, because the friend is jointly and severally liable.

Question 42

During the defendant's trial for embezzlement, the defense calls a witness to testify as to the defendant's reputation for honesty and veracity. The prosecution objects.

Should the court allow the testimony?

(A) Yes, because the prosecution put the defendant's character for truthfulness in issue by filing charges against him.

(B) Yes, because it is admissible character evidence.

(C) No, because a party cannot bolster the testimony of his witness until he has been impeached.

(D) No, because the evidence is inadmissible hearsay.

Question 43

A mother died, bequeathing all of her property to a trustee "to pay the income to my husband for life, and to distribute the principal to my son and daughter if they graduate from college. If they do not graduate from college, then the principal shall be distributed to charity." Subsequently, the son and the daughter graduated from college.

Upon their graduation from college, the interests of the son and the daughter in the trust principal would be classified as:

(A) Tenants in common to a vested remainder.

(B) Joint tenants to a vested remainder.

(C) Tenants in common to a fee simple absolute.

(D) Tenants by the entirety to a fee simple absolute.

Question 44

Citing traffic concerns, a city passed an ordinance prohibiting residents from holding meetings in their homes with more than 15 persons unrelated to the resident. A resident of the city who belonged to a religious group with 50 members allowed the group to hold weekly services at his home. Between 30 and 40 people attended meetings at the resident's home each week. A neighbor of the resident who was upset by the number of cars parked in front of her home on the day of the services contacted the police. Police officers investigated and the resident admitted that he was holding services in his home in violation of the ordinance. When he refused the officers' requests to cease holding such services, they issued him a citation.

At his trial on the citation, how should the court rule on the resident's claim that application of the ordinance to him violates his right to the free exercise of religion?

(A) The ordinance is unconstitutional as applied to the resident because it does not include a religious exemption.

(B) The ordinance is unconstitutional as applied to the resident because traffic concerns are not compelling interests that justify an interference with religion.

(C) The statute is constitutional as applied to the resident because the constitution does not protect religious practices, only religious beliefs.

(D) The statute is constitutional as applied to the resident because the burden on his religion was incidental.

Question 45

The police obtained a valid arrest warrant for the defendant. A reliable informant told the police that the defendant was staying at a friend's house until "the heat was off." Without having obtained a search warrant, the police went to the friend's house, knocked on the door, and asked the friend if the defendant was there. The friend replied that the defendant had been staying at the house for a few days but had left a few hours ago. The police pushed open the door and began searching for the defendant. They found him hiding in a closet and arrested him.

Is the arrest valid?

(A) No, because a search warrant was required.

(B) No, because one cannot be arrested at the third party's home.

(C) Yes, because the defendant has standing to complain about the search of his friend's home.

(D) Yes, because the police had a valid arrest warrant.

Question 46

A landowner conveyed his land to his wife, son, and daughter "as joint tenants with right of survivorship." The daughter then conveyed her interest to a friend. The wife subsequently executed a will devising her interest to the daughter. Then the son mortgaged his interest to a lender, who promptly and properly recorded the mortgage. The wife died, then the daughter's friend died, leaving a will that bequeathed her entire estate to the daughter. The daughter and the son survived.

If the jurisdiction follows the title theory, who owns what interest in the land?

(A) The lender owns the fee simple.

(B) The lender and the daughter own unequal shares as tenants in common.

(C) The son and the daughter own unequal shares as tenants in common.

(D) The son and the daughter own equal shares as joint tenants.

Question 47

A student started a small fire in a trash can in the men's room at his university. His plan was to set off the school's fire alarms so that he could break into the computer lab and steal a laptop computer while the building was being evacuated. The student was stopped after he had set the fire and was attempting to smash in the glass on the computer lab door. The fire was quickly extinguished and no serious damage was done to the building by the fire beyond some charring on the walls in one stall of the men's room. A statute in the jurisdiction extends the crime of arson to buildings other than dwellings.

Which of the following best describes the crimes of which the student could be properly convicted?

(A) Larceny only.

(B) Larceny and attempted arson.

(C) Attempted larceny and arson.

(D) Arson only.

Question 48

A small business owner decided to retire, so she offered her long-time employee a chance to buy the business for $1 million. She promised in writing to keep the offer open to him for 90 days and to give him enough time to secure financing once he accepted the offer. Over the next few days, the employee cashed out all his retirement accounts and took a second mortgage on his home to raise the funds to purchase the business. When he approached the business owner to discuss the details of the sale, she said that she changed her mind and was revoking her offer because she did not want to retire after all.

Was the owner's revocation of her offer proper?

(A) Yes, because it was an offer that could be revoked at will.

(B) No, because the owner created an option contract by promising to keep the offer open for 90 days.

(C) No, because the employee detrimentally relied on the offer.

(D) No, because the offer constitutes a merchant's firm offer.

Question 49

In a lawsuit over ownership of stereo equipment between two roommates, the plaintiff testified that he purchased the equipment one year ago for his DJ business. The defendant offers the testimony of a clerk at the electronics store where the equipment was purchased. The clerk testifies that she remembers that the sale of the equipment occurred 10 months ago, not one year ago, because the purchase order was signed with such a distinctive signature. However, she cannot remember whether it was purchased by the defendant or the plaintiff.

If the plaintiff objects to this testimony, should the trial court admit it?

(A) Yes, because the purchase order is a past recollection recorded.

(B) Yes, because the purchase order is a business record.

(C) No, because the date of purchase is a collateral matter.

(D) No, because the content of the purchase order is hearsay not within any exception.

Question 50

An accountant employed by the Federal Communications Commission was offended by various jokes and cartoons that employees would post in the office cafeteria. The Commission did not have any rules regarding what employees could post in the cafeteria, and none of the cartoons were pornographic or harassing. Nevertheless, the accountant lodged a number of complaints with his supervisor that went unheeded. Finally, the accountant posted his own notice chastising the hypocrisy and immorality of the agency for allowing such cartoons when it was charged with ensuring a standard of decency on the public airwaves. The notice prompted a great deal of debate among employees and a great deal of displeasure on the part of the accountant's supervisor, particularly after it was posted on another employee's blog and received some media attention. A labor contract between the agency and the clerical workers union contained a policy providing for termination of union employees only for certain specified grounds, but the accountant was not a member of the union and was not covered by the policy or any other employment agreement.

Which of the following statements is most accurate regarding the agency's right to dismiss the accountant?

(A) The accountant has a liberty interest in the exercise of his First Amendment rights that entitles him to a hearing to contest the grounds of his dismissal.

(B) The accountant has a property interest as a public employee that precludes him from being fired without notice and an opportunity to respond.

(C) The accountant has no right to a hearing because his statements were not an expression of views on public issues.

(D) The accountant has both a liberty interest and a property interest tha entitles him to a pre-termination evidentiary hearing.

MIXED SUBJECT SET 8 SUBJECT GUIDE

1. Criminal Law
2. Evidence
3. Contracts
4. Real Property
5. Constitutional Law
6. Torts
7. Contracts
8. Real Property
9. Evidence
10. Criminal Law
11. Real Property
12. Contracts
13. Evidence
14. Constitutional Law
15. Criminal Law
16. Real Property
17. Torts
18. Evidence
19. Constitutional Law
20. Contracts
21. Real Property
22. Evidence
23. Constitutional Law
24. Criminal Law
25. Real Property
26. Criminal Law
27. Constitutional Law
28. Evidence
29. Torts
30. Criminal Law
31. Real Property
32. Constitutional Law
33. Contracts
34. Evidence
35. Torts
36. Constitutional Law
37. Criminal Law
38. Real Property
39. Evidence
40. Contracts
41. Torts
42. Evidence
43. Real Property
44. Constitutional Law
45. Criminal Law
46. Real Property
47. Criminal Law
48. Contracts
49. Evidence
50. Constitutional Law

MIXED SUBJECT ANSWERS - SET 8

Answer to Question 1

(A) The police officers had the right to enter the building without a warrant because exigent circumstances existed as a result of the shooting. Like arrests, evidentiary searches and seizures must be reasonable to be valid under the Fourth Amendment. Reasonable usually means that the police must have obtained a warrant before conducting the search unless the situation falls into one of the six exceptions to the warrant requirement, one of which is an exception based on hot pursuit, evanescent evidence, or other emergencies. A shooting is deemed to create an emergency justifying a warrantless entry to search premises to preserve the life of a person thought to be on the premises and in immediate danger. Therefore, the officers had a right to enter the building without a warrant. Because the officers were legitimately on the premises, they had a right to seize all illegal items in plain view. Thus, (C) and (D) are wrong. (B) is wrong because the fact that the officers were acting in their official function is not enough to allow them to enter a building without a warrant.

Answer to Question 2

(A) The testimony is admissible to impeach the testimony of the defendant's spouse. The credibility of a witness can be impeached by showing that the witness has made prior statements that are inconsistent with some material part of her present testimony. Here, the friend is prepared to testify that the defendant's spouse stated that she had not been driving the car at the time of the incident, a fact that would be material to the allegations in the lawsuit and inconsistent with the spouse's trial testimony. Thus, the friend's testimony is admissible for impeachment purposes. (B) is incorrect. Extrinsic evidence of bias is not admissible unless a foundation has been laid—the witness must first be questioned about the facts that show bias on cross-examination. If the witness, on cross-examination, admits to the facts claimed to show bias, then the trial judge may allow the extrinsic evidence to be introduced. Here, nothing suggests that the spouse was cross-examined as to the facts tending to show bias; thus, this is an incorrect ground for admitting the testimony. (C) is incorrect because a witness ordinarily may be impeached by either cross-examination or extrinsic evidence. Here, the prosecution is seeking to impeach the defendant's spouse by extrinsic evidence of her prior inconsistent statement, and the evidence will be admissible for that purpose. (D) is incorrect because the opportunity to explain or deny the statement can be given subsequent to the friend's testimony; it does not need to be given prior to her testimony.

Answer to Question 3

(C) The grocery store can hold the child to the contract because food is a necessity and the child told the store manager that she had lost her lunch and needed the food. Although an elementary school-age child is a minor (the age of majority in most jurisdictions is 18), and minors lack the legal capacity to contract, there is an exception for necessities: A minor is bound to pay the reasonable value of necessities. Food being a necessity, the child would be bound to repay the grocery store for the lunch. (A) is wrong because the presence of a third party is not essential to enforce the contract. (B) is irrelevant. (D) is wrong because even though it is true that the contract did not have to be evidenced by a writing signed by the party to be charged to be valid—because the contract was not for the sale of goods valued at $500 or more—choice (D) does not address the child's minority, the issue on which this question turns.

Answer to Question 4

(D) The buyer's best argument would be that the deed is void because the son signed it. A valid deed requires a writing containing a description of the land and parties, words of intent, and the grantor's signature. Here, the signature on the deed was forged. A defective deed may be ***voidable***, which means that it would be set aside only if the property had not been conveyed to a bona fide purchaser, or it could be ***void***, meaning that the deed would be set aside regardless of the property having passed to a bona fide purchaser. Deeds obtained by means of, among other things, duress, undue influence, or mistake are considered voidable. Deeds that were forged, never delivered, or obtained by fraud in the factum are void. Here, although the father seems to have ratified the conveyance and the buyer was a bona fide purchaser, the deed is void because the signature was forged. (A) is incorrect. A deed obtained by duress would be merely voidable, and in any case, the pressure caused by rapidly dropping values is not the duress that is contemplated by the common law rule. Duress for voidability purposes means pressure that is brought by an individual or entity in order to procure the deed. (B) is incorrect. Although a deed must identify the parties, courts will presume that the person taking delivery is authorized to fill in the name of the grantee. In the absence of the son's forgery—*i.e.*, if the landowner had executed and handed the deed to the buyer—all the buyer would have had to do was fill in his name and the deed would be valid. (C) is incorrect because a recitation of the consideration for the conveyance is not required to make a deed valid.

Answer to Question 5

(C) The statute is a constitutional restriction on speech is a public forum. The conduct related to speech can be restricted through reasonable time, place, and manner regulations. To be reasonable, such a regulation must be content neutral and narrowly tailored to serve an important government interest, and leave open alternative channels of communication. The statute here does not have any content rules. The state administrator must issue the permits to the first 10 people or organizations who apply, regardless of message; the administrator has no discretion here. The statute also appears to be narrowly tailored to achieving the purpose of facilitating access to the capitol building, and it allows other ways of protesting (*e.g.,* standing more than 100 feet from the building). (A) is incorrect. If the purpose of the statute is to facilitate access to the building, a 10-permit limit seems reasonable; more than 10 people as close as 10 feet away from the capitol doors could impede access (and if the permit is issued to organizations, there may be even more than 10 people). (B) is incorrect for a similar reason. [*See, e.g.,* Hill v. Colorado (2000)—upholding a prohibition of approaching within eight feet of persons attempting to enter abortion facilities] (D) is incorrect; the rule is just the opposite. Capitol grounds and their walkways are traditional public forums.

Answer to Question 6

(D) Violation of the ordinance will not bar or reduce recovery by the younger brother. When an applicable statute establishes a duty of care, a tortfeasor's conduct will be governed by that statutory duty of care. Similarly, a plaintiff's contributory negligence may be established by his violation of a statute under the same principles. However, for the manufacturer to be able to assert the statute as a defense (to establish contributory negligence of the plaintiff), it will have to show that the statute was designed to prevent the type of harm that occurred. In all likelihood, the statute was intended to protect the hikers, horseback riders, and bicyclists who use the trails from injury caused by vehicles on the trails, and to protect the trails from being damaged by vehicles, rather than to prevent the type of accident that occurred here. Even if the statute were applicable, it was the older brother, not the younger brother, who violated the statute by operating the vehicle, and there is no basis for imputing the older brother's negligence to the younger brother. Hence, the violation of the statute would not bar or reduce recovery by the younger brother. Thus, (A) is wrong. (B) is wrong. Even if it were shown that he knew of the ordinance, it would not bar his recovery because it is inapplicable here, as discussed above. (C) is wrong because there are no facts to show that the prohibition against vehicular traffic was limited to the hours the park was open.

Answer to Question 7

(C) The grandson was an intended beneficiary whose rights to collect the $10,000 had not vested before the contract was modified. Therefore, he could not enforce the agreement between his grandfather and the friend. Courts generally look to a number of factors in determining whether a third party is an intended beneficiary or an incidental beneficiary, and are more likely to find intended beneficiary status when: (i) the third party is expressly designated in the contract; (ii) performance is to be made directly to the third party; (iii) the third party has any rights under the contract; and (iv) the third party stands in such a relationship to the promisee that one could infer that the promisee wished to make an agreement for the third party's benefit. If the court determines that a third party is an intended beneficiary, it must then decide whether his rights have vested, which is necessary to enforce the contract. Vesting occurs when the beneficiary: (i) manifests assent to the promise in a manner invited or requested by the parties; (ii) brings suit to enforce the promise; or (iii) materially changes position in justifiable reliance on the promise. Here, the grandson was an intended beneficiary because he was expressly designated in the contract, repayment of the loan was to be made directly to him, and he had a relationship with his grandfather (*i.e.,* the promisee) that would lead one to infer that the grandfather wished to make the agreement for his grandson's benefit. However, the grandson's rights had not vested because neither his grandfather nor the friend told him of the arrangement, so he could not have manifested assent to it; he did not bring suit to enforce the promise prior to the modification of the contract; and he did not materially change his position in justifiable reliance on the promise, because he did not know about the agreement between the parties when he bought the car. Thus, (C) is correct and (B) is incorrect. (A) is incorrect because although the grandson was indeed an intended beneficiary of the contract, that alone would not be enough to enforce the contract where his rights had not vested prior to the contract's modification. (D) is incorrect because the general rule regarding the vesting of rights in a third party applies to a donee beneficiary (*i.e.,* a third party in a contract in which the promisee's primary intent in contracting is to confer a gift on the third party) as well as to a creditor beneficiary, so long as he is an intended beneficiary to the contract.

Answer to Question 8

(C) The granddaughter will win because she has a profit. A profit is a nonpossessory interest in land, allowing the grantee to enter on the land and remove resources of the land, in this case, fish and game. Moreover, the profit can be conveyed from the original grantee to a third party, as it was here from the neighbor to her granddaughter. A profit can be terminated in one of several ways, such as by abandonment or misuse, but the facts here do not indicate that termination has occurred. (D) is incorrect. Although the warranty deed used the word "privilege" to describe the interest that was being conveyed, the additional use of the words "covenant" and "shall run with the land" evidences an intent on the part of the original landowner to create more than a bare license to hunt and fish. Otherwise, such a license would have been revocable at the will of the landowner, and would have been extinguished once the neighbor conveyed her lot to her granddaughter. (A) is not as good an answer as (C). Although easements and profits are similar, an easement is an interest allowing the holder to use the land, while a profit specifically allows the holder to remove resources. An easement would not have included the right to hunt and fish on the builder's land. (B) is incorrect, because an irrevocable license requires the holder to have a privilege, in reliance on which she has invested substantial moneys or labor. That is not the situation under these facts.

Answer to Question 9

(B) The objection should be sustained because the testimony of the witness is irrelevant. Generally, a defendant may introduce evidence of his good character to show his innocence of the alleged crime. However, the evidence must be relevant; *i.e.*, it must have some tendency to make the existence of any fact that is of consequence to the determination of an action more probable than it would be without the evidence. Here, the defendant is charged with arson and there is nothing to indicate that the defendant's honesty is at issue. Therefore, the witness's testimony is inadmissible because it is irrelevant. (A) is incorrect. Hearsay is an out-of-court statement offered to prove the truth of the matter asserted. However, reputation of a person's character in the community is an exception to the hearsay rule. Therefore, the witness's statements regarding the defendant's reputation falls under that exception to the hearsay rule. (C) is incorrect because only the defendant can put his character at issue; the prosecution cannot initiate evidence of the defendant's character. Furthermore, filing criminal charges against a person does not put his character at issue. (D) is incorrect because reputation evidence is admissible to establish a character trait only when the trait sought to be established is pertinent to the crime charged. Here, the defendant's reputation for honesty and veracity is not pertinent to the crime of arson.

Answer to Question 10

(C) The defendant should not be convicted of battery. Battery is a general intent crime that can be established with a mental state of recklessness. Additionally, all crimes require a voluntary act on the part of the actor. Here, the epileptic seizure would negate both the voluntary act and the culpable mental state. Thus, (C) is the correct answer. (A) and (B) are wrong. Although (A) correctly states that even a light punch is an offensive touching, it does not take into consideration that the act must be voluntary. Similarly, (B) correctly identifies battery as a general intent crime, but it too does not take into consideration the requirement of a voluntary act. (D) is wrong because a physical injury (or any injury at all) is not required for battery. Any offensive touching suffices.

Answer to Question 11

(B) The bakery's right to use the driveway is an easement appurtenant. An easement is deemed appurtenant when the right of special use benefits the holder of the easement in its physical use or enjoyment of another tract of land. For an easement appurtenant to exist, there must be two tracts of land: the dominant tenement has the benefit of the easement, and the servient tenement is subject to the easement right. Here, the bakery's easement is appurtenant because its use and enjoyment of the western parcel is benefited by the right to use the driveway; thus, the easement is appurtenant. (A) is incorrect because an easement in gross is acquired independent of the ownership and enjoyment of another tract of land; there is no dominant tenement. (C) and (D) are incorrect because the bakery's easement is ***in writing*** and is therefore express rather than implied. An easement by necessity is created by implied grant or reservation when the owner of a tract of land sells a part of the tract and by this division deprives one lot of access to a public road or utility line. An easement implied from an existing use (quasi-easement) exists if, prior to the time a tract is divided, a use exists on the "servient part" that is reasonably necessary for the enjoyment of the "dominant part" and the parties intended the use to continue after division of the property. Here, although the western and eastern parcels were once a unified tract of land, there is no need to resort to an implied easement because the coffee shop expressly granted the bakery an easement in the driveway.

Answer to Question 12

(A) Performance of a preexisting legal duty does not constitute consideration sufficient to support a contract. Even the slightest change in the consideration given by the promisee will suffice to overcome the preexisting legal duty rule. Here, absolutely no new or different consideration was given by the builder. Thus, (A) is correct. (B), (C), and (D) are incorrect. (B) is incorrect because this was not a one-sided bargain where one of the parties to the contract had substantially superior bargaining power and could dictate the terms of the contract to the other party with inferior bargaining power. The wealthy landowner was undoubtedly a sophisticated shopper and could certainly have chosen another builder to do the job. Thus, this is not a case of unconscionability. (C) is incorrect because it is immaterial whether the Statute of Frauds is satisfied if there is, as here, a failure of consideration. (D) is incorrect. The fact that the modification was made in good faith may be relevant in a contract for the sale of goods because the U.C.C. permits modifications without consideration, but that rule is not applicable here.

Answer to Question 13

(A) The court should rule that the testimony is admissible as substantive, nonhearsay evidence. Hearsay is an out-of-court statement offered to prove the truth of the matter asserted, and is inadmissible unless it falls within an exception to the hearsay rule. However, admissions by a party-opponent are admissible nonhearsay. An admission is any statement made or act done that amounts to a prior acknowledgment of one of the facts at issue. An admission is admissible if it was made by an agent of a party with authority to speak on behalf of the party. Here, the bakery's manager, an agent of the bakery, admitted during the preliminary hearing that the bakery's employee was at fault for the fire. This is an admission by an agent of a party and is admissible nonhearsay. Therefore, (A) is correct and (D) is incorrect. (B) is incorrect. Under the former testimony exception to the hearsay rule, the testimony of a now unavailable witness given at another hearing is admissible in a subsequent trial if there is a sufficient similarity of parties and issues so as to provide sufficient opportunity for cross-examination. As discussed, the testimony of the court reporter is not hearsay and the exception does not apply. However, even if the testimony were hearsay, the former testimony exception would still not apply because the criminal charges against the gang member are not related to the civil suit between the plaintiff and defendant, and there was never any opportunity to cross-examine the manager as to his statement. (C) is incorrect because the best evidence rule applies only when the material contents of a document are sought to be proved. The rule does not apply to these facts because the manager's testimony exists independently of the transcript.

Answer to Question 14

(D) The factors articulated by the *Lemon* case are most relevant. The Establishment Clause restricts government action respecting the establishment of religion. If government takes an action that tends toward the establishment of religion and the action does not prefer one religious sect over another, the determination of whether the action is valid generally is made under the *Lemon* test.

The action will be upheld only if it has a secular purpose, its primary effect neither advances nor inhibits religion, and it does not produce excessive government entanglement with religion. (A) and (B) are incorrect because they each involve factors affecting the validity of government action under the Free Exercise Clause. Under the Free Exercise Clause, government action that incidentally burdens religious practices (*i.e.,* laws of general application) are upheld despite the interference with the religious practice. Also, under the Free Exercise Clause, courts may question the sincerity of a litigant's beliefs, but not the truth of his beliefs. (C) is incorrect because it gives the factors that are used to assess an Establishment Clause claim involving a sect preference, and there is no sect preference here.

Answer to Question 15

(B) If the hitman was insane, the wife cannot be said to have conspired with him to commit the murder. A conspiracy consists of: (i) an agreement between two or more persons; (ii) an intent to enter into an agreement; and (iii) an intent to achieve the objective of the agreement. The parties must agree to accomplish the same objective by mutual action. This agreement requires a meeting of at least two "guilty minds"; *i.e.,* two persons who are actually committing themselves to the scheme. If the hitman was insane, then he lacked the capacity to intentionally enter into an agreement to kill the husband and to intend to achieve the murder. Under this circumstance, the wife was the only one who was actually committed to the crime and who intended to bring it about. Because there was no meeting of the wife's "guilty mind" with at least one other, the wife cannot be convicted of conspiracy under the common law rule. (A) is incorrect because a defendant can be tried and convicted of both conspiracy and the crime she commits pursuant to the conspiracy (here, attempted murder). (C) is incorrect because a conviction of conspiracy does not require that all parties be tried and convicted. While an ***acquittal*** of all persons with whom a person is alleged to have conspired precludes conviction of the remaining defendant, that is not the case here. The hitman was not acquitted. Also, note that a state's decision to discontinue prosecution would not be deemed to be an acquittal, and thus most likely a state's ***inability*** to prosecute because of a co-conspirator's death would not be an acquittal. (D) is incorrect for two reasons: (i) withdrawal from a conspiracy is not a defense to a charge of conspiracy, and (ii) withdrawal is a defense to ***subsequent crimes*** committed by other members of the conspiracy only if the withdrawing party performs an affirmative act notifying all members of the conspiracy in time for them to have the opportunity to abandon their plans. Here, the wife notified the priest, but took no further action to thwart the conspiracy. Thus, she has no defense to the conspiracy, and it is unlikely that merely telling a priest would be a sufficient withdrawal as to subsequent crimes.

Answer to Question 16

(A) The friend and the daughter own the home as co-tenants. A joint tenancy is an estate between two or more co-tenants who have a right of survivorship—when one joint tenant dies, the property is freed from her concurrent interest and the survivor or survivors retain an undivided right in the property. An inter vivos conveyance by one joint tenant of his undivided interest destroys the joint tenancy so that the transferee takes the interest as a tenant in common and not as a joint tenant. Here, when the brother conveyed his interest to the friend, the joint tenancy between the brother and the sister was severed. At that point, the friend and the sister held title to the home as tenants in common. The adopted daughter then inherited the sister's interest upon the sister's death. Because delivery of a deed cannot be canceled, the friend's return and subsequent destruction of his deed has no effect. Thus, (A) is correct and (C) is incorrect. (B) is incorrect because the brother has transferred his interest to the friend. As stated above, the destruction of the friend's deed has no effect on his interest. For the brother to have his interest back, the friend would have to reconvey by deed to him. (D) is incorrect because when the brother conveyed his interest to the friend, the joint tenancy was severed and the interest became a tenancy in common. Because a tenancy in common has no right of survivorship, when the sister died, her interest passed to her daughter as her heir.

Answer to Question 17

(B) Res ipsa loquitur will be most helpful against the designer. Res ipsa loquitur means the thing speaks for itself. It is appropriate in situations where an injury does not usually occur unless someone was negligent and the plaintiff does not know which of the defendants caused the injury. While res ipsa loquitur is not always available where more than one person may have been in control of the instrumentality causing the injury, it is available in a case where a particular defendant had the power of control over the site of the injury. Even if the homeowner does not know why the deck collapsed, the deck's designer, who was supervising the construction, would be responsible and res ipsa loquitur could be used. (A) is not correct because the doctrine of respondeat superior imposes vicarious liability on an employer for the tortious conduct of its employee. That doctrine would be helpful against the building company for any negligence by its employees, but not against the designer because the workers were not the designer's employees. (C) and (D) are incorrect because the doctrines of contribution and indemnity pertain to how the responsibility of the loss is apportioned or shifted among the defendants after the plaintiff has recovered his judgment. They are not relevant to the homeowner's recovery.

Answer to Question 18

(D) The testimony is inadmissible. A party cannot bolster the testimony of a witness until the witness has been impeached. Here, plaintiff's counsel is seeking to introduce the sister's prior statement, which is consistent with her in-court testimony, to prove she is telling the truth. The testimony is inadmissible for this purpose because the sister has not been impeached. Therefore, (D) is correct. (A) is incorrect. A prior consistent statement is admissible if offered to rebut a charge that a witness is lying. Here, the credibility of the sister has not been attacked; therefore, there is no justification for bolstering her credibility. (B) is incorrect. While the statement would not be hearsay if it is not being offered to prove the truth of the matter asserted, it is nevertheless inadmissible because it is improperly offered to bolster the credibility of the witness. (C) is incorrect. There is no indication that plaintiff's counsel asked any leading questions. Furthermore, leading questions are sometimes permitted on direct examination (*e.g.*, when the witness is hostile).

Answer to Question 19

(B) The woman must allege that she pays federal income taxes and that the use of federal funds in this manner is improper under Congress's taxing and spending power. In general, a taxpayer has no standing to challenge the expenditure of federal funds. The major exception to this rule is where the taxpayer alleges that the expenditure was enacted under Congress's taxing and spending power, and exceeds some specific limitation on that power, in particular the Establishment Clause. Here, by providing federal tax money to parochial schools, there may be excessive entanglement with religion and thus a violation of the Establishment Clause. Thus, the woman would have standing to contest this federal expenditure. The woman would not have to have children to make this challenge. However, she would have to be a taxpayer. Thus, (A), (C), and (D) are wrong.

Answer to Question 20

(C) Under the doctrine of substantial performance, contracts governed by the common law are enforceable despite minor breaches. The contract here—to build a manufacturing plant—is governed by the common law. In determining whether a breach is minor or substantial, courts look to whether the party received the substantial benefit of the bargain. Here, the manufacturer got a plant that was, perhaps, better than the one called for in the contract. Therefore, the contract will be enforceable under the doctrine of substantial performance. (A) is incorrect because the perfect tender doctrine applies only to contracts for the sale of goods—not to common law contracts. (B) is incorrect because the doctrine of waste is a property concept; it does not apply to contracts. Indeed, in contracts, a party can sue for nominal damages when, as here, a breach has not caused a monetary injury. Here the breach appears to have benefitted the manufacturer. (D) is incorrect because quasi-contract provides a remedy in some situations in which a contract fails (or is absent) and the defendant would be unjustly enriched as a result. The doctrine is not applicable here because, as discussed above, the contract will not fail due to a minor breach.

Answer to Question 21

(D) If the buyer prevails it will be because he is a bona fide purchaser. The jurisdiction's recording act is a notice statute. Under a notice statute, a subsequent bona fide purchaser (*i.e.*, a person who gives valuable consideration and has no actual, record, or inquiry notice of the prior instrument) prevails over a prior grantee who failed to record. Here, the developer failed to record its deed. Thus, the buyer will prevail if he is a bona fide purchaser. The buyer did not have actual notice of the developer's interest in the land, nor record notice of the developer's unrecorded deed. Because the land was still vacant, the buyer also did not have inquiry notice. Thus, assuming the buyer paid value for the land, he is a bona fide purchaser. (A) is wrong because the recording act is a notice statute. The buyer would prevail against the developer even if the buyer had not recorded (in contrast to the result under a race-notice statute). (B) is wrong because the developer's return of its deed does not affect its interest. The developer loses under the recording act because the buyer is a bona fide purchaser. (C) is a misstatement of law. A general warranty deed is one in which the grantor covenants against title defects created both by herself and all prior titleholders, while a quitclaim deed conveys whatever interest, if any, the grantor has in the property. Neither has priority over the other.

Answer to Question 22

(B) The question on cross-examination regarding the witness's honesty is an appropriate impeachment method. Under Federal Rule 608, a witness may be interrogated on cross-examination with respect to any act of misconduct that is probative of truthfulness (*i.e.*, demonstrates dishonesty). Lying on a job application would be such an act. (A) is incorrect because juvenile offenses are generally not admissible for impeachment purposes in civil cases (the judge has the discretion to admit such evidence in criminal cases). (C) is incorrect because the Federal Rules do not allow a conviction to be used to impeach if the pardon was based on innocence. (D) is incorrect because a record of an arrest cannot be used to impeach a witness—an actual conviction is required.

Answer to Question 23

(D) Under the Equal Protection provisions of the Due Process Clause of the Fifth Amendment, Congress may not engage in any activity that promotes segregation. Here, by providing funds to a scouting group that engages in segregation, Congress has violated the Due Process Clause of the Fifth Amendment, and this would thus be the strongest argument. (A) and (B) are incorrect because, while the discrimination might be by a private entity and members of private entities generally may associate with whom they like, by providing funding for the private entity, Congress is supporting discrimination in violation of the Fifth Amendment Due Process Clause. (C) is incorrect because the Constitution generally prohibits only action by the government. In some cases, private action might be considered state action (*e.g.*, where the government is entangled with the private action). It is unclear whether the scouts' actions here would be considered government action. In any case, the Equal Protection Clause would not apply against the federal government, making (D) a better answer choice.

Answer to Question 24

(A) The court need not overturn the conviction. A conviction will not necessarily be overturned merely because improperly obtained evidence was admitted at trial. Rather, the harmless error test applies, so a conviction can be upheld if the conviction would have resulted despite the admission of improperly obtained evidence. On appeal, the government bears the burden of showing beyond a reasonable doubt that the admission was harmless. In the instant case, there was plenty of other evidence—a security camera recording, eyewitnesses, and physical evidence recovered from the crime scene—that ties the defendant to the crime. Hence, the burden of proving harmless error beyond a reasonable doubt would be met under these facts. Thus, (A) is correct, and (C) is incorrect. (B) is incorrect because it implies that some lesser standard applies when the judge make findings of fact rather than a jury. The standard remains the same—the government must show, beyond a reasonable doubt, that the error was harmless. (D) is an overbroad and incorrect statement of the law.

Answer to Question 25

(C) The friend owns the land. A joint tenancy is a concurrent estate in land in which each co-tenant has an undivided right in the property and a right of survivorship—when one joint tenant dies, the property is freed of his concurrent interest and the survivor retains an undivided right in the property that is no longer subject to the interest of the deceased co-tenant. An inter vivos conveyance by one joint tenant, even a "secret" deed that is to take effect only upon the grantor's death, severs a joint tenancy. However, although acceptance (presumed or otherwise) usually "relates back" to the date of delivery of the deed in escrow, many courts refuse to relate back an acceptance where it would defeat the rights of intervening third parties, such as surviving joint tenants. Thus, the grantee's acceptance of the deed ***after*** the grantor's death does ***not*** relate back to defeat the right of survivorship. Here, the grandson did not accept the deed until after the landowner's death. In the meantime and because of that death, the friend's right to the whole property had accrued to her as the surviving joint tenant. Thus, the grandson has no interest in the land, and (A), (B), and (D) are incorrect. Note that if the landowner's conveyance had been effective, (B) rather than (A) would have been the correct answer. Upon severance of a joint tenancy by inter vivos conveyance, the new tenant holds as a tenant in common with the remaining joint tenant, and not as a joint tenant.

Answer to Question 26

(B) The janitor is guilty of larceny, which consists of the taking and carrying away of the tangible personal property of another by trespass, with intent to permanently deprive the person of his interest in the property. The janitor's actions meet this definition. (A) is wrong because the janitor was not the employee responsible for the candy money. Embezzlement requires the fraudulent conversion of property of another by a person in lawful possession of that property. Here the janitor was never in lawful possession of the money so it was not an act of embezzlement. (C) is also wrong. Motive is not what distinguishes larceny from robbery. Robbery is defined as a taking of personal property of another from the other's person or presence, by force or intimidation, with the intent to permanently deprive her of it. Robbery is essentially an aggravated form of larceny in which the taking is accomplished by force or threat of force. Here there was no force involved. (D) is wrong because, even though the employees were on their honor to contribute money for the candy, the money was not just abandoned by them. The money was exchanged for candy, originally purchased by the company, and thus belonged to the company at the time the janitor took it.

Answer to Question 27

(C) Federal district courts are courts of limited jurisdiction and only hear cases in which there is a federal question involved or those in which there is diversity of citizenship and the amount in controversy exceeds $75,000. In these facts, the company is alleging that the state statute violates the Commerce Clause by placing an undue burden on interstate commerce. Thus, a federal question based on the United States Constitution is involved here. (A) is wrong because the purpose of the Eleventh Amendment is to protect the sovereignty of a state by preventing lawsuits against that state being brought in a federal court; the appeal in this case deals only with the constitutionality of a state statute. (B) is wrong because federal courts may also decide whether state laws violate the United States Constitution. (D) is wrong under these facts; even if there is diversity of citizenship, there is no amount in controversy alleged in these facts.

Answer to Question 28

(C) The doctor may testify. An expert's opinion may be based on one or more of the following sources of information: (i) facts that he knows from his own observation, (ii) facts presented in evidence at the trial and submitted to the expert, or (iii) facts not in evidence that were supplied to the expert out of court and which are of a type reasonably relied upon by experts in the particular field in forming opinions on the subject. Here, the doctor's testimony will be based on facts presented in evidence at the trial. Thus, (C) is correct. (A) is incorrect because personal examination by the doctor is not required in order to provide expert testimony as to the plaintiff's injuries. (B) is incorrect because whether the plaintiff's injuries will prevent her from ever working again is an issue that requires specialized knowledge to assist the jury in its determination; it is not an issue left for the jury to ultimately decide. (D) is incorrect because the doctor's qualification as an expert is based on his specialized knowledge, skill, experience, etc. Personal examination of the plaintiff is not a prerequisite to testifying as an expert.

Answer to Question 29

(A) The motion by the patient's attorney should be granted, because the statute of limitations is tolled under the circumstances. The general rule in malpractice actions is that the patient must know of the injury before the statute of limitations begins to run. Here, the subsequent physical examination is the first indication of the negligence. The statute would begin to run only from the time of that examination, and would have been tolled until that point in time. Thus, (A) is correct and (C) is incorrect. (B) is incorrect because there is no established rule to that effect. (D) is incorrect because the tolling of the statute of limitations would apply to both the surgeon and the hospital.

Answer to Question 30

(C) The cashier can be convicted of conspiracy in a unilateral jurisdiction even though the minor can be convicted of neither solicitation nor conspiracy. Under the unilateral approach adopted by the Model Penal Code, the crime of conspiracy is shown by proof that the defendant agreed with another to commit a crime, even if the other person does not share the commitment, and does not require proof of an actual agreement between two or more persons. Thus, the fact that no other party to the conspiracy could be found guilty does not prevent the defendant from being convicted of conspiracy. Here, the fact that the minor is a member of the class that the statute was designed to protect prevents him from being found guilty of conspiracy. (B) is therefore incorrect. However, this fact has no bearing on the cashier's liability for conspiracy under the unilateral approach. Thus, (C) is correct and (D) is incorrect. (A) is incorrect because the crime of solicitation is treated the same as conspiracy. If the solicitor could not be guilty of the completed crime because of legislative intent to exempt him, he cannot be guilty of solicitation of the crime. Because the minor is a member of the class intended to be protected by the statute, he cannot be found guilty of soliciting the cashier to complete it.

Answer to Question 31

(D) The court should render judgment for the brother and sister because the mortgage does not encumber the fee simple. A life tenant is entitled to all the ordinary uses and profits of the land, which includes encumbering his own interest, but he cannot lawfully do any act that would injure the interests of the remaindermen. Permissive waste occurs when the life tenant allows the land to fall into disrepair or fails to take reasonable measures to protect the land. Although a life tenant is obligated to pay interest on any encumbrances of the fee simple estate to the extent of the income or profits from the land (or in their absence to the extent of the reasonable rental value of the land), he is liable for ***both*** principal and interest payments if the encumbrance is on the life estate alone. Here, because the son did not obtain the consent or joinder of the remainderman when he mortgaged the land, the mortgage attaches only to the life estate. Thus, the remaindermen (the brother and sister) are not liable for the mortgage payments. (A) is incorrect because the son made improvements rather than repairs to the land. Although a life tenant is obligated to preserve the land and structures in a reasonable state of repair, to the extent of the income or profits from the land (or in their absence to the extent of the reasonable rental value of the land), he is under no obligation to make permanent improvements on the land. (B) is incorrect because remaindermen are obligated to pay the principal of a debt only if the debt encumbers the entire fee simple estate. Here, only the life estate is encumbered. (C) is incorrect because ameliorative waste, which occurs when the use of the property is substantially changed but the change increases the value of the property, may have been an appropriate cause of action for the brother and sister to bring against the son for the improvements, but it does not affect the bank's rights.

Answer to Question 32

(B) The strongest argument is that the minimum wage law applies to both private sector and state employees. Generally, the Tenth Amendment provides that powers not delegated to the federal government are reserved to the states. Under the Tenth Amendment, the court will usually uphold federal legislation that applies both to the private sector and to state governments, but will generally not uphold attempts by Congress to regulate the states as states. Here, the federal minimum wage law applies to all private and government employers. Thus, it will be upheld. (C) is therefore incorrect because extending minimum wage laws to legislative staffers does not interfere with the Constitutional guarantee of a republican form of government. (A) is incorrect because the Necessary and Proper Clause alone does not furnish authorization for federal laws. Congress must be acting in the exercise of one of its express powers, and (A) ***only*** deals with the Necessary and Proper Clause. (D) is incorrect because the General Welfare Clause is a congressional ***taxing and spending*** authorization and is not related to minimum wage requirements.

Answer to Question 33

(B) The hospital's best theory to recover the $50,000 would be promissory estoppel (detrimental reliance). Under section 90 of the Second Restatement, a promise is enforceable, even without consideration, if the promisor reasonably expects to induce action or forbearance and such action or forbearance is in fact induced. (The remedy may be limited as justice requires.) Here, the father called the hospital's president and promised to donate $50,000 to the hospital. Based on that promise, and the president's knowledge that the father was a wealthy philanthropist who could make good on the promise and had donated generously to other worthy causes, the hospital's board of directors authorized the hospital president to purchase a new respirator for $50,000, which she did. The father should have reasonably expected to induce such action, and such action was in fact induced. Therefore, the father was estopped from not performing. (A) is incorrect because in most jurisdictions "past" or "moral" consideration is not sufficient consideration because it was not bargained for. If something was already given or performed before the promise was made, it will not satisfy the "bargain" requirement because it was not given in exchange for the promise. Here, the doctors had already saved the daughter's life when the father made his offer; the father's promise was not made to induce the doctors to act, nor did the doctors act to induce the father's promise. Thus, (A) is not correct. (C) is not correct because there is nothing in the facts to suggest that the father engaged in fraud in the inducement, *i.e.*, that he made his promise knowing he had no intention of keeping it; rather, he simply changed his mind. Fraud in the inducement occurs when one party induces another to enter into a contract by asserting information he knows to be untrue, and the innocent party justifiably relies on the fraudulent misrepresentation. In such cases, the contract is voidable by the innocent party. (D) is incorrect because, although it is true that the father's offer was definite and certain, there can still be no contract absent consideration.

Answer to Question 34

(C) The court will not order the defendant to produce the report. Communications between an attorney and client, made during professional consultation, are privileged from disclosure. A business report prepared as a communication from client to attorney is privileged. Here, the manager prepared the report at the request of the restaurant's attorney. As such, the report constitutes a privileged communication between an attorney and client and its production is not required. Thus, (C) is correct and (A) is incorrect. (B) is incorrect because the best evidence rule is inapplicable here. That rule requires that where the terms of a writing are material, the original or its duplicate must be produced. Here, the copy of the report would have the same effect as the original, but the report is privileged and therefore does not have to be produced. (D) is incorrect because a report may be discovered by the opposing party even if it contains hearsay.

Answer to Question 35

(B) The attorney will prevail. Defamation is actionable if the plaintiff proves defamatory language, "of or concerning" the plaintiff, publication by the defendant to a third person, and damage to the plaintiff's reputation. The statement at issue may be defamatory on its face, or the defamatory meaning may be established by additional facts (innuendo). In the present case, the doctor is alleging that the attorney implied that he failed to inform the patient that he was not board-certified when he did the surgery, making the bare statement, "Doctors who are not board-certified need to notify their patients regarding their true qualifications" defamatory by innuendo. However, the truth of the statement is a complete defense to a defamation action. Even though it is true that the doctor is board-certified in dermatology, the context in which the attorney made his statement was the interview concerning malpractice in a cosmetic surgery procedure, and the doctor did not have a board certification in plastic surgery. With all the additional facts considered, the attorney's statement is not actionable defamation. Therefore, (C) is incorrect. (A) is incorrect because, although the statement did concern a judicial proceeding, it was not made as part of the proceedings, and thus is not privileged. (D) is incorrect because, as explained above, the doctor also must show defamatory language, publication, and damage to reputation in order to establish a prima facie case for defamation, and the attorney can raise truth as a defense.

Answer to Question 36

(C) The best argument is that the taxpayer lacks standing. Generally, taxpayers lack standing to challenge federal appropriations. There is an exception for expenditures violating the Establishment Clause, but that is not the case here. (A) also is a good answer, but it is not as good as (C). (C) stops the case at its inception. While (A) correctly states that the spending measure here is a valid exercise of the federal police power, such an argument would be made later in the case. (B) is wrong because the doctrine of separation of powers does not prevent the courts from enjoining unconstitutional activities by Congress. (D) is wrong because the spending appropriation represents a federal question, so diversity is not required.

Answer to Question 37

(D) The motorist will not be guilty of murder because she acted in self-defense. At common law, murder is the unlawful killing of another human being with malice aforethought. Malice aforethought exists if the defendant: (i) intends to kill; (ii) intends to inflict great bodily injury; (iii) acts in reckless indifference to an unjustifiably high risk to human life; or (iv) intends to commit a felony. A person may use deadly force in self-defense if (i) she is without fault; (ii) she is confronted with unlawful force; and (iii) she is threatened with imminent death or great bodily injury. The majority rule is that there is no duty to retreat. Here, all three prongs for a valid self-defense claim are present. The defendant was without fault in creating the carjacking, and she was obviously confronted with unlawful force, in that the carjacker was pointing a gun at her. Such threatened force clearly is also "deadly" and "imminent." Thus, the defendant's killing was not "unlawful" as required by the definition for common law murder. (A) is incorrect because, although the majority rule is that a person may not use deadly force in defense of personal property, a person may use deadly force in self-defense. Here, the defendant was justified in using deadly force in self-defense, as explained above. (B) is also incorrect. The felony murder rule historically has been used to impute malice to the victim. As such, courts have imposed some limitations on the felony murder rule. Some courts will limit the felonies to "inherently dangerous" felonies, while others will require the felony to be dangerous as committed. Here, the felony of carrying a concealed handgun is not an inherently dangerous felony, in that the felony could be carried out without the resort to violence. Furthermore, there is no indication from the facts that the defendant used the concealed handgun in a dangerous manner. As a result, most courts probably would not convict the defendant of felony murder absent some unlawful misuse of the gun. This is especially true given that the defendant was acting in lawful self-defense. (C) is an incorrect statement of the law; deadly force generally may not be used in defense of property.

Answer to Question 38

(A) Telling the neighbor about owning the lot would be most helpful to the homeowner. Establishing title by adverse possession requires the possessor to show (i) actual and exclusive possession that is (ii) open and notorious, (iii) adverse, and (iv) continuous for the statutory period. Mowing the vacant lot regularly would be an act consistent with open and notorious possession. That along with the homeowner's communication of hostility—which means simply that the homeowner is possessing without the neighbor's permission—ought to establish open and notorious adverse possession. (B) is incorrect. The placement of the underground dog fence without the neighbor's knowledge means that the possession of the property is not open and notorious. That the homeowner's dog occasionally went over into the vacant lot does not result in open and notorious possession by the homeowner. (C) is incorrect, because constructive possession of part of a tract of land is sufficient to title to the whole only if there is reasonable proportion between the part actually possessed and the whole of the tract. Landscaping that crosses over a few feet into the vacant lot is not likely to rise to the level of possession of the whole. (D) is incorrect, because the state of mind of the homeowner is irrelevant in determining whether the possession is hostile. The only consideration is whether he was actually in possession without the true owner's permission.

Answer to Question 39

(C) The court will allow the witness to testify as to the testator's handwriting simply because he is familiar with it by virtue of his former business relationship with the testator. As long as such a foundation is laid to show familiarity with the handwriting, a lay opinion is permissible. Thus, because the witness became familiar with the testator's handwriting when they worked together, he will be permitted to testify that the handwriting on the instruments is that of the testator. (A) is incorrect because expert testimony is not required for handwriting identification. Because the witness's testimony is based on his previous familiarity with the testator's handwriting, it will be admissible as nonexpert opinion testimony. (B) is incorrect because a proper foundation has been laid. To lay a foundation for nonexpert opinion testimony, it must be shown that the witness had the opportunity to observe the event that forms the basis of the opinion. The defense has established that the witness was familiar with the testator's handwriting because he had seen it on various business documents. This is sufficient foundation for his testimony. (D) is incorrect because his interest in the outcome of the will is irrelevant to his competency as a witness (though it may affect the weight and credibility given to his testimony).

Answer to Question 40

(C) The woman can recover $10,000, the difference between her contract salary and the salary of the position she was offered. When there is a breach of an employment contract by the employer, the standard measure of the employee's damages is based on the full contract price. Thus, (B) is incorrect because damages are based on the contract price, not the going rate for the position in the area. However, under these facts, (A) is also incorrect. The nonbreaching party has a duty to mitigate her damages. In an employment contract, if the employer breaches, the employee is under a duty to use reasonable care in finding a position of the same kind, rank, and grade in the same locale. The position need not pay the exact same wage. Here, the woman did not mitigate her damages when she failed to accept similar employment offered by another school. When a party fails to mitigate, she will not be allowed to recover those damages that might have been avoided by mitigation after the breach. Even though the woman failed to mitigate her damages, this does not mean she is entitled to no relief as stated in (D). Had the woman taken the replacement position, her damages still would have been $10,000, so that is the amount she is entitled to recover.

Answer to Question 41

(D) The cousin can collect all of her damages from the friend. When two tortfeasors combine to proximately cause an indivisible injury to a plaintiff, the tortfeasors each will be jointly and severally liable for the entire injury. This means that each is liable to the plaintiff for the entire damage incurred. Here, the driver and his friend acted negligently and the cousin suffered injuries as a result; thus, she can recover all of her damages from the friend. (A) is incorrect. Some states have enacted statutes abolishing joint and several liability for pain and suffering damages; however, there is no such statute in this case. (B) is incorrect. While the driver and the friend may not have acted in concert (*i.e.*, by agreement), that is not necessary to create joint and several liability for an indivisible injury. It is enough that the negligence of the two tortfeasors combined to cause the plaintiff's injuries. (C) is incorrect because an injury can be considered divisible only if it is possible to identify the portion of injury that is caused by each defendant. In this case, the accident was a single occurrence that caused a single set of injuries to the cousin.

Answer to Question 42

(B) The defendant can put his character in issue by calling a witness to testify to his good reputation for the trait involved. Here, the defendant is offering the testimony of a witness as to his reputation for honesty and veracity, which is a trait directly in issue in his embezzlement charge. Therefore, the testimony should be allowed, and the prosecution will have the opportunity to rebut the testimony on cross-examination. (A) is incorrect because only the defendant can put his character in issue, and the filing of criminal charges does not have the effect of putting the defendant's character in issue. (C) is incorrect because there is no impeachment issue here and the defense is not attempting to bolster the testimony of its witness (which is generally done after the credibility of the witness is attacked on cross-examination), but rather to offer an opinion as to the defendant's character. (D) is incorrect because, to the extent that the witness's testimony is hearsay, it falls within the exception to the hearsay rule for reputation evidence of a person's character.

Answer to Question 43

(A) Upon their graduation, the interests of the son and the daughter in the trust principal would be classified as tenants in common to a vested remainder. A remainder is classified as contingent if its taking in possession is subject to a condition precedent. Here, because the condition precedent—that the son and the daughter graduate from college—has been satisfied, the son and the daughter's contingent remainder has "vested." Also, at common law, it was held that any conveyance to two or more persons was presumed to create a joint tenancy unless a contrary intention was clearly expressed. But today all courts hold that such a conveyance creates a tenancy in common. To create a joint tenancy, words such as "as joint tenants with right of survivorship" must normally be used to show the necessary intent. Thus, the son and the daughter are tenants in common to a vested remainder. (B) is therefore wrong. (C) is wrong because the son and the daughter's estate is in a remainder interest, not a fee simple absolute, because the facts do not indicate that the life tenant (the husband) has died. (D) is wrong for the same reason and, additionally, because a tenancy by the entirety can be held only by a husband and wife, which is not the case here.

Answer to Question 44

(D) The court should rule that the statute is constitutional as applied to the resident. The statute here raises a free exercise issue. The Free Exercise Clause provides that government shall not interfere with the free exercise of religion. However, the Supreme Court currently interprets this prohibition narrowly. States are permitted to adopt regulations that incidentally interfere with religious practice or belief. The Clause only prevents the states from targeting religious practice. Because the ordinance here applies to all meetings (not just religious meetings), and nothing in the facts suggests that the ordinance was adopted to prevent the resident or anyone else from holding a religious meeting in his home, the ordinance is valid. (A) is incorrect because the Supreme Court has held that laws of general application need not include an exemption for religious conduct. (B) is incorrect because it is based on the former test for free exercise questions—formerly, government action that interfered with religious practice was said to be justified only if it was necessary to achieve a compelling interest. As discussed above, that is no longer the test. (C) is incorrect because it is not true. Religious practices are protected, but only to the extent that government cannot prohibit conduct just because it is religious. [*See, e.g.,* Church of the Babalu Aye, Inc. v. Hialeah (1993)—city could not outlaw religious slaughter of chickens while allowing similar nonreligious slaughter]

Answer to Question 45

(A) The arrest is not valid because a search warrant was required. Absent exigent circumstances, the police executing an arrest warrant may not search for the subject of the warrant in the home of a third party without first obtaining a separate search warrant for the home. Thus, (A) is correct and (D) is incorrect. (B) is incorrect because it is too broad. A person can be arrested at the home of a third party, but the police generally cannot enter the third party's home without consent unless they have a search warrant for the home. (C) is incorrect because, as an overnight guest, the defendant does have standing to complain about the warrantless entry into the home.

Answer to Question 46

(B) The lender and the daughter own unequal shares as tenants in common. Creation of a joint tenancy requires four unities: (i) time (interests must vest at the same time); (ii) title (interests must be acquired by the same instrument); (iii) interest (interests must be of the same type and duration); and (iv) possession (interests must give identical rights to enjoyment). When property is held in joint tenancy by three or more joint tenants, a conveyance by one of them destroys the joint tenancy only as to the conveyor's interest. The other joint tenants continue to hold in joint tenancy as between themselves, while the grantee holds her interest as a tenant in common with them, because she does not share the unities of time or title with the joint tenants (*i.e.*, her interest vested at a different time and was acquired by a different instrument). Here, the wife, the son, and the daughter owned the property as joint tenants. When the daughter conveyed her interest to the friend, the joint tenancy was severed as to the daughter's interest. At that point, the wife and the son each held one-third interests as joint tenants because, as between themselves, the four unities were preserved. The friend did not share the unities of time or title with the wife and the son. Thus, the friend took a one-third interest as a tenant in common rather than as a joint tenant. Because this jurisdiction follows the title theory, the son's mortgage also severed the joint tenancy. The minority of states following the title theory regard a mortgage as an actual transfer of title to the property. Thus, a mortgage by one joint tenant transfers the legal title of the joint tenant to the mortgagee (the lender). This action destroys the unity of title and severs the joint tenancy. On the other hand, in a lien theory state (majority), a mortgage is considered a lien on title—one joint tenant's execution of a mortgage on his interest does not, by itself, sever a joint tenancy until default and foreclosure proceedings have been completed. Here, when the son executed the mortgage, title was transferred to the lender, severing the joint tenancy again. At that point, the wife, the lender, and the friend each held one-third interests ***as tenants in common*** because each interest was acquired at a different time and by a different title. An interest in a tenancy in common is freely alienable by inter vivos and testamentary transfer, is inheritable, and is subject to claims of the tenant's creditors. The only "unity" involved is possession: Each tenant is entitled to possession of the whole estate. Thus, when the wife died, her interest passed under her will to the daughter. Likewise, when the friend died, her interest passed to the daughter. Thus, the lender holds a one-third interest as a tenant in common with the daughter, who holds the remaining two-thirds interest. (A) is incorrect because the daughter also has an interest in the property (*see* above). When one joint tenant dies, the right of survivorship operates to free the property of her interest; the surviving joint tenants retain an undivided right in the property. Although a will is inoperative as to joint tenancy property because the decedent's rights in the property evaporate at the instant of death, a will may effectively dispose of an interest held in a tenancy in common, as discussed above. Here, although the wife executed her will while the property was still held in joint tenancy, a will is ambulatory (effective only at death), and at her death the wife held her interest as a tenant in common. Thus, it passed to the daughter under the will. (C) and (D) are incorrect because, as explained above, the son has no interest.

Answer to Question 47

(C) The student is guilty of the crime of arson and of attempted larceny. At common law, arson was defined as the malicious burning of the dwelling of another. The mens rea required for arson is malice, which is broader than the intent required for specific intent crimes. The defendant need not have intended to burn down the building; it is sufficient if he intended a burning that creates an obvious fire hazard to the building. Here, the student's intent was to set off the fire alarm so that the building would be evacuated. Nevertheless, he intended to start a fire with reckless disregard of a high risk that it would cause damage to the building. The risk or hazard is not that the building will burn down, merely that damage to the structure from a burning will occur. The "burning" required for arson does not require significant damage to the building; a charring of the combustible material is sufficient. Here, the wall of a stall in the men's room was charred. This satisfies the "burning" requirement. The common law requirement that the structure be a dwelling has been broadened by the statute in this question to include other buildings. Thus, the student's conduct satisfies all of the elements of the crime of arson. The student is also guilty of attempted larceny. Common law larceny requires a taking and carrying away of the personal property of another by trespass with intent to permanently deprive (or for an unreasonable time) the other of his interest in the property. Here, the student planned to take and carry away a laptop computer by trespass (*i.e.,* without permission) and with the intent to permanently deprive the university of it. However, he cannot be convicted of a completed larceny because he never actually took the laptop. (A) and (B) are therefore incorrect. At common law, the crime of attempted larceny required both a specific intent by the actor to commit a larceny and an act that put the defendant in close proximity to completing the crime. The Model Penal Code and most state criminal codes modify the "proximity" test for the act requirement, instead requiring an act that constitutes a "substantial step" towards commission of the crime. Here, the student intended to do what he did in order to commit a larceny for which he had the requisite intent. Also, he was apprehended after he set a fire to cause the building's evacuation and while he was smashing the glass on the computer lab door. Together, these acts satisfy the act requirement for attempt liability, regardless of which test is employed. Thus, the student is liable for attempted larceny and arson, making (C) correct and (D) incorrect.

Answer to Question 48

(A) The owner's revocation of her offer was proper because the offer could be revoked at will.

Generally, offers can be revoked at will by the offeror, even if she has promised not to revoke for a certain period of time. There are limitations on the offeror's power to revoke, but none of those exceptions apply in this case. (B) is incorrect because an option contract requires that the offeree give consideration for the promise by the offeror to keep the offer open, and no consideration is indicated by the facts. (C) is also incorrect. Detrimental reliance can limit an offeror's power to revoke where the offeror could reasonably expect that the offeree would rely to his detriment on the offer, and the offeree does so rely. However, this usually is limited to those situations in which the offeror would reasonably contemplate reliance by the offeree in using the offer before it is accepted; *e.g.*, when a general contractor uses a subcontractor's bid in making its own offer. Here, the offer itself included a promise by the owner to give the employee time to secure financing after the offer was accepted. Therefore, the owner had no reason to anticipate that the employee would take immediate steps to raise the purchase money before he even accepted the offer. (D) is incorrect because these facts are not an example of a merchant's firm offer. A merchant's firm offer does not apply to any offer by a merchant; it applies only to an offer under the U.C.C. for the sale of goods where a signed writing gives assurances that the offer will be held open.

Answer to Question 49

(C) Testimony as to the date of purchase should not be admitted because its minimal relevance is substantially outweighed by considerations of waste of time and confusion of the issues. The actual date of purchase has no bearing on the issue of ownership, but instead is offered to cast doubt on the plaintiff's credibility. However, when a witness makes a statement not directly relevant to the issues in the case, the rule against impeachment on a collateral matter bars his opponent from proving the statement untrue either by extrinsic evidence or by a prior inconsistent statement. As noted previously, the clerk's statement as to the date on which he purchased the panels is not directly relevant to any other issue in the case. Thus, (C) is correct. (A) is incorrect. The past recollection recorded exception to the hearsay rule permits a party to offer into evidence a writing made by a witness whose memory cannot be refreshed. The purpose of the writing would be to prove the facts contained therein to which the witness cannot testify due to insufficient memory. Here, the clerk has not stated that she has insufficient recollection of the events to which she is testifying, she is simply referring the purchase order due to the unusual signature. Additionally, the defense is not attempting to introduce the purchase order into evidence. Thus, the purchase order does not constitute a past recollection recorded. (B) is incorrect for the same reason. A record of any act, transaction, occurrence, or event is admissible as proof of that act, transaction, occurrence, or event if made in the regular course of business. Here, the purchase order is not being offered into evidence and a passing reference to it does not affect the clerk's testimony. (D) is incorrect because the clerk is not testifying to the content of the purchase order. Rather, she is simply testifying to the date of purchase from her own memory. Thus, the hearsay nature of the contents of the purchase order is not at issue.

Answer to Question 50

(A) If the accountant is fired, he has a right to a hearing to determine whether his First Amendment rights were violated by his dismissal. Under the Due Process Clause of the Fifth Amendment, a person has a liberty interest in the exercise of specific rights provided by the Constitution, including freedom of speech. A government employee may not be fired for expressing his views regarding public issues, but can be fired for speech that disrupts the employer's policies or undermines the employer's authority. Under the Court's expansive interpretation of what a public issue is in this context [*see* Rankin v. McPherson (1987)], the accountant's statement would probably qualify. At the very least, he can make enough of a showing that his termination violates his free speech rights to be entitled to a hearing on the issue under procedural due process principles. [*See* Givhan v. Western Line Consolidated School District (1979)] (B) is wrong because the accountant does not appear to have a property interest in his job. A public employee who is subject to removal only for "cause" has a property interest in his job and must be given notice of the charges against his that are to be the basis for his job termination, and a pretermination opportunity to respond to those charges. Here, however, the accountant did not have a property interest in his job. He could have been dismissed for no reason at all. He was not covered by the labor contract between the agency and its clerical workers, and there appears to be no other basis for him to claim an entitlement to continued employment. (C) is wrong because the accountant is entitled to a hearing as long as he can raise a prima facie claim that his speech, which was regarding an issue important to the perception of his agency, was on a public issue and therefore protected by the First Amendment. (D) is wrong for two reasons: As discussed above, the accountant does not have a property interest in his job. Also, due process does not necessarily entitle him to a pretermination evidentiary hearing; a post-termination evidentiary hearing is probably sufficient. [*See* Cleveland Board of Education v. Loudermill (1985)]

Released Multistate Questions and Analytical Answers

CONSTITUTIONAL LAW QUESTIONS

Question 1

A newly enacted criminal statute provides, in its entirety, "No person shall utter to another person in a public place any annoying, disturbing or unwelcome language." Smith followed an elderly woman for three blocks down a public street, yelling in her ear offensive four-letter words. The woman repeatedly asked Smith to leave her alone, but he refused.

In the subsequent prosecution of Smith, the first under this statute, Smith will:

(A) Not prevail.

(B) Prevail, because speech of the sort described here may not be punished by the state because of the First and Fourteenth Amendments.

(C) Prevail, because though his speech may be punished by the state, the state may not do so under this statute.

(D) Prevail, because the average user of a public street would think his speech/action here was amusing and ridiculous rather than "annoying," etc.

Question 2

Congressional legislation regulating the conditions for marriages and divorces would be most likely upheld if it:

(A) Applied only to marriages and divorces by members of the armed services.

(B) Applied only to marriages performed by federal judges and to divorces granted by federal courts.

(C) Implemented an executive agreement seeking to define basic human rights.

(D) Applied only to marriages and divorces in the District of Columbia.

Question 3

Assume for the purposes of this question that you are counsel to the state legislative committee that is responsible for real estate laws in your state. The committee wants you to draft legislation to make all restrictions on land use, imposed by deeds (now or hereafter recorded), unenforceable in the future so that public land-use planning through zoning will have exclusive control in matters of land use.

Which of the following is ***least*** likely to be a consideration in the drafting of such legislation?

(A) Compensation for property rights taken by public authority.

(B) Impairment of contract.

(C) Sovereign immunity.

(D) Police power.

Questions 4-6 are based on the following fact situation:

Congress provides by statute that any state that fails to prohibit automobile speeds of over 55 miles per hour on highways within the state shall be denied federal highway construction funding. The state of Atlantic, one of the richest and most highway-oriented states in the country, refuses to enact such a statute.

4. Which of the following potential plaintiffs is most likely to be able to obtain a judicial determination of the validity of this federal statute?

   (A) A taxpayer of the United States and the state of Atlantic who wants his state to get its fair share of his tax monies for highways, and fears that, if it does not, his state taxes will be increased to pay for the highway construction in the state of Atlantic that federal funds would have financed.

   (B) Contractors who have been awarded contracts by the state of Atlantic for specified highway construction projects, which contracts are contingent on payment to the state of the federal funds to which it would otherwise be entitled.

(C) An automobile owner who lives in the state of Atlantic and regularly uses its highway system.

(D) An organization dedicated to keeping the federal government within the powers granted it by the Constitution.

5. The best argument that can be made in support of the constitutionality of this federal statute is that:

(A) The states conceded their authority over highways to the national government when the states accepted federal grants to help finance the highways.

(B) The federal government can regulate the use of state highways without limitation because the federal government paid for most of their construction costs.

(C) Reasonable legislators could believe that the 55 mile-per-hour speed limit will ensure that the federal money spent on highways results in greater benefit than harm to the public.

(D) A recent public opinion survey demonstrates that 90% of the people in this country support a 55 mile-per-hour speed limit.

6. The federal statute relating to disbursement of highway funds, conditioned on the 55 mile-per-hour speed limit, is probably:

(A) Unconstitutional.

(B) Constitutional only on the basis of the spending power.

(C) Constitutional only on the basis of the commerce power.

(D) Constitutional on the basis of both the spending power and the commerce power.

Questions 7-8 are based on the following fact situation:

A recently enacted state law forbids nonresident aliens from owning more than 100 acres of land within the state and directs the state attorney general to bring an action of ejectment whenever a nonresident alien owns such land. Zane, a nonresident alien, has obtained title to 200 acres of land in the state, and he brings an action in federal court to enjoin the state attorney general from enforcing the statute. The defendant moves to dismiss the complaint.

7. The best argument for Zane is that:

(A) States are forbidden by the Commerce Clause from interfering with the rights of nonresidents to own land.

(B) The state's power to restrict alien rights is limited by the federal power to control foreign relations.

(C) The state statute adversely affects Zane's right to travel.

(D) The 100-acre restriction means that aliens cannot engage in farming operations requiring larger amounts of land.

8. The federal court should:

(A) Dismiss the action, because under the Constitution, nonresident aliens may not sue in federal court.

(B) Dismiss the action, because a state has plenary power to determine the qualifications for landholding within its boundaries.

(C) Hear the action, because the United Nations Charter forbids such discrimination.

(D) Hear the action, because a federal question is presented.

Question 9

Zall, a resident of the state of Paxico, brought suit in federal district court against Motors, Inc., a Paxico corporation. Zall seeks recovery of $12,000 actual and $12,000 punitive damages arising from Motors's sale to him of a defective automobile. Zall's suit is based only on a common law contract theory.

From a constitutional standpoint, should the federal district court hear this suit on its merits?

(A) Yes, because Article III vests federal courts with jurisdiction over cases involving the obligation of contracts.

(B) Yes, because it is an action affecting interstate commerce.

(C) No, because this suit is not within the jurisdiction of an Article III court.

(D) No, because there is no case or controversy within the meaning of Article III.

Questions 10-11 are based on the following fact situation:

The state of Missoula has enacted a new election code designed to increase voter responsibility in the exercise of the franchise and to enlarge citizen participation in the electoral process. None of its provisions conflict with federal statutes.

10. Which of the following is the strongest reason for finding unconstitutional a requirement in the Missoula election code that each voter must be literate in English?

    (A) The requirement violates Article I, Section 2 of the Constitution, which provides that representatives to Congress be chosen "by the people of the several States."

    (B) The requirement violates Article I, Section 4 of the Constitution, which gives Congress the power to "make or alter" state regulations providing for the "times" and "manner" of holding elections for senators and representatives.

    (C) The requirement violates the Due Process Clause of the Fourteenth Amendment.

    (D) The requirement violates the Equal Protection Clause of the Fourteenth Amendment.

11. The Missoula election code provides that in a special-purpose election for directors of a state watershed improvement district, the franchise is limited to landowners within the district, because they are the only ones directly affected by the outcome. Each vote is weighted according to the proportion of the holding of that individual in relation to the total affected property. The best argument in support of the statute and against the application of the "one person, one vote" principle in this situation is that the principle:

    (A) Applies only to election of individuals to statewide public office.

    (B) Does not apply where property rights are involved.

    (C) Does not apply because the actions of such a district principally affect landowners.

    (D) Does not apply because of rights reserved to the states by the Tenth Amendment.

Questions 12-14 are based on the following fact situation:

The state of Yuma provides by statute, "No person may be awarded any state construction contract without agreeing to employ only citizens of the state and of the United States in performance of the contract."

12. In evaluating the constitutionality of this state statute under the Supremacy Clause,

which of the following would be most directly relevant?

(A) The general unemployment rate in the nation.

(B) The treaties and immigration laws of the United States.

(C) The need of the state for this particular statute.

(D) The number of aliens currently residing in Yuma.

13. If the Yuma statute is attacked as violating the Commerce Clause, which of the following defenses is the ***weakest***?

(A) The statute will help protect the workers of the state of Yuma from competition by foreign workers.

(B) The statute will help ensure that workers with jobs directly affecting the performance of public contracts are dedicated to their jobs.

(C) The statute will help ensure a continuously available and stable work force for the execution of public contracts.

(D) The statute will help ensure that only the most qualified individuals work on public contracts.

14. Suppose the state supreme court declares the statute to be unconstitutional on the ground that it violates the Privileges and Immunities Clause of the Fourteenth Amendment to the federal Constitution and the Equal Protection Clause of the state constitution. If the state seeks review in the United States Supreme Court, which of the following statements is most accurate?

(A) The United States Supreme Court may properly review that decision by certiorari only.

(B) The United States Supreme Court may properly review that decision by appeal only.

(C) The United States Supreme Court may properly review that decision by appeal or certiorari.

(D) The United States Supreme Court may not properly review that decision.

Questions 15-16 are based on the following fact situation:

The state of Champlain enacts the Young Adult Marriage Counseling Act, which provides that, before any persons less than 30 years of age may be issued a marriage license, they must receive at least five hours of marriage counseling from a state-licensed social worker. This counseling is designed to ensure that applicants for marriage licenses know their legal rights and duties in relation to marriage and parenthood, understand the "true nature" of the marriage relationship, and understand the procedures for obtaining divorces.

15. Pine, aged 25, contemplates marrying Ross, aged 25. Both are residents of the state of Champlain. Pine has not yet proposed to Ross because he is offended by the counseling requirement.

Pine sues in federal court seeking a declaratory judgment that the Young Adult Marriage Counseling Act is unconstitutional. Which of the following is the clearest ground for dismissal of this action by the court?

(A) Pine and Ross are residents of the same state.

(B) No substantial federal question is presented.

(C) The suit presents a nonjusticiable political question.

(D) The suit is unripe.

16. In a case in which the constitutionality of the Young Adult Marriage Counseling Act is in issue, the burden of persuasion will probably be on the:

(A) Person challenging the law, because there is a strong presumption that elected state legislators acted properly.

(B) Person challenging the law, because the Tenth Amendment authorizes states to determine the conditions on which they issue marriage licenses.

(C) State, because there is a substantial impact on the right to marry, and that right is fundamental.

(D) State, because there is a substantial impact on the discrete and insular class of young adults.

Question 17

A statute of the state of Tuscarora made it a misdemeanor to construct any building of more than five stories without an automatic fire sprinkler system.

A local construction company built, in Tuscarora, a 10-story federal office building. It constructed the building according to the precise specifications of a federal contract authorized by federal statutes. Because the building was built without the automatic fire sprinkler system required by state law, Tuscarora prosecutes the private contractor.

Which of the following is the company's strongest defense to that prosecution?

(A) The state sprinkler requirement denies the company property or liberty without due process.

(B) The state sprinkler requirement denies the company equal protection of the laws.

(C) As applied, the state sprinkler requirement violates the Supremacy Clause.

(D) As applied, the state sprinkler requirement violates the Obligation of Contracts Clause.

Question 18

A state accredits both public and private schools, licenses their teachers, and supplies textbooks on secular subjects to all such schools. Country Schoolhouse, a private school that offers elementary and secondary education in the state, denies admission to all non-Caucasians.

In a suit to enjoin as unconstitutional the continued racially exclusionary admissions policy of the Country Schoolhouse, which of the following is the strongest argument ***against*** the school?

(A) Because education is a public function, the Country Schoolhouse may not discriminate on racial grounds.

(B) The state is so involved in school regulation and support that the Equal Protection Clause of the Fourteenth Amendment is applicable to the school.

(C) The state is constitutionally obligated to eliminate segregation in all public and private educational institutions within the state.

(D) Any school with teachers who are licensed by the state is forbidden to discriminate on racial grounds.

Question 19

A federal statute requires United States civil service employees to retire at age 75. However, that statute also states that civil service employees of the armed forces must retire at age 65.

Prentis, a 65-year-old civil service employee of the Department of the Army, seeks a declaratory judgment that would forbid his mandatory retirement until age 75.

The strongest argument that Prentis can make to invalidate the requirement that he retire at age 65 is that the law:

(A) Denies him a privilege or immunity of national citizenship.

(B) Deprives him of a property right without just compensation.

(C) Is not within the scope of any of the enumerated powers of Congress in Article I, Section 8.

(D) Invidiously discriminates against him on the basis of age in violation of the Fifth Amendment.

Question 20

Congress passes a law regulating the wholesale and retail prices of "every purchase or sale of oil, natural gas, and electric power made in the United States."

The strongest argument in support of the constitutionality of this statute is that:

(A) The Constitution expressly empowers Congress to enact laws for "the general welfare."

(B) Congress has the authority to regulate such products' interstate transportation and importation from abroad.

(C) Congress may regulate the prices of every purchase and sale of goods and services made in this country, because commerce includes buying and selling.

(D) In inseverable aggregates, the domestic purchases or sales of such products affect interstate or foreign commerce.

Question 21

Congress enacted a statute providing that persons may challenge a state energy law on the ground that it is in conflict with the federal Constitution in either federal or state court. According to this federal statute, any decision by a lower state court upholding a state energy law against a challenge based on the federal Constitution may be appealed directly to the United States Supreme Court.

The provisions of this statute that authorize direct United States Supreme Court review of specified decisions rendered by lower state courts are:

(A) Constitutional, because congressional control over questions of energy use is plenary.

(B) Constitutional, because Congress may establish the manner by which the appellate jurisdiction of the United States Supreme Court is exercised.

(C) Unconstitutional, because they infringe the sovereign right of states to have their supreme courts review decisions of their lower state courts.

(D) Unconstitutional, because under Article III of the Constitution, the United States Supreme Court does not have authority to review directly decisions of lower state courts.

Question 22

Congress enacts a criminal statute prohibiting "any person from interfering in any way with any right conferred on another person by the Equal Protection Clause of the Fourteenth Amendment."

Application of this statute to Jones, a private citizen, would be most clearly constitutional if Jones, with threats of violence, coerces:

(A) A public school teacher to exclude black pupils from her class, solely because of their race.

(B) Black pupils, solely because of their race, to refrain from attending a privately owned and operated school licensed by the state.

(C) The bus driver operating a free school bus service under the sponsorship of a local church to refuse to allow black pupils on the bus, solely because of their race.

(D) The federal official in charge of distributing certain federal benefits directly to students from distributing them to black pupils, solely because of their race.

Questions 23-24 are based on the following fact situation:

All lawyers practicing in the state of Erewhon must be members of the State Bar Association, by order of the state supreme court. Several state officials serve on the Bar Association's Board of Bar Governors. The Board of Bar Governors authorizes the payment of dues for two staff members to the Cosmopolitan Club, a private dining club licensed to sell alcoholic beverages. The Cosmopolitan Club is frequented by affluent businessmen and professionals and by legislators. It is generally known that the purpose of the membership of the Bar Association staff is to enable them to go where members of the "elite" meet and to lobby for legislation in which the Bar Association is interested. The State Association has numerous committees and subcommittees concerned with family law, real estate law, unauthorized practice, etc., and its recommendations often influence state policy. Some committee meetings are held at the Cosmopolitan Club. The club is known to have rules which restrict membership by race, religion, and sex.

Plaintiffs, husband and wife, who are members of the Erewhon Bar Association, petition the Board of Bar Governors to adopt a resolution prohibiting the payment of club dues to and the holding of meetings of the Bar Association or its committees at places that discriminate on the basis of race, religion, or sex. After substantial public discussion, the Board of Bar Governors, by a close vote, fails to pass such a resolution. These events receive extensive coverage in the local newspapers. Plaintiffs bring an action in federal court seeking an injunction against such payments and the holding of meetings in such places as the Cosmopolitan Club.

23. The strongest argument for Plaintiffs is:

(A) Private rights to discriminate and associate freely must defer to a public interest against discrimination on the basis of race, religion, or sex.

(B) The failure of the State Bar Association to pass a resolution forbidding discrimination on the basis of race, religion, or sex constitutes a denial of equal protection.

(C) The State Bar Association is an agency of the state and its payment of dues to such private clubs promotes discrimination on the basis of race, religion, and sex.

(D) The State Bar Association's payment of dues to such private clubs promotes discrimination on the basis of race, religion, and sex.

24. Which of the following actions should a federal district court take with respect to jurisdiction?

(A) Hear the case on the merits, because a federal claim is presented.

(B) Hear the case on the merits, because the expenditure of state funds in support of segregation is forbidden by the Fifth Amendment.

(C) Abstain from jurisdiction, because the constitutional issue should be litigated first in a state court.

(D) Dismiss the case for lack of jurisdiction, because the issue of Bar Association activities is solely within the domain of state law.

Question 25

Congress enacts a statute punishing "each and every conspiracy entered into by any two or more persons for the purpose of denying black persons housing, employment, or education, solely because of their race."

Under which of the following constitutional provisions is the authority of Congress to pass such a statute most clearly and easily justifiable?

(A) The Obligation of Contracts Clause.

(B) The General Welfare Clause of Article I, Section 8.

(C) The Thirteenth Amendment.

(D) The Fourteenth Amendment.

Question 26

A federal criminal law makes it a crime for any citizen of the United States not specifically authorized by the President to negotiate with a foreign government for the purpose of influencing the foreign government in relation to a dispute with the United States.

The strongest constitutional ground for the validity of this law is that:

(A) Under several of its enumerated powers, Congress may legislate to preserve the monopoly of the national government over the conduct of United States foreign affairs.

(B) The President's inherent power to negotiate for the United States with foreign countries authorizes the President, even in the absence of statutory authorization, to punish citizens who engage in such negotiations without permission.

(C) The law deals with foreign relations and therefore is not governed by the First Amendment.

(D) Federal criminal laws dealing with international affairs need not be as specific as those dealing with domestic affairs.

Question 27

A state statute requires that all buses which operate as common carriers on the highways of the state shall be equipped with seat belts for passengers. Transport Lines, an interstate carrier, challenges the validity of the statute and the right of the state to make the requirement.

What is the best basis for a constitutional challenge by Transport Lines?

(A) Violation of the Due Process Clause of the Fourteenth Amendment.

(B) Violation of the Equal Protection Clause of the Fourteenth Amendment.

(C) Unreasonable burden on interstate commerce.

(D) Difficulty of enforcement.

Question 28

Congress passes an act requiring that all owners of bicycles in the United States register them with a federal bicycle registry. The purpose of the law is to provide reliable evidence of ownership to reduce bicycle theft. No fee is charged for the registration. Although most stolen bicycles are kept or resold by the thieves in the same cities in which the bicycles were stolen, an increasing number of bicycles are being taken to cities in other states for resale.

Is this act of Congress constitutional?

(A) Yes, because Congress has the power to regulate property for the general welfare.

(B) Yes, because Congress could determine that, in inseverable aggregates, bicycle thefts affect interstate commerce.

(C) No, because most stolen bicycles remain within the state in which they were stolen.

(D) No, because the registration of vehicles is a matter reserved to the states by the Tenth Amendment.

Question 29

A statute of the state of Lanape flatly bans the sale or distribution of contraceptive devices to minors. Drugs, Inc., a national retailer of drugs and related items, is charged with violating the Lanape statute.

Which of the following is the strongest constitutional argument Drugs, Inc., could make in defending itself against prosecution for violation of this statute?

(A) The statute constitutes an undue burden on interstate commerce.

(B) The statute denies minors one of their fundamental rights without due process.

(C) The statute denies Drugs, Inc., a privilege or immunity of state citizenship.

(D) The statute violates the First Amendment right to freedom of religion because it regulates morals.

Question 30

Congress enacted a law prohibiting the killing, capture, or removal of any form of wildlife upon or from any federally owned land.

Which of the following is the most easily justifiable source of national authority for this federal law?

(A) The Commerce Clause of Article I, Section 8.

(B) The Privileges and Immunities Clause of Article IV.

(C) The Enforcement Clause of the Fourteenth Amendment.

(D) The Property Clause of Article IV, Section 3.

Question 31

The President of the United States recognizes the country of Ruritania and undertakes diplomatic relations with its government through the Secretary of State. Ruritania is governed by a repressive totalitarian government.

In an appropriate federal court, Dunn brings a suit against the President and Secretary of State to set aside this action on the ground that it is inconsistent with the principles of our constitutional form of government. Dunn has a lucrative contract with the United States Department of Commerce to provide commercial information about Ruritania. The contract expressly terminates, however, "when the President recognizes the country of Ruritania and undertakes diplomatic relations with its government."

Which of the following is the most proper disposition of the Dunn suit by the federal court?

(A) Suit dismissed, because Dunn does not have standing to bring this action.

(B) Suit dismissed, because there is no adversity between Dunn and the defendants.

(C) Suit dismissed, because it presents a nonjusticiable political question.

(D) Suit decided on the merits.

Question 32

Congress passes an Energy Conservation Act. The Act requires all users of energy in this country to reduce their consumption by a specified percentage, to be set by a presidential executive order. The Act sets forth specific standards the President must use in setting the percentage and detailed procedures to be followed.

The provision that allows the President to set the exact percentage is probably:

(A) Constitutional, because it creates a limited administrative power to implement the statute.

(B) Constitutional, because inherent executive powers permit such action even without statutory authorization.

(C) Unconstitutional as an undue delegation of legislative power to the executive.

(D) Unconstitutional, because it violates the Due Process Clause of the Fifth Amendment.

Question 33

The federal government has complete jurisdiction over certain park land located within the state of Plains. To conserve the wildlife that inhabits that land, the federal government enacts a statute forbidding all hunting of animals in the federal park. That statute also forbids the hunting of animals that have left the federal park and have entered the state of Plains.

Hanson has a hunting license from the state of Plains authorizing him to hunt deer anywhere in the state. On land within the state of Plains located adjacent to the federal park, Hanson shoots a deer he knows has recently left the federal land.

Hanson is prosecuted for violating the federal hunting law. The strongest ground supporting the constitutionality of the federal law forbidding the hunting of wild animals that wander off federal property is that:

(A) This law is a necessary and proper means of protecting United States property.

(B) The animals are moving in the stream of interstate commerce.

(C) The police powers of the federal government encompass protection of wild animals.

(D) Shooting wild animals is a privilege, not a right.

Question 34

A state statute makes fraud for personal financial gain a crime. Jones was convicted of violating this statute on three separate occasions. Following his most recent conviction, he professed to have undergone a religious conversion and proclaimed himself to be the divine minister of "St. Rockport," an alleged messiah who would shortly be making his appearance on earth. Jones solicited cash donations from the public to support his efforts to spread the word of St. Rockport and his coming appearance on earth.

Following complaints by several contributors who claimed he defrauded them, Jones was again charged with fraud under this state statute. The charge was that Jones "should have known that his representations about St. Rockport were false and, therefore, that he made them solely to collect cash donations for his personal gain." A witness for the prosecution in Jones's trial stated that Jones had admitted that, at times, he had doubts about the existence of St. Rockport. Jones was the only religious minister prosecuted for fraud under this state statute.

The strongest constitutional defense that Jones could assert would be that this prosecution:

(A) Deprived him of the equal protection of the laws because other religious ministers have not been charged under this statute.

(B) Denied him procedural due process because it placed upon Jones the burden of rebutting evidence, submitted by the state, of his bad faith in raising this money.

(C) Denied him rights conferred by the Obligation of Contracts Clause by preventing him from taking money from persons who wished to contract with him to spread the word of St. Rockport.

(D) Denied him the free exercise of religion in violation of the First and Fourteenth Amendments because it required the state to determine the truth or falsity of the content of his religious beliefs.

Questions 35-37 are based on the following fact situation:

As part of a comprehensive federal aid-to-education program, Congress included the following provisions as conditions for state receipt of federal funds: (1) Whenever textbooks are provided to students without charge, they must include no religious instruction and must be made available on the same terms to students in all public and private schools accredited by the state educational authority. (2) Salary supplements can be paid to teachers in public and private schools, up to 10% of existing salary schedules, where present compensation is less than the average salary for persons of comparable training and experience, provided that no such supplement is paid to any teacher who instructs in religious subjects. (3) Construction grants can be made toward the cost of physical plants at private colleges and universities, provided that no part of the grant is used for buildings in which instruction in religious subject matters is offered.

35. Federal taxpayer Allen challenges the provision that allows the distribution of free textbooks to students in a private school where religious instruction is included in the curriculum. On the question of the adequacy of Allen's standing to raise the constitutional question, the most likely result is that standing will be:

    (A) Sustained, because any congressional spending authorization can be challenged by any taxpayer.

    (B) Sustained, because the challenge to the exercise of congressional spending power is based on a claimed violation of specific constitutional limitations on the exercise of such power.

    (C) Denied, because there is insufficient nexus between the taxpayer and the challenged expenditures.

    (D) Denied, because, in the case of private schools, no state action is involved.

36. Federal taxpayer Bates also challenges the salary supplements for teachers in private schools where religious instruction is included in the curriculum. On the substantive constitutional issue, the most likely result is that the salary supplements will be:

    (A) Sustained, because the statute provides that no supplements will be made to teachers who are engaged in any religious instruction.

    (B) Sustained, because to distinguish between private and public school teachers would violate the Free Exercise Clause of the First Amendment.

    (C) Held unconstitutional, because some religions would benefit disproportionately.

    (D) Held unconstitutional, because the policing of the restriction would amount to an excessive entanglement with religion.

37. Federal taxpayer Bates also challenges the construction grants to church-operated private colleges and universities. The most likely result is that the construction grants will be:

    (A) Sustained, because aid to one aspect of an institution of higher education not shown to be pervasively sectarian does not necessarily free it to spend its other resources for religious purposes.

    (B) Sustained, because bricks and mortar do not aid religion in a way forbidden by the Establishment Clause of the First Amendment.

    (C) Held unconstitutional, because any financial aid to a church-operated school strengthens the religious purposes of the institution.

    (D) Held unconstitutional, because the grants involve or cause an excessive entanglement with religion.

Question 38

Leonard was the high priest of a small cult of Satan worshippers living in New Arcadia. As a part of the practice of their religious beliefs, a cat was required to be sacrificed to the glory of Satan after a live dissection of the animal in which it endured frightful pain. In the course of such a religious sacrifice, Leonard was arrested on the complaint of the local Humane Society and charged under a statute punishing cruelty to animals.

On appeal, a conviction of Leonard probably will be:

(A) Sustained, on the grounds that belief in or worship of Satan does not enjoy constitutional protection.

(B) Sustained, on the grounds that sincere religious belief is not an adequate defense on these facts.

(C) Overturned, on the grounds that the constitutionally guaranteed freedom of religion and its expression was violated.

(D) Overturned, on the grounds that the beliefs of the cult members in the need for the sacrifice might be reasonable, and their act was religious.

Question 39

Congress enacts a law providing that all disagreements between the United States and a state over federal grant-in-aid funds shall be settled by the filing of suit in the federal district court in the affected state. "The judgment of that federal court shall be transmitted to the head of the federal agency dispensing such funds, who, if satisfied that the judgment is fair and lawful, shall execute the judgment according to its terms."

This law is:

(A) Constitutional, because disagreements over federal grant-in-aid funds necessarily involve federal questions within the judicial power of the United States.

(B) Constitutional, because the spending of federal monies necessarily includes the authority to provide for the effective settlement of disputes involving them.

(C) Unconstitutional, because it vests authority in the federal court to determine a matter prohibited to it by the Eleventh Amendment.

(D) Unconstitutional, because it vests authority in a federal court to render an advisory opinion.

Question 40

A statute authorizes a specified federal administrative agency to issue rules governing the distribution of federal grant funds for scientific research. The statute provides that, in issuing those rules, the agency must follow procedures and substantive standards contained in the statute. In a severable provision, the statute also provides that otherwise valid rules issued by the agency under authority delegated to it by this statute may be set aside by a majority vote of a designated standing joint committee of Congress.

The provision of this statute relating to the power of the designated standing joint committee of Congress is:

(A) Constitutional, because it is a necessary and proper means of ensuring that the rules issued by this agency are actually consistent with the will of Congress.

(B) Constitutional, because discretionary money grants authorized by statute are privileges, not rights, and, therefore, Congress has greater freedom to intervene in their administration than it has to intervene in the administration of regulatory laws.

(C) Unconstitutional, because it denies equal protection of the laws to members of Congress who are not appointed to the joint legislative committee authorized to set aside rules of this agency.

(D) Unconstitutional, because it authorizes a congressional change of legal rights and obligations by means other than those specified in the Constitution for the enactment of laws.

CONSTITUTIONAL LAW ANSWERS

Answer to Question 1

(C) The statute at issue is void for vagueness. If a criminal law or regulation fails to give persons reasonable notice of what is prohibited, it may violate the Due Process Clause. This principle is applied somewhat strictly when First Amendment activity is involved in order to avoid the chilling effect a vague law might have on speech (*i.e.,* if it is unclear what speech is regulated, people might refrain from speech that is permissible for fear that they will be violating the law). Here, the statute does not give reasonable notice as to what language is being prohibited, and no court decisions have limited its construction. Thus, it is impermissibly vague, and Smith will prevail. Therefore, (A) incorrectly states that Smith will not prevail. (B) is incorrect because it is too broad a statement. First Amendment freedoms are not absolute; for instance, obscenity may be punished under a properly drawn statute. The problem here is that it cannot be determined what speech is being prohibited. (D) is incorrect because there is no ***constitutional*** "average person test."

Answer to Question 2

(D) (D) is the "safest" answer because Congress has the same legislative authority over the District of Columbia as a state legislature has over matters internal to its state. This clearly includes the authority to regulate marriage and divorce. It could be argued that Congress's military and war powers could sustain (A); that Congress's power to regulate the jurisdiction of federal courts could sustain (B); that Congress's power over external affairs, which includes the power to implement executive agreements, could sustain (C), but these arguments are more speculative than that for (D).

Answer to Question 3

(C) (A) is incorrect because, depending upon specific applications of the proposed legislation, a "taking of property," requiring just compensation, could result. This would raise the issue as to whether the governmental action amounts to a taking (in which case the state must fairly compensate the owner of property) or a regulation (in which case there is no need for compensation), and would certainly be a consideration in the drafting of the subject legislation. (B) is incorrect because the proposed legislation could be seen as constituting a prohibited retroactive impairment of contract rights. (D) is incorrect because questions of "taking" often arise in connection with the state's exercise of its police power (*i.e.*, the power to legislate for the health, welfare, or safety of the people). (C) appears least relevant because the proposed legislation does not seem to contemplate suits against the state.

Answer to Question 4

(B) In order to have standing, a person must usually show a direct and immediate personal injury due to the challenged government action. The claimant must be in a position to demonstrate a concrete stake in the outcome of the suit and a direct impairment of his own constitutional rights. The contractors in (B) satisfy the criteria. The plaintiffs in (C) and (D) do not. As to (A), federal taxpayers generally have no standing to challenge the validity of federal expenditures; in any event, the federal taxpayer here is not complaining of any added tax burdens. State taxpayers may challenge the validity of state programs that involve measurable state expenditures, but here it is a federal program whose constitutionality is in issue and, in any event, the state expenditure is only hypothetical.

Answer to Question 5

(C) (A) is incorrect because the mere acceptance of federal money to help pay for highways does not amount to a concession of authority over such highways. Federal authority over the highways must be derived from a specific source, rather than from the mere supplying of funds for the highways. Thus, (B) also is incorrect. (D) is incorrect because the constitutionality (or lack thereof) of an exercise of federal legislative power is in no way based on public opinion. (C) is correct because Congress has power to condition federal spending if Congress reasonably finds that the spending program is for the general welfare. Even where Congress otherwise has no power to regulate an area, it can use its spending power to so regulate by requiring entities that accept government money to act in a certain manner.

Answer to Question 6

(D) (D) is correct, because Congress clearly has the right to place conditions on appropriated funds under the spending power and because highways fall within the purview of interstate commerce and are thus subject to Commerce Clause regulation. Few cases have ever declared a generally applicable federal statute based on commerce power to be an unconstitutional interference with state functions, and spending power conditions were upheld in *South Dakota v. Dole* (1987). It follows that (A), (B), and (C) are incorrect.

Answer to Question 7

(B) (B) is an accurate statement of constitutional doctrine. Congress has plenary power over aliens. A state or local law that is based on alienage is subject to strict scrutiny (*i.e.*, a compelling state interest must be shown to justify disparate treatment). When, as with the state law here at issue, state action regulates aliens, Congress's plenary power over aliens arising from its power over naturalization is more directly implicated than Congress's commerce power; thus (B) is a better choice than (A). (C) is incorrect because the state law does not penalize anyone for exercising the right to travel from state to state. (D)'s relevance is remote, at best.

Answer to Question 8

(D) The federal judicial power extends to cases arising under the Constitution of the United States. (D) is correct because the recently enacted state law discriminates against aliens, and many state discriminations against aliens have been held unconstitutional. Thus, there is a federal question. (A) is incorrect because aliens are permitted to bring certain actions in federal court challenging constitutionally suspect governmental action. (B) is incorrect because a state's regulation of land ownership may not be exercised in a manner that runs afoul of constitutional parameters. (C) is incorrect because, even assuming that there is a United Nations charter provision on point, this would not give the court jurisdiction; there must be a federal question.

Answer to Question 9

(C) The court should not hear this suit on the merits because Article III courts are not empowered to hear suits between citizens of the same state where no federal question jurisdiction is involved. Article III lists the cases to which federal jurisdiction extends. It includes suits arising under federal law, and suits between citizens of two or more states. Zall's suit against Motors involves two citizens of the state of Paxico and no federal question is raised. No provision of Article III covers such a suit. Thus, Zall should have brought suit in Paxico state court. (A) is incorrect because the Contracts Clause deals with state ***legislation*** impairing contracts and no such legislation is implied by the facts. Article III has no general provision for suits involving the obligation of contracts. (B) is incorrect because while it might be said that the action can affect interstate commerce and thus is subject to federal regulation, absent such federal regulation, there is no basis under Article III for jurisdiction. Article III does not provide for federal court jurisdiction in all cases affecting interstate commerce. (D) is incorrect because a "case or controversy" exists. The case or controversy requirement only prohibits federal courts from rendering advisory opinions, such as where the case is moot or unripe, or the parties are not truly adverse. The parties here are clearly adverse and there is a real, live controversy; the only thing missing is a basis for federal court jurisdiction.

Answer to Question 10

(D) The Fourteenth Amendment prevents states from discriminating against the exercise of "fundamental rights," one of which is the right to vote, unless the state shows a compelling interest. The English requirement suggests discrimination against the right to vote of people who cannot speak English. (A) is clearly inapplicable. (B) is clearly incorrect. (C) may be correct, but it is not as good as (D). Note that the Supreme Court has not specifically decided whether a "discriminatory purpose" is required for a violation of the Fifteenth Amendment's bar against governmental racial discrimination in voting.

Answer to Question 11

(C) When a governmental body establishes voting districts for the election of representatives, the number of persons in each district may not vary significantly ("one person, one vote"). This principle applies to almost every election where a person is being elected to perform normal governmental functions. However, the government can limit the class of persons who are allowed to vote in an election of persons to serve on a special purpose government unit if the unit has a special impact on the class of enfranchised voters. The watershed improvement districts referred to in this question are so specialized that election of their directors is not subject to the "one person, one vote" principle. These districts disproportionately affect landowners and do not perform general governmental functions. Thus, (C) is correct. (A) is incorrect because "one person, one vote" has a broader reach than merely election to statewide office. As noted above, the principle applies to almost every election for the performance of normal governmental functions. (B) is incorrect because conditioning the right to vote on property ownership normally would be invalid under the Equal Protection Clause. Only certain special purpose elections can be based on property ownership. (D) incorrectly implies that "one person, one vote" does not apply to states. In fact, the principle is binding on states through the Equal Protection Clause of the Fourteenth Amendment.

Answer to Question 12

(B) An act of Congress or federal regulation supersedes any state or local action that actually conflicts with the federal rule, whether by commanding conduct inconsistent with that required by the federal rule, or by forbidding conduct that the federal rule is designed to foster. The conflict need not relate to conduct; it is sufficient if the state law interferes with achievement of a federal objective. In addition, note that Congress has exclusive power over naturalization and denaturalization. Thus, United States treaties and immigration laws would supersede an inconsistent state law, making them relevant to the constitutionality of the state Yuma statute. (A), (C), and (D) all refer to some perceived justification for the statute. However, they are irrelevant because, even if a state law was enacted for a valid purpose, it will be rendered void if it conflicts with federal law.

Answer to Question 13

(A) The acknowledgment that the statute will protect Yuma workers from outside competition is the weakest defense because it indicates that the law has a discriminatory impact. State legislation that is challenged on Commerce Clause grounds (i) must not discriminate against out-of-state competition to benefit local economic interests, and (ii) must not be unduly burdensome. A discriminatory law will be valid only if it furthers an important ***noneconomic*** state interest and there are no reasonable alternatives available, whereas a nondiscriminatory law will be valid as long as the legitimate state interests outweigh the burden on interstate commerce. Here, choices (B), (C), and (D) all attempt to provide a nondiscriminatory rationale for the statute, making it easier to pass muster under the Commerce Clause, while choice (A) amounts to a concession by the state that the statute discriminates in favor of state economic interests, making it more likely to be invalidated.

Answer to Question 14

(D) The Supreme Court will hear a case from a state court only if the state court judgment turned on federal grounds. The Court will refuse jurisdiction if it finds adequate and independent non-federal grounds to support the state decision. The nonfederal grounds must be adequate in that they are fully dispositive of the case, so that even if the federal grounds are wrongly decided, it would not affect the outcome of the case. Also, the nonfederal grounds must be independent. If the state court's interpretation of its state provision was based on federal case law interpreting an identical federal provision, the state law grounds for the decision is not independent. Here, the state supreme court rested its decision on the ground of violation of the state constitution, without any interpretation based on an identical federal provision. Thus, the decision is supported by adequate and independent nonfederal grounds, and the Supreme Court should refuse jurisdiction. (A), (B), and (C) are all based on the incorrect premise that the Supreme Court may somehow properly review the decision.

Answer to Question 15

(D) This issue would not be considered ripe because there is no real harm or immediate threat of harm. If Pine and Ross were actually engaged to be married, refused to undergo the counseling, and then requested that a license be issued, the issue would be ripe, because at that point they would have been denied the license on the basis of the statute. As it is, they have not even come to the point of requesting a license. (A) is wrong because diversity is not the only basis for federal jurisdiction. (B) is wrong because there is a substantial federal question—the right to marry is part of the constitutionally protected right of privacy. (C) is wrong because no political question is presented. Political questions include those issues committed by the Constitution to another branch of government and those inherently incapable of resolution and enforcement by the judicial process.

Answer to Question 16

(C) Where a fundamental right, such as the right to marry, is substantially affected, the state bears the burden of persuading the court that the statute in question is necessary to achieve a compelling or overriding government purpose. (A) is wrong because there is no presumption that state legislators acted properly. Also, as can be seen from the analysis at the beginning of this answer, (A) places the burden on the wrong party. (B) also places the burden on the wrong party. In addition, the Tenth Amendment provides that all powers not delegated to the federal government by the Constitution are reserved to the states. The Tenth Amendment does not authorize states to place unconstitutional burdens on fundamental rights. (D) is wrong, because "young adults" are not a discrete and insular class entitled to judicial scrutiny of laws that arguably require equal protection under the law.

Answer to Question 17

(C) Whenever Congress acts within the scope of a delegated power such as that of the Commerce Clause, the Supremacy Clause renders any conflicting state or local law or action void. Thus, as applied, the state sprinkler requirement violates the Supremacy Clause. (A) is wrong because a substantive due process claim would be almost guaranteed to fail, since business regulation is now invariably sustained as reasonable state action under the Due Process Clause. (B) is wrong because classifications that relate only to matters of economics or social welfare (not fundamental rights) and do not employ suspect or quasi-suspect classifications are almost always upheld. The classification of building story size is not arbitrary. (D) is wrong because the contract has not been breached, so no Obligation of Contracts Clause issue is presented.

Answer to Question 18

(B) Race is a "suspect category" under the Equal Protection Clause, but the Fourteenth Amendment does not apply to purely private acts of discrimination. However, if state action is found, the clause can be invoked against Country Schoolhouse. State action can be found in the actions of seemingly private individuals who (i) perform exclusive public functions or (ii) have significant state involvement in their activities. (B) states an example of significant state involvement and is, therefore, correct. (A) is wrong because to be state action, the activity must be both a traditional and exclusive government function. Education does not so qualify. The Supreme Court has only found running a town and running an election for public office to be such exclusive government functions. (C) is wrong because the statement is overbroad. Only intentional discrimination will be found to create discriminatory classifications calling for strict scrutiny. (D) is wrong because state involvement must be "significant" to trigger state action. Mere licensure is generally not "significant."

Answer to Question 19

(D) Prentis's strongest argument would be that his Fifth Amendment due process rights have been abridged. While the Equal Protection Clause of the Fourteenth Amendment only applies to state action, it is clear that arbitrary or invidious discrimination by the federal government violates the Due Process Clause of the Fifth Amendment. Thus, there are really two equal protection guarantees. Since age is not a suspect category, this legislation would only be subject to the rational basis test. Because other civil service employees can work until the age of 75, Prentis would have an argument that the state had invidiously discriminated against him on the basis of age. His argument would probably fail, but is the "strongest" argument of the four alternatives given. (A) is wrong because employment is not a privilege or immunity of national citizenship. (B) is wrong because, where a public employee holds his position at the will of an employer, there is no property interest in continued employment. Since Prentis was dismissed on the basis of his age, rather than for cause, he had no property interest in continued employment. (C) is wrong because under the Necessary and Proper Clause, Congress may do anything that is arguably appropriate to relate to a federal interest.

Answer to Question 20

(D) This would be the strongest argument in support of the constitutionality of this statute. Article I, Section 8, Paragraph 3 empowers Congress to "regulate commerce with foreign nations and among the several states, and with the Indian tribes." Only rarely has a modern case invalidated a federal law regulating nongovernmental persons because it exceeded the commerce power. (A) is wrong because Congress does not have a general welfare power to regulate all activity in this country. (B) is wrong because it would not justify the statute at issue. (C) is wrong because it overstates congressional power by failing to connect the activity to "commerce."

Answer to Question 21

(B) Congress has the power to regulate and limit the appellate jurisdiction of the Supreme Court. Thus, the statute here, which was enacted by Congress, properly authorizes direct appeal of a specified decision to the Supreme Court. (A) is incorrect because there is nothing to support the proposition that Congress has plenary control over matters involving energy use. Also, (A) does not address the issue of jurisdiction of the Supreme Court. (C) is incorrect because states possess no such sovereign right. Federal review of state acts (whether they be executive, legislative, or judicial) is well established. (D) is incorrect because Article III actually provides that the Supreme Court shall have appellate jurisdiction under such regulations as Congress shall make.

Answer to Question 22

(A) Application (A) is the most clearly constitutional. Section 1 of the Fourteenth Amendment guarantees equal protection; it applies directly only to "state action," which is most clearly indicated in answer (A). Thus, answers (B) and (C) are not as clearly constitutional. Answer (D) is incorrect because the Fourteenth Amendment does not directly apply to federal action. Congress's power to prohibit federal acts would be easier to justify under Article I (*e.g.,* as necessary and proper to carry out the spending power). Thus, (D) is not as clear a Fourteenth Amendment case as (A).

Answer to Question 23

(C) Race is a suspect classification under the Equal Protection Clause. However, the Fourteenth Amendment only applies if there is action by a state or local government office, or a private individual whose behavior meets the requirement of "state action." State action exists where seemingly private individuals (i) perform exclusive public functions, or (ii) have significant state involvement in their activities. "State action" also exists where a state affirmatively facilitates, encourages, or authorizes acts of discrimination by its citizens. However, there must be some sort of affirmative act by the state approving the private action. It is not enough that the state merely permits the conduct to occur. Under these facts, several state officials serve on the Bar Association's Board of Bar Governors. Furthermore, the state supreme court requires all lawyers to be members of the State Bar Association. Thus, the State Bar Association does not operate independently of the state and, therefore, Plaintiffs' strongest argument would be to demonstrate that "state action" is involved in payment of dues by the Association to private clubs that discriminate. Thus, (C) is correct. (A) is wrong because "state action" is required to invoke the antidiscrimination protections of the Fourteenth Amendment. Only the Thirteenth Amendment's ban on badges or incidents of slavery applies to purely private actions. (B) is wrong because the failure of the Association to pass a resolution forbidding discrimination does not, in and of itself, constitute a denial of equal protection, and the argument for state action being present is much weaker than in option (C). (D) is wrong because, unless it is shown that the Association is an instrumentality of the state or closely intertwined with state action, the mere fact of its payment of dues to such private clubs will not invoke the Equal Protection Clause. (C) is the only answer that clearly focuses on the state action issue.

Answer to Question 24

(A) The court should hear the case on the merits. Federal judicial power extends to all cases and controversies arising under the Constitution, laws, or treaties of the United States. Because the activities of the State Bar Association present a federal claim arising under the Equal Protection Clause of the United States Constitution, the federal district court should hear the case on its merits. Therefore, (A) is correct. (B) is wrong because it is the Fourteenth Amendment that applies to the states. The Fifth Amendment Due Process Clause forbids ***federal*** discrimination. (C) is wrong because the doctrine of abstention is applicable when a federal constitutional claim is premised on an unsettled question of state law. These facts present no such unsettled state law question. (D) is wrong because the Bar Association's activities encroach on federally protected constitutional rights and, therefore, are not solely within the domain of state law, nor are there any "adequate and independent state grounds" here.

Answer to Question 25

(C) (C) is correct because the Thirteenth Amendment addresses private acts of racial discrimination. (D) is incorrect because the Supreme Court has not recognized any power of Congress to regulate private persons under Section 5 of the Fourteenth Amendment. (A) is incorrect because the Obligation of Contracts Clause prohibits states from impairing contractual obligations. Thus, this clause is inapplicable to this case. (B) is incorrect because the General Welfare Clause authorizes Congress to spend to provide for the common defense and general welfare. There is no connection between this clause and the statute at issue.

Answer to Question 26

(A) Congress has the power to declare war, raise and support armies, provide for and maintain a navy, and spend to provide for the common defense and general welfare, as well as the power to make all laws that are necessary and proper for carrying into execution the foregoing powers or any other federal power (including the power of the President and Senate to enter into treaties in conformity with Article II). Pursuant to these enumerated powers, Congress can take preventive measures against activities that may cause international misunderstandings, which in turn may lead to war, as well as against endeavors to undermine the government. The statute here shows a congressional intent to ensure that only properly authorized persons negotiate with foreign governments, and it is a legitimate means of implementing Congress's powers. (B) is incorrect because, although the President has broad discretion in foreign affairs, it is doubtful that such discretion would include the authority to unilaterally punish citizens who encroach on that discretion, absent legislative authorization to impose such punishment. (C) and (D) are incorrect because they are based on the mistaken notion that laws dealing with foreign affairs need not pass constitutional muster.

Answer to Question 27

(C) A challenge based on interstate commerce would be most effective. Sometimes a nondiscriminatory law that regulates commerce may place a burden on interstate commerce. Such a law will be invalidated if the burden on interstate commerce outweighs local interests. This is a case-by-case balancing test, and it is by no means clear that the law in question ***would*** be ruled invalid. However, the Commerce Clause issue is the only answer where there is any reasonable likelihood that the legislation could be declared invalid. Thus, (C) is the correct answer. (A) is wrong because no fundamental right is involved and, therefore, the mere rationality test is applied, and the law will be upheld if it is rationally related to any conceivable legitimate end of government. The seat belt law clearly meets this minimal standard and any challenge based on due process would surely fail. (B) is wrong because the legislation does not involve a fundamental right, a suspect classification, or a quasi-suspect classification. In equal protection analysis, if any other classification is involved, the action will be upheld unless the challenger proves that the action is not rationally related to a legitimate government interest. Transport Lines cannot carry such a burden of proof. (D) is wrong because a constitutional challenge should be based on the infringement of rights guaranteed by the Constitution. Difficulty of enforcement is not relevant here.

Answer to Question 28

(B) Congress may regulate any activity, local or interstate, which either in itself, or in combination with other activities, has a substantial effect upon interstate commerce. Here, although most stolen bicycles remain within the state in which they were stolen, the cumulative effect of many instances of stolen bicycles being transported across state lines for resale could be felt in interstate commerce. It follows that (C) is incorrect. (A) is incorrect because Congress has the power to ***spend*** for the general welfare. The ***property power*** involves the disposal and acquisition of property belonging to the United States, and is not at all relevant to this question. (D) is incorrect because the Tenth Amendment reserves to the states those powers not delegated to the United States nor prohibited to the states by the Constitution. As noted above, the power to regulate commerce is conferred upon Congress by the Constitution. Thus, this matter is not reserved to the states.

Answer to Question 29

(B) The purchase of contraceptives is encompassed by the fundamental right of privacy. Because this statute contains no procedural safeguards, it denies minors a fundamental right without due process. Because Drugs, Inc., may assert the minors' rights, (B) is the correct answer. (A) is incorrect because there does not appear to be an undue burden on interstate commerce. (C) is incorrect because the statute does not treat state residents differently from out-of-state residents. (D) is nonsensical. *Note:* Under the Supreme Court's decisions regarding the sale of contraceptives to minors, the best possible answer would have been that the statute violated equal protection because it denied a fundamental right to a class of persons (minors) without sufficient justification. Since that answer was not given, the due process answer (which mentioned fundamental rights) was the best choice.

Answer to Question 30

(D) It has been held that the Property Clause empowers Congress to protect wildlife wandering onto federally owned lands. (B) is incorrect because the Privileges and Immunities Clause of Article IV pertains to discrimination by states against out-of-state citizens. (A) is incorrect because the commerce power is not as ***easy a way to justify*** the law as is the property power, which clearly and literally applies here (note the wording of the question). (C) is incorrect because the enabling clause of the Fourteenth Amendment gives Congress the power to enforce the amendment by appropriate legislation. The Fourteenth Amendment, which prevents the states from depriving any person of life, liberty, or property without due process of law and equal protection of the law, is not at issue here.

Answer to Question 31

(C) A federal court will not decide political questions, which are: (i) those issues committed by the Constitution to another branch of government; and (ii) those issues inherently incapable of resolution and enforcement by the judicial process. Political questions include those regarding the conduct of foreign relations. Based on Supreme Court cases, the recognition of and establishment of diplomatic relations with a foreign country appear to be political questions. Thus, (D) is incorrect. (A) and (B) are incorrect because Dunn will be injured economically by the actions of the President and Secretary of State. Therefore, Dunn can demonstrate such a concrete stake in the outcome of this controversy as to ensure the adversariness which sharpens the presentation of issues.

Answer to Question 32

(A) Legislative power can be delegated to executive officers and/or administrative agencies. Any delegated power must not be uniquely confined to Congress. The delegation must include intelligible standards for action by the delegatee. The statutory provision here meets these criteria for a permissible delegation. It follows that (C) is incorrect. (B) is an incorrect statement of law. Even if the executive had the inherent power, that would not make the legislation constitutional. (D) is incorrect because this statute does not represent arbitrary governmental action. It serves a proper governmental purpose and provides for specific standards and procedures relative to its implementation.

Answer to Question 33

(A) In addition to its enumerated powers, Congress possesses auxiliary powers that are necessary and proper to carrying out all powers vested in the federal government. The statute here at issue is necessary and proper to carry out Congress's property power. By proscribing even the hunting of animals that have left the federal park, the statute will help protect the wildlife, which is property belonging to the United States. (B) is not the "strongest ground" because nothing in the facts points to interstate commerce. (C) is incorrect because the police power is a power of state government, not the federal government. (D), as a general statement of law, is incorrect. Also, it apparently is based on the rejected "right" vs. "privilege" distinction relative to deprivation of liberty and property without procedural due process, an issue not raised by these facts.

Answer to Question 34

(D) Jones's strongest defense is that the statute violates his free exercise of religion. The Free Exercise Clause forbids government from making laws that prohibit the free exercise of religion. The Court has held that this means that the government may not punish a person for his or her religious beliefs. In determining what is a religious belief, the court may delve into the sincerity of the belief, but it may not find religious beliefs to be false. Thus, the prosecution here may be unconstitutional because it was based on the alleged falsity of a religious belief. (A) could be correct but it is not as good a basis as (D). Under the Equal Protection Clause, government must not unreasonably discriminate against similarly situated people. If a law discriminates (on its face or in its application) on the basis of a suspect class or where a fundamental right is involved, the law will be held invalid unless it is narrowly tailored to achieve a compelling government interest. Here, the law interferes with freedom of religion (a fundamental right), but it is not clear from this one prosecution that the law is being applied in a discriminatory manner. Therefore, (D) is a better answer. (B) is incorrect because the Due Process Clause requires only that the prosecution prove each element of a crime. Once the prosecution proves an element, there is no due process violation in having the defendant rebut the evidence; otherwise no one could ever be convicted of a crime. (C) is wrong because it is not clear that there was a Contract Clause violation. The Contract Clause forbids the retroactive impairment of contract rights unless the impairment is narrowly tailored to meet an important government interest. Here, the statute was apparently in existence when Jones "contracted" with his donors (although presumably the donations were gratuitous and not contractual). Thus, there is no retroactive impairment of contract. Moreover, even if this were a retroactive impairment, it could be argued that it was justified because preventing fraud is an important government interest. In any case, this clearly is not as good a defense as (D).

Answer to Question 35

(B) The general rule is that people do not have standing as taxpayers to challenge the way tax dollars are spent because their interest is too remote. However, there is an exception to the general rule. A federal taxpayer has standing to challenge federal appropriations and spending measures if she can establish that the challenged measure: (i) was enacted under Congress's taxing and spending power; and (ii) exceeds some specific limitation on the power. To date, the only limit that the Supreme Court has found on the taxing power is the Establishment Clause. Here, Allen's challenge is based upon such an Establishment Clause matter. Hence, the exception applies and (B) is correct. (A) is incorrect because it is overbroad. Only spending falling within the exception described above may be challenged by taxpayers. (C) is incorrect because sufficient "nexus" is a concept applied to state taxation of interstate commerce—a state can tax only those persons with a sufficient relationship to the state. Here, the complaint is not that Allen is being taxed, but that the tax money is being spent in violation of the Constitution. (D) is wrong. First, state action ***is*** involved—the government is giving money for textbooks. Second, standing depends on whether the party has a concrete stake in the outcome of the litigation and is not dependent on whether the action complained of is state action.

Answer to Question 36

(D) The salary supplements probably will be held unconstitutional. The controlling case in this area is *Lemon v. Kurtzman* (1971), which determined that supplements to salaries of teachers in religious school raised "excessive entanglement" problems. The current Establishment Clause test is that the government program must: (i) have a secular purpose; (ii) have a primary effect that neither advances nor inhibits religion; and (iii) not produce excessive government entanglement with religion. The instant case raises both "primary purpose" and, from the policing of the restriction on use of the funds, "entanglement" problems. Option (D) goes most directly to the issue in question and is, therefore, correct. (A) is incorrect because it does not consider the "entanglement" problems of the "no religious instruction" restriction. The answer given in option (A) goes only to the "secular purpose" issue. (B) is incorrect because: (i) no "free exercise" issues are involved here; and (ii) distinguishing between public and private schools ***avoids*** Establishment Clause problems. (C) is incorrect because the facts do not indicate disproportionality. Even if disproportionality can be assumed, the courts have elected to invalidate similar laws on the basis of the three-pronged test discussed above rather than couching the issues in terms of "sect preference."

Answer to Question 37

(A) The Supreme Court applies the Establishment Clause prohibitions less strictly when the benefited institution is a religiously affiliated college or hospital rather than a grade or secondary school. The Court will uphold a government grant of aid to such a college or hospital as long as the government program requires that the aid be used only for nonreligious purposes and the recipient so agrees in good faith. Option (A) most nearly approximates this test and is, therefore, correct. (B), on the other hand, is incorrect because it is overbroad. "Bricks and mortar" may not be used, *e.g.,* to build a college chapel. (C) is incorrect because it is overbroad in another direction. Certain grants (*e.g.,* state-approved textbooks, transportation to and from school, expenses of compiling state-required data) have been allowed even for grade and secondary schools. (D) is incorrect because the Supreme Court has found that no excessive entanglement is involved when government funds are used to build "secular" buildings at colleges and universities.

Answer to Question 38

(B) Leonard's conviction will be sustained because states can prohibit or regulate conduct in general, and this is true even if the prohibition or regulation happens to interfere with a person's religious practices. The Free Exercise Clause cannot be used to challenge a neutral law of general applicability (such as the law against cruelty to animals) unless it can be shown that the law was motivated by a desire to interfere with religion. [*See* Church of the Lukumi Babalu Aye, Inc. v. Hialeah (1993)] A law that regulates the conduct of all persons, as this statute appears to do, can be applied to prohibit the conduct of a single person even if the person's religious beliefs prohibit him from complying with the law. (A) is incorrect because the constitutional protection of religious beliefs does not require that the belief arise from a traditional, or even an organized, religion. Beliefs in Satan could have constitutional protection. (C) is wrong for the reasons given in the analysis of option (B). (D) is incorrect because the reasonableness of religious beliefs is not a suitable subject for constitutional inquiry. The courts may not, for example, declare a religion to be "false." The courts may inquire into the sincerity of religious belief, but the reasonableness of the belief is not relevant.

Answer to Question 39

(D) Federal courts are barred from rendering advisory opinions. The legislation here calls for a federal court to transmit to the head of a federal agency an opinion regarding the proper disbursement of federal funds, and the agency head is not required to follow the opinion. This would be an advisory opinion. (A) is incorrect because it fails to consider the necessity for a case and controversy prior to the exercise of federal judicial power. (B) may be a true statement, but the rendition of advisory opinions by a federal court is not a permissible method to settle disputes involving the spending of federal monies. (C) is incorrect because the Eleventh Amendment pertains to suits brought against a state by citizens of that or any other state. Such a suit is not at issue here.

Answer to Question 40

(D) The provision is unconstitutional. The Supreme Court has found "legislative vetoes" to be unconstitutional because they are not subject to presidential review and they violate the separation of powers guaranteed by the federal Constitution. The mechanism set up here has even less basis for constitutionality because the legislative veto that the Supreme Court held unconstitutional at least envisioned votes by one or both full houses of Congress (rather than a mere committee). (A) is incorrect because the Necessary and Proper Clause does not allow Congress to exceed its powers or violate the separation of powers. It merely allows Congress to adopt laws necessary and proper to the powers granted by the Constitution. (B) is incorrect because there is no such rule. Furthermore, the Supreme Court has generally abandoned the "privileges vs. rights" dichotomy. (C) is incorrect because the Equal Protection Clause applies only to actions by the states. Moreover, since no fundamental right or suspect class is involved, the discrimination here would be upheld as long as it is rational.

CONTRACTS QUESTIONS

Questions 1-2 are based on the following fact situation:

Addie, who has been in the painting and contracting business for 10 years and has a fine reputation, contracts to paint Boone's barn. Boone's barn is a standard red barn with a loft. The contract has no provision regarding assignment.

1. If Addie assigns the contract to Coot, who has comparable experience and reputation, which of the following statements is correct?

   (A) Addie is in breach of contract.

   (B) Boone may refuse to accept performance by Coot.

   (C) Boone is required to accept performance by Coot.

   (D) There is a novation.

2. If Addie assigns the contract to Coot and thereafter Coot does not meet the contract specifications in painting Boone's barn, Boone:

   (A) Has a cause of action against Addie for damages.

   (B) Has a cause of action only against Coot for damages.

   (C) Has a cause of action against Addie for damages, only after he has first exhausted his remedies against Coot.

   (D) Does not have a cause of action against Addie for damages because he waived his rights against Addie by permitting Coot to perform the work.

Questions 3-5 are based on the following fact situation:

Johnston purchased 100 bolts of standard blue wool, No. 1 quality, from McHugh. The sales contract provided that Johnston would make payment prior to inspection. The 100 bolts were shipped and Johnston paid McHugh. Upon inspection, however, Johnston discovered that the wool was No. 2 quality. Johnston thereupon tendered back the wool to McHugh and demanded return of his payment. McHugh refused on the ground that there is no difference between No. 1 quality wool and No. 2 quality wool.

3. Which of the following statements regarding the contract provision for preinspection payment is correct?

   (A) It constitutes an acceptance of the goods.

   (B) It constitutes a waiver of the buyer's remedy of private sale in the case of nonconforming goods.

   (C) It does not impair a buyer's right of inspection or his remedies.

   (D) It is invalid.

4. What is Johnston's remedy because the wool was nonconforming?

   (A) Specific performance.

   (B) Damages measured by the difference between the value of the goods delivered and the value of conforming goods.

   (C) Damages measured by the price paid plus the difference between the contract price and the cost of buying substitute goods.

   (D) None, since he waived his remedies by agreeing to pay before inspection.

5. Can Johnston resell the wool?

   (A) Yes, in a private sale.

   (B) Yes, in a private sale but only after giving McHugh reasonable notice of his intention to resell.

(C) Yes, but only at a public sale.

(D) No.

Questions 6-8 are based on the following fact situation:

Duffer and Slicker, who lived in different suburbs 20 miles apart, were golfing acquaintances at the Interurban Country Club. Both were traveling salesmen—Duffer for a pharmaceutical house and Slicker for a widget manufacturer. Duffer wrote Slicker by United States mail on Friday, October 8:

> I need a motorcycle for transportation to the country club, and will buy your Sujocki for $1,200 upon your bringing it to my home address above [stated in the letterhead] on or before noon, November 12 next. This offer is not subject to countermand.
>
> Sincerely,
>
> [signed] Duffer

Slicker replied by mail the following day:

> I accept your offer and promise to deliver the bike as you specified.
>
> Sincerely,
>
> [signed] Slicker

This letter, although properly addressed, was misdirected by the postal service and not received by Duffer until November 10. Duffer had bought another Sujocki bike from Koolcat for $1,050 a few hours before.

Koolcat saw Slicker at the Interurban Country Club on November 11 and said: "I sold my Sujocki to Duffer yesterday for $1,050. Would you consider selling me yours for $950?" Slicker replied, "I'll let you know in a few days."

On November 12, Slicker took his Sujocki to Duffer's residence; he arrived at 11:55 a.m. Duffer was asleep and did not answer Slicker's doorbell rings until 12:15 p.m. Duffer then rejected Slicker's bike on the ground that he had already bought Koolcat's.

6. In Duffer's letter of October 8, what was the legal effect of the language: "This offer is not subject to countermand"?

   (A) Under the Uniform Commercial Code, the offer was irrevocable until noon, November 12.

   (B) Such language prevented an effective acceptance by Slicker prior to noon, November 12.

   (C) At common law, such language created a binding option in Slicker's favor.

   (D) Such language did not affect the offeror's power of revocation of the offer.

7. In a lawsuit by Slicker against Duffer for breach of contract, what would the court probably decide regarding Slicker's letter of October 9?

   (A) The letter bound both parties to a unilateral contract as soon as Slicker mailed it.

   (B) Mailing of the letter by Slicker did not, of itself, prevent a subsequent effective revocation by Duffer of his offer.

   (C) The letter bound both parties to a bilateral contract, but only when received by Duffer on November 10.

   (D) Regardless of whether Duffer's offer had proposed a unilateral or a bilateral contract, the letter was an effective acceptance upon receipt, if not upon dispatch.

8. What is the probable legal effect of Koolcat's conversation with Slicker and

report that he (Koolcat) had sold his Sujocki to Duffer on November 10?

(A) This report had no legal effect because Duffer's offer was irrevocable until November 12.

(B) Unless a contract had already been formed between Slicker and Duffer, Koolcat's report to Slicker operated to terminate Slicker's power of accepting Duffer's offer.

(C) This report had no legal effect because the offer had been made by a prospective buyer (Duffer) rather than a prospective seller.

(D) Koolcat's conversation with Slicker on November 11 terminated Duffer's original offer and operated as an offer by Koolcat to buy Slicker's Sujocki for $950.

Questions 9-10 are based on the following fact situation:

Tortfeasor tortiously injured Victim in an auto accident. While Victim was recovering in Hospital, Tortfeasor's liability insurer, Insurer, settled with Victim for $5,000. Victim gave Insurer a signed release and received a signed memorandum wherein Insurer promised to pay Victim $5,000 by check within 30 days. When Victim left Hospital two days later, Hospital demanded payment of its $4,000 stated bill. Victim thereupon gave Hospital his own negotiable promissory note for $4,000, payable to Hospital's order in 30 days, and also, as security, assigned to Hospital the Insurer settlement memorandum. Hospital promptly assigned for value the settlement memorandum and negotiated the note to Holder, who took the note as a holder in due course. Subsequently, Victim misrepresented to Insurer that he had lost the settlement memorandum and needed another. Insurer issued another memorandum identical to the first, and Victim assigned it to ABC Furniture to secure a $5,000 credit sale contract. ABC immediately notified Insurer of this assignment. Later it was discovered that Hospital had mistakenly overbilled Victim by the amount of $1,000 and that Tortfeasor was an irresponsible minor.

9. If Victim starts an action against Insurer 40 days after the insurance settlement agreement, can Victim recover?

(A) Yes, because his attempted assignments of his claim against Insurer were ineffective, inasmuch as Insurer's promise to pay "by check" created a right in Victim that was too personal to assign.

(B) No, because he no longer has possession of Insurer's written memorandum.

(C) No, because Tortfeasor's minority and irresponsibility vitiated the settlement agreement between Victim and Insurer.

(D) No, because he has made at least one effective assignment of his claim against Insurer, and Insurer has notice thereof.

10. In view of Tortfeasor's age and irresponsibility when Insurer issued his liability policy, can Holder and ABC Furniture recover on their assignments?

(A) Neither can recover because Victim, the assignor, is a third-party beneficiary of the liability policy, whose rights thereon can be no better than Tortfeasor's.

(B) Neither can recover unless Insurer knowingly waived the defense of Tortfeasor's minority and irresponsibility.

(C) Neither can recover because the liability policy, and settlement thereunder, are unenforceable because of Tortfeasor's minority.

(D) Either Holder or ABC Furniture, depending on priority, can recover as assignee (or subassignee) of Victim's claim because the latter arose from Insurer's settlement agreement, the latter agreement not being vitiated by Tortfeasor's minority and irresponsibility when he obtained the policy.

Question 11

On January 15, Carpenter agreed to repair Householder's house according to certain specifications and to have the work completed by April 1. On March 1, Householder's property was inundated by flood waters which did not abate until March 15. Householder could not get the house in a condition which would permit Carpenter to begin the repairs until March 31. On that date Carpenter notified Householder that he would not repair the house.

Which one of the following facts, if it was the only one true and known to both parties on January 15, would best serve Carpenter as the basis for a defense in an action brought against him by Householder for breach of contract?

(A) Carpenter's busy schedule permitted him to work on Householder's house only during the month of March.

(B) Any delay in making the repairs would not seriously affect Householder's use of the property.

(C) The cost of making repairs was increasing at the rate of 3% a month.

(D) The area around Householder's property was frequently flooded during the month of March.

Question 12

In a telephone call on March 1, Adams, an unemployed, retired person, said to Dawes, "I will sell my automobile for $3,000 cash. I will hold this offer open through March 14." On March 12, Adams called Dawes and told her that he had sold the automobile to Clark. Adams in fact had not sold the automobile to anyone. On March 14, Dawes learned that Adams still owned the automobile, and on that date called Adams and said, "I'm coming over to your place with $3,000." Adams replied, "Don't bother. I won't deliver the automobile to you under any circumstances." Dawes protested, but made no further attempt to pay for or take delivery of the automobile.

In an action by Dawes against Adams for breach of contract, Dawes probably will:

(A) Succeed, because Adams had assured her that the offer would remain open through March 14.

(B) Succeed, because Adams had not in fact sold the automobile to Clark.

(C) Not succeed, because Dawes had not tendered the $3,000 to Adams on or before March 14.

(D) Not succeed, because on March 12, Adams had told Dawes that he had sold the automobile to Clark.

Question 13

Carver is a chemical engineer. She has no interest in or connection with Chemco. Carver noticed that Chemco's most recent publicly issued financial statement listed, as part of Chemco's assets, a large inventory of a certain special chemical compound. This asset was listed at a cost of $100,000, but Carver knew that the ingredients of the compound were in short supply and that the current market value of the inventory was in excess of $1 million. There was no current public quotation of the price of Chemco stock. The book value of Chemco stock, according to the statement, was $5 per share; its actual value was $30 per share.

Knowing these facts, Carver offered to purchase from Page at $6 per share the 1,000 shares of Chemco stock owned by Page. Page and Carver had not previously met. Page sold the stock to Carver for $6 per share.

If Page asserts a claim based on misrepresentation against Carver, will Page prevail?

(A) Yes, because Carver knew that the value of the stock was greater than the price she offered.

(B) Yes, if Carver did not inform Page of the true value of the inventory.

(C) No, unless Carver told Page that the stock was not worth more than $6 per share.

(D) No, if Chemco's financial statement was available to Page.

Questions 14-15 are based on the following fact situation:

In a written contract Singer agreed to deliver to Byer 500 described chairs at $20 each F.O.B. Singer's place of business. The contract provided that "neither party will assign this contract without the written consent of the other." Singer placed the chairs on board a carrier on January 30. On February 1, Singer said in a signed writing, "I hereby assign to Wheeler all my rights under the Singer-Byer contract." Singer did not request and did not get Byer's consent to this transaction. On February 2, the chairs, while in transit, were destroyed in a derailment of the carrier's railroad car.

14. In an action by Wheeler against Byer, Wheeler probably will recover:

    (A) $10,000, the contract price.

    (B) The difference between the contract price and the market value of the chairs.

    (C) Nothing, because the chairs had not been delivered.

    (D) Nothing, because the Singer-Byer contract forbade an assignment.

15. In an action by Byer against Singer for breach of contract, Byer probably will:

    (A) Succeed, because the carrier will be deemed to be Singer's agent.

    (B) Succeed, because the risk of loss was on Singer.

    (C) Not succeed, because of impossibility of performance.

    (D) Not succeed, because the risk of loss was on Byer.

Question 16

After several days of negotiations, Ohner wrote to Plummer: "Will pay you $3,000 if you will install new plumbing in my office building according to the specifications I have sent you. I must have your reply by March 30." Plummer replied by a letter that Ohner received on March 15: "Will not do it for less than $3,500." On March 20, Plummer wrote to Ohner: "Have changed my mind. I will do the work for $3,000. Unless I hear from you to the contrary, I will begin work on April 5." Ohner received this letter on March 22 but did not reply to it. Plummer, without Ohner's knowledge, began the work on April 5.

Which of the following best characterizes the legal relationship between Ohner and Plummer as of April 5?

(A) A contract was formed on March 20 when Plummer posted his letter.

(B) A contract was formed on March 22 when Ohner received Plummer's letter.

(C) A contract was formed on April 5 when Plummer began work.

(D) There was no contract between the parties as of April 5.

Questions 17-18 are based on the following fact situation:

On January 15, in a signed writing, Artisan agreed to remodel Ohner's building according to certain specifications, Ohner to pay the agreed price of $5,000 to Artisan's niece, Roberta Neese, as a birthday present. Neese did not learn of the agreement until her birthday on May 5.

Before they signed the writing, Artisan and Ohner had orally agreed that their "written agreement will be null and void unless Ohner is able to obtain a $5,000 loan from the First National Bank before January 31."

17. For this question only, assume that Ohner was unable to obtain the loan and, on January 31, phoned Artisan and told him, "Don't begin the work. The deal is off." In an action for breach of contract brought against Ohner by the proper party, will Ohner be successful in asserting as a defense his inability to obtain a loan?

    (A) Yes, because obtaining a loan was a condition precedent to the existence of an enforceable contract.

    (B) Yes, because the agreement about obtaining a loan is a modification of a construction contract and is not required to be in writing.

    (C) No, because the agreement about obtaining a loan contradicts the express and implied terms of the writing.

    (D) No, because Ohner is estopped to deny the validity of the written agreement.

18. For this question only, assume that Ohner obtained the loan, that Artisan completed the remodeling on May 1, and that on May 3, at Artisan's request, Ohner paid the $5,000 to Artisan. If Neese learns of Ohner's payment to Artisan on May 5, at the same time she learns of the written Artisan-Ohner contract, will she succeed in an action against Ohner for $5,000?

    (A) Yes, because she is an intended beneficiary of the written Artisan-Ohner contract.

    (B) Yes, because the written Artisan-Ohner contract operated as an assignment to Neese, and Artisan thereby lost whatever rights he may have had to the $5,000.

    (C) No, because Neese had not furnished any consideration to support Ohner's promise to pay $5,000 to her.

    (D) No, because on May 3, Artisan and Ohner effectively modified their written contract, thereby depriving Neese of whatever rights she may have had under that contract.

Questions 19-20 are based on the following fact situation:

When Esther, Gray's 21-year-old daughter, finished college, Gray handed her a signed memorandum stating that if she would go to law school for three academic years, he would pay her tuition, room, and board, and would "give her a $1,000 bonus" for each "A" she got in law school. Esther's uncle, Miller, who was present on this occasion, read the memorandum and thereupon said to Esther, "and if he doesn't pay your expenses, I will." Gray paid her tuition, room, and board for her first year but died just before the end of that year. Subsequently, Esther learned that she had received two "As" in the second semester. The executor of Gray's estate has refused to pay her anything for the two "As" and has told her that the estate will no longer pay her tuition, room, and board in law school.

19. In an action by Esther against Miller on account of the executor's repudiation of Gray's promise to pay future tuition, room, and board, which of the following would be Miller's strongest defense?

    (A) The parties did not manifestly intend a contract.

    (B) Gray's death terminated the agreement.

    (C) The agreement was oral.

    (D) The agreement was divisible.

20. In an action against Gray's estate for $2,000 on account of the two "As," if the only defense raised is lack of consideration, Esther probably will:

(A) Succeed under the doctrine of promissory estoppel.

(B) Succeed on a theory of bargained-for exchange for her father's promise.

(C) Not succeed, because the $1,000 for each "A" was promised only as a bonus.

(D) Not succeed, because Esther was already legally obligated to use her best efforts in law school.

Question 21

Zeller contracted in writing to deliver to Baker 100 bushels of wheat on August 1 at $3.50 per bushel. Because his suppliers had not delivered enough wheat to him by that time, Zeller on August 1 had only 95 bushels of wheat with which to fulfill his contract with Baker.

If Zeller tenders 95 bushels of wheat to Baker on August 1, and Baker refuses to accept or pay for any of the wheat, which of the following best states the legal relationship between Zeller and Baker?

(A) Zeller has a cause of action against Baker, because Zeller has substantially performed his contract.

(B) Zeller is excused from performing his contract because of impossibility of performance.

(C) Baker has a cause of action against Zeller for Zeller's failure to deliver 100 bushels of wheat.

(D) Baker is obligated to give Zeller a reasonable time to attempt to obtain the other five bushels of wheat.

Questions 22-23 are based on the following fact situation:

On May 1, Selco and Byco entered into a written agreement in which Selco agreed to fabricate and sell to Byco 10,000 specially designed brake linings for a new type of power brake manufactured by Byco. The contract provided that Byco would pay half of the purchase price on May 15 in order to give Selco funds to "tool up" for the work; that Selco would deliver 5,000 brake linings on May 31; that Byco would pay the balance of the purchase price on June 5; and that Selco would deliver the balance of the brake linings on June 30.

On May 10, Selco notified Byco that it was doubtful whether Selco could perform because of problems encountered in modifying its production machines to produce the brake linings. On May 15, however, Selco assured Byco that the production difficulties had been overcome, and Byco paid Selco the first 50% installment of the purchase price. Selco did not deliver the first 5,000 brake linings on May 31, or at any time thereafter; and on June 10, Selco notified Byco that it would not perform the contract.

22. Which of the following correctly states Byco's rights and obligations immediately after receipt of Selco's notice on May 10?

(A) Byco can treat the notice as an anticipatory repudiation, and has a cause of action on May 10 for breach of the entire contract.

(B) Byco can treat the notice as an anticipatory repudiation, and can sue at once to enjoin an actual breach by Selco on May 31.

(C) Byco has no cause of action for breach of contract, but can suspend its performance and demand assurances that Selco will perform.

(D) Byco has no cause of action for breach of contract, and must pay the installment of the purchase price due on May 15 to preserve its rights under the contract.

23. Which of the following is ***not*** a correct statement of the parties' legal status

immediately after Selco's notice on June 10?

(A) Byco has a cause of action for total breach of contract because of Selco's repudiation, but that cause of action will be lost if Selco retracts its repudiation before Byco changes its position or manifests to Selco that Byco considers the repudiation final.

(B) Byco can bring suit to rescind the contract even if it elects to await Selco's performance for a commercially reasonable time.

(C) Byco can await performance by Selco for a commercially reasonable time, but if Byco awaits performance beyond that period, it cannot recover any resulting damages that it reasonably could have avoided.

(D) Byco has a cause of action for breach of contract that it can successfully assert only after it has given Selco a commercially reasonable time to perform.

Questions 24-25 are based on the following fact situation:

The Kernel Corporation, through its president, Demeter Gritz, requested from Vault Finance, Inc., a short-term loan of $100,000. On April 1, Gritz and Vault's loan officer agreed orally that Vault would make the loan on the following terms: (1) the loan would be repaid in full on or before the following July 1 and would carry interest at an annual rate of 15% (a lawful rate under the applicable usury law); and (2) Gritz would personally guarantee repayment. The loan was approved and made on April 5. The only document evidencing the loan was a memorandum, written and supplied by Vault and signed by Gritz for Kernel, that read in its entirety:

April 5

In consideration of a loan advanced on this date, Kernel Corporation hereby promises to pay Vault Finance, Inc., $100,000 on September 1.

Kernel Corporation
by /s/ Demeter Gritz
Demeter Gritz, President

Kernel Corporation did not repay the loan on or before July 1, although it had sufficient funds to do so. On July 10, Vault sued Kernel as principal debtor and Gritz individually as guarantor for $100,000, plus 15% interest from April 5.

24. At the trial, can Vault prove Kernel's oral commitment to repay the loan on or before July 1?

(A) Yes, because the oral agreement was supported by an independent consideration.

(B) Yes, because evidence of the parties' negotiations is relevant to their contractual intent concerning maturity of the debt.

(C) No, because such evidence is barred by the preexisting duty rule.

(D) No, because such evidence contradicts the writing and is barred by the parol evidence rule.

25. At the trial, can Vault prove Gritz's oral promise to guarantee the loan?

(A) Yes, because Gritz signed the memorandum.

(B) Yes, because, as president of the debtor-company, Gritz is a third-party beneficiary of the loan.

(C) No, because there was no separate consideration for Gritz's promise.

(D) No, because such proof is barred by the Statute of Frauds.

Question 26

Osif owned Broadacres in fee simple. For a consideration of $5,000, Osif gave Bard a written option to purchase Broadacres for $300,000. The option was assignable. For a consideration of $10,000, Bard subsequently gave an option to Cutter to purchase Broadacres for $325,000. Cutter exercised his option.

Bard thereupon exercised his option. Bard paid the agreed price of $300,000, and took title to Broadacres by deed from Osif. Thereafter, Cutter refused to consummate his purchase.

Bard brought an appropriate action against Cutter for specific performance, or, if that should be denied, then for damages. Cutter counterclaimed for return of the $10,000.

In this action, the court will:

(A) Grant money damages only to Bard.

(B) Grant specific performance to Bard.

(C) Grant Bard only the right to retain the $10,000.

(D) Require Bard to refund the $10,000 to Cutter.

Questions 27-28 are based on the following fact situation:

Mater, a wealthy widow, wishing to make a substantial and potentially enduring gift to her beloved adult stepson, Prodigal, established with the Vault Savings and Loan Association a passbook savings account by an initial deposit of $10,000.

27. For this question only, assume the following facts. The passbook was issued solely in Prodigal's name; but Mater retained possession of it, and Prodigal was not then informed of the savings account. Subsequently, Mater became disgusted with Prodigal's behavior and decided to give the same savings account solely to her beloved adult daughter Distaff. As permitted by the rules of Vault Savings and Loan, Mater effected this change by agreement with Vault. This time she left possession of the passbook with Vault. Shortly thereafter, Prodigal learned of the original savings account in his name and the subsequent switch to Distaff's name.

    If Prodigal now sues Vault Savings and Loan for $10,000 plus accrued interest, will the action succeed?

    (A) Yes, because Prodigal was a third-party intended beneficiary of the original Mater-Vault deposit agreement.

    (B) Yes, because Prodigal was a constructive assignee of Mater's claim, as depositor, to the savings account.

    (C) No, because Prodigal never obtained possession of the passbook.

    (D) No, because Prodigal's right, if any, to the funds on deposit was effectively abrogated by the second Mater-Vault deposit agreement.

28. For this question only, assume the following facts. The passbook was issued by Vault to Mater solely in her own name. That same day, disinterested witnesses being present, she handed the passbook to Prodigal and said, "As a token of my love and affection for you, I give you this $10,000 savings account." Shortly thereafter, she changed her mind and wrote Prodigal, "I hereby revoke my gift to you of the $10,000 savings account with Vault Savings and Loan Association. Please return my passbook immediately. Signed: Mater." Prodigal received this letter but ignored it, and Mater died unexpectedly a few days later.

    In litigation between Prodigal and Mater's estate, which of the following is a correct statement of the parties' rights with respect to the money on deposit with Vault?

(A) The estate prevails, because Mater's gift to Prodigal was revocable and was terminated by her death.

(B) The estate prevails, because Mater's gift to Prodigal was revocable and was terminated by her express revocation.

(C) Prodigal prevails, because he took Mater's claim to the savings account by a gratuitous but effective and irrevocable assignment from Mater.

(D) Prodigal prevails, because his failure to reject the gift, even if the assignment was revocable, created an estoppel against Mater and her estate.

Questions 29-30 are based on the following fact situation:

On October 1, Toy Store, Inc., entered into a written contract with Fido Factory, Inc., for the purchase at $20 per unit of 1,000 mechanical dogs, to be specially manufactured by Fido according to Toy Store's specifications. Fido promised to deliver all of the dogs "not later than November 15, for the Yule shopping season," and Toy Store promised to pay the full $20,000 price upon delivery. In order to obtain operating funds, Fido as borrower entered into a written loan agreement on October 5 with the High Finance Company. In relevant part, this agreement recited, "Fido Factory hereby transfers and assigns to High Finance its (Fido Factory's) October 1 mechanical dog contract with Toy Store, as security for a 50-day loan of $15,000, the advance and receipt of which are hereby acknowledged by Fido Factory. . . ." No copy of this agreement, or statement relating to it, was filed in an office of public record.

On October 15, Fido notified Toy Store, "We regret to advise that our master shaft burned out last night because our night supervisor let the lubricant level get too low. We have just fired the supervisor, but the shaft cannot be repaired or replaced until about January 1. We can guarantee delivery of your order, however, not later than January 20." Toy Store rejected this proposal as unacceptable and immediately contracted with the only other available manufacturer to obtain the 1,000 dogs at $30 per unit by November 15.

29. For this question only, assume that on November 1, Toy Store sues Fido for damages and alleges the above facts, except those relating to the Fido-High Finance loan agreement. Upon Fido's motion to dismiss the complaint, the court should:

(A) Sustain the motion, because Fido on October 15 stated its willingness, and gave assurance of its ability, to perform the contract in January.

(B) Sustain the motion, because Toy Store's lawsuit is premature in any case until after November 15.

(C) Deny the motion, because Toy Store's complaint alleges an actionable tort by Fido.

(D) Deny the motion, because Toy Store's complaint alleges an actionable breach of contract by Fido.

30. For this question only, assume that by November 16, Fido, without legal excuse, has delivered no dogs, and that Toy Store has brought no action against Fido. In an action brought on November 16 by Toy Store against High Finance Company because of Fido's default, Toy Store can recover:

(A) Nothing, because the October 5 assignment by Fido to High Finance of Fido's contract with Toy Store was only an assignment for security.

(B) Nothing, because no record of the October 5 transaction between Fido and High Finance was publicly filed.

(C) $10,000 in damages, because Toy Store was a third-party intended beneficiary of the October 5 transaction between Fido and High Finance.

(D) $10,000 in damages, because the October 5 transaction between Fido and High Finance effected, with respect to Toy Store as creditor, a novation of debtors.

Question 31

In March, when Ohm was 17, Stereo delivered to Ohm a television set. At that time Ohm agreed in writing to pay $400 for the set on July 1, when he would reach his 18th birthday. Eighteen is the applicable statutory age of majority, and on that date Ohm was to receive the proceeds of a trust. On July 1, when the reasonable value of the television set was $250, Ohm sent Stereo a signed letter stating, "I'll only pay you $300. That is all the set is worth."

In an action against Ohm for money damages on July 2, what is the maximum amount that Stereo will be entitled to recover?

(A) Nothing.

(B) $250, the reasonable value of the set.

(C) $300, the amount Ohm promised to pay in his letter of July 1.

(D) $400, the original sale price.

Question 32

Ann leased commercial property to Brenda for a period of 10 years. The lease contained the following provision: "No subleasing or assignment will be permitted unless with the written consent of the lessor." One year later, Brenda assigned all interest in the lease to Carolyn, who assumed and agreed to perform the lessee's obligations under the terms of the lease. Ann learned of the assignment and wrote to Brenda that she had no objection to the assignment to Carolyn and agreed to accept rent from Carolyn instead of Brenda. Thereafter, Carolyn paid rent to Ann for a period of five years. Carolyn then defaulted and went into bankruptcy. In an appropriate action, Ann sued Brenda for rent due.

If Ann loses, it will be because there was:

(A) Laches.

(B) An accord and satisfaction.

(C) A novation.

(D) An attornment.

Questions 33-34 are based on the following fact situation:

Furrow leased in writing a 100-acre farm from Quark for five years at $2,000 per year, with an option to purchase "five acres of the land for $10,000 cash" at the end of the lease term. Before the lease was executed, Quark orally promised to have a five-acre parcel surveyed before the end of the lease term. Furrow took possession of the farm and paid the rent for five years. During the fifth year, having decided that he would exercise the purchase option, Furrow planted several fruit trees and built a large grain silo on the property. At the end of the term, Furrow tendered Quark $10,000 and demanded a conveyance, but Quark repudiated the option agreement and retook possession of the farm. He had never had the five-acre parcel surveyed.

33. In an action by Furrow against Quark for specific performance of the option agreement, which of the following is Quark's best defense?

    (A) The option part of the agreement is unenforceable because it lacked a separate consideration.

    (B) The description of the property to be sold in the parties' written agreement is too indefinite to permit the remedy sought.

    (C) Quark's failure to have the five-acre parcel surveyed was failure of a condition precedent to his own duty of performance.

(D) The option part of the agreement is unenforceable under the parol evidence rule.

34. Assume for this question only that Quark is not liable to Furrow for breach of a land-sale contract. In an action by Furrow against Quark for the reasonable value of the improvements that Furrow added to the farm, which of the following theories would best support Furrow's claim?

(A) Quasi-contract, for benefits unofficiously and non-gratuitously conferred upon Quark by Furrow.

(B) Tort, for conversion by Quark in retaking possession of the improvements.

(C) Breach of trust by Quark as trustee of a resulting trust of the improvements.

(D) Breach by Quark of an implied-in-fact promise (manifested by his retaking possession of the farm and improvements) to compensate Furrow for the improvements.

Questions 35-36 are based on the following fact situation:

On January 2, Hugh Homey and Sue Structo entered into a written contract in which Structo agreed to build on Homey's lot a new house for Homey, according to plans and specifications furnished by Homey's architect, Barbara Bilevel, at a contract price of $200,000. The contract provided for specified progress payments and a final payment of $40,000 upon Homey's acceptance of the house and issuance of a certificate of final approval by the architect. Further, under a "liquidated damages" clause in the agreement, Structo promised to pay Homey $500 for each day's delay in completing the house after the following October 1. Homey, however, told Structo on January 2, before the contract was signed, that he would be on an around-the-world vacation trip most of the summer and fall and would not return to occupy the house until November 1.

35. For this question only, assume the following facts: Because she was overextended on other construction jobs, Structo did not complete the house until October 15. Homey returned on November 1 as planned and occupied the house. Ten days later, after making the $40,000 final payment to Structo, Homey learned for the first time that the house had not been completed until October 15.

If Homey sues Structo for breach of contract on account of the 15-day delay in completion, which of the following will the court probably decide?

(A) Homey will recover damages as specified in the contract, *i.e.*, $500 multiplied by 15.

(B) Homey will recover his actual damages, if any, caused by the delay in completion.

(C) Having waived the delay by occupying the house and making the final payment, Homey will recover nothing.

(D) Homey will recover nothing because the contractual completion date was impliedly modified to November 1 when Homey on January 2 advised Structo about Homey's prospective trip and return date.

36. For this question only, assume the following facts: Structo completed the house on October 14 and, when Homey returned on November 1, requested the final payment of $40,000 and issuance of a certificate of final approval by the architect, Bilevel. Homey, however, refused to pay any part of the final installment after Bilevel told him, "Structo did a great job and I find no defects worth mentioning, but Structo's contract price was at least $40,000 too high, especially in view of the big drop in housing values within the past 10 months. I will withhold the final certificate, and you just hold on to your money."

If Structo sues Homey for the $40,000 final payment after Bilevel's refusal to issue a final certificate, which of the following will the court probably decide?

(A) Structo wins, because nonoccurrence of the condition requiring Bilevel's certificate of final approval was excused by Bilevel's bad-faith refusal to issue the certificate.

(B) Structo wins, but, because all contractual conditions have not occurred, her recovery is limited to restitution of the benefit conferred on Homey, minus progress payments already received.

(C) Homey wins, provided he can prove by clear and convincing evidence that the fair-market value of the completed house is $160,000 or less.

(D) Homey wins, provided he can prove by clear and convincing evidence that total payments to Structo of $160,000 will yield a fair net profit.

CONTRACTS ANSWERS

Answer to Question 1

(C) Although this assignment of rights would result in the performance of personal services, the nature of the personal service described here appears to be routine rather than unique and thus the duty is delegable. Note also that the contract contains no language restricting assignment or delegation. (Note also that language "assigning the contract" may be construed to include a delegation of duties.) Thus, Boone (the obligee) would be required to accept performance by the delegate (Coot). Therefore, (B), which states that Boone may refuse to accept such performance, is incorrect. Because the contract does not prohibit Addie's assignment thereof, (A) incorrectly states that such assignment renders Addie in breach. (D) is incorrect because a novation substitutes a new party for an original party to the contract, and requires the assent of all parties, and completely releases the original party. The facts here do not indicate that Boone agreed to any such new arrangement.

Answer to Question 2

(A) The delegator remains personally liable on his contract, even if the delegate has expressly assumed the duties. Thus, Addie remains liable for any defective performance of the painting. (B) and (C) each are based on the incorrect assumption that the obligee is required to look to the delegate for a remedy in the event of defective performance. As explained above, the obligee (Boone) may hold the delegator (Addie) liable on the contract. (D) is incorrect because the facts do not indicate that Boone accepted performance by a new party with knowledge that there was an intent to substitute that party for an original party to the contract. Therefore, Boone did not waive his rights against Addie.

Answer to Question 3

(C) Because Johnston promised to pay without inspecting the goods, he had no right to inspect ***prior to payment***. If payment is due before inspection, the fact that the goods are defective does not excuse nonpayment, unless the defect appears without inspection or there is fraud in the transaction. However, the buyer is not prevented from inspecting the goods after making payment, and thereafter pursuing all available remedies for defective performance. (D) is incorrect because, as explained above, nothing prevents a buyer from promising to pay prior to inspection. (A) is incorrect because the contractual provision at issue does not constitute an acceptance. There is no acceptance until Johnston has had an opportunity to inspect. (B) also incorrectly implies that the provision effectuates a waiver of the buyer's rights.

Answer to Question 4

(C) Where the seller does not deliver or the buyer properly rejects or revokes acceptance of tendered goods, the buyer's basic remedy is the difference between the contract price and either the market price or the cost of buying replacement goods (cover). (C) reflects the latter measure of damages. (A) is incorrect because specific performance is only available where the goods are unique or in other proper circumstances. Here, the wool does not appear to be unique. (B) is incorrect because it sets forth a measure of damages that is properly applicable where the buyer accepts goods that breach one of the seller's warranties; here, the goods have not been accepted. (D) is incorrect because, as explained in the answer to the preceding question, agreeing to pay before inspection does not waive any of the buyer's rights.

Answer to Question 5

(B) Where the buyer has paid for goods which are nonconforming, and the seller has refused the buyer's offer to restore the goods and the buyer's demand for repayment, the buyer may resell the goods and credit the proceeds to the amount owed by the seller (under the same rules that apply to a seller's resale of wrongfully rejected goods). The buyer may sell at either a public or private sale; but if it is a private sale, reasonable advance notice must be given to the seller. [U.C.C. §§2-711(3), 2-706(2), (3)] (A) and (C) each incorrectly limit the sale to being either private or public. (D) incorrectly states that the sale is not permitted at all.

Answer to Question 6

(D) Generally, offers are revocable unless the offeror receives consideration to keep the offer open. If a ***merchant*** signs a written offer giving assurances that it will be held open, the offer is irrevocable for the stated period or for a reasonable time if no period is stated. Here, the language at issue would probably be interpreted as a promise not to revoke; however, the offeror (Duffer) is not a merchant (*i.e.*, he does not deal in goods of the kind being sold). Thus, in the absence of consideration being given for this promise, it remains revocable. (A) is incorrect because, although there is a sale of goods, neither of the parties is a merchant, and hence, the "firm offer" provision of the U.C.C. does not apply. (B) makes no sense because the very terms of the offer state that Slicker can accept prior to noon on November 12. (C) is incorrect because no consideration was given for the promise not to countermand.

Answer to Question 7

(B) Duffer's letter would be construed as an offer that unambiguously calls for completion of performance, rather than a promise, as the only manner of acceptance. This would be an offer for a unilateral contract. An offer for a unilateral contract cannot be accepted by promising to perform. Hence, Slicker's letter of October 9 by itself wouldn't prevent Duffer from revoking his offer. (A) is wrong because a unilateral contract is created only on completion of performance of the bargained-for act, not by simply mailing a purported acceptance. (C) is wrong because the offer was for a unilateral contract. (D) is wrong because, as a response to an offer to enter into a unilateral contract, the promise to perform had no legal effect regardless of when it was received.

Answer to Question 8

(B) An offer is effectively revoked when the offeree acquires knowledge that the offeror has made an inconsistent contract with another, whether such knowledge is obtained from the offeror or some independent source. (A) is wrong because there was no consideration for the promise to keep the offer open. (C) makes no sense. Whether Slicker's power of accepting the offer is terminated does not depend on the fact that the offer was made by a prospective buyer rather than a prospective seller. (D) is incorrect insofar as it states that the November 11 conversation was also an offer to purchase; the wording used by Koolcat ("would you consider . . .") seems too preliminary in nature and thus more an invitation than an offer.

Answer to Question 9

(D) An assignor may not enforce rights against an obligor that have been previously assigned, as is the case here. An assignment establishes privity of contract between the obligor and the assignee while extinguishing privity between the obligor and assignor. Thus, the assignee replaces the assignor as the real party in interest, and the assignee alone is entitled to performance under the contract. (A) is incorrect because a promise to pay by check does not create a right too personal to assign. An attempted assignment is invalid where the rights "assigned" would result in the obligor having to perform unique personal services to someone other than the original obligee. Paying by check does not constitute such a personal service. (B) is incorrect because possession of the memorandum of settlement has no bearing on the effectiveness of an assignment. (C) is wrong because minority does not vitiate a contract, but makes it ***voidable*** by the minor. Furthermore, insurance contracts usually cannot be voided by minors.

Answer to Question 10

(D) Insurance contracts usually cannot be voided by infants. Thus, the liability insurance, and settlement agreement arising out of it, are valid. (A) seems to be based on the incorrect assumption that, because of Tortfeasor's minority at the time the liability policy was issued, Insurer might not be bound on the contract of insurance. Actually, the effect of a contract entered into between an infant and an adult is that the contract is voidable by the infant but binding on the adult. Thus, there is no question that Tortfeasor has rights under the liability policy. (B) assumes that Tortfeasor's minority constitutes a defense. As explained above, this is incorrect. (C) is incorrect for the same reason.

Answer to Question 11

(A) If both parties knew of Carpenter's schedule limitation at the time the contract was entered into, the supervening flood would discharge the duty to perform by impossibility, because no one could have performed during the month of March. The requirement that the impossibility must arise after the contract was entered into has been met. Since the impossibility is temporary, it could be argued that the impossibility only suspends contractual duties rather than discharging them. However, if it was specifically understood that the only time for performance was the month of March, then the contract should be discharged by impossibility. (B) is wrong because this would actually argue for a continuing duty on the part of Carpenter to make the repairs. (C) is wrong because it would not be relevant. With no additional facts, Carpenter could have begun performance in January and incurred no extra costs. (D) is wrong because it does not speak to whether Carpenter could have performed either before or after March.

Answer to Question 12

(D) On March 12, Adams terminated his offer by communicating his revocation to the offeree before Dawes had accepted. Since the revocation was directly communicated to the offeree, it was immediately effective. Because the offer was revoked, Dawes no longer had any power of acceptance. (A) is wrong because Adams's assurance did not create an option contract. Dawes gave no value for an option contract, and Adams did not assure Dawes that the offer would remain open to her personally until March 14, but only that the offer would remain open generally until that date. (B) is wrong because Adams's failure to sell the car is of no import. Adams's statement clearly communicated the intent to revoke the offer and thus terminated the offer to Dawes. (C) is wrong because even if Dawes had tendered the $3,000 on March 13, Adams need not have conveyed the automobile because he had already terminated the offer.

Answer to Question 13

(C) Carver had no duty to disclose to Page the true value of the stock. If, however, Carver had represented that the stock was not worth more than $6 a share, this would have constituted material misrepresentation and no contract would result. (A) is wrong because Carver's knowledge of the true value did not create a duty to disclose that knowledge. (B) is wrong because there was no duty to inform Page of the true value of the inventory. (D) is wrong because if Carver had misrepresented the value of the stock, availability of Chemco's financial statement to Page would not relieve Carver of liability.

Answer to Question 14

(A) Since the contract stipulated F.O.B. Singer's place of business, the risk of loss passed to Byer on January 30 when Singer placed the chairs on board a carrier. Thus, the loss of the chairs must be borne by Byer, and Singer is entitled to the contract price. Wheeler, as Singer's assignee, is entitled to the contract price. (B) is wrong as this is the measure where the buyer refuses the goods and the seller then resells them to someone else. Here, since the chairs do not exist any more, the measure of damages would be the entire contract price. (C) is wrong because the contract stipulated F.O.B. Singer's place of business. If it had not so stated, the statement in (C) would be correct. (D) is wrong because, absent circumstances suggesting otherwise, a clause prohibiting the assignment of "the contract" will be construed as barring only the delegation of the assignor's duties, not the assignment of the right to receive payment.

Answer to Question 15

(D) In a contract that specifies that delivery is F.O.B. (free on board) a particular point, the F.O.B. point is the delivery point. If the contract is F.O.B. the seller's place of shipment, the seller need only, at his expense and risk, put the goods in the hands of the carrier. If the contract is F.O.B. destination, the seller must, at his expense and risk, tender delivery of the goods at the designated destination. Here, the risk of loss had passed to Byer because the contract specifically stated that delivery was to be F.O.B. Singer's place of business. (A) and (B) are incorrect because, as explained above, the terms of the contract establish that the risk of loss was not on Singer. (C) is wrong because Singer had already performed by delivering the chairs to the carrier.

Answer to Question 16

(D) No contract was formed between the parties because Plummer gave Ohner a counteroffer rather than an acceptance. If the language had been different, this might have been an acceptance conditioned on higher payment, but given the wording, there were no clear words of acceptance. The making of the counteroffer made acceptance of the original offer impossible, and since Ohner never accepted the counteroffer, no contract was formed between the parties. (A) is wrong because at that point Plummer no longer had power of acceptance on the original offer. (B) is wrong because if Plummer's writing had been a valid acceptance, it would have been valid upon posting under the mailbox rule. (C) is wrong because Ohner's original offer was to be accepted by reply rather than by conduct, and it terminated when Plummer made his counteroffer.

Answer to Question 17

(A) A condition precedent is one which must occur before an absolute duty of immediate performance arises in the other party. Here, because performance was expressly conditioned upon Ohner's obtaining a loan and since that loan was refused, no duty to perform exists. (B) is wrong because the agreement was made before the signing of the contract. (C) is wrong because the agreement does not contradict and is in addition to the meaning of the written contract. (D) is wrong because Ohner is not attempting to deny the validity of the written agreement.

Answer to Question 18

(D) Parties to a contract may modify it by mutual assent. While consideration is necessary to modify a contract, courts usually find consideration to be present in that each party has limited his right to enforce the original contract on its own terms. On May 3, the parties modified the original contract by making other arrangements for payment which were then met. This modification served to discharge the terms in the original contract regarding payment, so Neese has no claim to the $5,000. (A) is wrong because even though Neese was an intended beneficiary of the contract, her rights in it had not vested when the modification was made on May 3, because she had not yet learned of the contract. (B) is wrong because the contract was not assigned to Neese. Rather, she was an intended beneficiary of the contract. (C) is wrong because an intended beneficiary need not furnish any consideration, so long as the original contract is supported by consideration.

Answer to Question 19

(C) Miller's strongest argument is that since the contract, by its own terms, could not be performed within a year, it was subject to the Statute of Frauds and should have been in writing. Since it was not, it is void under the Statute of Frauds. (A) would be a possible argument, but it is not as strong as the Statute of Frauds argument. Further, it would probably fail as there does appear to be manifest intent to contract. (B) is wrong because if there was a valid contract, it would not have been terminated by Gray's death. Rather, Gray's estate would have been liable for the monies owed. (D) is wrong because this was not a divisible contract.

Answer to Question 20

(B) Esther's argument would be that her hard work academically constituted her consideration for the agreement. It is not required that consideration be economic in nature. (A) is wrong because if the only defense is lack of consideration, Esther should keep arguing on contractual terms. Even in arguing under the doctrine of promissory estoppel, Esther would have to establish that she relied on the promise to her detriment. (C) is wrong because the "bonus" provision was an integral part of the contract. (D) is wrong because there is no legal duty to try one's hardest in academic pursuits, so Esther had no preexisting duty to excel.

Answer to Question 21

(C) Since Baker contracted for 100 bushels on August 1, Zeller had a contractual duty which was breached by the tendering of only 95 bushels. Baker has a cause of action for that breach. (A) is wrong because substantial performance does not excuse total performance of contractual duties. (B) is wrong because discharge by impossibility only occurs where impossibility is objective. The fact that Zeller only had 95 bushels created a subjective rather than an objective impossibility of performance, and thus did not excuse his breach. (D) is wrong because Baker was entitled to performance on August 1.

Answer to Question 22

(C) Under Article Two of the U.C.C., Selco's notice of May 10 would be considered an action which increases the risk of nonperformance, but does not clearly indicate that performance will not be forthcoming. Thus, it will not immediately be treated as a repudiation. The notice constitutes reasonable grounds for insecurity, entitling Byco to demand adequate assurance of due performance. Until Byco receives such assurance, it may suspend its own performance. (C) is the only answer embodying these principles. (A) and (B) are incorrect because they treat Selco's notice as an anticipatory repudiation. (D) is incorrect because it implies that Byco may not suspend its own performance until receipt of adequate assurances.

Answer to Question 23

(D) Selco's notice of June 10 made it clear that it was unable or unwilling to perform. In such circumstance, the aggrieved party may: (i) await performance for a commercially reasonable time; (ii) resort to any remedy for breach even though he has also urged the other party to perform; or (iii) suspend his own performance. The repudiating party may, at any time before his next performance is due, withdraw his repudiation unless the other party has canceled, materially changed her position in reliance on the repudiation, or otherwise indicated that she considers the repudiation final. From the foregoing, (A), (B), and (C) are clearly correct statements of the parties' legal status after June 10. (D) is an incorrect statement (and, thus, the correct answer) because, in actuality, Byco may assert its cause of action immediately, without giving Selco a commercially reasonable time to perform.

Answer to Question 24

(D) Where the parties to a contract express their agreement in a writing with the intent that it embody the full and final expression of their bargain, any other expressions made prior to or contemporaneous with the writing are inadmissible to vary the terms of the writing. This is the parol evidence rule. In this case, the memorandum clearly states the time of repayment as September 1. If Vault were permitted to prove Kernel's oral commitment to repay the loan by July 1, this would be permitting the introduction of an expression prior to the writing, to vary the terms of the writing. (A) is incorrect because the parol evidence rule bars evidence of the oral agreement regardless of whether such agreement was supported by consideration. (B) is incorrect because the memorandum contains no ambiguity requiring further exposition of the parties' intent. (C) is incorrect because the preexisting duty rule relates to the issue of consideration, which is not at issue here.

Answer to Question 25

(D) The Statute of Frauds provides, inter alia, that a promise to answer for the debt or default of another must be in writing, except where the main purpose of the promisor is to serve a pecuniary interest of his own. Gritz's oral promise to guarantee the loan falls within the ambit of the Statute. Proof of such promise is barred, regardless of whether it was supported by separate consideration. Thus, (C) is incorrect. (A) is incorrect because Gritz signed the memorandum in his capacity as president of Kernel, not in an individual capacity. (B) is incorrect because Gritz, as president of Kernel, appears to be a mere employee, not someone with an ownership interest. There is no indication that Gritz will benefit from the loan.

Answer to Question 26

(B) Specific performance is appropriate where the legal remedy is inadequate. The legal remedy is inadequate where land is the subject of the contract. Although theoretically the seller of land will be fully compensated by money damages, the courts will usually grant specific performance to the seller, because land is considered unique. Thus, (A) is incorrect. Although Bard did not have title to Broadacres at the time he entered into the option contract with Cutter, he did own the option to buy the property. By exercising his option under his agreement with Osif, Bard could have obtained title to Broadacres. This, in turn, would have enabled Bard to convey to Cutter, if the latter exercised his option. Thus, Bard could have been compelled to perform. Because Bard is able to perform, and Cutter has exercised his option for purchase of the land, the case is an appropriate one for specific performance. Only (B) reaches this conclusion.

Answer to Question 27

(D) Prodigal was a third-party beneficiary of the original Mater-Vault deposit agreement. A third-party beneficiary's rights do not vest (*i.e.*, are modifiable) until he: manifests assent to the promise, brings suit to enforce the promise, or materially changes position in justifiable reliance on the promise. None of these vesting acts occurred before the modification here; in fact, Prodigal did not even know of the first contract until after the modification. Thus, his rights had not vested, and the terms of the second Mater-Vault deposit agreement control the disposition of the funds. Thus, (A) is incorrect. (B) is incorrect, because even if Prodigal were an assignee, this gratuitous assignment would be revocable. (C) is incorrect because Prodigal's rights could have vested without obtaining possession of the passbook.

Answer to Question 28

(C) This question involves an assignment. Generally, a gratuitous assignment is revocable. However, an assignment is irrevocable if a token chose involving the rights to be assigned (*e.g.*, a savings account passbook) is delivered. In such a case, the assignor loses both the right and the power to revoke. (C) is the only alternative that embodies these principles. (A) and (B) are wrong because they are based on the revocability of the gift. (D) is wrong because there is no showing of detrimental reliance on the part of Prodigal. Thus, there is no estoppel.

Answer to Question 29

(D) Where the other party's words, actions, or circumstances make it clear that she is unwilling or unable to perform, the aggrieved party may, inter alia, resort to any remedy for breach. By informing Toy Store that the shaft cannot be repaired or replaced until January, Fido has made it clear that it is unable to perform by the agreed-upon date of November 15. This is a material breach, because the contract indicates that delivery must be made in time for the Christmas shopping season. Thus, Toy Store is entitled to bring an action for damages. Thus, (B) is incorrect. (A) is incorrect because performance by January does not satisfy Fido's contractual undertaking. (C) is incorrect because, although Fido's night supervisor may have been negligent, it is clear that the appropriate cause of action against Fido is based on breach of its contractual agreement to deliver the dogs by November 15.

Answer to Question 30

(A) An assignment of "the contract" or an assignment in similar general terms is an assignment of rights and, unless the language or the circumstances (as in an assignment for security) indicate the contrary, it is also a delegation of performance of the assignor's duties. Here, the October 5 assignment constituted an assignment for security, pursuant to which only Fido's rights, not its duties, under its contract with Toy Store were transferred. (B) is incorrect because even if the October 5 transaction had been filed, this would not change the fact that High Finance had not assumed Fido's duties under the contract. (C) is incorrect because Toy Store was never intended to benefit from this assignment for security. (D) is incorrect because High Finance was not substituted as a new party in place of Fido, nor did Toy Store consent thereto, both of which are requirements for a novation.

Answer to Question 31

(C) A contract entered into by a minor is voidable at his election. Upon reaching majority, the minor may affirm, *i.e.*, choose to be bound by the contract. If he retains the benefits of the contract after reaching majority, he is liable for the fair market value of the goods. Here, Ohm, who contracted to pay for the television while still an infant, could have chosen to avoid the entire contract. However, upon reaching majority, Ohm not only retained the set, but expressly affirmed the contract to the extent of $300. Therefore, Stereo may recover against Ohm on the contract, but only to the extent that he has chosen to be bound ($300). Thus, (C) is correct. (A) is wrong because Ohm affirmed the contract after reaching 18 and so must pay for the set. (B) is wrong because Ohm expressly agreed to pay more than fair market value. (D) is wrong because Ohm was not liable on the contract made while he was a minor.

Answer to Question 32

(C) If Ann loses it will be because there was a novation. A novation occurs when a new contract substitutes a new party to receive benefits and assume duties that had belonged to one of the original parties under the terms of an old contract. All the parties must agree to the substitution. A novation discharges the old contract. The elements of a valid novation are: (i) a previous valid contract; (ii) an agreement among all parties, including the new party to the new contract; (iii) the immediate extinguishment of contractual duties as between the original parties; and (iv) a valid and enforceable new contract. When lessor Ann wrote to Carolyn agreeing to accept rent and Carolyn began to do so, a new contract was formed, and Ann's rights against Brenda were extinguished. (A) is incorrect because laches is not available here. Laches is an equitable defense available when a party delays in bringing an equitable suit and the delay prejudices the defendant. The action here (for back rent) is at law, not equity. Moreover, nothing in the facts indicates that Ann delayed in bringing her action. Thus, laches is not available. (B) is incorrect because there was no accord and satisfaction. An accord occurs when the parties to a contract agree to substitute a different duty for an existing duty under the contract. Satisfaction occurs when the new duty is performed. There was no new duty here; rather, the parties agreed to substitute a new party under an existing contract (a novation). (D) is incorrect because attornment arises when the tenant agrees to accept a new landlord, and here Ann remained the landlord at all times.

Answer to Question 33

(B) Quark's best defense is that the description is too indefinite. Specific performance will not be granted unless there is an enforceable contract. For a contract for the sale of land to be enforceable, there must be an adequate description of the subject property. A description of "five acres" from a 100-acre tract is not sufficient because it does not describe which five acres were intended. Thus, specific performance will not be available. (A) is incorrect because the option agreement was a term of the contract between Quark and Furrow. As such, it was fully supported by the consideration (payment of the rent) on the contract. It was not an additional agreement requiring further consideration. (C) is incorrect because a condition precedent is one that must occur before an absolute duty of immediate performance arises in the other party. The survey was not such a condition. When Furrow tendered the $10,000 for the five acres, Furrow had a duty to perform. Nowhere in the contract itself, or extrinsically, is there an indication that Furrow's option may not be exercised until a survey is made. (D) is incorrect because the option term of the contract is a part of the written contract and does not require proof via parol evidence.

Answer to Question 34

(A) Quasi-contract is the best theory because a quasi-contract action to recover restitution is the standard remedy to avoid unjust enrichment in the case of a failed contract. Here, Furrow did not intend to gratuitously confer a benefit on Quark, but rather he conferred the benefit in reliance on Quark's promise that Quark would convey five acres to Furrow. If Quark were allowed to keep the benefits under such conditions, he would be unjustly enriched. (B) is incorrect because conversion deals with the wrongful taking or retention of chattels. Here, the fruit trees became part of the land and so were not chattels. Moreover, it was not wrongful for Quark to keep the trees since they were affixed to his property. (C) is incorrect because resulting trusts arise only where an attempted trust has failed. There was no attempt to create a trust here. (D) is incorrect because the general rule is that at the end of a lease, the owner is entitled to keep any improvements that the tenant has made that have become securely affixed to the premises. Retaining such property does not imply a promise to pay for the improvements.

Answer to Question 35

(B) Homey will only be able to recover his actual damages; the liquidated damages clause is unenforceable because it constitutes a penalty. A liquidated damages clause will be enforced only if: (i) damages in case of breach were difficult to ascertain at the time the contract was made, and (ii) the amount agreed upon was a reasonable approximation of what the damages would be. The liquidated damages clause here fails the second test. The facts indicate that Homey knew that he would not be moving into the new house until November. Thus, there is no reason for assuming that Structo's late performance would cause any damages until November. The $500 a day late fee during October can thus only be viewed as a penalty. Therefore, the liquidated damages clause will be unenforceable and Homey will be able to collect only actual damages. (C) is incorrect because there was no valid waiver here. For a waiver of rights to be valid, one must at least know of the rights being waived. Here, Homey did not know of Structo's late performance when Homey paid. Thus, the payment cannot constitute a waiver of Homey's rights arising from the late performance. (D) is incorrect—there was no enforceable modification here—because of the parol evidence rule. The parol evidence rule prohibits a party to a written contract from bringing into court evidence of prior or contemporaneous oral communications that seek to vary the terms of the written contract. Here, the oral statement was made before the written contract was signed, and the evidence seeks to vary the completion date provided in the written contract. This will not be allowed under the parol evidence rule. Thus, Structo will not be able to bring in evidence seeking to vary the written date.

Answer to Question 36

(A) Structo will win because the condition of the architect's certificate will be excused by Bilevel's bad faith. While the issuance of the certificate was an express condition precedent to Homey's duty to pay, the condition will be excused by Homey's hindrance. If a party having a duty of performance that is subject to a condition wrongfully prevents the condition from occurring, the condition will be excused. Here, Homey's duty of payment was subject to the condition precedent that Bilevel issue a certificate of approval, and Homey wrongfully hindered the occurrence of the condition by agreeing to allow Bilevel to not issue the certificate for an improper reason—Structo had done all that it was obliged to do under the contract properly and the only reason for refusing the certificate is that Bilevel and Homey believe the price Homey agreed to is now too high. This is not a valid reason for withholding the certificate. Thus, the condition of the certificate will be excused and Structo can collect the full $40,000. (B) is incorrect because, as explained above, the condition of the architect's certificate will be excused. Thus, the contract is fully enforceable. (C) and (D) are incorrect because, as explained above, the contract is fully enforceable. Thus, Homey will have to pay the contract price. It is not a defense that the price is higher than it should have been at current prices.

CRIMINAL LAW QUESTIONS

Question 1

In which of the following situations is Defendant's claim of intoxication most likely to result in his being found not guilty?

(A) Defendant is charged with manslaughter for a death resulting from an automobile accident. Defendant, the driver, claims he was so drunk he was unable to see the other car involved in the accident.

(B) Defendant is charged with assault with intent to kill Watts, as a result of his wounding Watts by shooting him. Defendant claims he was so drunk he did not realize anyone else was around when he fired the gun.

(C) Defendant is charged with armed robbery. He claims he was so drunk he did not know whether the gun was loaded.

(D) Defendant is charged with statutory rape, after he had sexual intercourse with a girl aged 15, in a jurisdiction where the age of consent is 16. Defendant claims he was so drunk he did not realize the girl was a minor.

Question 2

Jackson and Brannick planned to break into a federal government office to steal food stamps. Jackson telephoned Crowley one night and asked whether Crowley wanted to buy some "hot" food stamps. Crowley, who understood that "hot" meant stolen, said, "Sure, bring them right over." Jackson and Brannick then successfully executed their scheme. That same night they delivered the food stamps to Crowley, who bought them for $500. Crowley did not ask when or by whom the stamps were stolen. All three were arrested. Jackson and Brannick entered guilty pleas in federal court to a charge of larceny in connection with the theft. Crowley was brought to trial in the state court on a charge of conspiracy to steal food stamps.

On the evidence stated, Crowley should be found:

(A) Guilty, because, when a new confederate enters a conspiracy already in progress, he becomes a party to it.

(B) Guilty, because he knowingly and willingly aided and abetted the conspiracy and is chargeable as a principal.

(C) Not guilty, because, although Crowley knew the stamps were stolen, he neither helped to plan nor participated or assisted in the theft.

(D) Not guilty, because Jackson and Brannick had not been convicted of or charged with conspiracy, and Crowley cannot be guilty of conspiracy by himself.

Question 3

Jack and Paul planned to hold up a bank. They drove to the bank in Jack's car. Jack entered while Paul remained as lookout in the car. After a few moments, Paul panicked and drove off.

Jack looked over the various tellers, approached one and whispered nervously, "Just hand over the cash. Don't look around, don't make a false move—or it's your life." The teller looked at the fidgeting Jack, laughed, flipped him a dollar bill, and said, "Go on, beat it." Flustered, Jack grabbed the dollar and left.

Paul's best defense to a charge of robbery would be that:

(A) Jack alone entered the bank.

(B) Paul withdrew, before commission of the crime, when he fled the scene.

(C) Paul had no knowledge of what Jack whispered to the teller.

(D) The teller was not placed in fear by Jack.

Question 4

Adam and Bailey, brothers, operated an illicit still. They customarily sold to anyone unless they suspected the person of being a revenue agent or an informant. One day when Adam was at the still alone, he was approached by Mitchell, who asked to buy a gallon of liquor. Mitchell was in fact a revenue officer. After Adam had sold him the liquor, Mitchell revealed his identity. Adam grabbed one of the rifles that the brothers kept handy in case of trouble with the law, and shot and wounded Mitchell. Other officers, hiding nearby, overpowered and arrested Adam.

Shortly thereafter, Bailey came on the scene. The officers in hiding had been waiting for him. One of them approached him and asked to buy liquor. Bailey was suspicious and refused to sell. The officers nevertheless arrested him.

Adam and Bailey were charged with conspiracy to violate revenue laws, illegal selling of liquor, and battery of the officer.

On the charge of battery, which statement concerning Adam and Bailey is true?

(A) Neither is guilty.

(B) Both are guilty.

(C) Adam is guilty but Bailey is not, because the conspiracy had terminated with the arrest of Adam.

(D) Adam is guilty but Bailey is not, because Adam's act was outside the scope of the conspiracy.

Question 5

Dent, while eating in a restaurant, noticed that a departing customer at the next table had left a five-dollar bill as a tip for the waitress. Dent reached over, picked up the five-dollar bill, and put it in his pocket. As he stood up to leave, another customer who had seen him take the money ran over to him and hit him in the face with her umbrella. Enraged, Dent choked the customer to death.

Dent is charged with murder. He requests the court to charge the jury that they can find him guilty of voluntary manslaughter rather than murder. Dent's request should be:

(A) Granted, because the jury could find that Dent acted recklessly and not with the intent to cause death or serious bodily harm.

(B) Granted, because the jury could find that being hit in the face with an umbrella constitutes adequate provocation.

(C) Denied, because the evidence shows that Dent intended to kill or to cause serious bodily harm.

(D) Denied, because the evidence shows that Dent provoked the assault on himself by his criminal misconduct.

Question 6

Brown suffered from the delusion that he was a special agent of God. He frequently experienced hallucinations in the form of hearing divine commands. Brown believed God told him several times that the local Roman Catholic bishop was corrupting the diocese into heresy, and that the bishop should be "done away with." Brown, a devout Catholic, conceived of himself as a religious martyr. He knew that shooting bishops for heresy is against the criminal law. He nevertheless carefully planned how he might kill the bishop. One evening Brown shot the bishop, who was taken to the hospital, where he died two weeks later.

Brown told the police he assumed the institutions of society would support the ecclesiastical hierarchy, and he expected to be persecuted for his God-inspired actions. Psychiatrist Stevens examined Brown and found that Brown suffered from schizophrenic psychosis, that in the absence of this psychosis he would not have shot the bishop, and that because of the psychosis Brown found it extremely difficult to determine whether he should obey the specific command that he do away with the bishop or the general commandment "Thou shalt not kill"; Brown was charged with murder.

If Brown interposes an insanity defense and the jurisdiction in which he is tried has adopted only the *M'Naghten* test of insanity, then the strongest argument for the defense under that test is that:

(A) Brown did not know the nature of the act he was performing.

(B) Brown did not know that his act was morally wrong.

(C) Brown did not know the quality of the act he was performing.

(D) Brown's acts were the product of a mental disease.

Question 7

In which of the following situations is Defendant most likely to be guilty of common law murder?

(A) During an argument in a bar, Norris punches Defendant. Defendant, mistakenly believing that Norris is about to stab him, shoots and kills Norris.

(B) While committing a robbery of a liquor store, Defendant accidentally drops his revolver, which goes off. The bullet strikes and kills Johnson, a customer in the store.

(C) While hunting deer, Defendant notices something moving in the bushes. Believing it to be a deer, Defendant fires into the bushes. The bullet strikes and kills Griggs, another hunter.

(D) In celebration of the Fourth of July, Defendant discharges a pistol within the city limits in violation of a city ordinance. The bullet ricochets off the street and strikes and kills Abbott.

Question 8

Dutton, disappointed by his eight-year-old son's failure to do well in school, began systematically depriving the child of food during summer vacation. Although his son became seriously ill from malnutrition, Dutton failed to call a doctor. He believed that as a parent he had the sole right to determine whether the child was fed or received medical treatment. Eventually, the child died. An autopsy disclosed that the child had suffered agonizingly as a result of the starvation, that a physician's aid would have alleviated the suffering, and that although the child would have died in a few months from malnutrition, the actual cause of death was an untreatable form of cancer.

The father was prosecuted for murder, defined in the jurisdiction as "unlawful killing of a human being with malice aforethought." The father should be:

(A) Acquitted, because of the defendant's good faith belief concerning parental rights in supervising children.

(B) Acquitted, because summoning the physician or feeding the child would not have prevented the child's death from cancer.

(C) Convicted, because the father's treatment of his son showed a reckless indifference to the value of life.

(D) Convicted, because the child would have died from malnutrition had he not been afflicted with cancer.

Question 9

Vance had cheated Dodd in a card game. Angered, Dodd set out for Vance's house with the intention of shooting him. Just as he was about to set foot on Vance's property, Dodd was arrested by a police officer who noticed that Dodd was carrying a revolver. A statute in the jurisdiction makes it a crime to "enter the property of another with the intent to commit any crime of violence thereon."

If charged with attempting to violate the statute, Dodd should be found:

(A) Not guilty, because the statute defines an attempt crime and there cannot be an attempt to attempt.

(B) Not guilty, because to convict him would be to punish him simply for having a guilty mind.

(C) Guilty, because he was close enough to entering the property and he had the necessary state of mind.

(D) Guilty, because this is a statute designed to protect the public from violence, and Dodd was dangerous.

Questions 10-15 are based on the following fact situation and require you to assume that you are in either a TYPE A or a TYPE B jurisdiction:

TYPE A. The homicide statute in this jurisdiction reads in part as follows:

Murder is the unlawful killing of a human being with malice aforethought. Such malice may be express or implied. It is express when there is manifested a deliberate intention unlawfully to take away the life of a fellow creature. It is implied when no considerable provocation appears or when the circumstances attending the killing show an abandoned and malignant heart. Every person guilty of murder shall suffer death or confinement in the state prison for life, at the discretion of the jury trying the same.

TYPE B. The homicide statute in this jurisdiction reads in part as follows:

Murder is the unlawful killing of a human being with malice aforethought. Such malice may be express or implied. It is express when there is manifested a deliberate intention unlawfully to take away the life of a fellow creature. It is implied when no considerable provocation appears or when the circumstances attending the killing show an abandoned and malignant heart. All murder that is perpetrated by willful, deliberate, or premeditated killing or that is committed in the perpetration of or attempt to perpetrate arson, rape, robbery, or burglary is murder of the first degree. All other kinds of murders are of the second degree. Every person guilty of murder in the first degree shall suffer death or confinement in the state prison for life, at the discretion of the jury trying the same. Every person convicted of murder in the second degree shall be confined in the state prison for life.

Both TYPE A and TYPE B jurisdictions have a statute reading as follows:

Manslaughter is the unlawful killing of a human being without malice. It is of two kinds:

1. Voluntary—upon a sudden quarrel or heat of passion.

2. Involuntary—in the commission of an unlawful act, not amounting to a felony; or in the commission of a lawful act that might produce death in an unlawful manner or without due caution and circumspection.

Manslaughter is punishable by imprisonment in the state prison not exceeding 15 years.

Victor and Defendant were 16 and 17, respectively. Both were old enough to be legally responsible for a crime in the particular jurisdiction. By prearrangement they met at the Dairy Shoppe, a teenage hangout. They were depressed. It had been raining for some days, and school had been out for several weeks. Defendant asked Victor if he would like to play Russian roulette. They played with a revolver, as they had done before. The cylinder of the revolver had six chambers, from which they would remove all but one cartridge. One of them would then spin the cylinder, point the revolver at the other's head, and fire it. With six chambers and one cartridge, the odds were 5 to 1 that the revolver would not fire.

Defendant obtained the revolver from his parents' bedroom. Adam, his father, kept the revolver in the bedroom at all times. Adam repeatedly bragged that he kept a loaded revolver in his room. Defendant took the revolver from the bedroom. He had done this before. He took out all but one cartridge, placed the others in his pocket, and then proceeded to the Dairy Shoppe.

Victor agreed to play Russian roulette. Defendant, pointing the revolver at Victor's head, pulled the trigger. Nothing happened. Victor then spun the cylinder and pointed the revolver at Defendant's head. He pulled the trigger. Nothing happened. Defendant spun the cylinder and pointed the revolver at Victor's head. He pulled the trigger. The gun fired. He was heard to exclaim: "Victor, Victor, I didn't think it would shoot! I'm sorry!" Victor died en route to the hospital.

10. Defendant is charged with murder in a TYPE A jurisdiction. Which of the following is the soundest result?

    (A) Not guilty, because consent is a complete defense.

    (B) Not guilty, because the negligence of Adam is a complete defense.

    (C) Guilty of murder.

    (D) Guilty of involuntary manslaughter.

11. Defendant is charged with first degree murder in a TYPE B jurisdiction. Which of the following is Defendant's soundest theory of defense?

    (A) Laws making a 17-year-old liable for any homicide are unconstitutional as imposing a cruel and unusual punishment.

    (B) A revolver with only one of its six chambers loaded is not a deadly weapon, and its use therefore cannot prove deliberate killing.

    (C) Defendant, because of his youth, could not have the malice aforethought required for murder.

    (D) Defendant is guilty of murder, but his deed does not fall within the definition of first degree murder.

12. Defendant is charged with murder in a TYPE A jurisdiction. The trial judge can properly charge the jury on which of the following theories?

    (A) Involuntary manslaughter only.

    (B) Murder and involuntary manslaughter.

    (C) Murder and voluntary manslaughter.

    (D) First degree murder, second degree murder, and involuntary manslaughter.

13. Defendant is charged with murder in a TYPE A jurisdiction. Which of the following is the soundest argument of the prosecutor?

    (A) Defendant's actions demonstrated an abandoned and malignant heart because he knew his act might cause death or great bodily harm.

    (B) The homicide is a felony murder since Victor's death was the result of an assault with a deadly weapon.

    (C) Defendant by definition is not a juvenile and can be found guilty of a capital crime.

    (D) The negligence of Adam is not a supervening cause which will relieve Defendant of liability.

14. Defendant is charged with first degree murder in a TYPE B jurisdiction. Defendant's best argument for acquittal of first degree murder would be that:

    (A) He committed no arson, rape, robbery, or burglary.

    (B) He did not deliberate or premeditate.

    (C) Victor consented to the homicide.

    (D) He did not deliberate, premeditate, or commit a first degree felony murder.

15. Assuming statutes covering the following offenses, in a TYPE A jurisdiction Adam, the father, can be most appropriately charged with:

    (A) Assault with a deadly weapon.

    (B) Contributing to the delinquency of a minor.

    (C) Murder.

    (D) Voluntary manslaughter.

Questions 16-17 are based on the following fact situation:

Linda was 15 years old, but she appeared and acted older. When asked, she always said she was 22, and she carried false identification saying she was that old. She frequented taverns and drank heavily. One evening in a bar she became acquainted with Duke. He believed her when she told him her claimed age. They had several drinks and became inebriated. Later, they drove in Duke's car to a secluded spot. After they had necked for a while, Duke propositioned Linda and she consented. Before Duke achieved penetration, Linda changed her mind, saying, "Stop! Don't touch me! I don't want to do it." When Duke did not desist, Linda started to cry and said, "I am only 15." Duke immediately jumped from the car and ran away. Duke was indicted for attempted rape, assault with intent to rape, contributing to the delinquency of a minor, and attempted statutory rape. The age of consent in the jurisdiction is 16.

16. If the contributing charge were based on a statute reading, "Whoever shall commit an act affecting the morals of a minor under 16 years of age shall be deemed guilty of contributing to the delinquency of a minor and shall be punished by imprisonment in the state penitentiary for a period not to exceed 5 years," Duke's best legal defense would be that:

    (A) The statute is unconstitutionally vague.

    (B) Linda consented to his actions.

    (C) He was entrapped by Linda's appearance.

    (D) He did not intend to contribute to her delinquency.

17. With respect to the contributing charge under the statute set out in the question above, proof by Duke that he was so inebriated that he could not have formed a criminal intent would be a:

    (A) Good defense, because the charge requires a specific intent.

    (B) Good defense, because at least a general criminal intent is required for every offense.

    (C) Poor defense, because contributing to the delinquency of a minor is an offense against a child.

    (D) Poor defense, because the state of mind of the defendant is irrelevant to this offense, so long as he was legally sane.

Questions 18-20 are based on the following fact situation:

Adams, Bennett, and Curtis are charged in a common law jurisdiction with conspiracy to commit larceny. The state introduced evidence that they agreed to go to Nelson's house to take stock certificates from a safe in Nelson's bedroom, that they went to the house, and that they were arrested as they entered Nelson's bedroom.

Adams testified that he thought the stock certificates belonged to Curtis, that Nelson was improperly keeping them from Curtis, and that he went along to aid in retrieving Curtis's property.

Bennett testified that he suspected Adams and Curtis of being thieves and joined up with them in order to catch them. He also testified that he made an anonymous telephone call to the police alerting them to the crime and that the call caused the police to be waiting for them when they walked into Nelson's bedroom.

Curtis did not testify.

18. If the jury believes Adams, it should find him:

    (A) Guilty, because there was an agreement and the entry into the bedroom is sufficient for the overt act.

    (B) Guilty, because good motives are not a defense to criminal liability.

    (C) Not guilty, because he did not have a corrupt motive.

    (D) Not guilty, because he did not intend to steal.

19. If the jury believes Bennett, it should find him:

    (A) Guilty, because there was an agreement and the entry into the bedroom is sufficient for the overt act.

    (B) Guilty, because he is not a police officer and thus cannot claim any privilege of apprehending criminals.

    (C) Not guilty, because he did not intend to steal.

    (D) Not guilty, because he prevented the theft from occurring.

20. If the jury believes both Adams and Bennett, it should find Curtis:

    (A) Guilty, because there was an agreement and the entry into the bedroom is sufficient for the overt act.

    (B) Guilty, because he intended to steal.

    (C) Not guilty, because a conviction would penalize him for exercising his right not to be a witness.

    (D) Not guilty, because Adams and Bennett did not intend to steal.

Questions 21-25 are based on the four case summaries below. For each question, select the case that would be most applicable as a precedent:

(A) *Commonwealth v. Mason.* Two brothers see a wealthy neighbor's pedigreed dog on the street. They take the dog home, intending to conceal it until the owner offers a reward. Held, guilty of larceny.

(B) *Saferite v. State.* Two young men saw a motor car on the street with the keys in the ignition lock. They drove the car to a neighboring town with the intention, they said, of visiting the wife of one of them. The car was wrecked on their way back. Conviction for larceny reversed.

(C) *People v. Noblett.* Defendant, a tenant of a city apartment, advertised it for sublease. Will agreed to sublease for three months, and on March 12 paid Defendant $550, the total agreed rental. Will was to receive possession on March 20, but possession was never given him. Held, not guilty of common law larceny.

(D) *King v. Pear.* From a stablekeeper, Defendant hired a horse to go to Sutton and back, saying he would be back at 8 p.m. He did not return. Investigation showed that Defendant had given a false address, and that he had sold the horse the same day. Conviction of larceny affirmed.

21. Davis paid Realtor $500 as down payment on a house. That night, Davis broke into a hardware store and took a brace and bit. Davis broke into Realtor's office and used the tools to open the safe, where he had seen Realtor place the $500. The safe was empty. Davis's fingerprints on the tools, left lying in front of the safe, led to his arrest. He is charged with larceny of the tools.

22. Smith placed a newspaper advertisement reading, "Wanted: responsible man to collect for large firm. $500 security required. Address Box 66, Times." Vincent answered the ad and was called on by Smith, who said he represented Ames Advertising Agency. He took Vincent to the office of the company (a large actual firm), but as they were about to enter the building Smith said, "There is Mr. Ames now," and introduced him to a companion of Smith who impersonated Ames. The result of the conversation was that the false Ames agreed to hire Vincent. It was agreed that Vincent would draw $500 from the bank to put up as security, and that this money would be placed in a bank and Vincent given a certificate of deposit in his own name. They went to the bank where Vincent gave Smith the money, after which Smith and "Ames" disappeared. Smith was later charged with larceny.

23. Jones, angry at a neighbor with whom he had quarreled, for revenge surreptitiously removed a piece of stone statuary from the neighbor's garden and concealed it in his garage. He intended to replace it a day or two later, after giving the neighbor a chance to feel bad over its being stolen. Suspecting who was guilty, the neighbor had Jones arrested and charged with larceny.

24. Harris, a heroin addict, broke into a home and took several cameras and watches, which he promptly pawned to obtain cash with which to purchase a "fix." Harris was later charged with larceny of the cameras and watches.

25. Allison told Mark that he, Allison, was the legal representative for a syndicate that had a photoelectric machine for making counterfeit money, and to prove that the money was good enough to "pass anywhere," Allison showed what he said was one of the counterfeit $10 bills. He said that if Mark would invest $1,000, the syndicate would pay him counterfeit money in the amount of $10,000. Mark paid the $1,000 to Allison, who then disappeared. Allison is caught and charged with larceny.

Question 26

Ted frequently visited Janet, his next-door neighbor. Janet was separated from her husband, Howard. Howard resided with his mother but jointly owned the house in which Janet resided. Late one night, Ted and Janet were sitting on the bed in Janet's bedroom drinking when Howard burst through the door and told Ted, "Get out!" When Ted refused, Howard challenged him to go outside and "fight it out." Ted again refused. Howard then pulled a knife from his pocket and lunged at Ted. Ted grabbed a lamp, struck Howard on the head, and killed him. Ted is charged with murder.

On a charge of murder, Ted should be found:

(A) Not guilty, because Ted had as much right as Howard to be in the house.

(B) Not guilty, because Howard attacked Ted with a deadly weapon.

(C) Guilty, because Ted's presence in Janet's bedroom prompted Howard's attack.

(D) Guilty, because Ted's failure to obey Howard's order to leave the house made him a trespasser.

Question 27

Defendant is charged with assault and battery. The state's evidence shows that Victim was struck in the face by Defendant's fist.

In which of the following situations is Defendant most likely to be ***not guilty*** of assault and battery?

(A) Defendant had been hypnotized at a party and ordered by the hypnotist to strike the person he disliked the most.

(B) Defendant was suffering from an epileptic seizure and had no control over his motions.

(C) Defendant was heavily intoxicated and was shadow boxing without realizing that Victim was near him.

(D) Defendant, who had just awakened from a deep sleep, was not fully aware of what was happening and mistakenly thought Victim was attacking him.

Question 28

Donna was arrested and taken to police headquarters, where she was given her *Miranda* warnings. Donna indicated that she wished to telephone her lawyer and was told that she could do so after her fingerprints had been taken. While being fingerprinted, however, Donna blurted out, "Paying a lawyer is a waste of money because I know you have me."

At trial, Donna's motion to prevent the introduction of the statement she made while being fingerprinted will most probably be:

(A) Granted, because Donna's request to contact her attorney by telephone was reasonable and should have been granted immediately.

(B) Granted, because of the "fruit of the poisonous tree" doctrine.

(C) Denied, because the statements were volunteered and not the result of interrogation.

(D) Denied, because fingerprinting is not a critical stage of the proceeding requiring the assistance of counsel.

Question 29

Driving down a dark road, Defendant accidentally ran over a man. Defendant stopped and found that the victim was dead. Defendant, fearing that he might be held responsible, took the victim's wallet, which contained a substantial amount of money. He removed the identification papers and put the wallet and money back into the victim's pocket.

Defendant is ***not guilty*** of:

(A) Larceny, because he took the papers only to prevent identification and not for his own use.

(B) Larceny, because he did not take anything from a living victim.

(C) Robbery, because he did not take the papers by means of force or putting in fear.

(D) Robbery, because he did not take anything of monetary value.

Question 30

Tom had a heart ailment so serious that his doctors had concluded that only a heart transplant could save his life. They therefore arranged to have him flown to Big City to have the operation performed.

Dan, Tom's nephew, who stood to inherit from him, poisoned him. The poison produced a reaction which required postponing the journey. The plane on which Tom was to have flown crashed, and all aboard were killed. By the following day, Tom's heart was so weakened by the effects of the poison that he suffered a heart attack and died.

If charged with criminal homicide, Dan should be found:

(A) Guilty.

(B) Not guilty, because his act did not hasten the deceased's death, but instead prolonged his life by one day.

(C) Not guilty, because the deceased was already suffering from a fatal illness.

(D) Not guilty, because the poison was not the sole cause of death.

Questions 31-32 are based on the following fact situation:

Statutes in the jurisdiction define criminal assault as "an attempt to commit a criminal battery" and criminal battery as "causing an offensive touching."

As Edward was walking down the street, a gust of wind blew his hat off. Edward reached out, trying to grab his hat, and narrowly missed striking Margaret in the face with his hand. Margaret, fearful of being struck by Edward, pushed Edward away.

31. If charged with criminal assault, Edward should be found:

    (A) Guilty, because he caused Margaret to be in apprehension of an offensive touching.

    (B) Guilty, because he should have realized he might strike someone by reaching out.

    (C) Not guilty, because he did not intend to hit Margaret.

    (D) Not guilty, because he did not hit Margaret.

32. If charged with criminal battery, Margaret should be found:

    (A) Guilty, because she intentionally pushed Edward.

    (B) Guilty, because she caused the touching of Edward whether she meant to do so or not.

    (C) Not guilty, because a push is not an offensive touching.

    (D) Not guilty, because she was justified in pushing Edward.

Question 33

A state statute makes it a felony for any teacher at a state institution of higher education to accept anything of value from a student at the same institution. Monroe, a student at the state university, offered Professor Smith, his English teacher, $50 in exchange for a good grade in his English course. Smith agreed and took the money. Professor Smith and Monroe are tried jointly for violation of the state statute. Professor Smith is charged with violating the statute and Monroe with aiding and abetting him.

Monroe's best argument for a dismissal of the charge against him is that:

(A) A principal and an accessory cannot be tried together, since the principal must be convicted first.

(B) He cannot be an accessory, since he is the victim of the crime.

(C) The legislature did not intend to punish the person giving the thing of value.

(D) He did not assist Professor Smith in violating the statute.

Question 34

In which of the following situations is Defendant most likely to be guilty of larceny?

(A) Defendant took Sue's television set, with the intention of returning it the next day. However, he dropped it and damaged it beyond repair.

(B) Defendant went into Tom's house and took $100 in the belief that Tom had damaged Defendant's car to that amount.

(C) Mistakenly believing that larceny does not include the taking of a dog, Defendant took his neighbor's dog and sold it.

(D) Unreasonably mistaking George's car for his own, Defendant got into George's car in a parking lot and drove it home.

Question 35

Which of the following is most likely to be found to be a strict liability offense?

(A) A city ordinance providing for a fine of not more than $200 for shoplifting.

(B) A federal statute making it a felony to possess heroin.

(C) A state statute making it a felony to fail to register a firearm.

(D) A state statute making the sale of adulterated milk a misdemeanor.

Question 36

Which of the following is ***least*** likely to be the underlying felony in a prosecution for felony murder?

(A) Arson.

(B) Manslaughter.

(C) Attempted rape.

(D) Burglary.

Question 37

Rimm and Hill were fooling around with a pistol in Hill's den. Rimm aimed the pistol in Hill's direction and fired three shots slightly to Hill's right. One shot ricocheted off the wall and struck Hill in the back, killing him instantly.

The most serious crime of which Rimm can be convicted is:

(A) Murder.

(B) Voluntary manslaughter.

(C) Involuntary manslaughter.

(D) Assault with a dangerous weapon.

Question 38

Defendant, a worker in a metal working shop, had long been teasing Vincent, a young colleague, by calling him insulting names and ridiculing him. One day Vincent responded to the teasing by picking up a metal bar and attacking Defendant. Defendant could have escaped from the shop. He parried the blow with his left arm, and with his right hand struck Vincent a blow on his jaw from which the young man died.

What is the most serious offense of which Defendant could be properly convicted?

(A) Involuntary manslaughter.

(B) Voluntary manslaughter.

(C) Murder.

(D) None of the above.

Question 39

Alford was a suspect in a homicide committed during a robbery of a liquor store. Barber was a friend of Alford. Police telephoned Barber and asked if he would help locate Alford. Barber agreed and met the police officers at headquarters later that night.

After a discussion during which police asked questions about Alford and the homicide, Barber said that he wanted to get something "off his chest" and advised the officers that he was in on the robbery but that Alford had shot the owner of the store without his permission or prior knowledge. The officers then for the first time gave Barber his *Miranda* warnings.

Barber was indicted for felony murder. He moved to prevent the introduction of his statement into evidence. His motion should be:

(A) Granted, because Barber was effectively in custody and entitled to receive *Miranda* warnings at the beginning of the discussion.

(B) Granted, because Barber's right to counsel and due process were violated by the interrogation at police headquarters.

(C) Denied, because his statement was freely and voluntarily given and he was not entitled to *Miranda* warnings.

(D) Denied, because by visiting headquarters voluntarily, Barber waived his right to have *Miranda* warnings at the beginning of the discussion.

CRIMINAL LAW ANSWERS

Answer to Question 1

(B) Voluntary intoxication is a defense to a crime that requires ***intent*** (assault with intent to kill), and in (B) the intoxication prevented Defendant from formulating the intent to commit the crime. (A) and (D) are incorrect because voluntary intoxication is no defense to crimes involving recklessness or strict liability. (C) is incorrect because Defendant's intoxication did not prevent him from formulating the purpose or intent to commit the crime.

Answer to Question 2

(C) Crowley should be found not guilty because what he did was commit the crime of ***receiving*** stolen property knowing it to be stolen. This crime would not be necessary if the mere agreement to purchase the loot after another had already stolen it were enough to make the purchaser a conspirator. (A) is wrong. The point of law stated is accurate enough, but it assumes that simply by agreeing to buy the stamps, Crowley joined in the conspiracy to steal them. (B) is wrong because Crowley did not aid and abet the conspiracy to commit larceny because that conspiracy had already accomplished its target object, the stealing of the stamps. (D) is wrong. It is true that one may not conspire with himself. But it is not true that one who does enter into a conspiracy with one or more people cannot be convicted unless the others are at least charged with the conspiracy. If only one conspirator is prosecuted, however, the prosecution must show that, in fact, others were involved with the defendant on trial.

Answer to Question 3

(D) Paul's best defense is that Jack did not commit a robbery. Robbery is in effect a larceny from the person, committed by force or fear. Here, force was threatened, not actually used. Had the teller felt any apprehension that Jack would use a gun if he did not do what he was told, this would be "fear" even though the victim remained cool and poised while complying with the demands, and knew that as long as he did so, no force would be used. In this case, however, it is obvious that the teller felt no fear at all. (Paul's crime was ***attempted*** robbery.) (A) is wrong. Paul was an accomplice to Jack. He would incur vicarious liability for crimes committed by Jack. (B) is wrong. Paul would be an accomplice to attempted robbery (and perhaps larceny) because he did not repudiate his assistance before fleeing; thus, he did not effectively withdraw. (C) is wrong. We are told that Paul and Jack planned to hold up a bank. It is not necessary that the accomplice know all the precise details of how this is to be carried out. It suffices that Paul knew that Jack would use the threat of force to obtain property permanently.

Answer to Question 4

(B) Battery is an unlawful application of force to the person of another resulting in bodily injury or an offensive touching. Adam's shooting and wounding of Mitchell meets all the elements of the crime. Thus, Adam is guilty of battery. Bailey is also guilty of battery because Adam conspired with Bailey to operate an illegal still, and each co-conspirator is liable for the crimes of all other co-conspirators if: (i) the crimes were committed in furtherance of the objective of the conspiracy; and (ii) the crimes were a natural and probable consequence of the conspiracy (*i.e.,* foreseeable). The battery was committed in furtherance of the conspiracy (to keep the still in operation) and was foreseeable because the conspirators kept guns on the site in case of trouble with the law, and the wounding of a peace officer would be a "natural and probable" consequence. Thus, (B) is correct, and it follows that (A) must be incorrect. (C) is wrong because even if the conspiracy was terminated by Adam's arrest, the battery occurred before the arrest, when the conspiracy was clearly ongoing. Bailey made no legally effective withdrawal prior to the battery, and he remains liable for Adam's act. (D) is wrong because, as discussed above, the battery was in furtherance of the objective of the conspiracy and a foreseeable consequence of the conspiracy.

Answer to Question 5

(B) The existence of adequate provocation may reduce a killing to voluntary manslaughter. Being subjected to a serious battery is frequently recognized as constituting adequate provocation. Here, the jury should decide whether being hit in the face with an umbrella qualifies. (A) is incorrect because a finding that Dent acted recklessly would not necessarily suffice to reduce the crime to voluntary manslaughter. Provocation is the key. (C) is incorrect because to the extent that Dent intended to kill or to cause serious bodily harm, he was acting in the wake of a sudden and intense passion that caused him to lose his self-control, which would make voluntary manslaughter applicable. (D) is incorrect because it is questionable whether Dent's taking of the money that had been left for the waitress constituted sufficient reason for the customer to hit him in the face with an umbrella. Thus, the jury should be allowed to consider voluntary manslaughter as an option.

Answer to Question 6

(B) The traditional *M'Naghten* rule provides that a defendant is entitled to acquittal if the proof establishes that: (a) a disease of the mind; (b) caused a defect of reason; (c) such that the defendant lacked the ability at the time of his actions to either: (i) know the wrongfulness of his actions; or (ii) understand the nature and quality of his actions. (B) is the best answer here, because this option goes directly to the wrongfulness issue and is supported by the facts, which indicate Brown's moral dilemma. His conclusion that direct orders from God overrode the general prohibition against killing indicates that Brown did not know the wrongfulness of his act. (A) and (C) are incorrect because the *M'Naghten* test speaks of nature ***and*** quality, and each of these options contains only one of these two elements. In addition, the facts are less likely to support an assertion that Brown was ignorant of either the nature or quality of his act than that he did not understand it was wrong. (D) is wrong because mental disease is but one element of the *M'Naghten* test. Acts that occur as a "product of mental disease or defect" fall under the insanity defense in jurisdictions that apply the *Durham* rule, which is substantially broader than *M'Naghten*.

Answer to Question 7

(B) The defendant is guilty of felony murder in this fact situation, since even an accidental killing committed during the course of a felony constitutes common law murder. Malice is implied from the intent to commit the underlying felony. Since defendant did have the requisite intent to commit the robbery with no defense to cut off liability, he would be liable at common law for the accidental death as well. (A) is wrong, since this fact situation would give the defendant a possible self-defense claim, and if that failed, it would be manslaughter, not common law murder. (C) is wrong because here there was no malice aforethought. At most, the defendant would be guilty of involuntary manslaughter. (D) is not as good a choice as (B) because a jury could find that there was no malice aforethought. Defendant then would be guilty only of misdemeanor manslaughter while committing an "unlawful act," not common law murder.

Answer to Question 8

(B) Dutton would have to be acquitted because his actions did not cause the death of the child. (A) is wrong because the defendant's beliefs about his rights are irrelevant. If the child had died of malnutrition, the defendant's good faith belief concerning parental rights in supervising children would have been of no help to him. (C) is wrong because that reckless indifference did not cause the child's death. (D) is wrong because the child did not actually die from malnutrition.

Answer to Question 9

(C) Vance could not be convicted of actually violating the statute because he did not enter the property of another. However, since he was approaching the property with the requisite state of mind, he could be charged with attempting to violate that statute. (A) is wrong because the statute does not define an attempt crime. Entering onto the property of another is an affirmative action. (B) is wrong because entering the property of another with the intent to commit a crime of violence constitutes more than merely "having a guilty mind." (D) is wrong because it is overbroad and overly subjective.

Answer to Question 10

(C) Defendant's conduct qualifies as a killing with "an abandoned and malignant heart" because it exhibited a reckless indifference to the "very high" risk of death or serious injury. (A) is wrong because consent is not a defense to acts involving serious bodily injury. (B) is wrong because the misconduct of Adam is not a defense to homicide. (D) is wrong because the manslaughter statute requires that the killing be without malice. Here, malice is implied from Defendant's "abandoned and malignant heart."

Answer to Question 11

(D) Since the felony murder rule is not involved here, the only theory of first degree murder available would be that killing was "willful, deliberate, or premeditated." First degree murder requires an actual intent to kill, which Defendant lacked. (A) is wrong under common law. At common law, it was possible to convict a seven-year-old of a crime. Also, there is nothing under this statute to indicate that a 17-year-old could not be convicted of a crime. Nor is youthfulness (of a defendant over the age of 14) a legally recognized source of "mitigating" a criminal homicide to manslaughter. Hence, (C) is wrong. (B) is wrong because a revolver is a deadly weapon and intentional use of it would support an inference that Defendant intended to kill.

Answer to Question 12

(B) This is the best alternative. The choice as to whether this behavior is wanton or reckless (murder) or criminal or gross negligence (involuntary manslaughter) is best left to the jury. Hence, it would be wrong to instruct the jury "only" on involuntary manslaughter, and thus (A) is incorrect. (D) is wrong because the question relates to a Type A jurisdiction where murder is not divided into degrees. (C) is wrong as there is no way that Defendant would be guilty of voluntary manslaughter, which would involve an unjustified, unexcused but mitigated, intentional homicide. Defendant did not intend to kill or seriously injure.

Answer to Question 13

(A) This question tests your understanding of the "abandoned and malignant heart" terminology still found in many murder statutes. (B) is wrong because "assault with a deadly weapon" is not the "independent" or "collateral felony" required for the felony murder rule. (C) and (D) are wrong because they do not concern issues that would be the most relevant to the murder charges. Both of these cover responses to defenses raised by the defendant rather than a necessary element to be proved by the prosecutor.

Answer to Question 14

(D) This answer covers all the possible ways to commit a first degree murder under a Type B statute (felony murder ***and*** premeditative or deliberate). Hence, both (A) and (B) are incomplete and wrong. (C) is wrong because consent of the victim will not excuse, mitigate, or reduce the level of a criminal homicide.

Answer to Question 15

(B) This is the only possible charge. Although the 17-year-old son is old enough to be "legally" responsible for a crime, he is still a minor, and the father's bragging about a loaded revolver in his room could be deemed contributory to his delinquency. At best, the father's act was "criminally" negligent, and therefore any liability on the father's part would not rise above the level of involuntary manslaughter. Therefore, (C) is wrong; merely leaving a loaded gun about is not an "abandoned and malignant heart" situation. (D) is also wrong; the father did not kill Victor as a result of a sudden quarrel or in the heat of passion. (A) is wrong because the father did not assault anyone and also because the assault charge would merge into the murder charge.

Answer to Question 16

(A) The best defense is challenging the statute, because all of the other choices do not offer defenses. Linda's consent is irrelevant under the statute, as is her appearance of being older. Duke's intent is likewise irrelevant under this type of statute, which is a strict liability statute. Therefore, his only possible challenge is that the statute is void for vagueness because it does not apprise a defendant of which acts are proscribed.

Answer to Question 17

(D) This is a strict liability crime. Voluntary intoxication is no defense to crimes of strict liability because a defense that negates intent is not a defense to a strict liability crime. Thus, (D) is the correct answer and (A) is incorrect. (B) is misleading because voluntary intoxication is an insufficient defense to general intent offenses. (C) is irrelevant.

Answer to Question 18

(D) Adams is not guilty if he did not intend to achieve the objective of the conspiracy—*i.e.,* to permanently deprive the owner of his property, since Adams thought that Curtis was the owner and that Nelson was improperly keeping the certificates from Curtis. (A) is incorrect because an agreement and overt act are insufficient for conspiracy if Adams did not have the intent to commit larceny. (B), while a correct statement of law, is irrelevant to the required specific intent element. The corrupt motive doctrine is a minority view requiring conspirators to know that their objective is illegal. However, (C) is inapplicable to these facts since Adams had no intent to commit larceny.

Answer to Question 19

(C) The crime of conspiracy requires that each conspirator intend to achieve an unlawful goal. If the jury believes Bennett, he must be found not guilty because he did not intend to achieve an unlawful goal. (A) is therefore incorrect. (D) is incorrect because Bennett's act of prevention would not have excused the conspiracy if he had the proper mental state. (*Note:* The Model Penal Code recognizes such a defense.) (B) is incorrect because the privilege to apprehend criminals is not in issue here.

Answer to Question 20

(D) If the jury believes both Adams and Bennett, neither could be guilty of conspiracy because of absence of intent. Therefore, Curtis could not be guilty of conspiracy at common law because there was never an agreement to achieve an unlawful purpose. (A) is wrong because there was never an agreement between two or more persons. (B) is incorrect because intent is but one element of conspiracy—there must also be an agreement. (C) is a nonsensical statement.

Answer to Question 21

(A) Case squib (A) is the most applicable. Case squib (A) illustrates that the state of mind required for larceny is satisfied when the defendant intends to deal with the property in a manner that involves a substantial risk of loss to the owner, such as intending to sell the property back to the owner or hold it until a reward is offered. In this question, Davis used the tools to break open a safe. While he probably never intended to keep the tools, he also never intended to return them either—he did not care whether the hardware store ever got the tools back. Thus, the charge of larceny here is based on an intent to deal with the property in a manner that involves a high risk of loss to the owner, just as in squib (A). Squib (B) is not as applicable because the decisive element there was the defendants' intent only to borrow the car and to return it within a reasonable time. Squibs (C) and (D) are inapplicable because they involved a taking by means of false representations, which is not the case here.

Answer to Question 22

(D) Squib (D) is the most applicable precedent. That squib establishes that the "trespassory" aspect of the taking is satisfied when the victim consents to defendant's taking possession of the property only as a result of defendant's misrepresentations. In this question, Vincent transferred possession of the $500 as a result of the false representations of Smith. Squib (C) is not applicable because it establishes that one obtaining ***title*** to property as a result of false representations is not guilty of larceny. Here, Vincent only transferred ***possession*** of the $500—he was expecting to receive a certificate of deposit for it.

Answer to Question 23

(B) Squib (B) is most applicable because it establishes that an intent to borrow another's property without permission for a short period of time is not sufficient for common law larceny. Here, Jones took the statuary with the intent to return it within a day or two. Despite his vindictive motive, Jones would not be liable for larceny if the jury decides that he did not intend to keep it for an unreasonable length of time. Regardless of the verdict, squib (B) is the most applicable precedent. Squib (A) is not applicable because the defendants in that case were not planning to return the dog until the owner offered a reward, which is not the case here.

Answer to Question 24

(A) Squib (A) is most applicable. That case squib establishes that an intent to deal with another's property in any manner that creates a substantial risk of loss of the property is a sufficient intent for larceny. Here, Harris's conduct in pawning the property after taking it from the owner created a substantial risk of loss to the owner—enough to make Harris liable for larceny. Squib (B) is inappropriate because pawning the property negates any intent to return it. Squibs (C) and (D) are inapplicable because there were no misrepresentations in this case.

Answer to Question 25

(C) Case squib (C) is most applicable because it establishes that common law larceny does not apply in the fact situation here. In squib (C), the decisive element is that the victim, Will, gave the cash to the defendant with the intent that he keep it (*i.e.,* with the intent to convey title to the cash to defendant in exchange for possession of the apartment). As a result, defendant was not guilty of common law larceny of the cash because more than possession was transferred. Similarly, here Mark passed ***title*** to the money to Allison based on Allison's false representations. Squib (C) is therefore more applicable than squib (D) because (C) establishes that common law larceny does not apply in this case.

Answer to Question 26

(B) It seems clear from the facts that Ted has killed in self-defense. Even if striking Howard with the lamp were seen as the use of deadly force, it was necessary in response to the latter's use of deadly force. (A) is simply irrelevant. (C) might have been relevant to a defense for Howard if he had killed Ted, but it is irrelevant to the facts of this case. (D) is a misstatement of law.

Answer to Question 27

(B) Battery is a general intent crime that may be satisfied by a showing of recklessness or criminal negligence. (B) involves facts that are most clearly inconsistent with the defendant having any mental state whatever. Alternatively, (B) is to be preferred because it most clearly indicates that there was not a willed act, since convulsive acts are not considered to be voluntary. Even while in a hypnotic state, Defendant's striking Victim was a voluntary physical movement. (A) is therefore incorrect. (C) is wrong because voluntary intoxication is not a defense to crimes requiring recklessness. (D) is inapplicable because, although he was mistaken as to Victim's actions, Defendant willed himself to hit Victim.

Answer to Question 28

(C) Answer (A) is to be rejected because the request for the attorney means interrogation must cease and not that the attorney be produced immediately. In this case, interrogation had not yet begun. (B) is inapplicable since there is no suggestion that the arrest was unlawful. (D) is accurate but nonsensical. It is the introduction of the statement, not the fingerprints, that is in issue. The best answer is (C), because truly volunteered statements are not the product of custodial interrogation.

Answer to Question 29

(C) It is clear that the taking was not achieved by the use of force, an element of robbery. (It would be different if Defendant had run down the victim with the intent to appropriate his property.) (A) and (B) are based on mistaken legal premises and are thus incorrect. The Defendant's motive is irrelevant, and larceny does not require a taking from a living person. (D) might be accurate at common law but modern statutes normally include documents as being property subject to larceny and thus, robbery.

Answer to Question 30

(A) Dan should be found guilty. The problem here is whether Dan caused Tom's death. Dan's act was not only the "but for" cause but also, since the death as it happened was the natural and foreseeable result, the "proximate" cause. The fact that other preexisting conditions contributed to the death does not absolve Dan. Therefore, (D) is incorrect. (B) is irrelevant to whether Dan committed murder. (C) is a misstatement of the facts relating to Tom's "serious" illness. Moreover, an act that hastens an inevitable result is still a legal cause of that result.

Answer to Question 31

(C) The statute defines assault as "an attempt to commit a battery." Attempts require the specific intent to commit the crime. We are told Edward had no such intent. Hence, (C) is the best answer. Thus, (A) and (B) are incorrect. (D) is incorrect because an assault is an attempt to cause an offensive touching, and thus it would not be necessary for him to actually hit Margaret.

Answer to Question 32

(D) There is no doubt that Margaret committed a battery. Hence, (C) is to be rejected. The question is whether it was justified. Since she is permitted to use nondeadly force when she reasonably believes such is necessary to avoid the danger of harm from an aggressor and the facts indicate this was her position, the best answer is (D). (A) is incorrect because, even though her conduct was intentional, she has a defense of self-defense. (B) is incorrect because of her justification for the pushing.

Answer to Question 33

(C) A court, in enforcing a criminal statute, will construe legislative intent in assessing criminal liability. If a statute defines a crime in a way that necessarily involves more than one participant and provides for the liability of only one participant, it is presumed that the legislative intent was to immunize the other participant from liability as an accomplice (*e.g.,* the buyer in an illegal sale of drugs is neither guilty of being an accessory to the sale nor in a conspiracy with the seller). Further, the rule of lenity requires that an ambiguous criminal statute must be strictly construed in favor of the defendant. (A) is wrong because those who provide inducement for a crime that requires two parties are not accessories. Further, Monroe was not an accessory at common law because accessories were not present when the crime was committed. (B) is wrong because Monroe is not the victim; the state is. (D) is wrong because Monroe did assist Professor Smith in violating the statute by offering him the $50.

Answer to Question 34

(C) Answer (A) is wrong because we are told Defendant did not have the requisite intent to steal. (B) is incorrect because Defendant's mistake may have gone to civil law—his right to use self-help in recovering a debt—rather than to the former type of mistake. (D) is to be rejected because of the facts; Defendant did not intend to steal the property of another. (C) is the best answer because Defendant's mistake is as to the coverage of the criminal law and that is not an excuse.

Answer to Question 35

(D) A strict liability offense does not require awareness of all of the factors constituting the crime. Strict liability offenses are generally part of a regulatory scheme. They generally involve a relatively low penalty. Here, (A) and (B) are incorrect because the offenses described do not appear to be part of a regulatory scheme. Also, they appear to require awareness of all of the factors constituting the crime; *i.e.,* a defendant probably could not be convicted under (A) without an awareness that he was shoplifting, and a defendant probably could not be convicted under (B) without an awareness that he possessed heroin. (C) presents a closer question. The offense described in (C) appears to be part of a scheme to regulate firearms. The offense described in (D) is part of a scheme to regulate the sale of milk for the purpose of protecting the public from the threat of consumption of tainted milk. Such statutes, in protecting the public health and safety, almost always provide for culpability, regardless of the seller's knowledge of the tainted nature of the product. Also, the statute in (D) describes a misdemeanor, meaning that a violation thereof carries a lesser penalty than does violation of the felony statute in (C). Consequently, because (D) fits more closely the classic concept of a strict liability offense, it is a better answer than (C).

Answer to Question 36

(B) Manslaughter will not serve as the underlying felony in a felony murder prosecution. The felony murder rule can be applied only where the underlying felony is independent of the killing. With a felony such as manslaughter, there is ordinarily no intent to commit a felony independent of the killing itself; hence, felony murder does not apply. In contrast, the other crimes listed would satisfy the requirement that the defendant intend to commit an underlying felony. One who is guilty of arson (choice A) would have intended that a burning take place. Attempted rape (choice C) requires the intent to perform an act which, if achieved, would constitute rape. Burglary (choice D) requires intent to commit a felony at time of entry.

Answer to Question 37

(A) Rimm can be convicted of murder because the way Rimm employed the firearm was sufficient to fulfill the "malice" requirement for murder. Murder is the unlawful killing of a human being with malice aforethought. Malice aforethought may be express or implied. In addition to obvious malice situations where there is intention to kill, malice is implied where there is: (i) intent to inflict great bodily injury; (ii) reckless indifference to an unjustifiably high risk to human life (also called acting with "an abandoned and malignant heart"); or (iii) felony murder situations. Here, Rimm's firing of the gun when aimed slightly to the side of Hill in an enclosed room (where ricochet was likely) constituted acting with reckless disregard of an unjustifiably high risk to human life. Rimm's malice is thus implied. (B) is incorrect because the provocation that would reduce murder to voluntary manslaughter is not present in the facts. (C) is incorrect because Rimm's activities could be found to be more dangerous than "criminal negligence." (D) is incorrect. Although Hill's conduct of aiming a pistol at Rimm and firing could constitute assault with a deadly weapon, the more serious crime of which Rimm can be convicted is murder, because Hill was killed by Rimm's reckless conduct.

Answer to Question 38

(D) Defendant acted in self-defense and, therefore, should not be convicted of a homicide. A person may use deadly force in self-defense if: (i) he is without fault; (ii) he is confronted with unlawful force; and (iii) he is threatened with imminent death or great bodily harm. All three elements are present under these facts. Because Vincent initiated the attack, he will be considered the aggressor, and Defendant will be deemed "without fault." Mere teasing words should not be sufficient to deem Defendant the aggressor, but even if the words were such a provocation, Vincent's sudden escalation of the fight into one involving deadly force would allow Defendant to use force in his own defense. Unlawful force is defined as force that constitutes a crime or a tort. Vincent's attack with the metal bar so qualifies. The defendant must reasonably believe that he is threatened with imminent death or great bodily harm if he does not respond with deadly force. Defendant had such a reasonable belief. Furthermore, Defendant had no duty to retreat under the prevailing rule. It follows that (A), (B), and (C) are incorrect, because Defendant's use of deadly force was justified by self-defense.

Answer to Question 39

(C) *Miranda* warnings are required only where the accused has made a statement during custodial interrogation. Barber voluntarily complied with a request to come to police headquarters, where he was not arrested and was free to leave. During his discussion with the police officers, he voluntarily made a spontaneous inculpatory statement. Thus, he was not entitled to *Miranda* warnings, and (A) is incorrect. (B) is incorrect because, in circumstances such as these, the right to counsel would attach only if there was a custodial police interrogation. "Interrogation" refers not only to express questioning, but also to other words or actions reasonably likely to elicit an incriminating response from the suspect. However, routine questions that the police had no reason to believe would elicit an incriminating response do not constitute an interrogation. Also, there is no due process violation arising from the making of a free and voluntary statement. (D) is incorrect primarily because Barber was not entitled to *Miranda* warnings simply by visiting the police station. Thus, he had nothing to waive. However, even if Barber was entitled to the warnings, the facts do not indicate a waiver. A waiver must be knowing, voluntary and intelligent. Merely agreeing to visit police headquarters does not constitute a knowing, voluntary, and intelligent waiver of *Miranda* warnings.

EVIDENCE QUESTIONS

Questions 1-2 are based on the following fact situation:

Paula sued for injuries she sustained in a fall in a hotel hallway connecting the lobby of the hotel with a restaurant located in the hotel building. The hallway floor was covered with vinyl tile. The defendants were Horne, owner of the hotel building, and Lee, lessee of the restaurant. The evidence was that the hallway floor had been waxed approximately an hour before Paula slipped on it, and although the wax had dried, there appeared to be excessive dried wax caked on several of the tiles. Horne's defense was that the hallway was a part of the premises leased to Lee over which he retained no control, and Lee denied negligence and alleged contributory negligence.

1. Lee offered to prove by Marks, the restaurant manager, that in the week immediately preceding Paula's fall at least 1,000 people had used the hallway in going to and from the restaurant, and Marks had neither seen anyone fall nor received reports that anyone had fallen. The trial judge should rule this evidence:

   (A) Admissible, because it tends to prove that Paula did not use the care exercised by reasonably prudent people.

   (B) Admissible, because it tends to prove that Lee was generally careful in maintaining the floor.

   (C) Inadmissible, because Marks's testimony is self-serving.

   (D) Inadmissible, because it does not bear on the issue of Lee's exercise of due care on this specific occasion.

2. If Paula offered to prove that the day after she fell, Horne had the vinyl tile taken up and replaced with a new floor covering, the trial judge should rule the evidence:

   (A) Admissible, because it is relevant to the issue of whether Horne retained control of the hallway.

   (B) Admissible, because it is relevant as to the issue of awareness of the unsafe condition of the hallway at the time of Paula's fall.

   (C) Inadmissible, because there was no showing that the new floor covering would be any safer than the old.

   (D) Inadmissible, because to admit such would discourage a policy of making repairs to prevent further injury, regardless of fault.

Question 3

Powers sued Debbs for battery. At trial, Powers's witness, Wilson, testified that Debbs had made an unprovoked attack on Powers.

On cross-examination, Debbs asks Wilson about a false claim that Wilson had once filed on an insurance policy. The question is:

(A) Proper, because the conduct involved untruthfulness.

(B) Proper, provided that the conduct resulted in conviction of Wilson.

(C) Improper, because the impeachment involved a specific instance of misconduct.

(D) Improper, because the claim form would be the best evidence.

Question 4

In a tort action, Fisher testified against Dawes. Dawes then called Jones, who testified that Fisher had a bad reputation for veracity. Dawes then also called Weld to testify that Fisher once perpetrated a hoax on the police.

Weld's testimony is:

(A) Admissible, because a hoax involves untruthfulness.

(B) Admissible, provided that the hoax resulted in conviction of Fisher.

(C) Inadmissible, because it is merely cumulative impeachment.

(D) Inadmissible, because it is extrinsic evidence of a specific instance of misconduct.

Questions 5-6 are based on the following fact situation:

Peters sued Davis for $100,000 for injuries received in a traffic accident. Davis charges Peters with contributory negligence and alleges that Peters failed to have his lights on at a time when it was dark enough to require them.

5. Davis calls Bystander to testify that Passenger, who was riding in Peters's automobile and who was injured, confided to him at the scene of the accident that "we should have had our lights on." Bystander's testimony is:

   (A) Admissible as an admission of a party-opponent.

   (B) Admissible as a statement against interest.

   (C) Inadmissible, because it is hearsay not within any exception.

   (D) Inadmissible, because it is opinion.

6. Davis offers to have Bystander testify that he was talking to Witness when he heard the crash and heard Witness, now deceased, exclaim, "That car doesn't have any lights on." Bystander's testimony is:

   (A) Admissible as a statement of present sense impression.

   (B) Admissible, because Witness is not available to testify.

   (C) Inadmissible as hearsay not within any exception.

   (D) Inadmissible, because of the Dead Man's Statute.

Questions 7-8 are based on the following fact situation:

Owner and his employee, Driver, consult Attorney about a motor vehicle collision resulting in a suit by Litigant against Owner and Driver as joint defendants. Attorney calls Irving, his investigator, into the conference to make notes of what is said, and those present discuss the facts of the collision and Owner's insurance. Owner thereafter files a cross-claim against Driver for indemnity for any damages obtained by Litigant.

7. Litigant calls Driver to testify in Litigant's case-in-chief to admissions made by Owner in the conference. On objection by Owner, the court should rule that Driver's testimony is:

   (A) Admissible, because of the presence of persons in the conference other than Attorney and Owner.

   (B) Admissible, because Driver is an adverse party in the lawsuit.

   (C) Inadmissible, because of the attorney-client privilege.

   (D) Inadmissible, because the best evidence is Irving's notes of the conference.

8. Driver calls Irving in his defense against the cross-claim. He seeks to have Irving testify to admissions made by Owner in the conference. On objection by Owner, the court should rule Irving's testimony:

   (A) Admissible, because the attorney-client privilege does not apply, in suits between those conferring with him, to joint consultations with an attorney.

   (B) Admissible, because the attorney-client privilege does not apply to testimony by one who does not stand in a confidential relationship with the person against whom the evidence is offered.

(C) Admissible, because the conference was not intended to be confidential, since it concerned anticipated testimony in open court.

(D) Inadmissible, because Owner has not waived the attorney-client privilege.

Questions 9-11 are based on the following fact situation:

Pemberton and three passengers, Able, Baker, and Charley, were injured when their car was struck by a truck owned by Mammoth Corporation and driven by Edwards. Helper, also a Mammoth employee, was riding in the truck. The issues in *Pemberton v. Mammoth* include the negligence of Edwards in driving too fast and in failing to wear glasses, and of Pemberton in failing to yield the right of way.

9. Pemberton's counsel proffers evidence showing that shortly after the accident, Mammoth put a speed governor on the truck involved in the accident. The judge should rule the proffered evidence:

(A) Admissible as an admission of a party.

(B) Admissible as res gestae.

(C) Inadmissible for public policy reasons.

(D) Inadmissible, because it would lead to the drawing of an inference on an inference.

10. Pemberton's counsel seeks to introduce Helper's written statement that Edwards, Mammoth's driver, had left his glasses (required by his operator's license) at the truck stop which they had left five minutes before the accident. The judge should rule the statement admissible only if:

(A) Pemberton first proves that Helper is an agent of Mammoth and that the statement concerned a matter within the scope of his agency.

(B) Pemberton produces independent evidence that Edwards was not wearing corrective lenses at the time of the accident.

(C) Helper is shown to be beyond the process of the court and unavailable to testify.

(D) The statement was under oath in affidavit form.

11. Mammoth's counsel seeks to have Sheriff testify that while he was investigating the accident he was told by Pemberton, "This was probably our fault." The judge should rule the proffered evidence:

(A) Admissible as an admission of a party.

(B) Admissible, because it is a statement made to a police officer in the course of an official investigation.

(C) Inadmissible, because it is a mixed conclusion of law and fact.

(D) Inadmissible, because it is hearsay not within any exception.

Question 12

In a contract suit between Terrell and Ward, Ward testified that he recalls having his first conversation with Terrell on January 3. When asked how he remembers the date, he answers, "In the conversation, Terrell referred to a story in that day's newspaper announcing my daughter's engagement." Terrell's counsel moves to strike the reference to the newspaper story.

The judge should:

(A) Grant the motion on the ground that the best evidence rule requires production of the newspaper itself.

(B) Grant the motion, because the reference to the newspaper story does not fit within any established exception to the hearsay rule.

(C) Deny the motion on the ground that the court may take judicial notice of local newspapers and their contents.

(D) Deny the motion on the ground that a witness may refer to collateral documents without providing the documents themselves.

Question 13

In Peel's personal injury action, Wilson, a physician who had no previous knowledge of the matter, sat in court and heard all of the evidence about Peel's symptoms and conditions.

Wilson is called to give her opinion whether Peel's injuries are permanent. May Wilson so testify?

(A) Yes, provided she first identifies the data on which her opinion is based.

(B) Yes, because an expert may base her opinion on facts made known to her at the trial.

(C) No, because she has no personal knowledge of Peel's condition.

(D) No, because permanence of injury is an issue to be decided by the jury.

Questions 14-15 are based on the following fact situation:

Rider, a bus passenger, sued Transit Company for injuries to his back from an accident caused by Transit's negligence. Transit denies that Rider received any injury in the accident.

14. Rider's counsel seeks to introduce an affidavit he obtained in preparation for trial from Dr. Bond, who has since died. The affidavit avers that Dr. Bond examined Rider two days after the Transit Company accident and found him suffering from a recently incurred back injury. The judge should rule the affidavit:

    (A) Admissible as a statement of present bodily condition made to a physician.

    (B) Admissible as prior recorded testimony.

    (C) Inadmissible, because it is irrelevant.

    (D) Inadmissible, because it is hearsay not within any exception.

15. Transit Company calls Observer to testify that right after the accident, Rider told him that he had recently suffered a recurrence of an old back injury. The judge should rule Observer's testimony:

    (A) Admissible as an admission of a party-opponent.

    (B) Admissible as a spontaneous declaration.

    (C) Inadmissible, because it is irrelevant.

    (D) Inadmissible, because it is hearsay not within any exception.

Question 16

Patty sues Mart Department Store for personal injuries, alleging that while shopping she was knocked to the floor by a merchandise cart being pushed by Handy, a stock clerk, and that as a consequence her back was injured.

Handy testified that Patty fell near the cart but was not struck by it. Thirty minutes after Patty's fall, Handy, in accordance with regular practice at Mart, had filled out a printed form, "Employee's Report of Accident—Mart Department Store," in which he stated that Patty had been leaning over to spank her young child and in so doing had fallen near his cart. Counsel for Mart offers in evidence the report, which had been given him by Handy's supervisor.

The judge should rule the report offered by Mart:

(A) Admissible as res gestae.

(B) Admissible as a business record.

(C) Inadmissible, because it is hearsay not within any exception.

(D) Inadmissible, because Handy is available as a witness.

Question 17

Pace sues Def Company for injuries suffered when Pace's car collided with Def Company's truck. Def's general manager prepared a report of the accident at the request of the company's attorney, in preparation for the trial, and delivered the report to the attorney. Pace demands that the report be produced.

Will production of the report be required?

(A) Yes, because business reports are not generally privileged.

(B) No, because it is a privileged communication from client to the attorney.

(C) No, because such reports contain hearsay.

(D) No, because such reports are self-serving.

Question 18

At the trial of Davis for a murder that occurred in Newtown, the prosecution called Waite, who testified that she saw Davis kill the victim. Davis believed that Waite was 600 miles away in Old Town, engaged in the illegal sale of narcotics, on the day in question. On cross-examination by Davis, Waite was asked whether she had in fact sold narcotics in Old Town on that date. Waite refused to answer on the ground of self-incrimination.

The judge, over the prosecutor's objection, ordered that if Waite did not testify, her direct testimony should be stricken.

The order to testify or have the testimony stricken can best be supported on the basis that:

(A) Waite had not been charged with any crime and, thus, could claim no privilege against self-incrimination.

(B) Waite's proper invocation of the privilege prevented adequate cross-examination.

(C) The public interest in allowing an accused to defend himself or herself outweighs the interest of a nonparty witness in the privilege.

(D) The trial record, independent of testimony, does not establish that Waite's answer could incriminate her.

Question 19

Alex and Sam were arrested for holding up a gas station. They were taken to police headquarters and placed in a room for interrogation. As a police officer addressing both started to give them *Miranda* warnings prior to the questioning, Alex said, "Look, Sam planned the damned thing and I was dumb enough to go along with it. We robbed the place—what else is there to say?" Sam said nothing. Sam was escorted into another room and a full written confession was then obtained from Alex.

If Sam is brought to trial on an indictment charging him with robbery, the fact that Sam failed to object to Alex's statement and remained silent after Alex had implicated him in the crime should be ruled:

(A) Admissible, because his silence was an implied admission by Sam that he had participated in the crime.

(B) Admissible, because a statement of a participant in a crime is admissible against another participant.

(C) Inadmissible, because under the circumstances there was no duty or responsibility on Sam's part to respond.

(D) Inadmissible, because whatever Alex may have said has no probative value in a trial against Sam.

Question 20

Pack sued Donlon for slander, alleging that Donlon had publicly accused Pack of being a thief. In his answer, Donlon admitted making the accusation, but alleged that it was a true statement.

At trial, Donlon offers evidence that Pack stole a ring worth $10,000 from a jewelry store.

Evidence concerning this theft should be:

(A) Admitted, because specific instances of conduct may be proved when character is directly in issue.

(B) Admitted, because Pack's actions constituted a felony.

(C) Excluded, because character must be shown by reputation or opinion.

(D) Excluded, because its relevance is substantially outweighed by the danger of unfair prejudice.

Question 21

In a suit attacking the validity of a deed executed 15 years ago, Plaintiff alleges mental incompetency of Joe, the grantor, and offers in evidence a properly authenticated affidavit of Harry, Joe's brother. The affidavit, which was executed shortly after the deed, stated that Harry had observed Joe closely over a period of weeks, that Joe had engaged in instances of unusual behavior (which were described), and that Joe's appearance had changed from one of neatness and alertness to one of disorder and absentmindedness.

The judge should rule Harry's affidavit:

(A) Inadmissible as opinion.

(B) Inadmissible as hearsay not within any exception.

(C) Admissible as an official document.

(D) Admissible as an ancient document.

Question 22

Park brought an action against Dan for injuries received in an automobile accident, alleging negligence in that Dan was speeding and inattentive. Park calls White to testify that Dan had a reputation in the community for being a reckless driver and was known as "Daredevil Dan."

White's testimony is:

(A) Admissible as habit evidence.

(B) Admissible, because it tends to prove that Dan was negligent at the time of this collision.

(C) Inadmissible, because Dan has not offered testimony of his own good character.

(D) Inadmissible to show negligence.

Question 23

In Polk's negligence action against Dell arising out of a multiple-car collision, Witt testified for Polk that Dell went through a red light. On cross-examination, Dell seeks to question Witt about her statement that the light was yellow, made in a deposition that Witt gave in a separate action between Adams and Baker. The transcript of the deposition is self-authenticating.

On proper objection, the court should rule the inquiry:

(A) Admissible for impeachment only.

(B) Admissible as substantive evidence only.

(C) Admissible for impeachment and as substantive evidence.

(D) Inadmissible, because it is hearsay not within any exception.

Questions 24-25 are based on the following fact situation:

Price sued Derrick for injuries Price received in an automobile accident. Price claimed Derrick was negligent in (a) exceeding the posted speed limit of 35 m.p.h., (b) failing to keep a lookout, and (c) crossing the center line.

24. Bystander, Price's eyewitness, testified on cross-examination that Derrick was wearing a green sweater at the time of the accident. Derrick's counsel calls Wilson to testify that Derrick's sweater was blue. Wilson's testimony is:

    (A) Admissible as substantive evidence of a material fact.

    (B) Admissible as bearing on Bystander's truthfulness and veracity.

    (C) Inadmissible, because it has no bearing on the capacity of Bystander to observe.

    (D) Inadmissible, because it is extrinsic evidence of a collateral matter.

25. Derrick testified in his own behalf that he was going 30 m.p.h. On cross-examination, Price's counsel did not question Derrick with regard to his speed. Subsequently, Price's counsel calls Officer to testify that, in his investigation following the accident, Derrick told him he was driving 40 m.p.h. Officer's testimony is:

    (A) Admissible as a prior inconsistent statement.

    (B) Admissible as an admission.

    (C) Inadmissible, because it lacks a foundation.

    (D) Inadmissible, because it is hearsay not within any exception.

Question 26

Drew is charged with the murder of Pitt. The prosecutor introduced testimony of a police officer that Pitt told a priest administering the last rites, "I was stabbed by Drew. Since I am dying, tell him I forgive him." Thereafter, Drew's attorney offers the testimony of Wall that the day before, when Pitt believed he would live, he stated that he had been stabbed by Jack, an old enemy.

The testimony of Wall is:

(A) Admissible under an exception to the hearsay rule.

(B) Admissible to impeach the dead declarant.

(C) Inadmissible, because it goes to the ultimate issue in the case.

(D) Inadmissible, because irrelevant to any substantive issue in the case.

Question 27

Post sued Dean for personal injury alleged to have been caused by Dean's negligence. A major issue at trial was whether Post's disability was caused solely by trauma or by a preexisting condition of osteoarthritis.

Post called Dr. Cox, who testified that the disability was caused by trauma. On cross-examination, Dr. Cox testified that a medical textbook entitled *Diseases of the Joints* was authoritative and that she agreed with the substance of passages from the textbook that she was directed to look at, but that the passages were inapplicable to Post's condition because they dealt with rheumatoid arthritis rather than with the osteoarthritis that Post was alleged to have.

Dean then called his expert, Dr. Freed, who testified that, with reference to the issue being litigated, there is no difference between the two kinds of arthritis. Dean's counsel then asks permission to read to the jury the textbook passages earlier shown to Dr. Cox.

The judge should rule the textbook passages:

(A) Admissible only for the purpose of impeaching Cox.

(B) Admissible as substantive evidence if the judge determines that the passages are relevant.

(C) Inadmissible, because they are hearsay not within any exception.

(D) Inadmissible, because Cox contended that they are not relevant to Post's condition.

Question 28

Pratt sued Danvers for injuries suffered by Pratt when their automobiles collided. At trial, Pratt offers into evidence a properly authenticated letter from Danvers that says, "Your claim seems too high, but, because I might have been a little negligent, I'm prepared to offer you half of what you ask."

The letter is:

(A) Admissible as an admission by a party-opponent.

(B) Admissible as a statement against pecuniary interest.

(C) Inadmissible, because Danvers's statement is lay opinion on a legal issue.

(D) Inadmissible, because Danvers's statement was made in an effort to settle the claim.

Question 29

Parker sued Dodd over title to an island in a river. Daily variations in the water level were important.

For many years Wells, a commercial fisherman, kept a daily log of the water level at his dock opposite the island in order to forecast fishing conditions. Parker employed Zee, an engineer, to prepare graphs from Wells's log.

Wells was called to testify to the manner in which he kept the log, which had been available for inspection. His testimony should be:

(A) Excluded on a general objection because not admissible for any purpose.

(B) Excluded on a specific objection that it calls for hearsay.

(C) Admitted to support the credibility of Wells and Zee as witnesses.

(D) Admitted as part of the foundation for admission of Zee's graphs.

Question 30

Polk sued DeVore on a written contract. In her case-in-chief, DeVore testified that she withdrew from the contractual arrangement, as the contract permitted, by notifying Polk by means of a letter. She testified that she put the letter in an envelope, with proper postage, addressed to Polk at his place of business, and that she placed it in a United States Post Office mailbox.

In rebuttal, Polk testified that he got his mail each day from a locked post office box and that he had never received any such letter. There was no other evidence relating to receipt of the notice letter.

When the case is ready to go to the jury, the trial judge should:

(A) Withdraw from the jury's consideration the issue of whether Polk received the notice.

(B) Instruct the jury that it may presume that Polk received the notice.

(C) Instruct the jury that it should find that Polk received the notice.

(D) Submit the case to the jury without instruction concerning a presumption of receipt.

Question 31

Park sued Dent for breach of an oral contract which Dent denied making. Weston testified that he heard Dent make the contract on July 7. Dent discredited Weston, and Park offers evidence of Weston's good reputation for truthfulness.

The rehabilitation is most likely to be permitted if the discrediting evidence by Dent was testimony that:

(A) Weston had been promoting highly speculative stocks.

(B) Weston had been Park's college roommate.

(C) Weston had attended a school for mentally retarded children.

(D) Weston had been out of town the whole week of July 4-10.

Question 32

In a will case, Paula seeks to prove her relationship to the testator Terrence by a statement in a deed of a gift from Terrence, "I transfer to my niece Paula . . ." The deed was recorded pursuant to statute in the office of the county recorder and is kept there. Paula calls Recorder, who authenticates an enlarged print photocopy of the deed. The photocopy was made from the microfilm records kept in Recorder's office pursuant to statute.

The photocopy is:

(A) Admissible as a record of a document affecting an interest in property.

(B) Admissible as recorded recollection.

(C) Inadmissible as hearsay not within any recognized exception.

(D) Inadmissible as not the best evidence.

Question 33

Alice was held up at the point of a gun, an unusual revolver with a red-painted barrel, while she was clerking in a neighborhood grocery store. Dennis is charged with armed robbery of Alice.

The prosecutor calls Winthrop to testify that, a week after the robbery of Alice, he was robbed by Dennis with a pistol that had red paint on the barrel. Winthrop's testimony is:

(A) Admissible as establishing an identifying circumstance.

(B) Admissible as showing that Dennis was willing to commit robbery.

(C) Inadmissible, because it is improper character evidence.

(D) Inadmissible, because its probative value is substantially outweighed by the danger of unfair prejudice.

Question 34

Darden was prosecuted for armed robbery. At trial, Darden testified in his own behalf, denying that he had committed the robbery. On cross-examination, the prosecutor intends to ask Darden whether he had been convicted of burglary six years earlier.

The question concerning the burglary conviction is:

(A) Proper if the court finds that the probative value for impeachment outweighs the prejudice to Darden.

(B) Proper, because the prosecutor is entitled to make this inquiry as a matter of right.

(C) Improper, because burglary does not involve dishonesty or false statement.

(D) Improper, because the conviction must be proved by court record, not by question on cross-examination.

Question 35

Pitt sued Dow for damages for injuries that Pitt incurred when a badly rotted limb fell from a curbside tree in front of Dow's home and hit Pitt. Dow claimed that the tree was on city property and thus was the responsibility of the city. At trial, Pitt offered testimony that, a week after the accident, Dow had cut the tree down with a chainsaw.

The offered evidence is:

(A) Inadmissible, because there is a policy to encourage safety precautions.

(B) Inadmissible, because it is irrelevant to the condition of the tree at the time of the accident.

(C) Admissible to show the tree was on Dow's property.

(D) Admissible to show the tree was in a rotted condition.

Question 36

In litigation over the estate of Baggs, who died intestate, Payton, who is 18 years old, claimed to be Baggs's niece and entitled, therefore, to a share of his large estate. In support of her claim, Payton offered in evidence a Bible, properly identified as having belonged to Baggs's family, in the front of which was a list of family births, marriages, and deaths. The list recorded Payton's birth to Baggs's oldest sister.

To prove that Payton is Baggs's niece, the Bible listing is:

(A) Admissible as an ancient document.

(B) Admissible as a family record.

(C) Inadmissible, because it is hearsay not within any exception.

(D) Inadmissible, because there was no showing of firsthand knowledge by the one who wrote it.

Question 37

Paulsen sued Daly for nonpayment of a personal loan to Daly, as evidenced by Daly's promissory note to Paulsen. Paulsen called Walters to testify that he knows Daly's handwriting and that the signature on the note is Daly's. On direct examination, to identify himself, Walters gave his name and address and testified that he had been employed by a roofing company for seven years.

During presentation of Daly's case, Daly called Wilson to testify that she is the roofing company's personnel manager and that she had determined, by examining the company's employment records, that Walters had worked there only three years.

The trial judge should rule that Wilson's testimony is:

(A) Inadmissible, because it is not the best evidence.

(B) Inadmissible, because it is impeachment on a collateral question.

(C) Admissible as evidence of a regularly conducted activity.

(D) Admissible as tending to impeach Walters's credibility.

Question 38

In a civil suit by Pine against Decker, Decker called Wall, a chemist, as an expert witness and asked him a number of questions about his education and experience in chemistry. Over Pine's objection that Wall was not shown to be qualified in chemistry, the trial court permitted Wall to testify as to his opinion in response to a hypothetical question.

On cross-examination, Pine asked Wall if he had failed two chemistry courses while doing his graduate work. The answer should be:

(A) Admitted, because it is relevant to the weight to be given Wall's testimony.

(B) Admitted, because specific acts bearing on truthfulness may be inquired about on cross-examination.

(C) Excluded, because the court has determined that Wall is qualified to testify as an expert.

(D) Excluded, because Wall's character has not been put in issue.

EVIDENCE ANSWERS

Answer to Question 1

(D) The testimony of Marks presents a problem of relevance. When evidence that relates to a time, event, or person other than the time, event, or persons directly involved in the controversy being litigated is offered, the relevance of that evidence is suspect. However, such evidence may be relevant if it is probative of the material issue involved, and if such probative value outweighs the risk of confusion or unfair prejudice. Specifically, the evidence being offered here is evidence of the absence of similar accidents. Many courts are reluctant to admit evidence of the absence of similar accidents or complaints to show absence of negligence, or lack of a defect. Thus, (D) correctly concludes that the testimony cannot be admitted to show that, at the time of Paula's injury, Lee was exercising due care. For the same reason, (B) is incorrect in stating that the evidence may be used to show that Lee was generally careful in maintaining the floor. (A) is incorrect because, if this type of evidence cannot be used to show that the defendant was not negligent, then it certainly cannot be used to show that the plaintiff was negligent. (C) is incorrect because the fact that evidence may be self-serving does not render it inadmissible; virtually all evidence is self-serving to its proponent, or else it would not be offered by that party.

Answer to Question 2

(A) The law encourages the repair of defective conditions that cause injury. Thus, evidence of repairs or other precautionary measures made following an injury is inadmissible to prove negligence or culpable conduct. However, such evidence may be admissible for other purposes. One such purpose is to show ownership or control, since it is unlikely that a stranger would make repairs. Here, Horne has denied that he had control of the hallway in which the injury occurred. Thus, evidence that he had a new floor covering placed in the hallway is relevant to show that he did in fact have control of the subject premises. This conclusion is accurately reflected in (A). (B) is incorrect because it points precisely to a reason why the evidence might ***not*** be admissible (*i.e.,* it tries to use the evidence to show that Horne was negligent). (D) is incorrect because proof of ownership or control is, as detailed above, an exception to the general rule that evidence of subsequent repairs is inadmissible. Regarding (C), we have already established that the evidence is admissible to show control. Whether the new floor covering is actually safer than the old will not change this result.

Answer to Question 3

(A) A witness may be interrogated upon cross-examination, in the discretion of the court, with respect to any act of misconduct that is probative of truthfulness, regardless of whether the witness was convicted as a result of the "bad act." Thus, (A) is correct. (B) is incorrect because, although it arrives at the correct conclusion that the question is proper, it incorrectly requires that the misconduct have resulted in a conviction. (C) is incorrect because impeachment may be based on specific acts of misconduct. (D) is incorrect because such specific acts of misconduct can only be elicited on cross-examination of the witness; extrinsic evidence is not permitted.

Answer to Question 4

(D) A witness may be interrogated upon cross-examination, in the discretion of the court, with respect to any act of misconduct that is probative of truthfulness, regardless of whether the witness was convicted as a result of the "bad act." Such specific act of misconduct ***can only be elicited on cross-examination*** of the witness. Extrinsic evidence is not permitted. Weld's testimony would constitute extrinsic evidence of a specific instance of misconduct. Thus, (D) is correct. It follows that (A) and (B) are incorrect. (C) is incorrect because there is no rule limiting cumulative impeachment.

Answer to Question 5

(C) Hearsay is a statement, other than one made by the declarant while testifying at the trial or hearing, offered in evidence to prove the truth of the matter asserted. Bystander's testimony as to Passenger's statement is offered to prove the truth of the matter asserted therein; *i.e.*, that Peters did not have his lights on and was thus contributorily negligent. Therefore, the statement is not admissible unless it comes within one of the hearsay exceptions. (A) is incorrect because Passenger is not a party, and there is no indication either that Peters adopted Passenger's statement or that Peters and Passenger had such a relationship that would render the statement a vicarious admission by Peters. (B) is incorrect because the statement against interest exception requires that the declarant be unavailable as a witness. Passenger does not appear to be unavailable. Also, the statement does not seem to be against the interest of Passenger (although it certainly is against the interest of Peters). (D) is incorrect because the matter is one about which laypersons regularly form opinions.

Answer to Question 6

(A) Witness's statement is hearsay but within the present sense impression exception to the hearsay rule. This exception comes into play when a person perceives some event that is not particularly shocking, yet that person nevertheless is moved to comment on what he perceived at the time of receipt of the sense impression or immediately thereafter. Here, the statement conveys what Witness perceived at the time of the accident; thus, it is allowed into evidence as a present sense impression. Because the statement falls within one of the hearsay exceptions, (C) is incorrect. (B) is incorrect because, for the present sense impression exception, the declarant's availability is immaterial. (D) is incorrect because a Dead Man's Statute prohibits testimony as to a personal transaction or communication with a decedent when such testimony is offered against the representative or successors in interest of the deceased. This question does not involve a suit against a decedent's estate.

Answer to Question 7

(C) A communication is confidential, for purposes of the attorney-client privilege, if it was not intended to be disclosed to third persons, other than those to whom disclosure would be in furtherance of the rendition of legal services to the client. Also, where a lawyer acts for two parties, the privilege can be claimed in a suit between either or both of the parties and third persons. Here, Attorney's investigator is someone to whom disclosure was in furtherance of the rendition of legal services. Thus, any statements made in Irving's presence will still be confidential. In addition, the fact that Owner made statements in the presence of a joint client does not deprive those statements of the protection of the attorney-client privilege. For these reasons, (A) is incorrect in holding the privilege inapplicable because of the presence of third persons in the conference. (B) is incorrect because Driver and Owner are both defendants in Litigant's suit, and communications made by joint clients are privileged as against third parties. (D) is incorrect because the best evidence rule does not apply to these facts. According to the rule, in proving the terms of a writing, where the terms are material, the original writing must be produced. Testimony is not offered here to prove the contents of Irving's notes.

Answer to Question 8

(A) Where a lawyer acts for joint clients, no privilege can be invoked in a suit between the two parties, as they could not have desired nor could they have expected confidentiality as between themselves in a joint consultation. There is a suit (a cross-claim) between Owner and Driver.

Thus, in this suit, Owner cannot claim the privilege as to statements made during the joint conference. Therefore, (A) is correct. (B) is wrong because where a privilege attaches, the holder can prevent disclosure by anyone. (C) is incorrect because the lack of confidentiality arises from the fact that the two litigants participated in a joint conference, rather than from the fact that the conference related to testimony to be given in open court. (D) reaches the incorrect conclusion that the testimony is inadmissible, because the privilege has not been waived. As explained above, the requisite confidentiality is missing.

Answer to Question 9

(C) Evidence of repairs or other precautionary measures made following an injury is inadmissible to prove negligence or culpable conduct. This is because public policy encourages people to make such repairs. Such evidence ***is*** admissible for other purposes, *e.g.*, to prove ownership or control. Here, we are told that the issues involve negligence. Thus, the evidence as to the speed governor is being offered to prove culpable conduct or negligence, and therefore is inadmissible. (A) and (B) each incorrectly conclude that the evidence is admissible. (D) makes absolutely no sense.

Answer to Question 10

(A) The statement by Helper is one made by the declarant (Helper) other than while testifying at the trial, offered to prove the truth of the matter asserted (*i.e.*, that Edwards was not wearing his glasses at the time of the accident). This presents a hearsay issue. However, an admission by a party-opponent is not considered hearsay under the Federal Rules. Here, the party-opponent is Mammoth Corporation, while the statement is by an employee of Mammoth. Statements by an agent concerning any matter within the scope of his agency, made during the course of the employment relationship, are not hearsay and are admissible against the principal. Thus, (A) correctly states that the statement is admissible only if Helper is an agent of Mammoth and the statement concerned a matter within the scope of the agency. (B) is incorrect because admissibility of the statement is not dependent on independent corroboration of the truth thereof. (C) is incorrect because unavailability of the declarant is not a prerequisite for an admission of a party-opponent. (D) is incorrect because an admission need not be under oath in order to be admissible.

Answer to Question 11

(A) As detailed in the answer to the preceding question, an admission by a party-opponent is nonhearsay under the Federal Rules. An admission is a statement made or act done that amounts to a prior acknowledgment by one of the parties of a relevant fact. Here, a fact in issue is whether Pemberton failed to yield the right of way. Pemberton's statement to Sheriff acknowledges fault. Thus, the testimony as to the statement is admissible as an admission by a party-opponent of Mammoth's. Because the evidence is not considered hearsay, (D) incorrectly concludes that it ***is*** hearsay. (B) is incorrect because statements made in such a manner may be inadmissible multiple hearsay. (C) is incorrect because the admissibility of the testimony centers on a party's admission of a relevant fact. The declarant's use of the word "fault," which may be a legal conclusion, does not affect the admissibility of the statement.

Answer to Question 12

(D) Pursuant to the best evidence rule, when proving the terms of a writing (where the terms are material), the original writing must be produced. The rule does not apply to writings of minor importance to the matter in controversy. Thus, a witness may refer to collateral documents without providing the documents themselves. Here, the newspaper issue is tangential. As a result, there is no need to produce the newspaper. Therefore, (A) incorrectly concludes that the best evidence rule requires production of the newspaper. (B) is wrong because the newspaper story is not offered to prove the truth of its contents. (C) is incorrect because courts may take judicial notice of the ***existence*** of a local newspaper (a matter of common knowledge within the community) but not the ***contents*** of articles appearing therein.

Answer to Question 13

(B) An expert's opinion may be based upon one or more of three possible sources of information: (i) facts that he knows from his own observation; (ii) facts presented in evidence at the trial and submitted to the expert; or (iii) facts not in evidence that were supplied to the expert out of court, which facts are of a type reasonably relied upon by experts in the particular field in forming opinions on the subject. (B) correctly refers to (ii), above, as a proper source of information for the expert. (A) is incorrect because, where an expert bases her opinion on facts made known to her at the trial, the expert need not disclose the reasons for the opinion on direct examination unless the court orders it. (C) is incorrect because, although personal observation is one of the sources upon which an expert opinion may be based, it is not the only such source. (D) is incorrect because permanence of injury is an issue that requires specialized knowledge to assist the jury.

Answer to Question 14

(D) The statement is inadmissible hearsay. Hearsay is an out-of-court statement offered in evidence to prove the truth of the matter asserted. Here, the affidavit is being offered to prove that Rider incurred a recent back injury. Because Dr. Bond is dead, the adverse party is denied the opportunity to cross-examine him and test the veracity of his statement. Furthermore, the statement falls within no recognized exception to the hearsay rule. Thus, (D) is correct. (A) is incorrect because declarations of present bodily condition are statements made contemporaneously with the symptoms. Here, the affidavit was prepared later in contemplation of trial. It does not contain Rider's contemporaneous statements regarding his symptoms, but rather the physician's observation that Rider suffered from a recent back injury. Hence, the statement does not fall within the exception. (B) is incorrect because the former testimony exception requires that the statement be given during formal proceedings and under oath by a witness subject to cross-examination. (C) is incorrect because the statement relates to a time, event, or person in controversy. Whether Rider's back injury was an old or a recent injury is such a matter in controversy. Hence, the statement is relevant.

Answer to Question 15

(A) An admission by a party-opponent is considered nonhearsay under the Federal Rules. An admission is a statement that amounts to a prior acknowledgment by one of the parties to an action of one of the relevant facts. If the party said or did something inconsistent with his contentions at trial, the law regards him as estopped from preventing its admission into evidence. (A) is correct because Rider's statement that his back injury was a recurrence of an old injury is inconsistent with his assertion that the injury resulted from the recent accident. (B) is wrong because a spontaneous declaration (or "excited utterance") must concern the immediate facts of a startling occurrence. Rider's statement does not refer to the accident itself. Nor is it clear from the facts that the statement was made under the stress of the excitement. (C) is wrong because the statement relates to a time, event, or person in controversy (*i.e.*, whether Rider's back injury resulted from Transit Company's negligence). Hence, it is relevant. (D) is wrong because (as noted in the discussion of option (A), above) an admission by a party-opponent is nonhearsay under the Federal Rules of Evidence.

Answer to Question 16

(C) The report is hearsay, as it is a statement, not made by the declarant while testifying at the trial, offered to prove the truth of the matter asserted. Thus, the report is inadmissible unless it comes within a hearsay exception. The only applicable exception is the business records exception, under which a writing or record made as a memorandum of any act, transaction, occurrence, or event is admissible as proof of such act, etc., if made in the regular course of a business, and if it was the regular course of such business to make it at the time of the act, or within a reasonable time thereafter. Many courts exclude self-serving employee accident reports that are prepared primarily for litigation by someone with a strong motive to misrepresent. Under the Federal Rules, courts have discretion to exclude a business record if the source of information indicates a lack of trustworthiness. The report at issue was prepared primarily for litigation purposes by Handy, who had a strong motive to misrepresent the facts. Therefore, the report is sufficiently lacking in trustworthiness so as to not qualify for admission as a business record. Because the report is inadmissible, (A) and (B) are incorrect for concluding that it is admissible. (D) is incorrect because unavailability is not germane to the business records exception.

Answer to Question 17

(B) Communications between attorney and client, made during professional consultation, are privileged from disclosure. A business report prepared as a communication from client to attorney is privileged. Here, Def's general manager prepared the report at the request of the company's attorney. This report constitutes a privileged, confidential communication between a client (Def Company) and its attorney. Therefore, production of the report will not be required. (A) is incorrect because the facts indicate that this particular business report is of a privileged nature. (C) and (D) are wrong because the fact that a report contains hearsay or is self-serving does not prevent its discovery by the opponent.

Answer to Question 18

(B) Waite's invocation of the privilege meant that Davis could not cross-examine her on a critical issue in the case. If Waite actually was in Old Town, she could not have witnessed the murder, and her testimony would be impeached. Because she cannot be adequately cross-examined on this matter, her testimony should be stricken in its entirety. (A) is wrong because it is not necessary for a person to have been charged with a crime in order to claim a privilege against self-incrimination. (C) is wrong because a non-party's privileges are not outweighed by the rights of the accused. (D) is wrong because it is not necessary for one claiming a privilege against self-incrimination to establish that she would actually be self-incriminated by her testimony.

Answer to Question 19

(C) Under the Fifth Amendment to the United States Constitution, a witness cannot be compelled to testify against himself. A prosecutor may not comment on a defendant's silence after being arrested and receiving *Miranda* warnings. The warnings carry an implicit assurance that silence will carry no penalty. Thus, Sam's silence after Alex's incriminating statement is inadmissible against Sam and (C) is correct. It follows that (A) is incorrect. The self-incrimination privilege negates the "adoptive admission" doctrine, and failure to reply to an accusation or statement made by police in a criminal case can almost never be used as an implied admission of a criminal act. (B) is wrong because the statement is overbroad, and because the issue of admissibility involves Sam's silence (which is protected by the Fifth Amendment) rather than Alex's confession. (D) is an incorrect statement of fact. Alex's statement relates to a time, person, or event in controversy, and thus is relevant and obviously has probative value. However, the issue of admissibility in this question involves Sam's silence and not Alex's statement. Thus, option (D) is unresponsive to the call of the question.

Answer to Question 20

(A) Evidence concerning the theft should be admitted because specific instances of conduct may be proved when character is directly in issue. Although character evidence, including evidence of specific acts, is generally inadmissible in a civil case, there is an exception where character is directly in issue. In defamation cases, character is always in issue, and evidence is admissible as to the trait in question. Here, the issue is whether Pack is a thief. Evidence of acts of theft by Pack are admissible. (B) is wrong because whether the act is a felony is only important if it is offered as a prior conviction to attack the character for truthfulness of a testifying witness. Any act of theft, felony or misdemeanor, would be admissible here to show that Pack is a thief; it is not being offered for impeachment purposes. (C) is incorrect because, under the Federal Rules, any of the types of character evidence (reputation, opinion, or specific acts) may be used to prove character when character is directly in issue. (D) is wrong because the evidence is central to the ultimate issue in the case—the truth of Donlon's statement. Its relevance could not be greater and could not be substantially outweighed by the danger of unfair prejudice.

Answer to Question 21

(B) Harry's affidavit is inadmissible. Hearsay is an out-of-court statement offered in evidence to prove the truth of the matter asserted. Here, the affidavit is an out-of-court statement Plaintiff seeks to introduce to prove that Joe was incompetent when he conveyed the property. Hence, it is hearsay. The affidavit does not fall within any recognized exception to the hearsay rule. Hence, (B) is correct. (A) is wrong because opinion testimony by lay witnesses is admissible when: (i) it is rationally based on the perception of the witness; and (ii) it is helpful to a clear understanding of testimony or to the determination of a fact in issue. Opinions of laypersons as to the general appearance or condition of a person are generally admissible. The problem here does not involve "opinion," but rather the fact that the affidavit is hearsay. (C) is wrong because the affidavit does not qualify as an official document. The official records exception to the hearsay rule covers records, reports, statements, or data compilations of public offices and agencies made by, and within the scope of duty of, the public employee. Harry and his affidavit have no such official standing. (D) is wrong because the affidavit is 15 years old, and the Federal Rules of Evidence require that a document be at least 20 years old to qualify as an "ancient document." (It should also be noted that statements affecting an interest in property are not subject to the 20-year rule. However, the affidavit is not a deed, a will, or a document that otherwise disposes of property. Therefore, it does not qualify under the exception.)

Answer to Question 22

(D) White's testimony is inadmissible to show negligence. Evidence of character to prove the conduct of a person in the litigated event is generally not admissible in civil cases, because the slight probative value of character is outweighed by the danger of prejudice, the possible distraction of the jury from the main question in issue, and the possible waste of time required by examination of collateral issues. There is an exception to this general rule when a person's character itself is one of the issues in the case. Here, Dan's character is not in issue. Thus, the general rule applies, and (D) is correct. (A) is incorrect because habit describes one's regular response to a specific set of circumstances. Here, however, what is involved is character evidence rather than habit evidence. Character describes one's disposition with respect to general traits (*i.e.*, Dan's reputation in the community as a reckless driver). (B) is wrong because reputation evidence in civil cases is admitted only for the purpose of proving character. Negligence of Dan on a particular occasion does not raise character issues. (C) is wrong because it applies the general rule for criminal cases, and the case in question is a civil one.

Answer to Question 23

(C) Under Federal Rule 801(d)(1), Witt's statement made in the earlier deposition is considered nonhearsay as a prior inconsistent statement made by a witness while testifying under oath at some prior proceeding, and thus is admissible as substantive proof. It can be admitted for impeachment purposes so long as a proper foundation is laid. Federal Rule 613 requires that the witness must be first examined "so as to give him an opportunity to explain or deny" the allegedly inconsistent statement unless "the interests of justice otherwise require." (A) is wrong because this was a former statement made under oath, is considered not to be hearsay, and is admissible as substantive proof. (B) is wrong because so long as a proper foundation is laid, it can be introduced for impeachment purposes as well. (D) is wrong because it is not hearsay.

Answer to Question 24

(D) Where a witness makes a statement not directly relevant to the issues in the case, the opponent is barred from proving the statement untrue either by extrinsic contradictory facts or by a prior inconsistent statement. The color of the sweater worn by Derrick is collateral to the issues in this case. Thus, allowing testimony contradicting Bystander's testimony on this matter would raise the possibility of unfair surprise, confusion of issues, and inefficient use of the court's time. For these reasons, Wilson's testimony is inadmissible. (A) is wrong because nothing in the facts indicates that the color of Derrick's sweater is of consequence to the action. (B) and (C) are wrong because even if the evidence has some bearing on the witness's credibility, it is excluded because of possible confusion of issues or waste of time.

Answer to Question 25

(B) The statement made by Derrick to Officer is an admission by a party-opponent (*i.e.*, a statement that amounts to a prior acknowledgment by a party of one of the relevant facts). We are told that the rate of speed at which Derrick was traveling is in issue. Thus, Derrick's statement that he was driving 40 m.p.h. comes in as an admission. (D) is wrong because, under the Federal Rules, an admission is not hearsay. (A) is wrong because an admission is admissible whether or not it discredits later testimony. (C) is wrong because no foundation is necessary for the admission into evidence of an admission by a party-opponent.

Answer to Question 26

(B) Where an out-of-court statement is admitted into evidence under one of the exceptions to the hearsay rule, the party against whom the statement has been admitted may impeach the credibility of the declarant. The declarant's credibility may be attacked by evidence that would be admissible if the declarant had testified. The testimony of Wall is admissible to show that Pitt made a statement that was inconsistent with the statement related by the police officer. (A) is incorrect because impeachment evidence is ***excluded*** from the hearsay rule. (C) refers to the traditional rule prohibiting expert witnesses from expressing opinions on the ultimate issue in the case. This rule has been repudiated by the Federal Rules. Also, this case does not involve expert testimony. In addition, the testimony does not relate an opinion. For these reasons, (C) is incorrect. (D) is wrong because Pitt's credibility is crucial to Drew's culpability.

Answer to Question 27

(B) The Federal Rules allow for substantive admissibility of learned treatises, if such treatises are called to the attention of the expert witness upon cross-examination or relied upon by her during direct examination and they are established as reliable authority by the testimony or admission of the witness, or by other expert testimony, or by judicial notice. This is an exception to the hearsay rule. Here, the medical textbook was called to the attention of Dr. Cox on cross-examination, and she testified that it was authoritative. Thus, the passages from the textbook are admissible as substantive evidence. It logically follows that (A) and (C) are incorrect. (D) is incorrect because it is not Dr. Cox's job to determine the relevancy of proffered evidence.

Answer to Question 28

(D) Evidence of compromises or offers to compromise a claim disputed as to either liability or damages is inadmissible to prove liability for or invalidity of a claim. Also, any conduct or statement made in the course of negotiating a compromise is inadmissible. It follows that (A) and (B) are incorrect. (C) is incorrect because, were it not for the rule excluding offers of compromise, the statement would be an admission of a party-opponent. Such an admission can be in the form of an opinion.

Answer to Question 29

(D) Zee's graphs are demonstrative evidence, offered to illustrate the daily variations in water level at issue here. Because the graphs are reproductions of the data contained in Wells's log, Wells's testimony regarding the compilation of the log is necessary to determine whether the graphs are based on a foundation strong enough to justify their admission into evidence. It follows that (A) is incorrect. (B) is incorrect because this is not hearsay. Wells is going to testify to the manner in which he kept the log, not to an out-of-court statement offered to prove the truth of the matter asserted. (C) is incorrect because, generally, credibility may not be bolstered until it has been impeached.

Answer to Question 30

(D) A letter shown to have been properly addressed, stamped, and mailed is presumed to have been delivered in the due course of mail. Under the Federal Rules, such a presumption is overcome when the party against whom it is directed produces sufficient evidence contradicting the presumed fact. Here, DeVore's testimony raises a presumption of due delivery of the notice letter. However, Polk, by his testimony, has produced enough evidence to rebut this presumption. Thus, when the case goes to the jury, the judge should not instruct the jury regarding a presumption of receipt, because that presumption is gone. (A) is incorrect because the jury must determine questions of fact, such as whether Polk received the notice. (B) is incorrect because, as explained above, there is no longer a presumption that Polk received the notice. (C) is incorrect because it goes even further than to call for a presumption. Rather, it calls for a "conclusive" presumption, which cannot be rebutted by contrary evidence. Such a presumption runs afoul of the Federal Rules, which permit a presumption to be rebutted.

Answer to Question 31

(D) A witness's good reputation for truth and veracity may be shown after attack. However, only under certain circumstances will it be proper. (A) is not correct because selling speculative stocks does not need the response of good reputation for truth. (B) is not correct because good reputation for truth and veracity does not refute bias. (C) is not correct since attending a school for the mentally retarded does not go to credibility. (D) is a fundamental attack going to the credibility of Weston's entire testimony. It is thus the best answer.

Answer to Question 32

(A), (C) (A) and (C) were both given credit by the examiners. (B) is wrong because for past recollection recorded there must be a record made at or near the event by someone with firsthand knowledge who has no present recollection but who can say it was accurate when written. That is not present here. (D) is wrong because the best evidence rule requires the production of the original unless it is accounted for. Photocopies would be admissible, absent a genuine dispute about the authenticity of the original or other unfairness. Either (A) or (C) could be correct depending upon interpretation. This is a document affecting an interest in property. Statements in documents affecting an interest in property are admissible if they are "relevant to the purpose of the document." If one interprets the statement that the recipient of the deed of gift is related to the donor to be "relevant to the purpose of the document," then (A) would be correct. If not, then (C) would be correct.

Answer to Question 33

(A) Other crimes or wrongs are not generally admissible. They may be shown, however, to prove identity (among a few other relevant things). Other crimes are admissible on identity only when they are highly individual and amount to a "signature." Red paint on a gun is individual enough to qualify. Thus, (A) is right and (D) is wrong. (B) is an incorrect theory. Having a red gun does not show anything about the defendant's willingness to commit a crime. (C) is wrong, too. This is not character evidence.

Answer to Question 34

(A) The Federal Rules allow impeachment by: (i) any felony conviction, if the trial judge decides that the probative value of the conviction outweighs its prejudicial effect; and (ii) conviction of any other crime requiring proof or admission of an act of dishonesty or false statement. The prior conviction is usually shown either by direct or cross-examination of the witness or by introducing a record of the judgment. It follows that (D) is incorrect. (C) is incorrect because impeachment may be accomplished by showing any felony conviction (if the probative value outweighs the prejudicial effect), not just by showing conviction of crimes involving dishonesty or false statement. (B) is incorrect because it fails to account for the need to find that the probative value outweighs the prejudicial effect.

Answer to Question 35

(C) The evidence is admissible to show that the tree was on Dow's property. While evidence of repairs made following an accident is generally inadmissible to prove negligence or culpable conduct under Federal Rule 407, such evidence may be introduced to show ownership or control, since a stranger would hardly make repairs. (A) is wrong because while there is such a public policy, in this case a valid exception applies. (B) is wrong because the evidence is not being introduced to show the condition of the tree at the time of the accident. (D) is wrong because Dow's cutting down of the tree cannot be admitted to show the tree was in a rotted condition. This would contravene the policy of the rule, which has the purpose of encouraging people to make such repairs.

Answer to Question 36

(B) The Bible listing is admissible as a family record. Federal Rule of Evidence 803(13) provides a specific exception to the hearsay rule allowing admission of family records, such as family Bibles, genealogies, engravings, etc. A family Bible with a record of births and deaths is exactly the type of document intended by this exception. (A) is incorrect because the inscription concerning Baggs's niece is less than 20 years old. (C) is incorrect because the hearsay exception described above applies to the family Bible. (D) is incorrect because there is no such foundational requirement in the exception to the hearsay rule. The family Bible is considered to have inherent indicia of trustworthiness. The Bible has been properly identified as having belonged to Baggs's family, and there is no reason to consider the inscription untrustworthy.

Answer to Question 37

(B) Where a witness makes a statement not directly relevant to the issues in the case, the rule against impeachment on a collateral matter applies to bar the other side from proving the statement untrue by extrinsic evidence or by a prior inconsistent statement. Here, the actual number of years during which Walters was employed by the roofing company is irrelevant to the genuineness of Daly's signature on the note. Thus, this is a collateral matter, and Daly will not be permitted to impeach Walters on it. (D) then is incorrect. (C) is incorrect, not only because Wilson's testimony is irrelevant to any issue in the case, but also because such testimony is not evidence of a regularly conducted activity. (A) is incorrect. Although the witness is testifying orally about matters contained in a writing (the employment records), the records here are collateral to the issue being litigated. Accordingly, the collateral document exception applies and the best evidence rule is inapplicable.

Answer to Question 38

(A) The credibility of an expert witness may be attacked by cross-examining him as to: (i) his general knowledge of the field in which he is claiming to be an expert; and (ii) his particular knowledge of the facts upon which his opinion is based. Pine's question on cross-examination relates to Wall's general knowledge of the field of chemistry. This bears directly on the weight to be given Wall's testimony. Thus, (A) is correct. (C) is incorrect because any determination of Wall's qualifications as an expert does not preclude an attack on his credibility or on the weight to be given the opinion. (B) and (D) are incorrect because the question relates to neither Wall's truthfulness nor his character.

REAL PROPERTY QUESTIONS

Questions 1-3 are based on the following fact situation:

Sue owned a five-acre tract of land, one acre of which had previously been owned by Opal, but to which Sue had acquired title by adverse possession. Sue contracted to convey the full five-acre tract to Peg, but the contract did not specify the quality of title Sue would convey.

1. Suppose Peg pays the purchase price and accepts a deed. Subsequently, Sue's title to the one acre proves inadequate and Opal ejects Peg from that acre. Peg sues Sue for damages. Which of the following statements applies most accurately to the determination of Peg's rights?

   (A) Sue's deed was fraudulent.

   (B) The terms of the deed control Sue's liability.

   (C) The only remedy available for breach of warranty of title is rescission.

   (D) Peg's rights are based on the implied covenants that the title conveyed shall be marketable.

2. Suppose Sue's contract had called for the conveyance of "a good and marketable title." Pursuant to that contract, Peg paid the purchase price and accepted a deed from Sue containing no covenants of title. Sue's title to the one acre subsequently proved defective and Peg was ejected by Opal. Peg sued Sue. Which of the following results is most likely?

   (A) Peg will win, because Sue's deed was fraudulent.

   (B) Peg will win, because the terms of the deed control Sue's liability.

   (C) Sue will win, because the terms of the deed control her liability.

   (D) Sue will win, because the deed incorporates the terms of the contract.

3. Suppose that before closing, the house on the property had been totally destroyed by fire. In determining the rights of Sue and Peg, the court would most likely consider the doctrine of equitable:

   (A) Marshaling.

   (B) Sequestration.

   (C) Subrogation.

   (D) Conversion.

Question 4

Owens contracted to sell a tract of land, Overlea, to Painter by general warranty deed. However, at the closing Painter did not carefully examine the deed and accepted a quitclaim deed without covenants of title. Painter later attempted to sell Overlea to Thompson, who refused to perform because Owens had conveyed an easement for a highway across Overlea before Painter bought the property.

Painter sued Owens for damages. Which of the following arguments will most likely succeed in Owens's defense?

(A) The existence of the easement does not violate the contract.

(B) The mere existence of an easement that is not being used does not give rise to a cause of action.

(C) Painter's cause of action must be based on the deed and not on the contract.

(D) The proper remedy is rescission of the deed.

Question 5

Lord leased a warehouse building and the lot on which it stood to Taylor for a term of 10 years. The lease contained a clause prohibiting Taylor from subletting his interest.

Can Taylor assign his interest under the lease?

(A) Yes, because restraints on alienation of land are strictly construed.

(B) Yes, because disabling restraints on alienation are invalid.

(C) No, because the term "subletting" includes "assignment" when the term is employed in a lease.

(D) No, because even in the absence of an express prohibition on assignment, a tenant may not assign without the landlord's permission.

Question 6

The following facts concern a tract of land in a state which follows general law. Each instrument is in proper form, recorded, marital property rights were waived when necessary, and each person named was adult and competent at the time of the named transaction.

1. In 1940, Oleg, the owner, conveyed his interest in fee simple "to my brothers Bob and Bill, their heirs and assigns as joint tenants with right of survivorship."

2. In 1950 Bob died, devising his interest to his only child, "Charles, for life, and then to Charles's son, Sam, for life, and then to Sam's children, their heirs and assigns."

3. In 1970 Bill died, devising his interest "to my friend, Frank, his heirs and assigns."

4. In 1972 Frank conveyed by quitclaim deed "to Paul, his heirs and assigns, whatever right, title, and interest I own."

Paul has never married. Paul has contracted to convey marketable record title in the land to Patrick. Can Paul do so?

(A) Yes, without joinder of any other person in the conveyance.

(B) Yes, if Charles, Sam, and Sam's only child (Gene, aged 25) will join in the conveyance.

(C) No, regardless of who joins in the conveyance, because Sam may have additional children whose interests cannot be defeated.

(D) No, regardless of who joins in the conveyance, because a title acquired by quitclaim deed is impliedly unmarketable.

Questions 7-8 are based on the following fact situation:

Oscar, the owner in fee simple, laid out a subdivision of 325 lots on 150 acres of land. He obtained governmental approval (as required by applicable ordinances) and, between 1968 and 1970, he sold 140 of the lots, inserting in each of the 140 deeds the following provision:

> The Grantee, for himself and his heirs, assigns and successors, covenants and agrees that the premises conveyed herein shall have erected thereon one single-family dwelling and that no other structure (other than a detached garage, normally incident to a single-family dwelling) shall be erected or maintained; and, further, that no use shall ever be made or permitted to be made other than occupancy by a single family for residential purposes only.

Because of difficulty encountered in selling the remaining lots for single-family use, in January 1971, Oscar advertised the remaining lots with prominent emphasis: "These lots are not subject to any restrictions and purchasers will find them adaptable to a wide range of uses."

7. Payne had purchased one of the 140 lots and brought suit against Oscar to establish that the remaining 185 lots, as well as the 140 sold previously, can be used only for residential purposes by single families. Assuming that procedural requirements have been met, to permit adjudication of the issue Payne has tendered, which of the following is the most appropriate comment?

(A) Oscar should win because the provision binds only the grantee.

(B) The outcome turns on whether a common development scheme had been established for the entire subdivision.

(C) The outcome turns on whether there are sufficient land areas devoted to multiple family uses within the municipality to afford reasonable opportunity for all economic classes to move into the area so as to satisfy the standards of equal protection of the law.

(D) Payne should win under an application of the doctrine, which requires construction of deeds, to resolve any doubt against the grantor.

8. Suppose that Oscar sold 50 lots during 1971 without inserting in the deeds any provisions relating to structures or uses. Doyle purchased one of the 50 lots and proposes to erect a service station and to conduct a retail business for the sale of gasoline, etc.

Pringle purchased a lot from Boyer. Boyer had purchased from Oscar in 1968 and the deed had the provision that is quoted in the fact situation.

Pringle brings suit to prevent Doyle from erecting the service station and from conducting a retail business.

In the litigation between Pringle and Doyle, which of the following constitutes the best defense for Doyle?

(A) Oscar's difficulty in selling with provisions relating to use establishes a change in circumstances which renders any restrictions which may once have existed unenforceable.

(B) Enforcement of the restriction, in view of the change of circumstances, would be an unreasonable restraint on alienation.

(C) Since the proof (as stated) does not establish a danger of monetary loss to Pringle, Pringle has failed to establish one of the necessary elements in a cause of action to prevent Doyle from using his lot for business purposes.

(D) The facts do not establish a common building or development scheme for the entire subdivision.

Question 9

Odum owned Brightacre (a tract of land) in fee simple. He conveyed it "to Pike, his heirs and assigns; but if Farley shall be living 30 years from the date of this deed, then to Farley, his heirs and assigns."

The limitation "to Farley, his heirs and assigns" is:

(A) Valid, because Farley's interest is a reversion.

(B) Valid, because the interest will vest, if at all, within a life in being.

(C) Valid, because Farley's interest is vested subject to divestment.

(D) Invalid.

Questions 10-11 are based on the following fact situation:

Trease owned Hilltop in fee simple. By his will, he devised as follows: "Hilltop to such of my grandchildren who shall reach the age of 21; and by this provision I intend to include all grandchildren whenever born." At the time of his death, Trease had three children and two grandchildren.

10. Courts hold such a devise valid under the common law Rule Against Perpetuities. What is the best explanation of that determination?

(A) All of Trease's children would be measuring lives.

(B) The rule of convenience closes the class of beneficiaries when any grandchild reaches the age of 21.

(C) There is a presumption that Trease intended to include only those grandchildren born prior to his death.

(D) There is a subsidiary rule of construction that dispositive instruments are to be interpreted so as to uphold interests rather than to invalidate them under the Rule Against Perpetuities.

11. Which of the following additions to or changes in the facts of the preceding question would produce a violation of the common law Rule Against Perpetuities?

(A) A posthumous child was born to Trease.

(B) Trease's will expressed thc intention to include all afterborn grandchildren in the gift.

(C) The instrument was an inter vivos conveyance rather than a will.

(D) Trease had no grandchildren living at the time of his death.

Question 12

Assume for the purposes of this question that you are counsel to the state legislative committee that is responsible for real estate laws in your state. The committee wants you to draft a statute, governing the recording of deeds, that fixes priorities of title, as reflected on the public record, as definitely as possible.

Which of the following, divorced from other policy considerations, would best accomplish this particular result?

(A) Eliminate the requirement of witnesses to deeds.

(B) Make time of recording the controlling factor.

(C) Make irrebuttable the declarations in the deeds that valuable consideration was paid.

(D) Make the protection of bona fide purchasers the controlling factor.

Questions 13-15 are based on the following fact situation:

Owen held in fee simple Farmdale, a large tract of vacant land. The state wherein Farmdale is situated has a statute which provides, in substance, that unless the conveyance is recorded, every deed or other conveyance of an interest in land is void as to a subsequent purchaser who pays value without notice of such conveyance. The following transactions occurred in the order given.

First: Owen conveyed Farmdale, for a fair price, to Allred by general warranty deed. Allred did not immediately record.

Second: Owen executed a mortgage to secure repayment of a loan concurrently made to Owen by Leon. Leon had no notice of the prior conveyance to Allred and promptly recorded the mortgage.

Third: Owen, by general warranty deed, gratuitously conveyed to Niece, who promptly recorded the deed.

Fourth: Allred recorded his deed from Owen.

Fifth: Niece, by general warranty deed, conveyed Farmdale to Barrett. Barrett had no actual notice of any of the prior transactions, paid full value, and promptly recorded the deed.

13. Asserting that his title was held free of any claim by Barrett, Allred instituted suit against Barrett to quiet title to Farmdale. If Barrett prevails, it will be because:

(A) Allred's prior recorded deed is deemed to be outside Barrett's chain of title.

(B) Barrett's grantor, Niece, recorded before Allred.

(C) As between two warranty deeds, the later one controls.

(D) Barrett's grantor, Niece, had no notice of Allred's rights.

14. Asserting that his title was held free of any claim by Leon, Allred instituted suit against Leon to quiet title to Farmdale. Judgment should be for:

    (A) Allred, because Leon is deemed not to have paid value.

    (B) Allred, because a mortgagee is not a subsequent purchaser within the meaning of the statute mentioned.

    (C) Leon, because he recorded before Allred.

    (D) Leon, because he advanced money without notice of Allred's rights.

15. Assume for this question only that Niece had not conveyed to Barrett. After Allred recorded his deed from Owen, Allred, asserting that Allred's title was held free of any claim by Niece, instituted suit against Niece to recover title to Farmdale. Judgment should be for:

    (A) Niece, because she had no notice of Allred's rights when she accepted the deed from Owen.

    (B) Niece, because she recorded her deed before Allred recorded his.

    (C) Allred, because Niece was not a bona fide purchaser who paid value.

    (D) Allred, because he had paid value for Farmdale and had no actual or constructive notice of the deed to Niece.

Questions 16-17 are based on the following fact situation:

Ogden was the fee simple owner of three adjoining vacant lots fronting on a common street in a primarily residential section of a city which had no zoning laws. The lots were identified as Lots 1, 2, and 3. Ogden conveyed Lot 1 to Akers and Lot 2 to Bell. Ogden retained Lot 3, which consisted of three acres of woodland. Bell, whose lot was between the other two, built a house on his lot. Bell's house included a large window on the side facing Lot 3. The window provided a beautiful view from Bell's living room, thereby adding value to Bell's house.

Akers erected a house on his lot. Ogden made no complaint to either Akers or Bell concerning the houses they built. After both Akers and Bell had completed their houses, the two of them agreed to and did build a common driveway running from the street to the rear of their respective lots. The driveway was built on the line between the two houses so that one-half of the way was located on each lot. Akers and Bell exchanged right-of-way deeds by which each of them conveyed to the other, his heirs and assigns, an easement to continue the right of way. Both deeds were properly recorded.

After Akers and Bell had lived in their respective houses for 30 years, a new public street was built bordering on the rear of Lots 1, 2, and 3. Akers informed Bell that, since the new street removed the need for their common driveway, he considered the right-of-way terminated; therefore, he intended to discontinue its use and expected Bell to do the same. At about the same time, Ogden began the erection of a six-story apartment house on Lot 3. If the apartment house is completed, it will block the view from Bell's window and will substantially reduce the value of Bell's lot.

16. In an action brought by Bell to enjoin Akers from interfering with Bell's continued use of the common driveway between the two lots, the decision should be for:

    (A) Akers, because the termination of the necessity for the easement terminated the easement.

    (B) Akers, because the continuation of the easement after the change of circumstances would adversely affect the marketability of both lots without adding any commensurate value to either.

(C) Bell, because an incorporeal hereditament lies in grant and cannot be terminated without a writing.

(D) Bell, because the removal of the need for the easement created by express grant does not affect the right to the easement.

17. In an action brought by Bell to enjoin Ogden from erecting the apartment building in such a way as to obstruct the view from Bell's living room window, the decision should be for:

(A) Bell, because Ogden's proposed building would be an obstruction of Bell's natural right to an easement for light and air.

(B) Bell, because Bell was misled by Ogden's failure to complain when Bell was building his house.

(C) Ogden if, but only if, it can be shown that Ogden's intention to erect such a building was made known to Bell at or prior to the time of Ogden's conveyance to Bell.

(D) Ogden, because Bell has no easement for light, air, or view.

Question 18

Morgan conveyed Greenacre, her one-family residence, to "Perez for life, remainder to Rowan, her heirs and assigns, subject, however, to First Bank's mortgage thereon." There was an unpaid balance on the mortgage of $10,000, which is payable in $1,000 annual installments plus interest at 6% on the unpaid balance, with the next payment due on July 1. Perez is now occupying Greenacre. The reasonable rental value of the property exceeds the sum necessary to meet all current charges. There is no applicable statute.

Under the rules governing contributions between life tenants and remaindermen, how should the burden for payment be allocated?

(A) Rowan must pay the principal payment, but Perez must pay the interest to First Bank.

(B) Rowan must pay both the principal and interest payments to First Bank.

(C) Perez must pay both the principal and interest payments to First Bank.

(D) Perez must pay the principal payment, but Rowan must pay the interest to First Bank.

Question 19

Anders conveyed her only parcel of land to Burton by a duly executed and delivered warranty deed, which provided:

> To have and to hold the described tract of land in fee simple, subject to the understanding that within one year from the date of the instrument said grantee shall construct and thereafter maintain and operate on said premises a public health center.

The grantee, Burton, constructed a public health center on the tract within the time specified and operated it for five years. At the end of this period, Burton converted the structure into a senior citizens' recreational facility. It is considered by all parties in interest that a senior citizens' recreational facility is not a public health center.

In an appropriate action, Anders seeks a declaration that the change in the use of the facility has caused the land and structure to revert to her. In this action, Anders should:

(A) Win, because the language of the deed created a determinable fee, which leaves a possibility of reverter in the grantor.

(B) Win, because the language of the deed created a fee subject to condition subsequent, which leaves a right of entry or power of termination in the grantor.

(C) Lose, because the language of the deed created only a contractual obligation and did not provide for retention of property interest by the grantor.

(D) Lose, because an equitable charge is enforceable only in equity.

Question 20

Homer conveyed his home to his wife, Wanda, for life, remainder to his daughter, Dixie. There was a $20,000 mortgage on the home, requiring monthly payment covering interest to date plus a portion of the principal.

Which of the following statements about the monthly payment is correct?

(A) Wanda must pay the full monthly payment.

(B) Wanda must pay a portion of the monthly payment based on an apportionment of the value between Wanda's life estate and Dixie's remainder.

(C) Wanda must pay the portion of the monthly payment that represents interest.

(D) Dixie must pay the full monthly payment.

Questions 21-22 are based on the following fact situation:

The owner of Newacre executed and delivered to a power company a right-of-way deed for the building and maintenance of an overhead power line across Newacre. The deed was properly recorded. Newacre then passed through several intermediate conveyances until it was conveyed to Sloan about 10 years after the date of the right-of-way deed. All the intermediate deeds were properly recorded, but none of them mentioned the right-of-way.

Sloan entered into a written contract to sell Newacre to Jones. By the terms of the contract, Sloan promised to furnish an abstract of title to Jones. Sloan contracted directly with Abstract Company to prepare and deliver an abstract to Jones, and Abstract Company did so. The abstract omitted the right-of-way deed. Jones delivered the abstract to his attorney and asked the attorney for an opinion as to title. The attorney signed and delivered to Jones a letter stating that, from the attorney's examination of the abstract, it was his "opinion that Sloan had a free and unencumbered marketable title to Newacre."

Sloan conveyed Newacre to Jones by a deed which included covenants of general warranty and against encumbrances. Jones paid the full purchase price. After Jones had been in possession of Newacre for more than a year, he learned about the right-of-way deed. Sloan, Jones, Abstract Company, and Jones's attorney were all without actual knowledge of the existence of the right-of-way prior to the conveyance from Sloan to Jones.

21. If Jones sues Abstract Company for damages caused to Jones by the presence of the right-of-way, the most likely result will be a decision for:

    (A) Jones, because Jones was a third-party creditor beneficiary of the contract between Sloan and Abstract Company.

    (B) Jones, because the abstract prepared by Abstract Company constitutes a guarantee of Jones's title to Newacre.

    (C) Abstract Company, because Abstract Company had no knowledge of the existence of the right-of-way.

    (D) Abstract Company, because there was no showing that any fraud was practiced upon Jones.

22. If Jones sues Sloan because of the presence of the right-of-way, the most likely result will be a decision for:

    (A) Jones, because Sloan is liable for his negligent misrepresentation.

    (B) Jones, because the covenants in Sloan's deed to Jones have been breached.

(C) Sloan, because Jones relied upon Abstract Company, not Sloan, for information concerning title.

(D) Sloan, because Sloan was without knowledge of any defects in the title to Newacre.

Question 23

Testator devised his farm "to my son, Selden, for life, then to Selden's children and their heirs and assigns." Selden, a widower, had two unmarried adult children.

In an appropriate action to construe the will, the court will determine that the remainder to the children is:

(A) Indefeasibly vested.

(B) Contingent.

(C) Vested subject to partial defeasance.

(D) Vested subject to complete defeasance.

Questions 24-25 are based on the following fact situation:

Ohner holds title in fee simple to a tract of 1,500 acres. He desires to develop the entire tract as a golf course, country club, and residential subdivision. He contemplates forming a corporation to own and to operate the golf course and country club; the stock in the corporation will be distributed to the owners of lots in the residential portions of the subdivision, but no obligation to issue the stock is to ripen until all the residential lots are sold. The price of the lots is intended to return enough money to compensate Ohner for the raw land, development costs (including the building of the golf course and the country club facilities), and developer's profit, if all of the lots are sold.

Ohner's market analyses indicate that he must create a scheme of development that will offer prospective purchasers (and their lawyers) a very high order of assurance that several aspects will be clearly established:

1. Aside from the country club and golf course, there will be no land use other than for residential use and occupancy in the 1,500 acres.

2. The residents of the subdivision will have unambiguous right of access to the club and golf course facilities.

3. Each lot owner must have an unambiguous right to transfer his lot to a purchaser with all original benefits.

4. Each lot owner must be obligated to pay annual dues to a pro rata share (based on the number of lots) of the club's annual operating deficit (whether or not such owner desires to make use of club and course facilities).

24. In the context of all aspects of the scheme, which of the following will offer the best chance of implementing the requirement that each lot owner pay annual dues to support the club and golf course?

(A) Covenant.

(B) Easement.

(C) Mortgage.

(D) Personal contractual obligation by each purchaser.

25. Of the following, the greatest difficulty that will be encountered in establishing the scheme is that:

(A) Any judicial recognition will be construed as state action which, under current doctrines, raises a substantial question whether such action would be in conflict with the Fourteenth Amendment.

(B) The scheme, if effective, renders title unmarketable.

(C) One or more of the essential aspects outlined by Ohner will result in a restraint on alienation.

(D) There is a judicial reluctance to recognize an affirmative burden to pay money in installments and over an indefinite period as a burden that can be affixed to bind future owners of land.

Question 26

Oaks, the owner of Blackacre, conveyed a right-of-way to United Utility "for the underground transportation of gas by pipeline, the location of right-of-way to be mutually agreed upon by Oaks and United Utility." United Utility then installed a six-inch pipeline at a location selected by it and not objected to by Oaks. Two years later, United Utility advised Oaks of its intention to install an additional six-inch pipeline parallel to and three feet laterally from the original pipeline. In an appropriate action, Oaks sought a declaration that United Utility has no right to install the second pipeline.

If Oaks prevails, it will be because:

(A) Any right implied to expand the original use of the right-of-way creates an interest that violates the Rule Against Perpetuities.

(B) The original installation by United Utility defined the scope of the easement.

(C) Oaks did not expressly agree to the location of the right-of-way.

(D) The assertion of the right to install an additional pipeline constitutes inverse condemnation.

Question 27

Martinez, a widower, owns in fee simple a ranch, Ranchacre. Martinez has one child, Enrique, who is married. Enrique has one child, Ana Maria, who is also married but has no children. In an effort to dispose of Ranchacre to his descendants and to honor a request by Ana Maria that she be skipped in any such disposition, Martinez conveys Ranchacre to his son, Enrique, for life with the remainder to Ana Maria's children in fee simple.

What interest, if any, is created in favor of Ana Maria's unborn children at the time of the conveyance?

(A) A contingent remainder.

(B) A vested remainder subject to divestment.

(C) A springing use.

(D) None.

Question 28

While hospitalized, Marsh requested her attorney to draw a deed conveying her home to her son, Simon. While Marsh remained in the hospital, the deed was drawn, properly executed, and promptly and properly recorded. On being informed of the existence of the deed, Simon told his mother, "I want no part of the property; take the deed right back." Marsh recovered and left the hospital, but shortly thereafter, before any other relevant event, Simon died intestate.

Marsh brought an appropriate action against Simon's heirs to determine title.

If Marsh wins, it will be because:

(A) The court will impose a constructive trust to carry out the intent of the deceased son.

(B) The presumption of delivery arising from the recording is not valid unless the grantee has knowledge at the time of the recording.

(C) Simon's declaration was a constructive reconveyance of the land.

(D) There was no effective acceptance of delivery of the deed.

Question 29

Andres conveyed Applewood Farm "to Bogatz, her heirs and assigns, so long as the premises are used for residential and farm purposes, then to Cohen and his heirs." The common law Rule Against Perpetuities, unmodified by statute, is part of the law of the jurisdiction in which Applewood Farm is located.

As a consequence of the conveyance, Cohen's interest in Applewood Farm is:

(A) Nothing.

(B) A valid executory interest.

(C) A possibility of reverter.

(D) A right of entry for condition broken.

Question 30

Metterly, the owner in fee simple of Brownacre, by quitclaim deed conveyed Brownacre to her daughter, Doris, who paid no consideration for the conveyance. The deed was never recorded. About a year after the delivery of the deed, Metterly decided that this gift had been ill-advised. She requested that Doris destroy the deed, which Doris dutifully and voluntarily did. Within the month following the destruction of the deed, Metterly and Doris were killed in a common disaster. Each of the successors in interest claimed title to Brownacre.

In an appropriate action to determine the title to Brownacre, the probable outcome will be that:

(A) Metterly was the owner of Brownacre, because Doris was a donee and therefore could not acquire title by quitclaim deed.

(B) Metterly was the owner of Brownacre, because title to Brownacre reverted to her upon the voluntary destruction of the deed by Doris.

(C) Doris was the owner of Brownacre, because her destruction of the deed to Brownacre was under the undue influence of Metterly.

(D) Doris was the owner of Brownacre, because the deed was merely evidence of her title, and its destruction was insufficient to cause title to pass back to Metterly.

Question 31

By her validly executed will, Sallie devised a certain tract of land to her son, Ben, for his life with remainder to such of Ben's children as should be living at his death, "Provided, however, that no such child of Ben shall mortgage or sell, or attempt to mortgage or sell, his or her interest in the property prior to attaining 25 years of age; and, if any such child of Ben shall violate this provision, then upon such violation his or her interest shall pass to and become the property of the remaining children of Ben then living, share and share alike."

Sallie's will included an identical provision for each of her four other children concerning four other tracts of land. The residuary clause of the will gave the residuary estate to Sallie's five children equally. Sallie died and was survived by the five children named in her will and by 11 grandchildren. Several additional grandchildren have since been born.

In an action for a declaration of rights, it was claimed that the attempted gifts to Sallie's grandchildren were entirely void and that the interests following the life estates to Sallie's children passed to the children absolutely by the residuary clause.

Assuming that the action was properly brought with all necessary parties and with a guardian ad litem appointed to represent the interests of unborn and infant grandchildren, the decision should be that:

(A) The attempted gifts to grandchildren are void under the Rule Against Perpetuities.

(B) The attempted gifts to grandchildren are void as unlawful restraints on alienation.

(C) The provisions concerning grandchildren are valid and will be upheld according to their terms.

(D) Even if the provisions against sale or mortgage by the grandchildren are void, the remainders to grandchildren are otherwise valid and will be given effect.

Questions 32-33 are based on the following fact situation:

Meadowview is a large tract of undeveloped land. Black, the owner of Meadowview, prepared a development plan creating 200 house lots in Meadowview with the necessary streets and public areas. The plan was fully approved by all necessary governmental agencies and duly recorded. However, construction of the streets, utilities, and other aspects of the development of Meadowview has not yet begun, and none of the streets can be opened as public ways until they are completed in accordance with the applicable ordinances of the municipality in which Meadowview is located.

College Avenue, one of the streets laid out as part of the Meadowview development, abuts Whiteacre, an adjacent one-acre parcel owned by White. Whiteacre has no access to any public way except an old, poorly developed road which is inconvenient and cannot be used without great expense. White sold Whiteacre to Breyer. The description used in the deed from White to Breyer was the same as that used in prior deeds except that the portion of the description which formerly said, "thence by land of Black, northeasterly a distance of 200 feet, more or less," was changed to "thence by College Avenue as laid out on the Plan of Meadowview North 16° East 201.6 feet," with full reference to the plan and as recording data.

Breyer now seeks a building permit which will show that Breyer intends to use College Avenue for access to Whiteacre. Black objects to the granting of a building permit on the grounds that he has never granted any rights to White or Breyer to use College Avenue. There are no governing statutes or ordinances relating to the problem. Black brings an appropriate action in which the right of Breyer to use College Avenue without an express grant from Black is at issue.

32. The best argument for Black in this action is that:

(A) Breyer's right must await the action of appropriate public authorities to open College Avenue as a public street, since no private easements arose by implication.

(B) The Statute of Frauds prevents the introduction of evidence which might prove the necessity for Breyer to use College Avenue.

(C) Breyer's right to use College Avenue is restricted to the assertion of a way by necessity and the facts preclude the success of such a claim.

(D) Breyer would be unjustly enriched if he were permitted to use College Avenue.

33. The best argument for Breyer in this action is that:

(A) There is a way by necessity over Meadowview's lands to gain access to a public road.

(B) The deed from White to Breyer referred to the recorded plan and therefore created rights to use the streets delineated on the plan.

(C) Sale of lots in Meadowview by reference to its plan creates private easements in the streets shown on the plan.

(D) The recording of the plan is a dedication of the streets shown on the plan to public use.

Question 34

Lester, the owner in fee simple of a small farm consisting of 30 acres of land improved with a house and several outbuildings, leased the same to Tanner for a 10-year period. After two years had expired, the government condemned 20 acres of the property and allocated the compensation award to Lester and Tanner according to their respective interest so taken. It so happened, however, that the 20 acres taken embraced all of the farm's tillable land, leaving only the house, outbuildings, and a small woodlot. There is no applicable statute in the jurisdiction where the property is located nor any provision in the lease relating to condemnation. Tanner quit possession and Lester brought suit against him to recover rent.

Lester will:

(A) Lose, because there has been a frustration of purpose which excuses Tanner from further performance of his contract to pay rent.

(B) Lose, because there has been a breach of the implied covenant of quiet enjoyment by Lester's inability to provide Tanner with possession of the whole of the property for the entire term.

(C) Win, because of the implied warranty on the part of the tenant to return the demised premises in the same condition at the end of the term as they were at the beginning.

(D) Win, because the relationship of landlord and tenant was unaffected by the condemnation, thus leaving Tanner still obligated to pay rent.

Question 35

Allen and Barker are equal tenants in common of a strip of land 10 feet wide and 100 feet deep which lies between the lots on which their respective homes are situated. Both Allen and Barker need the use of the 10-foot strip as a driveway, and each fears that a new neighbor might seek partition and leave him with an unusable five-foot strip.

The best measure to solve their problem is:

(A) A covenant against partition.

(B) An indenture granting cross-easements in the undivided half interest of each.

(C) A partition into two separate five-foot-wide strips and an indenture granting cross-easements.

(D) A trust to hold the strip in perpetuity.

Question 36

Santos agreed to sell and Perrine agreed to buy a described lot on which a single-family residence had been built. Under the contract, Santos agreed to convey marketable title subject only to conditions, covenants, and restrictions of record and all applicable zoning laws and ordinances. The lot was subject to a 10-foot side line setback originally set forth in the developer's duly recorded subdivision plot. The applicable zoning ordinance zones the property for single-family units and requires an 8.5-foot side line setback.

Prior to closing, a survey of the property was made. It revealed that a portion of Santos's house was 8.4 feet from the side line.

Perrine refused to consummate the transaction on the ground that Santos's title is not marketable. In an appropriate action, Santos seeks specific performance.

Who will prevail in such an action?

(A) Santos, because any suit against Perrine concerning the setback would be frivolous.

(B) Santos, because the setback violation falls within the doctrine of *de minimis non curat lex*.

(C) Perrine, because any variation, however small, amounts to a breach of contract.

(D) Perrine, because the fact that Perrine may be exposed to litigation is sufficient to make the title unmarketable.

REAL PROPERTY ANSWERS

Answer to Question 1

(B) Every land sale contract (not deed) contains an implied warranty of marketable title. For bar examination purposes, title acquired by adverse possession is unmarketable. However, the buyer's acceptance of a deed discharges the seller's contractual obligation to furnish marketable title, and leaves the buyer with remedies only on the covenants in the deed. (D) is wrong because a deed contains no implied covenant of marketability. (A) is wrong because it is not supported by the facts, and (C) is an incorrect statement of law; a buyer can choose to rescind, sue for damages for breach, get specific performance with abatement of the purchase price, or, in some jurisdictions, require the seller to quiet title.

Answer to Question 2

(C) Acceptance of a deed discharges the seller's liability on the contract. Since the deed here contained no covenants of title, it was a quitclaim deed. Conveyances under a quitclaim deed give the buyer only that which the seller owns. If Sue did not own the one acre she believed that she had acquired by adverse possession, then her quitclaim deed conveyed only the four remaining acres to Peg. Thus, Peg cannot prevail and (B) and (D) are wrong. (A) is not supported by the facts.

Answer to Question 3

(D) Once a land sale contract is signed, the doctrine of equitable conversion applies, making the buyer the equitable owner of the property. Under the majority view, the risk of loss then rests on the buyer; Peg must pay the purchase price. Thus, (D) is correct and the other choices are incorrect. Note that if Sue had insured the house for loss by fire, most courts would require her to give Peg credit, in the amount of the insurance proceeds, against the purchase price.

Answer to Question 4

(C) Painter's acceptance of the deed constituted a discharge of Owens's liability on the contract. A quitclaim deed contains no warranties and conveys only what the seller owns—here, property encumbered by an easement. Therefore, (C) is correct and (D) is inapplicable since there was no breach. (A) and (B) are not valid defenses, since existence of the easement was violative of the contract. The contract contained an implied warranty of marketable title, which generally means an unencumbered fee simple with good record title. An easement is an encumbrance. Note that if Owens had conveyed a general warranty deed to Painter, it would have contained a covenant against encumbrances.

Answer to Question 5

(A) Anti-transfer covenants are strictly construed; therefore, a prohibition against subleasing does not prevent assignment, and (C) is thus incorrect. (D) is wrong because an anti-assignment covenant must be express. Regarding (B), disabling restraints on a legal interest are always void. However, lease provisions restricting assignments and subleases are valid restraints. These are considered promissory restraints, breach of which will void an attempted assignment or transfer. Thus, (B) is wrong.

Answer to Question 6

(A) Oleg expressly conveyed a fee simple to Bob and Bill as joint tenants with the right of survivorship. Since the joint tenancy was not severed, Bill became the owner in fee simple at the instant of Bob's death. Bob's will was not effective until his death, at which time he no longer had an interest in the property; the act of making a will containing a testamentary devise of the land is not sufficient to sever the joint tenancy. Hence, Bob's attempt to devise his interest was inoperative, and (B) and (C) are thus incorrect. (D) is wrong because conveyance by quitclaim deed does not render title unmarketable.

Answer to Question 7

(B) If Oscar had a scheme for an exclusively residential subdivision, the court could ***imply*** a reciprocal negative servitude limiting the remaining lots to the same use. Reciprocal negative servitudes are implied only when the sales begin. Since all 140 lots already sold contain the covenant restricting the land use to single-family residential dwellings, a common scheme will be implied. Any subsequent purchaser will be bound by the covenant if there was notice. The appearance of an area containing only single-family residences is sufficient to constitute inquiry notice. Hence, (A) is wrong. (C) is incorrect because covenants are a private land use control. (D) is wrong because the issue does not concern construction of the deeds.

Answer to Question 8

(D) If Oscar had no uniform development scheme, there is no basis for implying a residential restriction in Doyle's deed. (A) is not the best defense because selling difficulties probably do not establish changes such as would render enforcement of the covenants inequitable. (B) is wrong because restraints upon use (as opposed to restraints upon alienation) of land are valid and enforceable. (C) is wrong because monetary loss is irrelevant in an action to establish an implied equitable servitude.

Answer to Question 9

(B) Pike had a fee simple subject to a shifting executory interest in Farley. If Farley lives 30 more years, the fee simple will shift to him. Therefore, (B) is correct and (D) is wrong. The Rule Against Perpetuities requires that the interest vest, if at all, within 21 years after a life in being and, using Farley's life as the measuring life, it is clear that his interest will vest, if at all, within his lifetime. (A) is wrong because a reversion occurs by operation of law when a grantor conveys less than the entire estate. Here, Odum transferred a fee simple in Brightacre to either Pike or Farley; there was no interest left to revert to Odum. (C) is wrong because an executory interest is not vested.

Answer to Question 10

(A) The class of Trease's grandchildren would close at the death of his last surviving child, who was necessarily a life in being at Trease's death (when the gift took effect); the gift would then vest (or fail) within 21 years thereafter. (C) is wrong because the express language of the will controls. The rule of convenience is used to determine when a class closes only absent an express intent to include all persons described no matter when born. Since Trease expressed such an intention, the rule is inapplicable and (B) is incorrect. (D) is wrong because the gift is valid without resort to preferential rules of construction.

Answer to Question 11

(C) If Trease had made the gift by inter vivos conveyance, he might have had another child thereafter who would not have been a life in being at the creation of the interest (and whose children might have reached 21 after the permissible perpetuities period). (A) is wrong because the Rule Against Perpetuities allows for periods of gestation. (B) is wrong because it changes nothing; the will already expresses an intention to include afterborn grandchildren. Further, (B) and (D) are wrong because all of Trease's grandchildren would be born to his children, who were lives in being at his death.

Answer to Question 12

(B) Priorities based on time of recording would protect most persons obtaining an interest in land that is timely recorded. Since the purpose of recordation is to give notice to others of a conveyance of title, prospective purchasers could easily determine the status of the title. Furthermore, priorities based on recording generally protect bona fide purchasers. (D) is wrong because simply protecting bona fide purchasers would not assure an accurate reflection of priority of title on the public record (*e.g.*, "notice" statutes). (A) and (C) alone have no bearing on priority of title. Moreover, they are misstatements of law; witnesses to a deed are generally unnecessary and no recital of consideration is required for a valid deed.

Answer to Question 13

(A) A subsequent grantee has constructive knowledge of all prior recorded deeds except those outside of his chain of title. (B) and (D) are wrong because Niece's recordation would be relevant only if she had been a bona fide purchaser who could "shelter" Barrett. Under the shelter rule, a person who takes from a bona fide purchaser will prevail against any interest that the bona fide purchaser would have prevailed against—even if the grantee knew of the prior unrecorded interest. However, donees are not bona fide purchasers and, thus, are not protected. (C) is wrong because the state statute governs priority of title.

Answer to Question 14

(D) Leon will prevail because he had no actual or constructive notice of the conveyance to Allred, since it was not recorded at the time of the mortgage. A mortgagee who gives a concurrent loan is considered a purchaser for value within state recording acts. Hence, (A) and (B) are incorrect. (C) is wrong because the statute is a pure notice statute, which does not require that the subsequent purchaser be the first to record to protect his rights against a ***prior*** purchaser.

Answer to Question 15

(C) Judgment should be for Allred. Under the statute, unrecorded conveyances are void only as against bona fide purchasers. Since Niece took by a gratuitous conveyance, her prior recordation without notice is irrelevant. Thus, (A) and (B) are incorrect because Niece is not protected by the recording statute. (D) is incorrect because, absent a bona fide purchaser, priority is determined by the first-in-time rule.

Answer to Question 16

(D) Because the easement was validly created and recorded, the removal of the need for the easement does not affect the continuing right to the easement. (A) is wrong because there is no such automatic termination. If the parties had failed validly to create the easement in this case, a court might still have found an easement by necessity. If that had been the case, the end of the necessity would result in the expiration of the easement. But that was not the case here. Because an easement was created and recorded, the fact that the easement is no longer necessary has no bearing on its continued existence. The easement could be terminated by release or abandonment, but Bell does not wish to terminate the easement. (B) is wrong because an easement is a right that exists even if it adversely affects the marketability of land. (C) is wrong because easements can be terminated in ways other than by a writing. For example, Bell could abandon his easement by long nonuse accompanied by intent to abandon.

Answer to Question 17

(D) Bell has no claim because he had no easement for light, air, or view. (A) is wrong because there is no "natural right" to an easement for light and air. (B) is wrong because Bell's building of his house has no relationship to whether an easement for light and air was created. (C) is wrong because even if Ogden had no plans, at the time of his conveyance to Bell, to erect such a building, no easement for light and air would automatically be created. Bell could have requested and could have been granted an easement for light, air, or view, but there is no evidence that he did so.

Answer to Question 18

(A) A life tenant is obligated to pay interest on any encumbrances to the extent of the income or profits from the land. He does not, however, have to pay anything on the principal. The remainderman, here Rowan, must pay off the principal in order to protect her own interests. (B) is wrong because Rowan is only liable for the principal. (C) is wrong because Perez is only liable for the interest payments. (D) is wrong because it reverses the duties of the life tenant and the remainderman.

Answer to Question 19

(C) Anders could have constructed a deed such that she would have retained a property interest in the parcel of land, but she did not do so. Rather, she only created a contractual obligation which was met in the first five years after the conveyance. Because she retained no property interest, she has no claim to the land. (A) is wrong because this could have been a determinable fee only if durational language, such as "for as long as," "while," "during," or "until," had been used in the deed. Because it was not, no possibility of reverter was created in Anders. (B) is wrong because the grantor did not reserve the right to terminate the grantee's estate on the happening of a specified condition subsequent, and thus reserved no right of entry for condition broken. (D) is wrong because it has been stated that Anders has instituted an appropriate action, so it is assumed that she is in the proper court. In any event, the contract or covenant obligation of Burton would probably be enforceable both at law (for damages) and in equity (for an injunction). In most jurisdictions today the same court could order either remedy.

Answer to Question 20

(C) The application of a basic allocation rule is involved here. A life tenant is obligated to pay interest on any encumbrances on the land to the extent of the income or profits from the land (or in their absence to the extent of the reasonable rental value of the land). However, she does not have to pay anything on the principal of the debt: reversioners or remaindermen must pay the principal in order to protect their interests. Thus, (C) is correct because it applies the rule correctly. (A) is incorrect because Dixie must make the portion of the monthly payment allocated to principal. (B) is wrong because the allocation between life tenant and remainderman is a simple allocation between interest and principal and hence the actual value of the life estate and the remainder are not considered. (D) is wrong because Wanda must make the portion of the monthly payment allocated to interest.

Answer to Question 21

(A) Jones was the intended third-party creditor beneficiary of the contract between Sloan and the Abstract Company to prepare and deliver the abstract. Abstract Company is liable because it failed to uncover the existence of the right-of-way deed which was in the chain of title. Jones should recover because he was the intended beneficiary. (B) is wrong because Abstract Company is liable on breach of its contract to describe accurately the state of the record title. It gave no title guarantee. (C) is wrong because, while Abstract Company may have had no actual knowledge of the deed, it had a contractual duty to find any encumbrances in the record chain of title. (D) is wrong because fraud is not necessary for a showing of breach of contract.

Answer to Question 22

(B) Sloan conveyed a deed including covenants of general warranty and against encumbrances. Because an encumbrance exists in the form of the right-of-way, Sloan is in breach of the covenant against encumbrances. (A) is wrong because Sloan was diligent in his attempt to establish clear title through the Abstract Company. (C) is wrong because it was Sloan and not the Abstract Company which actually made the covenant against encumbrances. (D) is wrong because Sloan covenanted that there were no encumbrances at all. It makes no difference whether he had any actual knowledge of such encumbrances.

Answer to Question 23

(C) Because the remainder is created in a class of persons (*i.e.*, Selden's children) that is certain to take on the termination of the preceding estate, but is subject to diminution by reason of other persons becoming entitled to share in the remainder (*i.e.*, additional children that Selden could sire), the remainder is vested subject to partial defeasance (or divestment). This is also sometimes called a vested remainder subject to open. (A) is wrong because an indefeasibly vested remainder must not be subject to being diminished in size, which could be the case if Selden has more children. (B) is incorrect because the remainder here is not subject to a condition precedent or in favor of unborn or unascertained persons. Hence, it is not contingent. (D) is wrong because a vested remainder subject to complete defeasance arises when the remainderman is in existence and ascertained and his right to possession and enjoyment is subject to being defeated by the happening of some condition subsequent. Under the facts, Selden's children or their heirs under all circumstances will be entitled to a portion of the fee.

Answer to Question 24

(A) A covenant is the best choice because a real covenant, normally found in deeds, is a written promise to do something on the land or a promise not to do something on the land. Real covenants run with the land at law, which means that subsequent owners of the land may enforce or be burdened by the covenant. In cases where the covenant involves a promise to pay money, the majority rule is that if the money is to be used in a way connected with the land, the burden will run with the land. The most common example is a covenant to pay a homeowners' association an annual fee for maintenance of common ways, parks, etc., in a subdivision. Such a situation is analogous to the golf course and country club dues presented in the facts. (B) is incorrect because the holder of an easement has the right to use a tract of land (called the servient tenement) for a special purpose but has no right to possess and use the land. The annual dues requirement does not constitute the right to use another's land for a special purpose. (C) is incorrect because a mortgage is a security interest in real estate (usually to secure a promise to repay a loan represented by a promissory note). The payment of dues does not result in a security interest in the golf course, and is thus inapplicable to the facts. (D) is wrong because a personal contractual obligation by each purchaser does not bind subsequent purchasers, who would, therefore, be under no obligation to pay the annual dues.

Answer to Question 25

(D) (D) is the correct answer by a process of elimination. (A) is incorrect because there is no racial discrimination or other constitutionally questionable activity presented in the facts. (B) is wrong because marketable title is title reasonably free from doubt. Generally, this involves either defects in the chain of title or encumbrances that might present an unreasonable risk of litigation. The dues scheme is not such an encumbrance. (C) is incorrect because the scheme does not impose a direct restraint on alienation of the fee. There are no disabling restraints, forfeiture restraints, or promissory restraints on transferability of property. Thus, by a process of elimination, (D) presents the greatest obstacle to establishing the scheme, even though a majority of courts today allow real covenants that require payment of an annual fee for maintenance of common ways, parks, etc.

Answer to Question 26

(B) If Oaks prevails, it will be because the original installation defined the scope of the easement. The scope of the easement depends on the intent of the parties. In determining the intent of the parties, the courts look at the subsequent conduct of the parties respecting the arrangement as well as the language of the instrument. Here, the instrument states the location is to be mutually agreed upon. Oaks and United agreed to the original pipeline and its location, but have not agreed upon the location of the second set of pipes. The parties' subsequent conduct could also lead to the conclusion that the first installation was the full extent of what the parties intended. (A) is incorrect because the Rule Against Perpetuities has absolutely no application to these facts. The easement was vested when it was created, and easements are presumed to be perpetual. (C) is incorrect because Oaks will be deemed to have acquiesced in the location of the original easement. (D) is wrong because inverse condemnation is the term for a landowner's lawsuit for damages to recover for a governmental taking without exercising its formal power of eminent domain (*e.g.,* regulatory takings that deprive the owner of all economically viable uses of the property). Even if United were a government agency and this were a regulatory taking, inverse condemnation would not be correct since Oaks is seeking an injunction, not compensation.

Answer to Question 27

(A) A remainder is a future interest created in a transferee that is capable of becoming a present interest upon the natural termination of the preceding estates created in the same disposition. A contingent remainder is a remainder that is subject to a condition precedent, or a remainder that is created in favor of unborn or unascertained persons. Here, Ana Maria's unborn children will take a remainder, because their interest will become a present interest upon the natural termination of the preceding estate (upon Enrique's death). Because this remainder is created in favor of unborn and unascertained persons, it is contingent. A vested remainder subject to divestment arises when the remainderman is in existence and ascertained and his interest is not subject to any condition precedent, but his right to possession is subject to being defeated by some condition subsequent. (B) is incorrect because the remaindermen are neither in existence nor ascertained. A springing use is a form of executory interest (a future interest in a transferee that is not capable of taking on the natural termination of the preceding estate). (C) is incorrect because Ana Maria's children's interest will become a present interest upon the natural termination of the preceding estate. Finally, because (A) is correct, (D) is obviously incorrect.

Answer to Question 28

(D) If Marsh wins, it will be because there was no effective acceptance of delivery of the deed. There must be acceptance by the grantee to complete a conveyance. Although acceptance is presumed, this presumption is rebutted by evidence of rejection. Here, Simon expressly rejected the conveyance, and therefore, title never passed to Simon. (A) is incorrect because a constructive trust presumes that Simon had legal title. As discussed above, title did not pass to Simon. Furthermore, even had title passed, a constructive trust would probably be inappropriate here. Constructive trust is the appropriate remedy for unjust enrichment, and there is no indication of any wrongdoing under these facts. (B) is an incorrect statement of law. If the grantor intends the recording of the deed to be the final act in vesting title in the grantee, such recording creates a presumption of delivery even though the grantee did not know of the recordation. (C) is wrong because there is no such thing as a constructive reconveyance. Had Simon accepted the deed and then changed his mind, he would have had to execute a new deed to reconvey the property back to Marsh.

Answer to Question 29

(A) Cohen's interest purports to be an executory limitation. However, Cohen cannot take the land until such time as the premises are no longer used for residential and farm purposes. This could happen more than 21 years after the death of Bogatz or Cohen, the relevant lives in being. Thus, this interest violates the Rule Against Perpetuities. It follows that (B), (C), and (D) are incorrect. Note also that, regarding (C) and (D), possibilities of reverter and rights of entry for condition broken are future interests left in a ***grantor***. Cohen is not a grantor.

Answer to Question 30

(D) The deed, once it has been delivered, is merely evidence of its own existence, and its destruction does not cause any change in the title. Doris therefore continued to own the property. (A) is wrong because a title can be acquired by a quitclaim deed and that is true, even though the grantee has paid no consideration. (B) is wrong because destruction of the deed does not cause title to revert. (C) is wrong because there is no evidence of undue influence, and, in any event, destruction of the deed would cause no change in the status of the title.

Answer to Question 31

(D) The question is somewhat confusing, since there are really two gifts to grandchildren. The first is the vested remainder in the grandchildren that follows Ben's life estate. The second is the executory interest that is given to the other grandchildren if one of the grandchildren purports to mortgage or sell in violation of the condition. This latter gift is void both as a violation of the Rule Against Perpetuities and as an unlawful restraint on alienation. It violates the Rule because by its terms it could purport to vest possession in the "other" grandchildren more than 21 years after the termination of a life in being. However, these objections apply only to the second of the two gifts to the grandchildren. The first gift, that is, the remainder to them, is entirely valid. The language dealing with the restraint on alienation would probably be stricken by the court, leaving the initial gift intact. (D) is the answer that best expresses this result.

Answer to Question 32

(A) The best argument is that Breyer's rights depend on the existence of a public street. (B) is wrong because no issue of the Statute of Frauds is present. There has been no purported conveyance to Breyer of rights in the street by anyone who owns such rights. (C) is wrong because, if a public street exists, Breyer need not assert a way of necessity. (D) is wrong because there is no legal objection to the enrichment that results if persons other than the dedicator are permitted to use a public street.

Answer to Question 33

(D) The dedication argument is Breyer's strongest, although even it is not likely to be successful unless and until the city bodies accept the dedication. (A) is wrong because Breyer does not need a way of necessity, since he has other access to his land. (B) is wrong because the deed from White to Breyer, while referring to the plan, used it only as a boundary reference and did not create any rights to the use of the streets. (C) is wrong because, while the sale of lots by reference to a plan does create private easements in the streets, the easements serve only the lots in the subdivision plan itself and not such land as Whiteacre that is outside the plan.

Answer to Question 34

(D) In a partial condemnation case, the landlord-tenant relationship continues, as does the tenant's obligation to pay the entire rent for the remaining lease term. (A) is wrong because the law of landlord and tenant traditionally refuses to recognize frustration of purpose as a ground for termination of a lease. (B) is wrong because the covenant of quiet enjoyment can be breached only by actions of the landlord and not those of a third party, such as the government. (C) is wrong because, while the tenant generally is obligated to return the premises in the same condition as when received (except for ordinary wear and tear), that obligation would not be considered breached by the actions of a third party such as the government.

Answer to Question 35

(C) Partition and cross-easements is the best approach because the holder of an easement has the right to use a tract of land (called the servient tenement) for a special purpose, but has no right to possess and enjoy the tract of land. Typically, easements are created to give their holder the right of access over a tract of land. An easement is deemed appurtenant when the right of special use benefits the holder in his physical use or enjoyment of another tract of land. For an easement appurtenant to exist, there must be ***two tracts*** of land. The dominant tenement has the benefit of the easement, and the servient tenement is subject to the easement right. One consequence of appurtenance is that the benefit passes with transfers of the benefited land, regardless of whether the easement is mentioned in the conveyance. Partition is necessary to create the required two tracts of land. (A) is incorrect because a covenant not to partition is personal to the parties and thus subsequent owners will not be bound by the covenant. It is also wrong because under the principles of the Rule Against Restraints on Alienation, the courts will enforce prohibitions against partition by any one co-tenant only if the restriction is to last for a reasonable time. (B) is wrong because, as noted above, easements appurtenant require two tracts of land. As long as the strip remains undivided, a new neighbor, as a tenant-in-common, would have the right to partition the strip and thus terminate the cross-easement. (D) is incorrect because a trust in perpetuity would violate the Rule Against Restraints on Alienation. The effect of the trust would be to create a disabling restraint.

Answer to Question 36

(D) Generally, an existing violation of a zoning ordinance renders title unmarketable. Here, the location of the house in relation to the side line setback exposes Perrine to the threat of litigation, both for violation of the zoning ordinance and for violation of a restriction in the recorded subdivision plot. Regardless of the likelihood that such litigation may be initiated, and of the likelihood that Perrine would ultimately prevail, he cannot be required to "buy a lawsuit." Thus, (D) is the correct answer. It follows that (A) and (B) are incorrect. (C) is incorrect because it fails to address the issue of unmarketability of title through exposure to potential litigation, which forms the basis for Perrine's refusal to consummate the transaction.

TORTS QUESTIONS

Questions 1-2 are based on the following fact situation:

Innes worked as a secretary in an office in a building occupied partly by her employer and partly by Glass, a retail store. The two areas were separated by walls and were in no way connected, except that the air conditioning unit served both areas and there was a common return-air duct.

Glass began remodeling, and its employees did the work, which included affixing a plastic surfacing material to counters. To fasten the plastic to the counters, the employees purchased glue, with the brand name Stick, that was manufactured by Steel, packaged in a sealed container by Steel, and retailed by Paint Company.

In the course of the remodeling job, one of Glass's employees turned on the air conditioning and caused fumes from the glue to travel from Glass through the air conditioning unit and into Innes's office. The employees did not know that there was common ductwork for the air conditioners. Innes was permanently blinded by the fumes from the glue.

The label on the container of glue read, "DANGER. Do not smoke near this product. Extremely flammable. Contains Butanone, Toluol, and Hexane. Use with adequate ventilation. Keep out of the reach of children."

The three chemicals listed on the label are very toxic and harmful to human eyes. Steel had received no reports of eye injuries during the 10 years that the product had been manufactured and sold.

1. If Innes asserts a claim against Paint Company, the most likely result is that she will:

   (A) Recover if she can recover against Steel.

   (B) Recover, because Innes was an invitee of a tenant in the building.

   (C) Not recover, unless Paint Company was negligent.

   (D) Not recover, because the glue came in a sealed package.

2. If Innes asserts a claim against Glass, the most likely result is that she will:

   (A) Recover, because a user of a product is held to the same standard as the manufacturer.

   (B) Recover, because the employees of Glass caused the fumes to enter her area of the building.

   (C) Not recover, because Glass used the glue for its intended purpose.

   (D) Not recover, because the employees of Glass had no reason to know that the fumes could injure Innes.

Questions 3-4 are based on the following fact situation:

When Denton heard that his neighbor, Prout, intended to sell his home to a minority purchaser, Denton told Prout that Prout and his wife and children would meet with "accidents" if he did so. Prout then called the prospective purchaser and told him that he was taking the house off the market.

3. If Prout asserts a claim against Denton for assault, Prout will:

   (A) Recover if Denton intended to place Prout in fear of physical harm.

   (B) Recover, because Denton's conduct was extreme and outrageous.

   (C) Not recover if Denton took no action that threatened immediate physical harm to Prout.

   (D) Not recover, because Prout's action removed any threat of harmful force.

4. If Prout asserts a claim against Denton for intentional infliction of emotional distress, Prout will:

   (A) Recover if Prout suffered severe emotional distress as a consequence of Denton's conduct.

   (B) Recover, because Denton intended to frighten Prout.

   (C) Not recover, because Denton made no threat of immediate physical harm to Prout or his family.

   (D) Not recover if Prout suffered no physical harm as a consequence of Denton's conduct.

Question 5

Doctor, a licensed physician, resided in her own home. The street in front of the home had a gradual slope. Doctor's garage was on the street level, with a driveway entrance from the street.

At two in the morning, Doctor received an emergency call. She dressed and went to the garage to get her car and found a car parked in front of her driveway. That car was occupied by Parker, who, while intoxicated, had driven to that place and now was in a drunken stupor in the front seat. Unable to rouse Parker, Doctor pushed him into the passenger's side of the front seat and got in on the driver's side. Doctor released the brake and coasted the car down the street, planning to pull into a parking space that was open. When Doctor attempted to stop the car, the brakes failed to work, and the car crashed into the wall of Owner's home, damaging Owner's home and Parker's car and injuring Doctor and Parker. Subsequent examination of the car disclosed that the brake linings were badly worn. A state statute prohibits the operation of a motor vehicle unless the brakes are capable of stopping the vehicle within specified distances at specified speeds. The brakes on Parker's car were incapable of stopping the vehicle within the limits required by the statute. Another state statute makes it a criminal offense to be intoxicated while driving a motor vehicle. The state follows traditional contributory negligence rules.

If Parker asserts a claim against Doctor for his injuries, Parker will probably:

(A) Recover, because Doctor was negligent as a matter of law.

(B) Recover, because Doctor had no right to move the car.

(C) Not recover, because his brakes were defective.

(D) Not recover, because he was in a drunken stupor when injured.

Question 6

Construction Company contracted to build a laundry for Wash Company on the latter's vacant lot in a residential area. As a part of its work, Construction Company dug a trench from the partially completed laundry to the edge of a public sidewalk; waterlines were to be installed in the trench. Because of the contour of the land, the trench was dug to a depth ranging from seven to nine feet. Construction Company did not place any barriers around the trench and permitted it to lie open for almost a week while waiting for the delivery of water pipes. This was known to Wash Company, but it raised no objection.

During the time the trench was open, a series of heavy rains fell, causing five feet of surface water to gather in the bottom of the trench. While this condition existed, five-year-old Tommy, who was playing on the vacant lot with friends, stumbled and fell into the trench. Robert, an adult passerby, saw this and immediately lowered himself into the trench to rescue Tommy. However, his doing so caused the rain-soaked walls of the trench to collapse, killing both him and Tommy.

In a claim for wrongful death by Tommy's administrator against Construction Company, the most likely result is that plaintiff will:

(A) Recover, because the defendant left the open trench unprotected.

(B) Recover, because construction companies are strictly liable for inherently dangerous conditions.

(C) Not recover, because Tommy was a trespasser.

(D) Not recover, because Tommy's death was a result of the collapse of the trench, an independent intervening cause.

Question 7

Philip was a 10-year-old boy. Macco was a company that sold new and used machinery. Macco stored discarded machinery, pending sale for scrap, on a large vacant area it owned. This area was unfenced and was one-quarter mile from the housing development where Philip lived. Macco knew that children frequently played in this area and on the machinery. Philip's parents had directed him not to play on the machinery because it was dangerous.

One day Philip was playing on a press in Macco's storage area. The press had several wheels, each geared to the other. Philip climbed on the largest wheel, which was about five feet in diameter. Philip's weight caused the wheel to rotate, his foot was caught between two wheels that were set into motion, and he was severely injured.

A claim for relief was asserted by Philip through a duly appointed guardian. Macco denied liability and pleaded Philip's contributory fault as a defense.

In determining whether Macco breached a duty to Philip, which of the following is the most significant?

(A) Whether the press on which Philip was injured was visible from a public way.

(B) Whether the maintenance of the area for the storage of discarded machinery was a private nuisance.

(C) Whether the maintenance of the area of the storage of discarded machinery was a public nuisance.

(D) Whether Macco could have eliminated the risk of harm without unduly interfering with Macco's normal operations.

Question 8

Householder hired Contractor to remodel Householder's kitchen. She had learned of him through a classified advertisement he placed in the local newspaper. During the telephone conversation in which she hired him, he stated he was experienced and qualified to do all necessary work. Because of his low charge for his work, they agreed in writing that on acceptance of his job by Householder, he would have no further liability to her or to anyone else for any defects in materials or workmanship, and that she would bear all such costs.

Householder purchased a dishwasher manufactured by Elex Company from Dealer, who was in the retail electrical appliance business. The washer was sold by Dealer with only the manufacturer's warranty and with no warranty by Dealer; Elex Company restricted its warranty to 90 days on parts and labor. Contractor installed the dishwasher.

Two months after Householder accepted the entire job, she was conversing in her home with Accountant, an acquaintance who had agreed to prepare her income tax return gratuitously. As they talked, they noticed that the dishwasher was operating strangely, repeatedly stopping and starting. At Householder's request, Accountant gave it a cursory examination and, while inspecting it, received a violent electrical shock which did him extensive harm. The dishwasher had an internal wiring defect that allowed electrical current to be carried into the framework and caused the machine to malfunction. The machine had not been adequately grounded by Contractor during installation; if it had been, the current would have been led harmlessly away. The machine carried instructions for correct grounding, which Contractor had not followed.

If Accountant asserts a claim based on strict liability against Elex Company for damages, the probable result is that Accountant will:

(A) Recover, because the dishwasher was defectively made.

(B) Recover, because Elex Company is vicariously liable for the improper installation.

(C) Not recover, because he assumed the risk by inspecting the machine.

(D) Not recover, because he was not the purchaser.

Question 9

Diner, a drive-in hamburger and ice cream stand, recently opened for business in the suburban town of Little City. Diner's business hours are from 9 a.m. to midnight. It is in an area that for 15 years has been zoned for small retail businesses, apartment buildings, and one- and two-family residences. The zoning code specifies that "small retail businesses" include "businesses where food and drink are dispensed for consumption on the premises." Diner was the first drive-in in Little City. For seven years Mr. and Mrs. Householder have owned and lived in their single-family residence, which is across the street from Diner.

On opening day a brass band played in the parking lot of Diner until midnight, and the noise of cars and the usual activity as a result of the new business prevented the Householders from getting to sleep until well after midnight, long after their usual time. Diner is heavily patronized during the day and night by high school students. The noise of cars, the lights of the cars, the lights illuminating the parking lot at Diner, and the noise from the loudspeaker of the ordering system prevented the Householders from sleeping before midnight. Paper cups, napkins, and other items from the drive-in are regularly blown into the Householders's front yard by the prevailing wind. The traffic to and from Diner is so heavy on the street in front of their house that the Householders are afraid to allow their small children to play in the front yard.

The Householders have asserted a claim against Diner based on private nuisance.

The most likely effect of the fact that the Householders were in the area before Diner is that it:

(A) Requires that the Householders' interest be given priority.

(B) Is irrelevant because of the zoning ordinance.

(C) Is irrelevant because conforming economic uses are given priority.

(D) Is some, but not controlling, evidence.

Questions 10-11 are based on the following fact situation:

In City of State Y, Maple Street is a local public thoroughfare, designated as a one-way street for northbound traffic. Pine Street is a public thoroughfare, designated as a one-way street for eastbound traffic. Maple and Pine Streets intersect at right angles. The intersection is controlled by traffic lights. There are two sets of lights, one at the northeast corner and one at the northwest corner, for traffic on Maple Street. There are two sets of lights, one at the northeast corner and one at the southeast corner, for traffic on Pine Street.

Trucker was making a delivery to a market on the east side of Maple Street, just north of its intersection with Pine Street. There being insufficient space for his truck and enclosed trailer, he parked it with the rear of the trailer extending entirely across the crosswalk on the north side of the intersection. The height of the trailer was such that it entirely obscured the traffic light on the northeast corner from the view of traffic moving east on Pine Street. Unknown to Trucker, the traffic light at the southeast corner was not functioning, because a collision 72 hours earlier had knocked down the pole from which the light was suspended.

Visitor, on his first trip to City, was driving east on Pine Street. Not seeing any traffic light or pole, he entered the intersection at a time when the light was red for eastbound traffic and green for northbound traffic. Driver, proceeding north on Maple Street and seeing the green light, entered the intersection without looking for any cross traffic and struck Visitor's car. Driver received personal injuries, and Visitor's car was damaged severely as a result of the impact.

Statutes of State Y make it a misdemeanor (1) to park a motor vehicle so that any part projects into a crosswalk and (2) to enter an intersection contrary to a traffic signal.

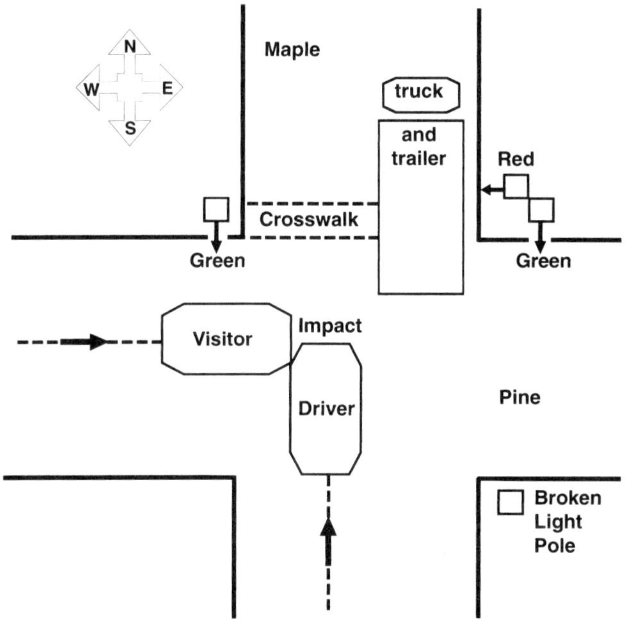

10. If Driver asserts a claim against Trucker and establishes that Trucker was negligent, the likely result is that Trucker's negligence is:

    (A) A legal but not an actual cause of Driver's injuries.

    (B) An actual but not a legal cause of Driver's injuries.

    (C) Both an actual and a legal cause of Driver's injuries.

    (D) Neither an actual nor a legal cause of Driver's injuries.

11. If Driver asserts a claim against City, the theory on which he has the best chance of prevailing is that City:

    (A) Is strictly liable for harm caused by a defective traffic signal.

    (B) Was negligent in not replacing the broken pole within 72 hours.

    (C) Had an absolute duty to maintain installed signals in good operating order.

    (D) Created a dangerous trap by not promptly replacing the broken pole.

Question 12

Henry hated Wanda, his former wife, for divorcing him and marrying John a short time thereafter. About a month after Wanda married John, Henry secretly entered Wanda and John's rented apartment during their absence by using a master key. Henry placed a microphone behind the bookstand in the bedroom of the apartment and drilled a hole in the nearby wall, with the result that the microphone appeared to be connected with wires going into the adjoining apartment. Actually, the microphone was not connected to anything. Henry anticipated that Wanda would discover the microphone in a few days and would be upset by the thought that someone had been listening to her conversations with John in their bedroom.

Shortly thereafter, as he was putting a book on the stand, John noticed the wires behind the bookstand and discovered the hidden microphone. He then called Wanda and showed her the microphone and wires. Wanda fainted and, in falling, struck her head on the bookstand and suffered a mild concussion. The next day John telephoned Henry and accused him of planting the microphone. Henry laughingly admitted it. Because of his concern about Wanda and his anger at Henry, John is emotionally upset and unable to go to work.

If Wanda asserts a claim against Henry based on infliction of mental distress, the fact that John was the person who showed her the microphone will:

(A) Relieve Henry of liability, because John was careless in so doing.

(B) Relieve Henry of liability, because John's conduct was the immediate cause of Wanda's harm.

(C) Not relieve Henry of liability, because Henry's goal was achieved.

(D) Not relieve Henry of liability, because the conduct of a third person is irrelevant in emotional distress cases.

Questions 13-14 are based on the following fact situation:

Peter was rowing a boat on a mountain lake when a storm suddenly arose. Fearful that the boat might sink, Peter rowed to a boat dock on shore and tied the boat to the dock. The shore property and dock were the private property of Owner.

While the boat was tied at the dock, Owner came down and ordered Peter to remove the boat because the action of the waves was causing the boat to rub against a bumper on the dock. When Peter refused, Owner untied the boat and cast it adrift. The boat sank.

Peter was wearing a pair of swimming trunks and nothing else. He had a pair of shoes and a parka in the boat, but they were lost when Owner set it adrift. Peter was staying at a cabin one mile from Owner's property. The only land routes back were a short rocky trail that was dangerous during the storm, and a 15-mile road around the lake. The storm continued with heavy rain and hail, and Peter, having informed Owner of the location of his cabin, asked Owner to take him back there in Owner's car. Owner said, "You got here by yourself and you'll have to get back home yourself." After one hour the storm stopped, and Peter walked home over the trail.

13. A necessary element in determining if Peter is liable for a trespass is whether:

(A) Owner had clearly posted his property with a sign indicating that it was private property.

(B) Peter knew that the property belonged to a private person.

(C) Peter had reasonable grounds to believe the property belonged to a private person.

(D) Peter had reasonable grounds to believe his boat might be swamped and might sink.

14. If Peter asserts a claim against Owner for loss of the boat, the most likely result is that Owner will:

(A) Have no defense under the circumstances.

(B) Prevail, because Peter was a trespasser ab initio.

(C) Prevail, because the boat might have damaged the dock.

(D) Prevail, because Peter became a trespasser when he refused to remove the boat.

Questions 15-16 are based on the following fact situation:

Dave is a six-year-old boy who has a well-deserved reputation for bullying younger and smaller children. His parents have encouraged him to be aggressive and tough. Dave, for no reason, knocked down, kicked, and severely injured Pete, a four-year-old. A claim has been asserted by Pete's parents for their medical and hospital costs and for Pete's injuries.

15. If the claim is asserted against Dave's parents, the most likely result is they will be:

(A) Liable, because parents are strictly liable for the torts of their children.

(B) Liable, because Dave's parents encouraged him to be aggressive and tough.

(C) Not liable, because a child under seven is not liable in tort.

(D) Not liable, because parents cannot be held liable for the tort of a child.

16. If the claim is asserted against Dave, the most likely result is Dave will be:

(A) Liable, because he intentionally harmed Pete.

(B) Liable, because, as a six-year-old, he should have known his conduct was wrongful.

(C) Not liable, because a child under seven is not liable in tort.

(D) Not liable, because he is presumed to be under his parents' control and they have the sole responsibility.

Questions 17-18 are based on the following fact situation:

Mrs. Ritter, a widow, recently purchased a new uncrated electric range for her kitchen from Local Retailer. The range has a wide oven with a large oven door. The crate in which Stove Company, the manufacturer, shipped the range carried a warning label that the stove would tip over with a weight of 25 pounds or more on the oven door. Mrs. Ritter has one child—Brenda, age three. Recently, at about 5:30 p.m., Brenda was playing on the floor of the kitchen while Mrs. Ritter was heating water in a pan on the stove. The telephone rang and Mrs. Ritter went into the living room to answer it. While she was gone Brenda decided to find out what was cooking. She opened the oven door and climbed on it to see what was in the pan. Brenda's weight (25 pounds) on the door caused the stove to tip over forward. Brenda fell to the floor and the hot water spilled over her, burning her severely. Brenda screamed. Mrs. Ritter ran to the kitchen and immediately gave her first aid treatment for burns. Brenda thereafter received medical treatment.

Brenda's burns were painful. They have now healed and do not bother her, but she has ugly scars on her legs and back. Brenda's claim is asserted on her behalf by the proper party.

17. If Brenda asserts a claim based on strict liability against Local Retailer, she must establish that:

(A) Local Retailer did not inform Mrs. Ritter of the warning on the crate.

(B) The stove was substantially in the same condition at the time it tipped over as when it was purchased from Local Retailer.

(C) Local Retailer made some change in the stove design or had improperly assembled it so that it tipped over more easily.

(D) Local Retailer knew or should have known that the stove was dangerous because of the ease with which it tipped over.

18. If Brenda asserts a claim based on strict liability against Stove Company, she must establish that:

(A) The defendant negligently designed the stove.

(B) Stoves made by other manufacturers do not turn over with a 25-pound weight on the oven door.

(C) The defendant failed to warn the Ritters that the stove would turn over easily.

(D) The stove was defective and unreasonably dangerous to her.

Question 19

Paulsen was eating in a restaurant when he began to choke on a piece of food that had lodged in his throat. Dow, a physician who was sitting at a nearby table, did not wish to become involved and did not render any assistance, although prompt medical attention would have been effective in removing the obstruction from Paulsen's throat. Because of the failure to obtain prompt medical attention, Paulsen suffered severe brain injury from lack of oxygen.

If Paulsen asserts a claim against Dow for his injuries, will Paulsen prevail?

(A) Yes, if the jurisdiction relieves physicians of malpractice liability for emergency first aid.

(B) Yes, if a reasonably prudent person with Dow's experience, training, and knowledge would have assisted Paulsen.

(C) No, because Dow was not responsible for Paulsen's condition.

(D) No, unless Dow knew that Paulsen was substantially certain to sustain serious injury.

Questions 20-21 are based on the following fact situation:

Parents purchased a new mobile home from Seller. The mobile home was manufactured by Mobilco and had a ventilating system designed by Mobilco with both a heating unit and an air conditioner. Mobilco installed a furnace manufactured by Heatco and an air conditioning unit manufactured by Coolco. Each was controlled by an independent thermostat installed by Mobilco. Because of the manner in which Mobilco designed the ventilating system, the first time the ventilating system was operated by Parents, cold air was vented into Parents' bedroom to keep the temperature at 68° F (20° C). The cold air then activated the heater thermostat, and hot air was pumped into the bedroom of Child, the six-month-old child of Parents. The temperature in Child's room reached more than 170° F (77° C) before Child's mother became aware of the condition and shut the system off manually. As a result, Child suffered permanent physical injury.

Claims have been asserted by Child, through a duly appointed guardian, against Mobilco, Seller, Heatco, and Coolco.

20. If Child's claim against Seller is based on negligence, the minimum proof necessary to establish Seller's liability is that the ventilating system:

(A) Was defective.

(B) Was defective and had not been inspected by Seller.

(C) Was defective and had been inspected by Seller, and the defect was not discovered.

(D) Was defective, and the defect would have been discovered if Seller had exercised reasonable care in inspecting the system.

21. If Child's claims against Mobilco, Heatco, and Coolco are based on strict liability in tort, Child will probably recover against:

(A) Mobilco only, because the ventilating system was defectively designed by Mobilco.

(B) Heatco only, because it was the excessive heat from the furnace that caused Child's injuries.

(C) Mobilco and Heatco only, because the combination of Mobilco's design and Heatco's furnace caused Child's injuries.

(D) Mobilco, Heatco, and Coolco, because the combination of Mobilco's design, Heatco's furnace, and Coolco's air conditioning unit caused Child's injuries.

Question 22

Hank owned a secondhand goods store. He often placed merchandise on the sidewalk, sometimes for short intervals, sometimes from 7 a.m. until 6 p.m. Pedestrians from time to time stopped and gathered to look at the merchandise. Fred had moved into an apartment that was situated immediately above Hank's store; a street-level stairway entrance was located about 20 feet to the east. On several occasions, Fred had complained to Hank about the situation because not only were his view and peace of mind affected, but also his travel on the sidewalk was made more difficult. Fred owned and managed a restaurant two blocks to the west of his apartment and made frequent trips back and forth. There was a back entrance to his apartment through a parking lot; this entrance was about 200 feet farther in walking distance from his restaurant. Once Fred complained to the police, whereupon Hank was arrested under a local ordinance which prohibited the placing of goods or merchandise on public sidewalks and imposed, as its sole sanction, a fine for its violation.

One day, the sidewalk in front of Hank's store was unusually cluttered because he was cleaning and mopping the floor of his shop. Fred and his 15-year-old son, Steve, saw a bus they wished to take, and they raced down the stairs and onto the cluttered sidewalk in front of Hank's store, Fred in the lead. While dodging merchandise and people, Fred fell. Steve tripped over him and suffered a broken arm. Fred also suffered broken bones and was unable to attend to his duties for six weeks.

If, prior to the day of his personal injuries, Fred had asserted a claim based on public nuisance for injunctive relief against Hank for his obstruction of the sidewalk in violation of the ordinance, the defense on which Hank would have most likely prevailed is that:

(A) Fred consented to the obstruction by continuing to rent his apartment.

(B) The violation of the ordinance was not unreasonable.

(C) Remedy of abatement by self-help was adequate.

(D) There was no claim for special damage.

Question 23

The city of Metropolis has an ordinance that makes it an offense, punishable by fine, for the owner of a dog to permit the dog to run unleashed on a public way.

Smythe, a police officer, observed a small dog running loose in the street. As Smythe picked the dog up, Nelson, who was seated in her car lawfully parked at the curb, called out, "Oh, thank you, Officer, for returning Fido." Smythe asked Nelson whether the dog was hers, and when she acknowledged ownership, he asked to see her driver's license. Nelson gave her name and address, but she refused to produce a driver's license. Smythe then told her to produce her driver's license if she did not want to go to jail. Nelson responded by saying, "Isn't this ridiculous?" Smythe took her by the arm and said, "Let's go. You are under arrest."

Nelson cried out that Smythe was hurting her but he refused to release her arm, and she struck him with her free hand. Smythe then dragged Nelson from her car, forced her into his squad car, and took her to the police station.

The incident took place on the street in front of the apartment where Nelson and her aged father, Joplin, lived. Smythe did not know that Joplin had observed what took place from a window in the apartment.

If Nelson's father, Joplin, asserts a claim against Smythe for the intentional infliction of emotional distress, will Joplin prevail?

(A) Yes, if Smythe's acts caused Joplin severe emotional distress.

(B) Yes, if it is found that Smythe's behavior was extreme and outrageous with respect to Nelson.

(C) No, because Smythe did not know that Joplin was watching.

(D) No, because Joplin was not within the zone of physical danger.

Questions 24-25 are based on the following fact situation:

Gasco owns a storage facility where flammable gases are stored in liquefied form under high pressure in large spherical tanks. The facility was constructed for Gasco by Acme Company, a firm that specializes in the construction of such facilities. After the facility had been in use for five years, an explosion in the facility started a large fire that blanketed the surrounding countryside with a high concentration of oily smoke and soot.

Farber owns a large truck farm near the facility. His entire lettuce crop was destroyed by oily deposits left by the smoke.

24. If Farber asserts a claim against Gasco for the loss of his lettuce crop and is unable to show any negligence on the part of Gasco, will Farber prevail?

    (A) Yes, because the operation of the storage facility was an abnormally dangerous activity.

    (B) Yes, because the intrusion of the smoke onto Farber's farm amounted to a trespass.

    (C) No, if the explosion was caused by internal corrosion that reasonable inspection procedures would not have disclosed.

    (D) No, if the explosion was caused by negligent construction on Acme's part.

25. If Farber asserts a claim against Acme Company for the loss of his lettuce crop, will Farber prevail?

    (A) No, if Acme did not design the storage facility.

    (B) No, because Acme was an independent contractor.

    (C) Yes, because the operation of the storage facility was an abnormally dangerous activity.

    (D) Yes, if the explosion resulted from a defect of which Acme was aware.

Question 26

Siddon worked as a private duty nurse and on occasion worked in Doctors' Hospital. The hospital called Registry, the private duty referral agency through which Siddon usually obtained employment, and asked that in the future she not be assigned to patients in Doctors' Hospital. Registry asked the hospital why it had made the request. Doctors' Hospital sent a letter to Registry giving as the reason for its request that significant amounts of narcotics had disappeared during Siddon's shifts from the nursing stations at which she had worked.

If Siddon asserts a claim based on defamation against Doctors' Hospital, Siddon will:

(A) Recover, because the hospital accused Siddon of improper professional conduct.

(B) Recover if Siddon did not take the narcotics.

(C) Not recover if narcotics disappeared during Siddon's shifts.

(D) Not recover if the hospital reasonably believed that Siddon took the narcotics.

Question 27

When Mary Weld visited Dugan's Alleys to participate in the weekly bowling league competition held there she brought her two-year-old son, Bobby, along and left him in a nursery provided by Dugan for the convenience of his customers. The children in the nursery were normally supervised by three attendants, but at this particular time, as Mary Weld knew, there was only one attendant present to care for about 20 children of assorted ages.

About 30 minutes later, while the attendant was looking the other way, Bobby suddenly started to cry. The attendant found him lying on his back, picked him up, and called his mother. It was later discovered that Bobby had suffered a skull fracture.

If a claim is asserted against Dugan on Bobby's behalf, will Bobby prevail?

(A) Yes, because Dugan owed the child the highest degree of care.

(B) Yes, because a two-year-old is incapable of contributory negligence.

(C) No, unless Dugan or his employees failed to exercise reasonable care to assure Bobby's safety.

(D) No, if Mary Weld assumed the risk by leaving Bobby in the nursery.

Question 28

Dever drove his car into an intersection and collided with a fire engine that had entered the intersection from Dever's right. The accident was caused by negligence on Dever's part. As a result of the accident, the fire engine was delayed in reaching Peters's house, which was entirely consumed by fire. Peters's house was located about 10 blocks from the scene of the accident.

If Peters asserts a claim against Dever, Peters will recover:

(A) That part of his loss that would have been prevented if the collision had not occurred.

(B) The value of his house before the fire.

(C) Nothing if Dever had nothing to do with causing the fire.

(D) Nothing, because Dever's conduct did not create an apparent danger to Peters.

Question 29

Purvis purchased a used car from Daley, a used-car dealer. Knowing them to be false, Daley made the following statements to Purvis prior to the sale:

Statement 1. This car has never been involved in an accident.

Statement 2. This car gets 25 miles to the gallon on the open highway.

Statement 3. This is as smooth-riding a car as you can get.

If Purvis asserts a claim against Daley based on deceit, which of the false statements made by Daley would support Purvis's claim?

(A) Statement 1. only.

(B) Statement 2. only.

(C) Statements 1. and 2. only.

(D) Statements 2. and 3. only.

Question 30

Customer, age 20, went into Store at approximately 6:45 p.m. to look at some suits that were on sale. The clerks were busy, and one of them told him that he should wait on himself. Customer selected three suits from a rack and went into the dressing room to try them on. Signs posted on the walls of the Store state that closing time is 9 p.m.; however, because of a special awards banquet for employees, Store was closed at 7 p.m. on this day. The employees, in a hurry to get to the banquet, did not check the dressing rooms or turn off the lights before leaving. When Customer emerged from the dressing room a few minutes after 7 p.m., he was alone and locked in. Customer tried the front door but it was secured on the outside by a bar and padlock, so he went to the rear door. Customer grabbed the doorknob and vigorously shook the door. It did not open, but the activity set off a mechanism that had been installed because of several recent thefts committed by persons who had hidden in the store until after closing time. The mechanism sprayed a chemical mist in Customer's face, causing him to become temporarily blind. The mechanism also activated an alarm carried by Store's employee, Watchman, who was just coming to work. Watchman unlocked the front door, ran into the store, and grabbed Customer. Customer, who was still unable to see, struck out at this person and hit a metal rack, injuring his hand. Watchman then identified himself, and Customer did the same. After assuring himself that Customer was telling the truth, Watchman allowed him to leave.

If Customer is to prevail on a claim against Store based on battery from the use of the chemical spray, Customer must establish that:

(A) He suffered severe bodily harm.

(B) The spray mist was an offensive or harmful contact.

(C) He suffered severe emotional distress.

(D) His conduct was not a factual cause of the chemical's spraying him.

Question 31

Dock had been the unsuccessful suitor of Mary, who had recently announced her engagement to Paul. Angered by her engagement, Dock sent Mary the following letter: "I hope you know what you are doing. The man you think you love wears women's clothes when at home. A Friend."

The receipt of this letter caused Mary great emotional distress. She hysterically telephoned Paul, read him the letter, and told him that she was breaking their engagement. The contents of the letter were not revealed to others. Paul, who was a young attorney in the state attorney's office, suffered serious humiliation and emotional distress as a result of the broken engagement.

If Paul asserts a claim against Dock based on defamation and it is proved that Dock's statement was true, such proof will be:

(A) A defense by itself.

(B) A defense only if Dock was not actuated by malice.

(C) A defense only if Dock reasonably believed it to be true.

(D) No defense by itself.

Question 32

Auto Company, a corporation, was a small dealer in big new cars and operated a service department. Peter wanted to ask Mike, the service manager, whether Auto Company would check the muffler on his small foreign car. Peter parked on the street near the service department with the intention of entering that part of the building by walking through one of the three large entrances designed for use by automobiles. There was no street entrance to the service department for individuals, and customers as well as company employees often used one of the automobile entrances.

As Peter reached the building, he glanced behind him to be sure no vehicle was approaching that entrance. Seeing none, he walked through the entrance, but immediately he was struck on the back of the head and neck by the large overhead door which was descending. The blow knocked Peter unconscious and caused permanent damage.

Peter did not know how the door was raised and lowered; however, the overhead door was operated by the use of either of two switches in the building. One switch was located in the office of the service manager and the other was located near the door in the service work area for the convenience of the mechanics. On this occasion, no one was in the service work area except three Auto Company mechanics. Mike, who had been in his office, and the three mechanics denied having touched a switch that would have lowered the door. Subsequent investigation showed, however, that the switches were working properly and that all of the mechanisms for moving the door were in good working order.

If Peter asserts a claim based on negligence against Auto Company, Peter probably will:

(A) Recover, because Auto Company is strictly liable under the circumstances.

(B) Recover, because an employee of Auto Company was negligent.

(C) Not recover, because Peter was a licensee.

(D) Not recover, because Peter assumed the risk.

Questions 33-34 are based on the following fact situation:

Si was in the act of siphoning gasoline from Neighbor's car, in Neighbor's garage and without his consent, when the gasoline exploded and a fire followed. Rescuer, seeing the fire, grabbed a fire extinguisher from his car and put out the fire, saving Si's life and Neighbor's car and garage. In doing so, Rescuer was badly burned.

33. If Rescuer asserts a claim against Si for personal injuries, Rescuer will:

    (A) Prevail, because he saved Si's life.

    (B) Prevail, because Si was at fault in causing the fire.

    (C) Not prevail, because Rescuer knowingly assumed the risk.

    (D) Not prevail, because Rescuer's action was not a foreseeable consequence of Si's conduct.

34. If Rescuer asserts a claim against Neighbor for personal injuries, Rescuer will:

    (A) Prevail, because he saved Neighbor's property.

    (B) Prevail, because he acted reasonably in an emergency.

    (C) Not prevail, because Neighbor was not at fault.

    (D) Not prevail, because Rescuer knowingly assumed the risk.

Question 35

Telco, a local telephone company, negligently allowed one of its telephone poles, located between a street and a sidewalk, to become termite-ridden. Rhodes, who was intoxicated and driving at an excessive rate of speed, lost control of her car and hit the weakened telephone pole. One week later, the pole fell and struck Walker, a pedestrian who was walking on the sidewalk. The pole fell because of the combination of the force of the impact and the pole's termite-ridden condition.

If Walker asserts a claim against Telco and Rhodes, will Walker prevail?

(A) Yes, against Telco but not Rhodes.

(B) Yes, against Rhodes but not Telco.

(C) Yes, against Telco and Rhodes, each for one-half of his damages.

(D) Yes, against both Telco and Rhodes for the full amount of his damages.

Question 36

While on a hiking trip during the late fall, Page arrived toward the end of the day at a clearing where several similar cabins were located, none of which was occupied. One of the cabins belonged to Levin, Page's friend, who had given Page permission to use it. Page entered one of the cabins, which she thought was Levin's, and prepared to spend the night. In fact the cabin was owned, not by Levin, but by Dwyer.

When the night turned cold, Page started a fire in the stove. Unknown to Page, there was a defect in the stove that allowed carbon monoxide fumes to escape into the cabin. During the night the fumes caused serious injury to Page.

If Page asserts a claim against Dwyer for her injury, will Page recover?

(A) Yes, if Dwyer knew that the stove was defective.

(B) Yes, if Dwyer could have discovered the defect in the stove by a reasonable inspection.

(C) No, because Dwyer had no reason to anticipate Page's presence in the cabin.

(D) No, unless Page needed to use the cabin for her own protection.

Question 37

A group of children, ranging in age from 8 to 15, regularly played football on the common area of an apartment complex owned by O'Neill. Most of the children lived in the apartment complex, but some lived elsewhere. O'Neill knew that the children played on the common area and had not objected.

Peter, a 13-year-old who did not live in the apartment complex, fell over a sprinkler head while running for a pass and broke his leg. Although Peter had played football on the common area before, he had never noticed the sprinkler heads, which protruded one inch above the ground and were part of a permanently installed underground sprinkler system.

If a claim is asserted on Peter's behalf, Peter will:

(A) Prevail, if the sprinkler head was a hazard that Peter probably would not discover.

(B) Prevail, because O'Neill had not objected to children playing on the common area.

(C) Not prevail, because Peter did not live in the apartment complex.

(D) Not prevail, unless the sprinkler heads were abnormally dangerous to users of the common area.

Question 38

Chemco designed and built a large tank on its premises for the purpose of storing highly toxic gas. The tank developed a sudden leak and escaping toxic gas drifted into the adjacent premises, where Nyman lived. Nyman inhaled the gas and died as a result.

In a suit brought by Nyman's personal representative against Chemco, which of the following must be established if the claim is to prevail?

I. The toxic gas that escaped from Chemco's premises was the cause of Nyman's death.

II. The tank was built in a defective manner.

III. Chemco was negligent in designing the tank.

(A) I. only.

(B) I. and II. only.

(C) I. and III. only.

(D) I., II., and III.

Question 39

Plummer, a well-known politician, was scheduled to address a large crowd at a political dinner. Just as Plummer was about to sit down at the head table, Devon pushed Plummer's chair to one side. As a result, Plummer fell to the floor. Plummer was embarrassed at being made to look foolish before a large audience but suffered no physical harm.

If Plummer asserts a claim against Devon for damages because of his embarrassment, will Plummer prevail?

(A) Yes, if Devon knew that Plummer was about to sit on the chair.

(B) Yes, if Devon negligently failed to notice that Plummer was about to sit on the chair.

(C) No, because Plummer suffered no physical harm along with his embarrassment.

(D) No, if in moving the chair Devon intended only a good-natured practical joke on Plummer.

Question 40

In 1956, Silo Cement Company constructed a plant for manufacturing ready-mix concrete in Lakeville. At that time Silo was using bagged cement, which caused little or no dust. In 1970, Petrone bought a home approximately 1,800 feet from the Silo plant. One year ago, Silo stopped using bagged cement and began to receive cement in bulk shipments. Since then at least five truckloads of cement have passed Petrone's house daily. Cement blows off the trucks and into Petrone's house. When the cement arrives at the Silo plant, it is blown by forced air from the trucks into the storage bin. As a consequence, cement dust fills the air surrounding the plant to a distance of 2,000 feet. Petrone's house is the only residence within 2,000 feet of the plant.

If Petrone asserts a claim against Silo based on nuisance, will Petrone prevail?

(A) Yes, unless using bagged cement would substantially increase Silo's costs.

(B) Yes, if the cement dust interfered unreasonably with the use and enjoyment of Petrone's property.

(C) No, because Silo is not required to change its industrial methods to accommodate the needs of one individual.

(D) No, if Silo's methods are in conformity with those in general use in the industry.

TORTS ANSWERS

Answer to Question 1

(A) Because Steel had no notice that the product would cause eye injuries, an action against Steel must be predicated on strict liability, not negligence. The strict duty in such cases extends to any supplier in the distributive chain. Thus, if Steel, the manufacturer of the glue, is liable, then Paint Company, the retailer, may also be subject to liability. Conversely, if there is a determination that Steel did not manufacture an unreasonably dangerous product, then there will be no basis for holding the retailer liable. (B) is incorrect. It addresses Innes's status as a foreseeable victim of the fumes. However, it fails to address the basic issue of liability. Innes could be a foreseeable victim, yet she still must establish the unreasonably dangerous character of the product. (C) is incorrect because negligence is irrelevant to a strict liability action, which Innes can pursue against Paint Company as a commercial supplier. (D) is incorrect because the dangerous character of the glue emanates from its properties during use, not its packaging. The fact that Paint Company had no opportunity to inspect the product is irrelevant to its liability.

Answer to Question 2

(D) Innes probably cannot recover against Glass. An action against Glass would have to be based on the actions of its employees. Because it was not functioning as a commercial supplier in this case, it cannot be held liable on a strict liability theory. A successful action against it must be based on negligence. The employees had no notice of the dangerous character of the glue, nor were they even aware of the common ductwork. Therefore, a cause of action for negligence will not lie against the employees, and obviously will not lie against Glass. (A) is an incorrect statement of the law. (B) is incorrect. The employees did cause the fumes to enter Innes's area of the building. However, as has been shown, they were unaware of the damage the fumes could cause, or that they were sending fumes into the other area. (C) is incorrect because use of a product for its intended purpose does not negate the possibility of liability. If Glass's employees acted negligently while using the product for its intended purpose, Glass could be held vicariously liable for their actions.

Answer to Question 3

(C) Prout will not recover if Denton's conduct did not threaten immediate physical harm. A prima facie case for tortious assault requires that the defendant create a reasonable apprehension in the plaintiff of ***immediate*** harmful or offensive contact to the plaintiff's person. Threats of ***future*** harm do not give rise to an action for assault. (A) is incorrect because mere intent to place in fear of physical harm is not enough. There must be a creation of reasonable apprehension of immediate harm. (B) is incorrect; extreme and outrageous conduct is an element of intentional infliction of emotional distress, but not of assault. (D) is incorrect because it is irrelevant, and later actions would not vitiate any threat of immediate harm.

Answer to Question 4

(A) Prout will recover if he suffered severe emotional distress. The tort of intentional infliction of emotional distress requires: (i) an act by defendant amounting to extreme and outrageous conduct; (ii) intent to cause severe emotional distress or recklessness as to the effect of the conduct; (iii) causation; and (iv) damages. If Prout suffered severe emotional distress resulting from Denton's conduct (which was extreme and outrageous and, at the very least, reckless), he can recover from Denton. (B) is incorrect because intent, without more, does not establish intentional infliction of emotional distress. (C) is incorrect because immediate threat of physical harm is an element of assault rather than intentional infliction of emotional distress. (D) is incorrect because, even though actual damages are required to win a case grounded on intentional infliction of emotional distress, physical injuries are not required.

Answer to Question 5

(C) Parker will not prevail because at common law Parker's contributory negligence will completely bar his right to recover. Parker was contributorily negligent because he was operating a car with defective brakes in violation of the statute. (A) is wrong because Parker was not in the class intended to be protected by the statute. It was Parker's obligation to ensure that the brakes complied with the statute. (B) is incorrect because the existence of an emergency, presenting little time for reflection, may be considered as among the circumstances under which the defendant acted (*i.e.,* he must act as the reasonable person would act in the same emergency). Applying this criterion, Doctor was justified in moving the car. (D) is incorrect because a person who is injured while intoxicated does not automatically lose a cause of action against the person causing the injury. In addition, the harm in this case was not the type of harm which the drunk driving statute was designed to prevent.

Answer to Question 6

(A) (A) is correct because leaving the trench uncovered was the proximate cause of Tommy's death. Generally, rescuers are viewed as foreseeable intervening forces, and the original tortfeasor will be liable for their negligence. (B) is wrong as a matter of law. Construction companies are subject to strict liability based on the same criteria applied to other companies and individuals. The activity must be deemed abnormally dangerous to subject the party performing the activity to strict liability. Leaving the trench uncovered was negligent, but it is not abnormally dangerous. (C) is wrong because under the attractive nuisance doctrine, the defendant had a duty to exercise ordinary care to avoid reasonably foreseeable harm to children caused by artificial conditions on the property. The fact that children played on the vacant lot made it possible for the defendant to anticipate infant trespassers. The defendant also knew of the dangerous condition, and the expense of covering the trench would be slight in comparison with the magnitude of the risk. (D) is incorrect, because even if the collapse of the trench was unforeseeable, Construction Company's conduct still threatened to cause injury, and most courts find liability where there is a foreseeable result of an unforeseeable cause.

Answer to Question 7

(D) The most significant factor pertains to the burden on Macco to eliminate the danger. Under the attractive nuisance doctrine, most courts impose on a landowner the duty to exercise ordinary care to avoid reasonably foreseeable risks of harm to children caused by artificial conditions on the property. To assess this special duty on the landowner, the plaintiff must show, among other things, that the expense of remedying the situation is slight compared with the magnitude of the risk. Choice (D) most closely reflects that requirement. (A) is incorrect because most jurisdictions no longer require that the child plaintiff be lured onto the property by the dangerous condition. Thus, whether the press was visible from a public way would only be relevant to show that the trespass was foreseeable, and here the facts indicate that the landowner was already aware that children played on the machinery. (B) and (C) are incorrect because the doctrine of attractive nuisance is distinct from nuisance law. The landowner may be liable even if the danger is neither a public nor a private nuisance as to adjoining landowners.

Answer to Question 8

(A) Accountant will recover because the dishwasher was defective. A prima facie products liability action based on strict liability in tort requires: (i) an absolute duty owed by a commercial supplier;

(ii) production or sale of a defective product; (iii) actual and proximate cause; and (iv) damages. Accountant can make such a case because he need not prove that the defendant was at fault in selling or producing a defective product—only that the product in fact is so defective as to be "unreasonably dangerous." The product also must have reached the user without substantial change in the condition in which it is supplied. The fact that the dishwasher had an internal wiring defect causing the machine to malfunction is a sufficient basis to impose strict liability. Any negligence by Contractor as an intermediary does not void the manufacturer's liability. Suppliers must anticipate reasonably foreseeable uses even if they are misuses. (B) is wrong because Contractor was an independent contractor with no relationship to Elex Company that vicarious liability would support. (C) is wrong even though assumption of risk may sometimes be successfully raised in strict liability cases. Here, Accountant did not know of the risk and did not voluntarily assume it. (D) is incorrect because privity is not required to bring a strict liability action. A majority of courts extend protection not only to buyers, but also to members of the buyer's family, guests, friends, and employees of the buyer, as well as foreseeable bystanders.

Answer to Question 9

(D) Absent a valid defense, a defendant may not cause a substantial, unreasonable interference with a neighbor's use or enjoyment of his property. Whether the Householders were there before or after Diner opened does not control the result; plaintiffs' right to the reasonable use or enjoyment of their land is the test. (A) is wrong because the fact that one type of land use was entered into before another is relevant but not conclusive evidence as to reasonableness of use. (B) is wrong because a use permitted under a zoning ordinance may be shown to be unreasonable. (C) is a misstatement of law.

Answer to Question 10

(C) Driver's injuries were actually caused by Trucker since they would not have occurred "but for" Trucker's negligent parking. Trucker was also the legal (proximate) cause of Driver's injuries. It was foreseeable that an eastbound car might proceed into the intersection when the traffic signal was obstructed and possibly collide with another car possessing the right of way—a foreseeable result caused by a foreseeable intervening force. Therefore, (A), (B), and (D) are incorrect.

Answer to Question 11

(B) Nothing in the facts indicates that City was under an absolute duty to maintain its traffic poles. Hence, (A) and (C) are incorrect. (D) states no legal theory for Driver's claim and so is not as good an answer as (B). The best theory for Driver is that City was negligent in not replacing the broken pole within 72 hours.

Answer to Question 12

(C) Henry intended to cause Wanda the severe emotional distress that did, in fact, result from his outrageous conduct. Hence, his conduct satisfies the prima facie case and (C) is the correct response. John's conduct was a foreseeable response to Henry's act and hence did not break the chain of causation leading to the result intended by Henry. Thus, (B) is wrong. (A) is unsupported by the facts, and (D) is a misstatement of law; if the third person's conduct was unforeseeable, it may affect the defendant's liability.

Answer to Question 13

(D) Although Peter intended to go onto Owner's property, his entry was privileged if Peter believed it was necessary to protect himself and/or his boat. Note that this privilege is qualified in that Peter must pay for any damage he caused to Owner's property. (A), (B), and (C) are incorrect because knowledge that the land is privately owned is irrelevant to the privilege of necessity.

Answer to Question 14

(A) The privilege to invade land as a private necessity supersedes the occupant's right to protect the property from invasion; hence, the landowner is liable to the invader for any harm suffered if entry is denied. (C) is wrong because Owner could have recovered for injury to his dock, but had no right to resist Peter's entry. (B) and (D) are incorrect because Peter's entry was privileged.

Answer to Question 15

(B) Parents may be liable for ***negligence*** for failing to prevent the tortious conduct of their children. Further, if parents know of their child's propensity to harm, they have a duty to exercise due care to control the child's behavior. Here, they did just the opposite. Hence, (D) is wrong. (C) is wrong because children are considered capable of committing torts. (A) is wrong because parents' liability is based on ***negligence***.

Answer to Question 16

(A) A child is liable for his intentional torts whether or not he knows of their "wrongfulness." Hence, (B) is incorrect. (C) is wrong because there is no minimum age for capacity to commit torts. Children generally are deemed to have the capacity to form the intent to commit intentional torts. (D) is wrong because parents are not vicariously liable for their children's torts.

Answer to Question 17

(B) Brenda must establish the facts in (B) because to hold the commercial supplier strictly liable for a product defect, the product must be expected to, and must in fact, reach the user or consumer without substantial change in the condition in which it is supplied. (A) is wrong because warnings are only one consideration in determining whether a product is in a "defective condition unreasonably dangerous" as required for strict liability purposes. Strict liability can apply even if the customer is informed of the warnings. (C) is wrong because it goes to an issue of negligence on the retailer's part. It is unnecessary for a retailer to affirmatively contribute to the defectiveness of the product for strict liability to apply. (*See* the analysis of option (B), above.) (D) is incorrect because in a strict liability case it is unnecessary to prove that the defendant was at fault in selling or producing a dangerous product—only that the product is in fact so defective as to be unreasonably dangerous. Thus, plaintiff need not show that Local Retailer was aware or should have been aware of the danger. Options (A), (C), and (D) all deal with fault on Local Retailer's part, and are, therefore, wrong in a strict liability analysis.

Answer to Question 18

(D) Brenda must show that the stove had an unreasonably dangerous defect to establish a breach of duty by the manufacturer. To establish a prima facie case based on strict liability in tort, the plaintiff must prove: (i) strict duty owed by a commercial supplier; (ii) breach of that duty; (iii) actual and proximate cause; and (iv) damages. To establish breach of duty for a strict liability action, the plaintiff need not prove that the defendant was at fault in selling or producing a dangerous product—only that the product in fact is so defective as to be "unreasonably dangerous." (A) is wrong because negligence need not be proven in a strict liability case. (B) is wrong because the availability of safer product alternatives is only one factor to be considered by the courts in determining whether a product is defective. (C) is incorrect because even though the warnings may well have been inadequate because they were placed on the crate rather than on the stove itself, the role of instructions and warnings is but one of many factors the courts will consider in determining the defective nature of a given product.

Answer to Question 19

(C) At issue is Dow's duty to Paulsen. Generally, the law imposes no duty to affirmatively act for the benefit of others. There are exceptions to this rule—*e.g.,* one who places another in a position of peril must use reasonable care to aid that person; one who gratuitously acts for the benefit of another thereby assumes a duty to act like an ordinary reasonable person. None of the exceptions is applicable to the case at bar. Therefore, (B) and (D) are clearly incorrect. The "Good Samaritan" statute, described in (A), generally exempts from liability medical personnel who voluntarily and gratuitously render emergency treatment. However, it does not ***require*** them to provide such treatment. Thus, (A) is incorrect.

Answer to Question 20

(D) Under a negligence analysis, the defendant's conduct must fall below the standard of care expected of a reasonable person under like circumstances. In the instant case, Seller had a duty, at the time of transfer of possession of the home to Parents, to disclose concealed, unreasonably dangerous conditions, of which he knew or had reason to know, and of which he knew Parents were ignorant and not likely to discover on reasonable inspection. Thus, if Seller did not know of a defect in the ventilating system, and could not have discovered the defect through reasonable care, a cause of action for negligence would not lie. (B) and (C) imply that Seller would be liable in negligence merely for failure to inspect or for failure to discover the defect upon inspection. However, there must also be a showing that a reasonable inspection would have disclosed the defect. Consequently, (B) and (C) are incorrect. (A) is more appropriate to a strict liability case, since it does not even mention the necessity for knowledge or discovery of the defect. Therefore, it is an incorrect alternative.

Answer to Question 21

(A) The issue is causation. But for Mobilco's defective design of the ventilating system, the injury to Child would not have occurred. Since Child can trace the injury to a defect in the ventilating system that existed when it left Mobilco's control, cause in fact is established. The same concepts of proximate cause which govern negligence actions are applicable to strict liability actions for defective products. Child's injury is the direct result of Mobilco's defective design, which is the cause in fact of the injury. Thus, proximate cause is established. Heatco's furnace and Coolco's air conditioning unit contained no defects and did not cause injury to Child. As the facts make clear, both units were controlled by a thermostat independent of the units themselves. Thus, (B), (C), and (D) are incorrect.

Answer to Question 22

(D) Hank would prevail in the absence of a claim for special damage. Public nuisance is an act that unreasonably interferes with the health, safety, or property rights of the ***community***. Recovery is available for public nuisance only if a private party has suffered some unique damage not suffered by the public at large. Thus, without a claim of special damage by Fred, Hank would be able to defend against Fred's public nuisance suit. (A) is wrong because it is a form of the largely discredited "coming to the nuisance" defense. Fred is entitled to the reasonable use and enjoyment of his leasehold. Remaining in the apartment does not constitute "consent." (B) is incorrect because the ordinance is enforceable against Hank even if his violation is "reasonable." This option is a "distractor," designed to lure you into wrongfully applying the "unreasonable interference" test from ***private*** nuisance cases. (C) is incorrect because only one who has suffered some unique damage has a privilege to abate a public nuisance by self-help. In the absence of such unique damage, a public nuisance may be abated or enjoined only by public authority.

Answer to Question 23

(C) Where the defendant intentionally causes severe physical harm to one person, and another person suffers severe emotional distress because of that person's relationship to the injured party, problems of intent and causation arise. To sustain a claim for intentional infliction of emotional distress under such circumstances, the plaintiff generally must show: (i) he was present when the injury occurred to the other person; (ii) he is a close relation of the injured person; and (iii) the defendant knew that the plaintiff was present and a close relation to the injured person. In the case at bar, we do not know that Nelson suffered severe physical harm. However, we do know that Smythe was unaware that Joplin observed the incident. (A) and (B) are incorrect, because they ignore the issue of whether Smythe knew that Joplin was watching. (D) is incorrect, because the term "zone of physical danger" is more appropriate to an action for ***negligent*** infliction of emotional distress.

Answer to Question 24

(A) An activity may be characterized as abnormally dangerous if it (i) creates a foreseeable risk of serious harm even when reasonable care is taken by the actors; and (ii) is not a matter of common usage in the particular community. In such cases, the duty owed is an absolute duty to make safe the condition. Liability will be imposed for any injuries to persons or property resulting from the condition. Pursuant to the foregoing criteria, Gasco's operation of the storage facility constitutes an abnormally dangerous activity, subjecting Gasco to liability for damage caused by the explosion, regardless of any negligence on the part of Gasco. Thus, (C) is incorrect. (D) is incorrect because any negligence on the part of Acme will not absolve Gasco of liability for maintenance of an abnormally dangerous condition. (B) is incorrect because where, as here, no physical object enters the plaintiff's land, a court will generally treat the matter as a nuisance case or one involving strict liability if an abnormally dangerous activity is involved, rather than as a trespass case.

Answer to Question 25

(D) Acme, as the manufacturer of the facility, owed a duty of due care to any foreseeable plaintiff. Farber, whose farm is located near the facility, is a foreseeable plaintiff. Therefore, if the explosion resulted from a defect of which Acme was aware, Acme would be liable to Farber for the resultant loss of his lettuce crop. (B) is incorrect because Acme's status as an independent contractor relative to Gasco has no bearing on the duty owed by Acme to Farber. (A) is incorrect because Acme will be liable for manufacturing the facility with knowledge of a defect, regardless of the identity of the facility's designer. (C) is incorrect because Acme was the ***manufacturer***, rather than the ***operator***, of the facility.

Answer to Question 26

(D) In a defamation action, a defendant may assert a claim of qualified privilege for statements made in the interest of the publisher of the statement, the recipient of the statement, or both. The privilege will be lost only if the statement is not within the scope of the privilege or if it was made with malice (*i.e.*, knowledge of falsity or reckless disregard of truth or falsity). In this case, Hospital's response to Registry on a matter of common interest was within the scope of the privilege. Thus, (D) is correct because Hospital's reasonable belief would negate any malice on its part. (A) is incorrect, because the accusation alone does not establish defamation when a claim of qualified privilege is raised. (B) is incorrect, because the falsity of the statement does not dispose of the question of qualified privilege. (C) is incorrect, because the disappearance of the narcotics does not, by itself, establish a reasonable belief on the part of the hospital that Siddon was responsible for the disappearance.

Answer to Question 27

(C) (A) is incorrect because Dugan owed the child the duty to act as an ordinary, prudent, reasonable person—not the "highest degree of care." (B) is incorrect because, even if a two-year-old were incapable of contributory negligence, the plaintiff could prevail only if the defendant or his employees were negligent—*i.e.*, failed to exercise reasonable care to ensure the plaintiff's safety. Because (C) reflects this principle, it is the correct answer. (D) is incorrect because, even if Mary assumed the risk, the mother's assumption of risk will not be imputed to the plaintiff-child.

Answer to Question 28

(A) In negligently causing the collision with the fire engine, it was foreseeable that Dever's actions could cause injury to someone else (*e.g.*, a local resident who the fire engine would be unable to reach because of the accident). Peters, whose house was located only 10 blocks from the scene of the accident, falls within the foreseeable zone of danger. It follows that (D) is incorrect. (C) is incorrect because, even if Dever was not involved in causing the fire, his negligence caused the delay in the arrival of the fire engine. In turn, this delay may well have caused all or part of the damage suffered by Peters. (B) is incorrect because it assumes, without a factual basis, that Dever's negligence caused the entire loss. (A) is correct because it recognizes that Dever breached a duty of due care owed to Peters, and that Dever will be liable for that part of Peters's damages that was actually and proximately caused by Dever's breach of duty.

Answer to Question 29

(C) A cause of action for deceit requires: (i) a false representation of a material past or present fact; (ii) scienter; (iii) intent to induce reliance; (iv) causation; (v) justifiable reliance; and (vi) damages. Generally, reliance upon false statements of opinion, value, or quality is unjustified. Here, Daley's statements regarding the car's not having been involved in an accident and the gasoline mileage constitute knowingly false representations of material fact that will form the basis of a cause of action for deceit. Thus, statements 1. and 2. are correct. Statement 3., regarding the smooth ride of the car, is an opinion, upon which Purvis would not be justified in relying. Consequently, statement 3. would not support Purvis's claim for deceit. Therefore, (C) is correct, and (A), (B), and (D) are wrong.

Answer to Question 30

(B) In order to establish a prima facie case for battery, Customer must show (i) an act by the defendant Store that brings about harmful or offensive contact to Customer's person, (ii) intent by Store to bring about such contact, and (iii) causation. (B) is correct since this is one of the elements necessary to establish a battery. (A) is wrong because there need not be severe bodily harm for a battery to occur. The contact may be merely offensive without causing any bodily injury.

(C) is wrong because there need not be any emotional distress for a battery to occur. (D) is wrong because Customer's conduct of vigorously shaking the door was indeed the factual cause of the spray. However, there was causation on the Store's part in the sense of the Store having set in motion a force that would bring about a harmful or offensive contact to Customer's person where there was any attempt to open the door.

Answer to Question 31

(A) Truth is an absolute defense to a claim of defamation. (B) is wrong because it is irrelevant whether Dock made the statement out of malice as long as the statement was in fact true. (C) is wrong because it is equally irrelevant whether Dock reasonably believed the statement to be true. The fact that the statement is true is the only requirement for the defense to prevail. (D) is wrong for the reason that (A) is correct. Note that Paul's claim is based on defamation. Even though Dock can defend the defamation action by showing that the statement is true, Paul might nonetheless be able to successfully assert a cause of action based on intentional infliction of emotional distress.

Answer to Question 32

(B) (B) is correct because res ipsa loquitur applies. When the facts are such as to strongly indicate that the plaintiff's injuries resulted from the defendant's negligence, the trier of fact may be permitted to infer the defendant's liability. The circumstantial evidence doctrine of res ipsa loquitur requires the plaintiff to show: (i) the accident causing his injury is of the type that would not normally occur unless someone was negligent; (ii) the negligence was attributable to the defendant; and (iii) the plaintiff was free from negligence. All of these elements are satisfied from the facts of this case. Because the switches and the doors were found to be in good working order, the injury can reasonably be inferred to be attributable to one of Auto Company's employees, because they had access to the switches. (A) is wrong because strict liability applies to abnormally dangerous activities that cannot be performed without risk of serious harm no matter how much care is taken. The operation of the door cannot be characterized as abnormally dangerous. (C) is incorrect because the owner has a duty to exercise reasonable care in the conduct of "active operations" (such as opening and closing the door) for the protection of licensees known to be on the property. (D) is incorrect because to have assumed the risk, the plaintiff must have known of the risk and voluntarily assumed it. Peter had no reason to know of any risk involving the overhead door and consequently could not assume it.

Answer to Question 33

(B) It is foreseeable that where a defendant's wrongful conduct places him in a position of peril, a rescuer may suffer injuries while reasonably attempting to aid him, *i.e.,* "danger invites rescue." Hence, (B) is correct and (D) is incorrect. (C) is wrong because a rescue is not a "voluntary" assumption of the risk. (A) is not a reason for imposing liability.

Answer to Question 34

(C) Since Neighbor's conduct did not endanger Si, Neighbor owed no duty to Si or his rescuer. Generally, there is no duty owed to an undiscovered trespasser such as Si, whose conduct was unforeseeable. (A) and (B) are wrong because the facts that Rescuer acted reasonably or saved Neighbor's property are irrelevant to the issue of Neighbor's duty. (D) is wrong because an act of rescue is not an assumption of the risk.

Answer to Question 35

(D) Telco and Rhodes are liable for the full amount as joint tortfeasors. In cases where there are joint tortfeasors and the injury suffered is not divisible, each tortfeasor will be jointly and severally liable for that injury. The rule of joint and several liability applies even where (as in the case described by the facts) each defendant acted entirely independently. Both defendants were negligent and contributed to the injuries suffered by the plaintiff when the pole fell. (A) is incorrect because Telco's prior negligence has no effect on Rhodes's liability. Her conduct was the direct cause of the foreseeable harmful result of the pole falling; the fact that it did not happen immediately is irrelevant. (B) is incorrect because Rhodes's reckless driving was not a superseding intervening force that would cut off Telco's liability for its original negligence. Because of Telco's negligence, it was foreseeable that the pole would fall. The fact that it was caused by another's reckless conduct, whether foreseeable or unforeseeable, does not cut off Telco's liability. (C) is incorrect because there is no basis to divide the plaintiff's injuries as 50% caused by Telco and 50% caused by Rhodes.

Answer to Question 36

(C) Page will not recover because she was an unforeseeable plaintiff to whom Dwyer owed no duty. A duty of care is owed only to foreseeable plaintiffs. A trespasser is not a foreseeable plaintiff unless the landowner has discovered her presence or should reasonably know of trespassers who constantly cross over a section of his land. Neither of these situations is indicated by the facts. Thus, Page was an undiscovered trespasser to whom no duty is owed. Dwyer was under no obligation to inspect his premises to determine if trespassers were entering his cabin. (A) is incorrect. Because Dwyer owed no duty to Page, it is irrelevant whether Dwyer knew that the stove was defective. (B) is incorrect for the same reason. Dwyer had no duty to inspect the appliances in his cabin to make it safe for undiscovered trespassers. (D) is incorrect because it mitigates Page's liability for trespass but has no effect on Dwyer's duty to Page.

Answer to Question 37

(A) Most courts impose upon a landowner the duty to exercise ordinary care to avoid reasonably foreseeable risk of harm to children caused by artificial conditions on his property. Under the general rule, the plaintiff must show: (i) that there is a dangerous condition present on the land that the owner is (or should be) aware of; (ii) that the owner knows or should know that young persons frequent the vicinity of this dangerous condition; (iii) that the condition is likely to cause injury because of the child's inability to appreciate the risk; and (iv) that the expense of remedying the situation is slight compared to the magnitude of the risk. If the sprinkler head was a hazard that Peter would probably not discover, it would meet the requirements for a showing of attractive nuisance, and O'Neill would be liable. (B) is incorrect because O'Neill would continue to be responsible even if he had objected to the children playing on the common area. (C) is incorrect because it is of no consequence where Peter lived. (D) is incorrect because there is a higher standard of care where attractive nuisances to children are concerned.

Answer to Question 38

(A) The only proposition that must be established is that the gas caused Nyman's death. The storage of highly toxic gas is an activity for which strict liability is imposed. Proposition I. relates to an element required in a strict liability case, while propositions II. and III. relate to additional matters that might be necessary to prove if negligence were the issue. In strict liability the plaintiff need only prove: (i) the nature of the defendant's activity imposes an absolute duty to make safe; (ii) the dangerous aspect of the activity was the actual and proximate cause of the plaintiff's injury; and (iii) damages. Abnormally dangerous activities fall into the strict liability category because they: (i) create a foreseeable risk of serious harm even when reasonable care is exercised by all actors; and (ii) are not matters of common usage in the community. The storage of toxic gas is such an activity. Nyman's personal representative need only prove that the escaping toxic gas was the cause of Nyman's death. It follows that (B), (C), and (D) are incorrect because they state propositions that need not be proved for the plaintiff to recover in a strict liability case.

Answer to Question 39

(A) Devon's knowledge that Plummer was about to sit on the chair makes his action a battery. A prima facie case for battery requires an act by defendant that brings about harmful or offensive contact to plaintiff, intent on the part of defendant to do the act, and causation. Here, Devon's act in pulling out Plummer's chair brought about offensive contact to Plummer. The causation element is satisfied not only by direct contact but also by indirect contact. Here, since Devon set in motion the events that brought about the offensive contact, causation exists. The intent element is satisfied if defendant knew with substantial certainty the consequences of his act. Here, if Devon knew that Plummer was about to sit on the chair, he also knew with substantial certainty that Plummer would fall if the chair were moved. Thus, Plummer will prevail on a battery cause of action. (B) is incorrect because Devon's negligence would not suffice for battery, and the only alternative cause of action based on negligence is negligent infliction of emotional distress, which requires that defendant's negligent conduct cause some physical injury to plaintiff. Here, Plummer suffered no physical harm. (C) is incorrect because the prima facie case for battery does not require physical harm to be shown. Even if Plummer cannot prove any actual damages, he will be entitled to a judgment for nominal damages. (D) is incorrect because it merely states Devon's motive for moving the chair. Regardless of the fact that Devon did not have an evil motive or intend to cause injury, he knew with substantial certainty that his conduct would cause an offensive contact to Plummer; this satisfies the intent requirement for battery.

Answer to Question 40

(B) Petrone will prevail if the cement dust constituted an unreasonable interference. For a private nuisance to be actionable, defendant's conduct must amount to a substantial, unreasonable interference with plaintiff's use and enjoyment of property. The operative language in the choice is "interfered unreasonably," and in most MBE nuisance questions such language usually can be found in the correct choice. (A) is incorrect because, even though a balancing test is sometimes used in nuisance cases, mere increased costs is not a sufficient justification to allow continued unreasonable interference with plaintiff's rights. (C) is incorrect because the number of individuals affected is not determinative of whether a nuisance exists. (D) is similarly incorrect; conformity to general methods in the industry will not preclude Silo from being liable for nuisance.

barbri®

Step 5: MBE Simulated Final Exam

MULTISTATE ADVANTAGE™
100 QUESTION EXAM

PLEASE DO NOT TAKE THIS EXAM UNTIL ASSIGNED IN YOUR PACED PROGRAM™

To be used in conjunction with the Summer 2011 and Winter 2012 BARBRI Bar Review Courses

SFE

barbri®

MBE Simulated Final Exam

100 QUESTION EXAM

Time—3 hours

You will be given three hours to work on this test. Be sure that the question numbers on your answer sheet match the question numbers in your test book. You are not to begin work until the supervisor tells you to do so.

Your score will be based on the number of questions you answer correctly. It is therefore to your advantage to try to answer as many questions as you can. Give only one answer to each question; multiple answers will not be counted. If you wish to change an answer, erase your first mark completely and mark your new choice. Use your time effectively. Do not hurry, but work steadily and as quickly as you can without sacrificing your accuracy.

YOU ARE TO INDICATE YOUR ANSWERS TO ALL QUESTIONS ON THE SEPARATE ANSWER SHEET PROVIDED.

DIRECTIONS

Each of the questions or incomplete statements in this test is followed by four suggested answers or completions. You are to choose the ***best*** of the stated alternatives. Answer all questions according to the generally accepted view, except where otherwise noted.

For the purpose of this test, you are to assume that Articles 1 and 2 of the Uniform Commercial Code have been adopted. You should assume that the 2001 revision to Article 1 has been adopted, but that the 2001 and 2003 proposed amendments to Article 2 have not been adopted.

The Federal Rules of Evidence are deemed to control.

The terms "Constitution," "constitutional," and "unconstitutional" refer to the federal Constitution unless indicated to the contrary.

You are also to assume that there is no applicable statute unless otherwise specified; however, survival actions and claims for wrongful death should be assumed to be available where applicable. You should assume that joint and several liability, with pure comparative negligence, is the relevant rule unless otherwise indicated.

DO NOT OPEN THE TEST UNTIL YOU ARE INSTRUCTED TO DO SO.

Simulated Final Exam

1. Ⓐ Ⓑ Ⓒ Ⓓ	26. Ⓐ Ⓑ Ⓒ Ⓓ	51. Ⓐ Ⓑ Ⓒ Ⓓ	76. Ⓐ Ⓑ Ⓒ Ⓓ
2. Ⓐ Ⓑ Ⓒ Ⓓ	27. Ⓐ Ⓑ Ⓒ Ⓓ	52. Ⓐ Ⓑ Ⓒ Ⓓ	77. Ⓐ Ⓑ Ⓒ Ⓓ
3. Ⓐ Ⓑ Ⓒ Ⓓ	28. Ⓐ Ⓑ Ⓒ Ⓓ	53. Ⓐ Ⓑ Ⓒ Ⓓ	78. Ⓐ Ⓑ Ⓒ Ⓓ
4. Ⓐ Ⓑ Ⓒ Ⓓ	29. Ⓐ Ⓑ Ⓒ Ⓓ	54. Ⓐ Ⓑ Ⓒ Ⓓ	79. Ⓐ Ⓑ Ⓒ Ⓓ
5. Ⓐ Ⓑ Ⓒ Ⓓ	30. Ⓐ Ⓑ Ⓒ Ⓓ	55. Ⓐ Ⓑ Ⓒ Ⓓ	80. Ⓐ Ⓑ Ⓒ Ⓓ
6. Ⓐ Ⓑ Ⓒ Ⓓ	31. Ⓐ Ⓑ Ⓒ Ⓓ	56. Ⓐ Ⓑ Ⓒ Ⓓ	81. Ⓐ Ⓑ Ⓒ Ⓓ
7. Ⓐ Ⓑ Ⓒ Ⓓ	32. Ⓐ Ⓑ Ⓒ Ⓓ	57. Ⓐ Ⓑ Ⓒ Ⓓ	82. Ⓐ Ⓑ Ⓒ Ⓓ
8. Ⓐ Ⓑ Ⓒ Ⓓ	33. Ⓐ Ⓑ Ⓒ Ⓓ	58. Ⓐ Ⓑ Ⓒ Ⓓ	83. Ⓐ Ⓑ Ⓒ Ⓓ
9. Ⓐ Ⓑ Ⓒ Ⓓ	34. Ⓐ Ⓑ Ⓒ Ⓓ	59. Ⓐ Ⓑ Ⓒ Ⓓ	84. Ⓐ Ⓑ Ⓒ Ⓓ
10. Ⓐ Ⓑ Ⓒ Ⓓ	35. Ⓐ Ⓑ Ⓒ Ⓓ	60. Ⓐ Ⓑ Ⓒ Ⓓ	85. Ⓐ Ⓑ Ⓒ Ⓓ
11. Ⓐ Ⓑ Ⓒ Ⓓ	36. Ⓐ Ⓑ Ⓒ Ⓓ	61. Ⓐ Ⓑ Ⓒ Ⓓ	86. Ⓐ Ⓑ Ⓒ Ⓓ
12. Ⓐ Ⓑ Ⓒ Ⓓ	37. Ⓐ Ⓑ Ⓒ Ⓓ	62. Ⓐ Ⓑ Ⓒ Ⓓ	87. Ⓐ Ⓑ Ⓒ Ⓓ
13. Ⓐ Ⓑ Ⓒ Ⓓ	38. Ⓐ Ⓑ Ⓒ Ⓓ	63. Ⓐ Ⓑ Ⓒ Ⓓ	88. Ⓐ Ⓑ Ⓒ Ⓓ
14. Ⓐ Ⓑ Ⓒ Ⓓ	39. Ⓐ Ⓑ Ⓒ Ⓓ	64. Ⓐ Ⓑ Ⓒ Ⓓ	89. Ⓐ Ⓑ Ⓒ Ⓓ
15. Ⓐ Ⓑ Ⓒ Ⓓ	40. Ⓐ Ⓑ Ⓒ Ⓓ	65. Ⓐ Ⓑ Ⓒ Ⓓ	90. Ⓐ Ⓑ Ⓒ Ⓓ
16. Ⓐ Ⓑ Ⓒ Ⓓ	41. Ⓐ Ⓑ Ⓒ Ⓓ	66. Ⓐ Ⓑ Ⓒ Ⓓ	91. Ⓐ Ⓑ Ⓒ Ⓓ
17. Ⓐ Ⓑ Ⓒ Ⓓ	42. Ⓐ Ⓑ Ⓒ Ⓓ	67. Ⓐ Ⓑ Ⓒ Ⓓ	92. Ⓐ Ⓑ Ⓒ Ⓓ
18. Ⓐ Ⓑ Ⓒ Ⓓ	43. Ⓐ Ⓑ Ⓒ Ⓓ	68. Ⓐ Ⓑ Ⓒ Ⓓ	93. Ⓐ Ⓑ Ⓒ Ⓓ
19. Ⓐ Ⓑ Ⓒ Ⓓ	44. Ⓐ Ⓑ Ⓒ Ⓓ	69. Ⓐ Ⓑ Ⓒ Ⓓ	94. Ⓐ Ⓑ Ⓒ Ⓓ
20. Ⓐ Ⓑ Ⓒ Ⓓ	45. Ⓐ Ⓑ Ⓒ Ⓓ	70. Ⓐ Ⓑ Ⓒ Ⓓ	95. Ⓐ Ⓑ Ⓒ Ⓓ
21. Ⓐ Ⓑ Ⓒ Ⓓ	46. Ⓐ Ⓑ Ⓒ Ⓓ	71. Ⓐ Ⓑ Ⓒ Ⓓ	96. Ⓐ Ⓑ Ⓒ Ⓓ
22. Ⓐ Ⓑ Ⓒ Ⓓ	47. Ⓐ Ⓑ Ⓒ Ⓓ	72. Ⓐ Ⓑ Ⓒ Ⓓ	97. Ⓐ Ⓑ Ⓒ Ⓓ
23. Ⓐ Ⓑ Ⓒ Ⓓ	48. Ⓐ Ⓑ Ⓒ Ⓓ	73. Ⓐ Ⓑ Ⓒ Ⓓ	98. Ⓐ Ⓑ Ⓒ Ⓓ
24. Ⓐ Ⓑ Ⓒ Ⓓ	49. Ⓐ Ⓑ Ⓒ Ⓓ	74. Ⓐ Ⓑ Ⓒ Ⓓ	99. Ⓐ Ⓑ Ⓒ Ⓓ
25. Ⓐ Ⓑ Ⓒ Ⓓ	50. Ⓐ Ⓑ Ⓒ Ⓓ	75. Ⓐ Ⓑ Ⓒ Ⓓ	100. Ⓐ Ⓑ Ⓒ Ⓓ

Question 1

A 15-year-old sophomore high school student became pregnant, and the school board required her to attend a special program for pregnant students instead of her regular classes. The girl did not want to attend a special program; rather, she wanted to attend her regular classes.

She sued the school district in federal district court, demanding that she be allowed to attend her regular classes. Before her case came to trial, the girl gave birth to the child. Subsequently, the district reinstated her in her regular classes.

When her suit comes before the federal district court, the court should:

(A) Dismiss, because she is no longer pregnant.

(B) Dismiss, because she is no longer required to attend the special classes.

(C) Hear the case on the merits, because she may get pregnant again before she graduates from the high school.

(D) Hear the case on the merits, because it impacts the right to privacy, which is an important federal issue.

Question 2

A car was pulled over for speeding and the police officer ordered the driver to step out and move away from the car. The officer subsequently searched the glove compartment of the car and found an illegal handgun.

Which of the following would ***not*** be a valid basis for the search of the glove compartment?

(A) The officer had a reasonable suspicion that the driver was dangerous.

(B) The officer properly placed the driver under arrest and secured him in the back of the squad car before conducting the search.

(C) The officer properly placed the driver under arrest, impounded the vehicle, and then conducted a standard inventory search.

(D) The officer had probable cause to believe that the vehicle contained illegal narcotics.

Question 3

A resident living near a factory brought a private nuisance action against the factory, alleging that emissions from the factory's smoke-stack were aggravating her sinus condition and interfering with the use and enjoyment of her property.

What is the most relevant factor in the factory's defense of the lawsuit?

(A) The plaintiff moved to her current residence after the factory's smokestack was releasing that level of emissions.

(B) No other residents of that neighborhood have complained about the factory.

(C) The factory complies with local zoning ordinances.

(D) No particulate matter from the emissions has landed on the plaintiff's property.

Question 4

In early July, the owner of a toy store entered into a contract with a craftsman for the purchase of 25 hand-carved wooden rocking horses for the holiday sales season. The agreement failed to state a delivery date for the horses. After several months went by without any word from the craftsman, the owner forgot about the agreement. On October 15, the owner ordered a quantity of mass-produced resin-based rocking horses to sell in his store for the upcoming holiday season. One week later, the craftsman arrived at the toy store with a truck carrying the horses and demanded payment, but the toy store owner refused, stating that he already had more than enough rocking horses to sell. The craftsman sued the owner for breach of contract.

May the craftsman enforce the contract?

(A) No, because the contract was missing an essential term, the delivery date, at the time of formation.

(B) No, because so much time had passed without word from the craftsman that the toy store owner had reasonable grounds for insecurity and was entitled to cancel the contract and mitigate his damages.

(C) Yes, because the delivery date was reason-able given the nature of the goods.

(D) Yes, because the craftsman accepted the contract by completing the hand-carved horses.

Question 5

The defendant wanted to borrow his neighbor's car to go shopping for lawnmowers. Knowing that the neighbor was out of town for the weekend, the defendant opened the neighbor's garage door and took a car key that the neighbor hid in an old coffee can for emergencies. Once inside, the defendant, mistakenly believing that larceny applied only to the taking of items valued at over $100, decided to take the neighbor's lawnmower (worth $75) in order to trade it in on a new mower. However, on the way to the store with the mower, he was involved in an automobile accident, totaling the car.

In a common law jurisdiction, the defendant is guilty of larceny of:

(A) Both the car and the mower.

(B) Neither the car nor the mower.

(C) The car, but not the mower.

(D) The mower, but not the car.

Question 6

A proprietor of a business in a small town who had a very antagonistic relationship with the mayor was denied a renewal of his business license. At a village council meeting that was closed to the public, the proprietor engaged in a heated argument with the mayor and demanded to know why his business license had not been renewed. The mayor truthfully declared that it was due to reports that the business was conducting illegal gambling on the premises. The mayor had received such reports but had not yet had them investigated. Council members at the meeting later voted to overturn the mayor's decision and renew the license. After a subsequent investigation, the reports were determined to be false.

In a defamation action by the proprietor against the mayor, the proprietor will:

(A) Prevail, because the mayor had demonstrated malice toward the proprietor.

(B) Prevail, because the mayor had neglected to investigate the reports before making the statement.

(C) Not prevail, because the mayor's statement was oral and the proprietor did not suffer special damages from the statement.

(D) Not prevail, because the proprietor had demanded an explanation for why his license was denied.

Question 7

A landowner conveyed his farm "to my daughter for life, and on her death to her children in equal shares." At the time of the conveyance the daughter had one child, the landowner's grandson. A few years later, the grandson struck a pedestrian with his vehicle. The pedestrian obtained a judgment against the grandson for damages. The jurisdiction has no applicable statute on the matter.

Is the grandson's interest in the farm subject to sale to satisfy the pedestrian's judgment?

(A) Yes, because the grandson's after-acquired title inures to the benefit of the pedestrian.

(B) Yes, because the grandson's interest is subject to involuntary transfer.

(C) No, because the daughter may have more children.

(D) No, because contingent remainders are not transferable inter vivos.

Question 8

The defendant was on trial for possession of methamphetamines. Charges against the drug dealer who sold the pills to the defendant were dropped in exchange for his testimony against the defendant. The defendant denied knowing that the pills he purchased were illegal drugs. At trial, the drug dealer testified that he told the defendant before the sale that the pills were illegal methamphetamines. The drug dealer died on the stand, prior to the defense counsel's opportunity to cross-examine him. The defense counsel moved for admission of the drug dealer's testimony at the defendant's pretrial hearing that he told the defendant that the pills were not illegal. The prosecutor had an opportunity to cross-examine the drug dealer during the hearing.

Should this testimony be admitted?

(A) No, because the drug dealer cannot be cross-examined about his current testimony.

(B) No, because the drug dealer's prior statement was hearsay not within an exception.

(C) Yes, but only to impeach the credibility of the witness.

(D) Yes, to impeach the credibility of the witness and as substantive evidence.

Question 9

During summer months, thousands of tourists regularly visited a state's capital to see its many sites. Because the city had few outdoor water fountains, a number of vendors had taken advantage of the situation by selling water out of coolers set up on the sidewalks of the city.

After receiving several complaints regarding the clutter associated with the water vendors, the city council passed an ordinance, effective immediately, prohibiting persons from selling bottled water out of coolers on the sidewalks between the hours of 8 a.m. and 6 p.m., Monday through Friday.

A vendor had been selling water on the sidewalks of the city for the past three years. He sold his water for $1 less per bottle than other water vendors because his water bottles were adorned with religious messages, and his reduced price helped the dissemination of his religious message. Sixty percent of the vendor's sales were made on weekdays between 8 a.m. and 6 p.m. On learning of the ordinance, the vendor sought to enjoin its enforcement in federal district court on the basis that it is unconstitutional.

In this suit, the court will probably:

(A) Reach the merits of the vendor's challenge to the ordinance, because it interferes with his right to earn a living under the Privileges and Immunities Clause of Article IV.

(B) Reach the merits of the vendor's challenge, because enforcement of the ordinance will interfere with his business, and the rights of the public are linked to the vendor's rights.

(C) Decline to hear the case, because the ordinance has not yet been enforced against him.

(D) Decline to hear the case, because the ordinance constitutes a reasonable time, place, and manner restriction on speech and association.

Question 10

A drug dealer was persuaded by his public defender to plead guilty to possession of marijuana, even though the drug dealer believed that the seizure of the marijuana was illegal. He pleaded guilty while protesting that he was innocent. The judge accepted the plea after determining that it was voluntary and intelligent. After the drug dealer was released on bail prior to sentencing, he was advised by a civil attorney that he could sue the arresting police officer to recover damages for an illegal search and seizure of the marijuana.

Is the civil attorney correct?

(A) No, because the guilty plea was voluntary.

(B) No, because a guilty plea is binding, whether or not it was voluntary.

(C) Yes, because the drug dealer protested his innocence.

(D) Yes, because the drug dealer did not waive his Fourth Amendment claims when he pled guilty.

GO ON TO THE NEXT PAGE

Question 11

A brother and a sister owned a parcel of land as joint tenants with right of survivorship. The brother and the sister entered into an installment contract for the sale of the property "as joint tenants with right of survivorship and not as tenants in common." The buyer promised to pay $50,000 down, to pay $10,000 per year for five years, and then to secure a mortgage and pay the balance of the $150,000 purchase price. The week before the buyer made his final $10,000 payment and closed on the mortgage for the $50,000 balance, the brother died. His will bequeathed his entire estate to his wife. The jurisdiction has no applicable statute on the matter.

To whom should the proceeds be distributed, and who must sign the deed conveying the land to the buyer?

(A) The sister is entitled to $60,000, and only the sister must sign the deed.

(B) The sister is entitled to $55,000, the wife is entitled to $5,000, and the sister and the wife must sign the deed.

(C) The sister is entitled to $30,000, the wife is entitled to $30,000, and the sister and the wife must sign the deed.

(D) The sister is entitled to $30,000, the wife is entitled to $30,000, and only the sister must sign the deed.

Question 12

In a state where gaming is legal, a professional gambler ran up a tab of $50,000 at his favorite casino. Pursuant to a longstanding agreement between the gambler and the casino, once the gambler's tab reached $50,000 he was required to repay the debt in five monthly installments of $10,000 before putting any additional charges on his tab. After making three repayments, the gambler approached the casino owner and offered an immediate payoff of $15,000 in cash as payment in full. The casino owner had a cash flow problem and needed the money, so he agreed. The gambler made the cash payment of $15,000 that same day. A few days later, the casino owner demanded $5,000 from the gambler.

Does the casino owner have a right to collect $5,000 from the gambler?

(A) Yes, because the gambler had a preexisting duty to pay the full $50,000.

(B) Yes, because the casino owner acted under duress when he accepted the immediate payoff of $15,000 in cash as payment in full for the gambler's debt.

(C) No, because there was a discharge by release.

(D) No, because there was an accord and satisfaction.

Question 13

A patient met with a surgeon prior to a surgical procedure that would involve the implantation of a medical device in the patient's artery. The surgeon advised the patient of risks and benefits, but she did not advise him that there was a 1% chance of a defect occurring in the manufacturing process of the medical device that would cause the device to break during the surgery. The patient gave his consent and underwent the surgery. The medical device did break during surgery as a result of the manufacturing defect, causing damage to his artery. The patient then underwent additional surgery that repaired the damage. He subsequently learned about the 1% risk of the medical device breaking.

In a malpractice action by the patient against the surgeon, which of the following questions will ***not*** be at issue?

(A) Would a reasonable person have refused consent on learning of the 1% risk of failure?

(B) Could the manufacturing process have been modified to eliminate the 1% risk of failure?

(C) Did the patient make a full recovery from the surgery?

(D) Would the patient have refused consent had he known of the 1% risk of failure?

Question 14

A buyer entered into a contract with a seller to purchase a parcel of land for $140,000. Because the buyer had only fair credit, the buyer was able to obtain financing from a bank only in the amount of $90,000, secured by a mortgage on the land. Due to a clerical error, the bank's mortgage was not immediately recorded. Without notifying the bank, the buyer went to the seller a few days later and obtained a loan for the remaining $50,000, secured by a mortgage on the land. The next day, the bank discovered the error and recorded its mortgage. The following day, the seller recorded his mortgage. A statute in the jurisdiction provides: "No unrecorded conveyance or mortgage of real property shall be good against subsequent purchasers for value without notice, who shall first record."

Who has the prior lien?

(A) The bank, because the bank recorded its interest.

(B) The bank, because the bank has a purchase money mortgage.

(C) The seller, because the seller did not have notice of the bank's interest when he executed his mortgage on the land.

(D) The seller's interest and the bank's interest are equal in priority because they are both purchase money mortgages.

Question 15

A city has a permanent display of passages from various political and religious documents on plaques along the side of its municipal building, including the Declaration of Independence, the Ten Commandments, and the lyrics to the Star Spangled Banner. The city has added the documents over time when they have been donated by various civic groups. Members of a religious organization that worships the planet Mars donated to the city a plaque containing their basic creed and requested that the plaque be displayed along with the other plaques on the side of the municipal building. The city refused to display the plaque, and the organization that donated the plaque brought suit against the city, claiming that its rights to freedom of speech were being violated by the city's refusal to include the plaque along with the others.

How should the court rule?

(A) For the city, because the plaque would constitute government speech and the city may pick and choose among messages it wishes to convey.

(B) For the city, because of the religious basis of the organization's message.

(C) For the organization, because the city allowed other religious messages to be displayed.

(D) For the organization, because the city's decision was based on the content of the plaque, unless the city has a compelling reason for its refusal.

Question 16

A thief sold some stolen goods to a dealer. Several weeks later, the police raided the dealer's store and arrested him. In this raid, the police seized the goods the thief sold to the dealer and a record book in which the dealer had recorded this transaction. However, at the dealer's subsequent trial for receiving stolen goods, the charges against him were dismissed when the court ruled that the search warrant had been improperly issued.

The police were able to trace the stolen goods to the thief because of fingerprint identification and the information contained in the dealer's record book. At his trial, the thief made a motion to suppress the stolen goods and record book.

The judge should:

(A) Grant the motion, because the evidence is the fruit of the poisonous tree in that the search of the dealer's store was improper.

(B) Grant the motion, because the trial court in the dealer's case has already ruled that the evidence was improper.

(C) Deny the motion, because the thief has no standing to object to the search.

(D) Deny the motion, because the thief's fingerprints on the stolen goods were what led to his identification.

Question 17

A store ordered $2,000 worth of clocks from a large clock supplier. The day before the clocks were delivered to the store, while the clocks were in the hands of a carrier, the supplier learned that the store was insolvent. The supplier contacted the store and told its owner that it would not be making the delivery due to the store's insolvency. The store owner told the supplier that he would pay cash for the clocks at the time of delivery, but the supplier still refused to make the delivery.

If the store sues the supplier for breach of contract, the store will:

(A) Prevail, because the goods were in transit to the store by a carrier.

(B) Prevail, because the store owner said that he would pay cash for the clocks at the time of delivery.

(C) Not prevail, because the store was insolvent.

(D) Not prevail, because the store demonstrated a prospective inability to perform.

Question 18

During the defendant's trial for battery, a witness testified that he did not see the altercation but that he heard an eyewitness shout, "A fight! The man in the red shirt just punched the man in the yellow shirt in the face!" Previous evidence has established that the defendant was wearing a red shirt. The defendant offers to call a witness who will testify that he spoke with the eyewitness the day after the altercation and that the eyewitness said, "The man in the yellow shirt was punching the man in the red shirt." The eyewitness cannot be found to testify.

Should this evidence be admitted?

(A) Yes, because it is the former testimony of an unavailable witness.

(B) Yes, because it impeaches the credibility of the eyewitness.

(C) No, because the eyewitness is not available to explain or deny his prior inconsistent statement.

(D) No, because it is inadmissible hearsay.

Question 19

A landowner owned two adjoining parcels of land containing a number of lakes. She conveyed the eastern parcel, which contained a campground, to a fisherman. The deed transferring the parcel granted to the fisherman "and to invited guests of the campground all hunting and fishing rights and use of the lakes on the western parcel for the benefit of the campground." Subsequently, the fisherman assigned his hunting and fishing rights to a hunter. When the landowner discovered the hunter hunting and fishing on her land, she brought an appropriate action to declare his rights void.

If the court rules for the landowner, it will be because the fisherman's right to hunt and fish on the western parcel is:

(A) A profit appurtenant.

(B) A profit in gross.

(C) An easement in gross.

(D) A license.

Question 20

A state enacted a gross receipts tax on all businesses operating in that state. The tax was a proportional tax based on revenue derived by businesses in the state. A leading manufacturer of widget assembly devices had its corporate headquarters and most of its manufacturing plants in the state. Its products were sold to widget users throughout the country.

If the company challenges the constitutionality of the state's assessment of the tax against it, what is its strongest argument?

(A) Eighty percent of its revenue is derived from purchases of its products by the federal government.

(B) The tax applies to revenue derived from all of the company's manufacturing plants, including those not located in the state.

(C) The state also imposes a use tax on component parts purchased by the company outside of the state to make its widget assembly devices that is equivalent to the state's sales tax for similar purchases within the state.

(D) Sales taxes are imposed by other states on the company's widget assembly devices sold in those states.

Question 21

The defendant was on trial for possession of marijuana with intent to deliver. The defendant claimed that she had been set up and testified that she was not the owner of the marijuana. In support of her defense, defense counsel wishes to present testimony from the defendant's long-time neighbor that the defendant has a reputation for being a law-abiding citizen, and that, in his opinion, the defendant would never become involved with drugs. The prosecutor objects to the testimony in its entirety.

How should the court proceed?

(A) Admit the testimony regarding the defendant's reputation for being law-abiding, but exclude the testimony regarding the neighbor's opinion that she would not be involved with drugs.

(B) Exclude the testimony regarding the defendant's reputation for being law-abiding, but admit the testimony regarding the neighbor's opinion that she would not be involved with drugs.

(C) The testimony should be admitted in its entirety.

(D) The testimony should be excluded in its entirety.

Question 22

A woman owed her auto mechanic $2,000. The debt remained unpaid until any claim for its repayment became barred by the statute of limitations. The woman then agreed in writing to pay the mechanic $1,500, but failed to pay him.

If the mechanic sues the woman for the $1,500, will the court rule in his favor?

(A) Yes, because the woman's promise to pay the $1,500 is in writing.

(B) Yes, because the woman had a preexisting legal duty to pay the mechanic.

(C) No, because the woman's promise to pay the $1,500 is not supported by consideration.

(D) No, because there has not been part performance.

Question 23

A robber attempted an armed robbery of a liquor store with an accomplice. A police officer arrived at the scene and shot and killed the robber's accomplice, who had been guarding the door with a gun and had not obeyed the officer's command to drop the weapon. Meanwhile, the store owner pulled out a gun and shot at the robber but missed. The robber then killed the store owner in self-defense before he could fire a second shot.

In most jurisdictions, the robber is guilty of felony murder for the death of:

(A) The store owner and the accomplice.

(B) The store owner only.

(C) The accomplice only.

(D) Neither the store owner nor the accomplice.

Question 24

A father executed a will, devising his land "to my son and my daughter, share and share alike." The following year, the son died intestate, leaving a child as his only heir. Subsequently, the father and the daughter were involved in a plane crash. The father died immediately. The daughter died the following week, leaving a will that bequeathed her entire estate to her husband. The jurisdiction has the following statute: "A bequest to a descendant of the testator who predeceases the testator passes instead to the predeceasing beneficiary's surviving descendants."

Who owns the land?

(A) The son's child owns all of the land in fee simple.

(B) The daughter's husband owns all of the land in fee simple.

(C) The son's child and the daughter's husband each own an undivided one-half interest in the land.

(D) The son's child and the daughter's husband each own one-half of the land.

Question 25

A tenant remained in possession of the house she was renting after her lease term had expired, prompting the landlord to begin eviction proceedings. While the tenant was still in the house, a heavy snowfall covered the driveway, requiring her to shovel the driveway so she could get her car out of the garage. Shortly after she finished shoveling, the tenant's neighbor used a snowblower to blow all of the snow from his driveway onto the tenant's driveway. Consequently, the tenant had to shovel it again before she could get her car out.

A trespass action against the neighbor can be brought by:

(A) Just the landlord, because the tenant no longer had a right to possession of the property.

(B) Just the tenant, because the neighbor blew the snow onto her driveway.

(C) Just the tenant, because the neighbor interfered with her use of the driveway.

(D) Both the landlord and the tenant.

Question 26

Following their divorce, the plaintiff and defendant were engaged in a bitter custody battle over their two children. The plaintiff is seeking to testify as to statements made by the defendant prior to the divorce in which she had told him that she did not feel that she could properly care for the children by herself. The defendant objects, alleging that the statements are privileged as a confidential communication made during the marriage.

The court should find that the statements are:

(A) Admissible, because the privilege does not apply.

(B) Admissible, because the privilege terminates on divorce.

(C) Inadmissible, because the plaintiff has a motive to lie.

(D) Inadmissible, because the statements were confidential and made during the marriage.

GO ON TO THE NEXT PAGE

Question 27

In late January, the manager of a grocery store announced via flyers and in the local newspaper that he would award a $700 in-store gift certificate to any shopper who generated more than $3,000 in sales on their store credit card for goods purchased in the store in the month of February.

A woman with a large family who regularly shopped at the store decided that she had a good chance to win the contest, so she bought a large deep freezer for $300 so she could buy food in bulk and store it at home. She then began buying large quantities of food and racking up purchases on her store credit card that were substantially higher than her usual monthly expenditures.

About two weeks later, the store manager realized that receipts for the month thus far had not increased enough to justify the cost of awarding the gift certificate, so he again put up flyers and took out an ad in the local newspaper, this time to announce that the contest was canceled. Although the woman saw the flyers, she continued to make larger than normal purchases at the store. At the end of the month, she had totaled more than $3,000 in purchases on her store credit card, but the store manager declined to give her the gift certificate.

If the woman sues for breach of contract, will she prevail?

(A) No, because the revocation was made in the same manner as the offer and, therefore, was effective.

(B) No, because the woman knew that the offer had been revoked.

(C) Yes, because she relied on the store's promise when she purchased the freezer.

(D) Yes, because the offer could not be revoked as to the woman once she had begun to perform.

Question 28

As part of a redevelopment plan, a developer purchased a parcel of land and constructed a condominium complex thereon. The deeds to each of the units prohibited any owner from (i) failing to occupy the unit as the owner's principal place of residence for any period, and (ii) leasing the unit at any time for any reason. The restrictions, which were also contained in the contracts that all owners signed, were designed to foster an owner-occupied environment in the redevelopment area. Subsequently, a current owner of a condo unit obtained a job transfer to another state. When he attempted to lease his unit to a friend, the condominium association filed an action for declaratory and injunctive relief.

Should the court grant the injunction?

(A) Yes, because any restrictions may be imposed on the transfer of a condominium unit if they are agreed to by the parties.

(B) Yes, because reasonable partial restraints on alienation are enforceable.

(C) No, because any total restraint on a fee simple interest is void.

(D) No, because the restriction violates the Fair Housing Act.

Question 29

To combat a drought that was threatening the water supply of metropolitan areas in the southeastern portion of the United States, legislation was introduced suspending a portion of the Endangered Species Act. The suspension would allow water to be retained in reservoirs instead of being released to protect endangered fish and fresh-water mussels that live in streams below the reservoirs. The bill also directed the expenditure of $5 billion to fund a solar desalinization plant to convert ocean water into drinking water to serve the drought stricken area. Congress passed the legislation by a nearly unanimous vote in both houses. The day after the bill was passed, the President vetoed the portion of the bill authorizing the expenditure of $5 billion to build a desalinization plant and signed the remainder of the bill.

If a senator from a drought-stricken state seeks to challenge the President's actions in federal court, will she likely succeed?

(A) Yes, because the President does not have the power to exercise a line item veto.

(B) Yes, because when legislation is passed by more than a two-thirds vote in both houses of Congress, it prospectively overrides the President's veto power.

(C) No, because the senator lacks standing to challenge the President's veto.

(D) No, because the President vetoed the bill within 10 days of its passage.

Question 30

An elderly aunt devised her land to a charity "because my nephew has been stealing from me." When the nephew, who had been caring for the aunt, discovered the will, he threatened to withdraw his care unless she conveyed the land to him. The nephew obtained a blank deed and filled in the description of the land and the parties' names. Under "consideration" he wrote, "past and future care." The aunt signed the deed and the nephew recorded it. Subsequently, the nephew sold the land for market value to a buyer who was unaware of the nephew's threat to the aunt. The buyer recorded her deed. Last month, the aunt died.

If the charity brings suit to impose a constructive trust on the land, will it prevail?

(A) Yes, because "past and future care" is not adequate consideration.

(B) Yes, because the deed to the nephew was void.

(C) No, because the land has been adeemed.

(D) No, because the buyer is a bona fide purchaser.

Question 31

The plaintiff brought a breach of contract suit against the defendant, alleging that the defendant paid for only 25 cases of baseball cards even though the order was for 50. The defendant claimed that only 25 cases were delivered to his store. The plaintiff then introduced a shipping bill from a freight company showing that pickup had been made from the plaintiff on 50 cases.

May the defendant now compel the plaintiff to introduce the remainder of the record, showing that the freight company had only 25 cases of baseball cards on its truck?

(A) Yes, after a proper foundation is laid.

(B) Yes, because fairness dictates that it should be considered contemporaneously with what the plaintiff is offering.

(C) No, because the information is irrelevant to the case.

(D) No, because the record would constitute inadmissible hearsay.

Question 32

A developer constructed several small stores in a commercial district. She received a bid from a contractor to install awnings on the front windows of the stores. The developer had heard that the contractor did shoddy work, but the price was right and the contractor expressly assumed all of the risk of any liability. The developer subsequently sold one of the stores to a barber. A few months later, an awning collapsed without warning, injuring a customer who was about to enter the barbershop.

An investigation by the building inspector revealed that the awning collapsed because the brackets used by the contractor were chcaper and weaker than the required brackets, although they looked the same. The developer and the contractor are now both bankrupt.

If the customer sues the barber for his injuries, the customer is likely to:

(A) Prevail, because the barber had a nondelegable duty to keep the premises safe for those customers and those passing by.

(B) Prevail, because the developer did not exercise reasonable care in hiring the contractor to install the awnings.

(C) Not prevail, because the contractor assumed all of the risks from his work.

(D) Not prevail, because the barber had no opportunity to oversee the contractor's actions.

Question 33

A defendant is on trial for a federal offense. The government has subpoenaed crucial documents from the defendant's bookkeeper that will clearly incriminate the defendant.

May the defendant invoke her Fifth Amendment privilege against self-incrimination to prevent the documents from being admitted?

(A) Yes, because the documents will incriminate the defendant.

(B) Yes, because the documents belong to the defendant; the bookkeeper merely has custody of them.

(C) No, because the Fifth Amendment privilege applies only to compelled testimony.

(D) No, unless the documents contain records that the defendant was required by law to maintain.

Question 34

A member of an out-of-town yacht club agreed to buy a luxury boat from a local yachtsman, a boat which the parties referred to as "the 'Lady' boat" throughout their preliminary negotiations. The yachtsman owned two boats—"Lady Be Good" and "Lady Luck." The yachtsman's intent was to sell "Lady Luck," while the club member intended to buy "Lady Be Good," which the club member knew was once owned by the club member's favorite celebrity. The club member was unaware of the existence of "Lady Luck." The written contract for the yachtsman's "Lady" boat included a sale price of $100,000. When the yachtsman delivered "Lady Luck" to the club member's slip, the club member saw that it was not the boat he had intended to purchase and refused to accept delivery.

If the club member sues the yachtsman for specific performance to compel him to deliver "Lady Be Good," and the yachtsman countersues to compel the club member to accept delivery of "Lady Luck," who should prevail?

(A) The yachtsman, because in the case of a latent ambiguity in the contract, the intent of the seller controls.

(B) The club member, because the yachtsman knew that he had two "Lady" boats at the time the contract was formed.

(C) Neither party, because an ambiguity existed at the time the contract was formed, and the parties did not intend the same meaning.

(D) Neither party, because money damages would be sufficient.

Question 35

The police department of a small city has jurisdiction within the city limits and over a defined portion of the surrounding rural communities within the county. A farmer lives in one of the rural communities receiving police protection from the city. The farmer does not pay any tax to the city directly, but a portion of the farmer's county property tax is turned over by the county to the city in order to support the city's police department.

The farmer's property was vandalized several times over the past several months, and the farmer became unhappy with the police protection that the city was providing. After his complaints to the police department and city hall did not improve the situation, the farmer wanted to vote against the mayor in the next election, but a city ordinance provides that only residents of the city may vote in city elections.

If the farmer brings a suit to compel the city to allow him to vote in the city's mayoral election, is he likely to prevail?

(A) No, because the resident voting limitation appears to be rationally related to a legitimate government interest.

(B) No, but only if the city can prove that the resident voting limitation, which affects a fundamental right, is necessary to a compelling interest.

(C) Yes, because the resident voting limitation violates the Privileges or Immunities Clause of the Fourteenth Amendment.

(D) Yes, because the resident voting limitation constitutes an instance of taxation without representation.

Question 36

In separate lawsuits, the driver of a car and the passenger both sued the defendant for injuries sustained when the defendant's car struck the driver's car. In the passenger's lawsuit, he testified that he was not paying attention to the other cars on the road at the time of the accident, but offers into evidence the prior deposition testimony of the driver. At that deposition, the driver had testified that she noticed the defendant's car swerving in the lane next to her and suddenly crossing into her lane and colliding with her car. The driver had moved out of state shortly after her lawsuit concluded. No attempt was made to locate the driver or procure her attendance.

Should the court admit the deposition testimony over the defendant's objection?

(A) Yes, because the statement was made under oath at a prior deposition.

(B) Yes, under the former testimony exception to the hearsay rule.

(C) No, because it is hearsay not within any exception.

(D) No, because the passenger and the driver filed separate lawsuits and therefore are not co-parties.

Question 37

A tenant had been leasing an apartment from a landlord for more than 10 years. There was no written lease; however, the parties had agreed orally, at the beginning of the rental, what the rent would be per month. The tenant left a check for each month's rent in the landlord's mailbox on the first day of that month, without fail. On September 10, the landlord handed the tenant a handwritten note stating that the lease was to be terminated effective that October 1. On October 1, the tenant placed a check for the rent in the landlord's mailbox, and the landlord brought an action for unlawful detainer against the tenant.

Who is likely to prevail?

(A) The tenant, because in the absence of a statute, six months' notice of termination is required.

(B) The tenant, because a full month's notice is required.

(C) The landlord, because there is no written lease, and therefore this is a tenancy at will and only reasonable notice is required.

(D) The landlord, because this is a tenancy at sufferance, and therefore no notice is required to end the tenancy.

Question 38

A hiker was passing by an isolated farmhouse one evening when she noticed flames coming from a shed attached to the house, which was dark and apparently unoccupied at the moment. The property on which the house was located was protected by a barbed wire fence, but the hiker happened to have a pair of wire cutters with her, so she cut through the barbed wire fence and entered the property. She put out the fire with a garden hose before it spread to the house.

The hiker is:

(A) Liable for trespass, because she damaged the landowner's property.

(B) Liable for trespass, because the landowner was entitled to protect his property with the barbed wire fence.

(C) Not liable for trespass, because the landowner will be deemed to have consented to the hiker's conduct.

(D) Not liable for trespass, but she has to pay for fixing the barbed wire fence.

Question 39

A woman entered into a written contract with her local wigmaker to pay $2,000 for a long silver wig, which was in fashion at the time. The wigmaker completed the wig by the date he had promised, but by that time silver wigs were out of style, and the woman refused to accept the wig or pay for it. The wigmaker spent $200 in making the wig, but because the wig was so out of fashion, the best he could do in good faith was to sell the wig to a Halloween store for $20.

If the wigmaker sues the woman, what is the most he can recover?

(A) $1,980.

(B) $1,800.

(C) $1,780.

(D) $180.

Question 40

A young prosecutor was assigned to a widely publicized murder case in which many people believed that the police might have arrested an innocent person for the crime. After interviewing the defendant and reviewing the files, the prosecutor agreed with that opinion, and told her supervising attorney that she thought that the defendant was innocent. The supervisor instructed the prosecutor to keep her opinions to herself, put on the best case she could, and let the jury decide the issue of guilt. At the first hearing of the case, the prosecutor told the judge that, in her opinion, the defendant was innocent. Immediately after the hearing, the supervising attorney fired the prosecutor for insubordination. After exhausting all administrative remedies available to her, the prosecutor filed suit in federal court, claiming that her firing violated the First Amendment because it was triggered by her expression of belief on a matter of public concern.

How should the court rule?

(A) For the prosecutor, because a government employee cannot be fired for stating an opinion on a matter of public concern.

(B) For the prosecutor, because the prosecutor's right to comment on a matter of public concern in this case outweighs the government's interest in efficiency.

(C) For the government, because the courts give government employers wide deference whenever employees speak critically of government action.

(D) For the government, because the speech occurred while the employee was performing her official duties.

Question 41

The defendant was invited over to a friend's house one night for drinks. The friend told the defendant that he wanted to show him a pistol that he had stolen. After showing him the pistol, they decided to go out to a bar. As they got to the defendant's car, the defendant realized that he had left his coat in the house and told the friend that he was going back to get it. The defendant opened the front door and went to the room where his coat was. As the defendant picked up his coat, he saw the stolen pistol on the table. He quickly picked it up, put it in his pocket, and returned to his car.

In a common law jurisdiction, the defendant could be convicted of:

(A) Both larceny and burglary.

(B) Burglary only.

(C) Larceny only.

(D) Neither larceny nor burglary.

Question 42

The plaintiff brought suit against the defendant for injuries sustained when she was struck by the defendant's car while crossing the street. The defendant denied liability, claiming that the plaintiff crossed against the light. To establish liability, the plaintiff offers into evidence the hospital record from her visit to the emergency room, in which she stated that the defendant failed to come to a complete stop at a red light when the plaintiff entered the crosswalk. The physician who made the entry still works at the hospital but has not been called to testify.

If the defendant objects to the evidence, the court should rule that it is:

(A) Admissible, under the business records exception.

(B) Admissible, because the plaintiff is subject to cross-examination as to her statement.

(C) Inadmissible, because the emergency room physician is available to testify.

(D) Inadmissible, as hearsay not within any exception.

Question 43

At an intersection, a motorist's car struck the car of a mother who was driving her teenage son to school. The mother was killed in the collision. The mother's estate brought a wrongful death action against the motorist on behalf of the mother's son and daughter, her sole heirs. At trial, evidence introduced by the estate established that the motorist drove through a red light at the intersection. Evidence introduced by the motorist showed that the son was showing his mother a video on his phone just before the collision occurred.

The evidence introduced by the motorist:

(A) May be used against the estate to show that the mother was contributorily negligent.

(B) May be used against the estate to show that both the mother and the son were contributorily negligent.

(C) May not be used against the estate, because a parent's contributory negligence is not imputed to her children.

(D) May not be used against the estate, because the mother's inattentive driving was a foreseeable intervening force and does not cut off the motorist's liability.

Question 44

An investor entered into a written agreement to purchase a parcel of land from a seller for $50,000, with closing to take place on July 1. Two weeks before the date set for closing, the investor entered into a written agreement to sell the same parcel of land to a buyer for $100,000, with closing to occur on August 1. On July 1, the investor received a deed to the land and informed the buyer that she would not be proceeding with their deal because she had received a better offer.

If the buyer sues for specific performance, judgment will likely be for:

(A) The buyer, because he did not know the investor was purchasing the land from the seller for less than its market value.

(B) The buyer, because the investor had marketable title at the time the buyer sought to enforce the contract.

(C) The investor, because she had no title to the land as of the date she entered into the agreement with the buyer.

(D) The investor, because her agreement with the buyer was fraudulent to the seller at the time it was entered into, and therefore unenforceable.

Question 45

An astronomer who had studied the moon for more than 20 years became convinced that the moon began sending him messages revealing how to achieve an afterlife. The astronomer created a website where he shared the secrets that the moon had revealed. He gained a sizeable following. A wealthy follower convinced the astronomer that they should build an observatory to serve as the national headquarters for the astronomer and his followers. The observatory was built, and the astronomer continued to study the moon from the observatory. He also held weekly meetings at the observatory at which he revealed the continuing messages that he received from the moon. Some followers attended the meetings regularly, and some watched the meetings via an Internet feed. After receiving his first state property tax bill for the observatory, the astronomer applied for a state property tax exemption that was available for houses of worship. After conducting an investigation, the state denied the observatory tax exempt status.

The astronomer filed suit to overturn the denial. The state moved for a summary judgment, arguing that the exemption is available only for houses of worship and that, because the astronomer and his followers do not belong to a recognized religion, the observatory is not eligible for the exemption as a matter of law.

How should the court rule on the motion?

(A) Grant the motion, because the astronomer and his followers are not members of a recognized religion.

(B) Grant the motion, because the exemption is a law of general application and such laws need not include religious exemptions.

(C) Deny the motion, because the astronomer should be allowed to prove whether his beliefs occupy a place in his life parallel to that occupied by orthodox religious beliefs.

(D) Deny the motion, because a court cannot question a person's religious beliefs.

Question 46

On January 1, a car salesman offered to sell an antique car to a collector for $35,000 cash on delivery. The collector paid the car salesman $100 to hold the offer open for a period of 25 days. On January 4, the collector called the car salesman and left a message on his answering machine, asking him whether he would consider lowering the price to $30,000. The car salesman played back the message the same day but did not reply. On January 9, the collector wrote the car salesman a letter, telling him that he could not pay more than $30,000 for the antique car, and that if the car salesman would not accept that amount, he would not go through with the deal. The car salesman received this letter on January 10 and again he did not reply. The car salesman never heard from the collector again.

The offer that the car salesman made to the collector on January 1 terminated:

(A) On January 4, when the collector made a counteroffer.

(B) On January 9, when the collector mailed to the car salesman what amounted to a rejection.

(C) On January 10, when the car salesman received from the collector what amounted to a rejection.

(D) On January 25, when the 25-day option expired.

Question 47

The plaintiff sued the defendant for injuries resulting from a car accident. At trial, the plaintiff's witness testified that the defendant ran a red light and then hit the plaintiff's car.

Which of the following is the court most likely to allow to impeach the credibility of the witness?

(A) A record of a juvenile offense.

(B) A question on cross-examination asking whether the witness lied on a recent job application.

(C) A certified copy of a conviction for robbery five years ago for which the witness has since been proved innocent and pardoned.

(D) A record of an arrest one week ago for criminal trespass.

Question 48

The defendant and the victim, both of whom were drinking, got into a heated exchange of words in a bar. After several minutes, both calmed down and continued drinking. When the victim started to stagger out of the bar after several more hours, the defendant yelled an insult directed at the victim and picked up a chair as if he were going to strike the victim. However, the defendant immediately dropped the chair when the victim turned around. The defendant was charged with assault, and defends on the basis that he was so intoxicated at the time that he did not realize what he was doing.

Which of the following would be ***least*** helpful to this defense?

(A) Assault is a general intent crime in the jurisdiction.

(B) Assault is a specific intent crime in the jurisdiction.

(C) The victim was intoxicated at the time of the assault.

(D) The victim did not take the threat seriously.

Question 49

A young man borrowed his mother's car to go on a job interview. He was running late and made a left turn directly in front of a taxicab without looking. The cab driver was busy talking on his cell phone and did not see the man until it was too late, so the two cars collided. Had the cab driver been paying proper attention, he could have avoided the accident. The cab's passenger was injured in the accident.

The cab's passenger asserted a claim against the young man's mother for personal injuries. The jurisdiction retains the common law rule pertaining to the liability of car owners for the conduct of drivers.

The passenger will:

(A) Recover, because a car owner is vicariously liable for the tortious acts of the driver.

(B) Recover, because the cab driver's negligence will not be imputed to the passenger.

(C) Not recover, because the immediate cause of the collision was the cab driver's cell phone use.

(D) Not recover, because the jurisdiction retains the common law rule.

Question 50

A group of doctors filed suit in federal court against the United States government to challenge a new statute that places caps on the amount that doctors, hospitals, clinics, and other medical facilities may charge patients to perform specifically enumerated procedures. The government filed a motion to dismiss the doctors' suit, arguing that the doctors lack standing to pursue their case.

Which of the following is ***least*** relevant in determining whether the doctors have standing?

(A) A ruling in the doctors' favor would result in removal of the price caps.

(B) Enforcement of the price caps would reduce the doctors' profits by an average of 4%.

(C) The statute placing the caps on the enumerated procedures provides that doctors shall have standing to challenge the price caps.

(D) Eighty percent of all doctors charged more for the specified procedures than the price caps allow.

Question 51

A teacher brought a battery action against a student. At trial, the evidence established that the teacher was kicked by the student in the leg.

What additional fact established at trial will likely prevent the teacher from recovering?

(A) The student was only six years old and weighed 200 lbs less than the teacher.

(B) Because of a medical condition affecting his leg, the teacher did not feel the contact made by the student.

(C) The student swung his leg up to avoid a mouse on the floor.

(D) The teacher had lawfully taken possession of the student's cellphone during class but refused to return it when class ended.

Question 52

Police went to a warehouse in response to a report of a gunshot. There they found the defendant standing over the victim's body. They immediately arrested the defendant and gave him *Miranda* warnings. The defendant immediately requested an attorney. The defendant eventually was charged with murder and brought to trial. At trial, the defendant testified in his own defense. He claimed that he was in the warehouse alone when he was attacked by the victim, and that he shot the victim in self-defense. The prosecution, on cross-examination, asked the defendant why he did not tell the police when they arrived there that he had shot the victim in self-defense. The defendant's attorney objected to this question, but he was overruled. The defendant was unable to give a satisfactory answer, and the prosecution suggested that he was lying. The defendant was convicted.

Does the defendant have grounds to appeal his conviction on the basis of the prosecutor's cross-examination?

(A) Yes, because the defendant's request for an attorney relieved him of the obligation to talk with the police while he was in custody.

(B) Yes, because post-arrest silence constitutes the defendant's exercise of his *Miranda* rights, which carry an implicit assurance that silence will carry no penalty.

(C) No, because the defendant's silence when the police arrived is tantamount to a prior inconsistent statement that may be used for impeachment purposes.

(D) No, because by taking the stand, the defendant waived any right he may have had not to testify against himself.

GO ON TO THE NEXT PAGE

Question 53

The owner of a custom jewelry supply shop placed an order with a manufacturer for 500 pairs of sterling silver "posts" of the type that are used to make pierced earrings. However, when the manufacturer started to fill the order, it had only 450 pairs of sterling silver posts available.

The manufacturer shipped the 450 pairs of sterling silver posts to the shop owner, plus 50 pairs of higher-priced 10-karat gold posts, without making any adjustment in price. The manufacturer enclosed a note with the order, explaining to the shop owner that it was sending the last of the sterling silver posts in stock, plus the 50 10-karat gold posts to accommodate the buyer.

Did the manufacturer's shipment constitute an acceptance of the shop owner's offer?

(A) Yes, and the shop owner may not reject the substituted goods because they are of comparable or greater value.

(B) Yes, although it is also a breach of the contract under the perfect tender doctrine.

(C) No, because it is a counteroffer that the shop owner is free to accept or reject.

(D) No, because it is a breach of the contract under the perfect tender doctrine.

Question 54

A landowner died, devising her property "to my sister for life, then to my son." A small stream divided the property into a one-acre lot and a quarter-acre lot. The sister moved into the home on the one-acre lot. To access the quarter-acre lot, the sister installed a footbridge. Ten years later, the bridge had deteriorated and was no longer safe to use. After the sister refused to repair the bridge, the son filed a suit against the sister for damages. The jurisdiction has no applicable statute on the matter.

In such action, should damages be awarded to the son?

(A) No, because the sister has no obligation to repair the bridge.

(B) No, because the son's interest has not yet come into possession.

(C) Yes, because the sister changed the property, even though her change likely increased the value of the property.

(D) Yes, because the sister did not keep the bridge in a reasonable state of repair.

Question 55

The mayor of a small city decided that he would like to start each city council meeting with a nonsectarian prayer. Several city council members and citizens objected to the proposal, claiming that it would violate the Establishment Clause of the First Amendment. The mayor argued that it would not constitute the establishment of a religion because he would invite clerics from all of the different religious sects to take turns giving the prayer at the meetings. When the council members still objected, the mayor asked the city attorney to research the constitutionality of his proposal.

How should the attorney advise the mayor?

(A) The proposal is constitutional, because by varying the clerics who will give the prayer, it does not constitute an establishment of religion.

(B) The proposal is constitutional, because there is a long history in this country of allowing prayer at legislative sessions.

(C) The proposal is unconstitutional, because it has no secular purpose.

(D) The proposal is unconstitutional, because its primary effect advances religion.

Question 56

A professional athlete was involved in a car accident after leaving his team's stadium following a game, and a child was killed. The child's parents brought a wrongful death lawsuit against the athlete, which eventually was settled. A reporter for a sports gossip website accurately reported that, as part of the legal settlement, the athlete was required to seek counseling for alcoholism. The website reporter incorrectly believed that she had received this information from a press release by the athlete's agent, but in fact it had been supplied by an unauthorized source, and no public information was released of the terms of the settlement. The athlete brought a privacy action against the website reporter based on the public disclosure of private facts.

If the website reporter prevails, it will be because:

(A) The facts stated were true.

(B) The publication involved a matter of public interest.

(C) The report was based on a judicial proceeding.

(D) The website reporter reasonably believed that the athlete had consented to release of this information.

Question 57

The defendant and the victim got into a minor verbal altercation, concluding with the defendant lightly shoving the victim. The victim lost his balance and struck his head on the pavement, causing serious bodily injury. The defendant was charged with battery, which is defined in the jurisdiction as "purposely or knowingly causing serious bodily injury to another."

Should the defendant be convicted of battery?

(A) No, because the defendant did not know that the victim would be seriously injured.

(B) No, because the defendant did not strike a serious blow to the victim.

(C) Yes, because the defendant purposely shoved the victim.

(D) Yes, because the victim suffered serious bodily injury.

Question 58

The plaintiff sued the defendant, alleging that the defendant allowed her dogs to roam onto the plaintiff's land and cause significant damage to his landscaping. The defendant denied the allegations and called a witness to testify on her behalf. The witness testified on direct examination that she visited the defendant every day and that the defendant never allowed her dogs to leave the perimeter of her property. On cross-examination, the plaintiff's counsel presented the witness with a letter written by the witness to a friend in which she expressed her dismay that the defendant allowed her dogs to roam throughout the neighborhood. The plaintiff's counsel requests that the witness read the letter to herself prior to cross-examination. The defendant objects.

May the witness refer to the letter?

(A) Yes, to refresh her recollection prior to being cross-examined.

(B) Yes, because it is a past recollection recorded.

(C) No, because it has not been formally offered into evidence.

(D) No, because the witness has not claimed any inability to remember.

Question 59

Congress enacted a statute imposing an additional 2% national retail sales tax on all goods sold in the United States. The purpose of the tax was to fund unemployment payments during the recession. An association of newspaper and book publishers sued to remove the tax from newspaper and book publications, claiming that the tax placed an unconstitutional burden on the freedom of speech and press.

Assuming that the association has standing, it:

(A) Wins the lawsuit, because only states have the taxing authority over retail sales.

(B) Wins the lawsuit, because Congress may not impose taxes that chill the freedom of expression.

(C) Loses the lawsuit, because Congress has plenary power to tax.

(D) Loses the lawsuit, because a tax imposed to fund unemployment payments during a recession serves a compelling interest of the federal government.

Question 60

A masked magician contracted with a casino to perform magic tricks six nights a week on the casino floor for $2,000 per week. The contract did not contain an assignment provision. One weekend, the magician came down with flu, so he asked his apprentice to perform in his place. The two signed a written assignment agreement that the apprentice would fully take the magician's place under the terms of the contract for the next week. Excited about the opportunity, the apprentice told the casino's manager of the deal, but no one else knew. During that week, the apprentice wore the magician's costume and mask and performed all of the magician's tricks. No one in the casino noticed the difference. When the magician regained his health, he and the apprentice had a falling out and the magician refused to pay the apprentice. The apprentice went to the casino with the assignment agreement and demanded his pay for the prior week's performances. The magician claimed that he was still the one entitled to payment under the contract.

Who should the casino pay for the prior week's performances?

(A) The apprentice, because he told the manager about the arrangement.

(B) Neither, because the magician breached the contract with the casino.

(C) The magician, because he is the original party to the contract with the casino and no one in the casino could tell that it was not him performing.

(D) The magician, because personal services cannot be delegated.

Question 61

A mother properly executed a deed, purporting to convey a parcel of land to her son. The mother gave the deed to her son for his birthday. A week later, the son decided that he should not have accepted such an expensive gift and told his mother so, suggesting that she devise the land to him by will rather than by deed. Instead, the mother executed a will, devising the land to "my son and daughter, share and share alike." Two years later, the mother died. The next day, the son found the deed in his desk drawer and recorded it.

Who has title to the land?

(A) The son and the daughter, because the son did not pay valid consideration for the land.

(B) The son and the daughter, because the will is evidence that the mother did not intend to pass title to the son only.

(C) The son, because the deed was recorded by him.

(D) The son, because the deed was delivered to him.

Question 62

After a heavy snow and ice storm, a shopkeeper posted signs on his store's front windows saying, "Beware of falling ice." A chunk of ice fell off the store's roof and hit a customer on the sidewalk in front of the store, causing her to suffer a concussion. The customer was texting on her cell phone and was not looking at her surroundings, and did not see the signs.

The customer sued the shopkeeper for her injuries in a jurisdiction that retains traditional contributory negligence rules. The above facts were established at trial. At the conclusion of the proofs, both parties moved for a directed verdict.

The trial judge should:

(A) Grant the customer's motion, because the shopkeeper breached his duty to her to make the dangerous condition safe rather than to just post a warning.

(B) Deny both motions and submit the case to the jury.

(C) Grant the shopkeeper's motion, because he owed no duty to the customer on the sidewalk for natural conditions.

(D) Grant the shopkeeper's motion, because the evidence establishes that the customer was contributorily negligent in not paying attention to her surroundings.

Question 63

The defendant was on trial for burglary. At the conclusion of the prosecution's case, the defendant called a neighbor as his first witness. The neighbor testified that the defendant was with him at an out-of-town sporting event at the time of the burglary. On cross-examination, the prosecutor asked the neighbor, "Weren't you on a jury that acquitted the defendant of another criminal charge?"

If the judge sustained an objection to this question, the most likely reason would be that:

(A) The question is leading.

(B) The question goes beyond the scope of direct examination.

(C) The probative value of the answer would be substantially outweighed by its tendency to mislead.

(D) A proper foundation was not laid.

Question 64

A scientist who had worked in a secret government biological weapons laboratory for 15 years was laid off when funding for the lab was eliminated by Congress. After unsuccessfully looking for another job, the scientist wrote a book detailing some aspects of his research in hopes that it would sell well in the scientific community. After reviewing the book before its publication, the government requested that the scientist edit out certain material that the government thought might jeopardize national security. When the scientist refused to make the requested changes, the government filed suit to enjoin publication of the book.

Which of the following standards should the court apply in determining whether to grant the injunction?

(A) Because the scientist's work involved national security—a compelling national interest—the scientist must prove that there is no rational basis for the injunction.

(B) The court should presume that the injunction would be unconstitutional unless the government can convince the court that the injunction is necessary.

(C) If the scientist's book is truthful and not misleading, it is protected commercial speech and cannot be restricted unless the scientist contractually agreed not to reveal his work.

(D) The injunction cannot be issued unless it presents a clear and present danger of imminent lawlessness.

Question 65

An engineering firm was having difficulty finding qualified engineers because most universities could not afford the costly hardware needed to train top engineering students. The firm's president wrote a letter to the dean of a highly respected university in the area, offering to provide, at cost, "all the necessary electronic drafting tables your university needs" for use in its engineering degree program. The dean received the letter and immediately mailed an acceptance. Two weeks later, before the dean had taken any other action, he received another letter from the firm president explaining that the firm was in the midst of an unforeseen financial crisis and it could not provide the drafting tables to the university at cost after all.

If the dean, on the university's behalf, brings an action for breach of contract against the engineering firm, who will prevail?

(A) The engineering firm, because the dean took no action in reliance on the offer.

(B) The engineering firm, because the contract is illusory—no additional students will necessarily apply to the engineering degree program.

(C) The dean, because the engineering firm is classified as a merchant under the U.C.C. and its offer was therefore irrevocable.

(D) The dean, because there is an enforceable contract between the parties.

Question 66

A bartender and a patron were arguing over an upcoming football game. Their argument grew heated, and the bartender reached over the bar and pushed the patron's shoulder. Enraged, the patron picked up a beer bottle, smashed it, and lunged over the bar. He pinned the bartender against the wall and swung the broken glass toward the bartender's throat. The bartender managed to grab a baseball bat he kept hidden under the bar and hit the patron, causing the patron to fall and strike his head on the edge of a table. The patron died as a result and the bartender was charged with manslaughter in a jurisdiction that recognizes the "imperfect self-defense" doctrine.

Should the bartender's claim of self-defense succeed?

(A) No, because the bartender started the fight by shoving the patron.

(B) No, because the bartender did not attempt to retreat before swinging the bat.

(C) Yes, because the patron escalated the fight when he lunged at the bartender with the broken glass.

(D) Yes, because the jurisdiction recognizes the "imperfect self-defense" doctrine.

GO ON TO THE NEXT PAGE

Question 67

To satisfy a debt owing to her friend, a granddaughter executed and delivered to the friend a warranty deed to a vacant tract of land. The friend promptly and properly recorded his deed. Shortly thereafter, the friend built a house on the property and has lived there since. The granddaughter did not actually own the vacant tract of land at the time. Her grandfather was the record title holder, but he had promised to leave the land to her. Later, the grandfather died and his will devised the land to the granddaughter. Pressed for money, the granddaughter sold the land to a creditor by warranty deed, which it promptly and properly recorded. Although the creditor paid full value for the land, it did not conduct a title search of the land before accepting the deed. Both the friend and the creditor now claim ownership of the land. The jurisdiction in which the land is located has the following statute: "No unrecorded conveyance or mortgage of real property shall be good against subsequent purchasers for value without notice unless the conveyance is recorded."

Who has title to the land?

(A) The friend, because the creditor did not conduct a title search.

(B) The friend, because the creditor was not a purchaser for value without notice of the friend's interest.

(C) The creditor, because of the doctrine of estoppel by deed.

(D) The creditor, because the deed from the granddaughter to the friend was not in the chain of title.

Question 68

A patient went to a dermatologist for treatment of a skin condition on his face that had resisted standard treatment. The dermatologist prescribed a new topical antibiotic cream that was recommended by her associate. She gave the patient instructions on how and when to apply the cream but did not discuss potential side effects. The patient purchased the cream at his local pharmacy and applied it as instructed. Shortly thereafter his skin turned a distinct shade of green and he felt a strong burning sensation when he tried to wash it off. The color took almost a week to fade away, during which time he avoided going out in public and took time off from work.

The cream was packaged with a lengthy printed insert that detailed a number of possible side effects of varying degrees of probability. A "green pallor" and "irritation" were listed as uncommon side effects. The patient sued the dermatologist for prescribing the medicine and established the above facts. He also testified that he would not have taken the medicine had he been informed of all of the potential side effects.

If the patient does not prevail, it will be because:

(A) A reasonable person in the patient's position would have used the cream even when told of the potential side effects.

(B) The printed insert that came with the cream listed possible side effects similar to the reaction the patient experienced.

(C) The severity of the reaction the patient experienced was unforeseeable.

(D) The jurisdiction does not apply a "national" standard of care to specialists.

Question 69

A state statute provided that only residents of the state can be granted a license to practice medicine within the state. The statute was passed after a series of well-publicized mistakes by a nonresident physician led to a public consensus that nonresidents were less likely to be familiar with the medical standards followed in the state, making them more likely to commit malpractice. A respected surgeon who lived and was licensed in a neighboring state was offered and accepted the position of chief surgeon at a hospital in the state with the residency statute. Because he lived only 20 minutes away from the hospital, he did not wish to move. He filed an action in federal court challenging the residency requirement, alleging that the statute discriminated against nonresidents in violation of the Privileges and Immunities Clause of Article IV.

The federal court is likely to find that the statute is:

(A) Constitutional, because the state has a substantial justification for the discriminatory treatment.

(B) Constitutional, because a license to practice medicine is not a "privilege" under the Privileges and Immunities Clause.

(C) Unconstitutional, because the state does not have a substantial justification for the discriminatory treatment.

(D) Unconstitutional, because the discrimination is not necessary to promote a compelling state interest.

Question 70

An artist received permission to display some of his paintings in the lobby of his town's library. The librarian really liked one of the paintings and offered the artist $200 for it. The artist accepted the offer and payment in advance from the librarian, and told her that he would deliver the painting to her at the end of the month when his display came down. A few days later, however, an eccentric millionaire in the town who was unaware of the agreement between the librarian and the artist offered to buy the painting for $200,000. The artist quickly agreed and promptly gave the millionaire the painting. When the librarian found out, the artist offered to paint her another similar painting or return her money, but the librarian was not satisfied.

If the librarian sues for specific performance to gain possession of the painting, will she be successful?

(A) Yes, because a painting is one of a kind.

(B) Yes, because the librarian contracted to buy the painting first and paid for it.

(C) No, because the artist offered to return the money or paint the librarian another similar painting.

(D) No, because the millionaire bought the painting in good faith.

Question 71

An investor financed the purchase of a parcel of land with a $500,000 loan from a bank, secured by a mortgage on the land. After an unsuccessful search to find a developer to subdivide and build homes on the land, the investor leased the existing home to a tenant for five years. During the fourth year of the lease, the investor defaulted on the bank loan. The bank brought a foreclosure action, joining the investor and the tenant in the proceeding. The land was sold to a buyer at the foreclosure sale for the outstanding amount of the loan. After the buyer obtained a judgment in an ejectment action against the tenant, the tenant brought an appropriate action for damages against the investor.

As between the tenant and the investor, for whom should the court rule?

(A) The tenant, because failure to include a necessary party results in the preservation of that party's interest despite foreclosure and sale.

(B) The tenant, because the investor breached the covenant of quiet enjoyment.

(C) The investor, because a landlord may assign the rents and reversion interest that she owns to a third party.

(D) The investor, because the doctrine of constructive eviction protects tenants only against the landlord's actions.

Question 72

The defendant is on trial for murder. During the trial, the prosecution offers into evidence a properly authenticated affidavit summarizing the results of the defendant's fingerprint test, as proof that the fingerprints on the murder weapon are those of the defendant. The affidavit was prepared pursuant to statute by the lab technician that conducted the test. The defendant objects to the evidence.

How should the court rule?

(A) Admissible, because the affidavit satisfies the best evidence rule.

(B) Admissible, because the affidavit is a business record.

(C) Admissible, because the affidavit was prepared pursuant to statute.

(D) Inadmissible, because the defendant's rights under the Confrontation Clause are violated.

Question 73

As part of a plea agreement, the defendant pleaded guilty at a pretrial hearing to possession of stolen goods, because she knew that the police had recovered the goods and could thereby link her to the crime. Unbeknownst to the defendant, however, the search and seizure of the stolen property was conducted without a warrant, and no exception to the warrant requirement applied. During the negotiation of the plea agreement, the defendant admitted her guilt and provided considerable factual details of the crime, but she was never provided with *Miranda* warnings before making the statements. At the hearing, the defendant's attorney failed to recognize that the search and seizure was unconstitutional or request a copy of the warrant, and thus failed to advise the defendant that the stolen property could be suppressed. The defendant was convicted and sentenced in accordance with the plea agreement.

Can the defendant move to withdraw her guilty plea?

(A) Yes, because no *Miranda* warnings were given before the defendant provided details of the commission of the crime.

(B) Yes, because the representation by the defendant's attorney was ineffective.

(C) No, because the defendant's statement in which she admits guilt would make the admission of the stolen property cumulative.

(D) No, because a guilty plea may not be withdrawn after sentencing if the government lives up to its end of the plea agreement.

Question 74

A rancher kept his cattle in a fenced enclosure on his property. The rancher's neighbor, who raised sheep and chickens, was driving his tractor negligently and lost control of it, causing it to run over the rancher's fence and knock down a section of it. The neighbor meant to alert the rancher about the break but forgot by the time he got back to his barn. A few hours later, a small herd of the rancher's cattle wandered through the hole in the fence onto the neighbor's property. The cattle were peacefully munching on hay left out for the sheep when the neighbor's sheepdog began barking loudly and harrying the cattle, nipping at their heels. The cattle became agitated and stampeded over the neighbor's property, trampling a number of chickens in an enclosure. The neighbor sued the rancher for the death of his chickens.

Is the neighbor likely to prevail in this lawsuit?

(A) Yes, because the owner of trespassing livestock is strictly liable for damages caused by the trespass.

(B) Yes, because the herd of cattle had dangerous propensities.

(C) No, because the rancher could not reasonably foresee that the cattle would escape.

(D) No, because the neighbor's dog caused the cattle to stampede.

Question 75

A state passed a law prohibiting liquor manufacturers from falsely advertising or misrepresenting facts about alcohol to the public. A brewery's advertising in the state claimed that its beer had only 45 calories per bottle and was great for individuals trying to lose weight. After performing tests on the beer and finding that it had 145 calories per bottle, the state filed suit against the brewery for violating the state law. The brewery filed a motion to dismiss the state's action, claiming that the state law is unenforceable because it is preempted by the Federal Liquor Labeling Act, which was passed by Congress to inform the public of the health risks of intoxicating liquors and provided that no prohibition based on alcohol and health may be imposed under state law with respect to the advertising or promotion of alcoholic beverages.

The motion should be:

(A) Denied, because a violation of the state statutory duty not to deceive has nothing to do with the health risks regulated by federal law.

(B) Denied, because the states have special power to enact liquor regulations under the Twenty-First Amendment.

(C) Granted, because a valid act of Congress or federal regulation supersedes any state or local action that actually conflicts with the federal rule.

(D) Granted, because Congress intended to occupy the entire field of alcohol regulation, thus precluding any state regulation.

Question 76

The owner of a store in a small beach town contacted a manufacturer about buying 100 Adirondack chairs. The parties reduced their agreement to sell and buy the 100 chairs to a signed writing that contained all of the essential terms, as well as a merger clause. When the chairs were delivered to the store owner, she discovered that they were not "Adirondack chairs," as she understood that term and as that term was commonly used, but a different style of chair altogether that was manufactured in the Adirondack region of New York. The store owner refused delivery, and the manufacturer sued the store owner for breach of contract, arguing that he complied with the terms of the contract.

Will the store owner be allowed to introduce evidence of the meaning of the term "Adirondack chair"?

(A) Yes, because the parol evidence rule does not apply to subsequent modifications.

(B) Yes, because of the dispute between the parties over the meaning of the term "Adirondack chair."

(C) No, because the written agreement of the parties was a complete integration.

(D) No, because the contract was for a sale of goods between merchants.

Question 77

A defendant was charged with murdering his boss. After obtaining a valid search warrant and executing a valid search of the defendant's office, an officer found a love letter from the defendant's wife to his boss describing their sexual relations. The letter stated, "I can no longer hide my love for you from my husband. I intend to tell him about us and leave him for you." At trial, the officer seeks to testify about the contents of the letter as proof of the defendant's motive for killing his boss.

The defense counsel should object on which of the following grounds?

(A) The letter was not authenticated as being from the defendant's wife.

(B) The testimony violates the best evidence rule.

(C) The testimony is hearsay not within any exception.

(D) The probative value of the evidence is substantially outweighed by the danger of unfair prejudice.

Question 78

A landlord leased her home to a tenant for 10 years. The lease provided, "On payment of the purchase price of $100,000 during the lease term or any renewal term, the landlord covenants and agrees to convey the said home to the tenant, his successors and assigns, by a recordable instrument having good and marketable title in fee simple." Five years later, the tenant assigned the remainder of the lease term to a friend with the landlord's consent. Six months ago, the friend sought to exercise the option to purchase the home for $100,000, but the landlord refused. The friend brought an appropriate action for specific performance. The jurisdiction in which the home is located follows the common law Rule Against Perpetuities.

For whom should the court rule?

(A) The landlord, because the option violates the Rule Against Perpetuities.

(B) The landlord, because the option is not assignable.

(C) The friend, because the option is enforceable.

(D) The friend, because he exercised the option within the perpetuities period.

Question 79

An equestrian left his horse with a stable while he went on vacation. When he returned, he went to the stable to pick up his horse and was informed by the stable that the bill was $500. The equestrian told the stable that he would have to go home and get more money. The equestrian believed that he was being overcharged by the stable; instead of paying the stable, he arranged to have a neighbor pick up the horse from the stable. The neighbor thought that the stable bill had been paid and the equestrian had a right to the horse; thus, the neighbor took the horse without the stable's knowledge. Halfway to the equestrian's house, the neighbor decided to keep the horse and rode away on it to his own home.

Is the neighbor guilty of larceny in taking the horse from the stable?

(A) Yes, because the equestrian had not paid the stable bill.

(B) Yes, because the stable had possession of the horse.

(C) No, because the equestrian was the rightful owner of the horse.

(D) No, because he did not know that the stable had not been paid its stable bill.

Question 80

During the defendant's trial for assault and battery, he called to the stand a witness to testify that the victim was the aggressor and the defendant was acting in self-defense. During cross-examination, the prosecution asked the witness if he embezzled funds from his employer five years ago. The witness denied any such activity, and in rebuttal the prosecution seeks to call to the stand the witness's former employer to testify that the witness did in fact embezzle funds during the employment. The defense objects to the testimony.

Should the court sustain the objection?

(A) Yes, because extrinsic evidence of prior bad acts is not permissible.

(B) Yes, because the prior bad act of a witness is relevant only if the witness was convicted.

(C) No, because the offense occurred less than 10 years ago.

(D) No, because the alleged misconduct is probative of truthfulness.

Question 81

A student purchased a chemistry set from the manufacturer through its website. The set contained printed warnings instructing users to mix the chemicals only according to the formulas provided. Nevertheless, the student combined a variety of chemicals in an attempt to make an adhesive remover. The chemicals he mixed generated toxic fumes, which caused him to suffer lung damage. The student brought a strict liability action against the manufacturer.

If the manufacturer prevails, it will be because:

(A) Manufacturing chemistry sets is not an abnormally dangerous activity.

(B) It was not economically feasible to modify the chemistry set to make it less dangerous.

(C) The manufacturer used the utmost care in the process of manufacturing the chemistry set.

(D) The student failed to follow the instructions when he mixed the chemicals.

Question 82

A developer purchased a 25-acre tract of land abutting an industrial park. The property was rezoned for mixed residential and commercial use and subdivided into 50 half-acre lots. The developer sold the 30 lots furthest from the industrial park to buyers using deeds that restricted the lots to residential use. Only 15 of those lots were improved with single-family homes. Over the next 10 years, the owners of the other 15 lots constructed commercial buildings on their land. Five years later, the developer sold the remaining 20 lots to an investor who planned to erect a shopping mall on the land. An original owner of one of the lots with a single-family home objects to the investor's proposed use.

If the investor is permitted to build the shopping mall, it will be because:

(A) The neighborhood has significantly changed.

(B) The servitude has been abandoned.

(C) Nonuse is sufficient to terminate a servitude.

(D) The zoning ordinance preempts the restrictive covenant.

Question 83

On March 1, a widget manufacturer and a retailer entered into a written contract whereby the manufacturer agreed to sell and the retailer agreed to buy 10,000 widgets at a price of $10,000. Due to slow sales, the manufacturer was operating its factory at only 50% capacity and had ample inventory on hand. Delivery and payment was set for May 1. On April 1, the retailer told the manufacturer that he had no need for the widgets after all and would not accept delivery of them on May 1. After notice to the retailer, the manufacturer sold the widgets to another buyer a week later for $11,000, the market price at the time. On May 1, the market price of the widgets dropped to $8,000. The manufacturer's cost to produce and deliver the widgets was $7,000.

The manufacturer sued for breach of contract. At the time of the trial, the market price of widgets was $9,000. The court ruled in the manufacturer's favor, and found that its sale of the widgets to the subsequent buyer was done in good faith and in a commercially reasonable manner, and that there were no incidental damages or expenses saved as a result of the breach.

What amount of damages should the court award to the manufacturer?

(A) Nothing.

(B) $1,000.

(C) $2,000.

(D) $3,000

Question 84

The plaintiff brought suit against a train company for the death of her husband, a passenger on a train that crashed, alleging that her husband died due to the negligence of the defendant. Immediately after the crash, an agent from a federal transportation safety board investigated the accident. The agent issued a report concluding that the accident occurred due to the engineer operating the train at an excessive speed. The plaintiff seeks to admit into evidence the report. The defendant objects on the ground that the report is hearsay.

How should the court rule?

(A) Overrule the objection, because the report is self-authenticating.

(B) Overrule the objection, because the report is a public record.

(C) Sustain the objection, because the investigator who prepared the report must testify unless he is unavailable and the defendant had an opportunity to cross-examine him.

(D) Sustain the objection, because the report is hearsay not within any exception.

Question 85

Congress declared war on a nation in Asia. Congress also passed a statute making it a crime to make public statements in support of the Asian nation and against the United States. A United States citizen subsequently spoke out against the war at a rally in front of a federal building. During her speech, the citizen urged people to "smash the windows of the federal building like U.S. troops are doing" in the Asian nation. Several members of the frenzied crowd did as the speaker urged. The speaker was immediately arrested and charged with violating the statute.

Can the speaker successfully defend by asserting that the statute violates her First Amendment speech rights?

(A) Yes, because the statute is substantially overbroad.

(B) Yes, because her speech involved core political speech.

(C) No, because she incited imminent lawless action.

(D) No, because the ongoing war constitutes a compelling interest that justifies the statute.

Question 86

At the defendant's trial for murder, facts were introduced that the defendant acted in the heat of passion. After a lengthy trial, the defendant was convicted of manslaughter. On appeal, the conviction was reversed on procedural grounds. The state immediately moved to retry the defendant, again bringing murder charges against her. The defendant moved to strike the murder charge, and the court refused to grant the motion. After the second trial, the defendant was again convicted of the lesser charge of manslaughter. The defendant appeals the second conviction, claiming that it violated her constitutional rights.

May the second conviction stand?

(A) No, because the state could not refile charges after the acquittal.

(B) No, because the state could not retry the defendant for murder under the circumstances.

(C) Yes, because the state could retry the defendant because the manslaughter conviction was overturned.

(D) Yes, because the defendant was reconvicted of the lesser charge again, so any error was harmless.

Question 87

Some teenage boys were canoeing on a river when their canoe overturned. A nearby fisherman overheard the teens' cries for help and immediately dove into the river to rescue them. The fisherman hit his head on some hidden rocks and suffered a head injury.

If the fisherman sues the teens to recover damages and prevails, it will be because:

(A) The jurisdiction has adopted a "Good Samaritan" statute.

(B) The teens put themselves in danger by not paying attention to the rocks and currents in the river.

(C) The jurisdiction imposes a duty of care toward unforeseeable plaintiffs.

(D) The jurisdiction does not impose a duty of care toward unforeseeable plaintiffs.

Question 88

A landowner conveyed her vacant parcel of land "to my neighbor and his heirs, but if the land is sold to a non-Christian person, the grantor has a right to enter and retake the premises." Five years later, the landowner died, leaving her daughter as her sole heir. The following year, the neighbor sold the land to an atheist. The atheist built a single-family home on the land. Fifteen years later, the daughter brings suit to eject the atheist from the land. The period required to establish title by adverse possession in the jurisdiction is 10 years.

If the court rules for the atheist, it will be because:

(A) He acquired title to the land by adverse possession.

(B) The daughter is estopped from bringing her claim.

(C) The landowner's right of entry is not descendible.

(D) The condition subsequent is unenforceable.

Question 89

An East Coast seller of knockoff French handbags and a discount department store chain buyer in the Midwest entered into a contract whereby the seller would sell to the department store 1,000 of a specific brand of its handbags for a price of $20 apiece, with the seller delivering the handbags "F.O.B. Chicago CSX Terminal." The handbags were sent by rail to Chicago; midway through the trip, the freight car that was carrying the handbags was struck by lightning and caught fire, destroying the handbags.

If the seller brings suit against the buyer, which has refused to pay the contract price for the handbags, the seller will:

(A) Prevail, and recover the full contract price.

(B) Prevail, but the seller's recovery will be limited to the profits it would have realized under the contract.

(C) Not prevail, because the risk of loss had not yet passed to the buyer.

(D) Not prevail, because destruction of the subject matter without fault of either party discharges both parties of their obligations under the contract.

Question 90

An obsessive fan was heartbroken when her favorite actor announced his engagement to a well-known actress. The fan waited for the couple outside of a nightclub. When they arrived, the fan raised a gun and fired it at the actress, but as she fired, the actor's bodyguard spotted the gun and knocked it to one side. The bullet grazed the bodyguard's hand, causing minor injuries, and lodged in the actor's chest. Through prompt emergency medical treatment, the actor survived the shooting.

The fan may be charged with attempted murder of:

(A) The actress.

(B) The actor.

(C) The actress and the actor.

(D) The actress, the actor, and the bodyguard.

Question 91

Congress created a seven-member safety commission to investigate and make recommendations to Congress for new fireworks safety laws, to make further rules for establishing safety and performance standards, and to prosecute violations of these safety standards. The chairman of the commission was appointed by the President. Three members were selected by the Speaker of the House of Representatives, and three members were selected by the President pro tempore of the Senate. An organization with proper standing seeks to enjoin enforcement of the commission's rules.

Which of the following presents the strongest constitutional argument that thc organization can make against the validity of the commission?

(A) The commerce power does not extend to activities occurring solely within a state.

(B) Legislative power may not be delegated by Congress to an agency in the absence of clear guidelines.

(C) The organization is denied due process of law because it is not represented on the commission.

(D) The commission lacks authority to enforce its standards, because some of its members were appointed by Congress.

Question 92

A driver and his passenger were involved in an accident with another car. They consulted a lawyer regarding their claim and decided to file a suit against the other driver. The lawyer's paralegal attended the consultation. The passenger subsequently sued the driver on a cross-complaint. Prior to trial, the paralegal left the lawyer's employ. At trial, the driver's lawyer called his former employee, the paralegal, to take the stand. The paralegal will testify regarding the passenger's statements to the lawyer at the initial consultation that he was arguing with the driver at the time of the collision.

The testimony is:

(A) Admissible, because the paralegal's presence destroyed the attorney-client privilege.

(B) Admissible as an admission.

(C) Inadmissible, because it is protected by the attorney-client privilege.

(D) Inadmissible, because it is hearsay.

Question 93

The CEO of a pharmaceutical company wanted to reward his top salesperson. He knew that the salesperson's daughter was applying to medical school, so he met with them both and told them that he entered into a contract with the dean of admissions at a prestigious medical school that would guarantee admission to the daughter. The CEO did not disclose that the consideration for this contract was actually an illegal bribe. The daughter submitted her application only to that school and did not send applications to any other schools. Shortly thereafter, the dean of the medical school was removed from his position for other misconduct. The replacement dean denied the daughter admission based on her mediocre grades and test scores, and the deadline had passed for submitting applications to other schools that might have admitted her.

Can the daughter successfully sue the CEO and the medical school for any damages she has suffered?

(A) Yes as to both the CEO and the medical school, because the daughter is a third-party beneficiary whose rights were vested.

(B) Yes as to the CEO, because the daughter detrimentally relied on the contract when she did not apply anywhere else.

(C) Yes as to the medical school, because the medical school breached the contract when it refused to admit her.

(D) No as to both the CEO and the medical school, because the daughter was only a gratuitous beneficiary.

Question 94

An investor owned a parcel of land subject to a covenant prohibiting construction of a two-story residence in order to protect the view from the neighbor's adjoining lot. The investor's parcel was also benefited by an easement in a driveway that ran over the adjoining lot to the investor's property. Fifteen years ago, a trespasser entered the investor's land and constructed a two-story residence. The trespasser also used the driveway over the adjoining lot to access the residence. Last month, the neighbor sold his lot to a buyer by a deed containing the covenant but omitting the easement. The buyer contacted her lawyer regarding her right to recover damages for the obstructed view caused by the two-story residence and to prohibit the trespasser from using the driveway. The period of time necessary to establish title by adverse possession in the jurisdiction is 10 years.

What should the lawyer tell the buyer concerning the enforceability of the covenant and the trespasser's right to use the driveway?

(A) The covenant is enforceable, and the trespasser has a right to use the driveway.

(B) The covenant is enforceable, but the trespasser has no right to use the driveway.

(C) The covenant has been terminated, but the trespasser has a right to use the driveway.

(D) The covenant and the easement have been terminated.

Question 95

A consumer bit into a hamburger at a restaurant and cut her gum on a piece of bone in the meat. The bone was over an inch long. The consumer sued the meat processor in strict liability and negligence. At trial, she presented evidence that the processor supplied the ground beef that the restaurant used to make its hamburgers and that she was injured from the piece of bone in the meat. The meat processor presented evidence that restaurant employees prepared the hamburger patties by hand from the ground beef supplied by the processor, and asserted that one of the employees would have found the piece of bone had they made a reasonable inspection of the meat while preparing it. At the close of the evidence, the meat processor moved for a directed verdict on the consumer's negligence claim.

Based on the facts above, the court should:

(A) Grant the motion, because the consumer has failed to show negligent conduct by the meat processor.

(B) Grant the motion, because the restaurant employees' failure to inspect the meat and discover the bone cuts off the processor's negligence liability.

(C) Deny the motion, because the jury could find that the bone was in the ground beef as a result of negligence by the processor.

(D) Deny the motion, because the jury could find that the processor was more at fault than the restaurant.

Question 96

The defendant was on trial for the crime of reckless homicide after allegedly running over the victim with his car and killing him. The defendant testified that he was not driving recklessly. Defense counsel wants to call to the stand the defendant's colleague, who regularly shares rides with the defendant to and from work, to testify to his reputation for careful driving and for truthfulness.

Should the testimony be admitted?

(A) The testimony regarding the defendant's reputation as a careful driver should be excluded, but the testimony regarding his truthfulness should be admitted.

(B) The testimony regarding the defendant's reputation as a careful driver should be admitted, but the testimony regarding his truthfulness should be excluded.

(C) The testimony should be excluded in its entirety.

(D) The testimony should be admitted in its entirety.

Question 97

A pop musician of modest fame offered to sell his first guitar, the one he played as a teenager before he became famous, to a devoted fan for $2,000. The fan paid the musician $50 to keep the offer open for 60 days. Thirty days later, the musician suddenly died. The administrator of his estate found a copy of the agreement and informed the fan that the offer was revoked. Nevertheless, after the value of the musician's paraphernalia skyrocketed due to his death, the fan contacted the administrator to proceed with the sale for $2,000 just before the 60-day period expired. At that time the value of the guitar was estimated to be $50,000. The administrator refused to sell the guitar to the fan for $2,000, so the fan sued the estate for breach of contract.

Is the court likely to rule in the fan's favor?

(A) Yes, because he had an option contract that survived the musician's death.

(B) Yes, because an offer may be effectively revoked only by direct communication from the offeror, and the offeror is dead.

(C) No, because the option terminated by operation of law on the musician's death.

(D) No, because the offer was revoked by the musician's estate, which had the power to do so after the musician's death.

Question 98

A state located in the southern half of the United States experienced a strong influx of retirees, due in part to its mild winters and in part to the generous health benefits that the state historically provided to its elderly residents who fell below the federal poverty line. The state's Office of Budget Management determined that the influx of retirees would bankrupt the state's health care benefit fund within five years. To preserve the fund and ensure the health of its citizens, the state revised its health care statute to make persons ineligible for coverage until they have lived in the state for at least one year.

If a retiree who was denied benefits because she just moved to the state challenges the constitutionality of the statute in federal court, is she likely to prevail?

(A) No, because the state has a compelling interest in maintaining the fiscal integrity of its health care fund.

(B) No, because the states do not have a constitutional duty to provide health care benefits to retirees even if they fall below the federal poverty line.

(C) Yes, because the requirement improperly burdens the right of interstate travel in violation of the Equal Protection Clause of the Fourteenth Amendment.

(D) Yes, because the requirement deprives some retirees of certain privileges and immunities in violation of the Privileges and Immunities Clause of Article IV.

Question 99

A driver arrested for DUI was booked and read *Miranda* warnings. He refused to answer any questions and was arraigned in night court. He then requested an attorney and was provided with one. Later that night, after the attorney left, a bartender arrived at the police station to complain that he was beaten up by the driver. The driver had not made bail and was still in police custody, so the police took the driver from his cell, read him *Miranda* warnings, and questioned him about the fight. The driver admitted to beating up the bartender.

The interrogation about the fight was:

(A) Not proper under either the Fifth or Sixth Amendment.

(B) Not proper under the Fifth Amendment, but proper under the Sixth Amendment.

(C) Proper under the Fifth Amendment, but not proper under the Sixth Amendment.

(D) Proper under both the Fifth and Sixth Amendments.

Question 100

A consumer purchased a grass trimmer from a hardware store. He took it out of the box and assembled it according to the instructions. He noticed that there were bolts and screws left over and some joints that could have accepted additional fasteners, but he just discarded the extra hardware. As he was using the trimmer, the housing came apart and a hard piece of plastic flew off. His neighbor, who was standing nearby, was struck in the eye by the piece of plastic and suffered permanent injuries.

The neighbor sued the hardware store and the manufacturer of the trimmer in a strict liability action. Through discovery, it was determined that the instructions omitted a critical step in the assembly process that would have used the extra hardware, which is why the housing came apart, and that the manufacturer had received some complaints about the instructions previously. The hardware store had no knowledge of any complaints with any of the manufacturer's products.

As to the hardware store, the neighbor will:

(A) Recover, because the manufacturer had reason to know that the design was defective because of faulty instructions.

(B) Recover, because the consumer's failure to recognize the improper assembly does not cut off the store's liability.

(C) Not recover, because the neighbor is not a consumer and can only recover against the manufacturer of the product.

(D) Not recover, because the hardware store had no opportunity to inspect the product and no reason to anticipate that the instructions were faulty.

STOP

Explanatory Answers

ANSWER KEY AND SUBJECT KEY

Answer		Subject	Answer		Subject
1.	C	Constitutional Law	51.	C	Torts
2.	B	Criminal Law/Procedure	52.	B	Criminal Law/Procedure
3.	B	Torts	53.	C	Contracts
4.	C	Contracts	54.	A	Real Property
5.	D	Criminal Law/Procedure	55.	B	Constitutional Law
6.	D	Torts	56.	B	Torts
7.	B	Real Property	57.	A	Criminal Law/Procedure
8.	D	Evidence	58.	D	Evidence
9.	B	Constitutional Law	59.	C	Constitutional Law
10.	D	Criminal Law/Procedure	60.	A	Contracts
11.	A	Real Property	61.	D	Real Property
12.	D	Contracts	62.	B	Torts
13.	B	Torts	63.	C	Evidence
14.	A	Real Property	64.	B	Constitutional Law
15.	A	Constitutional Law	65.	D	Contracts
16.	C	Criminal Law/Procedure	66.	C	Criminal Law/Procedure
17.	B	Contracts	67.	B	Real Property
18.	B	Evidence	68.	A	Torts
19.	A	Real Property	69.	C	Constitutional Law
20.	B	Constitutional Law	70.	D	Contracts
21.	C	Evidence	71.	B	Real Property
22.	A	Contracts	72.	D	Evidence
23.	B	Criminal Law/Procedure	73.	B	Criminal Law/Procedure
24.	C	Real Property	74.	C	Torts
25.	B	Torts	75.	A	Constitutional Law
26.	A	Evidence	76.	B	Contracts
27.	D	Contracts	77.	B	Evidence
28.	B	Real Property	78.	C	Real Property
29.	C	Constitutional Law	79.	D	Criminal Law/Procedure
30.	D	Real Property	80.	A	Evidence
31.	B	Evidence	81.	B	Torts
32.	D	Torts	82.	B	Real Property
33.	C	Criminal Law/Procedure	83.	D	Contracts
34.	B	Contracts	84.	B	Evidence
35.	A	Constitutional Law	85.	A	Constitutional Law
36.	C	Evidence	86.	B	Criminal Law/Procedure
37.	B	Real Property	87.	B	Torts
38.	C	Torts	88.	D	Real Property
39.	A	Contracts	89.	C	Contracts
40.	D	Constitutional Law	90.	A	Criminal Law/Procedure
41.	C	Criminal Law/Procedure	91.	D	Constitutional Law
42.	D	Evidence	92.	B	Evidence
43.	B	Torts	93.	B	Contracts
44.	B	Real Property	94.	C	Real Property
45.	C	Constitutional Law	95.	C	Torts
46.	D	Contracts	96.	B	Evidence
47.	B	Evidence	97.	A	Contracts
48.	A	Criminal Law/Procedure	98.	C	Constitutional Law
49.	D	Torts	99.	D	Criminal Law/Procedure
50.	C	Constitutional Law	100.	B	Torts

Answer to Question 1

(C) The court should hear the case on the merits. A real, live controversy must exist at all stages of review, not merely when the complaint is filed. If a true controversy no longer exists, the court will dismiss the complaint as moot. A case becomes moot, for example, when a party can no longer be affected by the challenged statute. Here, even though the girl is no longer pregnant, she can get pregnant again, at which time she will be affected by the policy once again. Thus, the harm to the girl (being taken out of regular classes) is capable of repetition but evading review because by the time the case comes to trial, the girl may have given birth, miscarried, or had an abortion. (C) is therefore correct. (A) is incorrect because, as discussed, she may become pregnant again prior to graduation from high school. (B) is incorrect because, as discussed, the harm is capable of repetition. Specifically, if the girl gets pregnant again prior to graduation from high school, she will be required to attend the special classes again. (D) is incorrect because it is irrelevant. The fact that an important federal issue might be involved does not negate the "case or controversy" requirement.

Answer to Question 2

(B) The search of the glove compartment would not be valid if the officer had placed the driver under arrest and secured him in the back of the squad car. After arresting the occupant of a vehicle, the police may search the interior of the vehicle incident to the arrest if (i) the arrestee is unsecured and still may gain access to the interior of the vehicle, or (ii) the police reasonably believe that evidence of the offense for which the person was arrested may be found in the vehicle. Here, if the officer secured the arrested driver in the back of the squad car, the first basis for permitting the search incident to arrest no longer applies (and there are no facts to support the second basis). Hence, there would be no grounds under (B) to support the search of the glove compartment. (A) is incorrect because, under the stop and frisk exception, an officer may order the occupant of a vehicle out of the car and search the passenger compartment if the officer reasonably believes that the occupant may be dangerous. (C) is incorrect because once a vehicle has been impounded, the police may conduct an inventory search as part of standard procedure. (D) is incorrect because, under the automobile exception, the police may search a vehicle without a warrant if they have probable cause to do so, and they may seize any contraband that they find.

Answer to Question 3

(B) The most relevant factor in the factory's defense is that no one else in the neighborhood has complained. A private nuisance is a substantial, unreasonable interference with another private individual's use or enjoyment of her property. To constitute a substantial interference, the activity must be offensive, inconvenient, or annoying to an average person in the community. It will not be characterized as substantial if it is merely the result of the plaintiff's hypersensitivity. Here, if no other residents of the plaintiff's neighborhood have complained about the emissions, that indicates that the interference may not be substantial, and that the lawsuit may stem just from the plaintiff's hypersensitivity caused by her sinus condition. (A) is incorrect because the fact that the plaintiff "came to the nuisance" would not preclude her from recovering. Even though the factory was emitting the same level of emissions before she moved to the property, she can recover as long as she shows a substantial and unreasonable interference. (C) is incorrect because compliance with government authority is not a defense to a private nuisance action. The fact that the factory complies with zoning requirements may be some evidence as to the reasonableness of the activity but it is not determinative, nor is it as persuasive as showing that the emissions did not interfere with anyone else's use of their property. (D) is incorrect because particulate matter landing on the plaintiff's property would be necessary for establishing a trespass action but not a nuisance action. The interference may be substantial and unreasonable even though there was no physical invasion of the plaintiff's property

Answer to Question 4

(C) The craftsman will prevail because the delivery date was reasonable given the nature of the goods and the time for their sale. The key to forming a contract for the sale of goods is the quantity term. If other items are missing from the agreement, Article 2 has "gap filler" provisions to fill in the missing terms. Under these "gap filler" terms, if the time for delivery is not specified, delivery is due within a reasonable time. It is reasonable to take several months to hand-carve 25 wooden rocking horses; hence, the contract is enforceable. (A) is incorrect because, as discussed above, the mere lack of a specific delivery date is not fatal to a contract. (D) is incorrect because the language in choice (D) deals with acceptance of an offer for a unilateral contract. The facts of the question clearly state that the parties formed a bilateral contract with promises on both sides, so acceptance of the contract is not at issue. (B) is incorrect because it also does not match the facts given. When a party has reasonable grounds to believe that the other party will be unable or unwilling to perform, the innocent party may suspend his performance until he receives adequate assurances from the other party. But here the toy store owner did not request assurances, or even inquire at all about the progress of the horses; the facts state that he simply forgot about the contract. His action in ordering the plastic horses was not a deliberate act to mitigate his damages from not receiving the wooden horses. Had he actually inquired about the contract, presumably the craftsman could have informed him of his progress on making the horses and that he was able and willing to perform.

Answer to Question 5

(D) The defendant is guilty of larceny of the mower, but not the car. Larceny is the taking and carrying away of the personal property of another by trespass with the intent to permanently (or for an unreasonable time) deprive the other of his interest in the property. The intent to permanently deprive may be found when the defendant intends to use the property in such a manner as to create a substantial risk of loss. As to the mower, the defendant took and carried away the mower with the intent to permanently deprive his neighbor of it. The defendant's mistake as to the coverage of the criminal law does not negate his intent to commit the crime, and thus provides no mistake of law defense. Thus, (B) and (C) are incorrect. However, the defendant is not guilty of larceny of his neighbor's car because he did not have the intent to permanently deprive the neighbor of the car; rather, his intent was to borrow the car. Furthermore, merely driving a car does not constitute a use that creates a substantial risk of loss sufficient to find the intent to permanently deprive the neighbor of the car. As a result, (A) and (B) are incorrect.

Answer to Question 6

(D) The proprietor will not prevail because he will be deemed to have consented to the defamation. Consent is a complete defense to a defamation action. Apparent consent may be implied where a reasonable person would infer consent from the plaintiff's actions. Here, the proprietor can establish a prima facie case of defamation because the mayor, in the presence of council members, repeated allegations of illegal activity by the proprietor. (Keep in mind that a republisher of defamatory statements will be held liable to the same extent as the original publisher even if he states the source or states that he does not believe the defamation.) However, by demanding a response at the council meeting as to why his business license was not renewed, the proprietor impliedly consented to a statement of the basis for the decision, which the mayor provided. (A) is incorrect. While malice in the sense of ill will would have negated a qualified privilege at common law, it is irrelevant to a consent defense. (B) is incorrect. If the proprietor's alleged illegal activity is deemed to be a matter of public concern, most states would require him to show that the mayor made the statement negligently, which this choice addresses. However, the mayor can still raise the defense of consent. (C) is not as good a choice as (D) because the statement might qualify as slander per se. Spoken defamation requires pleading and proof of special damages unless the defamation falls into a slander per se category. Here, the allegation of illegal gambling at the proprietor's business may either qualify as a crime of moral turpitude or adversely reflect on how he conducts his business, obviating the need to show special damages as part of the prima facie case.

Answer to Question 7

(B) The grandson's interest in the farm is subject to involuntary transfer to satisfy the pedestrian's judgment. If a future interest can be transferred voluntarily by its owner, it is also subject to involuntary transfer; *i.e.*, it can be reached by the owner's creditors by appropriate process. At common law and in all jurisdictions today, all types of vested remainders are fully transferable during life. Here, the grandson has a vested remainder subject to open in the land. Because the grandson could assign this interest, his creditors may also reach it. (A) is incorrect because the doctrine of estoppel by deed is inapplicable here. Under the doctrine, the subsequent acquisition of title by a debtor who had no interest in the land automatically inures to the benefit of a creditor if the creditor properly recorded her judgment. Here, however, the grandson has an interest in the farm—a vested remainder subject to open. Although his possession is postponed until the daughter's death, his interest is a ***present*** interest, reachable by creditors. (C) is incorrect because the fact that the daughter may have more children, who would partially divest the grandson's interest, does not affect the ability of the grandson's creditors to reach his interest in the farm. (D) is incorrect because, although contingent remainders are not transferable inter vivos at common law and thus not subject to involuntary transfer, the grandson's interest in the farm, as discussed above, is vested rather than contingent.

Answer to Question 8

(D) The statement is admissible as substantive evidence and as impeachment evidence. For purposes of impeaching the credibility of a witness, a party may show that the witness has, on another occasion, made statements that are inconsistent with some material part of his present testimony. This can be done by cross-examination or extrinsic evidence. Extrinsic evidence of the witness's prior inconsistent statement ordinarily is admissible only if the witness is, at some point, given an opportunity to explain or deny the allegedly inconsistent statement. This foundation requirement may be dispensed with, however, where "the interests of justice otherwise require" (as where the witness has left the stand and is not available when his prior inconsistent statement is discovered). Here, the drug dealer's testimony is admissible to impeach his credibility because the interests of justice require it (*i.e.*, he could not be cross-examined at the current trial because he died). The drug dealer's testimony at the pretrial hearing also qualifies as substantive evidence because it is not barred by the hearsay rule. Hearsay is an out-of-court statement offered into evidence to prove the truth of the matter asserted. Here, the drug dealer's original out-of-court statement (that the drugs are not illegal) was admissible as nonhearsay at the pretrial hearing (offered just to show its effect on the hearer). Now the question is whether the testimony at the pretrial hearing is hearsay. That testimony may be considered hearsay because it is being offered for its truth, *i.e.*, that the dealer told the defendant that the drugs were legal. However, the former testimony exception to the hearsay rule applies. Under that exception, the testimony of a now unavailable witness given at another hearing or in a deposition taken in accordance with the law is admissible in a subsequent trial if there is sufficient similarity of parties and issues so that the opportunity to develop testimony or cross-examine at the prior hearing was meaningful. The exception applies here because the testimony was given under oath at another hearing of the same proceeding where there was a meaningful opportunity to cross-examine, and, because he died, the declarant is now unavailable to be cross-examined on his present testimony. Thus, the testimony is admissible as substantive and impeachment evidence. (A) is incorrect because, as stated above, the circumstances here permit the court to dispense with the cross-examination requirement. (B) is incorrect because, even though the statement may be hearsay, the statement is admissible under the former testimony exception to the hearsay rule. (C) is not as good a choice as (D) because the statement also is admissible as substantive evidence, as discussed above.

Answer to Question 9

(B) The court will reach the merits of the case because the vendor has standing. A person who challenges governmental action in federal court on constitutional grounds must have standing to raise the constitutional issue. A person has standing only if he can demonstrate a concrete stake in the outcome of a controversy and that the governmental action at issue impairs his own rights. A plaintiff may also assert third-party rights if he has suffered an injury and that injury adversely affects his relationships with third parties, resulting in an indirect violation of their rights. Here, enforcement of the ordinance will effectively destroy 60% of the vendor's business and cut down on the dissemination of his religious message. Thus, the vendor is faced with an immediate and direct threat of injury. This injury will also affect the vendor's relationship with those who purchase water from him on the sidewalk, because now he will be unable to sell them water with religious messages when they need it (physically, or, perhaps, metaphysically). (A) is incorrect. Although, as discussed above, the vendor has standing, the constitutional issue involved here is not the Privileges and Immunities Clause of Article IV. That Clause prohibits discrimination by a state against nonresidents that impacts a fundamental right, such as the conduct of commercial activities. Here, while the ordinance involves commercial activity, nothing in the ordinance treats nonresidents differently from residents. (C) is incorrect because the vendor does not have to be charged with violating the law to challenge its constitutionality. Nothing suggests that the law will not be enforced against him if he tries to continue selling his water; hence, he is faced with an immediate and direct threat of injury. (D) is incorrect because it goes to the merits and is a fact question that must be resolved at trial. The vendor will argue that the water ordinance impinges on his First Amendment freedoms of speech and religion. The city may defend such a claim by arguing that the water ordinance constitutes a reasonable time, place, and manner restriction on First Amendment activities. However, such an argument would not be a reason for declining jurisdiction; rather, it is a fact issue that must be determined at trial.

Answer to Question 10

(D) The civil attorney is correct. The Supreme Court has ruled that a defendant's guilty plea neither admits the legality of the incriminating search nor waives Fourth Amendment claims in a subsequent civil damages action challenging the constitutionality of the incriminating search. [Haring v. Prosise (1983)] Therefore, although the drug dealer pled guilty, he may still bring civil claims challenging the constitutionality of the search performed by police officers. (A) is incorrect. If the guilty plea was not voluntary, the plea itself would be invalid, but it would have no bearing on the drug dealer's ability to bring a civil claim for Fourth Amendment violations. (B) is incorrect because a guilty plea is not binding if it is not voluntary. However, as expressed above, the voluntariness of the plea has no bearing on the drug dealer's ability to bring a civil claim for Fourth Amendment violations. (C) is incorrect because it is irrelevant. A plea may be valid even though a defendant protests his innocence, as long as the plea was made voluntarily and intelligently. The defendant can bring a civil action regardless of whether he protested his innocence in court.

Answer to Question 11

(A) The entire $60,000 proceeds should be distributed to the sister, and only the sister must sign the deed conveying the land to the buyer. A joint tenancy is a concurrent estate in land in which each co-tenant has an undivided right in the property and a right of survivorship—when one joint tenant dies, the property is freed of his concurrent interest and the survivor retains an undivided right in the property that is no longer subject to the interest of the deceased co-tenant. If one joint tenant conveys his interest, the joint tenancy is severed. The new tenant holds as a tenant in common with the remaining joint tenant, so that there is no longer a right of survivorship. In states following the common law view, an executory contract to sell entered into by ***all*** joint tenants does ***not*** sever the joint tenancy. The joint tenancy continues in both the right to the proceeds and the retained legal title. Other jurisdictions proceed on the doctrine of equitable conversion and hold that the executory contract converts the joint tenants' ownership rights to a mere contract right to receive the purchase price (which they hold as tenants in common because of the statutory presumption favoring such tenancies). The legal title to the land, retained for security purposes, is also held to be in tenancy in common. Here, the brother and the sister contracted to sell the parcel of land "as joint tenants with right of survivorship and not as tenants in common." Because the jurisdiction follows the common law, the joint tenancy continued, and on the brother's death the sister's right to the proceeds and legal title were freed of his interest. Note that even if the jurisdiction followed the doctrine of equitable conversion, the sister would argue that the contract language "as joint tenants with right of survivorship and not as tenants in common" rebuts the presumption favoring tenancies in common. Thus, the sister is entitled to the entire $60,000 proceeds and only her signature is required to convey title to the buyer. (B), (C), and (D) are incorrect because the brother's wife has no interest in the proceeds or title; the brother's interest evaporated on the brother's death.

Answer to Question 12

(D) The casino owner cannot collect from the gambler. There was a valid accord and satisfaction, discharging the gambler's obligations under the contract. An accord is the agreement under which one party agrees to accept some other, different performance from the other party than he would have received under the existing contract. An accord, like other contracts, must be supported by consideration. The casino owner's willingness to take a ***lesser amount*** in exchange for an ***earlier repayment*** of a mutually agreed upon amount, is sufficient as mutual consideration. Payment of a smaller sum than due is sufficient consideration for a promise by a creditor to discharge a debt because the consideration was ***different*** (*e.g.,* immediate payment before the last payment was due). Thus, there was consideration supporting the accord. The satisfaction of the accord occurred on the payment of the $15,000 cash. Satisfaction discharges both the accord and the original contract. (A) is incorrect because, while it is true that the gambler had a preexisting legal duty to pay $50,000, the slight change in the consideration is an exception to the rule that a preexisting legal duty cannot constitute valid consideration. (B) is incorrect because the casino owner's decision to take less than the full amount of the debt because of a cash flow problem does not rise to the level of duress. Duress is typically not found where one party merely takes economic advantage of the other's pressing need to enter into a contract. (C) is incorrect because a discharge by release is an agreement to release a party from liability; in other words, it is a contract not to sue. Here the parties were seeking to change the terms of their agreement. They were not attempting to release either party from the contract or agreeing not to sue.

Answer to Question 13

(B) The manufacturer's ability to eliminate the risk of failure is not at issue in the patient's malpractice action against the surgeon. The patient is suing the surgeon for negligence, which requires a showing of (i) duty, (ii) breach of duty, (iii) actual and proximate causation, and (iv) damages. A physician proposing a course of treatment or a surgical procedure has a duty to provide the patient with enough information about its risks to enable the patient to make an informed consent. Question (A) is at issue because, if an undisclosed risk was serious enough that a reasonable person in the patient's position would have withheld consent to the treatment, the doctor has breached this duty. The question in (D) is at issue for establishing actual cause. If the patient can establish that, but for the surgeon's failure to disclose, he would have refused consent, he can establish actual causation. The question in (C) is at issue in establishing the element of damages. Even though the facts state that the additional surgery repaired the damage from the device breaking, the patient still suffered damage from having to undergo an additional surgery. Whether he fully recovered from the surgery impacts the amount of damages he can recover. (B) is the correct choice because it is not relevant to the action against the surgeon. Whether the manufacturer could have eliminated the risk of failure may be at issue in a product liability action against the manufacturer, but is not at issue in the malpractice action against the surgeon. There is nothing to suggest that the surgeon had any influence over the manufacturing process or that she had an option to select a medical device from a different manufacturer.

Answer to Question 14

(A) The bank's mortgage lien is prior to the seller's mortgage lien because the bank recorded its interest. This jurisdiction has a race-notice statute, under which a subsequent bona fide purchaser (*i.e.*, a person, including a mortgagee, who gives valuable consideration and has no notice of the prior instrument) prevails over a prior grantee only if he records before the prior grantee. Here, the seller did not record his interest before the bank recorded its interest. Thus, the bank prevails. (B) is incorrect because the fact that the bank's interest is a purchase money mortgage does not establish the bank's priority. A purchase money mortgage, given when the mortgagor buys the property, is considered to have priority over non-purchase money mortgages executed at about the same time, even if the other mortgages are recorded first. As between two purchase money mortgages, the priority rules are designed for the typical situation where each mortgagee knows of the other's interest and the recording statute does not come into play. Here, the seller's interest is also a purchase money mortgage, and neither mortgagee had notice of the other. Thus, the recording statute would apply and provide the bank with priority. (C) is incorrect because the seller is not protected by the jurisdiction's recording act due to his failure to record first. However, (C) would be the correct answer in a notice jurisdiction, where a subsequent bona fide purchaser prevails over a prior grantee regardless of whether he records at all. Notice is measured ***at the time of conveyance***. Thus, the fact that the bank recorded one day before the seller does not put the seller on record notice because the seller did not have such notice at the time his mortgage was executed. (D) is incorrect because, even if the purchase money priority rules were applicable, the seller's interest would have priority because it was a purchase money mortgage given to the vendor of the property and the other purchase money mortgage was given to a third-party lender, the bank. In any case, as discussed above, the recording statute is applicable here and provides the bank with priority.

Answer to Question 15

(A) The court should rule for the city. A permanent display on a government building constitutes government speech, even if the display was originally donated by a private entity. The government generally is free to choose which messages it will and will not convey, absent some other constitutional proscription. (B) is incorrect. Just because a message may have had origins in a religion does not prevent the government from adopting the message. Otherwise, the government might not be able to urge concepts against stealing and killing, because those concepts can be said to have originated in religion. (C) is incorrect for the reasons stated with regard to (B). Moreover, because the display on the municipal building is varied, it does not run afoul of Establishment Clause prohibitions. [*See, e.g.,* Van Orden v. Perry (2005)—upholding display of the Ten Commandments along with 17 other monuments and 21 other historical markers on state capitol grounds] (D) is incorrect because it applies the standard that is applicable to government regulation of private speech; that standard is not applicable to government speech.

Answer to Question 16

(C) The court should deny the motion because the thief had no standing to object to the search. A person challenging the admissibility of seized evidence must have standing to do so. As a general rule, standing requires a person to have a reasonable expectation of privacy in the place being searched or the item being seized. One may not challenge a search or seizure by claiming that another person's constitutional rights have been violated. Here, the thief had no ownership interest in the dealer's store. He had no legitimate expectation of privacy with respect to it; *i.e.*, he was not present when the search was made, and he had no ownership interest in the stolen goods. Thus, he lacks the standing to object to their illegal seizure. (A) and (B) are incorrect because, while the dealer does have such standing and was successful in having the evidence suppressed at his trial, what occurred at the dealer's trial is not relevant to the thief's motion. (D) is incorrect because the only evidence containing the thief's fingerprints were the stolen goods. If it is found that these items were illegally seized, it would follow that the evidence arising out of this illegal seizure, including the thief's fingerprints, was also illegally seized.

Answer to Question 17

(B) The store will prevail in its action. The rule under Article 2 of the U.C.C. is that a seller must deliver goods to an insolvent buyer if the buyer tenders cash for their payment. Because the store owner told the supplier that he would pay cash for the clocks on delivery, the supplier was bound to deliver the clocks to the store, and the seller's failure to do so was a breach of contract. (A) is wrong because a seller may stop delivery of goods even if they are in the possession of a carrier or other bailee when he discovers that the buyer is insolvent. (C) is wrong because, while the seller would have the right to stop delivery of the clocks due to the store's insolvency had the store not tendered cash for their payment, the store owner did do so here. (D) is wrong because the store did not demonstrate a prospective inability to perform by virtue of its insolvency status, because the store owner had the money to pay for the clocks and told the supplier that he would, in fact, pay cash for them on delivery. A prospective failure to perform involves conduct or words that raise doubts that the party will perform. Here, the store owner's words indicate that he ***would*** perform when the time comes.

Answer to Question 18

(B) The evidence is admissible for impeachment purposes as the prior inconsistent statement of a hearsay declarant. Statements made by hearsay declarants can be impeached to the same extent as those of an in-court witness; thus, a statement of the declarant made at any time that is inconsistent with his hearsay statement may be offered into evidence for impeachment purposes. Here, the eyewitness's subsequent statement is inconsistent with his hearsay statement and is therefore admissible to discredit that prior statement. (A) is incorrect. Generally, the former testimony of an unavailable declarant can be admitted into evidence, even if it contains hearsay, if it was given during another hearing or deposition. Here, the statement was not made during another hearing or in a deposition. Thus, it does not qualify as former testimony. (C) is incorrect. Generally, a prior inconsistent statement is admissible only if the witness is given the opportunity to explain or deny the statement. However, this rule does not apply to hearsay declarants. Hearsay statements are often admissible at trial after the declarant has died or is otherwise unavailable, and the declarant need not be given an opportunity to explain or deny statements that are inconsistent with his hearsay statement. (D) is incorrect because the statement is not being offered as substantive evidence to prove the truth of the matter asserted. Rather, it is being offered for purposes of impeachment and is therefore admissible.

Answer to Question 19

(A) If the court rules for the landowner, it will be because the fisherman's right to hunt and fish on the western parcel is a profit appurtenant. A profit is a nonpossessory interest in land that entitles the holder of the profit to enter on the servient tenement and take the soil or a substance of the soil (*e.g.*, minerals, timber, oil, or game). Like an easement, a profit may be appurtenant or in gross. If the profit exists to serve a dominant estate, the profit is appurtenant and can only be transferred along with the dominant estate. Conversely, if the profit does not exist to serve a dominant estate, it is a profit in gross and may be transferred separate and apart from the dominant estate. Here, the fisherman has a profit with respect to the game on the western parcel. Because the profit is "for the benefit of the campground" on the eastern parcel, it is appurtenant rather than in gross because it serves the dominant estate (the eastern parcel). Thus, the fisherman's assignment of the profit to the hunter is void. (B) is incorrect because it supports the ***hunter's*** rather than the landowner's claim. As discussed above, if the profit were in gross, it could have been transferred to the hunter. (C) is incorrect because the fisherman has a profit rather than an easement. Like a profit, an easement is a nonpossessory interest in land. However, the holder of an easement only has the right to ***use*** the servient land and not to remove the soil or products of the soil therefrom (including game). (D) is incorrect because, as explained above, the fisherman's interest ***is*** alienable, whereas a license is personal to the licensee and therefore not alienable. The problem here is that the fisherman did not transfer the dominant parcel with the profit, and thus the attempted transfer of the profit appurtenant alone is void.

Answer to Question 20

(B) The company's strongest argument is that the state's application of the tax to all of its manufacturing plants violates the Commerce Clause. States may impose "doing business" taxes, such as a gross receipts tax, on companies engaged in interstate commerce as long as the tax does not discriminate against or unfairly burden interstate commerce. A tax will impose an unfair burden unless (i) the activity taxed has a substantial nexus to the taxing state, (ii) the tax is fairly apportioned, and (iii) the tax fairly relates to the services provided by the state. Here, the fact that the tax applies to revenue derived from the company's plants located in other states strongly suggests that it imposes an unfair burden, because those plants may be potentially subject to a similar tax in those states, and the relationship between the tax and services provided by the state in which the company is located is very tenuous with regard to the out-of-state plants. (A) is not as strong an argument because the tax is not levied directly against federal government property. Nondiscriminatory, indirect taxes levied by a state on the federal government or its property are permissible if they do not unreasonably burden the federal government. Here, the tax is not even on the products purchased by the federal government, but only on the company doing business with it. The fact that the costs of the tax may be passed on to the government through the price of the products does not impose an unreasonable burden. (C) is wrong because the use tax is a different type of tax than the gross receipts tax, and does not appear to be invalid. A use tax on users of goods purchased out of state is permissible as long as it is nondiscriminatory and otherwise does not unfairly burden interstate commerce. Although a use tax is directed at goods passing through interstate commerce, it is permissible if the use tax burden on the goods purchased out of state is equivalent to the sales tax burden on goods purchased within the state, as suggested by choice (C). (D) is wrong because the fact that sales taxes are imposed on the company's products in other states does not by itself suggest the invalidity of the state's gross receipts tax, which is a different type of tax that is not being imposed directly on the transactions that other states are taxing. Hence, the argument that it constitutes an unfair burden on interstate commerce is not as strong.

Answer to Question 21

(C) Both the neighbor's testimony regarding the defendant's reputation for being law-abiding and his opinion that the defendant would not be involved with drugs should be admitted. The accused in a criminal case may introduce evidence of her good character to show her innocence of the alleged crime. However, when a defendant puts her character in issue by calling a qualified witness to testify her good character, the testimony must relate to the trait involved in the case, and is limited to reputation or personal opinion testimony. Here, the defendant is on trial for a drug charge and is claiming that the drugs were not hers, thereby putting at issue both her character trait for obeying the law and her disposition towards drug involvement. Because the neighbor's testimony was limited to reputation and opinion evidence and did not mention specific acts, such character evidence is admissible. (A) and (D) are incorrect because the opinion evidence is admissible. (B) and (D) are incorrect because the reputation evidence is admissible.

Answer to Question 22

(A) The court should award the mechanic the $1,500 because the woman's promise to pay him that amount is in writing. A promise to pay a legal obligation barred by law, in this case, by the statute of limitations, is enforceable. If a past obligation, such as a debt, would be enforceable except for the fact that a technical defense to enforcement stands in the way (*e.g.,* statute of limitations), the courts will enforce a new promise if it is in writing ***or*** there has been part performance. Here, the promise is in writing, so it can be enforced. (B) is incorrect because the woman's preexisting legal duty to pay the mechanic terminated when the statute of limitations ran out. (C) is incorrect because the mechanic can enforce this agreement without further consideration on the woman's part. (D) is incorrect because, as stated above, the promise can be enforced because it is in writing, even though there has been no part performance.

Answer to Question 23

(B) The robber is guilty of felony murder of the store owner only. This choice represents an exception to the general rule that almost any death occurring in the course of a felony is felony murder. In the majority of jurisdictions, the robber would not be held guilty of felony murder for a justifiable killing of a co-felon by a police officer. The *Redline* view (the majority position) holds that the killing of a felon by a police officer to prevent the felon's crime or escape cannot be the basis for felony murder. Thus, (A) and (C) are incorrect. (C) and (D) are incorrect because a person has no right of self-defense when he is the aggressor, and especially if he is engaged in a felony. The store owner, who was the victim of this felony, had the right to use at least the threat of force against the robber. Because the death occurred in the course of the felony, and the robber had no right of self-defense, he is guilty of felony murder, as well as deliberate premeditated murder.

Answer to Question 24

(C) The son's child and the daughter's husband each own an undivided one-half interest in the land. At common law, if a will beneficiary died before the testator, the gift to the beneficiary was void. However, this jurisdiction has an anti-lapse statute, which saves the gift for the predeceasing beneficiary's descendants if the beneficiary himself is a descendant of the testator. Here, when the son died, his one-half interest in the land passed to his child under the anti-lapse statute. When the daughter died, her one-half interest in the land, which she was entitled to upon the father's death when his will took effect, passed through her estate (not the anti-lapse statute) to her husband. Moreover, a conveyance to two or more persons is presumed to create a tenancy in common rather than a joint tenancy unless an intention to create a right of survivorship is clearly expressed. Each co-tenant has the right to possess all portions of the property; no co-tenant has the right to exclusive possession of any part. Therefore, the son's child and the daughter's husband each own an undivided one-half interest in the land as tenants in common. (A) and (B) are wrong because neither the child nor the husband owns all of the land in fee simple. (D) is wrong because the child and the husband each own an ***undivided*** one-half interest, which is a one-half interest as to the entire tract, as opposed to one-half of the land, which would be ***all*** interest in a one-half part of the tract.

Answer to Question 25

(B) Only the tenant may bring a trespass action against the neighbor. Trespass to land is an interference with the right of possession of the land. It requires (i) an act of physical invasion of the plaintiff's real property by the defendant, (ii) intent on the defendant's part to bring about the physical invasion, and (iii) causation. Here, the tenant can allege that the neighbor knowingly blew all of the snow from his driveway onto the tenant's driveway, causing an invasion of the tenant's possession of her property. (A) and (D) are incorrect because an action for trespass may be maintained by anyone in actual or constructive possession of the land, even if that possession is without title or legal right. One who is not in possession, however, generally has no right to sue for trespass, and the landlord would not have a right to sue here because the tenant is in actual possession of the land. While some modern cases allow a landlord to bring a damages action against a trespasser for injury to the landlord's interest (*i.e.*, for any permanent damage to the property), there was no such injury in this case. Hence, the landlord is not entitled to sue for trespass because he has suffered no interference with his right to possession. (C) is incorrect because trespass is an interference with possession of the land rather than use and enjoyment (which would be the basis of a nuisance action). The tenant could bring a trespass action even if the snow blown onto the property did not interfere with her use of the driveway.

Answer to Question 26

(A) The court should find that the statements are admissible. The privilege for confidential marital communications provides that a party has a privilege to refuse to disclose, and to prevent another from disclosing, confidential communications made between spouses during the marriage.

However, the privilege does not apply in actions between the spouses. Because this is an action between the spouses, the privilege does not apply and the testimony is admissible. Thus, (A) is correct and (D) is incorrect. (C) is incorrect. The plaintiff would have to be cross-examined as to any potential bias or motive to lie; the mere possibility of such a motive does not automatically preclude his testimony. (D) is incorrect because the privilege survives divorce. Here, the statements were made during the marriage and the privilege would apply even though the parties are now divorced.

Answer to Question 27

(D) The woman will prevail in her breach of contract suit because she began performing before the store manager canceled the contest, making the offer irrevocable as to her. A unilateral contract is one in which the offer requests performance rather than a promise to perform, and under the First and Second Restatements, as well as the U.C.C., once performance has begun the offer cannot be revoked as to that performer. Here, the woman began performing when she purchased the deep freezer and began buying much larger than normal quantities of food with the intent of winning the contest. At that point in time, the offer became irrevocable as to her. (A) is incorrect because, even though the offer could be revoked as to others who had not yet begun to perform, and revocation in the same manner as the offer is generally effective, as stated above, the offer was irrevocable as to the woman because she had begun performing. (B) is incorrect because, as discussed above, the attempted revocation was ineffective as to the woman, so she is entitled to continue her performance even though she was aware of the revocation notice. (C) is incorrect because this is a breach of contract action. Detrimental reliance is an element of a promissory estoppel remedy that is sought when there is a defect in the formation of a contract. She could enforce the contract even if she had not purchased the freezer, because she had begun making substantially larger purchases before the attempted revocation; conversely, if all she had done was purchase the freezer and had not yet made any credit card purchases before the revocation, she could only rely on a promissory estoppel theory.

Answer to Question 28

(B) The court should grant the injunction because the restriction is an enforceable reasonable partial restraint on alienation. Because condominium unit ownership is treated as fee ownership, the ordinary rules against restraints on alienation apply. A partial restraint is one that purports to restrict the power to transfer to specific persons, by a specific method, or until a specific time. Such restraints, if for a reasonable purpose, are likely to be upheld. Here, the restriction is a partial restraint because an owner is prohibited from transferring an interest by a lease agreement to a tenant. Moreover, the purpose of the restriction is to foster an owner-occupied environment in the redevelopment area, which is reasonable. Thus, the restraint is enforceable. (A) is incorrect because it is too broad. Although reasonable restraints may be imposed on the transfer of a condominium unit, total restraints and discriminatory restraints are unenforceable, even if agreed to by the parties. (C) is incorrect because the restriction is not a total restraint on alienation. Nothing prohibits the owner from selling or otherwise conveying fee simple ownership of the unit to the friend. He is merely prohibited from leasing it. (D) is incorrect because the restriction does not violate the Fair Housing Act. The Fair Housing Act prohibits discrimination in the sale or rental of housing on grounds of race, ethnic origin, religion, sex, family status, or disability. Here, there is no such discrimination.

Answer to Question 29

(C) The senator will not succeed because she lacks standing to challenge the veto. The Supreme Court has held that members of Congress lack standing to challenge a law authorizing the President to exercise a line item veto, reasoning that the injury is not concrete and personal, but rather is institutional in that it is shared by all members of Congress. The same rationale likely would apply to the senator's challenge here. (A) is incorrect even though it is a true statement. The Supreme Court has ruled that the President has no power to exercise a line item veto because it violates the Presentation Clause of the United States Constitution. However, (A) is not the best choice here because the senator is not a proper person to bring the challenge. (B) is incorrect. Although Congress may override a President's veto with a two-thirds vote of each house, the override may not be done prospectively; it must take place after the veto. (D) is incorrect because, while it is true that the President exercised his veto power within a proper time frame, the veto here was improper because, as explained above, it was of only part of the bill. The reason the senator will fail is that she lacks standing to challenge the veto.

Answer to Question 30

(D) The charity will not prevail in a suit to impose a constructive trust on the land because the buyer is a bona fide purchaser. A deed is voidable if it is executed by a minor or incapacitated person or is obtained through fraud in the inducement, duress, undue influence, mistake, or breach of fiduciary duty. Undue influence exists where (i) influence is exerted on the grantor, (ii) the effect of the influence is to overpower the mind and free will of the grantor, and (iii) the product of the influence is a deed that would not have been executed but for the influence. A voidable deed will be set aside only if the property has not passed to a bona fide purchaser (*i.e.*, a purchaser who pays valuable consideration and takes without notice). Here, although the nephew's acts may not have risen to the level of duress, they likely constitute undue influence. His threat of cessation of care caused the aunt to convey the land to him, when her desire was to devise the land to a charity. Thus, the deed is voidable. However, because the buyer paid market value for the land without notice of the circumstances surrounding the aunt-nephew deed, the deed will not be set aside. (A) is incorrect because consideration is not required in order to make a deed valid. (B) is incorrect because the deed was voidable rather than void. Deeds considered void include those that are forged, were never delivered, or were obtained by fraud in the factum; none of those apply here. (C) is incorrect because, although specifically devised property that is no longer in the testator's estate at her death is adeemed, the charity would have prevailed in its suit to impose a constructive trust on the land if it had not been conveyed to a bona fide purchaser. A constructive trust is an equitable remedy imposed by a court to prevent an unjust enrichment of one person at the expense of another as the result of wrongful conduct, such as fraud, undue influence, or breach of fiduciary duty. Here, the nephew would have been unjustly enriched if he were allowed to retain title to land he acquired through undue influence. However, this remedy was "cut off" by the nephew's conveyance to the buyer, a bona fide purchaser.

Answer to Question 31

(B) The defendant may compel the plaintiff to introduce the remainder of the record. When part of an act, conversation, or writing is introduced into evidence, the Federal Rules provide that the adverse party may compel the proponent of the evidence to introduce any part thereof that ought, in fairness, to be considered contemporaneously with it. Here, the remainder of the shipping record that supports the defendant's position should be introduced at the same time as the part introduced by the plaintiff. (A) is incorrect because no foundation need be laid for another part of a record that has already been introduced. (C) is incorrect because Federal Rule 106 does not require proof of relevance. The standard is fairness. In any case, the remainder of the record appears to be relevant to the defendant's claim. (D) is incorrect because, although it is hearsay, a shipping record from a freight company very likely falls within the business records exception to the hearsay rule.

Answer to Question 32

(D) The customer is not likely to prevail because the barber had no opportunity to oversee the contractor's work. A property owner owes a duty to those adjacent to the premises to take due precautions to protect them from dangerous conditions, and owes invitees on the premises a duty to make reasonable inspections to discover and make safe any dangerous conditions. Further, that duty cannot be delegated to an independent contractor; the owner remains vicariously liable. However, nothing in the facts establishes that the barber breached his duty to the customer. There was nothing wrong with the brackets evident from a reasonable inspection, and the awning collapsed without warning. Further, the barber was not involved in hiring or supervising the contractor and would not be responsible for the contractor's negligence. Hence, because no facts point to negligence by the barber, the customer is not likely to prevail. (A) is incorrect even though it is true that a business owner would be vicariously liable to customers and passersby injured by the negligent work of an independent contractor that he hired. Here, however, the barber did not engage the contractor and is not responsible for the contractor's conduct. (B) is similarly incorrect. While the developer arguably was negligent in hiring a contractor who does shoddy work, her negligence will not be imputed to the barber. (C) is incorrect because it is irrelevant. Had the barber hired the contractor, the fact that the contractor contractually assumed all of the risks of liability would not preclude the customer from recovering against the barber.

Answer to Question 33

(C) The documents will be admitted. The privilege against self-incrimination bars the government from procuring ***compelled testimony***. Here, the act of producing the documents does not involve testimonial self-incrimination. Documents are considered to be real or physical evidence, not testimonial evidence, and thus are outside the scope of the privilege. Thus, (A) is incorrect. (B) is irrelevant because the documents are beyond the scope of the privilege, regardless of who owns them. (D) is incorrect because it is irrelevant. Records required by statute that have a lawful administrative purpose are not protected by the Fifth Amendment.

Answer to Question 34

(B) The club member should prevail, because the yachtsman knew that he had two "Lady" boats and the club member did not. This is a case of ambiguous contract language, because the expression of the parties' agreement (here, to purchase the yachtsman's "Lady" boat) is open to two different interpretations. In cases where one party is aware of the ambiguity and the other party is not at the time of contracting, a contract will be enforced according to the intent of the party who was unaware of the ambiguity. In this case, the yachtsman owned two boats, each with the word "Lady" in its name, but he intended to sell the boat known as "Lady Luck." The club member, on the other hand, intended to buy the boat known as "Lady Be Good" and was unaware that the yachtsman owned a second boat called "Lady Luck." The club member did not know that an ambiguity existed at the time the contract was formed, while the yachtsman, of course, knew that he owned two boats with the word "Lady" in its name, and thus knew of the ambiguity. Therefore, the contract will be enforced in accordance with the club member's intention to purchase "Lady Be Good," because he was the party who was unaware of the ambiguity. Hence, (A) is incorrect because it is an incorrect statement of the law, which is correctly stated above. (C) is incorrect because an ambiguity alone does not void a contract; there are different rules as to whether a contract containing an ambiguity is or is not voided. It depends on who knew of the ambiguity at the time the contract was formed. If neither party, or if both parties, are aware of the ambiguity, no contract would be formed unless both parties intended the same meaning. Here, because one party knew of the ambiguity and the other did not, the contract is still enforceable. (D) is incorrect because "Lady Be Good" is a rare or unique item, having been owned by the club member's favorite celebrity. When an item is rare or unique, money damages are inadequate. Specific performance is the proper remedy.

Answer to Question 35

(A) The farmer is not likely to prevail because the rational relationship test applies. Although the right to vote is a fundamental right, laws prohibiting nonresidents from voting are generally valid, provided that they meet the minimal scrutiny, or "rational basis," standard. Under this standard, a law will be upheld as long as it is rationally related to a legitimate government interest. Limiting the voters in a city's mayoral election to residents of the city serves the interests of efficiency and prevents persons with little personal interest in the city from voting. Thus, a court would likely uphold the ordinance. (B) is incorrect because it sets out the strict scrutiny standard. While voting is a fundamental right and governmental action affecting fundamental rights generally is reviewed under strict scrutiny, that is not the case with laws limiting voting to residents. (C) is incorrect. The Privileges or Immunities Clause of the Fourteenth Amendment prohibits a state from denying its citizens certain privileges or immunities of national citizenship. The voting restriction here does not affect any national right, except, perhaps, the right to travel. Even if that right is impacted here, as discussed above, the Supreme Court has approved limiting the right to vote to residents. (D) is incorrect. While "no taxation without representation" was a rallying cry for the war of independence, it is broader than the constitutional doctrines applicable here.

Answer to Question 36

(C) The court should not admit the deposition testimony. The driver's statement is hearsay because it is being offered to prove the truth of the matter asserted—that the defendant's car crossed lanes and struck her car. Because it is hearsay, the statement is admissible only if it falls within an exception to the hearsay rule. Here, there are no exceptions under which to admit the deposition transcript. (A) and (B) are incorrect because the former testimony exception to the hearsay rule does not apply. This exception allows the prior statement of a declarant to be admitted into evidence if the statement was made under oath at a prior deposition or proceeding. There must be a sufficient similarity of parties and issues. The exception applies, however, only if the declarant is unavailable to testify. For the absent driver to be "unavailable" here as defined by the Federal Rules, the passenger must show that he has been unable to procure her attendance or testimony by process or other reasonable means, and here no attempt was made to procure her attendance. As such, the deposition transcript is inadmissible under this exception and the driver should be subpoenaed to testify on behalf of the plaintiff. (D) is incorrect because the driver and the passenger need not be co-parties. There was a sufficient similarity of parties and issues because both lawsuits were against the same defendant and arose from the same car accident. Hence, if the driver were unavailable, the former testimony exception likely would apply.

Answer to Question 37

(B) The tenant will prevail because a full month's notice is required. In this case, there was no written lease outlining the terms of the tenancy, but only an oral agreement regarding the payment of monthly rent. That led to the creation of a periodic—here, a monthly—tenancy. The termination date of a periodic tenancy is uncertain, until notice of termination is given. For a tenancy that is less than a year in duration, such as this, notice must be given a full period in advance of the termination. Although the landlord gave notice, because the lease was monthly, the landlord was required to provide a full month's notice of termination. (A) is incorrect because six months' notice would be required for a tenancy from year to year, but this tenancy was a month-to-month tenancy. (C) is incorrect. A tenancy at will arises from an agreement between the parties that either party may terminate the tenancy at any time. However, in the absence of a specific agreement to create a tenancy at will, regular rent payments will lead to the tenancy being treated as a periodic tenancy. (D) is incorrect. Tenancies at sufferance arise from a tenant wrongfully holding over after the termination of a tenancy. It is true that no notice is necessary in order to terminate such a tenancy. Nothing in the facts presented, however, allows the conclusion that the tenant was wrongfully holding over when the landlord gave notice.

Answer to Question 38

(C) The hiker is not liable for trespass. A defendant is not liable for an otherwise tortious act if the plaintiff has been deemed to consent. Consent may be implied by law where action is necessary to save an important interest in person or property, such as in an emergency situation where the plaintiff is not in a position to consent but a reasonable person would conclude that consent would be given. Here, consent will be implied by law for the hiker's trespass because it was reasonable to conclude that the landowner would have consented to having the fire put out. (D) is incorrect because the hiker does not have to pay for fixing the barbed wire fence because her privilege to enter onto the property is not qualified. Under the privilege of necessity, a person may interfere with the property of another where the interference is reasonably and apparently necessary to avoid threatened injury from a natural or other force and where the threatened injury is substantially more serious than the invasion that is undertaken to avert it. A trespass to benefit the person or property of the trespasser or a third person has only a qualified privilege under the private necessity doctrine, so that the trespasser must pay for any injury she causes. However, the privilege is absolute when the trespass is undertaken for the benefit of the person or property of the landowner, as was the case here. (A) is incorrect both because the hiker is not liable for trespass and because trespass does not require damage to the property—absent the hiker's defense, she would be liable for trespass even if she had not damaged the fence. (B) is incorrect because the landowner's right to protect his property is superseded by the hiker's right to enter the property to put out the fire.

Answer to Question 39

(A) The most the wigmaker can recover is $1,980, the contract price of $2,000 minus the resale price of $20. When a buyer breaches the contract by refusing to accept the goods, the seller's basic damages are either the difference between the contract price and the market price or the difference between the contract price and the resale price of the particular goods, plus incidental damages, if any. (B) is incorrect because it represents a lost profits measure of damages. Here, the seller is not a lost volume seller and can recover the higher amount based on the difference between contract and resale price. (C) is incorrect because it is reducing the wigmaker's recovery both by his cost to create the wig, which reduces recovery only in damages based on lost profit, and by the resale price, which reduces recovery only in the standard measure of damages. (D) is incorrect because the wigmaker can recover more than just his costs minus the resale price. Because the woman breached the contract, the wigmaker can recover his expectation damages, which will put him in the position he would have been in had the contract been performed.

Answer to Question 40

(D) The court should rule for the government. A government employee may be punished for speech that is made pursuant to his official duties, even if the speech touches on a matter of public concern. [*See* Garcetti v. Ceballos (2009)—no First Amendment protection for speech of government employees on the job and within the scope of their duties] Here, although the possible innocence of the defendant is certainly a matter of public concern, the speech here occurred while the prosecutor was performing official duties (*i.e.*, attending a hearing). Thus, (D) is correct and (A) is incorrect. (B) is incorrect both because the result is wrong and because no weighing is needed. (B) states the test that is used for comments made by employees regarding matters of public concern and not made as part of the employee's official duties. Therefore, it is inapplicable here. (C) is incorrect because it is overbroad. Deference is granted to a government employer only if the speech is made while the employee is performing official duties or, if the speech does not involve official duties, is not addressing a matter of public concern.

Answer to Question 41

(C) In a common law jurisdiction, the defendant is guilty of larceny, but not burglary. At common law, larceny is the taking and carrying away of the tangible personal property of another by trespass with the intent to permanently (or for an unreasonable time) deprive the other of the property. Larceny is a trespass against ***possession***, not ownership, and therefore, in most jurisdictions, a defendant can be convicted of larceny even when he takes property from someone who only has possession of that property because of some wrongful act. Thus, the defendant is guilty of larceny when he took the stolen pistol from his friend's house, and (B) and (D) are incorrect. However, the defendant would not be guilty of burglary. At common law, burglary is the breaking and entering of the dwelling of another at nighttime with the intent of committing a felony therein. In the instant case, the defendant did not enter the house with the intent to steal the pistol. Furthermore, a breaking requires a trespass. If the defendant has consent to enter, his use of force to gain entry is not a breaking. Thus, although opening a shut door may be enough to constitute a breaking, it would not be a breaking under these facts, because the defendant presumably had consent to enter to retrieve his coat. Therefore, (A) and (B) are incorrect.

Answer to Question 42

(D) The court should rule that the statement is inadmissible hearsay. Hearsay is an out-of-court statement offered to prove the truth of the matter asserted, and is inadmissible unless it falls within an exception to the hearsay rule. Hearsay within hearsay refers to an out-of-court statement that contains other hearsay, and is admissible only if both the outer hearsay and the inner hearsay fall within an exception to the hearsay rule. Here, the hospital record itself is hearsay, and the plaintiff's statement contained within the record is also hearsay. Therefore, both the record and the statement contained within the record must fall within an exception to the hearsay rule to be admissible. Neither the hospital record nor the statement within it falls within any exception to the hearsay rule; hence, the record is inadmissible. (A) is incorrect because a hospital record can qualify as a business record only to the extent that it is related to the medical diagnosis or treatment of a plaintiff. Here, the statement that the defendant did not stop at the red light is not related to the plaintiff's treatment, and is therefore inadmissible under the business records exception. (B) is incorrect. Prior declarations of a witness on the stand may be hearsay because they were not subject to contemporaneous cross-examination. Here, the plaintiff's statement in the hospital record was not subject to cross-examination, and the plaintiff is offering that statement as evidence rather than testifying at trial as to what happened. (C) is incorrect because it only addresses one of the hearsay issues. The testimony would still be inadmissible hearsay if the physician testified because the physician would be testifying as to the plaintiff's statement, which does not fall within any exception to the hearsay rule.

Answer to Question 43

(B) The evidence may be used against the estate to show that both the mother and the son were contributorily negligent. In a wrongful death action, recovery is allowed only to the extent that the deceased could have recovered in the action had she lived. Had the mother lived, her recovery likely would have been barred or reduced because of her contributory negligence. The estate's recovery of damages will be similarly impacted. (A) is incorrect because the evidence also may be used against the estate to show that the son was contributorily negligent. While defenses against potential beneficiaries did not bar a wrongful death action under traditional rules, a contributorily negligent beneficiary would recover nothing. In most comparative negligence jurisdictions, the negligent beneficiary's recovery would be reduced by his fault, reducing the overall award granted to the estate. Hence, the evidence may be used to show that the son also was contributorily negligent. (C) is incorrect. While it is true that a parent's contributory negligence is not imputed to her children, their recovery will be barred or reduced in a wrongful death action by the estate because it is a derivative action, and the mother would have had her recovery against the motorist barred or reduced had she lived, as discussed above. (D) is incorrect because the woman's conduct is analyzed as if it were contributory negligence by a plaintiff, which is never characterized as an intervening force by a third party.

Answer to Question 44

(B) The buyer will most likely prevail in a suit for specific performance because the investor had marketable title at the time the buyer sought to enforce the contract. There is an implied warranty in every land sale contract that at closing the seller will provide the buyer with marketable title; *i.e.*, title that is free from questions that might present an unreasonable risk of litigation. An inability to establish a record chain of title will generally render the title unmarketable. Here, although the investor did not have marketable title at the time she entered into the agreement with the buyer, the warranty only requires that the investor be able to deliver marketable title at the closing. When the buyer brought the action for specific performance, the investor held marketable title to the land. Thus, (C) is incorrect. (A) is incorrect because the purchase price paid by the investor is irrelevant. (D) is incorrect because it is not fraudulent to buy property for resale.

Answer to Question 45

(C) The court should deny the motion. The question here might be categorized as an Establishment Clause question with a sect preference (the state is preferring "recognized" religious sects over others), but before we can reach that point, we must first decide whether the astronomer's beliefs are religious at all, and that is probably the province of the Free Exercise Clause. The Free Exercise Clause restricts government interference with the exercise of religion. Under current precedents, the Clause strongly protects religious beliefs. The government may not punish religious beliefs, at least not unless it is necessary to achieve a compelling interest. Thus, if the astronomer's beliefs are religious, the government probably cannot discriminate against his beliefs merely because they are not shared by a recognized religion. The only choice here that deals with whether the astronomer's beliefs are religious is (C). (A) is incorrect because the Free Exercise Clause does not protect only recognized religions. The courts must be open to new religious beliefs. (B) is incorrect because it is based on the standards for judging religiously motivated conduct. The standard for judging the validity of government action that incidentally interferes with religious conduct is far more deferential to the government than the standards for restrictions on religious beliefs. (D) is incorrect because it is overbroad. While the courts cannot judge the truth of religious beliefs (as they often are a matter of faith rather than fact), they can judge the sincerity of religious belief. Thus, the court could judge whether the astronomer's beliefs were merely a ploy to obtain tax exempt status.

Answer to Question 46

(D) The car salesman's offer terminated on January 25, when the 25-day option expired. An option is a distinct contract in which the offeree gives consideration for a promise by the offeror not to revoke an outstanding offer. The collector paid the car salesman $100 to hold the offer open for a period of 25 days, and the offer could not be terminated before that time, not even by the offeree (here the collector). (A) is incorrect because the collector's words did not amount to a counteroffer because they merely inquired as to whether the collector would consider lowering his price; the words were not unequivocal. (Even if this were a counteroffer, it would not extinguish the car salesman's offer, because of the option, as explained above.) (B) is incorrect because, as discussed above, even a rejection by the offeree will not terminate the option. Also, if the communication were effective as a rejection, it would be effective when received by the offeror. (C) is incorrect because, as discussed above, even unequivocal words of rejection by the offeree will not extinguish an option, absent detrimental reliance on the part of the offeror, which was not the case here.

Answer to Question 47

(B) The question on cross-examination regarding the witness's honesty is an appropriate impeachment method. A witness may be interrogated on cross-examination with respect to any act of misconduct that is probative of truthfulness (*i.e.*, demonstrates dishonesty). Lying on a job application would be such an act. Thus, (B) is a proper method of impeaching the witness's credibility. (A) is incorrect because juvenile offenses are generally not admissible for impeachment purposes in civil cases. (C) is incorrect because a conviction cannot be used to impeach a witness if he has been pardoned based on innocence. (D) is incorrect because a record of an arrest cannot be used to impeach a witness—an actual conviction is required.

Answer to Question 48

(A) It would be least helpful to the defendant's defense if assault were a general intent crime in the jurisdiction. Although courts have not always clearly defined "general intent," the mental state required for the material elements of the offense is analogous to "recklessness" under the Model Penal Code—a conscious disregard of a substantial or unjustifiable risk that the material element exists or will result from his conduct. Thus, the defendant need not be certain that his conduct will cause the result or that the attendant circumstances required by the crime exist; it is enough if he is aware of a high likelihood of that result or circumstance. In contrast, a specific intent crime requires the doing of an act with a conscious intent or objective. Most importantly for the defendant, defenses such as voluntary intoxication are not recognized as defenses to general intent crimes but are for specific intent crimes. If the jurisdiction treats assault as a specific intent crime, the defendant's intoxication could be used to show that he was incapable of forming the requisite intent. Thus, it would be helpful to defendant if the jurisdiction treated assault as a specific intent crime, making (B) incorrect and (A) correct. (C) is incorrect because it might be helpful for the defendant if the victim were intoxicated. In theory, the victim could have been so intoxicated that he did not notice the threat of harm, which would negate the "reasonable apprehension" element of the crime of assault. For much the same reason, (D) would also be helpful to the defendant. If the victim did not take the threat seriously, there would be no apprehension of imminent bodily harm, negating an element of the crime.

Answer to Question 49

(D) The passenger will not recover because the jurisdiction has not changed the common law rule. The common law rule is that an automobile owner is not liable for torts committed by another person driving the automobile. (A) is therefore wrong. By statute or judicial precedent, many states have imposed liability on a car owner for the tortious conduct of an immediate family member driving the car (family car rule) or for the tortious conduct of anyone driving the car with consent (permissive use rule). This jurisdiction, however, has not changed the common law rule. Nor is a parent vicariously liable for the negligence of her child. (B) is wrong even though it is a true statement. The cab driver's negligence will not be imputed to the passenger, but the passenger cannot prevail against the car owner because of the absence of vicarious liability. (C) is wrong because negligence on the part of both the young man and the cab driver were actual and proximate causes of the collision.

Answer to Question 50

(C) The least helpful argument is that the statute setting the price caps provides that doctors shall have standing to challenge them. Standing is a jurisprudential doctrine designed to limit the cases federal courts will hear to those brought by parties with a true interest in the litigation. Standing requires a party to have a concrete stake in the outcome of the litigation. While Congress can, by statute, create new rights, injury to which may be sufficient for standing, Congress may not simply confer standing. Thus, an argument simply that the statute confers standing on the doctors is not very helpful. (A) is incorrect because one of the requirements to establish standing is redressability. An argument that a ruling in a party's favor will eliminate the party's injury is the essence of redressability. (B) is incorrect because a party has standing only if he can show that he has suffered an injury in fact. The injury does not have to be great—it need only be a specific injury not suffered by all persons. An argument that the doctors' profits will be reduced by an average of 4% is a sufficiently concrete injury to establish standing. (D) is incorrect because a party has standing only if there is a causal connection between the injury and the conduct of which he complains. The fact that 80% of all doctors charged more than the price caps allow for the specified procedures subject to the caps shows a causal link between the statute and the doctors' reduction in income. Thus, (D) would help the doctors establish standing.

Answer to Question 51

(C) Establishing that the student swung his leg up to avoid a mouse on the floor will likely prevent the teacher from recovering for battery because it appears to negate the student's intent. Battery requires (i) an act by the defendant that brings about harmful or offensive contact to the plaintiff's person, (ii) intent on the part of the defendant to bring about such contact, and (iii) causation. While the defendant need not intend an injury, he must at a minimum know with substantial certainty that a harmful or offensive contact will result from his action. Here, if the student's action of swinging his leg up was reflexive to avoid contact with the mouse, it would not appear to be triggered by an intent to cause contact with the teacher. Absent any other evidence of an intent to cause the contact, the teacher will not prevail. (A) is incorrect because the teacher does not need to establish that the student did, or could have, harmed him. As long as the student intentionally caused an offensive contact to the teacher, the teacher can establish a battery action and recover at least nominal damages. Furthermore, a six-year-old is capable of committing an intentional tort. (B) is incorrect because a person may recover for battery even though he is not conscious of the harmful or offensive contact when it occurs. Because the evidence established that the teacher was kicked by the student, the teacher can recover even though he was not aware of it at the time. (D) is incorrect because the teacher's retention of the student's cellphone does not authorize the student to use force against teacher. When another's possession of the defendant's property began lawfully, the defendant may use only peaceful means to recover the chattel. Even if the teacher were no longer entitled to retain the student's cellphone at the end of class, the student was not entitled to use force to recover it.

Answer to Question 52

(B) The defendant can challenge his conviction because the prosecution's comment on the defendant's silence was improper. After arrest, a defendant has the right to an attorney and the right to remain silent. The exercise of those rights cannot be used against the defendant at trial. The Supreme Court has held that the prosecution cannot comment to the jury on the fact that an arrested defendant exercised the privilege against self-incrimination after being given *Miranda* warnings. Hence, when the prosecution, at trial, asked the defendant why he had not told the police about his self-defense claim right away, the prosecution was improperly using the defendant's exercise of a constitutional right against him. (A) is not entirely accurate. Even if the defendant had not asked for an attorney, he could have invoked the privilege against self-incrimination and refused to talk while in custody. Thus, (A) is not as good an answer as (B), which speaks directly to the reason the conviction can be challenged. (C) is incorrect. Even though his silence might give rise to the inference that the story was fabricated, the arrested defendant has the right to remain silent and to consult with an attorney, and the exercise of those rights cannot be used against him. (D) is incorrect. By testifying, he waived his right to be silent at the trial; he did not waive his right to silence before the trial.

Answer to Question 53

(C) The shipment did not constitute an acceptance. The manufacturer's shipment of both conforming and nonconforming goods along with a note explaining that the nonconforming goods were being offered as an accommodation to the buyer constitutes a counteroffer, which the shop owner is free to accept or reject. Hence, (D) is incorrect. If the counteroffer is accepted, a contract is thereby created. Under U.C.C. section 2-206(1)(b), a shipment of nonconforming goods by a seller is not an acceptance of the buyer's offer if the seller seasonably notifies the buyer that the shipment is offered only as an accommodation to the buyer. If the seller had merely shipped the nonconforming goods without the explanatory note, the shipment would have been both an acceptance of the buyer's offer, creating a bilateral contract, and a breach of the contract. In that case, (B) would have been the correct answer. Under the perfect tender rule, if goods or their tender of delivery do not conform to the sales contract ***in any respect,*** the buyer may reject the whole, accept the whole, or accept any commercial unit or units and reject the rest, subject to the seller's right to cure. (A) is incorrect for that same reason: The perfect tender rule, and not the concept of comparable worth, applies to contracts for the sale of goods.

Answer to Question 54

(A) Damages should not be awarded to the son because the sister has no obligation to repair the footbridge. A life tenant is entitled to all the ordinary uses of the land, but cannot lawfully do any act that would injure the interests of the remainderman. Here, failing to maintain the bridge does not injure the son's remainder because at the inception of the life estate, the property did not contain a bridge. Thus, the sister cannot be charged with waste. (B) is incorrect because a future interest holder need not wait until his interest comes into possession to sue the life tenant for waste. (C) is incorrect because the sister has not substantially changed the use of the property.

Ameliorative waste occurs when the use of the property is ***substantially*** changed, but the change increases the value of the property. The addition of a footbridge where no bridge existed prior to the inception of the life estate does not constitute a substantial change in use of the property. (D) is incorrect because, although a life tenant is obligated to preserve the land and structures in a reasonable state of repair, the duty does not extend to minor improvements made by the life tenant herself.

Answer to Question 55

(B) The attorney should advise the mayor that the proposal is constitutional. The First Amendment prohibits government establishment of religion, and this prohibition has been applied to the states through the Fourteenth Amendment Due Process Clause. Generally, under the Establishment Clause, if government action involving religion does not include a sect preference, it is tested under the *Lemon* test: it will be valid only if (i) it has a secular purpose; (ii) its primary effect neither advances nor inhibits religion; and (iii) it does not produce excessive government entanglement with religion. While it may seem that starting a legislative meeting with a prayer would not pass the *Lemon* test, the Supreme Court has held that because of the long history of legislative prayer in America, such prayers do not constitute an establishment of religion, and it is permissible for a legislative body to hire a chaplain and to begin sessions with a prayer. [Marsh v. Chambers (1983)] (A) is incorrect because it is incomplete; the mere fact that government action does not have a sect preference does not alone make it constitutional under the Establishment Clause. (C) and (D) are incorrect because they run counter to the decision in *Marsh*, discussed above.

Answer to Question 56

(B) If the website reporter prevails, it will be because the publication involved a matter of public interest. The invasion of privacy action based on public disclosure of private facts requires the following elements: (i) publication or public disclosure by defendant of private information about the plaintiff, and (ii) the matter made public is such that its disclosure would be highly offensive to a reasonable person. However, publication in such a case may be privileged if the matter is one of legitimate public interest, as long as it is made without malice (*i.e.*, knowledge of falsity or reckless disregard for the truth). Here, the professional athlete may very well be considered a public figure, but, even if he is not, his conduct of possibly driving from his team's stadium while intoxicated and striking and killing a child would appear to be a matter of public interest. The facts indicate that the report was not made with malice, and therefore would be privileged. (A) is incorrect because an action for public disclosure of private facts is permitted even if the facts disclosed were true. (C) is incorrect. While a defendant has no liability for matters of public record, nothing in the facts indicates that the terms of the settlement were part of the public record, and no public information was released about the terms of the settlement. (D) is incorrect because, while consent is a defense to an invasion of privacy action, a reasonable mistake as to whether consent was given is not a valid defense.

Answer to Question 57

(A) The defendant should not be convicted of battery. Under the statute's fault standards, a defendant must have acted purposely (*i.e.*, with conscious intent) or knowingly (*i.e.*, with knowledge to a substantial certainty) as to the harmful result. The apparent inference to be drawn from the facts is that the defendant did not consciously desire, nor contemplate to a practical certainty, the ***serious*** injury to the victim that actually occurred. Had the defendant intended to cause such severe harm, he no doubt would have dealt the victim a strong blow rather than simply giving the victim a light shove. Therefore, as to the nature of the result, the defendant did not act with "purpose" or "knowledge" as those terms are defined in the Model Penal Code and modern criminal codes. (B), while close, is not as good of an answer as (A) because it does not address the state of mind issue in the problem. A light shove might be sufficient for a battery as defined under a different set of facts (*e.g.*, if the defendant believes that the victim would fall down stairs with a light shove). (C) is incorrect because it addresses the act but not the result. As defined in this question, battery must not only be committed by a purposeful act, but also be done with a "purposeful" or "knowing" state of mind as to the result. (D) is incorrect for much of the same reason—the state of mind requirement also applies to the result, as discussed above. The injury must have been purposely or knowingly caused, and that concept is not contained within choice (D).

Answer to Question 58

(D) The witness may not refer to the letter. Generally, a memorandum can be used to refresh the recollection of a witness, to substitute for forgotten testimony, or on cross-examination. Here, the plaintiff's counsel can use the letter to impeach the witness's testimony because it is a prior inconsistent statement. To do so, he can cross-examine her as to the contents of the letter (as opposed to having her read it to herself prior to cross-examination, as he attempted to do) to show that she has made statements contrary to her testimony, thereby discrediting her testimony. (A) is incorrect because refreshing recollection does not apply. A witness may use a writing for the purpose of refreshing her present recollection while she is testifying, but here the witness has testified and has not claimed any inability to remember the facts about which she testifies (B) is similarly incorrect. If the witness states that she has an insufficient recollection of events even after consulting a writing, the writing may be read into evidence as a recorded recollection. Again, however, there is no indication of insufficient recollection. Therefore, there is no basis for the plaintiff's counsel to ask her to read the letter to herself prior to beginning cross-examination. (C) is incorrect because the memorandum does not need to be offered into evidence; a witness may simply refer to it to refresh recollection prior to giving her testimony.

Answer to Question 59

(C) The association will lose the lawsuit because Congress has plenary power to tax. Article I, Section 8 of the Constitution gives Congress the "plenary" or exclusive power to raise revenue through the imposition of taxes. A tax measure will be upheld if it bears some reasonable relationship to revenue production or if Congress has the power to regulate the taxed activity. (A) is incorrect because the sales tax is nowhere reserved to the states under the Constitution. (B) is incorrect because the press can be subject to general business taxes that are not based on content or targeting a small category of publishers. (D) is incorrect because, as discussed above, the government has no burden to prove that the tax is necessary to any compelling government interest.

Answer to Question 60

(A) The casino should pay the apprentice for his performance because the assignment agreement established privity of contract with the casino. While most contractual rights may be assigned and contractual duties delegated, duties involving personal judgment or skill typically cannot be delegated. The type of personal services contract involved here would not be delegable, but the casino waived the nondelegability by accepting the apprentice's performance after being apprised of the delegation. The casino manager's knowledge will be imputed to the casino. Hence, the assignment agreement between the magician and apprentice is valid, and the casino must pay the apprentice under the contract. (B) is incorrect because of the waiver by the casino. Had the casino refused the apprentice's performance, the magician would be in breach. (C) is incorrect because the effect of the assignment is to establish privity of contract between the obligor (the casino) and the assignee (the apprentice) while extinguishing privity between the obligor and the assignor (the magician). The assignee then replaces the assignor as the real party in interest and he alone is entitled to performance under the contract. The fact that no one could tell that the magician was not on stage does not change the legal status of the parties. (D) is incorrect because (i) some personal services contracts are delegable, and (ii) the nondelegability of this contract was waived here, as discussed above.

Answer to Question 61

(D) The son has title to the land because the deed was delivered to him. A deed must be delivered to be valid. Delivery is presumed if the deed is: (i) handed to the grantee, (ii) acknowledged by the grantor before a notary, or (iii) recorded. Title passes to the grantee upon effective delivery. Thus, destroying the deed or returning it to the grantor has no effect; such an act constitutes neither a cancellation nor a reconveyance. Moreover, there must be acceptance by the grantee in order to complete a conveyance. Most courts will infer the grantee's acceptance if the conveyance is beneficial to him. However, all courts will consider evidence that is contrary to the presumption or inference. Here, the son's statement that he should not have accepted such a gift occurred ***after*** the conveyance was complete, *i.e.*, after the deed was handed to the son and he did not object. (A) is incorrect because a deed may validly convey land by inter vivos gift (*i.e.*, without consideration) as long as there is donative intent, delivery, and acceptance, all of which are present here. (B) is incorrect because delivery refers to the grantor's intent that the deed have some present operative effect. Here, the mother possessed the requisite intent at the time of the conveyance. The fact that she changed her mind later is irrelevant, because delivery cannot be cancelled. (C) is incorrect because recording a deed has no effect on its validity. Here, the deed to the son is valid because it was delivered to him and he accepted it.

Answer to Question 62

(B) The court should deny both motions and submit the case to the jury. While the general rule is that a possessor of land owes no duty to those off the premises for natural conditions, a landowner may be liable for damage caused by unreasonably dangerous artificial conditions or structures abutting adjacent land. This probably would apply to ice collecting on the roof of a building and injuring passersby on the sidewalk. Here, the customer was on the sidewalk and was struck by the ice from the roof of the shopkeeper's store, which suggests a potential breach of the shopkeeper's duty. Nevertheless, it is a question for the jury whether the warning signs were sufficient to satisfy the shopkeeper's duty here, or what other steps he could have taken to eliminate the danger. Also, the jury will need to determine whether the customer could have avoided the injury had she been paying attention, because a finding of contributory negligence will prevent her recovery in this jurisdiction. (A) is incorrect because it will be a jury question whether the shopkeeper breached his duty to the customer. Also, while it appears that the customer was not on the shopkeeper's premises at the time she was injured, the result would be no different even if the sidewalk were part of the shopkeeper's premises. The shopkeeper owes a duty to his customers, as business invitees, to make reasonable inspections to discover dangerous conditions and make them safe. However, in some cases a reasonable warning will satisfy that duty. Again, it will be up to the jury to determine whether the warning signs were sufficient under the circumstances. (C) is incorrect because, as discussed above, the shopkeeper may have owed a duty for the ice falling from his roof. (D) is incorrect because, even assuming that the customer acted negligently by not paying attention, nothing establishes that the negligence was a cause of her injury. Even had she seen the signs, she would not necessarily have been aware of the ice about to hit her, and may not have taken a different path if she was trying to enter the store. As stated above, the jury will need to determine whether her conduct constituted contributory negligence that was a cause of her injury, which would bar her recovery under the law of the jurisdiction.

Answer to Question 63

(C) If the judge sustains an objection to the question, it will likely be because the probative value of the answer would be substantially outweighed by its tendency to mislead. Jurors are incompetent as witnesses, but only as to the case in which they are currently sitting or at a later time to impeach their verdict. This is not the case here. The evidence could be excluded, however, under Rule 403 if the judge determines that the probative value of the evidence would be substantially outweighed by its tendency to mislead. (A) is wrong because a leading question is permitted on cross-examination. (B) is wrong because the question goes to bias, so it cannot be excluded on the issue of scope of direct examination. (D) is wrong because no foundation is necessary for this type of question.

Answer to Question 64

(B) The government must convince the court that the injunction is necessary. The government seeks to prohibit dissemination of speech before it is being made—a prior restraint. Prior restraints are not favored in our political system. Most cases hold that a prior restraint will not be tolerated unless the government can show that the prior restraint is narrowly tailored to achieve a compelling, or at least significant, government interest. This, in essence, is a presumption that the injunction should not be granted unless the government can make the required showing. (A) is incorrect because it puts the burden on the scientist of showing that the injunction is not necessary. As discussed above, the government has this burden even if we assume that a matter of national security is involved. (C) is incorrect because it treats the book only as commercial speech. A prior restraint may be imposed—even on truthful commercial speech—if the restraint is necessary to achieve a compelling or significant government interest. Preventing dissemination of secret biological weapons research would constitute a compelling interest. (D) is incorrect because it too is based on the wrong standard. It states the standard for advocating the use of force or violation of law, and here the facts involve a prior restraint.

Answer to Question 65

(D) The dean will prevail, because his letter of acceptance created an enforceable contract. Requirements contracts, such as this one, are recognized as sufficiently definite to be enforced. In a requirements contract, a buyer promises to buy from a certain seller all of the goods it requires, and the seller agrees to sell that amount to the buyer. Here, the university promised to use the engineering firm's electronic drafting tables in its program, which it will be required to buy, albeit at cost. (A) is incorrect because the dean does not need to establish reliance on the offer to keep it open; he accepted the offer and a binding contract exists. (B) is incorrect because the contract is not illusory; each party is bound by its promise to the other party, so the requisite mutuality exists. The university agreed to buy the engineering firm's drafting tables, and the engineering firm agreed to sell the appropriate drafting tables to the university at cost. Although it is possible that no additional students will apply to the engineering program, both parties stood ready to perform their duties under the contract. (C) is incorrect because the rule on a merchant's firm offer applies only when the merchant signs a written offer giving assurances that he will hold the offer open for a stated time period; in such cases, the offer is irrevocable for the stated period or for a reasonable time period if no period is stated (not to exceed three months). An option contract is not created automatically when a merchant makes an offer—the intent to create an option contract must be expressly stated in writing, which did not happen here.

Answer to Question 66

(C) The bartender should succeed in his self-defense claim. Generally, one who begins a fight has no right to use force in self-defense, but when the victim of an initial aggression suddenly escalates a "minor" fight into one involving deadly force and does so without giving the aggressor the chance to withdraw, the aggressor may use force in his own defense. Here, the bartender merely pushed the patron on the shoulder over their disagreement about an upcoming football game. This was a minor disagreement. The patron then suddenly escalated the fight by lunging toward the bartender's throat with a potentially deadly weapon, a broken glass bottle, without giving the bartender an opportunity to withdraw. At that point the bartender had the right to respond with force, even deadly force, in self-defense. (A) is incorrect because, as stated above, the sudden escalation of the fight by the patron allowed the bartender to regain his right of self-defense. (B) is incorrect because, even if retreat were possible, the majority rule is that there is no duty to retreat before using deadly force. As discussed above, the bartender regained his right to use deadly force when the patron unlawfully escalated the fight. (D) is incorrect because the "imperfect self-defense" doctrine merely reduces a murder to manslaughter (in some jurisdictions) when the defendant acts unreasonably in using deadly force. It does not establish self-defense to manslaughter.

Answer to Question 67

(B) The friend has title to the land because the creditor had notice of the friend's interest in the land and thus was not a bona fide purchaser for value. When a grantor purports to convey property that he does not own, his subsequent acquisition of title to that property vests in the grantee under the doctrine of estoppel by deed. Hence, this doctrine would provide the friend with title once the granddaughter acquired the land. Most courts, however, hold that this is personal estoppel, which means that title inures to the grantee's benefit only as against the grantor, not a subsequent bona fide purchaser (*i.e.*, a purchaser who gives valuable consideration and has no notice of the prior instrument). If the grantor transfers her after-acquired title to an innocent purchaser for value, the bona fide purchaser gets good title. Here, however, the creditor was not a bona fide purchaser. The fact that the friend built a home and was living on the property gave the creditor constructive notice of the friend's interest. If the possession is unexplained by the record, the subsequent purchaser is charged with knowledge of whatever an inspection of the property would have disclosed and anything that would have been disclosed by inquiring of the possessor. Therefore, the creditor is charged with knowledge of the friend's possession and with what the friend would have told the creditor about his possession; *i.e.*, that the property was conveyed to him by the granddaughter prior to her conveyance to the creditor. Consequently, the creditor does not qualify as a bona fide purchaser. (A) is incorrect because no one has a legal duty to perform a title search, although a subsequent purchaser will be charged with the notice that such a search would provide. There is a split of authority as to whether the original grantee's recordation of the deed imparts sufficient notice to prevent a subsequent purchaser from being a bona fide purchaser, but the majority view is that it does not because the deed is not in the subsequent purchaser's chain of title. Here, the creditor would not be charged with record notice of the friend's deed because it was not in the chain of title. But the failure to perform a title search is not what prevents the creditor from being a bona fide purchaser; it is the fact that the creditor is on inquiry notice arising from the friend's possession of the land. (C) is incorrect because the estoppel by deed doctrine is what provides the friend with title to the land, as discussed above. It does not benefit the creditor. (D) is incorrect because, as discussed above, the creditor is not a bona fide purchaser despite the deed not being in the chain of title. Note that the statute here is a notice statute, under which a subsequent bona fide purchaser prevails over a prior grantee who failed to record, but the doctrine of estoppel by deed governs the outcome.

Answer to Question 68

(A) If the patient does not prevail, it will be because a reasonable person in the patient's position would have used the cream even after being told of the potential side effects. As part of the physician's duty of care, a doctor proposing a course of treatment has a duty to provide the patient with enough information about its risks to enable the patient to make an informed consent to the treatment. If an undisclosed risk was serious enough that a reasonable person in the patient's position would have withheld consent to the treatment, the doctor has breached her duty. Here, whether the dermatologist breached her duty to the patient by not warning him of possible side effects would be determined ultimately by the trier of fact using a reasonable person standard. A determination that a reasonable person in the patient's position would have consented to using the cream even after being informed of the potential side effects would preclude the patient from prevailing. (B) is not as good a choice as (A) because the listing of side effects on a lengthy and detailed printed insert does not necessarily satisfy the dermatologist's duty to provide enough information for the patient to make an informed consent. Information that is buried in a lengthy insert may not be read through by a reasonable person, so the dermatologist may have had a duty to verbally disclose side effects, and she will have breached that duty if a reasonable person in the patient's position would have withheld consent to the treatment if given the information. (C) is incorrect because the dermatologist could be liable regardless of the severity of the reaction the patient experienced. If she should have warned about the particular side effects the patient experienced even though they are ordinarily less severe, the fact that the patient suffered an unforeseeably severe reaction to the medicine does not relieve her from liability. (D) is incorrect. Even if the jurisdiction requires only that the dermatologist exercise the knowledge and skill of a physician in good standing in similar communities, rather than apply a national standard typically used for specialists, that does not establish whether the duty was breached here. The duty issue here is whether she provided the patient with enough information to allow him to make an informed consent, for which the factor in (A) is determinative.

Answer to Question 69

(C) The statute is likely unconstitutional because the state does not have a substantial justification for the statute. The Privileges and Immunities Clause of Article IV protects against discrimination by a state in favor of its own citizens when it affects a fundamental right, such as the pursuit of a livelihood. Any statute that results in such discrimination violates the Clause unless the state shows that it has a substantial justification for the discriminatory treatment. In effect, it must show that nonresidents either cause or are part of the problem it is attempting to solve, and that there are no less restrictive means to solve the problem. Here, the state statute clearly discriminates against nonresidents in favor of residents. The reason offered by the state to justify the discrimination, *i.e.*, that nonresident physicians are less likely to be familiar with the medical standards imposed by the state, does not meet the test of substantiality required here. The state can find less restrictive means to ensure that all physicians are familiar with its medical standards. Accordingly, (A) is incorrect. (B) is incorrect, because a "privilege" under the Privileges and Immunities Clause includes those professions that are important to the national economy, which the practice of medicine clearly is. (D) is incorrect because it states the wrong standard. The state does not have to show a compelling interest for the discrimination.

Answer to Question 70

(D) The librarian will not be successful because the millionaire purchased the painting in good faith. A nonbreaching party may seek specific performance if the legal remedy, *i.e.*, damages, is inadequate. Damages are generally inadequate when the subject matter of the contract is rare or unique, such as a painting. However, if the subject matter of a contract has already been sold to another, who purchased for value and in good faith, the right to specific performance is cut off. Here, the millionaire purchased the painting without knowing of the deal between the artist and the librarian, so the millionaire was a bona fide purchaser. The sale to the millionaire cut off the librarian's right to specific performance. (A) is incorrect because, even though specific performance ordinarily would be available, the artist can raise the equitable defense of sale to a bona fide purchaser, as discussed above. (B) is incorrect for the same reason. The artist will be liable for breach of contract when he fails to deliver the painting to the librarian, but she cannot obtain specific performance. (C) is incorrect because, as stated above, damages are not considered adequate when the subject matter is unique.

Answer to Question 71

(B) The court should rule for the tenant because the investor breached the covenant of quiet enjoyment. There is implied in every lease a covenant that neither the landlord nor someone with paramount title will interfere with the tenant's quiet enjoyment and possession of the premises. The covenant of quiet enjoyment may be breached by actual eviction—where the landlord or paramount title holder excludes the tenant from the entire leased premises. Having been deprived of possession of the entire premises, the tenant may treat the lease as terminated, and his liability for further rent under the lease is discharged. The tenant may also collect damages from the landlord for breach of covenant. Here, because foreclosure destroys all interests junior to the mortgage being foreclosed, the tenant's lease was wiped out by the bank's foreclosure. The buyer obtained paramount title at the foreclosure sale and properly evicted the tenant from the premises. Thus, the investor is in breach of the covenant of quiet enjoyment and the tenant can recover damages from her. (A) is incorrect because it misstates the facts. Although failure to include a necessary party results in the preservation of that party's interest despite foreclosure and sale, the tenant was joined in the foreclosure proceedings. (C) is incorrect because the investor did not assign the rents and her reversion interest to the buyer. Although an assignee is liable to the tenants for performance of all covenants made by the original landlord, nothing in the facts indicates the buyer purchased the land subject to the lease. Moreover, the fact that the buyer obtained an ejectment order from the court shows that she did ***not*** take title subject to the lease. (D) is incorrect because the doctrine of constructive eviction is inapplicable here. The doctrine provides that if the landlord does an act or fails to provide some service that she has a legal duty to provide, and thereby makes the property uninhabitable, the tenant may terminate the lease and seek damages. The acts that cause the injury must be by the landlord or her agent, the premises must be uninhabitable, and the tenant must vacate within a reasonable time. Here, the tenant was evicted by a paramount title holder and did not leave because the premises were uninhabitable. Thus, the fact that the investor did not effect the eviction is irrelevant.

Answer to Question 72

(D) The court should rule that the evidence is inadmissible. A criminal defendant has the constitutional right, under the Confrontation Clause, to confront and cross-examine the witnesses against him. Affidavits summarizing the findings of forensic analysis are testimonial in nature and cannot be offered against a defendant unless the preparer is unavailable and the defendant previously had an opportunity to cross-examine. Here, admission of the affidavit precludes the defendant from cross-examining the lab technician, and there is no evidence suggesting that the technician is unavailable. Thus, the affidavit is inadmissible—the lab technician must be brought in to testify as to the findings of the fingerprint test. (A) is incorrect because the fact that the affidavit is an original does not, by itself, make it admissible. Admissibility still violates the defendant's rights under the Confrontation Clause. (B) is incorrect because, even if the affidavit qualifies as a business record, it is inadmissible in this case under the Confrontation Clause. (C) is incorrect because the report, even if prepared pursuant to statute, is still inadmissible because it violates the Confrontation Clause.

Answer to Question 73

(B) The defendant can move to withdraw her plea. Ordinarily it is difficult to collaterally attack a guilty plea after sentencing when the plea is seen as an intelligent choice among the defendant's alternatives. Notwithstanding, a plea may be attacked after sentencing in certain circumstances; *e.g.,* if there was ineffective assistance of counsel. Ineffective assistance of counsel undercuts the assumption of an intelligent choice among the defendant's alternatives on the advice of counsel. Therefore, a defendant may successfully attack a guilty plea on the ground that she received ineffective assistance of counsel if, but for the counsel's errors, the defendant probably would not have pleaded guilty and instead would have insisted upon going to trial. Here, the facts indicate that the defendant pleaded guilty because she believed that the government lawfully seized evidence that would implicate her in the crime. Had the defendant's counsel requested a copy of the search warrant, as most defense lawyers would have done, the defendant would have discovered that the evidence might be suppressed, and thus would not as readily have pleaded guilty. Hence, (B) is correct. (A) is incorrect because any admissions made during plea negotiations are inadmissible at trial. The fact that the defendant was not *Mirandized* before such statements would not be a basis for overturning the plea agreement. (C) is incorrect because a defendant's admissions during plea negotiations also would not save a plea agreement for the government. Admissions during plea agreements would not cure a defective plea agreement. (D) is incorrect as an overbroad statement. A plea agreement may be attacked after sentencing in certain circumstances.

Answer to Question 74

(C) The neighbor is not likely to prevail. The owner of trespassing animals is strictly liable for the damage they cause as long as it was reasonably foreseeable. Here, because the neighbor's negligence allowed the cattle to escape, the rancher will ***not*** be strictly liable for the damages from his trespassing livestock. While the rancher could be liable for negligence, nothing in the facts suggests that the rancher should have foreseen that the neighbor would knock down the fence; hence, the rancher was not negligent and will not be liable to the neighbor. (A) is incorrect because, as stated above, it is an incorrect statement of law under these facts. The rancher will not be strictly liable for the damages from his trespassing livestock under these facts. (B) is incorrect. For domestic animals such as cattle, the owner may be liable for injuries caused by a particular animal's dangerous propensities, which refers to propensities more dangerous than normal for that species. Nothing in the facts indicates that the herd of cattle had dangerous propensities. (D) is incorrect because the neighbor would not prevail even if the cattle caused the damage on their own without being harried by the dog. The rancher is not liable because the neighbor's negligence allowed the cattle to escape.

Answer to Question 75

(A) The motion should be denied. A state law may fail under the Supremacy Clause, even if it does not conflict with federally regulated conduct or objectives, if it appears that Congress intended to occupy the entire field, thus precluding any state or local regulation. Congress may indicate preemptive intent through a statute's express language (express preemption) or through the statute's structure and purpose (implied preemption). In *Altria Group, Inc. v Good* (2009), the Court concluded that federal regulation of advertising for health and safety "has nothing to do with" the state's regulatory interest in preventing fraudulent advertising. Here, the laws do not actually conflict even thought the same subject matter is being regulated by the federal government and the state. Hence, (C) is incorrect. (B) is a true statement, but not the reason why the motion should be denied. The Twenty-First Amendment does not prohibit Congress from controlling economic transactions involving liquor under the Commerce Clause, and Commerce Clause legislation regarding liquor has supremacy despite the Twenty-First Amendment. (D) is incorrect because the express preemption must unequivocally establish, on its face or as part of its legislative history, an intention to fully preempt the field which the labeling act does not. Here, the federal law merely addresses a health and safety issue.

Answer to Question 76

(B) The store owner will be allowed to introduce parol evidence of the meaning of the term "Adirondack chair" because there is a dispute as to its meaning. If there is uncertainty or ambiguity in the written agreement's terms or a dispute as to the meaning of those terms, parol evidence can be received to aid the factfinder in reaching a correct interpretation of the agreement. (A) is incorrect because a subsequent modification of the agreement is not in issue. There is a dispute as to the interpretation of a term in the original agreement. (C) is incorrect because, while it is probably true that the writing is a complete integration, that fact will not affect the admissibility of the evidence regarding the meaning of "Adirondack chair." Whether the writing was intended as a final expression of the contract or was a complete integration is important when parol evidence is sought to change the agreement, but the parties in this case are not trying to modify, add to, or subtract from the original written agreement. Instead, they are merely seeking clarification of a material term in the agreement. Parol evidence on this matter is admissible even if the writing is a complete integration. (D) is incorrect because the rule is not different for merchants with respect to interpreting a material term. In fact, Article 2 of the U.C.C. is even more liberal in allowing, even in the absence of ambiguity, terms to be explained or supplemented by permitting evidence of course of dealing, usage of trade, and course of performance.

Answer to Question 77

(B) The defense counsel should object because the officer's testimony violates the best evidence rule. Under the best evidence rule, the original writing must be produced when proving the material terms of that writing. Secondary evidence of the writing, such as oral testimony regarding the writing's contents, is permitted only after it has been shown that the original is unavailable for some reason other than by serious misconduct of the proponent. Here, the terms of the letter are material and no justification has been given for why it cannot be produced. Thus, the original letter must be produced and the officer's testimony violates the best evidence rule. (A) is wrong because, even assuming that authentication was not proper, it does not matter whether the letter is genuine or a forgery because the purpose for admitting it is to show motive. (C) is wrong because the statement is not being offered for its truth. Hearsay is an out-of-court statement offered to prove the truth of the matter asserted. Here, the statement is not being offered to prove that the defendant's wife was going to leave him, but rather to show that the defendant had motive to murder his boss. Therefore, it is not hearsay. (D) is wrong because any prejudicial impact that the evidence may have is greatly outweighed by its probative value in showing the defendant's motive.

Answer to Question 78

(C) The court should rule for the friend because the option is enforceable. The Rule Against Perpetuities provides that no interest in property is valid unless it must vest, if at all, not later than 21 years after one or more lives in being at the creation of the interest. Options to purchase generally are subject to the Rule, so that an option that might be exercised later than the end of the perpetuities period is void. However, the Rule does not apply to options connected to leaseholds. Thus, the option does not violate the Rule and (A) is incorrect. (B) is incorrect because an option generally is considered a running covenant, exercisable by an assignee in the absence of contrary intent. Here, the lease provides that the option may be exercised by "the tenant, his successors and assigns," and the landlord gave her consent to the tenant's assignment to the friend. Thus, there is no evidence of contrary intent as to the friend's right to exercise the option. Note also that the tenant did not separate the option from the leasehold estate (which could make it subject to the Rule Against Perpetuities). The tenant assigned the entire leasehold. (D) is incorrect because the fact that the friend exercised the option within the perpetuities period is irrelevant. Even if the option were subject to the Rule, it would not be saved by this fact. The test by which the invalidity of an interest is shown is not whether it actually vests within the period, but rather whether it might not vest within the perpetuities period; if so, it is void.

Answer to Question 79

(D) The neighbor would not be guilty of larceny when he took the horse from the stable because the neighbor did not have the mens rea necessary for the crime. Common law larceny required the trespassory taking and carrying away of personal property in the possession of another, with the intent to permanently (or for an unreasonable time) deprive the other of lawful possession. The intent to permanently deprive was often referred to by the courts as the "intent to steal." If the actor believed that he had a right to the property or was taking the property on behalf of someone who had that right, the actor could not be found guilty of larceny because there would be no intent to permanently deprive another of lawful possession. Because the neighbor thought the bill had been paid and the horse rightfully belonged to the equestrian, the neighbor did not have the "intent to steal" necessary for larceny at the time he took the horse from the stable. (A) is wrong. Even though the bill had not been paid, the neighbor is not guilty if he believed the equestrian had a lawful right to the horse. (B) is wrong. Even though the horse was in the possession of the stable, the neighbor is not guilty if he believed the equestrian had a lawful right to the horse. (C) is wrong because a person can be guilty of larceny of his own property if another person (usually a bailee) has a superior right to possession of the property at the time of the taking.

Answer to Question 80

(A) The court should sustain the objection. Generally, a witness can be interrogated on cross-examination with respect to any activity that is probative of truthfulness, even if it did not result in a conviction. However, extrinsic evidence of the misconduct is not permitted; the examiner is limited to cross-examination of the witness. Therefore, if the witness denies the misconduct, the examiner cannot introduce other evidence. Here, the witness was asked on cross-examination about having embezzled funds from his employer. The witness denied the allegation and there is no evidence of a conviction. While embezzling is probative of truthfulness, the prosecution must accept the witness's denial and is not permitted to offer into evidence the testimony of the employer to rebut the witness's denial. Therefore, the testimony is inadmissible. (B) is incorrect because, as discussed above, evidence of conduct that is probative of truthfulness is admissible even if there was no conviction. Furthermore, extrinsic evidence of a conviction is typically shown by introducing a record of the judgment. Although permissible, proof of conviction by testimony is less likely to be allowed by the judge because it may be too time consuming and more prejudicial than proof by record of the conviction. (D) is incorrect because the mere fact that the conduct is probative of truthfulness does not guarantee admissibility; extrinsic evidence is still prohibited. (C) is incorrect because the 10-year rule applies only if there was a conviction, and in this case there was none.

Answer to Question 81

(B) If the manufacturer prevails, it will be because the product was not defectively designed. In most jurisdictions, a product can be the basis for a products liability action if the product was in a dangerous condition unreasonably dangerous to users. For design defects, the plaintiff usually must show a reasonable alternative design, *i.e.*, that a less dangerous modification or alternative was economically feasible. If it was not economically feasible to modify the chemistry set to make it less dangerous, the product was not defectively designed. Hence, (B) provides a basis for the manufacturer to prevail. (A) is incorrect because, while it may be true, it is not applicable to the student's action. The student was not hurt by the manufacturer's activity of manufacturing chemistry sets; he was hurt by the product itself during his use of it. Even if the manufacture of chemistry sets were an abnormally dangerous activity, the student would have to show that the set itself was a defective product to recover. (C) is incorrect because the manufacturer's care in manufacturing the product is irrelevant in a products liability action based on strict liability. The plaintiff need prove only that the product was so defective as to be unreasonably dangerous. (D) is incorrect because the student's contributory negligence in failing to follow the instructions would not be the basis for the manufacturer prevailing. Most comparative negligence states apply their comparative negligence rules to strict products liability actions. Hence, in a pure comparative negligence jurisdiction, any negligence on the plaintiff's part would only reduce his recovery and not bar it. *Note*: Even if the question indicated that the jurisdiction here applied traditional contributory negligence rules to strict products liability actions, the result would be no different. In strict products liability actions in those jurisdictions, the plaintiff's ordinary contributory negligence in failing to discover or guard against the danger is not a defense. While voluntarily and unreasonably encountering a known risk is a defense in those jurisdictions, there is no indication here that the student knew of the fumes that would be generated by mixing those chemicals or that he had even read the warnings and instructions that came with the set.

Answer to Question 82

(B) If the investor is permitted to build the shopping mall, it will be because the servitude has been abandoned. If a benefited party acquiesces in a violation of the servitude by one burdened party, he may be deemed to have abandoned the servitude as to other burdened parties. Here, there is no evidence that the original owner objected to the 15 lots being developed as commercial properties. Thus, she cannot enforce an implied servitude against the investor. (A) is incorrect because the doctrine of changed neighborhood conditions is inapplicable here. Under the doctrine, if the neighborhood has changed significantly since the time the servitude was created, with the result that it would be inequitable to enforce the restriction, injunctive relief will be withheld. Here, the industrial park existed ***prior to*** the subdivision. The only change has occurred within the subdivision itself, but it will be permitted because the servitude has been abandoned by acquiescence. (C) is incorrect because mere nonuse is insufficient to terminate a servitude. To terminate the servitude, the nonuse must be combined with other evidence of intent to abandon it. (D) is incorrect because the zoning ordinance does not preempt the restrictive covenant. The restrictive covenant, permitting only residential use, would prevail over the less restrictive zoning ordinance.

Answer to Question 83

(D) The court should award the manufacturer $3,000 as lost profits. When a buyer anticipatorily breaches a contract for the sale of goods, the seller's basic damages are either the difference between the contract price and the market price as of the time for performance or the difference between the contract price and resale price. If neither of these measures puts the seller in as good a position as performance would have, and the seller is a lost volume seller, the seller may recover lost profits plus incidental damages. Here, the manufacturer, by virtue of the fact that it can manufacture as many widgets as it can sell and has ample inventory on hand, is a lost volume seller. The difference between the contract price and the market price on May 1 (the time for performance) was $2,000. The difference between the contract price and the resale price is $0 because it sold them for more than the contract price. Neither of those measures puts the manufacturer in as good a position as it would have been had the retailer performed under the contract. In that case, the manufacturer would have had $3,000 profit from the sale to the retailer, as well as a $4,000 profit from the sale to the subsequent buyer. The facts state that there are no incidental damages. Thus, the manufacturer should be awarded the $3,000 in lost profit as damages. (A) is incorrect because it is based on the difference between the contract price and the resale price. Because the manufacturer sold the widgets for more than the contract price, its damages would be zero under this calculation. The manufacturer, however, is a lost volume seller and this measure of damages does not put the manufacturer in as good a position as it would have been had the retailer performed. Thus, the manufacturer is entitled to lost profits. (B) is incorrect because it represents the difference between the market price at trial and the contract price. That is not the correct measure of damages in any case unless the trial date precedes the date for performance. That is not the case here and would not be the correct answer even if it were, because the manufacturer is entitled to lost profits. (C) is incorrect. This figure represents the difference between the market price and the contract price at the time for performance, but, like the resale price measure, does not put the manufacturer in as good a position as it would have been had the retailer performed. In any case, that measure would not apply because the manufacturer had already resold the widgets. Alternatively, $2,000 represents the difference between the manufacturer's lost profit of $3,000 and the extra profit of $1,000 that it made on resale of the widgets because of the higher market price. Again, however, because the manufacturer is a lost volume seller and could have made that sale anyway, the extra profit will not be deducted from its lost profits damages.

Answer to Question 84

(B) The court should overrule the objection because the report, prepared by a federal agency, falls within the public record exception to the hearsay rule. The report on the accident constitutes hearsay because it is an out-of-court statement offered to prove the truth of the matter asserted—that the accident happened because the engineer was going too fast. However, an exception to the hearsay rule applies for public records, which avoids having public agents leave their jobs to testify to acts done in their official capacity. This exception includes, in civil actions, factual findings (including opinions and conclusions) resulting from an investigation made pursuant to authority granted by law, unless the sources of information and other circumstances indicate lack of trustworthiness. Here, the report was made by the government investigator and there is nothing to suggest that it is not trustworthy. Thus, the report should be admissible. (A) is incorrect because the fact that a document is self-authenticating is not enough to admit it into evidence and does not address the hearsay objection. (C) is incorrect. The investigator need not testify because the report falls within an exception to the hearsay rule. Nor would the Confrontation Clause require the investigator's testimony because this is not a criminal case against the defendant. (D) is incorrect because, as stated above, the hearsay exception for public records applies.

Answer to Question 85

(A) The speaker may successfully defend on overbreadth grounds. If a regulation of speech punishes a substantial amount of protected speech, judged in relation to the regulation's plainly legitimate sweep, the regulation is facially invalid and cannot be enforced against anyone—not even against a person who is engaging in an activity that is not constitutionally protected. The statute here falls within this rule. It makes ***any*** public statement in support of the Asian nation a crime. (B) is incorrect because the mere fact that the speaker's speech was political in nature does not exempt it from regulation. Although the Supreme Court might protect core political speech more than other forms of speech, even political speech is subject to reasonable regulation (*e.g.,* reasonable time, place, and manner restrictions). Thus, if the statute here were valid, the fact that the speaker's speech was politically motivated would do nothing to aid in the speaker's defense. (C) is incorrect because a statute regulating speech that is substantially overbroad cannot be enforced even against a person whose conduct is not constitutionally protected. The First Amendment does not protect speech that encourages imminent lawless action, and the speaker's speech seems to fall within this category. Nevertheless, because the statute is substantially overbroad, it cannot be enforced against the speaker. (D) is incorrect because the statute is unenforceable for the reasons stated above. If the statute were not unenforceable for overbreadth, the mere fact that the war might be a compelling interest for regulating certain speech is not alone sufficient to negate the speaker's First Amendment rights. As the statute regulates the content of speech, the government would also have to show that the regulation is necessary to achieving the compelling interest. Choice (D) is missing that element.

Answer to Question 86

(B) The second conviction will not stand. The Double Jeopardy Clause prohibits retrying a defendant whose conviction has been reversed on appeal for any offense more serious than that for which she was convicted at the first trial. This right is violated by retrial for a more serious offense, even if at the second trial the defendant is only convicted of an offense no more serious than that for which she was convicted at the first trial. Thus, (B) is correct because the state could not retry the defendant for murder. (A) is an incorrect statement of the law. The state may retry the defendant, subject to the limitation discussed above. (C) is incorrect. Although a retrial is permissible, the retrial is subject to the limitation discussed above. (D) is also incorrect. Such a violation of the Double Jeopardy Clause is not considered to be harmless even if the defendant is convicted of the same lesser offense again.

Answer to Question 87

(B) If the fisherman prevails, it will be because the teens acted negligently by not paying attention to the rocks and currents in the river. Under the principal that danger invites rescue, a rescuer is a foreseeable plaintiff. The teens owed the fisherman a duty of care because he undertook to rescue them. By negligently placing themselves in a position of danger that might invite a rescue, the teens breached a duty to any rescuer who suffered injury from a rescue attempt, as long as the attempt was not reckless. Here, the fisherman can prevail if the teens were negligent by failing to pay attention to the rocks and currents, because there is no indication that he acted recklessly and because he suffered damages in the rescue attempt. (A) is wrong because a typical Good Samaritan statute protects the rescuer from liability for negligence; it does not affect the liability of those being rescued. (C) and (D) are wrong because the unforeseeable plaintiff problem does not apply here; a rescuer is deemed foreseeable as long as the rescue is not reckless.

Answer to Question 88

(D) If the court rules for the atheist, it will be because the condition subsequent is unenforceable. A fee simple subject to a condition subsequent is created when the grantor retains the power to terminate the estate of the grantee on the happening of a specified event. On the happening of that event, the estate of the grantee continues until the grantor exercises her power of termination (right of entry) by bringing suit or making reentry. Here, the landowner conveyed a fee simple subject to a restriction against selling to non-Christian persons, retaining a right of entry. The right of entry passed to the daughter on the landowner's death, and the daughter exercised this right by bringing an ejectment action against the atheist after the condition was violated. However, the daughter's right of entry cannot be enforced in court because such judicial action would be discriminatory state action forbidden by the Fourteenth Amendment. The condition may also violate the Fair Housing Act by imposing a restriction in a deed that discriminates on the basis of religion. Thus, the invalid condition is stricken and the atheist owns the land in fee simple. (A) is incorrect because, as the fee simple owner of the land, the atheist need not resort to adverse possession. However, if a valid condition subsequent had been contained in the grant, the atheist would not prevail on this claim. The statute of limitations for adverse possession does not begin to run against the holder of a right of entry until the holder asserts the right. Before then, no cause of action arises because the grantee's continued possession of the land is proper. (B) is not as strong an answer as (D) because, rather than asserting in defense of enforcement of the condition that he expended substantial funds in reliance on his interest in the land, the atheist's better argument would be that the condition itself is unenforceable. (C) is incorrect because a right of entry is descendible in all states.

Answer to Question 89

(C) The seller bore the risk of loss at the time the handbags were destroyed and, therefore, it will not prevail in its suit against the buyer. This contract is governed by the Uniform Commercial Code ("U.C.C.") because it involves the sale of goods. Under the U.C.C., the risk of loss falls on the buyer or seller according to the terms of their contract. Here, the contract called for the seller to deliver the handbags "F.O.B. (free on board) Chicago CSX Terminal." When a contract has an F.O.B. delivery term, the seller is obligated to get the goods to the destination indicated and make a reasonable contract for freight if the destination indicated is not the buyer's place of business. The seller has the risk of loss until the goods make it to the F.O.B. destination, and thereafter the buyer has the risk. Here, the destruction occurred before the seller got the goods to the F.O.B. destination (Chicago), so the risk of loss remained with the seller. Hence, the seller, and not the buyer, is in breach (for nondelivery). (A) would be correct if the seller did not have the risk of loss, because a nonbreaching seller's remedy for destroyed goods is the contract price. However, as explained above, the seller bore the risk of loss at the time the handbags were destroyed. (B) would be incorrect even if the seller did not have the risk of loss, because merely awarding a nonbreaching seller the profits on a contract where the goods are destroyed rather than the full contract price will cause him a loss, because he had to pay for the manufacture or purchase of the goods and would not be recovering those goods. (D) is incorrect because the U.C.C. governs this contract, and the U.C.C. risk of loss rules modify the common law rule that destruction of the subject matter without fault of either party discharges both parties of their obligations under the contract.

Answer to Question 90

(A) The fan should be charged with the attempted murder of her original target, the actress. A criminal attempt is an act that, although done with the intention of committing a crime, falls short of completing the crime. The fan fired a gun at the actress; her intentional use of a deadly weapon permits an inference that she had the intent to kill the actress. If her plan had succeeded, she would have been guilty of murder. (B), (C), and (D) are incorrect because the fan did not have the intent to kill the actor. Had the fan actually killed the actor, her intent to kill the actress could have been transferred to make her guilty of murdering the actor, but the doctrine of transferred intent does not apply to an attempt. (D) is also incorrect because the fan did not have intent to kill the bodyguard.

Answer to Question 91

(D) The strongest argument is that the commission lacks authority to enforce its standards. The Appointments Clause of the Constitution permits Congress to vest appointments of inferior officers only in the President, the courts, or the heads of departments. Enforcement is an executive act; therefore, Congress cannot appoint members of a commission that exercises enforcement powers. In these facts, the safety commission consists of some members appointed by Congress. This commission therefore violates the Appointments Clause of the Constitution because it has enforcement powers, since it can prosecute violations. Legislative power can be delegated even under vague guidelines without creating an unconstitutional delegation. Thus, (B) is incorrect. (A) is incorrect because the commerce power extends to many activities occurring solely within a particular state, if, taken as a whole, the activities in question have a substantial economic effect on interstate commerce. There is no constitutional provision requiring that a party or group to be regulated be represented on the commission that regulates it. (C) is therefore incorrect.

Answer to Question 92

(B) The testimony is admissible. This is the statement of the passenger, a party-opponent, and can be admitted as an admission. An admission is a statement made or act done that amounts to a prior acknowledgment by one of the parties to an action of one of the relevant facts. Here, the driver's lawyer is seeking to admit the passenger's statement that he was arguing with the driver when the collision occurred. The testimony relates to the issue of fault and is admissible as an admission. (A) and (C) are incorrect. The attorney-client privilege protects from disclosure communications between a client and an attorney made during professional consultation. The privilege applies even if the communication is made in the presence of an agent of the attorney. The privilege does not apply, however, in suits between two parties represented by the same attorney. Here, the privilege would apply despite the paralegal's presence because she is an agent of the lawyer. It does not, however, apply in the suit between the driver and passenger because they were represented by the same attorney. (D) is incorrect because admissions are admissible nonhearsay.

Answer to Question 93

(B) The daughter can successfully sue the CEO for her damages because she detrimentally relied on the contract when she did not apply anywhere else. This is a third-party beneficiary contract involving a donee beneficiary. The CEO (the promisee) entered into a contract with the medical school (the promisor) to grant a benefit to the daughter (the third-party beneficiary). Because the CEO entered into the contract to reward his salesperson, the daughter is a donee beneficiary to the contract. The rights of a donee beneficiary vest when the beneficiary materially changes position in justifiable reliance on the promise. Here, the daughter did not send applications to any other schools in reliance on the CEO's promise, so her rights vested. But because a third-party beneficiary's rights are derivative, the promisor may raise any defense against the third-party beneficiary that it would have against the promisee, including illegality. Because the payment for the daughter's admission was actually an illegal bribe, the daughter cannot enforce the contract against the medical school as a third-party beneficiary, so both (A) and (C) are incorrect. The daughter could successfully sue the CEO, however. When a promisee tells the donee beneficiary of the contract and should foresee reliance by the beneficiary, and the beneficiary reasonably relies to her detriment, the beneficiary can sue the promisee directly under a promissory estoppel/detrimental reliance theory, even though the beneficiary cannot sue the promisee as a third-party beneficiary. Hence, (D) is incorrect.

Answer to Question 94

(C) The covenant has been terminated, but the trespasser has a right to use the driveway. To establish title by adverse possession, the possessor must show (i) an actual entry giving exclusive possession that is (ii) open and notorious, (iii) adverse (hostile), and (iv) continuous throughout the statutory period. Here, the trespasser has acquired title to the investor's land by adverse possession. The trespasser's possession was clearly actual and exclusive, as he did not share possession with the investor or the general public. His possession was open and notorious, as the construction of a residence is a use that the usual owner would make of the land. His possession was hostile because he did not enter with the investor's permission. Finally, the trespasser possessed the property for 15 years, five years more than the requisite period. If the possessor uses the land in violation of a covenant for the limitations period, he takes title free of the covenant. Here, the trespasser constructed a two-story residence in violation of the covenant and resided there longer than the limitations period. Thus, he takes title to the parcel free of the covenant, and (A) and (B) are incorrect. Regarding the easement, if the servient parcel is transferred, its new owner takes it subject to the burden of the easement, unless she is a bona fide purchaser with no notice of the easement. There are three ways the person who acquires the servient land might have notice of the easement: (i) actual knowledge, (ii) notice from the visible appearance of the easement on the land, and (iii) notice from the fact that the document creating the easement is recorded in the public records. Here, the facts do not indicate whether the easement was recorded, thus imparting constructive notice, but the buyer has at least inquiry notice of the easement because the driveway running to the other property over the buyer's lot was visible at the time of sale. Thus, she is not a bona fide purchaser and takes the lot subject to the easement. Because the benefit of the easement automatically passes with title to the dominant parcel, the trespasser acquired the right to use the easement when he acquired title by adverse possession. Thus, (B) and (D) are incorrect.

Answer to Question 95

(C) The court should deny the motion because the jury could find that the processor was negligent on the evidence presented. To prove breach of duty in a products liability case based on negligence, the plaintiff must show (i) negligent conduct by the defendant leading to (ii) the supplying of a defective product by the defendant. Defective food products are treated as manufacturing defects—the product is defective if it is dangerous beyond the expectation of the reasonable consumer. To show negligence in a manufacturing defect case, the plaintiff may invoke res ipsa loquitur. To rely on that doctrine, the plaintiff must show that the injury is the type that would not normally occur absent negligence and that it usually occurs because of the negligence of the manufacturer (and that the injury was not attributable to the plaintiff). Here, the jury could find that a piece of bone over an inch long in ground beef was a dangerous defect that would not have occurred without negligence on the part of the meat processor. Hence, the processor's motion should be denied and the case sent to the jury. (A) is wrong because, as discussed above, the plaintiff may rely on res ipsa loquitur to establish negligence. (B) is wrong because, even if the restaurant employees were negligent in not finding the bone, an intermediary's failure to discover a defect is not a superseding cause, and the defendant who created the defect will remain liable. (D) is wrong because the relative fault of the joint tortfeasors is not a basis for denying a directed verdict motion. The processor would be liable even if it were less at fault than the restaurant; the basis for denying its motion is to allow the jury to determine whether, and to what extent, it was at fault.

Answer to Question 96

(B) The testimony regarding careful driving is admissible; the testimony regarding truthfulness is inadmissible. In a criminal case, a defendant may call a qualified witness to testify to the defendant's good reputation and opinion ***for the trait involved*** in the case. Here, the defendant's character for being a reckless driver is directly at issue, and testimony on that issue is admissible. However, the evidence regarding his truthfulness should be excluded because his veracity for truthfulness is not at issue in a reckless homicide case. Furthermore, a party may not bolster or accredit the testimony of a witness unless the relevant trait has been attacked. While truthfulness is a relevant trait to rehabilitate a witness whose credibility has been impeached, there is no indication in these facts that the defendant's credibility was challenged. Thus, the reputation testimony for truthfulness is inadmissible. (A) and (C) are wrong because, as stated above, the portion of the testimony relating to the defendant's reputation as a careful driver is admissible. (A) and (D) are wrong because, as stated above, testimony relating to the defendant's truthfulness is not admissible

Answer to Question 97

(A) The fan should win because an option contract is not terminated by operation of law on the offeror's death. An option is a distinct contract in which the offeree gives consideration for the promise by the offeror not to revoke an outstanding offer. While ordinarily an offer is terminated if either of the parties dies prior to acceptance, an offer that was irrevocable for a period of time because of an option contract survives the offeror's death, and the offer may be accepted at any time during the option period. (B) is incorrect because it misstates the law and the facts. Revocation of an offer does not have to be by direct communication of the offeror. An offer may be effectively terminated if the offeree receives correct information from a reliable source of acts of the offeror that would indicate to a reasonable person that the offeror no longer wishes to make the offer. Furthermore, the musician's estate stands in his stead, and the estate can directly communicate the revocation to the fan. (C) is incorrect because it states the general rule for offers, and this case involves an option contract, which is an exception to the general rule that an offeror can revoke an offer at will regardless of a promise to the contrary. Here that promise was supported by $50 in consideration and, thus, could not be revoked. (D) is incorrect because, even though the musician's estate stands in the shoes of the musician, the offer cannot be revoked because it is an option, as discussed above.

Answer to Question 98

(C) The court will likely find that the one-year residency requirement is unconstitutional because it burdens the right to travel. An individual has a fundamental right to travel from state to state, and a state law that is designed to deter persons from moving into the state is likely to violate the Equal Protection Clause. When a state uses a durational residency requirement (a waiting period) for dispensing benefits, that requirement normally should be subject to the strict scrutiny test, and usually will be found not to have satisfied the test. One such requirement that has been invalidated on this basis is a one-year waiting period for state-subsidized medical care, such as the one here. [*See* Memorial Hospital v. Maricopa County (1974)] (A) is incorrect. The Supreme Court has specifically held that a state's interest in fiscal integrity is not sufficient to justify a one-year waiting period for welfare or health benefits. (B) contains a true statement—the states have no constitutional duty to provide health care benefits for those below the poverty line. However, once a state chooses to provide such benefits, it may not do so in a manner that violates the Constitution, and as explained above, the restriction here violates the right to travel. (D) is incorrect because the privileges and immunities protection of Article IV prohibits discrimination by a state against nonresidents when fundamental national rights are involved. Here, the restriction differentiates between residents.

Answer to Question 99

(D) The questioning was proper under both the Fifth and Sixth Amendments. Under the Fifth Amendment, the driver did not request counsel when dealing with the assault and battery interrogation. The police are not required to call his attorney unless the driver specifically requested an attorney. On the DUI charge, he did not request an attorney until after his arraignment—at that point, an invocation of the right to counsel falls under the Sixth Amendment and is specific to that offense. Therefore, the interrogation about the fight was proper under the Fifth Amendment, and (A) and (B) are incorrect. As for the Sixth Amendment, the right to an attorney is offense-specific. While the driver asked for an attorney on the DUI charge, he did not ask for one on the assault and battery charge. Therefore, his request for an attorney did not automatically follow from the DUI charge to the assault and battery charge. Moreover, there has not yet been a formal charge on the assault and battery issue, so the driver does not have a right to an attorney under the Sixth Amendment until formal proceedings on that charge have begun. Thus, the interrogation was proper under the Sixth Amendment, and (A) and (C) are incorrect.

Answer to Question 100

(B) The neighbor will recover against the hardware store. In a products liability action based on strict liability, the plaintiff need show only (i) an absolute duty owed by a commercial supplier, (ii) production or sale of a defective product, (iii) actual and proximate cause, and (iv) damages. Here, the hardware store is in the chain of supply of the product. The product was defective because the instructions omitted a critical part of the assembly process. Finally, the omission was an actual and proximate cause of the neighbor's injury, allowing him to recover against the hardware store. As indicated by choice (B), an intermediary's negligent failure to recognize the danger does not cut off the supplier's strict liability. (A) is incorrect because the manufacturer's awareness of the faulty instructions does not affect whether the hardware store will be liable. The hardware store was not aware of any problems with the product, but it is nevertheless liable as a commercial supplier. (C) is incorrect. The neighbor, as a bystander, is within the foreseeable zone of danger and is therefore a foreseeable plaintiff who can recover in this action. (D) is incorrect because the fact that the hardware store was not at fault and had no opportunity to inspect is irrelevant. It is liable because it is a commercial supplier of a defective product and the neighbor is suing under a strict liability theory.

Lecture Review

CONSTITUTIONAL LAW

Question 1

A 15-year-old sophomore high school student became pregnant, and the school board required her to attend a special program for pregnant students instead of her regular classes. The girl did not want to attend a special program; rather, she wanted to attend her regular classes.

She sued the school district in federal district court, demanding that she be allowed to attend her regular classes. Before her case came to trial, the girl gave birth to the child. Subsequently, the district reinstated her in her regular classes.

When her suit comes before the federal district court, the court should:

(A) Dismiss, because she is no longer pregnant.

(B) Dismiss, because she is no longer required to attend the special classes.

(C) Hear the case on the merits, because she may get pregnant again before she graduates from the high school.

(D) Hear the case on the merits, because it impacts the right to privacy, which is an important federal issue.

Question 9

During summer months, thousands of tourists regularly visited a state's capital to see its many sites. Because the city had few outdoor water fountains, a number of vendors had taken advantage of the situation by selling water out of coolers set up on the sidewalks of the city.

After receiving several complaints regarding the clutter associated with the water vendors, the city council passed an ordinance, effective immediately, prohibiting persons from selling bottled water out of coolers on the sidewalks between the hours of 8 a.m. and 6 p.m., Monday through Friday.

A vendor had been selling water on the sidewalks of the city for the past three years. He sold his water for $1 less per bottle than other water vendors because his water bottles were adorned with religious messages, and his reduced price helped the dissemination of his religious message. Sixty percent of the vendor's sales were made on weekdays between 8 a.m. and 6 p.m. On learning of the ordinance, the vendor sought to enjoin its enforcement in federal district court on the basis that it is unconstitutional.

In this suit, the court will probably:

(A) Reach the merits of the vendor's challenge to the ordinance, because it interferes with his right to earn a living under the Privileges and Immunities Clause of Article IV.

(B) Reach the merits of the vendor's challenge, because enforcement of the ordinance will interfere with his business, and the rights of the public are linked to the vendor's rights.

(C) Decline to hear the case, because the ordinance has not yet been enforced against him.

(D) Decline to hear the case, because the ordinance constitutes a reasonable time, place, and manner restriction on speech and association.

Question 50

A group of doctors filed suit in federal court against the United States government to challenge a new statute that places caps on the amount that doctors, hospitals, clinics, and other medical facilities may charge patients to perform specifically enumerated procedures. The government filed a motion to dismiss the doctors' suit, arguing that the doctors lack standing to pursue their case.

Which of the following is ***least*** relevant in determining whether the doctors have standing?

(A) A ruling in the doctors' favor would result in removal of the price caps.

(B) Enforcement of the price caps would reduce the doctors' profits by an average of 4%.

(C) The statute placing the caps on the enumerated procedures provides that doctors shall have standing to challenge the price caps.

(D) Eighty percent of all doctors charged more for the specified procedures than the price caps allow.

Question 59

Congress enacted a statute imposing an additional 2% national retail sales tax on all goods sold in the United States. The purpose of the tax was to fund unemployment payments during the recession. An association of newspaper and book publishers sued to remove the tax from newspaper and book publications, claiming that the tax placed an unconstitutional burden on the freedom of speech and press.

Assuming that the association has standing, it:

(A) Wins the lawsuit, because only states have the taxing authority over retail sales.

(B) Wins the lawsuit, because Congress may not impose taxes that chill the freedom of expression.

(C) Loses the lawsuit, because Congress has plenary power to tax.

(D) Loses the lawsuit, because a tax imposed to fund unemployment payments during a recession serves a compelling interest of the federal government.

Question 29

To combat a drought that was threatening the water supply of metropolitan areas in the southeastern portion of the United States, legislation was introduced suspending a portion of the Endangered Species Act. The suspension would allow water to be retained in reservoirs instead of being released to protect endangered fish and fresh-water mussels that live in streams below the reservoirs. The bill also directed the expenditure of $5 billion to fund a solar desalinization plant to convert ocean water into drinking water to serve the drought stricken area. Congress passed the legislation by a nearly unanimous vote in both houses. The day after the bill was passed, the President vetoed the portion of the bill authorizing the expenditure of $5 billion to build a desalinization plant and signed the remainder of the bill.

If a senator from a drought-stricken state seeks to challenge the President's actions in federal court, will she likely succeed?

(A) Yes, because the President does not have the power to exercise a line item veto.

(B) Yes, because when legislation is passed by more than a two-thirds vote in both houses of Congress, it prospectively overrides the President's veto power.

(C) No, because the senator lacks standing to challenge the President's veto.

(D) No, because the President vetoed the bill within 10 days of its passage.

Question 91

Congress created a seven-member safety commission to investigate and make recommendations to Congress for new fireworks safety laws, to make further rules for establishing safety and performance standards, and to prosecute violations of these safety standards. The chairman of the commission was appointed by the President. Three members were selected by the Speaker of the House of Representatives, and three members were selected by the President pro tempore of the Senate. An organization with proper standing seeks to enjoin enforcement of the commission's rules.

Which of the following presents the strongest constitutional argument that the organization can make against the validity of the commission?

(A) The commerce power does not extend to activities occurring solely within a state.

(B) Legislative power may not be delegated by Congress to an agency in the absence of clear guidelines.

(C) The organization is denied due process of law because it is not represented on the commission.

(D) The commission lacks authority to enforce its standards because some of its members were appointed by Congress.

Question 20

A state enacted a gross receipts tax on all businesses operating in that state. The tax was a proportional tax based on revenue derived by businesses in the state. A leading manufacturer of widget assembly devices had its corporate headquarters and most of its manufacturing plants in the state. Its products were sold to widget users throughout the country.

If the company challenges the constitutionality of the state's assessment of the tax against it, what is its strongest argument?

(A) Eighty percent of its revenue is derived from purchases of its products by the federal government.

(B) The tax applies to revenue derived from all of the company's manufacturing plants, including those not located in the state.

(C) The state also imposes a use tax on component parts purchased by the company outside of the state to make its widget assembly devices that is equivalent to the state's sales tax for similar purchases within the state.

(D) Sales taxes are imposed by other states on the company's widget assembly devices sold in those states.

Question 75

A state passed a law prohibiting liquor manufacturers from falsely advertising or misrepresenting facts about alcohol to the public. A brewery's advertising in the state claimed that its beer had only 45 calories per bottle and was great for individuals trying to lose weight. After performing tests on the beer and finding that it had 145 calories per bottle, the state filed suit against the brewery for violating the state law. The brewery filed a motion to dismiss the state's action, claiming that the state law is unenforceable because it is preempted by the Federal Liquor Labeling Act, which was passed by Congress to inform the public of the health risks of intoxicating liquors and provided that no prohibition based on alcohol and health may be imposed under state law with respect to the advertising or promotion of alcoholic beverages.

The motion should be:

(A) Denied, because a violation of the state statutory duty not to deceive has nothing to do with the health risks regulated by federal law.

(B) Denied, because the states have special power to enact liquor regulations under the Twenty-First Amendment.

(C) Granted, because a valid act of Congress or federal regulation supersedes any state or local action that actually conflicts with the federal rule.

(D) Granted, because Congress intended to occupy the entire field of alcohol regulation, thus precluding any state regulation.

Question 98

A state located in the southern half of the United States experienced a strong influx of retirees, due in part to its mild winters and in part to the generous health benefits that the state historically provided to its elderly residents who fell below the federal poverty line. The state's Office of Budget Management determined that the influx of retirees would bankrupt the state's health care benefit fund within five years. To preserve the fund and ensure the health of its citizens, the state revised its health care statute to make persons ineligible for coverage until they have lived in the state for at least one year.

If a retiree who was denied benefits because she just moved to the state challenges the constitutionality of the statute in federal court, is she likely to prevail?

(A) No, because the state has a compelling interest in maintaining the fiscal integrity of its health care fund.

(B) No, because the states do not have a constitutional duty to provide health care benefits to retirees even if they fall below the federal poverty line.

(C) Yes, because the requirement improperly burdens the right of interstate travel in violation of the Equal Protection Clause of the Fourteenth Amendment.

(D) Yes, because the requirement deprives some retirees of certain privileges and immunities in violation of the Privileges and Immunities Clause of Article IV.

Question 35

The police department of a small city has jurisdiction within the city limits and over a defined portion of the surrounding rural communities within the county. A farmer lives in one of the rural communities receiving police protection from the city. The farmer does not pay any tax to the city directly, but a portion of the farmer's county property tax is turned over by the county to the city in order to support the city's police department.

The farmer's property was vandalized several times over the past several months, and the farmer became unhappy with the police protection that the city was providing. After his complaints to the police department and city hall did not improve the situation, the farmer wanted to vote against the mayor in the next election, but a city ordinance provides that only residents of the city may vote in city elections.

If the farmer brings a suit to compel the city to allow him to vote in the city's mayoral election, is he likely to prevail?

(A) No, because the resident voting limitation appears to be rationally related to a legitimate government interest.

(B) No, but only if the city can prove that the resident voting limitation, which affects a fundamental right, is necessary to a compelling interest.

(C) Yes, because the resident voting limitation violates the Privileges or Immunities Clause of the Fourteenth Amendment.

(D) Yes, because the resident voting limitation constitutes an instance of taxation without representation.

Question 69

A state statute provided that only residents of the state can be granted a license to practice medicine within the state. The statute was passed after a series of well-publicized mistakes by a nonresident physician led to a public consensus that nonresidents were less likely to be familiar with the medical standards followed in the state, making them more likely to commit malpractice. A respected surgeon who lived and was licensed in a neighboring state was offered and accepted the position of chief surgeon at a hospital in the state with the residency statute. Because he lived only 20 minutes away from the hospital, he did not wish to move. He filed an action in federal court challenging the residency requirement, alleging that the statute discriminated against nonresidents in violation of the Privileges and Immunities Clause of Article IV.

The federal court is likely to find that the statute is:

(A) Constitutional, because the state has a substantial justification for the discriminatory treatment.

(B) Constitutional, because a license to practice medicine is not a "privilege" under the Privileges and Immunities Clause.

(C) Unconstitutional, because the state does not have a substantial justification for the discriminatory treatment.

(D) Unconstitutional, because the discrimination is not necessary to promote a compelling state interest.

Question 15

A city has a permanent display of passages from various political and religious documents on plaques along the side of its municipal building, including the Declaration of Independence, the Ten Commandments, and the lyrics to the Star Spangled Banner. The city has added the documents over time when they have been donated by various civic groups. Members of a religious organization that worships the planet Mars donated to the city a plaque containing their basic creed and requested that the plaque be displayed along with the other plaques on the side of the municipal building. The city refused to display the plaque, and the organization that donated the plaque brought suit against the city, claiming that its rights to freedom of speech were being violated by the city's refusal to include the plaque along with the others.

How should the court rule?

(A) For the city, because the plaque would constitute government speech and the city may pick and choose among messages it wishes to convey.

(B) For the city, because of the religious basis of the organization's message.

(C) For the organization, because the city allowed other religious messages to be displayed.

(D) For the organization, because the city's decision was based on the content of the plaque, unless the city has a compelling reason for its refusal.

Question 85

Congress declared war on a nation in Asia. Congress also passed a statute making it a crime to make public statements in support of the Asian nation and against the United States. A United States citizen subsequently spoke out against the war at a rally in front of a federal building. During her speech, the citizen urged people to "smash the windows of the federal building like U.S. troops are doing" in the Asian nation. Several members of the frenzied crowd did as the speaker urged. The speaker was immediately arrested and charged with violating the statute.

Can the speaker successfully defend by asserting that the statute violates her First Amendment speech rights?

(A) Yes, because the statute is substantially overbroad.

(B) Yes, because her speech involved core political speech.

(C) No, because she incited imminent lawless action.

(D) No, because the ongoing war constitutes a compelling interest that justifies the statute.

Question 40

A young prosecutor was assigned to a widely publicized murder case in which many people believed that the police might have arrested an innocent person for the crime. After interviewing the defendant and reviewing the files, the prosecutor agreed with that opinion, and told her supervising attorney that she thought that the defendant was innocent. The supervisor instructed the prosecutor to keep her opinions to herself, put on the best case she could, and let the jury decide the issue of guilt. At the first hearing of the case, the prosecutor told the judge that, in her opinion, the defendant was innocent. Immediately after the hearing, the supervising attorney fired the prosecutor for insubordination. After exhausting all administrative remedies available to her, the prosecutor filed suit in federal court, claiming that her firing violated the First Amendment because it was triggered by her expression of belief on a matter of public concern.

How should the court rule?

(A) For the prosecutor, because a government employee cannot be fired for stating an opinion on a matter of public concern.

(B) For the prosecutor, because the prosecutor's right to comment on a matter of public concern in this case outweighs the government's interest in efficiency.

(C) For the government, because the courts give government employers wide deference whenever employees speak critically of government action.

(D) For the government, because the speech occurred while the employee was performing her official duties.

Question 64

A scientist who had worked in a secret government biological weapons laboratory for 15 years was laid off when funding for the lab was eliminated by Congress. After unsuccessfully looking for another job, the scientist wrote a book detailing some aspects of his research in hopes that it would sell well in the scientific community. After reviewing the book before its publication, the government requested that the scientist edit out certain material that the government thought might jeopardize national security. When the scientist refused to make the requested changes, the government filed suit to enjoin publication of the book.

Which of the following standards should the court apply in determining whether to grant the injunction?

(A) Because the scientist's work involved national security—a compelling national interest—the scientist must prove that there is no rational basis for the injunction.

(B) The court should presume that the injunction would be unconstitutional unless the government can convince the court that the injunction is necessary.

(C) If the scientist's book is truthful and not misleading, it is protected commercial speech and cannot be restricted unless the scientist contractually agreed not to reveal his work.

(D) The injunction cannot be issued unless it presents a clear and present danger of imminent lawlessness.

Question 45

An astronomer who had studied the moon for more than 20 years became convinced that the moon began sending him messages revealing how to achieve an afterlife. The astronomer created a website where he shared the secrets that the moon had revealed. He gained a sizeable following. A wealthy follower convinced the astronomer that they should build an observatory to serve as the national headquarters for the astronomer and his followers. The observatory was built, and the astronomer continued to study the moon from the observatory. He also held weekly meetings at the observatory at which he revealed the continuing messages that he received from the moon. Some followers attended the meetings regularly, and some watched the meetings via an Internet feed. After receiving his first state property tax bill for the observatory, the astronomer applied for a state property tax exemption that was available for houses of worship. After conducting an investigation, the state denied the observatory tax exempt status.

The astronomer filed suit to overturn the denial. The state moved for a summary judgment, arguing that the exemption is available only for houses of worship and that, because the astronomer and his followers do not belong to a recognized religion, the observatory is not eligible for the exemption as a matter of law.

How should the court rule on the motion?

(A) Grant the motion, because the astronomer and his followers are not members of a recognized religion.

(B) Grant the motion, because the exemption is a law of general application and such laws need not include religious exemptions.

(C) Deny the motion, because the astronomer should be allowed to prove whether his beliefs occupy a place in his life parallel to that occupied by orthodox religious beliefs.

(D) Deny the motion, because a court cannot question a person's religious beliefs.

Question 55

The mayor of a small city decided that he would like to start each city council meeting with a nonsectarian prayer. Several city council members and citizens objected to the proposal, claiming that it would violate the Establishment Clause of the First Amendment. The mayor argued that it would not constitute the establishment of a religion because he would invite clerics from all of the different religious sects to take turns giving the prayer at the meetings. When the council members still objected, the mayor asked the city attorney to research the constitutionality of his proposal.

How should the attorney advise the mayor?

(A) The proposal is constitutional, because by varying the clerics who will give the prayer, it does not constitute an establishment of religion.

(B) The proposal is constitutional, because there is a long history in this country of allowing prayer at legislative sessions.

(C) The proposal is unconstitutional, because it has no secular purpose.

(D) The proposal is unconstitutional, because its primary effect advances religion.

CONTRACTS

Question 4

In early July, the owner of a toy store entered into a contract with a craftsman for the purchase of 25 hand-carved wooden rocking horses for the holiday sales season. The agreement failed to state a delivery date for the horses. After several months went by without any word from the craftsman, the owner forgot about the agreement. On October 15, the owner ordered a quantity of mass-produced resin-based rocking horses to sell in his store for the upcoming holiday season. One week later, the craftsman arrived at the toy store with a truck carrying the horses and demanded payment, but the toy store owner refused, stating that he already had more than enough rocking horses to sell. The craftsman sued the owner for breach of contract.

May the craftsman enforce the contract?

(A) No, because the contract was missing an essential term, the delivery date, at the time of formation.

(B) No, because so much time had passed without word from the craftsman that the toy store owner had reasonable grounds for insecurity and was entitled to cancel the contract and mitigate his damages.

(C) Yes, because the delivery date was reasonable given the nature of the goods.

(D) Yes, because the craftsman accepted the contract by completing the hand-carved horses.

Question 53

The owner of a custom jewelry supply shop placed an order with a manufacturer for 500 pairs of sterling silver "posts" of the type that are used to make pierced earrings. However, when the manufacturer started to fill the order, it had only 450 pairs of sterling silver posts available.

The manufacturer shipped the 450 pairs of sterling silver posts to the shop owner, plus 50 pairs of higher-priced 10-karat gold posts, without making any adjustment in price. The manufacturer enclosed a note with the order, explaining to the shop owner that it was sending the last of the sterling silver posts in stock, plus the 50 10-karat gold posts to accommodate the buyer.

Did the manufacturer's shipment constitute an acceptance of the shop owner's offer?

(A) Yes, and the shop owner may not reject the substituted goods because they are of comparable or greater value.

(B) Yes, although it is also a breach of the contract under the perfect tender doctrine.

(C) No, because it is a counteroffer that the shop owner is free to accept or reject.

(D) No, because it is a breach of the contract under the perfect tender doctrine.

Question 27

In late January, the manager of a grocery store announced via flyers and in the local newspaper that he would award a $700 in-store gift certificate to any shopper who generated more than $3,000 in sales on their store credit card for goods purchased in the store in the month of February.

A woman with a large family who regularly shopped at the store decided that she had a good chance to win the contest, so she bought a large deep freezer for $300 so she could buy food in bulk and store it at home. She then began buying large quantities of food and racking up purchases on her store credit card that were substantially higher than her usual monthly expenditures.

About two weeks later, the store manager realized that receipts for the month thus far had not increased enough to justify the cost of awarding the gift certificate, so he again put up flyers and took out an ad in the local newspaper, this time to announce that the contest was canceled. Although the woman saw the flyers, she continued to make larger than normal purchases at the store. At the end of the month, she had totaled more than $3,000 in purchases on her store credit card, but the store manager declined to give her the gift certificate.

If the woman sues for breach of contract, will she prevail?

(A) No, because the revocation was made in the same manner as the offer and, therefore, was effective.

(B) No, because the woman knew that the offer had been revoked.

(C) Yes, because she relied on the store's promise when she purchased the freezer.

(D) Yes, because the offer could not be revoked as to the woman once she had begun to perform.

Question 46

On January 1, a car salesman offered to sell an antique car to a collector for $35,000 cash on delivery. The collector paid the car salesman $100 to hold the offer open for a period of 25 days. On January 4, the collector called the car salesman and left a message on his answering machine, asking him whether he would consider lowering the price to $30,000. The car salesman played back the message the same day but did not reply. On January 9, the collector wrote the car salesman a letter, telling him that he could not pay more than $30,000 for the antique car, and that if the car salesman would not accept that amount, he would not go through with the deal. The car salesman received this letter on January 10 and again he did not reply. The car salesman never heard from the collector again.

The offer that the car salesman made to the collector on January 1 terminated:

(A) On January 4, when the collector made a counteroffer.

(B) On January 9, when the collector mailed to the car salesman what amounted to a rejection.

(C) On January 10, when the car salesman received from the collector what amounted to a rejection.

(D) On January 25, when the 25-day option expired.

Question 97

A pop musician of modest fame offered to sell his first guitar, the one he played as a teenager before he became famous, to a devoted fan for $2,000. The fan paid the musician $50 to keep the offer open for 60 days. Thirty days later, the musician suddenly died. The administrator of his estate found a copy of the agreement and informed the fan that the offer was revoked. Nevertheless, after the value of the musician's paraphernalia skyrocketed due to his death, the fan contacted the administrator to proceed with the sale for $2,000 just before the 60-day period expired. At that time the value of the guitar was estimated to be $50,000. The administrator refused to sell the guitar to the fan for $2,000, so the fan sued the estate for breach of contract.

Is the court likely to rule in the fan's favor?

(A) Yes, because he had an option contract that survived the musician's death.

(B) Yes, because an offer may be effectively revoked only by direct communication from the offeror, and the offeror is dead.

(C) No, because the option terminated by operation of law on the musician's death.

(D) No, because the offer was revoked by the musician's estate, which had the power to do so after the musician's death.

Question 65

An engineering firm was having difficulty finding qualified engineers because most universities could not afford the costly hardware needed to train top engineering students. The firm's president wrote a letter to the dean of a highly respected university in the area, offering to provide, at cost, "all the necessary electronic drafting tables your university needs" for use in its engineering degree program. The dean received the letter and immediately mailed an acceptance. Two weeks later, before the dean had taken any other action, he received another letter from the firm president explaining that the firm was in the midst of an unforeseen financial crisis and it could not provide the drafting tables to the university at cost after all.

If the dean, on the university's behalf, brings an action for breach of contract against the engineering firm, who will prevail?

(A) The engineering firm, because the dean took no action in reliance on the offer.

(B) The engineering firm, because the contract is illusory—no additional students will necessarily apply to the engineering degree program.

(C) The dean, because the engineering firm is classified as a merchant under the U.C.C. and its offer was therefore irrevocable.

(D) The dean, because there is an enforceable contract between the parties.

Question 22

A woman owed her auto mechanic $2,000. The debt remained unpaid until any claim for its repayment became barred by the statute of limitations. The woman then agreed in writing to pay the mechanic $1,500, but failed to pay him.

If the mechanic sues the woman for the $1,500, will the court rule in his favor?

(A) Yes, because the woman's promise to pay the $1,500 is in writing.

(B) Yes, because the woman had a preexisting legal duty to pay the mechanic.

(C) No, because the woman's promise to pay the $1,500 is not supported by consideration.

(D) No, because there has not been part performance.

Question 34

A member of an out-of-town yacht club agreed to buy a luxury boat from a local yachtsman, a boat which the parties referred to as "the 'Lady' boat" throughout their preliminary negotiations. The yachtsman owned two boats—"Lady Be Good" and "Lady Luck." The yachtsman's intent was to sell "Lady Luck," while the club member intended to buy "Lady Be Good," which the club member knew was once owned by the club member's favorite celebrity. The club member was unaware of the existence of "Lady Luck." The written contract for the yachtsman's "Lady" boat included a sale price of $100,000. When the yachtsman delivered "Lady Luck" to the club member's slip, the club member saw that it was not the boat he had intended to purchase and refused to accept delivery.

If the club member sues the yachtsman for specific performance to compel him to deliver "Lady Be Good," and the yachtsman countersues to compel the club member to accept delivery of "Lady Luck," who should prevail?

(A) The yachtsman, because in the case of a latent ambiguity in the contract, the intent of the seller controls.

(B) The club member, because the yachtsman knew that he had two "Lady" boats at the time the contract was formed.

(C) Neither party, because an ambiguity existed at the time the contract was formed, and the parties did not intend the same meaning.

(D) Neither party, because money damages would be sufficient.

Question 76

The owner of a store in a small beach town contacted a manufacturer about buying 100 Adirondack chairs. The parties reduced their agreement to sell and buy the 100 chairs to a signed writing that contained all of the essential terms, as well as a merger clause. When the chairs were delivered to the store owner, she discovered that they were not "Adirondack chairs," as she understood that term and as that term was commonly used, but a different style of chair altogether that was manufactured in the Adirondack region of New York. The store owner refused delivery, and the manufacturer sued the store owner for breach of contract, arguing that he complied with the terms of the contract.

Will the store owner be allowed to introduce evidence of the meaning of the term "Adirondack chair"?

(A) Yes, because the parol evidence rule does not apply to subsequent modifications.

(B) Yes, because of the dispute between the parties over the meaning of the term "Adirondack chair."

(C) No, because the written agreement of the parties was a complete integration.

(D) No, because the contract was for a sale of goods between merchants.

Question 89

An East Coast seller of knockoff French handbags and a discount department store chain buyer in the Midwest entered into a contract whereby the seller would sell to the department store 1,000 of a specific brand of its handbags for a price of $20 apiece, with the seller delivering the handbags "F.O.B. Chicago CSX Terminal." The handbags were sent by rail to Chicago; midway through the trip, the freight car that was carrying the handbags was struck by lightning and caught fire, destroying the handbags.

If the seller brings suit against the buyer, which has refused to pay the contract price for the handbags, the seller will:

(A) Prevail, and recover the full contract price.

(B) Prevail, but the seller's recovery will be limited to the profits it would have realized under the contract.

(C) Not prevail, because the risk of loss had not yet passed to the buyer.

(D) Not prevail, because destruction of the subject matter without fault of either party discharges both parties of their obligations under the contract.

Question 12

In a state where gaming is legal, a professional gambler ran up a tab of $50,000 at his favorite casino. Pursuant to a longstanding agreement between the gambler and the casino, once the gambler's tab reached $50,000 he was required to repay the debt in five monthly installments of $10,000 before putting any additional charges on his tab. After making three repayments, the gambler approached the casino owner and offered an immediate payoff of $15,000 in cash as payment in full. The casino owner had a cash flow problem and needed the money, so he agreed. The gambler made the cash payment of $15,000 that same day. A few days later, the casino owner demanded $5,000 from the gambler.

Does the casino owner have a right to collect $5,000 from the gambler?

(A) Yes, because the gambler had a preexisting duty to pay the full $50,000.

(B) Yes, because the casino owner acted under duress when he accepted the immediate payoff of $15,000 in cash as payment in full for the gambler's debt.

(C) No, because there was a discharge by release.

(D) No, because there was an accord and satisfaction.

Question 39

A woman entered into a written contract with her local wigmaker to pay $2,000 for a long silver wig, which was in fashion at the time. The wigmaker completed the wig by the date he had promised, but by that time silver wigs were out of style, and the woman refused to accept the wig or pay for it. The wigmaker spent $200 in making the wig, but because the wig was so out of fashion, the best he could do in good faith was to sell the wig to a Halloween store for $20.

If the wigmaker sues the woman, what is the most he can recover?

(A) $1,980.

(B) $1,800.

(C) $1,780.

(D) $180.

Question 83

On March 1, a widget manufacturer and a retailer entered into a written contract whereby the manufacturer agreed to sell and the retailer agreed to buy 10,000 widgets at a price of $10,000. Due to slow sales, the manufacturer was operating its factory at only 50% capacity and had ample inventory on hand. Delivery and payment was set for May 1. On April 1, the retailer told the manufacturer that he had no need for the widgets after all and would not accept delivery of them on May 1. After notice to the retailer, the manufacturer sold the widgets to another buyer a week later for $11,000, the market price at the time. On May 1, the market price of the widgets dropped to $8,000. The manufacturer's cost to produce and deliver the widgets was $7,000.

The manufacturer sued for breach of contract. At the time of the trial, the market price of widgets was $9,000. The court ruled in the manufacturer's favor, and found that its sale of the widgets to the subsequent buyer was done in good faith and in a commercially reasonable manner, and that there were no incidental damages or expenses saved as a result of the breach.

What amount of damages should the court award to the manufacturer?

(A) Nothing.

(B) $1,000.

(C) $2,000.

(D) $3,000

Question 70

An artist received permission to display some of his paintings in the lobby of his town's library. The librarian really liked one of the paintings and offered the artist $200 for it. The artist accepted the offer and payment in advance from the librarian, and told her that he would deliver the painting to her at the end of the month when his display came down. A few days later, however, an eccentric millionaire in the town who was unaware of the agreement between the librarian and the artist offered to buy the painting for $200,000. The artist quickly agreed and promptly gave the millionaire the painting. When the librarian found out, the artist offered to paint her another similar painting or return her money, but the librarian was not satisfied.

If the librarian sues for specific performance to gain possession of the painting, will she be successful?

(A) Yes, because a painting is one of a kind.

(B) Yes, because the librarian contracted to buy the painting first and paid for it.

(C) No, because the artist offered to return the money or paint the librarian another similar painting.

(D) No, because the millionaire bought the painting in good faith.

Question 17

A store ordered $2,000 worth of clocks from a large clock supplier. The day before the clocks were delivered to the store, while the clocks were in the hands of a carrier, the supplier learned that the store was insolvent. The supplier contacted the store and told its owner that it would not be making the delivery due to the store's insolvency. The store owner told the supplier that he would pay cash for the clocks at the time of delivery, but the supplier still refused to make the delivery.

If the store sues the supplier for breach of contract, the store will:

(A) Prevail, because the goods were in transit to the store by a carrier.

(B) Prevail, because the store owner said that he would pay cash for the clocks at the time of delivery.

(C) Not prevail, because the store was insolvent.

(D) Not prevail, because the store demonstrated a prospective inability to perform.

Question 93

The CEO of a pharmaceutical company wanted to reward his top salesperson. He knew that the salesperson's daughter was applying to medical school, so he met with them both and told them that he entered into a contract with the dean of admissions at a prestigious medical school that would guarantee admission to the daughter. The CEO did not disclose that the consideration for this contract was actually an illegal bribe. The daughter submitted her application only to that school and did not send applications to any other schools. Shortly thereafter, the dean of the medical school was removed from his position for other misconduct. The replacement dean denied the daughter admission based on her mediocre grades and test scores, and the deadline had passed for submitting applications to other schools that might have admitted her.

Can the daughter successfully sue the CEO and the medical school for any damages she has suffered?

(A) Yes as to both the CEO and the medical school, because the daughter is a third-party beneficiary whose rights were vested.

(B) Yes as to the CEO, because the daughter detrimentally relied on the contract when she did not apply anywhere else.

(C) Yes as to the medical school, because the medical school breached the contract when it refused to admit her.

(D) No as to both the CEO and the medical school, because the daughter was only a gratuitous beneficiary.

Question 60

A masked magician contracted with a casino to perform magic tricks six nights a week on the casino floor for $2,000 per week. The contract did not contain an assignment provision. One weekend, the magician came down with flu, so he asked his apprentice to perform in his place. The two signed a written assignment agreement that the apprentice would fully take the magician's place under the terms of the contract for the next week. Excited about the opportunity, the apprentice told the casino's manager of the deal, but no one else knew. During that week, the apprentice wore the magician's costume and mask and performed all of the magician's tricks. No one in the casino noticed the difference. When the magician regained his health, he and the apprentice had a falling out and the magician refused to pay the apprentice. The apprentice went to the casino with the assignment agreement and demanded his pay for the prior week's performances. The magician claimed that he was still the one entitled to payment under the contract.

Who should the casino pay for the prior week's performances?

(A) The apprentice, because he told the manager about the arrangement.

(B) Neither, because the magician breached the contract with the casino.

(C) The magician, because he is the original party to the contract with the casino and no one in the casino could tell that it was not him performing.

(D) The magician, because personal services cannot be delegated.

CRIMINAL LAW

Question 23

A robber attempted an armed robbery of a liquor store with an accomplice. A police officer arrived at the scene and shot and killed the robber's accomplice, who had been guarding the door with a gun and had not obeyed the officer's command to drop the weapon. Meanwhile, the store owner pulled out a gun and shot at the robber but missed. The robber then killed the store owner in self-defense before he could fire a second shot.

In most jurisdictions, the robber is guilty of felony murder for the death of:

(A) The store owner and the accomplice.

(B) The store owner only.

(C) The accomplice only.

(D) Neither the store owner nor the accomplice.

Question 66

A bartender and a patron were arguing over an upcoming football game. Their argument grew heated, and the bartender reached over the bar and pushed the patron's shoulder. Enraged, the patron picked up a beer bottle, smashed it, and lunged over the bar. He pinned the bartender against the wall and swung the broken glass toward the bartender's throat. The bartender managed to grab a baseball bat he kept hidden under the bar and hit the patron, causing the patron to fall and strike his head on the edge of a table. The patron died as a result and the bartender was charged with manslaughter in a jurisdiction that recognizes the "imperfect self-defense" doctrine.

Should the bartender's claim of self-defense succeed?

(A) No, because the bartender started the fight by shoving the patron.

(B) No, because the bartender did not attempt to retreat before swinging the bat.

(C) Yes, because the patron escalated the fight when he lunged at the bartender with the broken glass.

(D) Yes, because the jurisdiction recognizes the "imperfect self-defense" doctrine.

Question 5

The defendant wanted to borrow his neighbor's car to go shopping for lawnmowers. Knowing that the neighbor was out of town for the weekend, the defendant opened the neighbor's garage door and took a car key that the neighbor hid in an old coffee can for emergencies. Once inside, the defendant, mistakenly believing that larceny applied only to the taking of items valued at over $100, decided to take the neighbor's lawnmower (worth $75) in order to trade it in on a new mower. However, on the way to the store with the mower, he was involved in an automobile accident, totaling the car.

In a common law jurisdiction, the defendant is guilty of larceny of:

(A) Both the car and the mower.

(B) Neither the car nor the mower.

(C) The car, but not the mower.

(D) The mower, but not the car.

Question 79

An equestrian left his horse with a stable while he went on vacation. When he returned, he went to the stable to pick up his horse and was informed by the stable that the bill was $500. The equestrian told the stable that he would have to go home and get more money. The equestrian believed that he was being overcharged by the stable; instead of paying the stable, he arranged to have a neighbor pick up the horse from the stable. The neighbor thought that the stable bill had been paid and the equestrian had a right to the horse; thus, the neighbor took the horse without the stable's knowledge.

Halfway to the equestrian's house, the neighbor decided to keep the horse and rode away on it to his own home.

Is the neighbor guilty of larceny in taking the horse from the stable?

(A) Yes, because the equestrian had not paid the stable bill.

(B) Yes, because the stable had possession of the horse.

(C) No, because the equestrian was the rightful owner of the horse.

(D) No, because he did not know that the stable had not been paid its stable bill.

Question 41

The defendant was invited over to a friend's house one night for drinks. The friend told the defendant that he wanted to show him a pistol that he had stolen. After showing him the pistol, they decided to go out to a bar. As they got to the defendant's car, the defendant realized that he had left his coat in the house and told the friend that he was going back to get it. The defendant opened the front door and went to the room where his coat was. As the defendant picked up his coat, he saw the stolen pistol on the table. He quickly picked it up, put it in his pocket, and returned to his car.

In a common law jurisdiction, the defendant could be convicted of:

(A) Both larceny and burglary.

(B) Burglary only.

(C) Larceny only.

(D) Neither larceny nor burglary.

Question 57

The defendant and the victim got into a minor verbal altercation, concluding with the defendant lightly shoving the victim. The victim lost his balance and struck his head on the pavement, causing serious bodily injury. The defendant was charged with battery, which is defined in the jurisdiction as "purposely or knowingly causing serious bodily injury to another."

Should the defendant be convicted of battery?

(A) No, because the defendant did not know that the victim would be seriously injured.

(B) No, because the defendant did not strike a serious blow to the victim.

(C) Yes, because the defendant purposely shoved the victim.

(D) Yes, because the victim suffered serious bodily injury.

Question 90

An obsessive fan was heartbroken when her favorite actor announced his engagement to a well-known actress. The fan waited for the couple outside of a nightclub. When they arrived, the fan raised a gun and fired it at the actress, but as she fired, the actor's bodyguard spotted the gun and knocked it to one side. The bullet grazed the bodyguard's hand, causing minor injuries, and lodged in the actor's chest. Through prompt emergency medical treatment, the actor survived the shooting.

The fan may be charged with attempted murder of:

(A) The actress.

(B) The actor.

(C) The actress and the actor.

(D) The actress, the actor, and the bodyguard.

Question 48

The defendant and the victim, both of whom were drinking, got into a heated exchange of words in a bar. After several minutes, both calmed down and continued drinking. When the victim started to stagger out of the bar after several more hours, the defendant yelled an insult directed at the victim and picked up a chair as if he were going to strike the victim. However, the defendant immediately dropped the chair when the victim turned around. The defendant was charged with assault, and defends on the basis that he was so intoxicated at the time that he did not realize what he was doing.

Which of the following would be ***least*** helpful to this defense?

(A) Assault is a general intent crime in the jurisdiction.

(B) Assault is a specific intent crime in the jurisdiction.

(C) The victim was intoxicated at the time of the assault.

(D) The victim did not take the threat seriously.

Question 2

A car was pulled over for speeding and the police officer ordered the driver to step out and move away from the car. The officer subsequently searched the glove compartment of the car and found an illegal handgun.

Which of the following would ***not*** be a valid basis for the search of the glove compartment?

(A) The officer had a reasonable suspicion that the driver was dangerous.

(B) The officer properly placed the driver under arrest and secured him in the back of the squad car before conducting the search.

(C) The officer properly placed the driver under arrest, impounded the vehicle, and then conducted a standard inventory search.

(D) The officer had probable cause to believe that the vehicle contained illegal narcotics.

Question 16

A thief sold some stolen goods to a dealer. Several weeks later, the police raided the dealer's store and arrested him. In this raid, the police seized the goods the thief sold to the dealer and a record book in which the dealer had recorded this transaction. However, at the dealer's subsequent trial for receiving stolen goods, the charges against him were dismissed when the court ruled that the search warrant had been improperly issued.

The police were able to trace the stolen goods to the thief because of fingerprint identification and the information contained in the dealer's record book, and charged the thief with larceny. Prior to trial, the thief made a motion to suppress the stolen goods and record book.

The judge should:

(A) Grant the motion, because the evidence is the fruit of the poisonous tree in that the search of the dealer's store was improper.

(B) Grant the motion, because the trial court in the dealer's case has already ruled that the evidence was improper.

(C) Deny the motion, because the thief has no standing to object to the search.

(D) Deny the motion, because the thief's fingerprints on the stolen goods were what led to his identification.

Question 52

Police went to a warehouse in response to a report of a gunshot. There they found the defendant standing over the victim's body. They immediately arrested the defendant and gave him *Miranda* warnings. The defendant immediately requested an attorney. The defendant eventually was charged with murder and brought to trial. At trial, the defendant testified in his own defense. He claimed that he was in the warehouse alone when he was attacked by the victim, and that he shot the victim in self-defense. The prosecution, on cross-examination, asked the defendant why he did not tell the police when they arrived there that he had shot the victim in self-defense. The defendant's attorney objected to this question, but he was overruled. The defendant was unable to give a satisfactory answer, and the prosecution suggested that he was lying. The defendant was convicted.

Does the defendant have grounds to appeal his conviction on the basis of the prosecutor's cross-examination?

(A) Yes, because the defendant's request for an attorney relieved him of the obligation to talk with the police while he was in custody.

(B) Yes, because post-arrest silence constitutes the defendant's exercise of his *Miranda* rights, which carry an implicit assurance that silence will carry no penalty.

(C) No, because the defendant's silence when the police arrived is tantamount to a prior inconsistent statement that may be used for impeachment purposes.

(D) No, because by taking the stand, the defendant waived any right he may have had not to testify against himself.

Question 99

A driver arrested for DUI was booked and read *Miranda* warnings. He refused to answer any questions and was arraigned in night court. He then requested an attorney and was provided with one. Later that night, after the attorney left, a bartender arrived at the police station to complain that he was beaten up by the driver. The driver had not made bail and was still in police custody, so the police took the driver from his cell, read him *Miranda* warnings, and questioned him about the fight. The driver admitted to beating up the bartender.

The interrogation about the fight was:

(A) Not proper under either the Fifth or Sixth Amendment.

(B) Not proper under the Fifth Amendment, but proper under the Sixth Amendment.

(C) Proper under the Fifth Amendment, but not proper under the Sixth Amendment.

(D) Proper under both the Fifth and Sixth Amendments.

Question 33

A defendant is on trial for a federal offense. The government has subpoenaed crucial documents from the defendant's bookkeeper that will clearly incriminate the defendant.

May the defendant invoke her Fifth Amendment privilege against self-incrimination to prevent the documents from being admitted?

(A) Yes, because the documents will incriminate the defendant.

(B) Yes, because the documents belong to the defendant; the bookkeeper merely has custody of them.

(C) No, because the Fifth Amendment privilege applies only to compelled testimony.

(D) No, unless the documents contain records that the defendant was required by law to maintain.

Question 73

As part of a plea agreement, the defendant pleaded guilty at a pretrial hearing to possession of stolen goods, because she knew that the police had recovered the goods and could thereby link her to the crime. Unbeknownst to the defendant, however, the search and seizure of the stolen property was conducted without a warrant, and no exception to the warrant requirement applied. During the negotiation of the plea agreement, the defendant admitted her guilt and provided considerable factual details of the crime, but she was never provided with *Miranda* warnings before making the statements. At the hearing, the defendant's attorney failed to recognize that the search and seizure was unconstitutional or request a copy of the warrant, and thus failed to advise the defendant that the stolen property could be suppressed. The defendant was convicted and sentenced in accordance with the plea agreement.

Can the defendant move to withdraw her guilty plea?

(A) Yes, because no *Miranda* warnings were given before the defendant provided details of the commission of the crime.

(B) Yes, because the representation by the defendant's attorney was ineffective.

(C) No, because the defendant's statement in which she admits guilt would make the admission of the stolen property cumulative.

(D) No, because a guilty plea may not be withdrawn after sentencing if the government lives up to its end of the plea agreement.

Question 10

A drug dealer was persuaded by his public defender to plead guilty to possession of marijuana, even though the drug dealer believed that the seizure of the marijuana was illegal. He pleaded guilty while protesting that he was innocent. The judge accepted the plea after determining that it was voluntary and intelligent. After the drug dealer was released on bail prior to sentencing, he was advised by a civil attorney that he could sue the arresting police officer to recover damages for an illegal search and seizure of the marijuana.

Is the civil attorney correct?

(A) No, because the guilty plea was voluntary.

(B) No, because a guilty plea is binding, whether or not it was voluntary.

(C) Yes, because the drug dealer protested his innocence.

(D) Yes, because the drug dealer did not waive his Fourth Amendment claims when he pled guilty.

Question 86

At the defendant's trial for murder, facts were introduced that the defendant acted in the heat of passion. After a lengthy trial, the defendant was convicted of manslaughter. On appeal, the conviction was reversed on procedural grounds. The state immediately moved to retry the defendant, again bringing murder charges against her. The defendant moved to strike the murder charge, and the court refused to grant the motion. After the second trial, the defendant was again convicted of the lesser charge of manslaughter. The defendant appeals the second conviction, claiming that it violated her constitutional rights.

May the second conviction stand?

(A) No, because the state could not refile charges after the acquittal.

(B) No, because the state could not retry the defendant for murder under the circumstances.

(C) Yes, because the state could retry the defendant because the manslaughter conviction was overturned.

(D) Yes, because the defendant was reconvicted of the lesser charge again, so any error was harmless.

EVIDENCE

Question 31

The plaintiff brought a breach of contract suit against the defendant, alleging that the defendant paid for only 25 cases of baseball cards even though the order was for 50. The defendant claimed that only 25 cases were delivered to his store. The plaintiff then introduced a shipping bill from a freight company showing that pickup had been made from the plaintiff on 50 cases.

May the defendant now compel the plaintiff to introduce the remainder of the record, showing that the freight company had only 25 cases of baseball cards on its truck?

(A) Yes, after a proper foundation is laid.

(B) Yes, because fairness dictates that it should be considered contemporaneously with what the plaintiff is offering.

(C) No, because the information is irrelevant to the case.

(D) No, because the record would constitute inadmissible hearsay.

Question 58

The plaintiff sued the defendant, alleging that the defendant allowed her dogs to roam onto the plaintiff's land and cause significant damage to his landscaping. The defendant denied the allegations and called a witness to testify on her behalf. The witness testified on direct examination that she visited the defendant every day and that the defendant never allowed her dogs to leave the perimeter of her property. On cross-examination, the plaintiff's counsel presented the witness with a letter written by the witness to a friend in which she expressed her dismay that the defendant allowed her dogs to roam throughout the neighborhood. The plaintiff's counsel requests that the witness read the letter to herself prior to cross-examination. The defendant objects.

May the witness refer to the letter?

(A) Yes, to refresh her recollection prior to being cross-examined.

(B) Yes, because it is a past recollection recorded.

(C) No, because it has not been formally offered into evidence.

(D) No, because the witness has not claimed any inability to remember.

Question 47

The plaintiff sued the defendant for injuries resulting from a car accident. At trial, the plaintiff's witness testified that the defendant ran a red light and then hit the plaintiff's car.

Which of the following is the court most likely to allow to impeach the credibility of the witness?

(A) A record of a juvenile offense.

(B) A question on cross-examination asking whether the witness lied on a recent job application.

(C) A certified copy of a conviction for robbery five years ago for which the witness has since been proved innocent and pardoned.

(D) A record of an arrest one week ago for criminal trespass.

Question 8

The defendant was on trial for possession of methamphetamines. Charges against the drug dealer who sold the pills to the defendant were dropped in exchange for his testimony against the defendant. The defendant denied knowing that the pills he purchased were illegal drugs. At trial, the drug dealer testified that he told the defendant before the sale that the pills were illegal methamphetamines. The drug dealer died on the stand, prior to the defense counsel's opportunity to cross-examine him. The defense counsel moved for admission of the drug dealer's testimony at the defendant's pretrial hearing that he told the defendant that the pills were not illegal. The prosecutor had an opportunity to cross-examine the drug dealer during the hearing.

Should this testimony be admitted?

(A) No, because the drug dealer cannot be cross-examined about his current testimony.

(B) No, because the drug dealer's prior statement was hearsay not within an exception.

(C) Yes, but only to impeach the credibility of the witness.

(D) Yes, to impeach the credibility of the witness and as substantive evidence.

Question 80

During the defendant's trial for assault and battery, he called to the stand a witness to testify that the victim was the aggressor and the defendant was acting in self-defense. During cross-examination, the prosecution asked the witness if he embezzled funds from his employer five years ago. The witness denied any such activity, and in rebuttal the prosecution seeks to call to the stand the witness's former employer to testify that the witness did in fact embezzle funds during the employment. The defense objects to the testimony.

Should the court sustain the objection?

(A) Yes, because extrinsic evidence of prior bad acts is not permissible.

(B) Yes, because the prior bad act of a witness is relevant only if the witness was convicted.

(C) No, because the offense occurred less than 10 years ago.

(D) No, because the alleged misconduct is probative of truthfulness.

Question 18

During the defendant's trial for battery, a witness testified that he did not see the altercation but that he heard an eyewitness shout, "A fight! The man in the red shirt just punched the man in the yellow shirt in the face!" Previous evidence has established that the defendant was wearing a red shirt. The defendant offers to call a witness who will testify that he spoke with the eyewitness the day after the altercation and that the eyewitness said, "The man in the yellow shirt was punching the man in the red shirt." The eyewitness cannot be found to testify.

Should this evidence be admitted?

(A) Yes, because it is the former testimony of an unavailable witness.

(B) Yes, because it impeaches the credibility of the eyewitness.

(C) No, because the eyewitness is not available to explain or deny his prior inconsistent statement.

(D) No, because it is inadmissible hearsay.

Question 63

The defendant was on trial for burglary. At the conclusion of the prosecution's case, the defendant called a neighbor as his first witness. The neighbor testified that the defendant was with him at an out-of-town sporting event at the time of the burglary. On cross-examination, the prosecutor asked the neighbor, "Weren't you on a jury that acquitted the defendant of another criminal charge?"

If the judge sustained an objection to this question, the most likely reason would be that:

(A) The question is leading.

(B) The question goes beyond the scope of direct examination.

(C) The probative value of the answer would be substantially outweighed by its tendency to mislead.

(D) A proper foundation was not laid.

Question 96

The defendant was on trial for the crime of reckless homicide after allegedly running over the victim with his car and killing him. The defendant testified that he was not driving recklessly. Defense counsel wants to call to the stand the defendant's colleague, who regularly shares rides with the defendant to and from work, to testify to his reputation for careful driving and for truthfulness.

Should the testimony be admitted?

(A) The testimony regarding the defendant's reputation as a careful driver should be excluded, but the testimony regarding his truthfulness should be admitted.

(B) The testimony regarding the defendant's reputation as a careful driver should be admitted, but the testimony regarding his truthfulness should be excluded.

(C) The testimony should be excluded in its entirety.

(D) The testimony should be admitted in its entirety.

Question 21

The defendant was on trial for possession of marijuana with intent to deliver. The defendant claimed that she had been set up and testified that she was not the owner of the marijuana. In support of her defense, defense counsel wishes to present testimony from the defendant's long-time neighbor that the defendant has a reputation for being a law-abiding citizen, and that, in his opinion, the defendant would never become involved with drugs. The prosecutor objects to the testimony in its entirety.

How should the court proceed?

(A) Admit the testimony regarding the defendant's reputation for being law-abiding, but exclude the testimony regarding the neighbor's opinion that she would not be involved with drugs.

(B) Exclude the testimony regarding the defendant's reputation for being law-abiding, but admit the testimony regarding the neighbor's opinion that she would not be involved with drugs.

(C) The testimony should be admitted in its entirety.

(D) The testimony should be excluded in its entirety.

Question 26

Following their divorce, the plaintiff and defendant were engaged in a bitter custody battle over their two children. The plaintiff is seeking to testify as to statements made by the defendant prior to the divorce in which she had told him that she did not feel that she could properly care for the children by herself. The defendant objects, alleging that the statements are privileged as a confidential communication made during the marriage.

The court should find that the statements are:

(A) Admissible, because the privilege does not apply.

(B) Admissible, because the privilege terminates on divorce.

(C) Inadmissible, because the plaintiff has a motive to lie.

(D) Inadmissible, because the statements were confidential and made during the marriage.

Question 92

A driver and his passenger were involved in an accident with another car. They consulted a lawyer regarding their claim and decided to file a suit against the other driver. The lawyer's paralegal attended the consultation. The passenger subsequently sued the driver on a cross-complaint. Prior to trial, the paralegal left the lawyer's employ. At trial, the driver's lawyer called his former employee, the paralegal, to take the stand. The paralegal will testify regarding the passenger's statements to the lawyer at the initial consultation that he was arguing with the driver at the time of the collision.

The testimony is:

(A) Admissible, because the paralegal's presence destroyed the attorney-client privilege.

(B) Admissible as an admission.

(C) Inadmissible, because it is protected by the attorney-client privilege.

(D) Inadmissible, because it is hearsay.

Question 77

A defendant was charged with murdering his boss. After obtaining a valid search warrant and executing a valid search of the defendant's office, an officer found a love letter from the defendant's wife to his boss describing their sexual relations. The letter stated, "I can no longer hide my love for you from my husband. I intend to tell him about us and leave him for you." At trial, the officer seeks to testify about the contents of the letter as proof of the defendant's motive for killing his boss.

The defense counsel should object on which of the following grounds?

(A) The letter was not authenticated as being from the defendant's wife.

(B) The testimony violates the best evidence rule.

(C) The testimony is hearsay not within any exception.

(D) The probative value of the evidence is substantially outweighed by the danger of unfair prejudice.

Question 36

In separate lawsuits, the driver of a car and the passenger both sued the defendant for injuries sustained when the defendant's car struck the driver's car. In the passenger's lawsuit, he testified that he was not paying attention to the other cars on the road at the time of the accident, but offers into evidence the prior deposition testimony of the driver. At that deposition, the driver had testified that she noticed the defendant's car swerving in the lane next to her and suddenly crossing into her lane and colliding with her car. The driver had moved out of state shortly after her lawsuit concluded. No attempt was made to locate the driver or procure her attendance.

Should the court admit the deposition testimony over the defendant's objection?

(A) Yes, because the statement was made under oath at a prior deposition.

(B) Yes, under the former testimony exception to the hearsay rule.

(C) No, because it is hearsay not within any exception.

(D) No, because the passenger and the driver filed separate lawsuits and therefore are not co-parties.

Question 42

The plaintiff brought suit against the defendant for injuries sustained when she was struck by the defendant's car while crossing the street. The defendant denied liability, claiming that the plaintiff crossed against the light. To establish liability, the plaintiff offers into evidence the hospital record from her visit to the emergency room, in which she stated that the defendant failed to come to a complete stop at a red light when the plaintiff entered the crosswalk. The physician who made the entry still works at the hospital but has not been called to testify.

If the defendant objects to the evidence, the court should rule that it is:

(A) Admissible, under the business records exception.

(B) Admissible, because the plaintiff is subject to cross-examination as to her statement.

(C) Inadmissible, because the emergency room physician is available to testify.

(D) Inadmissible, as hearsay not within any exception.

Question 84

The plaintiff brought suit against a train company for the death of her husband, a passenger on a train that crashed, alleging that her husband died due to the negligence of the defendant. Immediately after the crash, an agent from a federal transportation safety board investigated the accident. The agent issued a report concluding that the accident occurred due to the engineer operating the train at an excessive speed. The plaintiff seeks to admit into evidence the report. The defendant objects on the ground that the report is hearsay.

How should the court rule?

(A) Overrule the objection, because the report is self-authenticating.

(B) Overrule the objection, because the report is a public record.

(C) Sustain the objection, because the investigator who prepared the report must testify unless he is unavailable and the defendant had an opportunity to cross-examine him.

(D) Sustain the objection, because the report is hearsay not within any exception.

Question 72

The defendant is on trial for murder. During the trial, the prosecution offers into evidence a properly authenticated affidavit summarizing the results of the defendant's fingerprint test, as proof that the fingerprints on the murder weapon are those of the defendant. The affidavit was prepared pursuant to statute by the lab technician that conducted the test. The defendant objects to the evidence.

How should the court rule?

(A) Admissible, because the affidavit satisfies the best evidence rule.

(B) Admissible, because the affidavit is a business record.

(C) Admissible, because the affidavit was prepared pursuant to statute.

(D) Inadmissible, because the defendant's rights under the Confrontation Clause are violated.

REAL PROPERTY

Question 7

A landowner conveyed his farm "to my daughter for life, and on her death to her children in equal shares." At the time of the conveyance the daughter had one child, the landowner's grandson. A few years later, the grandson struck a pedestrian with his vehicle. The pedestrian obtained a judgment against the grandson for damages. The jurisdiction has no applicable statute on the matter.

Is the grandson's interest in the farm subject to sale to satisfy the pedestrian's judgment?

(A) Yes, because the grandson's after-acquired title inures to the benefit of the pedestrian.

(B) Yes, because the grandson's interest is subject to involuntary transfer.

(C) No, because the daughter may have more children.

(D) No, because contingent remainders are not transferable inter vivos.

Question 54

A landowner died, devising her property "to my sister for life, then to my son." A small stream divided the property into a one-acre lot and a quarter-acre lot. The sister moved into the home on the one-acre lot. To access the quarter-acre lot, the sister installed a footbridge. Ten years later, the bridge had deteriorated and was no longer safe to use. After the sister refused to repair the bridge, the son filed a suit against the sister for damages. The jurisdiction has no applicable statute on the matter.

In such action, should damages be awarded to the son?

(A) No, because the sister has no obligation to repair the bridge.

(B) No, because the son's interest has not yet come into possession.

(C) Yes, because the sister changed the property, even though her change likely increased the value of the property.

(D) Yes, because the sister did not keep the bridge in a reasonable state of repair.

Question 88

A landowner conveyed her vacant parcel of land "to my neighbor and his heirs, but if the land is sold to a non-Christian person, the grantor has a right to enter and retake the premises." Five years later, the landowner died, leaving her daughter as her sole heir. The following year, the neighbor sold the land to an atheist. The atheist built a single-family home on the land. Fifteen years later, the daughter brings suit to eject the atheist from the land. The period required to establish title by adverse possession in the jurisdiction is 10 years.

If the court rules for the atheist, it will be because:

(A) He acquired title to the land by adverse possession.

(B) The daughter is estopped from bringing her claim.

(C) The landowner's right of entry is not descendible.

(D) The condition subsequent is unenforceable.

Question 11

A brother and a sister owned a parcel of land as joint tenants with right of survivorship. The brother and the sister entered into an installment contract for the sale of the property "as joint tenants with right of survivorship and not as tenants in common." The buyer promised to pay $50,000 down, to pay $10,000 per year for five years, and then to secure a mortgage and pay the balance of the $150,000 purchase price. The week before the buyer made his final $10,000 payment and closed on the mortgage for the $50,000 balance, the brother died. His will bequeathed his entire estate to his wife. The jurisdiction has no applicable statute on the matter.

To whom should the proceeds be distributed, and who must sign the deed conveying the land to the buyer?

(A) The sister is entitled to $60,000, and only the sister must sign the deed.

(B) The sister is entitled to $55,000, the wife is entitled to $5,000, and the sister and the wife must sign the deed.

(C) The sister is entitled to $30,000, the wife is entitled to $30,000, and the sister and the wife must sign the deed.

(D) The sister is entitled to $30,000, the wife is entitled to $30,000, and only the sister must sign the deed.

Question 37

A tenant had been leasing an apartment from a landlord for more than 10 years. There was no written lease; however, the parties had agreed orally, at the beginning of the rental, what the rent would be per month. The tenant left a check for each month's rent in the landlord's mailbox on the first day of that month, without fail. On September 10, the landlord handed the tenant a handwritten note stating that the lease was to be terminated effective that October 1. On October 1, the tenant placed a check for the rent in the landlord's mailbox, and the landlord brought an action for unlawful detainer against the tenant.

Who is likely to prevail?

(A) The tenant, because in the absence of a statute, six months' notice of termination is required.

(B) The tenant, because a full month's notice is required.

(C) The landlord, because there is no written lease, and therefore this is a tenancy at will and only reasonable notice is required.

(D) The landlord, because this is a tenancy at sufferance, and therefore no notice is required to end the tenancy.

Question 78

A landlord leased her home to a tenant for 10 years. The lease provided, "On payment of the purchase price of $100,000 during the lease term or any renewal term, the landlord covenants and agrees to convey the said home to the tenant, his successors and assigns, by a recordable instrument having good and marketable title in fee simple." Five years later, the tenant assigned the remainder of the lease term to a friend with the landlord's consent. Six months ago, the friend sought to exercise the option to purchase the home for $100,000, but the landlord refused. The friend brought an appropriate action for specific performance. The jurisdiction in which the home is located follows the common law Rule Against Perpetuities.

For whom should the court rule?

(A) The landlord, because the option violates the Rule Against Perpetuities.

(B) The landlord, because the option is not assignable.

(C) The friend, because the option is enforceable.

(D) The friend, because he exercised the option within the perpetuities period.

Question 71

An investor financed the purchase of a parcel of land with a $500,000 loan from a bank, secured by a mortgage on the land. After an unsuccessful search to find a developer to subdivide and build homes on the land, the investor leased the existing home to a tenant for five years. During the fourth year of the lease, the investor defaulted on the bank loan. The bank brought a foreclosure action, joining the investor and the tenant in the proceeding. The land was sold to a buyer at the foreclosure sale for the outstanding amount of the loan. After the buyer obtained a judgment in an ejectment action against the tenant, the tenant brought an appropriate action for damages against the investor.

As between the tenant and the investor, for whom should the court rule?

(A) The tenant, because failure to include a necessary party results in the preservation of that party's interest despite foreclosure and sale.

(B) The tenant, because the investor breached the covenant of quiet enjoyment.

(C) The investor, because a landlord may assign the rents and reversion interest that she owns to a third party.

(D) The investor, because the doctrine of constructive eviction protects tenants only against the landlord's actions.

Question 19

A landowner owned two adjoining parcels of land containing a number of lakes. She conveyed the eastern parcel, which contained a campground, to a fisherman. The deed transferring the parcel granted to the fisherman "and to invited guests of the campground all hunting and fishing rights and use of the lakes on the western parcel for the benefit of the campground." Subsequently, the fisherman assigned his hunting and fishing rights to a hunter. When the landowner discovered the hunter hunting and fishing on her land, she brought an appropriate action to declare his rights void.

If the court rules for the landowner, it will be because the fisherman's right to hunt and fish on the western parcel is:

(A) A profit appurtenant.

(B) A profit in gross.

(C) An easement in gross.

(D) A license.

Question 82

A developer purchased a 25-acre tract of land abutting an industrial park. The property was rezoned for mixed residential and commercial use and subdivided into 50 half-acre lots. The developer sold the 30 lots furthest from the industrial park to buyers using deeds that restricted the lots to residential use. Only 15 of those lots were improved with single-family homes. Over the next 10 years, the owners of the other 15 lots constructed commercial buildings on their land. Five years later, the developer sold the remaining 20 lots to an investor who planned to erect a shopping mall on the land. An original owner of one of the lots with a single-family home objects to the investor's proposed use.

If the investor is permitted to build the shopping mall, it will be because:

(A) The neighborhood has significantly changed.

(B) The servitude has been abandoned.

(C) Nonuse is sufficient to terminate a servitude.

(D) The zoning ordinance preempts the restrictive covenant.

Question 28

As part of a redevelopment plan, a developer purchased a parcel of land and constructed a condominium complex thereon. The deeds to each of the units prohibited any owner from (i) failing to occupy the unit as the owner's principal place of residence for any period, and (ii) leasing the unit at any time for any reason. The restrictions, which were also contained in the contracts that all owners signed, were designed to foster an owner-occupied environment in the redevelopment area. Subsequently, a current owner of a condo unit obtained a job transfer to another state. When he attempted to lease his unit to a friend, the condominium association filed an action for declaratory and injunctive relief.

Should the court grant the injunction?

(A) Yes, because any restrictions may be imposed on the transfer of a condominium unit if they are agreed to by the parties.

(B) Yes, because reasonable partial restraints on alienation are enforceable.

(C) No, because any total restraint on a fee simple interest is void.

(D) No, because the restriction violates the Fair Housing Act.

Question 44

An investor entered into a written agreement to purchase a parcel of land from a seller for $50,000, with closing to take place on July 1. Two weeks before the date set for closing, the investor entered into a written agreement to sell the same parcel of land to a buyer for $100,000, with closing to occur on August 1. On July 1, the investor received a deed to the land and informed the buyer that she would not be proceeding with their deal because she had received a better offer.

If the buyer sues for specific performance, judgment will likely be for:

(A) The buyer, because he did not know the investor was purchasing the land from the seller for less than its market value.

(B) The buyer, because the investor had marketable title at the time the buyer sought to enforce the contract.

(C) The investor, because she had no title to the land as of the date she entered into the agreement with the buyer.

(D) The investor, because her agreement with the buyer was fraudulent to the seller at the time it was entered into, and therefore unenforceable.

Question 94

An investor owned a parcel of land subject to a covenant prohibiting construction of a two-story residence in order to protect the view from the neighbor's adjoining lot. The investor's parcel was also benefited by an easement in a driveway that ran over the adjoining lot to the investor's property. Fifteen years ago, a trespasser entered the investor's land and constructed a two-story residence. The trespasser also used the driveway over the adjoining lot to access the residence. Last month, the neighbor sold his lot to a buyer by a deed containing the covenant but omitting the easement. The buyer contacted her lawyer regarding her right to recover damages for the obstructed view caused by the two-story residence and to prohibit the trespasser from using the driveway. The period of time necessary to establish title by adverse possession in the jurisdiction is 10 years.

What should the lawyer tell the buyer concerning the enforceability of the covenant and the trespasser's right to use the driveway?

(A) The covenant is enforceable, and the trespasser has a right to use the driveway.

(B) The covenant is enforceable, but the trespasser has no right to use the driveway.

(C) The covenant has been terminated, but the trespasser has a right to use the driveway.

(D) The covenant and the easement have been terminated.

Question 30

An elderly aunt devised her land to a charity "because my nephew has been stealing from me." When the nephew, who had been caring for the aunt, discovered the will, he threatened to withdraw his care unless she conveyed the land to him. The nephew obtained a blank deed and filled in the description of the land and the parties' names. Under "consideration" he wrote, "past and future care." The aunt signed the deed and the nephew recorded it. Subsequently, the nephew sold the land for market value to a buyer who was unaware of the nephew's threat to the aunt. The buyer recorded her deed. Last month, the aunt died.

If the charity brings suit to impose a constructive trust on the land, will it prevail?

(A) Yes, because "past and future care" is not adequate consideration.

(B) Yes, because the deed to the nephew was void.

(C) No, because the land has been adeemed.

(D) No, because the buyer is a bona fide purchaser.

Question 61

A mother properly executed a deed, purporting to convey a parcel of land to her son. The mother gave the deed to her son for his birthday. A week later, the son decided that he should not have accepted such an expensive gift and told his mother so, suggesting that she devise the land to him by will rather than by deed. Instead, the mother executed a will, devising the land to "my son and daughter, share and share alike." Two years later, the mother died. The next day, the son found the deed in his desk drawer and recorded it.

Who has title to the land?

(A) The son and the daughter, because the son did not pay valid consideration for the land.

(B) The son and the daughter, because the will is evidence that the mother did not intend to pass title to the son only.

(C) The son, because the deed was recorded by him.

(D) The son, because the deed was delivered to him.

Question 24

A father executed a will, devising his land "to my son and my daughter, share and share alike." The following year, the son died intestate, leaving a child as his only heir. Subsequently, the father and the daughter were involved in a plane crash. The father died immediately. The daughter died the following week, leaving a will that bequeathed her entire estate to her husband. The jurisdiction has the following statute: "A bequest to a descendant of the testator who predeceases the testator passes instead to the predeceasing beneficiary's surviving descendants."

Who owns the land?

(A) The son's child owns all of the land in fee simple.

(B) The daughter's husband owns all of the land in fee simple.

(C) The son's child and the daughter's husband each own an undivided one-half interest in the land.

(D) The son's child and the daughter's husband each own one-half of the land.

Question 67

To satisfy a debt owing to her friend, a granddaughter executed and delivered to the friend a warranty deed to a vacant tract of land. The friend promptly and properly recorded his deed. Shortly thereafter, the friend built a house on the property and has lived there since. The granddaughter did not actually own the vacant tract of land at the time. Her grandfather was the record title holder, but he had promised to leave the land to her. Later, the grandfather died and his will devised the land to the granddaughter. Pressed for money, the granddaughter sold the land to a creditor by warranty deed, which it promptly and properly recorded. Although the creditor paid full value for the land, it did not conduct a title search of the land before accepting the deed. Both the friend and the creditor now claim ownership of the land. The jurisdiction in which the land is located has the following statute: "No unrecorded conveyance or mortgage of real property shall be good against subsequent purchasers for value without notice unless the conveyance is recorded."

Who has title to the land?

(A) The friend, because the creditor did not conduct a title search.

(B) The friend, because the creditor was not a purchaser for value without notice of the friend's interest.

(C) The creditor, because of the doctrine of estoppel by deed.

(D) The creditor, because the deed from the granddaughter to the friend was not in the chain of title.

Question 14

A buyer entered into a contract with a seller to purchase a parcel of land for $140,000. Because the buyer had only fair credit, the buyer was able to obtain financing from a bank only in the amount of $90,000, secured by a mortgage on the land. Due to a clerical error, the bank's mortgage was not immediately recorded. Without notifying the bank, the buyer went to the seller a few days later and obtained a loan for the remaining $50,000, secured by a mortgage on the land. The next day, the bank discovered the error and recorded its mortgage. The following day, the seller recorded his mortgage. A statute in the jurisdiction provides: "No unrecorded conveyance or mortgage of real property shall be good against subsequent purchasers for value without notice, who shall first record."

Who has the prior lien?

(A) The bank, because the bank recorded its interest.

(B) The bank, because the bank has a purchase money mortgage.

(C) The seller, because the seller did not have notice of the bank's interest when he executed his mortgage on the land.

(D) The seller's interest and the bank's interest are equal in priority because they are both purchase money mortgages.

TORTS

Question 51

A teacher brought a battery action against a student. At trial, the evidence established that the teacher was kicked by the student in the leg.

What additional fact established at trial will likely prevent the teacher from recovering?

(A) The student was only six years old and weighed 200 lbs less than the teacher.

(B) Because of a medical condition affecting his leg, the teacher did not feel the contact made by the student.

(C) The student swung his leg up to avoid a mouse on the floor.

(D) The teacher had lawfully taken possession of the student's cellphone during class but refused to return it when class ended.

Question 25

A tenant remained in possession of the house she was renting after her lease term had expired, prompting the landlord to begin eviction proceedings. While the tenant was still in the house, a heavy snowfall covered the driveway, requiring her to shovel the driveway so she could get her car out of the garage. Shortly after she finished shoveling, the tenant's neighbor used a snowblower to blow all of the snow from his driveway onto the tenant's driveway. Consequently, the tenant had to shovel it again before she could get her car out.

A trespass action against the neighbor can be brought by:

(A) Just the landlord, because the tenant no longer had a right to possession of the property.

(B) Just the tenant, because the neighbor blew the snow onto her driveway.

(C) Just the tenant, because the neighbor interfered with her use of the driveway.

(D) Both the landlord and the tenant.

Question 38

A hiker was passing by an isolated farmhouse one evening when she noticed flames coming from a shed attached to the house, which was dark and apparently unoccupied at the moment. The property on which the house was located was protected by a barbed wire fence, but the hiker happened to have a pair of wire cutters with her, so she cut through the barbed wire fence and entered the property. She put out the fire with a garden hose before it spread to the house.

The hiker is:

(A) Liable for trespass, because she damaged the landowner's property.

(B) Liable for trespass, because the landowner was entitled to protect his property with the barbed wire fence.

(C) Not liable for trespass, because the landowner will be deemed to have consented to the hiker's conduct.

(D) Not liable for trespass, but she has to pay for fixing the barbed wire fence.

Question 6

A proprietor of a business in a small town who had a very antagonistic relationship with the mayor was denied a renewal of his business license. At a village council meeting that was closed to the public, the proprietor engaged in a heated argument with the mayor and demanded to know why his business license had not been renewed. The mayor truthfully declared that it was due to reports that the business was conducting illegal gambling on the premises. The mayor had received such reports but had not yet had them investigated. Council members at the meeting later voted to overturn the mayor's decision and renew the license. After a subsequent investigation, the reports were determined to be false.

In a defamation action by the proprietor against the mayor, the proprietor will:

(A) Prevail, because the mayor had demonstrated malice toward the proprietor.

(B) Prevail, because the mayor had neglected to investigate the reports before making the statement.

(C) Not prevail, because the mayor's statement was oral and the proprietor did not suffer special damages from the statement.

(D) Not prevail, because the proprietor had demanded an explanation for why his license was denied.

Question 56

A professional athlete was involved in a car accident after leaving his team's stadium following a game, and a child was killed. The child's parents brought a wrongful death lawsuit against the athlete, which eventually was settled. A reporter for a sports gossip website accurately reported that, as part of the legal settlement, the athlete was required to seek counseling for alcoholism. The website reporter incorrectly believed that she had received this information from a press release by the athlete's agent, but in fact it had been supplied by an unauthorized source, and no public information was released of the terms of the settlement. The athlete brought a privacy action against the website reporter based on the public disclosure of private facts.

If the website reporter prevails, it will be because:

(A) The facts stated were true.

(B) The publication involved a matter of public interest.

(C) The report was based on a judicial proceeding.

(D) The website reporter reasonably believed that the athlete had consented to release of this information.

Question 13

A patient met with a surgeon prior to a surgical procedure that would involve the implantation of a medical device in the patient's artery. The surgeon advised the patient of risks and benefits, but she did not advise him that there was a 1% chance of a defect occurring in the manufacturing process of the medical device that would cause the device to break during the surgery. The patient gave his consent and underwent the surgery. The medical device did break during surgery as a result of the manufacturing defect, causing damage to his artery. The patient then underwent additional surgery that repaired the damage. He subsequently learned about the 1% risk of the medical device breaking.

In a malpractice action by the patient against the surgeon, which of the following questions will ***not*** be at issue?

(A) Would a reasonable person have refused consent on learning of the 1% risk of failure?

(B) Could the manufacturing process have been modified to eliminate the 1% risk of failure?

(C) Did the patient make a full recovery from the surgery?

(D) Would the patient have refused consent had he known of the 1% risk of failure?

Question 68

A patient went to a dermatologist for treatment of a skin condition on his face that had resisted standard treatment. The dermatologist prescribed a new topical antibiotic cream that was recommended by her associate. She gave the patient instructions on how and when to apply the cream but did not discuss potential side effects. The patient purchased the cream at his local pharmacy and applied it as instructed. Shortly thereafter his skin turned a distinct shade of green and he felt a strong burning sensation when he tried to wash it off. The color took almost a week to fade away, during which time he avoided going out in public and took time off from work.

The cream was packaged with a lengthy printed insert that detailed a number of possible side effects of varying degrees of probability. A "green pallor" and "irritation" were listed as uncommon side effects. The patient sued the dermatologist for prescribing the medicine and established the above facts. He also testified that he would not have taken the medicine had he been informed of all of the potential side effects.

If the patient does not prevail, it will be because:

(A) A reasonable person in the patient's position would have used the cream even when told of the potential side effects.

(B) The printed insert that came with the cream listed possible side effects similar to the reaction the patient experienced.

(C) The severity of the reaction the patient experienced was unforeseeable.

(D) The jurisdiction does not apply a "national" standard of care to specialists.

Question 62

After a heavy snow and ice storm, a shopkeeper posted signs on his store's front windows saying, "Beware of falling ice." A chunk of ice fell off the store's roof and hit a customer on the sidewalk in front of the store, causing her to suffer a concussion. The customer was texting on her cell phone and was not looking at her surroundings, and did not see the signs.

The customer sued the shopkeeper for her injuries in a jurisdiction that retains traditional contributory negligence rules. The above facts were established at trial. At the conclusion of the proofs, both parties moved for a directed verdict.

The trial judge should:

(A) Grant the customer's motion, because the shopkeeper breached his duty to her to make the dangerous condition safe rather than to just post a warning.

(B) Deny both motions and submit the case to the jury.

(C) Grant the shopkeeper's motion, because he owed no duty to the customer on the sidewalk for natural conditions.

(D) Grant the shopkeeper's motion, because the evidence establishes that the customer was contributorily negligent in not paying attention to her surroundings.

Question 87

Some teenage boys were canoeing on a river when their canoe overturned. A nearby fisherman overheard the teens' cries for help and immediately dove into the river to rescue them. The fisherman hit his head on some hidden rocks and suffered a head injury.

If the fisherman sues the teens to recover damages and prevails, it will be because:

(A) The jurisdiction has adopted a "Good Samaritan" statute.

(B) The teens put themselves in danger by not paying attention to the rocks and currents in the river.

(C) The jurisdiction imposes a duty of care toward unforeseeable plaintiffs.

(D) The jurisdiction does not impose a duty of care toward unforeseeable plaintiffs.

Question 49

A young man borrowed his mother's car to go on a job interview. He was running late and made a left turn directly in front of a taxicab without looking. The cab driver was busy talking on his cell phone and did not see the man until it was too late, so the two cars collided. Had the cab driver been paying proper attention, he could have avoided the accident. The cab's passenger was injured in the accident.

The cab's passenger asserted a claim against the young man's mother for personal injuries. The jurisdiction retains the common law rule pertaining to the liability of car owners for the conduct of drivers.

The passenger will:

(A) Recover, because a car owner is vicariously liable for the tortious acts of the driver.

(B) Recover, because the cab driver's negligence will not be imputed to the passenger.

(C) Not recover, because the immediate cause of the collision was the cab driver's cell phone use.

(D) Not recover, because the jurisdiction retains the common law rule.

Question 74

A rancher kept his cattle in a fenced enclosure on his property. The rancher's neighbor, who raised sheep and chickens, was driving his tractor negligently and lost control of it, causing it to run over the rancher's fence and knock down a section of it. The neighbor meant to alert the rancher about the break but forgot by the time he got back to his barn. A few hours later, a small herd of the rancher's cattle wandered through the hole in the fence onto the neighbor's property. The cattle were peacefully munching on hay left out for the sheep when the neighbor's sheepdog began barking loudly and harrying the cattle, nipping at their heels. The cattle became agitated and stampeded over the neighbor's property, trampling a number of chickens in an enclosure. The neighbor sued the rancher for the death of his chickens.

Is the neighbor likely to prevail in this lawsuit?

(A) Yes, because the owner of trespassing livestock is strictly liable for damages caused by the trespass.

(B) Yes, because the herd of cattle had dangerous propensities.

(C) No, because the rancher could not reasonably foresee that the cattle would escape.

(D) No, because the neighbor's dog caused the cattle to stampede.

Question 81

A student purchased a chemistry set from the manufacturer through its website. The set contained printed warnings instructing users to mix the chemicals only according to the formulas provided. Nevertheless, the student combined a variety of chemicals in an attempt to make an adhesive remover. The chemicals he mixed generated toxic fumes, which caused him to suffer lung damage. The student brought a strict liability action against the manufacturer.

If the manufacturer prevails, it will be because:

(A) Manufacturing chemistry sets is not an abnormally dangerous activity.

(B) It was not economically feasible to modify the chemistry set to make it less dangerous.

(C) The manufacturer used the utmost care in the process of manufacturing the chemistry set.

(D) The student failed to follow the instructions when he mixed the chemicals.

Question 95

A consumer bit into a hamburger at a restaurant and cut her gum on a piece of bone in the meat. The bone was over an inch long. The consumer sued the meat processor in strict liability and negligence. At trial, she presented evidence that the processor supplied the ground beef that the restaurant used to make its hamburgers and that she was injured from the piece of bone in the meat. The meat processor presented evidence that restaurant employees prepared the hamburger patties by hand from the ground beef supplied by the processor, and asserted that one of the employees would have found the piece of bone had they made a reasonable inspection of the meat while preparing it. At the close of the evidence, the meat processor moved for a directed verdict on the consumer's negligence claim.

Based on the facts above, the court should:

(A) Grant the motion, because the consumer has failed to show negligent conduct by the meat processor.

(B) Grant the motion, because the restaurant employees' failure to inspect the meat and discover the bone cuts off the processor's negligence liability.

(C) Deny the motion, because the jury could find that the bone was in the ground beef as a result of negligence by the processor.

(D) Deny the motion, because the jury could find that the processor was more at fault than the restaurant.

Question 100

A consumer purchased a grass trimmer from a hardware store. He took it out of the box and assembled it according to the instructions. He noticed that there were bolts and screws left over and some joints that could have accepted additional fasteners, but he just discarded the extra hardware. As he was using the trimmer, the housing came apart and a hard piece of plastic flew off. His neighbor, who was standing nearby, was struck in the eye by the piece of plastic and suffered permanent injuries.

The neighbor sued the hardware store and the manufacturer of the trimmer in a strict liability action. Through discovery, it was determined that the instructions omitted a critical step in the assembly process that would have used the extra hardware, which is why the housing came apart, and that the manufacturer had received some complaints about the instructions previously. The hardware store had no knowledge of any complaints with any of the manufacturer's products.

As to the hardware store, the neighbor will:

(A) Recover, because the manufacturer had reason to know that the design was defective because of faulty instructions.

(B) Recover, because the consumer's failure to recognize the improper assembly does not cut off the store's liability.

(C) Not recover, because the neighbor is not a consumer and can only recover against the manufacturer of the product.

(D) Not recover, because the hardware store had no opportunity to inspect the product and no reason to anticipate that the instructions were faulty.

Question 3

A resident living near a factory brought a private nuisance action against the factory, alleging that emissions from the factory's smokestack were aggravating her sinus condition and interfering with the use and enjoyment of her property.

What is the most relevant factor in the factory's defense of the lawsuit?

(A) The plaintiff moved to her current residence after the factory's smokestack was releasing that level of emissions.

(B) No other residents of that neighborhood have complained about the factory.

(C) The factory complies with local zoning ordinances.

(D) No particulate matter from the emissions has landed on the plaintiff's property.

Question 32

A developer constructed several small stores in a commercial district. She received a bid from a contractor to install awnings on the front windows of the stores. The developer had heard that the contractor did shoddy work, but the price was right and the contractor expressly assumed all of the risk of any liability. The developer subsequently sold one of the stores to a barber. A few months later, an awning collapsed without warning, injuring a customer who was about to enter the barbershop.

An investigation by the building inspector revealed that the awning collapsed because the brackets used by the contractor were cheaper and weaker than the required brackets, although they looked the same. The developer and the contractor are now both bankrupt.

If the customer sues the barber for his injuries, the customer is likely to:

(A) Prevail, because the barber had a nondelegable duty to keep the premises safe for those customers and those passing by.

(B) Prevail, because the developer did not exercise reasonable care in hiring the contractor to install the awnings.

(C) Not prevail, because the contractor assumed all of the risks from his work.

(D) Not prevail, because the barber had no opportunity to oversee the contractor's actions.

Question 43

At an intersection, a motorist's car struck the car of a mother who was driving her teenage son to school. The mother was killed in the collision. The mother's estate brought a wrongful death action against the motorist on behalf of the mother's son and daughter, her sole heirs. At trial, evidence introduced by the estate established that the motorist drove through a red light at the intersection. Evidence introduced by the motorist showed that the son was showing his mother a video on his phone just before the collision occurred.

The evidence introduced by the motorist:

(A) May be used against the estate to show that the mother was contributorily negligent.

(B) May be used against the estate to show that both the mother and the son were contributorily negligent.

(C) May not be used against the estate, because a parent's contributory negligence is not imputed to her children.

(D) May not be used against the estate, because the mother's inattentive driving was a foreseeable intervening force and does not cut off the motorist's liability.